GOOD FAITH IN SALES

AUSTRALIA
LBC Information Services
Sydney

CANADA and USA
Carswell
Toronto

NEW ZEALAND
Brooker's
Auckland

SINGAPORE and MALAYSIA
Thomson Information (S.E. Asia)
Singapore

Good Faith in Sales

by Reziya Harrison
of Lincoln's Inn, Barrister

London
Sweet & Maxwell
1997

Published in 1997 by
Sweet & Maxwell Limited, 100 Avenue Road,
Swiss Cottage, London NW3 3PF
Computer set by Interactive Sciences Ltd, Gloucester
Printed and bound in Great Britain by Hartnolls Ltd, Bodmin

No natural forests were destroyed to make this product;
only farmed timber was used and replanted.
A CIP catalogue record for this book is
available from the British Library.

ISBN 0421 58570 6

FOREWORD

In *The Double Dealer*, one of Congreve's characters observes that "Conscience and law never go together". The opposite view was taken by Trollope's elderly attorney, Mr Grey, in *Mr Scarborough's Family* when, summarising his professional creed at the end of a long career, he said: "I am sure that the law and justice may be made to run on all-fours. I have been so proud of my country as to make that the rule of my life". The same difference of perception is evident in the courts themselves. Many judges will sternly declare: "This is a court of law, not a court of morals". But many more judges will strive to reach a decision which reflects their view of the substantial merits of the case.

These differences of perception in large part reflect different views of what one contracting party owes to another during the negotiation and on the making of a contract, and while it is being performed. On one extreme view, the language of the contract (oral or written) is all. The courts should on this view be very slow to imply terms which the parties have not expressed for themselves, and then only if such implication is necessary to give the contract business efficacy. If, in the current vernacular, this strict approach to construction enables one party to rip the other off, or take him for a ride, or hold him to ransom, that is too bad. The victim should have thought more carefully, or taken better advice, before making the deal in the first place. He has made his bed and must lie on it. The courts are not there to mend any man's bargain.

The alternative view is that contracting parties owe each other not merely a negative duty to refrain from deceiving each other but a positive duty of good faith, sometimes expressed as a duty to play fair, or come clean, or put one's cards face upwards on the table.

The difference between these competing views essentially lies in differing perceptions of the role of good faith in the law of contract: what in this context does good faith mean? does it give rise to a duty? when does the duty begin and end? what does the duty require of the parties?

In offering answers to these questions this book is by no means neutral. It argues the case, strongly and persuasively, for recognition of an expanded concept of contractual good faith, going far beyond the limited role which many contemporary English lawyers would assign to it. But unlike many authors with a message, Reziya Harrison rests her argument not on unsubstantiated assertion but on a meticulous, critical and scholarly analysis of the precedents, both in equity and at law, and both here and abroad. Conscious, no doubt rightly, that an expanded doctrine of good faith will be viewed by some with suspicion, as a new-fangled import from continental Europe, the author is at pains to show that the roots of such a doctrine lie deep in our history, embodied in precedents many of which will be unfamiliar to all save the most learned. But there will be few of her conclusions, it is thought, which would startle Lord Mansfield, the greatest of all Chief Justices — and perhaps the most important influence in the development of our commercial law.

This book addresses, with learning and historical perspective, the most important contractual issue of our time. As Gladstone wrote in the late 1880s, with reference to Irish Home Rule and the Tory voter, "We only ask him to *think*". That is the demand which this book makes of its readers. Those who rise to the challenge will be richly rewarded, and may never see the law in quite the same light again.

The Lord Chief Justice of England
The Right Hon. The Lord Bingham of Cornhill

Royal Courts of Justice
Strand WC2
January 15, 1997.

PREFACE

"Good faith" and fair dealing

This book is about misleading conduct by sellers and buyers. It shows how the courts, starting in the eighteenth century, have developed methods by which they can apportion responsibility for such conduct and ensure fairness between the parties. The courts in so doing have not tried to proscribe every kind of bad conduct, as modern statutes tend to do, but have developed rules for what is acceptable conduct, in the light of the parties' reasonable expectations. 'Good faith" is the label attached to these judge-made rules.

"Good faith" nowadays has a *fuzzy* sound to the ears of English lawyers. For that reason, I have often used the term "fair dealing". However, the traditional label "good faith" cannot be abandoned; that would be to obscure the historical roots of the fair dealing principles and a proper understanding of them. The expression "good faith" is used in the older cases: it is still a recognised legal term in civil-law countries: the civil-law concept and our own English concept of good faith have a shared ancestry. Lord Mansfield introduced good faith to England before it became part of the law of France.

It is a pity that good faith sometimes sounds to present-day English lawyers like a vague, literary concept. The truth is that it is a technical legal term. It is every bit as technical as terms like "equity", "transfer", "convey", all of which possess everyday meanings in addition to the technical legal one; and rather more technical than terms like 'unconscionable" "extortionate" or "unreasonable".

A word of caution may be needed about certain everyday expressions incorporating the words "good faith". The legal opposite of good faith is not bad faith: it is a breach of good faith, or a lack of good faith. "Bad faith" normally means a deliberate misrepresentation or a deliberate misuse of a power; which is not at all the territory of good faith. Also, the expression, "I did it in good faith", has come to mean something like the opposite of its true legal meaning. Commonly, it is used by people who may have been in breach of their duty of good faith: the person using it feels he ought to escape blame, sometimes because he did not have actual knowledge, sometimes because he thinks he holds an office that requires him to practise obfuscation. At all events it should never be taken to mean, "I observed the good faith rules".

About this book

This book is intended chiefly as a textbook for lawyers, especially practitioners. I hope, however vainly, that there may also be some non-lawyers, for instance, businessmen and businesswomen who are concerned in sale transactions and may feel able to read or consult this book. It is difficult to see why this kind of law, which governs all our buying and selling transactions, should be thought of as accessible only to lawyers. To keep matters simple, I have tried to omit all expressions like "sed quaere" and "cadit quaestio"; and the risky enterprise has been attempted of explaining the cases in the appendices, and how they fit, or occasionally do not fit, with the principles under discussion. I have tried to eschew the law-as-plumbing-manual style of textbook writing, now happily going out of fashion. As far as possible, gnomic utterances followed by long strings of case references have been avoided.

The appendices

The text may be read with little or no recourse to the appendices of source material. The appendices are intended for reference, and although it is certainly possible, and by no means without utility, to read them through from beginning to end, a gripping read is not guaranteed.

Since lawyers do not live for a thousand years, any more than anyone else, I have felt that slightly more, and fuller, reference to cases would be an advantage to them. The cases are the sources of good faith law. A large number of the important good faith cases are in the English Reports, which many people do not possess, or do not find readily accessible. Also, since this is a relatively new topic for English lawyers in this century, it is useful and important to be able to survey the field rather more widely than would be usual in other subjects.

The appendices form a longish section at the end of each chapter. There are notes of some cases of interest, with quotations from judgments where these may be thought to shed light on the topic, together with occasional comment. It is certainly not intended to discourage anyone from looking up the cases in the normal way.

The cases are in chronological order. I think it is a help to see how the law has developed; and, sometimes, where it went off course for a while. The present approach of lawyers to cases is all too often what one may call a "timeless senior-common room approach", as though the court were in an Oxbridge senior common room with all the eighteenth, nineteenth and twentieth century judges present, holding views assumed to be prima facie capable of being reconciled one with another. This is to ignore the reality of the historical development of principles by our judges over the centuries. It is particularly unfortunate in any search for the development of fair-dealing or good-faith principles in English law. This development took place over a period of time, and in a changing historical and social context. To read the sources can be remarkably illuminating — that is, the cases on each topic, running from somewhere around the end of the eighteenth century till the present day.

Case references have been printed in bold in the text, where the case appears in an Appendix. The page and place on the page of quotations from judgments is normally not given: many of the cases noted are older cases, which are relatively short compared with modern ones, and in which the passage can be easily found; so this particular piece of lawyerly usage has been felt unnecessary. There will be found, quite freely italicised by me, in the Appendix and elsewhere any passage in a judgment quoted that seems specially illuminating or relevant to good faith. These italics were not in the original, and where this happens it has been expressly noted.

It may be found unusual that there are many early cases. No one should disdain these. If we are looking for proper explanation of a recently developed principle, for instance, Mareva injunctions, we look to the relatively recent period when the principle began to be developed by the courts. The same approach has been followed here. Good faith principles were for the most part developed in the late eighteenth and early to mid nineteenth centuries. The cases from that period explain it.

The book should be up to date up until November, 1996.

It may interest readers to know that there is an illustrious exemplar for the practice of collecting relatively large amounts of source material — Lord Eldon: see *Butcher v. Butcher** in which he spoke of tracing:

> "the Doctrine from beginning to end through all the Cases; as has been my Habit; which I hope will produce at least this Degree of Service; that I shall leave a Collection of Doctrine and Authority, that may prove useful".

Finally, it is hoped that those who think there are faults and omissions in this book (as there will undoubtedly be) will bear them with patience. The self-imposed task of attempting to write a new book, rather than an edition of an existing one, is exciting; and I have found it enjoyable beyond expectation. The penalty, no doubt, is that one is vastly more likely than normal to be guilty of omissions and errors of fact or judgment. I hope this book may still prove useful, and that such sins, if not little ones, will at least be forgiven.

Acknowledgements

I should like to express my gratitude to Mr Justice Lightman, and to Jonathan Rayner James Q.C. of 5 New Square, Lincoln's Inn, for taking the time from their busy judicial and professional lives, respectively, to read and comment helpfully on substantial parts of this book in draft. I hope I have profited properly from their comments. They are not in the least responsible for the errors that remain. I should also like to thank Nicholas Bamforth of Robinson College, Cambridge, for reading and commenting most helpfully on Chapter 9, Dealings with the Vulnerable Buyer or Seller. My thanks are also owed for various acts of kindness — mainly drawing useful cases or articles to my attention — to Sir Anthony Mason, former Chief Justice of Australia, to Glenn Campbell of 11 Old Square, Lincoln's Inn, to my ex-pupil Nicolai Eatwell, to Anne de Moore of Somerville College, Oxford, to Sian Thomas of 11 Old Square and to Martin Mann Q.C. and Amanda Harington of 24 Old Buildings, Lincoln's Inn; to Philip Bovey of the

* (1812) 1 V. & B. 79; 35 E.R. 31.

Department of Trade and Industry for kindly letting me have copies of a number of useful articles; to Ashley Holmes, Consumers' Association, for letting me have the correct wording of the Association's reference to the European Court; and to the staff of Sweet & Maxwell for their patient and professional overseeing of the publishing of this book.

Since I do not profess to be any kind of philosopher, I am extremely grateful to Professor Stephen Hallowell, of St Andrew's University, Fife, Scotland, for checking the section in Chapter 2 and Appendix on the influence of Aristotle, Aquinas and the natural lawyers; and to my son Tom Harrison for kindly arranging this. Neither is responsible for any philosophical or other errors which may remain. I am also grateful to Professor Barry Nicholas for kindly casting an eye over the section on France in Chapter 18, Do we need Good Faith anyway?

My thanks are also due to the Librarians and their staffs of Lincoln's Inn Library and the Bodleian Law Library, for their never-failing helpfulness, courtesy, and professionalism; to the Librarian and staff of the London Library, to which it is a privilege to belong; and to the Librarian of the Codrington Library at All Souls College, use of which is an experience as gratifying to the eye as the mind.

I should like, finally, to record a huge debt of gratitude to my husband, Martin Harrison, for his encouragement, enthusiasm for the topic, and practical help. He is not a lawyer. He has tested the book's accessibility to non-lawyers by reading a substantial part of the main text in draft. Habitually in command of more elegance of style than I possess, he has also pointed out a number of infelicities of language and content which I have attempted to remedy. I should also like to thank my daughter Frances Harrison, and my son Tom Harrison (who has been kind enough also to read and comment on a part of the book in draft), for their encouragement in this as in all my other endeavours.

Reziya Harrison
Lincoln's Inn
March 1997

CONTENTS

TABLE OF CASES

Entries in **bold** indicate paragraphs devoted to discussion of case

Wood v. Abrey (1818) 3 Madd. 417; 56 E.R. 558 .... 9.22, 9.30, **9.69**

TABLE OF STATUTES

Entries in **bold** indicate paragraphs devoted to discussion of the statute or section

TABLE OF STATUTORY INSTRUMENTS

Entries in **bold** indicate paragraphs devoted to discussion of the statutory instrument

TABLE OF EUROPEAN LEGISLATION

TABLE OF FOREIGN LEGISLATION

Part 1

THE QUEST FOR GOOD FAITH

CHAPTER 1

THE NEW REGULATIONS AND THE OLD LAW: COALS TO NEWCASTLE?

Les conventions légalement formées . . . doivent être executées de bonne foi"[1]

"*. . . The governing principle is applicable to all contracts and dealings. Good faith forbids either party by concealing what he privately knows, to draw the other into a bargain, from his ignorance of that fact, and his believing the contrary. But either party may be innocently silent as to grounds open to both to exercise their judgment upon.*"[2]

INTRODUCTION

The Historical Perspective

No good faith in English law?

1.01 It is customary for English lawyers to say "We do not have a principle of good faith in English law". The Department of Trade and Industry subscribe to this view, it would seem. In the First Consulation Document on the Implementation of the EC Directive on Unfair Terms in Consumer Contracts[2a] the following sentence appears in paragraph 2 of the Introduction:

> "The main effect of the Directive will be to introduce for the first time a general concept of fairness into the UK law of contract."

[1] Art. 1134 of the French Code Civil Dalloz edition 1994/5; see also Chap. 18. Do we need good faith anyway? for French good–faith provisions affecting the formation of the contract.

[2] Lord Mansfield in ***Carter v. Boehm*** (1766), noted in Chap. 4, Insurance and Surety Transactions.

[2a] [1993] O.J. L95/29

This sentence would seem, contrary to popular belief, to be quite wrong. In fact, the general position is much more accurately, if briefly, set out in the judgment of Bingham L.J., as he then was, in *Interfoto v Stiletto.*[3]

> "[The civil law principle of good faith] does not simply mean that [the parties to a contract] should not deceive each other, a principle which any legal system must recognise; its effect is perhaps most aptly conveyed by such metaphorical colloquialisms as "playing fair", coming clean" or "putting one's cards face upwards on the table." It is in essence a principle of fair and open dealing. . . .
>
> English law has, characteristically, committed itself to no such overriding principle but has developed piecemeal solutions in response to demonstrated problems of unfairness."

1.02 Bingham L.J., went on to give examples, referring to Equity's intervention to strike down unconscionable bargains, to Parliament's intervention to regulate the imposition of exemption clauses and the form of certain hire purchase agreements, to the common law's contribution by holding that certain classes of contract require the utmost good faith, and to the law on penalties. He probably did not mean the list to be exhaustive. He went on:

> "The tendency of the English authorities has, I think, been to look at the nature of the transaction in question and the character of the parties to it; to consider what notice the party alleged to be bound was given of the particular condition said to bind him; and to resolve whether in all the circumstances it is fair to hold him bound by the condition in question. This may yield a result not very different from the civil law principle of good faith, at any rate so far as the formation of the contract is concerned."

This tendency to develop piecemeal solutions, looking at each matter individually, may well have tended to obscure the existence of the principles by which English courts have acted the past, and to some extent, still act. There is to be found in English case law, more particularly in the late eighteenth and the nineteenth century case law, a reasonably consistent set of fair dealing principles, or implied contractual terms of fair dealing, as incidents of certain types of contracts. It is, however, true also that these principles are to a considerable extent unrecognised now. This does not mean they do not exist. They do, and are good law—and much-needed law.

How did we mislay good faith?

1.03 That our fair dealing principles are no longer acknowledged as such stems perhaps from a number of reasons. There is first, the historical

[3] [1989] Q.B. 433 at 439. It is appreciated that this case is becoming rather over-quoted since the coming into force of the Unfair Terms Regulations 1994, but no apology is made for quoting it again: there are at present few

division of our courts into Equity and Common Law courts, and the consequent somewhat eccentric (for nowadays) division of barristers' and then solicitors' practices between Chancery (now including commercial but not shipping law and not the full range of insurance law) on the one hand and Common Law or Commercial (including shipping Law and the full range of insurance law) on the other. Thus, there may be some Chancery barristers who do not have a very detailed awareness of the principles obtaining in insurance law, for example. Conversely, it would be relatively unusual for many practitioners in commercial sets to have much knowledge of the rules of fairness which apply in conveyancing transactions. Yet both types of barrister operate in a similar market; both have business clients as well as private clients. The synthesis of knowledge might have been useful. One casualty of this division has been a deeper appreciation of insurance law's important development of implied terms of precontractual disclosure. Another has perhaps been a lack of understanding of the true scope (and indeed, even the Latin meaning,) of the maxim *caveat emptor*.

1.04 Apart from Lord Mansfield's contribution in the eighteenth century, and the remarkable development around the mid-nineteenth century of implied terms of fair dealing in sales of goods and intellectual property, probably the main source of fair-dealing terms in contracts was the old Courts of Equity. One would thus expect that the Chancery Bar and in particular, the Chancery judges, would be enthusiastic proponents of the presumption of fair dealing, and the consequent implication of fair dealing terms and fair dealing constructions.[4] This is not really so. One can but speculate about the reasons why.

Thus, relative ignorance of implied terms of fair dealing can seem to breed a kind of macho hostility to fair dealing principles. "Hard cases make bad law"; and "Law has little to do with justice" are phrases that trip readily off the tongues of many practising barristers. It does not seem always to have been so. Fairness and justice seem to have been thought-related concepts. Literalism was not always king.

1.05 Nor was it always the case, as it is now, that English law was regarded as best kept undefiled by mention of any save a little Commonwealth and occasionally United States authority. The tendency to cite Australian law, of course, has been wholly beneficial. However, there was a time when the French law of obligations was regarded as relevant and influential, and certainly proper to be mentioned to a judge in a commercial case. In a leading case on the sale of goods, *Eichholz v. Bannister*,[5] counsel felt it possible to mention to the court the relevant law in France and America. The same thing happened in *Morley v. Attenborough*.[6] Most members of the Bar would agree that probably the men in white coats would be summoned if any of us had the temerity to try such a thing in court these days. Yet in 1822,

judicial insights into an English law of good faith which are there to be quoted.

[4] See Chap. 2.

[5] (1864) 17 C.B. (N.S.) 708.

[6] (1849) 3 Ex. 500.

Best J. (as he then was), in the Court of Common Pleas, in *Cox v.Troy*[7], a case about whether an acceptance of a bill of exchange might be withdrawn before it was communicated to the holder, first remarked that there was no express English authority on the point, and then said:

> "But the authority of Pothier [the French jurist] is expressly in point. That is as high as can be had, next to the decision of a Court of Justice in this country. It is extremely well known that he is a writer of acknowledged character; his writings have been constantly referred to by the Courts, and he is spoken of with great praise by Sir William Jones in his Law of Bailments, and his writings are considered by that author equal in point of luminous method, apposite examples, and a clear mainly style, to the works of Littleton the laws of this country. We cannot, therefore, have a better guide than Pothier on this subject."

1.06 The language is of its period, but this should not obscure the startling fact that the writing of Pothier was regarded by a judge who was in effect a Commercial Court judge of the day as highly persuasive authority. Pothier's views were hugely influential in France in his day, and contributed to the making of Napoleon's Code Civil. His work became so popular in England that his Law of Obligations was translated into English in 1806. It would be surprising for this to have happened if we had not had our own nascent, home-grown notion of good faith in those days. Contract doctrine and contract terms were in the course of development in England at the time Pothier wrote. It would also be surprising, given that barristers and judges would no doubt have been then a much smaller, more enclosed circle than now, and would have been able to take for granted certain reading in common, if imported notions of fair dealing had not been taken up at all. Our law of contract diverged from the French one, of course, when it became accepted that consideration was necessary for a binding contract. It was by no means the case that we abandoned every other import into contract law. Fair dealing terms remained alive and well, and proved capable of considerable development in England, as will be seen.

1.07 One might suppose that when England was a major commercial power its law would have been developed on complacently isolationist lines. Curiously, the opposite seems to have been the case. It is now, in our period of relative decline in commercial importance, that we have an essentially isolationist system of contract law in which literal interpretation of the (increasingly many) words used in written documents is the prevailing approach. Other countries have a law of good faith. Almost alone, England does not—*or so it is said*.

1.08 How then did good faith go out of fashion here? The reason may partly have been the administrative problems experienced by the chancery courts in the nineteenth century, the effects of which were graphically described by Dickens in *Bleak House*. These problems may

[7] (1822) 5 B & A. 474 at 481.

perhaps have contributed to some stifling of creative thinking at the Chancery Bar of the time, and a general sense among Chancery and other judges that the Chancery past was not good news: Another reason may well have been the growing influence of the logical positivist philosophers such as Hume, who were out of tune with the law on fair dealing, with the latter's Aristotelian emphasis on purpose, and on "natural" terms.[8] If "good" can be anything a society chooses to define as good, then lawyers are not going to find much guidance in principles. Far better to stick to grammatical interpretation of documents. The parties are king; this is their charter, freely entered into. Too bad, if they did not realise what it entailed. Too bad, if they could not in practice have realised. Thus, we have had growing enthusiasm among many of the judiciary for what is regarded as bargain maintenance at the cost of social or other fairness. The latter has tended in recent years to be regarded as something "namby pamby", verging on the dangerously metaphysical, and certainly best left to Parliament. The question of what the bargain really was remains neglected.

1.09 When did we lose good faith? It is probably wrong to overemphasize the reaction against Lord Mansfield by Lord Kenyon and others. Lord Mansfield's successors may well have been concerned rather more to keep the distinction between the Common Law courts' and the Equity courts' traditional jurisdiction than to nip in the bud any introduction of good faith concepts in English law. As to the alleged reaction against Lord Mansfield, in *Butcher v. Butcher*[9] Lord Eldon, commenting on the suggestion that "fraud" should mean the same in law as in Equity, said:

> "To that Doctrine I do not agree. Though in modern Times, and particularly during the Period, in which I have been engaged in this Hall, a strong Inclination has been evident to say, that whatever is Equity ought to be Law; an Opinion, acted upon especially by Mr Justice *Buller*; who persuaded Lord *Mansfield* to act upon it, until it was reformed by Lord *Kenyon*, with the Assistance of the same very able Judge, as he certainly was; yet the clear Doctrine of Lord *Hardwicke* and all his Predecessors was, that there are many Instances of Fraud, that would affect Instruments in Equity; of which the Law could not take Notice; and this Class of Cases is one Instance."

There was indeed a reaction against good faith in this country, but it seems to have been much later, roughly from the late 1870's onwards. The precise reasons would probably form a book in their own right, but one can speculate.

The Judicature Act 1873, merging the Equity and Common Law jurisdictions in England provided a background, simply, we may suspect, because of the shifting for position which ensued quite naturally as a result.

1.10 More important, perhaps, was the new enthusiasm for legislation:

[8] See, *e.g.* Gordley, *The Philosophical Origins of Modern Contract Doctrine* (1991) and Atiyah, *The Rise and Fall of Freedom of Contract* (1979).

[9] (1812) 1 Ves. & B. 79; 35 E.R. 31.

there was really remarkably little legislation before that period, no doubt because Parliament did not have the requisite capacity. However, the introduction of the railways meant that legislation was necessary to protect the public travelling on them and to make sure that the railway companies accepted responsibility for the safety of the travelling public. "Social" legislation had also earlier become necessary to deal with the financially scandalous who had taken advantage of the new joint-stock companies for their own gain.[10] A number of Acts proved necessary; as often happens, each well-meaning new Act spawning a number of interpretation problems, and about the time that these were ironed out, it would be thought that another Act might be a good idea; and so on. Good faith concepts alone could hardly cope with the new and artificial construct represented by the joint-stock company, at all events after it had developed into more or less the creation we have come to know, if not really to love, today. Perhaps because it was not until after the Judicature Act 1873 that companies really began to be regarded as ordinary investments, and by then good faith was rapidly going out of fashion, no real thought was given to the application of good faith principles to the sale of shares. The fact that banking partnerships remained the norm, with special statutory help, and that the Partnership Act became law in 1892, tells us something about the early lack of respectability of joint-stock companies. One has the impression from the cases as much as from Dickens, that for much of the century, companies were regarded as thoroughly unsound raffish outfits, fit only for speculators who did not mind that sort of thing. Take, for example, for what may be a typical early nineteenth-century view of proper investment policy, the delightful case of *Rothschild v. Brookman*[11] in which Lord Wynford said:

> "I am very sorry to say, that, with respect to one of the parties in this case, it is perfectly clear that he is a most desperate gambler in the funds, and he has met with that fate which most of those meet with who become such gamblers. For I believe whenever a man puts his foot into the Stock Exchange, not being a member of that Stock Exchange, his ruin is certain, and the only question is a question of time. Therefore that has happened to this Plaintiff which generally happens: for, according to the statement, he has been completely ruined."

Perhaps, then, the nature of the social legislation required to deal with "gamblers" and others paved the way for the rather curious idea that all broadly "social" effects should thenceforward be achieved by legislation rather than the imposition of moral rules of reasonable expectation.

1.11 One would have expected nonetheless that where good faith had already been fully established, it would have flourished still. The obvious place to look for good faith or fair dealing terms is in transactions concerning real property—the only really safe and respectable invest-

[10] There is essentially no kind of latterday financial problem which was not to be found in one guise or another at some stage in the last two centuries.

[11] (1831) 2 Dow. & Cl. 188; (noted more fully in Chap. 15 Remedies).

ment for most of the nineteenth century. (It is odd to think that good faith may well have originated as a kind of protection-of-investors policy as much as a morally-based one.) One does indeed find the good faith rules best developed in sale of land cases in the first half of the nineteenth century, albeit in parallel with the newer development of good faith terms by the Common Law courts in regard to sale of goods. It may be that a major reason why they survived beyond the end of the century only in what are seen as isolated pockets is the introduction of an Act in 1874 called the Vendor and Purchaser Act. This provided a new summary (that is, speedy) method of having questions of title looked at by the court and their validity or otherwise determined, and was extremely popular. However, the Act effectively ruled out the taking of any good faith points by excluding from the procedure any points which tended to attack the validity of the contract. It may be that the courts could easily have interpreted the good-faith points as merely defining what the contract was—probably a more accurate approach to the operation of good faith. They did not, perhaps partly because, while Mr Justice Fry had written a textbook about specific performance, no-one had written a book explaining the operation of good faith. Thus, good faith points become rarer and rarer, even on their traditional ground; and even there, increasingly likely to be seen as an unexplained anomaly.

1.12 Those, then, are some of the reasons which may be identified for the reaction against good faith at the end of the nineteenth century. It may be that there are others. The deadening effect of statute is noted below, in regard to the Sale of Goods Act 1893 (which has of course survived with little change to the present day.) A period of economic boom also, as happened at the end of the nineteenth century, quite simply meant that people needed the main good faith remedy of rescission much less. Rescission is most beneficial in times of economic decline. This can be seen today, for example, from the facts of *William Sindall v. Cambridgeshire County Council*[12] where the defective land, the subject of a decision to rescind which in the end was declared ineffective by the Court of Appeal, had gone from some £5,000,000 in value at the time of purchase to some £3,000,000 when the defect was discovered about 18 months later and some £1,000,000 by the time the appeal was heard. The opening up of the prairies after the end of the American Civil War had flooded the market with cheap wheat and caused a huge decline in the price of land from which it took decades to recover. Dealings in land diminished in consequence. Small wonder, perhaps, that people turned to investment in the new companies; or on the whole thought that their claims were best framed in damages rather than rescission or compensation.

1.13 There may also have been (dare one suggest) a group reaction by the majority of Common Law judges after the Judicature Act 1873 against what were perceived as difficult doctrines to pick up. It is surprising perhaps, given that the Common Law judges were and are the inheritors of Lord Mansfield who introduced good faith to this country. However, the normal course of events one finds in each area

[12] [1994] 1 W.L.R. 1016.

of law covered by this book as the century progresses is first that the good faith doctrine is introduced (or if there is a similar more ancient doctrine already in existence, given a new look) at the beginning of the nineteenth century; then it is developed and flourishes until some time towards the end of that century, at which point a curious uncertainty develops, together with curious shifts of approach.[13] Sometimes in the same case in the Court of Appeal there are to be found both good faith based judgments and judgments based on the new literalism sitting side by side. There was a great deal of—rather suspect—historical "explanation" of the jurisdiction originally exercised by the Courts of Equity. This seems to have had two notable unconscious tendencies: (1) to give to the Courts of Equity a much less focused, general discretion than they had in fact ever claimed as far as can be seen; and (2) to limit their exercise of their good faith jurisdiction to occasions when specific performance had been sought. In fact the early Lord Chancellors in the late eighteenth and early nineteenth century were extremely careful to avoid arrogating to themselves a wide general discretion of any kind. A wide general discretion is in fact only needed to correct the wilder injustices brought about by a mainly literalist approach. The early Lord Chancellors neither needed nor wanted such a wide discretion: they thought there would be "no safety for mankind" if they did not operate according to rules which could be predicted, as good faith rules can be. Nor was adherence to good faith rules limited to the exercise of the discretion to give or withhold specific performance: when specific performance had been refused, the Equity courts if they thought fit went on to grant rescission. The idea that after granting or withholding specific performance they always left the parties to their remedy at law[14] is simply incorrect: that was merely an option for the Equity Courts in cases where they did not think the defect quite bad enough for rescission, since they had not (for practical reasons: no jury) the jurisdiction to give damages. Good faith points were often a major factor in their granting of rescission; and the granting of rescission would be to them an entirely separate question from specific performance. In any case, good faith points were not always exclusive to Equity courts: they were sometimes adopted, as far as can be seen, as a matter of comity between the two divisions, by Common Law judges dealing with real property transactions: as, for example, in well-known case of *Flight v. Booth*[15] which was a decision not of an equity judge, but a common law judge, Tindal C.J.[16]

[13] For a broadly similar historical perception in the field of mortgages, see Nicholas Bamforth, *Lord MacNaghten's Puzzle: The Mortgage of Real Property* in *English Law in Current Legal Problems.*

[14] See *e.g. Faruqi v. English Real Estates* [1979] 1 W.L.R. 963.

[15] (1834) 1 Bing N.C. 370.

[16] For a fuller discussion of Equity's original jurisdiction, see Chap. 5, Sale of Land.

The return of good faith?

1.14 As we have seen, for a number of reasons, good faith has not flourished in England except in isolated pockets, not recognised for what they are, during the whole of this century thus far. Instead, we have had a literalist approach to contracts, increasingly long contracts, and a positive ocean of legislation, in which even lawyers may sometimes fear to swim. It may be thought that this is responsible for much of the burgeoning cost of civil litigation which is reasonably the subject of current concern. Curiously, no-one seems yet to have considered the role of substantive contract law in increasing the cost of litigation. Today, we are revisited by fair dealing, or good faith principles, this time packaged as an European Community requirement, stated to be in order to facilitate the free movement of goods and services in the Community. There may be a tendency to minimise the effect of European Directives embodying good faith requirements, such as the Directive given effect in our law as the Unfair Terms in Consumer Contract Regulations 1994,[17] and to confine their operation. It would in fact be useful if instead we were to embrace them, and take the opportunity to reacquaint ourselves with our own subtle and carefully-wrought English law of fair dealing or good faith. If nothing else, it will serve to elucidate and flesh out the real meaning the Regulations may bear in our legal system which is very different from those in Europe.

In any event, one may venture to think that our own law of good faith or fair dealing has certain evident merits which the Unfair Terms Regulations 1994 do not have, and therefore should have independent recognition. For example, our equitable and common law terms of fair dealing do not seek to draw rigid—and sometimes unjust—distinctions between the consumer and the business. When a consumer is put to financial detriment, he suffers. When a company is put out of business, hundreds if not thousands of employees lose their jobs. Why should a company or a business of any kind be less deserving of fair dealing than a natural person? Further, the literalist interpretation of contracts means, it may be suspected, an increased burden on insurance companies and the courts. Take the example of a professional person. His contract with a company contains a lot of small print about his obligations. On a literalist interpretation he may be in breach of a small print obligation. He considers this to be unfair or misleading so he takes the company to court. He loses. He pays up and he or his insurers sue his solicitor for not advising him of the likely effect of the small print. The Regulations do not help the professional in technical breach: he is a business, not a "consumer". Yet, a good faith interpretation of the contract might well have limited his obligations within bounds that he could reasonably anticipate. That would have meant no claim on the insurers, one action less, and the windfall "loss" to the company foregone without ill effect.

1.15 It may be hoped that this book will help to show that the Unfair Terms Regulations 1994 are in truth a matter of carrying coals to

[17] S.I. 1994, No. 3159.

Newcastle. English principles of fair dealing may indeed have developed piecemeal, and are only recognised piecemeal; but they have continued to exist as a reasonably coherent body of identifiable principle and are by no means beyond rediscovery. In one or two areas social change may have affected the underlying factual assumptions; in others specially fashioned fair-dealing rules are needed to meet new situations. Here, it may be hoped, our own law could acknowledge social change and allow the fair-dealing rules to be developed accordingly. We rather need a latterday Lord Mansfield or two.

Looking for good faith

1.16 English law's principles of fair dealing certainly do not emerge in an easily packaged state. The reason for this is the very nature of our system of precedent itself. This system proceeds, as everyone knows, by development of principle from argued cases. The underlying principle of the judgment, in its surrounding factual background, is then followed, in similar cases, or "distinguished" It is no doubt a good system. It is capable of changing, as circumstances change. Further, a system of precedent has the appeal of the Biblical parables—it enables one to see an abstraction not purely as an abstraction, but in the factual setting which gave rise to it. Continental lawyers complain, it is said, that our judgments are ridiculously discursive. Discursiveness, within reason, is a good thing. We are enabled to know not only what principle has been established, but to a large extent, why. We can envisage the problem in a human way, and follow the probable course of the judge's reaction to the fact-situation before him or her. This helps us to understand the principle, in its application to the facts. A code, even a simple, well-drafted, code, like the Code Civil, the Sale of Goods Act 1893, or the Law of Property Act 1925, is an abstract affair, by comparison.

1.17 It has been said that a system of precedent has the illustrative appeal of the Biblical parables. It can on occasion begin to have something of their ambiguity also. We have frequently enshrined, as authorities for a particular proposition, a number of cases which go back to the period when the doctrine of contract was in the making, namely the eighteenth and early nineteenth century, and earlier still in the case of contracts for the sale of land. This is fine, but we need to remember the social conditions in which the cases were set—which were of course too well known in their day to need explaining, but are now all too easily forgotten. A system whereby we derive the ratio or principle from the particular case does presuppose a reasonably well-informed attempt to put oneself into the shoes of an eighteenth or early nineteenth century judge, where necessary, and into the prevailing social conditions.

1.18 If we do not remember, for example, that a man who did not obtain a warranty from a horse dealer was either a fool, or someone who everyone knew had paid a considerably lower price simply *because* he was taking an appreciable risk, we cannot properly understand an everyday dealing which was as common as the purchase of secondhand cars is nowadays. We are liable then to make mistakes about the principle inherent in the cases. An example of the blind application of a precedent which depended on social conditions of the time is the statement which one finds in textbooks on the law of fitness for purpose of furnished/unfurnished accommodation: a sort of legal magic is accorded, it would seem, to the presence of furniture, while what was probably the true ratio of these cases, in their own period, passes unnoticed. The authors of such books are not to be criticised: we are all guilty of such things. It is likely the true *ratio* was that in such cases there was an implicit—and reasonable—reliance on the landlord to draw attention to any physical defects. This implicit reliance was allowed its due weight. Implicit reliance, or reasonable expectation, is central to the English law of fair dealing or good faith.

1.19 Again, an early precedent may depend on some other aspect of the body of law of the time. It can happen that a general statement may not have been meant to be taken as a wholly general statement, but as a statement applied in its legal context. That context changes; yet the earlier precedent begins to be applied blindly, without regard for the principle behind it. An example of this is probably the law as it is conceived to be regarding rescission of a contract for the sale of land for innocent misrepresentation after the contract has been executed. The rule is believed to be that this is impossible, unless there was fraud in the sense of dishonesty on the part of the vendor, or a total or near-total failure of consideration. No-one is quite sure why this should be an inflexible rule, and it seems thoroughly unfair if a defect is discovered after completion which could not be discovered before by reasonable investigation; but the conventional advice is that it is inflexible. The rule derives primarily from dicta of two members of the House of Lords in *Wilde v. Gibson*[18] in 1848, and from other general-sounding statements in later cases. It appears on analysis that all these earlier cases were focusing on particular aspects of the facts which rendered rescission inappropriate; they were not in fact enunciating any general rule about what should happen after completion in all cases.[19] There is thus no reason in principle now why a mistake *which can only be discovered after completion* should be any different from a mistake discovered after contract and before completion. The inappropriate reliance on precedents with insufficient guidance about the principles involved has led us astray. We have not appreciated the principles which lay behind the law on rescission for misrepresentation or for breach of the fair-dealing duty of candour and accuracy, as it has been labelled in this book. This is a duty to avoid half-truths and misleading words or conduct.

1.20 English law, as is evident, is not much about general principles; we do not, as the French do, start with elegant statements of principle and work out the law from these. Nonetheless, we ought not to avoid stating—elegantly or otherwise—those principles whereby fair

[18] (1848) 1 H.L.C. 605; 9 E.R. 897.

[19] See Chap. 16, Rescission of Executed Sales for a fuller explanation of this.

dealing terms are implied in the decided cases. We need to put back the principle into precedent in this area; or maybe one should say, draw out the principle from the precedents. Precedent ought not to mean either blind adherence to the factual basis of an older case without appreciation of the underlying principle, nor yet the length of a judge's foot, or in modern parlance, his personal view of "the merits" or, to put it colloquially, "how it grabs the court". The latter in particular means lengthier hearings, more expense to litigants, and more uncertainty as to what the law really is. Judicial discretions—formal or informal—lengthen hearing times. The near-irrelevant might, just might, be grist to the discretion-mill.

1.21 As is well known, the House of Lords in a leading case on implied terms, *Liverpool City Council v. Irwin*,[20] held that a term was to be implied that the landlord was to take reasonable care to keep the staircase and means of access to the flats in the block concerned in reasonable repair and usability. Lord Wilberforce referred to the distinction drawn by the House of Lords in *Lister v Romford Ice and Cold Storage Co Ltd*[21] between (1) a search for an implied term such as might be necessary to give "business efficacy" to the particular contract and (2) "a search, based on wider considerations, for such a term *as the nature of the contract might call for*, or *as a legal incident of this kind of contract*." He therefore held that a reasonable obligation on the part of the landlord to maintain the common parts was placed upon the landlord by "the nature of the contract, and the circumstances"—in other words, an implied term of the second type he referred to. And there we are. No further guidance is given by him. Lord Cross, agreeing with Lord Wilberforce, does not give us much guidance either. He said[22]:

> "When it implies a term in a contract the court is sometimes laying down a general rule that in all contracts of a certain type—sale of goods, master and servant, landlord and tenant and so on—some provision is to be implied unless the parties have expressly excluded it. In deciding whether or not to lay down such a prima facie rule the court will naturally ask itself whether in the general run of such cases the term in question would be one which it would be reasonable to insert. Sometimes, however, there is no question of laying down any prima facie rule applicable to all cases of a defined type but what the court is being asked to do is to rectify a particular—often a very detailed—contract by inserting in it a term which the parties have not expressed. Here it is not enough for the court to say that the suggested term is a reasonable one the presence of which would make the contract a better or fairer one; it must be able to say that the insertion of the term is necessary to give . . . "business efficacy" to the contract . . ."

1.22 Lord Salmon did not advert to the distinction between the two types of implied term. Lord Edmund-Davies accepted the submission of the

[20] [1977] A.C. 239.
[21] [1957] A.C. 555.
[22] *ibid*. at 257.

tenants' counsel that the obligation was placed on the landlord in all lettings of multi-storey premises such as those concerned. There was no further exegesis. Nobody looked further back, as far as can be seen, than the decision in *Lister v. Romford Ice and Cold Storage Ltd.*[23] The passage relied on in that case was from the speech of Lord Simonds[24]:

> "For the real question becomes, not what terms can be implied in a contract between two individuals who are assumed to be making a bargain in regard to a particular transaction or course of business; we have to take a wider view, for we are concerned with a general question, which, if not correctly described as a question of status, yet can only be answered by considering the relation in which the drivers of motor vehicles and their employers generally stand to each other. Just as the duty of care, rightly regarded as a contractual obligation, is imposed on the servant, or the duty not to disclose confidential information . . . or the duty not to betray secret processes . . . just so the question must be asked and answered whether in the world in which we live today it is a necessary condition of the relation of master and man that the master should, to use a broad colloquialism, look after the whole matter of insurance . . ."

It is all very puzzling. How does Lord Simonds "necessary condition of the relationship" turn into Lord Cross's term which it would be "reasonable to insert" in the general run of cases? And can one really be sure that the implied term they did uphold in the case was actually "necessary" in the business efficacy/officious bystander sense: it has justly been said on occasions that it would not seem so. How do we recognise Lord Cross' "contracts of a certain type" and how do we recognise what their implied terms are or ought to be? Why should it matter all that whether the contract is "of the nature of" master and servant, or landlord and tenant, or of some other nature? Has "status" any real relevance today? Anyway, we have all sorts of new "natures" of contract now: why should a type of contractual relationship be left out in the cold from the point of view of implied terms simply because it is not one of the old contractual or "status" relationships?

1.23 In the field of real property law there are fairly frequently to be found statements such as "equity will not permit . . ." or "equity presumes . . ." or "a vendor may not . . ." Can equity have only presumed/ permitted that which was "called for" by "the nature of the contract" and if so, how did it first come to be decided that the nature of the contract did call for it? Might it not be a rather circular process? "These are implied where the nature of the contract calls for it." "And when is that?" "It is when the nature of the contract calls for it." It may seem in fact that the nature of the contract could only be said to call for an implied term if you presuppose a basic standard of fair dealing. Is fair dealing therefore the key?

One can be forgiven for thinking that land law, where one finds

[23] [1957] A.C. 555.
[24] *ibid.*, at 576.

fair dealing terms, is perhaps a law unto itself; a kind of backwater where strange historical implied terms were allowed to roam as a species of licensed dinosaur, permitted to range free within the bounds of their native reservation, so long as they do not presume to venture out. "It is different with land law", is a thread one finds in some of the cases. Yet there has always been the fact, acknowledged by modern textbooks in a general way, that in the field of sale of goods, there had been implied terms, apparently alive and flourishing in the everyday mercantile world, as late as the last decade of the nineteenth century. These were codified by the Sale of Goods Act 1893. Once codified, this background was eventually more or less forgotten. If the Act's implied terms have ever been "called for by the nature of the contract" in sales of goods, then it must be in some sense that by no means leaps out at the reader.

1.24 The cases on pre-Sale of Goods Act implied terms yield some interesting information. Terms appeared to be implied not merely in the case of goods, but occasionally in the case of intellectual property rights also: no-one seemed to bother to distinguish particularly. Further, as the nineteenth century progressed, the courts, Common Law courts, let us remember, appeared to be ready to imply terms with remarkable facility. Since the nature of sales of goods was changing, it was hardly possible to point to an old historical "status" requirement of any implied term. Certainly no-one seems to have done this. There does not seem to have been any overall "nature" attributed to sales of goods. Nor did the courts simply decide what was "reasonable"; or at least, they certainly did not describe what they were doing in that way. Different categories or "natures" of sale were approached differently. Sometimes, the court would simply consider the meaning of a word: its primary meaning, and its underlying implications. If the word had in it a secondary implication, reasonably understood, a term was implied accordingly. More often, they would consider the circumstances of the sale, and make implications from these. In the nineteenth century, sales of goods were becoming commercialised: while once most sales had been in markets overt, where title passed anyway, by then a more sophisticated retail trade was developing. The courts implied terms about this new retail trade. The first such was that a vendor who was in possession of the goods and sold them thus, without disclaimer of ownership, was *making a statement by conduct*: he "sold as his own" and thereby warranted title. This warranty could be displaced by circumstances—you would be a fool to expect a warranty of title from a sheriff, or a pawnbroker. But otherwise, it was a general rule. The idea of a statement by conduct is rarely met nowadays; yet perhaps it should be revived as a more than theoretical possibility. There is a philosophical article which makes the point that a man with a bicycle carrying a bucket, a long ladder and a piece of chamois leather probably does not need to make a verbal statement to the effect that he is a window cleaner! He is making a statement by conduct and silence.

1.25 Then again, the courts thought it was clearly necessary for a buyer to examine the goods where possible. He should not expect a premium for his laziness. But where the buyer *could not* examine the goods, whether because they had yet to be manufactured for his purposes, or because of inaccessibility, then certain terms were often implied: that the goods should be whatever they were said to be—a ship should be something you could reasonably describe as a ship, for example; that if a vendor undertook to have something manufactured for a particular purpose specified by the buyer, the thing should be reasonably fit for the purpose; but if the buyer gave his own detailed specifications (relied on his own skill and judgment), then it only had to correspond to those. The buyer was taking on himself the risk of suitability for the purpose in the latter case.

1.26 An attempt has been made in this book to draw out the principles whereby terms are implied as incidents of sale contracts, and to show that, in fact, there is little difference in the operation of these principles as between the different categories of sales. Insurance sales are a special case, but this is because of the circumstances in which insurance is taken out, rather than because they are a separate, different category of sale. The balance shifts between vendor and purchaser in the different types of sale mainly by reason of the relative ease or difficulty the buyer has in protecting himself. Where he cannot be expected to find out the necessary points by doing his homework, using due diligence, making normal inquiries, etc., the vendor's conduct is scrutinised more carefully. A reasonable expectation by the purchaser of fair dealing by the vendor shifts easily into a purchaser's *right* to fair-dealing by the vendor. The vendor's silence can sometimes be perilous if he has the means of knowing of a defect, and the buyer has not. Moreover, what he does say will be easily construed as an invitation to the buyer to rely on him, as we shall see. There is a full duty of disclosure in insurance sales because the seller, in that case, is obliged to rely on the buyer, and has virtually no access himself to *any* of the relevant information. In other cases the duty of disclosure is limited, and becomes what has been called the duty of candour and the duty of accuracy: the duty to avoid misleading omissions, the duty to express accurately that which you know, either if asked by the buyer, or sometimes spontaneously, whether or not asked, if the buyer has no means of finding it out for himself.

1.27 Nor is the vendor's duty to the buyer (or the buyer's to the vendor where this applies) always at an end after the sale. When the vendor retains some power to influence what has been sold: for example, a landlord who retains the freehold, a seller who retains the right to approve buildings, etc. or who retains next-door land: these after-sale relationships have been held to be subject to various implied terms, reflecting in different ways the original main purpose of the contract or clause in question.

Perhaps the vendor wants to exclude the fair-dealing terms. This is not so easy a task as might be supposed. He can do it, but the job of excluding *must itself be done fairly*. If he does so by means of a lot of ambiguous small print, he is taking a legal risk. If on the other hand he points out the exclusion in reasonably clear terms, likely to be understood by the actual purchaser that he has ("know your purchaser" is another fair-dealing rule) then he is safe legally, but perhaps at risk commercially. "I will sell you this land or goods (or pension), but I have to tell you it will be subject to important and unimportant incidents, which may more or less severely affect your ability to use it for the purpose we both intend you to use it for" will tend to have a diminishing effect on the price. And quite right too.

1.28 As has been said, the duty is a mutual one. Thus, especially in the later chapters of this book, the expressions the "seller or defining party" on the one hand, and the "buyer or inquiring party" on the other, will sometimes be found. In this way, in insurance cases and surety cases, the buyer is the one with the good faith duty, not the seller: it is the seller who has to rely (to a lesser extent in surety cases where there is a healthy duty of inquiry on him as to what he can reasonably be expected to find out) on the buyer for information about the terms which affect the risk: that is, both the nature of the risk and how likely the risk is to crop up—both equally important. The party *who must inquire* is the party who is owed the duty in general; the other party, usually the seller, is the one *who describes or defines what it is he is parting with.*

Notice

The counterpart of good faith

1.29 It may seem surprising that in a book about implied terms of good faith/fair dealing there is a chapter on Knowledge and Notice, and frequent mention of the buyer's duty of due diligence. The buyer's duty of due diligence has considerable importance in the proper working of good faith principles. It is an essential counterpart, without which good faith would have developed, perhaps, as the woolly sort of doctrine of some people's imaginings. The whole point about fair-dealing principles is that they are based on a doctrine of objectively reasonable expectations. The buyer or inquiring party will expect fair dealing: candour and accuracy in what is said, and in certain circumstances, spontaneous disclosure. Conversely, the seller or defining party will not expect (unless specifically asked) to have a duty to tell the buyer about what he could perfectly well find out for himself by making reasonable and normal pre-contractual investigations. Where the buyer fails to make such investigations, or fails to follow up facts which are on their face puzzling or inconsistent, he is quite simply deemed to have thought to himself, "Well, I won't bother to investigate, because I shall simply take the risk of whatever the investigations would have revealed." Notice is simply the doctrine of deemed knowledge of such matters. The scope of the underlying duty, however, needs to be examined if the scope of good faith is to be seen accurately: there is a tension between the two, but the territory of the two counterpart principles is quite carefully mapped out.

CHAPTER 2

THE LEGAL NATURE OF THE DUTY OF GOOD FAITH?

"The rationale of the rule imposing a duty of utmost good faith on the insured is that matters material to the risk are generally speaking peculiarly within his knowledge. In so far as matters are peculiarly within the insurer's knowledge, as in Lord Mansfield's example of the arrived ship, principle and fairness requires the imposition of a similar duty on the insurer. Indeed, it is difficult to imagine a more retrograde step, subversive of the standing of our insurance law and our insurance markets, than a ruling today that the great judge erred in Carter v Boehm, 3 Burr. 1905 in stating that the principle of good faith rests on both parties . . ."[1]

"Dans chaque contrat l'on doit distinguer trois choses: celles qui sont de l'essence du contrat, celles qui sont seulement de sa nature, et celles qui sont purement accidentelles. 6. Les choses qui sont de l'essence du contrat, sont celles sans lesquelles ce contrat ne peut subsister; faute de l'une de ces choses, ou il n'y'a pas du tout de contrat, ou c'est une autre espèce du contrat.

Par exemple, il est de l'essence du contrat de vente qu'il y ait une chose qui soit vendue."

"Les choses qui sont seulement de la nature du contrat sont celles qui, sans être de l'essence du contrat, en font partie quoique les parties contractantes ne s'en point expliquées; en un mot les choses qui sont sous-entendues par la loi, l'usage, etc.

Ces choses tiennent un milieu entre les choses qui sont de l'essence du contrat, et celles qui sont accidentelles au contrat; et elles diffèrent des unes et des autres. Elles diffèrent des choses qui sont de l'essence du contrat, en ce que le contrat peut subsister sans elles; et qu'elles peuvent être exclues du contrat par la convention des parties; et elles diffèrent des choses accidentelles au contrat, en ce qu'elles font partie du contrat sans avoir été expressément convenues . . ."[2]

[1] Steyn J. at first instance in *Banque Keyser v. Skandia* [1990] 1 Q.B. 665 at 701.
[2] Pothier, *Traité des Obligations* (1835 ed.) Part I, Chap. I s.5.

SCOPE OF THE DUTY

What kind of a duty is it?

2.01 So, we have the rationale of the duty. Steyn J. was talking only about insurance contracts; but the duty of fair dealing/good faith is properly seen as more pervasive than that—as indeed Lord Mansfield saw it. But what kind of a duty is it? How is it to be classified? The question has arisen mainly in the context of the duty of good faith in insurance contracts. The courts have over the years expressed a number of somewhat tentative views: essentially the contest has been between

(1) an implied term of the contract;
(2) a condition precedent to liability under the contract; or
(3) simply a body of rules, arising outside the contract, imposed originally by the courts of equity, to prevent imposition.

Towards the end of the last century the discussion seems to have been differently structured: there were those who thought the duty arose because its breach was a species of fraud ("legal" or "equitable" fraud—cp note the expression "a fraud on the power"—as opposed to "moral" fraud which actually connoted dishonesty); and those who thought it arose contractually in some sense, though not a sense which seems to have been defined in much detail.[3] "Legal" fraud suffered some ups and downs in esteem in legal circles, perhaps losing respectability gradually over the years but retaining some adherents until it received its final *coup de grace* (as an expression: the substance described remained[4]) in the House of Lords decision in *Derry v. Peek*.[5]

Breach of duty of disclosure *per se* does not sound in damages

2.02 It can at all events be said that a breach of the duty of disclosure, in its full-blown insurance form, whatever its nature, does not *per se* and in the absence of statute[6] give rise to a direct right in damages if breached. This has been held by the House of Lords in *Banque Financière v. Westgate* (formerly *Banque Keyser v. Scandia*).[7]

Is it an implied term (but not sounding in damages *per se*)?

2.03 In the Court of Appeal in *Banque Keyser v. Scandia*[8] Slade L.J., giving the judgment of the court, gave what Lord Templeman in the House

[3] See the Appendix to this chapter.
[4] See *Low v. Bouverie* [1891] 3 Ch. 82.
[5] (1889) 14 App. Cas. 337.
[6] See the Law of Property (Miscellaneous Provisions) Act 1989 abolishing the good-faith look alike Rule in *Bain v. Fothergill*; and the Misrepresentation Act 1967.
[7] [1990] 2 A.C. 249.
[8] [1990] 1 Q.B. 665 at 727.

of Lords called "cogent reasons" for this. The interesting judgment of Slade L.J. merits further study if one is searching for an analysis of the duty. The judgment was naturally directed to the damages question which was before the court. The proper classification of the duty of disclosure was looked at in that context alone. Logically, the fact that the duty does not give rise to a right in damages is separate from the related, but distinct question whether it can give rise to an implied term of the contract, a condition precedent to the contract, or is simply a rule made by the court. While Slade L.J.'s judgment does appear to make general statements about the nature of the duty, it does not in fact offer cogent reasons for a *further conclusion* (not in fact required or reached) that the duty of good faith may not operate as an implied term of a special sort (albeit one which does not sound in damages).

2.05 Slade L.J. dealt in turn with the arguments which had been put up by counsel for an implied term sounding in damages. These were:

(1) The principle applied by Steyn J. in the court below—which was simply *ubi jus, ibi remedium*—something of a last resort, no doubt. Steyn J. had not, however, regarded the duty of good faith as an implied term of a contract, at all events *in the sense which the banks had sought to do this*, nor a fiduciary duty, nor a tortious one, but simply part of a "body of rules". Thus, Slade L.J. found it difficult to see how as a matter of legal analysis the breach of the term could sound in damages. This approach could be thought somewhat question-begging, although logical enough within its confines: damages only arise in contract, fiduciary relationships, or tort; this is not contract, a fiduciary relationship or tort, therefore no damages are allowed.

(2) The substitute argument before the Court of Appeal, that the duty was an implied term of all contracts of insurance, supported by the wording of section 17 of the Marine Insurance Act 1906.[9] Slade L.J. thought simply that the wording of section 17 did not on its true construction lead to that conclusion, since it made no mention of damages but did mention the right to avoid the contract. The only comment one may make on this is that both the argument and the decision dealing with it perhaps exemplify the demerits of the over-technical arguments on construction of deeds and statutes which are common in courts nowadays. Elegant linguistic arguments may be constructed, and in turn rejected by the court on similarly elegant, linguistic grounds, without scratching the surface of the real issue.

(3) The argument based on the old practice prior to 1936 whereby the insurer had a right to an affidavit disclosing the ship's papers, once an action making a claim under the policy had been commenced. It had been said by Hirst J. in *Black King Shipping Corporation v. Massie*[10] that this practice (which was

[9] The principles apply outside pure marine insurance also: ***London Assurance v. Mansel*** (1879) 11 Ch. D. 363.

[10] [1985] 1 Lloyd's Rep. 437 at 511.

obviously necessary at a time when automatic discovery in an action was not available) was clearly founded on a general duty of the utmost good faith in insurance contracts. Slade L.J. simply said of the submission of counsel built on the above (that in all cases the duty of the utmost good faith is based on such an implied term):

"We did not find this line of argument compelling. It may be that on the particular facts of some cases (though by no means necessarily all) the duty of post-contractual disclosure can be said to arise under the terms of the preceding contract. However, it by no means follows that the duty of pre-contractual disclosure arises under the contract rather than the general law."[11]

2.06 This part of Slade L.J.'s judgment probably deals with Hirst J.'s judgment in a less than satisfactory manner: the ships' papers cases were said by Hirst J. to have been based on the general duty of good faith owed in insurance cases; which duty was of course hardly limited to post-contractual disclosure. This point was thus simply side-stepped by the court.

The fourth argument, which related only to the importance of a term sounding in damages, is omitted here.

(5) The argument (which is no doubt correct as far as it goes) that the duty of disclosure was simply an example of a term implied by the general law as an incident in contracts of this kind.[12]

This argument was rejected by Slade L.J. by the following route: If he thought it was an implied term, he could see no reason in principle why it should not sound in damages, but he thought "the weight of authority and principle" was against it being an implied term. Thus, Slade L.J. in reality relied heavily on certain earlier decisions he mentioned as constituting this "weight of authority and principle". These were:

(a) Lord Esher in his dissenting judgment in the Court of Appeal in *Blackburn, Low v. Vigors*[13] who had thought it was a condition precedent to the right of the assured to insist on the performance of the contract.

(b) The House of Lords in that case, which had possibly or probably endorsed Lord Esher's view.

(c) In *Merchants and Manufacturers Insurance Co Ltd v. Hunt*[14] Luxmoore L.J. (with whom Scott L.J. agreed), who considered that in the case of positive misrepresentation the right to avoid a contract, whether of insurance or not, depends not on any implied term of the contract but arises by reason of the jurisdiction originally exercised by the courts of equity to prevent imposition.

[11] [1990] 1 Q.B. 665 at 777.

[12] See *Lister v. Romford Ice and Cold Storage Co Ltd* [1957] A.C. 555.

[13] (1886) 17 Q.B.D. 553.

[14] [1941] 1 K.B. 295.

(d) the dictum of Lord Atkin in *Bell v. Lever Brothers*[15] which supports the view that the duty arises otherwise than out of contract. He had said " . . . In such cases [contracts of the utmost good faith] the duty [of good faith] does not arise out of contract; the duty of a person proposing an insurance arises before a contract is made, so of an intending partner."

(e) *March Cabaret Club & Casino Ltd v. London Assurance*[16] in which May J. had said: "in my judgment the duty to disclose is not based upon an implied term in the contract of insurance at all; it arises outside the contract."

2.07 Slade L.J. also made some points in regard to the damages claim:

(i) that it would be difficult to award damages in cases where the actual insurer would not have been induced, though the prudent one would.[17]

(ii) that the duty to disclose material facts is an absolute one.

> "It attaches with equal force whether the failure is attributable to 'fraud, carelessness, inadvertence, indifference, mistake, error of judgment or even to [the] failure to appreciate its materiality': see *E.R. Hardy Ivamy, General Principles of Insurance Law*, 5th ed. (1986) p. 156 and the cases there cited. A decision that the breach of such an obligation in every case and by itself constituted a tort if it caused damage could give rise to great potential hardship to insurers and even more, perhaps, to insured persons".[18]

It does seem that the last points are limited to the damages question and do not shed any light on the wider question of the nature of the duty of good faith/disclosure.

The cases relied on above, which arguably do have some bearing on the wider question have a weakness: the relevant parts of the judgments comprise for the most part more or less cursory statements: they do not condescend to much in the way of reasoning to support the belief that the duty was not an implied term in some sense. Thus, the "weight of authority" has on examination more than a flavour of the "What I tell you three times is true" approach.[19] See the Appendix to this chapter for a fuller note of the cases.

Analysis

2.08 It seems, with respect to Slade L.J., that the "weight of authority" leans towards the duty being, when required, an implied term of the contract of *some kind*. It is not clear that the distinctions adverted to

[15] [1932] A.C. 161 at 227.

[16] [1975] 1 Lloyd's Rep. 169.

[17] See now the House of Lords' decision in *Panatlantic Insurance v. Pine Top Insurance* [1995] 1 A.C. 501, and the Court of Appeal in *St Paul Insurance v. McConnell* [1996] 2 All E.R. 96.

[18] [1990] 1 Q.B. 665 at 781.

[19] Lewis Carroll, *Hunting of the Snark*.

in the above cases are especially helpful in the search for the true nature of the duty of good faith/disclosure.

The distinction between matters arising "outside the contract" and "inside the contract"

2.09 This is remarkably superficial. After all, an implied term which arises by reason of a custom in the trade, for example, arises "outside the contract" yet is incorporated in the contract so as to become "inside the contract". Why should not a duty of disclosure or good faith behave likewise?

The distinction between matters arising before the contract and after the contract

2.10 This distinction suffers from the same problems as that in paragraph 2.09. Where the "factual matrix" is taken into account in construing a term of the contract, the factual matrix which existed before the contract is being given effect after the contract is made, in interpreting it. Where a purchaser of land purchases land in its actual state and condition, it is the actual state and condition just before the contract which is referred to. In a sense, all contractual terms are based on matters which "arise before the contract": they are negotiated and/or inspected before the point of time when formal agreement is reached.

The supposed distinction between terms imposed originally by the courts of Equity to prevent oppression, and other terms

2.11 This seems to fly in the face of history. Lord Mansfield was a common lawyer: his expounding of the duty of disclosure in the great common law case of *Carter v. Boehm*[20] had nothing to do with the jurisdiction exercised by the Courts of Equity. The good faith principles affecting sales of goods which came to be codified in the Sale of Goods Act 1893 were developed in Common Law and in effect, commercial courts. No doubt the jurisdiction of Equity to prevent "surprise" or oppression of various sorts will have operated in parallel. This was especially the case in sales such as sales of land, which a seller might think to be a candidate for equity's special remedy of compensation with specific performance of contracts which might prove to be slightly broken, the compensation being awarded to the purchaser where appropriate to make up to him for lesser breaches. The case of dealings with the vulnerable is another, somewhat special case.

2.12 The more natural conclusion, surely, is that both courts were applying similar principles. Indeed, it has been suggested elsewhere that the tendency to diminish the role of good faith, and to describe it as all part of what has, in this book, been labelled "Equity's supposed

[20] (1766), noted in the Appendix to Chap. 4, Insurance and Surety Transactions.

discretionary fudge"[21] was something which started for the first time at the end of the last century, and may have had rather more to do with a desire to facilitate the new fashion for literalism by pushing older doctrines to one side than with a real desire to explain the basis on which the older doctrines were operated. If this is right, to label the duty "equitable" tells us nothing useful about its nature. Further, it may be said that the label is itself something of a part-disclosure, as tending to obscure the real participation in and contribution to the doctrine made by the Common Law courts. Meanwhile, we revert to Slade L.J.'s judgment.

The distinction between an implied term, sounding in damages, and a condition precedent to liability, which does not sound in damages

2.13 The problem about this distinction is that it is not a true one. Not even all ordinary express terms of contracts do sound in damages: some do and some do not. (And conditions precedent are in fact terms of the contract, not something popping up "from outside".) Those terms which do not sound in damages are normally what one might call administrative terms or "machinery", in contrast to the substantive terms of the contractual promise. They are there, for example, to elucidate the boundaries of the contractual promises made. Conditions precedent or subsequent are probably a particular sub-set of these administrative terms. At the risk of being obvious, these are terms which add an if-content; that is, they delimit by means of a contingency which is normally not in the control of the parties themselves. A condition precedent prevents the contract or a part of it ever coming into being in certain circumstances, but not in others: a condition subsequent similarly terminates the continued existence of the contract in whole or in part. Their purpose is, in a sense, solely to unmake the contract; they are an inbuilt contractual time bomb, with the trigger held by people or forces outside the contract. Nonetheless, they have contractual force: they are effective to destroy the contract because it has been agreed that should be done in those circumstances. They are thus one kind of delimiting term in a contract. Parcels clauses in a conveyance or agreement for the sale of land are another, although they are also the kind of term which does sound in damages. They are two sides of a coin. If the description or measurement includes Blackacre but does not include Whiteacre, you know what you are and are not entitled to receive. The question of damages only arises if you do not receive Blackacre; but this does not mean the clause has not an administrative sense, in which you learn that the contract does not include Whiteacre, also.

Fair-dealing duty: a contractual measuring device

2.14 Presumptions of fair dealing, together with other administrative clauses, are perhaps best seen as the contract's measuring devices.

[21] See further Chap. 5, Sale of Land.

They set bounds, they have the potential to "destroy" the areas of non-contract as well as to define the areas of contract. "Destroy" is not however the accurate description of what they do; outside the area in which the contract operates there is simply no contract. It is not that anything has been destroyed, it never existed in that place.

An analogy, though with a difference, may be found in rent review clauses—another type of administrative term. The parties have agreed that a rent increase should take place at stated intervals. However, they have agreed it on the footing or basis that certain machinery be operated, and certain assumptions (for example, willing vendor and purchaser, improvements to be disregarded, etc. be made). The failure to operate the machinery may "destroy" the landlord's right to an increased rent, but it is not properly speaking "destroying" any part of "the contract", merely putting up a flag saying, "This contract does not operate in this territory".

And so it is with the implied machinery of good faith. Where it is not normal or reasonable for buyer or seller to check on what he is getting, and he has to rely on the other party, his reasonable expectations on matters as to which he has so relied are as much a part of the contract as the expressed terms. Thus, the presumption of fair dealing has contractual effect in two distinct ways:

(i) *it is used to interpret contractual provisions*; and
(ii) *it is used to imply a term where there is no appropriate existing contractual provision at all.*

Very few people would willingly contract on the footing that important matters they cannot discover are not disclosed to them, at all events without a substantial reduction in price for the risk they are shouldering. Good faith rules are the parties' presumed alter egos.

Slade L.J.'s distinction between a "rule of law" or "an incident of certain types of contract" on the one hand and an implied term of the contract on the other

2.15 This is probably an unnecessary distinction. It is almost certainly merely a matter of shifting around labels rather than a matter of substance. If one labels "implied term" something which excludes for example the duty of good faith/disclosure, then that is what one has done. It would be a delusion to suppose anything more than an elective labelling exercise has taken place. If the presumption of good faith/disclosure in fact has contractual force, whether as an underlying rule of construction or where necessary as an implied term, then it seems more sensible to accept that it does. See for example, the judgment of Steyn J. in the *Banque Keyser* case at first instance.[22] He said:

> "The plaintiffs cited a number of decisions in which courts have referred to the implied obligation or duty of an insured to make a fair disclosure. These observations were not made in the context of the issue now under consideration, and do not assist in decid-

[22] *Banque Keyser SA v. Skandia* [1990] 1 Q.B. 665 at 702.

ing the concrete issue before me. After all, it is often said that a term is implied in a contract when in truth a positive rule of contract law is applied because of the category in which a particular contract falls."

Later, again, reference having been made to the *Black King*[23] case, a decision of Hirst J. referred to above, Steyn J. said:

> "In my respectful view the actual decision in that case is concerned with the scope of the duty of the utmost good faith on special facts, and not with the question whether it is a rule of positive law, *or an implied term in the sense of a term derivable from the terms of the particular contract, read in the light of the subject matter and contextual scene.* In my respectful view the body of rules, which are described as the uberrima fides principle, are rules of law developed by the judges. The relevant duties apply before the contract comes into existence, and they apply to every contract of insurance. In my judgment it is incorrect to categorise them as implied terms, *in the sense in which the plaintiffs seek to do so.*"[24]

Not implied terms in the sense of a term derivable from the terms of a particular contract . . .

2.16 It is interesting that Steyn J. (as he then was) a judge deserving the utmost respect, has in fact drawn back from simply saying "They are not implied terms." He has hedged his statement: they are not implied terms in the sense *of a term derivable from the terms of the particular contract, read in the light of the subject matter and contextual scene*; they are not implied terms in the sense the plaintiffs seek. He seems to leave open the possibility that they might be some other kind of implied term. He may well have been right to do so.

More about the duty of fair dealing

2.17 The implied duty, or presumption, of fair dealing, then, is in some cases, such as insurance and some surety cases, a duty to give information where appropriate. This duty is crucial at the formation of the contract. It arises in insurance cases where one intending party is obliged to rely on the good faith or fair dealing of the other party for most information relevant to the contract. In the case of ordinary sales such as sales of land, as will be seen, it arises because the buyer, though not needing to rely on the seller to quite such an extent, is nevertheless in a relatively disadvantaged position as regards information. Thus, the duty is more limited than in insurance sales; it is a duty to be candid (for example, avoiding misleading half-truths)

[23] [1985] 1 Lloyd's Rep. 437.
[24] Italics supplied.

and to be accurate (not trying to tie buyers up in fuzzily worded conditions).

A judge-made presumption: also a contractual modifier and an implied term of a special sort

2.18 It would be right no doubt to call the duty a judge-made presumption, but it can also operate to supplement the contract, and thus may also be an implied term of a special sort. One may compare *the duty to mitigate*, which operates in the damages field in a very similar way, and indeed, one may speculate about possible good faith origins for that duty. It modifies and supplements the effect of a contract.

The duty has effect only when the contract is made

2.19 There is no duty to negotiate in good faith, unless and until a contract comes about: the duty "bites" when the contract is made.[25] Something rather like a contractual Judgment Day occurs at this point, exposing the seller's evasions, pregnant half-truths and the like, and penalising him for failing in his duty of good faith by deeming the contractual provisions to have included the duty of good faith. Where the contractual provision have been interpreted in the light of good faith he will sometimes be both in breach of the duty and consequently in breach of the express or implied contractual provisions *of the contract*. If so, the normal remedies will be applied, including damages where appropriate. Subject to that, damages are not the appropriate remedy, since they are seen as the proper compensation for the breach of a promise; while rescission is the only logical remedy for a factor which vitiates one party's consent to the contract.[26]

Some labels

2.20 We shall see later that the duty changes while the contractual relationship continues after the contract is made. It can then best be categorised as a duty, falling on the party who intends to exercise a right affecting the subject matter of the contract, to be loyal to the main purpose of the contract; or to be reasonable in the light of the natural assumptions as to the main purpose of the contract (in the sense of object or *telos*) which would have been made by the other party at the time of the contract. There has been some labelling in this book, with the intention, at least, of helping to clarify rather than confuse, and this later duty is labelled the *Duty of Loyalty*.

The duty which arises at the formation of the contract could no doubt be labelled a duty of disclosure, but since this is traditionally

[25] *cf.* the duty to mitigate which bites when a right to damages has accrued.

[26] It may be that Equity's power to award compensation is properly seen as of relevance here too, but full discussion of this topic is outside the scope of this book.

associated with the very full duty of "spontaneous" or un-asked, disclosure of all "material" facts in insurance cases (and to an extent, surety cases), it has in this book been labelled the twin *Duty of Candour and Accuracy*. This twin duty best describes the duty to give proper information or none at all about what is being sold in contracts outside the area of insurance and surety contracts. It does include a degree of "spontaneous" disclosure, but only in certain particular circumstances. It could no doubt also have been called the Duty not to Mislead[27]: "There is nonetheless a duty not to conduct oneself in such a way as to mislead." This otherwise sensible and descriptive label has been eschewed simply because it is wider than is called for by good faith: one can mislead while being fully fraudulent, one can mislead through lack of outside research before speaking and one can mislead (though it is not an entirely easy use of language) while being reasonably unaware of the facts which make what one is saying untrue. None of these is normally a breach of good faith, as will be seen.

Good faith—an overview of conclusions to be found in this book

2.21

(1) The duty of good faith or fair dealing as it applies in the formation of contracts of sale is normally a duty of candour and accuracy. The duty is a presumption of law (like the duty to mitigate damages). It thus operates both as an obligation in interpreting existing provisions and as an additional implied term where there are no relevant express terms to be interpreted.
(2) It does not operate as regards matters which it would be normal and possible for the buyer to investigate himself.
(3) Its effect may be expressly excluded, but the presumption of good faith, that is the duty of candour and accuracy, apply to the interpretation of any exclusion.
(4) A pre-contractual breach of the duty has no effect unless a contract is made. The effect on the parties only occurs when a contract is made.
(5) After the formation of the contract the application of good faith is broadly limited to a presumption of loyalty to the paramount or characteristic purpose of the contract. This may be applied in interpreting contractual provisions or implying terms where the seller and buyer remain in an after-sale relationship.
(6) The presumption of good faith may have an indirect effect on a party's entitlement or otherwise to damages for breach of a contract, by means of its interpretative effect on the contractual provisions.
(7) Subject as above, the remedy (apart from statute) for a breach

[27] *cf.* Bingham J. in *The Lutetian* [1982], 2 Lloyd's Rep. 140 (see Appendix to this Chapter) and see section 52 of the Australian Trade Practices Act 1974.

of the duty of good faith is rescission, or where applied, equitable compensation.

THE INFLUENCE OF ARISTOTLE, THOMAS AQUINAS AND THE "NATURAL LAWYERS" ON THE SHAPING OF ENGLISH GOOD-FAITH/FAIR DEALING TERMS

"The Natural Lawyers"

2.22 The reason the good-faith terms work in the way they do lies in their history—in the concept of the essential nature of contract that was current at the time English contract law was formed. The "natural lawyers" on the Continent wrote about the nature of contract. They were influenced by the "Glossators", the medieval jurists who had written commentaries on the Roman legal texts. These Glossators had brought their own philosophical baggage to their task—their reading of Aristotle and Thomas Aquinas.[28]

The "natural lawyers" developed these composite ideas in a practical way, concentrating on what exactly it is we do when we enter into a contract intended to be binding. There were perhaps two central concepts among others:

(1) the idea of "equality in exchange" as a necessary component of consent, and carrying with it the idea of a reasonable degree of equality of knowledge (and thus, sometimes the need for disclosure on the part of the seller or defining party);

(2) linked with it, the idea of a characteristic "end" or paramount purpose of the contract in question. This idea gives bounds to the contract, a permitted area within which it is to operate.

Both these concepts, with other "natural law" ideas such as *caveat emptor*, were taken up and developed by our judges. They worked out a sophisticated, practical system of good-faith/fair-dealing rules.

2.23 As has been noted in the Introduction, the reasons why these have been neglected in this century are a matter of speculation. However, we do not need to be deterred from taking them up again by a feeling that we are regressing thereby into our philosophical past (even assuming this were to be thought a regression). One does not need to subscribe to any particular philisophical school to find some of the natural law ideas seductive and surprisingly easy to understand: for example—the idea that you are pre-supposing a reasonable degree of equal access to knowledge when you agree to buy something; or the

[28] For the way in which the natural lawyers derived their approach ultimately from Aristotle via Thomas Aquinas and the Glossators who commented on the Emperor Justinian's Corpus Juris Civilis, see the interesting and eminently readable account in *Gordley, The Historical Origins of Modern Contract Doctrine* (1991).

idea that if you buy a pair of shoes, say, you are normally buying them for a characteristic "end", that is, to be walked in, whether or not this comes anywhere in the small print. We do not come to buying and selling in a vacuum: we bring to it, in practice if not in theory, our assumptions and the inferences based on our ordinary experience.

2.24 The following "Natural lawyers" from the continent were influential in England[29]:

(1) Grotius, *De Iure Belli et Pacis* (1654), translated into French with commentary by Barbeyrac, 1724.
(2) Pufendorf, *Of the Law of Nature and Nations* (English editions in 1710, 1729, 1749 and in abridged form in 1716) see Simpson, *op. cit.*
(3) Domat. *The Civil Law in its Natural Order together with the Publick Law* (published in translation by William Strahan, with comparative material, 1722 and 1739).
(4) Pothier, *Traité des Obligations*, (published in France in 1761–64, first English edition 1806 by Evans with comment (American edition 1802).
(5) Pothier, *Traité de Contrat de Vente*, published in English, 1839, ed L. S. Cushing, Boston.[30]
(6) Savigny, *System of the Modern Roman Law*. (Vol I translated by W. Holloway, was published in Madras in 1867. Professor Simpson[31] notes that Savigny's influence on English contract law seems to have been limited, perhaps because it came too late.)

Good faith ideas crossed the Channel

2.25 We may expect that the works of the "natural lawyers" which were popular enough in the original to achieve an English edition will have been *read*. They were read, and they were influential. They were meant to be read by ordinary educated people as well as lawyers. The methodical tracing of the natural-law influence on the nineteenth century barristers and judges who shaped contract law is plainly outside the scope of this book. For some relevant philosophical source materials and some reference to the influence of the various concepts, see, if desired, the appendix at the end of this book. For practical purposes, we need only remember that these ancient "natural law" concepts can be discerned, sometimes couched in language strikingly like the natural law original, in some of the late eighteenth and early nineteenth century judgments on good faith topics. Some of these are to be found in the Case Appendices to the various chapters of this book. That the

[29] See generally, *Simpson, "Innovation in Nineteenth Century Contract Law,"* 91 L.Q.R. 247.
[30] See *Simpson, op. cit.* Professor Simpson also notes *inter alia* that Evans also wrote *A Treatise on the Civil Law*, and *A General View of the Decisions of Lord Mansfield in Civil Causes.*
[31] *op. cit.*

ideas are not normally attributed need not cause us concern. It is a feature of English judgments that no need is apparently ever felt to give the attribution of striking phrases. Such phrases as "buying a lawsuit", "a flower in the desert", "a nod or a wink" recur from case to case seemingly as if newly thought up for the occasion; and, for an exposition which follows very closely indeed Pothier's *Traité des Obligations*, but, as is the norm, wholly without attribution, see Lord Diplock's account of primary and secondary obligations in *Photo Productions v. Securicors.*[32]

APPENDIX TO CHAPTER 2: SOME CASES OF INTEREST

***White v. Foljambe* (1805) 11 Ves. 337; 32 E.R. 1118**

2.26 Lord Eldon decided it as being *part of the meaning* or a matter of the description of a contract for the sale of a leasehold with no specific exceptions as to title that the vendor should have a good title.

Note. He obviously considered the indirect effect of the breach of good faith on the contractual terms of a contract might give a right to damages: he gave an example of a contract to sell the unencumbered freehold where the vendors were assignees, and did not have it in their power to do so. He envisaged the parties going to Law, where damages could be awarded.

***Deverell v. Lord Bolton* (1812) 18 Ves. Jun. 505; 34 E.R. 409**

2.27 The question was whether the vendor of a reversionary lease of a house in Upper Brook Street had to show good title. (It had been argued that "the probability of quiet enjoyment under it is exceedingly great; and it is also to be taken into consideration, that a marketable title to a house at the west end of the town is very seldom to be obtained."

Lord Eldon expressed the vendor's obligation in terms of his duty to describe accurately.

"The proposition, that the vendor of a leasehold interest cannot produce his lessor's title, is not to be represented as universally true. I know instances to the contrary. The vendor ought, therefore, where he sells with that restriction, to describe that it is the interest he has that is to be sold . . .

"when the Defendant's agent purchased under this particular without a fresh authority, no act done by him, unsanctioned by previous authority or subsequent approbation, can bind the Defendant either in Law or Equity . . ."

***Souter v. Drake* (1834) 5 B. & Ad. 991; 110 E.R. 1058**

2.28 Lord Denman C.J. having referred to the cases which decided that the lessee was entitled to have a good title said:

"All these were cases in equity arising on bills for specific performance: and Lord Eldon, and more particularly Sir W. Grant, both advert to the pos-

[32] [1980] A.C. 827. cp. Pothier, *Traité de Obligations*, para. 165.

sibility of a distinction between them and actions for damages to be recovered at law for breach of contract. We cannot however help thinking, that the opinions of these eminent Judges, and the decisions, especially that of *Purvis v. Rayer* (9 Price 488) are authorities upon the general question, whether it arise in a Court of Law or Equity, and that the true ground of refusing relief by a specific performance in these cases is, that the vendor by his contract was bound to make out a good title in all respects to the subject agreed to be sold, including the right of the lessor to demise, and that he had not done so. If that is his contract *he must equally fail in a Court of Law*, unless he can prove a performance of it on his part. And no reason occurs to us why, as the Courts of Law and of Equity would put the same construction on a contract for the sale of a freehold estate, they should do otherwise in respect of a contract for sale of a leasehold."

He referred to the cases, and to "the general understanding that a vendor is bound to make good title in all respects, upon the sale of a leasehold, unless the contrary is expressed," and said that the court had come to the conclusion "that, *unless there be a stipulation to the contrary, there is, in every contract for the sale of a lease, an implied undertaking to make out the lessor's title to demise, as well as that of the vendor to the lease itself, which implied undertaking is available at law as well as in equity*" . . .[33]

Ogilvie v. Foljambe (1817) 3 Mer. 53; 36 E.R. 21

2.29 Sir William Grant M.R. treated the right to a good title as "a right "not growing out of the agreement between the parties, but which is given by law". He called it collateral to the agreement. In the particular case, he found the plaintiff had waived this by his conduct.

Moens v. Heyworth (1842) 10 M. & W. 147; 152 E.R. 418

2.30 There was a throw-away *obiter* remark by Parke B.:

"The case of a policy of insurance does not appear to me to be analogous to the present; *those instruments are made upon an implied contract between the parties*, that everything material to the assured shall be disclosed by them. That is the basis on which the contract proceeds; and it is material to see that it is not obtained by means of untrue representation or concealment in any respect."[34] (The action Parke B. was trying had not been brought in contract but in tort.)

Proudfoot v. Montefiore (1867) L.R. 2 Q.B. 511

2.31 Cockburn C.J. said at 521:

". . . The insurer is entitled to assume, as the basis of the contract between him and the assured, that the latter will communicate to him every material fact of which the assured has, or, in the ordinary course of business, ought to have knowledge . . ." Cockburn C.J. also referred to the assumption above as "*the implied condition* on which the underwriter undertakes to insure".[35]

London Assurance v. Mansel (1879) 11 Ch.D. 363

2.32 There had been a failure by the assured to disclose that various life offices had declined his proposal.

[33] Italics supplied.
[34] Italics supplied.
[35] Italics supplied.

Jessel M.R. evidently considered the duty of disclosure to be of wider application than purely to contracts of insurance. He referred to the case of an application for a "special injunction"[36] as analogous (*Dalgleish v. Jarvie* 2 Mac. & G. 231, 243) and quoted Lord Cranworth, then Lord Commissioner Rolfe, as saying that such an application "is very much governed by the same principles which govern insurances, matters which are said to require the utmost good faith, "*uberrima fides*".[37]

***Thomson v. Weems* (1884) 9 App. Cas. 671**

2.33 The case concerned a misstatement in the proposal form for a life policy. (The assured had answered to the effect that he was temperate in his habits, though in fact he was, as Lord Watson primly put it, "in the habit of taking more drink than was good for him".)

Lord Blackburn said: "In policies of marine insurance I think it is settled by authority that any statement of a fact bearing upon the risk introduced into the written policy is, by whatever words and in whatever place, *to be construed as a warranty, and prima facie, at least that the compliance with that warranty is a condition precedent for attaching the risk*".[38]

***Blackburn, Low & Vigors* (i) in the Court of Appeal (1886) 17 Q.B.D. 553**

2.34 Lord Esher in his dissenting judgment referred to *Duer on Marine Insurance*, who "holds it is *part of the contract* that full disclosure shall be made, as well as that every representation shall be accurate." "But", Lord Esher said, "if this be correct, the contract should never be set aside or treated as void on the ground of concealment; the contract should stand and be treated as broken by the assured." Lord Esher preferred the view of another writer, Phillips, who wrote "The effect of a misrepresentation or concealment in discharging the underwriters does not seem to be merely on the ground of fraud[39] but also on the ground of a *condition* implied by the fact of entering into the contract, that there is no misrepresentation or concealment." Mr Arnould, another writer, had rejected the idea of "fraud" as a basis for the duty and instead endorsed the idea that "the practical doctrine" properly stated was "that it is an implied *condition* of the contract of insurance that it is free from misrepresentation or concealment, whether fraudulent or through mistake." Arnould had considered that what he called the "forfeiture" of the contract for misrepresentation or concealment was thus a forfeiture for breach of condition. Lord Esher endorsed these textbook views, saying "This seems to me to be the true doctrine. The freedom from misrepresentation or concealment is *a condition* precedent to the right of the assured to insist on the performance of the contract, so that on a failure of the performance of the condition the assured cannot enforce the contract."[40]

***Blackburn, Low v. Vigors* (ii) in the House of Lords (1887) 12 App. Cas. 531**

2.35 Lord Halsbury thought that it would not help very much in deciding the case if he attempted to solve the then-current controversy about "what is the

[36] *Ex parte*.
[37] Cp. the rule of disclosure when obtaining Mareva injunctions—no doubt governed by precisely the same principles.
[38] Italics supplied.
[39] A buzz-topic of the time; see above.
[40] (1886) 17 Q.B.D. 553 and 562.

true principle upon which the contract is avoided by concealment or misrepresentation, whether by considering it fraudulent or as an implied term of the contract . . .".

Lord Watson said "It is, in my opinion, *a condition precedent* of every contract of marine insurance that the insured shall make a full disclosure of all facts materially affecting the risk . . ."[41]
Lord Fitzgerald agreed both with Lord Halsbury and Lord Watson and with Lord Esher in the court below.[42]

***Joel v. Law Union* [1908] 2 K.B. 431 at 439**

2.36 In this well known case Lord Alverstone referred to Lord Blackburn's speech in *Brownlie v. Campbell* (1880) 5 App Cas 925 (a case about sale of land in Scotland) where he had described the duty of disclosure in insurance cases as an [underlying] understanding of the contract of insurance, and to *Moens v. Heyworth* (paragraph 2.26 above) (an implied term analysis).

***William Pickersgill v. London & Provincial Marine & General Insurance Co* [1912] 3 K.B. 614**

2.37 Hamilton J. considered he was bound by the decision in *Blackburn, Low v. Vigors* (above) in the House of Lords—especially by the decision of Lord Watson, to hold "in accordance with what has long been stated by the majority of approved text writers, that the rule imposing an obligation to disclose upon the intending assured does not rest upon a general principle of common law, but arises out of an implied condition, contained in the contract itself, precedent to the liability of underwriters to pay.[43]

***Bell v. Lever Brothers* [1932] A.C. 161 at 237**

2.38 Lord Atkin said "The range of authorities relating to some alteration in circumstances subsequent to the date of the contract do not, in my opinion, raise a question of mutual error or mistake; in them the formation of the contract is complete and binding, but subsequent events arise which critically affect the contract, but whose occurrence has not been provided for in the contract. However it may be stated, when relief from the contract is given, the Court, as it appears to me, rests such relief on an implied condition which forms part of a complete and binding contract, but which, on the happening of certain events, terminates the contract."

***Merchants & Manufacturers Insurance Co Ltd v. Hunt* [1941] 1 K.B. 295 at 312, 318**

2.39 Scott L.J. said regarding the implied term theory:
"On principle, it seems plain that the equitable jurisdiction to avoid a contract for misrepresentation cannot rest on such a foundation; . . . Even the common law duty of disclosure I find difficult to explain fully on the theory of its resting only on an implied term of the contract. If it did, it would not arise until the contract had been made; and then its sole purpose would be to unmake the contract". He went on to say that the language of the Marine Insurance Act 1906 and the Road Traffic Act with which he was concerned

[41] Italics supplied.
[42] Which of course leaves one none the wiser as to his views on the particular point under discussion. Lord MacNaghten simply said he agreed!
[43] [1912] 3 K.B. 614.

seemed to treat the duty as arising outside the contract and not as "mere implications inside the contract", but he felt he did not need to decide the question.

Luxmoore L.J. was satisfied that "in a case of positive misrepresentation, the right to avoid a contract, whether of insurance or not, depends not on any implied term of the contract but arises by reason of the jurisdiction originally exercised by the Courts of Equity to prevent imposition." However, in the case there was a "basis of the contract" clause, making the point unnecessary to decide.

***March Cabaret Club & Casino Ltd v. London Assurance* [1975] 1 Lloyd's Rep. 169**

2.40 May J. concluded (at 175) "in my judgment the duty to disclose is not based upon an implied term in the contract of insurance at all; it arises outside the contract; . . ."

***Tradax (Export) v. Dorada etc "The Lutetian"* [1982] 2 Lloyd's Rep. 140 at 157–8.**

2.41 The charterers had failed to pay the correct amount of hire at the right time, because they had made a mistake in calculating it. The owners thus became entitled to terminate the hire after 3 days. Bingham J., as he then was, held that the owners had not made a plain and unambiguous representation to the charterers that they would not withdraw the vessel, or that they would accept the payments made as timeous and sufficient, or that they were willing to extend the notice period. However, he accepted (save perhaps for the opening reference) the statement of principle in Spencer Bower and Turner, *Estoppel by Representation* (3rd ed.) p. 49 that "the parties to a transaction are entitled to assume, as against one another, omnia rite esse acta; each of them is entitled to suppose that the other has fully discharged all such obligations (if any) of disclosure or action against himself as may have been created by the circumstances . . ." If nothing is said "[the party to whom nothing is said] *is entitled to treat the representator's silence or inaction as an implied representation of the non-existence of anything which would impose, or give rise to, such a duty*, and, if he alters his position to his detriment on the faith of that representation, the representor is estopped from afterwards setting up the existence of such suppressed or undisclosed fact".

Bingham J. also referred to the very well-known dictum of Parke B. in *Freeman v. Cooke*[44]:

" . . . and conduct, by negligence or omission, where there is a duty cast upon a person, by usage of trade or otherwise, to disclose the truth, may often have the same effect."

He also cited Lord Wilberforce in *Moorgate Mercantile Co Ltd v. Twitchings*[45] as persuasive authority for the proposition "that the duty necessary to found an estoppel by silence or acquiescence arises where *a reasonable man would expect* the person against whom the estoppel is raised, *acting honestly and responsibly* to bring the new facts to the attention of the other party known by him to be under a mistake as to their respective rights and obligations. (He noted that Lord Wilberforce dissented on the outcome, and expressed the principle in proprietary terms appropriate to that case, but did not think that diminished the significance of what Lord Wilberforce said).

Bingham J. held that although the relationship of owner and charterer is

[44] (1848) 2 Ex. 654 [154 ER 652] at 663.
[45] [1977] A.C. 890.

not one of the utmost good faith, "*There is nonetheless a duty not to conduct oneself in such a way as to mislead. I have no doubt that the owners knew that the charterers believed they had paid the right amount. It was their duty, acting honestly and responsibly, to disclose their own view to the charterers.* They did not do so, and indeed thwarted the charterers' attempts to discover their views. Their omission to disclose their own calculation led the charterers to think, until a very late stage, that no objection was taken to the calculation. It would in my view be unjust in the circumstances if the owners could rely on the incorrectness of a deduction which they had every opportunity to point out at an early stage and which their failure to point out caused the charterers to overlook."[46]

Note. This case is particularly interesting on the nature of the duty of good faith. The attempt to link the doctrine of "concealment" to estoppel is interesting and perhaps a possible rationale of the original law about concealment or non-disclosure, or good faith. It also shows, no doubt absolutely rightly, that the duty to speak, where it arises, has been accepted on occasions as arising outside the insurance cases: see the other chapters on sales contained in Part 2 of this book. The owners had, it was held here, a duty to speak, if they perceived the charterers' belief. Another way of looking at it was that if they indulged in silence in circumstances when this could be misleading, they were in breach of their duty of good faith or fair dealing.

***Black King Shipping Corporation v. Massie* [1985] 1 Lloyd's Rep. 437**

2.42 This was a case in which the existence and extent of the *post-contractual* duty of disclosure in insurance cases had arisen. The owners had failed to give notice to the insurers that the ship was to visit a war zone on the Persian Gulf. Thus, it is unclear how far the judgment of Hirst J. is of relevance to the nature of the pre-contractual duty of disclosure. Hirst J. had however carefully considered what were called the "ship's papers" cases, that is, the cases which had held the insurer entitled to an affidavit of the ship's papers as soon as an action on a policy of insurance had begun. He thought that the right of the insurer to the affidavit, at a time when there was no pre-trial discovery, was based on the duty of good faith owed by the assured. He also relied on Willes J. in *Britton v. The Royal Insurance Co*[47] to the effect that a claim made under the policy had to be honestly made; and *Liberian Insurance Agency Inc v. Mosse*[48] in which it was held by Donaldson J. that the assured had to give notice under a "held covered" clause, expressly or impliedly seeking cover within a reasonable time of learning of the change of voyage or of the omission or the error in description; and a similar approach by McNair J. in *Overseas Commodities v. Style* [1958] 1 Lloyd's Rep. 546.[49]

***Bank of Nova Scotia v. Hellenic Mutual (The Good Luck)* [1992] 1 A.C. 233**

2.43 The insured was in breach of a promissory warranty in the contract of insurance not to send vessels into prohibited areas. It was held by the House of Lords (Lord Goff giving the judgment of the court) that the insurance contract was at an end once the insured committed a breach of the promissory warranty, and thus the insured became uninsured. The contract of insurance

[46] Italics supplied.
[47] (1866) 4 F. and F. 905.
[48] [1977] 2 Lloyd's Rep. 560.
[49] He also held at 512 that the same principle applied to ensure that claims were honestly made under the policy, citing the summing up in *Britton v. Royal Insurance Co* (above) and Baker Welford and Otter-Barry, *The Law relating to Fire Insurance*, (4th ed. 1948.)

was not at an end *ab initio* however, since certain liabilities would continue, such as a continuing liability to pay a premium.

Of interest is Lord Goff's reference to the use of the term "warranty" to signify a condition precedent.[50] "Section 33 of the 1906 Act reflects what has been described, in successive editions of Chalmers The Marine Insurance Act 1906, as the inveterate practice in marine insurance of using the term "warranty" as signifying a condition precedent."

Lord Goff then referred to Lord Blackburn's statement in *Thomson v. Weems*[51]: "in policies of marine insurance I think it is settled by authority that any statement of a fact bearing upon the risk introduced into the written policy is, by whatever words and in whatever place, to be construed as a warranty, and prima facie, at least that the compliance with that warranty is a condition precedent to the attaching of the risk."

[50] At 262.
[51] Para. 2.29, above.

PART 2

THE FORMATION OF THE CONTRACT: THE DUTY OF CANDOUR AND ACCURACY

CHAPTER 3

SALE OF PERSONAL PROPERTY: THE COMMON LAW COURTS' DEVELOPMENT OF GOOD FAITH TERMS

"Caveat emptor does not mean in law or Latin that the buyer must "take a chance", it means that he must "take care". It applies to the purchase of specific things, e.g. a horse or a picture, upon which the buyer can, and usually does, exercise his own judgment, it applies also whenever the buyer voluntarily chooses what he buys, it applies also where, by usage or otherwise, it is a term of the contract, express or implied, that the buyer shall not rely on the skill, or judgment of the seller."[1]

"The intention of the parties to any particular transaction may be gathered from their acts and deeds, in connexion with surrounding circumstances, as well as from their words; and the law therefore implies, from the silent language of men's conduct and actions, contracts and promises as forcible and binding as those that are made by express words, or through the medium of written material."[2]

"Il faut . . . distinguer le cas auquel le vendeur ignoroit le vice rédhibitoire, et le cas auquel il en avoit connoissance. Dans le premier cas, la garantie ne s'étend ordinairement qu'à la chose vendue; le vendeur est obligé de rendre à l'acheteur le prix qu'il lui en a coûté pour l'avoir, et il n'est pas obligé à la reparation du dommage que le vice de la chose vendue a causé à l'acheteur dans ses autres biens. Dans le second cas, lorsque le vendeur avoit connoissance du vice, il est en outre tenu de tous les dommages et intérêts que ce vice, dont il n'a pas averti l'acheteur a causés à celui ci dans ses autres biens . . .

[1] *Wallis v. Russell* (1902) 2 IR 585 at 615 *per* Fitzgibbon L.J.
[2] Addison, *Contracts* (1956 ed.) p. 48.

Le vendeur, quoiqu'il n'ait pas eu une connoissance formelle du vice de la chose vendue, est à cet égard réputé comme s'il avoit eue, lorsqu'ayant un légitime motif de soupçonner ce vice, il n'en rien dit à l'acheteur; car cette reticence est un dol ...". ... Il y a un cas auquel le vendeur, quand même il auroit ignoré absolument le vice de la chose vendue, est néanmoins tenu de la réparation du tort que ce vice a causé a l'acheteur dans ses autres biens: c'est le cas auquel le vendeur est un ouvrier ou un marchand qui vend des ouvrages de son art ou du commerce dont il fait profession: cet ouvrier ou ce marchand, est tenu de la réparation de tout le dommage que l'acheteur a souffert par le vice de la chose vendue, en s'en servant à l'usage auquel elle est destinée ... La raison est qu'un ouvrier, par la profession de son art, spondet peritium artis il se rend envers tous ceux qui contractent avec lui, responsable de la bonté de ses ouvrages, pour l'usage auquel ils sont naturellement destinés. Son impéritie ou défaut de connoissance dans tout ce qui concerne son art est une faute qui lui est imputée, personne ne devant professer publiquement un art, s'il n'a toutes les connoissances nécessaires pour le bien exercer. Il en est de même du marchand fabriquant ou non fabriquant: par la profession publique qu'il fait de son commerce, il se rend responsable de la bonté des marchandises qui'il débite, pour l'usage auquel elles sont destinées."[3]

INTRODUCTION

The pre-1893 implication of terms by the courts—does it matter today?

3.01 Why, it may be asked, do we need to look at the common law on sale of personal property prior to the Sale of Goods Acts 1893/1979 at all? The reason is that the development in the nineteenth century of the implied terms with which we are now familiar, at least as far as sales of chattels are concerned, is central to the understanding of implied terms of fair dealing/good faith. During the nineteenth century, as commerce became increasingly sophisticated, and trade in manufactured goods increased, the courts began to develop techniques for allocating the responsibility for disclosure of defects, both of title and of quality, as between seller and buyer. They did so by implying terms of good faith on the part of the seller in certain circumstances. Risk broadly went where responsibility ought to be: see the quotation from Pothier above for a French contemporary jurist's no doubt influential contribution. They did not call them "terms of good faith" or "allocation-of-risk terms" or "fair-dealing terms" (though see the quotation above from Addison); they tended simply to describe any other result as "fraudulent", or "a fraud on the purchaser",

[3] Pothier, *Contract de Vente* (1806), p. 125 *et seq.*

or quite simply to say that in the circumstances a "warranty", or statement made with contractual intent, should be implied. Nonetheless, what they developed were implied terms of good faith or fair-dealing: these can be seen as a doctrine of reasonable reliance where appropriate, by the buyer on the seller. Reasonable reliance on the skill and judgment of the seller is a crucial feature of these implied terms.

We have not, of late, recognised this especially. This is in large part because of the—wholly beneficial let it be said—impact of the Sale of Goods Act 1893, now the Sale of Goods Act 1979. The natural reaction to this, as to any statute codifying the common law, will have been, why bother with the underlying common law when you have a perfectly good statute? This is reasonable enough in the short term, but one needs to look behind this type of statute from time to time, if the law is not to be fossilised by the statute. A statute can cause what had until then been a lively development of the common law to be stopped in its tracks. After a generation or two the previous development of the law is forgotten; it is simply starved of oxygen by the smothering blanket of the statute's protection. It becomes virtually incapable of regeneration. We have then lost something vital from the law. The virtue of our system of judge-made law is that it can grow with the times. This is not a virtue possessed in the same degree by statutes. It does not matter, of course, in the main area covered by the statute; here, the sale of goods. The Act is acknowledged to be a rather good one. It is short; the gaps, which would nowadays be filled in by countless schedules requiring a wet towel and considerable application to understand, were supplied by the underlying common law. It works.

3.02 However, the loss of the common law does matter in the area not directly covered by the statute, the area as it were around the edges. The implication of terms of good faith—the relevance of the implied terms developed for the sale of goods to other personal property, such as intellectual property (originally regarded as not especially different from the sale of goods)—all these have lost the opportunity of growth. There are other examples of this deadening effect of statute to be found. The doctrine of marshalling, once known to "everybody" in the law and now regarded as somewhat recondite, was at once protected and smothered by a statute[4] which dealt with its main area of application only: the administration of assets of deceaseds' estates. The doctrine of good faith in insurance transactions proved more robust, but it is possible that the Marine Insurance Act 1906, although recognised as extending to non-marine insurance, may have hindered the proper recognition of the law of good faith in surety transactions and beyond. Dare one suggest that our law works better without too much assistance from statute? It would certainly be cheaper if we had shorter ones. At all events, in the interests of law today, this chapter takes a new look at the pre-1893 common law which underlies the Sale of Goods Act 1893/1979.

[4] Locke King's Act, the Real Estate Charges Act 1854 (see now s.35 of the Administration of Estates Act 1925 replacing it).

THE PRE-1893 IMPLIED TERMS

Fraud

3.03 A word or two of warning and explanation may be needed to start with. The older cases—especially those concerned with good faith—frequently use the word "fraud" in a sense which will be unfamiliar to the modern reader. "Fraud" did not during the nineteenth century by any means always connote fraud in the sense of dishonesty. We have developed a highly restrictive use of the word in this century—which *does* strictly connote dishonesty. "You aren't alleging fraud, are you?" is a question put by judges to barristers, usually with a degree of horror, as if it were being suggested that one were bringing fleas or the like into court. Usually one humbly says, "no", while privately thinking that the conduct complained of, if not fraudulent, certainly deserves some proper sign of opprobrium. For a considerable period in the nineteenth century it was not so. A number of lesser shades of unfair or "sharp" or even mildly irresponsible behaviour might be characterised as a *kind of fraud*.[5] We still retain a vestige of this usage in the expression "a fraud on the power", though "a fraud on the purchaser" is all but extinct. It was possible then to argue[6] that "legal fraud", or constructive fraud, might properly be labelled as fraud and attract similar sanctions. We do not need to become involved in this historical "legal/moral fraud" controversy: the legal fraud party was ultimately defeated, rightly or wrongly, in *Derry v. Peek*.[7] We should comfort ourselves with the thought that fraud is only a label after all. The fair-dealing rules concern themselves with the substance. This substance includes the conduct which constituted "legal fraud" among other lesser shades of doubtful conduct. We cannot assume that *Derry v. Peek* caused the conduct which had been characterised as "legal fraud" to disappear; and the underlying law was unscathed by *Derry v Peek*: see *Low v Bouverie*[8] and *Nocton v Lord Ashburton*.[9] Our need for rules that regulate it remains. The content of the common law's rules on fair dealing between vendor and purchaser of personal property does provide some of this regulation in a form which is easily manageable.

The process of implying terms

3.04 When anyone has bought something which proves unsatisfactory he naturally looks back to the pre-contractual negotiations. Did it look defective? Was the defect accessible to the buyer? How could a buyer

[5] See the discussion of this "grey innocence" in the section Eleven Shades of Ambiguity in Chap. 5 Sale of Land.

[6] Although it is fair to say there is often to be detected, even then, a party of opposition to the idea of fraud-without-dishonesty as a legal concept.

[7] (1889) 14 App, Cas. 337.

[8] [1891] 3 Ch. 82.

[9] [1914] A.C. 932.

be expected to know about it? What did the seller say about the goods? What was the purpose of the goods? How specific was the buyer about what he wanted? And so on. So it is equally natural that the implied terms of good faith are implied from the pre-contractual circumstances: from what is done, what is said, and from the circumstances generally. We are familiar with express representations and their effect, the main part of the law on which is now embodied in the Misrepresentation Act 1967. We think of a misrepresentation as inducing the contract. We are less familiar with the pre-contractual representation as warranty, a representation which becomes part of the contract. Lord Abinger C.B. defined this as

> "an express or implied statement of something which the party undertakes shall be part of a contract; and though part of the contract, yet collateral to the express object of it".[10]

These representations-as-warranties/contractual terms are the foundation of the implied terms in the Sale of Goods Act 1893. This approach, is of course, possible because a typical sale of goods is oral, or at worst, oral on terms that the buyer is handed a printed form with conditions.

Still less familiar to us are implied representations, inferred from a mixture of silence when good faith demands speech, and the pre-contractual circumstances. In the nineteenth century these too were readily inferred, and without them the common law and thus the Sale of Goods Act 1893 would look very different. When the pre-contractual circumstances suggested it, implied pre-contractual statements were readily regarded as terms of the contract, or warranties. This was done, essentially, in circumstances where the prudent buyer, who had done his homework to the extent that would be reasonable, nonetheless had to rely on the seller to disclose something to him. This might be something the seller actually knew. It might also be something of which the seller merely had the means of knowledge. If there was reasonable equality of access to relevant information, there was no need for reliance by the buyer: he could stand on his own feet. But what if he simply could not be expected to find out?

3.05 Addison, writing on Contracts in 1856, around the middle of the period of development of the implied terms under discussion, notes that a contractual statement is a matter of substance, not form: what (if anything) you label it, is unimportant. He then describes how certain contractual statements may be *implied*. First, he describes how the circumstances may yield the inference that the statement is in fact intended to have contractual force. Talking of express rather than implied statements, he says[11]:

> "Many representations and descriptions of the subject matter of a contract are *of such a nature and have been made under such circumstances, that the party making them may fairly be considered to warrant or vouch his knowledge of their truth and accuracy*, so as to be

[10] ***Chanter v. Hopkins*** (1838) 4 M. & W. 399; 150 E.R. 1484.
[11] At 126. Italics supplied.

> estopped from afterwards setting up his want of knowledge. *If the means of information are peculiarly within his reach, and he pretends to have informed himself upon the subject, and to know all about it, when in truth he knows nothing at all about it, he does in reality wilfully make a representation which he knows to be false, and is in principle guilty of wilful deception and fraud ...*"

He then goes on to deal with careless representations, where the purchaser thinks the vendor would know the truth, but the vendor may not have bothered to find out the truth, yet makes his statement nonetheless. Here there is a presumption of warranty, because the vendor has a peculiar opportunity to find out the truth. His examples come from the sale of land.

> "If the vendor of a house, or of the goodwill of a business, affirms the rent or the profit of the business to be 180*l*. per annum, whereas it is but 50*l*. per annum, or represents the business done on the premises to be greater than it really is, and so induces the purchaser to give more than the house or goodwill is worth, *this is a fraud upon the purchaser, although the statement may have been the result of mistake, because the amount of the rent, or of the annual profit of the trade, lies peculiarly within the private knowledge of the vendor*. He is *presumed* to warrant his knowledge of the fact, and it is his want of knowledge which constitutes the fraud. It must be imputed to him that he knew the fact, and whether he did, or not, is of no matter—"*he undertook to know, by undertaking to give the description*".[12]

3.06 He explains that where you do *not* presume that the vendor is making a statement intended to have contractual force, it will usually be found that the vendor and the purchaser have an equal opportunity to find out the truth.[13]

> "But there is no warranty as to the party's knowledge, or of the fact being as it is stated to be, if the representation is made concerning some matter, the knowledge of which lies *as much within the power of the one party as the other*, and its correctness or incorrectness may be ascertained by the party interested in knowing the truth by the exercise of ordinary inquiry and diligence, *and* the representation is not made for the purpose of throwing the latter off his guard and preventing him from making those inquiries and examination which every prudent person ought to make".[14]

3.07 Addison recognizes that a precontractual statement must be *material*. Not only must the statement be a significant one, but it is also

[12] Italics supplied. The words in quotation marks were taken from *Calverley v. Williams* (1790) I Ves. Jun. 212, a case concerning a conveyance of land, noted in Appendix to Chap. 5, Sale of Land.

[13] *cf.* the similar position regarding sureties: Chap. 4, Insurance and Surety Transactions.

[14] Italics supplied.

seen by him as a *sine qua non* that the value of the property sold must be materially affected by it. He lists the (to us by now familiar-sounding) exceptions to the general rule—mere puffs, mere statements of belief or opinion on which the buyer was to exercise his own judgment, as opposed to a positive affirmation or statement of a fact; cases where the buyer was not deceived; and unimportant or trifling misrepresentations, which would not have materially affected the value of the object purchased in the eyes of the purchaser and induced him to give a higher price.

The chapter from which the above passage is taken, it may be noted, is headed "Of Fraud and Deceit by and between Parties to Contracts"!

An early case on what became the implied term of fitness for purpose, *Jones v. Bright*,[15] was cited as an example of the kind of "fraud on the purchaser" which was apposite. The defendant in that case had simply undertaken to provide copper for sheathing a ship. Actions of this kind were at that time brought in deceit, and the plaintiff obtained damages on this basis.

3.08 The practice has been followed in this chapter as elsewhere of including some cases of interest in the Appendix. This has seemed useful even though these are hardly up-to-date cases.[16] The purpose of this chapter is not to set out the up to the minute position on the sale of goods, but to explore the essentially good faith nature of the underlying common law of sale of personal property generally. These pre-1893 cases laid the groundwork for the Sale of Goods Act 1893. This underlying common law also affected and has the power, save where statute has intervened, still to affect, the sales of miscellaneous personal property. For example, where an investor has adequately made known his purpose, such rights as a composite life assurance "package" may be covered by this underlying law. (See Article 11 of the Investment Services Directive, and comment thereto, in the Statutory Appendix).

Implied terms: Title

3.09 In earlier times, when most goods were sold in markets, a buyer would obtain good title by virtue of the market overt rule, so that there was little scope for the development of implied terms regarding title. Later, goods increasingly came from a wholesaler or manufacturer outside the immediate, familiar local community. Retail trade in something like the modern style developed. The buyer was less well placed to make inquiries about the goods: he was much more limited to what he actually saw. Over a period his worsened position received the protection of the courts, in a remarkably imaginative development of implied terms by Common Law judges to assist commerce.

15 (1829) 5 Bing. 533; 130 E.R. 1167.

16 For the current law on sale of goods, the standard textbooks should be referred to. Extracts from the Sale of Goods Act 1979 appear in the Statutory Appendix to this book.

Sales of Specific Goods or rights in existence

3.10 These are things which the buyer has usually had an opportunity of investigating for himself before purchase—"I want a pound of those apples" or, to take an actual nineteenth century example from the intellectual property field, "I wish to buy the copyright in your book "The Adventures of Monsieur Violet"; rather than "send me a pound of apples". It should be noted *apropos* Monsieur Violet that the nineteenth-century cases on sales of goods seem to draw little if any distinction between goods and other personal property rights. This is no doubt because the overriding principle of fair dealing could be expected to apply here too. It may also be worth observing that one main reason for the traditional categories in sales of goods such as specific/unascertained may be to reflect the degree of reliance which is to be expected by the buyer.

3.11 Deliberate fraud by the seller was an obvious let-out for the dissatisfied buyer. It was accepted from an early stage that where the seller had actual knowledge (or was *sciens*) at the time of the sale that the goods were not his or contained a material defect of quality, the buyer might return the goods.

"If, indeed, the representation was false to the knowledge of the party making it, this would in general be conclusive of fraud. . . ."[17]

In *Early v. Garrett*,[18] a case about the sale of land, Littledale J, said that where there was no warranty, the purchaser only had an action if he could show the vendor knew the true facts at the time of the sale,

> ". . . the scienter or fraud being the gist of the action where there is no warranty, for there the party takes upon himself the knowledge of the title to the horse and of his qualities."

However, the problem about the need to prove fraud is that the buyer is the least likely person in the world to have the necessary evidence to prove fraud. The increasing readiness of the courts to imply warranties will in time have made this difficult task unnecessary in most cases.

Implied representation from silence given appropriate circumstances

3.12 A contractual statement did not need to be express, but could be *inferred or deemed* where the seller was in possession of the goods and "sold the goods as his own". There was a presumption that a seller in possession of goods who sold or offered to sell *without express mention* of any third party rights was deemed to sell "as his own", or to give an implied warranty of title. A positive statement could thus be inferred from silence, when taken together with the kind of circumstances which gave out their own message unless contradicted.

[17] See ***Ormrod v. Huth*** (1845) 14 M. & W. 651; 153 E.R. 636 *per* Tindal C.J.

[18] 9 B. & C. 928; 109 E.R. 345. See also Co. Litt. 102A, 3 Rep. 22a, Noy's Maxims 42, Fitz, Nat. Brev. 94c in *Sprigwell v. Allen* Aleyn. 91, cited by Littledale J. In *Early v. Garrett* and earlier in *Wiliam v. Allison* 2 East. 469.

In the early case of *Medina v. Stoughton*[19] which was concerned with the sale of a lottery ticket, it was said that a seller who was *in possession of goods and sold them* "has affirmed the goods to be his own" and thus warranted the title.

Parke B. in *Morley v. Attenborough*[20] stated that where a vendor in possession sold goods as his own, it was "deemed equivalent" to a contractual statement (warranty). "Selling as his own" was a matter for the court to infer from the circumstances of the sale. Most practising barristers will have encountered resistance by judges to implications of this kind, on the ground that one is "trying to pile implication upon implication". We see that for his part, Parke B.—not a particularly "soft" judge—apparently found no difficulty in first implying that the seller was selling the goods as his own rather than anyone else's (from the fact of the seller being in possession at the time of the sale); *then* implying (from his silence on the question of title) a contractual statement that he had, and would pass on, the title to the goods.

Erle C.J. said, in *Eichholz v. Bannister*[21]:

> "If the vendor of a chattel *by word or conduct* gives the purchaser to understand that he is the owner, that tacit representation forms part of the contract, and that, if he is not the owner, his contract is broken . . . The sale of a chattel is the *strongest act of dominion* that is incidental to ownership."

The goods in question were in an open shop or warehouse. Note also the judgement Lee C.J. in *Ryall v. Rowles*.[22]

Relevance of price

3.13 Whether the inference from the vendor's silence could be made depended especially on certain particular pre-contractual circumstances. The price is one such. In argument in *Eichholz v. Bannister*[23] a statement of Chancellor Kent[24] was cited by Byles J. ": . . . if the seller has possession of the article, and he sells it as his own, and not as an agent for another and *for a fair price,* he is understood to warrant the *title*". Thus, no doubt, the sale for a ridiculously low price would be, in a sense, another implied statement, countering the effect of the general rule.

Relevance of the "very nature of the trade"

3.14 This seems to have been regarded as exceptionally important, if not virtually determinative. Certainly the impression one has from the nineteenth-century cases is that in certain common sale-scenarios the burden is on the seller to show that he did *not* warrant the title. That

[19] (12 W 3) Holt 208; 90 E.R. 1014.
[20] (1849) 3 Ex 500; 154 E.R. 943.
[21] (1864) 17 C.B. (N.S.) 708; 144 E.R. 284. Italics supplied.
[22] 1 Ves, Sen. 348; 27 E.R. 1074.
[23] (1864) 17 C.B. (N.S.) 708; 144 E.R. 284.
[24] 2 Comm. 478. Italics in original.

this is never expressed is perhaps because it was felt appropriate nonetheless to pay lip service to the supposedly overriding rule of *caveat emptor*. Yet this supposedly overriding rule was so easily and so often displaced that only a small vestige of it remained, as Lord Campbell commented in *Sims v. Marryat*.[25] Perhaps, too, it was felt necessary to emphasize the buyer's duty to make normal and necessary investigations, for policy reasons. The **kind** of goods the seller is selling could destroy (or create) an inference of "selling as his own" or of a contractual statement as to title. This is apparent from the consideration in *Eichholz v. Bannister*, above, of the kinds of trades which do *not* lend themselves to such an inference.

The mere fact that goods were sold from a *retail shop* seems to have come to be regarded as sufficient material from which to draw the inference of a warranty of title. Lord Campbell summarised the position in *Sims v. Marryat*[26] saying that the maxim *caveat emptor* did apply, but that the exceptions "well nigh eat up the rule. Executory contracts are said to be excepted; so are sales in retail shops or where there is a usage of trade; so that there may be difficulty in finding cases to which the rule would practically apply." The result was of course that in the majority of ordinary sales of specific goods, an inference was permitted without much ado, to the effect that the seller gave an express warranty of title by conduct.

3.15 Certain trades might *negative the inference*. In *Morley v. Attenborough*,[27] a sale of goods by a pawnbroker, it was held that there was no warranty of title. There were implied only from the nature of the pawnbroker's occupation (1) that the subject matter of the sale was a pledge and irredeemable, and (2) that the pawnbroker did not know (was "not cognisant of") any defect of title to it. See also the comment on *Morley v. Attenborough* by Erle C.J. in *Eichholz v. Bannister*.[28]

> "The pawnbroker, when he sells an unredeemed [pledge] virtually says,—I have under the provisions of the statute [39 & 40 G. 3, c. 99, s. 17] a right to sell. If you choose to buy the article, it is at your own peril."

Other examples of exceptions given by Erle C.J. in *Eichholz v. Bannister*,[29] including a sale by a sheriff of goods seized under a writ of *fi fa*, as in *Chapman v. Speller*.[30] He said:

> "The fact of the sale taking place under such circumstances is notice to buyers that the sheriff has no knowledge of the title to the goods; and the buyers consequently buy [presumably, that is, if they buy without investigation] at their own peril."

He went on to mention a case of the sale of a patent right, *Hall v.*

[25] (1851) 17 Q.B. 281; 117 E.R. 1287. See Appendix below.
[26] *ibid.*
[27] (1849) 3 Ex. 500; 154 E.R. 943.
[28] 17 C.B. (N.S.) 708, 144 E.R. 284.
[29] *ibid.*
[30] 14 Q.B. 62.

Conder[31] in which the seller only professed to sell the right he had, as an example of other contracts of sale which might "tacitly express the same sort of disclaimer of warranty."

Contractual statement not implied: seller out of possession

3.16 The *caveat emptor* rule was retained in this, no doubt relatively uncommon, situation. This is probably not surprising. We may suspect that "I will sell you those tomatoes in his shop over there", or the equivalent, could be expected to ring warning bells with most of us. Or, as it was more sedately put by Holt C.J. in the very early case, *Medina v. Stoughton*.[32]

> "there may be room to question the seller's title". . . .
> Where one having the possession of any personal chattel, sells it, the bare affirming it to be his amounts to a warranty, and an action lies on the affirmation; *for his having possession is a colour of title, and perhaps no other title can be made out; aliter* where the seller is out of possession, for there may be room to question the seller's title, and *caveat emptor* in such case. . . ."

Sales of Unascertained Goods or Rights

3.17 These are executory contracts, where the subject matter is unascertained (whether or not it is in existence at the time), and is afterwards to be "conveyed".[33] The expression "conveyance" seems to have been used in the sale of goods, to mean in the case of specific goods, simply the bargain and sale: while in the case of executory contracts, where the subject matter is unascertained, it may have meant the later delivery pursuant to the contract. See, for example the reference by Parke B. in *Eichholz v. Bannister*[34] to the sale of a specific ascertained chattel as operating to "transmit the property".

Warranty implied

3.18 It will be evident that the task of implying warranties was much less easy in the case of unascertained goods. The seller was not in possession, so the method of implying a warranty from his silent sale was hardly open to the courts. Nonetheless, by 1864 it was held that sales of unascertained goods also carried with them an implied warranty of title. The basis for this was a presumption about the parties" reasonable expectations of the sale and purchase: namely that *if nothing was said* on the subject of title, both parties *must have intended that the buyer should have full enjoyment and use of the goods*. Thus, this method of implication looked primarily to the overall purpose or aim

[31] (1857) 2 C.B. (N.S.) 22.
[32] 1 Salk 210; 91 E.R. 188. Italics supplied.
[33] See Per Parke B. in ***Morley v. Attenborough*** (1849) 3 Ex. 500; 154 E.R. 943.
[34] (1864) 17 C.B. (N.S.) 708; 144 E.R. 284.

of the transaction and deduced reasonable expectations from that.[35] In *Marley v. Attenborough*,[36] it was said that:

> "Unless the goods which the party could enjoy as his own, and make full use of, were delivered, the contract would not be performed. The purchaser could not be bound to accept if he discovered the defect of title before delivery; and if he did, and the goods were recovered from him, he would be not be bound to pay, or having paid, he would be entitled to recover back the price as on a consideration which had failed."

In *Allen v. Hopkins*,[37] the goods did not belong to the vendor, but to the executors of a certain deceased. The defendant had paid the executors, thinking them to be the true owners. The court held that the absence of title in the seller was a good defence by the purchaser to the seller's action for the price. Pollock C.B. said[38]:

> "I certainly can find no authority, and I have no recollection of ever hearing that doctrine applied to this case, that the buyer is bound to take care that the Plaintiff has a good title to the goods; and that, if it should turn out the Plaintiff has not a good title, the buyer of the goods should have taken care of that, before he made the contract, and therefore is bound by the contract, notwithstanding that he is able to prove that the seller had no title. The doctrine of *caveat emptor* applies not at all, as I apprehend, to the title of the Plaintiff, but to the condition of the goods."[39]

The original expression had after all been "*caveat emptor ne ius alienum emit*." (let him investigate lest he buys another's right)

Implied terms of quality and fitness for purpose

Principles of reasonable reliance by the buyer

3.19 In this area, still an extremely important one today, we are able to see clearly the way the fair dealing rule and the *caveat emptor* or "buyer-to-do-his-homework" rule worked in tandem. As one would expect, the balance is broadly in favour of the seller in the case of specific goods, which the buyer usually has the opportunity of examining. Conversely, it is broadly in favour of the buyer in the case of unascertained goods, where the seller is likely to have access to relev-

[35] *cf.* "a fraud on the power", where also the purpose or aim of the power is used to delimit the ways in which the power may be exercised. See also Chap. 11, the Post-sale Relationship, for the similar restraints on a vendor who retains power to influence the subject matter of the contract in one way or another.

[36] (1849) 3 Exch. 500; 154 E.R. 943.

[37] (1844) 13 M. & W. 94; 153 E.R. 39.

[38] *ibid* at 103.

[39] This last may have become accepted by 1844, but one must doubt if it had always been so.

ant knowledge about the goods and how they came into being and the buyer is not. Latent defects of course posed (and still pose) a particular problem with sales of goods as with all sales: should the risk of these be allocated to seller or buyer?

Latent to whom?

3.20 The expression "latent defect" contains a certain inherent ambiguity. Latent to whom? A defect may be latent on inspection by the buyer, in the sense that there is nothing obvious on the face of the goods. However, it may not be latent to the seller, if he has knowledge, or perhaps, the means of knowledge. Where the seller has merely received the goods from a grower or manufacturer, he is unlikely to have sufficient knowledge of the history of the goods to be in any better position than the buyer. The defect is likely to be truly latent to him. If on the other hand, he has known something about the process by which the goods came into being, typically if he has grown or manufactured them, he is likely to have actual or constructive knowledge of the defect. The nineteenth-century cases recognise this. Where the defect is deemed to be within the knowledge of the seller by virtue of his position, "latent" means latent to the buyer. The seller is responsible. If he did not know, he could have done. He could have protected himself. The fair dealing rules allocate the risk to him.

Specific goods

Equality of opportunity to find latent defect: no reliance and buyer takes risk

3.21 Where the seller is **not** the grower or manufacturer (these will have had at least constructive knowledge of the defects) and the buyer **has** had the opportunity to examine the goods or sample, the general rule is that the buyer takes the risk of defects, patent or latent. Thus, in cases covered by the general rule, the buyer had to bargain for a warranty if he wanted any better protection. However, the general rule is so set about with exceptions as hardly to be worthy of the name. See Mellor J, giving the judgment of the court in *Jones v. Just*,[40] a useful pre-Sale of Goods Act 1893 case in which the common law implied terms on sales were briefly summarised.

> "Where the goods are in esse [*existence*] *and may be inspected* by the buyer, and there is no fraud on the part of the seller, the maxim caveat emptor applies, *even though the defect which exists in them is latent, and not discoverable on examination*, at least *where the seller is neither the grower nor the manufacturer*."[41]

[40] (1868) L.R. 3 Q.B. 197.
[41] Italics supplied.

Horsfall v. Thomas[42] concerned a gun with a defective plug in it and a soft spot in the metal existed which rendered the gun defective. It was a patent defect, although perhaps not *very* patent. It was held in effect that the seller's liability in such cases should not depend on the good sense or otherwise of the purchaser who here had not bothered to examine the gun. The buyer lost. Bramwell B. said:

> "Now the manufacturer of an article is not always bound to point out its defects to the purchaser. If, indeed, there be a defect known to the manufacturer, and of which cannot be discovered on inspection, he is bound to point it out; but if there be a defect which is patent, and which the purchaser is as capable of judging as the manufacturer, he is not bound to call the attention of the purchaser to it."

3.22 The above principles applied also to sales of specific goods by sample, to the extent that it was up to the buyer to examine the sample. The case of *Parkinson v. Lee*[43] concerned the sale of hops by sample, where the seller was not the grower of the hops. Grose J. held that the buyer had an opportunity of judging by the samples "such as he finds them at the time. If he doubt the goodness, or do not choose to *incur any risk of a latent defect*, he may refuse to purchase without a warranty."[44] Without a warranty, in the absence of fraud on the part of the seller, the buyer simply obtained that which "passed in fact". Lawrence J. with whom Le Blanc J. agreed, considered that *by examining the sample*, the buyer bought *at his own risk of latent defect.*[45] (If, on the other hand, the seller had known, for example that cloth sold was badly fulled, then he would have been liable for the defect.

3.23 The cases stress the importance of the parties' respective *ability* to discover the defect. *Emmerton v. Mathews*[46] was a sale by a meat wholesaler in Newgate Market to a retail butcher of a carcase of meat which in fact turned out to be unfit for human consumption. This was not apparent until the meat was cooked, when it became black and had a very bitter taste. Pollock C.B. referred to *Chanter v. Hopkins*,[47] *Parkinson v. Lee*[48] and *Morley v. Attenborough*[49] as authority for the proposition that:

> "The undoubted general law is, that, in the absence of all fraud, *if a specific article be sold, the buyer having an opportunity of examining and selecting it*, the rule of "caveat emptor" applies ... and the plaintiff has to establish that, in the case of a salesman dealing with a retail butcher, there is an exception to the general rule,

[42] (1862) 1 H. & C. 90; 158 E.R. 813.
[43] (1802) 2 East 314; 102 E.R. 389.
[44] Italics supplied.
[45] Italics supplied.
[46] (1862) 7 H. & N. 586; 158 E.R. 604.
[47] 4 M. & W. 399.
[48] Above.
[49] Above.

> and that there is an implied warranty that the meat is fit for the purpose for which probably it is bought."

It was held that:

> "a salesman offering for sale a carcase with a defect, *of which he is not only ignorant, but has not any means of knowledge (the defect being latent)*" ... "does not as a matter of law impliedly warrant that the carcase is fit for human food, and is not bound to refund the price should it turn out to be so ..."[50]

3.24 In *Burnby v. Bollett*[51] the case turned on the fact that the seller was not a dealer in meat or a butcher, and had himself bought meat which was exposed for sale, and sold on to another. The court held that there was no implied term as to quality. Parke B., in the course of argument, said:

> "It is put for the plaintiff, whether, by reason of food being the subject of the sale this is not an exception to the general rule, so as to make the seller responsible on account of the common good, *though no care could have discovered the latent defect.* If the only obligation here was to use due diligence to see that it was not corrupt, the plaintiff cannot succeed."[52]

Thus, the seller's knowledge, actual *or presumed,* was relevant. Counsel had argued:

> "It is presumed in the case of the taverner or butcher, as in the case of the jeweller who sold a pebble for a bezar stone. The liability of such persons *arises from the opportunity they have, in dealing with the article, of knowing whether it is good or not.*"[53]

Hall v. Conder[54] is a case about the sale of a patent. The buyer complained that it was not new and was worthless. Williams J. delivered the judgment of the court; he said the worthlessness or otherwise was a matter equally within the knowledge of the defendant sellers and the plaintiff buyer. Similarly, as to the newness.

> "They had *the same means of inquiring into the fact, and learning whether it had been in use,* or the invention had been previously made known in England. Why, therefore, should we assume that the plaintiff meant to assert that the patent was indefeasible, and that the defendant purchased on that understanding, rather than that, each knowing what the invention was, and having equal means of ascertaining its value, they contracted for the patent such as it was, *each acting on his own judgment.*"[55]

It was thus held there was no express or implied warranty.

[50] Italics supplied.
[51] (1847) 16 M. & W. 644; 153 E.R. 1348.
[52] Italics supplied.
[53] Italics supplied.
[54] (1857) 2 C.B. (N.S.). 22; 140 ER, 318.
[55] Italics supplied.

Where the buyer has no opportunity or insufficient opportunity to inspect

3.25 Fair-dealing terms are presumed from the buyer's reasonable reliance on the seller's skill and judgment. The seller in this case takes the risk of latent defects. A term is implied in these circumstances that the thing should be merchantable, or reasonably fit for its use.

3.26 *Seller the manufacturer or dealer.* Where a seller undertakes to supply goods manufactured by himself, or in which he deals, but which the purchaser *has not had an opportunity of inspecting*, the implied term of merchantability was accepted fairly early. A relevant case is *Laing v. Fidgeon*[56] in which a quantity of saddles had been ordered to be shipped to Prince Edward's Island without the plaintiff's having had an opportunity of seeing them, and the seller was held liable for the defect.

In *Shepherd v. Pybus*[57] a barge was to be sold by the builder of it. The buyer had seen it during construction, but had not seen it when completed; and accordingly it was held that in these circumstances he had *relied on the skill and judgment* of the builder (the phrase which was picked up in the Sale of Goods Act 1893) to supply a barge *reasonably fit for use, or merchantable.*

Also referred to in argument in *Jones v. Just*[58] had been *Gardiner v. Gray*[59] in which Lord Ellenborough had said "*where there is no opportunity to inspect the commodity, the maxim of caveat emptor does not apply.*"[60] The goods sold had to answer the contract description.

3.27 *Seller not the manufacturer.* After initial doubts, the principle of reasonable reliance was applied. Where the seller is a merchant rather than a manufacturer, but the buyer still has no opportunity to inspect, the allocation of risk between the two is by no means straightforward in principle. Nonetheless the position here was eventually assimilated to that where the seller was the manufacturer, and again a term was implied in favour of the buyer that the goods should be merchantable, or reasonably fit for their purpose. Possibly this was because the seller was assumed to have a remedy against the manufacturer in such cases. In *Bigge v. Parkinson*[61] the Defendants had agreed to supply troop stores to the plaintiffs who had agreed with the East India Company to convey troops to Bombay. The troop stores were to be "guar-

[56] (1815) 4 Camp 169; 171 E.R. 55.
[57] 3 Man. & G. 868.
[58] Above.
[59] (1815) 4 Camp. 144; 171 E.R. 46.
[60] Italics supplied.
[61] (1862) 7 H. & N. 955; 158 E.R. 785.

anteed to pass survey of the East India Company's officers". It was held that that express warranty did not exclude the warranty implied by law that the stores should also be reasonably fit for the purpose for which they were intended. It had been argued that the implied warranty was more limited, arising only where:

(1) the article was not in existence but had to be manufactured; or
(2) where there was greater knowledge on the part of the seller than the buyer, and the buyer, relying on the seller, does not exercise his judgment; or
(3) where the seller was the manufacturer.

Cockburn C.J. retorted:

> "He [the seller] is nevertheless responsible, and must resort to his remedy against the manufacturer. Where a person undertakes to supply provisions and they are supplied in cases hermetically sealed, but turn out to be putrid, it is no answer to say that he has been deceived by the person from whom he got them."

The rule in favour of the buyer was, however, strictly confined to cases where the buyer had no opportunity to inspect the goods. It did not, for example, cover cases where he had been given an opportunity and not taken advantage of it.

Sales of a specific existing chattel by description: equality of opportunity to examine, no reliance

3.28 Where there is a sale by description of a definite existing chattel (for example "the ship Sarah"), the actual condition of which is capable of being ascertained by either party but which *neither* has in fact examined, there is no common law implied term as to quality. The buyer thus takes the risk. There is no reliance by the buyer on the seller, so there is no room for the application of the fair dealing rule. The chattel must, however, be in a condition *reasonably described by the description.* Note the decisions in *Jones v. Just*[62] and *Barr v. Gibson.*[63] In the latter case, the facts were as follows. A ship, the *Sarah,* which was on a voyage, was sold and assigned to the plaintiff, both seller and buyer being unaware that at the time of the sale the ship had run aground off Prince of Wales' Island. Parke B. held that in the bargain and sale of an existing chattel, by which the property passes, the law does not (in the absence of fraud) imply any warranty of the good quality or condition of the chattel so sold, relying on *Parkinson v. Lee.*[64] Accordingly, there was no implied term to the effect that the *Sarah* was seaworthy, or in a serviceable condition. However, this was a sale by description: that is the *Sarah* was sold as a ship, and had to be something which could properly be so called at the time of the contract.[65] It was held that the *Sarah* was, on the facts, a ship.

[62] (1868) L.R. 3 Q.B. 197, above.
[63] (1838) 3 M. & W. 390.
[64] (1802) 2 East. 314.
[65] *Bridge v. Wain* 1 Stark 504 and *Shepherd v. Kain* 5 B & Ald 240.

Sales of unascertained goods

Sales for a purpose made known to the seller

3.29 Where the buyer relies on the skill and judgment of the seller, there is a term of fitness for purpose implied. Where a manufacturer or dealer contracts to supply an article which he manufactures or produces or in which he deals, to be applied *for a particular purpose made known to him*, the buyer will normally have to rely on the manufacturer or dealer to see that it is fit for the purpose. The fair dealing rules thus allocate the risk to the seller as a general rule, and he then has the responsibility for providing the desired result. There are exceptions to this rule. There can be cases where the buyer does his own calculations and orders something to be made to his own specification. Clearly in such a case he does not rely on the skill and judgment of the manufacturer or dealer and there can be no application of the fair dealing rules.

If the manufacturer or dealer does not achieve the right result, at all events he will have had the means to achieve it. It is thus not unfair that the risk should be allocated to him rather than to the buyer; the converse would be grossly unfair to the buyer who can do nothing to influence the manufacturing process, of which he is usually ignorant. It is worth noting that, in a sense, the duty on the seller is a duty implied where nothing is said about the unsuitability of the thing for its purpose. A seller who wanted not to be liable for fitness for purpose would have to *tell the buyer of any defects rendering the thing unfit for its purpose.*[66]

3.30 The distinction between cases where the buyer trusted the seller's skill and judgment (or, as it was sometimes put, where the purpose becomes part of the description) and cases where he relied on his own specification could on occasions be a fine one. An example of a case where the liability was the seller's was the sale of the copper in *Jones v. Bright.*[67] The defendant, who knew the object for which the copper was wanted, said "I will supply you well." The seller's knowledge of the buyer's purpose, which was to sheath a ship, together with the foregoing statement, led to an inference (in the absence of specifications by the buyer as to how the copper should be manufactured) that the buyer relied on his skill and judgment. The copper had an intrinsic defect which resulted in its only lasting some four months, rather than the usual four years. Best C.J. began his reserved judgment:

> "It is the duty of the Court, in administering the law, to lay down rules calculated to prevent fraud; to protect persons who are necessarily ignorant of the qualities of a commodity they purchase; and to make it the interest of manufacturers and those who sell, to furnish the best article that can be supplied. The Court must decide with a view to such rules, although, upon the present

[66] Cp. the similar effect of Article 1643 of the French Code Civil cited at para. 18.15.

[67] (1829) 5 Bing. 533.

occasion, no fraud has been practised by the parties calling for decision."

The court had no difficulty in finding an implied term. Gaselee J. said:

> "Without inquiring whether the warranty here be express or implied, it is clear that where goods are ordered for a particular purpose, the law implies a warranty that they are fit for that purpose."

Thus, the product delivered did not, in marked contrast to *Chanter v. Hopkins* (below), answer the contract description which was arrived at by means of the inference. What had been ordered, on the true construction of the contract was *copper-for-sheathing-ships*.[68]

3.31 In *Brown v. Edginton*[69] a wine merchant had ordered a rope to raise pipes of wine from his cellar from a dealer in ropes, who also represented himself as a manufacturer of ropes. The dealer's foreman had taken dimensions and stated that the rope would need to be specially made. Tindal C.J. said:

> "It appears to me to be a distinction well founded, both in reason and on authority, that if a party purchases an article upon his own judgment, he cannot afterwards hold the vendor responsible, on the ground that the article turns out to be unfit for the purpose for which it was required; but if he relies upon the judgment of the seller, and informs him of the use to which the article is to be applied, it seems to me the transaction carries with it an implied warranty, that the thing furnished shall be fit and proper for the purpose for which it was designed."

He saw no distinction between a manufacturer (it had been conceded that had the dealer been in fact a manufacturer, there would have been liability) and a party who undertakes to get an article made.

Another of the judges, Erskine J., for his part stressed that here the rope was not in existence at the time of the contract, and continued: "If a purchaser himself selects the article, it has been held, that the mere fact that the vendor knows the use for which it was designed, will not raise an implied warranty, because the skill and judgment of the latter are not relied on in making the purchase." Maule J. agreed with the other two.[70]

Purpose made known but circumstances show no reliance by buyer: no term implied

3.32 Where a:

> "known described and defined article is ordered of a manufacturer, although it is stated to be required by the purchaser for a

[68] See para. 3.39 of the Appendix to this chapter for further extracts from this case.
[69] 2 Man & G. 279; 133 E.R. 751.
[70] See also ***Gray v. Cox*** (1824) 1 Car. & P. 184; 171 E.R. 1154.

> particular purpose, still if the known described and defined thing be actually supplied, there is no warranty that it shall answer the particular purpose intended by the buyer''.[71]

The fair dealing rules do not require it. In *Chanter v. Hopkins*,[72] the defendant was being sued for the price, which he had refused to pay, of a smoke-consuming boiler. He had written to the patentee of ''Chanter's smoke-consuming furnace,'' ''Send me your patent hopper and apparatus, to fit up my brewing copper with your smoke-consuming furnance''. The furnace proved in fact to be quite unsuitable for use in a brewery.

The plaintiff's counsel suggested that his case was on all fours with an order for a horse to draw the buyer's carriage, in which case, he suggested, there would obviously be an implied warranty; and Parke B. retorted:

> ''That is not the same case as this: there the seller knows the object for which the horse is wanted, and no particular horse is specified; but suppose the buyer said, ''send that bay horse in the third stall of your stable, to draw my carriage,'' then if it did not draw the carriage, it would be the buyer's concern.''

The buyer failed.

Lord Abinger C.B., incidentally, complained in his judgment in the above case about the way in which the purpose had been assimilated to the contract description in some of the cases. He felt that confusion had arisen about the meaning of the word ''warranty'', which was properly to be defined as:

> ''an express or implied statement of something which the party undertakes shall be part of a contract; and though part of the contract, yet collateral to the express object of it.''

In many cases, he complained, the word warranty was being used as a means to decide that there had been non-compliance with the contract by the seller, on the grounds that he had failed to provide something which answered the contract description, ''as if a man offers to buy peas of another, and he sends him beans''. The part-of-the-description approach certainly seems to have fallen out of favour eventually.

3.33 Thus, even though a buyer may make his purpose known to the seller, if he also gives a detailed description of the goods he required, it is easy to infer that he is not relying on the skill and judgment of the seller to achieve something reasonably fit for that purpose.

Ollivant v. Bayley[73] is a case which would seem to have been very much on the border line between the two. The plaintiff, who was the patentee of a two-colour printing machine, sued for the price of a machine which had been delivered to the defendant by him. The circumstances were as follows. The defendant had seen one at the plaint-

[71] Mellor J. in *Jones v. Just*, above.
[72] (1838) 4 M. & W. 399; 150 E.R. 1484.
[73] (1843) 5 Q.B. 288; 114 E.R. 1257.

iff's premises, but wanted a stronger one than that seen. The plaintiff gave him a memorandum in writing in which he stated "I undertake to make you a two- colour printing machine on my patent principle". The court (Lord Denman C.J. delivering the judgment of the court) held that here the buyer was relying on his own judgment, and not that of the seller.

THE FUTURE—WIDER APPLICATION OF THE COMMON LAW PRINCIPLES?

3.34 It is hoped this brief survey of the pre-1893 implied terms in sales of personal property will help to show how the fair dealing rules were implied essentially as rules of reasonable expectation. The survey should also show that the "nature of the transaction"[74] is a less simplistic affair than simple categories such as goods, intellectual property, insurance, pensions, land, etc. The type of transaction is chiefly relevant to see which of the buyer and the seller can be expected to have access to the relevant information about the subject matter of the sale. Information can give an unfair advantage if unequally available. The concept of equal availability may need to be re-examined, of course, in modern conditions. For example, the buyer was regarded as having done his homework sufficiently if he had simply looked at the goods, where this was possible. Even the Sale of Goods Act 1979 limits the buyer's risk to the defects which the examination he happens to have carried out ought to reveal. It may be that nowadays more sophisticated tests may be usual on the part of buyers in certain types of transaction. If and to the extent that this may be or become so, there is no prima facie reason why the buyer should not be deemed to have carried these out, and to have accepted any risk which should come his way if he does not. Chapters 5 and 6 cover the investigations which a buyer is deemed to have made in land and lease sales.

Another point which may be worth noting is that it is in this area that we see the germ of the modern statutory focus on the seller-in-the-course-of-a-business as contrasted with the buyer-who-buys-as-a-private-individual, or "consumer". The older cases concern themselves with the reality of access to information; while the current statutory dichotomy looks much more to the form, and thus runs the risk of neglecting the reality. The dealer or manufacturer was thought, as has been seen, to have access to the relevant information about the goods. That is why the fair dealing rules imposed obligations on him for the protection of the buying public, whether individual or otherwise (although of course we are looking at a period before the real rise of the joint stock companies). It is unclear why the business which has no access to the relevant knowledge about the article bought

[74] See *Liverpool City Council v. Irwin* [1977] A.C. 239.

should not be treated under the law in the same way as the individual who is similarly disadvantaged.

3.35 Finally, it has been seen that the underlying common law rules of reasonable expectation were applied to personal property generally, not confined to the sale of chattels alone. There were not in existence at the time that the implied terms of reasonable reliance were developed' the complex types of personal property which exist today, for example pension-linked or life- assurance-linked "packages" which sometimes contain financially damaging latent defects rendering them unsuitable for the buyer's purpose. There is however no reason why the underlying good-faith principle protecting the reasonable reliance of a buyer could not usefully be applied in this area. One may compare the imaginative step taken by the late nineteenth- century courts in applying the equitable principles developed in regard to dealings with the vulnerable individual buyer or seller to a vulnerable company vis à vis its promoters in *Erlanger's Case*[75] and *Lagunas Nitrate Co v. Lagunas Syndicate*[76] both noted in Chapter 9, Dealings with the Vulnerable Buyer or Seller.

APPENDIX: SOME CASES OF INTEREST

Parkinson v. Lee **(1802) 2 East. 314; 102 E.R. 389**

3.36 The buyer complained of defects in a sale of hops he had bought by sample. The seller, was to the knowledge of the buyer, not the grower. The grower had fraudulently watered them, to make them weigh more, and the effect of that is to make the hops heat and corrupt inside their bags, ultimately becoming quite unfit for sale. The buyer failed since the seller could not have known from inspection of the sample any more than the buyer had done.

Gardiner v. Gray **(1815) 4 Camp. 144; 171 E.R. 46**

3.37 Some bags of imported waste silk had been sold. The plaintiff had inspected samples of it but it was not a sale by sample. Lord Ellenborough held that: "under such circumstances, the purchaser has a right to expect a saleable article answering the description in the contract. Without any particular warranty, this is an implied term in every such contract. Where there is no opportunity to inspect the commodity, the maxim of *caveat emptor* does not apply. He cannot without a warranty insist that it shall be of any particular quality or fineness, but *the intention of both parties must be taken to be, that it shall be saleable in the market under the denomination mentioned in the contract between them. The purchaser cannot be supposed to buy goods to lay them on a dunghill.* The question then is, whether the commodity purchased by the plaintiff be of such a quality as can be reasonably brought into the market to be sold as waste silk?[77]

[75] 1877.
[76] (1899).
[77] He held it was not. Italics supplied.

Gray v. Cox **(1824) 1 Car. & P. 184; 171 E.R. 1154**

3.38 The action was brought by some copper merchants against their manufacturer who had sold some copper for sheathing a West India ship, and which had proved unfit for use after one voyage to Demerara and back. Abbott C.J. said that the jury should be directed that where a commodity having a fixed price or value (as opposed to a horse which does not) "is sold for a particular purpose, it must be understood that it is to be reasonably fit and proper for that purpose, and when I say reasonably fit and proper, I mean that a few defective sheets will not shew that it is not fit and proper."

Jones v. Bright **(1829) 5 Bing. 533; 130 E.R. 1167**

3.39 The plaintiff bought copper for sheathing a ship from the defendant's warehouse. The defendant knew the purpose for which the copper was wanted, and said "I will supply you well". In fact the copper had an intrinsic defect, and lasted only four months instead of the normal average of four years. The plaintiff, as was common at that time, brought an action in deceit, and obtained damages. Best C.J. said:

"It is the duty of the Court, in administering the law, to lay down rules calculated to prevent fraud; to protect persons who are necessarily ignorant of the qualities of a commodity they purchase; and to make it the interest of manufacturers and those who sell, to furnish the best article that can be supplied. The Court must decide with a view to such rules, although upon the present occasion, no fraud has been practised by the parties calling for decision.

. . . In a contract of this kind, it is not necessary that the seller should say, "I warrant;" it is enough if he says that the article which he sells is fit for a particular purpose . . .

"But I wish to put the case on a broad principle:—If a man sells an article, he thereby warrants that it is merchantable,—that it is fit for some purpose. This was established in *Laing v. Fidgeon*. If he sells it for a particular purpose, he thereby warrants it fit for that purpose; and no case has decided otherwise, although there are, doubtless, some dicta to the contrary. Reference has been made to cases on warranties of horses: but there is a great difference between contracts for horses and a warranty of a manufactured article. No prudence can guard against latent defects in a horse; but by providing proper materials, a merchant may guard against defects in manufactured articles; as he who manufactures copper may, by due care, prevent the introduction of too much oxygen . . .

The decisions, however, touching the sale of horses turn on the same principle. If a man sells a horse generally, he warrants no more than that it is a horse; the buyer puts no question, and perhaps gets the animal the cheaper. But if he asks for a carriage horse, or a horse to carry a female, or a timid and infirm rider, he who knows the qualities of the animal, and sells, undertakes, *on every principle of honesty*, that it is fit for the purpose indicated. The selling, upon a demand for a horse with particular qualities, is an affirmation that he possesses those qualities. So, it has been decided, if beer be sold *to be consumed at Gibraltar*, the sale is an affirmation that it is fit to go so far. Whether or not an article has been sold for a particular purpose, is, indeed, a question of fact; but if sold for such purpose, the sale is an undertaking that it is fit. As to the puffs to which allusion has been made, the Court has no wish to encourage them: they are mere traps for buyers; and if a case were to arise out of a contract made under such circumstances, and it were shewn that the article puffed was of inferior quality, when asserted to be of the best materials and workmanship, the seller would be bound to take it back, or make compensation in damages . . .

The law, then, resolves itself into this;—that if a man sells generally, he undertakes that the article sold is fit for some purpose; if he sells it for a particular purpose, he undertakes that it shall be fit for that particular purpose.

. . . the case is of great importance; because it will teach manufacturers that they must not aim at underselling each other by producing goods of inferior quality, and that the law will protect purchasers who are necessarily ignorant of the commodity sold".

Park J. agreed that it would be enough to show an implied warranty *from the nature of the dealing between the parties*. Burrough J. considered the case more one of fact than of law; and Gaselee J. agreed that "where goods are ordered for a particular purpose, the law implies a warranty that they are fit for that purpose."

***Chanter v. Hopkins* (1838) 4 M. & W. 399; 150 E.R. 1484**

3.40 The defendant wrote to the plaintiff "Send me your patent hopper and apparatus, to fit up my brewing copper with your smoke-consuming furance." Parke B. affirmed *Jones v. Bright* (above), which he regarded as authority that "if an order is given for an undescribed and unascertained thing, stated to be for a particular purpose, which the manufacturer supplies, he cannot sue for the price, unless it does answer the purpose for which it was supplied. The case may be illustrated by the example which has been already referred to. Suppose a party offered to sell me a horse of such a description as would suit my carriage; he could not fix on me a liability to pay for it, unless it were a horse fit for the purpose it was wanted for; but if I describe it as a particular bay horse, in that case the contract is performed by his sending that horse; and it appears to me that the present is a similar case. The order is [he quoted it as above]. The purchase is of a defined and well-known machine." The plaintiff thus lost.

***Allen v. Hopkins* (1844) 153 E.R. 39**

3.41 The goods turned out not to be owned at all by the vendor. Pollock C.B. said:

"It was put, in the course of argument, upon the ground of caveat emptor. I certainly can find no authority, and I have no recollection of ever hearing that doctrine applied to this case, that the buyer is bound to take care that the plaintiff has a good title to the goods; and that, if it turn out that the plaintiff has not a good title, the buyer of the goods should have taken care of that before he made the contract, and therefore is bound by the contract, notwithstanding he is able to prove that the seller had no title. The doctrine of caveat emptor applies not at all, as I apprehend, to the title of the plaintiff, but to the condition of the goods."

***Ormrod v. Huth* (1845) 14 M. & W. 651; 153 E.R. 636**

3.42 The sale was of some cotton by sample, warranting that the cotton would correspond to the sample but with no warranty about the sample, and the buyer had the opportunity to inspect the sample. The sample turned out to have had bad cotton in the middle where it was unlikely to be seen on inspection, but there was no evidence the seller knew about it. The buyer's action for a false and fraudulent representation failed before Tindal C.J. The buyer does not seem to have pleaded an implied warranty.

***Morley v. Attenborough* (1849) 3 Ex. 500; 154 E.R. 943**

3.43 The case concerned the question whether the seller of a pawned harp gave an implied warranty of title. The judgment of Parke B. is quoted at some length because it sheds particularly interesting light on the approach to the good-faith implication of terms which was developing.

"... the case was fully argued, and every authority cited and commented upon on both sides, bearing on the question, whether there is an implied warranty of title in the contract of sale of an article, or under what circumstances there is a liability on the part of the vendor to make good a loss by defect of title.

It is very remarkable that there should be any doubt, as that, certainly, is a question so likely to be of common occurrence, especially in this commercial country.... The bargain and sale of a specific chattel, by our law (which differs in that respect from the civil law), undoubtedly transfers all the property the vendor has, where nothing further remains to be done according to the intent of the parties to pass it. But it is made a question, whether there is annexed by law to such a contract, which operates as a conveyance of the property, an implied agreement on the part of the vendor, that he has the ability to convey. With respect to executory contracts of purchase and sale, where the subject is unascertained, and is afterwards to be conveyed, it would probably be implied that both parties meant that a good title to that subject should be transferred, in the same manner as it would be implied, under similar circumstances, that a merchantable article was to be supplied. Unless goods, which the party could enjoy as his own, and make full use of were delivered, the contract would not be performed. The purchaser could not be bound to accept if he discovered the defect of title before delivery, and if he did, and the goods were recovered from him, he would not be bound to pay, or, having paid, he would be entitled to recover back the price, as on a consideration which had failed. But when there is a bargain and sale of a specific ascertained chattel, which operates to transmit the property, and nothing is said about title, what is the legal effect of that contract? Does the contract necessarily import, unless the contrary be expressed, that the vendor has a good title? or has it merely the effect of transferring such title as the vendor has? According to the Roman law ... and in France ... and Scotland, and partially in America ... there is always an implied contract that the vendor has the right to dispose of the subject which he sells ...; but the result of the older authorities is, that there is by the law of England no warranty of title in the actual contract of sale, any more than there is of quality. The rule of caveat emptor applies to both; but if the vendor knew that he had no title, and concealed that fact, he was always held responsible to the purchaser as for a fraud, in the same way that he is if he knew of the defective quality ...

It may be, that as in the earlier times the chief transactions of purchase and sale were in markets and fairs, where the bona fide purchaser without notice obtained good title against all except the Crown ... the common law did not annex a warranty to any contract of sale. Be that as it may, the older authorities are strong to shew that there is no such warranty implied by law from the mere sale. In recent times a different notion appears to have been gaining ground ... and Mr Justice Blackstone says, "In contracts for sale it is constantly understood that the seller undertakes that the commodity he sells is his own; and Mr Wooddeson ... goes so far as to assert that the rule of caveat emptor is exploded altogether, which no authority warrants.

At all times, however, the vendor was liable if there was a warranty in fact; and at an early period, the affirming those goods to be his own by a vendor in possession, appears to have been deemed equivalent to a warranty ...

Some of the text writers drop the expression of "warranty" or "affirmation", and lay down in general terms, that if a man sells goods as his own, and the title is deficient, he is liable to make good the loss. ... Chancellor Kent ... says, "that in every sale of a chattel, if the possession be in another, and there be no covenant or warranty of title, the rule of caveat emptor applies, and the party buys at his peril; but if the seller has possession of the article, and he sells it as his own, and for a fair price, he is understood to warrant the title. From the authorities in our law, to which may be added the opinion of the late Lord Chief Justice Tindal, in *Ormrod v. Huth* ... it would seem that there is no implied warranty of title on the sale of goods, and that if there be no fraud, a vendor is not liable for a bad title, unless there is an express warranty, or an equivalent to it, by declarations or conduct; and the question in each case, where there is no warranty in express terms, will be, whether there are such circumstances as to be equivalent to such a warranty. Usage of trade, if proved as a matter of fact, would, of course, be sufficient to raise an inference of such an engagement; and without proof of such usage, the very nature of the trade may be enough to lead to the conclusion, that the person carrying it on must be understood to engage that the purchaser shall enjoy that which he buys, as against all persons. It is perhaps with reference to such sales or to executory contracts that Blackstone makes the statement above referred to.

Similar questions occur in cases as to the quality of goods, in which it is clear there is, by law, no implied warranty; yet, if goods are ordered of a tradesman, in the way of his trade, for a particular purpose, he may be considered as engaging that the goods supplied are reasonably fit for that purpose. We do not suppose that there would be any doubt, if the articles are bought in a shop professedly carried on for the sale of goods, that the shopkeeper must be considered as warranting that those who purchase will have a good title to keep the goods purchased. In such a case the vendor sells "as his own", and that is what is equivalent to a warranty of title. But in the case now under consideration, the defendant can be made responsible only as on a sale of a forfeited pledge eo nomine. Though the harp may not have been distinctly stated in the auctioneer's cataloque to be a forfeited pledge, yet the auctioneer had no authority from the defendant to sell it except as such. The defendant, therefore, cannot be taken to have sold it with a more extensive liability than such a sale would have imposed upon him; and the question is, whether, on such a sale, accompanied with possession, there is any assertion of an absolute title to sell, or only an assertion that the article has been pledged with him, and the time allowed for redemption has passed ...

In our judgment, it appears unreasonable to consider the pawnbroker, from the nature of his occupation, as undertaking anything more than that the subject of sale is a pledge and irredeemable, and that he is not cognisant of any defect of title to it. By the statute law ... he gains no better title by a pledge that the pawner had; and as the rule of the common law is that there is no implied warranty from the mere contract of sale itself, we think, that where it is to be implied from the nature of the trade carried on, the mode of carrying on the trade should be such as clearly to raise that inference. In this case we think it does not."

***Chapman v. Speller* (1850) 14 Q.B. 621; 117 E.R. 240**

3.44 The plaintiff's agent attended a sheriff's auction with the defendant. The defendant bought some goods at the auction, and the plaintiff bought what he had bought from him for somewhat more. It turned out there was no title to the goods; and the plaintiff claimed his money back. Patteson J. held that the plaintiff had in the circumstances no right to claim good title. *Morley v.*

Attenborough (paragraph 3.43 above) was thus not applied in these circumstances.

***Sims v. Marryat* (1851) 17 Q.B. 281; 117 E.R. 1287**

3.45 The plaintiffs were booksellers and publisher in Belfast, and the defendant was the sole executor of Captain Marryat who wrote among other books, one called *The Adventures of Monsieur Violet*. They decided that on the true construction of the correspondence forming the contract there had been an express warranty. Lord Campbell also commented on the law as to implied warranties. See text above at paragraph 3.14.

***Hall v. Conder* (1857) 2 C.B. (N.S.) 22; 140 E.R. 318**

3.46 The defendants agreed to buy *inter alia* a half of the plaintiff's English patent for his method of preventing boiler explosions. The defendants complained that they ought not to pay him the price because it emerged he was not the first inventor of the patent.

Williams J giving the judgment of the court said "With regard to the sale of ascertained chattels, it has been held that there is not any implied warranty of either title or quality, unless there are some circumstances beyond the mere fact of a sale, from which it may be implied. The law on this subject was fully explained by Parke B . . . in *Morley v. Attenborough* . . ." Here the worthlessness or otherwise of the patent was "a matter as much within the knowledge of the defendants as the plaintiff. They had the same means of inquiring into the fact, and of learning whether it had been in use, or the invention had been previously made known in England. Why, therefore, should we assume that the plaintiff meant to assert that the patent was indefeasible, and that the defendants purchased on that understanding, rather than that, each knowing what the invention was, and having equal means of ascertaining its value, they contracted for the patent such as it was, each *acting on his own judgment*.[78]

***Horsfall v. Thomas* (1862) 1 H.& C. 90; 158 E.R. 813**

3.47 The defence of fraud was set up to an action on a bill of exchange given for a gun manufactured by the plaintiff. The gun had a defect in the metal. This was apparent on a careful examination; but the plaintiff did not examine it.

Bramwell B. found that the manufacturer had not known of the defect, so the "only question is whether there was a suppression of anything which the plaintiffs were bound to make known to the defendant. Now the manufacturer of an article is not always bound to point out its defects to the purchaser. If, indeed, there be a defect known to the manufacturer, and which cannot be discovered on inspection, he is bound to point it out; but if there be a defect which is patent, and of which the purchaser is as capable of judging as the manufacturer, he is not bound to call the attention of the purchaser to it." The buyer lost his case.

***Eichholz v. Bannister* (1864) 17 C.B. (NS) 708; 144 E.R. 284**

3.48 The question of a warranty of title to the goods was in question here. The plaintiff bought certain pieces of material from the defendant's warehouse. A little later they turned out to have been stolen from a third party.

Erle C.J. affirmed the law as set out by Parke B. in *Morley v. Attenborough*

[78] Italics supplied.

(paragraph 3.43 above) namely that if the vendor of goods by word or conduct gives the purchaser to understand that he is the owner, that tacit representation forms part of the contract, and that if he is not the owner, his contract is broken. However, he pointed out that a tacit representation needed appropriate circumstances. "The pawnbroker, when he sells an unredeemed pledge, virtually says,—I have under the provisions of the statute . . . a right to sell. If you choose to buy the article, it is at your own peril. So, in the case of the sale by the sheriff of goods seized under a fi. fa. . .. The fact of the sale taking place under such circumstances is notice to buyers that the sheriff has no knowledge of the title to the goods; and the buyers consequently buy at their own peril. Many contracts of sale tacitly express the same sort of disclaimer of warranty. . . . These are some of the cases where the conduct of the seller expresses at the time of the contract that he merely contracts to sell such title as he himself has in the thing. But, in almost all the transactions of sale in common life, the seller by the very act of selling holds out to the buyer that he is the owner of the article he offers for sale. The sale of a chattel is the strongest act of dominion that is incidental to ownership. A purchaser under ordinary circumstances would naturally be led to the conclusion that by offering an article for sale, the seller affirms that he has title to sell, and that the buyer may enjoy that for which he parts with his money. . ..

He also spoke disparagingly of the alleged rule of *caveat emptor*, regarding it as based on slender authority:

"I think justice and sound sense require us to limit the doctrine so often repeated, that there is no implied warranty of title on the sale of a chattel. I cannot but take notice that, after all the research of two very learned counsel, the only semblance of authority for this doctrine from the time of Noy and Lord Coke consists of mere dicta. These dicta, it is true, appear to have been adopted by several learned judges . . . but I cannot find a single instance in which it has been more than a repetition of barren sounds, never resulting in the fruit of a judgment. This very much tends to shew the wisdom of Lord Campbell's remark in *Sims v. Marryat* [paragraph 3.45] that the rule is beset with so many exceptions that they well nigh eat it up. It is to be hoped that the notion which has so long prevailed will now pass away, and that no further impediment will be placed in the way of a buyer recovering back money which he has parted with upon a consideration which has failed."

Byles J. and Keating J. agreed. Byles J. said that not a single judgment had actually been based on *caveat emptor*: there had always been either declaration or conduct found.

"Thus the law stands that, if there be *declaration or conduct or warranty* whereby the buyer is induced to believe that the seller has title to the goods he professes to sell, an action lies for a breach. There can seldom be a sale of goods where one of these circumstances is not present. I think Lord Campbell was right when he observed that the exceptions had well nigh eaten up the rule."[79]

[79] Italics supplied.

CHAPTER 4

INSURANCE AND SURETY TRANSACTIONS

THE SELLER WHO MUST RELY ON THE BUYER

"No contract can be good, unless it be equal; that is, neither side must have an advantage by any means, of which the other is not aware. This being admitted of contracts in general, it holds with double force in those of insurance . . ."[1]

"If the defects in the subject matter of sale are patent, or such as might and should be discovered by the exercise of ordinary vigilance, and the buyer has an opportunity of inspecting it, the law does not require the seller to aid and assist the observation of the purchaser. Even a warranty will not cover defects that are plainly the objects of sense. Defects however, which are latent, or circumstances materially affecting the subject matter of the sale of which the purchaser has no means, or at least has not equal means, of obtaining knowledge, must, if known to the seller, be disclosed."[2]

"If the fact is one which ought to have been disclosed, the circumstance that it may not have been disclosed through mistake, ignorance, or forgetfulness, cannot be taken into consideration. It is immaterial that the concealment may not have been wilful or intentional, or with a view to private advantage."[3]

Introduction

4.01 Why have a chapter on disclosure covering insurance transactions at all, it may be asked? No one doubts that there is a duty of disclosure in insurance contracts; indeed the only doubt may be whether the

[1] Park J. in *A System of the Law of Marine Insurances* (8th ed., 1842) p. 403.
[2] Kerr, *A Treatise on Fraud and Mistake, as administered in the Courts of Equity* (1868) p. 58.
[3] Kerr, *op. cit.*, p. 53.

whole thing has not gone rather too far, perpetuating an unwholesome degree of uncertainty among assureds as to whether they are in fact covered as they thought or not. The insurance textbooks deal with this topic. All that is quite right and the reader is referred to these textbooks, too. This chapter is selective in its emphasis. This is a book on good faith or fair dealing principles. It covers also the sale of personal property, leases, land, company shares, insurance and surety/guarantee transactions, in order to show how these *work* in the different kinds of sales and in order to show how they differ according to the nature of the contractual subject matter. Accordingly, in this chapter, I do not mean to trespass unduly on ground that is already sufficiently well-trodden, and elegantly-trodden. There are, however, important and striking similarities (as well as differences) between the duty of disclosure in insurance cases and the duty of accuracy and candour, entailing some, but much less, disclosure, in contracts for the sale of other things such as land or a share in a business. A second point of importance for good-faith law is the way that surety/guarantee transactions occupy for the purpose of disclosure a shifting grey boundary between insurance sales and other sales, sometimes nearer to one, sometimes to another. Thirdly, it should be noted that some of the more detailed aspects of imputed knowledge through an agent are specifically dealt with in insurance transactions. The reader is cross-referred for this topic to Chapter 8. That chapter contains a general discussion of imputed and constructive notice[4] and the contribution made to this field by the insurance cases.

Insurance and surety transactions: common elements

4.02 In this chapter both surety cases (where property is put up as security for another's debt) and guarantee cases (where there is a simple promise to pay the debt if the other does not) are, for convenience of reference and because the distinction does not matter for present purposes, simply called "surety" cases or transactions.

Insurance and surety transactions have in common that the *seller or provider* is the party at risk. He has no independent means (the insurer) or has impaired means compared with the buyer (some sureties) of finding out many of the factors which bear on the risk. What has to be "inspected" is thus not the physical attributes, but risk-relevant information. The buyer not only has a better opportunity than the seller of "inspecting" these: in the case of sales of insurance policies in practice he often has the sole opportunity. Virtually all information tending to describe the risk is thus properly described as "latent" to the insurer; in some cases much important information describing the risk is similarly "latent" to the surety. The result has been that the law developed so as to shield the "buyer" (or, as a person in this position has often been termed in this book, the "inquiring party")

[4] Which the author increasingly came to see as a crucially important topic for understanding the operation of good faith terms.

from the inequality of information which there would otherwise be. The duty to disclose facts *material to the risk* took shape.

Due diligence—"common prudence"

(1) Insurers

4.03 Because the duty stems from the need to counteract damaging inequality of information, there is no duty of disclosure at all where and to the extent that it may reasonably be assumed that the insurer[5] can find out material facts for himself. Thus, there is no duty in the case of insurance policies to disclose material facts which the insurer *could find out for himself* by the exercise of "common prudence". He has first to exercise this, before he can start to complain about non-disclosure. His position is to this extent, not at all unlike that of a buyer in contracts for the sale of land, etc; he has to use due diligence. However, the duty of due diligence does not attract much attention in the case of insurance, since it is plainly a somewhat diluted one. In the nature of things, in a contract to indemnify against uncertain risks to arise in the future, on the basis of information mostly locked up in the mind of the would-be assured, there is not a lot to go out and investigate; thus the insurer's exercise of "common prudence" is no doubt largely exercised from his office chair, rather than by going out and looking at anything. It is likely, perhaps, to be limited to statistical, economic and current-affairs information of a general or trade nature. The amount of this which may be transmitted down the insurer's modem to his computer may well be much greater now than in the days of Lord Mansfield, but it remains limited, simply because of the circumstances in which most insurance transactions take place. Nonetheless, it is a real factor, narrowing the ambit of the assured's duty to disclose to a perceptible extent.

(2) Sureties

(a) The commercial surety

4.04 In the case of a surety, reasonable due diligence frequently enables him to be somewhat less vulnerable, to achieve more real equality of information. This depends enormously on the circumstances of the particular contract, however. A commercial surety, indeed, is not really specially vulnerable or specially uninformed as to risk-relevant factors *at all*; he can make any necessary inquiries about the debtor's financial well-being and ability to perform the contract before issuing a guarantee or performance bond. No doubt he will normally insist on seeing business accounts, company accounts, management accounts, etc., and can insist on seeing information from the debtor's

[5] Or surety.

bank if he regards this as likely to assist him in assessing the risk.[6] The dearth of applications by distressed guarantee companies to set their guarantees aside no doubt tells us something of their estimate of the court's probable reaction to a plea that risk-relevant information was not disclosed to them.

(b) The semi-domestic surety

4.05 The duty will arise where he or she *could not be expected to find out* the information in question for himself or herself provided this information is "within the knowledge" of the creditor. Something may also turn on the question whether the creditor or the debtor made the running in the transaction, that is, was the main one to communicate with the surety and the one who was the prime mover in requesting the surety.[7]

Wives and relatives of the debtor

4.06 It would seem to be unclear how far these parties must inform themselves. The cases tend not to distinguish clearly between the two distinct duties owed by each party—the duty on the part of the surety to make reasonable inquiries, and the narrow but real duty on the part of the creditor, to disclose certain material facts (as which see further below). Wives and relatives frequently give guarantees and stand as sureties for overdrafts. Reliance has often been placed in a rather literalist way on the first part of the statement of Lord Campbell in *Hamilton v. Watson*, a bank account guarantee case.[8]

> "Now the question is, what, upon entering into such a contract, ought to be disclosed? and I will venture to say, if your Lordships were to adopt the principles laid down, and contended for by the appellant's counsel here, that you would entirely knock up those transactions in Scotland of giving security upon a cash account, because no bankers would rest satisfied that they had a security for the advance they made, if, as it is contended, it is essentially necessary that every thing should be disclosed by the creditor that is material for the surety to know. If such was the rule, it would be indispensably necessary for the bankers to whom the security is to be given, to state how the account has been kept: whether the debtor was in the habit of overdrawing; whether he was punctual in his dealings; whether he performed his promises in an honourable manner;—for all these things are extremely material for the surety to know. But unless questions be particularly put by the surety to gain this information, I hold that it is quite unnecessary for the creditor, to whom the suretyship is to be given, to make any such disclosure; and I should think that this

[6] See, e.g. ***Trade Indemnity v. Workington Harbour and Dock Board*** [1937] A.C. 17.

[7] See ***Welton v. Somes*** (1888).

[8] (1844). Italics supplied. 12 Cl. & F. 109; 8 E.R. 1339.

might be considered as *the criterion whether the disclosure ought to be made voluntarily, namely, whether there is anything that might not naturally be expected to take place between the parties who are concerned in the transaction, that is, whether there be a contract, between the debtor and the creditor, to the effect that his position shall be different from that which the surety might naturally expect*; and if so, the surety is to see whether that is disclosed to him. But if there be nothing which might not naturally take place between these parties, then, if the surety would guard against particular perils, he must put the question, and he must gain the information which he requires." He thought it a probable expectation that the debtor would owe the bank something, so the guarantor failed to set his guarantee aside for this non-disclosure.

4.07 There may be problems about our relying on the case in any blanket sort of way.

(1) Its usefulness as a factual guide for the present day is somewhat limited by the fact that it pre-dated the kind of exhaustive credit information which is now available to commercial guarantors, and which *do* relate to punctuality in dealings and paying one's debts in an honourable manner;

(2) It by no means says that *no* overdraft situation need be disclosed, but gives rather vague guidance about what, if any, disclosure of overdrafts *should* be made by a creditor;

(3) It fails to explain in terms which translate easily into real life the kind of thing the guarantor would and would not reasonably expect;

(4) It has given rise to a degree of doubt about whether there must be a formal contract between the creditor and the debtor which contains terms which the guarantor would not expect, or whether an arrangement, a circumstance, or a fact which would not be expected is enough.

As to (4) above, the wider view (that a formal contract is not a prerequisite for the creditor's duty of disclosure to arise) has usually been taken to be the correct interpretation.[9] Once that problem is out of the way, it is clear that there is no duty on the surety to investigate for facts which he or she *would not naturally expect*, or as is perhaps better expressed in Gibbs C.J.'s phrase, "*unusual aspects of the transaction which are material to (or intrinsic to) the contract of guarantee*". There

[9] See Lord Chelmsford in ***Wythes v. Labouchere*** (1859) 3 De G. & J. 593; 44 E.R. 1397 ("some material part of the transaction itself between the creditor and his debtor"); A. L. Smith L.J.'s judgment and Romer L.J.'s judgment ("fact bearing on the exceptional risk") in ***Seaton v. Heath*** [1899] 1 Q.B. 782 (reversed on the facts only); Vaughan Williams L.J. in ***London General Omnibus Co v. Holloway*** [1912] 2 K.B. 72 "the non-disclosed fact"; Farwell L.J. in the same case ("matters which ought to have been communicated to him"); and Gibbs C.J. in the seminal Australian case of ***Commercial Bank of Australia v. Amadio*** (1983) 151 C.L.R. 147 "unusual aspects of the transaction".

is no prima facie reason why relatives and wives should be expected to have found out about these unusual aspects.[10]

Wives—a special case?

4.08 There is perhaps a degree of reluctance in English courts to allow that a wife or relative as intending surety may *not* be fixed with knowledge of all the actual facts of the husband's indebtedness, whether or not she could readily have found them out in practice and whether or not the indebtedness was on a scale which any intending guarantor would expect. One reason may have been the persistence of a tendency to treat non-working married women as if they had no independent existence, as if, as it has been put, the husband and wife were one person and that person was the husband. No doubt there is a feeling too that a married woman who is dependent on the husband has made no "real" contribution to the family wealth, which is derived from the husband's efforts in the marketplace, and thus it is not improper to treat the wealth, even if technically hers, as in some sense his. In good times the family business kept her in stockings and Volvo estates and flowers and wine: in bad times she should stand by it to the extent, if not of the shirt on her back, at least her share in the home.

One may have much sympathy with these feelings. However, there are perhaps good reasons why they should not be translated into "hard-line" decisions, so as to be allowed to prevail against the creditor's duty of disclosure to these semi-domestic sureties. The first is simply that the wife in such cases has little relevant power: she usually cannot easily obtain the information to know whether the risk is a proper one *she or her husband should take.*[11] It may be that she should be in no better position than him: she should nonetheless be in at least *as good a one* as regards relevant information. She is within the scope of Lord Mansfield's statement of principle, just as much as anyone else.

4.09 The second is that for what may in part be public policy reasons, to give young children a roof over their heads and so on, as much as to recognise women's share in contributing indirectly to the family wealth or absence of it, women's right to have a joint share in the family home, by express or imputed agreement with the husband, has been recognised by the law, even where this share has been directly acquired by the sole "economic" efforts of the husband. For the law to blow hot and cold, making exceptions where creditors are concerned cannot be right; either the share is real or it is not. If it is real, she must have the same right to protect or risk it as anyone else. No more, perhaps, but certainly no less.

The third reason is that it seems somewhat unfairly capricious if

[10] See also *Credit Lyonnais v. E.C.G.D.* [1996] 1 Lloyd's Rep. 200, in which Longmore J. followed the guidance of Gibbs C.J., albeit stressing "intrinsic".

[11] It is not uncommon for wives in these cases to say sadly, if only I had known what he was doing, I would at least not have let it go on so long.

the law is to confer a benefit in the shape of a right to preserve her property against creditors, on a wife whose husband happens to have been guilty of misrepresentation or of undue influence, while denying this benefit to the wife who may well have been equally ignorant of risk-relevant information but whose husband had chanced to do neither of those things, whose ignorance stems from the fact that no-one thought to tell her anything at all.

This is not to say that deciding in any given case what were "unusual circumstances" which she could not be expected to inform herself about will necessarily be a simple task. Meanwhile, the most helpful guidance as to the kind of circumstances which may be "unusual" probably remains that of Gibbs C.J. in the Australian case of *Amadio*.[12]

(3) Hybrid transactions midway between surety and insurance transactions

4.10 The duty of disclosure is seen in its purest form, and that most onerous to the buyer/defining party, in insurance contracts. When we come to surety contracts, we have to tailor-make the way the principle applies much more. For one thing, we can encounter contracts which are probably best described as hybrids between insurance and surety contracts anyway, and which may be nearer to insurance contracts. In these it may well be that the wide insurance-type duty may apply. In *Seaton v. Heath*[13] Romer L.J. said in the Court of Appeal that there was no hard and fast line for the purposes of the non-disclosure rule between contracts of insurance and contracts of guarantee, and pointed out that the cases where the duty of disclosure to the surety was found to be limited were cases where it was contemplated and intended that the surety would take upon himself the task of ascertaining[14] exactly what risk he was taking on. Where the risks to which the contract related could just as well be classified as insurance risks, the duty of disclosure was the same as in insurance contracts.

Relevance (material, intrinsic) and causation

(1) Surety transactions

"Material" and "intrinsic"

4.11 When the creditor does have to disclose, how much does he have to disclose? The scope of what is "material" or *relevant to the transaction* is limited (because of the quite wide normal scope of the surety's duty of diligence: see above) to that which the surety would not expect, or

[12] See further the Appendix to this chapter below for comment on this important case.
[13] [1899]. 1 Q.B. 782.
[14] From the debtor.

unusual material circumstances.[15] See, *e.g.* Lord Eldon in *Railton v. Mathews* who referred to "facts which ought to be communicated which would affect the situation of the parties . . . with a view to the advantage the parties were to receive"; see the second half of the statement of Lord Campbell in *Hamilton v. Watson* quoted above; and Lord Atkin in *Trade Indemnity v. Workington Harbour and Dock Board*, referred to at paragraph 4.53 below, who, on any view, considered the duty on a creditor to disclose to a guarantor did at all events extend to a positive duty to disclose any "unusual or abnormal characteristics".

The scope of what is "material" is expressly narrowed to that which is "intrinsic" to the surety transaction.[16] This use of the word "intrinsic" is likely to be intended to indicate that the duty is not the comprehensive insurance-type duty to disclose any facts even regarding outside events, which may be material to the risk, but simply facts which relate to the intended transaction itself. The real point about the addition of "intrinsic" is to emphasize that a guarantee is normally pointed at a smaller target than a typical insurance policy. An insurance insures typically against a much wider group of risks. With a health insurance, few symptoms are *irrelevant*: if I am guaranteeing a particular bank account, only matters which can be expected to have bearing on *that bank account* will be material. The label "intrinsic" seems to be owed to *Storey's Equity*,[17] in which it was said to "form the very ingredients of the contract" while extrinsic circumstances were those:

> "forming no part of it, but only accidentally connected with it, or rather bearing upon it, so as to enhance or diminish the price of the subject matter, or to operate as a motive to make or decline the contract."

Extrinsic circumstances might be the subject of disclosure in insurance cases, but not in surety cases. The purpose of the passage, and of the distinction, may thus be seen to be the contrast between the wide-ranging test of what is material, or relevant, in insurance transactions, and the narrower one in surety cases. The concept of a material fact forming "the very ingredients of a contract" certainly adds nothing of significance to "material" (or the plainer word "relevant"). It is suggested accordingly that the use of the extrinsic/intrinsic dichotomy is not to point out any inherent distinction of *principle* in the duty of disclosure as regards insurance and surety contracts, but to show that *in practice* the duty of disclosure in insurance contracts will cover matters such as moral hazard while in surety contracts the duty will generally be more limited.

4.12 There will be grey areas, where insurance and guarantee meet.[18]

[15] (1844) 10 Cl. & Fin. 935; 8 E.R. 993.

[16] See the judgments of Farwell L.J. and Kennedy L.J. in ***London General Omnibus Co v. Holloway*** [1912].

[17] 2 K.B. 72 and, more recently, Longmore J. in *Credit Lyonnais v. E.C.G.D.* [1996] Lloyd's Rep. 200.

[18] See above.

Being grey, they will be grey for "intrinsic" or "material" purposes also. The duty of good faith/fair dealing does not depend on labels but on the substance of the transaction.[19] It may be that there are cases such as *Seaton v. Heath* where the duty to disclose does become wider, despite the fact that a transaction falls technically on the guarantee side of the line.[20] When a person puts up security for an "all-monies" guarantee of a one-man business the resulting contract is technically thought to be a surety contract; when a firm affords professional indemnity cover to a professional person trading on his or her own, such as a barrister, this is termed insurance. One wonders whether the duty of good faith/disclosure on the part of the defining party should really be so very different in the two cases.

Finally, it would not be correct to suggest, for example, that the duty to disclose unusual circumstances only applies in "fidelity-bond" cases. This view is based on the fact that some of the cases[21] referring to the creditor's duty of disclosure to sureties/guarantors happen to be fidelity bond cases, or cases where the surety transaction was to secure another's fidelity in his employment. See, however, the *Workington Harbour* case, and see *Credit Lyonnais v. E.C.G.D.*,[22] above, a commercial guarantee case, for a firm *obiter* statement that the duty of disclosure is a general duty *as regards guarantees generally*.

"Material" (significant) and "material" (relevant): some distinctions

4.13 There is an ambiguity about the word "material".[23] "Material" may bear one of the two meanings above. The first usually comes without suffixes: the second often has "to" naturally coupled with it: the thing has to be material *to* something. There can sometimes be something of a slide between the two meanings. Something which is relevant, or "material to" is often going to possess at least in some degree the quality of reasonable significance or weightiness in regard to the transaction as a whole. This kind of "material", meaning "significant" is often relevant when considering questions of causation. The distinction between the two meanings is of some significance, nonetheless, simply because relevance and causation are different concepts.

"Material facts" in a surety contract are essentially no different from material facts in say, an expression of opinion regarding a seller's title, or a latent defect as to the land. The expression simply means *facts relevant to* the transaction. It says nothing about whether the prudent surety, or the actual surety, would be *induced* or *caused* to enter the contract thereby—or how material (significant) the material (relevant) facts are to his action. There might be something to be said for separa-

[19] See, *e.g.* Romer L.J. in ***Seaton v. Heath*** [1899] 1 Q.B. 782 below.
[20] See also Lord Atkin in the *Workington Harbour* case above [1937] A.C. 17.
[21] See the Appendix to this chapter.
[22] [1996] 1 Lloyd's Rep. 200.
[23] See Chap. 16 for discussion of this.

tion and plain labelling of the two elements—into relevant and causative, perhaps?[24]

Reliance or inducement element—

4.14 See Chapter 15, for the proposition that there is probably no significant distinction to be drawn between the two expressions "reliance" and "inducement", and indeed, any other similar causation-words. The question in surety cases is the same as in other cases of misrepresentation or breach of the good faith duty of accuracy or candour[25] whether the misrepresentation or omission *caused* the inquiring party to enter into the contract into which he entered. It may be put another way—if the statement had been accurate and full, would the inquiring party have entered into the contract, or would he have determined to enter into it on different terms, or not at all.

Levels of inducement, and "material" (serious enough to cause . . .)[26]

4.15 In surety contracts as with other contracts of sale, (see below, however, as to insurance) where the defect, misrepresentation, non-disclosure, etc. is of a material (meaning significant, this time) nature such that *it would influence a reasonable buyer or inquiring party* in deciding whether to enter into the transaction (whether at all or on the currently suggested terms) reliance may be presumed unless the defining party proves the contrary.[27] In other, less plain, cases, such as, for example cases of ambiguity where the statement made is true if taken in one sense, and only untrue in another which is not necessarily the overwhelmingly likely one, actual reliance must be proved by the Plaintiff.[28]

(2) Insurance transactions—relevance and causation

Material (relevant) facts v. common knowledge

4.16 The existence of the duty of disclosure is, as has been said, well known.[29] The duty is a remarkably full one, to disclose all *material (or relevant) facts*. There are certain exceptions to the duty. Matters which the underwriter *already knows* need not be repeated to him again. Matters of *common knowledge* are excepted.[30] The precise scope of this of course depends on a common sense view of what common knowledge

24 For the way in which the two were almost permitted to grow together in insurance law, at the risk of some confusion, see para. 4.17 below.
25 Described more fully in later chapters, *e.g.* Sale of Land.
26 See as to these Chap. 16, Remedies for Breach.
27 See *Smith v. Chadwick* [1882] 20 Ch. D. 27 and Chap. 5, Sale of Land.
28 See Chap. 5, Sale of Land. See also *C.T.I. v. Oceanus* [1984] 1 Lloyd's Rep. 476, for an account of the similar rule that prevailed in insurance cases until *Pan Atlantic v. Pine Top* [1995] 1 A.C. 501.
29 See the textbooks on insurance.
30 See above and see *Carter v. Boehm* (1766) 3 Burr. 1905; 97 E.R. 1162.

is expected of the parties at the time. The notion of what is common knowledge will probably change from time to time, so the old authorities are best read primarily for their statements of principle, not for statute-style definitions of common knowledge.

"Material" (relevant) and inducement: insurance cases

4.17 In the case of insurance, "material" has, by statute, the meaning ascribed to it in section 18(2) of the Marine Insurance Act 1906:

> "Every circumstance is material which would influence the judgment of a prudent insurer in fixing the premium, or determining whether he will take the risk."

This was intended to reproduce the effect of the then existing case law, and it was later accepted that it applied to insurance generally, not simply to marine insurance. The sub-section says, in effect, that the non-disclosure must be relevant to the calculation of the risk. Sales of insurance are about risk just as sales of land are about land. One could say there is nothing very unusual about the job done by the section. The problems perhaps reside in the innocuous-seeming words "influence the judgment . . .". We can unconsciously hark back to the confused overlapping meanings of material (relevant) and material (significant) and material (significant enough to cause . . .).

4.18 *Influence the judgment"* . . . "Material" has been held to mean something less than "decisive" in influencing the prudent insurer; see *C.T.I. v. Oceanus*[31] and see the House of Lords' decision in *Pan Atlantic Insurance v. Pine Top Insurance,*[32] also rejecting the "decisive influence" test in favour of something like "that he would want to take into account". This seems absolutely unexceptionable, if not positively predictable, given the wording of the section, and providing that the separation between relevance and causation is retained. Further, it has the merit of being similar to the test applied to the undisclosed "defect" in other sales. One has to remember that latent *facts about risks* are defects in a contract about risk, just as latent physical defects are defects in a contract to sell a physical object.

What *kind* of influence is *"influence"*? In *St Paul Insurance v. McConnell Insurance*[33] the Court of Appeal explored the meaning of influence[34] in insurance contracts a little further. They thought (and thought that the Court of Appeal in *CTI v. Oceanus*[35] had thought) it meant "which would have been taken into account" but not taken into account necessarily so that it had to lead to the premium being

[31] [1984] 1 Lloyd's Rep. 476.
[32] [1995] 1 A.C. 501.
[33] [1996] 1 All E.R. 96.
[34] Although they took it as exploration of "material" because of the two being in one casserole for the purposes of the section.
[35] Above.

raised. The judgment of Evans L.J. with whom the other agreed,[36] gives three reasons for the decision. These are:

(1) that "factors may not be 'clear-cut' in this way; the risk may be increased in some respects but decreased in others";
(2) that the duty of disclosure is a mutual one, not concerned with the proposer of insurance alone; and
(3) an argument which seeks to infer from section 18(3) of the 1906 Act, which provides that the insured need not disclose a circumstance which diminishes the risk, that such circumstances are nonetheless material, albeit not needing to be disclosed.

One may be doubtful about the last two reasons[37] but the first seems cogent, and the effect is the sensible one that "influence the judgement" remains firmly in the non-causative role that the House of Lords assigned it, and that fits the natural sense of the words used in the section.

4.19 *Inducement: what about the individual insurer?* Section 18(2) of the Marine Insurance Act 1906 does not deal specifically with the question of inducement of the individual insurer. It is difficult to see quite why it needed to do so. It could have been thought adequately covered by the general law.

The House of Lords in *Pan Atlantic Insurance v Pine Top Insurance*[38] has held that proof by the individual insurer that he was induced to enter into the contract of insurance is a prerequisite if the insurer is to be able to avoid the contract of insurance. This is because it is part of the general law of contract that this should be so.[39] The House of Lords rejected the view that to be material a fact needed *only* to have an influence on the mind of a hypothetical prudent insurer.

We may hope that their Lordships did not mean to displace—at least for non-insurance cases, the ability of the court to make inferences of fact that a non-disclosure, inaccurate, uncandid, etc. statement which was sufficiently serious would have influenced the reasonable (or prudent) buyer or inquiring party and thus may be assumed to have influenced the actual insurer, without need for further proof. There seems no reason to replace this healthy and time-saving approach with one where the time of the court is always, of necessity, taken up with formal proof of actual reliance—always very difficult *ex post facto* anyway.[40] Further, the inference of fact does not amount to a rigid rule: it merely shifts the burden of proof to the other side.

[36] *ibid.* 107.

[37] It is difficult to see the relevance of (2); (3) seems unrealistic, and in any case is in stark contrast to ***Carter v. Boehm***, above.

[38] [1995] 1 A.C. 501.

[39] See *e.g.* Lord Mustill's judgment at *ibid.* 549.

[40] See the comments of Buckley J. in *Broome v. Speak* [1903] 1 Ch. 586 (noted in the Appendix to Chap. 7, Sale of Company Shares) and ultimately affirmed by the House of Lords in *Shepheard v. Broome* [1904] A.C. 342.

Avoidance, rescission and compensation: the future?

4.20 Neither section 18(2) of the Marine Insurance Act 1906 nor the case law draws any other distinction between levels of gravity of non-disclosed facts—between those which would cause the insurer not to enter into the contract at all, and those which would merely cause him to fix a different, presumably higher, premium. The old equity courts acknowledged in cases of sale of land that came before them that both kinds of undisclosed defect were relevant, but graded them according to importance. They then drew a distinction between the grades for purposes of giving each practical effect. This they achieved mainly by means of separating out the first and more important of the two: this being variously described as "substantial" or "substantial and material" such that the "thing sold" was of a different nature from that contracted to be sold;[41] or such that "the whole substance and foundation of the contract" was affected.[42] Rescission was allowed to the party misled in such cases. In the other cases, where the defect was less important[43] they were able to preserve the slightly-broken contract, giving equitable compensation to make up for the new and less advantageous terms. In an insurance case equitable compensation[44] would no doubt be assessed by calculating all the premiums which would have been charged had the truth been known, and obliging the assured to pay the difference and interest to the insurer as a condition of being allowed to claim under the policy.[45] This power was traditionally associated with an application by a vendor or defining party for specific performance of the slightly-broken contract, with or without a cross-application by the buyer or inquiring party for rescission. It does not seem to have been *necessarily* associated with specific performance, but talked of simply as something equity was able to provide to *preserve contracts* without real injustice. The contracts which came before equity courts would have tended to be seeking one of Equity's special remedies such as specific performance, but "specific performance" in practice meant one of two things, when obtained: either the declaration that there had been no breach, or the declaration that there had been a breach but that equity would exercise its power to award compensation notwithstanding the breach. Since the Judicature Act 1873 has provided that equity's remedies are available in both courts, and in case of doubt should prevail, one must wonder whether compensation ought not to be reconsidered as an option in cases of less important non-disclosure.[46] Trivial non-disclosures,

[41] Sir G. J. Turner L. J. in *Ayles v. Cox* (1852) 16 Beav. 23; 51 E.R. 684.
[42] Lord Esher in *Re Terry and White's Contract* (1886) and see the Appendix to Chap. 5.
[43] Though short of trivial or minor, because in that case, no less than in insurance cases, it would not be "material" in either of the possible senses.
[44] If it were considered available.
[45] See the discussion of equity's power to preserve contracts by means of its power to do "substantial justice" in an imperfect world in Chap. 5.
[46] See para. 4.21 for the suggestion that s.2(2) of the Misrepresentation Act 1967 might be a possible vehicle for this.

where made part of the basis of the contract, and thus warranted, or made material by agreement, might be candidates for compensation in the same way.[47] It seems possible that some of the unease to which the duty of disclosure in insurance contracts gives rise is not so much due to the existence of the duty of good faith in these contracts, more due to the absence of equity's sticking plaster of compensation for less serious defects. Yet, this would seem to have been a self-imposed denial at all times since 1873.

4.21 It may be that an assured wishing to preserve his contract of assurance might nonetheless in appropriate cases consider bringing proceedings seeking an order that his contract be preserved, praying in aid section 2(2) of the Misrepresentation Act 1967. This section covers cases where it is claimed "in any proceedings arising out of the contract, that the contract ought to be or has been rescinded". The distinction between "avoid" which is the word traditionally used for rescission by an insurer[48] and "rescind" which is the word normally used by everyone else in a like position probably need not deter anyone. The distinction is not, arguably, as to a matter of any substance once the true good faith basis of the avoidance/rescission in both cases is appreciated: in both a party is electing to put an end to a contract which because of the breach of the applicable good-faith duties is something other than the bargain he had believed it to be. Section 2(2) of the Misrepresentation Act 1967 is normally thought of as providing a form of defence to a party against whom rescission is claimed (subject to the retrospective scrutiny of the court). Its use "as a sword" rather than as a shield would no doubt be novel but possibly none the worse for that. The "damages" referred to by the subsection which are to be awarded to the party whose rescission is retrospectively cancelled by the court may anyway be intended to refer to a form of equitable compensation.[49]

It is at all events a feature of insurance contracts that the non-disclosure may be of something relatively unimportant. The only check on the trivial is the lower standard of check provided by the question whether it would be taken into account *at all* by a prudent insurer. Even that is rendered nugatory in many cases by the use of "basis-of-the contract" clauses in insurance policies which have the effect of rendering all non-disclosures material. Consequently, an insurance policy provides the assured with cover which could well be thought of as containing an element of choice on the part of the

[47] Cp. the reference to the French Code des Assurances, Articles 113–119 in the Law Commission Working Paper, Non-disclosure in Insurance Contracts, p. 31, n. 96.

[48] *cf.* s.33 of the Marine Insurance Act 1906.

[49] Or what Millett L.J. in *Bristol & West v. Mothew* [1996] 4 All E.R. 698 has called equity's "restitutionary and restorative" remedy. See also the section on the 1967 Act in Chap. 17, Good Faith and the Misrepresentation Act 1967 and see further as to compensation the interesting article by McDermott, "Jurisdiction of the Court of Chancery to Award Damages" (1992) 108 L.Q.R. 652, drawing attention to the breadth of Equity's ancillary power to compensate, *e.g.* as regards the period between the time of breach and the time of the hearing.

insurer. It is likely this position will begin to change, as regards at least some insurance policies. The coming into force of The Unfair Terms in Consumer Contracts Regulations 1994 will in practice enable judges to give effect to insurance contracts in "consumer" insurances within the Regulations as if they operated without certain provisions unfair to the consumer.[50] It may be that insurers, faced with this, may welcome equitable compensation (by whatever route) in preference, as a solution providing fairness and reasonable certainty to both parties.

Insurance and surety contracts: some features both share with the general law of good faith:

(1) The effect of the parties' relative access to knowledge

4.22 The relative state of knowledge of the seller and buyer is relevant in ascertaining whether there has been non-disclosure.[51] In *Newbury v. Reliance*,[52] an insurance case, the assured was a specialist in motor racing while the underwriter was less specialised, underwriting a whole range of sports. This was held to impose a more stringent duty on the assured than would be normal; and on the facts he was found to have been guilty of non-disclosure. Surety cases will be governed by the general rule as to this, which similarly takes into account the parties' expertise or access to information: see Chapter 5, Sale of Land for examples. The liability of a defining party stops short with information "within one's knowledge"; nonetheless, in the case of an organisation with a number of branches and good access to computer-linked information this might nowadays cover quite a lot of information.

The *equal* availability of knowledge to both buyer and seller of insurance is treated in this way. Where the acquisition of the knowledge requires no effort by either to consult documents, etc, within his possession or control, it will rank as "common knowledge". Where it requires effort, for example looking at a daily report in one's office, the tendency of the courts has been to hold that the "seller"/insurer, or inquiring party (and perhaps also surety in a surety case) would have had no particular reason to make the effort, while the "buyer"/ assured, or defining party (and perhaps the creditor also in a surety case, by parity of reasoning) should have had reason to make it. So, in *London General Insurance Co v.General Marine Underwriters Insurance Co*,[53] the Lloyd's shipping list was equally available to both intending assured and insurers. The court held, however, that the assured had had a duty to look at it and disclose what it contained. The insurers had *no special reason to consult it* as to the ship in question. It may be that this rule could and should become less strict in time with the

[50] See commentary on these Regulations in Chap. 19.
[51] Compare the similar approach to the seller's duty of candour and accuracy in sales of physical objects, etc.
[52] [1994] 1 Lloyd's Rep. 83.
[53] [1921] 1 K.B. 104.

readily available access to computers which we all have. It does seem possible that where verification of the risk, say, on computer-accessible records, is the norm in the particular case of risk, matters which would have cropped up in the course of that verification might be held to be either common knowledge in the trade or presumptively known to the underwriter.

(2) No need to research material facts from outside information: "within his knowledge" sufficient

4.23 The focus is essentially on the knowledge that the defining party to the sale has within his possession or control at or shortly before entering into the contract.[54] It is not necessary for him to carry out a detailed investigation of relevant facts using outside information.[55] The reason is almost certainly to do with our reasonable expectation of a defining party or seller. We expect him to employ information "within his knowledge", that is, within his possession or control, before making statements to an intending buyer; but we do not generally expect him to go out and research the point from outside sources.[56] The insurer/inquiring party's position is precisely similar.

He is deemed to know that which is "within his knowledge" in the ordinary course of his business: for example, in *Foley v.Tabor*[57] Erle C.J. said:

> " . . . actual knowledge is not essential if the insurer knew he had the means of knowing the fact and it was within his knowledge."[58]

See also Clarke, *Law of Insurance,* citing US law to the effect that an insurer is there deemed to know what appears in his own records.

(3) A well-oiled system of access to information in one's possession or control is necessary

4.24 This is the other side of the coin. You are deemed to have a properly working information machine. You do not have to go outside it, or change its normal course just for the purposes of the transaction, but your own information-gathering process is deemed to work smoothly. Thus, if the head office of a bank, say, is intending to take a guarantee from a customer, the relevant knowledge actually held by its branches

[54] See *London General Insurance Co v. General Marine Underwriters Association* [1921] 1 K.B. 104, which also shows that where the information is within the knowledge of both assured and insurer, the balance tips in favour of the insurer, so that the assured's duty to disclose overrides.

[55] See *Australia and New Zealand Bank v. Colonial & Eagle Wharves* [1960] 2 Lloyd's Rep. 241.

[56] See also, for a discussion of various shades of blameworthiness in representation, Eleven Shades of Ambiguity in Chap. 5, Sale of Land.

[57] (1861) 2 F. & F.663.

[58] (2nd ed.) at p. 590, 239B2.

will, it is suggested, be imputed to it; but it will not need either to carry out a more detailed survey itself than any it has already or to instruct its branches to carry out a special investigation. As to insurance, section 19 of the Marine Insurance Act 1906 states:

> "... the agent must disclose to the insurer every material circumstance which is known to himself, and an agent to insure is deemed to know every circumstance which *in the ordinary course of business ought to be known by, or to have been communicated to, him....*"[59]

(4) Standard of materiality (relevance) objective, but in actual circumstances of sale.

4.25 In the well known insurance case of *Joel v. Law Union*[60] it was held that the standard was an objective one. In the surety case of *Railton v. Mathews*,[61] materiality was what the reasonable person (or the "person of good sense") *placed in the actual position of the assured* would have thought material.

(5) No-fault cases: no liability for non-disclosure where the defining party/seller could not have known about the fact in question

4.26 There is no liability in *no-fault* cases, or cases where the defining party could not have known the fact in question at the time of the sale. This will usually occur where there is no information "within the knowledge" of the defining party at the time of the sale which would have yielded the fact in question (and where he has not misrepresented the state of his knowledge in any way). This is also the case, typically in life assurance cases, where due to some defect of his own perception the defining party could not have been conscious of the fact in question at the time. Examples are the no-fault cases of *Swete v. Fairlie*[62] and *Fowkes v. Manchester & London Life Insurance Co.*[63] In both cases the assured could not have known the material fact in question, so there was no liability.[64]

(6) "Innocent" or mistaken motive for non-disclosure irrelevant

4.27 An "innocent" motive in non-disclosure, for example that the non-discloser genuinely thought the point unimportant, does not help the

[59] Italics supplied. See further as to agents, Chap. 8, Knowledge and Notice.
[60] [1908] 2 K.B. 431.
[61] Compare the similar approach to the seller in Chap. 5, Sale of Land.
[62] (1833) 6 C. & P. 1; 172 E.R. 1120.
[63] (1862) 3 F. & F. 440; 176 E.R. 198.
[64] See also *Wheelton v. Hardisty* (1857) 8 E. & B. 232, and ***Joel v. Law Union*** [1908] 2 K.B. 431. Compare the no-fault cases discussed in the section on rescission after completion of sales of land, in Chap. 16, Rescission of Executed Sales.

non-discloser. "Innocent" is in inverted commas, to emphasize that it is not total but relative innocence we are talking about here. See the discussion of Shades of Innocence in Chapter 5, Sale of Land. "I did it in good faith", which means simply, "I did not intend to deceive" affords no defence *per se*.[65] We are talking about the careless use of information in our possession or control, here; and thus, the putting into circulation of a statement containing a careless omission. To talk of this as "innocent" is to use a relative term. *Real* innocence is a defence in insurance and surety cases as in other cases where the duty of candour and accuracy are in question. Real innocence is when you blamelessly do not know; when you did not have any information within your knowledge from which you could know.[66] However, "grey innocence" or relative innocence is something else, and no defence.[67]

(7) Constructive, imputed and imputed-constructive knowledge

4.28 These topics are dealt with in Chapter 8, Knowledge and Notice. There is nothing unusual about the way in which they apply to agents of the assured and of sureties, as is recognised in the recent Court of Appeal case of *PCW Syndicates v. PCW Reinsurers*.[68]

APPENDIX TO CHAPTER 4: SOME CASES OF INTEREST

***Carter v. Boehm* (1766) 3 Burr. 1905; 97 E.R. 1162**
(Lord Mansfield's great good faith case)

4.29 The plaintiff had taken out insurance for the benefit of his brother, George Carter, the governor of Fort Marlborough in Sumatra against the fort being attacked by a foreign enemy. The insurers sought to avoid the policy, complaining that the fort was indefensible against foreign attack, was likely to be attacked by the French, and that the governor knew these material facts and ought to have disclosed them. Lord Mansfield stated:

[65] See *Private Eye*, March 6, 1996 commenting on the use of this phrase by some of those who gave evidence to the Scott Inquiry. *cf.* "in bad faith" which means "he intended to deceive", not, "he has failed to comply with his duty of good faith".

[66] See the preceding section.

[67] See ***Railton v. Mathews*** (1844) 10 Cl. & F. 935; 8 E.R. 993 and see the Appendix to this chapter. This was a fraud case, but the same principles were later held to apply where fraud was absent: see ***London General Omnibus Co v. Holloway*** [1912] 2 K.B. 72. See also ***Morrison v. Universal Marine Insurance Co*** (1873) L.R. 8 Ex. 40, where there had been a mistake or error of judgment in assessing the materiality of the information taken as a whole.

[68] [1996] 1 W.L.R. 1136.

"First, insurance is a contract upon speculation.

The special facts, upon which the contingent chance is to be computed, lie most commonly in the knowledge of the insured only: the underwriter trusts to his representation, and proceeds upon confidence that he does not keep back any circumstances in his knowledge, to mislead the underwriter into a belief that the circumstance does not exist, and to induce him to estimate the risque, as if it did not exist.

The keeping back such circumstances is a fraud, and therefore the policy is void. Although the suppression should happen by mistake, without any fraudulent intention; yet still the underwriter is deceived, and the policy is void, because the risque run is really different from the risque understood and intended to be run, at the time of the agreement. [Italics added.]

The policy would equally be void, against the underwriter, if he concealed: as, if he insured a ship on her voyage, which he privately knew to be arrived; and an action would lie to recover the premium.

The governing principle is applicable to all contracts and dealings.

Good faith forbids either party by concealing what he privately knows, to draw the other into a bargain, from his ignorance of that fact, and his believing the contrary.

But either party may be innocently silent, as to grounds open to both, to exercise their judgment upon. *Aliud est celare; aliud, tacere; neque enim id est celare quicquid reticeas; sed cum quod tuscias, id ignorare emolumenti tui causa velis eos, quorum intersit id scire.*

This definition of concealment, restraited to the efficient motives and precise subject of any contract, will generally hold to make it void, in favour of the party misled by his ignorance of the thing concealed."

He went on to list a number of matters about which the insured might be innocently silent:

"There are many matters, as to which the insured may be innocently silent—he need not mention what the under-writer knows—Scientia utrinque par pares contrahentes facit.

An under-writer can not insist that the policy is void, because the insured did not tell him what he actually knew; what way soever he came to the knowledge.

The insured need not mention what the under-writer ought to know; what he takes upon himself the knowledge of; or what he waves [sic] being informed of.

The under-writer needs not be told what lessens the risque agreed and understood to be run by the express terms of the policy. He needs not to be told general topics of speculation: as for instance—The under-writer is bound to know every cause which may occasion natural perils; as, the difficulty of the voyage—the kind of seasons—the probability of lightning, hurricanes, earthquakes, & c. He is bound to know every cause which may occasion political perils; from the ruptures of States from war, and the various operations of it. He is bound to know the probability of safety, from the continuance or return of peace; from the imbecility of the enemy, through the weakness of their counsels, or their want of strength, &c.

If an under-writer insures private ships of war, by sea and on shore, from ports to ports, and places to places, anywhere—he needs not be told the secret enterprizes they are destined upon; because he knows some expedition must be in view; and, from the nature of his contract, without being told, he waves the information. If he insures for three years, he needs not be told any circumstance to shew it may be over in two: or if he insures a voyage, with liberty of deviation, he needs not be told what tends to shew there will be no deviation.

Men argue differently, from natural phenomena, and political appearances: they have different capacities, different degrees of knowledge, and different intelligence. But the means of information and judging are open to both: each professes to act from his own skill and sagacity; and therefore neither needs to communicate to the other.

The reason of the rule which obliges parties to disclose, is to prevent fraud, and to encourage good faith. It is adapted to such facts as vary the nature of the contract; which one privately knows and the other is ignorant of, and has no reason to suspect.

The question therefore must always be "whether there was, under all the circumstances at the time the policy was under-written, a fair representation; or a concealment; fraudulent, if designed; *or though not designed, varying materially the object of the policy, and changing the risque understood to be run.*"[69]

On the facts, he found that the underwriter, who did not question any further, and after all, knew there was a danger of war (common knowledge in the trade, no doubt), was bound by the policy. Else, he felt, the rule would facilitate fraud by underwriters.

Toward the end of the case, Lord Mansfield added this.

"What has often been said of the Statute of Frauds may, with more propriety, be applied to every rule of law, drawn from principles of natural equity, to prevent fraud—"That it should never be so turned, construed, or used, as to protest, or be a means of fraud."

Note: Lord Mansfield's exposition of good faith is quoted in full because of its importance. We may see the debt he owes to Grotius, a natural lawyer—to the idea of equality in exchange, and the characteristic nature of the contract (see the references to Grotius' and other natural lawyers' influence in England in Chapter 2. There may also be inherent in the judgment the germ of the idea later taken up by Lord Eldon and others in contracts for the sale of land, that the concealment that causes the contract to be avoided is one that changes the nature of the contract; and that avoidance should be rejected in favour of a less drastic remedy where the concealment is less serious.

What is often not appreciated is that good faith is stated by Lord Mansfield to be a general principle, applicable to all contracts and dealings. He does not, of course, work out its application save to insurance contracts.

***R v. Wheatly* (1761) 3 Burr. 1125; 97 E.R. 746**

4.30 The defendant had been convicted of knowingly selling amber beer short of the due and just measure. He had delivered 16 gallons to the buyer instead of the 18 ordered. The defendant's counsel argued that this was merely a civil wrong, not an indictable offence.

Lord Mansfield explained that using false weights and measures or false tokens was a public offence.

"For these are deceptions that common care and prudence are not sufficient to guard against. So, if there be a conspiracy to cheat: for ordinary care and caution is no guard against this.

These cases are much more than mere private injuries: they are public offences. But here, it is a mere private imposition or deception: no false weights or measures are used; no false tokens given; no conspiracy; only an imposition upon the person he was dealing with, in delivering him a less quantity instead of a greater, which the other carelessly accepted. It is only a non-performance of his contract: for which non-performance, he may bring his action."

Mr Justice Wilmot, concurring, took the same line:

"This matter has been fully settled and established, and upon a reasonable foot. The true distinction that ought to be attended to in all cases of this kind,

[69] Italics supplied.

and which will solve them all, is this—that in such impositions or deceits where common prudence may guard persons against the suffering from them, the offence is not indictable, but the party is left to his civil remedy for the redress of the injury that has been done him: but where false weights and measures are used, or false tokens produced, or such methods taken to cheat and deceive, as people can not, by any ordinary care or prudence be guarded against, there it is an offence indictable. . . .

In the case now before us, the prosecutor might have measured the liquor, before he accepted it: and it was his own indolence and negligence if he did not. Therefor common prudence might have guarded him against suffering any inconvenience by the defendant's offering him less than he had contracted for."

Note: This general duty on the buyer to take care (and conversely the limits of the duty of good faith) emerge plainly from this different context. Where "common prudence" or "ordinary care and caution" will reveal the defect, the buyer must use just that, or take the risk of any defects which such investigations would have revealed.

Smith v. Bank of Scotland (1813) 1 Dow. 272, 292; 3 E.R. 697 (Surety bond)

4.31 The case concerned a surety bond obtained by the bank as to one Paterson, who was the Bank's agent at Thurso. The surety sought to set aside the bond, partly on grounds as to its due form, and partly because of fraud or undue concealment on the part of the Bank alleging that Paterson had been guilty of misconduct which the Bank was aware of or had strong reason to suspect.

Lord Eldon, Lord Chancellor, observed that the term fraud was a little harsh for circumstances like these, and the expression "concealment of material circumstances" had sometimes been used. He felt that if it could be proved the Bank knew or *had ground to believe* Paterson was not a good man, it should not be permitted to take advantage of its conduct if it had held him out as a trustworthy person.

Lord Redesdale agreed, and the matter was remitted to the court below.

Gladstone v. King (1813) 1 M. & S. 35; (Insurance: Imputed notice)

4.32 See Chapter 8, Knowledge and Notice for a note of this case.

Pidcock v. Bishop (1825) B. & C. 605; 107 E.R. 857

4.33 A surety guaranteed payment for certain pig iron by the buyer. What was not revealed to him was that the buyer would pay an additional 10s per ton, this additional amount to be applied in liquidation of an old debt due to one of the vendors.

Abbott C.J. said;

"I am of opinion that a party giving a guarantee ought to be informed of any private bargain made between the vendor and vendee of goods which may have the effect of varying the degree of his responsibility." He held the withholding of knowledge from the surety here "was a fraud upon him, and vitiated the contract."

Bayley J. said "It is the duty of a party taking a guarantee to put the surety in possession of all the facts likely to affect the degree of his responsibility; and if he neglect to do so, it is at his peril." . . . Here the contract to guaranty is void, because a fact materially affecting the nature of the obligation created by the contract was not communicated to the surety."

Holroyd J. said after outlining the facts:

"... The plaintiff and defendant therefore were not on equal terms. The former with the knowledge of a fact which necessarily must have the effect of increasing the responsibility of the surety, without communicating that fact to him, suffers hims to give the guarantee. That was a fraud upon the defendant, and vitiates the contract."

Littledale J. said:

"I think that a surety ought to be aquainted with the whole contract entered into with his principal. ..."

***Railton v. Matthews* (1844) 10 Cl. & Fin. 935; 8 E.R. 993 (Surety case: creditor's motive in non-disclosure irrelevant)**

4.34 This was another case where a surety sought to avoid a bond for a bank commission agent, on the grounds of previous material irregularities which had not been disclosed to the bank.

Lord Cottenham held that there could be a case of "improper concealment or non-communication of facts which ought to be communicated, which would affect the situation of the parties, even if it was not wilful and intentional, and with a view to the advantage the parties were to receive."

Lord Campbell said "undue concealment" meant omitting "to divulge [material] facts within their knowledge which they were bound in point of law to divulge". He said that it was immaterial whether the facts were concealed from one motive or another ... "because, to say that his obligations shall depend upon that which was passing in the mind of the party requiring the bond, appears to me preposterous; for that would make the obligation of the surety depend on whether the other party had a good memory, or whether he was a person of good sense, or whether he had the motive in his mind, or whether he was aware that those facts ought to be disclosed. The liability of a surety must depend upon the situation in which he is placed, upon the knowledge which is communicated to him of the facts of the case, and not upon what was passing in the mind of the other party, or the motive of the other party." A new trial was accordingly directed.

***Hamilton v. Watson* (1844) 12 Cl. & F. 109; 8 E.R. 1339 (Creditor's duty of disclosure limited)**

4.35 This has been adequately commented on for the most part in *Lee v. Jones* (below); and see the text above. The *ratio* of it is simply that a creditor is not under a duty to tell all facts to a surety which it may be material for him to know. Lord Campbell also explains that "you would entirely knock up those transactions in Scotland of giving security upon a cash account", if you had such a wide disclosure rule.

***North British Insurance Co v. Lloyd* (1854) 10 Ex. 523; 156 E.R. 545 (The non-disclosure must be material, or be fully fraudulent)**

4.36 A gentleman named Sir T. Brancker had obtained a loan from the plaintiff, putting up certain railway shares as security, on terms that if the shares fell below a certain amount Sir T. Brancker would either provide fresh ones or pay their value so as to leave a given surplus. By the end of the year the shares had fallen in value, but the plaintiffs gave Sir T. an extension of time, on his depositing certain further shares and an acceptance by his brother James of a bill of exchange for £2,000 for six months. At the end of a further year, the brother James proposed a guarantee by the defendant Lloyd and three others for £500 each, in place of his acceptance. The defendant executed the guarantee at the request of Sir T. He was however told neither of the acceptance, nor of its withdrawal. He alleged "constructive fraud", or "undue concealment".

Pollock C.B., giving the judgment of the court, held following Lord Campbell in *Hamilton v. Watson* (paragraph 4.35 above) that there was no duty in contracts of guarantee, as there was in contracts of insurance, to reveal *all* material facts. He considered that the cases cited to him, *Smith v. Bank of Scotland* (paragraph 4.31 above) and *Railton v. Mathews* (paragraph 4.34 above) were cases of actual fraud. He noted that the jury had found the undisclosed circumstance not to be material, but that notwithstanding that the plaintiff's counsel had pressed his point (it would seem on the basis that there was a full insurance-type duty of disclosure in such a case) and ended his judgment as follows.

"The non-disclosure of the circumstance of the change of security, even if it had been material, would not have vitiated the guarantee, unless it had been fraudulently kept back; and there was no ground to impute fraud in fact to the plaintiffs or their agents."

Note: Vaughan William L.J. in London General Omnibus Co (paragraph 4.46 below) says he finds it difficult to understand the passage at the conclusion of Pollock C.B.'s judgment. The heading above represents a possible view.

***Wythes v. Labouchere* (1859) 3 De G. & J. 593; 44 E.R. 1397**

4.37 The action was for relief from a bond of £30,000 given to the defendants as surety for Mr James McGregor. The claim in so far as relevant was that the defendants had concealed from him allegedly material facts, regarding McGregor's general financial relationship with the defendant bankers. These facts may perhaps be described as background facts to the transaction rather than relating to it directly.

In so far as relevant to concealment, Lord Chelmsford L.C. said that the case of the *North British Insurance Co* (paragraph 4.36 above) expressly decided that the obligation of the creditor to communicate even material circumstances that are known to him is not co-extensive with the rule that prevails in insurances upon ships and lives; and that unless the non-disclosure amounts to a *fraud upon the surety*, he is not entitled to relief. "The *concealment, too, must be of some material part of the transaction itself between the creditor and his debtor, to which the suretyship relates*. The creditor is under no obligation to inform the intended surety of matters as to the credit of the debtor, or of any circumstances *unconnected with the transaction* in which he is about to engage, which will render the position more hazardous."[70] For this and other reasons, the plaintiff failed.

Note: This stresses and affirms the narrower, more targeted duty of disclosure in surety cases. See the text above.

***Lee v. Jones* (1864) 17 C.B. (N.S.) 482; 144 E.R. 194 (Blackburn J.)**

4.38 This was an appeal against a decision of Erle C.J. A man named Packer was involved in selling coal for commission for the plaintiffs. He was supposed to hand over to the Plaintiffs within six days of the end of the month all the money he had received from sales. Packer fell into arrears to the extent of £1,271, so the plaintiffs asked him for a surety of £300. £100 of this was provided by the defendant. The defendant upon demand being made on him under the surety, pleaded "fraudulent concealment" by the plaintiffs of material facts, the main one being arrears. Crompton J., Channell B.,

[70] Italics supplied.

Blackburn J. and Shee J., affirmed the judgment (for the defendant surety) of the court below: Pollock C.B. and Bramwell B. dissented.

The surety agreement had simply recited the terms on which Packer earned commission, *without mentioning* the arrears. Thus, the effect could be that the defendant would become liable for his £100 as soon as the ink was dry on his signature.

Shee J. commented on the misleading language of the recital given the true facts. He quoted maxims about concealment.[71] He translates "The guilt of fraud is not in him only who, for the purpose of deceiving, uses obscure language, but in him who insidiously, and without appearing to do so, dissembles what he thinks." and[72] "To be silent is one thing, concealment is another. You may be silent respecting facts within your knowledge, without being guilty of concealment: you are guilty of it when the motive of your silence is a wish that others, for your advantage, should be ignorant of that which you know, and which it is for their interest that they should know."

He continued[73] "These definitions and maxims, *though cited in all the books on the contract of insurance are of much older date than any certain trace of that contract, and not more applicable to it than to the contract of guarantie.*"[74]

Blackburn J. dealt with the difference between contracts of insurance (in which all material circumstances known to the assured must be disclosed) and contracts of "guarantie". He emphasised the point made by the Chief Baron, "that, a surety is in general a friend of the principal debtor, acting at his request, and not at that of the creditor; and *in ordinary cases, it may be assumed that the surety obtains from the principal all the information which he requires; and I think that great practical mischief would ensue if the creditor were by law required to disclose everything material known to him, as in a case of insurance. If it were so, no creditor could rely upon a contract of guarantie, unless he communicated to the proposed sureties everything relating to his dealings with the principal, to an extent which would in the ordinary course of things be so vexatious and annoying to the principal and his friends, the intended sureties, that such a rule of law would practically prohibit the obtaining of contracts of suretyship in matters of business.*"

As regards sureties, he endorsed the narrower principle:

"*But I think, both on authority and on principle, that, when the creditor describes to the proposed sureties the transaction proposed to be guaranteed (as in general a creditor does), that description amounts to a representation, or at least is evidence of a representation, that there is nothing in the transaction that might not naturally be expected to take place between the parties to a transaction such as that described.*" He referred to the facts in the case and said "I think this was evidence of, or rather, if not qualified by other matters, amounted to a representation that there was nothing in the transaction between the Plaintiffs and Packer which might not in the ordinary course of affairs be expected to have taken place between them as parties to such a transaction."[75] Blackburn J. commented on Lord Eldon's judgment in *Smith v. Bank of Scotland* (paragraph 4.31 above) that the effect of Lord Eldon's judgment was that it was *so little to be expected* that a bank would continue in its service an agent who had already by breach of trust run into its debt, that the application for security amounted, as he said, to "holding him forth to the sureties as a trustworthy person.". He said that it must "*in every case depend upon the nature of the transaction, whether the*

[71] Dig 1.43 section 2 De Dolo malo.
[72] De Officiis 1.3, 12, 13(a).
[73] *ibid.* at 200.
[74] Italics supplied.
[75] Cp. for a modern example, Bingham J.'s statement in "*The Lutetian*" [1982] 2 Lloyd's Rep. 140 that a party was entitled to assume *omnia rite acta*.

fact not disclosed is such that it is impliedly represented not to exist" and that this must generally be a question of fact proper for a jury.[76] Bramwell B. and Pollock C.B. dissented. The remainder of the court agreed that there had been sufficient evidence of actual fraud for the case to have gone to the jury.

Note: This is an important case. Although on the facts, the case was held to be one where the concealment was fraudulent, the approach applies just as much in the case of ordinary, non-fraudulent misrepresentations: see below.

***Proudfoot v. Montefiore* (1867) L.R. 2 Q.B. 511 (Knowledge of agent imputed to principal)**

4.39 See Chapter 8, Knowledge and Notice for a note of this case.

***Morrison v. Universal Marine Insurance Co* (1873) L.R. 8 Ex. 40 and on appeal, 197. (Imputed notice)**

4.40 See Chapter 8, Knowledge and Notice for a note of this case.

***Davies v. London and Provincial Marine Insurance Co* (1878) 8 Ch.D. 469, 474 (Fry J.)**

4.41 Some friends of an individual had banded together to provide a bond for him, believing that he was otherwise in danger of being arrested at the instance of his employers. That was in fact *no longer the case* by the time the bond was provided. Fry J. said:

"The law upon that point [the duty of disclosure in such circumstances] seems to me to stand very much in this position. Where parties are contracting with one another, each may, unless there be a duty to disclose, observe silence even in regard to facts which he believes would be operative upon the mind of the other, and it rests upon those who say that there was a duty to disclose, to shew that the duty existed. Now *undoubtedly that duty does in many cases exist*. In the first place, if there be a pre-existing relationship between the parties, such as that of agent and principal, solicitor and client, guardian and ward, trustee and cestui que trust, then, if the parties can contract at all, they can only contract after the most ample disclosure of everything by the agent, by the solicitor, by the guardian, or by the trustee. The pre-existing relationship involves the duty of entire disclosure. In the next place, there are certain contracts which have been called contracts uberrimae fidei where, from their nature, the Court requires disclosure from one of the contracting parties. Of that description there are well-known instances to be found. One is a contract of partnership, which requires that one of the partners should disclose to the other all material facts. So in the case of marine insurance, the person who proposes to insure a ship or goods must make an entire disclosure of everything material to the contract. *Again, in ordinary contracts the duty may arise from circumstances which occur during the negotiation*. Thus, *for instance*, if one of the negotiating parties has made a statement which is false in fact, but which he believes to be true and which is material to the contract, and during the course of the negotiation he discovers the falsity of that statement, he is under an obligation to correct his erroneous statement; although if he had said nothing he very likely might have been entitled to hold his tongue throughout. So, again, if a statement has been made which is true at the time, but which during the course of the negotiations becomes untrue, then the person who knows that it has become untrue is under an obligation to disclose to the other the change of circumstances. . . ." Fry J. went on to quote from

[76] Italics supplied.

Lord Westbury in *Williams v Bayley*[77] that a contract of suretyship "should be based upon the free and voluntary agency of the individual who enters into it." In this type of contract *"Very little said which ought not to have been said, and very little not said which ought to have been said, would be sufficient to prevent the contract being valid."*[78] The agreement was rescinded.

Note: Fry J. appears to have been influential in the move towards the classification of certain relationships as relationships where a duty of good faith was to be expected. This approach has in the end and no doubt inadvertently, contributed to a kind of fossilisation of the live and flourishing good faith doctrines of our law as it then existed. We are in the habit of thinking of the specific relationships in his examples, principal and agent etc., as relationships of potential undue influence, relationships where the possessor of the information is in the position of a trustee. We have tended to concentrate on the potentiality for undue influence, without regard to the other point in these relationships—the unequal access to information. This is after all the whole point of the duty of good faith among partners. You have to trust a partner.

Another unfortunate aspect, for posterity, of this judgment by a distinguished judge is the prominence which he not unnaturally gave to cases where a representation made had become untrue to the knowledge of the maker. The facts of the case will have led him to dwell on this situation. It would be quite wrong to assume, as many probably have, that Fry J ever had the least intention of narrowing to such instances the situations in which the duty of fair dealing or good faith might compel pre-contractual disclosure. He gave examples: there is no indication whatever that he intended to limit his general statement to the subject matter of these examples.

***Blackburn Low & Co v. Vigors* (1887) 12 App. Cas. 531 (Imputed notice)**

4.42 See Chapter 8, Knowledge and Notice for a note of this case

***Welton v. Somes* (1888) 5 T.L.R. 46 (Overdraft/guarantee case)**

4.43 Two defendants gave a limited guarantee of a firm of coffee growers in Colombo. It was held that the bank was under no duty in this case to disclose the precise amount of the coffee firm's deficiency overdraft, given that it was apparent to the guarantors that there would be a deficiency. However, both Pollock B. and Manisty J. stressed as significant the fact that the guarantors had been in communication with the debtor and the guarantee had been given *not at the request of the bank but the debtor.*

***Seaton v. Heath* [1899] 1 Q.B. 782 (A.L. Smith L.J., Collins L.J. and Romer L.J.)**

4.44 The plaintiff insured the solvency of one Sir F. Seager Hunt for £15,000 which she had advanced to him. She did not disclose to her agent and thus to the insurers that she was charging him between 39 per cent and 40 per cent interest for the loan.

The judgments of the court all approach the problem from slightly different standpoints. A.L. Smith L.J. held that the contract in question was one of insurance and not of guarantee; that the non-disclosure rule applied to general insurance and not only to marine insurance; that inter alia the judge should have explained the term "exceptional risk", which he put to the jury, as exceptional in the sense that it in fact differed materially from what the *underwriters* on the facts disclosed might *naturally expect*; and ordered a new trial.

[77] L.R. 1 H.L. 200.

[78] Italics supplied. The expression was taken by Fry J. from Lord Eldon, in *Turner v. Harvey* Jac. 169; 37 E.R. 814.

Romer L.J. held that *there was no hard and fast line for the purposes of the non-disclosure rule between contracts of insurance and contracts of guarantee.* He pointed out that in general in contracts of guarantee where the party guaranteed is found to have owed no duty of disclosure to the guarantor, the contracts when examined will be found to have in substance, certain distinguishing features which contracts of insurance generally do not have: in particular[79] the circumstances will generally in this event point to the view that *"as between the creditor and surety it was contemplated and intended that the surety should take upon himself to ascertain exactly what risk he was taking upon himself".* Here, he considered *the present contract might with equal propriety be called a contract of insurance or a contract of guarantee; but "uberrima fides" was anyway required on the part of the insured.*

In the House of Lords[80] the decision was reversed on the facts. The House of Lords held that the non-disclosure of the rate of interest and the circumstances of the loan did not constitute a material fact, the risk in question being the risk as to Sir F. Seager Hunt's solvency, and the high rate of interest on the loan having, in their view, no bearing on this.

Note: No doubt this was a decision on the particular facts. It would perhaps be different nowadays, for example, if Sir F. Seager Hunt had had to pay a particularly high rate of interest, not because of an individual lender's decision, but because of his credit rating, or because of an unsatisfactory financial history, or in any other way which might represent a judgment by the market or a section of the market on his financial standing.

***Joel v. Law Union* [1908] 2 K.B. 431 (Test of materiality—what the reasonable person in the actual position of the assured would have thought material; good intentions irrelevant.)**[81]

4.45 The case concerned the answers given by the deceased assured to life insurers about her medical condition. The question was whether it was enough for her to have given her answers "in good faith", leaving out something she thought immaterial, if a reasonable person in her position would in fact have considered it material. It was held by the Court of Appeal that the test was what a reasonable person in her position would have thought material, not merely a matter of a decision reached in good faith. Fletcher Moulton L.J. quoted and endorsed Lord Blackburn in *Brownlie v. Campbell*[82] (a sale of land case):

"There is an obligation there to disclose what you know, and the concealment of a material circumstance known to you, whether you thought it material or not, avoids the policy."

He thought the further duty was analogous to a duty to do an act which you undertake with reasonable care and skill.

"A failure to do which amounts to negligence, which is not atoned for by any amount of honesty or good intention. The disclosure must be of all you ought to have realised to be material, not of that only which you did in fact realise to be so."

***London General Omnibus Co v. Holloway* [1912] 2 K.B. 72 (Vaughan Williams L.J., Farwell L.J., Kennedy L.J.)**

4.46 The plaintiff employers took a bond to guarantee the due performance of his duties by an employee. The bond was taken from the employee in ques-

[79] *ibid.* at 793.
[80] *sub nom. Seaton v. Burnand* [1900] A.C. 135.
[81] Cp. s.18(2) of the Marine Insurance Act 1906—"a prudent insurer."
[82] 5 App. Cas. 925 at 954.

tion. A surety bond was also taken from Mr Holloway. The plaintiffs did not reveal to Mr. Holloway the fact that the employee had previously taken the employer's money, which had been repaid by relatives. There was no fraud in the sense of dishonesty on their part in not revealing this.

Vaughan Williams L.J. stated[83]

(1) "It was suggested during the argument that although it may be true that, generally, it is not good law, except in the case of policies of insurance, to say that the non-disclosure of a fact within the knowledge of the person taking the security, material for the surety to know, will vitiate the security, yet it may be good law in a case where the *non-disclosed fact is of such a character that* the tribunal before which the question of the vitiation of the bond comes is of opinion that *the non-disclosure constitutes a misrepresentation by reason of the non-disclosed fact being inconsistent with a presumed basis of the contract of suretyship,* e.g. that the clerk whose fidelity or honesty is the subject of the security has not, to the knowledge of the person taking such guarantee, been guilty of a breach of honesty in the performance of the duties of the very office or service, fidelity and honesty in which is guaranteed." He went on to say that the honesty of such clerk, to the knowledge of the master, "is assumed by both parties to an ordinary contract of suretyship." ... *"Not to disclose such dishonesty is a misrepresentation, it may be innocently made, but still is a misrepresentation, because by non-disclosure the master must be assumed to be contracting on the assumption which I have just mentioned.*

(2) He considered the importance of the non-disclosed fact[84] might well be a question of fact for the jury or the judge sitting alone, the question of fact to put being, Would the surety have entered into this contract of suretyship if the non-disclosed fact had been disclosed to him?

(3) He commented on *Lee v. Jones* (paragraph 4.38 above) that that case concerned fraud, but he did not regard it as a statement that the misrepresentation *must* be fraudulent). He also commented on *Hamilton v. Watson* (paragraph 4.35 above), that Lord Campbell had merely said that the *bank manager* where a bank takes a security for one of its customers, is not bound to communicate to the proposed surety *every* information which, in relation to the suretyship, it may be material for him to know, and, if such information is not communicated, the surety is released. Lord Campbell had also said that disclosure was unnecessary *"unless questions be particularly put by the surety to gain this information"*; and "I should think that this might be considered as the criterion whether the disclosure ought to be made voluntarily, namely *whether there is anything that might not naturally be expected to take place between the parties who are concerned in the transaction,* that is, whether there be a contract between the debtor and the creditor, to the effect that his position shall be different from that which the surety *might naturally expect;* and if so, the surety is to see whether that is disclosed to him. . . ."[85] Vaughan Williams L.J. said that the contract spoken of by Lord Campbell was merely an example "of the general proposition that a creditor must reveal to the surety every fact which under the circumstances the surety would expect not to exist, for the omission to mention that such a fact does exist is

[83] *ibid*. at 77. Italics supplied.

[84] (Its materiality.)

[85] Italics supplied.

an implied representation that it does not. He said that such concealment was frequently described as "undue concealment".

4.47 Farwell L.J. thought the question was to consider whether there was in this case any ground for relief in equity before the Judicature Acts which could now be granted by the High Court. In a case like the present, innocent misrepresentation was sufficient to entitle the surety to relief in equity; fraud was unnecessary:

"although the doctrine by which uberrima fides is required in insurance cases is not applicable to the same extent in suretyship cases, still the surety is entitled to relief on the ground of non-disclosure of matters which ought to have been communicated to him, whether the non-communication was or was not innocent".

He had already commented that sureties had for very many years been favoured in equity, and that relief had been given to them from time to time on what has been called the clearest and most evident equity—Lord Eldon had called it in one case the "good faith of the contract".

He commented on the wide distinction between a case like the present, and those of *guarantees for overdrafts* given to bankers such as *Hamilton v. Watson* (paragraph 4.35 above) and *Wythes v. Labouchere* (paragraph 4.37 above). The distinction was that a surety *would naturally expect* that the principal debtor might overdraw, so there was nothing which needed to be disclosed to him (he explained Lord Campbell's comments in *Hamilton v. Watson* in this way.) He also mentioned as useful Story's distinction[86] between intrinsic and extrinsic circumstances: "the first forming the very ingredients of the contract, and the latter forming no part of it, but only accidentally connected with it, or rather bearing upon it, so as to enhance or diminish the price of the subject-matter, or to operate as a motive to make or decline the contract." The intrinsic circumstances require disclosure: the extrinsic do not, except in the case of insurance. Farwell L.J. said the reason was the plain exigencies of this class of transactions . . . "the underwriter . . . cannot as a rule, know, and but rarely has either *the time or the opportunity to learn by inquiry,* circumstances which are, or may be, most material to the formation of his judgment as to the acceptance or rejection of the risk, and as to the premium which he ought to require."[87]

Kennedy L.J. also affirmed the judgment in favour of the defendant. He accepted that "mere" non-disclosure of facts which it is material for a surety to know would not vitiate a contract of guarantee, but only a contract of insurance. He said that non-disclosure of intrinsic matters, according to Story, might vitiate a contract "only where there is some fiduciary *or other special and peculiar relation* to exist between the contracting parties.[88] Kennedy L.J. however must have defined "special and peculiar relation" widely, since he finally declared that *Railton v. Mathews* (paragraph 4.34 above) was authority for the proposition that the *peculiar relation* between guarantor and creditor or employer "justifies the importation into such a contract, as a condition of the liability of the surety, of the disclosure by the employer to the surety of any previous dishonesty of the servant known to the employer."

He referred to Lord Eldon in *Walker v. Symonds*[89] who distinguished between intentional concealment and actual concealment. The latter, said Kennedy L.J. was sufficient to dissolve the contract of suretyship in the case of a fidelity guarantee. He referred also to the way the matter was put by Story.[90]

[86] Story's Equity Jurisprudence, p. 210.
[87] Italics supplied.
[88] See per Fry J. in ***Davies v. London and Provincial Marine Insurance Co*** (1878) 8 Ch.D. 469 and para. 4.41 above.
[89] (1818) 3 Swans. 1 at 62; 36 E.R. 751.
[90] See Story's Equity Jurisprudence para. 215).

"If a party knowing himself to be cheated by his clerk, and, concealing the fact, applies for security in such a manner, and under such circumstances, as holds the clerk out to others as one whom he considers as a trustworthy person; and another person becomes his security, acting under the impression that the clerk is so considered by his employer; the contract of suretyship will be void; *for the very silence, under such circumstances, becomes expressive of a trust and confidence held out to the public, equivalent to an affirmation.*"[91]

Note: This case is cited at length because of its importance. The slightly confusing distinction adverted to between intentional concealment and actual concealment is probably just another way of saying that the duty of disclosure to a surety, where it arises, covers all facts within the knowledge of the creditor, or "buyer" of the guarantee: there does not have to be fraud, or any knowledge that the statement is false.

***National Provincial Bank v. Glanusk* [1913] 3 K.B. 335**

4.48 An owner of an estate had guaranteed his agent's debts to the Bank. It was held, on the facts, that the Bank had not had suspicions that the agent was acting dishonestly (which ought to have been disclosed) and the mere fact of the agent having an overdraft (which is what was left) need not be disclosed.

***Royal Bank of Scotland v. Greenshields* [1914] S.C. 259**

4.49 It was stressed in this cases in the Scottish Court of Session that although the creditor had no duty to reveal the mere fact of an overdraft, there would be a duty to speak if it was obvious to the creditor that the intended guarantor was labouring under a misapprehension. The Lord President said:

"The only circumstances in which I can conceive that a duty of disclosure would emerge, and a failure to disclose would be fatal to the Bank's case, would be where a customer put a question or made an observation in the presence and hearing of the bank-agent which necessarily and inevitably would lead anyone to the conclusion that the intending guarantor was labouring under a misapprehension with regard to the state of the customer's indebtedness."

Lord Mackenzie put the matter in a way which was less focussed on the facts of the case before them, and perhaps of more general usefulness:

"It is well-settled law that there is no obligation upon a bank-agent to disclose the position of his customer's account unless he is asked a specific question which imposes that obligation upon him, or unless circumstances emerge which put upon him the duty of making a full disclosure. The circumstances may be either that he volunteers a statement which is only half the truth, in which case the cautioner is entitled to say, "I was misled; I was entitled to assume that you were disclosing the whole truth," or—and this would be a case of ordinary fraud—if the intending cautioner makes a statement to the bank-agent, or in his presence, which plainly shows that he is entering into a transaction in an entire misapprehension of the facts of the case, then the bank-agent equally would be under an obligation, arising out of the circumstances of the case, to prevent the cautioner from being misled."

Note: the creditor's duty in this ordinary bank overdraft guarantee case is clearly being limited to the normal vendor's duty of candour and accuracy: see Chapter 5, Sale of Land for further examples of the working of the duty.

[91] Italics supplied.

***Greenhill v. Federal Insurance* [1927] 1 K.B. 65 (Lord Hanworth M.R., Scrutton L.J., Sargant L.J.) (Dictum of Park J about the underlying need for a degree of contractual equality approved by Court of Appeal in insurance case)**

4.50 A cargo of celluloid had been insured for a voyage across the Atlantic. Celluloid is very susceptible to damage by salt water. Some of the celluloid cargo proved to have been on deck, uncovered and exposed to salt water. It then remained at Halifax, uncovered on deck from November until the beginning of February. The question was whether the contract of insurance for the voyage onward was void for non-disclosure.

Scrutton L.J. referred to the duty of the assured to inform the underwriter of "everything that he is not taken as knowing, *so that the contract may be entered into on an equal footing*". He thought it as well expressed by Park J. as by anybody.[92]

"No contract can be good, unless it be equal; that is, neither side must have an advantage by any means, of which the other is not aware. This being admitted of contracts in general, it holds with double force in those of insurance . . ."

Scrutton L.J. found

(1) it was admitted to be material
(2) it was not disclosed
(3) there was a duty to disclose it
(4) the insurers had not waived disclosure.

Sargant L.J. and the Master of the Rolls agreed.

***London General Insurance Co v. General Marine Writers Association* [1921] 1 K.B. 104 C.A., standard of constructive knowledge required of assured:**

4.51 See Chapter 8, Knowledge and Notice, for a note of this case.

***Bank of Victoria v Mueller* [1925] VLR 642 (Notice to creditor of wife's vulnerability as guarantor)**

4.52 See Chapter 9, Dealings with the Vulnerable, for a note of this case.

***Trade Indemnity v. Workington Harbour and Dock Board* [1937] A.C. 17**

4.53 The case concerned a performance guarantee. Lord Atkin, with whom the others concurred, left open the question:

"whether in the formation of a contract of guarantee there is an obligation on the promisee to make a disclosure of material facts which would not exist in the formation of an ordinary contract." He went on: "There are decisions in the case of fidelity guarantees: *Railton v. Mathews* [paragraph 4.34 above] and *London General Omnibus Co v. Holloway* [paragraph 4.46 above] which would have to be examined if the point arose here for decision. But it is clear that in whatever way any duty to disclose arises and whether the promisee is under a positive duty to disclose material facts, which is one view, or is supposed to represent that the transaction sought to be guaranteed had no unusual or abnormal characteristics, making him the author of misrepresentation innocent or fraudulent as the case may be, which is another view, the duty or the implied representation will depend upon the particular circum-

[92] Park's *op. cit.*, Chap. 10 (which is headed "Of Fraud in Policies". At that time and for a considerable portion of the last century, "concealment" was always placed, loosely it may be, under the head of "fraud.") at p. 403 quoted also at the beginning of the chapter.

stances of each transaction." In this case there had been one outstanding feature, that the Dock Board made it absolutely plain that they left it to the proposed contractors to find out all the material facts, and made this plain in turn to the guarantors. Lord Atkin also said about this type of guarantee:

"For myself I doubt on the course of business alone whether a guarantor looks further than the skill and experience of the contractor to guard against risks of unknown difficulties in the performance of such a contract. . . . The guarantors are in such a case primarily concerned with the financial ability of the contractors to complete this contract whether it result in a loss or not."

***Westminster Bank v. Cond* [1940] 46 Com. Cas. 60**

4.54 Held by Tucker J. that in a guarantee of a debtor's debts to the bank, the mere existence of an overdraft need not, in the circumstances, be mentioned to the guarantor unless there was "anything to bring it to the notice of [the bank] that the existing overdraft was or could be a material matter for the consideration of Mr Cond in deciding whether or not he should sign the guarantee, for this reason: the bank already had ample cover in respect of the existing overdraft. They held the guarantees of two reputable gentlemen . . . What they wanted was further security for a further advance . . ."

Note: It will be seen that there may be a duty to disclose an existing overdraft to the debtor: a more flexible approach is being adopted.

***Cooper v. National Provincial Bank* [1946] K.B. 1**

4.55 Lord Campbell's criterion in *Hamilton v. Watson* (paragraph 4.35 above) was applied in the circumstances of the case again. A guarantor had guaranteed a Mrs Rolf's account with the bank. He claimed he had not appreciated that this would mean guaranteeing Mr Rolf also (an undischarged bankrupt) to an extent since she had given him authority to draw on her account. However, since the undertaking the guarantor had given to the bank made it clear that he could draw on it, there was no room for the guarantor to claim that *that which he would not naturally expect* was not disclosed to him by the bank.

***Union Bank of Australia v. Puddy* [1949] V.L.R. 242 (Australian Case)**

4.56 The case is of interest for the dictum of Fullagar J:

"If the creditor knows or would reasonably believe the surety to be acting upon a particular assumption of fact and knows that that assumption is unfounded, his conduct in not disclosing the truth may often be held to amount to a representation that the assumption is well founded."

***Australia & New Zealand Bank Ltd v. Colonial And Eagle Wharves Ltd* [1960] 2 Lloyd's Rep. 241**

4.57 This case settled or affirmed that the standard of care expected of the assured does not require him to carry out a detailed investigation before making his disclosure.

***Commercial Bank of Australia Limited v. Amadio* (1983) 151 C.l.R. 147 (Australian Case)**

4.58 This is rightly regarded as a seminal case. It was concerned with a dealing with vulnerable parties—an elderly migrant couple, not familiar with written English, who executed a mortgage of their property as security for their son's company's overdraft, relying on misrepresentations by him. See also Chapter

9, Dealings with the Vulnerable, for a note of the judgments dealing with that aspect of the case.

Gibbs C.J. felt that the dictum of Vaughan Williams L.J. in *London General Omnibus Co Ltd v. Holloway* (paragraph 4.46 above) to the effect that a creditor must reveal to the surety every fact which under the circumstances the surety would expect not to exist, was too broad. "To require a bank to make disclosure to a surety of the details of all unusual transactions which, to the knowledge of the bank, had taken place between the customer and third parties might prove to be both vexatious and misleading, as well as a breach of confidence. [He gave examples of [prima facie not material, but unusual aspects of the transaction] . . . It would be commercially unreal to suggest that a bank has a duty to reveal to a surety all the facts within its knowledge which relate to the transactions and financial position of a customer in any case where those transactions are out of the ordinary. The obligation is to reveal anything in the transaction between the banker and the customer which has the effect that the position of the customer is different from that which the surety would naturally expect, particularly if it affects the nature or degree of the surety's responsibility."

He then set out other circumstances which clearly were material from the sureties' point of view, such as the fact that there was an arrangement between the debtor and the bank that within three weeks the overdraft limit was to be reduced below the debit balance then existing; and that (within some unspecified but probably short time) the entire overdraft was to be cleared. He said:

"I find it impossible to suppose that a surety who undertook to meet the past and future liabilities of the company, and to give substantial security, would have expected that arrangement between the bank and the company included such unusual terms, which meant that the company was given merely a temporary respite, whereas the bank improved its existing and inadequate security. Further, there was the circumstance that the bank had not merely dishonoured the cheques, but had made itself a party to their selective dishonour, in an endeavour to maintain the facade of prosperity that the company, although insolvent, had erected . . ." Thus, he held that there had been disclosure which "*amounted to a misrepresentation* (albeit unintended) *of a material part of the transaction* between the bank and the company. . . ."[93]

Newbury v. Reliance [1994] 1 Lloyd's Rep. 83, Hobhouse J.

4.59 The case concerned prize indemnity insurance. Two points may be noted. First, the relative states of knowledge of the underwriter and the assured are relevant in deciding the amount of disclosure which is proper. In this case the individual dealing with the matter on behalf of the assured and the brokers were considered to be specialists in the field of motor racing with a particular expertise and knowledge. One of the partners of the firm had been a motor racing driver himself. Miss Clay, the underwriter, was prepared to underwrite indemnity risks in a whole range of sporting and other fields, but had no special knowledge of motor racing. Thus in the words of Hobhouse J.:[94]

"The position, therefore, on the broking of this risk to these underwriters was not factually the same as that which exists in other fields where the underwriter may be assumed to know already a large measure of the potentially material facts to the assessment of the risk and will only need to be informed about any special facts."

Secondly, where the presentation as a whole is such as not to give a fair

[93] Italics supplied.
[94] *ibid.* at 86.

picture of the risk, then there is no duty on the underwriter to make further inquiries, even though, as was argued for the assured, it was obvious that there was some relevant past history which might reveal relevant facts.[95] Hobhouse J. said[96]: "The obligation of an underwriter to make further enquiries only arises after a fair presentation has been made to him. He is entitled to assume that the risk has been presented to him in a fair fashion. Any other conclusion would, as Lord Justice Parker pointed out in the CTI case, emasculate the duty of the broker to make a disclosure of the material facts and would in effect reverse the burden of the obligations."

***Levett v. Barclay's Bank* [1995] 1 W.L.R. 1260**

4.60 This was a very strong case. Mr and Mrs Levett signed powers of attorney authorising the debtors to use their short-dated Treasury stock as security for a short-term loan from the bank to the debtors, which the latter intended to use in a development scheme in Ireland. Unknown to Mr and Mrs Levett, however, there was an agreement contained in the facility letter which was not disclosed to Mr and Mrs Levett, that the debt should be repaid by the sale of the security. It was held by Michael Burton Q.C. that the Bank had failed in its duty of disclosure or had impliedly misrepresented the position to Mr and Mrs Levett (the parties had agreed that no distinction need be drawn between the two for the purposes of the case). He held the terms of the facility letter contract were materially disadvantageous to Mr and Mrs Levett in a potentially disadvantageous way, and thus a non-disclosure they might rely on. He did not need to go into the question of the ambit in general of the duty of disclosure, because he was able to bring the case within the ambit of *Hamilton v. Watson* (paragraph 4.35 above) on the narrower interpretation of that case. Reliance was also placed on the statement of Gibbs C.J. in *Commercial Bank of Australia v. Amadio* (paragraph 4.58 above).

***PCW Syndicates v. PCW Reinsurers* [1996] 1 W.L.R. 1136**

4.61 See Chapter 8, Knowledge and Notice, for a note of this case.

***St Paul's Insurance v Mcconnell Insurance* [1996] 2 ALL E.R. 96**

4.62 See text at paragraph 4.18 above.

[95] Cp. lulling into a sense of false security, in other chapters, e.g. Chap. 5, Sale of Land, Chap. 8 Knowledge and Notice.
[96] *ibid.* at 90.

CHAPTER 5

SALE OF LAND: MISREPRESENTATION, MISDESCRIPTION, AMBIGUITY AND HALF-TRUTHS

"It is a general rule in Equity, founded on principles of honesty and the dictates of good sense, that if a person, generally speaking, offers anything for sale, the vendee . . . is entitled to see that the vendor has it with the qualifications, and in the way in which he . . . understood that he bought it, that is so as to afford him an assurance of having bought what he wanted, and meant to buy, or what was offered or professed to be sold—or he may reject the contract. In every common matter of business in life, that principle prevails. If a horse be sold by one person to another, and nothing be said about it on either side, the purchaser is entitled to have a sound horse delivered to him: and there are very many other familiar instances of the same kind, regarding the sale of chattels, which may be put in illustration of the generally prevailing principle in cases of this nature."[1]

"the concealment of material circumstances vitiates all contracts, upon the principles of natural law. A man, if kept ignorant of any material ingredient, may safely say it is not his contract."[2]

". . . there followed the costly ceremonial attendant—I will not say generally, let me rather say not very unusually—upon English purchases of land: a contract formally prepared and signed, then an abstract of title transmitted and perused, then objections, queries and requisitions—answer and replies, correspondence, embroilment, and a suit in Chancery."[3]

[1] Richards C.B. in ***Purvis v. Rayer*** (1821) 9 Price 488; 147 E.R. 159.
[2] Yates J., sitting with Lord Mansfield in *Hodgson v. Richardson* (1764) 1 Black W., 96 E.R. 268.
[3] Knight Bruce L.J. in *Denne v. Light* (1857) 8 De G.M. & G. 774; 44 E.R. 588.

"I impute no bad intention to the Plaintiff or his advisers, but I say that a man, knowing what this Plaintiff knew, who does not more fully express what he knows, does not do his duty."[4]

THE VENDOR'S DUTY OF CANDOUR AND ACCURACY

The importance of sales of land in the search for good faith principles

5.01 What follows is specific to sales of land. However, since, land was for centuries *the* investment the good faith rules applying to sales of land are crucially important. The rules are to be seen worked out in detail here in a way they are not anywhere else. When the sale of shares of companies from prospectuses began to be common, towards the end of the century, the good faith rules were simply the rules from sale of land, adapted to the new form of investment. The nature of the contract was different, and hence the way the good faith rules worked was different; but they built on the foundation already laid in sales of land.

Introduction

5.02 For those unfamiliar with conveyancing practice, in the sale of land there were traditionally, and still are, two stages: (1) the exchange of contracts; and (2) "completion", at which the price is handed over, the right to ownership of the land is handed over by means of a deed of conveyance or (more usually nowadays) transfer from the vendor to the purchaser, and the purchaser's "title", or ownership of the land is in most cases nowadays sent off to be registered at HM Land Registry so as to give public notice of the change of ownership.

Before the exchange of contracts stage it is usual for the purchaser to inspect the land (using a surveyor if he is prudent) and ask the vendor (and certain others, for example local authorities) questions about the land (traditionally called "Inquiries before Contract"). On formal exchange of contracts the two are bound to sell and to buy respectively. However, it is traditionally only at this stage, after the contract and before completion, that the purchaser starts to verify and check over the title deeds, sending the vendor "Requisitions on Title" or questions about his title or right to ownership of the land and the deeds which are said to prove this. It will be seen that as a result most title problems crop up after the formal contract has been entered into, while most problems of quality, description, etc, should crop up before the contract. Thus there is likely only to be complaint about defects of quality, etc, after the contract in two situations: first, where the purchaser has been too lazy to inspect the land and make usual

[4] Bacon V.-C. in *Heywood v. Mallalieu* (1883) 25 Ch. D. 357.

investigations; secondly, where the defect of quality has for some reason been difficult for the purchaser to find out about before contract. The background timetable for the purchaser's various pre-completion duties is important to bear in mind in reading this chapter and the cases referred to; the essential two-stage timetable is a long-established one and the cases on sale of land tend to presuppose a knowledge of it. Further, it can be important in understanding the reason for some of the judgments and in turn, the true basis of relief given by the courts for misrepresentation and misdescription in cases outside the sale of land. This is essentially a good faith basis: relief was given where there had been unfair dealing, leading the other party to be unfairly misled as to what he was buying. This was not just any unfair dealing, but a breach of the strictly limited principles of good faith or fair dealing laid down by the eighteenth and early to mid-nineteenth century courts.

5.03 Implied terms of the kind with which this book is concerned arise by virtue of "the nature of the contract". One needs accordingly to identify as far as possible in a general way the "nature" of sales of land. First, the sale of land is the sale of an ascertained, specific, subject matter. It is thus usually capable of reasonably accurate description; by contrast with, for example, the sale of a right to be covered against certain categories of risks which may arise in the future. On the other hand, description of land as a physical object requires considerable care: the point where the boundaries of my land end and someone else's begin can be a matter of debate in a way which is unthinkable in the case of a piece of machinery or a ship. Land is also different from most chattels in being something which may be crucially affected by its *history*: rights acquired by virtue of past happenings which may not have been thought about much at the time reach out to the present, preventing free use of the land by the purchaser. Thus, unsurprisingly, one finds that in the sale of land two problems predominate and have given birth to implied terms of good faith: (1) problems arising out of the land's history ("title" problems); and (2) questions about exactly what it is on the ground which the purchaser is getting (misdescription, misrepresentation, etc).

The fair dealing rules work differently in each case, although there is an area of overlap between the two, for example easement problems. Many of the cases mentioned below arise on a vendor's action for specific performance of the contract; some arise on a purchaser's action for rescission of the contract, and very occasionally, rescission of a completed sale. This is because the problems had mostly been spotted, as one would expect, before completion by conveyance or transfer. The Equity Courts sometimes allowed specific performance, sometimes allowed the purchaser rescission, and sometimes, feeling that damages (which they had not the power to give, being limited to compensation, which was something radically different) would be the appropriate remedy, left the parties to go to the common law courts for this.

5.04 It would not be accurate to say, as is sometimes suggested, that the good faith requirements arose in the course of the equity courts' discretionary jurisdiction to award specific performance, if by this it is meant that different good faith rules applied according to whether the vendor was seeking specific performance or the purchaser was seeking rescission.[5] Further, the Common Law courts applied the same good faith rules to contracts for the sale of land when these came before them.[6] There were differences between the courts, but not those differences. One tends to think of the Equity Courts operating as the Chancery Division does now, with virtually exclusive jurisdiction in cases concerning sales of real property. That was not so then; they were more like market stalls offering the consumer something different to choose from - different attitudes and above all different *remedies*. Thus, contracts for the sale of land might crop up in either kind of court. The really striking difference was that the Common Law courts could only find that the vendor had or had not performed his contract; they could not decide that he had not fallen short by much, and allow compensation or give "substantial justice" as the Equity Courts sometimes called their compensation jurisdiction, awarding compensation to the purchaser to make up to him for minor defects but preserving the contract. However, there seems to be no trace of difference in attitude between the two over the good faith rules to be implied in contracts for the sale of land.[7] Nor, perhaps, would one expect there to be. Only a generation or two had passed since Lord Mansfield's time.

1 *Title*

Implied term of good title a good faith term

5.05 Where the contract is silent about title, the rule is that the vendor has to show good title. This is considered to be something peculiarly within the knowledge of the vendor, who will normally have been associated with the property for a period, and peculiarly *outside* the knowledge of the purchaser. The courts in earlier times thought the vendor's advantage in the matter of special knowledge important as a justification of the implied term. Of the two, vendor and purchaser, the vendor was in the best position to know. The vendor was thus reasonably expected, one might say, to know the broad outlines of his title and to know whether he had any title or not. We may compare the attitude of the courts as regards the sale of chattels to "selling [goods] as his own"; the act of selling, without more, was an implied statement by conduct that the seller owned the thing being sold.

In *Stevens v. Adamson*,[8] which concerned an undisclosed then-equivalent to a "section 146 notice" in the sale of a leasehold, Abbott L.C.J. considered that a person putting up premises for sale was *bound*

[5] See below: Miscellaneous Points.
[6] See below: Some Questions.
[7] Save that the common law courts may at first have adopted a slightly more accepting attitude to "compensation clauses" in contracts for the sale of land: see Chap. 10, Excluding the Effect of the Fair-Dealing Terms.
[8] (1818) 2 Stark. 422; 171 E.R. 692.

to know of the notice and he felt, was required by the good faith which had to be exhibited in such transactions to communicate the fact of the notice to the purchaser.

Tindal C.J. in *Flight v. Booth*,[9] which concerned undisclosed restrictive covenants, said:

> "the lease being in the hands of the vendor, *he had peculiarly, and indeed exclusively, the means of knowledge* of the exact restrictions contained in it; the purchaser at the auction had none."[10]

Where the contract is silent about title, it is only binding on the purchaser in so far as there *is in fact good title* by the time of completion.[11] This was not merely a matter of Equity's intervention. Both common law courts and equity courts observed this implied term of good faith.

5.06 The courts often attached the implied term label to the duty to give good title but often also felt it needed to be differentiated in some way from other terms of the contract. Lord Eldon in *White v. Foljambe*[12] decided that it was *part of the meaning* of a contract for the sale of a leasehold that the vendor should have a good title, free from incumbrances—in other words a very similar approach to that applied in the course of evolution of implied terms on sales of chattels.[13] Lord Denman C.J. in *Souter v. Drake* also said[14]:

> ". . . the true ground of refusing relief by a specific performance in these cases is, that the vendor *by his contract was bound to make out a good title* in all respects to the subject agreed to sold, including the right of the lessor to demise . . . And no reason occurs to us why, *as the Courts of Law and of Equity would put the same construction on a contract for the sale of a freehold estate,* they should do otherwise in respect of a contract for the sale of a leasehold."[15]

He referred to the earlier cases, and said that the court had concluded:

> "that, unless there be a stipulation to the contrary, there is, *in every contract for the sale of a lease, an implied undertaking* to make out the lessor's title to demise, as well as that of the vendor to the lease itself, *which implied undertaking is available at law as well as in equity.*"[16]

5.07 In *Ogilvie v. Foljambe*,[17] on the other hand, Sir William Grant treated the right to a good title as a right "not growing out of the agreement

[9] (1834) 1 Bing. N.C. 370; 131 E.R. 1160.

[10] Italics supplied.

[11] See for an early example, *Farrer v. Nightingal* (1798) 2 Esp. 639; 170 E.R. 481, where the purchaser was held entitled to consider the contract at an end, and bring an action for the deposit as money had and received.

[12] (1805) 11 Ves. 337; 32 E.R. 1118.

[13] *cf.* Chap. 3, Sale of Personal Property.

[14] (1834) 5 B. & Ad. 991; 110 E.R. 1058.

[15] Italics supplied.

[16] *ibid.*

[17] (1817) 3 Mer. 53; 36 E.R. 21.

between the parties, but which is given by law''. He called it collateral to the agreement. The sale-of-goods implied terms were sometimes described as ''collateral'' to the main object of the contract.

By the time of *Ellis v. Rogers*,[18] Cotton L.J. felt uncertain whether it should be called a term of the contract or a collateral right. Perhaps the confusion arose from the notion, which may have begun to get around then, that it was rather irregular, so to speak, to have a term, implied or express, which did not sound in damages: see the discussion of the nature of the duty of good faith in Chapter 2. However, if one appreciates the de-limiting nature of the presumption of good faith, and terms thereby implied, which do not sound directly in damages, the problem disappears. Compare the implied term of good faith in insurance contracts, operating in a precisely similar way to the old good-title term, and arising for similar reasons—the superior access to knowledge of one typical party to a contract over the other.

The relevance of the now-defunct Rule in *Bain v. Fothergill*[19] to the good faith nature of the good title term

5.08 The implied-term analysis of the ''duty'' to give good title (really, like other good faith terms, a contingent duty only: if the duty is ''broken'': there is to that extent no contract; to the extent that the duty is fulfilled, the contract is binding; if no contract materialises the duty is irrelevant) is supported by the treatment traditionally afforded by the courts to vendors who had failed to disclose their absence of title. These vendors, we find, were never made to pay damages to the disappointed purchaser if it proved they had no title, unless they had actually *known* of the title defect and deliberately failed to disclose it. Instead, the contract was rescinded and the parties were restored to the state they were in before the contract or the *statu quo ante* the purchaser normally receiving back his deposit (at least after about the mid-nineteenth century) and his expenses of investigating title, while the vendor retained the land. This is precisely what one would expect in the case of an implied good faith term.

The Rule in *Bain v. Fothergill*, as it began to be called, has often been explained in more recent times simply as a piece of indulgence to vendors: the difficulty in knowing one's own title was so great, it is said, that they must have been allowed this special piece of indulgence. The obligation to deduce title undoubtedly *was* more onerous in earlier times—title for 60 years had to be deduced, the documents themselves tended to be more complicated than most present-day transfers, and there was no central register of title, so that the physical loss or destruction of deeds presented more of a problem. However, the idea that something should be done purely to help people out of commonly occurring difficulties is, possibly, a modern notion deriving from frequent state intervention in often lengthy statutes on behalf of

[18] (1885) 29 Ch. D. 661.
[19] (1874) L.R. 7 H.L. 158.

supposedly commercially disadvantaged categories of people.[20] We may doubt it would have occurred to the more stoical eighteenth and early to mid-nineteenth-century lawyers.

5.09 Nor does the idea of compassionate intervention here seem to be historically accurate. In *Flureau v. Thornhill*,[21] the Court of Common Pleas held that the purchaser of a piece of real property might not have damages for "the fancied goodness of the bargain, which he supposes he has lost".[22] Blackstone J. however, explained the reason why he might not have what we would now call "expectation damages". It was essentially no title, no contract. He said:

> "These contracts are merely upon condition, frequently expressed, but always implied, that the vendor has a good title. If he has not, the return of the deposit, with interest and costs, is all that can be expected . . ."

The good faith analysis of the good title term also fits more naturally with the thinking of the Courts of Equity in evolving their doctrine of compensation or "substantial justice" in cases of minor title defects or minor misrepresentations or misdescriptions: see below as to this doctrine, which applies both to the good faith terms about title and those about misrepresentation and misdescription, etc. A contract is what you agree to: when agreeing to X which you knew about you are also taken as agreeing to Y which you did not, *if* it is not going to make a crucial difference to the object of the contract, and if you could be compensated in money for the difference. Otherwise, the purchaser was not held to his contract. The way in which Equity operated its compensation or substantial justice jurisdiction was similar in the case both of material title flaws and material misdescription, etc., of the land sold: the purchaser had not agreed to *that* subject matter, so there was no agreement at all.

After the abolition of the Rule in *Bain v. Fothergill*: a choice of inconsistent remedies

5.10 The old Rule in *Bain v. Fothergill* prevailed, with growing numbers of "exceptions" over the years, until abolished by the passing of the Law of Property (Miscellaneous Provisions) Act 1989. This Act of course left untouched the implied term of good faith that the vendor must *have* title. The combined effect is thus curious: we now have a statutory right to loss-of-expectation damages for breach of contract even in the case of serious title defects, where the non-statutory law on its true analysis would have said there was no meeting of minds and no contract at all; and still does say that, to the extent that a

[20] These well-meaning statutes are often expressed in the kind of elaborate and lengthy form that makes these categories of people even more disadvantaged, since they cannot be expected to understand the helpful legislation without the assistance of a lawyer, and not always then.

[21] (1776) 2 Black, W. 1078; 96 E.R. 635.

[22] De Grey C.J.'s phrase.

purchaser may still obtain rescission if there is a substantial undisclosed title defect. The vendor is now, however, deemed by statute, in effect, to warrant that he has title. Perhaps it does not matter much in practice: with simplified conveyancing and the statutory registration of title there are fewer vendors who genuinely do not know their own title anyway and will encounter difficulties. The purchaser for his part has a choice of remedies: if his expectation damages are greater he may seek damages for the new implied or express term that there should be good title; and if his reliance damages are greater, for example because of a fall in the value of the land he has bought, he will still be able to rescind under the non-statutory law.[23]

2 *Mis-statements as to quality or extent of land*

Eleven shades of ambiguity

5.11 The misrepresentations or misleading statements in question here are statements about the quality (including rights over the land, often termed "incumbrances") or extent of the land; thus they may also be called misdescriptions. If I misrepresent the quality or size of something I am selling I am also misdescribing it: the two words are interchangeable.

The expressions misrepresentation or misdescription contain a certain ambiguity: they may mean false representations of what is the case (whether or not I know it) or false representations of my knowledge about what is the case. What causes the ambiguity is our uncertainty about the state of mind required in the vendor before we say, "That was definitely a misrepresentation". There are a number of relevant states of mind. Examples of these are given below, and for ease of collective reference they are awarded stars for blameworthiness, the most blameworthy receiving three stars, and the least blameworthy, or possibly not blameworthy at all, one star. The brackets which sometimes follow a statement contain the mental reservations or the circumstances of the author. Good faith is concerned with the middle-ranking category of blameworthiness—the two-star statements.

Seven shades of factual misrepresentation

5.12

(a) I know my statement is untrue.*
(b) I do not know if it is untrue or not (but do not care much either way).*
(c) I believe my statement is true (but that is because I have not bothered to consult the information in my possession or control: if I had I would have known it was untrue (or not wholly true)).**
(d) I believe my statement is true (but I am taking an unreason-

[23] As to the problems believed to prevent a party to a sale opting to rescind after completion, see Chapter 16, Rescission of Executed Sales.

able view of the information in my possession or control in so doing: most people with that information would think the statement untrue (not wholly true, etc.)).**

(e) I believe my statement is true (and it is true on the information in my possession or control, but if I had taken steps reasonably within my power to find out more, I would have discovered it was not true).*

(f) I believe my statement is true (but I have not mentioned to you that it is only a part of the truth)**

(g) I believe my statement is true (but it has two possible meanings and I have not mentioned to you which one I am taking it in).**

(2) Misrepresentations about one's own belief: four shades of ambiguity

5.13 The following are perhaps relevant:

(a) I believe that X is the case (but I have not consulted the information (*e.g.* documents, written material) in my possession about it).**

(b) I believe that X is the case (because Y has told me so but I know nothing about it myself).**

(c) I believe that X is the case (I have consulted the information in my possession about it, but that information for reasons unknown to you, only covers a part of the period or extent of my statement).**

(d) I believe that X is the case, I have consulted the information in my possession about it, and that information is much what you might expect me to have, but I have not taken active steps to seek out any other information about it.*

There is a sense, in which one does not even think of a statement as a misrepresentation *at all* if it is made by someone who honestly and *reasonably* believes it, even if in fact his belief proves to be wrong with hindsight. This is because we acknowledge that his statement was wrong but we think of it as *reasonably wrong*. The question is again one of our reasonable expectations. It will be seen that the two-star cases involve conduct which might mislead the other party. His reasonable expectations will almost certainly *not*, in normal circumstances have included the bracketed reservations. The one-star case is a different matter: there may be occasions there where the other party would expect me to take steps to find out; but more often perhaps, he will not so expect. It is a grey verging on white area. Our reasonable expectations are patchy, and inconsistent.

"Within his knowledge"

5.14 There is no fair dealing duty, in general, to research the basis of a statement about what is to be sold from what one might broadly call outside information. Good faith draws a tentative line ruling *in* relevant information inside one's possession or control and ruling *out* that which would need outside research, however easy it might be to undertake. The expression "within his knowledge" is frequently used to denote this. It has caused puzzlement, in these literal days. It plainly means something beyond actual knowledge, but what? The cases discussed in this chapter and elsewhere in this book give us the answer. Thus, inferences are often made that the vendor ought[24] to know, from the fact that he was *bound to have* relevant information within his possession. There is a presumption that he will have looked at relevant information. A seller of land will have looked at his title documents; either he or an agent can reasonably be expected to possess these. Similarly, he will reasonably be expected to know about all but the most trifling physical defects of his land, where its boundaries are, etc. If he does not know, who does, is the approach.

Suppose he does not in fact have the expected relevant information, or all the relevant information, in his possession? The answer in that case is, his duty of accuracy means that he must rebut the buyer's reasonable presumption so that the buyer *is not misled*. "All my records have been eaten by mice: you must take a chance on there being unregistered incumbrances over the land" may not be much of a selling point, but it gives accurate information to the buyer on a crucial aspect of what is to be sold him. It may indeed affect the price, but is it not right that it should? Since a seller has in general considerably superior access to information than a buyer, he is taken to know that the reasonable expectation of the buyer-recipient of his statement will be that his statements about what he is selling are made from knowledge of proper and usual sources of information.

5.15 It may be said, this is hard on a seller, in these days when anyone has *so much* information under his control. As has been said, when once documents were measured by the handful, now it may be the pantechnicon.[25] Then there is the information we have in our computer systems. If information is power, the corresponding responsibility may be to keep proper control of it so as to avoid misleading others. It may be, as suggested elsewhere, that lack of control over relevant information is a new or intensified type of vulnerability, properly giving rise to a new and greater responsibility in the possessor of the relevant information. At all events, the detailed working out of the sphere of this responsibility is likely to require further thought and informed decision by the courts. It is likely, one may suspect, to come up in future, if only in the sphere of the Unfair Contract Terms Regulations 1994. For example, over what period must a corporate body have control of information; and does the organisation as a whole have to be aware that the information in its control is missing vital parts that a buyer would expect to be there; or is it sufficient if the information *looks* complete to whichever individual agent

[24] The "ought" is not so much a moral judgment, more a term of reasonable expectation, as in "the train ought to be arriving about now".

[25] The then Sir Thomas Bingham M.R., President of the Chartered Institute of Arbitrators, giving the Holdsworth Club Lecture at the University of Birmingham on March 18, 1994. (The Price of Justice, printed in the *Journal of the Chartered Institute* (1994) pp. 239 *et seq.*)

of the corporation makes the statement? These questions were touched on in *William Sindall v. Cambridgeshire County Council*[26] in which it was thought that a seller would be bound to disclose that "the documents had been destroyed by enemy action or eaten by mice", but, rightly or wrongly, a fairly relaxed view was taken by Hoffmann L.J. of the non-disclosure in the past that a huge swathe of relevant documents had been destroyed, because the particular "reasonable conveyancer" employed by the County Council would not "realise they were inadequate for the purpose of answering the question".[27] Evans L.J., on the other hand, would have preferred not to be taken "as approving either corporate forgetfulness or collective amnesia of this sort."

5.16 We think of a statement, therefore, as misleading the other party when it is both wrong in fact, and made from a knowledge base which *confounds the other party's reasonable expectations*. It would probably not be true to say that the one-star statement does confound such reasonable expectations; it would only confound some people's in some circumstances. It is no doubt also true to say that we think of the three-star (fraudulent) statements as much more blameworthy, while we probably put the two-star statements somewhere a fair way below, calling them things like "careless", "unfair", or "misleading".

It is possible also for us to call two-star and one-star statements alike "innocent misrepresentations"; not in the sense that there is *no blame at all* to be attached to them, but in the sense that they are not deliberate untruths as the fraudulent statements are. In another sense, of course, the two-star statements are not innocent, or perhaps we would prefer to say, not wholly innocent: there is *some* blame attached to them; we do not feel the maker of the statement has really been at his best when making it, shall we say. There has been a lack of *candour*, or a lack of *accuracy*, at least. He has put something misleading into circulation when he need not have done.

The good faith approach to two-star misleading statements

5.17 The Courts of Equity, who first came to consider such matters as regards contracts which were not insurance contracts, since the state of a person's conscience, and thus his putatively blameworthy state of mind, came within their special purview, took much the view that is exemplified by the star system above. They too called broadly the area covered by the two-star statements careless, unfair, misleading, and the like, and required candour and accuracy from vendors and others in a similar position—that is, parties to a contract who had a responsibility for *defining what was sold*. They accepted that the defining party might well not have intended to mislead; but they did not accept that that was by any means the end of his responsibility. They used words of blame about his conduct, albeit *different* words of blame from those reserved for intentional misleading. They said such con-

[26] [1994] 1 W.L.R. 1016.

[27] But see the note of the case in the Appendix to Chap. 10: there had been an agreed formulation made by counsel.

duct amounted to a "fraud on the purchaser", when made by the vendor; or that it constituted "legal fraud"; which expression they contrasted with "moral fraud" or deceit, which meant the fully-fledged fraudulent cases given three stars above. On the other hand they certainly did not think vendors had to be right every time; they took a perfectly compassionate, common sense view of the information available to vendors of the time. A purchaser who complained about something which the vendor could never have known about did not get very far. Nor, if it came to that, did a purchaser who failed to make the normal investigations of the property he was buying (unless of course he had been misled as to the need for these or fobbed off by the vendor, as to which see below).

Misrepresentation and misdescription: a warning

5.18 The term misdescription is often used to denote a statement about the quality or extent of the land which becomes incorporated in the contract, in contrast to a statement about the quality or extent of the land which causes the contract but does not become incorporated in the contract, which is labelled a misrepresentation for this purpose. This is all right, as long as one remains aware of two important points.

(1) A false (which expression, as will shortly be seen, includes ambiguous or half-true) statement made before the contract will have no effect at all (other than no doubt to annoy the purchaser, and subject to the law on tortious misrepresentations) if a contract does not result;

(2) If a contract does result, a false statement made before the contract but not incorporated in it, and a false statement made in the contract itself will both *have a legal effect* but in slightly different ways. A statement in the contract which proves to be false will only be given effect in so far as the maker, usually the vendor, complied with his duty of good faith in making it. A pre-contractual false statement *not* incorporated in the contract

   (a) may be an additional part of the contract;
   (b) may shed light on the question whether the vendor has complied with his duty of good faith (for example in the event that the contract wording is ambiguous) or
   (c) may shed light on the question whether the purchaser knew or ought to have known the true state of affairs anyway (for example if it emerges that the vendor explained the truth to him anyway; or on the other hand, that the vendor made a statement lulling him into a false sense of security and thus deflecting him from normal investigations).

Both kinds of statement, that is those incorporated in the contract as well as those which are not, may cause the purchaser to be misled, to enter into a contract he had not expected and did not want. For practical purposes, the courts in the late eighteenth and early to mid-nineteenth century, when the good faith doctrines were being developed, did not differentiate between the two specially. The contrast is a late addition, and may have been connected with the belief which became widespread by the end of the last century that rescission for misrepresentation, etc., was not possible after completion of a contract for the sale of land. The focus of the courts which developed good faith principles was simply on the *practical effect of the contract wording*, taking into account what had been said and left unsaid, and done and left undone by the parties beforehand. Nor was there any special distinction made by the courts between the implied representation from silence that there would be good title, and any (usually positive) representations as to quality or extent of the land. In any case, something like an easement affecting land was right on the boundary: it was a matter both of title and of quality. Accordingly, misrepresentations about title will be included in the passage next following.

3 The vendor's duty of candour and accuracy: Misdescription/misrepresentation/part-true, tricky or ambiguous statements in or affecting the contract of sale

The duty arises normally when the vendor (or defining party) speaks (or writes) regarding what he is selling

5.19 The vendor (or person whom has sometimes been called the defining party, since he is not always the vendor) does not have, in theory, to speak at all: the duty is not a duty of spontaneous disclosure as in insurance cases and to an extent, surety cases. The vendor's duty of good faith in sales of land, unlike sales of personal property, arises rarely from silence in misleading circumstances, and almost always *when he does speak or write*; but this should not lead anyone to underestimate it. He is obliged, *if he describes what he sells*, to deal fairly with his purchaser by describing what is sold carefully and accurately; and to avoid sins of commission by avoiding anything which might mislead, and sins of omission by stating the whole of whatever point he is making—not for him the stance apparently taken by some of those who gave evidence to Lord Justice Scott in the Arms-to-Iraq Inquiry he undertook in 1996, that there is a lot of truth in a half- truth, and the like. There might be, but a vendor of land has always indulged in half-truths at his peril, as can be seen from the cases below.

Vendor's duty of good faith not fiduciary

5.20 The duty is in no way whatever a fiduciary duty: the sale of land has been firmly labelled an arm's-length transaction. Lord Eldon in *Turner v. Harvey*,[28] for example said:

"... the Court, in many cases, has been in the habit of saying,

[28] (1821) Jac. 169; 37 E.R. 814.

> that where parties deal for an estate, they may put each other at arm's length: the purchaser may use his own knowledge, and is not bound to give the vendor information of the value of his property."[29]

Lord Eldon's statement quoted, taken at face value, may be thought to mean that if a vendor keeps entirely silent about unsatisfactory features affecting the value, he is safe, even if he is keeping relevant knowledge to himself. This would be quite wrong. It is easy to misunderstand Lord Eldon's subtle pronouncement. The trouble was and is, that a vendor who wishes to sell his property is unlikely to get on very well if he *is* entirely silent. The scenario of an entirely silent vendor, who refuses to describe what land he is selling, is frankly an unlikely one. It would probably be naive to take Lord Eldon's classification of sales of land as much more than a figure of speech, meant to heighten the dramatic effect of the exceptions to the rule which come afterwards. (Compare the approach known as *occupatio* employed by Chaucer among others—"I will not tell of . . . and nor will I tell of. . . . and nor will I tell of. . . .!") Lord Eldon continues a little later[30]:

> "But a very little is sufficient to affect the application of that principle. If a word, if a single word be dropped which tends to mislead the vendor[31] that principle [safety for silent arm's length dealing] will not be allowed to operate."

His real point is in *this* passage: namely, the implied term that the contract does not extend to a misleading term. The purchaser's reasonable expectation of fair-dealing prevails. Vendors have of course in practice always described their property, and have often failed to come up to the stringent standards of candour and accuracy required by the fair-dealing rules. They have tried, after the contract, to rely on misleading descriptions against purchasers who reasonably thought they meant something else, and they have found that the courts have by and large been firm and unsympathetic.

In *Lachlan v. Reynolds*[32] Sir W. Page Wood V.C. said:

> "If there be one thing which the Court insists upon more than another *in dealings between vendor and purchaser* it is that there should be *perfectly good faith on the part of the vendor in the representations which he makes to the purchaser*".[33]

[29] We may assume that Lord Eldon is talking about the physical features of the property only; he was an upholder after all of the implied term that a vendor must give good title.
[30] *ibid.*
[31] In that case the purchaser happened to be the defining party.
[32] (1853) Kay 52; 69 E.R. 23.
[33] Italics supplied.

The good faith rules in operation: "fraud in the representation" to be avoided[34]

The Rule against Ambiguity: the vendor's duty of accuracy

5.21 A straightforwardly incorrect statement, whether about title or about the description of the land sold, is fairly obviously a breach of the duty of good faith on the part of the vendor. Less obvious and much more usual, especially nowadays, after around a century of literalism, is tricky or ambiguous language by the vendor. This is territory patrolled by good faith. If the purchaser was presumed to have been misled, or had actually been misled by such statements, he might either resist specific performance or seek rescission of the contract, depending on how "material"[35] the statement was.

The courts gradually began to draw a distinction for this purpose between statements which were literally true but misleading on the one hand, and those which were literally untrue on the other. In the latter case, it might be presumed that the purchaser had been misled by the statement.

(1) Ambiguous statements literally untrue

5.22 Where an unusual or local meaning was relied on this was counted as untrue.

In *Portman v. Mill*[36] a farm was described as having "349 acres or thereabouts". This was, in a sense, literally true: they turned out not to be normal acres, but "customary acres," working out at about 249 ordinary acres. The purchaser was held not bound to complete when there was so large a deficiency.

In *Stewart v. Alliston*[37] the purchaser was told that the "ground rent" of certain property was £40 a year. This was only true in a rather subjective sense: as Lord Eldon put it:

> "Would any man, seeing a house put up to auction . . . subject to a ground-rent lease, suppose that the word ground-rent meant rack-rent? The subject of the contract, therefore, does not answer the vendor's description of it . . ."

The purchaser was proceeding in the common law courts to recover his deposit, and Lord Eldon refused the vendor's application for an injunction to prevent this.[38]

[34] Lord Thurlow's expression, in *Lowndes v. Lane* (1789) 2 Cox Eq. Cas. 363; 30 E.R. 167.

[35] See below as to materiality.

[36] (1826) 2 Russ. 570; 38 E.R. 449.

[37] (1815) 1 Mer. 26; 35 E.R. 587.

[38] See also ***Farebrother v. Gibson*** (1857) 1 De G. & J. 602 though the purchaser there failed on the facts; ***Hughes v. Jones*** (1861) 3 De G.F. & J. 307 where "now or late in the several occupations of . . ." was held insufficiently "clear precise and definite" to denote tenancies for lives at low rents; ***Cox v. Coventon*** (1862) 31 Beav. 378; 54 E.R. 1185.

(2) Ambiguous statements literally true

5.23 In this case, the purchaser had to prove that he in fact relied on the false meaning. In considering the question of a purchaser's reliance the court would take into account matters which "are of such a kind as to be open to his [the purchaser's] observation."[39] *Lowndes v. Lane*[40] is an example of this kind of exercise. The case concerned the sale of some woods with a statement that they produced £250 a year. The purchaser accepted that this *could be* literally correct, but said it was so only if you assumed that the woods were "racked" beyond the normal course of husbandry; and would not be true at all if the woods were cut in the normal way. He said he had relied on the normal meaning of "produced" Lord Thurlow decided that in fact he had *not* relied on it, but on his own surveyor, whom he had sent down to examine the woods prior to the sale. However, Lord Eldon said that otherwise, if what the purchaser had said were true and he had relied on the more normal meaning, *"it would be a fraud in the representation, to be relieved against"*.[41]

In *Turner v. Harvey*,[42] Lord Eldon said:

> "It is not immaterial in cases like this to attend to the description of the property to be sold; for if one man understands an expression in one sense, and another in a different sense; though the Court must impute to both that they understood it in the right sense, yet if there has been any mistake, and especially *if the expression used by one party has at all misled the other*, it is always material in considering what a court of equity will do with the case".[43]

In *Leyland v. Illingworth*[44] Knight, Bruce and Turner L.JJ. considered that although there was "no direct misstatement in the particulars" a statement that a property was "well supplied with water" when in fact it had no water source of its own, was materially inaccurate, although a purchaser who knew the real state of the case would have nothing to complain of.[45]

The Duty of Candour—The Rule against Pregnant Half-truths

5.24 The problem about a half-truth is that it is, but is not known to be, pregnant with the unexpressed other half. A purchaser's problem thus arises when he does not know it is a part-truth, but supposes it to be the whole of the truth on a particular topic. The courts have held that in sales there is an implicit representation that the whole relevant

[39] Lord Thurlow in ***Lowndes v. Lane*** (1789) 2 Cox. Eq. Cas. 363; 30 E.R. 167.
[40] *ibid.*
[41] Italics supplied.
[42] (1821) above.
[43] Italics supplied.
[44] (1860) 2 De G.F. & J. 248; 45 E.R. 617.
[45] See also ***Swaisland v. Dearsley*** (1861) 29 Beav. 430; 54 E.R. 694; ***Bascombe v. Beckwith*** (1869) L.R. 8 Eq. 100; ***Denny v. Hancock*** (1870) 6 Ch. App. 1.

truth is told, that a mere pregnant half-truth[46] *is regarded as half a misrepresentation*. To the extent that the omission affects the description, the property is then held to be *incorrectly described*. The purchaser is deemed to have agreed to buy what was properly described, dealing fairly according to good faith principles; what is available in fact may well be radically different. The effect is thus to put the vendor in breach of contract—to a degree which may be small or large, depending on what falls to be omitted. The effect can also be seen as giving rise to **an ancillary duty of disclosure** on the part of the vendor in such cases.

See the well-known case of *Flight v. Booth*,[47] a good example of a pregnant part-true statement. Here the *implicit* representation in the particulars of sale was that the purchaser would have the leasehold property in Covent Garden subject only to the particular restrictions specifically mentioned (offensive trades, coffee house keeper, working hatter). These proved in fact to have been only a selection from a much longer list. The purchaser reasonably assumed that the whole truth would have been given him, not a mere part. The effect was drastic, in this particular case: the purchaser was held not obliged to take a lease at all, given the difference made to the thing purchased by the numerous additional restrictions on user which existed in fact. Tindal C.J. said:

> "Under such a state of facts, the purchaser may be considered as *not having purchased the thing which was really the subject of the sale*."[48]

Granger v. Worms[49] would seem to be another example of a pregnant half-truth. The question was whether the property sold should have included a summerhouse. The particulars actually said nothing about this; and there was no summerhouse on the demised premises since it had been pulled down; but since the summerhouse was described as part of the premises in the lease, the purchaser came under an obligation, which the vendor had not disclosed, to reinstate the summerhouse at the end of the lease. Lord Ellenborough allowed the purchaser to terminate the contract and recover back his deposit.[50]

[46] The expression is the author's, it does not occur in any case: it simply seemed a helpful label.
[47] (1838) 1 Bing (N.C.) 370; 131 E.R. 1160.
[48] Italics supplied.
[49] (1814).
[50] See also ***Dykes v. Blake*** (1838) 4 Bing (N.C.) 463; 132 E.R. 866; ***Price v. Macaulay*** (1852) 2 De G.M. & G. 331; 42 E.R. 903; ***Lachlan v. Reynolds*** (1853) Kay 52; 69 E.R. 23; ***Stanton v. Tattersall*** (1853) 1 Sim. & G. 529; 65 E.R. 231 (where a house was said to have a right of access from Pall Mall: in fact it had only an indirect access, through another house which itself was on Pall Mall); ***Caballero v. Henty*** (1874) 11 App. Cas. 232 and ***Coakes v. Boswell*** [1886] L.R. 9 Ch. 447. See further for the application of the duty of condour to a statement of opinion, ***Smith v. Land & House Property*** (1884) 28 Ch. D. 7 and ***Brown v. Raphael*** (1958) Ch. 636, a non-land case.

The Rule against Pregnant Half-Truths applied to summaries, etc.

5.25 If a vendor summarises a deed in his possession, or similar document, the summary has to be accurate, and has to cover all the points which are important from the purchaser's point of view. In *Cox v. Coventon*[51] it was said by Sir John Romilly that if the contents of a deed are set out in a general way, without reference to the document itself, then:

> "in order to sustain the contract, this account must not only be correct in itself as far as it goes, but must be such as to give the purchaser all the information as to the character of the property which it is essential he should possess."

Pregnant or misleading silence where circumstances lead to an inference contrary to that intended by silent vendor[52]

5.26 In *Bower v. Cooper*[53] it was held that a contract to sell land which did not express what interest what to be sold would import the whole of the vendor's interest in the premises.

It is likely, as mentioned at the beginning of the chapter, that the similar rule that a vendor should show good title unless he is able to point to a specific exclusion in the contract has a similar good faith basis.[54]

"Know your purchaser" applicable to test the duty of candour or accuracy

5.27 The vendor had not only to be accurate and candid in general; he had to express himself in terms which it could be anticipated would be understood by the kind of purchaser in question. In *Dykes v. Blake*[55] Tindal C.J. said—in terms which sound strikingly like the Unfair Contract Terms Regulations 1994:

> "Particulars and plans of this nature should be so framed as to convey clear information to the ordinary class of persons who frequent sales by auction; and they only become a snare to the purchaser, if after the bidder has been misled by them, the seller should be able to avail himself of expressions which none but lawyers could understand or attend to".[56]

[51] (1862) 31 Beav. 378; 54 E.R. 1185.
[52] Cp. the French legal concept of *reticence dolosive*.
[53] (1843) 2 Hare 408; 67 E.R. 168.
[54] Cp. *Smith v. Hughes* (1871) L.R. 6 Q.B. 597. and see ***Walters v. Morgan*** (1861) above.
[55] (1838) 4 Bing (N.C.) 463; 132 E.R. 866.
[56] See also ***Swaisland v. Dearsley*** (1861) 29 Beav. 430; 54 E.R. 694.

The good faith duty of candour may apply to the buyer too

5.28 Relevant cases are *Turner v. Harvey*[57] and *Philips v. Homfray*.[58]

Where there is a breach of the duty of candour or accuracy an innocent or mistaken motive is no defence

5.29 In *Dykes v. Blake*[59] Tindal C.J. accepted that the breach was unintentional on the part of the vendor.

In *Calverley v. Williams*[60] the rationale of the good-faith duty was explained thus by Lord Thurlow:

> "It must have been imputed to the owner, that he knew the parcels, which were let to *Groombridge*; for whether he did or not, he undertook to know by undertaking to give a description.[61]

In *Price v. Macaulay*[62] a representation made was that the reservoir and waterworks yielded a rent of £60. This was true, but not in the sense in which the purchaser might reasonably take it, because the water came over the land of a third party by permission only. Knight Bruce L.J. said "I do not impute wrong intention to anyone" but still refused the vendor in that case specific performance on the grounds that he had conducted himself with insufficient good faith.

Also relevant is the case of *Dimmock v. Hallett*[63] in which the court in setting aside the contract, disclaimed the notion that there had been actual fraud on the part of the vendor, but stressed his duty of good faith and said there had been nonetheless a lack of the requisite good faith on his part. The statement he had made as to the rent, though true as far as it went, was not the whole truth on the matter, and thus was calculated to mislead.

In *Denny v. Hancock*[64] the plan, taken in conjunction with what was on the ground, unintentionally had a misleading effect, and accordingly the purchaser was not compelled to complete.[65]

Lord Ellenborough in *Belworth v. Hassall*[66] said that "any fraud or material misdescription, though unintentional, would vacate the agreement"; and in *Stevens v. Adamson*[67] Abbott C.J. is noted as considering that "a person putting up premises for sale was bound to know how the premises were circumstanced".[68]

[57] (1821) above.
[58] (1871) 6 Ch. App. 770.
[59] (1838) above.
[60] (1790) 1 Ves. 210; 30 E.R. 306.
[61] Italics in original.
[62] (1852) 2 De G.M. & G. 331; 42 E.R. 903.
[63] (1866) 2 Ch. App. 21.
[64] (1870) 6 Ch. App. 1.
[65] See also ***Heywood v. Mallalieu*** (1883) 25 Ch. D. 357.
[66] (1815) 4 Camp. 140; 171 E.R. 45.
[67] (1818) 2 Stark 422; 171 E.R. 692.
[68] See also ***Leyland v. Illingworth*** (1860), 2 De G.F. & J. 248; 45 E.R. 617 in which Jessel M.R. imputed no fraudulent or dishonest intention to anyone; ***Bascombe v. Beckwith*** (1869) L.R. 8 Eq. 100 and ***Redgrave v. Hurd*** (1881) 20 Ch. D. 1.

Extended duty of good faith: exceptionally there may be a spontaneous duty to disclose one's own torts affecting the thing to be sold

5.30 The duty of good faith in sales can extend beyond the usual requirement for "the most perfect truth and the fullest disclosure" in what is actually said into a full-blown duty of spontaneous disclosure. It may be that one party to the sale has illicitly made *secret tests or investigations of the other's property* which materially affect his knowledge of the value, but which the other has no reason to suspect.[69] In *Phillips v. Homfray*[70] a case—unusually—about the *purchaser*'s duty of good faith, the purchaser of a colliery was also an adjoining land owner, and had secretly tunnelled through and abstracted a considerable amount of coal from the land to be bought. He argued that no damage would be suffered by the purchaser since the purchase price was calculated as if all the coal remained underground. The court however took the view that the unlawfully abstracted coal might well have had a higher price, and that in any event, since on the true facts the purchaser was buying a release from the consequences of his illicit act as well as the land itself, the vendor had to know about what had been done and have the opportunity to agree or otherwise.

Where the good faith duty does not operate: (i) what the purchaser knows

5.31 As we search for good faith terms we shall sometimes find the costs straining towards two objectives which sometimes seem to lie uneasily with each other. The courts were concerned to ensure that the purchaser should be properly diligent on his own behalf; they were also concerned the party with access to special knowledge (usually the vendor) should deal fairly. The latter duty was thus given its due limits by the former.

If the purchaser knows the truth, he does not need to rely on the seller, so the good faith duty falls away. Thus, where the contract to give good title would be *implied* rather than *express*, and where the purchaser is proved to have *known of* the title defect, the usual implied term is held not to arise, or to be displaced by inference. Where the contract to give good title is express, the purchaser's knowledge is taken to have the same effect; his knowing would not lead to any inference of acceptance in such circumstances.[71]

[69] *cf.* the example given in *Phillips v. Homfray* (1871), the case next referred to, of a picture restorer who uses his position to scrape off a part of the picture to reveal the true attribution.

[70] (1871) 6 Ch. App. 770.

[71] See, ***e.g. Re Gloag & Miller's Contract*** (1883) 23 Ch. D. 320. See also ***Rudd v. Lascelles*** [1900] 1 Ch. 815; and see ***Calverley v. Williams*** (1790) 1 Ves. 210; 30 E.R. 306, where the particulars of sale were ambiguous, but Lord Thurlow considered the purchaser really knew perfectly well what the vendor meant to sell. He said if they both *understood the same subject matter*, "then this pretence to have the whole conveyed is as contrary to good faith

(ii) Deemed (caveat emptor) *knowledge of purchaser*

5.32 The purchaser's actual knowledge is by no means the whole of the picture, however. *Caveat emptor* or let the buyer make proper investigations, the buyer's duty of due diligence, has been applied to confine the good faith duty within strict bounds. The Latin phrase, incidentally, means no more (or less) than "*take care*". It does **not** mean that the purchaser (or vendor) has to *take a risk* he cannot know about: only that he has to make normal and usual inquiries and inspections. "Caveat emptor does not mean in law or in Latin that the buyer must 'take a chance', it means that he must take care."[72] Taking care, however, is what the buyer (or "the inquiring party" to the sale contract) is obliged to do. The duty of good faith does not extend to readily obtained knowledge; so provided the vendor makes no lulling statements to deflect him, the lazy purchaser is lazy at his own risk. Hence, perhaps, the occasional eliptical confusion which has arisen about the meaning of the phrase *caveat emptor*: a buyer who did *not* do his homework certainly was taking a risk.

Thus, (in the absence of an express term as to title) if the title defect is manifesting itself physically in a way that makes the right evident to a purchaser, *e.g.* someone in unexplained occupation, or a path indicating an easement, etc., it is held to be binding on the purchaser. It is a "patent defect" which he ought to have seen. Because he ought to have seen it if he had taken normal and proper steps, he is taken to have accepted the risk of any defect he *could have found by normal inspection* and did not.[73] An example of the court's lack of sympathy for the lazy can be seen in the often-quoted trenchant comment of Lord Loughborough about the purchaser in *Bowles v. Round*[74] This purchaser had bought a 15-acre meadow at auction *without inspecting it first*. It had a footpath running across it which had become very wide over the years, so as to indicate clearly that a third party had or might have a right over it. Lord Loughborough said:

> "Certainly the meadow is very much the worse for a road going through it: but I cannot help the carelessness of the purchaser; *who does not choose to inquire. It is not a latent defect.*"[75]

The *caveat emptor* principle applies only to the normal investigation to be reasonably expected of the buyer: in *Dyer v. Hargrave*[76] a distinc-

upon his [the purchaser's] side, as the refusal to sell would be in the other case". See also ***Lowndes v. Lane*** (1789) 2 Cox Eq. Cas 363; 30 E.R. 167, where the vendor had sent his surveyor to look at some woods: "with that knowledge, I think it fell on him to take care of himself".

[72] Fitzgibbon L.J. in *Wallis v. Russell* (1902) 2 I.R. 585 at 615.

[73] See Chap. 8, Knowledge and Notice for a more detailed discussion of caveat emptor.

[74] (1800) 5 Ves. 508; 31 E.R. 707.

[75] Italics supplied. See below 5.37 for discussion of the proposition that the vendor has a duty to disclose all latent defects.

[76] (1805) 10 Ves. 505; 31 E.R. 707.

tion was drawn between defects a normal examination by a purchaser would have revealed, which the purchaser was deemed to have known about and defects which only an abnormally minute examination would have revealed, which were the subject of compensation.

Lulling statements by vendor: effect on caveat emptor—purchaser held to be reasonably deflected from investigations

5.33 The purchaser's duty of due diligence is itself narrowed or displaced if the vendor makes untrue or misleading statements: these may be held to have lulled the purchaser into a sense of security, so that he is reasonably deflected from investigation: see the (*obiter*) statement of Lord Ellenborough C.J. in *Vernon v. Keys*[77] explaining the basis of this, notionally at least in part in regard to fraudulent misrepresentation, since that was the thrust of the purchaser's action, but applicable generally to lulling remarks by the vendor.

> "A seller is unquestionably liable to an action of deceit, if he fraudulently misrepresent the quality of the thing sold to be other than it is in some particulars, which the buyer has not equal means with himself of knowing; or, if he does so, *in such a manner as to induce the buyer to forbear making the inquiries, which for his own security and advantage he would otherwise have made*".[78]

See *Pope v. Garland*,[79] in which Alderson B. said:

> "But if there is misrepresentation, so that the acuteness and industry of the purchaser is set to sleep, and he is induced to believe the contrary of what is the real state of the case, the vendor in such case is bound by that misrepresentation."

For a more modern example, see Eve J. in *Lee v. Rayson*[80]: the argument that the purchaser ought to have inspected the leases in question was rejected as not being open to the vendor, who had himself misstated these in the contract[81]

Duty to follow up puzzling facts

5.34 This duty is discussed in Chapter 8. Knowledge and Notice. It applies where appropriate to narrow the vendor's duty of good faith; the purchaser is fixed with knowledge of what he *would have* found out if he had looked into the puzzling facts.

[77] (1810) 12 East 632; 104 E.R. 246.
[78] Italics supplied.
[79] (1841) 4 Y. & C. Ex. 394; 160 E.R. 1059.
[80] (1917) 1 Ch. 613.
[81] See also, *e.g.* ***Re White and Smith's Contract*** [1896] 1 Ch. 637 where the purchaser's *caveat emptor* duty did not apply when he had not had an opportunity of inspecting the lease in question.

Lulling statements: Access to relevant information of purchaser and vendor important

5.35 The ability of the two parties to have access to relevant information relevant when considering whether the purchaser could in the circumstances be presumed to have relied on a lulling statement and thus been deflected from normal (*caveat emptor*) inquiries.

In *Clapham v. Shillito*[82] the Master of the Rolls, Lord Langdale, drew a distinction between cases where the vendor was in a superior position to the purchaser regarding information, and cases where it was obvious both were likely to be equally ignorant. In the latter case it would be rather hard on the vendor to presume that he had used his superior access to knowledge to lull the purchaser into a sense of false security.

> "If the subject is capable of being accurately known, and one party is, or is supposed to be, possessed of accurate knowledge, and the other is entirely ignorant, and a contract is entered into, after representations made by the party who knows, or is supposed to know, without any means of verification being resorted to by the other, it may well enough be presumed, that the ignorant man relied on the statements made by him who was supposed to be better informed; but if the subject is in its nature uncertain—if all that is to be known about it is a matter of inference from something else, and if the parties making and receiving representations on the subject have equal knowledge, and means of acquiring knowledge, and equal skill, it is not easy to presume, that representations made by one would have much or any influence upon the other".

Acceptance of defect by purchaser after discovering truth

5.36 Chapter 15 deals with the subject of acceptance by the purchaser of defects after contract.[83]

Is there a spontaneous duty on vendors to disclose latent defects anyway?

5.37 It is right that such a duty does implicitly exist as regards *title defects*. It is however mitigated in the case of patent defects, that is, title defects which leave visible signs of their presence on the ground, and thus may be seen before contract, by the purchaser's *caveat emptor* duty, or duty of due diligence. For example, in *Bowles v. Round*[84] which concerns a patent defect of title, it was held the purchaser, who ought to have seen it before the contract, could not complain about it.

[82] (1844) 7 Beav. 146; 49 E.R. 1019.

[83] See ***Burnell v. Brown*** (1820) 1 Jac. & W. 168; cp. ***Castle v. Wilkinson*** (1870) L.R. 5 Ch. 534 where the purchaser knew the defect before contract and thus was not misled, and ***Rudd v. Lascelles*** [1900] 1 Ch. 815.

[84] (1800)5 Ves. 508; 31 E.R. 707.

In *Cook v. Waugh*[85] there is an *obiter*[86] statement by the Vice Chancellor Sir John Stuart, "if a vendor or lessee is aware of some latent defect, and does not disclose it, the Court will consider him as acting in bad faith." However, it is not at all clear from this brief statement that the Vice Chancellor is referring to a spontaneous duty of disclosure, *unasked*. Indeed, since the Vice Chancellor referred to it as "the principle of that doctrine, which is very well established, and which I hope will never be weakened" it seems more likely he was referring implicitly to the doctrine which was indeed well-known, the duty of candour and accuracy *in what the vendor says*.

The case of *Yandle v. Sutton*[87] concerns a defect of title—an easement over a track, which was held latent in the sense that although the track was patent, the fact there was a right exercised over it by another owner was not. As Sargant J. put it:

> "I think he [the purchaser] is only liable to take the property subject to those defects which are patent to the eye, including those defects which are a necessary consequence of something which is patent to the eye."

The above cases do not really lend support to the idea of a wider general duty of *spontaneous disclosure of latent defects of pure quality or description*. It is probable that the vendor *is* technically allowed to remain silent about these, and is free from liability provided that he is successful in the delicate task of avoiding inaccuracies or half-truths. Half-truths of course do give rise to a duty of disclosure, but this, as stated above, is an ancillary duty which, generally arises only after there has been some positive communication made.

The standard to be expected of the purchaser

5.38 The standard of diligence is that of a "prudent and vigilant man" of the kind who is to be expected as a purchaser of that property; and in the actual circumstances of the sale. Thus, in *Dykes v. Blake*[88] below, the standard was that of "the ordinary class of persons who frequent sales by auction"; and the circumstances of a sale by auction were taken into account. It was said that it would be wrong to expect the purchaser in the case of such a sale to peruse the lease (which revealed the defect in question), since he might never have heard of the sale before the day it took place, and he could hardly be expected to "peruse it to any purpose" during the auction sale itself.

Also relevant is *Swaisland v. Dearsley*[89] in which Sir John Romilly, the Master of the Rolls said:

> "It is of the greatest importance and the duty of persons who put up property for sale by auction to describe it with perfect accu-

[85] (1860) Giff. 201; 66 E.R. 85.
[86] The purchaser failed on the facts.
[87] [1922] 2 Ch. 199.
[88] (1838) 4 Bing. (N.C.) 463; 132 E.R. 866.
[89] (1861) 29 Beav. 430; 54 E.R. 694.

racy, and not merely in such a way that a person, by drawing proper inferences from everything that is stated in the condition of sale, may be able to ascertain what it is that is sold."

He also took into account "the condition and situation in life" of the purchaser.

EQUITY AND COMMON LAW COURTS BEFORE THE JUDICATURE ACTS 1873: RELEVANT ASPECTS

Both common law and equity courts applied the good faith rules

5.39 The good faith rules were by no means a preserve of the equity courts. It would have been ridiculous if this had been so. Cases involving real property might come before either court, depending on the remedy wanted. A purchaser who considered that a vendor had broken his contract might bring his action in a common law court to have his deposit back as money had and received, or either party might seek damages. The common law courts could not relax the strict requirements of the contract, but the strict requirements were *defined by* the application of good faith—the presumption of the duty of candour and accuracy. This is much as one would expect given Lord Mansfield's famous introduction of good faith to the common law in *Carter v. Boehm.*[90] Good faith no doubt fitted very well with the Equity Courts' emphasis on conscience, but will hardly have been thought of as an equitable preserve. The common law courts could not, as the equity courts could, keep a slightly-broken contract in being and make up the difference by compensation. They were obliged to award damages, lacking the "healing power" of equity in regard to contracts. The equity courts on the other hand had not—or at all events, chose not to exercise—the power to award damages. There is also a suggestion in some of the cases that they may in any case often have felt that the common law courts' procedure, with a jury, was better able to come at the truth. Thus, on occasions, they opted to do nothing on an application for one of their special remedies, specific performance or rescission.[91]

The common law courts' application of good-faith rules to contracts (as distinct from the remedies then employed) was as far as may be judged indistinguishable from that of the equity courts. Whether they did so perceiving them to be equity's rules, or whether Lord

[90] (1766) 3 Burr. 1905; 97 E.R. 1162; see Chap. 4, Insurance and Surety Transactions.

[91] One may compare the procedure employed today of continuing "as if by Writ" in an action originally thought to involve few disputes of fact which becomes unexpectedly contentious.

Mansfield's tradition still lingered, is not clear. At all events, they did apply them.

Good faith duty to give good title in absence of specific exclusion recognised at common law

5.40 The case of *Gibson v. Spurrier*[92] was heard by Lord Kenyon. The good faith principle that a vendor who is silent on the question of title gives good title was adopted. Since the burden of the proof was on the vendor, and there was some doubt as to his unencumbered title at the time the question came before the court, Lord Kenyon permitted the purchaser to win. He was held "not obliged to buy a lawsuit".

In *Stevens v. Adamson*[93] the purchaser sued in *assumpsit* to recover his deposit. He had bought an assignment of a lease of a pub and other buildings at auction, only to find that he was at risk of forfeiture of his lease by the landlord, who had served the then-equivalent of a "section 146" notice to repair. Abbott L.C.J. affirmed the vendor's duty of good faith. The report notes:

> "Abbott L.C.J. was of opinion, that a person putting up premises for sale was *bound to know* how the premises were circumstanced . . . *In such transactions good faith was most essential*, and the vendor, or his agent, was bound to communicate to the vendee the fact of such notice".[94]

In *Purvis v. Rayer*[95] Richards C.B.[96] in the Court of Exchequer Chamber, affirming that the good-faith duty to give title applied to leaseholds as well as freeholds, put it on a broad general basis, perhaps unsurprisingly in the light of the interest beginning to be taken by the Common law courts in the rules for the sale of personal property.[97]

In *Belworth v. Hassall*[98] Lord Ellenborough confirmed that he would regard agreements as broken where there was a material breach of the duty of good faith. He said that "any fraud or material misdescription, though unintentional, would vacate the agreement".

Application in common law courts of vendor's duty of candour and accuracy in representations about quality

5.41 The case of *Flight v. Booth*[99] is well known in the Chancery Division and often cited in sale of land cases. The judge was a common law judge, Tindal C.J. It is evident that he accepted fully the development

[92] (1795) Peake Add. Cas. 49; 170 E.R. 190.
[93] (1818) 2 Stark. 422; 171 E.R. 692.
[94] Italics supplied.
[95] (1821) 9 Price 488; 147 E.R. 159.
[96] Sitting on Saturday July 28, 1821!
[97] See Chap. 3, Sale of Personal Property.
[98] (1815) 4 Camp. 140; 171 E.R. 692.
[99] (1834) 1 Bing. (N.C.) 370; 131 E.R. 1160.

of good faith principles made in the equity courts by Lord Eldon and others (although perhaps he was not quite prepared to become involved in a discussion about "equitable fraud", that troublesome label that bedevilled this topic in the mid nineteenth century). The case involved a "pregnant half-truth", to which his response was:

> "where the misdescription, although not proceeding from fraud, is in a material and substantial point, so far affecting the subject-matter of the contract that it may reasonably be supposed, that but for such misdescription, the purchaser might never have entered into the contract at all. Under such a state of facts, the purchaser may be considered as not having purchased the thing which was really the subject of the sale."[1]

Good faith and caveat emptor: equity's attitude to this also adopted by common law courts

5.42 In *Pope v. Garland*[2] Alderson B. affirmed that the common law courts would take the same attitude as the equity courts to the relationship between good faith and *caveat emptor*: lulling statements by a vendor such that a purchaser, believing them, was deflected from his normal duty to investigate what he was buying would narrow the purchaser's duty; he was entitled to believe what he was told.

Contrast between equity and common law courts: a marked divergence over remedies

Strict attitude at common law

5.43 The common law courts took a strict attitude to remedies. In *Farrer v. Nightingal*[3] Lord Kenyon held that a purchaser might have his deposit back as money had and received. The contract was held terminally broken by the vendor, who had only a six year lease of a pub, having said he had eight and a half years. It made no difference, in this court, that the vendor was prepared to give compensation in money for the difference. The common law courts' refusal to enter into questions of compensation is likely, as is the equity courts' refusal to award damages, to have had a common-sense procedural basis; the equity courts had a well-tried procedure of accounts and inquiries which was lacking in the common law courts. The equity courts' jurisdiction to save not very broken contracts with the sticking plaster of compensation required accurate, experienced assessment of compensation if it was not to wreak injustice. Indeed, even today the dis-

[1] See also ***Dykes v. Blake*** (1838) 4 Bing (N.C.) 463; 132 E.R. 866 in which Tindal C.J. took a similar attitude to another pregnant half-truth, and the earlier case of ***Granger v. Worms*** (1814) 4 Camp. 83.

[2] (1841) 4 Y. & C. Ex. 394; 160 E.R. 1059.

[3] (1798) 2 Esp. 639; 170 E.R. 481.

tinction persists: cases involving at all complicated accounts and inquiries are dealt with in the Chancery Division.

The equity courts: choice of remedies

5.44 Equity's options where a breach of the good-faith duty of candour and accuracy came before them were:

(1) to enforce the contract by means of a grant of specific performance with compensation for the breach of contract caused by the breach of the good faith duty; or
(2) to refuse specific performance but allow the claimant to seek damages, in an action in the common law courts. As has been seen, equity courts did not normally give damages;[4] this remedy only became possible for them (and the award of compensation in erstwhile common law courts, no doubt) after the reforms of 1873; or
(3) to grant rescission of the contract, so ruling out damages.

Equity's doctrine of specific performance with compensation: "substantial justice" for minor breaches of good faith

5.45 If a defect as to which the purchaser had been misled was relatively minor, the courts of equity made a practice of allowing a vendor to have specific performance on terms that he paid the purchaser compensation for the defect. For example in *Halsey v. Grant*,[5] Lord Erskine gave an example of a contract for a 99 year lease where the purchaser had only 97 or 98, where equity would simply order compensation for the defect, but preserve the contract. This was a jurisdiction exclusive to equity: as has been seen above, the common law courts could not do it at all, but were obliged to stick to the letter of the law.

Substantial justice: "materiality" (significance) of defect

5.46 Underlying equity's substantial justice discretion, was a principle or test which is unlikely to have been regarded as particularly discretionary, but most likely as a precondition for the operation of equity's option to preserve the slightly-broken contract: namely the question whether the defect was a "material defect."[6] This principle or test has been variously expressed—as where "the thing sold" has turned out to be "of a different nature from that contracted to be sold";[7] or such

[4] But see McDermott, The Jurisdiction of the Court of Chancery to Award Damages (1992) 108 L.Q.R. 652.
[5] (1806) 13 Ves. 73; 33 E.R. 22.
[6] ***Shackleton v. Sutcliffe*** (1847) 1 De G. & Sm 609; 63 E.R. 1217.
[7] *Ayles v. Cox* (1852) 16 Beav. 23; 51 E.R. 684.

as to "defeat the object and purpose of the contract";[8] or "material and substantial."[9]

Lord Erskine explained it in relation to the operation of the jurisdiction of the equity courts to give compensation for relatively minor defects in *Halsey v. Grant*.[10] He called it **substantial justice**; and expressed the aim of the court as *"preserving the substantial part of the contract, but not forcing upon the party something different [from that which he had agreed to take]."*[11] Compare Grotius *De Iure Belle et Pacis*,[12] who drew a distinction between what he labelled "precedent" and "accompanying" or "incidental" error: the first error giving rise to the contract, such that the contract in question would not have taken place but for the error: the second error which would not have prevented the contract taking place.

See also the then Master of the Rolls in *Dyer v. Hargrave*[13] who stated that the test for compensation was whether the purchaser was getting *"substantially that, for which he bargains."*[14] If he was, he was obliged to abide by his contract, albeit on the footing that he received compensation.

The test would seem to be a useful one. It provided a degree of predictability we lack at present. It could be used in the court's decision under section 2(2) Misrepresentation Act 1967. It is perhaps odd that it has not achieved recognition in this context, given that equity's powers have been available for all divisions of the High Court since 1873.

Substantial justice: some discretionary considerations as regards breaches of good faith

(1) Relevance of purchaser's actual purpose

5.47 It will be evident that the question whether the purchaser is getting substantially that for which he bargains involves: (a) an objective consideration of what the contract, on fair-dealing assumptions, actually described, as opposed to what in fact is available for him; and (b) an element which may be subjective to the purchaser—what he wanted the property for anyway.

This second element has nothing to do with good faith, except perhaps, where known to the vendor, as a "surrounding circumstance" against which to decide whether the defect was a substantial (or "material") one. The equity courts have, however, gone beyond the

[8] Tindal C.J. in *Robinson v. Musgrove* (1838) 2 M. & Rob. 92; 174 E.R. 225.
[9] (In *Re Fawcett and Holmes Contract* (1889) 42 Ch. D. 150. All three above cases are noted in the Appendix to Chap. 10, Excluding the Effect of the Fair-Dealing Terms.
[10] (1806) 17 Ves. 73; 33 E.R. 222.
[11] Italics supplied.
[12] Cited in Fry, *Specific Performance* (1858 ed. at p. 204, fn.) See Chap. 3 for further reference to Grotius' influence.
[13] (1805) 10 Ves. 505; 31 E.R. 707.
[14] Italics supplied.

pure assessment of good faith by the vendor in the exercise of their discretion; they also regarded as a relevant factor to the exercise of the substantial-justice jurisdiction the *purpose* for which the actual purchaser had contracted to buy. By knowing what his purpose had been it was possible to avoid saddling the purchaser with a defect which was perhaps unimportant in itself but was of proven importance to *him* for some reason to do with his use of the land. In this way the court might be sure that it was indeed, if it forced him to complete, giving him substantially that for which he had bargained, without injustice or undue hardship. The ascertainment of the purchaser's purpose *can* perhaps properly be classified as a part of the discretionary exercise involved in the court's discretion to grant specific performance. The objective ascertainment of the effect of the breach of the duty of candour or accuracy is not.

An example of the consideration of the purchaser's purpose is *Drewe v. Hanson.*[15] Lord Eldon had to consider the merits of a misdescribed purchase at an interlocutory stage. The purchase had been of a farm and some tithes of hay and corn. There was no problem with the corn tithes but the hay tithes were not as represented: half were in fact paid not to the owner of the land but to the vicar, and the other half were commuted for a payment of £2 per annum. Lord Eldon said in effect that he could not go so far as to say at that stage that the purchaser would *not* be obliged to accept compensation and go through with the contract.

> "... Suppose it proved, that this farm was taken *for the purpose of enjoying the corn tithe principally; that the hay tithe was a very small object*; great part of that capable of being taken in kind; but a small part, not much affecting the bargain ... *All those considerations are very material upon the question of compensation*; and it is impossible to determine now, that this will not be within the reach of some of the authorities a case for compensation." [16]

Thus, "the bargain" was seen as something with a purpose, and that purpose was the purchaser's—something which might work either for or against him when he wished to rescind the contract[17].

(ii) Relevance of difficulty in valuing difference in subject matter

5.48 Where the difference in subject matter between what had been intended to be bought and what was actually available was otherwise sufficiently immaterial for the court to order specific performance with compensation, any difficulty in valuing the difference might nonetheless tip the court's decision the other way. For example, in *Lord Brooke*

[15] (1802) 6 Ves. Jun. 675; 31 E.R. 1253.

[16] Italic supplied.

[17] See also ***Halsey v. Grant*** (1806) 13 Ves. 73; 33 E.R. 222 (above), in which the element of purpose was mentioned. This is not the "reasonable" purchaser's purpose, but the actual purchaser's.

v. Rounthwaite[18] a wood was sold with oak trees said to average approaching 50 feet in size. This proved incorrect, but the vendor was not allowed specific performance with compensation to the purchaser, because of the court's difficulty in knowing how the difference might be estimated, since the particulars of sale did not state how many trees per acre there were to begin with.

Again, the consideration of the difficulty in valuing *is* a step in the exercise of the equity court's choice of options. It has nothing to do with the assessment of the result of the breach of the duty of candour or accuracy.

Equity's other options: rescission or the damages option.

5.49 The equity courts could not only refuse an application for specific performance but could grant rescission of the contract, in the sense of setting it aside altogether and restoring the parties as far as possible to the state they were in before the contract.[19] They generally did this if the breach of the duty of candour was **material**. For a further discussion of the requirement of materiality in the context of recission, see the section on rescission in Chapter 15. A third option, a halfway house, was the damages option. Where they thought it appropriate, they would simply make no order either way, but allow the parties to seek damages (which as we have seen, the equity courts had no power to award) in a new action in the common law courts.[20]

Miscellaneous: some questions and misconceptions

Did the equity courts grant rescission of contracts for the sale of land when appropriate?

5.50 There has in more recent times been a suggestion that the early equity courts *never* went beyond the half-way point of refusing specific performance in the case of misdescription or misrepresentation; and did not technically **rescind** contracts, at least contracts for the sale of land, at all. It would follow that equity never regarded contracts as *broken* for breach of the duty of good faith. For example, Walton J. in *English Real Estates v. Faruqi*[21] stated:

> "... it appears to me that strictly the answer probably is that in accordance with the terms of the contract those requisitions had been sufficiently answered. Although at law the contract is a good one and the purchaser bound to take the title provided by the

[18] (1846) 5 Hare 298; 67 E.R. 926.

[19] See, *e.g.* ***Cadman v. Horner*** (1810) 18 Ves 10; 34 E.R. 221; and ***Farebrother v. Gibson*** (1857) 1 De G. & J. 602.

[20] See ***Savage v. Brocksopp*** (1811) 18 Ves. Jun 335; 34 E.R. 344; ***Wall v. Stubbs*** (1815) 1 Mad. 80; 56 E.R. 587.

[21] [1979] 1 W.L.R. 963.

> defendant, in equity that is not the case. Equity does not set aside a contract; it merely says first, that it will not grant specific performance of it and secondly, it will order the return of the deposit. As Megarry J pointed out in *Schindler v Pigault* (1975) 30 P & CR 328, whatever the technical effect of that may be, its practical effect is to put a complete end to the contract . . . I do not think that I can order the defendants to pay the plaintiff his costs of investigating the title of the property and of providing insurance, because it seems to me that I could do that only if it could be said that the defendants had *broken the contract at law, and at law, as I have already indicated, they have not done so. The plaintiff owes his position solely to the interposition of equity.*"[22]

Neither branch of this suggestion seems to be soundly based. After a while, the courts of equity did begin to order rescission of contracts where (1) there had been a breach of the duty of candour or the duty of accuracy and (2) because rescission is always a discretionary remedy, when they considered it right in the exercise of their discretion to do so, taking into account other factors such as the purchaser's purpose, and the difficulty in valuing.[23] The courts certainly had no hesitation in doing so on occasions: for example, in *Mortlock v. Buller*,[24] not a good-faith case but one concerning trustees' exercise of their power of sale, in which Lord Eldon adverted to the distinction "that Courts of Equity have always made, between ordering a contract to be rescinded and decreeing specific performance". He said:

> "... the distinction is always laid down, that there are *many cases*, in which the party had obtained a right to sue upon the contract at Law, and under such circumstances, that his conscience cannot be affected here, so as to deprive him of that remedy; and yet, on the other hand the Court, declaring, he ought to be at liberty to proceed at Law, will not actively interpose to aid him, and specifically perform the contract."[25]

Was the application of good faith "only" as a part of "Equity's discretion"?

5.51 This suggestion is made, for example, in Spry, *Equitable Remedies*[26] which, after mentioning contracts of insurance, contracts involving a fiduciary relationship, and *Dimmock v. Hallett*[27] states:

[22] Italics supplied.

[23] See the textbooks on specific performance for other factors which might be relevant to the decision whether or not to grant rescission.

[24] (1804) 10 Ves. 292; 32 E.R. 857.

[25] Italics supplied. See also **Farebrother v. Gibson** (1857) 1 De G. & J. 602 dealing with a case concerning the duty of accuracy, in which Turner L.J. said "... the Court might have refused to enforce the contract; it might even have rescinded it.

[26] (4th ed., 1990, p. 169.

[27] [1866] 2 Ch. App. 21.

"There are other cases of non-disclosure, however, where there is no ground for rescission because, for example, there is no definite duty of disclosure, but where nonetheless the non-disclosure in question is relevant in proceedings for an order of specific performance. In these cases *the non-disclosure is found to give rise to a discretionary consideration* that has more or less weight according to the various circumstances . . . the defendant may be able to establish circumstances that render it so unreasonable that performance be ordered in specie that the plaintiff is left to such remedies at law as he may possess. So a denial of relief may arise through a failure to disclose particular facts and matters. In these cases, however, *it is necessary that the failure to disclose the matters in question, and the consequent error or misapprehension of the defendant, should be such that performance of his obligations would bring about substantial hardship or unfairness that outweighs matters tending in favour of specific performance.*"[28]

This approach is somewhat suspect. The common law courts accepted and applied good faith principles as discussed above. Common law courts did not claim to use "Equity's discretions". The approach also confuses or runs together two essentially distinct matters: (1) the factors equity considered vitiated a contract, which might be quite objectively ascertained, such as a breach of the duty of candour or accuracy (also recognized by the common law courts) or the duty of fair-dealing to a vulnerable party; and (2) the discretionary factors that went to the choice of remedies, the question what to do about the breach. The breach of the duty of candour and accuracy, or the breach of the fair-dealing duty to a vulnerable party, had first to be established where applicable, before the "discretion" or options of equity could come into play at all.

It is true that since the burden of the proof was on the plaintiff to show that he was entitled to enforce the contract, a real doubt about this would cause him to be refused specific performance, even if he might ultimately prove not to be in breach of contract. This is not really a "discretionary" matter, either: see above for the similar approach to this by the common law courts.

It is therefore not true in any really meaningful sense to say that good faith rules were applied *as part of the Equity courts' discretion* to award or withhold specific performance. No doubt the question whether enforcing the contract in its (now ascertained) form with compensation for the defect would be forcing something different on the purchaser, would involve considerations which were properly labelled discretionary. But that arises afterwards, just as the question whether to order an inquiry into some specific matter only arises after the entitlement to compensation on one ground or another has first been determined. It is a matter of regret that the decidedly vague approach to the Equity courts' compensation jurisdiction exemplified above has tended to cause the good faith aspect of the question to become viewed as a kind of discretionary fudge.

[28] Italics supplied.

5.52 The well-known textbook on specific performance by Sir Edward Fry, which was first published in 1858, much nearer the time when the principles of specific performance were formulated by the courts of equity, does not seem to lend much support to the discretionary fudge approach. (Nor does it support the separate idea that equity courts did not or could not grant rescission in sale of land or other cases.) Fry has a number of chapters headed "Defences to the Suit". The main relevant ones for present purposes are perhaps "Want of Fairness", "Misrepresentation" and "Fraud". These do not list what we should really describe as discretionary considerations: they include factors *vitiating contracts*, which factors may thus attract the intervention of equity courts in actions for specific performance. "Want of Fairness" includes "improper suppression of a fact by one party from another" and dealings by fiduciaries. It is also evident that in most of the fiduciary cases and some of the improper suppression cases these factors are not merely defences to specific performance but would lead to setting aside the contracts. The chapter on Misrepresentation is explained as being about Misrepresentation *rendering the contract unconscionable*. Included are not only deliberate misrepresentations but misrepresentations which would be essentially breaches of the duty of candour and duty of accuracy; "for a man, before making a representation, ought not only not to know it to be untrue, he ought to know that it is true". The chapter "Of fraud" also covers a wider area than deliberately dishonest statements. It begins

> "Fraud is of course is a larger word than misrepresentation, and includes in it not only misrepresentations on the part of the vendor, which we have already considered, but also the unconscionable and deceptive dealing of either party to any contract."

It is clear from what follows that this includes "equitable fraud" or "legal fraud", that is breaches of the good-faith duty of candour and/or accuracy.[29]

5.53 There is no suggestion in the above chapters of Fry's first edition,[30] that these vitiating factors are subject to any discretion on the part of the court *in the modern sense*, that is, that the principle might apply but that the question whether it will or will not *be a defence* is up to the judge when he has heard all the circumstances. Instead, the principles are referred to in terms which are consistent with what is stated in this book. The questions the early equity courts asked themselves where there was in question a breach of the duty of candour and accuracy, or the fair-dealing duty to a vulnerable person, were

(1) Is there one of these contract-vitiating factors present?
(2) If there is, which of our options should we choose; is there anything here to be saved nonetheless?

The cases on breach of the fair dealing duty by vendors simply do not use the language of a modern discretion about whether it is a

[29] Fry says that "fraud" in this wide and all-embracing sense comes before courts of equity both as a ground for setting aside an executed contract, and as a defence to a suit for specific performance.

[30] *Specific Performance* (1st ed., 1858).

defence to specific performance or not: they refer to a fair dealing breach as a definite defence, giving rise either to compensation or to rescission. The only question in such cases is as between the two: whether the defect is sufficiently "material"[31] to prevent specific performance and/or allow the purchaser to rescind, or whether, by contrast, it is not "material" and thus a case for compensation.

Why did the courts in the 1880's and 1890's diminish the original role of good faith?

5.54 They did not say, so it is a matter of surmise. As mentioned in the Introduction, possible reasons are—the new-found belief in literalism via statute law in particular; perhaps the increasing influence of logical positivist philosophers, who will no doubt have seemed to possess considerable radical chic in comparison with the prevailing older, natural–law or Aristotelian principles; the feeling, perhaps, of many judges after the Judicature Acts that the spread of equity's doctrines and remedies to the common law courts would unsettle the common lawyers; a period of falling land prices but real prosperity in which there were fewer transactions in land and more in other forms of investment; and in land transactions the introduction of the Vendor and Purchaser Act 1874 which provided a summary and thus popular remedy, but discouraged any good-faith points outside pure title points since points tending to attack the validity of the contract were not allowed.

It is certainly likely that the idea of good faith as part of "Equity's discretions" stems from some judgments at the end of the nineteenth century. Fewer cases from this period than might be supposed do actually seek to confine good faith to specific performance cases: some which may seem at first blush to be doing so in one way or another prove on inspection to be no-fault cases, that is, cases where the vendor had not been in breach of his duty of good faith, because the defect was not to be found by purely looking at the information "within his knowledge"; and some are on a different point, such as the vendor's right to operate the vendor's rescission clauses which had become popular. However, there are comments in some of the cases at the end of the nineteenth century which do seem to seek to dwindle the role of good faith to a shadowy discretionary one. They tend to do so by means of a re-writing of history. It is always cogent in legal discussion if one can say "this has never been done", or, "this was only done in circumstances which could never apply to us". However, the credibility of this approach as taken by some judges at the end of the nineteenth century is plainly diminished by various demonstrably incorrect historical stances—such as the view that Equity courts had no jurisdiction to rescind contracts and/or always left the parties to their remedy at law where they declined to grant

[31] See above for discussion of this expression.

specific performance; and the view that good faith was anyway the equity courts' sole preserve.[32]

APPENDIX TO CHAPTER 5: SOME CASES OF INTEREST

***Buxton v. Lister* (1746) 3 Atk. 383; 26 E.R. 1020**

5.55 The Lord Chancellor who granted specific performance, on balance, said: "Nothing is more established in this court, than that every agreement of this kind [ie where specific performance is sought] ought to be certain, fair, and just in all its parts."

***Poole v. Shergold* (1786) 1 Cox 273 (Kenyon M.R.)**

5.56 Evidently by this date the rule existed that a vendor had to show a good title to freeholds.

***Lowndes v. Lane* (1789) 2 Cox Eq. Cas. 363; 30 E.R. 167 (*Caveat emptor* and the vendor's duty of accuracy)**

5.57 Lord Thurlow said, on the question how far the maxim *caveat emptor* was to be applied:

"For the sake of certainty in the transactions in the Court, I shall be willing to carry it to a great extent, but not to the extent of saying that it shall apply, where there is a *positive representation essentially material to the subject* in question, and which, at the same time, is *false* in fact. I must consider any fundamental mistake in the particulars of an estate as furnishing a case in which the purchaser will be entitled to have the mistake set right, if *recently applied for* . . . He certainly is bound to attend to all matters that are of such a kind as to be open to his observation. When this purchasor, therefore, comes here for relief, he must account for not observing the circumstances of this case sooner." He then explained the nature of the alleged deceit, which was that the statement that the woods produced £250 a year was only right if the woods were "racked" beyond the course of husbandry. He said that *if that were true, it would be a fraud in the representation, to be relieved against*; but in fact it was not true, the vendor *had* explained it; and further the purchaser had sent his own surveyors down, who had taken the view the woods had been cut in an improper manner. ". . . *with that knowledge* I think it fell on him to take care of himself . . ."[33] He granted an allowance, to be assessed by the Master, for another misrepresentation made by the vendor, as to the tithes.

***Calverley v. Williams* (1790) 1 Ves. 210; 30 E.R. 306 (Ambiguity literally true—need for evidence of purchaser's reliance on different meaning)**

5.58 The plaintiff Calverley sued for specific performance of a contract to sell a part of an estate which included "the lands in the possession of Groombridge". This was in fact seven acres, but the defendant had not meant to sell so much, and the particulars were ambiguous. Lord Thurlow, L.C. went into

[32] See above for discussion of these propositions.

[33] Some italics supplied.

the evidence, and concluded that the plaintiff did not really think he was obtaining the seven acres. He said in general, "No doubt, if one party thought, he had purchased *bona fide*, and the other party thought he had not sold, that is a ground to set aside the contract, that neither party may be damaged; as it is impossible to say, one shall be forced to give that price for part only, which he intended to give for the whole, or that the other shall be obliged to sell the whole, for what he intended to the price of part only. Upon the other hand, if both understood, the whole was to be conveyed, it must be conveyed. But again, if neither understood so, if the buyer did not imagine he was buying, any more than the seller imagined he was selling, this part, *then this pretence to have the whole conveyed is as contrary to good faith upon his side, as the refusal to sell* would be in the other case. The question is, does it appear to have been the common purpose of both to have conveyed this part? . . ." He went on to say that "It must have been imputed to the owner, that he knew the parcels, which were let to Groombridge; for whether he did or not, he undertook to know by undertaking to give a description."[34]

Gibson v. Spurrier (1795) Peake Add. Cas. 49; 170 E.R. 190 (Common law courts' application of good-faith rule as to title)

5.59 The plaintiff bought two lots near each other at auction. There was good title to one: the other was subject to a right of common every third year. He brought a common law action for money had and received. Lord Kenyon said "If there was any colour for his claim, [the witness claiming commons] that was sufficient to entitle the purchaser to avoid the bargain; he was *not obliged to buy a lawsuit*."[35] He also attached importance to the plaintiff's purpose in buying the land, which had possibly been to use both lots together.

Farrer v. Nightingal (1798) 2 Esp. 639; 170 E.R. 481 (Example of common law Courts' strict attitude to contractual terms describing property)

5.60 The vendor entered into a written agreement to sell a public house and the goodwill, reciting that he had eight and a half years of his lease. It emerged he only had six. Lord Kenyon said that it was correct for the buyer to consider the contract at an end, and to bring an action for money (paid in part performance of the contract) as money had and received. It made no difference that the vendor was prepared to make an allowance.

Note: the action for money had and received seems to have been the common law courts' version of the rescission of the contract allowed by Equity. The lack of sufficient title here attracted the remedy in effect of rescission, and since the court was not a Court of Equity, no question of Equity's doctrine of substantial justice arose.

Drewe v. Hanson (1802) 6 Ves. Jun. 675; 31 E.R. 1253 (Equity's compensation jurisdiction ("substantial justice"): relevance of purchaser's purpose to discretion)

5.61 Lord Eldon was considering in this case whether to continue an injunction restraining the Defendant from proceeding at law to recover his deposit on the purchase of some farms and the tithes of the parish of Bishop's Lincomb in Devonshire. It had emerged that half of the tithes of hay went to the vicar, and the other half were commuted by a payment of £2 per annum. Lord Eldon considered he had not enough evidence to be sure that the vendor might *not* obtain specific performance. He said, however, "In the case of an estate sold

[34] Some italics supplied.
[35] Italics supplied.

tithe-free it is a prodigiously strong measure in a Court of Equity to say, as a discrete exercise of its jurisdiction, that the contract shall be performed; the Defendant swearing positively, and proving, that he would have nothing to do with the estate, if not tithe-free. That, though a very strong proposition, does not come up to this case; for in those cases the Court probably speculates, that tithes and lands are the subjects of separate and accurate valuation; and the value of the one does not affect the other; and therefore, though there is a failure as to the tithes, a part only of the subject of the contract, the whole is not affected; as it would be, if the contract was for tithes only. Suppose it proved, that this farm was taken *for the purpose of enjoying the corn tithe principally; that the hay tithe was a very small object*; great part of that capable of being taken in kind; but a small part, not much affecting the bargain . . . the Court in such a case might decree upon the doctrine of compensation . . . [he went into the factual possibilities]. All those considerations are very material upon the question of compensation; and it is impossible to determine now, that this will not be within the reach of some of the authorities a case for compensation."[36]

Note: It is not apparent that the purchaser's purpose needs to be known to the vendor at the time of the contract.

***Bowles v. Round* (1800) 5 Ves. 508; 31 E.R. 707 (*Caveat emptor* and the good-faith duty to give title)**

5.62 The defendant who was objecting to specific performance of an auction sale of a 15 acre meadow on the grounds inter alia that it had a right of way across it—which turned out to be a footpath which had become very wide over the years. Lord Loughborough said "Certainly the meadow is very much the worse for a road going through it: but I cannot help the carelessness of the purchaser; who does not choose to inquire. *It is not a latent defect*."[37]

Note: the case has acquired a fame in later years as having been the foundation for the later doctrine that a vendor of land must in fact disclose all latent defects. This is doubted: see the text above.

***Dyer v. Hargrave* (1805) 10 Ves. 505; 31 E.R. 707. (Substantial justice; relevance of purchaser's purpose; operation of *caveat emptor* or due diligence principle where lulling statements by vendor)**

5.63 A 27-year lease of an estate was sold by auction, the house being said to be in good repair, and the farm in a high state of cultivation. Specific performance was ordered here at the request of the vendor, with compensation for a variance from the description. The Master of the Rolls said "The principle is, that, if he [the purchaser] vests *substantially that, for which he bargains*, he must take a compensation for a deficiency in the value . . ." A distinction was drawn for the purpose of compensation between defects which a minute examination might have discovered and variations which were perceptible on an ordinary inspection by the purchaser. *Caveat emptor* was applied to the defects the purchaser could have seen (and in fact in this case did see): he received compensation only for the other defects.

The Master of the Rolls also expressed a doubt (en passant) about the granting of compensation where there would be difficulties in fairly estimating this. *"Whether the Court ought to compel a Defendant to take compensation for that, which can hardly be estimated by pecuniary value, may admit of doubt."*[38]

[36] Italics supplied.
[37] Italics supplied.
[38] Italics supplied.

The relevance to the substantial justice jurisdiction of the purchaser's purpose for the land appears again in this case. The purchaser had not given evidence that he wanted to live in the house right away, so the disrepair might fairly be compensated in money. ("As to the repairs, unless it could be shewn, that the Defendant wanted possession of the house to live in at a given period, it is mere matter of pecuniary estimation.")

***Halsey v. Grant* (1806) 13 Ves. 73; 33 E.R. 222 (Operation of compensation ("substantial justice") jurisdiction)**

5.64 The vendor sued for specific performance. The agreement was for the sale of a parsonage house and about 79 acres of land, which proved to be subject to a perpetual rent-charge and some other payments. Lord Erskine L.C. said, "This case involves a principle of general importance. The authorities upon this subject are not so satisfactory as I could wish. I am therefore desirous of expressing my opinion with distinctness; that the principle may be understood.

If a Court of Equity can compel a party to perform a contract, that is substantially different from that, which he entered into, and proceed upon the principle of compensation, as it has compelled him to execute a contract substantially different, and substantially less than that, from which he stipulated, without some very distinct limitation of such a jurisdiction, having all the precision of law, the rights of mankind under contracts must be extremely uncertain. He adverted to the strict letter-of-the-law jurisdiction adopted by the common law courts and the quieting of these doubts, and the maintaining of their jurisdiction by the Courts of Equity. He said that the courts of equity could not confine their jurisdiction to cases of strict legal title.

"for another principle, equally beneficial, is equally well known and established; that equity does not permit the forms of law to be made instruments of injustice; and will interpose against parties, attempting to avail themselves of the rigid rule of law for unconscientious purposes. Where therefore advantage is taken of a circumstance, that does not admit a strict performance of the contract, *if the failure is not substantial, equity will interfere.* If, for instance, the contract is for a term of 99 years in a farm, and it appears, that the vendor has only 98 or 97 years, he must be nonsuited in an action [in a Court of Law]: but equity will not so deal with him; and if the other party can have the substantial benefit of his contract, that *slight difference being of no importance to him,* equity will interfere. Thus was introduced the principle of compensation; now so well established: a principle, which I have no disposition to shake."

He referred to another example, the lease of a farm, with immediate possession; where six months of the old lease were unexpired, and said:

"the lessee may not want it immediately. He may not look to an immediate entry. In that instance also equity will upon the same principle of compensation interfere. This is the perfection of our jurisdiction. If the rigid construction of the law were relaxed, there would be no safety: but the system is rendered perfect by this healing power of equity; preserving the substantial part of the contract, but not forcing upon the party something different; and the effect is **substantial justice**."[39]

Note: Lord Erskine's expression "substantial justice" has been adopted as a label for the power of equity to award specific performance with compensation in suitable cases. We may sympathise with his concern that such cases should not be left to the

[39] Italics and bold type supplied.

discretion of the court or "there would be no safety" (one sees all too well what he means, now we have many more discretions vested in the courts). It is also interesting that he thought the purchaser's purpose was an important matter—it was what the purchaser had bargained for, in a real, individual sense, that the court looked for. The question whether the purchaser's purpose had to be known to the vendor or not at the time of the contract was not discussed.

Vernon v. Keys **(1810) 12 East. 632; 104 E.R. 246 (The misrepresentation/ breach of good faith must be about the thing sold, not collateral surrounding circumstances)**

5.65 The vendor misrepresented during negotiations that his intended partners would not go any higher than his offer for certain buildings, trade and stock (which was not in fact right). However, this was not held a proper case for damages for deceit. Lord Ellenborough C.J. said, declaring the opinion of the court, "A seller is unquestionably liable to an action of deceit, if he fraudulently misrepresent the quality of the thing sold to be other than it is in some particulars, which the buyer has not equal means with himself of knowing; or if he does so, *in such a manner as to induce the buyer to forbear making the inquiries, which for his own security and advantage he would otherwise have made.* But is a buyer liable to an action of deceit for misrepresenting the seller's chance of sale, or the probability of his getting a better price for his commodity, than the price which such proposed buyer offers? I am not aware of any case, or recognized principle of law, upon which such a duty can be considered as incumbent upon a party bargaining for a purchase. It appears to be a false representation in a matter merely *gratis dictum by the bidder, in respect to which the bidder was under no legal pledge or obligation to the seller for the precise accuracy and correctness of his statement, and upon which, therefore, it was the seller's own indiscretion to rely.*" And in any case, it did not appear that the Plaintiff had sustained any damage.[40]

Note: (1) The confining of relevant misrepresentations to those made about the subject matter of the sale and where the vendor has special knowledge, excluding inter alia those made about the negotiating parties' state of mind, is reminiscent of the extrinsic/intrinsic distinction we meet in connection with the creditor's duty of disclosure to a surety.[41]

(2) *It echoes again the important idea that a misrepresentation made in such a way as to cause the buyer to forbear from making the inquiries he would otherwise have made can vitiate a sale. This idea is not confined to deliberate misrepresentations of the kind Lord Ellenborough was here concerned with.*

Cadman v. Horner **(1810) 18 Ves. 10; 34 E.R. 221 (Reference to Equity's power to rescind)**

5.66 The vendor complained that he had been induced to sell the property to the plaintiff (who was his agent) by misrepresentations as to the value of the estate and the costs of repairing houses on it. It was evident that the Master of the Rolls, Sir William Grant, was not able to form a final view of this rather strange case on the evidence, but was inclined to think that on the evidence before him there was some degree of misrepresentation, "operating to a certain, though a small, extent" and that "that misrepresentation disqualifies him from calling for the aid of a Court of Equity; where he must come, as it is said, with clean hands. He must, to entitle him to relief, be liable to no imputa-

[40] Italics supplied.

[41] See Chap. 4, Insurance and Surety Sales.

tion in the transaction."[42] He went on. "*This is not a case, where the Court is called upon to rescind an agreement, and to decree the conveyance, executed in pursuance of it, to be delivered up to be cancelled; which would admit a different consideration.*"[43]

Savage v. Brocksopp (1811) 18 Ves. Jun. 335; 34 E.R. 344 (Possible reason for equity's damages option)

5.67 Lord Eldon referred to "the practice of sending issues of fact to Courts of Law" *apropos* some remarks about evidential procedure. He remarked that it would "require more, to insist on having the contract delivered up, so as to prevent an action upon it."[44] In the instant case, the plaintiff sought to have the agreement delivered up, but on the facts, albeit these were in dispute, Lord Eldon considered it clear that he had not only not established that, but had not repelled the right to specific performance.

Note: See the suggestion in the text at paragraph 5.43, that one reason, possibly a major one, for the equity courts' decision to do nothing and leave the parties to their remedy at law would be the common law courts' better capacity to sift evidence of fact, presumably by means of a jury.

Granger v. Worms (1814) 4 Camp. 83; 171 E.R. 27 (Title defect: King's Bench court returns deposit to purchaser on good-faith grounds)

5.68 Leasehold premises were sold. The lease described part of the demised premises as being a summerhouse, and the particulars said nothing about it. There was a covenant to deliver up the demised premises in good repair at the end of the lease. The summerhouse had been pulled down by the time of the sale. Lord Ellenborough said simply that the plaintiff had a right to expect the summerhouse to be there, and allowed the purchaser to obtain back his deposit. The basis was said to be that as the summerhouse no longer existed "the consideration fails *on which*[45] he [the purchaser] paid the deposit".

Wall v. Stubbs (1815) 1 Mad. 80; 56 E.R. 587 (Example of equity courts' damages option (leaving the parties to their remedy at law))

5.69 The Vice Chancellor considered the evidence and thought that there had been a great misrepresentation as to the value of the estate, and observed that whether the misrepresentation was wilful or not; or of a fact latent, or patent, . . . such misrepresentation may be used to resist a specific performance unless the purchaser really knew the true facts. "In this case the Plaintiff must be left to his remedy at law. In a Court of law, on a proper case made, damages may be given commensurate to the injury the Plaintiff may have sustained; and *such Court can better examine into all the circumstances of a case like the present, in which there is contradictory evidence.* Money is all the Plaintiff seeks by his bill, as is the case in all bills by vendors, and money will be given him at law, if he is found entitled to it."[46]

[42] See also ***Viscount Clermont v. Tasburgh*** ((1819) para. 5.74, ***Wall v. Stubbs*** (1815)) (para. 5.69 below).
[43] Italics supplied.
[44] ***Cadman v. Horner*** para. 5.66, above.
[45] Italics supplied.
[46] Italics supplied.

Stewart v. Alliston **(1815) 1 Mer. 26; 35 E.R. 587 (The duty of accuracy: description relied on in its natural sense by purchaser)**

5.70 Premises were sold at a ground-rent lease of 40 guineas a year. The purchaser bought without looking at them, and relying wholly on the printed particulars. He found that in fact the £40 was the rack rent.

Lord Eldon said he would have great difficulty in decreeing specific performance "where the description is, at the least, of so ambiguous a nature that it cannot with certainty be known what it was that the purchaser imagined himself to be contracting for. But what, in fact, does the word mean . . .? Would any man, seeing a house put up to auction as a house to be sold subject to a ground-rent lease, suppose that the word ground-rent meant rack-rent? . . .

The subject of the contract, therefore, does not answer the vendor's description of it, and that in a point so material as to exclude the doctrine of compensation, which never ought to be applied to a case like the present". He refused the vendor an injunction preventing the purchaser from proceeding at law to recover his deposit.

Grant v. Munt **(1815) Coop. G. 173; 35 E.R. 520 (Compensation for patent defect, deemed latent by virtue of vendor's relevant misrepresentation)**

5.71 The vendor misrepresented to the purchaser that "all that would be required to be laid out in repairs of the said house and premises was about £5 for mending a cellar door." In fact the house was badly affected by dry rot. The Master of the Roll ordered compensation, it being apparent from the evidence that the dry rot was not "perfectly visible to everybody". (If it had been apparent on a normal examination, as opposed to an extra-minute one, *caveat emptor* would have applied).

Belworth v. Hassall **(1815) 4 Camp. 140; 171 E.R. 45 (Common law court reaches equitable result by relaxed construction; affirms good faith rules applicable)**

5.72 The agreement was for an eight year lease; the vendor had seven years seven months. Lord Ellenborough concluded the parties could be supposed to have meant seven years seven months, rather than exactly eight years. He also confirmed that "any fraud or material misdescription, though unintentional, would vacate the agreement" but the defendant might here have had substantially what he agreed to purchase.

Stevens v. Adamson **(1818) 2 Stark. 422; 171 E.R. 692 (Title defect: deposit returned by common law courts: comment on lack of good faith on part of vendor)**

5.73 The action was a common law action in assumpsit against the auctioneer in which the purchaser of a leasehold public house and other buildings at auction sued to recover his deposit. He had not been told by the auctioneer that the landlord had given notice that he would re-enter if the premises were not put into repair in three months' time. The report notes that "Abbott L.C.J., was of opinion, that a person putting up premises for sale was *bound to know* how the premises were circumstanced . . . *In such transactions good faith was most essential, and the vendor, or his agent, was bound to communicate to the vendee the fact of such notice*."[47]

[47] Italics supplied.

***Viscount Clermont v. Tasburgh* (1819) 1 Jac. & Walk. 112; 37 E.R. 318 (A vendor in breach of good faith may not rely on it to obtain specific performance with compensation)**

5.74 Premises were to be exchanged with vacant possession. The vendor's premises were in the occupation of tenants. The vendor accepted that he had accidentally misrepresented the position, but wanted specific performance with compensation. This he could not have since the misrepresentation had been his. The court affirmed however that there *were* cases where the contract was inoperative at law yet the equity courts would allow compensation.

"But this is only where there has been a perfect bona fide [sic] there is no case where this has been done at the instance of a Plaintiff, who has practised any misrepresentation."

***Burnell v. Brown* (1820) 1 Jac. & W. 168; 37 E.R. 339 (Acceptance of title defect by purchaser after acquiring relevant knowledge[48])**

5.75 There was a title defect, but the purchaser was held to have waived it by taking up possession of the estate after the abstract had been delivered which made the previously undisclosed reservation of shooting rights quite plain.

***Turner v. Harvey* (1821) Jac. 169; 37 E.R. 814 (Statement containing relevant omission relied on (by vendor)**

5.76 The sale was of a bankrupt's interest in right of his wife in an estate in which her interest came after her parents' life interest. The assignees in bankruptcy made the sale believing that the wife was still alive, while in fact she was dead, so that the only incumbrance on the estate was her elderly parents' life interest. The purchaser had been asked by the trustee-vendors about the health of the elderly parents: the purchaser (who knew the family) had replied accurately that they were alive and well, but omitted to mention that Mrs Everitt, the wife, was however dead. The difference in value between the assumed and the true basis would seem to have been at least 50 per cent. Lord Eldon said:

"It is not immaterial in cases like this to attend to the description of the property to be sold; for if one man understands an expression in one sense, and another in a different sense; though the Court must impute to both that they understood it in the right sense, yet if there has been any mistake, and especially if the expression used by one party has at all misled the other, it is always material in considering what a court of equity will do with the case. . . .

The Court, in many cases, has been in the habit of saying, that where parties deal for an estate, they may put each other at arm's length: the purchaser may use his own knowledge, and is not bound to give the vendor information of the value of his property.

As in the case that has been mentioned; if an estate is offered for sale, and I treat for it, knowing that there is a mine under it, and the other party makes no enquiry, I am not bound to give him any information of it; he acts for himself, and exercises his own sense and knowledge. But a very little is sufficient to affect the application of that principle. If a word, if a single word be dropped which tends to mislead the vendor, that principle will not be allowed to operate."

[48] *cf.* Chap. 15.

Purvis v. Rayer **(1821) 9 Price 488; 147 E.R. 159**

5.77 In this case it was decided for the first time (it had been in doubt since the time of Lord Mansfield) that the purchaser of a leasehold interest was entitled to have good title. The case was heard in the Common law Exchequer Chamber. Richards L.C.B. said (the passage is also quoted in full at p. 103, above):

"*It is a general rule in Equity, founded on principles of honesty and the dictates of good sense, that if a person, generally speaking, offers any thing for sale, the vendee, or he who becomes the purchaser, is entitled to see that the vendor has it with the qualifications, and in the way in which he, the vendee, understood that he bought it; that is, so as to afford him an assurance of having bought what he wanted, and meant to buy, or at least, what was offered or professed to be sold—or he may reject the contract.*[49] In every common matter of business in life, that principle prevails. If a horse be sold by one person to another, and nothing be said about it on either side, the purchaser is entitled to have a sound horse delivered to him: and there are very many other familiar instances of the same kind, regarding the sale of chattels, which may be put in illustration of the generally prevailing principle in cases of this nature."

He could not see why leaseholds should be an exception. He distinguished cases where the purchaser bought expressly on terms that the title would not be warranted. This was a case where the contract was not specially qualified in any relevant way.

Portman v. Mill **(1826) 2 Russ. 570; 38 E.R. 449 (Ambiguity treated as literally untrue and construed in favour of purchaser)**

5.78 A farm said to have 349 acres "or thereabouts" was sold but proved in fact to have been measured in "customary acres", which worked out about 100 acres less. There was a clause providing that any excess or deficiency in the quantity of acres should not vacate or affect the contract. The vendor was refused an inquiry into title: Lord Eldon said, "I can never agree that such a clause . . . would cover so large a deficiency in the number of acres as is alleged to exist here".

Flight v. Booth **(1834) 1 Bing. (N.C.) 370; 131 E.R. 1160 (Breach of good faith duty of candour avoids contract at common law)**

5.79 Leasehold premises in Covent Garden were sold subject to a covenant against offensive trades and with a proviso that the premises might not be let to a coffee-house keeper or working hatter. In fact, there were a large number of trades which were prohibited under the covenant in the lease. It was held by Tindal C.J. that even where the vendor had not been fraudulent, but merely negligent, the misdescription originating either from ignorance, inadvertence, or accident, (and even though the contract provided for compensation in the case of misdescription) the sale might be set aside "*where the misdescription, although not proceeding from fraud, is in a material and substantial point, so far affecting the subject-matter of the contract that it may reasonably be supposed, that, but for such misdescription, the purchaser might never had entered into the contract at all. Under such a state of facts, the purchaser may be considered as not having purchased the thing which was really the subject of the sale.*[50]

He said of the condition of sale requiring the purchaser to accept compensation, ". . . the very terms of the sixth condition of sale scarcely apply to a case where the difference of value is so uncertain and arbitrary as in the present

[49] Italics supplied.
[50] Italics supplied.

case. The condition, that the parties are to pay or allow a proportionate value according to the average, will comprehend a case where there is half an acre more or less than is described, or cases which resolve themselves into simple calculations of that nature; but how will it govern such a misstatement as the present? What action at law can be framed upon it? It would at least involve the purchasers in great difficulties. The lease being in the hands of the vendor, he had peculiarly, and indeed exclusively, the means of knowledge of the exact restrictions contained in it; the purchaser at the auction had none.''

Note: This is often referred to as a seminal case on misdescription. No doubt this is right, but it is built on the foundation laid by Lord Eldon and his Chancery predecessors. The point is not without importance: to take the applicable doctrines as being fully elaborated by Tindal C.J. for the first time would be to miss some useful guidance.

Dykes v. Blake **(1838) 4 Bing. (N.C.) 463; 132 E.R. 866 (Breach of good faith duty of candour and accuracy avoids sale at common law; even if no intention to deceive)**

5.80 The purchaser bought a villa and building plot at auction, subject to the reservation in another lot, which showed a plan and a reservation of other rights of way, but left out a reservation of a footway over the land bought. The footway was apparent from the lease of Lot 7, and there was a statement in the particulars that the lease might be seen at the vendor's office, and would be produced at the sale. The purchaser argued that it was an omission which no purchaser of reasonable caution or discernment would be likely to discover: that it would be wrong to expect him to have looked at the lease, since he might never have heard of the sale before the day it took place; he could not peruse the lease to any purpose during the business of the sale; and, as a reasonably prudent man, he was not bound to peruse it; he was entitled to rely on the particulars. Tindal C.J. agreed with the purchaser. He said the question was ''whether the Plaintiff [the purchaser] is at liberty, under the circumstances stated in the special case, to hold the contract of purchase into which he entered to be altogether void, and to recover back the money paid to the auctioneer as money had and received to his use''.[51] He said, ''And this will depend on the determination of two questions: first, whether the description of the premises in the printed particulars and plans exhibited at the time of the sale, upon the faith of which the Plaintiff made his purchase, was such that *a prudent and vigilant man* would enter into the contract without discovering the existence of the right of way over the land comprised in lot 13 [the building lot bought]; and secondly, whether such right of way being found to exist, renders the purchase altogether useless for the purposes for which it was made; or only brings it under the head of mis-description, so as to form the subject of compensation or equivalent under the ninth condition of sale [that if any mistake be made in the description of the premises, or any other error whatever shall appear in the particulars of the present sale, such mistake or error shall not annul the sale, but a compensation or equivalent shall be given or taken as the case may require].''

Tindal C.J. thought the plan omitting the right in question but mentioning others, would have lulled all suspicion to sleep, and that it was calculated, ''not simply to give no information, but actually to mislead.'' ''*Particulars and plans of this nature should be so framed as to convey clear information to the ordinary class of persons who frequent sales by auction; and they would only become a snare to the purchaser, if after the bidder has been misled by them, the seller should be able*

[51] *i.e.* the common law version of rescission.

to avail himself of expressions which none but lawyers could understand or attend to".[52] He concluded that the existence of the right "was not sufficiently disclosed to make it clear to persons of ordinary vigilance and caution," so that the contract was not binding on the plaintiff. He did not order compensation, because he thought the *object and purpose of the contract*, namely to use it as building ground, was entirely defeated by the existence of the right of way. He concluded by saying "We therefore think the mis-description, however unintentional, has been such as to justify the Plaintiff in saying, that the lots which the seller is ready to convey are not the lots which he purchased, and consequently that he may recover back with interest, the sums paid to the auctioneer."

Note: The case makes it clear that the innocent motive of the vendor in making the inaccurate statement/partial non-disclosure which he did is irrelevant. The duty to describe accurately what is to be sold is thus an implied fair-dealing term of any binding contract.

***Pope v. Garland* (1841) 4 Y. & C. Ex. 394; 160 E.R. 1059 (Common law court affirms good faith approach; reference to statements lulling the purchaser into a sense of security and thus narrowing the purchaser's duty of diligence)**

5.81 In this case the purchaser of a leasehold property subject to a number of leases sought to set aside the purchase on the grounds of lack of title, rather than resort to compensation under a condition providing for this. Alderson B. thought the duty of the purchaser who had notice of outstanding leases was to ask and ascertain what the terms were upon which the property was out on lease, "so that he may know precisely the nature of the property which he purchases, that is, whether he has certain rights upon it, or whether his rights are in any manner restricted. What is the difference in principle in purchasing a lease? The conditions under which the lease is framed are what make the land more or less valuable; just as in the other case the nature of the leases makes the land more or less valuable to a purchaser. . . . But *if there is misrepresentation, so that the acuteness and industry of the purchaser is set to sleep, and he is induced to believe the contrary of what is the real state of the case, the vendor in such case is bound by that misrepresentation. And that explains the case of Flight v. Booth . . . where the misrepresentation was as to the terms of a particular covenant, which when the covenant itself was produced, turned out to be of a much more stringent description. It appears to me that the party was bound in that case to take notice of the terms of the covenant in his particulars of sale; but on the contrary, his manner of stating it implied that was the whole restriction of the sort to which the lease was subject.*"[53] He thought however that the variations from the original contract might fairly be the subject of compensation here.

***Bower v. Cooper* (1843) 2 Hare 408; 67 E.R. 168 (Representation from silence—no part of the vendor's interest in land deemed kept back)**

5.82 The Vice-Chancellor held that a contract to sell land which did not express what interest was to be sold imported the whole of the defendant's interest in the premises. It is almost certainly an application of the duty of candour. The failure to mention limitations in the interest being sold would mislead the purchaser.

[52] Italics supplied.
[53] Italics supplied.

***Clapham v. Shillito* (1844) 7 Beav. 146; 49 E.R. 1019 (Question of inducement considered; constructive (due diligence) knowledge of purchaser; balance of access to information as between the two)**

5.83 The plaintiff sued for specific performance of an agreement for a lease of certain coal mines, the defendant alleging misrepresentation prior to the contract by the plaintiff.

The jury had found one alleged misrepresentation was not made by the plaintiff and the other was made but not relied on by the defendant. The Master of the Rolls, Lord Langdale said, "Cases have frequently occurred, in which upon entering into contracts, misrepresentations made by one party have not been, in any degree, relied on by the other party. If the party to whom the representations were made himself resorted to the proper means of verification, before he entered into the contract, it may appear, that he relied upon the result of his own investigation and inquiry, and not upon the representations made to him by the other party: or if the means of investigation and verification be at hand, and the attention of the party receiving the representations be drawn to them, the circumstances of the case may be such, as to make it incumbent on a Court of Justice to *impute to him a knowledge of the result, which, upon due inquiry, he ought to have obtained*, and thus *the notion of reliance on the representations made to him* may be excluded.

Again, when we are endeavouring to ascertain what reliance was placed on representations, we must consider them with reference to the subject-matter, and *the relative knowledge of the parties*. If the subject is capable of being accurately known, and one party is, or is supposed to be, possessed of accurate knowledge, and the other is entirely ignorant, and a contract is entered into, after representations made by the party who knows, or is supposed to know, without any means of verification being resorted to by the other, it may well enough be presumed, that the ignorant man relied on the statements made by him who was supposed to better informed; but if the subject is in its nature uncertain—if all that is to be known about it is matter of inference from something else, and if the parties making and receiving representations on the subject have equal knowledge, and means of acquiring knowledge, and equal skill, it is not easy to presume, that representations made by one would have much or any influence upon the other."[54] He saw no reason in the circumstances, to interfere with the jury's finding.

Note: What one might call, a trifle unwieldily, the "balance of access to information" is rightly stressed. It is likely to be the underlying rationale for the fair-dealing rules about full and accurate disclosure in all statements by vendors of land—the reasonable expectation of the purchaser. The vendor is "he who knows everything" while the relative ignorance of the purchaser makes reliance probable. In the eighteenth and nineteenth centuries, as has been repeated elsewhere in this book, land was the main investment: see the relative frequency of worries about tithes, rents, etc., and other investment-income problems in the older cases. Our investments tend to be securities and assurance policies of various kinds. There is perhaps no reason to suppose the old fair-dealing principle should not apply to these more modern subjects of investment. Insurance companies, building societies, banks and others have increasingly complex "products" as they often call them. There is no reason to suppose that they should have immunity from fair-dealing duties—whether by virtue of the Unfair Contract Terms Regulations 1994 where applicable, or by these ancient judge-made rules in other cases. It may be thought that the current system of self-regulation might work better (and possibly could consist in less bulky rulebooks?) if the duty at common law and in equity to explain the investments accurately and fully in

[54] Italics supplied.

language which can be understood by the actual customers they have were to be recognised.

***Lord Brooke v. Rounthwaite* (1846) 5 Hare 298; 67 E.R. 926 (Compensation ("substantial justice") jurisdiction: not applied where compensation impossible to estimate)**

5.84 The contract was for sale of an estate, described as a wood "with upwards of 65 acres of fine oak timber trees, the average size of which approached 50 ft". This proved incorrect, although it was not shown to have been a deliberately wrong statement. The action by the plaintiff vendor for specific performance with compensation was dismissed, it being impossible to estimate the compensation properly, since the particulars of sale did not say how many trees there were anyway.

***Price v. Macaulay* (1852) 2 De G.M. & G. 339; 42 E.R. 903 (Know your purchaser: duty of candour—partial disclosure grounds relief)**

5.85 A property was sold with a certain reservoir and waterworks yielding a yearly rental of £60; but in fact, the rent could not be relied on because the water came across the land of a third party by permission only. It was held this partial non-disclosure affecting the rent, albeit unintentional, amounted to a material misrepresentation as to the subject matter of the contract.

Knight Bruce L.J., said, "*I do not impute wrong intention to anyone; still, such a representation in the view of this Court must be considered a fraud . . .*" He also went into the question of the *kind of knowledge* on the part of the purchaser which would provide a defence to the vendor. . . . he [the vendor] must shew very clearly that the purchaser knew that to be untrue which was represented to him as true; for *no man can be heard to say that he is to be assumed not to have spoken the truth. . . . he* [the purchaser] *must be shewn clearly to have had information of the real state of the facts communicated to his mind.*[55]

Cranworth L.J. also referred to "the familiar principle that a vendor seeking specific performance ought to be optimae fidei". The vendor was refused specific performance.

Note: The know-your-purchaser principle is well expressed here: namely the principle that your duty in any disclosures you make is to be full and accurate, not in a vacuum, but so as to communicate the whole relevant truth clearly to the actual purchaser.

***Lachlan v. Reynolds* (1853) Kay. 52; 69 E.R. 23 (Vendor's good faith duty of candour affirmed: omission in description, contract rescinded)**

5.86 The particulars of sale of a house sold under the direction of the court stated that Lot 12 was "at present in the occupation of Mistress Clarke, at a rental of per annum £42." It emerged that Mrs Clarke was in fact in occupation adversely to the vendors! The purchaser did not complete but moved for leave to pay the balance of the purchase money into court, which was given. It was not clear that the vendors knew the truth about Mrs Clarke's occupation. Sir Page Wood, V.C., however, said. "If there be one thing which the Court insists upon more than another in dealings between vendor and purchaser it is that there should be *perfectly good faith on the part of the vendor in the representations which he makes to the purchaser.*[56] It would be strange indeed if, in sales made by the direction of the Court, this rule should be less stringent." He made an

[55] Italics supplied.
[56] Italics supplied.

order discharging the purchaser from the purchase, and ordered that the deposit be returned, that the purchaser account for any rent received, and be reimbursed the expenses of the purchase and of the reference to the court. He did not give interest because the deposit had not borne interest.

***Stanton v. Tattersall* (1853) 1 Sm. & G. 529; 65 E.R. 231 (Duty of candour and accuracy—ambiguous expression treated as literally untrue and reliance by purchaser inferred)**

5.87 This was the sale of a house which was said to have a right of access from Pall Mall and in fact only had an indirect right of access from Pall Mall, through a house which itself *was* in Pall Mall. The Vice Chancellor Sir John Stuart inquired whether the plaintiff had sworn that the misrepresentation (partial non-disclosure) above misled or deceived him, and the answer was that he had not; but he accepted the argument that as the defendants gave the false description of the property, the onus of proof lay on them to show that the misrepresentation, which was calculated to deceive, did not in fact deceive the plaintiff. The contract was rescinded "on the plain principle that what is presented to the purchaser as the subject-matter of his contract is something so different from what must be understood from the description in the particulars of sale" and the deposit returned.

***Farebrother v. Gibson* (1857) 1 De G & J.602; 44 E.R. 857 (The equity courts' choice of remedies mentioned)**

5.88 There was a condition of the sale that the house was in the occupation of a company under a lease. This was untrue: in fact the company was in occupation but the lease was held by some trustees for it. The purchaser was however held to his bargain: the implied term was shifted because the vendor had orally told him the true state of facts, or near enough, just before the sale.

Lord Justice Turner said if the matter had stood merely on the condition of sale "the Court might have refused to enforce the contract; *it might even have rescinded it.*"[57]

***Cook v. Waugh* (1860) Giff. 201; 66 E.R. 85 (Latent defect)**

5.89 The plaintiff failed on the facts. Sir John Stuart V.C., however, affirmed the well-established doctrine, which he hoped would never be weakened, "that if a vendor or lessor is aware of some latent defect, and does not disclose it, the Court will consider him as acing in bad faith."

Note: see comment on this case at paragraph 5.38.

***Leyland v. Illingworth* (1860) 2 De G.F. & J. 248; 45 E.R. 617[58] (Reliance by vendor on literal truth not allowed where the reasonable expectation aroused in the purchaser had been different)**

5.90 Jessel M.R. (in *Cato v. Thompson*, see paragraph 5.102) explained the case thus. "The representation in the particulars was that the premises were well supplied with water. They were well supplied with water, but only by a waterworks company. A purchaser who did not know the fact would have a right to say, 'When you told me that the property was well supplied with water, of course I understood you to mean that I should have an abundant supply of water without paying for it.' There was, however, no direct mis-

[57] Italics supplied.

[58] Mentioned by Jessel M.R. in *Cato v. Thompson* below.

statement in the particulars, and a purchaser who knew the real state of the case would have nothing to complain of."

The purchaser who had *relied on* the reasonable expectation engendered by the words used, had wanted compensation, which the vendor had declined to give. Knight Bruce L.J. held that the purchaser could be discharged from the contract, or, if he wished, receive compensation. He regarded the above statement as materially inaccurate, though he *did not impute fraudulent or dishonest intention to anyone.*

Turner L.J. agreed, relying on *Stewart v. Alliston.*[59] In that case Lord Eldon had emphasized what he called the ambiguous nature of the contract, given the meaning most purchasers ("would any man suppose . . .") would ascribe to the phrase used.

Note: The courts appear to use the same degree of opprobrium about both literally true and literally untrue ambiguous statements. The statement about the water here, despite its literal truth, is castigated as "materially inaccurate".

Walters v. Morgan (1861) 3 De G.F. & J. 718; 45 E.R. 1056 (Silence may ground relief if misleading in circumstances)

5.91 This was a defendant's action, in which he sought specific performance of a lease agreement. The case is really a vulnerable-sale case, interesting mainly because of the remarks about the vendor's limited duty made by Lord Campbell L.C. on appeal. He said,

"The ground on which I am of opinion that the decree ought to be supported is, that by the contrivance of the Plaintiff the Defendant was surprised and was induced to sign the agreement in ignorance of the value of his property. I most fully concur in the doctrine of concealment and misrepresentation as laid down by Lord Thurlow in *Fox v. Mackreth* [a fiduciary case], and qualified by Lord Eldon in *Turner v. Harvey* (above). There being no fiduciary relation between vendor and purchaser in the negotiation, the purchaser is not bound to disclose any fact exclusively within his knowledge which might reasonably be expected to influence the price of the subject to be sold. Simple reticence does not amount to legal fraud, however it may be viewed by moralists. But a single word, or (I may add) a nod or a wink, or a shake of the head, or a smile from the purchaser intended to induce the vendor to believe the existence of a non-existing fact, which might influence the price of the subject to be sold, would be sufficient ground for a Court of Equity to refuse a decree for a specific performance of the agreement.

So, *à fortiori*, would a contrivance on the part of the purchaser, better informed than the vendor of the real value of the subject to be sold, to hurry the vendor into an agreement without giving him the opportunity of being fully informed of its real value, or time to deliberate and take advice respecting the conditions of the bargain." It was set aside, on dealing-with-the-vulnerable grounds.[60]

[59] (1815) above.

[60] See further as to these Chap. 9, Dealings with the Vulnerable. The plaintiff had brought the lease to the defendant "cut and dry" and had urged him to sign, saying "you will trust to me for making a fair allowance if it should turn out more valuable." He had also employed his own solicitor to prepare the lease, and tried to get it signed by the defendant without his solicitor having seen it. "A purchaser who so conducts himself cannot be said to have proceeded with the *good faith* which even jurists require in such a transaction." Italics supplied.

Swaisland v. Dearsley (1861) 29 Beav. 430; 54 E.R. 694 (Duty of accuracy stressed: know your purchaser test to be applied)

5.92 This was a vendor's specific performance action. The particulars of sale were ambiguous. The purchaser put in sworn evidence he had relied on the ambiguity in "his" sense. Sir John Romilly, the Master of the Rolls, declined to grant the vendor specific performance. He said "But the principle upon which this Court proceeds in cases of mistake is this:—if it appears upon the evidence that there was, in the description of the property, *a matter on which a person might bonâ fide make a mistake, and he swears positively that he did make such mistake*, and his evidence is not disproved, this Court cannot enforce the specific performance against him. (He went on to say it was otherwise with a mistake not so occasioned.) He later said *"It is of the greatest importance and the duty of persons who put up property for sale by auction to describe it with perfect accuracy, and not merely in such a way that a person, by drawing proper inferences from everything that is stated in the condition of sale, may be able to ascertain what it is that is sold. Considering these circumstances, and considering also the condition and situation in life of the Defendant,*[61] which made him liable to fall into error . . . I do not think I ought, acting upon the regulated discretion with which the Court deals in matters of this description, to say that I can specifically enforce the contract against the Defendant."

Hughes v. Jones (1861) 3 De G.F. & J. 307 (Ambiguity in description grounds relief)

5.93 Another ambiguity in the description—property was said to be "now or late in the several occupations of Hugh Roberts and others". It was held that this language was insufficiently "clear precise and definite" to cover tenancies for lives at low rents, and the purchaser, who elected compensation, was allowed compensation.

Cox v. Coventon (1862) 31 Beav. 378; 54 E.R. 1185 (Vendor's duty if he summarises deeds to do so accurately and with full disclosure of essential information)

5.94 The point of interest is that Sir J. Romilly M.R., affirmed that if a property is sold subject to the provisions contained in a deed, and the deed is specially referred to, and the purchaser can examine the deed before sale, the purchaser is bound by everything in its contents; but if the vendor instead states what the contents of the deed are, the purchaser *"is not bound to examine the deed itself, but may reasonably trust to the representation of it contained in the particulars of sale as being a correct statement of its contents given by the vendor."* If the deed sets out a general account of the document, *"without referring to the deed itself for a more accurate knowledge of its contents"* then *"[I]n order to sustain the contract, this account must not only be correct in itself, as far as it goes, but must be such as to give the purchaser all the information as to the character of the property which it is essential he should possess"*.[62] He held that there was an important variation not communicated to the purchaser and the contract should not be specifically performed on the ground that the matter did not admit of compensation.

[61] Italics supplied.
[62] Italics supplied.

Dimmock v. Hallett [1866] 2 Ch. App. 21 (Vendor's duty of good faith in representations affirmed; purchaser discharged from contract altogether for vendor's partial disclosure)

5.95 An estate was sold at auction, and the particulars among other things stated that a particular farm was let at an annual rent of £290.15s a year, when in fact the tenant at that rent had given notice to quit and moved out, and the only new tenant who had been found paid only £225 and then rescinded his tenancy. No new tenant had been found. (There was a condition that mistakes in the description of the lots or any other error except as to the quantity of land, should not annul the sale but entitle the purchaser to compensation.)

Sir G.J. Turner L.J. said, "I am of opinion, therefore, that the particulars contain representations which were untrue, and calculated materially to increase the apparent value of the property. *The Court requires good faith in conditions of sale, and looks strictly at the statements contained in them.*"[63] And of the condition, he said "I think that such a condition applies to accidental slips, but not to a case like the present, where, though I do not mean to impute actual fraud, there is what in the view of a Court of equity, amounts to fraud—a misrepresentation calculated materially to mislead the purchaser."

Sir H.M. Cairns L.J. agreed and said "The statement as to the rent was calculated to mislead, and was not prepared with the good faith which is requisite in conditions of sale. I think that a misrepresentation of this nature affects the validity of the contract, and is not a matter for compensation, but entitles the Petitioner to be discharged."

Baskomb v. Beckwith (1869) L.R. 8 Eq. 100 (Vendor's duty of accuracy and candour ("most perfect truth and full disclosure") in his pre-contractual statements if he is to have specific performance; lack of intention to deceive irrelevant)

5.96 The M estate less a single retained plot was put up for sale, and so described that the purchaser would reasonably assume the whole estate was being sold, with nothing kept back. Covenants against any trade and any public house were to be entered into by all purchasers of lots. The purchaser of one of the lots, consisting of a mansion house 100 yards away from the excepted piece of land' was held entitled to resist specific performance unless the vendor would agree to bind his retained land by the same covenants. Lord Romilly M.R. attached importance to the evidence that the defendant bought the property in the firm belief that no pub or trade could be carried on anywhere on the estate. A pub at the distance of the retained plot would have had a very injurious effect on any lot in the vicinity, and would have seriously diminished the prices bid for them. "I think the Defendant bought Lot 1 *in the firm persuasion that no such use was to be made of this plot of ground, and that the acts of the Plaintiff's agents in framing the conditions of sale, as if including the whole estate without any reservation, and so framing and colouring the plan as to contribute to that belief,* are such that the Plaintiff cannot now compel the Defendant to execute the contract, if he insists on retaining this plot free from any restrictive covenants whatsoever. . . . *It is of the greatest importance that it should be understood that the most perfect truth and the fullest disclosure should take place in all cases where the specific performance of a contract is required, and that, if this fails, even without any intentional suppression, the Court will grant relief to the man who has been thereby deceived, provided he has acted reasonably and openly.*"[64] The

[63] Italics supplied.
[64] Italics supplied.

vendor was given the option of entering into a covenant as to his retained plot or having his bill dismissed.

Note: This is an example of an option given to the vendor by the equity courts when appropriate: to make his misrepresentation true or abide the consequences.

Denny v. Hancock (1870) 6 Ch. App. 1 (Duty of candour—misleading particulars)

5.97 A villa near London with two acres of land was sold by means of a plan which was drawn in a misleading way, so as to lead a purchaser to suppose that the boundary included some very fine trees bounded by an iron fence. These trees were not shown on the plan, but there was no real boundary of the property on the ground save some boundary posts which were easy to miss in the shrubbery, and which the purchaser did miss when he inspected the property. Sir W.M. James L.J. felt the mistake of the purchaser was caused by the plan together with the lack of a visible boundary in the right place. "I think that, independently of the plan, and on this latter ground alone, it would have required great consideration before a Court of Equity would have fixed the purchaser with this contract, which he swears he entered into in the belief that the property extended to its apparent boundary; but coupling the state of the property with the representation made by the plan, I am of opinion that it would not be according to the established principles of this Court to compel the purchaser to complete his contract." Sir G. Mellish L.J. agreed that the purchaser had been deceived by the plan regarding a material point, although he said he had the charity to suppose it was not deliberate. He said that since the mistake, which was a material one affecting the value of the property, had arisen through the negligence of the vendors' agents, the purchaser certainly could not be compelled to complete.

Castle v. Wilkinson (1870) L.R. 5 Ch. 534 at 537 (Purchaser's knowledge/acceptance of defect)

5.98 The vendor agreed to sell the land which he held in right of his wife for the joint lives of himself and his wife, and the wife refused to convey, and conveyed to someone else. The purchaser was not allowed specific performance against the husband for what he had, because it was held he was not at all misled, and the contract he wanted would be a different contract. The court distinguished cases where the vendor had expressly represented he could sell the fee simple; in such a case he would be compelled to convey that which he had in fact, if the purchaser opted for that.

Phillips v. Homfray (1871) 6 Ch. App. 770 (A special case?)

5.99 The owner of a colliery entered into a contract with an adjoining landowner to buy his land; but kept entirely silent about the fact that unbeknownst to the land owner, he had taken a considerable amount of coal from under it. The purchaser argued that no damage had been suffered because the sale would have been on the footing that the coal remained underground anyway. The court however considered that the extracted coal would have had a higher value than if it had remained underground. Lord Hatherley L.C. upheld the order of the court below refusing specific performance to the purchaser. He said,

"This Court requires the utmost good faith between buyer and seller, and will not specifically enforce a contract which is not entirely according to good faith.... The proposal which he [the purchaser] makes is not in reality a simple proposal for purchase of the property; it involves a buying-up of rights which the owner has acquired against him, and of which the owner is not aware. He is therefore bound to inform the owner of the circumstances of the case, and is not at liberty to enter into a contract without disclosing his commission of an act which has rendered him liable to certain consequences, and of which act the person with whom he is dealing has a right to be informed in order to know what course he is to adopt . . . I apprehend it would be an error to say generally that you cannot enforce a contract in this Court where the one party knows more of the value than the other does. It happens frequently in the purchase of pictures, for instance, that one party knows a great deal more of the value than the other, and yet the bargain is perfectly good. But I apprehend that the Vice-Chancellor meant his observations to be understood with reference to the circumstances of the particular case, and that when he says the vendors did not know the subject-matter of the contract, he means that they did not know that coal had been taken to the extent of 2000 tons, and that in that state of circumstances they could not be held to the bargain. If indeed, undervalue were shewn, this observation would naturally suggest itself: the case is not merely that the purchasers, being more experienced men, knew the value of the coal better than the vendors, but that the vendors being unable to gain access to the coal, the purchasers took advantage of an unlawful access to it in order to test its value, and did not communicate to the vendors the result. I apprehend that in such a case, the Court, whatever it might do as to cancelling the contract, certainly would decline to enforce it. The case would, I think, be something analogous to this: suppose a picture-dealer, employed to clean a picture, scrapes off a part of the picture to see if he can discover a mark which will tell him who is the artist, and thus finds a mark shewing it to be the work of a great artist; that would not be a legitimate mode of acquiring knowledge for the purposes of enabling him to buy the picture at a lower price than the owner would have sold it for had he known it to be the work of that artist."[65]

THE JUDICATURE ACT 1873

This fused the jurisdiction of equity and common law courts, but in case of choice gave equity's remedies precedence

***Caballero v. Henty* (1874) 9 Ch. App. 447 (Duty of candour—misleading description because of omission)**

5.100 The purchaser bought a public house at auction, said to be in the occupation of a tenant, but it had not been mentioned that the tenant was another brewer under a 21 year lease. The purchaser was held not to have constructive notice, and to have been right to resist specific performance.

THE CONVEYANCING ACT 1881

***Redgrave v. Hurd* (1881) 20 Ch. D. 1**

5.101 The defendant agreed to buy a house and solicitor's business, relying on the vendor's assurance that the business's gross returns were about £300 a

[65] He went on to say he did not dwell on the undervalue point, which had not been satisfactorily established on the evidence.

year. In fact they were only about £200 a year. The vendor sought specific performance and the purchaser sought to rescind. Jessel M.R. commented on the applicable law.

"As regards the rescission of a contract, there was no doubt a difference between the rules of Courts of Equity and the rules of Courts of Common Law—a difference which of course has now disappeared by the operation of the Judicature Act, which makes the rules of equity prevail. According to the decisions of Courts of Equity it was not necessary, in order to set aside a contract obtained by material false representation, to prove that the party who obtained it knew at the time when the representation was made that it was false. It was put in two ways, either of which was sufficient. One way of putting the case was, 'A man is not to be allowed to get a benefit from a statement which he now admits to be false. He is not to be allowed to say, for the purpose of civil jurisdiction, that when he made it he did not know it to be false; he ought to have found that out before he made it.' The other way of putting it was this: Even assuming that moral fraud must be shewn in order to set aside a contract, you have it where a man, having obtained a beneficial contract by a statement which he now knows to be false, insists upon keeping that contract. To do so is a moral delinquency: no man ought to seek to take advantage of his own false statements".

He went on to refer to the judgment of Lord Cairns in *Reese River Silver Mining Company v. Smith*,[66] which he said laid down the law as he had stated it. Baggallay L.J. agreed with Jessel M.R. on this latter point; and Lush L.J. agreed with both.

Note: The case is often cited as an post Judicature Act example of rescission being granted for a representation which was "innocent" in the sense that it was not alleged to be fraudulent. This is only remarkable if one assumes, wrongly, that it had never happened before. As has been seen above, rescission was only granted by courts of equity where there **had** *been at least the degree of fault constituted by a breach of the duty of good faith—whether the duty of candour (as it has been called in this book, or the duty of accuracy; and was granted as often as not where there was this degree of fault. Seen in this light, Jessel M.R. was doing nothing very remarkable in this case, merely doing what many equity judges had done before him. The vendor would have merited two stars in the exercise conducted above in the text: he had evidently not consulted the material available to him, yet had made a statement calculated to be relied on. (The fact that the purchase was of a share in a partnership is really neither here nor there: there is no doubt a duty of good faith as between partners, but it cannot be alleged that this duty seeps out into the negotiations for sale of a partnership share to an outsider.)*

Note also the affirmation by Jessel M.R. that it is not necessary for the vendor to know the purchaser is relying on his representation: it is enough if the representation is calculated to induce him to enter the contract. The purchaser will only be barred by full knowledge of the untruth of the representation, or an express statement. Lush L.J. put it similarly. "The onus probandi is on him [the vendor] to show that the other party waived it, and relied on his own knowledge."

Cato v Thompson (1882) 9 Q.B.D. 616 (Purchaser's knowledge of defect does not override an express covenant for freedom from incumbrances)

5.102 The purchaser bought expressly on terms that he should have a good marketable title. The land was in fact burdened with restrictive covenants restricting building. It was argued that the fact that he knew of the covenants meant he could not complain, but Jessel M.R. said.

"Now, where particulars contain a statement which is literally true, but

[66] (1869) L.R. 4 H.L. 64.

which is susceptible of another meaning, and such other meaning is more likely to be taken than the true one by a person reading the particulars, the purchaser if he knows nothing of the real facts, and understands the particulars in the other sense, is entitled to say that the vendor has deceived him; but if he knew the facts he has nothing to complain of." Thus, in cases which were literally true but taken by the purchaser in the belief that another possible sense of the words was the right one, knowledge on the part of the purchaser would bar any complaint by him. The case before him was not an ambiguity case, however: it was quite clear against the vendor.

Lindley L.J. and Bowen L.J. agreed and the purchaser was allowed to recover his deposit. Lindley L.J. added that if the purchaser's knowledge was allowed to prevail in this case, it would be contradicting a written contract by parol evidence. He said, "Parol evidence is admissible where you have a case of specific performance with compensation, but an express bargain to make a good title cannot be modified by parol evidence. Such evidence would be admissible in an action to reform the contract, but is not admissible for the purpose of construing it."

***Heywood v. Mallalieu* (1883) 25 Ch. D. 357 (Duty of candour; innocent motive irrelevant)**

5.103 An auction sale was subject to a printed condition in a common form that the lot was sold subject to any existing rights and easements of whatever nature. However the printed particulars made no mention of any easement or any claim to any easement. It emerged later that the plaintiff's solicitors had instructed surveyors to value the property, and they had received a letter from a Miss Walker asserting the existence of the right *inter alia* to use the kitchen of the property sold for washing and drying. The solicitor when informed of this decided not to make any further inquiry because he was not going to put other people on their guard about mere claims. Bacon V.C. said, *"I impute no bad intention to the Plaintiff or his advisers, but I say that a man, knowing what this Plaintiff knew, who does not more fully express what he knows, does not do his duty."*[67] The vendor's action for specific performance was dismissed, and the purchaser was given judgment for the return of his deposit with interest.

***Re Gloag & Miller's Contract* (1883) 23 Ch. D. 320 (Purchaser's acceptance of defect)**

5.104 Fry J. said "Two questions have been argued, (1) whether the purchaser's right to a good title is repelled by communications made to him or notice given to him by the vendor before the contract was signed; (2) whether the right to a good title has been to any extent waived by acts done by the purchaser subsequently to the contract.

In my view the law as to the first question stands in this way: When the contract is silent as to the title which is to be shewn by the vendor, and the purchaser's right to a good title is merely implied by law, that legal implication may be rebutted by shewing that the purchaser had notice before the contract that the vendor could not give a good title. If the vendor before the execution of the contract said to the purchaser, I cannot make out a perfect title to the property, that notice would repel the purchaser's right to require a good title to be shewn. But, if the contract expressly provides that a good title shall be shewn, then, inasmuch as a notice by the vendor that he could not shew a good title would be inconsistent with the contract, such a notice

[67] Italics supplied.

would be unavailing, and whatever notice of a defect in the title might have been given to the purchaser, he would still be entitled to insist on a good title. "The purchaser succeeded on this question.

On the second question, waiver [after the contract] of the right to insist on a good title, he drew a distinction between cases in which the objections to the title of which the purchaser knows are removable by the vendor, and cases in which they are irremovable, for example taking possession when the purchaser knows there is a mortgage will not amount to a waiver of his right to have the vendor pay off the mortgage; while the same act might amount to a waiver of some irremovable defect, for example shooting rights belonging to a third party. The purchaser was held to have waived the defect.

Brewer v. Brown [1884] 28 Ch. D. 309 (Duty of candour)

5.105 Sale particulars of a freehold villa in West Ham contained the following statement. "The garden is tastefully laid out and inclosed by a rustic wall, with tradesmen's side entrance." There was a condition that no mistake in the description of the premises or other error whatsoever in the particulars should annul the sale, but compensation should be given. The plaintiff entered into the contract with the intention, known to the defendant, of building cottages on the northern end of the garden (into which the side entrance opened) with that side entrance as their access. In fact the side wall did not belong to the property, and the right to use the side entrance was only on suffrance. The difference in value, on the plaintiff's own evidence, between the property with and without the wall, was only about £100 out of a purchase price of £1300. North J. thought the inference "anyone would draw" was the same as the plaintiff's inference, so that it was *"the vendor's duty to inform a person buying from him what the real state of things was"*, and whatever his duty might have been in other respects, it was all the more incumbent on him when he chose to put the misleading statement in the particulars. He found on the evidence that the plaintiff "believed he was buying this piece of land with the wall and with a frontage to the side road, and he contemplated the possibility of building on it. At any rate it is a piece of land that might be built upon, and what he would have if I gave him compensation would be a piece of land without a lateral frontage, and without the possibility of being built upon." That being so, he thought it was not a case for compensation, and the plaintiff was entitled to rescission. North J. said "I do not omit to notice that compensation can only be insisted on where there is a mistake in the description of the premise or error in the particulars. I do not think that accurately describes what took place in this case. Here *the omission is to state in the particulars something that was essential the vendor should tell the purchaser when entering into the contract of sale.*"[68] The purchaser was granted recissian of the contract.

Smith v. Land & House Property Corp [1884] 28 Ch. D. 7 (The duty of candour applied to a statement of opinion)

5.106 A hotel was sold with a representation in the particulars that it was let to a "most desirable tenant". In fact the tenant had paid his rent irregularly during the period within the vendor's knowledge. It was held that this was not a mere expression of opinion, but contained an *implied assertion*[69] that the vendors *knew of no facts leading to the contrary assertion*. Since it was established

[68] Italics supplied.
[69] See the stars exercise in the text at paragraph 5.11 *et seq.*

that the chairman of the purchaser would not have bought otherwise, the appeal against rescission was dismissed.

Bowen L.J. said; "It is material to observe that it is often fallaciously assumed that a statement of opinion cannot involve the statement of a fact. In a case where the facts are equally well-known to both parties, what one of them says to the other is frequently nothing but an expression of opinion. The statement of such opinion is in a sense a statement of a fact, about the condition of the man's own mind, but only of an irrelevant fact, for it is of no consequence what the opinion is. But *if the facts are not equally known to both sides, then a statement of opinion by the one who knows the facts best involves very often a statement of a material fact, for he impliedly states that he knows facts which justify his opinion*. Now a landlord knows the relations between himself and his tenant, other persons either do not know them at all or do not know them equally well, and if the landlord says that he considers that the relations between himself and his tenant are satisfactory, he really avers that *the facts peculiarly within his knowledge* are such as to render that opinion reasonable. Now are the statements here statements which involve a representation of material facts? They are statements on a subject as to which *prima facie* the vendors know everything and the purchasers nothing.... [The statement here] ... amounts at least to an assertion that nothing has occurred in the relations between the landlords and the tenant which can be considered to make the tenant an unsatisfactory one."[70] Fry L.J. and Baggallay L.J. delivered concurring judgments.

Note: See also Brown v. Raphael[71]*: an application of the principle outside the area of sales of land.*

***Coakes v. Boswell* (1886) 11 App. Cas. 232 (Duty of candour)**

5.107 The case concerned a sale under the direction of the court. The Earl of Selborne affirmed that he was proceeding on the ground the plaintiff was an ordinary purchaser standing in no special fiduciary relation to his vendor. "Every such purchaser is bound to observe good faith in all that he says or does, with a view to the contract, and (of course) to abstain from all deceit, whether by suppression of truth, or by suggestion of falsehood. But inasmuch as a purchaser is (generally speaking) under no antecedent obligation to communicate to his vendor facts which may influence his own conduct or judgment when bargaining for his own interest, no deceit can be implied from his mere silence as to such facts, unless he undertakes or professes to communicate them. *This, however, he may be held to do, if he makes some other communication which, without the addition of those facts, would be necessarily or naturally and probably misleading*." ... [72] On the facts neither he nor the others of the court thought there had been anything of that sort.

***Re Scott & Alvarez' Contract* [1895] 2 Ch. 603 (The new procedure outlawing good faith points; and the new orthodoxy about rescission: the decline of good faith begins)**

5.108 The vendor wanted specific performance and the purchaser wanted the return of his deposit. The contract for the sale of a leasehold property was subject to a condition that the purchaser should not make any objection or requisition in respect of the intermediate title to the lease, but should assume that an assignment of the lease vested in the assignees a good title for the

[70] Italics supplied.
[71] [1958] Ch. 636.
[72] Italics supplied.

residue of the term. This was a vendor and purchaser summons under the 1974 Act and since no good faith points might thus be taken, as tending to attack the validity of the contract, the effect was somewhat unsatisfactory. The age of literalism had to an extent begun, even in contracts for the sale of land. In the absence of good faith points, the contract was held technically to cover a bad title, so that the purchaser could not recover his deposit.[73]

The vendor was nonetheless not allowed specific performance.[74] Further, the by-then prevailing idea that the equity courts could not give rescission seems to have caused Lindley L.J. to consider he had no discretion to allow the purchaser to get back his deposit, either. (". . . I dissent", he said, "entirely from the proposition contended for by Mr Byrne, that since the Vendor and Purchaser Act, or since the Judicature Act, there is any difference now between the law on that point and the law before . . ."; but he seems to have made a difference.)

The other two Lord Justices agreed with Lindley L.J. without much useful discussion, that the parties should be "left to their remedy at law".

Note; It seems peculiary inappropriate that just now, after the Judicature Act 1873, when the only or main reason for "leaving the parties to their remedy at law"—the difference between the two jurisdictions—had actually disappeared, the courts should find this peculiarly money-wasting approach attractive.

Turner v. Green (1895) 2 Ch. 205

5.109 A compromise was reached at a time when one side knew and the other side did not, that the chief clerk of the court, before whom the summons for an account came on, had expressed the view that the summons ought to be dismissed. The defendant said he would not have agreed to the compromise had he known, and asked for it to be set aside. Chitty J. referred *inter alia* to *Walters v. Morgan*[75] and to the passage from Lord Campbell L.C.'s, judgment in that case quoted above, and continued, "That is a correct statement of the law, and one which, it appears to me, is not to be confined to the sale of lands or goods, but is of general application, except perhaps in the case of contracts requiring uberrima fides, which involve a duty to make full disclosure."

He refused to set aside the compromise.

Note. Chitty J. was a believer in the new literalism. His interpretation of the ambiguous passage above is consistent with this. Contrast the approach taken in Carlish v. Salt.[76]

Re White & Smith's Contract [1896] 1 Ch. 637 (Purchaser's caveat emptor duty of investigation only applies where he has had a fair opportunity of inspection, etc.)

5.110 Property was sold at auction containing no statement as to the covenants in the lease. The purchaser sought to rescind on finding that the lease contained onerous and unusual covenants. Stirling J. considered the question whether the purchaser should be fixed with constructive notice of the contents of the lease. He held that the purchaser had not necessarily had a fair opportunity of inspecting the lease within the meaning of the rule laid down in

[73] The property had been described as "a small, safe investment".

[74] Possibly it was felt that the misleading condition ought to prevent this: perhaps the idea that good faith was all part of the Equity courts' "discretionary fudge" was emerging now.

[75] (1861).

[76] (1906).

Reeve v. Berridge,[77] and *Hyde v. Warden*.[78] He also referred to the test for constructive notice set out in *Bailey v. Barnes*,[79] and *Ware v. Lord Egmont*,[80] in particular that a test was whether inquiry ought to have been made *"as a matter of prudence, having regard to what is usually done by men of business under similar circumstances."*[81]

Note: It is typical of the strange unease of the time that one finds the above impeccably good-faith case not long after the "new-look" case of Re Scott & Alvarez' Contract.[82]

***Rudd v. Lascelles* [1900] 1 Ch. 815 (Exceptional case: vendor's ignorance of her title known to purchaser displaces goodfaith obligation to give title)**

5.111 This was a vendor's specific performance action following sale of property by an open contract in correspondence. It appeared that the property was subject to certain restrictive covenants as to building and user. The plaintiff who had derived the property from her late husband, was, to the defendant's knowledge, practically ignorant as to her title, since the deeds were with mortgagees.

Farwell J. said both parties bought with their eyes open. He did not see how he could grant specific performance with compensation, since this would be of a new contract neither had intended to enter into. This was especially the case because there was no compensation clause. Although "a mere offer to sell real property prima facie implies that the vendor has the unincumbered fee simple therein, still, if the purchaser, as in this case, knows that the vendor is ignorant as to the title, he cannot set up any such implication as a representation inducing the contract."

In any case he thought the valuation difficulty here would rule out specific performance with compensation.

***Jacobs v. Revell* [1900] 2 Ch. 858 (*Flight v. Booth* applied)**

5.112 The land was described as bordering on a lake. The only part of the property to which a good title was shown did not border on a lake. Buckley J. reviewed authorities on compensation, *etc.*, impeccably and even reminded us that *Flight v. Booth*[83] (1834) was "at the root of cases of this class", by which one assumes he meant good faith cases. Since here there was no compensation clause, he held that the question was simply whether what was available was "substantially different from what he [the vendor] offered to sell". He thought it was, since there was no title to a material part of the land. He thus ordered rescission and the return of the deposit with interest. He dismissed the counterclaim for specific performance.

Note: Here we have a continued acceptance of the good faith obligation to give title, well after the Judicature Act 1873; and a court perfectly willing to grant rescission for the substantial absence of it.

[77] 20 QBD 523.
[78] (1877) 3 Ex. D. 72.
[79] [1894] 1 Ch. 25.
[80] 4 D.M. & G. 460.
[81] Italic supplied.
[82] See para. 5.108 above.
[83] (1834) 1 Bing (N.C.) 370; 131 E.R. 1160, para. 5.79, above.

Greenhalgh v. Brindley [1901] 2 Ch. 324 (A judge who sat on the fence about the good faith aspect of the case?)

5.113 The vendor (whose action for specific performance it was) had sold a house with windows overlooking land belonging to the local authority. He did not disclose to the purchaser that he had entered into a deed with the local authority acknowledging that he had no right (and in effect could not acquire one) of light over the land. It was held by Farwell J. that he could not give compensation, since "compensation is given in respect of the difference between the expressed subject matter of the contract and the property offered by the vendor as answering that description, and in this case there is none." He hedged his good faith bets, however: he did not give the vendor his costs, because he thought that given the vendor's special knowledge of his own position, he ought in fairness to have informed the purchaser that his position was not "the normal position of the vendor of a house".

Note. From a good-faith point of view the case is obviously inconsistent. If there was, as Farwell J. seems to have thought, a breach of the vendor's duty of candour, it is hard to see why the purchaser should not have received compensation. Merely not ordering him to pay the vendor's costs seems insufficient.

Re Puckett and Smith's Contract [1902] 2 Ch. 258 (*Flight v. Booth* applied)

5.114 This was a non-disclosure by the vendors, who were trustees of a former owner, of a culvert on the land sold. The purchaser had wanted the land for building, to the knowledge of the vendors; who had represented to him that it was suitable for building.

Collins M.R. held that the first question was whether it was contemplated by the parties and whether they were dealing on the basis that the land was reasonably capable of being made fit for building purposes. He thought that it was perfectly clear it was. He thought the second question was "Could the purchaser by reasonable inquiry and inspection have ascertained the existence of this culvert, which is in a very essential way a drawback to the use of the property for building purposes? He thought not. The plans gave no fair indication of its existence. Nor was it discoverable by reasonable inspection. Thirdly, was the culvert such a substantial defect as would within the meaning of the authorities alter the nature of the thing which he intended to buy, and oblige him to take a thing essentially different from that which he agreed to take. He applied *Flight v. Booth*[84] and held that the vendors had not shown a good title.

Stirling L.J. thought the question was not one of title, but of the "rule in *Flight v. Booth*"; and he thought that seeing the property was plainly sold to the purchaser for the purpose of building upon it, it was within this "rule". Cozens Hardy L.J. just said he agreed.

Carlish v. Salt [1906] 1 Ch. 335 (Another good faith decision)

5.115 The purchaser agreed to buy a tumbledown house in Portsmouth Street, Lincoln's Inn Fields. It was to be expected in the ordinary course of events that the house would be rebuilt. The vendor failed to disclose a party wall notice by the owner of the next-door house requiring the owner to shore up the party wall; and the award made thereafter requiring him to do so. The

[84] Above.

purchaser successfully claimed rescission of the contract and repayment of his deposit.

Joyce J.'s judgment is interesting and thoughtful. He rehearsed the facts that "mere silence as regards a material fact which the one party is not under an obligation to disclose to the other cannot be a ground for rescission or a defence to specific performance".[85] However, Joyce J. continued, "In the case of the sale of a chattel, the law as stated by Bramwell B. in *Horsfall v. Thomas* (1862) 1 H & C 90 is that if there be a defect known to the manufacturer, and which cannot be discovered on inspection, he is bound to point it out. Upon consideration of the authorities, I am of opinion that the vendor of real estate is under a similar obligation with respect to a material defect in his title, or in the subject of the sale, *which defect is exclusively within his knowledge, and which the purchaser could not be expected to discover for himself with the care ordinary used in such transactions.*"[86]

***Shepherd v. Croft* [1911] 1 Ch. 521**

5.116 Property was bought but found to have a covered-over watercourse, taking water from the road (ie not an easement). The vendors had known about it but not disclosed it. Specific performance with abatement was ordered.

Parker J. accepted that the defect was latent, but held that it was relatively trivial, not material enough to come within the "rule in *Flight v. Booth*". He considered that the old discretionary factor in specific performance cases, the purpose for which the purchaser purchased, would be a relevant factor in his decision as to whether it was substantial, albeit he thought this would only be so if it was known to the vendor.

Note: The remnants of good faith which are "allowed" to remain are seen to be selectively viewed at this period. The "rule in Flight v Booth*" has assumed great prominence, while the remainder of the good-faith rules have become shadowy and only recognised in the way that protruding angles of icebergs might be. Equity's two-part exercise is no longer appreciated. The objective inquiry into the terms of the contract viewed in the light of the duty of good faith, followed by the choice of remedies, taking into account for this purpose certain "discretionary" factors such as the purchaser's purpose, has been become a set of "factors" in a decision. The change has been awkwardly made; it is plainly felt unfair for the purpose of the purchaser to determine the decision if the vendor never knew of it, so the requirement that he should have known of the purpose, which does not seem to appear in the older cases at all, has been imported into it.*

***Rutherford v. Acton-Adams* [1915] A.C. 866**

5.117 This was a Privy Council case, on appeal from New Zealand. The respondent sold lands in New Zealand for £15,000 and livestock, *etc.*, for another £26,500. Before completion, the appellant complained that there had been a mistaken misrepresentation in negotiations as to the amount of fencing, said to be 232 miles, but actually only 164 miles. The written contract was silent about fencing. The appellant sought to have compensation with specific performance, by reason of the representation, deducting the amount of money involved, £3,570, from the balance to be paid on completion. Lord Haldane giving the judgment of the court, said,

[85] (Fry, *Specific Performance* (3rd edn.) p. 325, adopted in ***Turner v. Green*** above, para. 5.109.

[86] Italics supplied. He referred to *Edwards v. M'Leay* (1815) G. Coop. 308; 35 E.R. 568, on appeal (1818) 2 Swans. 287; 36 E.R. 625) (a good faith decision) and to other authorities.

"... As, shortly after the payment of the deposit, the purchaser entered into possession and has taken profits, rescission is now impossible. It is equally true that as there is no charge made of fraudulent misrepresentation, no claim can be made for damages for deceit. The only possible remedy open to the appellant is to claim compensation against the vendor for the deficiency in the mileage of fencing by invoking the well-known jurisdiction of a Court of Equity in cases of specific performance to order compensation for discrepancy between what was agreed to be conveyed and what can be conveyed." But the court thought compensation was inapplicable here, after completion (albeit without prejudice to the purchaser's claim for compensation) and where there had been what was termed a collateral misrepresentation.

Note: The case is not especially useful, since the reasons for the decision are not given fully, but it would seem to have been because on the facts there was no contractual promise by the vendor to give any particular amount of fencing.

***Lee v. Rayson* [1917] 1 Ch. 613**

5.118 This was an agreement for the sale of 13 houses, eight let at a ground rent of £11 per annum in pairs (so that each had double security) two at £11.10s. and three for £16.10s the three. In fact the rents were £5 for each of 12 houses and one at £6, and there were no pairs. It was held the purchaser was being offered something substantially different from that which he had contracted to buy. The compensation clause did not apply therefore, and the purchaser could have rescission. Eve J. thought that the fact that the rents had the same value as that which the purchaser had contracted for was not the only element, nor the dominant one, although it was something to be taken into account. He considered that Lord Eldon in *Knatchbull v. Grueber*[87] had indicated "the pertinent inquiry which has to be answered." (Lord Eldon had said "This Court is from time to time approaching nearer to the doctrine that a purchaser shall have that he contracted for, or not be compelled to take that which he did not mean to have.)" He went on to say,

"I take that to mean that what the Court has to do in such a case as I have here to deal with is to decide whether the purchaser is getting substantially that which he bargained for, or whether the vendor is seeking to put him off with something which he never bargained for, and in arriving at a conclusion on this question the Court is bound to consider every incident by which the property offered to be assured can be differentiated from that contracted for. If the sum of these incidents really alters the subject-matter, then the purchaser can repudiate the contract; if, on the other hand, the subject matter remains unaffected, or so little affected as to be substantially that which was agreed to be sold, then the purchaser must be held to his contract."

He also dealt with the argument raised that the purchaser ought to have inspected the leases by saying that it was not open to the vendor, having himself misstated the contents in the contract. The purchaser was allowed recission with interest.

Note: Good faith is still alive.

***Yandle v. Sutton* [1922] 2 Ch. 199**

5.119 Sargant J held that a defined track which was compatible with being a simple accommodation track for the land purchased was a latent defect, not a patent one. He said by way of a general observation, "In all these cases between vendor and purchaser, the vendor knows what the property is, and what the rights with regard to it are. The purchaser is generally in the dark.

[87] (1817) 3 Mer. 124; 36 E.R. 480.

I think, therefore, that, in considering what is a latent defect and what a patent defect, one ought to take the general view, that a patent defect, which can be thrust upon the purchaser, must be a defect which arises either to the eye, or by necessary implication from something which is visible to the eye. It would not be fair to hold that a purchaser is to be subjected to all the rights which he might have found out, if he had pursued an inquiry based upon that which was presented to his eye. I think he is only liable to take the property subject to those defects which are patent to the eye, including those defects which are a necessary consequence of something which is patent to the eye." The purchaser was allowed cancellation of his contract and the return of money paid under it.

Note: See text above on latent defects.

***Beyfus v. Lodge* [1925] Ch. 350 Russell J. (Breach of duty of candour)**

5.120 The vendor sued for specific performance of a contract for the sale of two leasehold houses. The contract was on terms that the purchaser should pay for any necessary repairs. There was a clause providing that the production of the last rent receipt should be conclusive evidence that the covenants had been performed. The vendors did not disclose that the landlords had served notices regarding disrepair. The particular individual who answered the inquiry was "in good faith"[88] but in fact a partner in the firm and one of the vendors knew that the notice had been served.

Russell J. held that the notices were something "directly affecting the value of the property which was within the vendors' knowledge, which the intending purchaser could not have ascertained, and which it *was the vendors' duty to disclose*. He declined to grant specific performance accordingly.

He considered however that the purchaser had failed to show a case *for the rescission of the contract*. There was a lot of distinguishing. He distinguished *Heywood v. Mallalieu*[89] and *Edwards v. Wickwar*[90] as being cases of imperfect title; the *Nottingham Patent Brick* case[91] as being a misrepresentation case inter alia. Here there was a condition providing that the deposit should be forfeited if the purchaser failed to comply with the conditions of sale. He also got into something of a muddle over good faith, saying "*There was no misrepresentation, there was, it is true, omission to disclose a material fact, but such omission rendered no stated fact untrue.*"[92]

Note: The waning in popularity and in understanding of the principles of good faith as applied in the old equity and common law courts has led to a curiously split decision. Unless the matter was not substantial, one would have thought rescission would have been appropriate.

***Re Belcham & Gawley's Contract* [1930] Ch. 56 (Breach of duty of condour but court opts for compensation rather than recession.)**

5.121 This case is a modern example of the application of the equitable doctrine of substantial justice. Regard was had to the fact that the purchaser's purpose, to make certain alterations to the house on the land, could be carried out perfectly well despite the defect. The property sold turned out to have two undisclosed public sewers running along one side of the property. The vendor agreed to give compensation, but declined to allow rescission of the contract.

[88] Presumably this means, he did not have actual knowledge.
[89] (1883) 25 Ch. D. 357.
[90] (1865) L.R. 1 Eq. 68.
[91] (1886) 16 Q.B. D. 778.
[92] Italics supplied.

The vendors had known about the sewers, but took the view that they were patent to inspection. (It is not clear whether the court agreed with this or not.) The purchaser was held to be getting substantially that which he contracted for, *provided he had compensation*.[93]

***Barnes v. Cadogan Development* [1930] 1 Ch. 479**

5.122 Property which was thought to be a good building site was sold, without disclosure of an obligation in a deed which provided for *inter alia* the stopping up of the street to which the site fronted and the making of a street bisecting the land sold. A closing order had been made as regards the former street, though not yet proceeded with. It was argued not on misrepresentation, *etc.*, (perhaps because of the presence of a condition precluding the purchaser from annulling the sale or claiming damages for an incorrect statement in the particulars) but on failure to give good title. *Neither vendor nor purchaser were aware of the closing order.* It was held that there was a good title, because the sale had been by mortgagees under their power of sale, and the deed had been by the owners of the land, so that the purchaser from the mortgagees would take free of it. Farwell J. considered, obiter, that innocent misrepresentation would have given no right to damages, only a right to have specific performance refused.

Note: Good faith is still alive.

***Bell v Lever Bros* [1932] AC 161**

5.123 Lord Atkin said, *obiter*, in the course of this well-known case, ". . . Ordinarily the failure to disclose a material fact which might influence the mind of a prudent contractor does not give the right to avoid the contract. The principle of caveat emptor applies outside contracts of sale. There are certain contracts expressed by the law to be contracts of the utmost good faith, where material facts must be disclosed; if not, the contract is voidable. Apart from special fiduciary relationships, contracts for partnership and contracts of insurance are the leading instances. In such cases the duty does not arise out of contract; the duty of a person proposing an insurance arises before a contract is made, so of an intending partner. Unless this contract can be brought within this limited category of contracts uberrimae fidei it appears to me that this ground of defence must fail I see nothing to differentiate this agreement from the ordinary contract of service; and I am aware of no authority which places contracts of service within the limited category I have mentioned."

Note: The point may well have been right as regards that case. One might have wished for a fuller and better exposition of the law on good faith.

***Brown v. Raphael* [1958] Ch. 636**

5.124 This important case, which is not well enough known, does not concern land but the sale of a reversion in a trust fund on the death of an annuitant. It is noted here because it followed *Smith v. Land and House Property*.[94] The sale was accompanied by a statement that the annuitant was believed to have

[93] Cp. *William Sindall PLC v. Cambridgeshire County Council* [1994] W.L.R. 1016, noted in the Appendix to Chap. 10, Excluding the effect of the Fair-dealing Terms, where some considerable degree of literalism in construction of Answers to Inquiries and Conditions of Sale was indulged in by the Court of Appeal, with the result that the unsuspecting purchaser of building land bisected by a 9-inch sewer got nothing at all, having only discovered the defect after completion.

[94] [1884] 28 Ch. D. 7.

no aggregable estate (for the purposes of death duty). The statement was made by a litigation clerk for the solicitors for the vendors.

Lord Evershed M.R. in the Court of Appeal held this was a statement of opinion, but was also two implicit statements of fact: (1) an assertion that it was the belief of the person making it; and (2) a statement by implication "that he knows facts which justify his opinion." Lord Evershed followed Bowen L.J. in the *Smith* case in adding a practical limitation for the application of the principle above: that this would apply where the facts were *not equally known to both parties*, as here (and no doubt in most sales, as the older cases thought). The implicit representation was untrue, and the purchaser had relied on it, so the appeal from rescission of the contract for "innocent" misrepresentation was dismissed.

***Becker v. Partridge* [1966] 2 Q.B. 155**

5.125 There was an undisclosed defect in title, that the lease was liable to be forfeited for breach of covenants in the head lease. The vendor did not know that, but the Court of Appeal, Danckwerts L.J. giving the judgment of the court, held that *he ought to have known*. They relied on Byrne J. in *Re Haedicke & Lipski's Contract*[95] for the proposition that the vendor has to disclose what is his duty to disclose; so that the purchaser was entitled to rescission. There was a condition that the purchaser should accept the vendor's title. This was held inapplicable, because the vendor must first have disclosed the defects of which he knew or ought to have known for such a special condition to have effect.

Note: an impeccable good faith decision.

***Laurence v. Lexcourt Holdings* [1978] 1 W.L.R. 1128**

5.126 See Chapter 6, Sales of Shorter Leases, for a note of this modern good faith decision.

***Faruqi v. English Real Estates Ltd* [1979] 1 W.L.R. 963 at 967**

5.127 See paragraph 5.50 above as to this case which temporarily perpetuates the narrow view of Equity's jurisdiction which became popular in the late nineteenth century following the Judicature Act 1873. However, the case is also an affirmation of the old know-your purchaser principle, applicable to exclusion clauses. Walton J. affirmed that such clauses must not only be accurate, so that "the trained conveyancer reading it, could know, after he had put on a wet towel and consulted all the works available precisely and exactly what the trouble was,"[96] but must also be expressed in such a way that an *ordinary* purchaser would understand what the difficulty was."

[95] [1901] 2 Ch. 666 noted in the Appendix to Chap. 10, Excluding the Effect of the Fair Dealing Rules.

[96] *cf. Williams v. Wood* (1868) 16 W.R. 1005.

CHAPTER 6

SALE OF SHORTER LEASES

Introduction

6.01 There is no essential difference between the purchase of shorter leases and the purchase of freehold land. What is most marked, however, about the cases on the purchase of leases is the emphasis on *caveat emptor*—the buyer's duty to carry out reasonable and normal investigations before buying. If anything, one has the sense that the courts tended after a while almost to overemphasize this, tending to obscure the operation of good faith principles. These good faith principles will have been needed much more rarely, since the transactions we are dealing with tended to be shorter and simpler to investigate anyway; but the principles were there nonetheless.

A reason for the emphasis on the purchaser's duty of due diligence may have been the desire to limit narrowly the early cases where it was held the landlord who let furnished premises under short leases, commonly a few months for the season, had a duty to speak if there was something about the premises rendering them unfit for human habitation. No doubt the courts had a reasonable enough fear that this indulgence might be taken to apply generally, so that hordes of careless purchasers would take to the law when disappointed with their leased premises.

6.02 The duty of good faith is not needed often in these shorter lease transactions, but it would not be right to suppose that it does not exist or has been excluded in some way. There is no justification in the cases for this view. These cases, for example, even go to the lengths of allowing a good-faith implication from silence[1] in circumstances where it has been impractical or impossible for the buyer to inspect, so that his duty of due diligence yields to a presumption of reasonable reliance on the vendor.[2] There is also to be found an impeccable modern example of the ordinary operation of the good-faith rules, concerning a misleading statement lulling the buyer into a sense of false security in *Laurence v. Lexcourt Holdings*.[3]

There are indeed statements to the effect that there is no implied term *per se* that the premises shall be fit for their purpose; these mean simply that the buyer is to inspect; that he cannot rely on a general

[1] See below.

[2] Compare the similar approach to dwelling houses in the course of construction: see Appendix.

[3] [1978] 1 W.L.R. 1128.

implied term.[4] This is not very surprising: even where the sale is of a chattel, it has been necessary both before and after the 1893 Sale of Goods Act to show that the purpose has been made known to the seller and that his skill and judgment were being relied on. The cases do not, however, take the further step of finding that the buyer is bound by defects he could not have found out, or denying him relief where he has been lulled into a false sense of security by something said by the seller, so that, relying on this, he has not investigated sufficiently, or where he has been misled by a failure on the part of the seller in his duty of accuracy or candour. *Caveat emptor* is a rule of reasonable expectation, not a blind, statute-like provision, and thus yields where appropriate to the circumstances, in this category of sale as elsewhere.

Purchaser's duty of due diligence

(1) Physical inspection

6.03 The purchaser should normally carry out a physical inspection of the premises before agreeing to take them. He is liable for any defects which such physical inspection would have revealed, whether or not he does so.

In *Hart v. Windsor*[5] the tenant had not in fact chosen to inspect the properly first. This may have been an underlying reason for the court's statement that the tenant, who had not inspected, had thus to be taken as bargaining for the premises, in whatever state they might be, and not the premises in any particular condition. The case is not authority for any proposition about circumstances when inspection was not possible.

In *Arden v. Pullen*[6] it was decided by implication that it was the tenant's duty to carry out a survey of the structure of the premises first, and if he chose not to, could not complain of defects which would have been revealed by that inspection.

In *Chappell v. Gregory*[7]—a case concerned with the structural condition of the premises, the question of a general implied term of fitness for purpose was considered and rejected, and the court stressed the tenant's opportunity to inspect the premises before taking them.

6.04 Also relevant is *Sutton v. Temple*.[8] The defect in that case was very nearly a latent defect, in which case perhaps there might, following the cases about furnished premises, have been a duty on the vendor to speak. But perhaps it was not quite latent: the traces of paint in the grass, which proved so fatal to the unfortunate tenant's cattle, would have been visible, it would seem, if only as faint specks in the grass.

[4] See now, however, the implied term as to drainage and hot water installations, *etc*, contained in s.11 of the Landlord and Tenant Act 1985.

[5] (1843) 12 M. & W. 68; 152 E.R. 1108.

[6] (1842) 10 M. & W. 321; 152 E.R. 492.

[7] (1863) 34 Beav. 250; 55 E.R. 631.

[8] (1843) 12 M. & W. 52; 152 E.R. 1108.

Of the court, Lord Abinger did not specifically rest his judgment on the opportunity the purchaser had had to inspect, but it may be suggested this was really the foundation of it. This can be deduced from his statement that *Smith v. Marrable*[9]—in which furnished premises on a short let were held to be subject to an implied fitness-for-purpose term—might not apply in a case where a party had had *an opportunity of personal inspection* of the house in question by himself or his agent.

> "Where the party has had an opportunity of personally inspecting a ready-furnished house by himself or his agent before entering on the occupation of it, perhaps the objection would not arise; but if a person take a ready-furnished house upon the faith of its being suitably furnished, surely the owner is under an obligation to let it in a habitable state. Common sense and common justice concur in that conclusion."

Thus, it seems possible, if not probable, that the defect in the grass *was* sufficiently evident to have been apparent to the purchaser or his agent on a thorough inspection before the contract.

Another member of the court in that case, Parke B, a "hard-liner", felt the crucial point was that one bought the *land* (as land, evidently, rather than with some particular purpose attached), so that no implied term that it should be fit for its purpose existed. This really does not mean any more than that no term should be *implied* without more. One finds this "he bought it as . . ." approach in sale of goods cases of the period: the test for a while being thought to be whether the purpose was or was not "part of the description" of what was bought. This approach was unsatisfactory, since it really provided no useful test at all: it was simply another way of putting the question; and ultimately it fell out of fashion. The other judges in the case simply agreed that *Smith v. Marrable*[10] was distinguishable and that no term of fitness for purpose should be implied. Thus, it is probably only Lord Abinger's judgment which gives any clue about the underlying rationale of this early and seminal case—the purchaser should survey the land thoroughly.

(2) Non-physical investigations

6.05 A purchaser must also carry out the usual and normal non-physical investigations. He must for example satisfy himself that the premises may legally be used, for example under the planning legislation, for the purpose for which he desires to use them. The fact that he has told the landlord of his purpose does not shift the burden. *Edler v. Auerbach*[11] will have turned on the assumption that the tenant will normally instruct a solicitor, who will look into the planning position.

The purchaser has also to carry out proper investigation of title through a solicitor where this would be normal. In *Hill v. Harris*[12] the

[9] (1843) above.
[10] (1843) above.
[11] [1950] 1 K.B. 359.
[12] (1965) 2 Q.B. 601.

fact that the landlord/vendor knew quite well the purpose for which the premises were to be used did not suffice to make him liable for its unsuitability for that purpose, given that the purchaser himself could have found out the problem by using due diligence. Russell L. J. said:

> "I myself would be very unwilling in any case to spell out a warranty on a matter to some extent related to title, when *the ordinary and prudent course of investigation of title* will in due course display the true position."[13]

The duty of candour and accuracy

6.06 See *Laurence v. Lexcourt Holdings*[14] for a modern application of the duty, relying on good faith cases to be found in Chapter 5, Sale of Land.

A particular application of the duty—furnished houses: a statement implied from silence in appropriate circumstances

Lettings of furnished houses appear to have been treated differently from unfurnished ones. It is thus an obvious place to search for any fair-dealing principles which may have been implied.[15] Furnished houses were to be fit at least for the purpose for which such premises are apparently leased, for example human habitation, in the case of residential leases. *Smith v. Marrable*[16] concerned a 5 or 6 weeks' lease where the premises were infested by bugs; and *Wilson v. Finch Hatton*[17] a three months' lease where the premises were unsuitable for human habitation by reason of the condition of the drains. The rationale for the rule applying to furnished leases, which became increasingly rigid, with less and less discussion of the true principles involved, is not entirely easy to find. The later approach, expressed in a number of cases, especially those in the early and middle part of this century, was simply acceptance, without discussion of principle, that it was well established that furnished houses were subject to a different rule, as though there were some unusual magic about furniture. This is evidently unsatisfactory; as one nineteenth- century commentator pointed out, the circumstances may show that a house may be clearly

[13] At 617, italics supplied.

[14] (1978) above.

[15] See the Landlord and Tenant textbooks for the statutory implied terms in leases at low rents contained in the Landlord and Tenant Act 1985. See also the useful account of existing statutory implied obligations, (ss. 8, 11 of the Landlord and Tenant Act 1985; s.4 of the Defective Premises Act 1972; s.35 of the Landlord and Tenant Act 1987) and their limited nature, in the Law Commission Report, Com 238, H.C. 236, Landlord and Tenant; Responsibility for the State and Condition of Property.

[16] (1843) above.

[17] (1877) Ex. D. 344.

intended for human habitation whether or not it is furnished. In *Bunn v. Harrison*[18] the Court of Appeal expressly left open the question whether an unfurnished house let for immediate occupation might not be subject to a similar implied term.

6.07 One may compare the statements thought to have been made by conduct in the sale of goods sphere; for example, the statement made by selling goods in a retail shop.[19] By parity of reasoning, the furniture will have showed that the purpose was in fact human habitation, so making unnecessary any express words from which a term could be implied. In such circumstances, silence on the part of the vendor would endorse the buyer's reasonable expectation of fitness: a statement expressly negativing it would be needed.[20] Some support for this view can also be derived from the judgment of Parke B, in *Hart v. Windsor*,[21] where in the event the court declined to apply a fair-dealing term in an unfurnished let. Parke B. felt that furnishing the house was in effect a statement by the landlord:

> "If the landlord furnishes the house, and by so doing holds it out as fit for immediate occupation, and secures to himself a greatly increased rent in consequence, that is a very different case."

A similar equation: furniture = a statement that the dwelling is fit to be lived in, seems to have been the basis of the decision in *Campbell v. Lord Wenlock*.[22]

The fact that inspection would have been impractical is likely to have been important in the furnished-lets rule. This would have been consistent with the way the fair-dealing rules were applied in other fields. The early cases on furnished lets concern short lets for the season, for six weeks or three months. Transport was more uncertain and took longer; and a long journey to inspect a house which was taken only for so short a time may have been regarded as impossible in practice. Thus, the basis on which the implied term perhaps became binding on the landlord may have included, originally at least, the purchaser's reasonable inability to investigate for himself. It was common at the time of *Smith v. Marrable*[23] (as we know from Jane Austen's and Trollope's novels and elsewhere) for people to take furnished houses for the season, and journeys of inspection first do not seem to figure.

6.08 It could be anticipated, on the other hand, that an intending tenant of an unfurnished house *would* inspect it, since it seems these were not sold with appurtenances such as grates or stoves. See for this piece of social knowledge, *Hart v. Windsor*,[24] in which the court recognised

[18] (1886) 2 T.L.R. 146.

[19] See Chap. 3, Sale of Chattels.

[20] C.p. the duty of disclosure in surety cases, of facts that the surety would not naturally expect; and see *Smith v. Hughes* (1871) L.R. 6 Q.B. 597 for a good explanation of the kind of circumstances where the duty arises.

[21] (1843) above.

[22] (1866) 4 F. & F. 716; 176 E.R. 760.

[23] (1843) above.

[24] (1843) above.

that an unfurnished house required to be put by the tenant into a state fit for habitation anyway; and the landlord's counsel had said in argument:

> "The landlord lets the mere fabric of the house, without grates or stoves or any articles of furniture, and it is the duty of the tenant to put the house in a habitable condition . . .".

Thus, the purchaser would need to visit before he took the house in order to measure for such things. Further, unfurnished houses would in the nature of things be taken for a longer term, so as to render a journey of inspection less unreasonable. The early cases on the subject, which are the ones to contain such discussion of principle as there is, certainly do seem frequently to stress the opportunity of inspection which the tenant had, although without seeking explicitly to infer any principle therefrom.

The rent at which the premises are let was in the early cases regarded as relevant to the question whether the term was to be implied or not. Again, this would be consistent with the development of the doctrine of reasonable reliance in the sale of goods field: there the fact that the goods were sold for a full price was a relevant factor.[25] It seems that there was in those days a large differential in price between furnished and unfurnished houses.[26]

Unfurnished houses in the course of construction: a comparable example of a statement implied from silence in the circumstances

6.09 We may compare a similar statement implied from silence in the circumstances, provided by the cases of sales (not necessarily on short leases) of unfurnished houses in the course of construction. In these the courts had no difficulty whatever in implying a term that *the work would be properly done,* and that they would be fit for human habitation when finished. They said this was purely *from the words* "in the course of construction", but the process is essentially one of implication from silence and the circumstances of construction, even if described as a process of grammatical amplification.[27]

Within his knowledge

6.10 Where a fair-dealing term does exceptionally arise, a landlord who "ought to have known" is regarded, in one instance at least, as one

[25] See Chap. 3, Sale of Personal Property. See also Parke B. in ***Hart v. Windsor*** (1843) who seems to have relied in part on the lower price asked for the unfurnished premises.

[26] Perhaps because insurance of the contents was not conveniently achieved then? See also ***Cruse v. Mount*** [1933] Ch. 278 for relevance of price.

[27] See ***Lawrence v. Cassel*** [1930] 2 K.B. 83; ***Miller v. Cannon Hill Estates*** [1931] 2 K.B. 113; ***Perry v. Sharon Development Co*** [1937] 4 All E.R. 390; ***Hancock v. Brazier*** [1966] 1 W.L.R. 1317. A vendor-builder is now liable in tort for dangerous defects even in an unfurnished house if he has constructed it himself: *Rimmer v. Liverpool City Council* [1985] Q.B. 1; and see *Targett v. Torfaen B.C.* [1992] 3 All E.R. 27.

who in fact knew. This is again precisely the way in which fair-dealing terms work in other sales.[28] Lord Abinger in *Smith v. Marrable*[29] seems to have envisaged that the unfitness for human habitation in that case might have been *"unknown perhaps to the landlord"* but it did not deter him from holding that the term of fitness for human habitation applied.

Honest belief, mistaken motive, etc., no excuse

6.11 An honest belief on the part of the vendor that the premises are fit for the purpose is no excuse, where a fitness for purpose term is to be implied, and they are not in fact fit.[30] Again, this is consistent with the good faith approach in other areas.

APPENDIX: SOME CASES OF INTEREST

Arden v. Pullen (1842) 10 M. & W. 321; 152 E.R. 492 (Duty of due diligence includes physical inspection; 3-year lease)

6.12 This was three-year lease of a house and premises, the tenant to keep the premises in as good repair and condition as they were at the start. The premises proved to have unsound foundations, built on marshy soil, which required underpinning, and extensive reconstruction. Alderson B. suggested in argument that *the tenant ought to examine the house before he takes it*. Lord Abinger C.B. held that *"unless there has been some fraud or improper concealment on the part of the plaintiff*, which is not suggested, the contract for letting this house was perfectly good."[31]

Alderson B. considered the contract was perfectly good also. He affirmed the rule laid down by Tindal C.J. in *Izon v. Gorton*[32] in which the latter had said that "the cases in which the tenant has been allowed to withdraw himself from the tenancy, and to refuse payment of rent, will be found to be cases where there has been either *error or fraudulent misdescription of the premises . . . or where the premises have been found to be uninhabitable by the wrongful act or default of the landlord himself*."[33] Gurney B. and Rolfe B. concurred.

Note: It seems that the faults will have been fairly apparent to the tenant on inspection. The italicised passage above does not make entirely clear the kind of exceptions envisaged by Alderson B. In particular, the scope of "error" or "improper concealment" is unclear. The expression "fraudulent concealment" was used on occasions in a wider sense than our modern one, to connote concealment of matters which ought to have been disclosed by virtue of the fair-dealing rules, whether or not the concealment was what we would now call dishonest.

[28] See, *e.g*, Chap. 4, Insurance and Surety Transactions, Chap. 5, Sale of Land, and Chap. 7, Sale of Company Shares.
[29] (1843) above.
[30] ***Charsley v. Jones*** (1889) 53 J.P. 280.
[31] Italics supplied.
[32] 5 Bing (N.C.) 501; 132 E.R. 1193.
[33] Italic supplied.

***Smith v. Marrable* (1843) 11 M. & W. 5; 152 E. R. 693 Short furnished lease; statement implied that habitable)**

6.13 Sir Thomas Marrable had agreed to take a furnished house at Brighton, No. 5 Brunswick Place, for five or six weeks. It proved to be infested by bugs.

Abinger C.B. had summed up to the jury in terms that *every house* must be taken to be let upon the implied condition that there was nothing about it so noxious as to render it uninhabitable. The Plaintiff moved for a new trial. Parke B. referred to earlier authorities, and held that they established the following position "... if the demised premises are incumbered with a nuisance of so serious a nature that no person can reasonably be expected to live in them, the tenant is at liberty to throw them up."

He said that it was not a matter of express contract, "it rather rests in an *implied condition of law*, that he undertakes to let them in a habitable state".

The remaining members of the court, Alderson B, Gurney B. and Lord Abinger C.B, agreed, Lord Abinger adding the following, 'Suppose, instead of the particular nuisance which existed in this case, the tenant discovered the fact—*unknown perhaps to the landlord*—that lodgers had previously quitted the house in consequence of having ascertained that a person had recently died in it of plague or scarlet fever; would not the law imply that he ought not be compelled to stay in it? I entertain no doubt whatever on the subject ..."[34]

***Hart v. Windsor* (1843) 12 M. & W. 68; 152 E.R. 1108 (3-year unfurnished lease; duty of due diligence prevails)**

6.14 It was held that there was no general implied warranty on a lease of an unfurnished house, or of land, that it is, or shall be reasonably fit for habitation or cultivation. There had been a three-year lease of a house, which proved to be infested by bugs. It was said that "the implied contract relates only to the estate, not the condition of the property." The basis of the judgments seems to have been in part that an unfurnished house required to be put into a state fit for habitation anyway. The landlord's counsel had said in argument "The landlord lets the mere fabric of the house, without grates or stoves or any articles of furniture, and it is the duty of the tenant to put the house in a habitable condition ..." In part, the court seems also to have been influenced by the low rent which unfurnished houses fetched. The landlord's Counsel had gone on to say, "If the lessor *furnishes the house, and by so doing holds it out as fit for immediate occupation*, and secures to himself *a greatly increased rent* in consequence, that is a very different case."[35]

Parke B. expressly distinguished the case of furnished houses, such as *Smith v. Marrable*[36], a decision he considered correct, saying that "it was the case of a fully-furnished house for a temporary residence at a watering-place." He stated that there was, "no implied warranty on a lease of a house, or of land, that it is, or shall be, reasonably fit for habitation or cultivation. The implied contract relates only to the estate, not the condition of the property."

***Sutton v. Temple* (1843) 12 M. & W. 52; 152 E. R. 1108 (Duty of diligence prevails; 6-month lease of grazing land)**

6.15 The purchaser had taken a six-month lease of 24 acres of eddish (grazing land) and stocked it. The cattle died because unbeknownst to the vendor, in

[34] Italics supplied.
[35] Italics supplied.
[36] Para 6.13 above.

the previous spring, paint with noxious residues (presumably lead?) had been tossed onto a manure heap, and the manure then sprinkled on the grass. On inspection, faint traces of paint were apparent in the grass. Lord Abinger—sitting in the hard-line Court of Exchequer—considered that *Smith v. Marrable*[37] (which he approved) was not applicable since in that case the contract had been (implicitly, it would seem: see above) for a house fit for immediate occupation. Counsel for the landlord had argued that anyway that was a case of a latent defect. Lord Abinger said that *the rule in Smith v. Marrable* might not apply in a case where a party had had *an opportunity of personal inspection* of the house in question by himself or his agent. Thus, it seems possible, if not probable, that the defect in the grass *was* sufficiently evident to have been apparent on a thorough inspection to the purchaser or his agent before the contract. Parke B, felt the crucial point was that one bought the *land* (as land, evidently, rather than with some particular purpose attached). The other judges all agreed that *Smith v. Marrable* was distinguishable.

Chappell v. Gregory (1863) 34 Beav. 250; 55 E.R. 631

6.16 The dispute was whether the landlord under an oral lease had verbally agreed to put the (unfurnished) house in question into a good state of repair. The question whether a term to this effect might also be implied was considered. Sir John Romilly M.R. said, "A promise by the landlord to put the house into a complete state of repair before the lease is executed, and upon the faith of which the lease is taken, is a distinct engagement which must be fulfilled by him. But, in the absence of such a promise, the man who takes a house from a lessor, *takes it as it stands;* it is his business to make stipulations beforehand, and if he does not, he cannot say to the landlord "This house is not in a proper condition, and you or your builder must put it into a proper condition which makes it fit for my living in." Here too, what seems to have been important was the opportunity the tenant had to inspect the house. Sir John said that not only was there no (general) implied warranty in the letting of a house, "but in this instance *the Defendant had, himself, previously inspected the house, and knew, or had the opportunities of knowing,*[38] what the condition was."

Campbell v. Lord Wenlock (1866) 4 F. & F. 716; 176 E.R. 760 (Another statement implied from silence in the circumstances of a furnished summer lease)

6.17 This was another house, No. 49 Eaton Place, which was let for the summer. Despite an express promise that it would be clean and ready for occupation, it was badly infested with bugs. Cockburn C.J. said he did not think it mattered whether there was an express condition that the house should be cleaned or not . . . "for if a house was let furnished, it could not be contended, surely, that it was not to be put into a fit state to receive the tenant?" . . . He did not see that it could make any difference whether the term was implied or express, because "it could scarcely be supposed that when a house was let ready furnished, it was to be let in a state so filthy and dirty that it was not fit for occupation".

It would seem thus that Cockburn C.J. implied a condition by means of a statement by conduct made by letting the house furnished for immediate occupation (see above). Although Cockburn C.J. did not mention it as part of

[37] Para 6.13 above.
[38] Italics supplied.

his reasoning, it does seem the tenant in this case *did not have an opportunity to reinspect, and thus will have been obliged to rely on the landlord.*

***Wilson v. Finch-Hatton* (1877) 2 Ex. D. 344 (Another statement implied from silence in the circumstances of a furnished three-month let)**

6.18 This was a let of a furnished family house for three months for the season. It was quite unsuitable for occupation by reason of the condition of the drains. It was held there was an implied term that it should be fit for human habitation. Pollock B. said rather vaguely that it was not a case which was governed by "the cases which refer to real property". However, he did *not* seem to be saying, as one might suppose, that because the furniture was in a sense goods, the law on sales of goods should be applied by analogy; since he expressly stated that he thought the case was *not* similar to *Jones v. Just*[39] which was an important sale-of-goods case.

He went on to say "... some of the incidents of this contract are analogous to those of the cases of supply of chattels there discussed, and it may therefore be observed that *the defect in this case was latent* and that the Defendant may be held to have *relied with reason on the assurance of the lessors* as to the condition of the house."[40] Note the assurance he refers to must be an assurance implied from the circumstances of letting a furnished house without saying anything more: there is certainly no evidence of any express assurance from the landlords. Thus, the case seems to rest on two pillars, the latent nature of the defect, and the reasonable reliance on an inferred statement from the circumstances and silence.

***Bunn v. Harrison* (1886) 2 T.L.R. 146**

6.19 In this case the Court of Appeal expressly left open the question whether there was an implied warranty of fitness in the case of an unfurnished house if it was to be let *for immediate occupation.*

***Charsley v. Jones* (1889) 53 J.P. 280**

6.20 It is no excuse that the landlord honestly believed the premises were habitable at the beginning of the tenancy, if in fact they were not so.

***Lane v. Cox* [1897] 1 Q.B. 415**

6.21 The Court of Appeal reaffirmed that there was no "law against" letting a house in a tumbledown condition.

***Collins v. Hopkins* [1923] 2 K.B. 617**

6.22 A furnished house had been inhabited by someone with consumption. The tenant was held not to be obliged to take it.

Note: There must have been some highly effective expert medical evidence in this case. A large part of the judgment is about the highly—and apparently enduringly—infectious nature of TB spores!

[39] (1868) L.R. 3 Q. B. 197, see Chap. 3 Sale of Personal Property.
[40] At 314 italics supplied.

***Lawrence v. Cassel* [1930] 2 K.B. 83 (Statement implied in circumstances of dwelling house under construction that work would be done properly)**

6.23 The court held that where the contract for the sale of a dwelling house in the course of erection contained express terms as to how the construction would be done, there was an implied term that the construction would be done properly. It was also held that although the conveyance did not contain any reference to the work, there was no merger of contract and conveyance, relying on *Palmer v. Johnson*.[41] In that case the court had held that a compensation clause relating to defects in the property survived a conveyance which contained no such compensation clause.)

***Miller v. Cannon Hill Estates* [1931] 2 K.B. 113 (Statement implied as above)**

6.24 A house was purchased in the course of construction. The vendor's oral statement that the house would be built of good material was held by the court to be a collateral oral term of the contract. Swift J. held also that where there was a duty to complete a house, the law would imply a further duty "that it shall be completed in an efficient and workmanlike manner and of proper materials." MacNaghten J. agreed that there would be an implied term, and thus did not find it necessary to consider whether there had been a collateral warranty or not.

Swift J. had commented on the rationale as he saw it for the different rule in the case of a completed house, where there is no implied contract that the house is necessarily fit for human habitation.

"That must be good sense, because a man who buys an empty house may not necessarily need it as a dwelling–house; he may be buying something which is almost in a state of ruin, knowing that he will have to restore it and pay a considerable amount of money for restoring it. He may buy a house which wants a new roof put on or which has other obvious defects of which he knows, and may have defects of which he does not know, and if he wants to buy a house which is fit for habitation, then he must expressly stipulate that the house shall be fit for habitation. He can always get an express warranty that an unfurnished house is fit for habitation, if he is prepared to pay the price which attaches to an unfurnished house which has such a warranty, rather than the price which a vendor is willing to take for an unfurnished house without such a warranty." By contrast, a contract such as the one before him was one where "the whole object, as both parties know, is that there shall be erected a house in which the intended purchaser shall come to live. It is *the very nature and essence of the transaction* between the parties that he will have a house put up there *which is fit for him to come into as a dwelling house.* It is plain that in those circumstances there is *an implication of law that the house shall be reasonably fit for the purpose for which it is required,*[42] that is for human dwelling."

Note: This reads like an attempt to justify the rule, which had become accepted without question by then, namely that unfurnished houses were not subject to any implied term of fitness for purpose. It is difficult to see why a person who buys a short lease of an unfurnished house with a fitted kitchen or bathroom, say, should not expect the kitchen or bathroom, at least, to be fit for its purpose, if no more is said. Similarly, there is no reason why a person who sells or lets a house for a full price with central heating or air conditioning or a swimming pool should not, if he says nothing about any defects, be regarded as making a statement by conduct/circum-

[41] (1884) 13 QBD 351; see Chap. 16 for a note of this case.

[42] Italics supplied.

stances that these are reasonably fit for their purpose. Thus, the vendor would, given appropriate circumstances, be at risk of the court implying a statement from his silence about such serious latent defects. Similarly, if a person buys a newly constructed house, it is hard to see why there should not similarly be an implied term at common law that this is fit for human habitation, requiring only furniture, curtains etc.

***Cruse v. Mount* [1933] Ch. 278**

6.25 Maugham J. applied *Hart v. Windsor*[43] and stressed the point made in that case, that unfurnished houses are constantly let in a very bad state, the state of repair being one which is reflected in the rent.

***Bottomley v. Bannister* [1932] 1 K.B. 458**

6.26 This was a house which was let unfurnished with an express condition that it should be fit for human habitation. The gas boiler serving the bathroom was one without a flue, but which was perfectly safe when a needle adjusting the flow of gas was properly regulated. The appliance was properly tested by the Gas company's inspector and left regulated at the correct flow. Nonetheless both tenants were found dead, and the flow adjustment set so as to allow a dangerous quantity of gas through. The action was brought in tort against the landlord on behalf of the estates of the deceased tenants for the benefit of their baby. Scrutton L.J. considered the tenant or his wife must have altered the regulator. He held that if the gas boiler was to be regarded as a chattel, it was not dangerous *per se*; and the vendor landlord, who did not know of the danger if the appliance was not properly regulated, could not be liable for not warning. If on the other hand, as he held, it was part of the realty, the landlord was again not liable. All three lords justices (the other two were Greer L.J. and Romer L.J.) referred to cases such as *Hart v. Windsor*[44] and *Lane v. Cox*[45] (above) as stating the well established English law. Scrutton L.J. applied Parke B.'s statement in *Hart v. Windsor*, to the effect that there was no term or condition implied by law "on the demise of real property only, that it is fit for the purpose for which it is let."[46]

Note. Thus, the dictum in Hart v. Windsor, which had related to particular facts before the court, had evidently begun to take on the appearance of a rule to be applied universally. This is unlikely to have been the intention in 1848.[47] *since the court then expressly approved Smith v. Marrable.*[48] *Accordingly, it seems likely that the true ratio of Bottomley v. Bannister is that a purchaser must take land with defects which he has had a reasonable opportunity of inspecting—that is, caveat emptor, or let the buyer use due diligence. It does not go so far as to state that a buyer who had no opportunity of inspection, or was misled by the vendor's breach of his duty of candour or accuracy, is similarly to be fixed with notice of defects.*

***Perry v. Sharon Development* [1937] 4 All E.R. 390 (C.A.)**

6.27 A purchaser bought land with "the dwelling house and premises erected or in the course of erection theron". The chimneys let in smoke and the walls

[43] Above, para. 6.14.
[44] Above, para. 6.14.
[45] Above, para. 6.21.
[46] This was so, he considered, even if the landlord had constructed the defects or was aware of their existence; but see now *Anns v. Merton BC* [1978] A.C. 728.
[47] See above.
[48] Above, para. 6.13.

let in damp. The court held that *as a matter of construction of the agreement by reference to the subject matter* a term must be implied that the house should be completely finished and ready for occupation. The judgment of MacKinnon L.J. is perhaps the most interesting: he felt, like the rest of the court, that the term was to be implied "from the words" above; but in addition, drew a distinction between a completed house, which may be examined by the purchaser, and where the maxim of *caveat emptor* applies, and an uncompleted one, where *the buyer naturally cannot inspect* the uncompleted parts. The case thus has a good-faith rationale.

***Davis v. Foots* [1940] 1 K.B. 116**

6.28 A flat was rented by a young couple. The defect in this case had been caused by the landlord. The couple were asked if they wanted a gas fire in one of the bedrooms, and said no, they did not. It was then taken out by the landlord's son in such a way that there was no gas tap left which could be turned off to prevent any gas escaping into the room. The husband, who was the legal tenant, died of asphyxiation; his wife became very ill, but recovered. She sued but failed to recover damages. MacKinmon L.J. cited Scrutton L.J. in *Bottomley v. Bannister*[49] and found the landlord not liable. He said "It is the tenant's business, when he takes possession of a house, *to discover and remedy any danger that may exist*. In this case quite obviously *it did not need the exercise of a great deal of care for anyone who was turning on the gas in a house where it had been turned off at the meter for some time, to go round the house and see that the various pipes into which the gas would be admitted were safe, and were not leaking*."[50] It is clear from the judgment of du Parcq L.J. that the defect concerned was not regarded by the court as a latent defect.

Note. This case is perhaps an example of the way the duty to use due diligence will depend on the times. Gas pipes were no doubt not as reliably constructed as in more recent times, so that it would seem to have been a normal part of inspection by a tenant to check the gas pipes and taps.[51]

***Edler v. Auerbach* [1950] 1 K.B. 359**

6.29 A house was let which could only be used for residential purposes, if it was to comply with the planning law, but which had been let with the intention known to both vendor and purchaser that it should be used as offices. There had been an "innocent" misrepresentation, but relief was thought to be barred by the "rule" in *Angel v. Jay*[52] Devlin J. held there was no implied warranty that the premises could be used as offices. Reliance was placed on Scrutton L.J.'s comments in *Bottomley v. Bannister*.[53] Devlin J. said "It is the business of the tenant, if he does not protect himself with an express warranty, to satisfy himself that the premises are fit for the purpose for which he wants to use them, whether that fitness depends on the state of their structure, the state of the law, or any other relevant circumstance."

[49] Para. 6.26 above.
[50] Italics supplied.
[51] The author once had a family holiday in a rented flat abroad where the main gas tap had to be turned on and off at the mains before and after using the gas cooker. These things evidently vary. It may be, perhaps, that nowadays a defect in the gas pipes such as that in ***Davis v. Foots*** might be regarded as latent at common law.
[52] See Chap. 16, Remedies for Breach of Good Faith Duties for this supposed rule.
[53] Para. 6.26 above.

Hancock v. Brazier **(1966) 1 W.L.R. 1317**

6.30 Lord Denning, following *Laurence v. Cassel,*[54] and *Miller v. Cannon Hill Estates*[55] held that "when a purchaser buys a house from a builder who contracts to build it, there is a threefold implication: that the builder will do his work in a good and workmanlike manner; that he will supply good and proper materials; and that it will be reasonably fit for human habitation. He held also that a condition of sale that 'The purchaser shall be deemed to buy with full notice in all respects of the actual state and condition of the property and shall take the property as it is' did not apply to exclude the purchaser's rights in this case.

"That condition applies merely to the contract for conveyance, not to the contract to erect the building. It does not apply to the building work. It does not derogate from the implied term that the builder will do his work well and with proper materials and that the house will be fit for human habitation."

Sleafer v. Lambeth B.C. **[1960] 1 Q.B. 43**

6.31 A weekly tenant of a flat fell down against an iron balustrade as a result of a defective front door handle, and sued the landlord for breach of an alleged implied term that the premises should be reasonably fit for habitation (and the door handle fit for use). The court again stressed that there was no such general implied term.

Hill v. Harris **[1965] 2 Q.B. 601 (Duty of due diligence stressed again; no good faith point argued)**

6.32 The buyers had agreed to take a sub-lease of a shop, intending to use it as a tobacconists shop. The sub-lease specified this user. However, the head lease, which the buyers had not looked at, did not allow it. The buyers brought an action for damages for breach of an implied warranty and the case really turned on that. The Court of Appeal held again that there was no general implied term that premises let would be fit for the purpose contemplated by the parties (but not specifically mentioned in the lease). The fact that both sides assumed the intended user was possible did not amount to a warranty, nor did a pre-contractual statement by the vendor's agent who had had no authority to make contractual statements.

Russell L. J. stressed the overall duty of the buyer to investigate before the contract, saying, "I myself would be very unwilling in any case to spell out a warranty on a matter to some extent related to title, *when the ordinary and prudent course of investigation of title will in due course display the true position.*"[56]

Note: It is to be noted that this was not an action for rescission, and no good faith point was argued. Contrast Laurence v. Lexcourt Holdings.[57]

Laurence v. Lexcourt Holdings **[1978] 1 W.L.R. 1128**

6.33 In this case there had been a statement lulling the buyers into a false sense of security. The buyers sought to set aside the lease. Dillon J. who unlike the

[54] Para. 6.23 above.
[55] Para. 6.24 above.
[56] Italics supplied.
[57] Para. 6.33 below.

court in *Hill v. Harris*[58] had had good faith cases cited to him, had no hesitation in applying these, and rescinding the lease. It should be noted this was not because the premises were unfit for their purpose, *per se*, but because of the lulling statement made by the vendors. The fact that they did not intend to deceive was held, in accordance with the good faith rules, to make no difference.

[58] Para. 6.32 above.

CHAPTER 7

SALE OF COMPANY SHARES

"In my opinion, the public, who are invited by a prospectus to join in any new adventure, ought to have the same opportunity of judging of everything which has a material bearing on its true character, as the promoters themselves possess. It cannot be too frequently or too strongly impressed upon those who, having projected any undertaking, are desirous of obtaining the co-operation of persons who have no other information on the subject than that which they choose to convey, that the utmost candour and honesty ought to characterize their published statements."[1]

GOOD FAITH PRINCIPLES APPLIED

Duty of good faith applied to sales from prospectuses

7.01 The principles of good faith developed in the sale of land were, naturally enough, applied to investment in shares in the new companies. As has been noted elsewhere, after the opening up of the prairies at the end of the American Civil War, the price of wheat fell, and land dropped greatly in value, so that there were fewer transactions in land. The new companies began to seem a worthwhile investment by contrast, despite the risk involved. The applicability of the duty of good faith to sales of shares from a prospectus was affirmed early on in the life of joint-stock companies, by Sir John Romilly. He expressed the good-faith duty *as a general contractual duty*.

In *Pulsford v. Richards*[2] he observed that the basis of the applicable principle was "the enforcement of a careful adherence to truth in all the dealings of mankind". "This principle", he said, "applies to all representations made on the faith of which other persons enter into engagements". His initial illustrations were taken from estoppel-type cases, but later in his judgment he gave examples taken from sale of land cases:

[1] Lord Chelmsford in ***Central Rly Co. of Venezuela v. Kisch*** (1867) L.R. 2 H.L. 99 at 113 17 Beav. 87; 51 E.R. 965.

[2] (1853) 17 Beav. 87; 51 E.R. 965.

"... but if the representation made be one which cannot be made good, the person deceived shall be at liberty, if he please, to avoid the contract. Thus, if a man misrepresent the tenure or situation of an estate, as if he sell an estate as freehold which proves to be copyhold or leasehold, or if he describes it as situate within a mile of some particular town, when, in truth, it is several miles distant, such a misrepresentation, as it cannot be made true, would, at the option of the party deceived, annul the contract."

7.02 In *Peek v. Overend. Gurney*[3]—a deceit case which marked a shocking fall from grace by a till-then respectable firm—Lord Cairns, with whom the others agreed, affirmed the jurisdiction to set aside contracts for want of good faith. He said:

"Mere non-disclosure of material facts, however morally censurable, however that non-disclosure might be a ground *in a proper proceeding at a proper time for setting aside on allotment or a purchase of shares*, would ... form no ground for an action in the nature of misrepresentation ... [i.e. damages for deceit]"

In the case of the latter type of action, there must at the least be "such a partial and fragmentary statement of fact, as that the withholding of that which is not stated makes that which is stated absolutely false."[4]

In *Central Rly Co. of Venezuela v. Kisch*[5] the House of Lords affirmed the jurisdiction to set aside contracts to take shares from a prospectus where there had been a want of good faith in the prospectus. The Lord Chancellor Lord Chelmsford affirmed the statement of principle made by the Vice-Chancellor in *New Brunswick and Canada Railway Co v. Muggeridge*[6] saying:

"It cannot be too frequently or too strongly impressed upon those who, having projected any undertaking, are desirous of obtaining the co-operation of persons who have no other information on the subject than that which they choose to convey, that the utmost candour and honesty ought to characterize their published statements."

7.03 In *Mair v. Rio Grande*[7] the statements in the prospectus were fraudulent, but Lord Shaw of Dunfermline stated that fraud was not an essential for an action to rescind the shares to succeed, and cited Turner L.J. in the *Re Reese River Company*[8] case (in which rescission had been granted for a breach of the duty of good faith). He continued:

"... for it is contrary to good faith and it partakes of fraud to hold a person to a contract induced by an untruth for which you yourself stand responsible. It is elementary that a party cannot

[3] (1873) L.R. 6 H.L. 277.
[4] Italics supplied.
[5] (1867) L.R. 2 H.L. 99.
[6] (1860) 1 Dr. & Sim. 363; 62 E.R. 418.
[7] (1913) A.C. 853.
[8] (1869) above.

> take advantage of a benefit derived from a contract sprung out of his own fraud, and I think it is equally sound that a party cannot take a benefit from a contract sprung out of a falsehood which he has placed before the other party as an inducing cause."

It will be seen, then, that the fair dealing duty of candour and accuracy on the part of sellers was (a) expressed as a general duty applicable to contracts and (b) applied to the sale of shares in companies from prospectuses.[9]

7.04 The application of fair dealing in company prospectuses could not be expected to be precisely the same as in sales of land. The differences which exist arise from the different nature of the subject matter, as is normal with fair-dealing terms. Land is a physical entity: the problems which arise and thus the good faith terms—relate to the difficulties of description of this physical entity and of title. If I buy a share in a trading company, I am buying a bundle of rights the value of which reflects (a) the underlying assets and (b) the skill which is exercised on them—the balance between these two varying from trade to trade. My share will be inherently liable to fluctuate in material aspects, to a much greater extent than land. Thus, the nature of the contract will dictate that the questions which concern a purchaser of shares will mostly be twofold.

First, since the investment value depends a great deal on the way the undertaking is run by those who have the day to day running of it, the purchaser will want to be reassured about them, about their probity, their judgment and their expertise.

7.05 Secondly and nowadays perhaps rather more crucially, there are the underlying assets. If these are land or machinery in this country, reasonable investigations are possible; but what of foreign assets—in the nineteenth century typically mines or railway projects, and now rather more often shares in Liechtenstein companies or the like; and what of intellectual property such as patent rights? These may all be extremely difficult to inspect or investigate satisfactorily.[10]

The purchaser, then, has the problem that the use of due diligence prima facie does him rather less good than due diligence in other contexts normally would. This risk is compounded by the fluctuating nature of shares. A buyer of land which drops in value by reason of some latent defect usually has left in his hands at least the physical entity represented by the land. Shares in a company, as we all know,

[9] For a further parallel with the duty as applied to sales of land, see also *Musselwhite v. Musselwhite* [1962] Ch. 964 in which the court recognised the similarity between sales of shares during the period between contract and registration and land sales between contract and completion.

[10] Cp. the Listing Particulars European Directive of March 17 1980, which makes special provision for the provision of information "regarding the extent to which the issuer is dependent . . . on patents or licences, industrial, commercial or financial contracts or new manufacturing processes, where such factors are of fundamental importance to the issuer's business or profitability." It similarly makes provision for "an estimate of economically exploitable reserves and expected period of working" in the case of mines, *etc.*

can disappear altogether, and indeed turn into a (limited) liability with breathtaking speed.

There is something, of course, which mitigates the effect of all this. A person who once becomes a shareholder acquires rights against the directors in regard to their management of the company. He can to some extent remedy defects in his investment in this way: he is not always stuck with once-and-for-all defects as tends to be the case with land. All these points are discernible as shaping the traditional fair-dealing terms applicability to prospectus sales.

What the purchaser wants to know from the prospectus

7.06 The difficulty the prospective purchaser of shares in a new company has, then, is in acquiring useful knowledge about those who will manage the company, and about the true nature of the underlying business and assets. This is recognised (and in modern times also statutorily recognised).[11] The prospectus sale represents perhaps the high point of a purchaser's inevitable ignorance. The company is always somewhat opaque to the purchaser, but much more so before the projected business has even begun. As Dickens' Martin Chuzzlewit shows, the prospective shareholders can see a prosperous-looking headquarters, sleek, impressively-suited directors and so on; they can (and should) consult the articles, but there their investigations will tend to stop, unless they are professionals.

The fair dealing rules' application to sales of shares in newly-formed companies is itself limited in time in one important way. The right to rescind which is the main fair dealing remedy must be claimed before the company is wound up: see *Oakes v. Turquand*,[12] on the need for due diligence). Further, the shareholder must in any event be extremely prompt about seeking relief: the rules about acquiescence are strictly applied in the case of companies, in order to give due weight to the interests of third parties who may buy the shares meanwhile.[13]

Non-prospectus sales: room for good faith?

(1) "Sid" or the non-professional shareholder

7.07 The duty of good faith was not developed to cover the sale of shares by an ordinary existing shareholder. The trend against the good faith principles at the end of the nineteenth century will have meant that people turned to statutory intervention, rather the application of good faith, by the time substantial trading in existing shares began to take place. Initially it may well have been felt that after the company had been trading for a while the shareholders would tend to gain more

[11] See below for comment on the present statutory regime.

[12] (1867) L.R. 2 H.L. 325.

[13] See further on Acquiescence, Chap. 15, Remedies for Breach of the Good-faith Duties.

knowledge of the real worth of the company for themselves. This may have been so, when companies were relatively simply constructed entities. In modern times, a solution is probably needed to address the relative ignorance of both vendor and purchaser of existing shares. A company's everyday persona is opaque to its shareholders (and sometimes even its directors: we frequently read in the press about a large concern where the managing director did not really know what was going on.[14] If he did not know what was going on, how much less could the hapless shareholders.

At present the fair dealing rules are virtually useless to aid a purchaser who buys securities from an ordinary, not specially expert or knowledgeable existing shareholder. An ordinary shareholder of a big company will not usually have sufficient information about the true activities of the concern in which he is participating. "Creative accounting" has perhaps to shoulder quite a lot of the blame for this, but the increasingly global involvement of most companies (a company may, for example, hold reserves in foreign currency even if it has no international offices) has also brought new opportunities for concealment (and new reasons for fluctuation in share price). The vanishing rubber plantations of the early prospectus cases have given way to more sophisticated vanishing foreign assets (sometimes themselves creatively accounted) of apparently popular and successful ongoing companies. An example is non-existent or exaggerated profits made abroad.[15]

7.08 The opaque nature of the undertaking being what it is, then, the individual shareholder who sells may thus be equally as ignorant of material problems as the buyer. Where this is so, the buyer cannot claim breach of the fair-dealing rules by the seller. Both are innocent buyers of pigs in pokes: the buyer is simply unlucky. He has unwittingly bought a risk.

Now there is nothing wrong with buying risks, but the courts have tended to feel in other areas that a person who does so should have the opportunity of knowing and understanding in advance precisely what kind of risk he is buying, as far as possible. This is after all what insurers do every day. It is curious, but the case, that inexperienced shareholders are currently encouraged to invest in shares, even though the enterprise is for them the equivalent of going to sea in a sieve. If it proves such a shareholder was misled by the accounts he cannot claim in negligence against the company's auditors. It has been held by the House of Lords in *Caparo v. Dickman*[16] that the accountants who draw up the company's accounts have in the normal case a duty only to the existing shareholders as a body and certainly not to pro-

[14] Since the first draft of this chapter was written we have had the Barings Bank disaster.

[15] Polly Peck's accounts are thought by at least one banker to have shown a profit in Northern Cyprus larger than Northern Cyprus's gross domestic product! See also the admirable description of various methods of disguising the company's true worth while satisfying all "small- print" accounting requirements, in T. Smith, *Accounting for Growth*, (1992).

[16] [1990] 2 A.C. 605.

spective new ones, save in special circumstances. Our inexperienced buyer cannot protect himself before he buys either, as we have seen, because the vendor too will usually only know what is in the accounts.

There is no prevalent mechanism whereby an intending purchaser of shares can demand answers to the equivalent of Enquiries before Contract adapted from those used in sales of land, from the vendor of shares. If the purchaser made a habit of doing this the vendor would in turn need to obtain answers from the company or its auditor. As a result, both the vendor and the company as his agent would assume some responsibility for providing the kind of full, accurate, information about the company's undertaking that a buyer of land is entitled to obtain. The good faith rules would apply to such statements.

7.09 No doubt shares need to be freely traded in the market, and a pre-contractual disclosure mechanism of precisely the kind prevalent with land would be impossibly cumbersome (though some form of standing answer would not be). The solution adopted at present is to aim for maximum "transparency" in the accounts, via the statutory audit of companies and an increasing number of statutory requirements as to the content of these, in order, it is hoped, to produce at one stroke better-informed vendors and better-informed shareholders generally. One may be sceptical about this approach. The statutory registration of title has after all reduced rather than eliminated problems encountered by the buyer of land. One must wonder whether a solution might not be to explore whether the company may not be[17] the vendor-shareholder's agent when it publishes accounts. In this case, the accounts would be a statement made on behalf of any selling shareholder to a prospective buyer. The duty of good faith would apply to these when the shareholder sold, as with other sales such as land: if the accounts failed to be full and accurate in what was said, if there was partial non-disclosure or misleading (even if literally true) statements as to a significant matter, the buyer might rescind, with salutary results for the company's next accounts (if any), no doubt.

An alternative might be for the courts to deem that certain information is "within the knowledge" of even the ordinary shareholder; that the buyer reasonably expects that any seller will have made it his business to find out certain material facts about the undertaking whether or not they are apparent from the statutory accounts. The existing shareholders are at least in a better position to find out than the buyer of shares.

(2) The professional seller

7.10 The expert, or professional seller may often have some knowledge about the shares he sells, and will therefore tend to describe them during the sale to some extent. The fair dealing rules may consequently come into play, to the advantage of a buyer from him. Statements made by a professional seller who is in breach of the duty of

[17] Or could be deemed by statute to be.

candour or accuracy may very well[18] not attract a remedy under the Misrepresentation Act 1967 which has for the most part been strictly confined to relief for positive misrepresentations. However, let us suppose that the defendant in *Smith New Court v. Scrimgeour Vickers*[19] (a case of fraudulent misrepresentation) had instead of indulging in positive misrepresentations regarding the shares, given the buyer information about them which was literally true, but only in a restricted, rather than the usual sense; or information which was ambiguous, but was relied on by the buyer in a different sense from the one claimed by the seller, or indulged in part-truths which were themselves literally true. These are all typical breaches of the twin good faith duty of candour and accuracy. In such a case the buyer could arguably have sought rescission on the grounds of breach of good faith by the seller. Information "within his knowledge", that is, knowledge which the broker ought[20] in the ordinary course of his business to have acquired, would also fall to be imputed to the seller, as in the other spheres of fair-dealing law.

Good faith/fair dealing rules as shown in the older prospectus cases

7.11 The older cases (there are few modern ones) are concerned for the most part, as one would expect, with the twin topics of interest to a buyer into a new company: who will be running it, and what are the underlying assets of the business. There are the prospectuses which promised directors of known standing in the community who mysteriously fail to materialise when the shares are allotted. There are foreign ventures: railways in Canada whose valuable concessions prove to be evanescent, the shrinking rubber plantation, etc. The law on rescission for breach of the fair-dealing rules remained fairly constant in principle, although the cases reveal a degree of tempering or working out of the detail of the application of the principle to the nature of the contract to take shares.

Good faith distinguished from deceit

7.12 Parallel with this, there was the development over a time of the law on deceit. Often a shareholder who took shares in a company which proved a disaster was faced with a winding up, and thus, being too late for rescission, had no practical remedy save an action in deceit against the promoters or promoter/directors. Deceit is outside the subject matter of this book. However, a few cases on deceit will be found noted in the Appendix to this chapter. The criteria for success in an action for rescission for breach of the good faith rules and an action for deceit were different. Deceit was[21] confined to statements

[18] But see the discussion in Chap. 17.
[19] [1996] 4 All E.R. 769, H.L.
[20] In the sense of "can be expected".
[21] See the well known case of ***Derry v. Peek*** [1889] 14 App. Cas. 337.

made by directors, *etc.*, which they knew to be false.[22] The action for rescission was based as before on a breach of the duty of good faith—whether of candour or accuracy. It thus covered statements which were not necessarily known to be untrue, but which were untrue according to the information which was "within the knowledge" of the vendor.[23] It would not be correct to suppose that the deceit duty in any sense swallowed up or narrowed the jurisdiction to set aside contracts to take shares where there had been a breach of the duty of good faith by the vendor. The two continued to coexist.[24] Where the plaintiff wanted damages he would have to prove the more stringent deceit requirements; where he wanted rescission it would be sufficient if he proved the lesser breach, whether only a positive but negligent representation, or a breach of the more stringent good-faith duty of candour and accuracy. For example, in *Karberg's Case.*[25] Lindley L.J. pointed out that in an action for rescission of a contract on the ground of misrepresentation, it is not necessary to prove knowledge by the defendant of its untruth.[26] For an application of the duty of good faith, in this instance the duty of candour, see the case of *Re Pacaya Rubber Co*,[27] in which the purchaser was allowed rescission for a pregnant half-truth.[28]

Good faith distinguished from the fiduciary duty of promoters who also sold something to the company they had formed

7.13 In 1878 the duty of a promoter was extended in certain circumstances into a new category: the fiduciary or "quasi-fiduciary". This fiduciary duty is quite distinct from the ordinary duty of good faith with which this chapter is concerned. It has been held to arise when there is between the promoters and the newly-formed company a relationship of the kind that elsewhere in this book is called a rely-on-me relationship: a relationship of trust and consequent vulnerability. The two important cases of *Erlanger v. New Sombrero Phosphate Company*[29] and *Lagunas Nitrate v. Lagunas Nitrate Syndicate*[30] are noted in Chapter 9, Dealings with the Vulnerable Buyer or Seller. The principles of law are precisely the same as those applied to any other party who is

[22] The three-star grade in Eleven Shades of Ambiguity, in Chap. 5, Sale of Land para. 5.11.
[23] The two-star statements in the section Eleven Shades of Ambiguity, in Chap. 5, Sale of Land, para. 5.11.
[24] See for an affirmation of this, and a useful historical account of the growth of joint stock companies in the nineteenth century, the article by Michael Lobban, *Nineteenth Century Frauds in Company Formation:* ***Derry v Peek*** *in context* (1996) L.Q.R. 287.
[25] [1892] 3 Ch. 1.
[26] See also the well-known misrepresentation case of ***Redgrave v. Hurd*** (1881) 20 Ch. D. 12.
[27] [1914] 1 Ch. 542.
[28] See also *Low v. Bouverie* [1891] 3 Ch. 82.
[29] (1878) 3 App. Cas. 1218.
[30] [1890] 2 Ch. 392.

trusted in regard to a transaction, and thus may not put his duty and interest in conflict with each other. The difficulty faced by the courts dealing with the cases was to work out the way in which these principles applied to the new creature represented by the company, whose nature was itself only gradually being worked out. It was held in these two cases that for the sale to the company to stand, the company must have had (1) the fullest information about the transaction and (2) a board of directors which was really independent and thus could judge independently and impartially. These are classic ways in which the courts have held that the locking-in factor, that factor which locks a person into his vulnerability[31] might be dispelled. Where there is a rely-on-me relationship of this kind, that is, where the promoters of the company act both for themselves and the company, typically in selling some property of their own to the newly formed company, the company will rank as a vulnerable person unless and until it has an independent body of directors and the promoters have candidly and accurately explained the material facts about the intended sale to these directors. The promoters who tried to occupy a dual role will have had a conflict of interest and duty, making them into "fiduciaries", or *people trusted not to do that*.[32] Thus, in *Erlanger's* Case, the duty of disclosure applicable to a fiduciary was said by Lindley L.J. (*obiter*) to apply, putting the promoters under a duty to disclose to the company fully and fairly all material facts which the company ought to know.

Extension of fiduciary duty to shareholders?

7.14 The shareholders have been spoken of on occasions as if they too had a right to set aside the dealing when the company was vulnerable. See Lord O'Hagan in *Erlanger's* Case[33] said:

> "But the privilege given them for promoting such a company for such an object [to afford them a profit on the sale of their rights in the island of Sombrero] involved obligations of a very serious kind. It required, in its exercise, the utmost good faith, the completest truthfulness, and a careful regard to the protection of the future shareholders."[34]

The references to the shareholders are, however, all strictly in the context of the rights between the promoters and the company (or the shareholders as a body), not the promoters and ordinary individual would-be shareholders who buy from a prospectus. The remaining judgments in both the two main cases refer only to the duty as owed to the company. It is possible in any case that some at least of the

[31] See Chap. 9, Dealings with the Vulnerable Buyer or Seller.
[32] See further Chap. 9.
[33] (1878).
[34] See also Lindley M.R. in ***Lagunas Nitrate Co v. Lagunas Syndicate*** (1899); and Cockburn C.J. in ***Twycross v. Grant*** (1877) a case on s.38 of the Companies Act 1867 the statutory provision aimed at preventing non-disclosure of contracts by the promoters with the company.

references to shareholders were made merely in order to emphasize that the entity consisting of the company was not to be regarded as comprised only of the puppet-directors who were appointed by the promoters.

Statements inducing a contract to take shares made by the directors or agents of the company: when binding on the company

7.15 Romer J. gave some general guidance in *Lynde v. Anglo-Italian Hemp Co.*[35]

> "It appears to me that, speaking generally, to make a company liable for misrepresentations inducing a contract to take shares from it the shareholder must bring his case within one or the other of the following heads:—
>
> (1.) Where the misrepresentations are made by the directors or other the general agents of the company entitled to act and acting on its behalf—as, for example, by a prospectus issued by the authority or sanction of the directors of a company inviting subscriptions for shares;
>
> (2.) Where the misrepresentations are made by a special agent of the company while acting within the scope of his authority—as, for example, by an agent specially authorized to obtain, on behalf of the company, subscriptions for shares. This head of course includes the case of a person constituted agent by subsequent adoption of his acts;
>
> (3.) Where the company can be held affected, before the contract is complete, with the knowledge that it is induced by misrepresentations—as for example, when the directors, on allotting shares, know, in fact, that the application for them has been induced by misrepresentations, even though made without any authority.
>
> (4.) Where the contract is made to the knowledge of the company on the basis of certain representations,[36] whether the particulars of those representations were known to the company or not, and it turns out that some of them were material and untrue—as, for example, if the directors of a company know when allotting that an application for shares is based on the statements contained in a prospectus, even though that prospectus was issued without authority or

[35] [1896] 1 Ch. 178.

[36] Luxmoore J. in *Collins v. Associated Greyhound Racecourses Ltd* [1930] 1 Ch. 1, relying on *Buckley on the Companies Acts* (10th edn.) p. 90, thought this must have been wrongly reported, and that it should read "Where the contract is made to the knowledge of the company or its agents on the basis of certain representations and", *etc.* Buckley's argument had been that the instances given of the fourth head were not apt unless the words "made on the basis" mean "made to the knowledge of the company on the basis".

> even before the company was formed, and even if its contents are not known to the directors."

There is no responsibility, for example by the directors, for statements put out without their knowledge, and which are not put out in the ordinary course of business of the company.[37]

The duty of good faith: candour and accuracy required on the part of a promoter in information he gives to intending purchasers.

7.16a The distinction between the twin duties of accuracy and candour is less easily drawn in the context of share sales. Frequently a statement will be regarded as inaccurate *and* a half-truth. In *New Brunswick, etc., Co v Muggeridge*[38] and see also above), the defendant who had agreed to take up shares sought to rescind the agreement (after the price had fallen) on the grounds of misrepresentation in the prospectus. The Vice-Chancellor, Sir R. T. Kindersley, said that the representations in the prospectus were "*inaccurate, and in that sense untrue.*"[39] He ascribed a wide meaning to misrepresentation in the context of rescission. He said:

> "And when I use the term misrepresentation, it would be more accurate to describe it as *a want of that full and true and complete representation which, in my opinion, ought to have been adopted* by persons issuing such a prospectus as this, and inviting persons to apply for shares on the faith of its representations."[40]

It was held to be enough if the natural meaning of the language used was untrue, even if there might have been a more specific meaning which the statement might have borne which would have been true. So seen, the statement contained a material part-disclosure. In *Central Rly Co. of Venezuela v. Kisch*[41] there was a positive misrepresentation found, but the duty to avoid misleading non-disclosure *inter alia* was affirmed; and in *Re Pacaya Rubber Co.*[42] rescission was granted for a statement which contained omissions so as to give a misleading overall picture.

The Duty of Candour

7.16a For an affirmation of this, see Malins V.-C. at first instance in *Re Scottish Petroleum Co*[43] who stated:

> "In all these transactions connected with the formation of com-

[37] See *Cargill v. Bower* (1878) 10 Ch. 502.
[38] (1860) 1 Dr. & Sm. 363; 62 E.R 418.
[39] Italics supplied.
[40] Italics supplied.
[41] (1867) L.R. 2 H.L. 99.
[42] [1914] 1 Ch. 542.
[43] (1881) 17 Ch.D. 373.

> panies the Court requires that there shall be straightforward, candid conduct."

The fate of the case in the Court of Appeal turned on the purchaser's acquiescence.

In *Re Reese River Company v. Smith*[44] rescission was granted for a statement of belief which omitted to reveal that it came from a third party and had not been verified in any way by the maker of the statement.

Common sense approach to the good faith duty

(1) General statements about the future of the projected company

7.17 The principles are tempered a little to take account of everyday reality. This is not due to any attempt on the part of the courts to render the good faith duty less applicable in sales of shares, but simply a common sense recognition that even an honest prospectus is bound to be written (a) about the future and (b) with a degree of hope and enthusiasm about the new business.

Thus, where it is reasonable to construe a prospectus as referring to events which the promoters believe will occur in the future, the courts will tend to do so, rather than construe the statement as one of existing fact. In *Hallows v. Fernie*[45] Lord Chelmsford said:

> "In construing a prospectus, the preliminary character of the document must always be taken into consideration. Everyone knows that it is intended to usher a company into existence, and not to describe its actual formation, no one is surprised to find that a future tense must be given to words in the past or present tense which it contains . . .
>
> This ought always to be borne in mind when a construction is required to be put upon the language of a prospectus, and unless it distinctly refers to what is actually existing at the time, it must be taken to represent what will be the state of things when the company is completely formed."

It is not a rule to be mechanistically applied, however; in *Karberg's Case*[46] the statement by the promoters that certain gentlemen had agreed to be members of the council of administration was found to be a statement of existing fact, rather than belief about the future.[47]

(2) Ebullient general descriptions

7.18 A passage which is properly seen merely as generally ebullient description will not be held to be a statement of specific fact. Sir John Romilly in *Jennings v. Broughton*[48] below said:

[44] (1867) L.R. 2 Ch. 604 and (1869) L.R. 4 H.L. 64.
[45] (1868) L.R. 3 Ch. App. 467.
[46] (1892) 3 Ch. 1.
[47] See also ***Re Pacaya Rubber Co.*** (1914) 1 Ch. 542.
[48] (1854) 17 Beav. 234; 51 E.R. 1023.

> "a distinction must be taken between that part of them [the statements] which gives a general description of the prospects and capabilities of the mine, and that part which gives a specific account of what is there to be seen."

It is likely that the same leniency would not be shown in the case of a statement about the future of an *ongoing* company: there the higher degree of knowledge on which to base such statements would probably bring a requirement that what was said took due account of such knowledge.

(3) False combined effect of document even if component parts of document literally true

7.19 It is enough if the effect of the document *as a whole* is untrue, even though each statement taken separately may be said to be literally true.

Lord Romilly in *Central Rly Co. of Venezuela v. Kisch*[49] said

> "It is in my opinion not merely by one or two statements in the prospectus, which are not borne out by the facts, that the matter ought to be tried, but by *the combined effect of them all* producing a result which would have misled any person who took shares upon the faith of the prospectus. . . ."[50]

Denman J. took a delightfully robust approach in *Edgington v. Fitzmaurice*,[51] the well-known deceit case.

> ". . . I do not think that in cases such as this it is incumbent upon the Court or upon the jury necessarily to look at each statement by itself without regard to the other statements. I think one can easily suggest cases, and that this may be such a case, in which taking one statement separately you might say there is nothing in it, or that there is very little in it, or much less than there is if you couple it with the other two. In all such cases, in considering the animus with which the statement was made, I think it is only common sense that, whether jury or Judge, you should look at the whole of the document together, and consider every statement in it with a view of forming a judgment as to the intention, and that it is not a fair way of dealing with these cases to say, I take statement A, there is nothing in it; I take statement B, there is nothing in it; and I take statement C, there is nothing in it—there is nothing in them if they stood alone, and therefore as you cannot make three nothings into something the whole thing falls to the ground. I think you must take the whole, together with its history, and then, it may be that there is just reason for holding statement A, statement B and statement C to be all inaccurate, and all falling within the definition of an actionable false statement. There may be cases in which that is so, though, if you had only one, the

[49] (1867) L.R. 2 H.L. 99.
[50] Italics supplied.
[51] (1885) 29 Ch. D. 459.

decision might be quite the other way as regards that one statement. It is quite certain that you must always take into consideration the surrounding facts of the case in construing every document, and not only so, but in considering the animus of the parties who issue that particular document."[52]

(4) An ambiguity which has no "natural meaning"

7.20 Where the ambiguity is not read naturally in any one sense, but is plainly ambiguous, the onus may sometimes be on the purchaser to find out which meaning is meant. In *Hallows v. Fernie*[53] Lord Chelmsford said:

> "I use the words 'clear and unequivocal' because it appears to me that there is a material distinction between the employment of words in a prospectus which can bear only one meaning and of those which are equivocal, and which different persons may interpret differently. In the latter case no prudent person would act upon his own construction without some inquiry. In construing a prospectus the preliminary character of the document must always be taken into consideration . . . He went on to say that 'if persons publishing a prospectus use such careless language that their statements literally read are untrue, although this literal sense is different from what they intended, this amounts to a misrepresentation, for which they may be responsible to any one who is deceived or injured by it.' However, he immediately qualified this as regards ambiguous statements which might be construed in a different manner by different minds. In this case it would not be right for the purchaser to act upon his own views without inquiry. "Because if the words are susceptible of different meanings, he is deceived, not by the words, but by his construction of them."

Nonetheless in *Smith v. Chadwick*[54] both Jessel M.R. in the Court of Appeal and Lord Blackburn in the House of Lords took the traditional approach as to this,[55] considering that it would be sufficient anyway if the plaintiff managed to prove that he had in fact been misled by the equivocal statement in question.

Lord Selborne in *Smith v. Chadwick*[56] in the House of Lords seemed to narrow the potential reliance of a purchaser on ambiguous statements very slightly, but probably so as to leave the above wide principle as to ambiguous statements essentially intact. He drew a distinction between on the one hand cases where the statement complained of, in the context in which it stands, could not be honestly intended

[52] See also Lord Halsbury to similar effect in ***Aaron's Reef v. Twiss*** [1896] A.C. 273, a fraudulent misrepresentation case.
[53] (1868) L.R. 3 Ch. App. 467.
[54] (1882) 20 Ch. D. 27 and (1884) 9 App. Cas. 187.
[55] See Chap. 5, Sale of Land for examples.
[56] (1884), above.

or reasonably understood in any other sense than the one complained of; and on the other cases where:

> "the words in the context in which they stand may have been honestly intended to bear another sense (in which they would be true) and *might reasonably have been so understood by an intelligent man of business* . . ."[57]

and where at the time the statement was made . . . the plaintiff "had notice that the defendants, who made the representation, did in fact allege such other sense to be the true one, and the sense which they intended."

Know your purchaser

7.21 The purchaser is taken to be the kind of purchaser likely for the transaction in question. See *Smith v. Chadwick*[58] in which Lord Selborne referred to the standard of understanding of the words in the prospectus as being that of "the intelligent man of business, aware of the current prices at that time of bar and plate iron." This will have been a socially accurate definition of the shareholder to be expected at the end of the nineteenth century. Whether it is so now is debatable. The range of potential shareholders is greater. We have the reasonable pension-fund manager on the one hand and "Sid" on the other.

"Within his knowledge"

7.22 Sir John Romilly in *Pulsford v. Richards*[59] (and see also above) affirmed that the duty of strict truthfulness to an intending purchaser may arise even in the absence of actual knowledge by the vendor. It applies where the persons who made the statement believed it to be true, but "in the due discharge of their duty they ought to have known [that it was untrue]." It applies also "if they had formerly known and ought to have remembered the fact which negatives the representation made." It may be doubted whether this goes further than the duty in the case of other sales, to know the information which you may reasonably be expected to have control of within your organisation (and any agent's to whom you have entrusted your business).

Innocent motive does not avail the vendor

7.23 In *Reese River Company v. Smith*[60] the directors had taken what proved to be an untrue statement on trust from their vendor, who proved to be fraudulent. This did not avail them at all, since they had foolishly omitted to state the limited foundation for this statement. In

[57] Italics supplied.
[58] (1884) 9 App. Cas. 187.
[59] (1853) 17 Beav. 87; 51 E.R. 965.
[60] (1867) L.R. 2 Ch. 604 (CA) and (1869) L.R. 4 H.L. 64 (HL), both noted below.

Karberg's Case[61] Lindley L.J. emphasized that in an action for rescission on the grounds of misrepresentation it was not necessary to prove knowledge by the defendant of the untruth of the statement made; and he referred to *Redgrave v. Hurd*[62] in which Jessel M.R. had stressed that for rescission purposes it was not necessary to prove that the vendor knew the statements were false.[63]

Reliance by purchaser/inducement

7.24 This is an essential element, as with other sales, if the purchaser seeks to rely on the absence of good faith in order to rescind his purchase. Sir John Romilly in *Pulsford v. Richards*[64] (and see also above), said it was essential that "the person deceived entered into the contract *on the faith of it*."[65]

The individual purchaser's actual state of experience or knowledge will be taken into account when the court is considering reliance by him on an untrue statement. In *Hallows v. Fernie*[66] the fact that the plaintiff was a shipping agent, a company secretary, and "not unaccustomed to dealings in shares" was taken into account.[67]

Inducement may be inferred where the breach of good faith is as to a material (significant) fact

7.25 *Pulsford v. Richards*,[68] and Jessel M.R.'s judgment in the Court of Appeal in *Smith v. Chadwick*,[69] the deceit action, together with Lord Blackburn's comments in the House of Lords, are relevant. Jessel M.R. said:

> "... on the question of the materiality of the statement, if the Court sees on the face of it that it is of such a nature as would induce a person to enter into the contract, or would tend to induce him to do so, or that it would be a part of the inducement, to enter into the contract, *the inference is, if he entered into the contract, that he acted on the inducement* so held out, and you want no evidence that he did so act ..."[70]

[61] [1892] 3 Ch. 1.
[62] (1881) 20 Ch. D. 1 (the case in which the Plaintiff was allowed to rescind, despite having made some of his own enquiries, essentially because lulled into a sense of false security by the vendor's statements).
[63] See also ***Mair v. Rio Grande*** (1913) A.C. 853, for an affirmation of the principles expressed in the ***Reese River Silver Mining Co*** case (1867) L.R. 2 Ch. 604.
[64] (1853) 17 Beav. 87; 51 E.R. 965.
[65] Italics supplied.
[66] (1868) L.R. 3 Ch. App. 467.
[67] See also the deceit case of ***Bellairs v. Tucker*** (1884) 13 Q.B.D. 562 where the plaintiff was a dealer in stocks and shares, and had formerly been a member of the Stock Exchange.
[68] (1853) above.
[69] (1882) 20 Ch. D. 27.
[70] Italics supplied.

Lord Blackburn felt this went a little too far, that it was not an inference of law, but an *inference of fact*, which might be made where appropriate, but did not essentially differ from Jessel M.R. otherwise.

In *Broome v. Speak*[71] a decision later affirmed by the Court of Appeal in *Shepheard v. Broome*,[72] a case on the omission to mention certain contracts in the prospectus as required by section 38 of Companies Act 1867, Buckley J. nonetheless commented:

> "It is unintelligible to say that a person relied upon a fact which he was not told, or relied on his not being told a fact, and when you call a man after the event to say whether, if he had known a further particular fact, he would have done something or not, speaking for myself, it is so difficult to say exactly what a few years ago you would have done under different circumstances, that I should regard that evidence as of very little value. Be the man the most honest man possible, it is so easy to be wise after the event, that it is difficult for any man to say what he would have done under circumstances which did not arise. It is too much to expect of him that he should be able to say fairly what he would have done under those altered circumstances. The test I think to be applied is—it has been so stated by Lord Halsbury, and was so stated in *Smith v. Chadwick* (1884) 9 App. Cas. 187, and will be found in many cases—that *if you find that the matter withheld is such as that if disclosed it reasonably would deter or tend to deter an ordinarily prudent investor from applying for the shares, then he is entitled to relief.*"[73]

Thus, it may perhaps be wise for a purchaser to put in some evidence about his reliance where possible. His position if he cannot be certain what he would have done is not desperate, provided that the non-disclosure was such that it would reasonably deter "an ordinarily prudent investor" from buying.[74]

The purchaser's duty of due diligence

(1) He is entitled to believe the vendor's words in their natural meaning.

7.26 To this extent, his duty of due diligence is, as with the land cases, deemed to be lulled to sleep. As the Vice-Chancellor said in *New Brunswick, etc., Co. v. Muggeridge*[75] the promoters had no right to turn round and say to the purchasers:

[71] [1903] 1 Ch. 586.
[72] [1904] A.C. 342.
[73] Italics supplied.
[74] Cp., however, as to insurance, the possibly different rule now laid down by the House of Lords in *Pan Atlantic Insurance v. Pine Top Insurance* [1995] 2 A.C. 501, see Chap. 4, Insurance and Surety Transactions, for discussion of this.
[75] (1860) 1 Dr. & Sim. 363; 62 E.R. 418.

"You ought to have been more prudent, more circumspect, more cautious, more vigilant; you ought, by applying your reasoning powers, to have concluded that our representations could not be true in the sense which the language we used in the prospectus naturally and fairly imports."

Cotton L.J. in the Court of Appeal in *Smith v. Chadwick*[76] re-affirmed what he had said in *Arkwright v. Newbold*,[77] that a person who issues a statement is not only answerable for what he in his own mind intended to represent, but is answerable for what anyone might reasonably suppose to be the meaning of the words he has used.

The purchaser should look at the articles of the company, and any other document he is referred to in the prospectus: see *Hallows v. Fernie*.[78]

Lord Cranworth in *Oakes v. Turquand*[79] thought that the purchaser should look at the memorandum in all cases:

"It is the duty of a person taking shares in a company to use all reasonable diligence in ascertaining the terms of the memorandum of association, which is in fact, his title deed."

Addendum

PUBLIC OFFERS OF SHARES—A NOTE ABOUT STATUTORY LIABILITY OF THE PERSONS RESPONSIBLE FOR INFORMATION CONTAINED IN THE LISTING PARTICULARS/PROSPECTUS

7.27 For statutory prospectus/listing requirements, etc., see *Palmer's Company Law* Vol. 5, C-115 and see the concise explanation of the statutory background by Lightman J. in the *Possfund* case.[80] The new statutory regime, which no-one could call simple, has come about as a result of European Directives. These have the primary purpose of harmonising the various existing practices as regards companies in the European Union, and probably a secondary purpose of encouraging sufficient disclosure to provide reasonable protection for investors. The disclosure requirements contain a considerable element of overlap with the law of good faith as described in this book. If the duty is not precisely the same, it is at all events first cousin at least to the twin good faith duty of candour and accuracy. Indeed, it may turn out after the statute has received the benefit of judicial interpretation that the

[76] (1882) 20 Ch. D. 27.
[77] (1881) 17 Ch. D. 301.
[78] (1868) L.R. 3 Ch. App. 467. See, however, Chap. 10, Excluding the Effect of the Fair dealing duty, for the position where he is not given a fair chance of reading the documents.
[79] (1867).
[80] *Possfund Custodian Trustees v. Diamond* [1996] 1 W.L.R. 135.

kinship is closer still. It is also possible that judicial interpretation could diminish the scope of the statutory duty. In that case, recourse to the old underlying good faith rules may be needed. This will also be needed when rescission is desired, rather than statutory compensation against the persons responsible for the Listing Particulars/prospectus.

There is a distinction made between listed and unlisted securities offered to the public. The provisions in each case are similar in most respects, so what follows centres on the rules regarding Listed Securities. These are shares which are listed in the Official List of the Stock Exchange.[81] The unlisted securities are those which are offered on the Unlisted Securities Market.

The scope of the information to be given

7.28 The information which is to be given for the admission of shares or convertible debt securities to listing is set out in Chapter 6 of the Listing Particulars and includes information about the persons responsible for the Particulars, the issuer and its capital, assets and liabilities, financial position and profits and losses, the management, and the recent development and prospects of the group. This is essentially the information which can be expected to be given in prospectuses anyway. It is rather like saying, The seller of land shall describe what he is selling. What gives the "bite" is the *standard* of good faith required on the basic subject matter.

What is the standard of good faith required?

(1) Investors and their professional advisers

7.29 The following appears under "Responsibility" in 5.5:

> "The issuer . . . must provide the Exchange with a letter signed by every director of the issuer (or his agent or attorney, with a copy of the authority of any such agent or attorney) confirming that the listing particulars include *all such information within their knowledge (or which it would be reasonable to obtain by making enquiries) as investors and their professional advisers would reasonably require and reasonably expect to find (regard being had to the matters mentioned in section 146(3) of the F[inancial] S[ervices] A[ct 1986]) for the purpose of making an informed assessment of the assets and liabilities, financial position, profits and losses and prospects of the issuer and of the rights attaching to the securities to which the listing particulars relate. . . .*"[82]

The expression "investors and their professional advisers" may be intended to bring in the eiusdem generis rule of construction. It is to

[81] See s.142 of the Financial Services Act 1986.

[82] Italics supplied.

be noted that the Unlisted Companies requirement[83] is "such information as *investors* would reasonably require". If so, the investor[84] may be deemed to possess the degree of financial sophistication appropriate to a professional adviser, whether or not he actually does. If the expression merely means "investors", it is difficult to see why the reference to professional advisers is needed at all. It is true there is no indication about the kind of professional adviser envisaged, and the standard of professional financial advisers in general covers a wide range of competence, but one supposes the expression "professional adviser" will be held to connote a reasonable degree of professional competence. So "Sid" may not understand what he is buying but nonetheless be held to have been given sufficient information. The good faith approach, which looks at the expected circumstances of the sale, and infers from those the kind of buyer to be expected, would perhaps be preferable, allowing the imposition of a stricter standard of disclosure in an issue of shares particularly likely to be subscribed to by unsophisticated members of the public.

(2) Liability for misleading statements and omissions as well as plain untruths

7.30 The statutory duty shares an important feature with the good faith duty. Section 150 of the Financial Services Act 1986 provides a remedy in damages against those responsible for the listing particulars "to any person who has acquired any of the securities in question and suffered loss in respect of them as a result of any *untrue or misleading statement* in [the listing particulars] or *the omission* from them of any matter required to be included." Thus, the statutory duty looks very like the twin good faith duties of accuracy and candour. It evidently covers statements which are literally true but misleading, and part truths which are misleading.[85]

(3) Basis of the statement: such enquiries as were reasonable

7.31 Section 151 of the Financial Services Act 1986 provides a defence to a person who reasonably believes

> "*having made such enquiries (if any) as were reasonable* that the statement was true and not misleading" [and certain other requirements] or where the statement purported to be made on the authority of an expert, if "he believed *on reasonable grounds* that

[83] See the Public Offers of Securities Regulations 1995 (S.I. 1995 No. 1537) reg. 9(1).

[84] Cp. good faith's buyer of *the kind to be expected.*

[85] Italics supplied. There is a similar duty in the case of prospectuses of companies on the Unlisted Securities market: see s.166 of the Financial Services Act 1986 as brought in in 1995 to replace a repealed section never brought into force, and reg. 14 of the Public Offers of Securities Regulations 1995 (S.I. 1995 No. 1537).

> the other person [the expert] was competent to make or authorise the statement . . ."[86]

This does not in terms define the scope of the inquiries the person must have made, and it is possible that the duty is a wider one than the seller's good-faith duty to investigate matters *within his knowledge*[87] before making descriptive statements about what is being sold to the buyer.[88] Compare the perhaps slightly different emphasis in the case of unlisted companies. The relevant regulations there require that the information is to be "such information [above] which is within the knowledge of any person responsible for the prospectus [See *ibid*. reg. 13 for these] or which it would be reasonable for him to obtain by making enquiries."

The wider duty imposed by the statute to go out and obtain information not at present within the maker's knowledge creates a difficulty. In order to put any bounds on this wider duty, recourse has been had to the word "reasonable". This in turn has introduced a wide discretion which could work either to expand the disclosure duty or to diminish it, depending on how it is interpreted, and meanwhile will create uncertainty. It is certainly arguable that a duty limited as is the good-faith duty to that which was "within his knowledge" might have been preferable, since it is much more readily capable of definition. See also Chapter 8, Knowledge and Notice, for the suggestion that modern trading conditions may in any case require a wider definition for the purposes of good faith of what is "within the knowledge" of the reasonable seller, where it would be normal for him to have access to certain outside information, for example on his daily computer screen.

(4) Standard of communication: in as easily analysable and comprehensible a form of possible

7.32 In the case of Publicly Listed Securities there is a requirement virtually identical with the good-faith requirement,[89] that the information must be "in as easily analysable and comprehensible a form as possible" and must be set out in words and figures, avoiding pictures, charts, graphs or other illustrations unless the Exchange is satisfied that it is the only way the relevant factual information can be clearly and fairly presented.

The "after-market" of a public offer: possible extension of the statutory duty?

7.33 There has been an interesting attempt made to extend prospectus liability to purchases (for example by those who were not allotted as many shares as they would have liked) called the "after-market

[86] Italics supplied.
[87] See Chap. 5 for reference to this concept.
[88] Reg. 9(2) of the Public Offers of Securities Regulations 1995.
[89] See, *e.g.*, Chap. 5, Sale of Land.

purchases" made in the immediate aftermath of the launch of a new company on the Unlisted Securities Market, whether by sale of the prospectus to prospective after-market purchasers, or by other means.[90] The case put was that commercial practice had now, more than a century after *Peek v. Gurney*[91] established an enlarged purpose for a normal prospectus; it was not confined to inducing investors to become placees, but extended to inducing the public to make what were self-explanatorily termed "after-market purchases". These after-market purchases were, it was argued, within the intended scope of the representation. A significant factor relied on was the requirement of the Stock Exchange for the entire prospectus to be printed on Extel cards for Extel Statistical Services Limited so that Extel could make the information available to all subscribers and investors who wanted to look at them. These circumstances, it was claimed, gave rise to a duty of care in tort. We do not yet have a definitive answer on this, since the above case came before the court on an application to strike out. The application to strike out was rejected by Lightman J., who considered the claim above was arguable.

If the claim succeeds, as it may, there will be an extension of the class who may claim damages against those responsible for the prospectus. There is likely to be an extension of the class who may claim rescission for a breach of the good-faith duty of candour and accuracy in statements made or omitted in a prospectus as well. If the after-market purchasers are within the prospectus representation, they are within it for all purposes. The position of the ordinary purchaser of shares[92] who comes along after the "after-market" and thus has no equivalent remedy will begin to seem even more unsatisfactory than at present.

APPENDIX: SOME CASES OF INTEREST

***Pulsford v. Richards* (1853) 17 Beav. 87; 51 E.R. 965**

7.34 The prospectus was issued for the formation of a company which was to construct a railway in Belgium. The prospectus said "They [the directors] have secured the services of a most able and efficient *directeur-gérant* in Belgium (Mr Chantrell), who will have an immediate interest in maintaining the strictest economy in the management and in the general prosperity of the concern."... "This grant [the railway grant] they [the directors] transfer to the company, subject to the reservations in favour of the fondateurs after mentioned". [There then followed a description of the way the profits of the undertaking were to be allocated, which was to include a reservation of com-

[90] See *Possfund Custodian Trustee v. Diamond* [1996] 2 All E.R. 774 a decision of Lightman J.

[91] (1873) L.R. 6, H.L. 377; and see also *Al Nakib v. Longcraft* [1990] 1 W.L.R. 1390.

[92] See above.

mission of 3 per cent on the capital to the fondateurs/directors.] The plaintiff took shares on the basis of the prospectus; and later, after he had become aware of all the facts, bought some more shares. He then sought rescission on the grounds that the prospectus was "fraudulent and void as between them and the Plaintiff".

Sir John Romilly, the Master of the Rolls, stated the applicable principles of equity thus: "The basis of this, as well as of most of the great principles on which the system of equity is founded, is *the enforcement of a careful adherence to truth in all the dealings of mankind*. The principle itself is universal in its application to these cases of contract. It affects not merely the parties to the agreement, but it affects also those who induce others to enter into it. It applies not merely to cases where the statements were known to be false by those who made them, *but to cases where statements, false in fact, were made by persons who believed them to be true, if in the due discharge of their duty, they ought to have known, or if they had formerly known and ought to have remembered the fact which negatives the representation made*. A strong illustration of this is to be found in the case of *Burrowes v. Lock*;[93] and in my opinion (as I held in the case of *Money v. Jorden*[94]) *This principle applies to all representations made on the faith of which other persons enter into engagements*, so that whether the representation were true or false, at the time when it was made, he who made it shall not only be restrained from falsifying it thereafter, but shall, if necessary, be compelled to make good the truth of that which he asserted."

7.35 "The results, however, which flow from the application of this principle, differ materially in different cases. In the case where the false representation is made by one who is no party to the agreement, entered into on the faith of it, the contract cannot be avoided, and all that equity can then do is to compel the person who made the representation to make good his assertion, as far as this may be possible. In cases, however, where the false misrepresentation is made by a person who is a party to the agreement, the power of equity is more extensive; *there the contract itself may be set aside if the nature of the case and condition of the parties will admit of it, or the person who made the assertion may be compelled to make it good*. The distinction between the cases where the person deceived is at liberty to avoid the contract, or where the Court will affirm it, giving him compensation only, are not very clearly defined. This question *usually* arises on the specific performance of contracts for the sale of property; and the principle which I apprehend governs the cases, although it is, in some instances, of very difficult application, and leads to refined distinctions, is the following, viz, that if the representation made be one which can be made good, the party to the contract shall be compelled or may be at liberty to do so; but if the representation made be one which cannot be made good, the person deceived shall be at liberty, if he please, to avoid the contract. Thus, if a man misrepresent the tenure or situation of an estate, as if he sell an estate as freehold which proves to be copyhold or leasehold, or if he describes it as situate within a mile of some particular town, when, in truth, it is several miles distant, such a misrepresentation, as it cannot be made true, would, at the option of the party deceived, annul the contract. But if the party be subject to incumbrances concealed from the purchaser, the seller must make good his statement and redeem those charges;

[93] (1805) 10 Ves. 470, a case where the point adverted to was that the "guilty party" had known but had forgotten the incumbrance in question, and was simply held to have knowledge of it.

[94] (1852) 15 Beav. 372. This was a case—an early estoppel case—in which a party had said he would never enforce a particular bond; and it was held that therefore he could not.

and even in the cases where the property is subject to a small rent not stated, or the rental is somewhat less than it was represented, the Court does not annul the contract, but compels the seller to allow a sufficient deduction from the purchase-money. *It does so on this principle—that, by this means, he, in fact, makes good his representation, and that the statement made was not such as, in substance,* deceived the purchaser as to the nature and quality of the thing he bought. With respect to the character or nature of the misrepresentation itself, it is clear that it may be positive or negative; that it may consist as much in the suppression of what is true as in the assertion of what is false; and it is almost needless to add that *it must appear that the person deceived entered into the contract on the faith of it.* To use the expression of the Roman law (much commented upon in the argument before me) it must be a representation *'dans locum contractui', that is, a representation giving occasion to the contract*: the proper interpretation of which appears to me to be the assertion of a fact on which the person entering into the contract relied, and in the absence of which, it is reasonable to infer, that he would not have entered into it; or the suppression of a fact, the knowledge of which, it is reasonable to infer, would have made him abstain from the contract altogether."[95]

7.36 He found on the facts that there had been no material omission. The fact that the directors had already allotted a number of shares to themselves was not important, since they might have done that afterwards anyway. The fact that Chantrell was to be paid a salary (even if one assumed it was excessive) was similarly not material since it was not a fact "that affected the intrinsic value of the undertaking. That depended on the line of the projected railway, the population, the commercial wealth and traffic of the places through which it was to pass, the difficulties of the construction and the costs of the lands required." He went on to say:

"Extravagance in the formation of a line of railway is, in my opinion, a question of liability of the individual directors to the shareholders, but not a ground for annulling the contract between them." . . . [He then referred to the directors' continuing duty, by virtue of the absence of all statement as to the costs by which the line was to be made: this meant that the directors were obliged to obtain the necessary services at fair and reasonable prices.] "That statement, whether expressed or implied, the directors shall be compelled to make good. Without that statement, the ordinary trust imposed upon directors, in their relations towards their shareholders, imposes this duty upon them. If, indeed, the case had been that a heavy irredeemable rental was, at all events, charged upon and payable out of the project, either to the Belgian Government or to some other persons, in addition to the cost of construction. . . . the case might have been different; because then the omission would have been of something affecting the value of the undertaking inherent to and inseparable from it, in addition to the formation of the line, which could not be known unless by express statement."

Jennings v. Broughton (1854) 17 Beav. 234; 51 E.R. 1023 (affirmed on appeal 5 De G.M. & G. 126; 43 E.R. 818)

7.37 This was another case in which a shareholder sought to rescind the contract to take shares, on the footing of alleged misrepresentations in the prospectus. Sir John Romilly the Master of the Rolls, repeated his observations in *Pulsford v. Richards*,[96] "that I entertain no doubt that persons who take shares upon the formation of a company and the directors who form it are contracting

[95] Some italics supplied.
[96] Para. 7.34 above.

parties, and that the prospectus and the advertisements issued by the directors are the representations, quae dant locum contractui". If these representations contain false statements which cannot be made good by the persons who made them, the person who took those shares on the faith of them may, in my opinion, avoid the contract and require the founders of the company to restore him to the position he was in when he took these shares." In the case before him he thought the question was "whether the prospectus and advertisements, so issued, contained such misrepresentation, or such suppression of existing facts, as, if the real truth had been stated, it is reasonable to believe that the Plaintiff would not have entered into the contract . . . But even if this should be determined in the affirmative, it will not be conclusive in the Plaintiff's favour, because, if the Plaintiff knew what the circumstances connected with the mine really were, and was cognizant of the fact that these representations were inaccurate, he cannot afterwards complain. And it is always to be borne in mind, in suits of this nature, that the burthen of proving that the representations were false, and that he acted on the faith of them, lies on the Plaintiff."

He went on to consider the representations in the case, observing "In considering the effect of these documents a distinction must be taken between that part of them which gives a general description of the prospects and capabilities of the mine, and that part which gives a specific account of what is to be there seen. With respect to the former it is fit to observe that the working of a mine is essentially a speculation of a doubtful character; that the most promising-looking mine may shortly become unproductive, that the most unfavourable appearances in a mine may rapidly disappear; and further, that this character is more prevalent in mines of lead, copper and tin, than in those of coal and ironstone." He concluded that the most the prospectus had done was to describe what was actually there in glowing and exaggerated colours, but had not misrepresented anything. He also attached weight to the fact that the plaintiff had made his own visits to the mine, and had asked searching questions form persons competent to give him correct information, and was given accurate information by them. The plaintiff thus failed.

***Rawlins v. Wickham* (1858) 3 De G. & J. 304; 44 E.R. 1285 (Partnership case)**

7.38 Misrepresentations were made by two partners to the plaintiff. The partnership agreement was set aside some three to four years after its inception. (The case is mostly about the statements made lulling him into a sense of security so that he had no reason to look at the partnership books.) It was found that there was legal (equitable) fraud on the part of one partner, a Mr Wickham, who had made a representation materially affecting the subject matter of the contract, so that, quoting Turner L.J. "he surely cannot be heard to say he knew nothing of the truth or falsehood of that which he represented, and still more surely he cannot be allowed to retain any benefit which he has derived if the representation he has made turns out to be untrue."

The fact that the plaintiff had had the means of knowledge was considered irrelevant by the Lord Justice Turner, who relied on a House of Lords decision in *Harris v. Kemble*[97] which although a specific performance case "and" accordingly "subject to the peculiar rules applicable to such cases, in which the Court exercises a discretion, though not an arbitrary discretion, and that the case is a direct decision only upon the question whether the Court will enforce specific performance where there has been a misrepresentation; still the remarks there made have an important bearing on all cases where the person

[97] (1827) 1 Sim, 111; 57 E.R. 520.

misled might have detected the misrepresentation." He also rejected an argument that the defendants should simply pay the difference—relying on *Clermont v. Tasburgh*[98] to the effect that there was a right to rescind; also on *Edwards v. M'Leay*.[99] (a completed sale of land which was set aside for a breach of good faith).

New Brunswick, etc., Co. v. Muggeridge (1860) 1 Dr. & Sim. 363; 62 E.R. 418 (Duty of accuracy and candour: breach treated as misrepresentation)

7.39 The plaintiff company sought specific performance against the defendant of his agreement to take up shares in the company, he having repudiated his contract after the price of the shares fell.

The Vice-Chancellor Sir R.T. Kindersley referred to the plea which had been put of misrepresentation in the prospectus regarding the land which was to belong to the shareholders. "*And when I use the term misrepresentation, it would be more accurate to describe it as a want of that full and true and complete representation which, in my opinion, ought to have been adopted by persons issuing such a prospectus as this, and inviting persons to apply for shares on the faith of its representations.*" He later referred to the representations as "*inaccurate, and in that sense untrue*". There was a statement that the company had succeeded in obtaining certain important advantages from the Colonial Government in New Brunswick, including a grant of a ten mile wide strip of land along the line amounting to 200,000 acres. In fact the prospectus omitted to mention that the land was only to be granted on completion of the line, and then only if it had not by then been granted away to settlers; while the impression given was that the shareholders would have it right away.

The Vice Chancellor said "... it appears to me that it is quite necessary to uphold this as a principle: that those who issue a prospectus holding out to the public the great advantages which will accrue to persons who will take shares in a proposed undertaking, and inviting them to take shares on the faith of the representations therein contained, are bound to state everything with strict and scrupulous accuracy, and not only to abstain from stating as facts that which is not so, but to omit no one fact within their knowledge the existence of which might in any degree affect the nature, or extent, or quality of the privileges and advantages which the prospectus holds out as inducements to take shares; and that they have no right to turn round upon those who refuse to fulfil their contracts to take shares and say to them, "You ought to have been more prudent, more circumspect, more cautious, more vigilant; you ought, by applying your reasoning powers, to have concluded that our representations *could not be true in the sense which the language we used in the prospectus naturally and fairly imports....*" He therefore dismissed the bill.[1]

Central Rly Co. of Venezuela v. Kisch (1867) L.R. 2 H.L. 99 (Duty of "the utmost candour and honesty" stressed)

7.40 Another case in which a purchaser of shares sought rescission on the grounds of various omissions and misrepresentations in the prospectus. The main misrepresentation described a contract for the building of a railway as entered into "at a price considerably within the available capital of the company". In fact it was in excess of the capital of the company.

The Lord Chancellor Lord Chelmsford emphasized the principle set out

[98] (1819) 1 Jac & W. 112; 37 E.R. 318.
[99] (1815) G. Coop. 308; 35 E.R. 568.
[1] But without costs "on account of the *laches* and negligence of the Defendant". Italics above supplied.

by Vice-Chancellor Kindersley in *New Brunswick and Canada Railway Co v. Muggeridge;*[2] and himself said that though "some high colouring, and even exaggeration, in the description of the advantages which are likely to be enjoyed by the subscribers to an undertaking, may be expected, yet no mis-statement or concealment of any material facts or circumstances ought to be permitted. In my opinion, the public, who are invited by a prospectus to join in any new adventure, ought to have the same opportunity of judging of everything which has a material bearing on its true character, as the promoters themselves possess. *It cannot be too frequently or too strongly impressed upon those who, having projected any undertaking, are desirous of obtaining the co-operation of persons who have no other information on the subject than that which they choose to convey, that the utmost candour and honesty ought to characterize their published statements.*"

Lord Cranworth agreed. Lord Romilly also agreed. He added that "It is in my opinion not merely by one or two statements in the prospectus, which are not borne out by the facts, that the matter ought to be tried, but *by the combined effect of them all producing a result which would have misled any person who took shares upon the faith of the prospectus.*"[3]

Re Reese River Company v. Smith (1867) L.R. 2 Ch. 604 (Duty of accuracy)

7.41 The House of Lords' decision is discussed at paragraph 7.47 below. A prospectus issued on the first day of registration of a new company stated that the company had agreed to purchase property in Nevada containing valuable claims, "some in full operation and making large daily returns." The directors had taken this statement effectively on trust from the vendor, who proved to be fraudulent.

Sir G.J. Turner L.J. said that the company had only itself to blame for making the statement without qualification. "If the company had confined themselves to saying, 'We have received reports from which we believe, and have reason to believe, that these mines are in full operation, and are making daily large returns,' it might, and no doubt would, have been very difficult for Mr Smith to be relieved from the contract, but the company, instead of thus referring to the information received, stated the circumstances as facts." He thought *Rawlins v. Wickham*[4] was decisive on the point, and thought on the facts that Mr Smith had not been guilty of laches.

Lord Cairns attached weight to the fact that the mines were not in this country, where independent inquiry would be made, and inspection might take place, but were at such a distance that the purchaser was obliged to rely on the statements in the prospectus. He thought also it was impossible to suppose that the directors had any reasonable ground for believing the statement they made.

Henderson v. Lacon (1867) L.R., 5 Eq. 249 (Rescission for positive misrepresentation after registration)

7.42 There had been a clear misrepresentation in the prospectus, namely that the directors and their friends had subscribed a large portion of the capital. This was quite untrue: they had subscribed none. Further there was an omission to state that the contractor's guarantie of $2\frac{1}{2}$ per cent was limited to £20,000. The court allowed the plaintiff the relief he sought, repayment of his money, removal from the register, and an injunction restraining the company

[2] Para. 7.39 above.
[3] Italics supplied.
[4] Para. 7.38 above.

from proceeding against him. This was after it had been ordered to be wound up.

***Hallows v. Fernie* (1868) L.R. 3 Ch. App. 467 (Duty of accuracy)**

7.43 Under the circumstances it was held there was no breach of the duty. The directors had issued a prospectus stating amongst other things that the company would commence trading with six screw steamships of 2200 tons and 300 horse-power each (having capacity for 2000 tons of cargo, leaving Liverpool once a months, *etc*; that the vehicles were guaranteed to steam ten knots, and being full rigged as clipper-sailing ships, were calculated to perform the voyage regularly from Falmouth to Rio in 25 days, *etc*; and that the articles of association might be seen at the offices of the company. The plaintiff complained first about the names of the directors, since in fact people not named in the prospectus had become directors; and secondly, that the company had no such ships as above, nor any contract for obtaining them.

Lord Chelmsford said:

"The question then to be decided is, does the prospectus announce to the public in clear and unequivocal language that the promoters of the company actually possessed, or had contracted for the possession of, six ships of the description mentioned, so as to be ready the moment the proper amount of shares were taken, to start the company?

In speaking of the language of the prospectus, I use the words "clear and unequivocal" because it appears to me that there is a material distinction between the employment of words in a prospectus which can bear only one meaning and of those which are equivocal, and which different persons may interpret differently. In the latter case no prudent person would act upon his own construction without some inquiry. In construing a prospectus the preliminary character of the document must always be taken into consideration. Every one knows that it is intended to usher a company into existence, and not to describe its actual formation, no one is surprised to find that a future sense must be given to words in the past or present tense which it contains. For instance, when we read in the prospectus in the present case the word "the company has been formed", we know that they can only mean, and can only be intended to mean, that the company is proposed to be formed for such objects, and in such a manner.

7.44 This ought always to be borne in mind when a construction is required to be put upon the language of a prospectus, and unless it distinctly refers to what is actually existing at the time, it must be taken to represent what will be the state of things when the company is completely formed."

He examined the words used, and thought that they were "very loosely and incautiously worded". ". . . if persons publishing a prospectus use such careless language that their statements literally read are untrue, although this literal sense is different from what they intended, this amounts to a misrepresentation, for which they may be responsible to any one who is deceived or injured by it.

I think, however, that this proposition must be confined to cases where the words used, whether taken alone or read with the context, are free from ambiguity. Because, if they may be construed in a different manner by different minds, it will be impossible to test the truth of any one man's assertion that he understood them in the sense in which they involved a misrepresentation. After the elaborate examination of this first part of the prospectus in the argument before me, its meaning cannot be regarded as so entirely free from doubt, that a person has a right, without inquiry, and acting entirely upon his own views of its proper construction, to purchase shares in the company and then complain that he has been deceived. Because, if the words are susceptible of different meanings, he is deceived, not by the words, but by his construction of them.

7.45 But if the obvious meaning of the prospectus is to represent things as existing which had no existence, and the Plaintiff meant to complain that he read it in this sense, and was deceived by it, he cannot obtain relief without distinctly alleging and proving that the particular statement was a material inducement to his purchasing his shares. It is not sufficient in a bill praying to be relieved from a contract for shares on the ground of its being induced by misrepresentation in a prospectus, to allege generally that the prospectus contains false statements, by which the Plaintiff was deceived and drawn into the contract, but the precise misrepresentation must be distinctly stated, and also that it formed a material inducement to the Plaintiff to take shares in the company."

He went on to comment that the plaintiff's first reason for wanting his money back was nothing to do with the six ships but because the Chilean government had not granted a subsidy to the company and that as to the statement about six ships, the plaintiff "might at any time have ascertained that it was not literally true by reference to the articles of association of the company, to which he was referred, and by which he agreed to be bound in the printed form which he used upon his application for shares." If a person purchases shares in a company upon the faith of a prospectus, and is referred to any document which will shew the untruth or inaccuracy of any of its statements, and chooses not to make use of his means of knowledge, but to continue in a state of wilful ignorance of the facts, he cannot afterwards be heard to complain that he has been deceived by the alleged misstatements.

7.46 In considering the question of knowledge or means of knowledge, it is important to see whether the Plaintiff was a person likely, through inexperience, to be misled by a prospectus, or to place implicit reliance upon all that it contains. He appears to be a shipping agent and secretary to a company, and not unaccustomed to dealings in shares. He nowhere alleges in his bill that he ever before put the construction upon the prospectus which he endeavours now to fasten upon it; nor does he anywhere state that it led him to the belief that the company had either procured ships, or had contracted for them, and that this belief led him to purchase his shares. . . .

I am satisfied, therefore, that the attempt to read the prospectus in the present tense as representing actual possession at the time it was issued, of the specified number of ships of a particular description, is an after-thought, and that the Plaintiff's case can only be established by his giving a sense to the prospectus which he never attributed to it before. But whatever may be the fair meaning of the prospectus, and even if the Plaintiff's construction of it is correct, he can only be entitled to succeed *secundum allegat et probat*. But he has not alleged, and he has failed to prove, that he read the prospectus in a sense which involved an untruth, that it led him into an erroneous belief of the existence of a certain state of facts, and that this belief was a material inducement to him to become a purchaser of shares in the company".

The plaintiff lost.

***Re Reese River Company v. Smith* (1869) L.R. 4 H.L. 64**

7.47 This was an appeal against the Lords Justices decision (see para. 7.41 above 1867 noted a different point) that it was too late to rectify the register after the winding up of the company. Their Lordships considered it was not, and that Mr Smith was entitled to an order that he be removed from the register despite the winding up. The only point of interest from the point of view of the duty of candour and accuracy is Lord Cairns' comments on "fraud" as contrasted with "fraud in the more invidious sense" where there was knowledge of the untruth. He said he had never entertained any doubt that the respondent was entitled to repudiate his shares in the company, nor that a fraud had been committed against him. "When I say 'a fraud', I do not enter into any question with regard to the imputation of what may be called fraud in the more invidious sense against the directors. I think it may be quite possible, as has been alleged, that they were ignorant of the untruth of the statements made in their prospectus. But I apprehend it to be the rule of law, that if persons take upon themselves to make assertions as to which they are ignorant whether they are true or untrue, they must, in a civil point of view, be held as responsible as if they had asserted that which they knew to be untrue."

***Peek v. Overend, Gurney* & Co (1873) L.R. 6 H.L. 277 (Breach of good faith and deceit contrasted)**

7.48 The action was not for rescission of the contract but for damages for deceit. Lord Chelmsford in effect thought the misrepresentation had not been made *to* the purchaser, who simply bought the shares in the open market after the prospectus had been issued and all original shares allotted. The judgments of Lord Chelmsford and the others draw a definite distinction between non-disclosure as the basis of an action for deceit, and non-disclosure as a basis for setting aside the contract. For example, Lord Cairns said "Mere non-disclosure of material facts, however morally censurable, *however that non-disclosure might be a ground in a proper proceeding at a proper time for setting aside an allotment or a purchase of shares,*[5] would in my opinion form no ground for an action in the nature of an action for misrepresentation. There must, in my opinion, be some active misstatement of fact, or at all events, such a partial and fragmentary statement of fact, as that the withholding of that which is not stated makes that which is stated absolutely false." He thought it was false; but that (in effect) the appellant was too remote from those who issued the prospectus to be able to claim on it.

***In re Coal Economising Gas Co, Gover's Case* (1875) 1 Ch.D. 182**

7.49 By then section 38 of the Companies Act 1867 had been enacted. This provided that: "every prospectus of a company, and every notice inviting persons to subscribe for shares in any joint-stock company, shall specify the dates and the names of the parties to any contract entered into by the company, or the promoters, directors, or trustees thereof, before the issue of such prospectus or notice, whether subject to adoption by the directors of the company or otherwise; and any prospectus or notice not specifying the same shall be deemed fraudulent on the part of the promoters, directors, and officers of the company knowingly issuing the same, as regards any person taking shares in the company on the faith of such prospectus, unless he shall have had notice of such contract." It did not enact that the contract for taking shares was to be rescinded on account of such concealment.

It was held by a majority that the particular omission was of no consequence; and further that the company as principal would not be liable to be deemed fraudulent within the statute merely because its agent might be. The section was also restrictively construed, so as to cover material concealment only. It was held however that the section did apply to a person who was not a promoter at the time he made the omitted contract, but became one

[5] Italics supplied.

afterwards. Brett J.'s dissenting judgment contains an interesting statement of the pre-1867-Act law. "Immediately before this section was passed the law was thus: if a subscription for shares in a company was obtained by a fraudulent misrepresentation, or by a fraudulent concealment so great as to make that which was stated in effect a misrepresentation, the company could not, either by action at law or in the course of any proceedings in equity, enforce payment of any call made in respect of such shares, and the shareholder could recover back money paid as for calls on those share, and the shareholder could obtain the removal of his name from the register of shareholders. *If a subscription for shares were obtained by a misrepresentation of facts, though not fraudulently made, a Court of Equiry would prevent the company from compelling payment of a call, would compel restitution of money paid for a call, and would remove the name from the register of shareholders.*[6] But for a mere non-disclosure, fraudulent or otherwise, which had not the effect of rendering that which was disclosed or stated a misrepresentation, however otherwise important for the consideration of an invited subscriber, there was no remedy either in law or equity if he became a registered shareholder."

Note: The contrast made is between fraud (three-star blameworthy statements); breaches of good faith (two-star blameworthy statements) and "mere" non-disclosures which if left undisclosed would have no effect on the representations made.

Twycross v. Grant (1877) 2 C.P.D. 469 (Idea that a vendor of his own property to a newly formed company who is also the promoter of the company is a "fiduciary" mooted.)

7.50 This was an action founded upon section 38 of the Companies Act 1867.[7] It was decided by a majority that the contract in question was to be disclosed, and that it did not matter that the promoters had genuinely not thought it important to disclose it—the non-disclosure did not in their view have to *be* fraudulent to be within the act; they merely had to know.

Cockburn C.J. said the case differed from *Gover's Case* in that here there was no doubt the contracts were entered into by the promoters, with a view to, and incidentally to its formation. . . ."Fully admitting that a person who sells to a company is no more bound to disclose how, or upon what terms, he acquired the subject-matter of the sale, than an ordinary vendor to an ordinary purchaser, *it seems to me that when the vendor adopts the character of a promoter, the matter assumes a very different aspect. A fiduciary or at all events, quasi-fiduciary, relation arises between him and the company. He is bound to protect its interests, and those of the shareholders. All his dealings with them, and for them, should be uberrimae fidei. He should conceal nothing from them which it is essential to them to know."* . . .[8]

Eaglesfield v. Marquess of Londonderry [1877] 4 Ch. D. 693 (Innocent motive irrelevant)

7.51 Jessel M.R. found that there were misrepresentations, and that the innocent motive of the directors made no difference; they had made the statement on the advice of their solicitor[9] and *Slim v. Croucher* 1 D.F. & J. 518 which were cases of forgotten knowledge; and thought this case was *a fortiori*. The Court of Appeal reversed the decision on the facts, finding that the purchaser was

[6] Italics supplied.
[7] See Gover's Case at para. 7.49 above for the text.
[8] Italics supplied.
[9] He referred to *Burrowes v. Lock* (1805) 10 Ves. 470; 32 E.R. 947.

not misled by the representation, because he knew precisely what kind of shares he was getting.

***Erlanger v. New Sombrero Phosphate Company* (1878) 3 App. Cas. 1218**

7.52 Chapter 9, Dealings with the Vulnerable Buyer or Seller, notes this important case at paragraph 9.91.

***In re Scottish Petroleum Company, Anderson's Case* (1881) 17 Ch. D. 373 (Duty of candour)**

7.53 The two Mr Andersons applied for shares relying on the prospectus which said that a Mr Gibson and a Mr Ross would be directors with a third. In fact both withdrew but the company did not issue a new prospectus; and allotted the shares to the two applicants and refused to give them their money back. Malins V.C. said that they could have it back. "In all these transactions connected with the formation of companies the Court requires that there shall be straightforward, candid conduct; and I think that straightforward and candid conduct required in this case that the persons who applied for shares on the faith of one state of things should have the option of retiring when a totally different state of things came into existence."

***Arkwright v. Newbold* (1881) 17 Ch. D. 301 (Deceit and good faith contrasted)**

7.54 The plaintiff bought shares in a paper manufacturing company relying on the prospectus. He retained them for two years, then brought an action for deceit, claiming that the statements in question in the prospectus were false by reason of an omission, that there had been an arrangement not amounting to a contract whereby the company was indirectly to do something the prospectus had said it would not do. Fry J. permitted him to recover, and awarded damages for the difference in value between what he received and what the prospectus would have led him to believe he was receiving. The losing side appealed.

James L.J. emphasized the difference between the two different wrongs and two different remedies "— between the question what mala praxis on the part of vendors and persons standing in a fiduciary position to a purchaser is sufficient to entitle the purchaser to rescind the contract, and the question what mala praxis is sufficient to enable him to maintain an action of deceit. There are a number of purely equitable considerations which arise when the Courts are dealing with actions to set aside contracts or conveyances which have been obtained by means of misrepresentation of a fact, or by means of concealment or suppression of a fact which in the opinion of the Court ought to have been stated. Those cases stand by themselves, and are entirely distinct from such a case as we have before us." He noted that "It has been conceded throughout that there was misconduct, that is to say, improper dealing between the vendors and the persons whom they procured to become directors—a kind of transaction against which the Courts always have, and I hope always will, very strongly set their faces. But we have to see whether there was, to use the language of Lord Cairns in *Peek v. Gurney*[10] that which must be proved, "Some active misstatement of fact, or, at all events, such a partial and fragmentary statement of fact as that the withholding of that which is not stated makes that which is stated absolutely false. "Supposing you state a thing partially, you may make as false a statement as much as if

[10] (1873) L.R. 6 H.L. 377.

you misstated it altogether. Every word may be true, but if you leave out something which qualifies it, you may make a false statement. For instance, if pretending to set out the report of a surveyor, you set out two passages in his report, and leave out a third passage which qualifies them, that is an actual misstatement. The statement made must be either in terms or by such an omission as I have stated an untrue statement, and no mere silence will ground the action of deceit." He went on to consider the facts here, and concluded there was no misstatement whatsoever.

7.55 Cotton L.J. agreed, saying that there was no such thing as an equitable action for deceit. "It is a common law action in which it is necessary to prove that a statement has been made which, to the knowledge of the person making it, was false, or which was made by him with such recklessness as to make him liable just as if he knew it to be false, and that the plaintiff acted on that statement to his prejudice or damage. . . . "mere omission, *even though such as would give reason for setting aside a contract,*[11] is not, in my opinion, if it does not make the substantive statements false, a sufficient ground for maintaining an action of deceit. This also must be borne in mind, that, in an action for setting aside a contract which has been obtained by misrepresentation, the Plaintiff may succeed, although the misrepresentation was innocent; but in an action of deceit the representation to found the action must not be innocent, that is to o say, it must be made either with knowledge of its being false, or with a reckless disregard as to whether it is or is not true."

Lush L.J. agreed, and pointed out, as did Cotton L.J., that the plaintiff had not stated he was misled, merely that the prospectus was deceptive. James L.J. then said that he agreed with Cotton L.J. that those who issue a prospectus are not liable to an action of deceit "because they do not mention a fact coming to their knowledge before the allotment of shares which falsifies a statement in the prospectus."

***Redgrave v. Hurd* (1881) 20 Ch. D. 1 (Jessel M.R., Baggalay L.J. and Lush L.J.)**

7.56 Chapter 5, Sale of Land, notes this case at paragraph 5.101.

***Smith v. Chadwick* (1882) 20 Ch. D. 27 (Deceit action, materiality and inducement considered)**

7.57 See paragraph 7.60 below for a note of the House of Lords' decision. The plaintiff took shares in a steel manufacturing company in reliance on the prospectus.

(1) The list of directors contained a Mr Grieve, who had not agreed to become director. Fry J. thought this was a false statement, though he did not know how much it operated on the mind of the plaintiff.

(2) There was a reference to a valuation of the stocks and shares at £301,000, followed by a statement about the method by which the purchase money for certain collieries was to be purchased. Fry J. thought this was a representation that the shares were the equivalent of the purchase money, and that all the land valued was to be bought. In fact three acres were excepted from the purchase.

(3) There was no mention of interest being payable on the instalments of the purchase price. This he thought also was a misstatement, since it was normal to mention interest.

(4) The "present value of the turnover or output of the entire works is

[11] Italics supplied.

over one million sterling per annum" was false, he held, and material, since the company had never had an actual output approaching anywhere near that.

On appeal it was argued that (1) was immaterial, (2) was immaterial, and no one could suppose the vendors would forego interest, (3) was misunderstood by the plaintiff: it meant that the works were capable of producing one million, not that they ever had, and anyway, the plaintiff had not shown that he understood the words in any different interpretation.[12]

7.58 Jessel M.R. said (at p. 44), "[n]ow, without repeating at full length what I have said in a recent case, I think the law on this subject is clear. A man may issue a prospectus, or make any other statement to induce another to enter into a contract, believing that his statement is true, and not intending to deceive; but he may through carelessness have made statements which are not true, and which he ought to have known were not true, and if he does so he is liable in an action for deceit;[13] he cannot be allowed to escape merely because he had good intentions, and did not intend to defraud. Again, on the question of the *materiality of the statement, if the Court sees on the face of it that it is of such a nature as would induce a person to enter into the contract, or would tend to induce him to do so, or that it would be a part of the inducement, to enter into the contract, the inference is, if he entered into the contract, that he acted on the inducement so held out, and you want no evidence that he did so act*; but even then you may shew that in fact he did not so act in one of two ways, either by shewing that he knew the truth before he entered into the contract, and therefore, could not rely on the misstatements; or else by shewing that he avowedly did not rely upon them, whether he knew the facts or not. He may by contract have bound himself not to rely upon them, that is to take the matter at his own risk whether they were true or false (which was the conclusion to which the House of Lords came in the recent case of *Brownlie v. Campbell*[14] . . . or he may state that he did not rely upon them in the witness box, which I think is so in one instance here. *But unless it is shewn in one way or the other that he did not rely on the statement the inference follows.*[15]

We now come to another class of cases, in which it is not obvious to the Court that the statement is material; and there may be several ways in which it may not be obvious. In the first place, the statement may be ambiguous; it may have one of two meanings, and the Court cannot decide which meaning it has. . . . In that case the Plaintiff must tell us what he relied on. It is for him to say, 'I relied on the statement in this meaning, that is the meaning I took; if it is ambiguous it is the fault of the Defendant, and relying on that I entered into the contract.' But if the Plaintiff will not tell us what he relied on; if he says to the Court 'Please to find out the meaning; I relied on the statements in the prospectus, and I relied upon them according to their meaning, whatever that meaning is'; surely that will not do. How can the Court find out that he has been deceived at all? The Court may think it means the very thing the Plaintiff did not think it meant, and then are they to say he has been deceived, because he took it in the wrong sense? That, of course, is impossible. That point of law, I think, will be found to have some application to the present case.

Again, in an action of deceit, even though the statement may be untrue, yet, if it was made in good faith, and the Defendant had reasonable ground

[12] The appellants cited ***Hallows v. Fernie*** (1868) L.R. 3 Ch. App. 467 and *Arkwright v. Newbold* (1881) 17 Ch. D. 301 in support of the proposition that this was necessary.
[13] See however, ***Derry v. Peek*** (1889) 14 App. Cas. 349.
[14] (1880) 5 App. Cas. 925.
[15] Italics supplied.

for believing it to be true, the Defendant will succeed. That again, it will be seen, has an application to this case also.

Finally, it is not every mis-statement, although untrue, and although untrue, in a sense, to the Defendant's knowledge, that will do. It may be that the mis-statement is trivial, so trivial as that the Court will be of opinion that it could not have affected the Plaintiffs mind at all, or induced him to enter into the contract; or it may be that although the means of knowledge were in the hands of the Defendant, yet the matter was minute, and required a careful examination, and there may have been reasonable grounds for the Defendant to believe that this statement was true, although he had those means of knowledge in his possession. In that way also he would be entitled to succeed."

7.59 He found against the plaintiff on the facts, stressing that the plaintiff had not troubled to put in evidence that he had been misled. He concluded with a quotation from Turner L.J. in *Jennings v. Broughton.*[16] "And, finally, I think that although it is the undoubted duty of this Court to relieve persons who have been deceived by false representations, it is equally the duty of this Court to be careful that in its anxiety to correct frauds, it does not enable persons who have joined with others in speculations to convert their speculations into certainties at the expense of those with whom they have joined."

***Smith v. Chadwick* (1884) 9 App. Cas. 187**

7.60 See paragraph 7.57 above for a note of the Court of Appeal's decision. Lord Selborne said that in an action of deceit the plaintiff had to establish,

"First, actual fraud, which is to be judged of by the nature and character of the representations made, considered with reference to the object for which they were made, the knowledge or means of knowledge of the person making them, and the intention which the law justly imputes to every man to produce those consequences which are the natural result of his acts: and, secondly, he must establish that this fraud was an inducing cause to the contract; for which purpose it must be material, and it must have produced in his mind an erroneous belief, influencing his conduct." (at p. 190)

He went on to consider the representation about the value of the turnover. He said the appellant's case would be made out if "in the context in which it stands, it could not be honestly intended or reasonably understood in any other sense. . . ." But it is otherwise, in my opinion, if the words in the context in which they stand may have been honestly intended to bear another sense (in which they would be true) and might reasonably have been so understood by an intelligent man of business, aware of the current prices at that time of bar and plate iron; and if at the time when that answer was given, the appellant had notice that the defendants, who made the representation, did in fact allege such other sense to be the true one, and the sense which they intended."

7.61 Lord Blackburn said that he did not quite agree with the way the Master of Rolls had stated the law. For his part, he considered that it was established[17] that in an action of deceit the plaintiff must not only allege but prove the damage he suffered by acting on the representations. "It is as to what is sufficient proof of this damage that I wish to make my remarks. I do not think it is necessary, in order to prove this, that the plaintiff always should be called as a witness to swear that he acted upon the inducement. At the time when *Pasley v. Freeman* . . . was decided, and for many years afterwards, he could not be so called. I think that if it is proved that the defendants with a view to induce the plaintiff to enter into a contract made a statement to the plaintiff

[16] (1853) 5 De G.M. & G. 140; 43 E.R. 818.

[17] *Pasley v. Freeman* (1789) 3 T.R. 51, 100 E.R. 450.

of such a nature as would be likely to induce a person to enter into a contract, and it is proved that the plaintiff did enter into the contract, it is a fair inference of fact that he was induced to do so by the statement. In *Redgrave v. Hurd*[18] ... the late Master of the Rolls is reported to have said it was an inference of law. If he really meant this he retracts it in his observations in the present case. I think it not possible to maintain that it is an inference of law. Its weight as evidence must greatly depend upon the degree to which the action of the plaintiff was likely, and on the absence of all other grounds on which the plaintiff might act (at p. 196). . . ."

***Bellairs v. Tucker* (1884) 13 Q.B.D. 562 (Deceit, balance of access to information relevant)**

7.62 The plaintiff was a dealer in stocks and shares, and had formerly been a member of the Stock Exchange. He bought shares in a company called the French Date-Coffee Company (date coffee was intended to be a substitute for coffee) relying on a prospectus which referred to the success attending the English sister company and then said "when a duty of 2d is payable, and the coffee sold at 1s per lb the directors feel justified in stating they confidently believe the profits of this company will be more than sufficient to pay dividends of at least 50% on the nominal capital. . . ." At this time the English company had not made any "profits" in a commercial sense. The plaintiff brought an action for deceit against the promoters of the French Date- Coffee Company Ltd after he had been called upon to pay in the winding-up.

Denman J. thought that on balance there was only a statement of belief in the future here and no misrepresentation. He relied on the experience of the plaintiff also, referring as to the relevance of this *inter alia* to *Hallows v. Fernie*,[19] and to Turner L.J. in *Kisch v. Venezuela Company*.[20–21] Manisty J. agreed, citing the Master of the Rolls in *Smith v. Chadwick*.[22]

***Edgington v. Fitzmaurice* (1885) 29 Ch. D. 459 (Deceit case, importance of consideration of statement as a whole stressed)**

7.63 The prospectus stated the objects of the company's issue of debentures, but omitted to mention that the real object of the loan was to enable the directors to pay off pressing liabilities. The plaintiff was partly influenced by a mistaken notion of his own, partly by the misrepresentation. Both Denman J. and the Court of Appeal held that this was enough, it had only to be a material misstatement of fact, it did not have to be the sole inducement.

Denman J. also had an interesting approach to the detail of the circular, "I do not think that in cases such as this it is incumbent upon the Court or upon the jury necessarily to look at each statement by itself without regard to the other statements. I think one can easily suggest cases, and that this may be such a case, in which taking one statement separately you might say there is nothing in it, or that there is very little in it, or much less than there is if you couple it with the other two in all such cases, in considering the animus with which the statement was made, I think it is only common sense that, whether jury or Judge, you should look at the whole of the document together, and consider every statement in it with a view of forming a judgment as to the intention, and that it is not a fair way of dealing with these cases to say, I

[18] 20 Ch. D. 1.
[19] Para 7.43, above.
[20–21] 34 L.J. Ch. 545 and 554.
[22] Para. 7.57, above.

take statement A, there is nothing in it; I take statement B, there is nothing in it; and I take statement C, there is nothing in it—there is nothing in them if they stood alone, and therefore as you cannot make three nothings into something the whole thing falls to the ground. I think you must take the whole, together with its history, and then, it may be that there is just reason for holding statement a, statement V and statement C to be all inaccurate, and all falling within the definition of an actionable false statement. There may be cases in which that is so, though, if you had only one, the decision might be quite the other way as regards that one statement. It is quite certain that you must always take into consideration the surrounding facts of the case in construing every document, and not only so, but in considering the animus of the parties who issue that particular document."[23]

***Derry v. Peek* (1889) 14 App. Cas. 337 (Deceit case)**

7.64 In this well-known case the House of Lords held definitively that a statement made honestly but without reasonable grounds was not fraudulent for the purposes of an action in deceit, although it might well be sufficient for the rescission of the contract.

***Karberg's Case* [1892] 3 Ch. 1 C.A. Rescission for positive misrepresentation)**

7.65 Mr Karsberg sought to rescind his contract with the company, relying on the representation by the promoters of the intended company two days before its incorporation, that certain persons, Lord Brabourne and Admiral Mayne, had agreed to be members of the council of administration. He took out the application a few days after discovering the truth, and a few months before the winding up of the company. It was held by the Court of Appeal that he might rescind, since on balance they thought the statement was not one of belief, but of present fact, and was untrue.

Lindley L.J. pointed out that the company, not having made the representation by itself or by its agents, is not liable in damages; "but as regards rescission of contract, the company is in the same position as if it had made the representation itself without knowing it to be untrue. But in an action for rescission of contract on the ground of misrepresentation, it is not necessary to prove knowledge by the defendant of its untruth: see *Redgrave v. Hurd*."[24]

The court held that "where a contract was rescinded, interest on money actually paid under it ought to be allowed, not by way of damages, but on the ground that the parties were to be restored as far as possible to their original position."

***Lynde v. Anglo-Italian Hemp Co.* [1896] 1 Ch. 178 (Statements by a company and its agents—guidance on responsibility)**

7.66 The Anglo-Italian Hemp Company was incorporated in November 1890, one of its objects being to buy certain hemp works at Ferrara. The company was promoted by gentlemen called Thomson and Waithman. One of the articles of association provided that the directors should adopt an agreement made a fortnight before the incorporation of the company made between these two and a trustee for the company. Neither became directors till about six months after the plaintiff had applied for and been allotted the shares;

[23] See also *Re Mount Morgan* (1887) 56 L.T. 622; *Re British Burma Lead Co.* (1887) 56 L.T. 814; and *Capel v. Sims* (1888) 58 L.T. 807.

[24] (1881) 20 Ch. D. 1.

but the plaintiff said that they had made a number of oral misrepresentations to him, on behalf of the company, inducing him to apply for the shares.

Romer J's guidance on the circumstances in which a company is made liable for others' statements is set out in the text at paragraph 7.15 above.

He held that the company knew that Waithman was applying to his friends to get them to subscribe for shares, but that did not make him the company's agent, nor put the company on inquiry as to whether he had made any, and if so, what representations to those friends. He thought it would lead to the most astonishing results if the mere awareness as above were enough to affect the directors with knowledge, or put them upon inquiry about the representations made. Further, it was not, like *Karberg*'s[25] case (so he thought), an application which was *on the basis of* any special or other representations made by Waithman.

Aaron's Reef v. Twiss [1896] A.C. 273 (Rescission for fraudulent misrepresentation; proof of inducement considered by Lord Halsbury)

7.67 Aaron's Reef Ltd was incorporated in January 1890 for the purpose of mining. A month after incorporation it acquired the right to work a mining concession in Venezuela by two deeds. The price was to be paid as to the first deed by paying half from the subscription of shares by the public until the price was paid, and then two-thirds of the moneys so received were to be paid till the price of the second deed was paid, retaining one third as working capital. The plaintiff company brought an action for calls on Captain Twiss's (the defendant's) shares. He sought rescission for fraudulent misrepresentations in the prospectus.

Lord Halsbury said *inter alia* on inducement "But I must protest against it being supposed that in order to prove a case of this character of fraud, and that a certain course of conduct was induced by it, a person is bound to be able to explain with exact precision what was the mental process by which he was induced to act." (at p. 280) He thought "I should say if I were a juryman that this was a very fascinating prospectus, and was calculated to induce any one who believed the statements in it to invest his money in the concern."

He also dealt with the argument that there was no specific allegation that was false. "I think one is entitled to look at the whole document and see what is meant taken together. . . ." (at p. 281) Again I protest, as I have said, against that [that you look at each specific allegation separately] being the true test. I should say, taking the whole thing together, was there false representation? I do not care by what means it is conveyed—by what trick or device or ambiguous language: all those are expedients by which fraudulent people seem to think they can escape from the real substance of the transaction. If by a number of statements you intentionally give a false impression and induce a person to act upon it, it is not the less false although if one takes each statement by itself there may be a difficulty in shewing that any specific statement is untrue." In fact he thought there were positively untrue statements anyway. He went on ". . . I wish to say for myself I do not think any particular form of words is necessary to convey a false impression. Suppose a person goes to a bank where the people are foolish enough to believe his words, and says, "I want a mortgage upon my house, and my house is not completed, but in the course of next week I expect to have it fully completed." (at p. 283) Suppose there was not a house upon his land at all, and no possibility, therefore, that it could be fully completed next week, can anybody say that that was not an affirmative representation that there was a house which was so near

[25] Para. 7.65, above.

to completion that it only required another week's work upon it to complete it? Could anybody defend himself if he was charged upon an indictment for obtaining money under false pretences, the allegation in the indictment being that he pretended that there was a house so near completion that it only required a week's work upon it, by saying that he never represented that there was a house there at all? . . ." (at p. 283)

7.68 Lord Watson considered "material matters". He said it sometimes required serious consideration. "The duty of disclosure is not the same in the case of a prospectus inviting share subscriptions as in the case of a proposal for marine insurance. In an honest prospectus many facts and circumstances may be lawfully omitted, although some subscribers might be of opinion that these would have been of materiality as influencing the exercise of their judgment. But the statement of a portion of the truth, accompanied by suggestions and inferences which would be possible and credible if it contained the whole truth, but become neither possible nor credible whenever the whole truth is divulged, is, to my mind, neither more nor less than a false statement. It was in that sense that the jury affirmed the suppression of all information with respect to the purchase of the concession to be material and fraudulent; because they thought, as I do, that such suppression was necessary in order to enable the company to manufacture a tempting bait for the unwary, and to submit to them a prospectus which was neither true nor honest."

***Lagunas Nitrate Co v. Lagunas Nitrate Syndicate* [1899] 2 Ch. 392**

7.69 Chapter 9, Dealings with the Vulnerable Seller or Buyer, notes this case at paragraph 9.96, and see also Chapter 15.

***Broome v. Speak* [1903] 1 Ch. 586 (Court of Appeal decision later affirmed by the House of Lords in *Shepheard v. Broome*;[26] *reliance considered*)**

7.70 This was a case on section 38 of the 1867 Act and on the Directors Liability Act 1890. Certain contracts had been omitted from the prospectus (in fact on the advice of counsel that they might be, but this did not avail the defendants). Buckley J.considered the question of reliance, in terms which were essentially approved although not specifically by reference to his judgment, in the Court of Appeal.

"It is unintelligible to say that a person relied upon a fact which he was not told, or relied on his not being told a fact, and when you call a man after the event to say whether, if he had known a further particular fact, he would have done something or not, speaking for myself, it is so difficult to say exactly what a few years ago you would have done under different circumstances, that I should regard that evidence as of very little value. Be the man the most honest man possible, it is so easy to be wise after the event, that it is difficult for any man to say what he would have done under circumstances which did not arise. It is too much to expect of him that he should be able to say fairly what he would have done under those altered circumstances. The test I think to be applied is—it has been so stated by Lord Halsbury, and was so stated in *Smith v. Chadwick*,[27] and will be found in many cases—that if you find that the matter withheld such as that if disclosed it reasonably would deter or tend to deter an ordinarily prudent investor from applying for the shares, then he is entitled to relief."

The Court of Appeal added nothing of interest.

[26] Para. 7.71 below; reliance considered
[27] (1884) 9 App. Cas. 187 para. 7.60, above.

***Shepheard v. Broome* [1904] A.C. 342 H.L.**

7.71 See paragraph 7.70 above, for a note of a point in the decision of the court of first instance. The appellant knew of certain material contracts, but did not disclose them in the prospectus. He took legal advice about it, but, as Lord Lindley said, "whether he was wrongly advised or whether he misunderstood the advice given is not clear." The decision of the Court of Appeal[28] was affirmed by the House of Lords.

***Mair v. Rio Grande* [1913] A.C. 853 (Rescission, good faith duty affirmed)**

7.72 The action was by a shareholder for rescission of his contract to take shares. He alleged that the statements in the prospectus were false and fraudulent. Lord Shaw of Dunfermline remarked that this need not be true of any of the directors for his action to succeed, and quoted Turner L.J. in the *Reese River Silver Mining Co.*[29] He went on that there was a further point. "Fraud is not far away from—nay, indeed, it must be that it accompanies—a case of any defendant holding a plaintiff to a bargain which has been induced by representations which were untrue; *for it is contrary to good faith and it partakes of fraud to hold a person to a contract induced by an untruth for which you yourself stand responsible.*[30] It is elementary that a party cannot take advantage of a benefit derived from a contract sprung out of his own fraud, and I think it is equally sound that a party cannot take a benefit from a contract sprung out of a falsehood which he has placed before the other party as an inducing cause."

***Re Pacaya Rubber Co* [1914] 1 Ch. 542 (Rescission action, importance of whole document stressed)**

7.73 A prospectus contained several important statements of facts, which they stated were based upon the report of an expert named Von Hassel. Astbury J. found that these statements, giving a general picture of a flourishing immediately payable rubber estate, were seriously misleading. Astbury J. quoted Lord Halsbury in *Aaron's Reef v. Twiss*,[31] "if you are looking to the language as only the language of hope, expectation, and confident belief, that is one thing; but (at p. 284) . . . you may use language in such a way as, although in the form of hope and expectation, it may become a representation as to existing facts." He also quoted Lord Shaw in *Mair v. Rio Grande*[32] saying,

"I do not deny that it would be possible for directors to apprise the public frankly in a prospectus that they dissociate themselves from one of their own number, and that with regard to him no warranty was given of the truth of what he represented or reported. This would make a peculiar document; but it might be done. Yet the doing of such a thing would require to be in the most clear and unambiguous terms, so as to constitute a specific warning to investors against doing that which otherwise anything under the hand of a director as such would warrant them in doing, namely, relying upon its accuracy and complete good faith." (at p. 868) The applicant was permitted rescission and removal of his name from the list of contributories. (The action was begun after a call was made on the applicant, but before the winding up.)

[28] ***Broome v. Speak*** [1903] 1 Ch. 586.
[29] (1867) L.R. 2 Ch. 604, para. 7.41, above.
[30] Italics supplied.
[31] [1896] A.C. 273.
[32] Para. 7.72, above.

CHAPTER 8

KNOWLEDGE AND NOTICE

"... Of purchasers without notice, and of presumptive notice ... "Mr Pigott the Conveyancer perused a Settlement, and afterwards drew another of the same Lands, but at such a Distance of Time that he had forgot the Contents of the former Settlement; and upon a Plea of a Purchasor without Notice on the latter Settlement, the question was, If this Notice to Mr Pigott of a Thing he had forgotten was sufficient to affect the Principal. And upon great Consideration, and upon examining Mr Pigott in Court, it was held by Lord Chan. King, assisted by several of the Judges, that it was not; for, when the Thing had slipt out of his Memory, he was as if he never had any Notice at all of the Thing. And Talbot, Lord C. in the Case of the Attorney General and Gower, said, no Man was obliged to remember a Thing for ever; and that this Determination was perfectly right ..."[1]

"It is said that this case is of great importance to the commercial world, and that the doctrine which it asserts will alarm bankers and others, who have advanced their money on the deposit of deeds, and who will find themselves exposed to the danger of having their securities affected by secret assignments. But the only effect of such a doctrine (if it really were new), would be to prevent persons obtaining advances of money with such facility on the deposit of their deeds, and whether any great mischief would result from a check being given to equitable mortgages of this description, may be questionable."[2]

"The purchaser bound himself by contract. He must be taken to have had present to his mind all those things of which he had notice, and those things which necessarily flowed from, and were incidental to, that notice."[3]

"The Court, therefore, receives evidence of the agency, and it receives evidence of the act of the principal, but it will not receive evidence whether the agent recollected the fact at the time or whether he commun-

[1] 2 Eq. Cases Abridged 682; 22 E.R. 573.
[2] The Lord Chancellor in ***Espin v. Pemberton*** (1859) 3 De G. & J. 547; 44 E.R. 1380.
[3] Lord Romilly M.R. in ***James v. Lichfield*** (1869) L.R. 9 Eq. 51.

icated it to his principal. It deals with those matters by way of irrebuttable presumption when the circumstances are known."[4]

NOTICE AND GOOD FAITH PRINCIPLES: TWO SIDES OF A COIN

8.01 It may seem slightly strange that there should be a chapter on the largely neglected topic of notice in a book about fair dealing terms. This chapter was not originally intended to be in the book. However, it eventually became evident that the attempt to grapple with notice had to be made. Doctrines about notice are at least as old as good faith rules, and are a necessary counterpoint to them. Good faith/fair dealing rules were never intended to permit a buyer to avoid doing his homework before buying; nor did they allow him to shelter behind a careless agent. Thus, the good-faith rules show a tension between the mutual reasonable expectations of the parties of each other. The defining party (that is, in most ordinary transactions the seller, but in, for example insurance and surety transactions the buyer), in all cases must fulfil at least a very high duty of accuracy in describing what he sells and in some cases must comply with a duty of "original" disclosure as well. On the other hand the "defining party" to a sale has reasonable expectations of the other, who may be labelled for this purpose the "inquiring party", (usually the buyer), but in the case of insurance and surety transactions the seller: see below. He (and any agent he employs) should look out for himself as far as he can, and make all reasonable and appropriate investigations and inquiries, as the nature of the contract dictates.

Notice rules operate in a very similar way to good-faith rules on the content of the contract: they operate as default rules to define what there is *in* the contract. What could be reasonably investigated by the inquiring party but is not, is deemed to be accepted by him; he is supposed by the courts to have shrugged his shoulders and said, Oh well, I will take the risk of that—not worth the bother of finding out. Now, he may in fact not have shrugged his shoulders at all, he may have got himself into a self-induced muddle of one sort or another. The courts do not go into what he keeps in his head: they are not concerned with the multitudinous reasons for being unreasonable which the inquiring parties/buyers may have in fact. Contracts of sale thus consist, in a sense, of both of these twin default rules of good faith and reasonable investigation, whereby the parties' reasonable expectations are fulfilled.

8.02 Finally, the presumptions about notice operate on the formation of the contract in precisely the same contingent way as the good faith rules do. It is only an inquiring party/buyer who does *not* reasonably investigate who brings down the default rules' operation upon himself: other, more careful people need not worry about this. Similarly,

[4] Fry J. in ***Kettlewell v. Watson*** (1882) 21 Ch. D. 709.

as we have seen, it is only a defining party/seller who does not comply with good-faith duties whose contractual performance shrinks to omit the area where he did not comply. In what follows the expressions "the buyer" and "the seller", will often be used for the inquiring and the defining party respectively, since the usual inquiring party is the buyer and the usual defining party is the seller. However, the application of the constructive notice (by operation of law) doctrine to insurance sales shows that the "buyer's" duty can in such cases be on the seller and vice versa; where the buyer is in effect defining what he is to buy, and the seller is the one who must trust. An alternative way to look at insurance transactions may be simply that the buyer of insurance is to be seen as the seller of risk, and because "risk" is essentially something that takes colour from the circumstances, thus has to describe precisely the boundaries of the risk he is selling.

Notice and knowledge

8.03 Notice and knowledge are crucially different concepts. Knowledge is what you actually know, commonly in the good faith sphere extended slightly (by another reasonable expectation presumption) to what is "within your knowledge," that is, that which you would know if you looked at the information you have in your desk, cupboard etc: see below. Notice concerns what you do *not* actually know, and often do not in the least wish to know. It was "brought to your notice" or you were "put on notice" of it, but you did not choose to know it, or failed to see it when it was under your nose. So it did not "come to your knowledge"; but—quite unlike the happier position of Dr Jowett, the one-time Master of Balliol[5]—you are deemed to have known it all the same.

The doctrine of notice is an ancient part of our law, and thus is judge-made—as are many, dare one say most, of the important underlying doctrines of English contract law. It is not any the worse for that. Judges may reasonably be expected to think a bit about the law: it is their equivalent of the carpenter's "nice bit of wood", handled often and one hopes with pleasure and appreciation. To suppose that there is something wrong with judge-made law is surely a little like finding fault with medical research which is carried out by qualified doctors. At all events, the doctrine of notice was mainly developed in the equity courts, unsurprisingly, since these tended to deal with the investment which required (and still requires) the most careful pre-contractual investigations—land. There was also, as has been seen, a parallel development in the common law courts in insurance cases, regarding the knowledge which the assured's agent had. The doctrine has been called a "subtle and difficult doctrine"[6] and so it is, in some

[5] "First come I, my name is Jowett
There's no knowledge but I know it
I am Master of this College
What I don't know isn't knowledge."

[6] Fry J. in ***Kettlewell v. Watson*** (1882) 21 Ch. D. 685.

ways, especially if one is conditioned—as we have perhaps come to be in recent decades and Fry J. was beginning to be—to expect contract law to be a matter of literalism—reading off words, like painting by numbers. But it is worth the effort. It is undoubtedly conceptual: but the concepts prove on inspection to be readily understandable and to owe a lot to common sense. See, however, below as to the confusion created by unsuitable labelling.

NOTICE: SOME LABELS AND SUBDIVISIONS—AN OVERVIEW

8.04 "Notice" is of several kinds. All of them are "penal" in the older sense of the world; that is, they all operate to the detriment of the person saddled with the unwelcome knowledge. The labels used are not entirely helpful. Judges have complained about them from time to time, with every justification. The labelling problem we have seen elsewhere is merely a matter of inadequately descriptive labels; here we have that, of course, but they are also inherently confusing. We start with the encompassing or global label: "constructive notice". This covers two categories: one is confusingly also called constructive notice; and the other is usually called imputed notice (though one sometimes finds it globally labelled, as it were, as "constructive notice"!). The global heading will be called "constructive notice (by operation of law)" and the first subdivision, "constructive (failure to investigate) notice". The second subdivision, notice through agents, will be called imputed notice.

There are other labels which crop up in this area. One is *"inferred notice"*. This is not a real category of notice at all, but a rolled-up expression, meaning a finding by the court that a person knew something because he had such compelling notice of it that the only inference is that he had actual knowledge of it. It is merely the normal operation of the power of the courts to infer a fact of any kind from indirect but compelling evidence. A person who sees and describes an event in a letter, say, may later deny it, or deny that he remembered the event the next day or next week, but the court can infer that he had actual notice of the event nonetheless. This inference may sometimes be described as inferred notice, as well as the more appropriate "inferred knowledge". It has nothing to do with constructive notice, but mention of it is included to avoid confusion. It is described by Lord Esher in *English & Scottish Mercantile Investment Co v. Brunton*[7]:

> "There is an inference of fact known to common lawyers which comes somewhat near to it. When a man has statements made to him, or has knowledge of facts, which do not expressly tell him of something which is against him, and he abstains from making further inquiry because he knows what the result would be—or,

[7] [1892] 2 Q.B. 700.

as the phrase is, he wilfully shuts his eyes"—then judges are in the habit of telling juries that they may infer that he did know what was against him. It is an inference of fact drawn because you cannot look into a man's mind, but you can infer from his conduct whether he is speaking truly or not when he says that he did not know of particular facts. There is no question of constructive notice or constructive knowledge involved in that inference; it is actual knowledge which is inferred."

(1) Constructive (failure to investigate) notice

8.05 The buyer is deemed to have done his homework ("used due diligence" is another expression) and achieved knowledge of whatever he would have learned thereby, whether or not he has in fact chosen to do his homework. Constructive notice is, as we have seen, simply *deemed knowledge* of something you do not know, but which you *ought* to have known about because you should have made inquiries. Why should you have made inquiries? Because any prudent businesslike person in your situation can be expected to have done so. You were "put on notice" by the circumstances which you had (actual) knowledge of. The expression "done his homework" is used in the subheading not because it occurs in any case (it does not) but because it seems to connote, in language we can understand, precisely the sort of reasonable diligence with which we are concerned, ie not specially wide-ranging, but simply diligence called for by the subject matter. See below as to the much lesser normal standard of diligence in "commercial" transactions.

(2) Imputed notice: the agent as conduit pipe of knowledge to the principal

8.06 This kind of notice occurs when you as principal do not have the knowledge in fact at all, but when it is known to a sufficiently general agent of yours *in the transaction* in question, and which, doing his duty, *he should have communicated to you* by the time in question. Each of these points will be explored in more detail below.

(3) Notice which is both imputed and constructive (failure to investigate)

8.07 This is knowledge of something you do not know, and your agent does not know either, but of which your agent has constructive (failure to investigate) notice as in (1) above and you have imputed constructive notice as in (2) above. The cases mostly simply rank this as "constructive notice", presumably in the global sense.

(4) Inferred actual knowledge of agent: imputed notice to principal

8.08 This is notice which leads to an inference of actual knowledge on the part of the agent which is then imputed to the principal on the usual conduit-pipe rule. This is, as has been seen, no more than an exercise of the court's normal power of inferring facts on the evidence before it; the principal is then deemed to know also, because, as we shall see, there is (with the exception only of fraud) to be no arguing about the conduit-pipe rule itself. Once it is shown that the agent had knowledge, whether actual or (within the proper limits) deemed, which had to be fed into the conduit pipe, the luckless principal has it too. The principal cannot be heard to say that the pipe was blocked and the knowledge never reached him. Again, the "conduit pipe" label is the author's: the metaphor simply seems helpful[8] in an area which remains a potential source of confusion.

(5) Actual knowledge of agent: imputed notice to principal

8.09 Where it is proved that the agent *had* actual knowledge, then (provided always he is the right kind of agent, is agent in that transaction, and the transaction imposes a duty on him to communicate the information in question to his principal) the notice is imputed to the principal also. This may seem too obvious for words, but is perhaps worth including to complete the set. One sometimes wonders if the possibility has been overlooked by those preparing cases.

Notice: un-labelled subdivisions: two senses of "another transaction"

8.10 It is worth pausing perhaps to remember that there are further subdivisions of notice which cut across the above categories and have effect in various ways.

8.11 *"Another transaction"* You may be affected with notice of something relating to *"another transaction"* in two senses. First there is "another transaction" in time: one in which you or your agent may have been involved, but which took place some time *before* the transaction you are immediately concerned with. Then, there is a transaction which is no doubt often also an earlier transaction in time, but which is additionally a transaction which took place between people who are strangers to you, and is "another transaction" in the sense that it was a transaction between strangers to your present transaction. Both are to be contrasted of course with *the kind of transaction in which you are actually engaged*, usually the purchase you are about to make or have made.

8.12 *The nature of the transaction: domestic, commercial or hybrid domestic/com-*

[8] Despite its plumbing overtones.

mercial. This classification perhaps relates mainly to the purpose, probably in the sense of "end" or "*telos*" of the transaction in question. For example, it would be unsurprising if notice in the case of guarantees differed greatly according to whether the debtor's and guarantor's purposes involved were *domestic, or hybrid domestic/commercial* or wholly *commercial*. A *Barclays Bank v. O'Brien*[9] surety will "sell" the guarantee of her husband's debts to a bank in return for the bank continuing to lend money to the husband. Her purpose is broadly domestic, while the purpose of the guaranteed husband or cohabitee is often a commercial purpose: eg to drag out the time of an ailing business against hope. Her guarantee is remunerated only by the continued loan by a bank or the like to her husband, and she is not normally paid anything by the husband, although she may no doubt expect to benefit indirectly in the future. It has features which are domestic and features which are commercial; although perhaps when questions of the wife's notice arise the domestic nature of the transaction is paramount, hence the deemed knowledge that husbands are often not very truthful to their wives about their business difficulties, and altogether too optimistic about the outcome of further or continued lending, which seems to have been underlying the House of Lords' statement in *Barclay's Bank v. O'Brien*[10] that in future lenders taking guarantees which appear detrimental to wives are to have notice of any "undue influence" by the husband, cohabitee etc. On the other hand, a purely commercial guarantee or performance bond, guaranteeing a contractor's ability to produce machinery, say, is sold to the employer as part of the obligations in the construction contract, after having been bought by the contractor from the bank or insurance company in quite a normal way, rather like an insurance policy, by the payment of a premium. One cannot envisage a successful claim to the effect that the provider was put on notice of the emotional pressure applied to the contractor by the employer, whatever the terms of the guarantee, and however much emotional pressure there may in fact have been. This may partly be that performance bonds are much less simple, one-purpose affairs, being often merely a part of a package offered by the contractor; partly also that the providers of the bond, unlike the Mrs O'Briens of this world, are not expected, and are under no moral or other pressure, to provide a bond at all except at the right price and as to a reasonably well-defined risk.

Sales of interests in land: section 199 Law of Property Act 1925

8.13 This provides in so far as material:

"(1) A purchaser[11] shall not be prejudicially affected by notice of —

[9] [1994] A.C. 180.

[10] [1994] A.C. [180].

[11] "Purchaser" means a purchaser in good faith for valuable consideration and includes a lessee, mortgagee or other person who for valuable consid-

(i) any instrument or matter capable of registration under the provisions of the Land Charges Act, 1925, or any enactment which it replaces, which is void or not enforceable as against him under that Act or enactment, by reason of the non-registration thereof;

(ii) any other **instrument** or matter or any **fact or thing unless**

(a) **it is within his own knowledge, or would have come to his knowledge if such inquiries and inspections had been made as ought reasonably to have been made by him; or**

(b) **in the same transaction with respect to which a question of notice to the purchaser arises, it has come to the knowledge of his counsel, as such, or of his solicitor or other agent, as such, or would have come to the knowledge of his solicitor or other agent, as such, if such inquiries and inspections had been made as ought reasonably to have been made by the solicitor or other agent . . .**

. . . **(3) A purchaser shall not by reason of anything in this section be affected by notice in any case where he would not have been so affected if this section had not been enacted.**"[12]

The section includes a part which is declaratory of the pre-1882 law on constructive notice (by operation of law)

8.14 The section is set out at length, because a substantial part of it is declaratory of the pre-1882 law on constructive notice (by operation of law; that is, both constructive (failure to investigate) notice and imputed notice).

The preamble to the Conveyancing Act 1882 described it as "An Act for further improving the practice of conveyancing", so it is perhaps likely that the bold-printed part of section 199 was intended to be confined to purchasers of interests in land. The marginal note to section 3 of the Conveyancing Act 1882 shows that a restriction of the existing law was intended to some extent. However, the Conveyancing Act 1882 was acknowledged to have set out the effect of the existing case law on constructive (failure to investigate) notice. See,

eration acquires an interest in property except that in Part I of [the Law of Property Act 1925] and elsewhere where so expressly provided "purchaser" only means a person who acquires an interest in or charge on property for money or money's worth; and in reference to a legal estate includes a chargee by way of legal mortgage; and where the context so requires "purchaser" includes an intending purchaser; "purchaser" has a meaning corresponding with that of "purchaser"; and "valuable consideration" includes marriage but does not include a nominal consideration in money."

This definition of "purchaser" reproduces s. 2 (viii) of the Conveyancing Act 1881, with amendments.

[12] Bold type added. The parts of the section printed in bold type are taken from the Conveyancing Act 1882.

for example, *Hunt v. Luck*[13] and *Molyneux v. Hawtrey*.[14] As regards imputed notice, it merely abolished the "recent memory" doctrine which had sprung up regarding imputed notice but which had not been part of the doctrine at its outset; and essentially accepted the other elements of the existing law regarding imputed notice, i.e. that an agent who has the requisite knowledge (which includes constructive (failure to investigate) knowledge in that transaction, has his knowledge imputed to his principal. Thereafter section 199 of the Law of Property Act 1925 made changes to the law regarding notice as regards registration of title, but retained the earlier section unchanged.

Does it matter whether section 3 of the 1882 Act was or was not confined to land?

8.15 In the light of the above, it probably does not matter for practical purposes (unless anyone were seeking seriously to revive the "recent memory" doctrine in a non-conveyancing case) whether the 1882 Act is confined to notice in the sphere of interests in land or not. Whether it is or not, we need the existing judge-made case law on constructive notice and imputed notice. The cases are necessary to explain and illustrate the 1882 and subsequent 1925 Act; just as the Sale of Goods Act 1893—another conceptual, non-literal Act—required knowledge of the nineteenth-century case law that came before it to flesh out and illustrate the principles involved.

CONSTRUCTIVE (FAILURE TO INVESTIGATE) NOTICE

The underlying duty to investigate

8.16 The duty to investigate shares certain characteristics with the fair dealing duty. The "breach" of the duty defines the area of a contract[15], but "breach" of the duty to investigate works against the buyer; while the fair-dealing duty usually works against the seller. A "breach" of the duty through, carelessness, laziness, *etc.*, brings no sanction in damages *per se*: it operates to redefine the respective obligations producing a differently defined contract from that which one had hoped.

[13] [1902] 1 Ch. 428.

[14] [1903] 2 K.B. 487. See also ***English and Scottish Mercantile Investment Company v. Brunton*** [1892] 2 Q.B. 700 affirming the doctrine of constructive (failure to investigate) notice as set out in 1841/3 in ***Jones v. Smith*** 1 Hare 61; 66 E.R. 943 and 1 Ph. 244; 41 E.R. 624.

[15] Cp. also the duty to mitigate which defines the recoverable damages.

Constructive knowledge (failure to investigate) notice

(i) Insurance

8.17 The duty varies according to the type of contract. Where there is a full duty of disclosure, like the one the buyer of insurance owes to the seller, the homework involves very little. The insurer is expected to keep in touch with "common knowledge" of which there is a greater quantity now accessible via his computer screen, than would have been available to an insurer in Lord Mansfield's day. He is expected to keep in touch also with the information which he is reasonably expected to be in touch with as the kind of insurer he is.[16]

(ii) Other sales

8.18 In the case of most other sales, for example of land, chattels, *etc.*, the buyer's duty is nearly always the less circumscribed one of taking *reasonable steps* to protect *himself* by inquiry. In the case of land he has to satisfy himself about the description as far as he can by inspecting it by himself or by a surveyor; as to the title of the owner to sell it, by making proper inquiry as to the title deeds and complaining at least about any missing link. In the case of sales of chattels, he had, even before the Sale of Goods Act 1893 to examine the chattel or the sample, where this could be done.

(iii) "Commercial" transactions which have to be concluded quickly

8.19 In these the court will tend not to assume that any particular type of inquiry is "normal". In *Manchester Trust v. Furness*[17], Lindley L.J. explained why the reasonable expectation of the buyer is different to an extent between land transactions and certain others (he was dealing with a charterparty):

> "In dealing with estates in land title is everything, and *it can be leisurely investigated*; in commercial transactions *possession is everything, and there is not time to investigate title* . . ."[18]

However, what both land and "commercial" transactions have in common is the remaining important duty on the buyer to follow up puzzling (or potentially "fishy") facts which present themselves.[19] If these are such that a normally cautious buyer would have been suspicious or puzzled by them, then any buyer will come under a duty to look into whatever it is further. In *London Joint Stock Bank v. Simmons*[20] this duty in commercial transactions was affirmed by the Court of Appeal. No doubt there will be an additional burden on an expert buyer, such as a stockbroker or financial agent, in this respect.

16 See further Chap. 4, Insurance and Surety Transactions.
17 [1895] 2 Q.B. 545.
18 Italics supplied.
19 See below, para. 8.23: puzzling facts must be followed up.
20 [1892] A.C. 221.

8.20 Lord Erskine in *Hiern v. Mill*[21] described constructive (failure to investigate) notice as the kind of notice which "from the nature of the transaction every person of ordinary prudence must have." It has been suggested towards the end of the nineteenth century that "the doctrine of constructive notice" ought not to be extended into commercial transactions: but it is evident[22] that this kind of comment meant no more than that the kind of inquiries which were normal in a "commercial" transaction would not be quite as leisurely as those which still take place in conveyancing transactions. It is not to be supposed they meant at all to suggest that puzzling features which might suggest that all was not well should not be followed up. It may be, in any case, that some of the more complex commercial "packages" developed in recent years do call for more leisurely, or at all events, more thorough, investigation.[23]

TWO KINDS OF CONSTRUCTIVE (FAILURE TO INVESTIGATE) KNOWLEDGE

8.21 There are in theory two kinds of constructive (failure to investigate) knowledge.

These are:

(1) "follow-on knowledge" where you become aware of something, some document for example, which will necessarily have an effect on your purchase, but it is unclear quite how much without making further inquiries; and

(2) "knowledge deemed through failure to investigate the puzzling facts", where you simply decide to make no inquiries or investigations, probably for fear of what you may find out if you do.

The Vice Chancellor Sir James Wigram put it as follows at first instance in *Jones v. Smith*[24]:

> "It is, indeed, scarcely possible to declare a priori what shall be deemed constructive notice, because, unquestionably, that which would not affect one man may be abundantly sufficient to affect another. But I believe I may, with sufficient accuracy for my present purpose, and without danger, assert that the cases in which constructive notice has been established, *resolve themselves into two classes:—First, cases in which the party charged has had actual notice that the property in dispute was, in act, charged, incumbered or in some way affected, and the Court thereupon bound him with constructive*

[21] (1806) 13 Ves. 114; 32 E.R. 729.

[22] See the Appendix to this chapter below.

[23] See for support for the view that the nature of the duty to investigate varies according to the kind of transaction (whether or not commercial). Millett J. *in Macmillan v. Bishopsgate Trust.* No. 3 [1995] 1WLR 978 at p. 1000 (also relying on *Barclays Banks v. O'Brien* [1994] 1 AC 180).

[24] (1841) 1 Hare 61; 66 E.R. 943.

> *notice of facts and instruments, to a knowledge of which he* ***would have been led*** *by an inquiry after the charge, incumbrance or other circumstances affecting the property of which he had actual notice; and, secondly, cases in which the Court has been satisfied from the evidence before it that the party charged had* ***designedly abstained from inquiry for the very purpose of avoiding notice.***[25]

The principles set out in *Jones v. Smith*[26] were re-affirmed by the Court of Appeal in *English & Scottish Investment Co v. Brunton.*[27] Lord Brougham, Lord Chancellor, put it without the subdivision, but essentially similarly, in *Kennedy v. Green*[28]:

> "... whatever is notice enough to excite attention, and put the party on his guard and call for inquiry, is also notice of everything to which it is afterwards found that such inquiry might have led, although all was unknown for want of the investigation."

Good faith, notice and the Sale of Goods Act 1979

8.22 *"In good faith"*. Section 61(3) Sale of Goods Act 1979 provides that a thing is deemed to be done in good faith if it is done honestly, whether or not it is done negligently. A buyer who is *not* "in good faith" will consequently have actual knowledge. This will include the kind of actual knowledge that a court may infer where the facts are such that it feels the buyer in question "must have known". "In good faith" is accordingly used here in its correct sense as a matter of English. (The phrase "I did it in good faith" is normally used to connote actual knowledge, not a breach of the good faith duties of accuracy and candour, which may happen despite perfect honesty.)

Obviously, once knowledge of a fact is proved, whether by direct evidence or by inference, that does not necessarily mean the absence of good faith in the above context. That will depend on the content of the knowledge. You have to know there is something wrong. This is not a subjective test. It does not help you that you have low standards and do not think the thing in question wrong at all. It is in effect a question of what the reasonable buyer, etc., is considered by the court to have felt. See the recent High Court of Australia case of *International Alpaca Management Pty v. Ensor*[29] also mentioned below. In this case it was pointed out that subjectively seeing nothing wrong with a proposal does not necessarily amount to honesty: there is an objective standard: and reference was made to the observations of Lord Nicholls about this objective standard in *Royal Brunei Airlines v.*

[25] Italics and bold type supplied.
[26] Above.
[27] [1892] 2 Q.B. 700.
[28] (1834) 3 My. & K. 699; 40 E.R. 266.
[29] (1995) ALR 561.

Tan.[30] ("Honesty is not an optional scale, with higher or lower values according to the moral standards of each individual . . .").

8.23 *"Without notice"*. (See sections 23, 24, and 25 Sale of goods Act 1979). There is no reason to carry over any part of the meaning of "good faith" into the separate expression "without notice". "Notice" therefore is prima facie to be taken as bearing its normal, wide meaning—constructive notice by operation of law (see above). It would thus cover imputed notice through an agent (who may have actual or constructive knowledge), and constructive (failure to investigate) knowledge of the kind regarded as appropriate for the transaction in question. No doubt since these are sales of goods not land or complex packages of personal rights, few if any investigative steps will be required in the normal case. The steps which may be required will be to follow up or inquire into circumstances which would appear "fishy" or puzzling to the normal buyer. If he fails to do so, he will be fixed with knowledge of what he would have found out if he had inquired into the puzzling facts presented to him.

It may be suggested that the bare word "notice" allows a narrower construction and should be taken as meaning only "constructive (failure to investigate) notice, excluding imputed notice. This is perhaps unlikely: there is no good reason why the buyer who uses an agent should escape a liability he would have had if he had done the transaction himself, and good public policy reasons why not.

"Without notice" was considered by Clarke J. in *Forsythe International Ltd v. Silver Shipping Ltd*[31] and in the Australian case of *International Alpaca Management Pty Ltd v. Ensor.*[32] Both courts relied on the statement of Neill J. in *Feuer Leather Corp v. Frank Johnstone & Sons*[33]:

> "For the purpose the court is concerned with actual notice and not with constructive notice."

Neill J. went on to state what a buyer did not have to do:

> "the court will not expect the recipient of goods to scrutinise commercial documents such as delivery notes with great care; (e) there is no general duty on a buyer of goods in an ordinary commercial transaction to make inquiries as to the right of the seller to dispose of the goods."

Neill J. in turn had founded himself on the judgment of Lindley L.J. in *Manchester Trust v. Furness*[34]. See also the earlier House of Lords case of *London Joint Stock Bank v. Simmons.*[35] Both Neill J.'s guidelines are in fact consistent with what is said in the text of this chapter, with *London Joint Stock Bank v. Simmons* (above) and with Lindley L.J.'s judgment interpreted in the light of *London Joint Stock Bank v. Simmons.* It would be wrong to take the futher step of assuming that, for

[30] [1995] 2 AC 378.
[31] [1994] 1 WLR 1334.
[32] (1995) ALR 561.
[33] [1981] Com L.R. 251.
[34] [1895] 2 Q.B. 39, noted at para. 8.112.
[35] [1892] A.C. 201, noted at para. 8.110.

example, the *Feuer Leather* case justifies the proposition that *no* duty to follow up puzzling facts exists in "commercial" as in other cases; or to suppose that in appropriate cases—complex transactions which would normally be investigated—there is not a duty to investigate and a corresponding risk of being fixed with constructive (failure to investigate) notice. The duty to investigate/scrutinise documents in minute detail is by no means to be expected of the buyer in an "ordinary commercial transaction" such as a sale of leather. That is all.[36]

The duty to investigate

(1) Normal diligence must be exercised before a contract

8.24 As has been said, the purchase calling most for diligent research is perhaps the purchase of land. In *Parker v. Brooke*[37] a purchaser who saw a deed was fixed with notice of a trust which was mentioned in the recitals to the deed, even though he had not looked at the trust deed. In *Taylor v. Stibbert*[38] a purchaser of land who knew that there were tenants on the land was held bound to enquire into the interests they had, and was thus fixed with knowledge of the interests they in fact had.

Similarly, in *Daniels v. Davidson*[39] Lord Eldon held that the purchaser of a public house who knew it was leased was deemed to know (because he should have enquired about) all the rights the tenant happened to have under an agreement with the landlord. This was particularly unfortunate for the purchaser, since it meant he was fixed with knowledge of an agreement the tenant had to buy the public house from the landlord.

Puzzling facts must be followed up

8.25 See *Kennedy v. Green*[40]. Here, the purchaser from the fraudulent agent would have been fixed with notice of the true state of affairs (but for the fraud) because his solicitor had failed to follow up the curious look of the mortgage discharge in question. Among other things, it had had a big blank space which could have been filled up by the holder in any manner he chose, and like a carelessly drawn cheque with extra writing in the gap, was "a circumstance to excite the greatest, the most jealous suspicion."

It is no excuse that the real facts prove to have been different from that of which the purchaser had notice. The purchaser should inquire

[36] See for a case where fobbing off by giving a reasonable answer to a query displaced the duty, *Greer v. Downs Supply Co* [1927] 2 KB 28.
[37] (1804) 9 Ves. 583; 32 E.R. 729.
[38] (1794) 2 Ves 437, 30 E.R. 713.
[39] (1809) 16 Ves. 249; 33 E.R. 978.
[40] (1834) 3 My. & K. 699; 40 E.R. 266, noted at para. 8.74.

into *any* puzzling facts which could indicate a problem with his purchase. In *Taylor v. Baker*[41] below the purchaser had notice of a judgment affecting the land, but in fact what affected the land proved to be a mortgage. This provided no excuse for him. He was fixed with knowledge of the mortgage.

(3) Problems which common or local knowledge shows exist in the particular subject matter may need to be followed up

8.26 This duty may arise out of common knowledge. Sir James refers, in *Jones v. Smith*[42] to a case named *Whitbread v. Jordan*[43] in which the buyer was fixed with notice of the common knowledge that public house tenants often gave mortgages to brewers. The buyer did not check and was fixed with a brewer's mortgage. It may be that the constructive notice of undue influence by husbands on wives which is now attributed to banks following *Barclay's Bank v. O'Brien*[44] is of this type.[45] Desperate spouses do not always tell the truth about their failing businesses to their wives/husbands; perhaps this statement, viewed simply as common knowledge, could provide a more rational basis of the constructive notice doctrine there described (perhaps not quite accurately) as a possible extension of the doctrine of constructive notice.

The limits of the duty to investigate

(1) Where reasonable diligence would not have found out the problem

8.27 In this case the buyer is safe. In *Jones v. Powles*[46] the Master of the Rolls absolved the buyer from the consequences of breach of the duty. The vendor had been in possession for a long time under a forged will; but "no reasonable diligence could have led to a discovery of the forgery." He was allowed to keep his purchase.

(2) Where inquiry has been made and the buyer has been fobbed off with a reasonable excuse

8.28 The buyer is also safe in these circumstances. A breach by the seller of the good faith rules may also have the effect of narrowing the ambit of the buyer's due diligence.[47]

[41] (1818) 5 Price 306; 146 E.R. 616.
[42] (1841) above.
[43] 1 You. & Col. 303.
[44] [1994] 1 A.C. 180.
[45] See the section on Third Parties in Chap. 9, Dealings with the Vulnerable Buyer Or Seller.
[46] (1834) 3 M. & K. 581; 40 E.R. 222.
[47] See below: The Duty of the Seller to deal fairly, as to both at para. 8.31 *et seq*.

What is a reasonable excuse?

8.29 The point, which was made clearer in a case of Sir James Wigram's, was that the buyer could accept the vendor's say-so in cases where the instrument or thing *might*, but would not *necessarily* affect his ownership. This developed into a formal rule over time. A marriage settlement obviously might affect any of a husband's property, but equally might not affect any particular property. The problem was, as explained by Sir James Wigram in *West v. Reid*,[48] that a line had to be drawn somewhere, else the buyer would be affected by constructive notice "of the contents of every instrument of the mere existence of which he has notice." In *West v. Reid*[49] the insurance office was also absolved from the accusation of notice of an assignment merely from the fact that all correspondence was directed to the solicitors for certain lenders to the owner of the policy, and all premiums were paid by them; these facts might, or might not, indicate a change of ownership of the policy. The reasonable excuse must be made in response to a question which is a reasonable question for the buyer to ask.[50]

(3) The buyer does not have to form the *right* view about ambiguous expressions in documents he does search.

8.30 See *Cordwell v. Mackrill*[51] below.

The Duty of the Seller to deal fairly

(1) Fobbing off inquiries, lulling buyer into sense of false security, ***etc.***

8.31 As we have already seen, the seller has a duty of candour and accuracy in speech and conduct. To say that he does not *have to* speak at all is no doubt right, but, in the real world, about as unhelpful as saying you can walk from London to Rome. You can, but few do. The non-speaking seller would not achieve many sales. So the seller has to deal fairly in what he says and does, and he usually does say and do things. A breach of his duty of fair dealing by the seller can affect the buyer's duty of due diligence in two ways. First, although the buyer has to be diligent, the seller must not put the buyer off the scent or mislead him in any way. If he does lull the buyer into a sense of false security in any way, the buyer who does not in fact enquire further into the subject matter of the falsely reassuring statement is normally deemed to have *relied on* the comforting words of the seller

[48] (1843) 2 Hare 249; 67 E.R. 104.
[49] *Ibid.*
[50] See ***Oliver v. Hinton*** [1899] 2 Ch. 264.
[51] (1765) 2 Eden. 344; 28 E.R. 930.

and been deflected from his own enquiries (whether or not this is in fact the case).[52]

In *Jones v. Smith*[53] the lender asked about whether the man's marriage settlement affected the security to be given, and was *told it did not*. He was held not to have notice even though it might have been *more* prudent to check up by looking at the settlement. The Vice-Chancellor emphasised that the buyer did not have to gain high marks, as it were, in a prudence test: he had to show himself to have been reasonably cautious.[54]

The silent vendor: fobbing off by misleading silence

8.32 The seller (and his agent) has to watch the quality of his silences in the presence of the buyer (and his agent). He must not—even by gesture, facial expressions, or whatever, encourage mistaken ideas of the buyer. *Smith v. Hughes*,[55] a pre Sale of Goods Act 1893 case which is often cited as showing that there is no "original" duty of disclosure on the part of the seller,[56] is in fact much more interesting for the way it explains how careful the seller must be not to mislead by speech *or conduct*. In that case Cockburn C.J. said:

> "If, indeed, the buyer, instead of acting on his own opinion, had asked the question whether the oats were old or new, or had said anything which *intimated his understanding that the seller was selling the oats as old oats, the case would have been wholly different*; or even *if he had said anything which shewed that he was not acting on his own inspection and judgment, but assumed as the foundation of the contract that the oats were old*, the silence of the seller, as a means of misleading him, might have amounted to a fraudulent concealment, such as would have entitled the buyer to avoid the contract." . . .[57]

"Acting on his own inspection and judgment" is reminiscent, of course, of the later wording of the Sale of Goods Act 1893, and shows the essentially good faith basis of the Act.

Fobbing off need not only be by silence with knowledge of the buyer's mistaken belief. There may be a representation *by certain acts in themselves*, which requires specifically to be *corrected by something said*. In *Re Valletort Laundry*[58] the act of a company director in depositing the company's title deeds with the bank was taken as an indication to the bank that he/the company had power to charge the property. See also Jessel M.R. in *Patman v. Harland*[59] on the representation made

[52] See the cases referred to at para. 5.31 *et seq.*, in Chap. 5, Sale of Land.
[53] (1841) 1 Hare 61; 66 E.R. 943.
[54] See also, *e.g.* ***Oliver v. Hinton*** [1899] 2 Ch. 264.
[55] (1871) L.R. 6 Q.B. 597.
[56] Which is true, but only as far as it goes: see Chap. 5, Sale of Land.
[57] Italics supplied.
[58] [1903] 2 Ch. 654.
[59] (1881) 17 Ch. D. 353.

by delivering an abstract of title without more, namely that it contains everything relevant to the title.

(2) A breach by the seller of the fair dealing rules narrows the buyer's duty to investigate accordingly.

8.33 The effect where the seller has failed in his duty, for example where a seller of land has failed in his duty of accuracy or has referred to some document without giving a fair opportunity to the buyer to look at it, is to narrow the buyer's duty to investigate so that it encompasses only that which has been plainly and accurately disclosed.

Caveat emptor, means, as we have seen, and as a Latin dictionary will tell us, Let the buyer take care, do his homework, be diligent. In answer to the notional buyer's question, But how diligent must I be?, the answer is[60] "The standard is that of the reasonable (sometimes the reasonably prudent) buyer, of the kind to be anticipated as buyer of that property, in the actual circumstances which happened." The court looks at what the buyer was told, and given to understand, and what correspondence and documents he had to form a judgement upon before the sale. If we are looking at information revealed at, say, an auction sale, the court will put itself into the shoes of the kind of buyer to be expected and ask itself whether he could have been expected to find out the defect in question, as a reasonably prudent buyer, at that sale. If he is found to fall short of what the reasonable buyer or inquiring party of the kind to be expected would have done, he is not permitted to profit from his own carelessness. He is assumed[61] to have done as much homework as he wanted to, and thereafter deliberately decided to take a risk on himself of whatever it was about the purchase that he did not investigate.

8.34 However, it is obviously unfair to impose a duty to investigate on the buyer when the scope of the contract itself would have been limited by the vendor's breach of the good faith rules to that which was properly described. Thus, the buyer's duty shrinks accordingly.

In *Hyde v. Warden*[62] the Court of Appeal limited the constructive notice that the purchaser had under an agreement for the grant of an underlease to those provisions of the original lease which he had *a fair opportunity of ascertaining.*

In *James v. Lichfield*,[63] on the other hand, the result for the purchaser was the exact opposite, because the purchaser had already come under a duty to follow up something which was necessarily a problem whose extent he was obliged to ascertain. This was because no question of lack of fair dealing by the vendor had arisen. The buyer knew there were tenancies, he omitted to inquire from them what their

[60] See Chap. 5, Sale of Land.
[61] See above para 8.01.
[62] (1877) 3 Ex D. 72.
[63] (1869) L.R. 9 Eq. 51.

rights were and was thus fixed with the whole extent of their actual interest.[64]

Notice and Registration of Title

8.35 Registration has been with us for longer than one might suppose. In the time of Queen Anne, an act was brought in requiring registration of deeds in the county of Middlesex: see *Le Neve v. Le Neve*.[65] In this case, Lord Hardwicke held that the doctrine of notice prevented registration of a later right taking precedence over an earlier one, when the owner of the later right knew or was deemed to know of the earlier one. A husband had resettled on his second wife property which he had earlier settled on his first wife and her children. The second transaction was registered but not the first. Lord Hardwicke said:

> "The operation of both acts of Parliament and construction of them is the same; and it would be a most mischievous thing, if a person taking that advantage of the legal form appointed by an act of Parliament, might under that protect himself against a person who had a prior equity of which he had notice ... The ground of it is plainly this. That the taking of a legal estate after notice of a prior right, makes a person *mala fide* purchaser; and not, that he is not a purchaser for a valuable consideration in every other respect. This is a species of fraud and *dolus malus* itself; for he knew the first purchaser had the clear right of the estate, and after knowing that, he takes away the right of another person by getting in the legal estate."

A similar approach was taken in *Sheldon v. Cox*[66] where the notice was imputed through the agent. Lord Northington, Lord Chancellor, commented that:

> "There is no difference between personal and constructive notice in its consequences, except as to guilt; if there was it would be very inconvenient; and notice would be avoided in every case, by employing an agent."

8.36 The above were cases respectively of actual and imputed knowledge. The impact of registration on constructive (failure to investigate) notice is something quite different. On this see *Agra Bank v. Barry*[67] in which the equitable mortgage in question had been registered at the Irish Land Registry, and the whole question of registration

[64] See also ***Re White & Smith's Contract*** [1896] Ch. 637; *Greenwood v. Leather Shod Wheel* [1900] 1 Ch. 421; ***Molyneux v. Hawtrey*** [1903] 2 K.B. 487; *In re Haedicke & Lipski's Contract* [1901] 1 Ch. 666; ***Lee v. Rayson*** [1917] 1 Ch. 613 and ***Flexman v. Corbett*** [1930] 1 Ch. 672.

[65] (1747) Amb. 436; 27 E.R. 291.

[66] (1764) Amb. 624; 27 E.R. 404.

[67] (1874) L.R. 7 H.L. 135.

and constructive (failure to investigate) notice was discussed fully and thoughtfully. As Lord Hatherley put, it it would be:

> "extraordinary to give priority to someone who had been careless enough not to register, against someone taking a subsequent instrument, although that person had neither himself, or through his solicitor, the slightest actual knowledge of the previous transaction . . ."

Lord Selborne felt it would be quite inconsistent with the policy of the Irish Register Act:

> "to hold that a purchaser or mortgagee is under any obligation to make any inquiries with a view to the discovery of unregistered interests. But it is quite consistent with that, that if he or his agent actually knows of the existence of such unregistered instruments when he takes his own deed, he may be estopped in equity from saying that, as to him, they are fraudulent."

8.37 Thus, it will be seen that there is a distinction for this purpose between *constructive (failure to investigate) knowledge*, which *cannot* be held against a later owner where the Register shows nothing relevant; and *actual knowledge* of the owner or of his agent, which can prevent reliance on the Register where there is knowledge. A case of actual knowledge preventing reliance on the Land Registration Act 1925, is the decision of Dillon J in *Lyus v. Prowsa Developments*[68]. Dillon J. was at pains to point out that his decision was not that it was fraud to rely on rights given by the Land Registration Act, but[69] that the fraud consisted in:

> "the first defendant reneging on a positive stipulation in favour of the plaintiffs in the bargain under which the first defendant acquired the land. That makes, as it seems to me, all the difference. It has long since been held, for instance, in *Rochefoucauld v. Boustead*[70] that the provisions of the Statute of Frauds 1677 . . . now incorporated in certain sections of the Law of Property Act 1925, cannot be used as an instrument of fraud, and that it is fraud for a person to whom land is agreed to be conveyed as trustee for another to deny the trust and relying on the terms of the statute to claim the land for himself . . .
>
> It seems to me that the same considerations are applicable in relation to the Land Registration Act 1925. If, for instance, the agreement . . . had expressly stated that the first defendant would hold Plot 29 upon trust to give effect . . . to the plaintiffs' agreement with the vendor company, it would be difficult to say that that express trust was overreached and rendered nugatory by the Land Registration Act 1925."

[68] [1982] 1 W.L.R. 1044.
[69] Echoing Lord Hardwicke in many ways.
[70] [1897] 1 Ch. 196.

IMPUTED (AGENTS') NOTICE

8.38 First, here is a nutshell description of the doctrine of imputed notice by the Lord Chancellor in *Wylie v. Pollen*[71]:

> "To affect the principal with notice, the agent's knowledge must have been derived in the particular transaction in hand, or be shewn to have been in that transaction present to his mind: and, further, it must have been knowledge of something material to the particular transaction, and something which it was the agent's duty to communicate to his principal . . .".

Affecting the principal with notice: The conduit pipe

8.39 As has been seen above, the transmission along the conduit pipe between agent and principal is automatic. Lord Hatherley in *Rolland v. Hart*[72] said:

> "It has been held over and over again that notice to a solicitor of a transaction and about a matter as to which it is part of his duty to inform himself, is actual notice to the client. *Mankind would not be safe if it were held that, under such circumstances, a man has not notice of that which his agent has actual notice of*. The purchaser of an estate has, in ordinary cases, no personal knowledge of the title, but employs a solicitor, and can never be allowed to say that he knew nothing of some prior incumbrance because he was not told of it by his solicitor.[73]
>
> "It cannot be left to the possibility or the impossibility of the man who seeks to affect you with notice being able to prove that your solicitor did his duty in communicating to you that which, according to the terms of your employment of him, was the very thing which you employed him to ascertain."

Or again, as Fry J, put it in *Kettlewell v. Watson*[74]

> "[the court] will not receive evidence whether the agent recollected the fact at the time or whether he communicated it to his principal. It deals with those matters by way of irrebuttable presumption when the circumstances are known."

The questions are consequently about what knowledge on the part of the agent goes into the pipe, who counts as an agent and when the deemed knowledge is deemed to arrive at the principal's end.

[71] (1863) 3 De. G. J. & Sm. 596; 46 E.R. 767.
[72] (1871) L.R. 6 Ch. App. 678.
[73] Italics supplied.
[74] (1882) 21 Ch. D. 709.

What knowledge is transmitted to the principal by the agent?

8.40 The agent's knowledge which is transmitted may be actual knowledge or constructive (failure to investigate) knowledge. Indeed, rather more cases of constructive notice are cases of imputed constructive notice than otherwise; that is, they relate to something not followed up, *etc.*, by the agent, not the principal himself. The knowledge imputed may be either knowledge which is derived (or "ought" to have been derived) from his acting in the particular transaction, or knowledge which he had before, but which is shown (that is, specifically proved) to have been present to his mind during the transaction[75] cited above). However, as to interests in land, note the restriction placed (rightly or wrongly) on the agent's knowledge by the Court of Appeal in *Halifax Building Society v. Stepsky*[76]: the expression "come to his knowledge" was construed so as to exclude any knowledge which was not derived for the first time from the transaction.[77]

The fraud exception

8.41 Fraud is deemed not to be transmitted to the principal by the agent. The rationale of this is the moderately common sense one that "He wouldn't tell him of his own fraud, would he;" but no doubt there is also an underlying feeling that it would be unfair to the innocent principal to saddle with him with deemed knowledge of his agent's fraud[78]. The Vice-Chancellor, in *Espin v. Pemberton* (1859)[79] put it this way:

> "... the commission of the fraud broke off the relation of principal and agent, or was beyond the scope of the authority, and therefore it prevented the possibility of imputing knowledge of the agent to his principal."

In *Kennedy v. Green*[80] Lord Brougham, Lord Chancellor, said:

> "Bostock was acting as Mr. Kirby's solicitor in the transaction, and although, generally speaking, the knowledge obtained by a man's attorney or agent fixes himself, if obtained while so employed, and on the same business ... yet it cannot here be said that Mr. Kirby is fixed with all which Bostock knew. For the fraud, practised by Bostock upon Mr. Kirby himself, was of course concealed from him ... and, therefore, I think we cannot, on this account alone, fix his client, Mr. Kirby ... with the know-

[75] See ***Wylie v. Pollen*** (1863) 3 De G. J. & Sm. 596; 46 E.R. 767.
[76] [1996] Ch. 207.
[77] Itself perhaps rather narrowly defined: see Appendix below.
[78] See ***Kennedy v. Green*** (1834) 3 My & K. 699; 40 E.R. 266; *Thompson v. Cartwright* (1863) 33 Beav. 178; 55 E.R. 335 and ***Cave v. Cave*** (1880) 15 Ch. D. 639 (all below) and *Armstrong v. Strain* [1952] 1 KB 232.
[79] (1859) 3 De G. & J. 547; 44 E.R. 1380. See also ***Re Hampshire Land*** [1896] 2 Ch. 743; *Belmont Finance Corporation Ltd v. Williams Furniture* Ltd [1979] Ch. 250; and *Houghton & Co*, v. *Nothard, Lowe & Wills* [1928] A.C. 1.
[80] (1834) above.

> ledge of his criminal proceedings. We must lay out of our view all the knowledge, the actual and full knowledge he had of his own fraud, and are not to hold Mr. Kirby as cognisant—I mean of course cognisant in law and constructively—of that, merely because his solicitor himself, the contriver, the actor, and the gainer of the transaction, knew it all well."

The fraud exception was affirmed by the Court of Appeal in regard to the codified duty to disclose in insurance cases arising under sections 18 and 19 of the Marine Insurance Act 1906.[81]

When is the knowledge deemed to arrive at the principal's end of things?

8.42 The answer to this is, when the "ordinary channels of intelligence in use" in the type of transaction concerned would have delivered the knowledge. See *Proudfoot v. Montefiore*[82] in which the owner was not allowed to take advantage of a specially slower than normal procedure used by his agent. In that case, an insurance disclosure case, the ordinary channels were those in use "in the mercantile world".

The same transaction: limitation of scope of knowledge deemed to be transmitted

8.43 The knowledge of the agent, to be imputed to the principal, must be *in the same transaction, and relating to the transaction*. In *Worsley v. the Earl of Scarborough*[83] the Lord Chancellor said *inter alia*:

> "It is settled, that notice to an agent or counsel *who was employed in the thing by another person, or in another business,* ***and*** *at another time, is no notice to his client,* who employs him afterwards; and it would be very mischievous if it was so, for the man of most practice and greatest eminence would then be the most dangerous to employ."[84]

In *Warrick v. Warrick*[85] Lord Hardwicke, Lord Chancellor also considered that (with the possible exception of cases where the agent acted for both mortgagor and mortgagee) the agent's knowledge had to be in the current transaction, and "relative to" it. He said:

> "It would be a pretty harsh thing to affect the lender of the money with all kind of knowledge which the agent may have of the title of the borrower; but still I will not lay it down as a general rule, that where the same person is concerned for the mortgagor and

[81] See *PCW Syndicates v. PCW Reinsurers* [1996] 1 All E.R. 774 and *Deutsche Ruckversicherung AG v. Walbrook Insurance Co. Ltd* [1996] 1 All E.R. 791.
[82] (1867) L.R. 2 Q.B. 511.
[83] (1746) 3 Atk. 392; 26 E.R. 1025.
[84] Italics in original.
[85] (1745) 3 Atk. 291; 26 E.R. 970.

mortgagee, that notice to such person will not be good constructive notice to the mortgagee.

But consider what kind of notice the defendant ... had: Mr Hawkins *had not notice at the time of the assignment, nor relative to this business, but before; even before the original mortgage ...*"[86]

When does "the transaction" begin?

8.44 The relationship of agency must first be constituted. Sir John Leach in *Mountford v. Scott*[87] said:

> "The agent stands in place of the principal; and notice therefore to the agent is notice to the principal; but he cannot stand in the place of the principal until the relation of principal and agent is constituted ..."

This relationship cannot be inferred but must be proved. In *Espin v. Pemberton*[88] the Lord Chancellor said:

> "I find it very difficult to accede to the proposition, however high may be the authority from which it proceed, that where a mortgagor is himself a solicitor, and prepares the mortgage deed, the mortgagor employing no other solicitor, the mortgagor must be considered to be the agent or solicitor of the mortgagee in the transaction. I think that there ought to be some consent on the part of the mortgagee to constitute this relation between them ..."

Agents for two parties to a transaction

8.45 The principles of imputed notice apply, of course, where there are two principals and one joint agent. What is unclear is quite how this operates in the early period, given that the instructions may not be given simultaneously. In *Fuller v. Benett*[89] the Vice-Chancellor noted that there was no dispute:

> "first that notice to the solicitor is notice to the client; secondly, that where a purchaser employs the same solicitor as the vendor he is affected with notice of whatever that solicitor had notice of in his capacity of solicitor for either vendor or purchaser in the transaction in which he is so employed; and thirdly, that the notice to the solicitor, which alone will bind the client, must be notice in that transaction in which the client employs him."

The Vice Chancellor also thought that in such a case:

> "a purchaser may be affected with notice of what the solicitor knew as solicitor for the vendor, although, as solicitor for the

[86] Italics supplied.
[87] (1818) 3 Madd. 34; 56 E.R. 422.
[88] (1859) 3 De G. & J. 547; 44 E.R. 1380.
[89] (1843) 2 Hare 405; 67 E.R. 162.

> vendor, he may have acquired his knowledge before he was retained by the purchaser."

It is unclear how far we may rely on this dictum, since the case itself is tainted by its reliance on the now outmoded (and in the case of land, overruled by statute) doctrine of "recent memory". However, Lord Hardwicke may have suggested something not dissimilar, in the case of *Warrick v. Warrick*[90]

> "but still I will not lay it down as a general rule, that where the same person is concerned for the mortgagor and mortgagee, that notice to such person will not be good constructive notice to the mortgagee."

In any case, it may well be that in such a transaction there is an implied consent by both, for practical reasons, to the relation back of all relevant knowledge between the agent and both principals, regardless of the exact date when each principal instructed the joint agent.[91]

When does the agency end?

8.46 It is perhaps not impossible for there to be circumstances in which an ex-agent is nonetheless a proper recipient of knowledge: in *Yasuda Fire & Marine Insurance v. Orion Marine Insurance*[92] Colman J. pointed out that an agency relationship need not arise by contract only, and may have obligations which continue after any contract is at an end.

The right kind of agent

8.47 Lord Halsbury in *Blackburn, Low v. Vigors*[93] said:

> "Some agents so far represent the principal that in all respects their acts and intentions and their knowledge may truly be said to be the acts, intentions, and knowledge of the principal. Other agents may have so limited and narrow an authority both in fact and in the common understanding of their form of employment that it would be quite inaccurate to say that such an agent's knowledge or intentions are the knowledge or intentions of his principal . . ."

The expression an "agent to know" has also been used in the case and has been taken up since. It is perhaps unhelpful, since the expression contains the question rather than the answer. However, it is helpful to consider Lord Halsbury's exclusion, for purposes of notice, of agents who have "so narrow and limited an authority both in fact and in the common understanding of their employment". Consideration of this phrase yields the idea that an agent must be reasonably expected

[90] (1745) above. See the passage quoted above.
[91] See however ***Halifax Building Society v. Stepsky*** [1996] Ch. 207; but the court did not have the opportunity of hearing full argument on the point.
[92] [1995] 2 Q.B. 174.
[93] (1887) 12 App. Cas. 531.

to be a part of the principal's business organisation, in some sense, *for the particular job* in which notice is given. For example, a barrister may have a plumber in his chambers installing central heating. The plumber would not be right person to receive notice of a legal matter; the barrister's clerk would. On the other hand, the plumber *would be* the right person to receive notice of some new regulation or requirement affecting heating installations in the area of the chambers, let us say. He is to be seen as a part of the barrister's organisation, his structure with which he confronts the world, as far as the heating project is concerned. Similarly the clerk is a part of his business structure for most purposes to do with his business as a barrister.

Agents who are employed for purely administrative tasks

8.48 Agents the scope of whose employment is restricted to purely administrative tasks, such as arranging for a deed to be executed, or drawing up (but not advising upon) a deed or the like form an exception from the class of agents whose knowledge may be imputed to the principal. In *Wylie v. Pollen*[94] solicitors entrusted with the execution of a deed were held to have no duty to communicate their knowledge relative to the transaction. In the cases of *In re Marseilles Extension Railway Company*[95] and *Kettlewell v. Watson*[96] the mere preparation of a deed was held not to give rise to any duty to pass on information.

The agent must have a duty to communicate the fact in question to the principal

8.49 This is simply shorthand for "he must have a duty to *investigate and communicate* the results to his principal. Another way of putting it is no doubt, *what is his job,* or what is he agent *to do*?[97] Clearly the fact of employing an agent is not going to widen the principal's duty to investigate, just as it normally will not narrow it either; they are part of the same organisation as far as the world is concerned. Thus, where neither principal nor agent have a duty to investigate, but the agent finds out something extraneous to his task, this is not imputed to the principal, because there is no reasonable expectation that it would be found out in the first place; it was not part of his job. Everything which the agent has a duty to investigate he has a duty to pass on, and is deemed to pass on.[98] As to the irrebuttable presumption see *Blackburn Law v. Vigors.* A simple approach might be to ask whether the principal (supposing him to have been acting for himself and had the expertise) would have been under a duty to find out the information in question. If so, the agent will have had the same duty, followed inevitably by the duty to pass it on.

[94] (1863) 3 De G.J. & Sm. 596; 46 E.R. 767.
[95] (1871) L.R. 7 Ch. App. 161.
[96] (1882) 21 Ch. D. 709.
[97] (1887) 12 App. Cas. 531.
[98] See para. 8.37 above.

Receiving notice and deciding upon acts

8.50 The fact that the agent is not the directing mind and will of the business does not matter in the least: he is a part of the structure of it. There would be a legitimate complaint if a message left with a part of the business reasonably expected to be taking messages had not reached the directing mind of the business. The directing mind is deemed to have notice of the message. Thus, it will be seen that there is a lesser degree of control necessary for receipt of knowledge from the outside, world than there is in cases where an actual or deemed act of the business in a positive sense is concerned.[99] There, considerations about the directing mind and will may well be relevant. It is hard to see how they can be relevant to the *receipt* of information by an agent. Again, it is a matter of reasonable expectation: we expect that decisions, or at least, decisions which go beyond the purely administrative such as how much copier paper to order, will be made by the directing mind and willed by the directing will. See further below under the section regarding incorporated bodies.

Does the agent need to be expressly authorised in fact to receive notices?

8.51 There may be a suggestion of this in Hoffmann L.J.'s judgment in *El Ajou v. Dollar Holdings*[99a], but he also seems to recognise that there may be ostensible authority. There is also a reference in the earlier case of *Re Hampshire Land*[99b] to a "duty imposed on him by the company . . . to receive the notice". However, the latter passage occurs while Vaughan Williams J. is attempting to summarise the effect of the yet earlier Court of Appeal case of *Re Marseilles Extension Railway*[1] and there is no trace of such an idea there, the emphasis being merely on the need to find out what task the agent was employed to carry out (the inference being, that he would normally be a proper recipient of notice of any kind in the course of that task). The likely answer, therefore, to the question above, is No, the agent in charge of the task (and his business organisation) may be taken to be a potential recipient of knowledge relating to his task, during the carrying out of his task, and it does not need some extra step to have happened authorising him, as it were, to open his communication channels to the outside world.

The sub-purchaser with notice who buys from a purchaser without notice: redemptive effect passed on

8.52 A purchaser in good faith and without notice of incumbrances has the effect of "cleansing" any sale on by him to a further purchaser,

[99] See *Hadenfayre v. British National Insurance* [1984] 2 Lloyd's Rep. 393 where the notice was simply a telephone message to the insurer's office.
[99a] (1994) 2 All E.R. 685.
[99b] [1896] 2 Ch. 743.
[1] (1871) L.R. 7 Ch. App. 161.

even if that purchaser has notice of the incumbrance or other defect in question. In *Lowther v. Carlton*[2] the reason for this rule was said to be simply a common sense one, that one could not "clog up" the sale of estates for ever.

The extent of notice: is the burden of notice as heavy for the person who takes something with notice as it would have been for his vendor?

8.53 The historically correct answer to this is certainly yes. Consider *Lowther v. Carlton*[3], *Earl Brook v. Bulkeley*[4] *Taylor v. Stibbert*[5] and the essentially public policy reasons for this. There are recent Court of Appeal decisions which appear to be to the contrary in the area of dealings with the vulnerable, to the extent at least that the person with notice is seen to have a lesser burden if he wants to *displace* the vulnerability than the original "undue influencer" would have had.[6] In these it was thought sufficient for the banks which had constructive notice of the possibility of undue influence by the husband simply to arrange for a solicitor to advise the wife and explain the nature and effect of the charge. This would be insufficient to displace the effect of the undue influence if the same steps had been taken by the husband[7]. It is right to say that cases such as *Tate v. Williamson*[8] were not cited to the court in any of the above decisions; and one may wonder if the decision, for example, in *Banco Exterior v. Mann*[9] would have been more in line with the dissenting judgment of Hobhouse L.J. had they been. Hobhouse L.J. clearly envisaged that the position of the bank would be no different, as regards displacing the vulnerability, from the position of the husband. Hobhouse L.J. said of the bank's steps:

> "No steps might be taken to ensure that the wife was signing the document as a result of the free exercise of her own will and not subject to any undue influence of the husband. . . . The steps taken by the bank simply did not address that aspect at all, which is *of the essence of the rebuttal of the presumption of undue influence.*"[10]

Bodies corporate—knowledge

8.54 Incorporated bodies, being abstractions, act through the agency of individuals. Cases on the knowledge or states of mind of various

[2] (1741) 2 Atk. 242; 26 E.R. 549.
[3] (1741) above.
[4] (1754) 2 Ves. 498; 28 E.R. 319.
[5] (1794) 2 Ves. 437; 30 E.R. 713.
[6] See *Bank of Baroda v. Shah* [1988] 3 All E.R. 24; *Massey v. Midland Bank* [1995] 1 All E.R. 929; and *Banco Exterior v. Mann* [1995] 1 All E.R. 936.
[7] See Chap. 9 Dealings with the Vulnerable Buyer or Seller.
[8] (1866) L.R. 2 Ch. App. 55 ref, and see Chap. 9, Dealings with the Vulnerable Buyer or Seller.
[9] above.
[10] Italics supplied.

kinds on the part of companies prove on analysis to concern two distinct kinds of state of mind:

(1) the knowledge required to do a positive act of some kind; and

(2) the kind of (relatively passive) knowledge which is gained when information is received.

Sometimes, of course, the kind of knowledge required may be both, as in *Meridian Global Securities v. Exchange Commission*[11] where the obligation to perform an act arose only after acquiring a particular kind of knowledge.

"Actual" or "anthropomorphic" knowledge

8.55 This is a species of quasi-individual knowledge. It occurs in cases where there is some provision applying to individuals, and it is felt that it ought to apply in a similar sort of way to a company. By a kind of fiction, therefore, acts which are done by a director or other agent of the company who may be seen to rank as the appropriate person for the company to have appointed to do the act or make the decision etc in question, are described as acts done with the "actual knowledge" of the company or in a quasi-individual sense, by the company. Metaphors abound in this area, the usefulness of which have been doubted, not without justification, by Lord Reid in *Tesco Supermarkets v. Nattrass*[12], Hoffmann L.J. in *El Ajou v. Dollar Holdings*[13] and Staughton L.J. in *PCW Syndicate v. PCS Reinsurers*[14]. An example of this kind of knowledge is *Lennard's Carrying Co Ltd v. Asiatic Petroleum Co Ltd*[15] in which a Mr Lennard was found to be sufficiently the "active spirit" of the company, or its "directing mind and will" to make the company liable in a sense which had some parity with the sense in which an individual would be liable. Further examples are *HMS Truculent, The Admiralty v. The Divina* (Owners)[16] and *The Lady Gwendolen*[17], *Tesco Supermarkets v. Nattrass*[18] *Tesco Stores v. Brent London Borough Council* (both similar cases)[19] *Re Supply of Ready-Mixed Concrete (No. 2)*[20], and to an extent, *Meridian Global v. Securities Commission*[21] all noted in the Appendix to this Chapter below. These have been noted although they do not strictly concern constructive notice, because it is as well to be clear that these cases are in something of a special class of their own, and do *not* affect the normal imputation of knowledge between principal and agent.

[11] [1995] 2 A.C. 500.
[12] [1972] 2 A.C. 153.
[13] [1994] 2 All E.R. 685.
[14] [1996] 1 W.L.R. 1136.
[15] [1915] A.C. 705.
[16] [1952] P.1.
[17] [1965] P. 294.
[18] [1972] A.C. 153.
[19] [1993] 1 W.L.R. 1037.
[20] [1995] 1 A.C. 456.
[21] [1995] 2 A.C. 500.

Actual or anthropormorphic knowledge and fraud

8.56 The "fraud exception" applies as between principal and agent only. Its application to companies where the fraud is that of a director who also may reasonably be seen as sufficiently an "active spirit" for the purpose, or a directing mind and will is unlikely. It would create a situation in which the liability for fraud of a company and an individual differed for no good reason. The idea that a director or employee's fraud may be attributed to the company not by an agent but by a directing mind of the company for the purpose in question has been supported in a cogent obiter statement by Staughton L.J. and probably supported by Rose L.J. in the Court of Appeal in *PCW Syndicates v. PCW Reinsurers*.[22]

The *Hampshire Land*[23] case was concerned with the agency principle only, as was *Houghton & Co v. Nothard Lowe & Wills*.[24]

(2) Imputed knowledge

8.57 This is the kind of knowledge a company as principal acquires through its agents. It works in precisely the same way as with any other principal and agent situation. Relevant cases are *In re Marseilles Extension Railway Co*[25], *In re Hampshire Land*[26] *Re Fenwick Stobart & Co. Ltd*[27] and *In re David Payne & Co.*[28] See also *PCW Syndicates v. Reinsavers*[29] and *Deutsche Rückversicherung AG v. Walbrook Insurance Co. Ltd.*[30]. Similarly, a principal who employs an agent which chances to be a company has the same liability for the knowledge, actual or constructive, which the company has or ought to have had as would have been the case had the company been an individual; in the above cases no trace of any different doctrine, or any desire for any different doctrine, can be discerned.

[22] [1996] 1 W.L.R. 1136.
[23] [1986] 2 Ch. 743.
[24] [1928] A.C. 1.
[25] [1871] L.R. 7 Ch. App. 161.
[26] [1896] 2 Ch. 743.
[27] [1902] 1 Ch. 507.
[28] [1904] 2 Ch. 608.
[29] [1996] 1 W.L.R. 1136.
[30] [1996] 1 W.L.R. 1152.

APPENDIX: SOME CASES OF INTEREST

***Lowther v. Carlton* (1741) 2 Atk. 242; 26 E.R. 549 (The cleansed transmission from the purchaser without notice to the purchaser with notice)**

8.58 Held by the Lord Chancellor that a purchaser with notice who bought from a purchaser without notice might shelter behind his vendor. The reason given was that "otherwise it would very much clog the sale of estates".

He went on, *obiter* it would seem, "If a counsel or attorney is employed to look over a title, and *by some other transaction, foreign to the busines in hand, has notice, this shall not affect the purchaser*; for if this was not the rule of the court, it would be of dangerous consequence, as it would be an objection against the most able counsel, because of course they would be more likely than others of less eminence to have notice, as they are engaged in a great number of affairs of this kind."[31]

***Warrick v. Warrick* (1745) 3 Atk. 291; 26 E.R. 970 (Imputed notice; not imputed from a different, earlier transaction)**

8.59 This was a case of Lord Hardwicke's. There had been a conveyance on mortgage of certain estates which had been settled under marriage articles, but the mortgagee insisted that he had not notice of the marriage articles or settlement. The plaintiff gave evidence that one Hawkins who was the attorney for the mortgagee, had about a year earlier seen the settlement (acting for some other party). Lord Hardwicke said:

"I take the case to be, that *Hawkins* was concerned on both sides, which is very frequent in the country.

It would be a pretty harsh thing to affect the lender of the money with all kind of knowledge which the agent may have of the title of borrower; but *still I will not lay it down as a general rule, that where the same person is concerned for the mortgagor and mortgagee*, that notice to such person will not be good constructive notice to the mortgagee.

But consider what kind of notice the defendant . . . had: Mr *Hawkins had no notice at the time of the assignment, nor relative to this business, but before; even before the original mortgage . . .*"[32]

He referred to the case of *Fitzgerald v. Fauconbarge(hord)*[33] and to *Worsley v. Earl of Scarborough*[34] in which it was held, the notice should be in the same transaction, and said, "This rule ought to be adhered to, otherwise it would make purchasers and mortgagees' titles depend altogether on the memory of their counsellors and agents, and oblige them to apply to persons of less eminence as counsel, as not being so likely to have notice of former transactions."

He pointed out that the transaction was one in which Hawkins had acted eighteen months earlier, and it seems had only incidentally seen the marriage settlement in question and said: "It is very probable that Hawkins might have forgotten it in this length of time, or which is much more likely, did not

[31] Italics supplied.
[32] Some italics supplied.
[33] (1729) Fitz. G. 207; 94 E.R. 722.
[34] (1764) 3 Atk 392; 26 E.R. 1025.

understand the rule of this court, but took the limitation for an absolute estate-tail."

He held that the mortgagee did not have imputed notice.

***Worsley v. The Earl of Scarborough* (1746) 3 Atk. 392; 26 E.R. 1025**

8.60 The Lord Chancellor said *inter alia* "It is settled, that notice to an agent or counsel *who was employed in the thing by another person, or in another business, and at another time, is no notice to his client*, who employs him afterwards; and it would be very mischievous if it was so, for the man of most practice and greatest eminence would then be the most dangerous to employ."

***Le Neve v. Le Neve* (1747) Amb. 436; 27 E.R. 291 (Imputed notice despite registration)**

8.61 This was a decision of Lord Hardwicke. One Edward Le Neve had married a first wife, Henrietta, and his father had covenanted in the marriage settlement to convey to them some property near Soho Square, for Edward for life, then for Henrietta for life to pay her £250 a year, and after their deaths to their issue as Edward should appoint.

Henrietta had died and Edward had married a wife named Mary, and had covenanted with *her* in his marriage settlement to convey the same estates near Soho Square to trustees, to pay Mary £150 for life if she survived him. The second settlement was registered but not the first. The children of Henrietta brought the action to set aside the second settlement in favour of their stepmother, on the ground that she had notice of the first articles through her solicitor. Lord Hardwicke referred to the Queen Anne statute requiring registration in the county of Middlesex and said that the doctrine of notice was unaffected by it. "The operation of both acts of Parliament and construction of them is the same; and it would be a most mischievous thing, if a person taking that advantage of the legal form appointed by an act of Parliament, might under that protect himself against a person who had a prior equity of which he had notice."

He referred to a number of prior cases, including *Blades v. Blades*,[35] a case of 1727, as to which he commented that the Court had said "that they would never suffer any Act of Parliament made to prevent fraud to be a protection to fraud". He said later:

"The ground of it is plainly this. That the taking of a legal estate after notice of a prior right, makes a person *mala fide* purchaser; and not, that he is not a purchaser for a valuable consideration in every other respect. This is a species of fraud and *dolus malus* itself; for he knew the first purchaser had the clear right of the estate, and after knowing that, he takes away the right of another person by getting the legal estate."

"It has been said, If this woman has been imposed on by her husband, she, instead of cheating, has been cheated. But then who ought to suffer? the person entrusting an agent, or a stranger who did not employ him? He certainly who trusts most ought to suffer most." He went on to say that if it was to be any excuse, it would make all the cases of notice very precarious: "for it seldom happens but the agent has imposed on his principal; and notwithstanding that, the person trusting ought to suffer for his ill-placed confidence."

[35] (1727) 1 Eq. Rep. 358; 21 E.R. 1100.

***Earl Brook v. Bulkeley* (1754) 2 Ves. 498 (The purchaser with notice is bound to the same extent that his vendor would have been)**

8.62 The purchaser from a tenant in tail had notice of an agreement by the latter to renew a lease which his father the tenant for life had covenanted to renew. It was held by the Lord Chancellor that the purchaser is similarly bound to renew. After noting the obligation of the tenant in tail, he said,

"If so, then I am of opinion, that is a sufficient consideration to bind him; and consequently it would go over, and bind the person who took the estate with notice of that obligation he had laid himself under. Then *on what terms is he bound to renew*? The plaintiff's bill is to indemnify and deliver himself from an action or suit in equity that might be brought against him by Bulkeley, and Bulkeley's bill is to have a lease made to him, or to have a satisfaction from the plaintiff. I must decree a performance of this agreement, and that a lease be made by Hulse agreeable to the prayer . . . Hulse, therefore, or his agent, having at time of the purchase, notice of the agreement between the plaintiff and Bulkeley, *is bound in equity to renew the lease*."[36]

***Sheldon v. Cox* (1764) Amb. 624; 27 E.R. 404 (Imputed notice (at that time: but see now section 199 of the Law of Property Act 1925) despite non-registration by first purchaser and registration by later purchaser)**

8.63 Dr Markham and Mr Salter were given power by an Act of Parliament to buy land in and around Dean's Yard, Westminster, "to build a square, &c. for the better accommodation of the school, &c. A barrister named Cox who appeared to have taken the management of the affair upon himself bought a parcel of ground with old houses on it from the Dean and Chapter of Westminster, and obtained a 99 year lease renewal under the act. He then gave a mortgage to a Colonel Sheldon for £3,500, giving him a declaration of trust as a security and delivering to him the renewed leases, but not registering the security. Cox then *inter alia* assigned certain of the houses he had built in the square by way of mortgage to Drummond and others. They had no actual personal notice of the mortgage to the plaintiff but they admitted in the pleadings that they had used Cox as their counsel and agent in the transactions. They registered their securities. Lord Northington, Chancellor, said as to the question whether they were affected through Cox with the Plaintiff's security that "it was a fixed and settled point, that notice to the agent was notice to the principal. Cox being owner of the estate makes no difference. He acted in different capacities; and it is the same as if they had been in different persons. There is no difference between personal and constructive notice in its consequences, except as to guilt; if there was, it would be very inconvenient; and notice would be avoided in every case, by employing an agent." And the fact that they had registered before the plaintiff made no difference to their being affected with notice of his mortgage.

Note: This case and Le Neve v. Le Neve[37] *are included because it is, thought helpful to see the quite cogent reasons why registration did not originally override either actual or imputed notice; and by implication, the extent of the change which was later made by statute.*

***Cordwell v. Mackrill* (1765–66) 2 Eden. 344; 28 E.R. 930 (Due diligence even if the purchaser then took the wrong view of an ambiguous expression)**

8.64 The question was whether a conveyance could be set aside against the purchaser on the grounds that he had seen the marriage articles and settlement

[36] Italics supplied.
[37] para. 8.61 above.

relating to the land conveyed and was thus affected by notice that the articles had not been properly performed, being at variance with the settlement made. The Lord Chancellor said, "A man must, indeed, take notice of a deed on which an equity, supported by precedents, the justice of which every one acknowledges, arises, as in the case of prior incumbrances; but not the mere construction of words, which are uncertain in themselves, and the meaning of which often depends upon their locality." The action failed

***Taylor v. Stibbert* (1794) 2 Ves. Jun. 437; 30 ER 713 (A purchaser with notice is bound in all respects as the vendor)**

8.65 A man named Wood settled the manor of Portswood on his son, retaining power to let during his life. He granted tenancies to Taylor for 99 years during the lives of Taylor and two others, but with a provision that he or his heirs would grant a new lease on the death of any of the three. Subsequently Wood and his son and the trustees of the settlement sold the estate to Stibbert, who was held to have constructive notice of the lease contents. The Lord Chancellor Lord Loughborough said, "The rule, that affects the purchaser is just as plain as that, which would entitle the Plaintiff to a specific performance against *Wood*: if he is a purchaser with notice, he is liable to the same equity, stands in his place, and is bound to do that, which the person, he represents, would be bound to do by the decree."

Thus Stibbert was bound to specifically perform the covenant in Taylor's lease and Stibbert "cannot say, he will do somewhat less than *Wood* engaged to do. The right against *Stibbert*, if any, is co-extensive with that against *Wood*."

Note The case is also authority for the proposition that the purchaser who knows there are tenants ought for his own protection to inquire into their estate.

***Parker v. Brooke* (1804) 9 Ves. 583; 32 E.R. 729**

8.66 Notice of a trust—the purchaser was affected with it from the recitals to a deed which set out the history of the matter which included the trust.

***Hiern v. Mill* (1806) 13 Ves. 114; 33 E.R. 237**

8.67 In this case an equitable mortgagee by deposit of title deeds was preferred to a purchaser. The latter was held to have constructive notice, because he knew the title deeds were with another, but did not investigate. Lord Erskine said,

"The doctrine of notice, as it affects purchasers, is of such immense consequence and extent, that I shall look through the cases upon that . . . The question as to *Arnold* [the purchaser] is, whether he is affected by notice in fact or law; upon which I shall look into the cases. There is something extraordinary as to the time, at which he became a purchaser. There is a marked distinction in this respect between a real estate and a personal chattel. The latter is held by possession: a real estate by title. Possession of an estate is not even *prima facie* title. It may be by lease, or only from year to year. The cases have gone upon that distinction. Is there any instance of a purchase upon mere possession? If the vendor, being asked, acknowledges to the purchaser, that the deeds are in the possession of another, who is to be postponed? Here is *crassa negligentia*; which, coupled with positive evidence of knowledge a year before the purchase, raises a case for a decree against [the purchaser] . . .

After having looked into the cases he said, "The only point, upon which I deferred my judgment in this case, is that of notice; which is of two sorts: *actual notice; which must be proved, as any other fact; and notice by construction of law, as, where notice to an agent is notice to the principal; if the agent* comes to the knowledge of the fact, while he is concerned for the principal, *and in the course of the very transaction, which becomes the subject of the suit* . . .

The rule as to notice, arising from Lis pendens, is a positive rule of law; made to prevent purchases of litigated titles. Another case is, *where the law imputes that notice, which from the nature of the transaction every person of ordinary prudence must necessarily have* . . .[38]

8.68 . . . It has been determined, that a purchaser, being told, particular parts of the estate were in possession of a tenant, without any information as to his interest, and taking for granted it was only from year to year, was bound by the lease that tenant had, which was a surprise upon him. That was rightly determined; for it was sufficient to put the purchaser upon inquiry, that he was informed the estate was not in the actual possession of the person with whom he contracted; that he could not transfer the ownership and possession at the same time; that there were interests, as to the extent and terms of which it was his duty to inquire."

After reference to another case he said, "No comparison can be made between these cases and the case now before the Court, with respect to the strength with which the principle applies. I repeat that land is held not by possession, but by title: not so as to personal chattels; for the common traffic of the world could not go on. Therefore a sale in Market overt changes the property of a chattel . . . But that is not so as to land; for no person in his senses would take an offer of a purchase from a man, merely because he stood upon the ground. It is not even *prima facie* evidence. He may be tenant by sufferance, or a trespasser. A purchaser must look to his title; and, if, being asked for the deeds, he acknowledges he has not got them, the purchaser is bound to farther inquiry."

***Daniels v. Davison* (1809) 16 Ves. 249; 33 E.R. 978 (Constructive (failure to investigate) notice)**

8.69 The vendor had agreed with a tenant to sell him the pub of which he was tenant; and then agreed to sell the land on which the pub stood to a purchaser. The purchaser was held bound not only by his tenancy but by the agreement the vendor had made with the tenant, because he knew there was a tenancy but did not inquire from the tenant what his rights were. Lord Eldon, Lord Chancellor, said,

"My opinion therefore, considering this as depending upon notice, is, that this tenant, being in possession under a lease, with an agreement in his pocket to become the purchaser, those circumstances altogether give him an equity, repelling the claim of a subsequent purchaser, who made no inquiry as to the nature of his possession."

***Gladstone v. King* (1813) 1 M. & S. 35; 105 E.R. 13 (Insurance: buyer derives imputed notice of disclosable fact through agent)**

8.70 The case concerned a claim made on a policy of insurance of a ship, the Richard. The insurers claimed that they ought not to be liable to pay in respect of damage to the ship's bottom, because the ship's captain had reason to suspect damage, after an incident in which the ship had been driven from her moorings and struck a rock. The owners themselves did not know about the possibility of damage, but the knowledge of their agent, the captain, was imputed to them, because, it was held, he was under a duty to inform them.

[38] Some italics supplied.

There was thus an implied exception out of the policy to the extent of this damage.

***Taylor v. Baker* (1818) 5 Price 306; 146 E.R. 616**

8.71 If a purchaser is told that there is a judgment affecting the land, that is notice of the judgment even though in fact what affects the land is a mortgage.

***Mountford v. Scott* (1818) 3 Madd. 34; 56 E.R. 422 ("Same transaction": original doctrine; consecutive agency by same solicitor: no imputed notice to later principal)**

8.72 Scott deposited a lease with the plaintiff as security. He subsequently granted Blake (who knew about the deposit) an underlease of the premises; and Blake assigned that underlease to a man named Warner. The same solicitor, Gyles, who had acted for Scott as vendor of the underlease to Blake later acted for Blake on his assignment to Warner. Warner also admitted that Gyles had acted for *him* as purchaser as well as for Blake as vendor on the assignment. Sir John Leach, the Vice Chancellor said that Warner was *not* affected with notice of either kind through his agent Gyles. First, there had been no duty upon Warner to inquire what had become of the original lease (that is the one which had been deposited) so there was no constructive notice; second there was no imputed notice by reason of the dual agency because the agency in which Gyles acquired the knowledge and the agency in which he acted for Warner were consecutive rather than simultaneous. "The agent stands in place of the principal; and notice therefore to the agent is notice to the principal; *but he cannot stand in the place of the principal until the relation of principal and agent is constituted: and as to all the information which he has previously acquired, the principal is a mere stranger.*"[38a]

Note: The law later took a different turn, and required to be corrected by statute: see below.

***Jones v. Powles* (1834) 3 M. & K. 581; 40 E.R. 222 (Constructive (failure to investigate) notice)**

8.73 The vendor had been in possession under a forged will, but he had been in possession a long time, the will appeared valid, and though the vendor had told an untruth, in the words of the Master of the Rolls, "no reasonable diligence could have led to a discovery of the forgery". Thus, the purchaser's legal estate was unaffected by notice.

***Kennedy v. Green* (1834) 3 My. & K. 699; 40 E.R. 266 (Fraud preventing imputed notice; constructive notice)**

8.74 The facts were that Mrs Kennedy, an elderly lady in full possession of her faculties, had a solicitor, James Bostock, in whom she reposed "more than the ordinary share of confidence" in the words of Lord Chancellor Brougham. Bostock was instructed by her to sell a sum of about £9,000 which she had in Consols and to invest it on mortgage securities. Bostock invested a part of her money on a mortgage on the security of two building subleases of some leasehold property of his own, then by a trick obtained her signature to what purported to be a discharge of the mortgage monies; then remortgaged the building leases to a Mr Kirby, his father in law. Mr Kirby trusted him, and

[38a] Italics supplied.

used him as his solicitor. Mr Kirby was thus also an innocent party. Lord Brougham, Lord Chancellor, said,

"The doctrine of constructive notice depends upon two considerations: first, that certain things existing in the relation or the conduct of parties, or in the case between them, beget a presumption so strong of actual knowledge that the law holds the knowledge to exist, because it is highly improbable it should not; and next, that policy and the safety of the public forbids a person to deny knowledge while he is so dealing as to keep himself ignorant, or so as that he may keep himself ignorant, and yet all the while let his agent know, and himself, perhaps, profit by that knowledge.

In such a case it would be most iniquitous and most dangerous, and give shelter and encouragement to all kinds of fraud, were the law not to consider the knowledge of one as common to both, whether it be so in fact or not. Under one or other of these heads, perhaps under both, comes the other principle, which is quite undeniable, that whatever is notice enough to excite attention, and put the party on his guard and call for inquiry, is also notice of everything to which it is afterward s found that such inquiry might have led, although all was unknown for want of the investigation."

These principles are so plain that they need not be supported by reference to authority, and they dispose of the present question.

"Bostock was acting as Mr. Kirby's solicitor in the transaction, and although, generally speaking, the knowledge obtained by a man's attorney or agent fixes himself, if obtained while so employed, and on the same business (for I do not at all differ from *Mountford v. Scott*[39], *Hiern v. Mill*[40] and the other cases) yet it cannot here be said that Mr. Kirby is fixed with all which Bostock knew. For the fraud, practised by Bostock upon Mr. Kirby himself, was of course concealed from him; and so we say would certainly be that other fraud which he had practised on Mrs. Kennedy. Indeed, that was only another part of the same fraud, another act of the same plot; and, therefore, I think we cannot, on this account alone, fix his client, Mr. Kirby, any more than his other employer, Mrs. Kennedy, with the knowledge of his criminal proceedings. We must lay out of our view all the knowledge, the actual and full knowledge he had of his own fraud, and are not to hold Mr. Kirby as cognisant—I mean of course cognisant in law and constructively—of that, merely because his solicitor himself, the contriver, the actor, and the gainer of the transaction, knew it all well."

8.75 However, he then went on to consider the situation on the footing that Bostock had *not* been fraudulent, and found that Mr. Kirby was fixed with constructive notice on that ground, which was that any solicitor would have seen that there were various unsatisfactory and curious things about the discharge: it bore the appearance of having been prepared in a hurry, and the receipt was unusual and not in the usual place, with a big blank space in between which could be filled up by the holder in any manner he chose. "This was, at once, a circumstance to excite the greatest, the most jealous suspicion. Had a check been originally written with an inch of blank to the left hand of the sum, would not all who saw it start at the risk run by the maker, and would not the maker, on his attention being drawn to it, nay, even the holder, take the precaution of drawing a line or two over the blank? But suppose a banker had discounted a check with a sum as "one hundred" interlined, would any judge direct any jury to let that banker recover against the maker, though full value had by him the banker been paid for it? All the cases have decided the contrary, and held that every unusual circumstance is a ground of suspicion, and prescribes inquiry; and I hold the receipt written here in a

[39] 3 Madd. 34, para. 8.72, above.
[40] 13 Ves. 114, para. 8.67, above.

way to enable any person to commit a gross fraud—a way for that reason never adopted—was abundant ground for suspicion, and demanded inquiry and explanation. When to this we add the further unusual circumstance of the party's name being written on the square below, and with a fold between it and the receipt, so that it was most probably written when the receipt was folded down, assuredly no one can hesitate in pronouncing that whoever, especially a man of business, looked at the deed, must have conceived such suspicions as to call for inquiry; and if he had inquired, Mrs. Kennedy would have told him that she knew of no receipt, and had received no money, and that the whole, consequently, was a fraud. Thus, taking Bostock to be merely an ordinary solicitor, employed by Mr. Kirby in settling this transaction for him, the deed was such as at once gave him notice that all was not right, and put him upon inquiring. That is notice to him and his employer of whatever the inquiry would have disclosed. Can it make the least difference that in this case Bostock abstained from making the inquiry, because he already knew the whole fraud, the tissue of which his own hands had woven? Can it alter the fact, or displace the point, on which the whole turns, of the existence of suspicious appearances, and the certainty that the inquiry, instigated by them, must have disclosed the truth, that this truth was already within the full knowledge of the person employed, and whom we are supposing to have examined the deed for his client? A difference it may make, but the difference is against, and not in favour of, the Defendant's argument.

Can it, again, make any difference in the case we are supposing of a solicitor employed to examine a deed, and having ground to suspect, and, suspecting, being bound to inquire as to its fraudulent concoction, that here, beside being so employed, he was himself the fabricator of the whole fraud, and only did not suspect, because he knew for certain the whole plot? A difference it may make, but that difference is against, and not in favour of, the Defendant's argument.

I therefore consider the case of constructive notice as here abundantly made out . . ."

Hargreaves v. Rothwell (1836) 1 Keen 154; 48 E.R. 265 (The "same transaction" doctrine goes awry)

8.76 A man named Nuttall granted an 800 year lease in 1827 to secure a loan by two Rothwells and another. In 1829 he conveyed the freehold of the property subject to the mortgage of 1827 to the plaintiff Hargreaves as security for his loan. In 1830 he granted a third mortgage over the property to the defendants, agreeing to hold the title deeds as security. The owner Nuttall became bankrupt, and the question of the second mortgagee, Hargreaves', priority over the third mortgagee arose. The notice alleged against the defendants was imputed notice by virtue of the fact that they had used a solicitor named Samuel Woodcock, who had been solicitor for the mortgagor and mortgagee in all three transactions.

The Master of the Rolls Lord Langdale considered "that where one transaction was closely followed by, and connected with another; or where it was clear, as in the case before the Court, that a previous transaction was present to the mind of the solicitor when engaged in another transaction, there was no ground for the distinction by which the rule, that notice to the solicitor is notice to the client, had been restricted to the same transaction."

Note: This was obviously a very strong case. It strikes one as curious however that the doctrine of constructive or inferred notice was not used to deal with the problem. At all events the "recent knowledge" doctrine in the case seems to have opened the floodgates, widening hugely the scope of the knowledge on the part of an agent which was imputed to his principal. This caused a widespread feeling that matters had gone too far; and the scope of imputed notice of this kind was restricted once again as far as interests in land were concerned by the Conveyancing Act 1882, and later section 199(1)(i)(b) of the Law of Property Act 1925. The better view, even for non-land cases, is probably that expressed in the earlier cases, which rule out the imputing of knowledge acquired in previous transactions, even for the same principal and relating to the same land.

***Jones v. Smith* (1841) 1 Hare 61; 66 E.R. 943 (Constructive notice: inquiry and reasonable excuse)**

8.77 Smith had inquired of a husband to whom he was about to advance money on the security of a mortgage of his property, whether he had made any marriage settlement affecting the property. He was assured that the settlement had only affected his wife's property, so Smith did not inquire further. On the question whether Smith had constructive notice of the fact that actually the husband's marriage settlement did affect his property, the Vice-Chancellor Sir James Wigram took the opportunity of examining and reviewing a large number of cases to establish the relevant principles. He said,

"It is, indeed, scarcely possible to declare *à priori* what shall be deemed constructive notice, because, unquestionably, that which would not affect one man may be abundantly sufficient to affect another. But I believe I may, with sufficient accuracy for my present purpose, and without danger, assert that the cases in which constructive notice has been established, resolve themselves into two classes:- First, cases in which the party charged has had actual notice that the property in dispute was, in act, charged, incumbered or in some way affected, and the Court has thereupon bound him with constructive notice of facts and instruments, to a knowledge of which he would have been led by an inquiry after the charge, incumbrance or other circumstance affecting the property of which he had actual notice; and, secondly, cases in which the Court has been satisfied from the evidence before it that the party charged had designedly abstained from inquiry for the very purpose of avoiding notice. How reluctantly the Court has applied, and within what strict limits it has confined, the latter class of cases, I shall presently consider.

The proposition of law, upon which the former class of cases proceeds, is not that the partly charged had notice of a fact or instrument, which, in truth, related to the subject in dispute without his knowing that such was the case, but that he had actual notice that it did so relate. The proposition of law, upon which the second class of cases proceeds, is not that the party charged had incautiously neglected to make inquiries, but that he had designedly abstained from such inquiries, for the purpose of avoiding knowledge—a purpose which, if proved, would clearly shew that he had a suspicion of the truth, and a fraudulent determination not to learn it. If, in short, there is not actual notice that the property is in some way affected, and no fraudulent turning away from a knowledge of facts which the *res gestae* would suggest to a prudent mind; if mere want of caution, as distinguished from fraudulent and wilful blindness, is all that can be imputed to the purchaser—there the doctrine of constructive notice will not apply; there the purchaser will, in equity, be considered, as in fact he is, a *bona fide* purchaser, without notice. This is clearly Sir Edward Sugden's opinion (Vend & Pur vol 13, pp 471, 472 ed 10); and with that sanction I have no hesitation in saying it is mine also".

8.78 He then reviewed a large number of cases, which he considered justified the principles he had set out. Among these was a particularly interesting case, (which Sir Edward Sugden considered a dangerous extension of the law on constructive notice)—*Whitbread v. Jordan*[41] This was a case in which the plaint-

[41] 1 You. & Col. 303; 160 E.R. 123.

iffs were brewers, and Jordan was a publican whom they supplied with beer. "It is," commented Sir James Wigram, "a practice almost amounting to a local custom for brewers in the metropolis to lend money to publicans whom they supply with beer, upon the security of an equitable deposit of their deeds." There was one Boulnois, a wine and spirit merchant, who had taken a mortgage of Jordan's property for an antecedent debt, without inquiring the brewers whether they had a mortgage of the property, even though he knew that they had lent money to Jordan.

The Vice-Chancellor thought the above case could in fact have been brought within his first principle. "For the evidence in support of the prevailing practice between brewers and publicans was so strong that, as against a wine and spirit merchant in the metropolis, who was aware of that practice, it could scarcely have been unjust to hold that a deposit of deeds was an inseparable incident to a large money credit existing between a brewer and a publican. And, if that reasoning were admissible, the notice which Boulnois has of Jordan's debt to the Plaintiff would be actual notice of a fact affecting his property." (The judge in the case had in fact rested his judgment on the fact that Boulnois had "studiously avoided" making the obvious inquiries which the facts of the case must have suggested "to any honest man using ordinary caution.") Nonetheless, the case is interesting on the "common knowledge" aspect of making reasonable inquiries.

Sir James Wigram did not think that the facts of the case before him were within the principles: the most that could be said against the lender here was that he had not used extreme caution: he could not be charged with culpable neglect. Accordingly, he was held not to have notice of the marriage settlement.

***West v. Reid* (1843) 2 Hare 249; 67 E.R. 104 (Constructive (failure to investigate) notice—insurance policy)**

8.79 A policy of insurance was assigned to a trustee as security for a loan. The lender's solicitor caused a memorandum to be entered at the offices of the insurance company directing correspondence to him, and paid all premiums thereafter on behalf of his client, but did not explain further. Later the assured became bankrupt, but the assignees in bankruptcy did not interfere with the arrangement. After the death of the bankrupt, it was held that the insurance office had insufficient notice of the assignment to effect any change of the interest.

The Vice Chancellor Sir James Wigram referred to his own judgment in *Jones v. Smith*[42] and corrected an impression he had been told had got about as a result of that, the idea that a fraudulent motive was necessary. Negligence might be evidence of [equitable] fraud, even if morally speaking, the party was perfectly innocent. "Negligence, as I understand the term, supposes a disregard of some fact known to a purchaser, which at least indicated the existence of that fact, notice of which the Court imputes to the purchaser."

He said he did not deny there could sometimes be difficulty in drawing the line between the two. "But the distinction is founded in principle, and the difficulty is one with which . . . Courts of Justice are in the daily habit of grappling; and the difficulty in principle is not distinguishable from that which occurs in every other case in which antagonist principles come into immediate conflict with each other". He continued "In short, let the doctrine of constructive notice be extended to all cases (it is in fact more confined . . . but) let it be extended to all cases in which the purchaser has notice that the property is affected, or has notice of facts raising a presumption that it is so,

[42] Above, para. 8.77.

and the doctrine is reasonable, thought it may sometimes operate with severity. But once transgress the limits which that statement of the rule imposes—once admit that a purchaser is to be affected with constructive notice of the contents of instruments not necessary to nor presumptively connected with, the title, only because, by possibility, they *may* affect it . . . and it is impossible, in sound reasoning, to stop short of the conclusion that every purchaser is affected with constructive notice of the contents of every instrument of the mere existence of which he has notice. A purchaser *must* be presumed to investigate the title of the property he purchases, and may, therefore, be presumed to have examined every instrument forming a link, directly or by inference, in that title; and that presumption I take to be the foundation of the whole doctrine. But it is impossible to presume that a purchaser examines instruments not directly nor presumptively connected with the title, only because they *may* by possibility affect it."

He thought the facts known to the insurance company were insufficient to raise any inference that the assured's interest in the policy had undergone any change.

Brotherton v. Hatt **(1843) 2 Vern. 574; 23 E.R. 973**

8.80 There were several mortgages, all "transacted at the shop of [particular scriveners], who were witnesses, and engrossed all the securities, and were in nature of agents to all the several lenders; and notice to the *agent* is good notice to the party, and consequently they that lend last must come last, having notice of what before was lent."

Note: See the note to Hargreaves v. Rothwell[43]*. This case will also have been overruled by the Conveyancing Act 1882 and by section 199 (1)(i)(b) of the Law of Property Act 1925*

Jones v. Smith **(1843) 1 Ph. 244; 41 E.R. 624 (The Lord Chancellor's decision in the case (see above, para. 8.77 for Sir James Wigram V.C.'s decision).)**

8.81 Wigram V.C. had held that the purchaser was not affected by notice of the settlement in those circumstances; and so did Lord Lyndhurst on appeal. Lord Lyndhurst said the conclusion the Vice-Chancellor came to was correct—that the transaction was fair, honest, and bona fide on part of Mr. Smith . . .

"The question therefore resolves itself into this, whether, where a party is informed of the existence of an instrument which may, but which does not necessarily, affect the property he is about to purchase, or upon which he is about to advance money, and it is at the same time stated that the instrument does not affect that property, but relates to some other property, whether, if he acts fairly and honestly, and believes that statement to be true, but it turns out in the result that he is misled, and that the instrument does relate to the property, he is under such circumstances to be fixed with notice of the contents of the instrument? Undoubtedly, where a party has notice of a deed, which from the nature of it must affect the property, or is told at the time that it does affect it, he is considered to have notice of the contents of that deed and of all other deeds to which it refers: but where a party has notice of a deed which does not necessarily—which may or may not—affect the property, and is told, that in fact it does not affect it but relates to some other property, and the party acts fairly in the transaction, and believes the representation to be true, there is no decision that goes the length of saying

[43] Para. 8.76, above.

that if he is misled he is fixed with notice of the instrument. I am not disposed to extend the doctrine of constructive notice . . ."

Later in the judgment he said, "I do not consider this a case of gross negligence: and I am of opinion that the party having acted *bonâ fide*, and having only omitted that caution which a prudent, wary, and cautious person might and probably would have adopted, is not to be fixed with notice of the instrument. I am satisfied he acted *bonâ fide* in the transaction . . .

Fuller v. Benett **(1843) 2 Hare 405; 67 E.R. 162**

8.82 The actual decision turned on the "recent knowledge" doctrine, and has been overruled by statute: see the comment to *Hargreaves v. Rothwell*[44]. However, it is of interest in that the Vice-Chancellor first rehearsed the general propositions which were **not** disputed: ". . . first that notice to the solicitor is notice to the client; secondly, that where a purchaser employs the same solicitor as the vendor he is affected with *notice of whatever that solicitor had notice in his capacity of solicitor for either vendor or purchaser in the transaction in which he is so employed*; and thirdly, that the notice to the solicitor, which alone will bind the client, must be notice *in that transaction in which the client employs him*."[45]

The Vice Chancellor also thought it was clear that where a solicitor is solicitor for two parties, in that case "a purchaser may be affected with notice of what the solicitor knew as solicitor for the vendor, although, as solicitor for the vendor, he may have acquired his knowledge before he was retained by the purchaser. Whatever the solicitor, during the time of his retainer, knows as solicitor for either party may possibly in some cases affect both, without reference to the time when his knowledge was first acquired." He was clearly referring to knowledge which came to the solicitor in that transaction, but before being instructed by the other party. This can be seen by the fact that he goes on to discuss something he is altogether less sure about: namely what he calls "previously acquired knowledge" which must refer to knowledge acquired in earlier transactions.

Note: This case is cited mainly because of the useful general statement of principle about the transmission of knowledge between vendor and purchaser through their joint agent; and deriving from the current transaction. This is a question which has been considered again in Halifax Building Society v. Stepsky.[46] *The basis for the cross-imputation of knowledge between the two parties to the transaction would no doubt be an implied consent by the earlier of the joint clients to disclosure of anything which had already occurred in the (now joint) transaction.*[47]

Penny v. Watts **(1849) 1 Mac. & G. 150; 41 E.R. 1220 (Purchaser's duty to follow up puzzling facts or be saddled with unwelcome deemed knowledge)**

8.83 The facts are too complicated for words; the reason the case is included is that it adverts to the fairly stringent due diligence duty which the purchaser is held to be under to inquire further, when *he has facts which seem puzzling and thus put him on notice*. It seemed the purchaser had married a widow who was entitled to an estate; but who had made a contract to leave it by will to her husband's niece, in return for the niece giving up a legacy for £2,000, charged on the estate, but not payable until after the widow's death. What

[44] (1836).
[45] Italics supplied.
[46] [1996] Ch. 207.
[47] See also comment below on ***Halifax Building Society v. Stepsky***, above.

the purchaser discovered was the niece's husband (the plaintiff in the case), who was in occupation, who said that because of the arrangement, he was in occupation of a part of the land as a sort of tenant. It was felt that his *presence* should have put the purchaser on notice. Lord Cottenham, Lord Chancellor, said that the purchaser had known about the release and the contract to leave the estate by will, and of course that the niece's husband was in occupation, but not looked into it further. The Lord Chancellor said,

"Now these two facts coming to the knowledge of the Defendant, one party giving up a valuable pecuniary benefit, and the other in lieu thereof devising a certain estate, I think it is not carrying the doctrine of the Court further than it has often been carried to say that, *knowing these facts, he was bound to enquire how these facts took place*, and that, as he knew that the one party gave up the legacy, and in lieu thereof the other party had devised the estate, he cannot afterwards, if the fact be proved, say that he had not that sort of knowledge which will affect him with constructive notice of that which, if the facts be proved to exist, will shew that the Plaintiff had an equitable title by contract to have the devised estates conveyed to him.[48] Lord Cottenham gave an example of a case which he said was similar: where A made an equitable mortgage to V, and gave a second security to C, telling him that he had given a judgment or warrant of attorney (ie not a security) to A for money borrowed, and it had been held that C having that knowledge, was bound to pursue the enquiry further, and if he had, he would have learned about the first mortgage on the land.

Hewitt v. Loosemore (1851) 9 Hare 449; 68 E.R. 586 (Constructive notice: fobbing off)

8.84 Robert Loosemore, a solicitor, had deposited a lease with the plaintiff to secure a loan and had then assigned the lease to the defendant John Loosemore. John Loosemore claimed that he had no notice of the lease. He had had no solicitor, the lease had been prepared by Robert Loosemore, but he had enquired where the lease was, and been told that he should have it shortly. The Vice-Chancellor Sir G.J. Turner held[49] that the defendant did *not* have constructive notice, since he had inquired for the deeds and been given a reasonable excuse.

"... the Court will not impute fraud, or gross or wilful negligence to the mortgagee if he has *bonâ fide* inquired for the deeds, and a reasonable excuse has been given for the non-delivery of them; but that the Court will impute fraud, or gross and wilful negligence to the mortgagee if he omits all inquiry as to the deeds.

... in transactions of sale and mortgage of estates, if there be no inquiry as to the title-deeds, which constitute the sole evidence of the title to such property, the Court is justified in assuming that the purchaser or mortgagee has abstained from making the inquiry, from a suspicion that his title would be affected if it was made, and is therefore bound to impute to him the knowledge which the inquiry, if made, would have imparted. But I think that where *bonâ fide* inquiry is made, and a reasonable excuse given, there is no ground for imputing the suspicion, or the notice which is consequent upon it."

Ware v. Lord Egmont (1854) 4 D.G.M. & G. 460; 43 E.R. 586 (Constructive (failure to investigate) notice))

8.85 The defendants had purchased land in respect of which the land tax had been redeemed, by means of funds belonging to an infant who died in

[48] Italics supplied.

[49] The other point of his decision, that the other side was deemed to act as the unrepresented party's solicitor was later overruled.

infancy, such that the plaintiff had (but for the sale) an equitable right to a rent-charge equivalent to the redeemed land tax. The purchaser had no actual notice of the right to the rent charge or the fact that it had ever been paid.

On the facts, Lord Cranworth L.C. thought that there was nothing really to put the purchaser on notice of anything wrong: there was a fund out of which the money *might* perfectly properly have been paid, and nothing to show that it was not, so as to give rise to the equitable right claimed. He said that it was "highly inexpedient for Courts of Equity to extend the doctrine[50]—to attempt to apply it to cases to which it has not hitherto been held applicable. *Where a person has actual notice of any matter of fact, there can be no danger of doing injustice if he is held to be bound by all the consequences of that which he knows to exist. But where he has not actual notice, he ought not to be treated as if he had notice, unless the circumstances are such as enable the Court to say, not only that he might have acquired, but also, that he ought to have acquired, the notice*[51] with which it is sought to affect him, that he would have acquired it but for his gross negligence in the conduct of the business in question.

The question, when it is sought to affect a purchaser with constructive notice, is not whether he had the means of obtaining, and might by prudent caution have obtained, the knowledge in question, but whether the not obtaining it was an act of gross or culpable negligence. It is obvious that no definite rule as to what will amount to gross or culpable negligence, so as to meet every case, can possibly be laid down. But I think it clear, that the imputation of gross negligence cannot fairly be fixed on a purchaser, merely because it did not occur to him or his advisers to inquire whether a transaction, legally valid and under which there had been long enjoyment (here it was for thirty-three years) might not have been so conducted in its origin as to have given to third persons equitable rights, of which there was no trace on the face of the abstract."

***James v. Lichfield* (1869) L.R. 9 Eq. 51**

8.86 A purchaser took a property which he knew to be in the occupation of a tenant. *He did not inquire*, but thought it was a tenancy from year to year. In fact it was a lease for 21 years. The purchaser sued to take the property with compensation.

Lord Romilly M.R. refused the purchaser relief on the grounds that he had constructive (want of due diligence) notice. He knew there was a tenancy, and should have found out what kind of tenancy. He relied on *Daniels v. Davidson*[52]

***Espin v. Pemberton* (1859) 3 De G. & J. 547; 44 E.R. 1380 (Imputed notice: agency/joint agency cannot be inferred; there must be actual consent by the principal to constitute the relationship**

8.87 The question was as to the priority between the equitable mortgagee by deposit of the lease of a house and the owner of the lease by virtue of a legal assignment of it. The Lord Chancellor, Lord Chelmsford, first complained about the "constructive notice" label when referring to what he said should be called either actual knowledge or imputed knowledge.

"The notice, which a client is supposed to receive through his solicitor, is generally treated as constructive notice. I think it would tend very much to clearness in these cases if it were classed under the head of actual notice. The notice which affects the principal through a solicitor does not depend upon

[50] [Of Constructive notice].
[51] Italic supplied.
[52] Above para. 8.69.

whether it is communicated to him or not. If a person employs a solicitor, who either knows or has imparted to him in the course of his employment some fact which affects the transaction, the principal is bound by the fact, whether it is communicated to or concealed from him. Constructive notice, properly so called, is the knowledge which the Courts impute to a person upon a presumption so strong of the existence of the knowledge, that it cannot be allowed to be rebutted, either from his knowing something which ought to have put him upon further inquiry, or from his wilfully abstaining from inquiry, to avoid notice. I should therefore prefer calling the knowledge which a person has, either by himself or through his agent, actual knowledge; or if it is necessary to make a distinction between the knowledge which a person possesses himself, and that which is known to his agent, the latter might be called imputed knowledge.

8.88 Was Pemberton, then who came to the transaction with a perfect knowledge of the Plaintiff's incumbrance, the solicitor of Browne? I find it very difficult to accede to the proposition, however high may be the authority from which it proceed, that where a mortgagor is himself a solicitor, and prepares the mortgage deed, the mortgagor employing no other solicitor, the mortgagor must be considered to be the agent or solicitor of the mortgagee in the transaction. I think that there ought to be some *consent* on the part of the mortgagee to constitute this relation between them. If the mortgagee is imprudent enough to entrust his interests to the mortgagor, being a solicitor, he may do so and take all the consequences. But he may not desire to have any solicitor, considering himself equal to his own protection; and if he omit to communicate this to the mortgagor, who is preparing the mortgage deed, the omission seems scarcely sufficient to constitute the mortgagor his solicitor.

But if the mortgagor, under these circumstances, becomes the solicitor of the mortgagee, it is hardly possible to stop short of applying all the consequences of the relation, and to refuse to impute the knowledge which the mortgagor possesses to his client the mortgagee. You cannot escape from this conclusion, unless you apply the principle of the case of *Kennedy v. Green*[53] and exclude this particular knowledge, because the mortgagor was committing a fraud in the transaction, which he could not be presumed to communicate. But I have already shewn that *imputed knowledge does not depend upon whether it is communicated or not*, and therefore the presumption of non-communication does not seem to be the proper principle to apply. I would rather say that *the commission of the fraud broke off the relation of principal and agent, or was beyond the scope of the authority, and therefore it prevented the possibility of imputing the knowledge of the agent to his principal.*[54]

Accordingly he decided because the solicitor Pemberton had never been consented to as Browne's solicitor, Browne had no imputed notice.

***Wylie v. Pollen* (1863) 3 De G.J. & Sm. 596; 46 E.R. 767 (Imputed notice: execution-only or merely ministerial agents do not "count" as agents for imputing knowledge to the principal)**

8.89 The solicitors for the transferees of a mortgage entrusted the execution of the deed by the mortgagors to another firm. It was held that the doctrine of constructive notice[55] would not extend to the knowledge of those who did such ministerial acts; and the knowledge in question being immaterial to the transfer would not have affected the main solicitors anyway.

The Lord Chancellor said he concurred with those Judges who thought that

[53] Above, para. 8.74.
[54] Italics supplied.
[55] Meaning what has been called imputed notice.

the doctrine of constructive notice should not be extended. "To affect the principal with notice, the agent's knowledge must have been *derived in the particular transaction in hand*, or be shewn to have been *in that transaction present to his mind*: and, further, it must have been knowledge of *something material to the particular transaction*, and something which it was the agent's *duty to communicate to his principal*; the whole doctrine of constructive notice resting on the ground of such a duty on the part of the agent."[56]

***Thompson v. Cartwright* (1863) 33 Beav. 178; 55 E.R. 335 (Fraudulent solicitor: no imputed notice to principal)**

8.90 The grantor of an annuity charged on his land covenanted, in a deed prepared by the solicitor for the grantee, that there were no incumbrances on it. It afterwards turned out that the solicitor who prepared the deed, with other persons, had a mortgage on the property.

The Master of the Rolls, Sir John Romilly referred first to *Kennedy v. Green*[57] (it appearing, it would seem, that the solicitor here *was* fraudulent) saying that it "establishes a very important principle, but one which must be very cautiously applied to the cases of notice of facts given to the solicitor employed by the client. That case establishes, that if the solicitor employed by the client was the actual perpetrator of a fraud, it is reasonably certain that he would not communicate that fact to his client, and that consequently the client cannot be treated as having had notice of that fact.

"I take the rule to be, generally, that the client must be treated as having had notice of all the facts which, in the same transaction, have come to the knowledge of the solicitor, and that the burthen of proof lies on him (the client) to shew that there is a probability, amounting to a moral certainty, that the solicitor would not have communicated that fact to his client." He thought here the grantor had discharged that burden. The case was later affirmed by the Lords Justices.

***Proudfoot v. Montefiore* (1867) L.R. 2 Q.B. 511 (Imputed knowledge (insurance): when knowledge deemed to be communicated to the principal)**

8.91 The particular question which arose here was the precise *time when* the agent's knowledge should be imputed to the principal. The owners had insured a cargo of madder at a time when in fact, unbeknownst to them, but known to their agent on the spot in Smyrna, the ship had been stranded and the cargo lost. If the agent had telegraphed the news, the owners would have known of the loss before insuring: in fact he deliberately wrote, rather than telegraphing, so that the owners might have the opportunity to insure first.

Cockburn C.J. giving the judgment of the court, held that the owners could not recover on the insurance.

". . . if an agent, whose duty it is, in the ordinary course of business, to communicate information to his principal as to the state of a ship and cargo, omits to discharge such duty, and the owner, in the absence of information as to any fact material to be communicated to the underwriter, effects an insurance, such insurance will be void, on the ground of concealment or misrepresentation. The insurer is entitled to assume, as the basis of the contract between him and the assured, that the latter will communicate to him every material fact of which the assured has, or, in the ordinary course of business, ought to have knowledge; and that the latter will take the necessary measures,

[56] Italics supplied.
[57] Above, para. 8.74.

by the employment of competent and honest agents, to obtain, through the ordinary channels of intelligence in use in the mercantile world, all due information as to the subject matter of the insurance. This condition is not complied with where, by the fraud or negligence of the agent, the party proposing the insurance is kept in ignorance of a material fact, which ought to have been made known to the underwriter, and through such ignorance fails to disclose it."

The court stressed that the decision was a policy decision, to prevent fraudulent concealment on the part of masters of vessels and agents at a distance, and any tendency on the part of owners to encourage this kind of behaviour. Since the owners had trusted or employed the agent, it was right that of the two innocent parties, the loss should fall on them.

Note: *"Ought" in "ought to have" above is likely to be used in the reasonable expectation sense, rather than the moral-obligation sense*[58]

***James v. Lichfield* (1869) L.R. 9 Eq. 51 (Constructive notice)**

8.92 Lord Romilly M.R. adopted the principle stated in argument in *Daniels v. Davison*[59] and adopted by the Lord Chancellor. "Whatever puts a purchaser upon inquiry shall be held notice; and if therefore he knows that a tenant is in possession, he is considered as having notice of the whole extent of his interest." Lord Romilly could not see that the purchaser was not similarly bound as against the vendor.

"If the purchaser, knowing of the tenancy, is bound to inquire, as regards the tenant, as to his interest in the land, and if the purchaser must be taken to be bound to know what would be the result of such inquiry as regards the tenant, why should he not be so bound as regards the vendor? and if the purchaser chooses to bind himself by agreement with this vendor, knowing of the tenancy, but without having accurately ascertained what was the extent and character of it, and what the results of such inquiry would have led to, he must, as it appears to me, be bound in the same manner as regards all other persons. I think, also, that no distinction can properly be drawn in a Court of Equity, on the ground that the matter rests in contract, and that the conveyance of the legal estate has not been made to him. The purchaser bound himself by contract. He must be taken to have had present to his mind all those things of which he had notice, and those things which necessarily flowed from, and were incidental to, that notice. He knew that *Allen* was tenant of this land; he was bound to inquire what the tenancy was unless he was willing to be bound by the tenancy whatever it was."

***In re Marseilles Extension Railway Co* (1871) L.R. 7 Ch. App. 161 (Company—imputed notice)**

8.93 A company named Crédit Foncier loaned money to the Marseilles Extension Railway Company, for a purpose which was not valid according to the constitution of the railway company. The two companies had the same solicitor and two directors in common. The question was whether the knowledge of the irregularity was to be imputed to Crédit Foncier by reason of this.

Sir G. Mellish L.J. said he could not think the fact that the Mr. Newbon who was a director of both companies had gone to the Crédit Foncier to negotiate the loan, could impute any knowledge to the latter. ". . . I cannot think that, because he was a common director to the two companies, we are on that

[58] Compare the example given in Chap. 5, "The train ought to be arriving around now" with, *e.g.* "You ought to return books to the library on time."

[59] (1809) 16 Ves. 249; 33 E.R. 978.

account to say that the one company has necessarily notice of everything that is within the knowledge of the common director, and *which knowledge he has acquired as director of the other company*. . . .

Then it is said that there was a common solicitor, and therefore everything known to one company must have been known to the other. Mr. *Heritage* is not called, and all that is said is, that he was the solicitor of both companies and used to attend their boards; but *what as matter of fact he actually knew*, or what conclusion he drew from what he knew, *we have no evidence* . . . I cannot see that there is any evidence at all when the loan was agreed upon that Mr. *Heritage* had begun to act or was acting as solicitor for the *Crédit Foncier*. He went with Mr. *Newbon* to negotiate the loan. That loan was only negotiated with Mr. *Grant*, the managing director of the *Crédit Foncier*, and the board as a board came to the resolution to make the loan, not, as far as appears, consulting Mr. *Heritage*, or employing him at all as their solicitor in the matter, but acting as commercial men upon their own discretion. No doubt it may have been part of the terms that there should be a mortgage, and Mr. *Heritage* may have been employed as their solicitor to draw up the mortgage deed. But I cannot think that is sufficient to affect the *Crédit Foncier* with notice of any improper mode in which this money was to be expended, even if Mr. *Heritage* had, which I cannot see that there is any evidence that he had, notice that it was to be expended for an improper purpose."[60]

Sir W.M. James L.J. agreed.

Note: There being no evidence of Mr. Heritage's actual knowledge during the transaction, the only point was imputed notice. Since he was not, as the court found, the agent for Crédit Foncier in that transaction, the question of imputed notice could not arise. It is interesting to note that merely drawing up the mortgage deed is treated as a purely administrative act, insufficient acting-as-agent to bring in the doctrine of imputed notice.[61]

Morrison v Universal Marine Insurance Co 1873 L.R. 8 Exch. 40 and on appeal, 197. (Insurance: imputed knowledge to buyer through agent who knew facts but formed a wrong deduction from them)

8.94 In this case the broker had formed a view on the balance of the evidence but did not reveal to the insurers the evidence on which he had formed that view. A ship, the Cambria, was to be insured. The owner sent this telegram to his broker: "Since writing Saturday, paragraph in Mercury "Cambria, quaere Cameo, from New Orleans, aground on North Breaker". Today's Mercury says: "The vessel on the North Breakers reported yesterday as the Cambria, is stated to be the Cameo from New Orleans." Can you find out at Lloyd's? Let me know by wire before acting." The broker tried to ascertain whether the ship was the Cambria or not, and decided it was not. Without intending any wrong, he did not pass any of this on to the underwriter. It was held there had been a concealment of a material fact.

Further, it was argued before the court that the material fact in question would have been apparent from the Lloyd's List. The Court of Exchequer held that it could not be assumed as a matter of law that the underwriters knew everything which was in the day's Lloyd's List. (The appeal was on a different point—whether the underwriters had elected to accept the new risk by continuing with the policy after they knew the true facts.)

[60] Italics supplied.

[61] C.p. ***Wylie v. Pollen*** (1863) 3 De G.J. & Sm 596; 46 E.R. 767.

***Agra Bank v. Barry* (1874) L.R. 7 H.L. 135 (Registration and constructive notice)**

8.95 The owner of an estate in Ireland granted an equitable mortgage over it by deposit of title deeds, then (through a new solicitor) permitted a legal mortgage to be taken out. The solicitor asked for the title deeds but the owner did not give them to him, saying they were at his house in Cork; but he gave him particulars, which did not include the fact of the equitable mortgage. The legal mortgage was registered at the Irish Land Registry.[62]

Lord Cairns, Lord Chancellor, referred to the system of registration in Ireland; and said:

"... by decisions which have now, as it seems to me, well established the law, and which it would not be, I think expedient in any way now to call in question, it has been settled that, notwithstanding the apparent stringency of the words contained in this Act of Parliament, still if a person in *Ireland* registers a deed, and if at the time he registers the deed either he himself, or an agent, whose knowledge is the knowledge of his principal, has notice of an earlier deed, which, though executed, is not registered, that which he actually effects will not give him priority over that earlier deed. And, my Lords, I take the explanation of those decisions to be that, which was given by Lord King in the case of *Blades v. Blades*[63], upwards of 150 years ago, the case which was mentioned just now at your Lordships' Bar. I take the explanation to be this, that inasmuch as the object of the statute is to take care that, by the fact of deeds being placed upon a register, those who come to register a subsequent deed shall be informed of the earlier title, the end and object of the statute is accomplished if the person coming to register a deed has, *aliunde*, and not by means of the register, notice of a deed affecting the property executed before his own. In that case the notoriety, which it was the object of the statute to secure, is effected, effected in a different way, but effected as absolutely in respect of the person who thus comes to register as if he had found upon the register notice of the earlier deed. If that is so, your Lordships will observe that those cases depend, and depend entirely, upon the question of *actual notice either to the principal, or to the agent* whose knowledge is the knowledge of the principal.[64]

8.96 But, my Lords, have authorities gone any farther than to the length which I have stated? Has it ever been decided, with regard to a Register Act such as that which prevails in *Ireland*, that negligence in not asking for the title deeds, or not taking up the title deeds, shall postpone a registered security? I am not going to say a word with regard to the effect of negligence of that kind in a country like *England*, where there is no general registration of deeds and no Act of Parliament like the Irish Act. But I am unable to discover any principle upon which mere negligence and mere failure to take all the securities that might be taken, could, in a country subject to a law like the *Irish Register Act*, postpone a registered deed."

He went on to except cases such as *Kennedy v. Green*[65] where there was

[62] In argument counsel referred (*inter alia*) to *Marjoribanks v. Hovenden* (1843) Drury temp. Sug. 11 in which a registered mortgage was held to have notice of the earlier unregistered one because the solicitor to the later mortgagee had a year earlier acted for the equitable mortgagee. However, that had been a case where it was proved the solicitor had had *actual knowledge*, not merely constructive notice, it was pointed out by counsel for the Bank.

[63] 1 Eq. Rep. 358.

[64] Italics supplied.

[65] (1834) 3 My. & K. 699; 40 E.R. 266.

"conduct so reckless, so intensely negligent, that you are absolutely unable to account for it in any other way than this, that, by reason of a suspicion entertained by the person whose conduct you are examining that there was a registered deed before his, he will abstain from inquiring into the fact, because he is so satisfied that the fact exists, that he feels persuaded that if he did inquire he must find it out." He did not express an opinion whether such conduct would or not be sufficient to prevail against registration; but he found nothing of that kind here.

Lord Hatherley agreed and felt that the fact of registration in Ireland made a difference to the standard of inquiry required. The fact of the register being free of encumbrances, and the fact he bona fide knew of none, must mean that a less strict search and inquiry was to be expected of the solicitor of his employer. He also thought it would be extraordinary to give priority to someone who had been careless enough not to register, against someone taking a subsequent instrument, "although that person had neither himself, or through his solicitor, the slightest actual knowledge of the previous transaction, which can only be brought home to him by the doctrine of imputed or constructive notice."

8.97 Lord Selborne pointed out that the duty to investigate title and inquire after deeds is a duty owed by the person who carried out the earlier transaction, but not a duty owed to the "possible holder of a latent title or security."

"It is merely the course which a man dealing *bona fide* in the proper and usual manner for his own interest, ought, by himself or his solicitor, to follow, with a view to his own title and his own security. If he does not follow that course, the omission of it may be a thing requiring to be accounted for or explained. It may be evidence, if it is not explained, of a design inconsistent with *bonâ fide* dealing, to avoid knowledge of the true state of the title. What is a sufficient explanation, must always be a question to be decided with reference to the nature and circumstances of each particular case; and among these the existence of a public registry, in a country in which a registry is established by statute, must necessarily be very material. It would, I think, my Lords, be quite inconsistent with the policy of the *Register Act*, which tells a purchaser or mortgagee that a prior unregistered deed is fraudulent and void as against a later registered deed—I say it would be altogether inconsistent with that policy to hold that a purchaser or mortgagee is under any obligation to make any inquiries with a view to the discovery of unregistered interests. But it is quite consistent with that, that if he or his agent actually knows of the existence of such unregistered instruments when he takes his own deed, he may be estopped in equity from saying that, as to him, they are fraudulent."

Hyde v. Warden (1877) 3 Ex. D. 72 (Constructive notice limited by vendor's breach of good faith duty)

8.98 It was held by the Court of Appeal (Lord Esher M.R., Fry and Lopes L.J.J.) that the purchaser under an agreement for the grant of an underlease has constructive notice of the provisions of the original lease only when he has had a fair opportunity of ascertaining what they were.

Twycross v. Grant (1877) 2 C.P.D. 469 (Due diligence required in share purchase)

8.99 Cockburn C.J. mentioned certain steps which would be expected of a purchaser of shares in a new undertaking. "Among the first things as to which a careful man, disposed to invest in an undertaking, would inquire, would be the adequacy of the capital to the intended purpose, adequacy of capital being essential to the success of an enterprise ...

The next point which a man would desire to ascertain would be the constitution and probable management of the company ..."

***Re Banister* (1879) 12 Ch. D. 131 (Good faith principles are seen narrowing the scope of constructive notice)**

8.100 See the Appendix to Chapter 5, Sale of Land for a note of the case, especially the well-known statement of Fry J. (whose decision was reversed on appeal, but on fresh evidence, and not differing on the applicable principles): "... a vendor, who means to exclude the purchaser from his common right to have a good title shewn, must do so by explicit and clear words.... if the vendor seeks to exclude the purchaser by a statement of fact, he must prove the statement to be true, and the statement of fact must be an honest and fair one; it must not for the purpose in hand be a part of the truth only ...

***Cave v. Cave* (1880) 15 Ch. D. 639 (Fraud breaking transmission)**

8.101 There was a family trust. A solicitor called Charles Cave became the sole trustee of the settlement. He paid the trust money into an account in the names of himself and his brother Frederick Cave, and bought freehold land at Wandsworth with it, conveying this to his brother Frederick Cave. Charles Cave acted for the settlement and for his brother as regards these conveyances. The defendant Chaplin then advanced money to Frederick Cave on a first mortgage of this Wandsworth land. Charles Cave acted on this transaction also. The question was whether Chaplin had notice of the fraud through his solicitor, Charles Cave. Other defendants advanced money, obtaining equitable mortgages. Frederick Cave became bankrupt ultimately, and the plaintiffs who were the beneficiaries of the estate, claimed priority against the defendants. The defendant Chaplin said that Charles Cave was party to a fraud, and the circumstances were such that it was impossible to conceive that the facts which were known to Charles Cave were communicated by him to his principal.

Fry J. held that the solicitor was clearly fraudulent, on the facts, and thus, following *Thompson v. Cartwright*[66], there was no notice to Chaplin. "I am bound to look at the terms of the mortgage in considering whether there was an intention on the part of the solicitors to commit a fraud, and, looking at it, the conclusion I had arrived at independently of them is strongly confirmed." Thus Chaplin obtained priority against the Plaintiff beneficiaries.[67]

***Patman v. Harland* (1881) 17 Ch. D. 353 (Due diligence)**

8.102 Jessel M.R. said that reasonable inquiry in the case of a leasehold meant looking at your lessor's title, and checking that it was a good one. He said as to marriage settlements (echoing earlier cases) that you would have constructive notice only if every marriage settlement *necessarily* affected all a man's land. He also added "I take it, under the modern practice, you are not bound to inquire, because the abstract furnished you is an abstract of every document affecting the land, and although you have been told that the man made a marriage settlement, you are not entitled to assume that the solicitor sup-

[66] (1863) 33 Beav. 178; 55 E.R. 335.

[67] The beneficiaries right as against the equitable mortgagees was different. Fry J. held the beneficiaries right to set aside the transactions was an equitable estate or interest, as opposed to a mere equity, and thus they had priority, being first in time.

pressed improperly the deed of settlement." He thought that if it had been the kind of constructive notice affected by being fobbed off or put off one's guard, then the lessee here would have been put off his guard, because the lease allowed the use the lessee proposed, and the vendor lessor thus knew about it, and thereby indirectly represented that it was possible.

Note: (1) It is interesting that the often-"modern" Jessel M.R. nonetheless supported the good faith duties of the vendor to the extent above.

(2) It is to be noted that the omission of a deed (provided presumably its absence was not part of the chain of title) from the abstract is tantamount to a statement that the deed is irrelevant. Similarly, no doubt, a failure to point out that the buyer's intended use of the land was not possible.[68]

Kettlewell v. Watson (1882) 21 Ch. D. 685 (The agent's job defines the area of relevant knowledge for the conduit pipe)

8.103 In this case it was held that an unpaid vendor of land need not obtain security for his lien, but may enforce it against sub-purchasers who have actual or constructive notice of it. There were two sub-purchasers in particular (the land was divided into small building lots): one who had allowed the purchaser's solicitor to prepare the conveyance to him, but had not relied on him in any other way, and had made no inquiries about the title or the deeds etc. It was held the duty of the solicitor in his case did not include telling him about the lien, so that he had no imputed notice.

There was another sub-purchaser who also made no inquiries himself and employed no solicitor of his own, but who left it to the purchasers "to manage the business" and they prepared the conveyance to him and charged him for it. It was held he *had thereby made them his general agents*, so that he did acquire notice. Fry J. said that the case turned on "the subtle and difficult doctrine of constructive notice".

"The constructive notice which is alleged is of two kinds . . ." and he referred to the distinction between constructive notice and imputed notice. He said he thought it desirable to state what he conceived to be the principle of law applicable to constructive notice. "The ground upon which the Courts have relieved against registered conveyances, or even against a prior legal title, seems to me to be fraud. The Court will not allow a man to avail himself of a legal estate which he has recovered, or of the right which he may have under a registered conveyance, when he, at the time he took the legal estate, or at the time of the registration of the conveyance, knew a fact which made it unconscionable for him to take the legal estate or to effect the registration. That unconscionable act requires, of course, the coincidence in the same person of the knowledge and of the act, because, if A. knows a thing, and B. does something inconsistent with A.'s knowledge, there is nothing fraudulent in the act; but, if A. knows something which renders it unconscionable for him to do the act, and he does it, then there is fraud. The fraud may be in an agent, he both knowing the fact and doing the act, in which case it may be unlawful for the principal to avail himself of the fraudulent act of his agent; or the fraud may be in the principal himself. The first question then which arises is, did the principal know of the charge? Then the next question is, *was is the agent's duty to communicate that fact to the principal? If it was, the Court always holds that he did communicate it, not because, in many cases, he did in fact communicate it, but because, as I understand it, it would be too dangerous to inquire whether the communication was really made; it would open the door to perjury.*

[68] See also **_Laurence v. Lexcourt Holdings_** and *Walker v. Boyle* and see *Smith v. Hughes* (1871) L.R. 6 Q.B. 597 for the occasions when silence can mean "All is well for what you have in mind".

Having found then that the agent both knew the fact and communicated it to his principal, the next step is to inquire whether the principal did an act which was unconscientious, having regard to the knowledge which the Court so imputes to him?"[69]... *"The Court, therefore, receives evidence of the agency, and it receives evidence of the act of the principal, but it will not receive evidence whether the agent recollected the fact at the time or whether he communicated it to his principal. It deals with those matters by way of irrebuttable presumption when the circumstances are known."*[70]

8.104 Fry J. then went on to describe the other kind of notice[71]. "I mean the notice said to be derived from the wilful shutting of the eyes to documents or to facts. That appears to me to rest really on the same principle, viz., that, if you see a man behaving in a way which shews that he desires to avoid knowing something, or having the knowledge of it brought home to him, then you conclude that he knew enough to make him desire not to have evidence of knowledge against him, and, therefore, it has been said that there may be negligence which amounts to fraud. That language has always seemed to me not strictly accurate. What a man does through negligence he does not do from a fraudulent motive. Fraud imports design and purpose; negligence imports that you are acting carelessly and without that design. But what is meant is this—that conduct which might be negligent, or which might be attributable to negligence, is really attributable to a design not to know any more, and is, therefore, an indication that you knew that of which you desired to avoid the evidence. I am perfectly aware that various Judges have expressed this principle in various ways, and that it is impossible to reduce to exact uniformity the principles which they have laid down, but it appears to me that the more recent authorities have gone back again to the true principle on which all these cases have proceeded. Thus in *Ratcliffe v. Barnard*[72](1). Lord Justice *James* referred to negligence of this sort as "wilful negligence which leads the Court to conclude that the person is an accomplice in the fraud". And in *Agra Bank v. Barry(2). Lord Selborne,* in addressing the House of Lords, said[73](3) that the negligence or omission to inquire after title deeds "may be evidence, if it is not explained, of a design inconsistent with *bona fide* dealing, to avoid knowledge of the true state of the title". In other words, what you require is, evidence shewing a desire or fixed purpose to avoid knowing more." Then he went on to refer to the *Kennedy v. Green*[74] presumption to the effect that fraud breaks the presumed chain of knowledge.

Note: We cannot be sure that the disquisition about fraud and "unconscionable conduct is all that helpful as a contribution to our knowledge of what notice is; but we may suspect it is relevant to the development (perhaps better described as non-development) in this century of the doctrine of notice in sales transactions. The fraud Fry J. was referring to seems probably to have been some kind of real or imagined "equitable fraud". The earlier cases do not bother about the basis of the doctrine being actual moral delinquency in an individual, however described: it seems to have been avowedly a default-doctrine of reasonable expectations, in order to supply in the formation of a contract what most people reasonably expect to be there. There is a degree of fault which is no doubt present, (see the section called Eleven Shades of Ambiguity, in Chapter 5 Sale of Land) but it is a failure to come up to the norm,

[69] He then cited passages from Lord Hardwicke in ***Le Neve v. Le Neve***. (1747) Amb. 436; 27 E.R. 291.
[70] Italic supplied.
[71] Constructive (failure to investigate) notice, although he may really be including some degree of inferred knowledge.
[72] L.R. 6 Ch. 652.
[73] (1874) L.R. 7 H.L. 135 at 157.
[74] (1834) 3 My. & K. 699; 40 E.R. 266.

the reasonable expectation of others, rather than any real moral fault. Fry J. was a distinguished judge. Nonetheless, we may suspect that the above passage is a part of the general shifting of position which took place in the 1880's and 90's following the advent of literalism, in which as many doctrines as possible were labelled "equitable". What seems to have happened[75] *with the "equitable" doctrines, formerly good faith/fair dealing doctrines was that they were reduced in status to ancillary matters, usually regarded (in the late nineteenth century, that is) as relevant only to equitable remedies such as specific performance. Here, there is of course no equivalent to specific performance which is possible for constructive or imputed notice. However, the focus on the supposedly "unconscionable" nature of an individual's conduct (the concept "unconscionable" was not normally applied to a failure to come up to reasonable expectations in earlier times in a case not involving a dealing with a vulnerable person) probably paves the way—consciously or unconsciously—for the eventual reduction in importance of the notice doctrine which took place around this time.*

***Re Cousins* (1886) 31 Ch. D. 671**

8.105 This case concerned section 3(1)(ii)(b) of the Conveyancing Act 1882[76]. The section's marginal note shows that it was clearly intended to restrict the doctrine of what is there called "constructive" notice. The marginal note however must mean constructive notice by operation of law, since the section in fact only restricts the doctrine of imputed notice, contenting itself with setting out the effect, unchanged,[77] of the doctrine of constructive (failure to investigate) notice. It provided as to imputed notice (see text above) that in order prejudicially to affect a purchaser with notice it must be "in the same transaction with respect to which a question of notice to the purchase arises" and that it has "come to the knowledge of his solicitor or other agent as such".

Matthew Cousins, the owner of a share of trust property (both real and personal) mortgaged it by deed in 1875 to a certain Dennis Pepper, not disclosing any prior charge to the mortgagee. The mortgagor served notice of the charge on the trustees in 1881. In fact at that date the share was subject (in so far as material) to a prior mortgage made in 1873 by deposit of title deeds to another person. Banks was solicitor (without fraud it would seem) for both Matthew Cousins and for parties in the later mortgage transaction, in which Cousins covenanted that he had good right to assign free from incumbrances. He had also acted for Cousins and for the earlier mortgagee in the earlier mortgage of the share. Notice of that earlier mortgage was said to have been put in a deed box by Banks, but it had been lost by the time of the later mortgage to Pepper, and it did not seem to have come to their knowledge. *There was no evidence before the court about what Banks did* in 1873, save that which could be inferred from the 1875 mortgage, that is, the covenant above.

Counsel for Pepper's executors argued that "whatever knowledge . . . may have been acquired by *Banks* in the previous dealings with the property is immaterial so far as *Pepper* is concerned, unless such knowledge is brought home to *Banks* as solicitor for *Pepper* in the transaction of June 1875. Counsel for the eventual assignee of the earlier mortgage argued that Banks would have had constructive notice if he had made proper inquiries; but his primary argument was that knowledge could be inferred on his part (and thus imputed to his principal) by reason of his employment both for Pepper and for the first mortgagee.

8.106 Chitty J. held that on such facts as he had before him he had to assume

[75] See Introduction, Chap. 1.
[76] Set out in the text at para. 8.13.
[77] Save as noted at para. 8.14.

Banks had made proper inquiries, asked for an abstract of title, and been satisfied with what it revealed; and further had to assume in the absence of other evidence that he was an honest solicitor, and thus *could not* have borne in mind the earlier incumbrance at the time he acted in regard to the 1875 one.

He then commented that section 3 of the Conveyancing Act 1882[78] was intended for the protection of purchasers to some extent—"the question is to what extent—against *that refined doctrine of imputed notice which had been found to work very grievous injustice to honest men, the notice being implied in a very refined manner, and brought home to a man who knew nothing about the matter, and who found that though he had acted perfectly honestly he was postponed by reason of the doctrine of the Court.*[79] Chitty thought the meaning of "come to the knowledge of his solicitor as such" was "come to the knowledge of the solicitor in the transaction as solicitor for the purchaser" (which of course includes mortgagee). He considered it was intended to remedy "the evil consequences of such a doctrine, as was well illustrated by *Hargreaves v Rothwell*"[80]. He said,

"A solicitor is employed who has had a considerable number of other transactions, and amongst them he has had a dealing with the particular estate which is under sale. He may or may not have a good memory, but according to the doctrine of that case notice was imputed to the client if there was such a distance only between the former transaction and the present transaction in which he was engaged as left the Court under the impression—it could not be much more than an impression—that the solicitor had actually remembered the former transaction; and in that way *knowledge was imputed to the solicitor, and then through the solicitor notice was imputed to the client*. That was too refined, and it is quite plain that the section put an end to that doctrine altogether . . ." He thought therefore it had put an end to the earlier mortgagee's case as well.[81]

On constructive notice, he said, "I think the solicitor is bound, as acting for a mortgagee, in a case such as that now before me, to ask what the title is, and to get some answer either in the shape of an abstract, or in the shape of a copy of the will and a statement of additional facts required to shew the title of the legatee who proposes to execute the mortgage. In some cases that is all that is necessary. In this case I cannot say that the prior incumbrance would have come to the knowledge of Banks if he had gone to Cousins . . . I ought not to infer that Cousins would have said that there was a prior incumbrance, but rather to infer that Cousins would have answered according to the statements that appear on his own deed . . ."

Note: The judgment of Chitty J. is quoted and noted rather fully so that we can be reasonably clear about what it in fact did and did not decide.

(1) *It seems to have been assumed rather than decided, that section 3 of the Conveyancing Act 1882 applied not only to interests in land, but interests in mixed property under trusts. This (if decided) is open to question: see the text above at 8.14.*

(2) *It decided that the 1882 Act prevented knowledge being imputed to a solicitor (and then further imputed in the normal way to the client)* ***merely because*** *he had had knowledge of the incumbrance in question on some previous occasion in which he had acted for one of the parties to the current transaction. As noted above, earlier cases had in any even taken the same view as*

[78] See para. 8.13 for the contents of that section.
[79] Italics supplied.
[80] (1836) 1 Keen 154; 48 E.R. 265 above.
[81] Italics supplied.

the statute: the doctrine of imputed notice upon imputed notice seems to date only from about 1834.

(3) *It* ***did not*** *decide:*

(a) *that* ***actual knowledge*** *in the solicitor while acting for both parties could not be imputed to the client. That knowledge would be imputed if the fact was learned for the first time during the new relationship is of course obvious. Less obvious, but also not decided by Chitty J., was the situation where the solicitor's evidence showed or admitted that he remembered the earlier transaction during the new relationship, but for some reason not amounting to fraud, (for example a mistaken view of his duty or because he forgot) did not mention it to his principal. The expression "come to his knowledge" prima facie covers all methods by which knowledge can come to one: remembering, learning from another, or a mixture of both.*

(b) *that* ***actual knowledge*** *may not be* ***inferred as a matter of fact*** *in the solicitor, and then imputed to the client in the usual way. (Chitty J. simply declined to do that, no doubt reasonably in the light of the wording of the deed, on the facts of the case.)*

(c) *that in a case where reasonable investigations would have yielded the knowledge in question (the mortgage of a trust share, of which notice needs to be given to the trustees, is something of a special case, after all) there would not have been constructive knowledge on the part of the solicitor, which would be imputed to the client in the usual way.*

(d) *precisely where the boundaries of the "same transaction" are where the parties jointly instruct the same solicitor, but do so one after another rather than simultaneously and the relevant knowledge is acquired during this gap*[82]

Blackburn Low & Co v. Vigors **(1887) 12 App. Cas. 531 (Insurance: scope of agent's knowledge to be imputed to buyer: limitation by "same transaction" and degree to which agent "represents the principal" (agent to know))**

8.107 The plaintiffs instructed agents to insure their whole line of ships. They then asked the same agents to reinsure one of their ships, the State of Florida. While acting as agents, these came to know of certain facts material to the reinsurance. They did not communicate these facts to the plaintiffs. The facts came to the agents' knowledge by chance, by reason of their being general agents for a third party. The plaintiffs did not reinsure through the first agent, but through another. The new agent knew nothing of the material facts in question.

Lord Halsbury L. C. rested his decision on the fact that the first agents were no longer the agents to know, at the time the reinsurance policy was effected. He also warned that not every agent had sufficiently wide authority that his knowledge bound the principal.

"I cannot but think that the somewhat vague use of the word "agent" leads to confusion. Some agents so far represent the principal that in all respects their acts and intentions and their knowledge may truly be said to be the acts, intentions, and knowledge of the principal. Other agents may have so limited and narrow an authority both in fact and in the common understanding of their form of employment that it would be quite inaccurate to say that such an agent's knowledge or intentions are the knowledge or intentions of his principal . . ."

Lord Watson, agreeing, drew a distinction for the purposes of the case

[82] As happened in ***Halifax Building Society v. Stepsky*** [1996] 2 Ch. 207.

between agents such as captains and ship agents on the one hand and brokers on the other. "The one class is specially employed for the purpose of communicating to him the very facts which the law requires him to divulge to his insurer; the other is employed, not to procure or furnish information concerning the ship, but to effect an insurance."

Lord Macnaghten drew the same distinction between ship agents, to whom the management of the vessel was entrusted: there was nothing unreasonable in imputing to a shipowner all the information which such an agent had at the time and might in the ordinary course of things have communicated to his employer.

Note: The questions are thus seen to be (1) was he an agent in the same transaction?; (2) what was he an agent **to do?**

***Reeve v. Berridge* (1888) 20 Q.B.D. 523 (Vendor's good faith duty of disclosure limits purchaser's constructive notice)**

8.108 An agreement had been made for the purchase of an existing lease. Fry L.J. delivering the judgment of the Court of Appeal affirmed that the purchaser was not bound by the contents of unusual covenants in the lease since he had not had a fair opportunity of inspecting it prior to the agreement. He noted that criticisms of the law as stated and of the earlier case *Hyde v. Warden*[83] had been addressed to the court, but affirmed the old law. He said, "... we cannot but observe that there is great practical convenience in requiring the vendor, who knows his own title, to disclose all that is necessary to protect himself, rather then in requiring the purchaser to demand an inspection of the vendor's title deed before entering into a contract, a demand which the owners of property would in some cases be unwilling to concede, and which is not, in our opinion, in accordance with the usual course of business in sales by private contract."

***English and Scottish Mercantile Investment Company v. Brunton* [1892] 2 Q.B. 700 (Constructive notice: fobbing off)**

8.109 A limited company issued debentures containing a restriction on the company's liberty to create any mortgage or charge in priority to the debentures. The company subsequently obtained a loan from the respondents on the security of an assignment to them of its interest in some monies due to it. The managing director of the company misled them into believing there was nothing in the debentures to affect the security. The respondents were thus held unaffected by notice.[84]

Lord Esher referred to the "constructive notice" argument which he said was wholly equitable and not known to the common law, although "There is an inference of fact known to common lawyers which comes somewhat near to it. When a man has statements made to him, or has knowledge of facts, which do not expressly tell him of something which is against him, and he abstains from making further inquiry because he knows what the result would be—or, as the phrase is, he wilfully shuts his eyes"—then judges are in the habit of telling juries that they may infer that he did know what was against him. It is an inference of fact drawn because you cannot look into a man's mind, but you can infer from his conduct whether he is speaking truly or not when he says that he did not know of particular facts. There is no question of constructive notice or constructive knowledge involved in that inference; it is actual knowledge which is inferred. Constructive notice or

[83] (1877) 3 Ex D. 72.

[84] Registration at Companies House would of course be a factor in a modern case.

knowledge, as I have said, is an equitable doctrine wholly; it is a doctrine not known to the common law, but it must now be dealt with and acknowledged by the Courts which administer the common law."

That being so, he applied *Le Neve v. Le Neve*.[85] pointing out that the debenture did not fall into the category of deeds which "must necessarily affect the property"; it might or might not affect the property and there had been misleading conduct. He referred to Lord Lyndhurst in *Jones v. Smith*[86] and Sir George Jessel M.R. in *Patman v. Harland*[87], pointing out that in that case the deed definitely affected the title, so it would have been no answer to tell him it did not; this was more like the marriage settlement cases, for example *Jones v. Smith*.[88]

Bowen L.J. also thought there was no constructive notice here. Kay L.J. said "I venture to say that the doctrine of constructive notice, if carefully applied and limited in the way pointed out by Wigram V.C.,[89] and Lord Lyndhurst[90], is a doctrine which will never defeat the ends of justice, but will promote them always. If we were to apply it as we are asked to apply it in this case, we should not only be extending it beyond what has been laid down in any previous case, but we should be extending it beyond the limits which Lord Lyndhurst and Wigram V.C. so carefully defined."

London Joint Stock Bank v. Simmons [1892] A.C. 201, H.L.

8.110 The question before the House of Lords was about whether the bank had received in good faith some negotiable instruments deposited with them as security by a broker with whom they dealt (but which negotiable instruments it turned out belonged to the plaintiff Simmons). The interest of the case lies in the relationship between good faith and constructive notice.

Lord Halsbury did not touch on this: he applied the statement of Abbott C.J.[91] that a holder of a negotiable instrument "has power to give title to any person honestly acquiring it", and held that on the facts there was nothing which could have raised the bank's suspicions about the transaction, so they were in good faith.

Lord Herschell relied on the similar statement of Parke B.,[92] "that the holder of bills of exchange indorsed in blank or other negotiable securities transferable by delivery could give a title which he himself did not possess to a bona fide holder for value" and Parke B.'s rejection of the suggestion in certain cases in which "care and caution in the taker of such securities has been treated as essential to the validity of his title besides and independently of honesty of purpose." He said also,

"One word I would say upon the question of notice, and being put upon inquiry. *I should be very sorry to see the doctrine of constructive notice introduced into the law of negotiable instruments. But regard to the facts of which the taker of such instruments had notice is most material in considering whether he took in good faith.* If there be anything wrong in the transaction, the taker of the instrument is not acting in good faith if he shuts his eyes to the facts presented to him and puts the suspicions aside without further inquiry".

Later, he affirmed again the duty to look into puzzling facts:

[85] (1747) Amb. 436; 27 E.R. 291.
[86] (1843) 1 Ph. 244; 41 E.R. 624.
[87] (1881) 17 Ch.D. 353.
[88] (1841) 1 Hare 61; 66 E.R. 943.
[89] ***Jones v. Smith*** at first instance, (1841) 1 Hare 61; 66 E.R. 943.
[90] ***Jones v. Smith*** an appeal, (1843) 1 Ph. 244; 41 E.R. 624.
[91] *Earl of Sheffield v. London Joint Stock Bank* (1888) 13 App. Cas. 333.
[92] *Foster v. Pearson* (1835) 1 Cr.M. & R. 849 at 855.

"I apprehend that when a person whose honesty there is no reason to doubt offers negotiable securities to a banker or any other person, the only consideration likely to engage his attention is, whether the security is sufficient to justify the advance required. And I do not think the law lays upon him the obligation of making any inquiry into the title of the person whom he finds in possession of them; *of course, if there is anything to arouse suspicion, to lead to a doubt whether the person purporting to transfer them is justified in entering into the contemplated transaction the case would be different, the existence of such suspicion or doubt would be inconsistent with good faith. And if no inquiry were made, or if on inquiry the doubt were not removed and the suspicion dissipated, I should have no hesitation in holding that good faith was wanting in a person thus acting."*[93]

***Bailey v. Barnes* [1894] 1 Ch 25**

8.111 The case concerned constructive (failure to investigate) knowledge as codified in the Conveyancing Act 1882: that is whether the purchaser had made "such inquiries and inspections ... as *ought reasonably*[94] to have made by him".

There had been an improper (not in good faith) exercise of a mortgagee's power of sale. The allegation was that the sub-purchaser (that is, the purchaser *from* the purchaser who had been in bad faith, had constructive (and imputed) notice by reason of facts known and not investigated by his solicitors. They had known that the property consisting of four houses was sold to the purchaser who had been in bad faith for £1,579 approximately each; and that about four months later a valuation for £8,700 was obtained. On the facts, the purchaser was held in good faith.

In the Court of Appeal, Lindley L.J. referred to section 21(2) of the Conveyancing Act 1881 which provided that a purchaser's title should not be impeachable on the ground that a mortgagee's power of sale was improperly or irregularly exercised; and said the question (against that background) was thus whether the purchaser, Lilley, had notice of the invalidity of the title of his vendor who bought from the mortgagee.

Lindley L.J. affirmed the law as stated by Lord Cranworth in *Ware v. Lord Egmont*[95] and by Wigram V.C. in his celebrated judgment in *Jones v. Smith*[96] About the Conveyancing Act 1882 (although perhaps he may have been talking only about constructive notice, not imputed notice) he said, "The Conveyancing Act 1882, really does no more than state the law as it was before, but its negative form shews that a restriction rather than an extension of the doctrine of notice was intended by the Legislature ..."

***Manchester Trust v. Furness* [1895] 2 Q.B. 539**

8.112 This concerned a charterparty which was referred to in the bill of lading. The bill of lading was signed by the master, and the plaintiffs made their claim under it, relying on the rule that the master's signature of the bill of lading is prima facie as agent for the shipowner. In this particular case, the charterparty, which the plaintiffs had not looked at, contained a restriction on his authority. The court held that what they termed "the equitable doctrine of constructive notice" should not be extended. Lindley L.J. (whose views on constructive notice were wholeheartedly agreed to by Lopes L.J. and Rigby L.J.) said,

[93] Italics supplied.
[94] Conveyancing Act 1882, s.3. Italics supplied.
[95] (1854) 4 D.M. & G. 460; 43 E.R. 586.
[96] (1841) 1 Hare 61; 66 E.R. 943.

"... there have been repeated protests against the introduction into commercial transactions of anything like an extension of those doctrines, and the protest is founded on perfect good sense. In dealing with estates in land title is everything, and it can be leisurely investigated; in commercial transactions possession is everything, and there is not time to investigate title; and if we were to extend the doctrine of constructive notice to commercial transactions we should be doing infinite mischief and paralyzing the trade of the country. That I am not going too far in making these observations will be found by turning to *English & Scottish Mercantile Investment Co v. Brunton*[97], and also to what Lord Herschell said about constructive notice in *London Joint Stock Bank v. Simmons.*[98] "as regards debentures and everything of that kind, and other commercial documents, the protest which I have been making has been made before, and I do not think it is likely to be made in vain."

Note: The expression "the doctrine of constructive notice" is beginning to be used to denote not the doctrine of constructive notice by operation of law, (that is in the wide or global sense), but constructive notice in the narrow (failure to investigate) sense. Although the duty to follow up puzzling facts where necessary (a subdivision of the latter, as has been seen) has been preserved (see above), there is here a failure to be clear about labelling, and a failure expressly to preserve the narrower duty. On its facts the case is no doubt unexceptionable in holding that a person does not expect that kind of restriction in a charterparty.

The failure to be clear is a matter of regret, but perhaps unsurprising in the literalist age that had now begun, which tended to be somewhat brusque with good faith doctrines, believing no doubt that all bad behaviour could be prevented by a sufficiently detailed statute outlawing seriatim all anticipated kinds of had behaviour. We now perceive this idea as open to considerable doubt. Commercial life was in the 1890's beginning to spawn more complex forms of transaction: the application of the old constructive notice doctrine to these new forms was bound to need care and some appreciation of the principles. No doubt there would not be a duty to investigate[99] *where there is a reasonable expectation (that is, in the circumstances of much everyday commercial life) that a purchaser will not carry out pre-contractual investigations. Also, the nature of many "commercial" transactions is that they are meant to be carried out very quickly.*

This will specially be the case where the nature of the right being bought is clear enough, and where it passes by possession, so that the need for patient uncovering of title, and detailed enquiry as to the precise boundaries of the purchase, are both unnecessary. It may ***not*** *be the case with some of the more complex "packages" now available.*

Thus the application of the doctrine of constructive alone notice is always going to be different according to the nature of the transaction: the "duty" of what one might call self-generated investigation (which is here being labelled "constructive notice" tout court) may occur relatively infrequently in simple "commercial" transactions.

***In re Hampshire Land Company* [1896] 2 Ch. 743 (Principles of imputed notice applied to company)**

8.113 The directors of a company had the power to borrow money on its behalf, up to a certain limit, beyond which they needed the consent of a general meeting. The directors borrowed from a society, but in fact there had been an irregularity in their power to borrow, because although they had the con-

[97] [1892] 2 Q.B. 700.
[98] [1892] A.C 201. "I should be very sorry to see the doctrine of constructive notice introduced into the law of negotiable instruments."
[99] See the text above.

sent of the general meeting, the notice summoning the meeting had been defective. The secretary of the company was also the secretary of the society which lent the money, and knew of the irregularity; and the question arose whether his knowledge could be imputed to the society.

Vaughan Williams J. held following Mellish L.J. in *In re Marseilles Extension Railway Company*[1] that the mere dual agency was insufficient to impute notice to the lender. He said "[w]here is the line to be drawn, or what is the test to be applied in order to say whether or not in each case the knowledge of the common officer is the knowledge of each company employing him? It seems to me that, broadly, the Lords Justices do draw the line thus, that the knowledge which has been acquired by the officer of one company will not be imputed to the other company, unless the common officer had some duty imposed upon him to communicate that knowledge to the other company, and had some duty imposed on him by the company which is alleged to be affected by the notice to receive the notice?"

Vaughan Williams L.J. rather curiously did not answer this question in the case. He distinguished cases where the duty to pass on information was express, and went on simply to hold that as there was no presumed duty to pass on his own fraud, so there was no presumed duty to pass on his own breach of duty at having committed an irregularity.

Note: One cannot be at all sure whether the tentative suggestion that the "fraud exception" regarding imputed knowledge could apply to the agent's own negligence is right. There is no earlier authority for it so far as is known. The case stands up perfectly well without it. It was not part of the dual agent's task to investigate such matters on the part of the lender company (and indeed these was no duty on the lender company either).[2]

***Re White & Smith's Contract* [1896] 1 Ch. 637**

8.114 This case shows how the scope of the purchaser's is affected with constructive notice is limited by the vendor's duty of fair dealing. It was held the purchaser did not have constructive notice of the contents of a lease, even though in fact that lease had been open for his inspection, because this fact had not been made clear, and he had consequently been unaware of it.

***Oliver v. Hinton* [1899] 2 Ch. 264 Constructive (failure to investigate) notice**

8.115 A solicitor named Hill deposited six title deeds to five houses with a widow named Caroline Oliver by way of equitable mortgage. He then executed a conveyance of three of the houses. The plaintiff in the action, who was his purchaser, employed only a former solicitor's clerk in the purchase. He did not ask for an abstract of title, but asked Hill about "the documents", and Hill said that he had them, but they would not be delivered up because they related to other property; and the clerk did not ask him to produce them.

Romer J. at first instance held that the purchaser who does not inquire into the title of his vendor at all, as here, will be affected with notice of what appears on the title.

On appeal, the judgment of Romer J. was upheld. Lindley M.R. said that the only person who acquired a title subsequent to the plaintiff's who could override her was "a bona fide purchaser for value without notice of her charge. But this does not include a purchaser for value who is so grossly negligent as to take none of the ordinary precautions which ought to be taken

[1] (1871) L.R. 7 Ch. App. 161.
[2] See ***In re David Payne & Co Ltd*** [1904] 2 Ch. 608.

in such a matter—who, in fact, takes no precautions whatever. He may be a bona fide purchaser for value without notice of a prior charge, but he is not entitled to the protection of the Court." He held that a purchaser who had "been guilty of such gross negligence as would render it unjust to deprive the prior incumbrancer of his priority" would be deprived of the protection of the legal estate.

Sir F.H. Jeune held that the gross negligence meant that although there was not "fraud actual" (no doubt in the sense of deliberate dishonesty) there was negligence so gross as to fix her with constructive notice.

Rigby L.J. stressed that although a fobbing-off answer to a reasonable question about the title deeds might let a purchaser off: it must be an answer *"to the question which under the circumstances it was reasonable that he should ask"*.[3] Here the vendor was not in terms ever asked to produce the title deeds. No proper inquiry had been made, which in his view was "just the same thing as if he had made no inquiry at all about the deeds."

***Hunt v. Luck* [1902] 1 Ch. 428**

8.116 The Court of Appeal affirmed the decision of Farwell J. This had been reached on the basis of the old law on the first branch (constructive notice) of section 3 of the Conveyancing Act 1882,[4] and was that the purchaser was not bound to enquire to whom a tenant paid his rent. Vaughan Williams L.J. drew attention to section 3(3) of the Act which said that "A purchaser shall not by reason of anything in this section be affected by notice in any case where he would not have been so affected if this section had not been enacted, and said "... the practical result is that the law prior to the Conveyancing Act can only be used as a shield, and not treated as going beyond the law contained in the code-like definition in s.3." The other two lord justices agreed.

***Re Fenwick, Stobart & Co Ltd* [1902] 1 Ch. 507 (Imputed notice—company)**

8.117 The case concerned notice of dishonour of a bill of exchange. Buckley J. said that the mere fact a particular man was secretary of the two companies concerned would not mean that he had notice in his capacity as secretary of the company which would have received the notice. *"What the Court has to see is whether the information he gets, as secretary of the one company, comes to him under such circumstances as that it is his duty to communicate it to the other company."*[5] Here he knew of the dishonour as secretary to the one company, but it was not his duty to communicate it to the second.

Note: It will be seen that the rule affecting imputed notice to the company is the same as in the case of other agents.

***Molyneux v. Hawtrey* [1903] 2 K.B.487**

8.118 This was a case about a lease with unusual covenants, which however the purchaser had *not had a fair opportunity to inspect;* so it could not be said he ought reasonably to have made further inquiries. Collins M.R. thought that section 3 of the Conveyancing Act 1882 "seems to me to leave the law applicable to such cases as this substantially on the same footing as before."

[3] Italics supplied.
[4] Set out (in bold type) in para. 8.13, above.
[5] Italics supplied.

Matthew L.J. thought regarding the Conveyancing Act 1882[6] that "*it seems to me that the effect of that enactment is very much to elucidate the principles upon which the applicability of the doctrine of constructive notice depends.*"[7]

Cozens-Hardy L.J. agreed, saying "*I think that the doctrine of law on this subject must now be treated as being nearly, if not quite, confined within the limits contained in the 3rd section of the Conveyancing Act 1882.*[8]

***Re Valletort Laundry* [1903] 2 Ch 654 (Constructive notice)**

8.119 Held[9] that a bank did *not* have notice of prior debentures which created floating charges by a company and which forbade the creation of any prior charge, merely because it actually held the debentures as security for other customers. It was held not unreasonable of the Bank not to inquire further as to the precise terms of the debentures, because it was anyway taking behind the debentures; and because the act of the managing director in depositing the title deeds with the bank amounted to a representation that he had power to do so ("*by such act represented that he had power to do so*").

Note: The italicised words are interesting. Jessel M.R. raised the same kind of possibility in Patman v. Harland[10]*: he thought the abstract of title was to be seen as a representation by the vendor that all relevant documents of title were there, so that any documents not obviously forming missing links in the chain (and thus within the purchaser's duty to investigate) would be covered by this representation.*

***In re David Payne & Co Ltd* [1904] 2 Ch. 608**

8.120 The case arose on an application by the liquidator of the above company to have a second mortgage debenture issued by the company to the Exploring Land and Minerals Company declared void, one of the supporting reasons for this being the knowledge of one Kolckmann, a member of a firm of stockbrokers who were agents of the lending company but who was also a director of the lending company, that the money to be lent was not going to be applied for the purposes of the company, which knowledge it was said should be imputed to the lending company.

The Court of Appeal, affirming Buckley J., held that his knowledge should *not* be imputed to the lending company. Vaughan Williams L.J.

(1) accepted that *Bradley v. Riches*[11] and *Kettlewell v. Watson*[12] supported the proposition that "it is not necessary that the agent should have acquired the knowledge at the time when he is acting as agent. It is sufficient if he afterwards acts as agent in respect of the matter as to which he has acquired the knowledge. It then becomes his duty to communicate to the company for which he is then acting the knowledge which he has previously acquired."

(2) held (referring to an earlier decision of his own, *In re Hampshire Land Co*[13] that that proposition had no application to the present case, because "at the moment when Kolckmann began acting on behalf of the company, the transaction was of such a nature that there was *no*

[6] Or at least the part regarding constructive notice which he quoted.
[7] Italics supplied.
[8] Italics supplied. Again, he may only have been referring to the first part, regarding constructive notice.
[9] But see now the statutory requirement to register company charges.
[10] (1881) 17 Ch. D. 353.
[11] (1878) 9 Ch. D. 189.
[12] (1882) 21 Ch. D. 685.
[13] [1896] 2 Ch. 743.

obligation on the part of the lending company to inquire to what purposes the borrowed money was going to be applied, and there was no obligation upon Kolckmann to receive or disclose any such information.[14]

Romer L.J. agreed (as did Cozens-Hardy L.J.) that the knowledge of Kolckmann could not be imputed to the lending company. Because the lending company was under *no duty to inquire into the transaction*, there was no duty upon Kolckmann to tell them what he knew about it: "it was knowledge of something which really did not concern the lending company as a matter of law".

Cozens-Hardy L.J. endorsed the way the point about the duty to inquire had been put by Buckley J. at first instance: "Where the power is merely a general power to borrow, limited only, as it must be, for the purposes of the company's business, I think the matter is to be treated in this way, that the lender cannot investigate what the borrower is going to do with the money; he cannot look into the affairs of the company and say, "Your purposes do not require it now; this borrowing is unnecessary; you must shew me exactly why you want it".

***Greenwood v. Leather Shod Wheel Co* [1900] 1 Ch. 421 (Constructive notice limited by vendor's good faith duty)**

8.121 A waiver clause in a company prospectus did not apply to matters not fairly disclosed to purchaser[15].

***Lennard's Carrying Co Ltd v. Asiatic Petroleum Co. Ltd* [1915] A.C. 705 ("Actual" knowledge of company in the sense of knowing and willing an act)**

8.122 By section 503 of the Merchant Shipping Act 1894 the owner of a British sea-going ship was not liable for damage to goods on board ship which were damaged or lost by fire where this happened without "his actual fault or privity".

The ship was owned by a limited company and managed by another. The House of Lords had no difficulty in finding that an active director in both companies, Mr. Lennard, was "*the active spirit*"[16] and the person whose knowledge of the vessel's unseaworthiness was to be attributed to the owner. Lord Haldane pointed out that a company being an abstraction, "its active and directing will must consequently be sought in the person of somebody who for some purposes may be called an agent, but who is really the directing mind and will of the corporation, the very ego and centre of the personality of the corporation." Thus, the company was liable because "*his action is the very action of the company itself*".[17]

Lord Dunedin agreed, also considering that Mr. Lennard was the "alter ego" of the company.

***Lee v. Rayson* [1917] 1 Ch. 613 (Constructive notice: duty of purchaser limited by vendor's good faith duty)**

8.123 Eve J. affirmed that although the purchaser had not inspected the leases which affected property he was buying, he was not bound to take the prop-

[14] Italics supplied.
[15] See Chap. 10 for a fuller note of this case.
[16] Italics supplied: Lord Haldane's phrase.
[17] Italics supplied.

erty subject to the actual terms of the leases, because the vendor had described them in a misleading manner.

***London General Insurance Co v. General Marine Underwriters Association* [1921] 1 K.B. 104, C.A. (Insurance: standard of constructive knowledge required of assured: test where knowledge available to both)**

8.124 The assured effected an insurance of a ship, not knowing that the ship had been lost the night before. In fact they had that morning received the Lloyd's casualty list showing the ship as lost, but had not had time to look at it. It was held that an assured is deemed to know that which in the ordinary course of his business he should have known. The policy was set aside in the circumstances. The insurers had access to the Lloyd's List also, but no special reason to consult it as to this ship, thus their opportunity of knowledge was disregarded.

***Flexman v. Corbett* [1930] 1 Ch. 672**

8.125 Maugham J. followed *Hyde v. Warden*[18] and *Reeve v. Berridge*[19].

***HMS Truculent, The Admiralty v. The S.S. Divina (Owners)* [1951] 2 All E.R. 968 ("Actual" knowledge of company in the sense of knowing and willing an act)**

8.126 This was an action to limit liability for damage caused by collision under section 503 of the Merchant Shipping Act 1894, which required the owner of the ship which caused the collision to show that the casualty happened without his "actual fault or privity". A Royal Navy submarine had collided with a fishing vessel because it had, in common with other Royal Navy submarines at the time, an inadequate system of navigation lights.

Willmer J., relying on the *Lennard*[20] case above, decided that the Third Sea Lord was for the purpose the alter ego of the owner.

***The Lady Gwendolen, Arthur Guinness, Son & Co (Dublin) Ltd) v. M.V. Freshfield (Owner)* [1965] P. 294 ("Actual" knowledge of company in the sense of knowing and willing an act)**

8.127 The Lady Gwendolen while on a voyage from Dublin to Liverpool collided with another ship. The collision was because of the negligence of the master of the Lady Gwendolen, in continuing in the channel in question in thick fog, and not using his radar. The question was whether the owners (whose main business was that of brewers), were privy to it. Since the relevant section, section 503 of the Merchant Shipping Act 1894 used the expression "actual fault", the fault had to be more than constructive fault, for which the master's negligence would be enough: there had to be something personal to the owner.

Further, the court pointed out that there must be an objective test of actual fault, which did not vary with the actual knowledge or competence of the company in question. Sellers L.J. said "It is no excuse for the plaintiffs that their main business was that of brewers . . .

In their capacity as shipowners they must be judged by the standard of conduct of the ordinary reasonable shipowner in the management and control of a vessel or of a fleet of vessels."

[18] (1877) 3 Ex D. 72.
[19] (1885) 20 Q.B.D. 523.
[20] [1915] A.C. 705.

Willmer L.J. said also that there had to be an objective test. The company could be in no better position than one whose main business was that of shipowning. "It seems to me that any company which embarks on the business of shipowning must accept the obligation to ensure efficient management of its ships if it is to enjoy the very considerable benefits conferred by the statutory right to limitation".

They held that the company for this purpose would at all events be someone in the management hierarchy, and no-one at all in that hierarchy had in fact carried out the functions necessary to see that the radar was used.

***Tesco Supermarkets v. Nattrass* [1972] A.C. 153; [1971] 2 W.L.R. 1166 ("Actual" knowledge of company in the sense of knowing and willing an act (the act to be carried out away from the centre of control))**

8.128 This concerned a provision of the Trade Descriptions Act 1968. Tesco was prosecuted under section 11(2) for displaying a notice that goods were "being offered at a price less than that at which they were in fact being offered . . ." A supermarket manager had accidentally failed to notice that it had run out of the washing powder advertised which was marked at 2s 11d and offered for sale instead the higher priced ones at 3s 11d. The question was whether Tesco could rely on a defence under section 24(10) that the act was caused by "another person" and that "he took all reasonable precautions and exercised all due diligence to avoid the commission of such an offence by himself or any person under his control." Thus, the real question here really was the directing, or responsible mind of the company.

Lord Reid commented on Denning L.J.'s metaphor of the human body with brain and hands[21]. He pointed out that it was unlikely, as had been suggested since, that the words were intended to apply to all servants of a company whose work is brain work, or who exercise some managerial discretion under the direction of superior officers of the company. He thought that the focus should be on those "who represent the directing mind and will of the company, and control what it does."[22] He continued: "I think that is right for this reason. Normally the board of directors, the managing director and perhaps other superior officers of a company carry out the functions of management and speak and act as the company. Their subordinates do not. They carry out orders from above and it can make no difference that they are given some measure of discretion. *But the board of directors may delegate some part of their functions of management giving to their delegate full discretion to act independently of instructions from them. I see no difficulty in holding that they have thereby put such a delegate in their place so that within the scope of the delegation he can act as the company.*[23] It may not always be easy to draw the line but there are cases in which the line must be drawn. *Lennard*'s case was one of them.

8.129 In some cases the phrase alter ego has been used. I think it is misleading. When dealing with a company the word alter is I think misleading. The person who speaks and acts as the company is not alter. He is identified with the company. And when dealing with an individual no other individual can be his alter ego. The other individual can be a servant, agent, delegate or representative but I know of neither principle nor authority which warrants the confusion (in the literal or original sense) of two separate individuals."

Lord Diplock said, "In my view, therefore, the question: what natural persons are to be treated in law as being the company for the purpose of acts

[21] In *H.L. Bolton (Engineering) Co. Ltd. v. T.S. Graham & Sons Ltd.* [1957] 1 Q.B. 159. See the ***Meridian*** case below at para. 8.135 *et seq.* for reference to this.

[22] Part of Denning L.J.'s phrase.

[23] Italics supplied.

done in the course of its business, including the taking of precautions and the exercise of due diligence to avoid the commission of a criminal offence, is to be found by identifying those natural persons who by the memorandum and articles of association or as a result of action taken by the directors, or by the company in general meeting pursuant to the articles, are entrusted with the exercise of the powers of the company. This test is in conformity with the classic statement of Viscount Haldane L.C. in *Lennard's Carrying Co Ltd v. Asiatic Petroleum Co. Ltd* . . .[24]

***Tesco Stores Ltd v. Brent London BC* [1993] 1 W.L.R. 1037 "Actual" knowledge of company in the sense of knowing and willing an act, such act to be carried out away from the centre of control**

8.130 A video film with an "18" classification had been sold in a Tesco store to a 14-year old boy. The question was whether the company might use the defence under the section 11(2)(b) of the Video Recordings Act 1984 that it did not have reasonable grounds to believe. . . .

Staughton L.J. pointed out that the section here was concerned, unlike *Tesco Supermarkets v. Nattrass*[25] with knowledge and information, rather than due diligence. It would be the employee at the shop till who would have the knowledge or reasonable grounds for belief. He also pointed out that if the contrary were right there would be a heavier burden under the Act on the Single handed shopkeeper. "I cannot believe that Parliament intended the large company to be acquitted but the single-handed shopkeeper convicted."

***El Ajou v. Dollar Holdings* [1994] 2 All E.R. 685, C.A.**

8.131 The plaintiff owned funds and securities which were under the control of an investment manager in Geneva. This manager was bribed to invest the plaintiff's money in fraudulent share selling schemes operated by three Canadians through two Dutch companies. The proceeds were channelled eventually back through Geneva, and some were invested in a London property project in conjunction with the first defendant. The first defendant was quite unconnected with the fraud, and simply required financial backing for a speculative building project. Points which arose were (1) whether the knowledge of a Mr. Ferdman, who played no active part in the first defendant's management, but who had *had a degree of involvement in the transaction*, was the knowledge of the first defendant in the quasi-individual (anthropomorphic) sense that companies may have knowledge or (2) whether his knowledge could be imputed to the first defendant, Dollar Holdings Limited. Mr. Ferdman was a non-executive director, and the chairman, of Dollar Holdings, but tended to act also for a Swiss company of his own.

(1) Company's own actual knowledge

8.132 Nourse L.J. quoted Millett J. who had referred to *Lennard's* case and had said of the persons who manage and control the company's actions "Their minds are its mind; their intention its intention; their knowledge its knowledge", and continued, "It is important to emphasize that the management and control is not something to be considered generally or in the round. It is necessary to identify the natural person or persons having management or control in relation to the act or omission in point. This was well put by Eveleigh J. in . . . *R v. Andrews Weatherfoil*[26] . . .:

[24] [1915] A.C. 705, see para. 8.122, above.
[25] Above para. 8.128.
[26] [1972] 1 ALL E.R. 65

"It is necessary to establish whether the natural person or persons in question have the status and authority which in law makes their acts in the matter under consideration the acts of the company so that the natural person is to be treated as the company itself."

Decided cases show that, in regard to the requisite status and authority, the formal position, as regulated by the company's articles of association, service contracts and so forth, though highly relevant, may not be decisive. Here Millett J. adopted a pragmatic approach. In my view he was right to do so, although it has led me, with diffidence, to a conclusion different from his own." He thought that Mr. Ferdman's knowledge *was* the company's.

Hoffmann L.J. thought also that Mr. Ferdman, who had in fact signed the agreement in question on behalf of the Dollar Holdings, was sufficiently the *directing mind and will of the company for this purpose,* even though he acted in a relatively informal way.

(2) *Imputed notice*

8.133 It had also been argued that Mr. Ferdman's knowledge ought to be imputed to the first defendant because he was its agent. This Nourse L.J. disagreed with (as did Hoffmann L.J.). Nourse L.J. thought that Mr. Ferdman had, on the facts of the case, no duty to communicate the information to the company. (See *Re Hampshire Land Co.*[27] and *Re Fenwick Stobart & Co Ltd, Deep Sea Fishery Co's Claim*[28].) He thought the case indistinguishable from *Re David Payne & Co Ltd, Young v. David Payne & Co Ltd*[29]

Hoffmann L.J. accepted that the principal has in some cases a duty to investigate or make disclosure, and this binds his agent also: as for example in *Gladstone v. King*[30]. He also accepted that there were cases where the agent had actual or ostensible authority to receive communications, as for example the insurance cases. This aspect was not, he thought, relevant here on the grounds that Mr. Ferdman was not, he considered, the agent for the right principal here. "Mr. Ferdman did not receive information about the frauds in his capacity as agent for DLH [Dollar Holdings]. He found it out while acting for the Canadians."

Thus, Hoffmann L.J. summarised "What it therefore comes to is that *Mr. Ferdman, an agent of DLH, had private knowledge of facts into which DLH had no duty to inquire*[31]. Mr. Beloff[32] said that Mr. Ferdman nevertheless owed DLH a duty to disclose those facts. He then submits that because he had such a duty, DLH must be treated as if he had discharged it.

I am inclined to agree that Mr. Ferdman did owe a duty, both as broker employed by DLH to find an investor and as chairman of the Board, to inform DLH that the Yulara money was the proceeds of fraud . . .

But Mr. Beloff's submission that DLH must be treated as if the duty had been discharged raises an important point of principle. In my judgment the submission is wrong. The fact that an agent owed a duty to his principal to communicate information may permit a court to infer as a fact that he actually did so. But *this is a rebuttable*

[27] [1896] 2 Ch. 743.
[28] [1902] 1 Ch. 507.
[29] [1904] 2 Ch. 608.
[30] (1813), 1 M. & S. 35; 105 E.R. 13.
[31] Italics supplied.
[32] Counsel for the plaintiff.

inference of fact and in the present case the judge found that Mr. Ferdman *did not disclose what he knew*[33] to anyone else acting on behalf of DLH. In some of the cases in the third of the categories I have mentioned, the fact that an agent with authority to receive a communication had a duty to pass the communication on to his principal is mentioned as a reason why the principal should be treated as having received it. I think, however, that the true basis of these cases is that communication to the agent is treated, by reason of his authority to receive it, as communication to the principal. I know of no authority for the proposition that in the absence of any duty on the part of the principal to investigate, information which was received by an agent otherwise than as agent can be imputed to the principal simply on the ground that the agent owed to his principal a duty to disclose it."

Note:

(1) *The judgments tend to be less clear than might be desirable in so far as they deal with the imputation of knowledge. What seems likely to have been the main determining factor in the case was the "same transaction" doctrine. On the face of it, it would seem that Mr. Ferdman must have acquired the knowledge at a point prior to his acting for DLH, so that his previous knowledge could not be imputed to DLH.*

(2) *It is not clear whether he may not, however, have had* ***actual knowledge*** *of puzzling facts, and had it during the transaction in which he acted for DLH. If this were the case, then it is difficult to see why that could not have been imputed to the principal: both or either would have had a duty to follow up puzzling facts which presented themselves during the transaction, and if either failed to follow them up, would be fixed with knowledge of what would have been found out.*[34]

(3) *We may perhaps feel some difficulty in following the precise aim of the passage in Hoffmann L.J.'s judgment to the effect that the communication from the agent to the principal is a rebuttable inference of fact, which may be rebutted by proof that he did not in fact communicate it. If the intention was for this to be a general principle, in regard to what has been called the conduit pipe, it would be wholly inconsistent with the principles expressed in earlier decisions. The presumption that the agent has passed on to the principal what it is his duty to pass on (provided he knows it actually or constructively in the transaction in which he is instructed) is in fact* ***irrebuttable.***[35] *The passage would seem perhaps more likely to be a reference to inferring actual knowledge in the principal, from the fact that the agent may have told him; in which case it does not, of course touch on the conduit pipe principle at all.*

Re Supply of Ready Mixed Concrete (No. 2) Director General of Fair Trading v. Pioneer Concrete (UK) Ltd **[1995] 1 A.C. 456 ("Actual" knowledge of company in the sense of knowing and willing an act)**

8.134 In this case a restrictive arrangement in breach of an undertaking by a company to the Restrictive Practices Court was made by executives of the company acting within the scope of their employment. The board knew nothing

[33] Italics supplied.

[34] See the text above at para. 8.38 for this kind of constructive knowledge of the agent being imputed to the principal.

[35] See the text above at para. 8.37, giving the public policy/prevention of fraud reasons for this rule.

of this, and had given directions that such arrangements were not to be made. The House of Lords however held in this case that the act and state of mind of an employee who entered into the arrangement should be attributed to the company. They did so by construing the undertaking against the background of the Restrictive Trade Practices Act 1976, and noting that it would hardly achieve its purpose otherwise.

***Meridian Global Funds Management Asia Ltd v. Securities Commission* [1995] 2 A.C. 500 (P.C.) ("Actual" knowledge of company in the sense of being an appropriate person to receive information (and give notice))**

8.135 The case came from New Zealand. It suffices to say that it concerned sections 20 (3) and (4) of the New Zealand Securities Act 1988. Subsection (4) required a certain notice to be given by a "person" as soon as the person "knows or ought to know" that the person is a substantial security holder [as defined] in a public company. The question was which kind of company employee's knowledge sufficed for the purpose. Lord Hoffmann gave the judgment of the Judicial Committee. Their Lordships' judgment is a model of clarity on this topic, if one may say so, and I set out the relevant passage at some length.

"The company's primary rules of attribution [that is, generally its constitution, typically the articles of association] together with the general principles of agency, vicarious liability and so forth are usually sufficient to enable one to determine its rights and obligations. In exceptional cases, however, they will not provide an answer. This will be the case when a rule of law, either expressly or by implication, excludes attribution on the basis of the general principles of agency or vicarious liability. For example, a rule may be stated in language primarily applicable to a natural person and require some act or state of mind on the part of that person "himself" as opposed to his servants or agents. This is generally true of rules of the criminal law, which ordinarily impose liability only for the actus reus and mens rea of the defendant himself. How is such a rule to be applied to a company?

One possibility is that the court may come to the conclusion that the rule was not intended to apply to companies at all; for example, a law which created an offence for which the only penalty was community service. Another possibility is that the court might interpret the law as meaning that it could apply to a company only on the basis of its primary rules of attribution, ie if the act giving rise to liability was specifically authorised by a resolution of the board or a unanimous agreement of the shareholders. But there will be many cases in which neither of these solutions is satisfactory; in which the court considers that the law was intended to apply to companies and that, although it excludes ordinary vicarious liability, insistence on the primary rules of attribution would in practice defeat that intention. In such a case, the court must fashion a special rule of attribution for the particular substantive rule. This is always a matter of interpretation; given that it was intended to apply to a company, how was it intended to apply? Whose act (or knowledge, or state of mind) was *for this purpose*[36] intended to count as the act etc of the company? One finds the answer to this question by applying the usual canons of interpretation, taking into account the language of the rule (if it is a statute) and its content and policy."

8.136 Lord Hoffmann then referred to various earlier authorities, and cast some doubt on the universal usefulness of the anthropomorphic metaphor, pervasive in this sphere, of the company's directing mind and will see Denning L.J.

[36] Italics in original.

in *HL Bolton (Engineering) Co Ltd v. TJ Graham & Sons Ltd*[37] "They have a brain and a nerve centre which controls what they do. They also have hands which hold the tools and act in accordance with directions from the centre."

The Judicial Committee considered "the question is one of construction rather than metaphysics". This being so, the answer was clear. "The policy of s. 20 of the 1988 Act is to compel, in fast-moving markets, the immediate disclosure of the identity of persons who become substantial security holders in public issuers. Notice must be given as soon as that person knows he has become a substantial security holder. In the case of a corporate security holder, what rule should be implied as to the person who knowledge for this purpose is to count as the knowledge of the company? Surely the person who, with the authority of the company, acquired the relevant interest. Otherwise the policy of the Act would be defeated. But their Lordships would wish to guard themselves against being understood to mean that whenever a servant of a company has authority to do an act on its behalf, knowledge of that act will for all purposes be attributed to the company."

Note: Perhaps the above judgment, sparklingly clear as it is, is very slightly flawed for general purposes by the fact that two "states of mind" on the part of the company are being implicitly run together: knowledge of the company in the sense of passive receipt of information by some individual appropriate for that purpose (it probably does not matter much whether this is "actual" or imputed); and the "actual" knowledge of the company in the sense of knowing and willing the act of giving the requisite notice.

***Halifax Building Society v. Stepsky* [1996] 2 W.L.R. 230**

8.137 In this case the same solicitor acted for husband and wife as mortgagors and for the Society as lender. The solicitor was told by the husband (who gave the instructions on behalf of husband and wife) of facts which would put the lender on notice that the transaction was not for the benefit of the wife, that is, that the loan was intended to be used to pay off various business debts of the husband's. The question was whether this knowledge, which was acquired a week before the solicitors started to act for the Society as well, was to be imputed to the Society as lender.

Morritt L.J. with whom the other two Lord Justices agreed, appears to have taken the line that "come to his knowledge" in section 199 of the Law of Property Act 1925[38] meant that it had to pop into his consciousness for the first time newborn, as it were, and had to do so while the solicitor was also solicitor for the lender. Thus, the knowledge did not qualify, even though it was "in the same transaction". It required not only to be that, but in the precise days of joint instruction.

Morritt L.J. also went on to add that he thought anyway if the solicitor's knowledge derived from the husband was to be imputed to the lender, it should also be imputed to the wife.[39]

Note: Some doubt may be felt about the ruling on section 199 of the Law of Property Act 1925, if only because it smacks of a literalism one feels to be inappropriate in a statute which codifies principles. It is not a list of factual do's and don'ts; and

[37] [1956] 3 All E.R. 624, a case however not on a company's knowledge, but on its "intention"

[38] See text above.

[39] Whether or not this would have excluded her from any defence would of course depend on the precise kind of misrepresentation proved to be made to her, and/or the undue influence involved. Her claim was somewhat sketchily deposed to, and the case proceeded on assumptions about these, so it is not clear how powerful an argument this would in fact have been.

is short, but needs to be applied in a way which is in accordance with the principles. The root problem perhaps is to reconcile the tension which arose in the circumstances between the "same transaction" and "solicitor as such". However, it is evident that the court did not have full submissions on the points involved from either counsel, so perhaps it is right simply to register a tentative question mark about this decision meanwhile.

CHAPTER 9

DEALINGS WITH THE VULNERABLE BUYER OR SELLER

"What has happened in Australia simply marks a return to underlying concepts and principles, more particularly the equitable concept of unconscionable conduct, and a restatement of principles designed to achieve greater fairness. The restatement of principles involves the application of broad standards rather than rigid formulae but the restatement of principles is none the worse for that. In more recent times, the Anglo-Australian lawyer has been more comfortable with rigid formulae than with broad standards presenting large issues of fact for determination. But rigid formulae do not achieve fairness: their object is certainty and predictability. Whether they have succeeded in attaining that object is another question. . . ."[1]

". . . this clear duty results from the rule of this Court, and throws upon him the whole onus of the case; that, if he will mix with the character of attorney that of vendor, he shall, if the propriety of the contract comes in question, manifest, that he has given her all that reasonable advice against himself, that he would have given her against a third person. It is asked, where is that rule to be found. I answer, in that great rule of the Court, that he, who bargains in matter of advantage with a person placing confidence in him is bound to shew, that a reasonable use had been made of that confidence; a rule applying to trustees, attorneys or any one else."[2]

"An equality of condition is a circumstance that is absolutely essential to the validity of any bargain. This is a principle which ought to be distinctly understood in London; if any man who is to be trusted places himself in a condition in which he has an opportunity of taking advantage of his employer, by placing himself in such a situation, whether acting fairly or not, he must suffer the consequence of his situation."[3]

[1] Sir Anthony Mason, former Chief Justice of Australia, "*Unfairness in Contracting: the Role of Equity and Good Conscience in Commercial Transactions*", paper given at Gray's Inn Hall on July 5, 1995.

[2] Lord Eldon in ***Gibson v. Jeyes*** (1801) 6 Ves. 278; 31 E.R. 1044.

[3] Lord Wynford in *Rothschild v. Brookman* (1831) S. Bligh N.S. 165; 5 E.R. 273 noted in the Appendix to Chap. 15.

"What has gone wrong? Their Lordships venture to think that the reason is that . . . there has been a tendency to cite, interpret and apply Lord Selborne L.C.'s formulation . . . as though it were a statute . . . This approach has been inimical to analysis of the underlying concept. Working within this constraint, the courts have found themselves wrestling with the interpretation of the individual ingredients . . . without examining the underlying reason why a third party . . . is being made liable at all."[4]

MAKING A MARKET OF ANOTHER MAN'S WEAKNESS

9.01 This chapter is about unfair dealings with the vulnerable, whether selling to them or buying from them. Such a label lacks that certain something a good legal label should have. However, one problem encountered in the search for any special rules about dealing with unusually vulnerable parties to a sale is the absence of any proper legal label for what one is looking for.[5] Various expressions are used. Some of the cases come under the heading of "undue influence"; some are called unconscionable bargains, unequal bargains, or "catching bargains". Some are called "abuse of confidence". A person may have difficulty with most of these, as labels. The concept of a "catching" bargain does not, perhaps, convey anything much to the average person now, and it hardly occurs even in the older cases. "Abuse of confidence" is in some ways more promising, were it not for the dual meaning which "confidence" has now. "Unconscionable bargains" (sometimes also called "unconscientious bargains") no doubt means something, but the meaning appears so wide that it may be unhelpful, and a lawyer will tend to avoid such wide phrases instinctively. "Palm-tree justice", will be his or her unspoken thought, and probably quite right too. It might after all be "unconscionable", viewed from one point of view, to buy shares in a company which made its profits out of the third-world poor. This would of course be nowhere near what what is meant in the cases by an unconscionable bargain. In any case, perhaps "conscience" is something fewer people nowadays will feel they have even an instinctive notion of: it begins perhaps to feel, to some, like a wholly optional virtue, or worse, an outmoded concept overdue for consignment to our literary past. Meanwhile, the wide overt meaning becomes unduly subjective—to the detriment of the litigant. Thus, it may be that when judges say, "The test is just what is unconscionable", they are in effect simply reserving a right to attach the label to anything they or the next judge happen to think deserves

[4] Parts of Lord Nicholls' remarks in *Royal Brunei Airlines v. Tan* [1995] 2 A.C. 378 at 386 B.

[5] Or at all events any label which would make sense to the modern Man on the Underground (or whatever the law's Mr/Mrs/Ms Average, the Man on the Clapham Omnibus, has turned into).

it[6] or a discretion under another name. (This may possibly be one reason why many cases on the topic take so "unconscionably" long to hear; nothing being definitely irrelevant to so wide a target; so that litigants will strive for days to catch the judge's ear with some particular piece of conduct embedded somewhere in the mass of material put in evidence, which it is hoped may achieve the winning stamp of "unconscionable".) Modern judges are easily seduced by these wide discretions masquerading as clear law. One seductive feature from a judicial point of view no doubt is that it is difficult actually to be wrong if the discretion is wide enough. Earlier judges saw the dangers. Lord Erskine in *Halsey v. Grant*[7] stated "This is the perfection of our jurisdiction. If the rigid construction of the law were relaxed, *there would be no safety ...*"[8]

9.02 "Unequal bargain" will not do as a label,[9] and see *Lloyd's Bank v. Bundy* for the misunderstandings arising from this label, attached by Lord Denning, with true historical insight, but unfortunately giving us insufficient analysis of the principles involved. This expression is unfortunate, as many have pointed out, in that it gives the idea that inequality between what is given and what is received in the bargain is what is being described. This, if correct, would obviously strike at the root of any sensible freedom of contract. In fact the principle is much, much narrower: it actually protects freedom of contract, only circumscribing the freedom to "rip off". A bargain may be unequal, and still a perfectly good one if the parties are reasonably equal in their negotiating positions, notably their access to relevant information about value, as will be seen. The inequality in point is the inequality in the parties' position in *arriving at* the bargain. "Undue advantage" is another expression, which occurs in the older cases; but perhaps it suffers from the same problem as "unequal bargain". Anyway, such labels have an inbuilt wobbliness about the essential point; which is surely to describe, however sketchily, what does actually come within the label, not merely to say that too much of some otherwise blameless ingredient (such as advantage) won't do. The phrase which is used in the Chapter title: "making a market of another man's weakness", is Lord Selborne's phrase,[10] noted below. There may be better phrases—and the search for one would perhaps be a good thing—but meanwhile Lord Selborne's is at least one with an appropriate descriptive content for the subject matter of this chapter.

[6] A decorous version of "What I tell you three times is true," Lewis Carroll, *Hunting of the Snark*.

[7] (1806) noted in the Appendix to Chap. 5, Sales of Land).

[8] He was talking about something regarded by some nowadays as highly "discretionary"—the equity courts' jurisdiction to preserve contracts, giving compensation and specific performance; but the old equity courts kept themselves firmly to a highly-regulated discretion, rather unlike the modern kind. Italics supplied.

[9] [1975] Q.B. 326.

[10] *Earl of Aylesford v. Morris* (1873) L.R. 8 Ch. App. 484.

The weakness has to determine the bargain

9.03 The point which the label "making a market of another man's weakness" does get across very well is that the *weakness has to be determinative of the bargain*: there has to be weakness, and it has to determine the bargain reached. Unless the weakness has this determinative quality, the bargain will not be set aside: the dealing with the vulnerable person will not be unfair.

Predators are always with us

9.04 Making a market of another man's weakness has not exactly gone out of fashion nowadays, one may venture to think. Some mis-sold pensions and life assurance policies may be one modern example; and some cases of bank sureties taken from wives, parents, and cohabitees may be another. Expectant heirs, however, who seem to have occasioned its first manifestations, are now confined to the pages of Trollope and the like for the most part. We need therefore to take a brief look at the evolution of this doctrine in the seventeenth century and beyond, and try to see the principles behind it.

Fair dealing/good faith attributes of principles

9.05 The principles which have been developed about dealings with the unusually vulnerable have relatively seldom been labelled "good faith" principles, but they are fair dealing principles: in *O'Rorke v. Bolingbroke*[11] Lord Blackburn said:

> "... Fraud in this cause, in my opinion, there is none; nor is there unfair dealing, including in those words every dealing by which one man having the means of getting a better bargain from another, effects the transaction by these means."

They have mostly lacked the good faith or fair dealing label, perhaps largely because the examples have arisen originally within the exclusive jurisdiction of equity to set aside contracts. They have thus been simply what "equity will not permit". Their breach has also often been what equity has called "fraudulent" in the sense in which that word was sometimes used then[12] or "unconscionable"—which may have been linked to good faith notions[13] However, it is also possible that the reason is simply that the law on dealing with the vulnerable, which is very ancient, pre-dated the influence in England of jurists such as Pothier, so the label never became quite so firmly attached to it. See now Millett L.J. in *Bristol & West Building Society v. Mothew*[14]

[11] (1877) noted below.
[12] See below.
[13] See Spence, *Equitable Jurisdiction of the Court of Chancery* (1846) Vol. 1 p. 411, cited in Finn.
[14] [1996] 4 All E.R. 698.

who *has* now, no doubt correctly, used the term "good faith" for the obligation of a "fiduciary" to be loyal to the relationship with his principal—the duty of loyalty, as he has labelled it.

In *Bristol & West Building Society v. Mothew*[15] Millett L.J. has warned against "unthinking resort to verbal formulae" in this branch of the law. Because of the importance of his judgment on this point, there follows a lengthy quotation from it. He said:

> "The expression "fiduciary duty" is properly confined to those duties which are peculiar to fiduciaries and the breach of which attracts legal consequences differing from those consequent upon the breach of other duties. Unless the expression is so limited it is lacking in practical utility. In this sense it is obvious that not every breach of duty by a fiduciary is a breach of fiduciary duty. I would endorse the observations of Southin J. in *Girardet v. Crease*[16] where she said:
>
> The word "fiduciary" is flung around now as if it applied to all breaches of duty by solicitors, directors of companies, and so forth . . . That a lawyer can commit a breach of the special duty [of a fiduciary] . . . by entering into a contract with a client without full disclosure and so forth is clear. But to say that simple carelessness in giving advice is such a breach is a perversion of words. These remarks were approved by La Forest J. in *Lac Minerals Ltd v. International Corona Ltd*,[17] where he said: ". . . not every legal claim arising out of a relationship with fiduciary incidents will give rise to a claim for a breach of fiduciary duty."
>
> Millett L.J. went on to say that the expression "fiduciary duty" was not appropriately applied to the duty of skill and care owed by, say, a solicitor to his client, which was the case before him. He cited in support Lord Browne-Wilkinson in *Henderson v. Merrett Syndicates Ltd*[18] who equated the duty of skill and care owed by "bailees, carriers, trustees, directors, agents and others", saying that they were all the same duty, and it was not their status or position which gave rise to the duty but the circumstances.
>
> Millett L.J. later defined a "fiduciary" as "someone who has undertaken to act for or on behalf of another in a particular matter in circumstances which give rise to a relationship of trust and confidence". "The distinguishing obligation of a fiduciary is the obligation of loyalty. The principal is entitled to the single-minded loyalty of his fiduciary. This core liability has several facets. A fiduciary must act in good faith; he must not make a profit out of his trust; he must not place himself in a position where his duty and his interest may conflict; he may not act for his own benefit or the benefit of a third person without the informed consent of his principal. This is not intended to be an exhaustive list, but it is sufficient to indicate the nature of

[15] *ibid.*
[16] (1987) 11 B.C.L.R. 2d 361.
[17] (1989) 61 D.L.R. (4th) at 28.
[18] [1994] 3 W.L.R. 761 at 799.

fiduciary obligations. They are the defining characteristics of the fiduciary."

How the good faith principles about dealings with the vulnerable came to be misunderstood

9.06 By the time the principles came to be clarified, it was natural to do so by means of examples as much as anything: the expectant heir, the person in a "humble station in life"; the solicitor, and so on. Next, it becomes forgotten that some of the principles were ever general ones in the first place. So does our law ossify, and then disappear. For example, despite the greatest respect for a distinguished former Vice-Chancellor, there have to have been better ways of approaching the case of *Cresswell v. Potter*[19] than to try to stuff twentieth century dealings with the vulnerable into the "poor and ignorant" straitjacket of the past.

> "... the euphemisms of the twentieth century may require the word 'poor' to be replaced by 'a member of the lower income group' or the like, and the word 'ignorant' by 'less highly educated'. The plaintiff ... is a Post Office telephonist.... The defendant told me that the plaintiff probably had a little saved, but not much; and there was evidence that her earnings were about the same as the defendant's and that these were those of a carpenter. The plaintiff also has a legal aid certificate....
>
> In those circumstances I think the plaintiff may properly be described as 'poor' in the sense used in *Fry v. Lane*[20] ... Further, although no doubt it requires considerable alertness and skill to be a good telephonist, I think that a telephonist can properly be described as 'ignorant' ..."

One or two exercises of that sort will probably suffice to see a fundamentally sound legal principle well on its way to oblivion. However sound the actual decision on the facts of the case, a principle of the kind we are concerned ought not to be treated as if it was a matter of coming within qualifying words, as within a statute. The influence of statute does not need to engender in lawyers a blinkered, small-print obsession. The law need not ossify, and need not disappear. Inequality in negotiating power is real, perhaps even more common now than in earlier centuries, and one really cannot think that legally aided telephonists have any monopoly of the victims' position. Faced, for example, with large powerful organisations, with better access to the vital (and increasingly complex) information relevant to a contract of sale or purchase of goods, services, land or rights, perhaps we are often, all of us, in a relatively humble station in life? A Lloyd's Name faced with his managing agent who silently forms the intention of putting him into high-risk business may not be exactly in a humble

[19] (1968) noted at [1978] 1 W.L.R. 255.

[20] (1888) 40 Ch. D. 312. For comment on the relatively crude exposition of the law given in this case, see Appendix.

"station in life"; indeed he will usually have been at least modestly wealthy, but his often greatly unequal access to crucial information has, no doubt, in some cases had a similar disabling effect in practice to the social awe felt by the spinster in *Baker v. Monk*[21] for the prosperous businessman who had twice been mayor of the town. Both the spinster and the Name will have made unequal bargains, which were unequal because their negotiating positions were—inescapably—unequal. The result was a market of the weakness of Miss Baker; and there will no doubt be markets of the weakness of others in a like position. Modern examples outside the field of "presumed undue influence"[22] are few. The case of *O'Sullivan v. Management Agency Ltd*[23] is an exception—the young, inexperienced music writer and the experienced publisher and agent. This is a pity. So, the quest to discover the real principles which apply to prevent a person making a market of another's weakness is, one may venture to think, a useful one.

The quest for the real principles

The author of this book is not alone in the feeling that a new analysis is called for. See in particular, Professor Birks and Chin Nyuk Yin's contribution to this branch of the law, seeking an X-factor, which in addition to the inequality of bargaining position, gives the victim the right to relief against the predator.[24]

Two types of vulnerability: "spontaneous" and "rely-on-me"

9.07 In this book a somewhat different emphasis is adopted as regards the analysis of the principles (subject as above). The most appropriate way to categorise the relevant vulnerability is considered to be by the circumstances of the *transaction* itself, and what these circumstances reveal about the parties' relative access to key information about the transaction, such as value.[25] The characteristics of the victim may, but

[21] (1864) 4 D.J. & S. 388; 46 E.R. 968, a delightful case, in part for the exquisite sense of period which it conveys.

[22] See below as to the way this topic fits into the subject matter of the chapter.

[23] [1985] Q.B. 428.

[24] Birks, *Introduction to Restitution*, (2nd ed.) Birks/Chin "On the Nature of Undue Influence", in *Good Faith and Default in Contract Law*, (ed., Beatson, 1995). They consider—in common with the views expressed in this chapter—(i) that fault on the part of the predator is not necessary, at all events save the implicit fault (which is not nothing) of accepting or agreeing to a contract with a vulnerable person; (ii) that "manifest disadvantage" is an unsatisfactory interloper into this area of the law.

[25] Birks/Chin seek the characteristics in the victim, who is said to exhibit "excessive dependence". If by this is meant some pre-existing state, common to all victims, one can only say that the cases do not seem to bear this out. See, *e.g.* below as to the rely-on-me type of vulnerability, which includes but is not limited to, the "nominate" relationships such as those of guardian and ward, doctor and patient, etc. It may be that the modern

need not be crucial. The degree of real equality of access to relevant information he has about the transaction is.[26] This is his real disadvantage, the X-factor which singles out transactions which should be set aside from those which are simply unequal, but perfectly proper bargains.

There are, none the less, two distinct main types of vulnerability on the part of the victims to be seen in the transactions. The first is the kind which arises in dealings which are between relative strangers. This *spontaneous vulnerability* is not in any sense induced by the other party: it arises purely out of the circumstances of the victim, and normally existed before the other party came on the scene at all. The victim may be a young lord or an inexperienced music writer, an over-awed spinster or a cunning, illiterate old man: he may be financially ignorant with no advisers; someone under pressure, usually from fear (for example, of imprisonment) or from pressure of debts; or he or she may be old, and/or relatively inexperienced, for example without knowledge of how to value the object sold or bought, or unable to understand the effect of a legal document. He or she is prey waiting for a predator.

9.08 The second kind of vulnerability may be called "induced" vulnerability or "*rely-on-me*" vulnerability. Here the victim is not specially vulnerable to people in general; but vulnerable purely because he or she is in a relationship which invites trust—whether expressly or by implication from the circumstances. A common example of this kind of vulnerability is of course the relationship of solicitor and client. Whom should one trust, if not one's solicitor? A ward will trust a guardian, similarly; a child will frequently still trust a parent, and in more deferential days certainly did. But a more informal or less anciently recognized situation may convey the message "You may rely on me," equally well. We tend to trust our managing agents or clerks, rightly or wrongly, and perhaps simply because we cannot in practice make sufficient checks. The need to trust is father to the duty to be trustworthy. It is in the nature of such managing agencies that the managing agent is down there doing his part of the job, while the principal is somewhere else. In earlier times, many people trusted their religious advisers;[27] and sometimes people like Miss Baker trusted those who held grander positions socially. What is common about all these relationships is that the victim, if there is one, has been *put off his guard*. He will not have checked on the other party, not because he was incapable of obtaining the necessary assistance, but because his trust prevented him from realising the *need* for it. His

over-emphasis on the supposed helplessness, excessive dependence, etc, of the victim stems as much as anything from a historically incorrect interpretation of the word "dominion" used in the older cases. The word has changed meaning over the period with which we are concerned.

[26] See the section dealing with the natural lawyers' influence on English law in Chap. 3, The Legal Nature of the Duty of Good Faith.

[27] Mr Baseley in *Haguenim v Baseley* (1807) 14 Ves 289; 33 E.R. 526 was both a clergyman and an unofficial managing agent.

trust may have stemmed from one of a number of things: the simple impracticability of checking, as suggested above; or again, what has been called the "rely-on-me" factor in the relationship: he believed he did not need to check but could trust the agent/guardian etc. The existence of the relationship of trust, however arrived at, was thus by its very existence a *locking-in* factor. The victim was weak, certainly, *because of his trust*, but more than that, he did not realise that he needed help, because he thought he was being looked after.

There is perhaps also a third category of vulnerability—the kind of induced vulnerability (or "actual undue influence" to use a traditional label) caused or contributed to by pressure on the victim directly exercised by the predator, *e.g.* by bullying, threats, etc. Here the assent of the victim is really so impaired as virtually to be non-existent in any real sense. It will be a matter of chance whether the victim's circumstances show him to be to some extent spontaneously vulnerable as well or whether he is a perfectly normally situated citizen who encounters an unfortunate influence. No doubt a lesser degree of pressure would be necessary in the former case than the latter. One may doubt that the courts are going to have much difficulty identifying and setting aside transactions found to have been entered into under this kind of pressure. The view taken in this book is that this kind of vulnerability therefore requires no additional comment.

Traditional categories of induced vulnerability unhelpful

9.09 The induced-vulnerability cases include cases which have been traditionally been labelled "undue influence" ("presumed undue influence" in so far as relevant for our purposes). These are differentiated[28] from "Abuse of confidence". Treatments of these topics are to be found in most textbooks dealing with the subject, and are mysteriously treated as different branches of the law.[29] This may be partly because of the over-emphasis which has developed on the existence of the status-relationships (guardian and ward, *etc.*) which are said to be "relationships of" presumed undue influence. It may also be because the sheer volume of undigested cases on the subject to be found in the textbooks by way of case references prevents working lawyers from gaining a proper appreciation of the topic. No reasoned justification for placing the "abuse of confidence" cases (primarily sales to or purchases from his solicitor by a client) in a separate category of their own seems to exist. There is nothing to be seen in the cases to justify the split. On the contrary, the courts at the time these principles were being developed appear to have been indifferent as to the label they attached to these cases.[30]

[28] See, *Barclay's Bank v. O'Brien* [1994] 1 A.C. 180.
[29] See also, *e.g. CIBC v. Pitt* [1994] 1 A.C. 200.
[30] See the examples given below at para. 9.09, and see the cases in the Appendix to the chapter.

Abuse of confidence cases simply examples of induced vulnerability

9.10 The true analysis is simply that the abuse of confidence cases are nothing other than particularly obvious cases of induced vulnerability. The true modern law on dealings with the vulnerable who are in a relationship of trust is thus much simpler than may be supposed. First, the same thread of principle runs through this *and* the presumed undue influence cases *and* the cases on dealings with the spontaneously vulnerable who are outside these relationships—making a market of the other person's weakness. Second, in the presumed undue influence cases and the abuse of confidence cases (in other words the category of *induced vulnerability* cases) it is a weakness the stronger party has previously *created* in the other (we need not call him the weaker) by accepting or agreeing or volunteering to take on the role of the trusted party—the solicitor, the adviser, *etc*. There is thus a shifting of the burden of proof. The law in this area is that once the transaction is questioned, and the requisite induced vulnerability is shown, the position of the defendant for practical purposes is similar to the seller of a reversion in the mid-nineteenth century, at the peak of the courts' enthusiasm for setting aside reversions. The plaintiff simply has to point to the relationship, question the transaction and sit back: it is then for the defendant to show that the transaction was a fair one: in other words, that *the vulnerability stemming from invited trust was in no way determinative of the bargain*. There is nothing unreasonable about this: if one seeks to be relied on, whether for professional or other profit or merely to satisfy one's own desire to manage other people's affairs (what used to be called "officious interference") one *ought* to be worthy of trust. If it is a professional relationship, no doubt the risk will also have been covered by insurance and paid for by all customers, just as happened with most sales of reversions by the mid nineteenth century.[31]

There are two defences for the trusted party who has been party to a sale or purchase with a vulnerable party. These, as the spontaneous vulnerability cases show also, are: (1) to show that the inequality gave no advantage, ie to show that there was no resulting disadvantage ("manifest"[32] or otherwise); or (2) to show that although there was a resulting advantage, the vulnerable party had lost any locking-in factor, for example by means of a cooling off period and proper outside advice, including where necessary legal or valuation advice or both. See as to the first *Edwards v. Burt*.[33] See as to the second *Hylton*

[31] See Lord Thurlow's comment noted by Lord Eldon "that insurance might now be made with so much ease and certainty", in the case of heirs apparent dealing with their expectancies: *Davis v. Duke of Marlborough* 2 Sw. 108 at 143; 36 E.R. at 567.

[32] Although it is to be doubted this extra word adds anything worth worrying about.

[33] 2 De G.M. & G. 55; 42 E.R. 791.

v. Hylton[34] ("If anything could make such a transaction supportable, it must be where there was a real and fair account"); and *Edwards v. Meyrick*[35] in which the solicitor had discharged the burden on him and shown that the parties had been "substantially at arm's length and on an equal footing".

The supposed requirement of manifest disadvantage to the plaintiff in "presumed undue influence" cases (but not "abuse of confidence" cases)

9.11 The requirement of "manifest disadvantage" has been imposed by the House of Lords' decision in *National Westminster Bank v. Morgan*.[36] Lord Scarman noted Cotton L.J.'s words in the gift case of *Allcard v. Skinner*,[37] about cases of what is called induced vulnerability in this chapter and presumed undue influence by traditional textbook writers:

> "... the court interferes, not on the ground that any wrongful act has in fact been committed by the donee, but on the ground of public policy, and to prevent the relations which existed between the parties and the influence arising therefrom being abused."

Lord Scarman pointed out that since that was a gift case, one could hardly expect Cotton L.J. to have mentioned disadvantage. Lord Scarman went on, however.

> "If, however ... Cotton L.J. ... should be understood as laying down that the transaction need not be one of disadvantage and that the presumption of undue influence can arise in respect of a transaction which provides 'reasonably equal benefits for both parties,' I have with great respect to say that in my opinion the Lord Justice would have erred in law: principle and authority are against any such proposition."
>
> "Like Dunn L.J.[38] I know of no reported authority where the transaction set aside was not to the manifest disadvantage of the person influenced ... Whatever the legal nature of the transaction, the authorities show that it must constitute a disadvantage sufficiently serious to require evidence to rebut the presumption that in the circumstances of the relationship between the parties it was procured by the exercise of undue influence."

Was Lord Scarman right?

9.12 Had he had submissions regarding the burden of proof[39] on the trusted party to show either that the transaction was fair just and

[34] (1754) 2 Ves. Sen. 547; 28 E.R. 349.
[35] (1842) 2 Hare 60; 67 E.R. 25.
[36] [1985] A.C. 686.
[37] (1887), 36 Ch. D. 145.
[38] In the court below.
[39] See above.

reasonable, or that the "victim" had been fully informed so had lost his "locking-in factor," no doubt he would have been right. As it is, his statement is so compressed as to be misleading. Further, it gives and has given the impression that the plaintiff has to prove that the transaction was manifestly disadvantageous to him; when in fact the burden of proof is, on the authorities up to that point, exactly the other way round—on the trusted party.

Spontaneous (un-induced) Vulnerability

A brief historical search for the principles

9.13 The law on spontaneous vulnerability in parties to sales is almost forgotten in this country. What follows therefore is a quest into history in search of its beginnings, and the principles developed, before setting out an analysis of the principles in more traditional form. This is not out of a delight in antiquarian matters.[40] It is simply because the principles governing dealings with the spontaneously vulnerable may best be seen in the older cases. Dealings with the already - vulnerable are the first thing to be looked at: dealings where the vulnerability has been induced by the other party logically come later.

The seventeenth century—vulnerability inferred from the circumstances of the transaction and the characteristics of the weaker party—the easily-led Lord Arglas.

9.14 The earliest case which appears below (though it is evident that it is by no means the earliest case on the topic) is the case of *The Earl of Arglas v. Muschampe*.[41] The principle is expressed as a well-established general principle by that date, and does not seem, at least as far as may be seen, to be confined to expectant heirs in particular. The Court in that case referred to the existence of "several Precedents in this Court, as well in the Reigns of Queen Elizabeth, King James, King Charles the First, as in his now Majesty's Reign, where Relief hath been given against over-reaching Bargains and Contracts made by young Heirs." This case is noted in some detail, because, although it was concerned with the sale of a contingent reversion, the principles on which the court acted are actually quite modern.

The Earl was entitled to an estate of his uncle if the uncle should die without male issue. Being "in Want of Money" he borrowed £100 from the defendant Muschampe, and gave him security in the form of a rentcharge of £300 per annum after the death of the then Earl of Arglas. The plaintiff, (who had succeeded to the earldom by the time of the action) "relying on the defendant's integrity sealed" the deeds, believing that the security would be void on repayment of the money

[40] Although some of the older cases combine clarity and a period charm.
[41] (1682–4) 2 Ch. Rep. 266; 21 E.R. 675.

lent. No copy of the deeds was given to him, nor was he given time to peruse them, and the court attached importance to this.[42]

The Court's judgment recited:

> "That Thomas Earl of Arglas, at the Time of this Bargain, was very young and of an easy Nature, and had forsaken his Wife and Friends and came to London, where he lived in Riot and Debauchery, and for the supply of his Expences therein, was this Bargain made, wherein it doth not appear he took the Advice of any Friends or Counsel, but relied wholly on the Defendant: That the Consideration of this Grant is very small, being but one Year's Purchase for a Rentcharge in Fee-simple, which is now happened in Possession; and the Over-Value, be it never so great, is not of it self sufficient Ground to set aside a Bargain, or whereupon this Court can presume Fraud: Yet it is a great Evidence of Fraud, where there are other Circumstances concurring, as there is in this Case."

9.15 As can be seen, Lord Arglas was not in any way simple, merely "of an easy nature"; by which is meant no more than "easily led" or "liable to be influenced".[43] The discrepancy in value itself, which was quite gross, was clearly the major factor in the court's decision to set aside the sale, but it was insufficient on its own; there had to be something else in addition. This proved to be his youth, and the absence of friends[44] to advise him. Mr Muschampe thus "made a market of" Lord Arglas's situation; turned it into extra cash. What Lord Arglas seems to have lacked, seen in modern terms, was any access to proper information about price. In many cases, this might have been his own fault. The particular problem he had, in common with many vulnerable parties, was that he had apparently not even any inkling that he ought to try to get access to such information, which meant that he was locked into his handicapped negotiating position and an obvious prey. Thus, the essential elements of the law on dealing with the vulnerable were discernible as early as the late seventeenth century.

The eighteenth century—Lord Hardwicke's "equitable fraud" and the land-man—a working class version of Lord Arglas

9.16 We go next to Lord Hardwicke, in the eighteenth century. The court now formulated the principle as a species of inferred "fraud".[45] Lord Hardwicke explained "fraud" in *Earl of Chesterfield v. Janssen*[46] in a sense which covered a range of conduct much wider than dishonesty.

[42] The cooling-off period is not a new idea.

[43] cp. Shakespeare, *3 Henry VI*, i. 171 "Have wrought the easy-melting King like wax" or Milton, *Comus*, 164 "wind me into the easy-hearted man, And hug him into snares" or Dryden, *Aeneid II*, 261 "With such deceits he gained the easy hearts".

[44] The court of that day will have meant not his cronies, but older friends.

[45] "Fraud" perhaps meant no more, here, than the *kind* of predatory conduct which would tend towards making a market of another man's weakness.

[46] (1751) 2 Ves. Sen. 125; 28 E.R. 82.

He explained, in effect, that fraud did not mean deceit or circumvention; it meant an unconscionable use of the power arising out of the circumstances and conditions[47] of the parties contracting "Fraud" was inferred from the circumstances of the contract, or the "nature of the bargain".

Lord Hardwicke said "There is always fraud presumed or inferred from the circumstances or conditions of the parties contracting: weakness on one side, usury on the other, or extortion, or advantage taken of that weakness. *There has been always an appearance of fraud from the nature of the bargain...*" Lord Hardwicke clearly felt he was extending the law by allowing "fraud" to be presumed from circumstances. "... this goes further than the rule of law; which is, that it must be proved, not presumed; but it is wisely established in this court to prevent *taking surreptitious advantage of the weakness or necessity of another: which knowingly to do is equally against the conscience as to take advantage of his ignorance*; a person is equally unable to judge for himself in one as the other."[48]

In fact Lord Hardwicke's comments were strictly *obiter*, in that Lord Chesterfield lost his case; and on the facts, was found to have affirmed the deal in question later. However, the importance of the case is that Lord Hardwicke set out the elements of the law preventing the making a market of another's weakness, in terms which were affirmed at the end of the nineteenth century, and remain good law today. Despite the liberal use of words like "conscience", the elements of the law are seen to be in place now; "taking surreptitious advantage of the weakness of another" is to precisely the same effect as Lord Selborne's phrase; and further the method, of inferring the relevant matters from the circumstances of the transaction, remains the only feasible approach.

The principle was certainly not confined, even in the eighteenth century, to expectant heirs. This can be seen from the case of *How v. Weldon & Edwards*.[49] The plaintiff in that case was a "land-man" on board one of the ships, which in 1745 "made the great capture which put into Kinsale in Ireland". The plaintiff agreed to sell his interest in the prize money, when he obtained it, to Weldon for what was acknowledged to be about a quarter of its true value. Weldon then assigned his rights to Edwards. The Master of the Rolls said that the plaintiff ought to be regarded in at least as favourable a light as a young heir. He said that the equity arose partly from the person entering into the transaction and partly from the price.[50] He also took judicial note of the fact that land-men were in general "a race of men loose and unthinking, who will almost for nothing part with what they have acquired perhaps with their blood." These generalisations about classes of person do rather plague the law on making a market

[47] As Lord Selborne was later to put in *Earl of Aylesford v. Morris* (1873) L.R. 8 Ch. App. 484.

[48] Italics supplied.

[49] (1754) 2 Ves. Sen, 516; 28 E.R. 330.

[50] Or undervalue.

of another man's weakness.[51] It is no doubt natural enough when one is considering something uncomfortably abstract such as the principle involved here to say "Oh of course, such and such a class of person is an obvious prey." It is easy, and natural, but it is unhelpful. It has tended to obfuscate the true principles of the law about dealings with the vulnerable.

The nineteenth century—the courts go too far for expectant heirs before the intervention of statute restores the position, and the principles are re-affirmed

9.17 During the nineteenth century there began to be quite an industry in setting aside sales of reversions and "post-obit" bonds on behalf of young heirs. The position was eventually reached where it was only necessary to show that a sale was of a reversion, and it could be set aside, even if the reversioner knew and understood perfectly well what he was doing, unless the buyer managed to prove to the court that he had given fair value. In *Shelly v. Nash*,[52] Sir John Leach the Vice-Chancellor declined to apply the rule to a sale by auction, explaining that he thought the circumstances of an auction avoided the mischief aimed at. In *Foster v. Roberts*,[53] a sale of a reversionary interest which was at a slight undervalue (£370 as opposed to £400), was set aside by Sir John Romilly, the Master of the Rolls, despite perfect bona fides on both sides.

Later in the mid-nineteenth century, an Act[54] was passed as to sales of reversions, to the effect that they were to be valid provided "made bona fide and without fraud or unfair dealing." The legal position thus once more reverted to that of the earlier cases (above): the weakness and the undervalue had to be proved once more, even in the case of sales of reversions.

O'Rorke v. Bolingbroke[55] re-affirmed the good faith principles. Lord Blackburn felt that there had to be either

(1) fraud (he did not specify which, but since he went on to consider unfair dealing separately, he probably meant "moral" fraud, or fraud in the sense of dishonesty;[56] or

(2) unfair dealing by the party getting the better bargain.

He said that in that case, on the evidence, there was no "*unfair dealing, including in those words every dealing by which one man having the means of getting a better bargain from another, effects the transaction* ***by these means***". He cited Lord Selborne also in *Earl of Aylesford v. Morris*.[57]

"and when the relative position of the parties is such as prima

[51] See below.
[52] (1818) 3 Madd. 417; 56 E.R. 494.
[53] (1861) 29 Beav. 467; 54 E.R. 708.
[54] (31 Vict, c.4).
[55] (1877) 2 App. Cas. 814.
[56] Which is how the word is used in courts in England today.
[57] (1873) L.R. 8 Ch. App. 484.

facie to raise this presumption, the transaction cannot stand unless the person claiming the benefit of it is able to repel the presumption by contrary evidence, proving it to have been in point of fact fair, just, and reasonable."

9.18 Lord Selborne in "*Earl of Aylesford v. Morris* (above) said that this was the rule applied to "the analogous cases of voluntary donations obtained for themselves by the donees, and to all other cases where influence, however acquired, has resulted in gain to the person possessing it at the expense of the person subject to it." He had gone on to say: "But it is sufficient for the application of the principle, if the parties meet under such circumstances as, in the particular transaction, to give the stronger party dominion over the weaker; and such power and influence are generally possessed, in every transaction of this kind, by those who trade upon the follies and vices of unprotected youth, inexperience, and moral imbecility."

Lord Hatherley in *O'Rorke v. Bolingbroke*[58] also said "It sufficiently appears that the principle on which Equity originally proceeded to set aside such transactions was for the protection of family property; but this principle being once established, the Court extended its aid to *all cases in which the parties to a contract have not met upon equal terms.* In ordinary cases each party to a bargain must take care of his own interest, and it will not be presumed that undue advantage or contrivance has been resorted to on either side; but in the case of the "expectant heir" or of persons under pressure without adequate protection, and in the case of dealings with uneducated ignorant persons, the burthen of shewing the fairness of the transaction is thrown on the person who seeks to obtain the benefit of the contract."

The twentieth century

9.19 It would be a neat way to finish this historical overview to be able to say that the influence of literalism had obscured the old principles. However, it is not quite as simple as that, in this particular area. The principles applicable to dealings with the vulnerable have become neglected rather than misunderstood. There are relatively few cases in England in this century which have been set aside using this jurisdiction. We had the beginning of a short-lived attempt to revive the jurisdiction by Lord Denning in *Lloyd's Bank v. Bundy*,[59] followed by the rejection of this (together with the invention of a new jurisdictional problem in the shape of manifest disadvantage; and the near-invention of another in the over-narrow definition of "dominion") in the later case of *National Westminster Bank v. Morgan*.[60] One senses a lost feeling, a feeling of alienation almost, in attempts like the latter case's to apply the old principles to modern situations. Let us hope

[58] (1877) 2 App. Cas. 814.
[59] [1975] Q.B. 326.
[60] [1985] A.C. 686.

this may change.[61] It is not likely, one fears, that the dearth of cases on dealings with the vulnerable means fewer people are making profits out of other people's weakness.

Part of this neglect of the old principles in this area may well be due to the sheer number of cases which exist, specially if one amalgamates—as the textbooks tend to do—the cases on gifts with the cases on bargains with the vulnerable. One may speculate also as to whether a liking for neat literalist rules is the reason for the extraordinary prominence given in this century to the relatively crude and narrow exposition to be found in *Fry v. Lane*[62] over the less modern-sounding but greatly more sophisticated and accurate account of the jurisdiction given by Lord Selborne in *Earl of Aylesford v. Morris*.[63] *Fry v. Lane*[64] is bound to have contributed noticeably to the lack of enthusiasm felt by many for a jurisdiction so based. However, perhaps in the end it is due to no more than a mood abroad among lawyers and judges in this country; a feeling that the law must be tough and literalist, while the courts have abjured their ancient role of "throwing a blanket of protection" round those in need of it, in the belief that Parliament will provide a suitable alternative in well-meaning statutes. In Australia, by contrast, the older cases on sale transactions with the vulnerable have not been allowed to languish unread, and the courts have retained their protective role in this sphere of contract law. One cannot but welcome cases such as the important *Commercial Bank of Australia v. Amadio*,[65] while wishing that they had happened in England.

Spontaneous Vulnerability: the true principles analysed

The Features of Vulnerability

9.20 There are a great many circumstances about the victim which may be thought to be candidates for the court's setting-aside jurisdiction. As Fullagar J. put it in the Australian case of *Blomley v. Ryan*[66]

> "The circumstances adversely affecting a party, which may induce a court of equity either to refuse its aid or to set a transaction aside, are of great variety and can hardly be satisfactorily classified. Among them are poverty or need of any kind, sickness, age, sex, infirmity of body or mind, drunkenness, illiteracy or lack of education, lack of assistance or explanation where assistance or explanation is necessary. The common characteristic seems to

[61] The case of ***Barclay's Bank v. O'Brien*** [1994] 1 A.C. 180 is a thoughtful and welcome step in the right sort of direction.

[62] (1888) 40 Ch.D. 312.

[63] (1873) L.R. 8 Ch. App. 484.

[64] Above.

[65] (1983) 151 C.L.R. 447.

[66] (1956) 999 C.L.R. 362, cited by Mason J. in *Commercial Bank of Australia v. Amadio* (above).

be that they have the effect of placing one party at a serious disadvantage vis a vis the other".

Formulations like this however leave the central problem unanswered: since weakness etc are not enough on their own, what is the X-factor that places the party at a serious disadvantage vis a vis the other?

The weakness: locking-in factor essential: "dominion" explained

9.21 The fact that a lot of the cases, old and new, emphasize the *class* of person under consideration[67] perhaps obscures one essential feature which must be present about the weakness: the factor which in this chapter is called *the locking-in factor*. The victim *must not know he is a victim*. Otherwise, he would not be a victim save by his own choice. As it is he is helpless to save himself and thus becomes locked into his weak position. It has been expressed by Lord Selborne in *Earl of Aylesford v. Morris*[68] as a relationship in which the circumstances are such as to give the stronger party "dominion" over the weaker. "Dominion" is a word sparingly used these days, less sparingly then. It perhaps meant no more, in modern terms, than an inbuilt negotiating advantage.[69] As Lord Hatherley put it in *O'Rorke v. Bolingbroke*,[70] equity would extend its aid to "all cases in which the parties to a contract have not met on equal terms." It did not mean, for example, that the aggressor party had to exercise a mesmeric influence over the victim, or that the victim had to be anything like a puppet of the aggressor.[71] Lord Scarman's approach in *National Westminster Bank PLC v. Morgan* represents a significant—albeit no doubt unconscious—narrowing of the law on making a market of another's weakness; and it is effected simply by a historically insensitive reading of the language used in the older cases.

The term "locking-in factor" is thus intended to denote the extra helplessness which compounds the unequal bargaining position of the victim, by his ignorance of the fact that he is helpless. Thus, he does none of the possible things open to him to help himself. The cases recognise that mere weakness, ignorance, *etc.*, is not enough; nor is it enough that the parties reached an unequal bargain. There is recognition to be found for the proposition that the something extra required is essentially that which has been labelled the locking-in factor. Expressions such as "not equal to protecting himself"; "not a free agent" or, more recently, "unable to make a worthwhile judgment as

[67] Expectant heirs, "loose and unthinking" land-men, *etc*.
[68] (1873) L.R. 8 Ch. App. 484.
[69] Cp. "Study thou the dominion of thyself . . .": Sir Thomas Browne.
[70] (1877) 2 App. Cas. 814.
[71] *c.f.* Lord Scarman's reference to "the relationships which may develop a dominating influence of one over another". *National Westminster Bank PLC v. Morgan* above at 709.

to what is in his best interests" are properly taken to refer to this kind of extra ingredient or added form of bargaining helplessness.

9.22 In *Evans v. Llewellin*[72] the Master of the Rolls, equating the jurisdiction in rely-on-me cases and cases of spontaneous vulnerability, said "all proceed upon the same general principle, and establish, that if the party is in a situation, in which he is not a free agent, and *is not equal to protecting himself*, this Court will protect him.[73]

In *Wood v. Abrey*[74] the Vice-Chancellor, Sir John Leach, said: "If a man who meets his purchaser on equal terms, negligently sells his estate at an under value, he has no title to relief in equity. But a Court of Equity will inquire whether the parties really did *meet on equal terms* ...[75]

In *Shelly v. Nash*[76] the Vice-Chancellor used the expression "in the power of [the predator]".

In *Commercial Bank of Australia v. Amadio*[77] Mason J. described the principle of "unconscionable conduct"[77a] in terms which can also be seen as referring, if obliquely, to the locking-in factor, in addition to the requirement for some kind of spontaneous vulnerability. He referred to;

> "the class of case in which a party makes unconscientious use of his superior position or bargaining power to the detriment of a party who suffers from some special disability or *is placed in some special situation of disadvantage* ... the will of the innocent party, even if independent and voluntary, is the result of the disadvantageous position in which he is placed and of the other party unconscientiously taking advantage of that position."

Later he referred to relief being granted when advantage is taken of an innocent party who, though not deprived of an independent and voluntary will, is *unable to make a worthwhile judgment as to what is in his best interest.*[78]

Further, one can deduce the existence of the locking-in factor by looking to see the steps necessary for the "predator" to show that he has taken if he is to uphold the bargain.[79] Evidently none of these steps will remove the party's basic ignorance, situation in life, *etc*: what they *are* directed to is removing the locking-in factor by making available the kind of independent, businesslike advice that a more sensible or less vulnerable person, without the locking-in helplessness, would have appreciated they needed in the first place.

[72] (1787) 1 Cox 333; 29 E.R. 1191.
[73] Italics supplied.
[74] (1818) 3 Madd. 417; 56 E.R. 558.
[75] Italics supplied.
[76] (1818) 3 Madd. 232.
[77] (1983) 151 C.L.R. 147.
[77a] The term which seems to be the label in Australia for the kind of vulnerability in sales and purchases now under discussion.
[78] Italics supplied *c.f. also Fullagar J, cited at para. 9.20 above, "lack of assistance or explanation where assistance or explanation is necessary".*
[79] See above.

Typical kinds of vulnerable situation

9.23 *"Weakness, necessity, ignorance"*[80] There are a number of specific kinds of vulnerability which occur in the cases, usually in combination. Fullagar J.[81] had eleven on my counting including the locking-in factor. Browne-Wilkinson J. in *Multiservice Bookbinding v. Mardon*[82] said the classic example of what he labelled an "unconscionable" bargain is where advantage has been taken of a young, inexperienced or ignorant person to introduce a term which no sensible well-advised person or party would have attempted, but he hastened to say that the jurisdiction was not limited to these. Lord Hardwicke has just three typical kinds of vulnerability: weakness, necessity, and ignorance; and perhaps so long as one translates these into a more modern idiom, they may help us as a kind of checklist at least, and will probably not work out so different in practice from Fullagar J.'s. The context of these abstract nouns needs to be added back to each one if they are to make much sense to modern ears. They are undoubtedly all simply examples of *bargaining weakness*, but since bargaining weakness is an abstraction, a look at some of the human faces it wears in practice may be thought useful.

Weakness

9.24 "Weakness" is something of a catch-all perhaps, but it must be remembered that it does not mean anything one would necessarily notice about the victim in the street, as it were: it is simply a built-in weakness as regards negotiating *the particular contract*. It is not a general quality, but a quality directed to the transaction which is in point.

Could the buyer under a standard form contract be capable of ranking as weak? The suggestion has been made, in effect, that the relevant kind of weakness for our purposes may exist in a buyer under a *standard-form contract*, particularly where the seller is part of a dominant group of businesses which is able more or less to dictate terms of sale, and where there is little or no choice for the buyer. In the Australian case of *Commercial Bank of Australia v. Amadio*.[83] Mason J. said:

> "Because times have changed new situations have arisen in which it may be appropriate to invoke the underlying principle. Take, for example, entry into a standard form of contract dictated by a party whose bargaining power is greatly superior, a relationship which was discussed by Lord Reid and Lord Diplock in *A Schroeder Music Publishing Co Ltd v. Macaulay*.[84] See also *Clifford Davis Management Ltd v. WEA Records Ltd*.[85] In situations of this kind it is necessary for the plaintiff who seeks relief to establish

[80] Lord Hardwicke in *Earl of Chesterfield v. Jansen* (1751) 2 Ves. Sen. 125; 28 E.R. 82. See para. 9.16 above.
[81] See para. 9.20, above.
[82] [1979] Ch. 84.
[83] (1983) 151 C.L.R. at 462.
[84] [1974] 1 W.L.R. 1308.
[85] [1975] 1 W.L.R. 61.

unconscionable conduct, namely that unconscientious advantage has been taken of his disabling condition or circumstances."[86]

The idea is an attractive and cogent one, which one may hope to see explored by the courts. The large concern offering standard terms has "dominion" in the old sense by reason of its superior position in the market, and the consumer is "weak" vis a vis that transaction. (There may also be a kind of economic "necessity" inhering in these transactions as well.) The locking-in factor will arise in this case probably less because of the victim's ignorance of his own weakness (which may or may not be the case) but one step beyond that. He is unable to save himself by his knowledge (if he has it), because he cannot do anything to change the terms of the contract if he needs the goods or services and cannot in practice obtain them from anyone else save on similar terms.

"Necessity"

9.25 This may mean being under economic pressure: the young heir whose father had "turned him out of doors" without his allowance because he had married below his station is an example; but it may also be a kind of emotional hemming- in, as in *Backhouse v. Backhouse*[87] in which the adulterous wife transferred the matrimonial home into her husband's sole name out of a sense of guilt, at a time of emotional strain at the break-up of the marriage. The successful plaintiff in *Gwynne v. Heaton*[88] who had married a servant girl and consequently been "turned out of doors" by his furious 81 year old father, was no doubt under emotional strain and possibly under economic pressure also[89].

9.26 *Necessity; Lack of "cooling-off period"* Simply being rushed into the deal may render the victim vulnerable (and contribute to the locking-in factor). In *Clarke v. Malpas*[90] this was important: the precipitancy of the transaction in the case of an unwell, elderly man, was commented on adversely. The significance of the cooling-off period is discussed below. (It probably needs to be re-labelled, cumbersomely, the cooling-off-and-consultation period.)

Ignorance

9.27 This is not ignorance in general, but ignorance for the purpose in point: for example, the proper valuation of difficult subject matter

[86] See also the Unfair Contract Terms Regulations 1994 and commentary, for the position of the "consumer" or individual private customer.

[87] [1978] 1 W.L.R. 243.

[88] (1778) 1 Bro. C.C.I.; 28 E.R. 949.

[89] See also ***Earl of Aylesford v. Morris*** and ***Berkley Freeman v. Bishop*** (1740) 2 Atk. 39 in which the court commented that it was the "necessity" (i.e, economic pressure) which young heirs are in for the most part, "which naturally lays them open to impositions of this kind."

[90] (1862) 31 Beav. 80; 54 ER. 968.

such as a reversion. It is certainly not education in a more general sense, the kind of school the plaintiff went to or whether he was a telephonist or the like; indeed one successful plaintiff in the seventeenth century,[91] was a (presumably rather unworldly) Proctor in Doctor's Commons.[92]

9.28 *Ignorance: youth* More specifically, *youth* seems to have been regarded as a kind of vulnerability *per se*, at all events when combined with the absence of proper advice from an friend, father or legal adviser. (Youth seems to have been regarded in the cases, interestingly, as extending to the twenties, but not beyond about thirty. Lord Guernsey in *Earl of Aylesford v. Morris*[93] was 21 and had no professional advice, nor were his father nor the family solicitors told of the transactions. Lord Arglas in *Earl of Arglas v. Muschampe*[94] was "very young" at the relevant time.

9.29 *Ignorance: business inexperience*

Temperament and degree of competence in business matters. This can be or contribute to vulnerability. A lack of basic education is also mentioned, as is "ignorance", but the text above discusses the limited sense of these. We have seen that Lord Arglas was "of an easy nature". Old Mr Gallimore in *Clarke v. Malpas*[95] was illiterate as well as "in a humble station in life" though he was also said to be possessed of "a low cunning, a peculiar jealousy with regard to his small property of three cottages", and there was evidence he was sharp-witted enough in regard to his rents. Thus, his ignorance problem would seem mainly to have been ignorance of real property valuation, rather than any more general defect of temperament such as unwariness or even lack of ordinary intelligence. Indeed, Sir John Romilly, the Master of the Rolls, in his judgment emphasized Mr Gallimore's unequal access to relevant knowledge as well as his illness and other factors:

> "In that state of the case it is impossible, in my opinion, to say that the Defendant has performed the obligation which rests on him, for in my opinion the burthen is upon him of proving that the bargain for a sale, at what I consider a very inadequate consideration, was entered into by Gallimore *carefully, deliberately, and with a knowledge of all the circumstances connected with it.*"[96]

In *Baker v. Monk*[97] the successful plaintiff was an elderly spinster

[91] ***Wiseman v. Beake*** (1690) 2 Vern 121. 23 E.R. 688.

[92] He was also nearly 40, but it is fair to say that the decision may well have been influenced by the gross undervalue in the case. As Lord Eldon put it in ***Gwynne v. Heaton*** (1778) (above), "Wiseman's case is not of so young a man, but the court was struck with the enormity of ten for one".

[93] (1873) (above).

[94] (1682) 2 Ch. Rep. 266; 21 E.R. 675, at 9.14. See note above and noted below.

[95] (1862) 31 Bear, 80; 54 E.R. 1067.

[96] Italics supplied

[97] (1864) 4 D.J. & S. 388; 46 E.R. 968.

"in humble life, of slender education", but it was not her education in general which was relevant; this was no relief for the educationally disadvantaged *per se*; the court was concerned at the fact that she had not realised (and had not therefore been in a position where she could check up) that the capitalised rental value of her dilapidated cottages did not reflect adequately the site value. It was thus a somewhat specialised, but *relevant ignorance* which mattered—her ignorance of the proper way to value real estate.

In *O'Sullivan v. Management Agency*[98] the plaintiff was a young music writer, wholly inexperienced in business or publishing (he had worked in the Post Office) doing business with a knowledgeable, sophisticated man and his companies. That the bargain reached was unequal was only a part of the picture: more crucial was the gross inequality in their respective negotiating power, by reason of the plaintiff's lack of relevant experience.

9.30 *Ignorance: pure lack of relevant information* The cases which stress the absence of relevant information about the transaction, whether about the value of what one is selling or buying, or about the consequences of a deed, are legion. This crucial feature has not received the attention it deserves, perhaps because of the neglect of sale and purchase cases, so that the slightly metaphysical "overbearing of will" aspect which generally suits the gift cases rather better has tended to predominate. This lack of information aspect of the cases may well be one that will (or should) assume even more importance in modern times, given the enormous imbalance in information available to specialists and to larger commercial concerns compared with that available to individuals and small businesses.[99]

Generalisations about classes of person

9.31 There is a sort of linguistic trap here. Membership of a class which usually behaves in a "loose and unthinking" way has been expressed as if it were in itself a type of vulnerability.[1] In fact, the real point here, despite being expressed in generalised terms, is simply that one

[98] [1985] Q.B. 428.

[99] See for specific emphasis on inequality of information ***How v. Weldon*** (1754) 2 Ves. Sen. 516; 28 E.R. 330; ***Hatch v. Hatch*** (1804) 9 Ves. 292; 32 E.R. 615; *Huguenin v. Basely* (1807) 14 Ves. 289; 33 E.R. 526 (*"the effect, nature and consequences" of the transaction were all unavailable to the plaintiff)*; ***Wood v. Downes*** (1811) 18 Ves. Jun. 120; 34 E.R. 263; ***Wood v. Abrey*** (1818) 3 Madd. 417; 56 E.R.558; ***Edwards v. Meyrick*** (1842) 2 Hare 60; 67 E.R. 25; ***Billage v. Southee*** (1852); 9 Hare 534; 68 E.R. 623; ***Savery v. King*** (1856) 5 H.L.C. 627; 10 E.R. 1046; ***Hesse v. Briant*** (1856) 6 D.M. & G. 623; 43 E.R. 1375; ***Baker v. Monk*** (1864) 4 D.J. & S. 388; 46 E.R. 968; ***Tate v. Williamson*** (1866) L.R. 2 Ch. App. 55; ***Erlanger v. New Sombrero Phosphate Co*** (1878) 3 App.Cas 1218 and ***McPherson v. Watt*** (1877) 3 App. Cas. 254.

[1] ***How v. Weldon & Edwards*** (1754) 2 Ves. Sen. 516; 28 E.R. 330; and see para. 9.16. above, and noted below. See also the generalisation about married women as a class among others in *Barclay's Bank v. O'Brien* [1994] 1 A.C. 180.

could not expect the plaintiff, in *his* circumstances, which may include having a particular job, or the like, to know he ought to check. Otherwise, such expressions would be irrelevant to the case in which they are used. We tend to use these generalised expressions which are overtly making a statement about inbuilt characteristics of a class or category of person, when we are in truth making a statement about the effect of certain *common circumstances* on that person: for example, "Women barristers seldom get on as well as men" which is not really intended to tell us anything about the women *per se*, merely about the usual effect or possible effect of their working circumstances. Consider also the recent notion that the purchaser of a dwelling house "of modest value" will rely on the building society's valuation.[2] This is really a rolled-up statement. What is really being said is first that one could not have expected Miss Smith herself to check up, because she had a modest income to go with her house of modest value and the expense would be likely to seem disproportionate to her, while her experience of business would probably not have been such as to warn her of the real risks of not obtaining a structural survey; and second that one could not expect anyone *else* in her position as regards those matters to check up either. Thus, the real point in *How*'s[3] case was not that Mr How was indelibly stamped with certain characteristics by reason of his being a landman: merely that Mr How's circumstances, in common with those of other landmen, were usually such that he would not (as perhaps proper sailors would) know much about the valuation of a prize. It is thus another way of saying that the plaintiff's circumstances led to an inference of a locking-in factor, or that the plaintiff was unlikely to have been competent enough in a business sense to negotiate on equal terms with the defendant. Lord Hardwicke would, one may suspect, simply have considered the circumstances and classified this as "ignorance".

9.32 Married women now seem to have been labelled as a class likely to possess particular characteristics, rather in the same way as landmen. In *Barclay's Bank v. O'Brien*,[4] it was held that as a class they[5] were likely—at least as regards third parties such as banks[6]—to possess an inbuilt vulnerability/locking-in factor vis a vis their husbands. Here, it was their susceptibility to emotional and perhaps also economic pressure exerted by their husbands which was being referred to. The approach is perhaps not as old-fashioned-male-chauvinist as it first strikes one: the married woman, even the sophisticated, competent, married woman will perhaps often be unlikely to check, likely to trust her husband rather in the way we trust managing agents or clerks—because she cannot in practice check up on him. It may be that if one tried hard one could squeeze this into Lord Hardwicke's "necessity",

[2] See *Smith v. Bush* [1990] 1 A.C. 831 *per* Lord Griffiths at 859.
[3] (1754) (above).
[4] [1994] 1 A.C. 180.
[5] Amongst others who were equally in a relationship of trust and confidence, known to the creditor, *e.g.* cohabitees.
[6] See below for the effect of unfair dealings with the vulnerable on third parties such as lenders.

but there is perhaps no need to make the effort. The linguistic trap has here had the effect of diverting our attention away from the circumstances of the kinds of husbands who run family companies or other businesses in which the wives play little or no part. It is no doubt correct law that there is no general presumption that a husband and wife relationship is one of presumed undue influence, such as parent and guardian. However, it is probable that insufficient thought has been given to the semi-agency relationship between a wife who benefits from the family business and the husband who actually runs it. The practical inability of the wife to check up is similar to that of most principals vis a vis their agents. Is there any real difference between a wife in such a position towards the husband running a family company and Miss Huguenin vis a vis the clergyman Mr Baseley who had constituted himself her informal agent? Both repose trust and confidence because the situation requires it. Miss Huguenin trusted Mr Baseley to manage her estates: wives in Mrs O'Brien's position trust their husbands to run the family company, in respect of which they have a claim for subsistence during the marriage, and on the assets of which they will have a claim on divorce. Thus, it may be suspected that the informal agency of the husband, with the impracticability of checking up by the wife, in fact gives rise, in appropriate circumstances, to an implicit "rely-on-me" or induced, vulnerability on the part of the wife.[7] On this view, it may simply have been the relatively large number of such informal agencies that occur by husbands for wives which Lord Browne-Wilkinson had in mind in *Barclay's Bank v. O'Brien.*[8]

How can a person ensure a valid transaction if he fears he is negotiating with a vulnerable party?

(i) Make it a fair transaction: remove the inequality in negotiating by obtaining, e.g. a joint valuation

9.33 The first way in which a transaction with a vulnerable party may be carried through with safety is to make sure, by taking appropriate advice from an independent third party such as a valuer that the transaction is indeed a fair one. In short, this approach removes the inequality in negotiating position. If this is done, the fact that another independent valuer or the like might have formed a different opinion is irrelevant. It is probable that the valuer will need to be jointly instructed to some extent, if only to ensure that the weaker party has the benefit of all the relevant information as to the transaction that the stronger party has. In *Edwards v. Burt*[9], the court discussed the measures a stronger party might use beforehand, if he was concerned that the transaction might be attacked. (The case occurred at a time

[7] It would work similarly with a husband who leaves certain aspects of business, say, to his lawyer or merchant-banker wife.

[8] [1994] 1 A.C. 180.

[9] (1852) 2 D. & G.M. & G. 55; 42 E.R. 791.

when there had developed an inflexible rule that purchasers of a reversionary interest from an expectant heir had to justify the transaction if it was impeached (see above), but the dictum is relevant to any case once the vulnerability has been established. Lord Cranworth said:

> "If previously to the sale of a reversionary interest, *the vendor and purchaser concur in ascertaining from persons of competent skill and having knowledge of the property, and of all the circumstances likely to influence value, a well-considered estimate of what the property would be likely to fetch on a sale, and act on that opinion,* we are far from meaning to decide that such a transaction could be afterwards impeached, merely because other surveyors should come to a conclusion different from that on which the parties had acted."[10]

It may well be that in cases where there is no joint instruction the same effect could be arrived at by an undertaking by the stronger party to make a statement to the valuer of all facts of relevance to value, risk, *etc.*, which are within his knowledge. This is an obvious common-sense necessity, at least in a case where the other party is unlikely to have access to such relevant facts: the independent advice will be limited in its efficacy to the facts known to the adviser. Note also Lord Kingsdown in *Smith v. Kay*[11]—a case of induced vulnerability in that there had been a misrepresentation and the victim had no independent advice—referring to the duty of those in a relationship giving "a power of influence" over the other,[12] to make "a free disclosure of every circumstance which it is important that the individual . . . should be apprised of."[13]

(ii) Displace the locking-in factor: warn him so that he may save himself

9.34 *Warning plus cooling-off and consultation period* The second precaution the stronger party may take is to displace not the pre-contractual vulnerability, but the locking-in factor; so that the vulnerable party is rendered a "free agent", as it has been expressed. This is obviously a riskier method if the stronger party wishes to retain a bargain which has or may have an element of undervalue, but is probably not impossible to achieve, given care and a high degree of honesty. The stronger party, it should seem, ought first to warn the vulnerable party carefully and accurately about his rights. This must mean the kind of explanation which explains or puts the victim on notice of the undervalue or possible undervalue or other disadvantage reasonably clearly: it is not probably not enough to indulge in vague warnings which could be misunderstood as relating to matters of pure form rather than practical importance such as "You really ought to consult a solicitor/surveyor" or "I hope you know what you are doing", or

[10] Italics supplied.
[11] (1859) 7 H.L.C. 750: 11 E.R. 299.
[12] Lord Cranworth's expression in the same case.
[13] See also below as to third parties' duty if they wish to avoid constructive notice.

the like. Warning is a matter of substance, not form. A cooling-off period is likely to be needed too. The cooling-off label is modern, the concept far from modern. The importance of the cooling-off period, or as the courts more often put it in earlier times, the avoidance of "surprise" or "precipitancy" was not only, in most cases, to allow the victim himself time to make a decision he had slept on, but also that it allowed him an appropriate amount of time in which he could then consult his more business-like friends or advisers about the wisdom of the deal. There is no requirement discernible in any of the cases that such advice has necessarily to be from a solicitor, and indeed, a solicitor may not always be the best person; for example, where the question is valuation rather than the legal effect of a transaction. Interestingly enough, this displacing of the locking-in factor was very much the approach of the House of Lords in the case of wives and others who stand surety for their husbands/cohabitees, *etc.*[14]: "reasonable steps" for a bank or other creditor include an explanation of "the risk she is running" and the urging to take independent advice. The danger perhaps is that a formulaic approach to "explaining" the risk she is running may prevail. This would not be right, whether the wife or person in a like position is treated purely as an ordinary surety or whether there are facts to put the Bank or other creditor on notice that she may be a vulnerable party by reason of the position occupied by her husband. For the duty of disclosure of certain unexpected features of the transaction to any intending surety, see Chapter 3, Insurance and Surety Transactions. For the duty of the person put on notice of a vulnerable transaction, and the proposition that the duty is coextensive with that of the original "predator", see Chapter 8, Knowledge and Notice.

In *Moody v. Cox & Hatt*[15] Scrutton L.J. said:

> "When the relation of solicitor and client occurs in the very transaction attacked . . . an independent solicitor should be employed by the client. It is called "putting him at arm's length." It might perhaps also be effected by a clear declaration of the position by the vendor, such as this: "Mind, I am going to get the highest price I can; be on your guard"; but the position would have to be made very clear in order to relieve the solicitor of obligations far exceeding those of an ordinary vendor, and is a position to be avoided."

Essentially it is the same approach: if you do not remove the inequality, then you must remove the locking-in factor, so that the other party knows he should be on his guard.

9.35 At the end of the eighteenth century, in *Evans v. Llewellin*[16] there had already been an accurate explanation to the plaintiff of his rights: the Master of the Rolls referred to the "caution" which had been delivered to the plaintiff by the defendant's solicitor, so it clearly contained an element of warning about the deal. The Master of the Rolls

[14] See ***Barclay's Bank v. O'Brien*** [1994] A.C. 180.
[15] [1917] 2 Ch. 71 at 89.
[16] (1787) 1 Cox 333; 29 E.R. 1191.

said that if the plaintiff had only been given time to go back and consult his friends (he had been slightly rushed into the deal without any cooling-off period) he would not have set the sale aside. Yet the sale in the case was certainly at an undervalue, so that the defendant would have been hard put to it to show that the transaction was "fair, just and reasonable". Accordingly, the defendant *would* have been allowed to keep his bargain if he had only taken this extra precaution. The plaintiff would then have been a "free agent": he might still have been vulnerable, but he would have lost the locking-in factor: he would have known that he was vulnerable, and so had a realistic opportunity to do something about it.

In *Clarke v. Malpas*, the plaintiff, Clarke, sued on behalf, of his testator, Josiah Gallimore[17], who had sold his three cottages to the defendant shortly before his death. The vulnerability was proved and stress was laid by the Master of the Rolls on the haste with which the affair was concluded: the matter was agreed after nine in the morning and completed before six that evening. The decision was affirmed by the Lords Justices, only varying a technical aspect of the relief ordered. Again, all that was really lacking was a cooling-off (and consultation) period in which the victim could be directed to go and consult his more knowledgeable friends.

The kind of independent advice required

9.36 There is a long line of authority to the effect that independent advice, if given to the victim before the transaction, will be adequate protection for the person wishing to take advantage of the transaction *only if the advice is sufficient (or sufficiently "competent")* to displace the victim's locking-in factor. It is not a formulaic matter at all, but a question of displacing a particular weakness. It is not a matter of course that the independent advice should be from a solicitor: sometimes a valuer will be more appropriate; sometimes an older friend will suffice[18] (see *Archerv. Hudson* as to the last). ". . . as to the last." . . . if this young lady had her trustees, or some friend or relation of the family, or somebody interested in her welfare . . .". Information about the nature of the transaction may suffice in some but by no means all cases: it will depend on what is necessary to displace the individual weakness.

In *Berdoe v. Dawson*[19] the *creditor's* solicitor, who had notice of the vulnerability of the two young men in question, had given them full information, and explained the nature of the transaction thoroughly. However this (which might have been more than enough in some cases) was held insufficient to displace their weakness, which was that they were totally under the control of their father, for whom they worked.

[17] (1862) 31 Beav. 80; 54 E.R. 968.
[18] 7 Beav. 551 at 565; 49 E.R. 1180 at 1185.
[19] (1865) 34 Beav. 603; 55 E.R. 768.

In *Tate v. Williamson*[20], the young man concerned had been advised to obtain independent advice from a solicitor, and had done so. This was disregarded by the Lord Chancellor: what had in fact been needed in that case was proper, full information about value, with full instructions from the intending buyer.

In *Wright v. Carter*[21], the Court of Appeal held that advice from a solicitor who was in a state of ignorance about the true financial condition of the intending donor plaintiff did not rank as "competent". The solicitor had not been in a position to do more than ask the plaintiff whether he knew what he was doing, whether he was making the gifts in question, and whether he was doing so of his own will and volition.

A similar attitude was taken, scrutinising the content of the advice, in *Bullock v. Lloyd's Bank*[22]. The adviser had failed to come up to the court's view of what would have been necessary in her case to displace her particular weakness.

In *Permanent Trustee Co of N.S.W. v. Bridgewater*[23] the Judicial Committee castigated the advice given to the victim there by an independent solicitor obtained by the intending buyer. "... the protective assistance which he afforded to Bridgewater was in fact nil."

See also *Boustany v. Pigott*[24] where the transaction was set aside even though Miss Pigott had in fact been given some advice about the disadvantages of the transaction she was contemplating entering, albeit the solicitor was not her usual family solicitor, and he proved to be prepared to settle the document for Miss Pigott despite advising against it.

Otherwise, the transaction if impugned, will have to be shown to be "fair, just and reasonable", with all the disadvantage of hindsight.

9.37 If neither of the above precautionary measures are taken, and taken adequately, the stronger party has to take his chances whether the court, on the evidence then before it, will consider that the transaction was in fact "fair, just and reasonable". In *Earl of Chesterfield v. Janssen*[25]. Lord Hardwicke had said that when the relative position of the parties was such as prima facie to raise the presumption of unfair dealing, the transaction could not stand unless the person claiming the benefit of it could prove it to have been "fair, just, and reasonable"; and in *Earl of Aylesford v. Morris*[26] that was confirmed by Lord Selborne. Whether it was fair, just and reasonable is a matter of fact, and is to be judged at the time of the contract.

[20] (1866) L.R. 2 Ch. App. 55.
[21] (1903) 1 Ch. 27.
[22] [1955] Ch. 317.
[23] [1936] 3 All E.R. 501.
[24] (1995) 69 P. & C.R. 298.
[25] (1751) 2 Ves. Sen. 125; 28 E.R. 82, see para. 9.16 above.
[26] (1873) L.R. 8 Ch. App. 484.

"Induced" or "Rely on me Vulnerability" (traditionally, Presumed Undue Influence and Abuse of Confidence)

9.38 The principles are essentially similar whether the vulnerable party has sold or bought property from the trusted one, or whether he or she has made a gift. However, since this book is concerned with sales, not gifts, the gift cases will be referred to only where strictly necessary. It is of course, obvious that although the principles are the same, their application will not be quite identical in the case of a gift and the case of a sale which is alleged to be disadvantageous. In the case of a gift, the spontaneous intention to make a gift, to indulge in what has been called "liberality",[27] is the only prerequisite. Thus, the gift cases tend to be preoccupied with the internal workings of the giver's mind, and the discussion can begin to smack of the metaphysical. In the case of a sale, the spontaneous intention to sell (or buy) is usually there: what is in question is how the intention to sell *on those particular terms* was produced; usually, why that price/rate of interest, etc., rather than another. Here we have to bear in mind (although cases of overlap may occur[28]) where the fact that the stronger party was a solicitor compounded the emotional pressure the victim was under and which arose from his being charged with forgery, that there is not anything specially "weak" about those whose vulnerability is induced: they may be and often are absolutely normal, upstanding, businesslike people. Their vulnerability arises from *invited trust* only. Thus, the disadvantageous terms of the bargain they agreed to will normally have been because of something defective about the information afforded to them on which to exercise their judgement, not because of something defective about *them*. In rare cases, there may have been a direct misrepresentation: much more often, there will have been simple non-disclosure by the trusted party of information affecting the value of what is bought or sold. Where there is a rely-on-me relationship, the purchaser (or seller) is absolved from the usual duty of due diligence: it is assumed that he will have been lulled into a sense of security by the relationship, and in consequence, will have failed to make the usual inquiries incumbent on a purchaser or vendor at arm's length.

In *Gibson v. Jeyes*[29], one of the seminal cases in this area, the plaintiff had a freely formed intention to sell, and the defendant hotly defended the annuity in question as being a perfectly reasonable price. However, since it was not proved that she, or her agent/attorney who was the counterparty, had the information on which to be sure she was getting the best price, the sale was set aside with interest. In *Wood v. Downes*[30] Lord Eldon, again emphasized the plaintiffs' *lack of information as to the nature and value of what they were selling*, and their dependence on the defendant for *information*. *Hesse v. Briant*[31] *McPher-*

[27] An Aristotelian concept, see Chap. 3.

[28] See, e.g. ***Walmsley v. Booth*** (1739) 2 Atk. 25; 26 E.R. 412.

[29] (1801) 6 Ves. 266; 31 E.R. 1044.

[30] (1811) 18 Ves. Jun. 120; 34 E.R. 263.

[31] (1856) 6 De G.M. & G. 623; 43 E.R. 1375.

son v. Watt[32] and *Moody v. Cox & Hatt*[33] (all noted below), are all solicitor-client transactions which stressed the lack of relevant information suffered by the plaintiffs and *Tate v. Williamson*[34] is a case of an unofficial adviser, in which the lack of information was again stressed.

The party trusted

9.39 The party trusted has often been termed a "fiduciary". This simply means "person trusted" and does not tell us what the person is trusted *for*.[35] It will be evident that the party trusted has to be in a position to make moderately significant decisions for the victim, typically a principal; and a person, however much trust is reposed in him, who has a purely administrative function in the transaction will perhaps rarely if ever rank as a party trusted for our purposes. I may trust my housekeeper or my piano tuner, but I do not normally invest them with sufficient discretion on my behalf to make either a "fiduciary" or relied-on or trusted party in the sense we are talking about, or to render me significantly vulnerable to their activities. Typical of the kind of relationships of trust are the broadly professional "relationships of confidence", such as solicitor and client, director and company, partner and co-partner, and principal and (many but not all) agents. However, an unofficial rely-on-me relationship will suffice and the cases show the party trusted may be an unofficial guardian, an unofficial estate/investment manager, and a trusted friend, for example. The essentials of the relationship have been well put by Mason J. in the Australian case of *Hospital Products Limited v. United States Surgical Corporation*.[36]

> "The critical feature of these relationship is that the fiduciary undertakes or agrees to act for or on behalf of or in the interests of another person in the exercise of a power or discretion which will *affect the interests of that other person in a legal or a practical sense*. The relationship between the parties is therefore one which gives the fiduciary a special opportunity to exercise the power or discretion to the detriment of that other person who is accordingly vulnerable to abuse by the fiduciary of his position. The expressions "for", "on behalf of", and "in the interests of" signify that the fiduciary acts in a "representative" character in the exercise of his responsibility, to adopt an expression used by the Court of Appeal."[37]

[32] [1877] 3 App. Cas. 254.

[33] [1917] 2 Ch. 71.

[34] (1866) L.R. 2 Ch. App. 55.

[35] See the House of Lords case of *Target Holdings v. Redfern* [1996] A.C. 421 which adopted a similarly flexible approach to compensation, and see the interesting note at (1996) 112 L.Q.R. 27 by C.E.F. Rickett of the University of Auckland.

[36] (1984) 156 C.L.R. 41. See that case also for a thoughtful exploration of the borderline between the contractual relationship and fiduciary relationship, where both may co-exist.

[37] Italics supplied

An alternative formulation is that of Finn[38]

> "A person will be a fiduciary in his relationship with another when and in so far as that other is entitled to expect that he will act in that other's interests or (as in a partnership) in their joint interest, to the exclusion of his own several interest. . . . A fiduciary
> (a) cannot misuse his position, or knowledge or opportunity resulting from it, to his own or to a third party's possible advantage; or
> (b) cannot, in any matter falling within the scope of his service, have a personal interest or an inconsistent engagement with a third party—unless this is freely and informedly consented to by the beneficiary or is authorized by law.[39]

Now, in *Bristol & West Building Society v. Mothew*[40] Millett L.J. has warned against "unthinking resort to verbal formulae" in this branch of the law. Because of the importance of his judgment on this point, there follows a lengthy quotation from it. He said:

> "The expression 'fiduciary duty' is properly confined to those duties which are peculiar to fiduciaries and the breach of which attracts legal consequences differing from those consequent upon the breach of other duties. Unless the expression is so limited it is lacking in practical utility. In this sense it is obvious that not every breach of duty by a fiduciary is a breach of fiduciary duty. . . ."

Millett L.J. went on to say that the expression "fiduciary duty" was not appropriately applied to the duty of skill and care owed by, say, a solicitor to his client. He cited in support Lord Browne-Wilkinson in *Henderson v. Merrett Syndicates Ltd*[41] who equated the duty of skill and care owed by "bailees, carriers, trustees, directors, agents and others", saying that they were all the same duty, and it was not their status or position which gave rise to the duty but the circumstances.

Millet L.J. later defined a "fiduciary" as "someone who has undertaken to act for or on behalf of another in a particular matter in circumstances which give rise to a relationship of trust and confidence".

> "The distinguishing obligation of a fiduciary is *the obligation of loyalty*. The principal is entiltled to the single-minded loyalty of his fiduciary. *This core liability has several facets. A fiduciary must act in good faith; he must not make a profit out of his trust; he must not place himself in a position where his duty and his interest may conflict; he may not act for his own benefit or the benefit of a third person without the informed consent of his principal*. This is not intended to be an exhaustive list, but it is sufficient to indicate the nature of fiduciary obligations. They are the defining characteristics of the fiduciary. . . ."[41a]

[38] *"Fiduciary Law and the Modern Commercial World"* in *Commercial Aspects of Trusts and Fiduciary Obligations*, ed. McKendrick, Clarendon Press.

[39] Based on Dean J.'s formulation in *Chan v. Zacharia* (1983) 53 A.L.R. 417.

[40] [1996] 4 All E.R. 698.

[41] [1994] 3 W.L.R. 761 at 799.

[41a] See note of case in Appendix for more detailed comment on the fiduciary's duty of good faith described, and on certain other aspects of the case.

Significance of independent advice

9.40 In the vast majority of the rely-on-me cases, the plaintiffs had no independent advice. In a sense, this is unsurprising, since it can be expected that the employment of an independent adviser would often have meant that the plaintiff did not think it necessary as it were to keep a dog and bark himself. However, the significance of *having* an independent adviser—on the rare occasions when there was one—should not be misunderstood. It was not (and is not) a magic formula by any means.[41b] The employment of independent advice is only a defence to the trusted party if it is the *kind of advice* which can be expected to *cure* the information lack, and in some cases also the inability to consult one's own interests for example because of parental control, *etc.* As to the limited significance of independent advice, an important case is *Tate v. Williamson*,[42] in which the young plaintiff not only was told to employ his own solicitor, he actually did so. However, since the problem was not as to the legal nature of the transaction, but its *value*, that was held insufficient: he had not employed a valuer, nor had he or the solicitor been told of the much higher valuation in fact obtained by Williamson. In the result, he lacked the crucial information on which he would have exercised his judgment.[43] Therefore, in practice, a party who is in a relationship of trust and enters into a sale transaction by which he benefits must ensure, just as in a case of spontaneous vulnerability, either:

(1) that an adviser whose expertise is calculated to ensure the victim's safety is employed, for example a valuer if the sale price turns on value, a solicitor if the question is the legal effect of a deed, and so on; or
(2) he must himself make a completely clean breast of all relevant information to the trusting counterparty.

If not, the victim may set the disadvantageous transaction aside.[44]

Is there any difference of principle or approach between the so-called "abuse of confidence" cases and the so-called "presumed undue influence" cases?

9.41 No difference of principle can be discerned, once one rids oneself of the notion that there is any magic in the stated "relationships of confidence" *per se*, apart from the element of trust involved rendering the victim vulnerable in that particular transaction. Further, the cases themselves seem not to differentiate—either between the "presumed undue influence" cases as to gifts on the one hand and sales on the

[41b] See above, para. 9.36, for the similar position as regards spontaneous vulnerability.
[42] (1866) L.R. 2 Ch. App 55, and see para. 9.36 above.
[43] See also ***Savery v. King*** (1856) 5 H.L.C. 627; 10 E.R. 1046.
[44] See now also the similar approach to this topic in the judgment of Millett L.J. in ***Credit Lyonnais v. Burch*** (1996), noted fully in the Appendix to this Chapter at para. 9.111.

other; or between the "abuse of confidence" cases on the one hand and the "presumed undue influence" cases on the other. Indeed, they only differentiate between spontaneous vulnerability cases such as sales to young heirs and induced vulnerability cases such as transactions with guardians or solicitors by means of one thing, the shifting of the burden of proof to the person in the position of trust. Note the famous reply of Sir Samuel Romilly in *Huguenin v. Baseley*,[45] in which after having earlier submitted that the doctrine of the "young heir" cases, which he called "public utility" was strikingly similar to a gift case such as the one in question, he finally submitted that the principle was a *general* one, applying to all the variety of relations in which dominion[46] may be exercised by one person over another. This statement of principle was later approved by Lord Eldon in *Dent v. Bennett*,[47] a "presumed undue influence" case involving a huge sum given to a medical adviser in return for a relatively small sum owed for medical services.[48]

The effect of dealings with the vulnerable on successors in title and third parties

(1) Volunteers

9.42 It is well established that the transaction may be set aside against volunteers who took either direct from the vulnerable party or via the predator. It is not necessary to show that the recipient had knowledge of the vulnerability; the gift is simply regarded as "tainted".[49] A company controlled by the donee of the "tainted" gift will count as the donee for practical purposes.[50]

(2) Knowledge or Notice

9.43 Otherwise, the third party must have had *notice* for the transaction to be successfully set aside against him. The question arises, Of what,

[45] (1807) 14 Ves. 273; 33 E.R. 526.

[46] See above, para 9.21, as to this meaning something more like "negotiating advantage."

[47] (1839) 4 My. 8 Cr. 269.

[48] See also ***Hylton v. Hylton*** (1754) 2 Ves. Sen. 547; 28 E.R. 349, which assimilated "undue influence", spontaneous vulnerability (or unconscionability, if you prefer that term), and "abuse of confidence"; ***Welles v. Middleton*** which spoke of spontaneous and induced vulnerability in the same breath; ***Hatch v. Hatch*** (1804), 9 Ves. 292; 32 E.R. 615, ***Billage v. Southee*** (1852) 9 Hare 534; 68 E.R. 623 and ***Smith v. Kay*** (1859) 7 H.L.C. 750; 11 E.R. 299, all noted below, which drew no distinction between abuse of confidence and undue influence.

[49] See ***Bainbrigge v. Browne*** (1881) 18 Ch. D. 188, *Debenham v. Ox* (1749) 1 Ves. Sen. 276; 27 E.R. 1029, ***Bridgman v. Green*** (1757) 2 Ves. Sen. 627; 28 E.R. 399 and ***Huguenin v. Basley*** (1807) 14 Ves. 289; 33 E.R. 526.

[50] See ***O'Sullivan v. Management Agency*** [1985]. Q.B. 428

exactly, should he have had notice? He must evidently know that there has been a sale or purchase or gift. He must also know or be deemed to know of the vulnerability of one of the parties involved in the transaction. This may arise in a number of ways. First, he may have actual knowledge that the relationship between buyer and seller was a relationship of confidence. That is sufficient[51]. Secondly, he may in principle have imputed knowledge through an agent. Thirdly he may have constructive (failure to investigate) or imputed- constructive (failure to investigate) knowledge;[52] It should be noted that the failure to follow up something puzzling or untoward is one type of constructive (failure to investigate) knowledge; the failure to take normal and usual precontractual steps for one's own protection is another. The former is the more likely to be the relevant kind of constructive (failure to investigate) knowledge the third party (typically but not necessarily a bank or lender) is likely to have.

Are wives a special case of constructive notice?

9.44 The case of wives has been thought to be a special one after *Barclays Bank v. O'Brien*.[53] Lord Browne-Wilkinson, giving the judgment of the court, said regarding the duty of third parties generally:

> "In particular, if the party asserting that he takes free of the earlier rights of another knows of certain facts which put him on inquiry as to the possible existence of the rights of that other and he fails to make such inquiry or take such other steps as are reasonable to verify whether such earlier right does or does not exist, he will have constructive notice of the earlier right and take subject to it."

He continued as regards wives in particular (though extending the principle to other relationships of trust and confidence):

> "Therefore where a wife has agreed to stand surety for her husband's debts as a result of undue influence or misrepresentation, the creditor will take subject to the wife's equity to set aside the transaction if the circumstances are such as to put the creditor on inquiry as to the circumstances in which she agreed to stand surety . . .
>
> Therefore in my judgment a creditor is put on inquiry when a wife offers to stand surety for her husband's debts by the combination of two factors: (a) the transaction is on its face not to the financial advantage of the wife; and (b) there is a substantial risk in transactions of that kind that, in procuring the wife to act as surety, the husband has committed a legal or equitable wrong that entitles the wife to set aside the transaction."

It would seem that on a true analysis Lord Browne Wilkinson is

[51] See *e.g. Maitland v. Irving* 15 Sim 437.
[52] See Chap. 8, Knowledge and Notice for a description of these.
[53] [1994] 1 A.C. 180.

not in fact laying down any special rule regarding wives[54]. He seems to have thought perhaps he was extending the law on constructive notice, if at least the test of constructive notice was that the third party had actually to know of the circumstances which give rise to a presumption of undue influence, as stated in *Bainbrigge v. Browne*[55] and *BCCI v. Aboody*[56].

9.45 This may be doubted. *Bainbrigge v. Browne*[57] was a case where the principles were not discussed at length but shortly stated, in so far as material, that the creditor had to have sufficient "notice of the circumstances under which the deed was executed". This, on the facts, he was held not to have. There is nothing specially amiss with the decision in its own circumstances. The facts known to the creditors appeared to be that the trustee for the plaintiffs was to join in the deed and that they were receiving advice, albeit from the father's solicitor; and they did *not* know that the plaintiffs were young and living at home with their father. It would be wrong to read too much into it, and doubly wrong to take it as giving a licence to ignore other cases on constructive notice of any variety. Slade L.J. in *Aboody*[58] simply applied what he took to be the principle in *Bainbrigge v. Browne*[59] without discussion.

Constructive notice deriving from failure to investigate puzzling features of a transaction is a well-established doctrine[60]. It must be a doctrine which takes account of everyday modern realities: one does not find features of a transaction puzzling in a vacuum, but bringing to it one's everyday knowledge of the degree to which husbands running businesses are likely to tell their wives about financial difficulties. Thus, *Barclay's Bank v. O'Brien*[61] is probably more deservedly seen as a justified development of the old law on constructive notice to take account of modern conditions, rather than an extension of any kind.

What must a third party do if he wants to be safe from a potential vulnerable dealing?

9.46 Has the third party, who fears he may have notice, a lighter burden if he wants to ensure the transaction is valid than the original predator party would have had? The answer to this, on the cases would seem to be no.[62] Once this is accepted, the nature of the independent advice

[54] One can be misled by the slightly Victorian-fiction attitude to wives which emerges here and there from the judgment: there may be doubt whether many working wives, or indeed non-working wives, will have been too gratified by the picture of wives as helpless preys to emotional pressure.

[55] (1881) 18 Ch. D. 188.

[56] [1990] 1 Q.B. 923.

[57] Above.

[58] Above.

[59] Above.

[60] See Chap. 8, Knowledge and Notice.

[61] [1994] 1 A.C. 180.

[62] See the cases cited in Chap. 8, Knowledge and Notice.

each the creditor or other third party needs to ensure the victim receives is much more readily appreciated. The advice must be such as will be likely to cure the actual problem.[63]

None of these above cases appears to have been cited to the Court of Appeal in the two recent cases of *Banco Exterior v. Mann*[64] and *Massey v. Midland Bank*[65], both induced–vulnerability cases, both of which in effect held that once a solicitor was known to have advised the vulnerable party in question the creditor was adequately protected, because he might *assume* the solicitor had done a sufficient job. These two cases seem to adopt an unnecessarily formulaic approach.[66] They are inconsistent both with the line of authority which holds that the party who takes with notice of vulnerability takes the same burden as the party who takes directly from the victim[67] and with the line of authority referred to above. Hobhouse L.J.'s dissenting judgment in *Banco Exterior v. Mann*[68] is to be noted. Note also, perhaps the well-known judgment of Dixon J. in the Australian case of *Yerkey v. Jones*:[69]

> "Nothing but independent advice or relief from the ascendancy of her husband over her judgment and will would suffice. If the creditor left it to the husband to obtain his wife's consent to become surety and no more is done independently of the husband than to ascertain that she understands what she is doing, then, if it turns out that she is in fact acting under the undue influence of her husband, it seems that the transaction will be voidable at her instance as against the creditor."

9.47 The question also arises whether the above two cases[70] are inconsistent with the guidance given by the House of Lords in *Barclay's Bank v. O'Brien*[71]. What Lord Browne Wilkinson said after setting out the applicable principles of constructive notice was:

> "It follows that unless the creditor who is put on inquiry takes reasonable steps to satisfy himself that the wife's agreement to stand surety has been properly obtained, the creditor will have constructive notice of the wife's rights.
>
> What, then are the reasonable steps which the creditor should take to ensure that it does not have constructive notice of the wife's rights, if any? Normally the reasonable steps necessary to

[63] See paras 9.36 and 9.40 above: The significance of Independent Advice, and the cases there cited.
[64] [1995] 1 All E.R. 936.
[65] [1995] 1 All E.R. 929. See also, *Bank of Baroda v. Rayarel* [1995] 2 F.L.R. 376 and *Midland Bank v. Serter* [1995] 1 F.L.R. 1034 on the solicitor who acts for the vulnerable party as well as the lender.
[66] See also *Banco Exterior v. Thomas* [1997] 1 All E.R. 46, for a similar approach.
[67] See above and Chap. 8
[68] [1995] 1 All E.R. 936, above.
[69] (1939) 63 C.L.R.
[70] *Banco Extérior v. Thomas*, above.
[71] [1994] 1 A.C. 180.

avoid being fixed with constructive notice consist of making inquiry of the person who may have the earlier right (ie the wife) to see whether such right is asserted. It is plainly impossible to require of banks and other financial institutions that they should inquire of one spouse whether he or she has been unduly influenced or misled by the other. But in my judgment the creditor, in order to avoid being fixed with constructive notice, can reasonably be expected to take *steps to bring home to the wife the risk she is running* by standing as surety and to advise her to take independent advice. As to past transactions, it will depend on the facts of each case whether the steps taken by the creditor satisfy this test. However for the future in my judgment a creditor will have satisfied these requirements if it insists that the wife attend a private meeting (in the absence of the husband) with a representative of the creditor at which she is *told of the extent of her liability as surety*, warned of the *risk she is running and urged to take independent legal advice*. . . . I should make it clear that I have been considering the ordinary case where the creditor knows only that the wife is to stand surety for her husband's debts. I would not exclude exceptional cases where a creditor has knowledge of further facts which render the presence of undue influence not only possible but probable. In such cases, the creditor to be safe will have to insist that the wife is separately advised."[72]

If one bears in mind that what is being set out is the application of a principle, and not a statute[73], the guidance given is wholly in accordance with principle and earlier authority. The task is no formulaic one for the creditor. The House of Lords some three centuries on is in effect echoing the dislike of Lord Mansfield in *Carter v. Boehm*[74] for "drawing in" a person to a contract through ignorance of the risk in fact being run. Make the transaction fair, or remove the locking-in factor by making the risk run clear, and point out that he or she can and should take independent advice. Thus, in the ordinary case (in all probability a wife whose chief vulnerability is the lack of information alone) she needs to be put in possession of really full information about the risk, and the likelihood of the risk maturing. "The extent of her liability" and "the risk she is running" are property seen as a supreme exercise in fair dealing by the creditor, rather than a formulaic gesture or two. If there are additional features of vulnerability, the duty may be a higher one, as stated.

[72] Italics supplied.

[73] See also Lord Nicholls' remarks in *Royal Brunei Airlines v. Tan* [1995] 2 A.C. 378, quoted at the beginning of the chapter.

[74] (1766) 3 Burr 1905; 97 E.R. 1162.

APPENDIX TO CHAPTER 9: SOME CASES OF INTEREST

***The Earl of Arglas v. Muschampe* (1682–4) 2 Ch. Rep. 266; 21 E.R. 675 (A victim?)**

DEALINGS WITH THE VULNERABLE BUYER OR SELLER

9.48 The Earl was entitled to an estate of his uncle if the uncle should die without male issue. Being "in Want of Money" he borrowed £100 from the defendants Muschampe, and gave the defendant security in the form of a rentcharge of £300 per annum after the death of the last Earl of Arglas. The Earl relying on the defendant's integrity sealed the deeds, believing that the security would be void on repayment of the money lent. No copy was given to the Earl, nor was he given time to peruse the deeds. The plaintiff, the victim's uncle said he was ready to pay the defendant the money lent with interest.

The court referred to the existence of "several Precedents in this Court, as well in the Reigns of Queen Elizabeth, King James, King Charles the First, as in his now Majesty's Reign, where Relief hath been given against overreaching Bargains and Contracts made by young Heirs." The court's judgment further recited, "That Thomas Earl of Arglas, at the Time of this Bargain, was very young and of an easy Nature, and had forsaken his Wife and Friends and came to London, where he lived in Riot and Debauchery, and for the supply of his Expences therein, was this Bargain made, wherein it doth not appear he took the Advice of any Friends or Counsel, but relied wholly on the Defendant: That the Consideration of this Grant is very small, being but one Year's Purchase for a Rent-charge in Fee-simple, which is now happened in Possession; and the Over-Value, be it never so great, is not of it self sufficient Ground to set aside a Bargain, or whereupon this Court can presume Fraud: Yet it is a great Evidence of Fraud, where there are other Circumstances concurring, as there is in this Case."

The plaintiff was granted relief "but in as much as his Lordship found by the Precedents, that in such Cases, this Court doth not turn any Loss upon the Defendant, but only correct the Excess and Extravagancy of such Bargain" the defendant was given back his £300 lent with interest at 6 per cent, and on payment thereof, the defendant was to reconvey the rent-charge to the plaintiff.

***Wiseman v. Beake* (1690) 2 Vern. 121; 23 E.R. 688**

9.49 Bonds ("statutes of great penalties") were entered into by the plaintiff "defeasanced for payment of ten for one, upon the death of his uncle". They were set aside even though the plaintiff was not young at the time but nearly 40, and was a professional man, a Proctor at Doctor's Commons; and further had acquiesced in the bonds during the lifetime of the testator. Still, the court ordered that he be relieved on payment of principal and interest only. This may have been a case where the huge undervalue virtually spoke for itself.

***Proof v. Hines* (1735) Cases T. Talbot 111; 25 E.R. 690 (Bond to litigation assistant)**

9.50 A bond obtained by the defendant's wife for her and husband's services in helping the plaintiff who was illiterate and poor with his action for a substantial estate was set aside on the grounds that it was obtained "under force and necessity"; and allowed to stand as security only for so much as had actually been laid out by the defendant, with interest.

Note: the early application of the doctrine may well have been the court's jurisdiction to set aside bonds.

Walmsley v. Booth (1739) 2 Atk. 25; 26 E.R. 412 (Lord Hardwicke, Lord Chancellor) (Bond to attorney)

9.51 One Japhet Crook was charged with forgery, and the defendant Mr Booth acted for him as his attorney, and obtained people to give bail for him. He executed a bond giving security for a gift by will which Crook also executed, in favour of Mr Booth. The recital purported to mention services and favours carried out by Booth. Lord Hardwicke said:[75]

"It has been said that *Japhet Crook* was a very cunning fellow, and a very great knave, and I believe it to be true; but the court must not consider the particular circumstances of the man, but the case in general . . .: for a person may be prosecuted for these very crimes, and yet be innocent; and it would be very mischievous if there was any encouragement given to an undue advantage taken of another under such circumstances".[76]

Lord Hardwicke set aside the bond, but ordered an inquiry into any extraordinary services that Booth might have rendered, and payment for what was justly due to Booth in this way to be made by Crook.

Note: this is evidently an example of vulnerability brought about by emotional pressures, i.e. Mr Booth was thought to be trading on the fear of a person charged with a serious criminal offence.

Berkley Freeman v. Bishop (1740) 2 Atk. 39; 26 E.R. 420 (Rationale for attitude to young heirs)

9.52 The Lord Chancellor laid down the rule that . . . "an heir of 22 or 23 years of age, if a dealer in horses, or other tradesmen, impose upon him, by selling at extravagant prices, in numberless instances, shall be relieved in this court, others if in a single instance only." He commented that it was "the necessity which young heirs are in for the most part, which naturally lays them open to impositions of this kind." and continued, "Where an extravagant price is charged for goods sold, and a mortgage is taken to secure it, the heir may be relieved so far as it stands as a security for the unjust gain; but after it is determined upon a *quantum meruit*, what was the real worth of the goods, the mortgage will still be binding upon the heir, for so much as is found by the verdict."

Cocking v. Pratt (1740) 1 Ves. Sen. 400; 27 E.R. 1105 (Daughter—parent transaction: daughter's ignorance of value stressed)

9.53 An agreement by daughter, four months after she came of age, as to the distribution of the personal estate of her late father was set aside. The Master of the Rolls stressed the daughter's lack of knowledge of the value of her estate, and the undervalue—in fact she had been entitled to £500 or £600 more than she received from her mother.

Debenham v. Ox (1749) 1 Ves. Sen. 276; 27 E.R. 1029 (Bond set aside even in favour of wrong-doing plaintiff)

[75] *Ibid.*
[76] Italics in original.

9.54 A bond was given by the plaintiff to the defendant's wife in consideration of the latter using her influence over the plaintiff's grandfather who was aged 82, to ensure that he made a will in the plaintiff's favour. Lord Hardwicke said that the court would set these transactions aside not for the plaintiff's sake, he was *particeps criminis*, but "because the objection, that infects the bond, arises from public consideration".

Note: he did not expatiate particularly; but the case was perhaps decided on the grounds that the defendant's wife was a third party who could not be permitted to benefit even indirectly from a transaction of undue influence. The idea that a gift obtained by undue influence was "tainted" in the hands of a third party can be seen in Bridgeman v. Green[77]

***Earl of Chesterfield v. Janssen* (1751) 2 Ves. Sen. 125; 28 E.R. 82**

9.55 As has been noted in the text, in this case Lord Hardwicke took the opportunity to clarify the basis of the law on dealings with the vulnerable.

***How v. Weldon & Edwards* (1754) 2 Ves. Sen. 516; 28 E.R. 330 (The land-man ignorant of the value of his prize)**

9.56 The plaintiff was a "land-man" on board one of the ships, which in 1745 "made the great capture, which put into Kinsale in Ireland". The plaintiff agreed to sell his interest in the prize money, when he obtained it, to the first defendant Weldon, for what was acknowledged to be about a quarter of its true value. Weldon then assigned his rights to the second defendant Edwards.

The court said that the plaintiff's equity against Weldon "is founded on the common and known principle, an instrument obtained from him by fraud and imposition". It seemed there had been *suggestio falsi* and *suppressio veri*, to some extent: the chances of the plaintiff not receiving the prize having been much exaggerated to him. "But", said the Master of the Rolls, "the more material part is from the other circumstances upon the general head of equity arising partly from the person with whom the transaction was, and beside the *value of the thing purchased*. It is reasonable to consider the vendor at least in as favourable a light as a young heir. I am warranted in saying that, by what has been often said in cases of this kind, and what has been done by the legislature itself; which has considered them [land-men] as a race of men loose and unthinking, who will almost for nothing part with what they have acquired perhaps with their blood; therefore are they restrained by two acts of parliament, the last of which was 20 G 2."

Then there was the price: "*though the inadequateness of the value will not of itself be sufficient to set aside the contract, yet it is a very material ingredient, and, with other things, will go a great way toward it.*"[78]

The deed was set aside, but to stand as a security for the amount bona fide advanced. It was also set aside against Edwards, because it was felt the inadequacy of the price had really *put him on notice so that he ought to have inquired further.*

***Hylton v. Hylton* (1754) 2 Ves. Sen. 547; 28 E.R. 349 (Lord Hardwicke, Lord Chancellor) (Gift case; indifference to labels)**

9.57 A transfer by a young man to his guardian (also the executor and trustee of his aunt's and half brother's estate under both of which he inherited) in return for an annuity of £60, was set aside. It was made just after he came of

[77] para. 9.58, below.
[78] Italics supplied.

age, and before he had been put in possession of his estate. The transaction was made freely and voluntarily. Lord Hardwicke said:

"Where a man acts as guardian, or trustee in nature of a guardian, for an infant, the court is extremely watchful to prevent that person's taking any advantage immediately upon his ward or *cestuy que* trust coming of age, and at the time of settling account or delivering up the trust; because an *undue advantage* may be taken. It would give an opportunity either by flattery or force, by good usage unfairly meant, or by bad usage imposed to take such advantage; and therefore *the principle of the court is of the same nature with relief in this court on the head of public utility*, as in bonds obtained from young heirs, and rewards given to an attorney pending a cause and marriage brocage bonds . . . All depend upon public utility; and therefore the court will not suffer it, though perhaps in a particular instance there may not be an actual unfairness."[79]

Certain particular circumstances had been relied on to take the matter out of the general rule. However, Lord Hardwicke did not think any of them assisted the defendant at all. The guardian appears to have given the impression that he would not part with the estate until he was sure of the grant. The young man was not in circumstances to grant the annuity. There was no account made up of the personal estate proved to have come to the defendant's hands. Lord Hardwicke said, *"Certainly, if any thing could make such a transaction supportable, it must be where there was a real and fair account . . ." Therefore, he set aside the settlement both "on the general rule and nature of this particular case, and the delusion and deception under which the plaintiff was"*.[80]

Note: the weakness here rendering the plaintiff vulnerable is no doubt his youth together with the rely-on-me factor constituted by the guardianship, only recently come to an end. This case is included to show that "undue influence" and "unconscionable" or "catching" bargains were all regarded as part of the same branch of the law.

***Bridgman v. Green* (1757) 2 Ves. Sen. 627; 28 E.R. 399 (Lord Chancellor); Wilm. 58 (Lord Commissioners) (Gift—tainted in hands of (volunteer) third parties)**

9.58 The facts appear more clearly from the hearing before the Lord Chancellor whose judgment was upheld by the Lords Commissioners.[81] The plaintiff had a butler called George Green who took advantage of the weakness of the plaintiff's understanding, and took a bond for £2,800 from the plaintiff to pay him an annuity if his wages were not paid, or if he were dismissed. George Green then together with an attorney, William Lock, procured various conveyances from the plaintiff; and a mortgage of his estate for £5,000, of which £3,000 was paid to George Green, £1,000 to Green's brother and £1,000 to Green's associate Lock.

Lord Commissioner Wilmot said when the case came before the Lords Commissioners[82]:

". . . this Court never did, nor even will annul donations merely because they are improvident, and such as a wise man would not have made, or a man of very nice honour would not have accepted: nor will this Court measure the

[79] Italics supplied.
[80] Italics supplied.
[81] Wilm 58.
[82] Noted as part of Sir Samuel Romilly's reply in *Huguenin v. Basely* 14 Ves. Jun. 273; 33 E.R. 526.

degrees of understanding; and say, that a weak man, provided he is out of the reach of a Commission [of lunacy], may not give as well as a wise man. But though this Court disclaims any such jurisdiction, yet, where a gift is immoderate, bears no proportion to the circumstances of the giver, "ubi modus non adhibetur, ubi non refertur ad facultatem" when no reason at all appears, or the reason given is falsified, and proved to be a fiction, and the giver is a weak man, of a facile easy temper, liable to be imposed upon, this Court will look upon such a gift with a very jealous eye, and very strictly examine the conduct and behaviour of the persons in whose favour it is made: if it see that any arts or stratagems, or any undue means have been used by them to procure such a gift, if it see the least speck of imposition at the bottom, or that the donor is in such a situation with respect to the donee, as may naturally give him an undue influence over him, if there be the least scintilla of fraud; in such a case, this Court will and ought to interpose; and by the exertion of such a jurisdiction, they are so far from infringing the right of alienation, which is the inseparable incident to property, that it acts upon the principle of securing the full, ample, and uninfluenced enjoyment of it."

He commented on the fact that the Plaintiff had given away a fifth of what he had, without any apparent motive whatsoever. He continued later "but when the gift bears no proportion to the situation of the giver, to his rank in life, and to his circumstances, and no cause is shewn which, according to the constitution of human nature, and the common and ordinary operations of mere love and esteem, might naturally beget such a bounty, it carries its own death wound, as Lord Hobart calls it, along with it, and proclaims itself upon view, to be the offspring of fraud and imposition."

Lord Commissioner Wilmot then went on to say that the plaintiff's gift of £5,000 was divided between Green and his wife, and Green's brother, and Lock the father. He thought they could not keep it, since it was tainted and infected with Green's undue influence.[83] The Lord Chancellor had merely described it as a barefaced and shameful transaction, and confirmed that it should be set it aside. He did not rely on the plaintiff's inability to manage his own affairs: he considered he was a very imprudent man, but not so weak as to be called a fool.

Note: The case is included mainly on account of the treatment of third parties deriving a benefit indirectly from the plaintiff; but it is also of interest as an example of the kind of concentration on the internal workings of the giver's mind (did they have a freely-formed intention of liberality?) which is characteristic of the gift cases, and quite uncharacteristic of the sale and purchase cases.

Gwynne v. Heaton **(1778) 1 Bro. C.C. 1; 28 E.R. 949 (Young, "necessitous" reversioner)**

9.59 The plaintiff's father was 81. The son was entitled in tail in reversion; but had been "turned out of doors", having offended his father by an "imprudent" marriage to a servant girl. Accordingly, the son was obliged to sell a reversionary annuity of £300 for £2300 and an annuity of £400 for the father's lifetime, and gave security.

The Lord Chancellor Lord Thurlow set the sale aside, warning however that mere inadequacy of price was insufficient to vitiate the contract. He was unhappy about the state of the evidence, but concluded that at the time the contract was negotiated, the life of the father, to the knowledge of the defendant, was only one or two year's purchase; while the calculations had been based on 17 years' purchase. He said, "To set aside a conveyance, there must

[83] It is unclear whether or not these third parties knew about the circumstances of the case: it is possible the "taint" overrode any question of knowledge.

be an inequality *so strong, gross, and manifest*, that it must be *impossible to state it* to a man of common sense, *without producing an exclamation at the inequality of it*''. He commented that the principle was looser than he would wish to see, but "to reverse the principles which had been laid down by successive great names would be to alter the rules of property". The deed was set aside, but the lender was to have the deeds as security and his costs of the redemption account, *etc.*

Note: This case evidences the requirement in spontaneous vulnerability cases to show inadequacy of price. There is no reason to suppose this is a requirement for the Plaintiff in induced vulnerability cases.

Evans v. Llewellin (1787) 1 Cox 333; 29 E.R. 1191 (Lack of cooling off/ consultation period)

9.60 The plaintiff was "in mean circumstances", was told of his rights (accurately) but not given a great deal of time to reflect, also had appeals made to his better nature and was offered what was for him a great sum of money (but below its true value) to relinquish his title to certain land. He had no independent advice.

The Master of the Rolls said, "there certainly may be cases put in which such confirmation [of what had been done] would be effectual, if proper time were allowed to the party, and due caution used in making him aware of the consequences . . . It is said he was cautioned by [the purchaser's solicitor]; it is true, and so far the parties did right; but they ought to have gone further; they should not have permitted the man to have made the bargain *without going to consult his friends; there was not sufficient locus penitentiae; there was no person present to give him advice; he was entirely in their hands, and surprised* at this unexpected acquisition of fortune."[84]

He noted that he had been called on for principles. He said, "However, here, I say, the party was taken by *surprise*; he had not sufficient time to act with caution; and therefore though there was no actual fraud, it is something like fraud, for an undue advantage was taken of his situation. The cases of infants dealing with guardians, of sons with fathers, all proceed on the same general principle, and establish this, that if the party is in a situation, in which he is not a *free agent*, and is *not equal to protecting himself*, this Court will protect him. He did not use "any harsh terms" because he did not think the case called for it; and gave no costs. He also said "indeed if the plaintiff had in fact gone back and consulted his friends, I should not have rescinded the transaction."[85]

Note: The case is of importance for two reasons:

(1) it stresses the need for a cooling-off/consultation period; and

(2) it overtly equates the jurisdiction in dealings for consideration with the vulnerable and in the cases of gifts.

Newman v. Payne (1793) 2 Ves. Jun. 199; 30 E.R. 593 (Referred to in argument in *Huguenin v. Baseley*[86]

9.61 A bond for £1,000 which the plaintiff had given to the defendant who was his attorney, and who had the general management of his affairs, and thus gained influence over him, was set aside. The defendant was allowed his proper fees. A horse which he had sold the plaintiff was to be valued, and if sold at an overvalue, the plaintiff was to be compensated accordingly. Lord

[84] Italics supplied.
[85] Italics supplied.
[86] (1807) 14 Ves. 289; 33 E.R. 526.

Loughborough, the Lord Chancellor based his decision on the fact that the defendant was an attorney, and an officer of the Court, rather than any rule particular to equity.

Note: This was a bargain, but because, it would seem, the rely-on-me element of the solicitor-client relationship made it unsafe, only the element of the transaction which amounted to normal payment for the solicitor's fees was allowed to stand. It is interesting to observe that the courts often allowed the transaction to stand in part despite setting aside the whole: as security for a loan made; or where an element was for fees for services rendered, as here.

Gibson v. Jeyes (1801) 6 Ves. 266; 31 E.R. 1044 (Lord Eldon, Lord Chancellor) (Duty of trusted party to shop around for prices)

9.62 Mrs Kerby, a widow aged over 70, gave £400 to the defendant Theophilus Jeyes who was her agent and an attorney. It was expressed to be in consideration of an annuity of £50 a year. He for his part gave her his bond in the penalty of £800, to secure it.[87] Mrs Kerby died three days after the first quarter became due. There was actuarial evidence on both sides, it being an issue whether the sum she paid was indeed an overvalue for the annuity. On this issue the Lord Chancellor thought that *reasonable and due diligence had not been exercised on her behalf* in that better terms might have been obtained for her. The transaction was set aside and the money returned with interest.

"If he will mix with the character of attorney that of vendor, he shall, if the propriety of the contract comes in question, manifest, that he has given her all that reasonable advice against himself, that he would have given her against a third person. It is asked, where is that rule to be found. I answer, in that great rule of the Court, that he, who bargains in matter of advantage with a person placing confidence in him is bound to shew, that a reasonable use has been made of that confidence; a rule applying to trustees, attorneys, *or any one else*."

Note: The case is mainly of interest for Lord Eldon's statement of principle, frequently referred to thereafter and quoted at the beginning of this chapter, which shows the duty is based on the position of invited trust of the solicitor, etc., but does not depend on the trusted party being in fact a solicitor or anything else. The duty to shop around for prices also shows the strictness with which invited trust was protected.

Hatch v. Hatch (1804) 9 Ves. 292; 32 E.R. 615 (Lord Eldon, Lord Chancellor) (Gift case, disclosure of information about value stressed)

9.63 A conveyance of an advowson to her guardian by a ward on becoming entitled was set aside. Lord Eldon referred to the lady's deafness—("for the purpose of conversing with her it was necessary to use the intercourse with the fingers") and said "*Under these circumstances a duty was imposed upon her guardian and her attorney to give her full information*. Her guardian, when she came of age, was in the enjoyment of the living. He therefore must have distinctly understood the value: not only the actual value at that time, but its improvable nature and quality. It is not like the case of a conveyance of an estate, yielding a certain rent, or stock, yielding dividends, or an annuity, a certain annual profit. *This is property of such a nature, that one party may be fully acquainted with the value, and no one else can have any correct information upon it except from that person*." He went on to note that the relationship of guardian continued after she came of age and until her marriage. He stated also that the Court would not permit gifts to guardians, attorneys, or trustees where these were purportedly bounty for the execution of antecedent duty. The

[87] He was aged 80!

court had to be quite satisfied, that the act is the result of fair, serious and well-informed consideration on the part of the ward, cestuy que trust etc, an "act of rational consideration, an act of pure volition, uninfluenced", rather than "the impulse of a mind, misled by undue kindess, or forced by oppression."[88]

Note: It plainly seems to have been important that the guardian here was the only person who understood properly the value of the living. This seems to have given rise to a duty of disclosure, necessary for a valid transaction.

Note: The above tends to support the idea that both these heads of equity—the transactions with those whose vulnerability was pre-existing and by those who had invited confidence, such as guardians, etc., were regarded as essentially part of the same branch of the law.

Wright v. Proud (1806) 13 Ves. Jun. 136; 33 E.R. 246 (Gift case; relief given by reason of informal relationship of confidence after the formal relationship had ceased)

9.64 The claim was to set aside a deed as having been obtained by fraud and undue influence from the plaintiff and one Lapworth Mills (by then deceased) by the defendants. The first defendant had been the keeper of an asylum in which Mills had been a patient for many years. At the time the transaction took place he was voluntarily resident there, and proposed the gift as a way to remunerate the kindness with which he had been treated.

The Lord Chancellor said, "The principle, upon which a transaction is set aside upon the relation between the parties, as between Guardian and Ward, has been extended to the case, where all accounts were previously settled; and the connection was at an end: the transaction appearing to have grown out of the influence, arising from the relation." In fact the deed was also fraudulent: it had been prepared by the donees' attorney and had misrepresented the interest the plaintiff had. The Lord Chancellor consequently declared the deed fraudulent and void.

Note: like Hatch v. Hatch[89], the case shows that it is the confidence reposed which gives the victim the right to question the transaction, rather than the existence of any formal relationship. In this case, there was after all, no formal relationship at all, merely the shadow of the old relationship and the real confidence reposed.

Welles v. Middleton (referred to in _Lady Ormond v. Hutchinson_ (1806) 13 Ves. Jun. 47; 33 E.R. 212) (Statement of principle differentiating between spontaneous and induced vulnerability, assimilating "abuse of confidence" and "undue influence"; _need for full disclosure by the trusted party stressed_)

9.65 The Lord Chancellor Erskine said, "The principle, upon which this Court acts, giving the relief in these cases, is plain; and, I think, not new. The jurisdiction is most beneficial, proceeding principally upon those confidential situations in life; in respect of which this Court assumes a guardianship over mankind: where a breach of confidence has been committed: advantage taken of men, unguarded, in particular situations, and under circumstances, such, that the Courts of Law, though fraud, according to the ordinary understanding of the term, is equally the subject of their jurisdiction, cannot give an adequate remedy: a Court of Equity, for instance, prohibiting a party from taking advantage of an instrument obtained under such circumstances ...

[88] Italics supplied.
[89] Para. 9.63 above.

Every case of this kind must stand upon its own circumstances; and the Court will try the application."

"The case of *Welles v. Middleton*[90] had no ingredient of fraud, but the deed was an instrument, which the policy of the Law would not sustain, and it was necessary to set aside upon the relation of the parties; the effect of which is, *that the Court has not sufficient evidence, that one party had given the other the benefit of all that knowledge, which from the situation, in which he stood, he ought to have supplied: the Court taking different views of contracts between such parties and between strangers.* The Defendants in that case were the attornies, and relations of the ancestor of the Plaintiffs; who were the heirs at law. The question was, whether notwithstanding all that advantage had been communicated, a deed of gift to an attorney could stand. The evidence was, that *Wilcox*, the ancestor, was of sufficient understanding to make the deed; that he made it knowing the contents; that it was deliberately read over to him; attested by respectable witnesses; and that he frequently afterwards recognized and admitted it. The Defendants had not done any thing immoral or dishonest; but the principle of that decision was the policy of the Law; founded upon the safety and convenience of mankind; a shield against advantage taken by persons in situations of confidence, preventing acts of bounty, which in other situations might have effect: but the deed being taken, while the character of attorney to the grantor remained, could not be permitted to stand without striking at the root of the principle."[91]

Note: The case is included to show the importance of the trusted party's disclosure so that there was "full knowledge"[92] *even in the gift cases; and the broad, sweeping nature of the principle, "a shield against advantage taken persons in situations of confidence . . .". This last would seem to leave no real room for distinctions between "abuse of confidence" cases and other "undue influence" cases. Indeed, in Hatch v. Hatch*[93] *the Lord Chancellor, Lord Eldon, referred to this case as being one in which Lord Thurlow's decree was affirmed eventually by the House of Lords and in which "all these cases relating to trustees, guardians, attornies, &c, were much considered, and the rule very strong laid down by Lord Thurlow".*

***Huguenin v. Baseley* (1807) 14 Ves. 273; 33 E.R. 526 (affirmed by the House of Lords; see 15 Ves. 180; 33 E.R. 722, Lord Eldon, Lord Chancellor) (*Gift to unofficial agent; requisite knowledge of "effect, nature and consequences" stressed; position of (volunteer) third parties who receive the gift considered*)**

9.66 The plaintiff was a widow who had certain estates in Oxfordshire and in Jamaica. She made a settlement of these on the defendant, who was a clergyman who had taken over the management of her affairs, and on his wife and children.

Lord Eldon held that the settlements ought to be set aside. He said[94], "To the question, whether, these instruments being such as I have represented them, the consequence is, that this Court shall undo them: *I answer, no; if they are the pure, voluntary, well understood, acts of her mind: but if they have not that character, if they are the result of her notion, that this is the true effect of that friendly assistance, that kind, providential, interference, to which she was looking, for the management of her affairs with advantage and facility to herself, if the conveyance*

[90] Stated by the Lord Chancellor from a M.S. note. See 12 Ves. 372, *Morse v. Royal*, and the note.)
[91] Italics supplied.
[92] Although it is unclear quite what knowledge was missing.
[93] Above, paragraph 9.63.
[94] *Ibid*. at 295.

was executed under the effect of that, which has always been considered in this Court as undue influence, if the deeds themselves, which are the best evidence, demonstrate, and if they are confirmed by extrinsic evidence, that they are not the pure, well understood, acts of her mind, this Court will undo them."

He continued later,[95] "Take it, that she intended to give it to him: it is by no means out of the reach of the principle. The question is, not, whether she knew what she was doing, had done, or proposed to do, but how the intention was produced: whether all that care and providence was placed round her, as against those, who advised her, which, from their situation and relation with respect to her, they were bound to exert on her behalf . . .

Repeating therefore distinctly, that this Court is not to undo voluntary deeds, *I represent the question thus: whether she executed these instruments not only voluntarily, but with that knowledge of all their effect, nature and consequences, which the Defendants Baseley and the attorney were bound by their duty to communicate to her, before she was suffered to execute them, and, though perhaps they were not aware of the duties, which this Court required from them in the situation, in which they stood, where the decision rests upon the ground of public utility, for the purpose of maintaining the principle it is necessary to* impute knowledge, *which the party may not actually have had*. These parties therefore cannot possibly hold the benefit of these instruments."[96]

The reply of Sir Samuel Romilly, her counsel, which became famous, is also quoted below, as an example of the typical "internal workings of the mind" approach to the gift cases. "*The relief stands upon a general principle, applying to all the variety of relations, in which dominion may be exercised by one person over another* . . . ."[97] He then quoted (*inter alia*) Wilmot C.J. in the court below in *Bridgman v. Green*[98]. Having said that English law did not draw a boundary between liberality and profusion, as did Roman law, Wilmot C.J. had continued "*Stat pro ratione voluntas*, is the law with us; and this Court never did, nor even will, annul donations merely as being unprovident, and such as a wise man would not have made, or a man of very nice honor have accepted: nor will this Court measure the degrees of understanding; and say, that a weak man, provided he is out of the reach of a Commission [on lunacy] may not give as well as a a wise man. But though this Court disclaims any such jurisdiction, yet, where a gift is immoderate, bears no proportion to the circumstances of the giver, where no reason appears, or the reason given is falsified, and the giver is a weak man, liable to be imposed upon, this Court will look upon such a gift with a very jealous eye; and very strictly examine the conduct of the persons, in whose favor it is made; and, if it sees, that any arts or stratagems, or *any undue means*, have been used, if it sees *the least speck of imposition at the bottom*, or that the donor is in such a situation with respect to the donee as may naturally give an undue influence over him, if there be the least *scintilla* of fraud, this Court will and ought to interpose."[99]

Note:

(1) *Mr Baseley was an unpaid agent, who had assumed the management of the plaintiff's affairs. This relatively informal agency sufficed, since as a result Mrs Huguenin placed her trust in Mr Baseley, apparently believing that the settlements on him would enable him to manage her affairs for her. (Would the agency be any different if he had been her husband?)*

(2) *Even in the case of a gift, Lord Eldon thought her lack of information crucial—"Knowledge of all their effect, nature and consequences". He seems to*

[95] *Ibid*. at 299.
[96] Italics supplied.
[97] Italics supplied.
[98] Para. 9.58, above.
[99] Italics in original.

have regarded this as a pre-requisite to the formation of a valid intention to be liberal[1].

(3) *The case is also of some interest on the position of third parties, specially those without knowledge of the undue influence who derive an advantage from the transaction.*[2] *The judgment of Wilmot C.J. in Bridgeman*[3] *on this question was cited by Lord Eldon, above. Lord Eldon noted that the wife and children of the defendant Baseley had not personally interfered in the transaction at all (although the plaintiff had made gifts direct to them) and continued*[4]. *"If therefore their estates are to be taken from them, that relief must be given with reference to the conduct of other persons; and I should regret, that any doubt could be entertained, whether it is not competent to a Court of Equity to take away from third persons the benefits, which they have derived from the fraud, imposition, or undue influence of others. The case of* Bridgeman v. Green[5] *is an express authority, that it is within the reach of the principle of this Court to declare, that interests, so gained, by third persons, cannot possibly be held by them; and Lord Hardwicke observes justly, that, if a person could get out of the reach of the doctrine and principle of this Court by giving interests to third persons, instead of reserving them to himself, it would be almost impossible ever to reach a case of fraud . . ." He then quoted Wilmot C.J. further.*

"There is no pretence, that Green's brother, or his wife, was party to any imposition, or had any due or undue influence over the Plaintiff: but does it flow from thence, that they must keep the money? No: whoever receives it must take it tainted and infected with the undue influence and imposition of the person receiving the gift: his partitioning and cantoning it out amongst his relatives and friends will not purify the gift, and protect it against the Equity of the person imposed upon. Let the hand receiving it be ever so chaste, yet, if it comes through a polluted channel, the obligation of restitution will follow it."

Wood v. Downes (1811) 18 Ves. Jun. 120; 34 E.R. 263 (Sale to solicitor; lack of information about value stressed)

9.67 The plaintiff William Wood, with his wife Frances, sought to set aside contracts and conveyances to Downes who had been their attorney and solicitor at the time. They actually sought a declaration that the conveyances might be declared fraudulent against them and an order that the conveyances should stand only as security for what was properly due by way of fees. They said *inter alia* that the conveyances were obtained by his influence and control, that they were *not acquainted with their rights, the nature and value of the estate*, that he advised them there was great doubt whether he could recover the estate for them; that he gave an inadequate price, and that no attorney was employed on behalf of the plaintiffs.

Lord Eldon granted the plaintiffs the relief they sought, and referred to a number of earlier cases. The latter *Hylton v. Hylton*[6] 2 Ves. Sen. 547, and *Hatch*

[1] *c.f.* "intention requires knowledge" in ***Billage v. Southee*** para 9.76 below.

[2] See the spate of articles on third parties following the decision in ***Barclay's Bank v. O'Brien*** [1994] 1. A.C. 180: in particular 1994 Conv. 140 (Thompson); 1994 Conv. 421 (Dixon and Harpum) and 1995 Conv. 250 (Sparkes).

[3] Above.

[4] *Ibid.* at 289.

[5] Above.

[6] 2 Ves. Sen. 547.

v. Hatch[7], laid down "as clear Law, that no attorney can take any thing for his own benefit from his client pending the suit, save his demand; and I add, that, as a guardian cannot take any thing from this ward pending the guardianship, or at the close of it, or at any period, until his influence has ceased to exist, the obligation upon an attorney to refrain from taking an extraordinary benefit is at least as strong."

Note: Hylton v. Hylton[8] *was a case in which there was consideration, and* Hatch v. Hatch[9] *was a gift case, and it is to be noted that Lord Eldon draws no distinction between the two cases. The courts tended to give judgments in a somewhat more referential way than is common nowadays ("This is an obvious case of negligence, would (in this mode) be expressed as 'This is an example of the well-known principle laid in down in* Donaghue v. Stevenson'*, as it were) so that it is perhaps important in understanding Lord Eldon's judgment that one takes on board the full flavour of* Hylton v. Hylton *and* Hatch v. Hatch. *In both these cases, as in* Wood v. Downes *itself, the court had emphasized the dependence of the giver/grantor on the guardian for true information as to the value of what was given. Thus, even though the approach to the case of* Wood v. Downes *is superficially by means of the status of the recipient (guardian, solicitor) the principle is as much or more one of unequal access to information about value. In short, the "rely-on-me" effect of the relationship between William and Frances Wood and their solicitor meant that their lack of information was presumed unless the contrary was shown (although in fact it formed an important part of their allegations in the case in any event).*

Montesqieu v. Sandys (1811) 18 Ves. 302 (purchase by solicitor allowed to stand)

9.68 A purchase by a solicitor of property other than the property with which he had been concerned as solicitor was not set aside, really because the evidence did not come up to what was alleged on the pleadings, but the Lord Chancellor Lord Eldon affirmed the principle (outlined by Sir Samuel Romilly) on the basis of *Gibson v. Jeyes*[10] and *Wood v. Downes*[11].

Wood v. Abrey (1818) 3 Madd. 417; 56 E.R. 558

9.69 The two Woods were respectively the tenant for life and the remainderman in tail, of certain estates. Both were in distressed circumstances. (The older Wood had become so poor that he had to take a job as a porter.) Abrey had bought a 21 year lease of the premises from the older Wood who was tenant for life, and had thereby become acquainted with its value. He accordingly offered to buy the estate for £400. The Woods "being unacquainted with the value of the estate, and in distress, complied with the proposal". There was evidence at trial that the price was a great undervalue. The Vice-Chancellor Sir John Leach set it aside, saying,

"With respect to value, mere inadequacy of price is of no more weight in equity than at law. If a man who meets his purchaser on equal terms, negligently sells his estate at an under value, he has no title to relief in equity. But a Court of Equity will inquire whether the parties really did meet on equal

[7] 9 Ves. 292.
[8] Above.
[9] Above, para. 9.63.
[10] Above, para. 9.63.
[11] Above, para. 9.67.

terms; and if it be found the vendor was in distressed circumstances, and that advantage was taken of that distress, it will avoid the I contract."

Note: This is a succinct early statement of the law in this area.

Shelly v. Nash **(1818) 3 Madd. 232; 56 E.R. 494**

9.70 The rule that was fast developing about the sale of reversions[12] was not applied to a sale of a reversion by auction. Sir John Leach, the Vice-Chancellor's comments, are worth noting.

"At law and in equity also, generally speaking, a man who has a power of disposition over his property, whether he sells to relieve his necessities or to provide for the convenience of his family, cannot avoid his contract upon the mere ground of inadequacy of price. A Court of Equity, however, will relieve expectant heirs and reversioners from disadvantageous bargains. In the earlier cases it was held necessary to shew that undue advantage was actually taken of the situation of such persons; but in more modern times it has been considered, not only that those who were dealing for their expectations, but those who were dealing for vested reversions also, were so exposed to imposition and hard terms, and so much in the power of those with whom they contracted, that it was a fit rule of policy to impose upon all who dealt with expectant heirs and reversioners, the *onus* of proving that they had paid a fair price, and otherwise to undo their bargains, and compel a reconveyance of the property purchased. The principle and the policy of the rule may be both equally questionable. Sellers of reversions are not necessarily in the power of those with whom they contract, and are not necessarily exposed to imposition and hard terms; and persons who sell their expectations and reversions from the pressure of distress, are thrown by the rule into the hands of those who are likely to take advantage of their situation; for no person can securely deal with them. The principle of the rule, however, cannot be applied to sales of reversion by *auction*. There being no treaty between vendor and purchaser, there can be no opportunity for fraud or imposition on the part of the purchaser. The vendor is in no sense in the power of the purchaser. The sale by auction is evidence of the market price. Being of this opinion, it is unnecessary for me to enter into a consideration of the evidence as to the inadequacy or adequacy of the price. It is said that pretended sales by auction may be used to cover private bargains; where such cases occur they will operate nothing."

Dent v. Bennett **(1839) 4 My. & Cr. 269; 41 E.R. 105 (Agreement to pay excessive lump sum to doctor)**

9.71 The plaintiff in the action sought to have an agreement allegedly signed by the plaintiff's testator delivered up to be cancelled and am injunction against any action at law being brought upon it. The Vice-Chancellor had granted the injunction, and the question was simply whether the agreement should be delivered up. By the agreement the testator had agreed to pay the defendant, who was his doctor, £25,000, both in return for his medical services in the future, and also by reason of the testator's gratitude for past services. The Lord Chancellor, Lord Cottenham, set the agreement aside, doubting that the testator signed it at all. The following passage from his judgment is however of particular interest as regards the principles involved.

"It was argued, upon the authority of the civil law and of some reported cases, that medical attendants were, upon questions of this kind, within that class of persons whose acts, when dealing with their patients, ought to be watched with great jealousy. Undoubtedly they are; *but I will not narrow the*

[12] see the text above at para. 9.17.

rule or run the risk of in any degree fettering the exercise of the beneficial jurisdiction of this Court by any enumeration of the description of persons against whom it ought to be most freely exercised."

He then cited with approval[13] the celebrated speech in reply of Sir Samuel Romilly in the gift case of *Huguenin v. Baseley*[14] "The relief stands upon a general principle, applying to all the variety of relations in which dominion may be exercised by one person over another . . ."

Lord Cottenham thought the signing of the paper, if the testator did sign it, was either produced by fraud, or "under such circumstances as render it the duty of a Court of Equity to protect the party signing it and his estate from being prejudiced by it."

Note:

(1) *The longer passage quoted above does tend to show that the "status" aspect of these cases, which as has been said receives rather more attention today than it deserves, was never paramount; it was the vulnerable position of the sick testator vis a vis his doctor.*

(2) *The case also shows that the borderline between gifts and sales is by no means a simple one: this transaction was overtly a sale of services, but the huge imbalance in the consideration meant that in practice the element of gift was paramount. Thus, Lord Cottenham naturally looked rather more to the gift cases, with their emphasis on the influencing power of the donee, than to the sale cases, which tended rather more to concentrate on unequal access to information about value.*

Edwards v. Meyrick (1842) 2 Hare 60; 67 E.R. 25 at 68 (Sale to solicitor)

9.72 The defendant Meyrick, a solicitor, became acquainted with the existence of a settlement under which the plaintiff was entitled to a property of considerable value. He was then instructed by the plaintiff to take various proceedings regarding the property, which were finally compromised. The plaintiff then granted a mortgage on two of his farms not connected with the proceedings, to secure the defendant's fees, and later sold them to the defendant. He later tried to set this aside.

On the facts, the case failed, since the solicitor there had given good value for the estate, and further, the action was brought after some years. The point was also made that the solicitor had to be the solicitor *in hac re*, that is, in some way involved as solicitor in the property sold to him. The court accepted this limitation of the principle, although giving it a liberal interpretation evidently, since it concluded that Mr Meyrick probably *was* solicitor *in hac re*. Nonetheless, in the circumstances, the court considered Mr Meyrick, who had proved he had given full value for the property he bought, was entitled to keep the property bought. Lord Eldon's statement of the law[15] was affirmed, but a know-your-purchaser principle applicable to these cases was stated by the court—that the duty of a buyer who was in a relationship of this kind varied according to the nature of the victim seller: there were various gradations, and Mr Meyrick's duty would have been a higher one, that is, presumably, would have extended beyond merely giving full value, if, for example the plaintiff had been elderly and/or mentally feeble.

Sir James Wigram, the Vice-Chancellor, considered that although the onus was on the solicitor to show the transaction was a fair one, since here there was no superadded weakness beyond that imposed by the relationship itself, the main duty on the solicitor was to show that he had given full information.

[13] Italics supplied

[14] para. 9.66 above.

[15] ***Wood v. Downes***, above para. 9.67.

"In other cases where an attorney has been employed to manage an estate he has been considered as bound to prove that he gave his employer the benefit of all the knowledge which he had acquired in his character of manager or professional agent, in order to maintain a bargain made for his own advantage . . . But, as the communication of such knowledge by the attorney will place the parties upon an equality, when it is proved that the communication was made, the difficulty of supporting the transaction is *quoad hoc* removed."

Sir James Wigram thus decided the solicitor had discharged the burden and that the parties had been "substantially at arm's length and on an equal footing".

Note: "Know your customer" is not new. The case shows that it was accepted by the mid-nineteenth century that the duty, at least of one who is trusted, to the other party in a sale will vary. What makes it vary is the degree of vulnerability (if any) of the other party to the sale.[16]

***Archer v. Hudson*(1844) 7 Beav. 551; 49 E.R. 1180**

9.73 A niece's standing surety for her uncle, shortly after she had come of age and been fully accounted to by her guardians, was set aside. The main interest of the case is in the passage about the kind of independent advice which might have prevented it.

Lord Langdale M.R. said, "I do not mean to say, that if this young lady had her trustees, or some friend or relation of the family, or somebody interested in her welfare, to advise and consult with, in the absence of the uncle and aunt, that the circumstance of her situation and the circumstance of the uncle's situation might not have been such, that this Court would have said that, having entered into this liability, she should be held by it."

The other point of interest is on the notice of her vulnerability which the creditor was held to have acquired. Lord Langdale said, "Mr Hauxwell, representing the bank, knew the relative position of the parties; he knew that the object was to obtain the liability of the child, for the benefit and accommodation of the uncle; he knew they were living together at the time. He went and assisted the uncle and aunt, both of whom were present at the very time. It therefore does not appear, that this young lady was ever severed from the influence which the uncle and aunt had over her, so as to enable her to form an adequate, full, and independent opinion as to what she ought in prudence to have done . . . but to say that Mr Hauxwell . . . a person with whom the uncle was dealing, the person through whom he is carrying on his business as a customer of the bank, by explaining to an inexperienced young woman who had just attained her age of twenty-one years the meaning of this note, offered anything like such a protection as would secure to her that free and independent judgment which she had a right to exercise, seems to me to go far beyond anything which has been proved in this case."

***Cooke v. Lamotte* (1851) 15 Beav. 234; 51 E.R. 527 (Sir John Romilly, MR) (Gift case, correct explanation of "dominion")**

9.74 The plaintiff sought to set aside a bond for £1,500 given by one Louisa Foster, then aged about 73, to her three nephews. Sir John Romilly held:

[16] A question which arises in this connection is whether the trusted party's duty is limited by what he in fact perceives about the other; or whether it extends also to constructive knowledge: what he ought to have perceived. It is probable that the reason the question does not seem to have been discussed in induced vulnerability cases is quite simply that the relationship itself will normally have meant that the trusted party had or could be assumed to have acquired all relevant knowledge about the other party.

"where those relations exist, by means of which a person is able to exercise a dominion over another, the Court will annul a transaction, under which a person possessing that power takes a benefit, unless he can shew that the transaction was a righteous one. It is very difficult to lay down with precision what is meant by the expression 'relation in which dominion may be exercised by one person over another.' That relation exists in the cases of parent, of guardian, of solicitor, of spiritual adviser, and of medical attendant, and *may be said to apply to every case in which two persons are so situated, that one may obtain considerable influence over the other.*"[17]

Sir John Romilly's decision took into account all the circumstances, and bearing in mind that Louisa Foster did not have a solicitor to explain the effect of the bond, he set it aside, on the grounds that she did not properly understand what she was doing.

Note: The relevance of the case for present purposes is the definition of "relation in which dominion may be exercised by one person over another": it becomes no more than one in which "considerable influence is possessed by one party over the other.[18]

***Edwards v. Burt* (1852) 2 De G.M. & G. 55; 42 E.R. 791 (How a buyer of a reversion might safeguard his position)**

9.75 This was during what one might almost call the craze for setting aside dealings in reversions, later calmed down by statute.[19] The only point of note for present purposes is the dictum about a way in which the buyer of the interest might be safe.

"If, previously to the sale of a reversionary interest, the vendor and purchaser concur in ascertaining from persons of competent skill and having knowledge of the property, and of all the circumstances likely to influence value, a well-considered estimate of what the property would be likely to fetch on a sale, and act on that opinion, we are far from meaning to decide that such a transaction could be afterwards impeached, merely because other surveyors should come to a conclusion different from that on which the parties had acted."

This had not been done, and since there was an undervalue, the court set the sales aside, and ordered that the land stand as security for the sums lent, to be reconveyed on repayment of these.

***Billage v. Southee* (1852) 9 Hare 534; 68 E.R. 623 (Excessive payment to surgeon; "abuse of confidence" and undue influence relationships assimilated)**

9.76 The plaintiff was a (somewhat sickly) shoemaker in Cambridge, and the defendant was his surgeon, who had attended him almost continuously for about eight years. He gave the defendant a promissory note for £325, which was much more than the amount he owed the defendant could possibly have

[17] Italics supplied. The expression "a righteous one" evidently came from Lord Eldon in ***Gibson v. Jeyes***, para. 9.62.

[18] Cp. Lord Scarman's contrasting reference to "relationships which develop a dominating influence" in ***National Westminister Bank v. Morgan*** (1985), noted in the text above.

[19] The Lord Justice Lord Cranworth said the rule on this subject had finally and distinctly been established by the House of Lords in *Lord Aldborough v. Trye* 7 Cl. & Fin. 436 clearly establishing that the purchaser of a reversionary interest, at least from an expectant heir, of from a person standing in the situation of an expectant heir, "is bound, if the transaction is impeached within a reasonable time, to satisfy the Court that he gave the fair market value for what he purchased.")

been. The transaction was thus nearly a gift of the £325. The Vice-Chancellor said this.

"No part of the jurisdiction of the Court [of Equity] is more useful than that which it exercises in watching and controlling transactions between *persons standing in a relation of confidence to each other*; and in my opinion this part of the jurisdiction of the Court cannot be too freely applied, either as to the persons between whom, or the circumstances in which, it is applied. The jurisdiction is founded on the principle of *correcting abuses of confidence*, and I shall have no hesitation in saying it ought to be applied, whatever may be the nature of the confidence reposed or the relation of the parties between whom it has subsisted. I take the principle to be one of universal application, and the cases in which the jurisdiction has been exercised—those of trustee and *cestui que* trust, *guardian and ward, attorney and client, surgeon and patient—to be merely instances of the application of the principle.*"

He considered that a relation of confidence subsisted, and that advantage had been taken of that confidence. . . . "It is said he intended to be liberal, and that this Court would not prevent him from being so; and no doubt it would not if such were his intention; but *intention imports knowledge*, and liberality imports the absence of influence; . . . and I see no evidence in this case either of knowledge or of the absence of influence; and where a gift is set up between parties standing in a confidential relation the *onus* of establishing it by proof rests upon the party who has received the gift." He set it aside, to remain only as security for what was owed in fact.[20]

Note: it may be seen that the Vice-Chancellor called this relationship one of confidence (a term more recently reserved for solicitor-client relationships), and the transaction an abuse of confidence, and declined to be much constrained by the various categories of relationships of presumed undue influence. He also referred to the "influence" inherent in the confidential relationship, thus tending to the conclusion[21] *that the "abuse of confidence" and "presumed undue influence" cases, to use the traditional labels, are not specially to be differentiated from each other.*

***Holman v. Loynes* (1854) 4 D.M. & G. 270; 43 E.R. 510 (Sale to solicitor; duty of solicitor to shop around stressed)**

9.77 A solicitor was engaged in relation to the sale of his client's property at auction, but only a small portion of it was sold. Sixteen months later, (and he had not been employed professionally during that period) he bought some of the unsold property. The consideration for it was partly the release of a debt for his fees, and partly an annuity, based on the assumption that the client was a healthy life. In fact he was of intemperate habits. The solicitor had made no special inquiries as to his client's state of health, and had not shopped around for better quotes. The Lord Chancellor, Lord Cranworth thought that the defendant ought to have endeavoured to get a considerably higher annuity for his client, by reason of the latter's intemperate habits. Turner L.J. felt the relation of solicitor and client had not ceased in the 16 months: he held "there was not any cessation of the relation, but only a cessation of the circumstances which were necessary to call the relation into action." He referred to Lord Eldon in *Wood v. Downes*[22] and said he saw no reason why the rule which applied to gifts should not equally in this respect apply to purchases. He commented that the rules of the court against gifts were absolute, and modified against a purchaser, but this was a question not

[20] Italics supplied.
[21] See text above.
[22] Para. 9.67 above.

of the extent of the rules, but upon the circumstances under which they are to be brought into operation.

Savery v. King **(1856) 5 H.L.C. 627; 10 E.R. 1046 (Mortgage of estates for benefit of father; independent advice must be sufficient to protect)**

9.78 A young man was persuaded by his father and the family solicitor who was also the mortgagee, to execute a disentailing deed followed by a mortgage of his interest to the solicitor, to secure the father's debt. Other transactions followed which will be omitted for present purposes. The solicitor was advised by a barrister who had drawn up the deeds that there should be "some person concerned" for the son, lest it be claimed that there was undue influence. The solicitor did not pass on this advice but sent the drafts to another solicitor to peruse on behalf of the son. He gave the solicitor no information or explanation as to the transaction which it was intended to carry into effect by the deeds, except such as was conveyed by the drafts themselves. The solicitor merely perused the deeds for the purpose of seeing that the same were in proper form, and returned them to the Appellant approved. This degree of "independent advice" did not prevent the Lord Chancellor, 'Lord Brougham', from setting aside the mortgage the son had entered into for the benefit of the father (though leaving the father's own mortgage untouched).

The Lord Chancellor said "The question is, whether before Richard had so bound his inheritance he had been duly and properly put on his guard as to the nature and consequences of what he was doing, so as to enable him to act independently and free from the influence of his father and the family solicitor.

A little later he asked "On these facts, then, can your Lordships see that due protection was thrown around Richard King; that the various suggestions which would occur to the minds of men of mature age and business-like habits, as to the prudence of the course which he was about to take, had been fairly presented to his mind, and that nevertheless he chose, for the purpose of relieving or assisting his father, to burthen his inheritance in favour of Savery, with the £10,000 due to Savery from the father? It is impossible to answer this question in the affirmative."

Note: This case is included here because it deals with the important question: what kind of independent advice is sufficient to protect the vulnerable party.[23]

Hesse v. Briant **(1856) 6 De G.M. & G. 623; 43 E.R. 1375 (Sale to another client of solicitor; absence of full information stressed)**

9.79 The parties were clients of the same solicitor; and Briant, the defendant, had given the solicitor an authority to sell certain property. Under this authority the solicitor sold it to Hesse. The Lord Chancellor refused specific performance of the agreement, because there had not been "that fair and open dealing between the parties which the relation in which they stood to each other demanded. Although, therefore, I do not lay it down that an agent cannot act for and bind opposing parties, yet it must appear that the principals were at arms' length in the transaction: and it would require a very strong case to make this out where, . . . a vendor and purchaser are together in the same house, but the vendor is excluded from the room where the negotiation is going on, and the agent *does not disclose to them both the whole nature of the dealing.*[24]

Note: The main feature of this case is again the lack of proper full information, it

[23] See also ***Tate v. Williamson***, para. 9.87 below.
[24] Italics supplied.

would seem as to value. The rely-on-me element provided by the solicitor-agent, will have lulled the weaker party into a sense of false security, so that he will not have exercised due diligence on his own behalf.

Smith v. Kay (1859) 7 H.L.C. 750; 11 E.R. 299 (Gift to solicitor; abuse of confidence and undue influence cases assimilated)

9.80 Kay was a young man "of fortune"; Smith was an attorney and solicitor (though not acting for Kay). Kay on the day after he came of age, gave a bond for over £12,000 and assigned some life policies to Smith. The case really proceeded on misrepresentation; but is of interest because the court felt that what Lord Cranworth called "the ordinary principle of the Court, which protects an infant, or any other person, under the influence, as it is called, of that other" would have done as well. The dicta about this are significant for three reasons: (1) because there is no distinction of principle drawn between the abuse of confidence (eg solicitor-client) cases, and the presumed undue influence cases (eg guardian—ward); (2) that in certain relationships such as those in (1) the confidence and the influence is rebuttably presumed; (3) that the primary duty on the person with "a power of influence" is a duty of disclosure of all matters likely to influence a person's decision as to the transaction.

Lord Cranworth said: "My Lords, there is, I take it, no branch of the jurisdiction of the Court of Chancery which it is more ready to exercise than that which protects infants and persons in a situation of dependance, as it were, upon others, from being imposed upon by those upon whom they are so dependant. The familiar cases of the influence of a parent over his child, of a guardian over his ward, of an attorney over his client, are but instances. The principle is not confined to those cases, as was well stated by Lord Eldon in the case of *Gibson v. Jeyes*[25] in which he says it is "the great rule applying to trustees, attornies, or any one else." Now, what does "any one else" mean? It is contended that it applies only to persons who stand in what is called a fiduciary relation. I believe, if the principle is examined, it will be found most frequently applied in such cases, for this simple reason, that the fiduciary relation gives a power of influence; but I could suggest fifty cases of fiduciary relation where the principle will not apply at all. If a man makes me trustee of an estate, to pay certain securities, and then ultimately to stand possessed of it for him, we deal with one another in purchase, or in any other way, perfectly at arm's length. I have no influence over him because I am his trustee. It is only a particular sort of trusteeship that gives the influence."

Lord Kingsdown said that he agreed "that it is not the relation of solicitor and client, or of trustee and *cestui que trust*, which constitutes the sole title to relief in these cases, and which imposes upon those who obtain such securities as these, the duty before they obtain their confirmation, of *making a free disclosure of every circumstance which it is important that the individual who is called upon for the confirmation, should be apprised of*. The principle applies to every case where influence is acquired and abused, where confidence is reposed and betrayed. The relations with which the Court of Equity most ordinarily deals, are those of trustee and *cestui que trust*, and such like. It applies specially to those cases, for this reason and this reason only, that from those relations the Court presumes confidence put and influence exerted. Whereas in all other cases where those relations do not subsist, the confidence and the influence must be proved extrinsically; but where they are proved extrinsically, the rules of reason and common sense, and the technical rules of a Court of Equity, are just as applicable in the one case as in the other."[26]

[25] 6 Ves. 266, 278, para. 9.62 above.
[26] Italics supplied.

Harrison v. Guest **(1855) 6 De G.M. & G. 424; 43 E.R. 1298 (Conveyance by a vulnerable party not set aside; cooling off period had been allowed, and independent advice urged)**

9.81 This was a transaction whereby Mr Hunt, an elderly man aged 71, agreed to convey his property to the defendant, in return for the defendant's agreeing to pay off the mortgage, and to let him lodge at one of the defendant's farm-houses and have free board, lodging and attendance for the rest of his life.[27] An undervalue was alleged, because in the event Mr Hunt only lived six weeks. However, the Lord Chancellor refused to set aside the sale. He noted that Mr Hunt was "rather a keen and cunning old man" who knew what he was about. Importance was attached to the fact that the purchaser had not hurried him into the deal at all, but suggested he take time to think it over, and had gone away for a fortnight; and that the purchaser had urged him to consult a solicitor.

Longmate v. Ledger **(1860) 2 Giff. 157; 66 E.R. 67 (Sale by a vulnerable party set aside: requirement for reasonable degree of equality in bargaining position)**

9.82 This was a sale at an undervalue by an old man of 72 who was "known to be of a weak and eccentric disposition, and at the time of the sale was without the assistance of a disinterested legal adviser". There were some doubts about his mental capacity. He also owed money to the purchaser, and was unduly anxious about that. The sale was set aside, the Vice-Chancellor commenting that the settled doctrine of this Court was that "in order to have a valid contract or conveyance of property there must be a reasonable degree of equality between the contracting parties." The sale was set aside, save that the property was to stand as security for the money actually advanced.

Foster v. Roberts **(1861) 29 Beav. 467; 54 E.R. 708**

9.83 This case occurred at a time when it was only necessary to show that a reversion had been sold at an undervalue to transfer the onus of showing that the price was a fair one to the buyer. Here there was an undervalue proved of £30 out of £400 which was held sufficient.

Clarke v. Malpas **(1862) 31 Beav. 80; 54 E.R. 968, affirmed on appeal, 4 De G.F. & J. 401 (Sale by a vulnerable party set aside: importance of cooling off/consultation period stressed)**

9.84 Clarke was the heir of one Josiah Gallimore who had sold a property to the defendant shortly before his death. It seemed that Josiah was a poor man "in a very humble station in life"; he was represented to be "an eccentric, weak minded and illiterate man, possessing however, a low cunning, a peculiar jealousy with regard to his small property of three cottages". Stress was laid by the Master of the Rolls on the haste with which the affair was concluded: the matter was agreed after nine in the morning and completed before six that evening. The decision was affirmed by the Lords Justices, only varying the technicality that the Master of the Rolls had simply ordered that the deed be cancelled and possession be delivered up, while the Lords Justices ordered a reconveyance.

[27] *i.e.* the equivalent of the modern sheltered rented flat and *c.f.* the modern French custom of "rents viageres".

***Baker v. Monk* (1864) 4 D.J. & S. 388; 46 E.R. 968 (Sale set aside: lack of information about value stressed)**

9.85 This was an appeal from the Master of the Rolls' decision, upheld by the Lords Justices. An elderly spinster "in humble life, of slender education" agreed to transfer her freehold property at Faversham, Kent, in return for an annuity of about nine shillings a week. The purchaser was a substantial tradesman in the town, who had once or twice been mayor, and his solicitors were used. The court considered that true value was not given, among other things because inadequate weight had been given to the site value of the land, as opposed to the rent that the somewhat dilapidated cottages on it would bring. Lord Justice Knight Bruce said given the relative positions and the undervalue, it was incumbent on the purchaser to show he had given full value to the unadvised and unassisted vendor; and he had not done so. Turner L.J. approved the principles laid down in *Evans v. Llewellin*[28], and felt that the plaintiff ought to have had more protection thrown around her by the purchaser.

Note: The idea that certain purchasers/vendors required to have "protection thrown around them" is a recurrent one in the older cases.

***Berdoe v. Dawson* (1865) 34 Beav. 603; 55 E.R. 768**

9.86 Two sons aged twenty-five and twenty-three gave security for their father's debt.

Sir John Romilly MR said, "The law is settled, that a person who takes a benefit obtained without consideration by a father from his child incurs the obligation, in the strongest possible sense of the word, of proving that the transaction as between the father and child was a righteous one. He must prove, not only that the son understood the transaction, but also that the benefit was not obtained from him by the undue exercise of the peculiar influence possessed by a father over his son."

In this case the creditor's solicitor gave them full information and explained everything to them. However, the two sons worked for their father in his business, and were totally under his control generally, so that was not enough to displace the burden. Note Sir John Romilly seems here to have regarded the creditor as automatically having notice; but this may simply be because he had known quite well of the father-son relationship, and thus will have had sufficient notice.

***Tate v. Williamson* (1866) L.R. 2 Ch. App. 55 (Sale to someone who assumes advisory role; independent solicitor for victim irrelevant because not given full information by trusted party)**

9.87 Mr Tate was aged 23, and being pressed for payment of his college debts, at a time when he was also estranged from his father. He asked his uncle for his assistance and advice in the matter, and the uncle deputed his son to meet him and help him. Mr Tate said he did not want to suggest a reduction in the debts, he thought his honour would suffer, but he would sell his half of the estate to which he was entitled to raise money. The cousin offered to buy it, and did buy it for £7,000, which was an undervalue. He told Mr Tate to get independent advice, but did not reveal prior to the sale that he had the property valued for £20,000. Held by Lord Chelmsford, the Lord Chancellor, that "it would be contrary to the principles upon which equity proceeds, in

[28] Above, para. 9.60.

judging of the dealings of persons in a fiduciary relation, to allow the purchase by the Defendant . . . to stand".

"I am satisfied that the Defendant had placed himself in such a relation of confidence, by his undertaking the office of arranging the intestate's [Mr Tate's] debts by means of a mortgage of his property, as prevented him from becoming a purchaser of that property without the fullest communication of all material information which he had obtained as to its value; that this openness and fair dealing were the more necessary when he was negotiating with an extravagant and necessitous young man, deprived at the time of all other advice, eager to raise money, and apparently careless in what manner it was obtained. . . . he cannot be permitted so to turn the confidence reposed in him to his own profit, and the sale ought to be set aside."

Mr Tate had in fact died, possibly of alcoholism, at the age of 24, so the relief granted was to his personal representatives. Mr Tate had consulted a solicitor as suggested.

Lord Chelmsford also made the following statement of principle about the courts of equity's jurisdiction over the dealings of "persons standing in certain fiduciary relations". "The principles applicable to the more familiar relations of this character have been long settled by many well-known decisions, but the Court have always been careful not to fetter this useful jurisdiction by defining the exact limits of its exercise. Wherever two persons stand in such a relation that, while it continues, confidence is necessarily reposed by one, and the influence which naturally grows out of that confidence is possessed by the other, and this confidence is abused, or the influence is exerted to obtain an advantage at the expense of the confiding party, the person so availing himself of his position will not be permitted to retain the advantage, although the transaction could not have been impeached if no such confidential relation had existed."

Note: The informal nature of this fiduciary relationship is one important point: the defendant had argued the principles only applied to more formal relationships such as guardian and ward, but this was rejected. Another point is regarding the nature of the independent advice which will cure the vulnerability. Here Mr Tate had actually been advised to use a solicitor, and did so, but this was held irrelevant, since there had not been full disclosure by the trusted party of the valuation he had obtained.

Earl of Aylesford v. Morris (1873) L.R. 8 Ch. App. 484 (Lord Hardwicke's original principles affirmed)

9.88 This was an appeal from the Vice-Chancellor. Lord Guernsey as he then was, the son of the Earl of Aylesford, obtained an advance from a money lender, taking by way of security his acceptances at three months for the sum advanced, with interest and discount together exceeding 60 per cent. These acceptances became due, and the process was repeated. Lord Guernsey had no professional advice, and neither his father nor the family solicitors were told of the transactions. The father died before the second set of bills became due and the new Earl commenced an action to set aside the bills.

Lord Selborne said "There is hardly any older head of equity than that described by Lord *Hardwicke* in *Earl of Chesterfield v. Janssen*[29] as relieving against the fraud "which infects catching bargains with heirs, reversioners, or expectants, in the life of the father," etc. Lord Selborne further quoted extensively from Lord Hardwicke's observations in *Earl of Chesterfield v. Janssen*[30], among other things the passage that "There is always fraud presumed or inferred from the circumstances or conditions of the parties con-

[29] (1751) 2 Ves. Sen. 125; 28 E.R. 82.
[30] *Ibid.*

tracting—weakness on one side, usury on the other, or extortion, or advantage taken of that weakness. There has been always an appearance of fraud from the nature of the bargain."

Lord Selborne said this was the rule applied to the analogous cases of voluntary donations obtained for themselves by the donees, and "to all other cases where influence, however acquired, has resulted in gain to the person possessing it at the expense of the person subject to it." He went on to say "But it is sufficient for the application of the principle, if the parties meet under such circumstances as, in the particular transaction, to give the stronger party dominion over the weaker; and such power and influence are generally possessed, in every transaction of this kind, by those who trade upon the follies and vices of unprotected youth, inexperience, and moral imbecility."

He commented later that Mr Morris here purposely abstained from making "any of those inquiries which every man would have made who was entering into a business transaction fairly and in good faith, without either an irrational disregard of his own security, or *a design to make his market of another man's weakness*"[31] (the origin of the phrase used in the chapter heading). The transaction was set aside, but since the appellant had not been proved to be guilty of deceit or circumvention, and the plaintiff "has no merits of his own to plead. He comes into Court to be relieved from the consequences of a course of very wilful and culpable folly and extravagance", he had to pay his costs in the Court below.

Note: in some ways the case is of importance for its resounding endorsement, with heavy quotations, of Lord Hardwicke's original exposition of the doctrine as to setting aside dealings with the vulnerable, in Lord Chesterfield v. Janssen[32]. *This case perhaps shows the timeless-senior-common-room approach at its most beneficial: it is as though the famous eighteenth-century judge Lord Hardwicke was an invisible extra judicial presence in this late nineteenth-century court.*

***O'Rorke v. Bolingbroke* (1877) 2 App. Cas. 814 (Sale of reversion allowed to stand despite lack of independent advice; principles in *Earl of Aylesford v Morris* (1873) (together with principles set out by Lord Hardwicke in *Earl of Chesterfield v Janssen* (1751) affirmed again).**

9.89 This was a sale of a reversion, which if the true state of the plaintiff's father's health had been known, would have been a sale at an undervalue. The young reversioner vendor had had no independent advice, which might have led to the ascertainment of the father's true state of health, but the purchase price was otherwise perfectly fairly arrived at. He lost his case.

Lord Hatherley, dissenting, essentially on the true complexion to be put on the facts, referred to the principles involved, but nonetheless commented usefully on the principles as follows:

"It sufficiently appears that the principle on which Equity originally proceeded to set aside such transactions was for the protection of family property; but this principle being once established, the Court extended its aid to *all cases in which the parties to a contract have not met upon equal terms*[33]. In ordinary cases each party to a bargain must take care of his own interest, and it will not be presumed that undue advantage or contrivance has been resorted to on either side; but in the case of the "expectant heir", or of persons under pressure without adequate protection, and in the case of dealings with uneducated ignorant persons, the burthen of shewing the fairness of the transaction is thrown on the person who seeks to obtain the benefit of the contract."

[31] Italics supplied.
[32] (1751) 2 Ves. Sen. 125; 28 E.R. 82.
[33] Italics supplied.

Lord Blackburn followed the principles stated by Lord Selborne in *Earl of Aylesford v. Morris*[34], that is to say, in effect the principles stated by Lord Hardwicke in *Earl of Chesterfield v. Janssen*[35] as being an accurate statement of the law as it stood then. He went on "Fraud in this cause, in my opinion, there is none, nor is *there unfair dealing, including in those words every dealing by which one man having the means of getting a better bargain from another, effects the transaction by these means*."[36]

Lord Gordon agreed with Lord Blackburn, on the evidence.

***McPherson v. Watt* (1877) 3 App. Cas. 254 (Purchase by solicitor; non-disclosure of information about value acquired by reason of role stressed)**

9.90 This was a Scottish case, in which the attorney for two sisters purchased their property, nominally for his brother, but in fact for himself. The House of Lords had no difficulty in setting the case aside, holding that the sisters were entitled to do so as of right, purely because the attorney was guilty of non-disclosure that he himself was the purchaser. (In fact there was evidence the sisters would have obtained independent advice if they had known.) Lord Blackburn pointed out that it may often be relevant in such cases that the agent will have acquired an *intimate knowledge of the property*, and will have an unfair advantage in consequence.

***Erlanger v. New Sombrero Phosphate Company* (1878) 3 App. Cas. 1218 (Application of principles to newly formed companies)**

9.91 A syndicate of people headed by a Baron Erlanger, a Paris banker, bought for £55,000 the lease of the island Sombrero in the West Indies. It had belonged to a company called the Sombrero Company, which had mined the beds of phosphate of lime which the island had, but the company got into difficulties and was wound up. The lease was sold for £110,000 to the New Sombrero Company, formed by the syndicate. They promoted the shares in it, without mentioning the previous purchase to the intending shareholders.

In the House of Lords, all their Lordships agreed that the contract to take the lease should be set aside, on the grounds that the syndicate stood in a fiduciary position to the new company. They considered the new company was not in a position to make an independent judgment, because the directors were chosen by the syndicate, so that it was in effect a puppet of the syndicate.[37]

(1) Lord Penzance set out the facts and drew two conclusions: "first, that the company never had an opportunity of exercising, through independent directors, a fair and independent judgment upon the subject of this purchase; and secondly, that this result was *brought about by the conduct* and contrivance of the vendors themselves. It was the vendors, in their character of promoters, who had the power and the opportunity of creating and forming the company in such a manner that with *adequate disclosures of fact, an independent judgment on the company's behalf might have been formed*.[38] But instead of so doing they used that power and opportunity for the advancement of their own interest. Placed in this position of unfair advantage over the company which they were

[34] Above.
[35] See text.
[36] Italics supplied.
[37] The judgments in so far as they deal with laches are referred to in Chap. 15.
[38] Italics supplied.

about to create, they were, as it seems to me, bound according to the principles constantly acted upon in the Courts of Equity, if they wished to make a valid contract of sale to the company, to nominate independent directors and fully disclose the material facts. . . .

A contract of sale effected under such circumstances is, I conceive, upon principles of equity liable to be set aside.

The principles of equity to which I refer have been illustrated in a variety of relations, none of them perhaps precisely similar to that of the present parties, but all resting on the same basis, and one which is strictly applicable to the present case. The relations of principal and agent, trustee and *cestui que trust*, parent and child, guardian and ward, priest and penitent, all furnish instances in which the Courts of Equity have given protection and relief against the pressure of unfair advantage resulting from the relation and mutual position of the parties, whether in matters of contract or gift; and this relation and position of unfair advantage once made apparent, the Courts have always cast upon him who holds that position, the burden of shewing that he has not used it to his own benefit."

(2) Lord Cairns L.C. dealt with the duty of promoters to a company which they propose to form. "They stand, in my opinion, undoubtedly in a fiduciary position. They have in their hands the creation and moulding of the company; they have the power of defining how, and when, and in what shape, and under what supervision, it shall start into existence and begin to act as a trading corporation. If they are doing all this in order that the company may, as soon as it starts into life, become, through its managing directors, the purchaser of the property of themselves, the promoters, it is, in my opinion, incumbent upon the promoters to take care that in forming the company they provide it with an executive, that is to say, with a board of directors, *who shall both be aware that the property which they are asked to buy is the property of the promoters, and who shall be competent and impartial judges as to whether the purchase ought or ought not to be made.*[39] I do not say that the owner of property may not promote and form a joint stock company, and then sell his property to it, but I do say that if he does he is bound to take care that he sells it to the company through the medium of a board of directors who can and do exercise an independent and intelligent judgment on the transaction, and who are not left under the belief that the property belongs, not to the promoter, but to some other person."

9.92 (3) Lord O'Hagan observed that the law permitted the promoters to sell their rights in the island of Sombrero on to a company which might afford them a profit on the transaction; and "provided the machinery by which the transfer of their interest might be equitably and beneficially effected for themselves and those with whom they meant to deal. But the privilege given them for promoting such a company for such an object, involved obligations of a very serious kind. It required, in its exercise, the utmost good faith, the completest truthfulness, and a careful regard to the protection of the future shareholders. The power to nominate a directorate is manifestly capable of great abuse, and may involve, in the misuse of it, very evil consequences to multitudes of people who have little capacity to guard themselves. Such a power may or may not have been wisely permitted to exist. I venture to have doubts upon the point. It tempts too much to fraudulent contrivance and mischievous deception; and, at least, it should be watched with jealousy and restrained from employment in such a way as to mislead the ignorant and the unwary. In all such cases the directorate nominated by the promoters should stand

[39] Italics supplied.

between them and the public, with such independence and intelligence, that they may be expected to deal fairly, impartially, and with adequate knowledge in the affairs submitted to their control. If they have not those qualities, they are unworthy of trust. They are the betrayers and not the guardians of the company they govern, and their acts would not receive the sanction of a Court of justice."

(4) Lord Blackburn said "My Lords, in this suit the Plaintiffs being a limited company . . . can only ask for relief on grounds affecting them in their corporate capacity. If individuals were deceived by misrepresentations a case might exist entitling such individuals to be personally relieved against the consequences of such misrepresentations, but the company would not have any title to be relieved on account of such misrepresentations to individuals, especially if the misrepresentations were made by those who at the time represented the company. All this is clearly stated by Lord Cottenham, in your Lordships' House, in *Vigers v. Pike*[40].

But inasmuch as corporations act by individuals who have the proper authority to manage their affairs, and by those who are duly appointed by that governing body to act as agents for the company, it may well happen that proof that the Defendants have deceived the individuals who form the governing body, or the agents appointed by them, is proof that they have deceived the corporation, and gives the corporation a substantive title to relief. And it may happen that the Defendants have corrupted, or unduly influenced, the governing body without deceiving them, so as to get the corporation to make a contract, from which the corporation, on proving such corruption or undue influence, has a right to relief. This again is stated by Lord Cottenham . . ."

He went on to say about the promoters:

"As promoters of a company they stood in a fiduciary position towards the company they were creating, and that [sic] the bargain between the promoters and that company could not stand unless more was done for the purpose of protecting the interest of that company than was done in this case."

He considered the Companies Act 1862, the fact that it imposed no duty on promoters, but gave them "an almost unlimited power to make the corporation subject to such regulations as they please, and for such purposes as they please, and to create it with a managing body whom they select, having powers such as they choose to give to those managers, so that the promoters can create such a corporation that the corporation, as soon as it comes into being, may be bound by anything, not in itself illegal, which those promoters have chosen. And I think those who accept and use such extensive powers, which so greatly affect the interests of the corporation when it comes into being, are not entitled to disregard the interests of that corporation altogether. They must make a reasonable use of the powers which they accept from the Legislature with regard to the formation of the corporation, and that requires them to pay some regard to its interests. And consequently they do stand with regard to that corporation when formed, in what is commonly called a fiduciary relation to some extent."

He made reference to *Gibson v. Jeyes*[41] and considered, on the evidence, that "an unreasonable use has been made of that confidence which the company did not indeed place in the promoters, for the company did not then exist, but which the Legislature did place in them for the company when it gave the promoters power to create it."

[40] 8 Cl. & Fin 562; 8 E.R. 220.
[41] (1801) 6 Ves. 278; 31 E.R. 1044.

***Bainbrigge v. Browne* (1881) 18 Ch. D. 188**

9.93 The three Bainbrigge children executed a deed charging their reversionary interests in the funds in their parents' marriage settlement with the payment of certain mortgage debts due from their father. The case is included which is of course not a sale but a surety case, because of the statement by Fry J. on the question of third parties' position. He said "Then the next point which arises is this, against whom does this inference of undue influence operate? Clearly it operates against the person who is able to exercise the influence (in this case it was the father) and, in my judgment, it would operate against every volunteer who claimed under him with notice of the equity thereby created, or with notice of the circumstances from which the Court infers the equity. But, in my judgment, it would operate against no others; it would not operate against a person who is not shewn to have taken with such notice of the circumstances under which the deed was executed."

Note: See at paragraph 9.45 above, as to this case. Although it undoubtedly gives a useful nutshell summary of the third party's position as to notice, it would be possible to place too much weight on it. It is primarily to be seen as a decision on its particular facts.

***Allcard v. Skinner* (1887) 36 Ch. D. 145**

9.94 A wealthy woman had entered a religious order which insisted on poverty. She gave a number of gifts to the Mother Superior. About six years after leaving the order, she commenced an action to set aside the gifts. The Court of Appeal by a majority dismissed the appeal on the ground of her laches and acquiescence. However, there was some discussion of the principle of undue influence, albeit firmly limited to the case of gifts.

Cotton L.J. considered the decisions of the Court of Chancery might be divided into two classes —" "First, where the Court has been satisfied that the gift was the result of influence expressly used by the donee for the purpose; second, where the relations between the donor and donee have at or shortly before the execution of the gift been such as to raise a presumption that the donee had influence over the donor. In such a case the Court sets aside the voluntary gift, unless it is proved that in fact the gift was the spontaneous act of the donor acting under circumstances which enabled him to exercise an independent will and which justifies the Court in holding that the gift was the result of a free exercise of the donor's will. The first class of cases may be considered as depending on *the principle that no one shall be allowed to retain any benefit arising from his own fraud or wrongful act.* In the second class of cases, the Court interferes, not on the ground that any wrongful act has in fact been committed by the donee, but on the ground of public policy, and to prevent the relations which existed between the parties and the influence arising therefrom being abused.[42]

Lindley L.J. also thought the cases could be subdivided into two somewhat overlapping groups: "First, there are the cases in which there has been some unfair or improper conduct, some coercion from outside, some overreaching, some form of cheating, and generally, *though not always,* some personal advantage obtained by a donee placed in some close and confidential relation to the donor."[43] He mentioned *inter alia Nottidge v. Prince* 2 Giff. 246 and *Lyon v. Home* L.R. 6 Eq 655, as belonging to this group.

The second group consists of cases *in which the position of the donor to the donee has been such that it has been the duty of the donee to advise the donor, or*

[42] Italics supplied.
[43] Italics supplied.

even to manage his property for him. In such cases the Court throws upon the donee the burden of proving that he has not abused his position, and of proving that the gift made to him has not been brought about by any undue influence on his part. In this class of cases it has been considered necessary to shew that the donor had independent advice, and was removed from the influence of the donee when the gift to him was made. *Huguenin v Baseley* was a case of this kind."[44]

He went on to stress that gifts are not to be set aside merely on the ground of "folly, imprudence, or want of foresight on the part of donors. "It would obviously be to encourage folly, recklessness, extravagance and vice if persons could get back property which they foolishly made away with, whether by giving it to charitable institutions or by bestowing it on less worthy objects. On the other hand, to protect people from being forced, tricked or misled in any way by others into parting with their property is one of the most legitimate objects of all laws; and the equitable doctrine of undue influence has grown out and been developed by the necessity of grappling with insidious forms of spiritual tyranny and with the infinite varieties of fraud."

He went on to mention the relevance of the size of the gift, where a person stands in a confidential relationship to the donor. The court would not set aside gifts for a small amount, simply on the ground that the donor had no independent advice. In such a case, some proof of the exercise of the influence of the donee must be given. "But if the gift is so large as not to be reasonably accounted for on the ground of friendship, relationship, charity, or other ordinary motives on which ordinary men act, the burden is upon the donee to support the gift."

Fry v. Lane (1888) 40 Ch. D. 312 (Sale by vulnerable party)

9.95 J.B. Fry sold Lane his interest in assets in which he had a one-fifth share under a will, subject to a tenancy for life in favour of his mother, who was thought to be aged around 70, for £170 less legal costs of £10. His brother George Fry sold his share to Lane for £270. Both sums were considerable undervalues, being no more than about 60 per cent of the true worth of the shares. The purchase price was calculated on a mistaken footing (known to the purchaser to be wrong by the time of the assignment), namely that two legacies of £250 remained to be deducted from the fund in which the brothers had their shares, when in fact one had already been paid out. Kay J. found that the transactions were entered into by both Frys under a material mistake of fact. He relied on a number of earlier cases and summed them up or purported to sum them up as follows: "The result of the decisions is that where a purchase is made from a poor and ignorant man at a considerable undervalue, the vendor having no independent advice, a Court of Equity will set aside the transaction . . . The circumstances of poverty and ignorance of the vendor, and absence of independent advice, throw upon the purchaser, when the transaction is impeached, the onus of proving, in Lord Selborne's words, that the purchase was "fair, just and reasonable".

Note: The case is in fact not particularly more interesting than many of the earlier sale cases involving vulnerable parties, nor is Kay J.'s summary of earlier cases anything other than a rather crude one. Perhaps its claim on the literalist twentieth century was its neat, easy, apparently general formula which Kay J. attempted to derive from the particular case. It would seem to be an unwarranted attempt to narrow the broad general principles set out in Earl of Aylesford v. Morris[45], *which case of course acknowledged its eighteenth century ancestry.*

[44] Italics supplied.
[45] (1873) L.R. 8 Ch. App. 484.

***Lagunas Nitrate Co v. Lagunas Nitrate Syndicate* [1899] 2 Ch. 392 (Another vulnerable newly formed company)**

9.96 The plaintiff company was promoted and formed by the directors of the defendant syndicate, in order to buy part of its property, consisting of nitrate works in Chile. The syndicate directors were to be the directors of the company also, and they prepared the articles of the new company nominating them, together with the prospectus and the purchase contract. Two years after the date of the contract and completion of the purchase, and after the nitrate had been worked from the date of the contract till the commencement of the action, the shareholders appointed a new independent board of directors, and brought an action against the syndicate and the directors for rescission of the contract, misrepresentation and misfeasance by the directors, breach of trust, and concealment of material facts; but did not allege fraud.

The Plaintiffs failed primarily because of their laches. The parts of the judgments dealing with this are noted in Chapter 15 Remedies for Breach of the Good Faith Duties.

In the court below, Romer J. held that the company was not entitled to rescission or damages. Dealing with the question of the fiduciary position of the promoting syndicate, he had felt the fact that they had disclosed their dual role was sufficient to absolve them from responsibility. He felt the conduct of the plaintiffs amounted to laches in any event. The Plaintiff company appealed.

(1) Lindley M.R. set out certain principles which he said were well-settled but in their application to this case, appeared to him to conflict with each other.

"The first principle is that in equity the promoters of a company stand in a fiduciary relation to it, and to those persons whom they induce to become shareholders in it, and cannot in equity bind the company by any contract with themselves without fully and fairly disclosing to the company all material facts which the company ought to know. *Erlanger v. New Sombrero Phosphate Co*[46] is the leading authority in support of this general proposition.

The second principle is that a company when registered is a corporation capable by its directors of binding itself by a contract with themselves as promoters if all material facts are disclosed. *Saloman v. Saloman & Co*[47] is the leading authority for this principle.

The third principle is that the directors of a company acting within their powers, and with reasonable care, and honestly in the interest of the company, are not personally liable for losses which the company may suffer by reason of their mistakes or errors in judgment. *Overend, Gurney & Co v. Gibb*[48] is the leading authority on this head.

A fourth principle is that a voidable contract cannot be rescinded or set aside after the position of the parties has been changed, so that they cannot be restored to their former position. Fraud may exclude the application of this principle, but I know of no other exception."

He considered that mere disclosure of the dual role was insufficient here. He found there was misrepresentation and concealment in the prospectus which the syndicate caused to be issued for the company. He also held that the fact that the directors of the nitrate company knew all the facts (in their capacity of directors of the syndicate) was irrelevant, since they were the persons with the duty to disclose them. *"To impute to the nitrate company the knowledge which the directors had acquired in another capacity, and which knowledge they did not*

[46] (1878) 3 App. Cas. 1218.
[47] [1897] A.C. 22.
[48] L.R. 5 H.L. 480.

disclose to any one, is neither law nor sense."[49] The company thus had the right to rescind, subject to questions of restoration of the parties to their original position.

9.97

(2) Rigby L.J. dissented on the question of laches. On the question of disclosure by the syndicate directors, he said: "The syndicate and its directors thus voluntarily placed themselves in a position in which the interest of the directors, both as directors of the syndicate and as to each on his own private account, must necessarily come into conflict with their duty as fiduciary agents for the company. This apparently made them all powerful, but the position, having regard to its consequences, was in reality a most unenviable one, as it left them, most properly, to be judged by a standard which it is next to impossible that any body of men could satisfy. The rules which apply as between independent vendors and independent purchasers have no longer any application, but other rules must apply.

It is an equitable rule, which has always been guarded and enforced with the utmost jealousy, that no fiduciary agent shall, under pain of consequences thoroughly well known and noticed below, intentionally place himself in a position in which his interest may conflict with his duty . . . *The equitable rule referred to does not in any way depend upon fraud or any presumption of advantage actually taken; indeed, it applies equally, even though it be shewn that no advantage has been taken. The rule is made general in order to prevent the danger arising from the difficulty of disproving in particular cases that duty has given way to interest: see per Lord Eldon in the leading case of Ex parte Lacey*".[50]

He also referred to *Gibson v. Jeyes*[51]. He went on to say (agreeing with Lindley M.R. on this point) that because the rule did not require advantage actually to be taken of the victim, he could not see why the fact that the articles made the fiduciary relation and the dual role plain could possibly be a defence for the syndicate. Like Lindley M.R. he thought the purchaser of shares in the company should not be treated as having waived the breach of trust until he knew all material facts (after the independent board of directors had been appointed).

On the way the rule about conflicts of duty and interest applied, he said. "The rule as to equitable interference was only necessary in order to get rid of some agreement at law (by actual contract or estoppel), and in cases within its operation the agreement at law, so far as it bound the offending party, was kept alive as against him, if it were thought by the beneficiaries more advantageous that the wrongdoers should be bound. In *ex Parte Lacey*[52], for instance, and in numberless cases which have followed it, the subject-matter of the inequitable purchase was set up for sale again on the terms that, if a larger bid were made, the beneficiaries were to have the benefit, but that if no large sum were bid, the purchaser should be held to his bargain. It is, indeed, one of the just and salutary branches of the rule that the party subjecting himself by his misconduct to the rule cannot make any advantage to himself out of it, but is bound by what he does if it turn out to his disadvantage.

. . . "The rule moreover specially applies where, as in this case, there was no full disclosure of all material facts. . . . *The completion of the contract by assignment would not in any way affect this right [to set aside], since any deeds executed for the purposes of completion would be tainted with the same weakness as the original agreement . . . The obligation to make a complete and candid disclosure of all material facts existed throughout the whole time during which they had the*

[49] cf. the similar position of agents in Chap. 8. Knowledge and Notice.
[50] (1802) 6 Ves. 625. Italics supplied.
[51] (1801) 6 Ves. 278; 31 E.R. 1044.
[52] 6 Ves. 625.

control of the affairs of the company, and could only have been fulfilled by calling a general meeting and laying before the shareholders at such meeting a full and complete disclosure of the material facts."[53]

Collins L.J. simply agreed with Romer L.J.

Note: For a later case of a dealing with a vulnerable company, see Gluckstein v. Barnes[54]. *There are a number of interesting questions discussed in this case.*

(1) *Is it enough for a fiduciary (person trusted) simply to reveal to the potential victim that he has a dual role? [No.]*

(2) *Does the dual knowledge of a person who holds two conflicting roles affect the role in which he is trusted by the victim? [No, because knowledge acquired as agent for another is not imputed to the principal in a separate principal and agent transaction].*

(3) *The case perhaps marks the beginning of a certain lack of precision about the role of those who are trusted in various ways. This is marked by the use of the term "fiduciary" which we meet around now. The syndicate members/original company directors were inevitably in a trusted role. This may therefore be called "fiduciary", probably meaning no more (or less) than "trusted". They happened to have a conflict between their duty as the trusted persons and their self-interest in relation to the contract. This made their fiduciary role dangerous and unsuitable, but did not, properly speaking, bring the fiduciary role into being (which is somewhat the impression given by the judgments) at all.*

It may be that the word "fiduciary" is a label we have relied on too much. One may well feel that the impression has got around that there is an automatic, ready-made role for "fiduciaries"; almost as if by poring over the word and understanding it properly we would know in any transaction what the duty owed by the fiduciary was. Once we recognise the word as simply meaning "trusted", its limited capacity is evident. The right question then naturally comes to us: "Trusted for what?"[55]

(4) *Lindley M.R.'s statement that there is a fiduciary relationship between (i) promoters and the company they form; (ii) promoters and the shareholders in that company is distinctly puzzling, unless "fiduciary" is being used in a very relaxed sense indeed. The first is fiduciary in the sense that the newly-formed company inevitably trusts and relies on the promoters: the second is that of seller to buyer, which is prima facie not fiduciary at all (except in the most relaxed sense of the word). Despite Lindley M.R.'s attribution of the composite statement to* Erlanger's Case[56], *there is in fact no trace of an idea that the promoters owe a fiduciary (as opposed to good-faith) duty to the prospective shareholders who buy from the prospectus; indeed Lord Blackburn goes out of his way to make it clear that the promoters' duty is to the company alone. The idea was taken up later by Vaughan Williams L.J. (but not the other two Lord Justices who based their decision on ordinary good-faith grounds) in* Leeds and Hanley Theatres of Varieties Limited[57].

Wright v. Carter [1903] 1 Ch. 27 (Shifting the burden: meaning of "competent" independent advice)

9.98 This was a case of gifts by a client to his solicitor. The solicitor had obtained an independent solicitor to advise the client. The latter solicitor was in a state

[53] Italics supplied.
[54] [1900] A.C. 240.
[55] See now for a new scepticism about the usefulness of the label "fiduciary", Millett L.J. in ***Bristol & West B.S. v. Mothew***.
[56] (1878) 3 App. Cas. 1218, above at para. 9.91.
[57] [1902] 2 Ch. 809.

of ignorance as to the plaintiff's true financial condition, and was not in a position to do more than ask the plaintiff whether he knew what he was doing, whether he understood he was making the reversionary gifts in question, and whether he was doing so of his own will and volition. The Court of Appeal held this was insufficient to constitute competent independent advice. Vaughan Williams L.J. said of one deed, "If and so far as competent independent advice was necessary to support the transaction, Mr Tarbet was manifestly not in a position to give it, for he knew really next to nothing about the plaintiff's affairs or of his financial condition."

The court thus set aside the deeds in so far as they gave gifts to the solicitor, but left them intact in so far as they benefited the plaintiff's children.

***Bullock v. Lloyd's Bank* [1955] Ch. 317; [1955] 2 W.L.R. 1**

9.99 Vaisey J. adopted a careful attitude to the advice given to a young woman in this case. She had been persuaded to settle her interest under a trust on protective trusts, and had had advice from her father's solicitor, but the advice was held insufficient. Vaisey J. said "Such a settlement as this is can in my judgment, only be justified after prolonged consideration, being made, as it was, by a young girl only just of age, and can only stand if executed under the advice of a competent adviser capable of surveying the whole field with an absolutely independent outlook, and who explains to the intending settlor, first, that she could do exactly as she pleased, and, secondly, that the scheme put before her was not one to be accepted or rejected out of hand but to be discussed, point by point, with a full understanding of the various alternative possibilities."

***Moody v. Cox & Hatt* [1917] 2 Ch. 71**

9.100 The plaintiff agreed to buy a pub called the Marquis of Granby and some other land from Hatt who was his solicitor, and Cox, who was Hatt's managing clerk, at what was shown later to be an overvalue.

Lord Cozens-Hardy MR adopted Lord Eldon's formulation of the duty in *Gibson v. Jeyes*.[58] "If he (the solicitor)" will mix with the character of attorney that of vendor, he shall, if the propriety of the contract comes in question, manifest, that he has given her all that reasonable advice against himself, that he would have given her against a third person." and "But, from the general danger the Court must hold, that if the attorney does mix himself with the character of vendor he must shew to demonstration, for that must not be left in doubt, that no industry he was bound to exert would have got a better bargain." Lord Cozens-Hardy based his judgment not on undue influence but the principle that "An attorney selling to a client or buying from a client is bound to disclose everything that is material, or may be material, to the judgment of his client before the transaction is completed." He went on to say "The duty to disclose is quite consistent with the absence of undue influence, and that is all that seems to me to be involved here."

He also considered it was irrelevant that the solicitor here was acting for the benefit of the trust of which he was trustee: he should not have put himself in a position where duty and duty conflicted.

Warrington L.J. said ". . . there exists, owing to the position of the solicitor towards his client, a fiduciary relationship which imposes upon him the obligation not only of observing the utmost good faith in dealing with his

[58] (1801) 6 Ves. 278; 31 E.R. 1044.

client, but of giving to the client such advice and such information as he would have given if he had not been personally, in his other capacity, interested in the matters arising between them."

Scrutton L.J. put the matter more generally. He said that in regard to certain relations and certain contracts, "a higher duty is imposed upon the parties, and they must not only tell the truth, but they must tell the whole truth so far as it is material and they must not only not misrepresent by words, but they must not misrepresent by silence if they know of something that is material. Some of those cases depend on the relation between the parties, and generally speaking, are cases where the relation is such that you have confidence reposed by one party and influence exercised by the other. In that class of relation of parties you may get the duty, first of all, that the party who has influence must make a full disclosure of everything that he know material to the contract; secondly, that the party who has the influence must not make a contract with the party over whom he has the influence unless he can satisfy the Court that that contract is an advantageous one to the other party. The second class of cases is one not depending on the relation of the parties, but depending on the nature of the contract; and a typical case of that kind is the contract of insurance, where to an underwriter who knows nothing comes an assured, a man who wants to be insured and who knows everything, and on him is imposed the duty of telling the man who knows nothing all that he knows, so that the underwriter may fix the premium. In the first class of relations that of solicitor and client is one of the obviously and constantly recognised examples. If a man who is in the position of solicitor to a client so that the client has presumably confidence in him, and the solicitor has presumably influence over the client, desires to contract with his client, he must make a full disclosure of every material fact that he knows, and must take upon himself the burden of satisfying the Court that the contract is one of full advantage to his client." He also adopted the statements of the law by Lord Eldon in *Gibson v. Jeyes*[59] and Lord Chelmsford in *Tate v. Williamson*[60].

***Bank of Victoria v. Mueller* [1925] V.L.R. 642 (Australian case)**

9.101 A wife gave a guarantee to the bank for the debts of her husband, who was hard-pressed financially. She knew she was signing a guarantee, and how much it was for, but did not understand the effect of it properly. Cussen J. considered she was not deprived of relief against the creditor. He held, altering to some extent the language of Lord Cranworth in *Owen v. Gutch & Homan* (1835) 17 Jur. 861; 10 E.R. 752, "without saying that in every case a creditor is bound to inquire in what circumstances his debtor has obtained the concurrence of a surety, it may safely be stated that, if the dealings are such as fairly to lead a reasonable man to the conclusion that the relation between the debtor and the surety and the advantage to be conferred by the latter are such that it is necessary as between these two that the matter should be fully understood by the surety, and if it appears that it was not understood, the surety may be entitled to equitable relief as against the creditor, even though he has given consideration."[61]

[59] (1801) 6 Ves. 266; 31 E.R. 1044.
[60] (1866) L.R. 2 Ch. App. 55.
[61] (1853) 17 Jur. 861; 10 E.R. 752.

***Permanent Trustee Co. of N.S.W. Ltd v. Bridgewater* [1936] 3 All E.R. 501 (JC on appeal from the Supreme Court of New South Wales) Sale by young mortgagor to mortgagee; mortgagee's solicitor's advice regarded as insufficiently protective**

9.102 Mr Murray, deceased, had been a moneylender in Sydney. Mr Bridgewater was a young Englishman who had arrived in Australia as an assisted emigrant, and had drifted from job to job, then learning that he had inherited under his grandfather's and father's will. There were problems as to the true interpretation of the grandfather's will, but the father's will was clear enough and in any event Bridgewater later agreed his interest in the grandfather's will at £1,450 with his mother. Mr Murray first lent him sums on his expectancy up to a total of £2,000 odd, then said he would purchase the whole of his interest in his grandfather's estate and the agreed interest in his father's estate for £125. He told him a solicitor must advise him, and a Mr Taylor acted for him, having been instructed on behalf of Murray to do so. Lord Russell giving the judgment of the court said of this "No suggestion is made against Mr Taylor's honesty, *but as will appear the protective assistance which he afforded to Bridgewater was in fact nil.*"[62] It seemed that Mr Taylor had seen Bridgewater, stated that he considered the price insufficient, and that Bridgewater had said he was determined to sell. Whereupon Mr Taylor read him the draft assignment and said he was rather a foolish young fellow. He then dictated a letter in which Bridgewater acknowledged that he had been advised against it; and Bridgewater executed the assignment.

Lord Russell having recited the facts said "From these facts it appears to their Lordships that Mr Taylor made no attempt to advise his youthful client, or to assist him in resisting the temptation to exchange his future prospects for immediate cash, or to counteract the pressure which must almost necessarily exist where a debtor is negotiating with one who is his creditor concerning the sale of property which already stands as security for a large indebtedness between them. He never even suggested making inquiries from insurance companies to see whether better terms were not obtainable. He simply accepted as irrevocable the young man's expressed determination to sell at the price which he had already agreed with his creditor, and contented himself with explaining the contents of the drat document which the creditor had prepared for that purpose."

It was set aside, and ordered that the balance remaining after Murray's loan and interest was paid off was to be paid to Bridgewater. Stress was laid on the following disquieting features. "The vendor was a young man not yet 22 years old, urgently in need of cash, and with no relation in the country to guide him. He was selling his expectant interests to a creditor who already had a powerful grip on them as security for his debt. The price was fixed between them alone. There was no bargaining or inquiry for a better market by anyone on the young fellow's behalf. The matter cut and dried, with draft assignment already prepared, was placed before Mr Taylor and was carried through without any real advice by him and almost without breathing space, in a few hours of a single day. A transaction carried out in these circumstances does not appear to their Lordships to be a purchase made in good faith and without unfair dealing."

Note: The case provides us with a modern example of Lord Arglas—the young man under financial pressure, with no access to the right information about the value of what he was selling, and no cooling-off and consultation period. Its other main interest is in the strict attitude to the "independent" advice given, and the willingness to inquire into it in the first place. Compare the more recent refusal to inquire into

[62] Italics supplied.

the content of advice given to to a wife by the husband's solicitors at the request of the bank in Banco Exterior v. Mann[63] *and* Massey v. Midland Bank PLC[64]. *It was held that the bank was entitled to assume the advice given by a solicitor was adequate, without inquiring into it. We may prefer the older, more careful attitude. If a party is put on notice of facts which indicate vulnerability, he ought to be under the same duty to displace the vulnerability by means of an agent as the original party to the relationship would have been; and no more entitled than him to any deeming provision that a solicitor will have displaced the vulnerability.*[65]

***Lloyd's Bank v. Bundy* [1975] Q.B. 326**

9.103 This is a well-known case. The defendant was an elderly farmer, who signed a series of charges to secure the overdraft of his son's company. Lord Denning held there was, on the facts, a relationship of confidentiality between the bank and the defendant, giving rise to a fiduciary duty of care which the bank had breached, so the transaction was set aside. It may be this decision would now be reached on other grounds[66]. Lord Denning said that the single thread running through (1) duress of goods (2) "unconscionable transactions" (3) "undue influence" and "undue pressure" and (4) salvage agreements was "inequality of bargaining power". (1) and (4) are outside the scope of this book, but it may well be thought that this judge, who had a greater sense of history than many, was right about the others. It is perhaps unfortunate that his explanation of the way the principle worked was both very short and open to misconstruction: and the result of this can be seen in *National Westminster Bank v. Morgan*[67].

***Commercial Bank of Australia v. Amadio* (1983) 1151 C.L.R. 447 (Australian case)**

9.104 See references in the text above to this important case. See also reference to the judgment of Gibbs C.J. in Chapter 4, Insurance and Surety Transactions.

***National Westminster Bank v. Morgan* [1985] A.C. 686**

9.105 A wife signed a second charge in favour of the bank to secure her husband's business indebtedness. The transaction was upheld by the House of Lords, which held the relationship between the wife and the bank had not been one of confidence, and further, that the transaction had not been one of "manifest disadvantage" to her, since she knew quite well this was the only way she would stand a chance of keeping the house. Lord Scarman, with whom the others agreed, said that counsel for the respondent had not relied on Lord Denning's general principle stated above. Lord Scarman said,

". . . in my view he was right not to do so. The doctrine of undue influence has been sufficiently developed not to need the support of a principle which by its formulation in the language of the law of contract is not appropriate to cover transactions of gift where there is no bargain. The fact of an unequal bargain will, of course, be a relevant feature in some cases of undue influence. But it can never become an appropriate basis of principle of an equitable doctrine which is concerned with transaction 'not to be reasonably accounted

[63] [1995] 1 All E.R. 936.
[64] [1995] 1 All E.R. 929.
[65] The topic of third-party constructive notice has been the subject of much academic discussion since ***Barclay's Bank v. O'Brien*** [1994] 1 A.C. 180.
[66] See ***Barclay's Bank v. O'Brien*** [1994] 1 A.C. 180.
[67] [1985] A.C. 686.

for on the ground of friendship, relationship, charity, or other ordinary motives on which ordinary men act" (Lindley L.J. in *Allcard v. Skinner* at 185). And even in the field of contract I question whether there is any need in the modern law to erect a general principle of relief against inequality of bargaining power. Parliament has undertaken the task—and it is essentially a legislative task—of enacting such restrictions upon freedom of contract as are in its judgment necessary to relieve against the mischief: for example, the hire-purchase and consumer protection legislation, of which the Supply of Goods (Implied Terms) Act 1973, Consumer Credit Act 1974, Supply of Goods and Services Act 1982 and Insurance Companies Act 1982 are examples. I doubt whether the courts should assume the burden of formulating further restrictions."

Note:

(1) *Lord Denning had rather gone out of fashion by this date. It is instructive to read the submissions made to the House of Lords in this case: they were based on the (somewhat inappropriate) cases about gifts. Perhaps as a consequence, the principle briefly alluded to by Lord Denning seemed to strike at the root of any regular system of contracting. Had the principles derived from the cases about sales been cited, one wonders if the result might not have been different. Further, there is the point made above: Lord Denning's very short explanation of the way the inequality of bargaining "thread" worked, did perhaps give the impression that this was a weapon being handed to anyone who did not fancy keeping their contract. It is possible that had the true principle, ruling out only those bargains where the vulnerable party was locked into a position of bargaining weakness, been isolated, the result might well have been different. It is also possible Lord Scarman's enthusiasm for legislation might not have survived legislation such as the Financial Services Act 1986. The idea that Parliament is the only proper source of "namby pamby" legislation to help people is relatively modern. Lord Eldon and the other early Chancellors thought the courts, not Parliament, were supposed to develop principles which protected contracting parties from imposition. It must be said that it is hard to see why the courts should not, where necessary, develop such principles, and at all events recognise those developed by earlier judges, who did not view their role in such narrow terms.*

(2) *This case also imposed the apparently additional requirement in undue influence cases that the plaintiff should show the transaction was "manifestly disadvantageous" to him. This requirement may be questioned, at all events in the induced vulnerability cases, and as something on which the plaintiff bore the burden. As can be seen from the cases cited above, the plaintiff had only to prove the relationship of trust, and it was for the trusted party to justify the transaction, either on the grounds that the plaintiff had formed a free and informed intention to make a gift or an undervalue transaction (the intention of liberality), or on the grounds that the transaction was a perfectly fair one (or, no doubt, not disadvantageous to the plaintiff). At all events, the need for a plaintiff to show manifest disadvantage has now been questioned by the House of Lords in* Barclay's Bank v. O'Brien[68], so the way may be open for a statement of the law which is more consistent with the approach in the older cases.

***O'Sullivan v. Management Agency* [1985] Q.B. 428**

9.106 This concerned a series of management agreements with the defendants. The first plaintiff was a young and unknown composer and performer of popular music, wholly inexperienced in business matters, while the third

[68] [1994] 1 A.C. 180.

defendant Mr Mills was an internationally recognised manager, producer and performer. He operated through and was a substantial shareholder in, a parent company, the first defendants, who were music agents, and two subsidiary companies, and other defendants who were publishing and record companies respectively. The judge found that the defendants were in a fiduciary position to the first plaintiff and that the agreements had been obtained through undue influence; and that they were also in restraint of trade. The case contains no statement of note on induced vulnerability per se, but is of interest on constructive notice and an important case on remedies[69].

On constructive notice, the point appealed was the finding of undue influence (and consequent account of profits) against Mr Mills companies.

Fox L.J. followed the statement in *Bridgman v. Green*[70] "whoever receives [the gift] must take it tainted . . ." and considered that the fact that consideration had been given in the case before him made no real difference to the principle, given that the companies, which were in the de facto control of Mr Mills and another, a Mr Smith, who dealt with the young plaintiff. He said "In those circumstances I think it would be quite unreal to regard the companies as being without notice of the facts."

Dunn and Waller L.J. simply thought the companies were in a direct fiduciary relationship with the plaintiff, through Mr Mills and Mr Smith, the companies' agents.

***Goldsworthy v. Brickell* [1987] Ch.378**

9.107 An elderly but perfectly competent farmer granted an advantageous tenancy to a neighbouring farmer who had been kind to him and whom he had come to trust. The Court of Appeal held that the transaction was, on the facts, manifestly disadvantageous to the plaintiff, and set it aside. They held that Lord Scarman had not intended to narrow the scope of the law on undue influence or what has (above) been called induced vulnerability—despite his use of the expression "dominating influence" which would seem to have done just that. What mattered was whether the defendant was in a position to exercise influence; or as Sir Raymond Evershed in *Tufton v. Sperni*[71], speaking of *Huguenin v. Baseley*[72] said "In other words, the relation must be one which makes it the duty of one party to take care of the other."

***BCCI v. Aboody* [1990] 1 Q.B. 923 (CA)**

9.108 A husband had exerted what has come to be called "actual" (or express) undue influence over a wife to make her sign a charge for the benefit of his company. Slade L.J. held that in a case of "actual" undue influence (as well as a case of presumed undue influence) the plaintiff must also show that the transaction was to his or her "manifest disadvantage".

Note: As observed already, there is now doubt about whether it really is necessary after all to prove "manifest disadvantage" following the well-known decision of the House of Lords in Barclay's Bank v. O'Brien[73].

[69] See further, Chap. 15, Remedies for Breach of the good Faith Duties.
[70] (1757) 2 Ves. Sen. 627; 28 E.R. 399.
[71] [1952] 2 T.L.R. 516.
[72] (1807) 14 Ves. 273; 33 E.R. 526.
[73] [1994] 1 A.C. 180.

***Barclay's Bank v. O'Brien* [1994] 1 A.C. 180**

9.109 This case and *CIBC v. Pitt*[74] are both now too well-known to require noting in substance.[75]

***Boustany v. Pigott* (1995) 69 P. & C.R. 298 (P.C.)**

9.110 This is not a case which would seem to make any special contribution to the law on the topic. The only points worth noting perhaps were that Miss Pigott, whose lease was set aside, was not "poor and ignorant", only "quite slow"; and that the Judicial Committee did accept the existence of the jurisdiction to set aside sale transactions with the vulnerable.[76]

***Credit Lyonnais v. Burch* (Court of Appeal, June 20, 1996, unreported save in New Law Digest).**

9.111 In this case the Credit Lyonnais was held to have had constructive notice of the "undue influence" exercised by Miss Burch's employer on her to agree to let her home stand as security for his firm's debts. She had not seen a solicitor of her own, but Millett L.J., in an interesting and thoughtful judgment, no doubt intended to dispel doubt on the topic among the legal profession, considered what the position would have been if she had. His judgement is cited at some length because of its importance. He said:

"Such advice is neither always necessary nor always sufficient. It is not a panacea. The result does not depend mechanically on the presence or absence of legal advice. I think that there has been some misunderstanding of the role which the obtaining of legal advice plays in these cases. . . .

It is well established that in such a case the court will examine the advice which was actually given. It is not sufficient that the solicitor has satisfied himself that the complainant understands the legal effect of the transaction and intends to enter into it. That may be a protection against mistake or misrepresentation: it is no protection against undue influence. . . ."

He pointed out that the the presumption of undue influence could only be rebutted by showing that "the complainant was either free from any undue influence . . . or had been placed, by the receipt of independent advice, in an equivalent position.[77] That involves showing that she was advised as to the propriety of the transaction by an adviser fully informed of all the material facts.[78]

". . . The cases show that it is not sufficient that she should have received independent advice unless she has acted on that advice; if this were not so, the same influence that produced her desire to enter into the transaction would cause her to disregard any advice not to do so. They also show that the solicitor must not be content to satisfy himself that his client understands the transaction and wishes to carry it out. His duty is to satisfy himself that the transaction is one which his client could enter into if free from improper

[74] [1994] 1 A.C. 200.

[75] See also references to the former in the text.

[76] See also *Hart v. O'Connor* [1985] A.C. 1000. For a much more sympathetic and fuller analysis of the case, see the article "Unconscionability as a vitating factor" by Nicholas Bamforth of Robinson College, Cambridge in (1995) L.M.C.L.Q. 538.

[77] *c.f.* the text above, where it has been put as making the transaction a fair one or removing the locking-in factor.

[78] See *Powell v. Powell* [1900] 1 Ch. 243; *Brusewitz v. Brown* [1923] N.Z.L.R. 1106; ***Permanent Trustee Co of New South Wales Ltd v. Bridgewater*** (1936) above; and *Bester v. Perpetual Trustee Co Ltd* [1970] 3 N.S.W.L.R. 30.

influence; and if he is not so satisfied to advise her not to enter into it, and to refuse to act further for her if she persists. He must advise his client that she is under no obligation to enter into the transaction at all and, if she still wishes to do so, that she is not necessarily bound to accept the terms of any document which has been put before her but (where this is appropriate) he should ascertain on her behalf whether less onerous terms might be obtained."

On the position of the creditor with notice, who wishes to avoid being fixed with constructive notice, he followed the line[79] that where a complainant has received independent legal advice "he is normally entitled to assume that the solicitor has discharged his duty and that the complainant has followed his advice." However, he then imposed a much heavier burden on the creditor than those words carry *per se* by continuing "But he cannot make any such assumption if he knows or ought to know that it is false." In the case before him the creditor "must have known that no competent solicitor could advise her to enter into a guarantee in the terms she did."

Note: The judgment does not quite impose a similar burden on the creditor with notice to that of the predator or undue influencer, that is, to show that the locking-in factor which renders the guarantor's bargaining position unequal has been displaced. However, it is a step in that direction. The creditor will probably now in practice have to look with some care at the information which the independent solicitor or other adviser has asked it for and in some cases, consider also whether the solicitor has attempted to negotiate a different form of guarantee for his client. If the information asked for is insufficient for a properly informed judgment to be formed about the wisdom of the transaction, the creditor will be at risk.

***Bristol & West Building Society v. Mothew* [1996] 4 All E.R. 698**

9.112 In this case the building society as intended mortgagee had shared a solicitor with the intended mortgagor. The society had instructed the solicitor *inter alia* that any proposal on the part of the intended mortgagor to create a second mortgage or otherwise borrow to finance part of the purchase price was to be reported to it, as was any incorrect information given in the solicitor's instructions, and any other matter which ought to be brought to the notice of the society as prospective mortgagee. The solicitor inadvertently omitted to mention to the society that there was to be a transfer to the new property of a second charge securing a small part of the debt (£3,350). The solicitor admitted that this omission was negligent. The transaction went through. The purchasers defaulted after making only small repayments. The society made a net loss on the sale.

The society claimed damages for breach of contract and further claimed to recover the entire loan, as having been allegedly paid away by the solicitors in breach of trust. The case came before the Court of Appeal on appeal from the order of Chadwick J. who had given judgment for damages to be assessed and for repayment of the entire loan, in respect of what he held to have been breach of fiduciary duty and of trust on the part of the solicitors.

The case was remitted to the court below for assessment of damages for negligence in accordance with *South Australia Asset Management v. York Montagu*.[80]

Millett L.J.'s judgment in so far as it dealt with the general label of "fiduciary" has been cited in the text above.

(i) Breach of fiduciary duty

Millett L.J. noted that the court was not concerned with the situation where

[79] Doubted in the text above—see para. 9.46 *et seq.*

[80] [1996] 3 All. E.R. 365

the fiduciary deals with his principal. "In such a case he [the principal] must prove affirmatively that the transaction is fair and that in the course of the negotiations he made full disclosure of all facts material to the transaction. *Even inadvertent failure to disclose will entitle the principal to rescind the transaction.*[81]

The fact that the solicitors were acting for the society and the purchasers was not in itself a breach of fiduciary duty: the society had consented to this. Had the solicitors breached their fiduciary duty of good faith? This duty was described as follows. "Even if a fiduciary is properly actying for two principals with potentially conflicting interests he must act in good faith in the interests of each and must not act with the intention of furthering the interests of one principal to the prejudice of those of the other . . ." Further, "He must not allow the performance of his obligations to one principal to be influenced by his relationship with the other. He must serve each as faithfully and loyally as if he were his only principal." So far, so good.

Millett L.J. went on, more questionably perhaps: "Conduct which is in breach of this duty need not be dishonest but it must be intentional. An unconscious omission which happens to benefit one principal at the expense of the other does not constitute a breach of fiduciary duty, though it may constitute a breach of the duty of skill and care. This is because the principle which is in play is that the fiduciary must not be inhibited by the existence of his other employment from serving the interests of his principal as faithfully and effectively as if he were the only employer." This was labelled the "no-inhibition" principle. It was made to depend on the fiduciary's belief: in other words, there had to be a kind of *mens rea.*

"Finally, the fiduciary must take care not to find himself in a position where there is an *actual* conflict of duty so that he cannot fulfil his obligations to one principal without failing in his obligations to the other: see *Moody v. Cox*[82] and *Commonwealth Bank of Australia v. Smith*[83] If he does, he may have no alternative but to cease to act for at least one and preferably both. The fact that he cannot fulfil his obligations to one principal without being in breach of his obligations to the other will not absolve him from liability. I shall call this 'the actual conflict rule'."

Since the Defendant firm had not "acted in bad faith" [*i.e.* in *deliberate* breach of its duty] it followed from the definition that it was not in breach of fiduciary duty.

(ii) Breach of trust

The society's instructions to the solicitor were not revoked before the money was applied for completion. Therefore, there was no breach of trust. The society's right to rescind for misrepresentation would have needed to be exercised: there was no automatic voiding of the payment.

Otton L.J. and Staughton L.J.-delivered concurring judgments.

Note:

(1) General comment.

The complaint (noted in the text to the chapter, above) about the too-ready labelling of "fiduciary situations without proper analysis must be whole-heartedly welcomed.

The actual analysis of the situation before the court may well be another matter. Is this perhaps another case of the court (which had no submissions about the ordinary good-faith duties of candour and accuracy, etc., before it) doing the right thing for the wrong reasons?

Since the judgment recognises that fiduciary and contractual duties (including, no

[81] Italics supplied.
[82] [1917] 2 Ch. 71; [1916–17] All. E.R. Rep. 548.
[83] (1991) 102 A.L.R. 453.

doubt, any duties arising out of the special relationship between seller and buyer) may co-exist in the same person, these submissions would perhaps not have come amiss. The concept of "fiduciary" duty has perhaps in the result been made to do work it should not have done, and the surprising mens rea doctrine invented to achieve a sensible result. The case, after all, involved two separate transactions: the sale by solicitors of legal services, and the loan on mortgage to the intended mortgagor. If a recognition of good faith duties on the part of solicitors selling their services (not obviously fiduciary any more than in a contract with a plumber to plumb in a washing machine) is injected into the analysis, we achieve precisely the same end result, but—it may be thought—on grounds that are both more understandable and more reconcilable with existing case law on dealings with the vulnerable by trusted persons/fiduciaries. This case law focuses on undisclosed private profit by the solicitor or other trusted party, not lack of disclosure of other matters.

(a) The solicitors' non-fiduciary good-faith duties.

In a two-client situation, the breach by the solicitor of the duty to tell the client of an actual conflict is—it is suggested—perhaps better seen as merely a breach of his good-faith duty of candour and accuracy, owed to his principal in the agency relationship. The effect of this breach (in circumstances where the good-faith duty is implied rather than express) will be an indirect effect on the contract of agency. The contract falls to be construed on the assumption that the solicitor has undertaken the good-faith duties. If he acts in breach of the contract as subject to these implied default duties, he pays damages. The contract for services is not vitiated ab initio. *The relevance of the other, quite distinct contract involved, the society's contract to lend on mortgage to the intended mortgagor, is not direct but indirect, i.e. to the society's damages against the solicitor.*

(b) The solicitors' "fiduciary" duty to a vulnerable client in a rely-on-me relationship.

The duty not to make a market of his client's induced weakness, or to make a personal profit out of the transaction in which he is engaged as solicitor unless there has been complete, fair, specific, disclosure to the client, is plainly a duty arising directly out of the rely-on-me relationship and the consequent vulnerability of the society. This is properly labelled "fiduciary" (in so far as the expression "fiduciary" continues to be thought helpful). It vitiates the transaction entered into in which the solicitor has been personally interested. It would never have happened but for the rely-on-me relationship. Therefore, unless the solicitor can show that the transaction was a fair one, or that the client had competent independent advice on a properly informed basis, the vitiated transaction will be set aside. Where this is not practicable, compensation is paid to put the client back in the position he would have been in but for the breach of duty. Nocton v. Lord Ashburton[84] *is an example of this kind of breach of duty. The compensation claimed, and granted, was the monetary equivalent of rescission.*[85] *It is assumed in the* Mothew *case, but without discussion, that the* Nocton *duty and duties that are (it is suggested) essentially good-faith duties are similar. This can be justified if it is permissible to assume that any duty owed by a "fiduciary" is a fiduciary duty, but we have been warned earlier in the judgment about the fallacy in this kind of reasoning. Since the duty not to impose unexpected and undisclosed limitations on what is sold applies to vendors who are* not *agents/fiduciaries, we may reasonably suppose it not to be fiduciary.*

(2) Does the existing case law support the Mothew analysis above?

(i) It is assumed in Millett L.J.'s judgment, without deep discussion, that a solicitor is in breach of his "fiduciary duty" to client A within the scope of Nocton v. Lord Ashburton[86] *if he fails to disclose to any extent an interest of another client, B, in*

[84] [1914] A.C. 932.

[85] The fact that the case confirmed the continued existence of other good-faith duties is important but irrelevant to the analysis.

[86] Above.

a joint transaction. It is questionable whether the duty described as breached in Nocton v. Lord Ashburton *really extends this far. In* Nocton v. Lord Ashburton, *which was cited by Millet L.J., the undisclosed interest was that of the solicitor himself. Similarly, in* Moody v. Cox & Hatt)[87] *also cited by Millett L.J. the client purchased (unwittingly) from his own solicitor and another.*

Is there is any precedent for the proposition that it ever could be a breach of fiduciary duty of the Nocton v. Lord Ashburton *kind on the part of a solicitor merely to fail (even with mens rea) to pass on information from one joint client to another who has an interest in knowing it? None is cited, and there must be some doubt whether any exists. The other cases cited in this Appendix about solicitors as trusted parties dealing with clients rendered vulnerable seem not to be cases of the* Mothew *type, but cases where the solicitor himself was the purchaser or vendor, whether on his own or jointly with others. See* Gibson v. Jeyes[88]; Wood v. Downes[89]; Montiesquieu v. Sandys[90] *in which the purchase was allowed to stand;* Edwards v. Meyrick[91]; Holman v. Loynes[92]; Hesse v. Briant[93]; McPherson v. Watt[94]; *as well as* Moody v. Cox & Hatt[95] *and* Nocton v. Lord Ashburton.[96] Hesse v. Briant[97] *was a case involving a solicitor acting for two clients with opposing interests, but that case was between the two clients, and only involved the solicitor tangentially. The court considered that there had not (through the agency of the joint solicitor) been "fair and open dealing" so that the solicitor as agent could not bind the vendor to the contract here. This is a point about notice, not about fiduciary duty. The breach in question was the vendor-client's breach of his ordinary good-faith duty of candour and accuracy to the purchaser-client, held not to be remedied by the fact that the two had shared a solicitor.*[98]

(iii) If it is right that there is no "fiduciary" duty of the Nocton v. Lord Ashburton *kind in the case where the person with the undisclosed interest is the joint client, rather than the solicitor, then it follows that there is no need for the (surely rather surprising) mens rea doctrine in this sphere at all. No authority was cited for it. In the cases of breach of fiduciary duty where the solicitor himself takes a benefit under the impugned transaction, there is no need for mens rea. Inadvertence, mistaken belief, and so on, will suffice to ground an action against the solicitor himself, as Millett L.J. has confirmed in* Mothew.

(iv) Is the no-conflict rule really based on "fiduciary" duty? The rule that a solicitor or other similar agent may not act initially for two parties with potentially conflicting interests without the informed consent of both is labelled a breach of "fiduciary" duty by Millett L.J. The breach of "fiduciary" duty here, if such it is, is indistinguishable in appearance from the breach of good faith owed by a vendor in circumstances where the purchaser could not be expected to find out about a defect in what was proposed to be sold him and which he could not be expected to find out about. Millett L.J. notes that there was no breach of this duty in the Mothew *case: the society knew perfectly well of the joint agency. However, this conclusion is ques-*

[87] [1917] 2 Ch. 71.
[88] Para. 9.62 above.
[89] Para. 9.67 above.
[90] Para. 9.68 above.
[91] Para. 9.72 above.
[92] Para. 9.77 above.
[93] Para. 9.79 above.
[94] Para. 9.90.
[95] Above.
[96] Above.
[97] Above.
[98] See also, on the point raised in this paragraph, the important recent case of the High Court of Australia, *Breen v. Williams* (1996) 138 A.L.R. 259. (Cp. however, the passage at p. 437 F–G of the judgment in the Privy Council case of *Clark Boyce v. Mouat* [1994] 1 A.C. 428.)

tionable: see Chapter 10: Excluding the effect of the Fair-dealing Terms, and cases therein cited; and see e.g. Erlanger v. New Sombrero Phosphate Co.[99] *and* Lagunas Nitrate v. Lagunas Syndicate,[1] *in the case of a trusted person proposing to make a private profit from the intended transaction). Whether one regards the no-conflict rule as an example of the ordinary good-faith duty or a fiduciary duty, it is likely that the client's consent to the joint agency will clearly (unless specifically excepted by a proper exclusion clause) have been deemed to be limited to circumstances in which no conflict of interest actually arose. It was consent to a potential, but not actual, conflict of interest.*

(3) Miscellaneous points

(i) Post-contractual non-disclosure

What was being alleged against the solicitors was non-disclosure of an actual cvonflict of interest, after the contract of agency between them and the society had already been entered into. Since the formation of the contract was perfectly valid (the problem not having arisen or been anticipated then, the breach of the no-conflict rule will have been a breach of the implied good-faith term (or good-faith lookalike) of the contract above. Accordingly it cannot be said to have vitiated the agency contract so as to render rescission of that the appropriate remedy (assuming any such client ever wanted it). The client's remedy against the solicitor would be damages for breach of the implied term of the agency contract. These would involve the usual questions of causation and would seem to give no special advantage to the claimant over and above damages for negligence.

(ii) A further question

What remedies in such circumstances does the client who has suffered by reason of the joint solicitor's non-disclosure have against the other client?

(a) If the circumstances are such that the other client (we will call him the vendor, for ease of identification) has had a "normal" vendor's good-faith duty of candour and accuracy and has been in breach of it there would be the right to rescission of that transaction *or compensation, depending on how serious the breach of the good-faith duty was. This would be because the breach of the good-faith duty would have vitiated the buyer client's consent to that contract* pro tanto. *The fact that the two had a joint agent in the person of the solicitor would not have cured the defect: see* Hesse v. Briant.[2]

(b) If the circumstances are that the vendor-client has no "normal" duty of good faith to reveal the fact in question (e.g. because the information in question, though relevant, did not relate to the subject matter of the sale), but the fact was nonetheless revealed to the joint solicitor, and something that the buying client ought to know, there would be a conflict of interest, and the solicitor would come under a duty to terminate the joint agency, but not, it seems, actually to tell the buyer client the information anyway. This duty would (it is suggested) be a good-faith duty implied in the contract of agency between the solicitor and the buying client. The consequences would be as in (i) above.

Barclays Bank v. Thomson [1996] _New Law Digest_ November 7, C.A.

9.113 The brief report summarises statements of the court to the following effect on the question of independent advice:

(1) A bank may rely on a solicitor's certificate even when the solicitor is

[99] Para. 9.91 above.
[1] Para. 9.96 above.
[2] Above.

also the lenders solicitor: *Massey v. Midland Bank*[3]; *Banco Exterior v. Mann*[4] and *Bank of Baroda v. Rayarel*.[5]

(2) A bank may rely on a solicitor's certificate as regards advice given to a signatory where the solicitor is also acting for the lender: *Midland Bank v. Serter*[6]; *Halifax Mortgages v. Stepsky*[7]. See also *BCCI v. Aboody*.[8]

The crucial question of the "competence" of the advice seems not to have been discussed as far as may be seen.

[3] [1995] 1 All. E.R. 929.
[4] [1995] 1 All. E.R. 936.
[5] [1995] 2 F.L.R. 376.
[6] [1995] 1 F.L.R. 1034.
[7] [1996] 2 W.L.R. 230.
[8] [1990] 1 Q.B. 923.

CHAPTER 10

EXCLUDING THE EFFECT OF THE FAIR-DEALING TERMS

"The court requires good faith in conditions of sale, and looks strictly at the statements contained in them."[1]

"There is a rule in English law that every man must be taken to know that which he has the means of knowing, whether he has availed himself of those means or not."[2]

"It standing so indifferent, we ought to construe it most strongly against the grantor."[3]

"I impute no bad intention to the Plaintiff or his advisers, but I say that a man, knowing what this Plaintiff knew, who does not more fully express what he knows, does not do his duty."[4]

THE GOOD FAITH DUTY APPLIES

Introduction

10.01 This chapter is about how a vendor may legitimately provide in his contract with the purchaser to *provide less* than he would otherwise (because of the fair dealing implied terms) be reasonably expected to do. This "providing-less" may be of two kinds: the purchaser may not receive the subject matter which he reasonably expected to receive but for the excluding clause; or he may find that there is some unwelcome extra in the package—a limitation of liability or an addition of extra risk. In what follows these providing-less clauses have been called "exclusion clauses"; but it should be understood that this expression, as used in this chapter, covers the kind of clause which

[1] Sir G.J. Turner L.J. in ***Dimmock v. Hallett*** (1866) 2 Ch. App. 21.
[2] Pollock C.B. in *Stewart v. London and NW Railway Co.* (1864) 33 L.J. Exch. 199.
[3] Scroggs C.J. in ***Manchester College v. Trafford*** (1678) 2 Show. 31.
[4] Bacon V.C. in ***Heywood v. Mallalieu*** (1883) 25 Ch. D. 357.

limits or cuts down the subject matter of the contract in any way, and is not confined to mere exclusions of liability or risk. Thus, an exclusion clause, in this sense, might affect the "core terms" in for example, the Unfair Contract Terms Regulations 1994[5] as well as other terms of the contract: it is the substance of the cutting down which is in point, not precisely where this occurs in the contract.

There is no reason whatever why the vendor should not expressly exclude the effect of the fair-dealing terms in either of the above ways, *provided he does so fairly*. This is simple to describe, but requires a considerable degree of attention—added perhaps to something of a sense of fair play—to achieve. An exclusion clause must itself be in plain language, likely to be understood by the kind of buyer to be expected[6] in the kind of conditions imposed by the actual sale. It must fairly point to the defect excluded if it is a specific one. Further, it must do so in a reasonably straightforward way, not leaving the purchaser to draw inferences, but putting the intended limitation squarely. If it is a general exclusion, there must be fair dealing of quite an advanced kind.[7] If it excludes a risk, then all risk-relevant information relating to that risk, whether in the possession of the vendor or his agent, must be revealed. If not, the exclusion clause simply does not bind the purchaser, however mortifying this may be to a vendor who seeks to hide behind obfuscatory general small-print material. It becomes a trap into which he himself falls. *On the other hand, a clause which is completely plain and understandable, and is clearly and fairly drawn to the customer or purchaser's attention, is binding however severe the terms of the exclusion clause.*

Is the exclusion a part of what was agreed with the customer at all?

10.02 Where an agreement is made by a mixture of writing and conduct, or by writing, conduct and orally, the exclusion of the fair dealing terms will normally be found (or not, as we shall see) in the part which is written. The first problem for a seller of goods or services who wants to exclude the fair dealing terms is to show that the exclusion was part of the contract in the first place. The "ticket cases" are the main seam for this particular part of the law. The seller of goods or services has to show that his customer has assented to the exclusion. This is easy enough, if he can show that the customer has read the exclusion, and acted upon it. There is express assent. However, the customer will often allege he has not read it, and most providers of goods or services are unlikely to be able to prove whether he has or not. A customer who has not read the condition *may nevertheless be bound by it*. Consent may often be implied from entering upon the

[5] See Chapter 19.

[6] The "person of ordinary vigilance and caution", to use Tindal C.J.'s phrase in ***Dykes v. Blake*** (1838) 4 Bing. (N.C.) 463; 132 E.R. 866.

[7] See further below.

contract with deemed or inferred knowledge of the clause. In *Harris v. Great Western Railway* Blackburn J. said[8]:

> "And though one of the parties may not have read the writing, yet, in general, he is bound to the other by those terms; and that, I apprehend, is on the ground that, by assenting to the contract thus reduced to writing, he represents to the other side that he has made himself acquainted with the contents of that writing and assents to them, and so induces the other side to act upon that representation by entering into the contract with him, and is consequently precluded from denying that he did make himself acquainted with those terms."

When is the customer's consent to the exclusion condition implied?

10.03 The courts considered this question, mainly in the "ticket" cases, and came up with the answer that it depended on three main factors:

(1) the extent to which the clause was one which was "usual", or could reasonably be anticipated in that kind of contract,
(2) whether reasonable steps had been taken to draw the attention of the purchaser to the clause; and
(3) "Know your purchaser" considerations.[9]

Usual and expected exclusion clauses

10.04 When the courts feel able to say that "everyone" expects exclusion clauses or conditions of that kind in that kind of contract, the buyer of goods or services is likely to be bound whether or not he has read the clause. The provider of the goods, services, etc., has the task of proving that it was expected. It is essentially a question of fact.

In *Lewis v. M'Kee*[10] the defendant, who was the consignee of a bill of lading, endorsed it to be delivered to a third party, and added a condition that the third party was to be responsible for all freight, dead freight and demurrage. The captain did not see the endorsement and the plaintiffs declined to be bound by it. Willes J. considered that a person receiving a bill of lading would not expect that kind of condition in it, so that he could not be said to have assented to the risk of that, only the normal conditions in a bill of lading. However, he said:

> ". . . If in the ordinary course of business a person were under the obligation of looking at a document before acting on the supposition that it was in order, and that the customary terms were stipulated for, it might be otherwise."

[8] (1876) 1 Q.B.D. 515.
[9] See Know your purchaser or customer, (para. 10.09 below.).
[10] (1869) L.R. 4 Exch. 58 noted in the Appendix to this chapter at para. 10.73.

Reasonable steps

10.05 Where the exclusion clause is *un*usual, one which the customer could not reasonably anticipate in that kind of contract, it will not be covered by the rules about implicit assent unless sufficient steps are taken to draw it to the attention of the customer. The exercise is not as easy as perhaps it sounds: it involves a certain degree of imaginative empathy on the part of the provider of services who wishes to be safe behind the fortress of his exclusions.

The presumed intention of the customer to take the risk covers only the sort of clauses which can be reasonably anticipated in that kind of contract, or "usual" clauses. This was explained by Byles J. in *Van Toll v. Southeastern Railway*[11]

> "... he [the customer who has put the conditions in his pocket without reading them] assents to it implicitly, whatever the terms may be, on two conditions. One of those conditions is, that the terms contained in the notice should be reasonable terms. I think that is essential. Suppose such a notice as this contained a condition to the effect that, whatever the nature or value of the goods, if the bailor does not claim them within two days, they shall belong absolutely to the railway company,—no one could say that, if the party put a notice of this kind into his pocket, he assented to such a stipulation as that.

See also Lord Dunedin in *Hood v. Anchor Line.*[12] He considered the question whether the clause or condition was usual was a prior question to the question whether the company had taken reasonable steps to bring the conditions to the customer's attention. He said:

> "But what is usual is in truth a question of fact. Accordingly it is in each case a question of circumstance whether the sort of restriction that is expressed in any writing (which, of course, includes printed matter) is a thing that is usual, and whether, being usual, it has been fairly brought before the notice of the accepting party."

10.06 In *Thompson v. LMS Railway*[13] Lawrence L.J. endorsed the view of Bramwell L.J. in *Parker*[14] that if the condition in the ticket were unreasonable the passenger would not be bound. Sankey L.J. agreed with Lawrence L.J. that unreasonable conditions would not form part of the implicit agreement made by the passenger. He gave an example[15] of an unreasonable condition whereby if the passenger's goods were not removed in 24 hours they would be forfeit to the railway company. However, he also endorsed the *obiter* views of Bramwell L.J. in his dissenting judgment (on the main issue) in *Parker v. South Eastern*

[11] (1862) 12 C.B. (N.S.) 75; 142 E.R. 1071.
[12] [1918] A.C. 837.
[13] [1930] 1 K.B. 41.
[14] (1877) 2 C.P.D. 416..
[15] No doubt derived from Blackburn J.'s example in *Van Toll v. Southeastern Railway Company* (1862).

Railway[16] and may thereby have added a further gloss. Bramwell L.J. had said in that case:

> "The truth is, people are content to take these things on trust. They know that there is a form which is always used—they are satisfied it is not unreasonable, because people do not usually put unreasonable terms into their contracts. If they did, then dealing would soon be stopped. Besides, unreasonable practices would be known. The very fact of not looking at the paper shews that this confidence exists . . . I think there is an implied understanding that there is no condition unreasonable to the knowledge of the party tendering the document and not insisting on its being read—no condition not relevant to the matter in hand."

Thus, it may be that the Court of Appeal's *obiter* view in *Thompson v. LMS Railway*[17] was also to the effect that the condition must be of "relevance to the matter in hand". It is not clear that it really adds very much to "usual and reasonable".

Reasonable steps may need to be quite stridently demanding of attention if the clause is unusual, and specially destructive of rights. In *Thornton v. Shoe Lane Parking*[18] Lord Denning commented on the lack of reasonable steps there, saying:

> "I do not pause to inquire whether the exempting condition is void for unreasonableness. All I say is that it is so wide and so destructive of rights that the court should not hold any man bound by it unless it is drawn to his attention in the most explicit way. It is an instance of what I had in mind in *J. Spurling v. Bradshaw*.[19] In order to give sufficient notice, it would need to be printed in red ink with a red hand pointing to it—or something equally startling."

10.07 Megaw L.J. on the same point, relying on Lord Dunedin in *Hood v. Anchor Line*[20] said that where the sort of restriction was a usual one in that kind of contract,

> "it may not be necessary for a Defendant to prove more than that the intention to attach some conditions has been fairly brought to the notice of the other party. *But at least where the particular condition relied on involves a sort of restriction that is not shown to be usual in that class of contract, a Defendant must show that his intention to attach an unusual condition of that particular nature was fairly brought to the notice of the other party.* How much is required as being . . . 'reasonably sufficient to give the plaintiff notice of the condition' depends upon the nature of the restrictive condition."
> He pointed out that the condition in question involved the abrogation of statutory rights as to occupier's liability, and con-

[16] Above.
[17] [1930] 1 K.B. 41.
[18] [1970] 2 Q.B. 163.
[19] [1956] 1 W.L.R. 461.
[20] [1918] A.C. 837.

sidered that there must be "some clear indication which would lead an ordinary sensible person to realise, at or before the time of making the contract, that a term of that sort, relating to personal injury, was sought to be included. I certainly would not accept that the position has been reached today in which it is to be assumed as a matter of general knowledge, custom, practice, or whatever is the phrase that is chosen to describe it, that when one is invited to go upon the property of another for such purposes as garaging a car, a contractual term is normally included that if one suffers any injury on those premises as a result of negligence on the part of the occupiers of the premises they shall not be liable."[21]

10.08 Finally, in *Interfoto v. Stiletto*,[22] a hire case of relevance here, the Court of Appeal agreed that an onerous condition in a photographic lending library's printed conditions, which provided that £5 per transparency per day was to be paid in the event of late return was not binding on the hirer. Dillon L.J. said:

"At the time of the ticket cases in the last century it was notorious that people hardly ever troubled to read printed conditions on a ticket or delivery note or similar document. That remains the case now. In the intervening years the printed conditions have tended to become more and more complicated and more and more one-sided in favour of the party who is imposing them, but the other parties, if they notice that there are printed conditions at all, generally still tend to assume that such conditions are only concerned with ancillary matters of form and are not of importance. In the ticket cases the courts held that the common law required that reasonable steps be taken to draw the other parties' attention to the printed conditions or they would not be part of the contract. It is, in my judgment, a logical development of the common law into modern conditions that it should be held, as it was in *Thornton v. Shoe Lane Parking Ltd*,[23] that if one condition in a set of printed conditions is particularly onerous or unusual, the party seeking to enforce it must show that that particular condition was fairly brought to the attention of the other party."

Bingham L.J. also held that where the plaintiff did not do what was necessary to draw what he called "an unreasonable and extortionate clause" fairly to the Defendants' attention, the Defendants would be "relieved from liability". The expression "relieved from liability" is perhaps unfortunate[24] since it obscures, the essential point of the earlier cases, which is that the customer cannot be taken to have assented to such clauses; and it is only in this sense that the court "relieves him" from a liability he never *had*, in truth, in the first place.

Conversely, where a condition of that kind *is* more usual in the kind

[21] Italics supplied.
[22] [1989] Q.B. 433.
[23] [1971] 2 Q.B. 163.
[24] See note on case in Appendix below.

of contract, it may not require much for the court to be satisfied that the purchaser's attention has been drawn to it. Thus, in *Thompson v. LMS Railway Co.*[25] the conditions on the back of the ticket were referred to in reasonably legible print on the face of the ticket, but the circumstances assisted the vendor also. As Sankey L.J. put it:

> "everybody familiar with the practice of the railway world knows the sort of conditions that are imposed upon people who take cheap tickets—sometimes they are drovers' tickets, sometimes they are tickets to enable workmen to go backwards and forwards, sometimes they are excursion tickets . . ."

(3) Know your purchaser or customer

10.09 First, "the customer or purchaser" means, as is usual in the context of good faith, not just anybody, but your likely customer or purchaser for your particular transaction. In a sale which is made on similar terms to large numbers of people, such as the sale of railway tickets, it means a typical class of customer: the kind of customer most likely to avail himself of the service in question. "Know your customer" is a necessity here.[26] Thus, it was said[27] in *Richardson, Spence & Co v. Rowntree*[28]

> "The ticket in question in this case was for a steerage passenger—a class of people of the humblest description, many of whom have little education and some of them none. I think, having regard to the facts here, the smallness of the type in which the alleged conditions were printed, the absence of any calling of attention to the alleged conditions and the stamping in red ink across them, there was quite sufficient evidence to justify the learned judge in letting the case go to the jury."

The dangers ensconced in small print are arguably less nice about class now; or at all events the "lower" class widens hugely, for example in the case of certain mortgage related packages, home income schemes and the like (even share purchase, perhaps): many more of us may consider ourselves "of the humblest description" vis a vis the hidden dangers of these investments.[29]

Physical obviousness

10.10 In general, the rule for "reasonable steps" is probably *"c'est le premier pas qui coute"* or "First impressions are what matter most". Putting

[25] [1930] 1 K.B. 41.

[26] Cp. the old Core Principles of the Financial Services legislation which contained the same rule, made explicit in these words.

[27] Somewhat *de haut en bas*, but this *was* the late nineteenth century.

[28] [1894] A.C. 217.

[29] See also Chap. 9, Dealings with the Vulnerable Seller or Buyer, for the suggestion that the use by a powerful organisation or group of organisations of certain provisions in standard-form contracts is capable of constituting a dealing with a vulnerable party.

the exclusion in much smaller print at the bottom of a larger-print upbeat piece about the advantages of rail travel (or whatever services are in question, including perhaps financial ones) just will not do. In *Butler v. Heane*[30] a carrier nailed a handbill to his door:

> "stating in large print the many advantages belonging to the waggon, and in a very small character at the bottom, that the owner would not be answerable for goods above the value of £5 unless entered as such and paid for accordingly."

As Lord Ellenborough said, the handbill "called the attention to everything that was attractive, and concealed what was calculated to repel customers". A carrier must "take care that everyone who deals with him is fully informed of the limits to which he confines it."

It is similarly fatal if the customer receives, say, a steamship ticket which appears complete on its face, bearing only the name of the ports between which it sailed, the conditions being printed on the back, with no reference to them in the front.[31]

The significance of the first marker

10.11 However, it has been held that it does not always matter, curiously perhaps, that the trail which would lead the customer eventually to actual knowledge of the conditions is a circuitous or difficult one, provided that the first flag or marker of the trail is conspicuous enough to be easily observed. In *Thompson v. LMS Railway*[32] the excursion ticket in question said on its face "Excursion. For conditions see back". On the back was a notice that the ticket was issued subject to the conditions in the defendant company's timetables and excursion bills. The excursion bills stated that they were subject to the conditions shown in the company's current timetables. The timetables, which cost 6d, finally contained the important exclusion clause! This coolly excluded liability for injury, however caused. The unfortunate customer thus had to make a search of the back of the ticket and two other documents, in the correct order, if she was to know of the exclusion. She was nonetheless held bound. The start of her trail was plainly marked; and possibly also, although this is not spelled out, the quest was not an appallingly difficult or impracticable one.[33] Otherwise, the decision would be in marked contrast with the good faith rules about leases, company documents and so on, being *reasonably available* to the buyer in the actual circumstances of the sale.[34]

No practical opportunity to reject exclusion clauses

10.12 If a customer has no practical opportunity to reject a set of conditions, this will tend to show the conditions were simply not part of

[30] (1810) 2 Camp. 415 170 E.R. 1202.
[31] See *Henderson v. Stevenson* (1875) L.R. 2 H.C. 470.
[32] [1930] 1 K.B. 41.
[33] Also, see 10.08, the condition was a fairly usual one.
[34] See also, No practical opportunity, *etc.*, at para. 10.12 below.

the contract in the first place. For example the printed conditions which are spewed out of a machine in a parking lot as the car is driven in may not be part of the contract.[35]

If the contractual terms are explained verbally to the customer in a way which differs from the printed conditions, the provider of services will not be able to rely on the printed conditions.[36] The printed conditions are either overridden by the later verbal statement[37] or may be taken to apply only to the contract as envisaged therein, not the contract as differently performed.[38]

Implied acceptance through an agent

10.13 Consent may be implied through the agency of another. In *Grand Trunk Railway of Canada v. Robinson*[39] Lord Haldane said, on the question whether the passenger had assented to the exclusion clause in the "special contract",

> "This he may be shown to have done either in person or through the agency of another. Such agency will be held to have been established when he is shown to have authorized antecedently or by way of ratification the making of the contract under circumstances in which he must be taken to have left everything to his agent. In such a case it is sufficient to prove that he has been content to accept the risk of allowing terms to be made without taking the trouble to learn what was being agreed to. The company may infer his intention from his conduct. If he stands by under such circumstances that it will naturally conclude that he has left the negotiation to the person who is acting for him, and intends that the latter should arrange the terms on which he is to be conveyed, he will be precluded by so doing from afterwards alleging want of authority to make any such terms as the law allows. Moreover, if the person acting on his behalf has himself not taken the trouble to read the terms of the contract proposed by the company in the ticket or pass offered, and yet knew that there was something written or printed on it which might contain conditions, it is not the company that will suffer by the agent's want of care. The agent will, in the absence of something misleading done by his company, be bound, and his principal will be bound through him. To hold otherwise would be to depart from the general principles of necessity recognized in other business transactions, and to render it impracticable for railway companies to make arrangements for travellers and consignors without delay and inconvenience to those who deal with them."

[35] See *per* Lord Denning in ***Thornton v. Shoe Lane Parking*** [1971]. 2.Q.B. 163.
[36] ***Mendelsohn v. Normand*** [1970] 1.Q.B. 177 and *Curtis v. Chemical Cleaning & Dyeing* [1951] 1 K.B. 805.
[37] *Curtis v. Chemical Cleaning & Dyeing.*
[38] ***Mendelssohn v. Normand***, above, *per* Lord Denning.
[39] [1915] A.C. 740 at 748.

He thought the agent had approbated the contract by travelling under it, and so could not reprobate it by claiming a right inconsistent with it.

Beyond "ticket" cases?

10.14 The kind of contract constituted by handing or sending a document containing conditions to the other party who assents by conduct does not seem to figure very often in modern reported cases. It is not clear why this is, because we all know it happens quite a lot. It is possible that one reason may simply be the usual compartmentalisation process of English law—"Those are ticket cases and this is not a ticket case, so I need not look at them." However, the case of *Interfoto v. Stiletto*[40] shows that this approach may be missing something, since the underlying principle remains relevant to sales of goods and services today, given appropriate circumstances.

These appropriate circumstances will probably include (1) the unexpectedness of the condition and (2) relatively little drawing of the victim's attention to the clause: in other words, the reasonable expectation of the offeree, together with reasonable steps to draw the exclusion to his attention will be what is important. Because the wider implications of the ticket cases may prove more useful to lawyers than might have been supposed, there are noted what may seem a surprisingly large number of "ticket" cases in the Appendix to this chapter. They have been put in with the cases which deal with exclusion clauses in already completed contracts. In theory the two are different in that the ticket cases are an exercise in determining what is included in the contract, while the exclusion clauses are about construing terms which are acknowledged to be "in" the contract, in the physical or literal sense at least. However the exercise carried out is in fact fairly similar for our purposes, and in both cases dependent on the buyer or customer's reasonable expectation. A vendor or provider of services can only ensure the buyer or customer has reasonable expectations to match the vender/provider's own desires by dealing fairly, and observing the duty of candour and the duty of accuracy, when excluding as much as when describing the subject matter of the contract.

Exclusion clause cases—various

10.15 The exclusion cases cover a wide area: they deal among other things with insurance policies, charter parties, land transactions, and the sale of shares. This is not surprising. The good faith principles governing exclusion clauses are general ones.[41]

[40] [1989] Q.B. 433.
[41] See, *e.g.*, Lindley L.J. in ***Re Terry & White's Contract*** (1886) 32 Ch.D.454, noted in the Appendix to this chapter at para. 10.89 and discussed below.

Relationship between the old *contra proferentem* rule and the good faith law on exclusion clauses

10.16 Where the two overlap, there seems to be little practical difference between them. The *contra proferentem* rule is narrower in ambit. The development of the duty of candour, with its dislike of misleading half-truths, seems not to have come under the *contra proferentem* head. Further, the operation of of the *contra proferentem* rule is traditionally confined to cases where the statement or exclusion is ambiguous on its face.[42] The ambiguity might extend to the type of document: if the proferens had not made the nature of the document sufficiently clear, the other party was allowed to treat it as the type of instrument most favourable to him.[43]

On the other hand, statements about the duty of accuracy and the need to avoid ambiguity are to be found under both. For example in the case of *Burton v. English*,[44] Bowen L.J. found it perfectly possible to base his judgment equally on *contra proferentem* and on exclusion-clause principles. More modern cases adopt an approach to *contra proferentem* that borrows more than a little from good faith rules.[45] In *Houghton v. Trafalgar Insurance*[46] Lord Denning said "he should not be allowed to cut it down by clever clauses of doubtful or ambiguous import".

Both have the same attitude to fault and knowledge: a vendor, or defining party, or grantor, or *proferens* may not plead "innocence" to any purpose where the relevant information for the purposes of the duty of candour or the duty of accuracy is *reasonably expected* to be within his knowledge. The point is not spelled out in the *contra proferentem* cases; it is just that no allowances ever seem to be made for "innocence"

The "*proferens*" was regarded as the party for whose benefit or protection the clause was introduced: it was a matter of substance, not who ranked technically as the grantor.[47] Some doubts have been expressed about this, by Staughton L.J. in *Youell v. Bland Welch*,[48] but he conceded that "No doubt diligent historical research would produce an answer."; and it does not appear that *Birrell v. Dryer*[49] was cited to the court.

It is possible that the reason for the existence of the two labels is

[42] See ***Birrell v. Dryer*** (1884) 9 App.Cas. 345; Lindley L.J. in ***Cornish v. Accident Insurance Co.*** (1889) 23 Q.B.D. 453; and ***London & Lancashire Insurance Co v. Bolands*** [1924] A.C. 836.

[43] ***Edis v. Bury*** (1827) 6 B. & C. 433; 108 E.R. 511; and ***Lloyd v. Oliver*** (1852) 18 Q.B. 471; 118 E.R. 178 at paras 10.49 and 10.62 respectively.

[44] (1883) 12 Q.B.D. 218.

[45] ***John Lee (Grantham) Ltd v. Railway Executive*** [1949] 2 All E.R. 581; ***Houghton v. Trafalgar Insurance*** [1954] 1 Q.B. 247 and ***Adams v. Richardson*** [1969] 1 W.L.R. 1645.

[46] [1954] 1 Q.B. 247.

[47] See Lord Watson in ***Birrell v. Dryer*** (above).

[48] [1992] 2 Lloyd's Rep. 127.

[49] Above.

purely historical; the ancient *contra proferentem* label predating[50] the newer, natural-law influenced developments in this area in the nineteenth century. Thus, while the more refined approach of the good-faith rules took over in cases of breach of the duty of candour, and while the duty of accuracy was extended to the avoiding of what one might call administrative unfairness, by ensuring the purchaser had a real opportunity to understand the true meaning of the exclusion, in more straightforward cases of evident ambiguity the contra proferentem rule continued to be applied.

Construing the Exclusion Clause

A good faith construction is presumed

10.17 Exclusion clauses are construed on the assumption that *good faith has been used*. The vendor is presumed to have complied with his duty of candour and of accuracy. If and to the extent that a clause is ambiguous, half-true, *etc.*, it is construed against the vendor. His contractual duty is limited to that which would have been the case had good faith been written into the contract explicitly.

Where there is a written contract signed by the purchaser, the latter cannot say (as in the contracts which are constituted by handing a printed document to a purchaser) that the clause is not included in his contract, because in a physical sense, it clearly is. The question becomes simply, given a reasonable expectation of fair dealing or good faith on the part of the vendor, *how would the purchaser have read this clause?*

There may be difficulty in defining a boundary between cases where the exclusion clause is cutting down something already defined as the contractual subject matter, and cases where the "exclusion clause" is a part of the definition of the contractual subject matter, albeit a part with a tendency to be cut down or limited in a way one would not naturally expect. Consider, for example a clause such as "The land is sold subject to all easements, quasi-easements, quit-rents. . . ." Does this mean "You are getting the land but it is subject to the following exclusions" or does it mean "You are getting what is left after the various easements etc have been, as it were, deducted." This distinction has not been given any special attention in what follows. The reason is that the same good faith rules apply to descriptions as apply to exclusions: so that compliance, or lack of compliance will be precisely the same in either case. Consequently, a degree of overlap on occasions in what follows with "substantive" chapters on the formation of various categories of contract, for example Sale of Land, Shares, *etc.*, has been unavoidable.

[50] See, *e.g.*, ***Davenport's Case*** (1610) 8 Co. Rep. 144b; 77 E.R. 693 and ***Seaman's Case*** (1610) Godb. 166; 78 E.R. 101, paras 10.44 and 10.45 in the Appendix to this chapter.

Exclusion clauses not construed "strictly"

10.18 The court does not construe these exclusion clauses "strictly" in the sense of "narrowly"—they are construed like any other clauses: but it does construe them *"strictly" in the sense of looking at them with care, assuming fair dealing and regarding them as of no effect* in so far as there has been a breach of the fair dealing duties of a vendor. A great many of the cases on the construction of exclusion clauses relate to the sale of land. Land, as has been emphasized earlier, was the major investment for most people during the majority of the nineteenth century. The early joint-stock companies were the province by and large of somewhat "fly" individuals: hence the importance of partnerships, in banking and the professions, until at least the end of the century. The general principles were thus bound to be particularly well worked out (although by no means exclusively worked out) in relation to land.

The construction of exclusion clauses examined

10.19 Lindley LJ made a number of points in *Re Terry & White's Contract*[51]

(1) He initially protested against the prevalent notion that these clauses were read by the court so as to apply in general only to comparatively trivial and unimportant errors, misstatements and misdescriptions.

(2) He then qualified this statement by saying however that it *was* true in "certain classes of cases".[52]

(3) He also said that conditions of sale, like all other contracts, must be construed *with reference to the subject-matter to which they relate, and upon the assumption that the parties to them are dealing fairly with each other.*

"Being deliberately prepared by the vendor, who knows much more of the subject-matter to which they relate than a purchaser usually knows, or can know, conditions of sale, where their language is at all ambiguous, or where the application of that language to the property sold gives rise to difficulty, are *always construed or applied in such a way as to prevent the vendor from dealing unfairly with the purchaser. But the same observations are true of all other contracts similarly circumstanced.*"[53]

Fair natural meaning

10.20 The reasonable expectation of the purchaser means that his natural reaction to the expression used will tend to be paramount. The court

[51] (1886) 32 Ch. D. 454.

[52] These may possibly have been (see Buckley J.'s suggestion in *Jacobs v. Revell* [1900]) 2 Ch. 858, those in which a vendor is seeking to force on a purchaser by means of conditions something *altogether different* from that which he had contracted to buy.

[53] Above.

will not extend the scope of any exclusion clause beyond what is the fair natural meaning.

In *Re Beyfus & Master's Contract*,[54] for example, a condition which stated "the description of the property in the particulars is believed to be correct, but if any error shall be found therein the same shall not annul the sale, nor shall any compensation be allowed in respect thereof." was held by the Court of Appeal to have no application beyond matters of pure *physical description*, and certainly not to cure a title defect.

Expressions of opinion: fair dealing factual basis for opinion assumed

10.21 A statement which is on its face a pure expression of opinion will not be construed as pure opinion: the underlying factual content is brought out and examined for compliance with good faith. In many cases where one party, for example the seller, has better access to relevant information, it will be assumed that the underlying facts *within the seller's knowledge*[55] must justify the opinion. If the facts which are proved to have been within his knowledge do not justify it then he is in breach of contract to that extent. The condition or contract will be taken as founded on the statement *as if made in good faith*. When the reality does not correspond with what was promised on the application of this test, the purchaser is entitled to the appropriate remedies for an untrue statement—he may take the contract without the condition, claiming damages for breach, or where appropriate he may rescind the contract.

In *Brown v. Raphael*[56] a sale of a reversion in a trust fund on the death of an annuitant, a statement of belief made on behalf of the vendor was so confined. This statement was that the annuitant was believed to have no aggregable estate (for the purposes of death duty). Lord Evershed in the Court of Appeal explained that this was both a statement of opinion and no less than two underlying statements of fact:

(1) an implicit assertion that it is in fact the belief of the person making it; and, more importantly,
(2) *that by implication* he knows facts which justify his opinion—in other words, that he has reasonable grounds for his belief.

In *Smith v. Land & House Property Corp*[57] the implied assertion underlying a statement of opinion was a negative one. A hotel had been put up for sale, it being stated in the particulars that it was let to a most desirable tenant. The court held that there was a (wholly untrue) implied assertion that the vendors *knew of no facts* leading to

[54] (1888) 39 Ch. D. 110.
[55] See Chap. 5, Sale of Land, para. 5.14 for discussion of this expression and what it connotes.
[56] [1958] Ch. D. 636, noted in the Appendix to Chap. 5, Sale of Land.
[57] (1884) 28 Ch. D. 7, noted in the Appendix to Chap. 5, Sale of Land.

the conclusion that he was not a desirable tenant, and allowed rescission of the contract.

The duty of accuracy applies to exclusion clauses

10.22 There is a duty to be accurate in what you are trying to exclude. The court has no time for fuzzy language in exclusion clauses. The vendor is supposed to express his meaning *so as to be plain* to the purchaser. As Fry J. said in *Re Banister*[58]

> "It is therefore, of course fair that the person who does know [the vendor/defining party] should express his meaning so as to be perfectly intelligible to the person who does not know.

Bacon V.C. said in *Heywood v. Mallalieu*[59]

> "I impute no bad intention to the Plaintiff or his advisers, but I say that a man, knowing what this Plaintiff knew, who does not more fully express what he knows, does not do his duty."

It must generally not require too much mental effort on the part of the purchaser. Sir John Romilly the Master of the Rolls said in *Swaisland v. Dearsley*[60]

> "It is of the greatest importance and the duty of persons who put up property for sale by auction to *describe it with perfect accuracy, and not merely in such a way that a person, by drawing proper inferences from everything that is stated in the condition of sale*, may be able to ascertain what it is that is sold. Considering these circumstances, and considering also the condition and situation in life of the Defendant, which made him liable to fall into error . . ."[61]

It must be specific. In *Nottingham Patent Brick & Tile Co v. Butler*[62] Lindley L.J. felt that the exclusion clauses/conditions in the contract might technically cover the specific blot, but that the vendor "ought to have used a condition *pointing to the blot much more specifically than the actual conditions have done*"[63] and because of this part-disclosure, rescinded the contract.

"Know your purchaser" is relevant

10.23 The exclusion clause should be framed so as to be clear to the *kind of buyer to be expected* ("the person of ordinary vigilance and caution")—not merely a trained lawyer or other expert.

[58] (1879) 12 Ch. D. 131.
[59] (1883) 25 Ch. D. 357.
[60] (1861) 29 Beav. 430; 54 E.R. 694, noted in Appendix to Chap. 5, Sale of Land.
[61] Italics supplied.
[62] (1886) 16 Q.B.D. 778.
[63] Italics supplied.

In *Dykes v. Blake*[64] Tindal C.J. said of a plan which revealed a defect not at all foreshadowed by the particulars:

> "Particulars and plans of this nature should be so framed as to convey clear information to the ordinary class of persons who frequent sales by auction; and they only become a snare to the purchaser, if after the bidder has been misled by them, the seller should be able to avail himself of expressions which none but lawyers could understand or attend to"

He held that the right there had been insufficiently disclosed to be apparent to "persons of ordinary vigilance and caution."

The exclusion clause must not presuppose special expertise or knowledge. In *Williams v. Wood*[65] Lord Romilly, the Master of the Rolls said:

> "The conditions of sale had been very carefully framed, and the facts were correctly stated, and so stated as to lead a practised lawyer to the legal inference that no title was shown in the vendor, but they were drawn in a way which would not lead an ordinary purchaser to this conclusion. Conditions of sale ought to be drawn in a perfectly fair and straightforward way, and ought distinctly to explain any difficulty of title."

The duty of candour

10.24 No part-disclosures or departures from the natural meanings of words are allowed to have effect in exclusion clauses, any more than they are in the main contract description.[66]

Circumstances are assumed to be those of the actual sale

10.25 The conditions in which the *actual sale* is held are the testing ground for the exclusion clause: the question asked is, would the purchaser have been able to understand the exclusion *in those conditions*.[67] See *Dykes v. Blake* in which the court considered the circumstances in which a purchaser would be, not at some hypothetical normal sale, but at the sale in question, which was an auction sale.

In *Torrance v. Bolton*[68] the exclusion clause was perfectly easy to understand *per se*, but produced *in circumstances* which were liable to lead to misunderstanding. The particulars said the property was freehold, subject only to a life tenancy of an elderly woman: the mortgages subject to which the property was sold only appeared in the

[64] (1838) 4 Bing. N.C. 463; 132 E.R. 866, also noted in the Appendix to Chap. 5, Sale of Land.
[65] (1868) 16 W.R. 1005, cited by Walton J. in ***Faruqi v. English Real Estates*** [1979] 1 W.L.R. 963, noted in the Appendix to this chapter.
[66] See, below, passim.
[67] Above.
[68] (1872) L.R. 14 Eq. 124.

conditions of sale, and these were only produced and read at the auction, not before. The purchaser did not take in the import of the condition properly, and was consequently allowed rescission.

Particular Instances

(1) Exclusion by means of another, fuller or separate document to be consulted by the purchaser

Fair opportunity to consult

10.26 If the exclusion clause requires that the purchaser should have consulted some document he must be given a fair opportunity of so doing. If the document is in another place, it must be practically possible for him to consult the extra document; for example the circumstances of an auction sale may mean that a buyer will not be able to call at a solicitor's office to examine deeds first.[69]

Summaries: Any attempt must be an accurate précis of it

10.27 In *Cox v. Coventon*[70] Sir J. Romilly, the Master of the Rolls, revealed that a vendor has to exercise extraordinary care and nice judgment if he wants to be safe when attempting to exclude what would otherwise be his liability by means of a reference in the main or first document. If not, he falls all too easily into a trap of his own making. If the vendor states what the contents of the deed are, the purchaser "may reasonably trust to the representation of it contained in the particulars of sale as being a correct statement of its contents given by the vendor."

The summary must also omit nothing of relevance

10.28 It must not only be accurate, but (unless it in terms directs the purchaser to read the deed or additional document) the duty of candour applies to prevent part-disclosure of anything of significance to the purchaser. If the main document sets out a general account of the deed, said Sir John Romilly[71] "without referring to the deed itself for a more accurate knowledge of its contents" then "in order to sustain the contract, this account must not only be correct in itself, as far as

[69] See ***Dykes v. Blake*** (1838) 4 Bing (N.C.) 463; 132 E.R. 866. See also *Cox v. Coventon* (1862) 31 Beav. 378; 54 E.R. 1185, listed in the Appendix to Chap. 5 in which Sir John Romilly explained that a vendor might properly make a property sold subject to the provisions of a deed, provided the deed was specifically referred to and there was time for the purchaser to look at it before the sale.

[70] (1862) 31 Beav. 378; 54 E.R. 1185.

[71] *ibid.*

it goes, but must be such as to give the purchaser *all the information as to the character of the property which it is essential he should possess.*"[72]

"Go and look at the fuller deed" has its dangers also

10.29 Even if the vendor makes the sale subject to the deed or other document, and requires the purchaser to go and consult this himself, he has to exercise his judgment about whether the deed itself is readily understandable by the purchaser of ordinary vigilance and caution who is not a trained lawyer: see above. There may well be cases when he may need to make a commercial decision that he would be better off simply pointing in plain language to the defect or risk he is worried about, or thinks the purchaser may be worried about.

(2) Exclusion by means of silence

10.30 Silence effectively counts as a half-truth where the reasonable expectation is that a cutting down etc of the whole would be expressly mentioned. For example, where the natural inference from the circumstances is that the seller is selling his entire interest in land, he may not keep silent and afterwards say he had never intended to sell so much. Note the case of *Bower v. Cooper*,[73] in which the rule was first expressed[74] that a vendor who does not expressly qualify his sale is deemed to be selling his entire interest in the land the subject matter of the sale. Note also the rule that where nothing is said, the vendor has to give vacant possession on completion of the sale of land, and, for example, *Cook v. Taylor*[75] affirming it.

(3) Exclusion of risk clauses

10.31 Exclusion- of -risk clauses are only binding to the extent that full and accurate disclosure has been made by the vendor of all facts bearing on the risk excluded. Such clauses are usually to be found as general exclusions covering an entire category of problem, apparently unascertained at the date of the contract.

Examples

10.32 *(1) Exclusion for misdescription of what is sold.* These are common in the sale of land, where, as we have seen, the task of description requires particular care. Such exclusions, if taken at face value, may potentially change the bargain reached out of all recognition—at all events given

[72] This may be a potential hidden danger in some cases about the "plain English" summaries of mortgagors' rights and duties which many building societies are now producing, with a view to complying with the Unfair Contract Terms Regulations 1994.
[73] (1843) 2 Hare 408; 67, E.R. 168 noted in the Appendix to Chap. 5, Sale of Land.
[74] See now s.63 of the Law of Property Act 1925.
[75] [1942] Ch. 349.

a very careless or a very ignorant vendor. An early exclusion clause or "condition of sale" referred to in the older cases[76] is:

> "If any mistake be made in the description of the premises, or any other error whatever shall appear in the particulars of the present sale, such mistake or error shall not annul the sale, but compensation or equivalent shall be given or taken as the case may require."

Such a clause was initially dis-applied where it could be said that the defect in question would materially interfere with the evident *purpose of the purchase*. In *Shackleton v. Sutcliffe*[77] land was sold described as fit for building. The condition was held altogether inapplicable to an easement which affected various parts of the land to be built on.

Later, the courts developed a somewhat different approach and this was applied consistently as regards this and other similar conditions: they had to be *founded on a duty of candid and accurate disclosure by the vendor of risk-relevant information within his knowledge.*[78] This risk-relevant information in contracts generally is limited to that *relevant to the risk to which the exclusion clause was directed*. There is no full duty of disclosure as with insurance purchases. The court is merely enforcing the reasonable expectation of the buyer as to the exclusion. The exclusion clauses were not to become the means of forcing the purchaser to take a risk, save after such full disclosure. Sir G.J. Turner in *Dimmock v. Hallett*[79] said:

> "The Court requires good faith in conditions of sale, and looks strictly at the statements contained in them."

10.33 The information about risk has not only to be conveyed: it must, in accordance with the fair-dealing rules, be accurately conveyed, so that a purchaser can understand it. There must be no partial non-disclosure, no misleading or ambiguous statements. In *Dimmock v. Hallett*[80] a condition excluding liability for misdescription was held not to apply to statements calculated to mislead the purchaser; these were not, it was said, in the good faith that the court requires of vendors who impose such conditions. The purchaser was accordingly allowed to rescind, on account of a partial non-disclosure by the vendor about a tenancy under which a farm on the estate was let, despite the existence of the condition.

In *Brewer v. Brown*[81] there was a condition in the sale of a house

[76] See now the possibly slightly more limiting Condition 16, National Conditions of Sale 20th edition "nor, save where . . . relates to a matter materially affecting the description value of the property, shall any damages be payable . . ." and compare the similar condition 7, Standard Conditions.

[77] (1847) 1 De G. & Sm. 609; 67 E.R. 1217.

[78] See the fuller discussion of the underlying factual basis of statements of opinion, *etc.*, in Chap. 5, Sale of land; see para. 5.14 of that chapter also for "within his knowledge".

[79] (1866) 2 Ch. App. 21, also noted in Appendix to Chap. 5, Sale of Land.

[80] (Above).

[81] (1885) 28 Ch. D. 309.

and land with a side entrance, that *no mistake in the description of the premises or other error whatsoever in the particulars should annul the sale, but compensation should be given*. The plaintiff entered into the contract with the intention, known to the defendant, of building cottages on a part of the land, with the side entrance as the access. The vendor had failed to mention that the side wall did not belong to the property, and that the right to use the side entrance was only on suffrance. The natural inference from the description of the property was that there was a right to the side entrance. The purchaser was granted rescission by North J. This was even though the difference in value was only about £100 out of a purchase price of £1300. The purchaser's intention to build had been taken into account as part of the rescission-or-compensation exercise[82]:

Given the natural inference any purchaser would draw from the description, it was, North J. said, "the vendor's duty to inform a person buying from him what the real state of things was".

In *Nottingham Patent Brick v. Butler*[83] there was *inter alia* a clause that

> "... any incorrect statement, error, or omission found in the particulars or these special conditions, is not to annul the sale, nor entitle the purchaser to be discharged from his purchase, nor is the vendor or purchaser to claim to be allowed any compensation in respect thereof."

Lindley L.J. felt that the vendor ought to have used wording which pointed much more specifically to the blot the vendor had in mind, so as to draw attention to it. The land was in fact encumbered by certain restrictive covenants. The vendor was not allowed specific performance.

10.34 *(2) "The property is sold subject to all easements, etc. ..."* This is a frequently used exclusion-of-risk clause in the sale of land. These clauses must, in accordance with the general principle set out above, be founded on an honest disclosure by the vendor of anything relevant to the risk to which the clause is directed which is within his or his agent's knowledge. If not, they are disregarded *pro tanto*.

In *Heywood v. Mallalieu*[84] an auction sale was subject to a common-form printed exclusion clause or condition, that the lot was sold *subject to any existing rights and easements of whatever nature*. No easement or claim to an easement was mentioned. It emerged later that the plaintiff's solicitors had instructed surveyors to value the property, and these surveyors had received a letter from a Miss Walker asserting the existence of the right *inter alia* to use the kitchen of the property sold for washing and drying. The solicitor when informed of this decided not to make any further inquiry because he was not going to

[82] See further as to the importance of the purchaser's purpose, the discussion of the equity courts' compensation jurisdiction in Chap. 5, Sale of Land.
[83] (1886) 16 Q.B.D. 778.
[84] (1883) 25 Ch. D. 357.

put other people on their guard about "mere claims". This honest misjudgment did not avail the vendor at all.

Note also *In Re Beyfus and Master's Contract*[85] mentioned above, in which Fry L.J. stressed that "we ought not to give an enlarged meaning to words which restrict the rights of a purchaser in relation to *a description which he has no opportunity of verifying*".[86]

10.35 *(3) Waivers of statutory or other rights*. There must be fair-dealing by the person who puts forward the waiver. Again, full, specific, disclosure of material facts bearing on the risk that are known to the vendor is a prerequisite, if the waiver clause is to be worth more than the paper it is written on.

In *Greenwood v. Leather Shod Wheel*,[87] the fair dealing principles were applied to a waiver clause purporting to exclude the purchaser's statutory rights to complain of certain non-disclosures in a contract to take up shares in a new company. It was held by the Court of Appeal, that there was insufficiently specific information given to the purchaser of risk-relevant information. Lindley M.R. said:

> ". . . in order to bind him [the person who takes shares] by election or agreement, he must be fairly dealt with; and his attention must be fairly drawn to the facts, or at all events the existence of facts, which confer the rights which he elects or agrees not to enforce."

Similarly, in *Cackett v. Keswick*,[88] another shareholder's case, Farwell J. said:

> "A man who desires to take advantage of a waiver clause must state the facts fairly. If he states that there may be contracts, he intends it to be inferred that he knows of none. It is immaterial whether he intended to deceive or not when he made the statement . . ."

He considered the Court of Appeal in the *Greenwood*[89] case had been applying the same principles to waiver clauses "as are applicable to ambiguous or misleading statements in conditions of sale or releases."

10.36 *(4) Exclusions for bad title*. Clauses which begin "Title shall commence with [a specific deed]. . . ."; and "the purchaser shall not investigate [further back in time than the date] . . .; or "no objection shall be made to . . ." are generally construed so as to leave the vendor's obligation to give *good* title intact. The court infers that the intention was merely to allow the vendor to limit the documents by which he proves his title, as opposed to the kind of title he proves by his documents. They are also construed as based on the assumption *that the vendor has told*

[85] (1888) 39 Ch. D. 110.
[86] Italics supplied.
[87] [1900] 1 Ch. 421 noted below.
[88] [1902] 2 Ch. 456.
[89] Above.

everything he knows which is relevant to the risk: if not, the clause cannot be relied on by him to that extent.

In *Phillips v. Caldcleugh*[90] the exclusion in regard to the sale of a freehold house was *inter alia* that the title should commence on April, 17 1860, and no purchaser should investigate, or take any objection in respect of the title prior to the commencement of the abstract. The purchaser was held entitled to a good title (the vendors had attempted to argue that it meant the purchaser should take such title as they had) and allowed to rescind because this could not be given.

In *Beioley v. Carter*[91] Lord Romilly, the Master of the Rolls, whose judgment was later upheld on this point, had stated in the court below:

> "I have always thought that where the vendor wishes to preclude the purchaser from taking a particular objection to the title, which must appear on the documents submitted to him, *it is essential that the vendor should, as a matter of good faith, point out, if not the objection itself, the nature of the objection, in the conditions of sale.*"[92]

10.37 *(5) Deeming clauses*. For example "The purchaser shall assume . . ."

These also have to be founded on fair dealing, and full disclosure of risk-relevant information as to the risk to which the clause is directed. There is thus an implication that these clauses are founded on a genuine and *well-founded* belief by the vendor in the correctness of the statement to be assumed or deemed. If they are founded on any erroneous statement of fact material to the risk, and the fact is within the knowledge of the vendor or his agent, then, however honest or well-intentioned the statement may have been[93]: the clause will be disregarded to that extent.

Brett L.J. in *Re Banister*[94] expressed the point as an *implied representation* in such clauses, that no facts are known to the vendor which would make the deemed statement inaccurate. One could as well put it the other way round: the vendor has to disclose all facts known to him which affect the risk, or he cannot rely on the clause. Brett L.J.'s words were:

> ". . . authorities shew that in a Court of Equity requirement or insistance that a certain state of things shall be assumed does by implication contain an assertion that no facts are known to the persons who require it which would make that assumption a wrong one according to those facts". It followed that "There is, therefore, an implied representation which arises from the insistance that certain matters should be assumed."

[90] (1868) L.R. 4 Q.B. 159.
[91] (1869) L.R. 4 Ch. App. 230.
[92] Italics supplied. See also *Re Haedicke & Lipski's Contract* [1901] 2 Ch. 666 and *Becker v. Partridge* [1966] 2 Q.B. 155.
[93] See ***Re Banister*** (1879) next mentioned.
[94] (1879) 12 Ch. D. 131.

Note also *Re Marsh and Earl of Granville*[95] in which Fry J. said:

> "... a vendor who desires to limit the rights of a purchaser must do so by explicit and plain conditions, and he must tell the truth, and all the truth, which is relevant to the matter in hand."

On appeal, Cotton L.J. said:

> "I think that the principle is this, that the Court will not compel a purchaser to take an estate with less than the ordinary title which the law gives him *unless the stipulation on which the vendor relies for the purpose of excluding what would otherwise be the purchaser's legal right is fair and explicit. I think that the test of its being fair and explicit is whether it discloses all facts within the knowledge of the vendor which are* ***material to enable the purchaser to determine whether or not he will buy*** *the property subject to the stipulation* limiting his right to the ordinary length of title."[96]

10.38 Note also *Re Davis & Cavey*[97] where a clause that no objection should be made in respect of anything contained in the lease to the vendors, and that the title should commence with that lease, was not allowed to prevail so as to permit the vendor to force on the purchaser (who had bought at auction without the opportunity to inspect the lease) an undisclosed bad title within his knowledge.

In *Harnett v. Baker*[98] a condition of sale required the purchaser to assume that a certain Dr Clarke was absolutely entitled to the beneficial ownership of the property in question at his death. In fact his title was not perfected for some time after his death. Sir R Malins V.C. said:

> "... it is clear that conditions of sale fairly and honestly made, not founded on any erroneous statement, are binding. But it is equally clear, and I think it is most important it should be understood, that although a vendor is at liberty to introduce special conditions of sale he must not make them the means of entrapping the purchaser, and *they must not be founded on any erroneous statement of fact. There must be fair and honest dealing in the transaction, and on that principle only special conditions are sanctioned.*"[99]

In *Charles Hunt v. Palmer*[1] a vendor who had misleadingly described a property as "valuable business premises" was not allowed to rely on a deeming condition which limited the business use, where he had not fully disclosed that which was within his knowledge and relevant to the purchaser's judgment.

10.39 *(6) Compulsory compensation clauses for any error, misdescription, etc.* There was initially something of a difference in approach to be

[95] (1882) 24 Ch. D. 11.
[96] Italics supplied. Cp. "material" in the Marine Insurance Act 1906.
[97] (1888) 40 Ch. D. 601.
[98] (1875) L.R. 20 Eq. 50.
[99] Italics supplied.
[1] [1931] Ch. 287, applying ***In re Davis & Cavey*** (above).

detected between the common law and equity courts as to these clauses that sought to exclude the purchaser's right to seek rescission of the contract (or, in the common law courts, to seek the return of his deposit as money had and received). In several early cases[2] the common law approach was that these clauses were to be upheld unless there had been deliberate deceit practised by the vendor. However, even at that time, they may have been scrutinised a little more carefully: Lord Ellenborough said in *Duke of Norfolk v. Worthy*[3] that nonetheless the court would always require an ample and substantial performance of the contract.

Later, both adopted a similar approach: they would construe the contract assuming compliance with good faith. As Lindley L.J. put it regarding exclusion clauses in sales generally[4]:

> "conditions of sale, like other contracts, must be construed with reference to the subject matter to which they relate and upon the assumption that the parties to them are dealing fairly with each other."

The good faith approach meant that the clause was to be applied literally, but was assumed not to apply to undisclosed defects which good faith dictated ought to have been disclosed, *and* which were "material [or 'substantial'] defects", or as Lord Esher put it in *Re Terry and White's Contract*[5] defects "affecting the whole substance and foundation of the contract".

10.40 In *Ayles v. Cox*[6] Sir John Romilly declined to apply a compensation clause on the grounds that the "thing sold" would be of a different nature from that contracted to be sold; in *Dimmock v. Hallett*[7] where the clause was not applied, and the contract discharged, because the undisclosed defect affected the validity of the contract"[8] or was a misrepresentation (though not deliberate) which was "calculated to mislead".[9] Sometimes an ordinary process of construction of the words, possibly somewhat *contra proferentem*, would be involved too, as in *Brewer v. Brown*[10] where a breach of good faith was not ranked as a "mistake" and thus was not covered by a compensation clause tied to mistakes, *etc*.

Meanwhile, in the common law courts, Tindal C.J. in *Robinson v. Musgrove*[11] was taking a similar line, declining to apply a compensation clause to a breach of good faith by the vendor, where this had

[2] See ***Duke of Norfolk v. Worthy*** (1808) 1 Camp. 337; 170 E.R. 977 and para. 10.47 of the Appendix of this chapter); *Leach v. Mullett* (1827) 3 Car. & P. 115; 172 E.R. 348; *Wright v. Wilson* (1832) 1 M. & Rob 207; 174 E.R. 71.
[3] (1808) 1 Camp. 337.
[4] See Appendix, para. 10.90.
[5] [1886] 32 Ch. D. 454.
[6] (1852) 16 Beav. 23; 51 E.R. 684.
[7] (1866) 2 Ch. App. 21.
[8] Sir H.M. Cairns L.J.
[9] Sir G.J. Turner.
[10] (1884) 28 Ch. D. 309.
[11] (1838) 2 M & Rob. 92; 174 E.R. 225.

the result that a substantial part of the thing contracted to be sold was not there (in contrast to a mere matter of value). In *Dykes v. Blake*,[12] he declined to apply the clause if the jury considered the defect rendered the land "altogether useless" for the purpose for which it was bought, in this case, as building land. He also declined to hold that the purchaser, having been lulled into a sense of false security by the vendor, had failed to comply with his duty of due diligence in investigating prior to the contract.

Innocent motive, accidental error, *etc.*, no defence to the vendor

10.41 Innocence, no intention to mislead, *etc.*, is no defence: note the case of *Re Banister*[13] mentioned above, in which the vendor was wholly innocent of any intention to mislead.

Note also *Heywood v. Mallalieu*[14] where an innocent misjudgement as to the import of the facts known did not at all avail the vendor; and *Cackett v. Keswick*[15] in which Farwell J. noted that it was immaterial whether or not the person putting forward the exclusion clause intended to deceive.

Breaches of the duty of accuracy or candour that are not material (meaning significant in relation to the purchase)

10.42 Reliance by the vendor on exclusion clauses may be permitted despite breach of his duty of accuracy and candour if the effect, notably on the value of what is sold, is not material.[16] To the same effect, note *Re Leyland and Taylor's Contract*,[17] although no doubt pronouncements about what is essentially good-faith law in a vendor and purchaser summons ought to be approached with caution[18] and para. 10.76n. of the Appendix to this chapter.

There is an unsatisfactory double meaning contained in the word "material": does it mean "significant to the purchaser" or "significant in relation to the contract"? It seems probable that the true rule is that a breach of the duty of accuracy or candour that is not "material" in the sense of significant in relation to the purchase, is *also* assumed in the absence of evidence to the contrary not to be "material" in the sense of material to the reasonable purchaser's judgment whether to enter into that contract or not. Thus, an immaterial (non-significant) breach of the duty of accuracy or candour will not avoid an exclusion clause save perhaps in cases where a purchaser proves (although this

[12] (1838) 4 Bing. (N.C.) 463; 132 E.R. 866.

[13] (1879) 12 Ch. D. 131.

[14] (1883) 25 Ch. D. 357.

[15] [1902] 2 Ch. 456 noted below.

[16] See ***Blaiberg v. Keeves*** (1906) which, however, is perhaps explicable on the alternative basis that the vendor had been entirely honest *and* had expressed himself with reasonable accuracy in any event.

[17] [1900] 2 Ch. 625.

[18] See the note to ***Re Scott and Alvarez' Contract*** [1895] 2 Ch. 603.

may not be entirely easy for him save perhaps in cases where he made a particular purpose known to the vendor at the time of the contract) that *he* would not in fact have entered into the contract if he had known the true basis. This would be consistent with the application of good-faith to clauses describing the subject matter of the contract.

Immaterial inaccuracies with reliance by purchaser: does the vendor have to know of the purchaser's reliance?

10.43 It is possible that in this case the vendor needs to have known, actually or constructively, of the purchaser's purpose for the purchaser to succeed. However, it would perhaps be consistent with the theoretical basis of good faith for the purchaser's reliance to be sufficient, even without knowledge by the vendor. This theoretical basis was seen to change somewhat during the nineteenth century as the influence of the French jurists and of natural law diminished and disappeared. The natural law principle was essentially that a contract was only properly assented to on the assumption and to the extent that there had in fact been good faith. The late-nineteenth century approach tended to be (although such statements were always expressed surprisingly tentatively) more concerned with the vendor's state of mind not at the time the contract was made but at the time the complaint was made: that it would be "against conscience" for a man to take advantage of a clause which he now (that is post-contract) knows to be untrue. In *Redgrave v. Hurd*.[19] Jessel M.R. said:

> "One way of putting the case was, 'A man is not to be allowed to get a benefit from a statement which he now admits to be false . . ."

The question is probably of limited practical importance anyway. A purchaser who comes along and tries to prove that a small point was of huge significance in his decision to enter the contract will normally be hard put to it to explain how it was that he never mentioned it to the vendor or his agent. Compare Lord Blackburn in *Smith v. Chadwick*[20] on the practical difficulties of providing credible evidence that one would not have entered into a particular contract if one had known the true basis; and the consequent common sense of relying on inferences about what would have influenced a (reasonable) purchaser.

[19] [1881] 20 Ch. D. 1.
[20] (1884) 9 App. Cas. 187 noted in the Appendix to Chap. 7, Sale of Shares.

APPENDIX TO CHAPTER 10: SOME CASES OF INTEREST

***Davenport's Case* (1610) 8 Co. Rep. 144b; 77 E.R. 693**

10.44 John Hastings Earl of Huntingdon possessed an advowson lasting 15 years which was appendant to a particular rectory which he also possessed at the time and by means of it granted the next avoidance (the vicarage when it fell vacant) of a church called Orton super montem to one Davenport for life. The Earl's successor in title surrendered his term in the rectory that is the "head" advowson to the Bishop of Oxford who was the reversioner. The question was what effect the surrender had on the earlier grant. It was held that it remained untouched, *inter alia* because otherwise "The grantor himself would derogate from his own grant, and would make it void at his pleasure, and that is against the rule of law, *sc.* that the grant of every one shall be taken most strongly against himself, and most beneficially for the grantee."

***Seaman's Case* (1610) Godb. 166; 78 E.R. 101.**

10.45 A lessee for 100 years made a lease for forty years to one Seaman if he should live so long, and afterwards leased the premises also to his son John, to take effect after Thomas Seaman for 23 years, to be accounted "from the date of these presents." The question was whether the lease to John should count from the date of the above disposition (in which case John got nothing) or from the end of the lease to Thomas. The jury held it was the latter, making it a good lease.

Cook C.J. said: "... if the limitation be not certain when the term shall begin, it shall be taken most beneficial, for the lessee."

***Manchester College v. Trafford* (1679) 2 Show. 31; 89 E.R. 774**

10.46 A lease was expressed to be for 21 years with a further covenant "that the lessee shall have the same for 21 years more after the expiration of the said term, and so from 21 years to 21 years until 99 years thence next ensuing shall be complete and ended". It was held the first 21 years should not be included in the covenant. Scroggs C.J. said, "... it standing so indifferent, we ought to construe it most strongly against the grantor."

***Duke of Norfolk v. Worthy* (1808) 1 Camp. 337; 170 E.R. 977 (Early common law court takes different approach from equity courts to application of compensation clause: upholds literal wording in the case of unintentional errors by vendor but not deliberate ones)**

10.47 There was a compensation clause as to misdescription or errors or misstatements in the particulars, which were not to vitiate the sale. The particulars stated the estate was only one mile from Horsham, when in fact it was three or four miles away.

Lord Ellenborough left the question of deliberate deceit to the jury; other wise, the contract was to be affirmed, although he should, in cases of this sort, "always require an ample and substantial performance of the particulars of sale, unless they were specifically qualified".[21]

[21] See also *Leach v. Mullett* (1827) 3 Car. & P. 115, which took a similar approach, in contrast to that of the equity courts; and Parke J. in *Wright v. Wilson* (1832) 1 M. & Rob. 207. But see Tindal C.J. in *Robinson v. Musgrove* (1838).

Munn v. Baker **(1817) 2 Stark 255; 171 E.R. 638 ("Ticket"-type case)**

10.48 Carriers had lost a parcel. They relied on large printed notices which had been stuck up in their counting house and warehouse and published in the Gazette which contained a limitation of liability. However, a paper containing a notice without any limitation had been handed to the person who delivered the parcel. Lord Ellenborough thought that there would have needed to be proof that the plaintiff had read the Gazette and considered that anyway the notice handed to the plaintiff's agent had nullified any other; and held that the defendants were bound by that notice which was least beneficial to themselves.

Edis v. Bury **(1827) 6 B. & C. 433; 108 E.R. 511** (*Contra proferentem* rule applied to category of document)

10.49 The defendant gave the plaintiff an instrument in writing which was not paid. It was doubtful whether it was a bill of exchange, in which case due notice of dishonour had to be proved, or a promissory note. Lord Tenterden said, "It is an instrument, therefore of a very ambiguous nature . . . . . . and I think that where a party issues an instrument of an ambiguous nature, the law ought to allow the holder, at his option, to treat it either as a promissory note or a bill of exchange."

Bayley J. agreed. Holroyd J. also agreed, adding "Besides, the words of an instrument are to be taken most strongly against the party using them; and therefore if there be any ambiguity in the words of this instrument, they ought to be construed favourably for the plaintiff, and against the defendant, who made the instrument . . ."

Hargreave v. Smee **(1829) 6 Bing. 244; 130 E.R. 1274**

10.50 A guarantee was as follows "I do hereby agree to guarantee the payment of goods to be delivered in umbrellas and parasols to John and Edward Agustus Smee, . . . according to the custom of their trading with you, in the sum of 200*l*."

Tindal C.J. confirmed that guarantees are not construed specially strictly but "With regard to other instruments the rule is, that if the party executing them leaves any thing ambiguous in his expressions, such ambiguity must be taken most strongly against himself."

The other judges delivered concurring judgments. Thus it was held to be a continuing guarantee.

Blackett v. Royal Exchange Assurance **(1832) at 2 C. & J. 244; 149 E.R. 106**

10.51 The words in an insurance policy were "free from average under 3l per cent". The underwriters claimed that this meant that each instance of damage had to be excluded if it was under 3 per cent even if the whole of the instances added up to more than 3 per cent: the insured claimed that the underwriters were liable for each instance of damage however small if the total added up to more than 3 per cent.

Lord Lyndhurst C.B. said: "The memorandum is in the nature of an exception. The policy is general, extending to all losses, the memorandum excepts losses where each or all, according to the construction to be put upon it, are under 3*l* per cent. The rule of construction as to exceptions is, that they are to be taken most strongly against the party for whose benefit they are introduced. The words in which they are expressed are considered as his words, and, if he do not use words clearly to express his meaning, he is the person who ought to be the sufferer . . . The words here are ambiguous . . . In the absence therefore, of usage and authority, it seems to us that we ought to rest upon the rule of construction we have mentioned, and according to that rule the defendants are responsible if the aggregate of different averages comes up to 3*l* per cent . . ."

Doe d. Sir W. Abdy v. Stevens **(1832) 3 B. & Ad. 299; 110 E.R. 112 (*Contra proferentem*: increased tendency to apply if effect ferocious)**

10.52 This concerned a question of construction of a right of forfeiture in a lease. Lord Tenterden CJ said: "It is a general rule of construction, that the words of a covenant must be taken most strongly against the covenantor, and that rule applies more strongly to a proviso for re-entry which *contains a condition that destroys or defeats the estate.*"[22]

Dykes v. Blake **(1838) 4 Bing. (N.C.) 463; 132 E.R. 866[23] (Good faith duty of candour expected; in absence condition not allowed operation)**

10.53 The purchaser bought a villa and building plot at auction, subject to the reservation in another lot, which showed a plan and a reservation of other rights of way, but left out a reservation of a footway over the land bought. The footway was apparent from the lease of Lot 7, and there was a statement in the particulars that the lease might be seen at the vendor's office, and would be produced at the sale. Sergeant Wilde for the plaintiff argued that it was an omission which a purchaser of reasonable caution or discernment would be unlikely to discover; that it would be wrong to expect the plaintiff to have looked at the lease, since the plaintiff might never have heard of the sale before the day it took place; he could not peruse the lease to any purpose during the business of the sale; and, as a reasonably prudent man, he was not bound to peruse it; he was entitled to rely on the particulars.

Tindal C.J. agreed. He said the question was: "whether the Plaintiff is at liberty, under the circumstances stated in the special case, to hold the contract of purchase into which he entered to be altogether void, and to recover back the money paid to the auctioneer as money had and received to his use. And this will depend on the determination of two questions: first, whether the description of the premises in the printed particulars and plans exhibited at the time of the sale, upon the faith of which the Plaintiff made his purchase, was such that a prudent and vigilant man would enter into the contract without discovering the existence of the right of way over the land comprised in lot 13 [the building lot bought], and secondly, whether such right of way being found to exist, renders the purchase altogether useless for the purposes for which it was made, or only brings it under the head of mis-description, so as to form the subject of compensation or equivalent under the ninth condition of sale."[24]

Tindal C.J. thought that the plan omitting the right in question, but mentioning others would have lulled all suspicion to sleep, and that it was calculated, "not simply to give no information, but actually to mislead." "Particulars and plans of this nature should be so framed as to convey clear information to the ordinary class of persons who frequent sales by auction;

[22] Italics supplied.

[23] Also noted in the Appendix to Chap. 5, Sale of Land.

[24] "That if any mistake be made in the description of the premises, or any other error whatever shall appear in the particulars of the present sale, such mistake or error shall not annul the sale, but a compensation or equivalent shall be given or taken as the case may require."

and they only become a snare to the purchaser, if after the bidder has been misled by them, the seller should be able to avail himself of expressions which none but lawyers could understand or attend to". He concluded that the existence of the right "was not sufficiently disclosed to make it clear to persons of ordinary vigilance and caution, and the contract was not binding on the Plaintiff". "He did not order compensation, because he thought the "*object and purpose of the contract*", namely to use it as building ground, was entirely defeated by the existence of the right of way.

Note: This early case (in a common law court) shows the stringent nature of the duty to be accurate: highlighting certain undoubted facts and omitting others is sufficiently misleading to enable the purchaser to escape the impact of the condition. It also shows the new attitude in the common law courts to compensation clauses.

Robinson v. Musgrove **(1838) 2 M. & Rob. 92; 174 E.R. 225 (Restrictive attitude of common law courts to clauses excluding fair dealing terms)**

10.54 There were two pro-vendor clauses in an auction contract: that all title objections not taken within 10 days should be deemed waived, and a compensation clause. The purchaser objected (albeit late) that the vendor's power of sale had not been validly exercised; and that the building on a part of the land could not possibly be described as a "substantial brick building" etc as described.

Tindal C.J. held that: "first, if any substantial part of the property purporting to be sold, turns out to have no existence, or cannot anywhere be found, that circumstance, in my opinion, entitled the plaintiff to rescind the contract *in toto*; even if you think that the defendant was not guilty of any fraudulent misrepresentation in that respect: deficiency in value may be fit matter for compensation, but not the total absence of one of the things sold."

He referred to the second complaint, and directed the jury as follows: "Was that a *bona fide* description, or not? If not—if you think that was an exaggerated description quite beyond the truth, and that the defendant was not acting *bona fide* when he gave that description of the premises, then I am of opinion that circumstance alone will entitle the plaintiff to rescind the contract even now, and to recover the deposit, notwithstanding the language of the ninth condition [the compensation clause]."

Bower v. Cooper **(1843) 2 Hare 408; 67 E.R. 168.[25] (Natural expectation from silence given due weight)**

10.55 The only noteworthy point about this is that the Vice-Chancellor held that a contract to sell land which did not express what interest was to be sold imported the whole of the defendant's interest in the premises.[26]

Borradaile v. Hunter **(1843) 5 M. & G. 639; 134 E.R. 715 (*Contra proferentem*)**

10.56 A life insurance policy contained an exception in case "the assured should die by his own hands, or by the hands of justice, or in consequence of a duel". He threw himself into the Thames and was drowned. The court held that the words meant self-inflicted death generally. However, Tindal C.J. affirmed the general principle saying, "It is to be observed, that the words of the proviso are the words, not of the assured, but of the insurers, introduced by themselves for the purpose of their own exemption and protection from liability;

[25] Noted also in the Appendix to Chap. 5, Sale of Land.

[26] See now s.62 of the Law of Property Act 1925.

both in reason and good sense, therefore, no less than upon acknowledged principles of legal construction, they are to be taken most strongly against those that speak the words, and most favourably for the other party . . ."

***Seaton v. Mapp* (1846) 2 Coll. 556; 63 E.R. 859 (Duty of accuracy)**

10.57 Executors sold a leasehold pub called the Dublin Castle in Camden Town. The purchasers argued that the vendor had not deduced title properly on the day fixed for possession to be given. There was a condition that the purchaser would not inquire into the lease "prior to the lease by which the premises were held". This was a lease dated 19 August, 1839. The purchasers requested sight of the original lease, dated 1822. Their objection was founded on the covenant in this original lease, which did not appear to have been complied with in the existing lease. The vendors argued that this was an objection relating to the prior lease the purchasers said it was the lease itself.

Knight Bruce V.C. said: "when a vendor sells property under stipulations which are against common right, and places the purchaser in a position less advantageous than that in which he otherwise would be, it is incumbent on the vendor to express himself with reasonable clearness; if he uses expressions reasonably capable of misconstruction, if he uses ambiguous words, the purchaser may generally construe them in the manner most advantageous to himself."

***Shackleton v. Sutcliffe* (1847) 1 De G. & Sm. 609; 63 E.R. 1217 (Equity courts applied good faith rules to compensation clauses)**

10.58 Land was sold described as fit for building and not stating in the particulars or conditions the existence of easements over the land. The Vice-Chancellor held that the title was defective by reason of the easements, the only questions being whether the purchaser, who lived in the neighbourhood, knew about the easements (which he did not, on the facts) and whether they were *material defects*. The plaintiffs said they were not material, and if they were, they would undertake to remove them, alternatively pay compensation. The Vice-Chancellor absolved the plaintiffs from fraud or unfair intention, but nonetheless refused to apply a compensation condition and refused specific performance. ("I should be applying the 14th condition of sale to a purpose and to an extent to which, in my judgment, it ought not to be treated as having been intended to be applicable.")

***Re Stroud* (1849) 8 C.B. 502; 137 E.R. 604**

10.59 This is noteworthy for the quotation, in argument, from *Broom's Maxims*.[27] "It is a general rule, that the words in a deed are to be construed most strongly contra preferentem—regard being had, however, to the apparent intention of the parties, as collected from the whole context of the instrument; for, as observed by Mr Justice Blackstone, the principle of self-preservation will make men sufficiently careful not to prejudice their own interest by the too extensive meaning of their words; and hereby all manner of deceit in any grant is avoided; for, men would always affect ambiguous and intricate expressions, provided they were afterwards at liberty to put their own construction upon them. Moreover, the adoption of this rule puts an end to many questions and doubts which would otherwise arise as to the meaning and intention of the parties, which, in the absence of it, might be differently construed by different

[27] 2nd ed., p. 456.

judges; and it tends to quiet possession, by taking acts and conveyances executed beneficially for the grantees and possessors."

Note: The above seems good judicial sense. Might there not, one ventures to suggest, be some lessons here for those judges worried about the increase in litigation?

Warde v. Warde **(1852) 16 Beav, 103; 51 E.R. 716 (*Contra proferentem*)**

10.60 A husband owned an estate in Warwickshire which was charged with a jointure in favour of his wife sold it, with a release of the jointure from her, in order to buy another one in Luton Hoo. He covenanted on the sale to charge instead such real estates "as he should thereafter acquire". He contended later that this did not apply to his new Luton Hoo estate, because at the time he gave the covenant, he was in the process of acquiring it, and indeed already owned it in equity.

Sir John Romilly M.R. said, "the principle of construction of covenants is, that they are to be construed most strongly against the covenantor, and most beneficially in favour of the covenantee."

The covenant was accordingly held to apply to any estate the husband did not yet own in law at its date, so as to bind the Luton Hoo estate.

Ayles v. Cox **(1852) 16 Beav. 23; 51 E.R. 684 (Good faith construction of compensation clause by Sir John Romilly M.R.: substantial defect)**

10.61 A compensation clause was held inapplicable by Sir John Romilly M.R. to a sale of copyhold land which was in fact freehold: this was because "the thing sold turns out to be of a different nature from that contracted to be sold."

Lloyd v. Oliver **(1852) 18 Q.B. 471; 118 E.R. 178 (*Contra proferentem* approach applied to ambiguity over category of document)**

10.62 This was an instrument which might have been a promissory note or a bill of exchange. *Edis v. Bury*[28] was cited by Lord Campbell C.J. in support of the proposition that the plaintiff might in such circumstances choose to treat the instrument as a promissory note.

Lindus v. Melrose **(1858) 3 H. & N. 177; 157 E.R. 434**

10.63 A promissory note was signed by three persons who described themselves as directors of a limited company. The question was whether they had made themselves personally liable or not. The court thought not, on the words of the instrument, but made clear that they did not mean "to break in upon the rule 'verba fortius accipiuntur contra proferentem', which however ought to be applied only where other rules of construction fail".

Cook v. Waugh **(1860) 2 Giff. 201; 66 E.R. 85**

10.64 The plaintiff failed on the facts, but Sir John Stuart V.C. referred to the well-established doctrine, which he hoped would never be weakened, "that if a vendor or lessor is aware of some latent defect, and does not disclose it, the Court will consider him as acting in bad faith."

Note: The idea that there was what one might call an "original" duty, that is, not one which was parasitic on some statement being made with bearing on the matter, to the effect that a latent defect had to be disclosed by the vendor seems to have caught

[28] Above, para. 10.49.

on to some extent in the second half of the nineteenth century, no doubt under the influence of the developing law on latent defects in sales of goods.[29]

***Cox v. Coventon* (1862) 31 Beav. 378; 54 E.R. 1185**[30]

10.65 This case sets out vendor's duty of accuracy where he refers to a deed and summarises its effect.

***Fowkes v. Manchester and London Assurance Association* (1863) 3 B. & S. 917; 122 E.R. 343**

10.66 An insurance policy and the declaration were read together by the court. Thus read, the declaration had the effect of putting a gloss on the meaning of "untrue statement" so that it meant "designedly untrue statement. The principle, which was said also to be known to the civil law, "verba chartarum fortius accipiuntur contra proferentem" was applied.

***Edwards v. Wickwar* (1865) L.R. 1 Eq. 68 (Vendor's duty of good faith in what he says (or omits) about his title affirmed and condition so construed)**

10.67 Conditions of sale protected a vendor from objections to a certain underlease or any other underlease prior to a specified date. This did not protect him from the purchaser's objections to another underlease not specified and which was known to the vendor at the time. Sir Page Wood V.C. said:

"It was the clear duty of the vendor to give the fullest information which he himself possessed as to the title. The object of special conditions of sale is to protect the vendor from inquiries which he himself may be unable to satisfy, and against objections which he cannot explain away. . . . I do not wish to lay down any different rule regarding sales under the direction of this Court from that which prevails generally, but certainly the principles on which such sales are conducted ought not to be more lax as to the complete bona fides required than those which are held to govern in other cases. Here it was plainly the duty of the parties to disclose the underlease, and it would be most mischievous to allow a vendor to suppress facts known to him affecting the title, and yet compel a purchaser to accept it."

***Johnson v. Edgware, etc., Rly.* (1866) 35 Beav. 480; [55] E.R. 982 (*Contra proferentem*)**

10.68 A landlord was empowered to resume possession of any part of the land demised in case it should be required by him "for the purpose of building, planting, accommodation or otherwise". Lord Romilly, the Master of the Rolls, held that this did not allow the resumption of possession of the land for a railway company. "Otherwise" was to be read *eiusdem generis*. He said the grant "must be taken most strongly against the lessor".

[29] See Chap. 5, Sale of Land, para. 5.37 for comment on this supposed duty. *cf.* also French Code Civil Article 1641, quoted in Chap. 18; Do we need Good Faith anyway?, at para. 18.14.

[30] Noted in the Appendix to Chap. 5, Sale of Land.

***Dimmock v. Hallett* (1866) 2 Ch. App. 21**[31]

10.69 An estate was sold at auction, and the particulars among other things stated that a particular farm was let at an annual rent of £290.15s a year, when in fact the tenant at that rent had given notice to quit and moved out, and the only new tenant who had been found paid only £225. There was a condition that *mistakes in the description of the lots or any other error except as to the quantity of land, should not annul the sale but entitle the purchaser to compensation.*

Sir G.J. Turner LJ said: "I am of opinion, therefore, that the particulars contain representations which were untrue, and calculated materially to increase the apparent value of the property. The Court requires good faith in conditions of sale, and looks strictly at the statements contained in them." . . . "I think that such a condition applies to accidental slips, but not to a case like the present, where, though I do not mean to impute actual fraud, there is what in the view of a Court of equity, amounts to fraud—a misrepresentation calculated materially to mislead the purchaser."

Sir H.M. Cairns L.J. agreed and said: "The statement as to the rent was calculated to mislead, and was not prepared with the good faith which is requisite in conditions of sale. I think that a misrepresentation of this nature affects the validity of the contract, and is not a matter for compensation, but entitles the Petitioner to be discharged."

***Henderson v. Stevenson* (1875) L.R. 2 (H.C.) 470 (Ticket case)**

10.70 A ticket for a steamship had on its face only the words "Dublin Whitehaven". On its back were printed conditions excluding liability for losses of any kind. The ship was wrecked on the Isle of Man. The House of Lords considered that the company had not taken reasonable steps to draw the passenger's attention to the condition, so that it did not bind him. The Lord Chancellor noted that there was no reference upon the face of the ticket to anything other than that which was written upon the face.

"Upon that which was given to the passenger, and which he read, and of which he was aware, there was a contract complete and self-contained without reference to anything *dehors*. Those who were satisfied to hand to the passenger such a contract complete upon the face of it, and to receive his money upon its being so handed to him, must be taken, as it seems to me, to have made that contract, and that contract only, with the passenger; and the passenger, on his part, receiving the ticket in that form, and without knowing of anything beyond, must be taken to have made a contract according to that which was expressed and shewn to him.

It seems to me that it would be extremely dangerous, not merely with regard to contracts of this description, but with regard to all contracts, if it were to be held that a document complete upon the face of it can be exhibited as between two contracting parties, and, without any knowledge of anything beside, from the mere circumstance that upon the back of that document there is something else printed which has not actually been brought to and has not come to the notice of one of the contracting parties, that contracting party is to be held to have assented to that which he has not seen, of which he knows nothing, and which is not in any way ostensibly connected with that which is printed or written upon the face of the contract presented to him. He went on to say it was a question of common sense. "Can it be held that when a person is entering into a contract containing terms which *de facto* he does not know, and as to which he has received no notice, that he ought to inform

[31] Also noted in the Appendix to Chap. 5; Sale of Land.

himself upon them? My Lords, it appears to me to be impossible that that can be held."

Lord O'Hagan referred to the recent legislation on railway and canal traffic, and considered that it was satisfactory that their decision was, he thought, in harmony with the policy of Parliament, to limit the power of companies to escape the proper consequences of their own misconduct or neglect. On the question, what more the company could have done to draw the condition to the passenger's attention, he said:

"One answer—and there might be many more—was supplied by some of the cases which he cited, and in which the signature of the passenger or consignor demonstrated conclusively his conscious and intelligent assent to the bargain by which it was sought to bind him. When a company desires to impose special and most stringent terms upon its customers, in exoneration of its own liability, there is nothing unreasonable in requiring that those terms shall be distinctly declared and deliberately accepted; and that the acceptance of them shall be unequivocally shewn by the signature of the contractor."

***Phillips v. Caldcleugh* (1868) L.R. 4 Q.B. 159 (Undisclosed title defect not excluded by restrictive condition)**

10.71 This was a sale of a freehold house, which actually proved to be encumbered with various covenants. There was a condition *inter alia* that the purchaser should not investigate, nor take any objection in respect of the pre-abstract title. (There was also a condition that no error or misstatement should annul the sale but the purchaser should be entitled to compensation.) The title problem was held not to be within the condition; and the purchaser was allowed to recover the deposit and the expenses of investigating title with interest.

***Beioley v. Carter* (1869) L.R. 4 Ch. App. 230 (Exclusion clauses must fairly state the problem to be binding)**

10.72 The judgment of Lord Romilly, the Master of the Rolls, was upheld. Lord Romilly had said: "I have always thought that where the vendor wishes to preclude the purchaser from taking a particular objection to the title, which must appear on the documents submitted to him, it is essential that the vendor should, as a matter of good faith, point out, if not the objection itself, the nature of the objection, in the conditions of sale."

***Lewis v. M'Kee* (1869) L.R. 4 Ex Ch. 58 (Ticket case)**

10.73 The defendant who was the consignee of a bill of lading, endorsed it to be delivered to a third party, an agent of his for the purposes of delivery, and added a condition that the third party was to be responsible for all freight, dead freight and demurrage. The captain put in sworn evidence that he had not seen the endorsement. The court held that the defendant was bound to prove that the plaintiffs (the carriers) had assented to his condition.

Willes J. delivering the judgment of the court said that the court threw no doubt on the principles acted upon in the earlier cases of *York, Newcastle, & Berwick Railway Company v. Crisp*[32] and *Van Toll v. South Eastern Railway Company*[33]); but distinguished them, in that in those cases the circumstances were such that the party handed the document could not be unaware of the terms which he was intended to be bound to. He continued:

[32] 23 L.J. (C.P.) 125.
[33] 12 C.B. (N.S.) 75; 142 E.R. 1071.

"And if one person seeks to impose on another a liability by contract, but chooses to abstain from reading the terms of the document in which the liability is sought to be expressed, he is in this dilemma. Either he has chosen to accept the terms without taking the trouble of informing himself what they are; or if not reading, he did not assent to the terms proposed, then no action lies, because one side has intended one thing; and the other a different thing, and the transaction is vitiated by mutual error. The first of these alternatives is probably the practical conclusion at which a jury would arrive. But here there is no such dilemma. The ship-owners were already entitled to receive freight on delivery of the goods; the contract they relied on was that contained in the bill of lading. The delivery taking place under circumstances in which it would, prima facie, have bound the defendant, the defendant shews, neither under the statute nor otherwise, a transfer of the liability to Watney & Keene, except by the plaintiff's assent. But he cannot rely on this; that which would have been proof of it if assented to, not having come to the knowledge of the plaintiffs. If in the ordinary course of business a person were under the obligation of looking at a document before acting on the supposition that it was in order, and that the customary terms were stipulated for, it might be otherwise. But the document here is a bill of lading . . . [and essentially not one where a condition of that kind would be expected]". The defendant's appeal accordingly failed.

Note: This early case raises the central problem about exclusion clauses: when are they really assented to by the other party so as to become part of the contract and when are they still mere wishes in the mind of the offeror.

Torrance v. Bolton (1872) L.R. 14 Eq. 124 (Exclusion clause not applied because insufficient opportunity to appreciate detail of defect)

10.74 The particulars of sale and the conditions of sale in an auction sale were to different effect: the former described the property as freehold and subject only to a life tenancy of someone in her seventieth year, the latter as subject to a mortgage. The conditions of sale were read at the auction, not being available for purchasers beforehand, but the plaintiff, who was deaf, did not hear them distinctly or pay real attention.

Sir R. Malins V.C. firmly rejected the argument that fraud had to be shown for a contract to be set aside in equity, and granted the purchaser rescission, labelling the ground for rescission "common mistake", but in fact qualifying this by saying. "And the mistake being one into which the Plaintiff has been led by the grossly negligent and improper mode in which the Defendant has conducted the sale, though I am satisfied there was no intention to mislead, the consequence is that the contract must be rescinded."

Taylor v. Liverpool and Great Western Steam Co. (1874) L.R. 9 Q.B. 546 (Bill of lading—_contra proferentem_)

10.75 A bill of lading contained an exception for acts of God, the Queen's enemies, pirates, robbers, thieves, vermin, barratry. . . . The question that arose was whether "thieves" included persons on board the ship, or had to mean persons from outside. Lush J. said: "The word is ambiguous, and being of doubtful meaning, it must receive such a construction, as is most in favour of the shipper, and not such as is most in favour of the the shipowner, for whose benefit the exceptions are framed; for it it was intended to give to it the larger meaning which is now contended for, the intention to give the shipowner that protection ought to have been expressed in clear and unambiguous language."

Archbald J. agreed with Lush J.

Section 9 of the Vendor and Purchaser Act 1874

10.76 "A vendor or purchaser of real or leasehold estate in England, or their representatives respectively, may at any time or times and from time to time apply in a summary way to a judge of the Court of Chancery in England in chambers, in respect of any requisitions or objections, or any claim for compensation, or any other question arising out of or connected with the contract (*not being a question affecting the existence or validity of the contract*) and the judge shall make such order upon the application as to him shall appear just, and shall order how and by whom all or any of the costs of and incident to the application shall be borne and paid. The first part of . . ."[34]

Note: this section is reproduced because of the effect it may have had on good faith law in England. As will be seen, cases brought under the Vendor and Purchaser Act 1874 began to crowd out other real property cases over the next few decades. Real property[35] *was a major investment then in the way that securities are today, so that it was broadly true to say that what affected real property cases affected property. The problem was that the procedure, which was summary and thus no doubt extremely attractive, seems to have discouraged plaintiffs from bringing good faith points as to quality, possibly because it was felt that these tended to attack the validity of the contract, while good faith title points were envisaged as a necessary part of the procedure of sifting title. At all events, it seems possible that the artificial prominence given to title points over quality points contributed to the demise of good faith at the end of the century. One can say, Title is different, but there is no good reason to deny general application to good faith points about quality. (Perhaps we could have a summary procedure for all good-faith points now?)*

At all events, good faith rules continued to be applied to exclusion clauses of various kinds at least in title applications, under the Act.[36]

Harnett v. Baker **(1875) L.R. 20 Eq. 50 (Good faith construction of condition affirmed by equity court)**

10.77 A condition of sale required the purchaser to assume that a certain Dr Clarke was absolutely entitled to the beneficial ownership of the property in question at his death. In fact his title was not perfected for some time after his death.

Sir R. Malins V.C. said ". . . it is clear that conditions of sale fairly and honestly made, not founded on any erroneous statement, are binding. But it is equally clear, and I think it is most important it should be understood, that although a vendor is at liberty to introduce special conditions of sale he must not make them the means of entrapping the purchaser, and they must not be founded on any erroneous statement of fact. There must be fair and honest dealing in the transaction, and on that principle only special conditions are sanctioned."

Harris v. GWR **(1876) 1 Q.B.D. 515 (Lush J, Mellor J., Blackburn J.) (Ticket case)**

10.78 The only point of note is one made by Blackburn J: "But if the bailor and bailee agree that the goods shall be deposited on other terms than those

[34] Italics supplied.
[35] See elsewhere in this book, passim.
[36] See *Re Marsh and Earl Granville* (1882) 24 Ch. D. 11, ***Re Davis and Cavey*** (1888) 40 Ch. D. 601, ***Re Sandbach and Edmondson's Contract*** [1891] 1 Ch. 99, ***Re Scott and Alvarez' Contract*** [1895] 2 Ch. 603 (although in the last two cases there was no breach of the good-faith duty), ***Re Leyland and Taylor's Contract*** [1900] 2 Ch. 625 (although

implied by law, the duty of the bailee, and consequently his responsibility, is determined by the terms on which both parties have agreed. And it is clear law that where there is a writing, into which the terms of any agreement are reduced, the terms are to be regulated by that writing. And though one of the parties may not have read the writing, yet, in general, he is bound to the other by those terms; and that, I apprehend, is on the ground that, by assenting to the contract thus reduced to writing, he represents to the other side that he has made himself acquainted with the contents of that writing and assents to them, and so induces the other side to act upon that representation by entering into the contract with him, and is consequently precluded from denying that he did make himself acquainted with those terms. But then the preclusion only exists when the case is brought within the rule so carefully and accurately laid down by Parke, B. in delivering his judgment of the Exchequer in *Freeman v. Cooke*,[37] that is, if he "means his representation to be acted upon, and it is acted upon accordingly: or if, whatever a man's real intentions may be, he so conduct himself that a reasonable man would take the representation to be true, and believe that it was meant that he should act upon it, and did act upon it as true."

***Parker v. South Eastern Railway Co.* (1877) 2 C.P.D. 416 (Ticket case)**

10.79 The plaintiff left his bag in the railway left luggage office. He was given a ticket, which he did not read; he said he thought it was a receipt. It had said "see back", and on the back were conditions, limiting the railway's liability for loss of baggage to baggage under £2 in value. The plaintiff's loss as a result of the theft of his bag was in excess of this.

Mellish L.J. thought the plaintiff would have been bound had he known that the ticket contained conditions. Since he did not, he would grant a new trial, the question to be put to the jury being not the question whether the plaintiff was under any obligation, in the exercise of reasonable and proper caution, to read or to make himself aware of the condition, but (since the Plaintiff was under no obligation to read the ticket) whether the railway company had done what was reasonably sufficient to give the plaintiff notice of the condition.[38]

Baggallay L.J. agreed. Bramwell L.J. (in the minority) delivered a thoughtful judgment also. He considered that if the clerk had said "Read that" as he put the ticket into the plaintiff's hands, it would have made a difference. "The truth is, people are content to take these things on trust. They know that there is a form which is always used—they are satisfied it is not unreasonable, because people do not usually put unreasonable terms into their contracts. If they did, then dealing would soon be stopped. Besides, unreasonable practices would be known. The very fact of not looking at the paper shews that this confidence exists . . . I think there is an implied understanding that there is no condition unreasonable to the knowledge of the party tendering the document and not insisting on its being read—no condition not relevant to the matter in hand."

He felt that what the clerk did *was* the equivalent of "Read that," since he put into the hands of the plaintiffs (there were two cases) a ticket which they knew contained printed matter and "in all good sense and reason must be

there the breach was insufficiently material), ***Re Haedicke and Lipinski's Contract*** [1901] 2 Ch. 666 affirmed by the Court of Appeal in ***Becker v. Partridge*** [1966] 2 Q.B. 155 and ***Re Brine and Davies Contract*** [1935] Ch. 388.

[37] 2 Ex. 654 at 663.

[38] He distinguished tickets which "everyone knows contain conditions", such as bills of lading.

supposed to relate to the matter in hand." So he must be held to consent to its terms.

***Taylor v. St Helen's Corporation* (1877) 6 Ch. D. 264**

10.80 In this case Jessel M.R., who seems sometimes to have flirted with the new literalism, doubted the maxim *contra proferentem*; however, as Chitty[39] points out, the cases relied on by him turn on the construction of wills, and in any case the House of Lords affirmed the *contra preferentem* maxim thereafter.[40]

***Re Banister* (1879) 12 Ch. D. 131**

10.81 The purchaser sought to have a contract for the sale of land rescinded. The contract had contained a condition that the *purchaser was to be satisfied with a declaration by a certain Esther Banister that she had held the land since 1835, on the footing that it was not accurately known how she acquired the property*. The purchaser discovered after the contract that she was a mortgagee in possession, and in a fiduciary character, as executrix under her father's will, so that the condition was misleading. Fry J. at first instance said:

"There are several things which are quite clear with regard to a contract founded on conditions of sale. One is this, that the vendor, who means to exclude the purchaser from his common law right to have a good title shewn, must do so by explicit and clear words. Another is, that, if the vendor seeks to exclude the purchaser by a statement of fact, he must prove the fact to be true, and the statement of fact must be an honest and fair one; it must not for the purpose in hand be a part of the truth only; it must, so far as that purpose is concerned, be the truth and whole truth. It must therefore not mislead an ignorant person. One of the main reasons why the Courts have treated conditions of sale in this way is, that the vendor is a person who knows, and he is stipulating with the purchaser, a person who does not know. It is therefore, of course fair that the person who does know should express his meaning so as to be perfectly intelligible to the person who does not know. Another thing equally plain is this, that where the conditions of sale are framed in bad faith, so as in effect to trap the purchaser, the Court will not hold him to be bound. It is also perfectly plain that, where the sale is under the direction of the Court, the Court will lean, if possible, to a more exact requirement of good faith and honesty on the part of the vendor; it will endeavour to insist upon that fair, straightforward, honest, open dealing which ought to characterise transactions between vendor and purchaser . . ." On the facts before him he found there had been no trap.

On appeal, on further evidence, Jessel M.R. also adopted the good faith principle. He said: "First of all, no one will doubt for a moment,—and the *dicta* on this subject are numerous—that in sales by the Court there should be as least as much good faith shewn towards the purchaser as, and perhaps a little more than, is required by ordinary vendors out of Court. The old Court of Chancery—and this Court is its successor—has always felt bound to see that purchasers are fairly and honestly dealt with in every respect . . . . "He went on to say that here an innocent misrepresentation by the conveyancing counsel of the Court, who was the vendor's agent, would rank as a misrepresentation by the vendor, and thus if it was shown that "the material statements made, which were either expressly or impliedly made, were untrue, the purchaser would not be held to be bound by the condition—that is, . . . bound

[39] *Contracts*, 27th edn. at 12–071 n. 18.
[40] See ***Neill v. Duke of Devonshire*** (1882) 8 App. Cas. 135.

to the extent of being compelled to take the title." He agreed with the argument that by putting in the condition asking the purchaser to assume that Esther Banister was entitled in fee simple in possession from 1835 on, the inferential statement was that "so far as he knew anything to the contrary, she was so seised and entitled in fee simple".

He felt, however, that there was a good holding title, and the purchaser was not entitled to ask for more.

10.82 Brett L.J. noted there was no want of good faith on the part of the vendor himself, since the unintentional misrepresentation had been by his agent. However, the conveyancing counsel of the court ranked as an agent of the vendor, and because of two doctrines of equity, he considered the purchaser entitled to rescission. These were:

(a) "the doctrine, that if there be a misrepresentation of facts, however innocently made, the Court of Equity will not enforce the performance of the contract" and
(b) "that the authorities shew that in a Court of Equity that requirement or insistance that a certain state of things shall be assumed does by implication contain an assertion that no facts are known to the persons who require it which would make that assumption a wrong one according to those facts,"; so that "There is, therefore, an implied representation which arises from the insistance that certain matters should be assumed."

Cotton L.J. drew a technical distinction between any entitlement of the purchaser to rescind on the ground of misrepresentation, and his entitlement to resist specific performance. He said the latter was in point here, although in practice there was no difference in the result. He considered the condition was misleading, and the purchaser entitled not to be compelled to buy. He said, "Now I take it that conditions of sale must be fair, and for the purposes of the present case I think one may lay down this, that in conditions of sale there must not be made any representation or condition which can mislead the purchaser as to the facts within the knowledge of the vendor ..." The question here was "whether or no it is shewn that there were within the knowledge of the vendor facts which made the 10th condition of sale a misleading condition."

He thought there were, in that the vendor had not understood the import of the facts he knew and had not disclosed them for that reason.

***Neill v. Duke of Devonshire* (1882) 8 App. Cas. 135 at 149 (*Contra proferentem* principle affirmed, at least in deeds for valuable consideration)**

10.83 The House of Lords accepted in passing that, as Lord Selbourne put it, "It is well settled that the words of a deed, executed for valuable consideration, ought to be construed, as far as they properly may, in favour of the grantee."

***Burton v. English* (1883) 12 Q.B.D. 218, C.A. (Restrictive construction of exclusion in charterparty)**

10.84 A charterparty contained a stipulation that the ship should be provided with a deck cargo if required, at full freight, but "at merchant's risk". It was held that "at merchant's risk" did not exclude general average contribution from the shipowners in respect of deck cargo jettisoned to save the ship. Brett M.R. said, "The stipulation is in favour of the shipowners, and is in restriction of their liability under their contract to carry. The general rule is that where there is any doubt as to the construction of any stipulation in a contract, one ought to construe it strictly against the party in whose favour it has been made." He held that general average contribution did not arise from an implied contract, but from the old Rhodian laws, which became incorporated into the law of England as the law of the ocean. Baggallay L.J. agreed.

Bowen L.J. based his judgment additionally on the rules about exclusion clauses: "There is in the second place another rule of construction which one would bring to bear upon this charterparty, and that is, that one must see if this stipulation which we have got to construe is introduced by way of exception or in favour of one of the parties to the contract, and if so, we must take care not to give it an extension beyond what is fairly necessary, because those who wish to introduce words in a contract in order to shield themselves ought to do so in clear words. . . ."

"But still, what is the sound principle to apply? Why, it is that those who wish to make exceptions in their own favour, and by which they are to be relieved from the ordinary laws of the sea, ought to do so in clear words . . ."

***Re Marsh and Earl Granville* (1882) 24 Ch.D.11**

10.85 The purchaser raised two objections to the title in a summons *under the Vendor and Purchaser Act 1874*. One failed, the other was successful. This one was his complaint that by a condition of sale the title was to begin with a conveyance of 1845, but that this conveyance proved to be a voluntary conveyance by someone who had declared himself a trustee, but with power reserved to revoke the trusts.

Fry J., at first instance, said, "The principles applicable to the decision of the question appear to me to be not in dispute. According to the view which I take, a vendor who desires to limit the rights of a purchaser must do so by explicit and plain conditions, and he must tell the truth, and all the truth, which is relevant to the matter in hand. The reason for this is twofold. In the first place, as I observed in *In re Banister*,[41] the vendor knows the condition of the title, and the purchaser does not, and that puts upon the vendor the burden of being very explicit in his description. In the next place, the descriptions in the contract, or conditions of sale, are the only materials which the purchaser has for deliberating upon before he enters into the purchase. He knows as much as is told him and no more, and, therefore, he ought to be put in possession of everything, so far as it is touched upon by the conditions of sale, which is likely to influence his mind in determining whether he will buy or not."

In the Court of Appeal, Baggallay L.J. said he did not think there was "such a full and explicit description of the deed given as he [the purchaser] was entitled to"; and Cotton L.J. said, "I think that the principle is this, that the Court will not compel a purchaser to take an estate with less than the ordinary title which the law gives him unless the stipulation on which the vendor relies for the purpose of excluding what would otherwise be the purchaser's legal right is fair and explicit. I think that the test of its being fair and explicit is whether it discloses all facts within the knowledge of the vendor which are material to enable the purchaser to determine whether or not he will buy the property subject to the stipulation limiting his right to the ordinary length of title."

Bowen L.J. agreed that the purchaser was not bound by the condition, and might insist on his requisition as to title. The result was that the title was not such as could be forced on him.

[41] 12 Ch.D. 131.

***Heywood v. Mallalieu* (1883) 25 Ch.D. 357 ("subject to any existing rights and easements of whatever nature" not extended to cover breach of good faith)**

10.86 An auction sale was subject to a printed condition in a common form that the lot was sold subject to any existing rights and easements of whatever nature. However, the printed particulars made no mention of any easement or any claim to any easement. It emerged later that the plaintiff's solicitors had instructed surveyors to value the property, and these surveyors had received a letter from a Miss Walker asserting the existence of a right inter alia to use the kitchen of the property for washing and drying. The solicitor dealing with the case, when informed, had decided not to make any further inquiry because he was not going to put other people on their guard about mere claims. The purchaser gave notice to terminate the contract for lack of title, while the vendor persisted in seeking specific performance, relying on the condition. The defendant purchaser obtained his judgment. Bacon V.C. said: "I impute no bad intention to the Plaintiff or his advisers, but I say that a man, knowing what this Plaintiff knew, who does not more fully express what he knows, does not do his duty."

***Brewer v. Brown* (1885) 28 Ch.D. 309 ("No mistake in the description . . . or other error shall annul . . .": strictly confined to mistakes not due to lack of good faith)**

10.87 Sale particulars of a freehold villa in West Ham contained the following statement. "The garden is tastefully laid out and inclosed by a rustic wall, with tradesmen's side entrance." There was a condition that no mistake in the description of the premises or other error whatsoever in the particulars should annul the sale, but compensation should be given. The plaintiff entered into the contract with the intention, known to the defendant, of building cottages on the northern end of the garden (into which the side entrance opened) with that side entrance as their access. In fact the side wall did not belong to the property, and the right to use the side entrance was only on suffrance. The difference in value, on the plaintiff's own evidence, between the property with and without the wall, was only about £100 out of a purchase price of £1,300. North J. thought the inference "anyone would draw" was the same as the plaintiff's inference, so that it was "the vendor's duty to inform a person buying from him what the real state of things was, and, whatever his duty might have been in other respects, it was all the more incumbent on him when he chose to put that statement [the above statement] in the particulars. "He found on the evidence that the plaintiff "believed he was buying this piece of land with the wall and with a frontage to the side road, and he contemplated the possibility of building on it. At any rate it is a piece of land that might be built upon, and what he would have if I gave him compensation would be a piece of land without a lateral frontage, and without the possibility of being built upon." That being so, he thought it was not a case for compensation, and the plaintiff was entitled to rescission. North J. said "I do not omit to notice that compensation can only be insisted on where there is a mistake in the description of the premises or error in the particulars. I do not think that accurately describes what took place in this case. Here the omission is to state in the particulars something that was essential the vendor should tell the purchaser when entering into the contract of sale."

***Birrell v. Dryer* (1884) 9 App. Cas. 345 (who is the proferens?)**

10.88 A policy of marine insurance contained an exception where there had been navigation in the St Lawrence between certain dates. The question arose whether the gulf of the St Lawrence river was included. The *contra proferentem* rule was held not applicable since the gulf was plainly included. Lord Selborne said, "I do not think that the evidence discloses any ambiguity or uncertainty, sufficient to prevent the application to this case of the ordinary rules and principles of construction ... There does not appear to me to be any necessity for resorting to presumptions in favour of or against either party, whether founded on the rule fortius contra proferentem, or on the onus of proving an exception from the general affirmative terms of this contract".

Lord Blackburn referred to the reliance which had been placed on the maxim. He said "I do not think the description of the district excluded can be considered as the words of one party more than the other. The shipowner knowing where he is likely to employ his ship, and that he does not intend to use her in some district, generally puts on the slip a description of that district in order to induce the underwriters to agree to a lower premium."

Lord Watson said about the argument that the underwriters were the proferentes "That the underwriters may be rightly held to be the proferentes with regard to many conditions in a policy I do not doubt; *whether they ought to be so held depends, in each case, upon the character and substance of the condition.*[42] In the present case there are many considerations which lead to the inference that the clause in question is not one constructed and inserted by the appellants alone, and for their own protection merely. It was, in point of fact, inserted in the contract by the agent of the respondents; and it is in form a warranty by them that their vessel will not be navigated in certain waters, a matter which it was entirely within their power to regulate. These consideration point rather to the respondents themselves being the proferentes; but I think the substance of the warranty must be looked to; and that, in substance, its authorship is attributable to both parties alike. The main object of the clause is to define the limits within which the vessel is to be kept whilst she is navigated under the policy; and that appears to me to be as much the concern of the shipowner as of the underwriters. To define the limits within which the vessel is to be navigated, for the purposes of a time policy, is, in principle, precisely the same thing as to describe the voyage for which a vessel is insured under an ordinary policy. In both cases it is a definition of the subject-matter of the insurance, a term of the contract, the settlement of which must, in my opinion, be regarded, in a case like the present, as the deliberate act of both parties.

Although the rule of construction *contra proferentem* may not apply, I think it was rightly argued for the respondents that, seeing the clause in question occurs in the shape of an exception from a leading term of the policy which gives the vessel leave to navigate in any waters, it can only receive effect in so far as it is plain and unambiguous. But I am not satisfied that there is any ambiguity, such as will avail the respondents, to be found in the clause when it is read as a whole".

Re Terry and White's Contract (1886) 32 Ch. D. 454 (Vendor and purchaser summons: more released attitude to recission clauses)

10.89 This was a summons by the purchaser *under the Vendor and Purchaser Act 1874* for specific performance with compensation, while the vendor wanted to rescind the contract under a term permitting him to do so. Land was sold in lots said to total over 4 acres. In fact this was an "innocent" misstatement, the total being about 3 acres. There were a number of conditions of sale including one which provided that "Each lot is believed and shall be taken to be correctly described as to quantity and otherwise ... and the respective

[42] Italics supplied.

purchasers ... shall be deemed to buy with full knowledge of the state and condition of the property as to repairs and otherwise, and no error, misstatment, or mis-description shall annul the sale, nor shall any compensation be allowed in respect thereof. There was also a right for the vendors to rescind if the purchaser should insist on any objection or requisition which the respective vendors should be unable, or on the ground of expense or otherwise unwilling to answer, comply with, or remove ...

Lord Esher complained about how wrongheaded the notion was that there were differences in the approach of the common law courts and the old courts of equity. Dealing with the summons itself, he said: "there having arisen a mistake, an innocent mistake, what are the rights of the parties?

Now I do not doubt that a Court of Equity would, if the mistake had been made by the vendor, as a general rule, though not always and invariably, have aided the purchaser to obtain specific performance, but giving compensation so as to make up for the mistake. If the mistake was so great as, in the opinion of the Court of Equity, to affect the whole substance and foundation of the contract, I believe that the Court would not have granted specific performance to the purchaser, but would have said that the contract was to be treated as if it had never existed. That was where there was not merely a large error, but where the error was *so great as to go to the whole foundation and substance of the contract, so that it would be impossible to conceive that the parties ever would have entered into the contract if the mistake had not existed*. But, where the vendor came for specific performance, and had made an error, I think that the Court of Equity never would grant him specific performance, if he had made a substantial error to the injury of the purchaser, and *would have left him to any remedy which he might have by bringing an action on the contract*. But it does not follow that the interpretation of the contract in the action, if the vendor had been left to bring his action at law, would have been different to the interpretation put upon the contract by the Court of Equity; the interpretation would have precisely the same, but he could not get in a Court of Common Law a remedy by way of specific performance.

10.90 Vendors finding themselves in this difficulty, that they could not get specific performance, and could not rescind the contract of their own accord—one party to a contract not being allowed to rescind it without the consent of the other—but that the purchaser could get specific performance against them with a compensation to be settled by the Court, desired to protect themselves, and it was in order to protect themselves against that which would have been the law without conditions of sale, that conditions of sale were put in to meet that state of the law.... How are they to be construed? To my mind they are to be construed in precisely the same manner in a Court of Law as in a Court of Equity. They are to be construed according to the ordinary interpretation of language as used in business, unless there is something in the contract or something in the subject-matter which obliges the Court—not which entitles the Court, but which obliges the Court—to read the language other than in its ordinary sense."[43]

Lindley L.J. also said that it was "necessary not to confound the principles or rules by which contracts are interpreted, with the principles or rules which guide the Court in enforcing or declining to enforce specific performance.

He said that the proposition that conditions such as the condition relating to mistakes only applied to "comparatively trivial and unimportant errors, mis-statements and misdescriptions" was not warranted as a general statement. "The proposition is only true in certain classes of cases."[44]

[43] Italics supplied.

[44] He did not explain what these classes of cases were. In *Jacobs v. Revell* (1900) it was suggested by Buckley J. that the class of cases he had in mind was the class of cases

. . . Conditions of sale, like all other contracts, must be construed with reference to the subject-matter to which they relate, and *upon the assumption that the parties to them are dealing fairly with each other*. Being deliberately prepared by the vendor, who knows much more of the subject-matter to which they relate than a purchaser usually knows, or can know, conditions of sale, where their language is at all ambiguous, or where the application of that language to the property sold gives rise to difficulty, *are always construed or applied in such a way as to prevent the vendor from dealing unfairly with the purchaser. But the same observations are true of all other contracts similarly circumstanced.*"[45]

He went on to deal with the cases which had been cited to him, and *inter alia* made it plain that where there had been a sufficiently serious fraud or misrepresentation, the whole contract was vitiated, including the condition in question.[46] However, he could see no reason in this case why the vendor could not rely on the rescission-clause, since it covered this kind of situation, and was not exercised "*mala fide* or without reason".[47]

Lopes L.J. dissented.

Note: The rescission clause seems to have been regarded as a mere substitute for what the court might have done anyway, rather than a special benefit to the vendor.

Nottingham Patent Brick & Tile Co v. Butler **(1886) 16 Q.B.D. 778 ("Any incorrect statement, error or omission . . . is not to annul the sale . . . nor . . . any compensation in respect thereof": pre-contractual statement literally true but in breach of good faith—purchaser allowed rescission despite conditions of sale preventing recission)**

10.91 The property sold turned out to be burdened with restrictive covenants, having been part of a building scheme. The vendor's solicitor, on being asked whether the land was not subject to restrictive covenants which prevented its use as a brickfield had said he was unaware of the defect in title. He omitted to mention that he had not read the earlier title deeds in his possession.

Lord Esher said that a Court of Equity would never have enforced a contract under such circumstances. He relied in the main on the positive misstatement as to the title by the vendor's solicitor prior to the contract.

Lindley L.J. said that he thought on the evidence the vendor himself was a bona fide purchaser for value without notice of the restrictive covenants, but even so, a purchaser might have been faced with litigation in which he would have to prove the absence of notice; and "It is to prevent purchasers from being embarrassed by any such chance of litigation that the Court of Chancery has never compelled a purchaser to take a title, which might be a good holding title, but which might possibly, and very probably, lead to an immediate litigation with some other person."

The question then arose whether the conditions might enable the vendor to escape. (These were inter alia ". . . any incorrect statement, error, or

"in which a vendor is seeking to force on a purchaser what he did not contract to buy. He was dealing with the equitable grounds for refusing specific performance." It is more likely perhaps that he was referring to the good faith construction of contracts of sale, since the subject matter at this point is construction, not equity's discretion. See also the next passage quoted, in which he affirms good faith principles of construction.

[45] Italics supplied.

[46] As, *e.g.* in ***Dimmock v. Hallett*** 2 Ch. App. 21.

[47] For a discussion of the court's control over the exercise of these clauses, see Chap. 12, The After-Sale Relationship.

omission found in the particulars or these special conditions, is not to annul the sale, nor entitle the purchaser to be discharged from his purchase, nor is the vendor or purchaser to claim to be allowed any compensation in respect thereof.") Lindley L.J. felt that the conditions might technically cover the specific blot, but that the vendor "ought to have used a condition pointing to the blot much more specifically than the actual conditions have done, and it would not be right to enforce specific performance of the contract without the attention of the purchasers having been much more closely drawn to the blot."

He thought the purchasers were entitled to rescind the contract and recover their deposit, he thought they were, because of the misrepresentation implicit in the partial disclosure of the blot.

"If there was nothing beyond that to which I have already alluded, I should have thought that they could not have got back their deposit. The case would have stood thus, that, if they had chosen, they could have completed, taking the title, which, in the circumstances which I have assumed, would be a good holding title, and, if they did not choose to do that, I do not think they would have been entitled to get back the deposit. But the case does not rest there. (He then referred to the misrepresentation, which he said was "such a misrepresentation tainting the whole of the contract"; and allowed the purchaser rescission and recovery of the deposit.) Lord Esher and Lopes L.J. agreed with Lindley L.J.

***Re Hargreaves and Thompson's Contract* (1886) 32 Ch. D. 454 (Decision widening scope of section 9 of the Vendor and Purchaser Act 1874, encouraging popularity of summary procedure)**

10.92 The Court of Appeal (Cotton, Lindley and Lopes L.J.J.) all agreed that the jurisdiction under section 9 of the Vendor and Purchaser Act 1874 was wide enough to allow them to order the return of the deposit and interest, in cases where the vendor had not shown good title.

Note: This case is noted merely as background. It increased the usefulness of the procedure under the Vendor and Purchaser Act 1874. For the relevance to good faith, see the note to section 9 of the Act above, noted at the year 1874.

***Re Beyfus and Master's Contract* (1888) 39 Ch. D. 110 (Vendor and purchaser summons: *contra proferentem* approach to condition)**

10.93 A house was offered for sale stated to be held under a lease dated July 11, 1845, with which title was to commence. There was a condition which stated "the description of the property in the particulars is believed to be correct, but if any error shall be found therein the same shall not annul the sale, nor shall any compensation be allowed in respect thereof." The property was in fact held on an underlease. The Court of Appeal (Lindley, Bowen and Fry L.J.J.) all held that the exclusion clause related only to the physical description of the property.

Bowen L.J. pointed out that an intending purchaser could satisfy himself by inspection whether the physical property had been described with sufficient accuracy, while he could not know of title defects till he had received the abstract.

Fry L.J. agreed, and said it was the natural meaning of the condition, but added a good faith reason also "because we ought not to give an enlarged meaning to words which restrict the rights of a purchaser in relation to a description which he has no opportunity of verifying."

***Re Davis and Cavey* (1888) 40 Ch. D. 601 (Vendor and purchaser summons: good faith rules applied to title defect)**

10.94 This was another Vendor and Purchaser summons. At an auction sale property described as "leasehold business premises" was sold, under conditions that no objection should be made in respect of anything contained in the lease to the vendors, and that the title should commence with that lease. No opportunity was given to the purchasers to inspect the lease, and the property was bought by a purchaser who had not seen it. It emerged that the lease actually contained covenants against carrying on any trade or business. The court held that the vendor could not force this on the purchaser.

The purchaser had also asked for his deposit back but was not allowed this. Stirling J. considered that *Re Hargreaves and Thompson's Contract*[48] allowed the return of the deposit in a summons under the section only where this would not entail an attack on the validity of the contract. Since there was in existence a condition of the contract that the purchaser was bound to make no objection to anything contained in the original lease, he would have to bring a separate action for the return of the deposit.

Note: This is a case which needs to be seen strictly in the light of the limited jurisdiction under the Vendor and Purchaser Act 1874, and not as in any way limiting the application of the good faith rules.

***Re Fawcett and Holmes Contract* (1889) 42 Ch. D. 150 (Condition of Sale allowed to "bite" because defect insufficiently substantial for rescission)**

10.95 This seems to have been an appeal by the purchaser from a vendor and purchaser summons. The contract was for the sale of land which proved to be subject to a personal covenant; and had also been misdescribed as to area (the contract sold 1372 square yds, but in fact 339 had already been sold off; however the land being sold was fenced, so that, as Fry L.J. said in argument, what you got was what you saw. The purchaser was obliged to complete, albeit with compensation, the defect being held insufficiently "material and substantial" to take the case out of the condition. The condition was "The description of the property is believed to be . . . correct but if any error . . . shall be found therein . . . shall not annul the sale.")

***Cornish v. Accident Insurance Co* (1889) 23 Q.B.D. 453 (*Contra proferentem* only where ambiguity)**

10.96 A policy of insurance contained an exception for accidents happening "by exposure of the insured to obvious risk of injury". The insured died through attempting to cross the main line of a railway in front of an approaching train. Lindley L.J. thought the case was within the exclusion. ". . . to ascertain the true meaning of the exception the whole document must be studied and the object of the parties to it must be steadily borne in mind. The object of the contract is to insure against accidental death and injuries, and the contract must not be construed so as to defeat that object, nor so as to render it practically illusory. . . . In a case on the line, in a case of real doubt, the policy ought to be construed most strongly against the insurers; they frame the policy and insert the exceptions. But this principle ought only to be applied for the purpose of removing a doubt, not for the purpose of creating a doubt, or magnifying an ambiguity, when the circumstances of the case raise no real difficulty." He thought the case plainly within the exception.

[48] (1886) 32 Ch. D. 454.

Re Sandbach and Edmondson's Contract [1891] 1 Ch. 99 Condition inserted honestly and without fault on the part of the vendor upheld despite significant effect on contract: application of good faith rules affirmed)

10.97 The purchaser was required to assume that a certain John Bouchier died intestate and without an heir before 1870. The vendor *had had reason to believe this to be true*, and had offered to search for proof of it at the purchaser's expense.

Lord Halsbury LC affirmed the judgment of the court below refusing specific performance. He said that the vendor was not obliged to *explain the legal effect of the assumption*, nor did it make any difference that the blot, if it was one, was very important. "I should quite agree that if there were an actual misstatement or such an imperfect statement of the facts as in the result makes what is stated untrue, the condition would be so tainted by falsehood that it could not be insisted on as against the purchaser misled by such taint of falsehood".

Richardson, Spence & Co v. Rowntree [1894] A.C. 217 (H.L.) (Ticket case)

10.98 *Parker v. SE Railway*[49] was affirmed. The passenger on a steamship had been given a ticket folded up so that no conditions were visible. The question before the House of Lords was whether there was sufficient evidence on which the jury could properly find, as they had, that the passenger had not known there were conditions, and that the company had not taken reasonable steps to draw them to her attention. Lord Ashbourne's judgment, concurring with the others, shows the way in which the circumstances of the sale were taken into account.

"The ticket in question in this case was for a steerage passenger—a class of people of the humblest description, many of whom have little education and some of them none. I think, having regard to the facts here, the smallness of the type in which the alleged conditions were printed, the absence of any calling of attention to the alleged conditions and the stamping in red ink across them, there was quite sufficient evidence to justify the learned judge in letting the case go to the jury."

Note: This approach is in some ways reminiscent of the older cases' approach to "undue influence" on women and vulnerable people. It is likely to be simply an affirmation of the Know your Purchaser rule that is prevalent in good faith law, that, when you have a duty to inform a purchaser, it is not the Man on the Clapham Omnibus, but the kind of purchaser you are in fact likely to have for those goods, services, etc.; and you will need to consider whether he or she is likely to be educated, not educated, in a hurry, short of money for inquiries, or whatever it may be. Compare also Smith v. Bush[50] *and the at-first-blush curiously limited approach to exclusion clauses in a building society surveyor's valuation (no exclusionary effect on a purchaser of low-cost houses).*

Re Scott and Alvarez' Contract [1895] 2 Ch. 603 (Deeming provision as to title: no breach of good faith, condition therefore applied but vendor refused a specific performance)

10.99 The vendor took out a vendor and purchaser summons for a declaration as to his title and for specific performance of the contract. It was held at first instance that his title was sufficient, given that his liability as to title was

[49] Above, para. 10.79.
[50] [1990] 1 A.C. 831.

restricted by a condition (set out below). The purchaser subsequently did further research into the title, and found it was in fact a bad title. *It did not appear that this was within the vendor's knowledge, actual, constructive or imputed.* Thus there was no want of good faith case which could be made against the vendor, who was truly innocent in the full sense of the word: the event making the title bad was a previous fraudulent transfer which he could not have known about. The purchaser obtained leave to appeal, seeking repayment of his deposit, and to put in the fresh evidence regarding the title, and the condition thus had to be considered by the court. The condition was that the purchaser should not make any objection or requisition in respect of the intermediate title to the lease of the property, but should assume that an assignment of the lease vested in the assignees a good title for the residue of the term.

The Court of Appeal held in its discretion that because the title was in fact entirely bad, the vendor might not have specific performance, since it would be wrong to force such a title on the purchaser; but the purchaser might not have the return of his deposit since there was, in the circumstances of the case, no breach at law.

The other two judges agreed, without much useful discussion.

Note: It is important to bear in mind that this was a no-fault case; and thus, that no implied term of good faith was argued, or could be argued, on behalf of the purchaser as regards title. In these circumstances, it would follow that the condition would bite according to its wording.

***Greenwood v. Leather Shod Wheel Co* [1900] 1 Ch. 421 (Deeming provision: good faith affirmed as general contractual principle)**

10.100 The Companies Act 1867, by section 38, enacted that every prospectus should specify the dates and names of the parties to any contract entered into by the company or the promoters, directors or trustees thereof, and that any prospectus which did not should be deemed "fraudulent" on the part of the promoters, directors and officers of the company knowingly issuing it.

The object with which the company was formed was to acquire and work certain patents for leather tyres for vehicle wheels. The prospectus listed orders etc in glowing terms, then in smaller print mentioned an agreement dated February 5, 1897, being an agreement for sale to the company, it said, "of the patents and rights at a profit". It then said "There may be other agreements as to the formation of the company, the subscription to the capital, or otherwise, to none of which is the company a party, and which may technically fall within section 38 of the Companies Act, 1867. Subscribers will be held to have had notice of all these contract and to have waived all right to be supplied with particulars of such contract, and to have agreed with the company, as trustees for the directors and other person liable, not to make any claims whatsoever or to take any proceedings under the said section, or otherwise in respect of any non-compliance therewith."

The plaintiff subscribed for shares, but then found, as he alleged, that the orders were merely trial orders; and further that a relevant agreement was omitted, and the small-print agreement misleadingly described.

Romer LJ said: "Assume that there was a contract by the plaintiff not to take advantage of the Act, how can you bind him when you state in your prospectus that there 'may be' other agreements when you knew there were? In your case you are a promoter knowing of this contract, and yet you put in a misleading statement that there 'may be' other agreements. That, surely, is not a case in which can say there is a waiver."

Lindley M.R. held that there was misrepresentation (about the orders) and material non-disclosure. "The principle of refusing to give effect to parts of documents so as to prevent successful deception by means of them is quite familiar in its application to general words in releases, and to catching conditions of sale. The refusal is based on ordinary principles of honesty, and is as applicable to tricky waiver clauses as to other tricky documents . . . in order to bind him [the person who takes shares] by election or agreement, he must be fairly dealt with; and his attention must be fairly drawn to the facts, or at all events the existence of facts, which confer the rights which he elects or agrees not to enforce. If his attention, instead of being drawn to such facts, is drawn from them, the attempt to catch him will fail."

***Re Leyland & Taylor's Contract* [1900] 2 Ch. 625 (Part-disclosure of defect ignored because non-disclosure not sufficiently material)**

10.101 The contract contained a condition that the purchaser should repay the vendor any expenses in complying with any requirement of the local authority in respect of various paving and other works, but did not mention that the local authority had served a notice to pave, flag and sewer the street opposite the cottages being sold. It was held by the Court of Appeal that the vendor's omission did not entitle the purchaser to compensation, since it was by no means clear that the works affected the value of the property at all. However, the purchaser would not, as it happened, have bought the property, or at all events not for the price paid, if he had known about the works; and the court left open the question whether it would have granted specific performance to the vendor in these circumstances, had the defect been a material one.

***Re Haedicke and Lipski's Contract* [1901] 2 Ch. 666 (Good faith construction of conditions affirmed: rescission granted to purchaser for undisclosed title defect)**

10.102 The conditions of sale provided that the purchaser would accept the vendor's leasehold title. It emerged that there were onerous and unusual covenants in the leases under which the property was held which had not been disclosed. The purchasers sought to rescind, the vendor objected and took out a vendor and purchaser summons. It was held by Byrne J. that the purchaser might rescind. Cases to the effect that the vendor was not entitled to limit his title by conditions phrased in general terms without specific disclosure were cited.[51]

Note: The point made by Byrne J. is correct, and specially worth nothing since there is perceptible confusion on occasions about the point; see Chapter 5, Sale of Land for a discussion of the idea that the good faith duty of candour and accuracy is only enforced as a matter of discretion, and as part of the discretion whether to grant or refuse specific performance. Byrne J.'s judgment was affirmed by the Court of Appeal in Becker v. Partridge.[52]

[51] *Bousfield v. Hodges* (1863) 33 Beav. 90; 55 E.R. 300. 90; *Jenkins v. Hiles* (1802) 6 Ves. 646; E.R. 1238 (see Lord Eldon's dictum on a vendor's duty). Byrne J. said that Lord Eldon in the latter case was dealing with a case of specific performance "*but the same principles as to the necessity for full disclosure apply*. I think the purchaser has a right to assume when a condition in the terms of that under discussion is inserted that the vendor has disclosed what it is his duty to disclose, and that the condition must be read as precluding objection upon that footing."

[52] At para. 10.117 below.

***Cackett v. Keswick* [1902] 2 Ch. 456 (Good faith construction of general waiver of statutory rights)**

10.103 The prospectus of a company failed to disclose a contract between the promoters and the future chairman of the company, whereby a firm of which he was a member was to receive 12,000 fully paid £1 vendor's shares, partly as commission for underwriting, and partly for the use of his name and that of the firm on the prospectus. It had been argued that the purchaser's right to complain was excluded by a waiver clause in the prospectus. This was as follows:

"There may also be various trade contracts and business arrangements in addition to [a specific agreement mentioned]. As these contracts and arrangements and the above-mentioned underwriting agreements may constitute contracts within the meaning of the 38th section of the Companies Act, 1867, (which provided for mention of certain contracts), applicants for shares shall be deemed to waive the insertion of the dates of and names of the parties to any such contracts, arrangements, or agreements, and shall accept the foregoing as a sufficient compliance with s. 38 of the Companies Act, 1867, or otherwise."

Farwell J. applied Romer L.J.'s statement in argument in *Greenwood v. Leather Shod Wheel Co.*[53] He continued: "A man who desires to take advantage of a waiver clause must state the facts fairly. If he states that there may be contracts, he intends it to be inferred that he knows of none. It is immaterial whether he intended to deceive or not when he made the statement; but if the element of unfairness is requisite, it is found when he insists that its effect is to make the other contracting party give up something of the existence of which the asserter knew, and the other contracting party was ignorant. As I read the judgments in *Greenwood v. Leather Shod Wheel Co*,[54] the decision, and the reasons given for it, involve the proposition that the statutory rights under the 38th section can be waived; that any waiver obtained by unfair dealing or trickery is void; that the person said to have waived must have sufficient information of what he was waiving; and that, apart from fraud, the same principles apply to waiver clauses as are applicable to ambiguous or misleading statements in conditions of sale or releases."

The Court of Appeal agreed. Stirling L.J. said ". . . when persons who issue a prospectus make statements in that prospectus with reference to the contracts, in respect of which the benefit of the statute is to be excluded, they must be such as to be in all respects well founded in fact, and fairly to convey to the mind of the intending shareholder the nature of the contracts which have been excluded."

All agreed that had not been done, and the appeal was dismissed.

***Blaiberg v. Keeves* [1906] 2 Ch. 175 (Reliance by vendor on condition allowed where inaccuracy not material and vendor had reasonably believed statement)**

10.104 Where the vendor had reasonably believed the statement in a risk-relevant condition to be true, and the inaccuracy made no material difference he was permitted to rely on it, even though in fact it was not strictly accurate. A sale of a house and shop in the Whitechapel Road described as freehold had a condition to the effect that it had been held on a 500 year lease from the manor of Stepney at a yearly rent of 1s, but had been assigned in 1828 free from the rent, which the vendor had never paid. In fact, the assignment had

[53] [1900] 1 Ch. 421, and para. 10.100 above.

[54] Above.

been free from the rent but subject to the lease, which mentioned the rent. However, it was proved at the hearing that no rent had in fact been paid for fifty years and there was no clear evidence that it had ever been paid, so that it was not unreasonable for the vendor to believe the property was freehold, and so to describe it. The purchaser was thus refused rescission.

Grand Trunk Railway of Canada v. Robinson [1915] A.C. 740

10.105 This case concerned another "special contract" for the carriage of a horse. The ticket had printed across it in red ink "Read this special contract". On the margin it said "Pass man in charge half fare." Lord Haldane said, on the question of the burden of proof on the company that the passenger assented to the special terms imposed, "This he may be shown to have done either in person or through the agency of another. Such agency will be held to have been established when he is shown to have authorized antecedently or by way of ratification the making of the contract under circumstances in which he must be taken to have left everything to his agent. In such a case it is sufficient to prove that he has been content to accept the risk of allowing terms to be made without taking the trouble to learn what was being agreed to.

The company may infer his intention from his conduct. If he stands by under such circumstances that it will naturally conclude that he has left the negotiation to the person who is acting for him, and intends that the latter should arrange the terms on which he is to be conveyed, he will be precluded by so doing from afterwards alleging want of authority to make any such terms as the law allows. Moreover, if the person acting on his behalf has himself not taken the trouble to read the terms of the contract proposed by the company in the ticket or pass offered, and yet knew that there was something written or printed on it which might contain conditions, it is not the company that will suffer by the agent's want of care. The agent will, in the absence of something misleading done by his company, be bound, and his principal will be bound through him. To hold otherwise would be to depart from the general principles of necessity recognized in other business transactions, and to render it impracticable for railway companies to make arrangements for travellers and consignors without delay and inconvenience to those who deal with them." He thought the passenger had approbated the contract by travelling under it, and so could not reprobate it by claiming a right inconsistent with it.

Roe v. R A Naylor Ltd [1917] 1 K.B. 712 (Ticket- case: application to timber sale with sold note—are the conditions misleading to the ordinary careful businessman?)

10.106 The Plaintiff was a builder. He bought timber from the defendants timber merchants. The following day the defendants' traveller left a sold note at the plaintiff's office listing the timber sold. On the left hand side of the note was printed "Goods are sold subject to their being on hand and at liberty when the order reaches the head office." The plaintiff checked the listing of timber but did not notice the condition. It emerged that the defendants did not have on hand two lots of the timber ordered. The Plaintiff brought an action for damages for breach of the contract to deliver timber. The reported case was heard on appeal from the county court.

Bailhache J, said: "I take the law to be that when the parties to a contract of sale exchange bought and sold notes, or when the seller hands to the buyer a sold note which is accepted by the buyer as being the contractual document, it is no part of the seller's duty to request the buyer to agree to the terms contained in the sold note or to call his attention to its terms. If the buyer accepts the sold note without reading it he does so at his own risk. He is bound by any conditions which may be in the note even if he has not read them. What are sometimes called the ticket cases are not in point; there seems to me to be a broad distinction between that class of case and the case of a contract of sale. There is, however, in my opinion, one exception to the rule that a buyer who accepts a sold note is bound by its terms even though he has not read them. The note may be misleading. The conditions may be so ambiguously worded that they may be read equally well in two different ways; or the conditions relied on by the seller may be placed in such a position in the document that a man or ordinary care and intelligence would not expect to find them there. For example, if the document contains a description of the articles dealt in by the seller, or a list of branch businesses, and mixed up with matter of that kind was a clause like the one in question or a strike clause, the purchaser might very reasonably say that he never expected to find an important condition of sale in that part of the document, and in a case of that sort he would not be bound by the condition. Nor would he be bound if the condition was printed in such small or illegible type as to be unreadable by a person of ordinary eyesight.

10.107 Therefore the question in the present case is whether this printed clause is a clause which is so printed that from its position in the document and the size of the type an ordinary careful business man, reading the document with reasonable care, might miss it. In order to escape being bound by a clause the buyer must be able to satisfy a judge or jury that the document was misleading in some or one of the ways which I have indicated, though possibly there may be others." He did not feel sure the county court judge had directed his mind to the right points, so ordered a new trial.

Atkin J agreed. He said: "When the question is whether a particular document has been assented to as containing contractual terms two points arise for consideration: First, has a contract been entered into on the terms of the written document? In order to decide that the question to be considered is, did the party offering the document convey to the other party that there were some written terms in the document? If the other party did not know of the existence of those written terms, then the question arises whether the first party took reasonable steps to inform him that the document contained some writing which was part of the contract. But there is another class of case in which by a clear course of business between the parties a certain document is understood to be the contract or to be a record of the terms of the contract. In that case the only question which can arise is whether the terms have been assented to. If a party signs the document he is taken to have assented to the terms contained in it. If, although he has not signed the document, he has received it without dissent, he would also prima facie be taken to have assented to the terms. But in both cases the issue might arise whether a particular clause was one of the terms so assented to. In that case the question would be, was the document in such a form that a reasonable man reading the document with reasonable care might and did fail to see that the particular clause in question formed part of the contractual terms? That is a question of fact. It is within one's experience that a document sometimes incorporates other documents containing statements in such a form that a printed contractual term might possibly be overlooked."

***Hood v. Anchor Line (Henderson Brothers) Ltd* [1918] A.C. 837 (H.L.) (Ticket case)**

10.108 The case concerned a ticket for a steamship journey from New York to Glasgow, which contained on the back a condition limiting liability for loss, injury or delay to £10. The ticket was in an envelope which had a finger on it, pointing to the words "Please read conditions of the enclosed contract." It was held that the company had taken reasonable steps to draw the condition to the passenger's attention, and although he had not read it, he could not be heard to say so.

Lord Haldane's judgment is especially interesting. He thought it might have been different if it been merely a case of inviting people to put a penny into an automatic machine and get a ticket for a brief journey. "In such a transaction men cannot naturally be expected to pause to look whether they are obtaining all the rights which the law gives them in the absence of a special stipulation. But when it is a case of taking a ticket for a voyage of some days, with arrangements to be made, among other things, as to cabins and luggage, I think ordinary people do look to see what bargain they are getting, and should be taken as bound to have done so and as precluded from saying that they did not know."

On the question of the relevance of the appellant's actual ignorance of the condition, Lord Haldane said: "The question is not whether the appellant actually knew of the condition. I have no doubt that he did not. The real question is whether he deliberately took the risk of there being conditions in the face of a warning sufficiently conveyed that some conditions were made and would bind him."

Lord Dunedin thought the question whether the condition was usual was a prior question to the question whether the company had taken reasonable steps. He did not elaborate. He said: "So far as the law is concerned, a contract of carriage may be constituted by writing or by parol, or may be inferred from the acquiescence of the carrier in the presence of the passenger on the conveyance. Contracts of carriage are not usually made by parol, nor are they usually embodied in signed writings. In so saying I am proceeding on common knowledge as to railways, stage-coaches and steamers. But what is usual is in truth a question of fact. Accordingly it is in each case a question of circumstance whether the sort of restriction that is expressed in any writing (which, of course, includes printed matter) is a thing that is usual, and whether, being usual, it has been fairly brought before the notice of the accepting party."

He thought in the circumstances of this case the finding of the court below should not be disturbed.

***London & Lancashire Insurance Co. v. Bolands* [1924] A.C. 836 (*Contra proferentem*).**

10.109 The case concerned the construction of an exception to an insurance policy. Lord Sumner referred to the maxim. He said: "It is suggested further that there is some ambiguity about the proviso, and that, under the various well-known authorities, upon the principle of reading words contra proferentes, we ought to construe this proviso, which is in favour of the insurance company, adversely to them. That, however, is a principle which depends upon there being some ambiguity—that is to say, some choice of an expression—by those who are responsible for putting forward the clause, which leaves one unable to decide which of two meanings is the right one."

In that case he thought the problem quite capable of being solved by the ordinary rules of grammar, so there was no ambiguity. The other judgments did not deal with the point.

***Thompson v. LMS Railway Co* [1930] 1 KB 41 (Ticket case)**

10.110 The plaintiff, who could not read, had a (cheap, half the usual price) ticket known as an excursion ticket taken for her by her niece. On the face of the ticket was printed in type as large as the other words "Excursion, For conditions see back." On the back, in reasonably legible print, was an exemption from any liability on the part of the railway company for personal injury. The jury found nonetheless that the terms had not been drawn to the plaintiff's attention: the appeal was about the question whether there was any evidence on which they could properly so find.

Lord Hanworth M.R. endorsed the approach of Swift J. in *Nunan v. Southern Railway Co*[55] as being the right approach in these cases to the question of the terms of the contract. Swift J. had said: "I am of opinion that the proper method of considering such a matter is to proceed upon the assumption that where a contract is made by the delivery, by one of the contracting parties to the other, of a document in a common form stating the terms upon which the person delivering it will enter into the proposed contract, such a form constitutes the offer of the party who tenders it, and if the form is accepted without objection by the person to whom it is tendered this person is as a general rule bound by its contents and his act amounts to an acceptance of the offer to him whether he reads the document or otherwise informs himself of its contents or not, and the conditions contained in the document are binding upon him"

That being so, he thought the contract bound the plaintiff, subject only to the question whether she had sufficient notice of the condition. He cited another ticket case exempting liability for luggage, *Stewart v. London and North Western Rly Co*[56] in which Pollock C.B. had said: "There is a rule in the English law that every man must be taken to know that which he has the means of knowing, whether he has availed himself of those means or not."

He distinguished *Parker v. South Eastern Railway Co*[57] on the grounds that there the cloakroom ticket might easily be taken to be a voucher: there was no need to have any terms and conditions at all; while here, clearly, it was necessary for there to be a ticket. He considered the case before him was on all fours with *Watkins v. Rymill*[58] in which Stephen J. had said: "The only question which can be called a question of fact is, whether giving a man a printed paper plainly expressing the conditions on which a keeper of a repository is willing to accept a carriage for sale on commission is or is not equivalent to asking the owner of the carriage to read that paper, with intent that he should read it when he has a fair opportunity of doing so. This, we think, is a question of law, to be answered in the affirmative."

Lawrence L.J. held that the ticket condition was sufficiently drawn to the plaintiff's attention, through her niece; and that the ticket conditions were not "tricky or illusory"; nor were any of them unreasonable.

Sankey L.J. agreed. He emphasized that the conditions were not unreasonable because "everybody familiar with the practice of the railway world knows the sort of conditions that are imposed upon people who take cheap tickets—sometimes they are drovers' tickets, sometimes they are tickets to enable workmen to go backwards and forwards, sometimes they are excursion tickets . . ."

***Charles Hunt v. Palmer* [1931] 2 Ch. 287 (Good faith rules applied where statements taken together were misleading)**

10.111 This was a vendors' specific performance action. The premises had been described as "valuable business premises"; but were sold subject to a condi-

[55] [1923] 2 K.B. 703.

[56] (1864) 33 L.J. Ex. 199.

[57] Above.

[58] (1882) 10 Q.B.D. 178.

tion that the leases might be inspected at the solicitors' offices and the purchaser should be deemed to have notice of the contents, whether or not he inspected them. Clauson J. relying on *In re Davis & Cavey*[59] refused specific performance, holding without much discussion that the misrepresentation of the vendors disentitled them from relying on the condition.

***Re Brine and Davies' Contract* [1935] Ch. 388 (Breach of good faith rules (part disclosure): reliance on deeming condition not permitted)**

10.112 A vendor sold property as registered freehold property without disclosing that the registered title was possessory only. Farwell J. held the condition was misleading, and therefore the vendor could not rely on the condition in the contract (that 'in default of timeous requisitions', the purchaser was deemed to have accepted the title'. He suggested that seeking to rely on such a condition gave rise to similar considerations as those which were relevant when a vendor was seeking specific performance.

***Chapelton v. Barry Urban District Council* [1940) 1 K.B. 532 (Ticket case (deckchair): no acceptance of conditions if document reasonably taken to be receipt)**

10.113 A slip containing an exclusion of liability for personal injury was given to the plaintiff when he hired a deckchair on the beach. The notice near the deckchairs said nothing about any exclusion. (The exclusion was on the back of the ticket with nothing on the front referring to it, but it does not seem this fact really began to assume significance, because the finding of the court rendered consideration of the notice-to-the-offeree question unnecessary.)

The Court of Appeal held that the ticket was reasonably taken by the plaintiff to be merely a receipt; and thus the exclusion was not properly drawn to his attention.

***John Lee & Son (Grantham) Ltd v. Railway Executive* [1949] 2 All E.R. 581 (Contra proferentem rules merged into good faith construction?)**

10.114 There was a clause in a tenancy agreement that the tenant should be responsible for loss "which but for the tenancy created . . . would not have arisen". Goods were damaged by fire. The Court of Appeal held that the above expression was intended only to cover liabilities which arose by reason of the relationship of landlord and tenant. Sir Raymond Evershed M.R. said: "Because of the extravagant result which the former view involves, I think that the latter construction is the one which the court ought to adopt. We are presented with two alternative readings of this document and the reading which one should adopt is to be determined, among other things, by a consideration of the fact that the defendants put forward the document. They have put forward a clause which is by no means free from obscurity and have contended that, on the view for which they argued, it has a remarkably, if not an extravagantly, wide scope, and I think that the rule *contra proferentem* should be applied and that the result is that the present claim is not one which obliges the first plaintiffs to give to the defendants a release and an indemnity." Somervell L.J. agreed and Denning L.J. did too. The latter said: "Above all, there is the vigilance of the common law which, while allowing freedom of contract, watches to see that it is not abused. It would, therefore, be a very serious question whether the defendants are free to exempt themselves in the wide terms which are here contended for . . ."

[59] (1888) 40 Ch. D. 601.

***Houghton v. Trafalgar Insurance Co. Ltd* [1954] 1 Q.B. 247 (Good faith/ *contra proferentem* rules applied to ambiguous clause in insurance policy)**

10.115 A clause in a motor insurance policy excepted liability for damage "caused or arising whilst the car is conveying any load in excess of that for which it was constructed". The car was a five-seater, but at the time of the accident had six people in it. The Court of Appeal refused to accede to the insurers' suggestion that they might escape liability by reason of the extra person. The Court thought the clause applied only where there was a specified weight limit which was exceeded, as with lorries.

Somervell L.J. said: "I think that it would need the plainest possible words if it were desired to exclude the insurance cover by reason of the fact that there was at the back one passenger more than the seating accommodation. All sorts of obscurities and difficulties might arise. I would like to add that if this or any other insurance company wishes to put forward a policy which will be inapplicable when an extra passenger is carried, I hope that they will print their provision in red ink so that the assured will have it drawn to his particular attention."

Romer L.J. said: "I think that any clause or provision that purports to have that effect ought to be clear and unambiguous so that the motorist knows exactly where he stands. This provision is neither clear nor unambiguous."

Denning L.J. said: "If the clause had such an interpretation I would regard it almost as a trap."

***McCutcheon v David MacBrayne Ltd* [1964] 1 W.L.R. 125 (Ticket case)**

10.116 A car which was shipped by the defendant from the Hebrides to the mainland was lost, the ship having sunk through the negligence of the defendants. When they accepted goods for shipping, their practice was to give a receipt which read "Passengers, passengers' luggage and livestock are carried subject to the conditions specified in the company's sailing bills, notices and announcements." The "risk note" contained conditions with a docket signed by the consignor agreeing to ship the goods "on the conditions stated above". However, on this occasion no risk note was signed, although the consignor had sometimes signed one in the past. Neither he nor his agent specifically knew what the conditions were, but they knew there were conditions which were normally imposed. The question was whether the previous (patchy) course of dealing sufficed, given that the conditions were in fact unknown to the consignor.

Lord Devlin said: "In my opinion, the bare fact that there have been previous dealings between the parties does not assist the respondents at all. The fact that a man has made a contract in the same form 99 times (let alone three or four times which are here alleged) will not of itself affect the hundredth contract in which the form is not used. *Previous dealings are relevant only if they prove knowledge of the terms, actual and not constructive, and assent to them.*[60] If a term is not expressed in a contract, there is only one other way in which it can come into it and that is by implication. No implication can be made against a party of a term which was unknown to him. If previous dealings show that a man knew of and agreed to a term on 99 occasions there is a basis for saying that it can be imported into the hundredth contact without an express statement. It may or may not be sufficient to justify the importation that depends on the circumstances; but at least by proving knowledge the essential beginning is made. Without knowledge there is nothing."

[60] Italics supplied.

***Becker v. Partridge* [1966] 2 Q.B. 155 (Good faith rules affirmed by Court of Appeal)**

10.117 There was a sale with an undisclosed defect in title: the lease was liable to be forfeited for breach of covenants in the head lease. The vendor did not know that, but the Court of Appeal held that he ought to have known, and relied on Byrne J. in *Re Haedicke & Lipski's Contract*[61] for the proposition that when a condition of this kind is inserted the *vendor has disclosed what it is his duty to disclose;*[62] so that the purchaser was entitled to rescission. The condition that the purchaser should accept the vendor's title was held inapplicable, the vendor having failed to disclose the defects of which he knew or ought to have known. The vendor had not known, because neither he nor his solicitors had exercised his right to inspect the superior underlease, but instead had accepted an oral assurance from the assignee's husband that no consent to an underletting was required.

Danckwerts L.J., giving the judgment of the court, said: "There is no doubt that by a clearly drawn special condition put in the contract by a vendor *who acts in good faith,*[63] and disclosing a possible defect in the title, the purchaser may be compelled to accept the title offered by the vendor. But the vendor must have disclosed the defects of which he knew. In this case the vendor did not know of the breaches which would give rise to forfeiture. But he ought to have known that such breaches might exist . . .

In our view the principle was stated by Lord Eldon in *Bousfield v. Hodges*[64] . . . namely that there should be no surprise upon the purchaser, and that there has been a full and fair representation as to the title on the part of the plaintiff."

Note: The case—though less well known that it should be—is an important modern case affirming the old good faith principle that actual knowledge of the truth by the vendor is not important where the truth is "within his knowledge"—that is, where he or his agent may reasonably be expected in the ordinary course of things to have had access to the relevant facts. The vendor has a duty which is ancillary to the making of any statement, description or condition in the contract, as it were to deal correctly with all the facts available to him and a further duty to produce the result, so correctly described, to the purchaser. It is otherwise if the vendor proves that the facts themselves really were not available to him or his agent, acting normally and properly in either case.

***Adams v. Richardson & Starling Ltd* [1969] 1 W.L.R. 1645 (*Contra proferentem*/good faith construction)**

10.118 This was a dry rot guarantee which contained ambiguities the supplier sought to rely on. Lord Denning inveighed against these clauses, saying: "He should not be allowed to limit it by clever clauses in small print—which, in 99 cases out of 100, the customer never reads."

Salmon L.J. said: "If the so-called guarantee purports to take away or cut down the customer's common law rights, it should be construed strictly contra proferentem. If, however, as in this case, the guarantee merely confers some possible additional benefit, however slight, it should certainly not be read in a restrictive sense, but it ought not to be read in a wider sense than it can fairly bear."

[61] [1901] 2 Ch. 666.
[62] Note, not limited to title.
[63] Italics supplied.
[64] (1863) 33 Beav. 90.

***Mendelssohn v. Normand Ltd* [1970] 1 Q.B. 177 (Ticket case (car parking): exclusion strictly construed)**

10.119 The conditions of a car park (which were accepted by the customer) involved the car being locked. The attendant however had asked the plaintiff to leave it unlocked, and promised to lock it. A suitcase was stolen. Lord Denning said that an exemption clause did not avail the garage, since it only applied to acts done in performance of the contract as agreed: the leaving the car unlocked was an entirely different way of performing the contract, and the clause, as a matter of construction, did not apply to that.

Edmund Davies L.J. agreed with Lord Denning. Phillimore L.J., approached the clause slightly differently, in effect holding that the representation nullified the effect of the exemption clause, as with *Curtis Chemical Cleaning and Dyeing Co.*[65]

***Thornton v. Shoe Lane Parking Ltd* [1971] 2 Q.B. 163 (Ticket case (car parking))**

10.120 Mr Thornton, who was "a free-lance trumpeter of the highest quality"[66] parked his car in the defendant's parking lot. There was a notice outside saying "All cars at owner's risk". He took a ticket from an automatic machine. When he went to collect the car, he himself was injured. On the back of the ticket, there were conditions, *inter alia* exempting the parking lot company from liability for injury to the customer.

In the Court of Appeal, Lord Denning thought the contract was concluded when the ticket was thrust out of the automatic machine, and it was too late to add conditions. As to the condition itself, (it had been admitted that reasonable steps were not taken to draw the conditions to the customer's attention) Lord Denning said: "I do not pause to inquire whether the exempting condition is void for unreasonableness. All I say is that it is so wide and so destructive of rights that the court should not hold any man bound by it unless it is drawn to his attention in the most explicit way . . . In order to give sufficient notice, it would need to be printed in red ink with a red hand pointing to it—or something equally startling."

Megaw L.J. relied, as to the question whether the defendant had done what was necessary to bring the condition to the attention of the plaintiff, on the words of Lord Dunedin in *Hood v. Anchor Line (Henderson Brothers) Ltd*[67]: whether it "is a thing that is usual, and whether, being usual, it has been fairly brought before the notice of the accepting party." He said that where the sort of restriction was a usual one in that kind of contract,

"it may not be necessary for a Defendant to prove more than that the intention to attach *some* conditions has been fairly brought to the notice of the other party. But at least where the particular condition relied on involves a sort of restriction that is not shown to be usual in that class of contract, a Defendant must show that his intention to attach an unusual condition *of that particular nature* was fairly brought to the notice of the other party. How much is required as being, in the words of Mellish L.J.,[68] "reasonably sufficient to give the plaintiff notice of the condition" depends upon the nature of the restrictive condition." He pointed out that the condition involved the abrogation of statutory rights as to occupier's liability, and considered that there must be "some clear indication which would lead an ordinary sensible person to realise, at

[65] [1951] 1 K.B. 805.
[66] Lord Denning's phrase.
[67] [1918] A.C. 837.
[68] 2 C.P.D. 416, 424.

or before the time of making the contract, that a term of that sort, relating to personal injury, was sought to be included. I certainly would not accept that the position has been reached today in which it is to be assumed as a matter of general knowledge, custom, practice, or whatever is the phrase that is chosen to describe it, that when one is invited to go upon the property of another for such purposes as garaging a car, a contractual term is normally included that if one suffers any injury on those premises as a result of negligence on the part of the occupiers of the premises they shall not be liable."

He also thought it important that the plaintiff had no practical opportunity of reading and rejecting the conditions. Sir Gordon Willmer agreed.

Faruqi v. English Real Estates Ltd [1979] 1 W.L.R. 963

10.121 See Chapter 5, Sale of Land for a note of this case; which applied good faith rules impeccably to a misleading condition, but nonetheless refused return of the deposit to a purchaser on questionable grounds.

Walker v. Boyle [1982] 1 W.L.R. 495

10.122 Mr Walker bought a house in Sussex from Mrs Boyle. In answer to an inquiry before contract as regards (*inter alia*) the existence of any boundary disputes relating to the property, she had answered "Not to the vendor's knowledge" (apart from reference to some minor matters which did not disturb Mr Walker). In fact there was an ongoing boundary dispute. Dillon J. granted Mr Walker the return of his deposit with interest. He held as follows:

(i) that the small print above the replies to the answers to the Inquiries, which read "These replies on behalf of the vendor are believed to be correct but accuracy is not guaranteed and they do not obviate the need to make appropriate searches, inquiries and inspections." was merely "a warning to a purchaser's solicitors to do what any experienced solicitor would know was his duty and make appropriate searches, inquiries and inspections, but it cannot prevent the answers that are given from being representations of fact." Accordingly he ignored those words.

(ii) that condition 17(1) of the *National Conditions of Sale* (19th ed.) which was incorporated in the contract of sale and which read "no error, mis-statement or omission in any preliminary answer concerning the property ... shall annul the sale, nor (save where the error, misstatement or omission is in a written answer and relates to a matter materially affecting the description or value of the property) shall any damages be payable, or compensation allowed by either party, in respect thereof" did not prevent Mr Walker from obtaining recission of the contract of sale. Dillon J. did not use the older, more accurate formulation excluding matters "within the vendor's knowledge" but accepted the submission of the purchaser's counsel that facts which the vendor knew or ought to have known were not within the condition. He relied on a number of good faith cases including *Flight v. Booth*,[69] *Nottingham Patent Brick and Tile Co. v. Butler*,[70] *Heywood v. Mallalieu*[71] and *Charles Hunt v. Palmer*,[72] this last relying in turn on *Re Davis & Cavey*[73]

[69] Para. 5.79, above.
[70] Para. 10.91, above.
[71] Para. 10.86, above.
[72] Para. 10.111, above.
[73] Para. 10.94, above.

(iii) in the alternative, he considered that condition 17 did not satisfy the requirement of reasonableness laid down by section 11, Unfair Contract Terms Act 1977,[74] amending section 3 of the Misrepresentation Act 1967.

***Interfoto v. Stiletto* [1989] Q.B. 433 C.A. (Application of "ticket" principles to contract for hire of transparencies)**

10.123 The plaintiff ran a photographic lending library. They lent out some transparencies to the defendants together with a delivery note containing printed conditions. One of these (which the defendant did not read) stipulated that the transparencies were to be returned in 14 days, failing which a fee of £5 plus VAT for each transparency would be charged for each day for which they were not returned.

Dillon L.J. said: "At the time of the ticket cases in the last century it was notorious that people hardly ever troubled to read printed conditions on a ticket or delivery note or similar document. That remains the case now. In the intervening years the printed conditions have tended to become more and more complicated and more and more one-sided in favour of the party who is imposing them, but the other parties, if they notice that there are printed conditions at all, generally still tend to assume that such conditions are only concerned with ancillary matters of form and are not of importance. In the ticket cases the courts held that the common law required that reasonable steps be taken to draw the other parties' attention to the printed conditions or they would not be part of the contract. It is, in my judgment, a logical development of the common law into modern conditions that it should be held, as it was in *Thornton v. Shoe Lane Parking Ltd*,[75] that if one condition in a set of printed conditions is particularly onerous or unusual, the party seeking to enforce it must show that that particular condition was fairly brought to the attention of the other party."

Bingham L.J. referred to the common law principle of good faith (see Chapter 1, Introduction) where an interesting passage from his judgment (now become positively ubiquitous since the coming into force of the Unfair Contract Terms Regulations 1994) is quoted. The court held the condition here had not been fairly brought to the attention of the hirer.

Note: If it were felt possible to criticise one of the few modern judgments which recognises that English law is not devoid of good faith concepts, there is perhaps one small point in Bingham L.J.'s judgment—the description of the way good faith operates. This owes perhaps slightly more to late nineteenth-century literalist orthodoxy than one would wish—that is, to the idea that any good faith principle was applied strictly as part of what elsewhere in this book is labelled equity's supposed discretionary-fudge approach. To speak of "relieving" a party from his contract for what are essentially good faith reasons may be less than satisfactory today: the essential good faith approach being, as has been seen, that the offending term simply never made it into the contract at all in the first place.

***William Sindall PLC v. Cambridgeshire County Council* [1994] 1 W.L.R. 1016**

10.124 The plaintiff was a building company, which bought a school playing field from the defendant County Council, with outline planning permission for 60 houses and 30 flats. Some eighteen months after transfer, it found by chance that a nine inch sewer ran diagonally across its planned housing estate. The

[74] See Statutory Appendix for this.
[75] [1971] 2 Q.B. 163.

plaintiff had taken all the normal precautions, but the manholes had been grassed over; and the sewer (although its status was unclear at first) did not appear on the map of public sewers. The contract had two exclusion clauses:

Condition 14 of the National Conditions of Sale 20th edition, "Without prejudice to the duty of the vendor to disclose all latent easements and latent liabilities known to the vendor to affect the property, the property is sold subject to any rights of way and water, rights of common and other rights, easements, quasi-easements, liabilities and public rights affecting the same." and Special Condition 17 was similar.

The Court of Appeal (Russell, Evans and Hoffmann L.J.J.) accepted (as—rightly or wrongly—did the parties) a slightly re-phrased formulation of the old expression used in the good-faith cases—"within the vendor's knowledge". Instead, the vendor's duty was said to be "to disclose all easements and incumbrances of which it had *knowledge or means of knowledge*. But subject to that important exception, it required the purchaser to take the risk of incumbrances which might affect its ability to use the land."

This new-style formulation had the unfortunate side effect of permitting a slide in meaning which probably caused a crucial good-faith point to be missed by the court. The County Council had within its records documents such as a letter of notice of the water authority's intention to build the sewer, which would have revealed the existence of the sewer. The relevant information about the sewer was thus within its possession, and would at one time have been within its knowledge. However, at the date of the transfer, the County Council had destroyed or lost many of its conveyancing records over its period of ownership. It had not mentioned this fact to the purchaser, nor the fact that their conveyancer would in practice be unable to check the records which an owner would reasonably be expected to have (this particular defendant also had a specific duty under the Local Government Act 1972 to make proper arrangements for the documents under its control). This last would clearly be within its knowledge, on any view. Thus, it had not told the whole truth relevant to the matter in hand to the purchaser[76] and on a traditional good faith formulation, the clauses should consequently not have applied to exclude the purchaser's claim to rescind or receive compensation or damages for the encumbrance represented by the sewer[77].

10.125 The slightly altered formulation managed to skew the whole tenor of the good-faith duty of the vendor to something a long way from the reasonable-expectation basis of these. The records were quite hard for the individual conveyancer entrusted with the handling of the transaction to find. It would not be unreasonable to suppose that he might not find it. The "means of knowledge" formulation naturally contains within it the question, Whose means? —; and thus points one to an individual by whose access to records the point is to be tested. It was therefore held that the Council, in its embodiment for the purpose as the individual conveyancer employed by it, did not have the means of knowledge. Accordingly the literal words of the clauses were to be applied. They were labelled "allocation of risk" clauses.

Note: The soundness of the decision as a paradigm for exclusion clauses of this kind in sales of land generally may be doubted. Indeed, Evans L.J. made it plain that his decision depended on the "means of knowledge" formulation, and he would not want the court's decision to be taken "as approving either corporate forgetfulness or collective amnesia of this sort". The duty of good faith would:

(a) be less stringent in the case of a large organisation with a lot of employees and records than that of an individual vendor; and

[76] See, *e.g.* ***Re Banister*** (1879) 12 Ch. D. 131 or ***Re Marsh and the Earl of Granville*** (1882) 24 Ch. D. 11.

[77] See also Chapter 16, Rescission of Executed Sales.

(b) would vary in a way which would defeat a buyer's reasonable expectation, since all would depend on the chance of whether the records were in a state where the individual would realise anything was wrong.

One may contrast the cases on the imputing of knowledge via an agent, where the duty to run a sufficiently well-oiled business so that information does not disappear is deemed to be the vendor or defining party's. The moral of the case may simply be that a "mere" change in the phrase used as a defining expression should perhaps be less readily accepted by courts and litigants alike: something which only appears to be a harmlessly modern translation of an old-fashioned phrase can inadvertently have built on it a whole edifice of "new" law. The case, interesting as it is, should probably be regarded as confined to its special facts.

***Witter (Thomas) v. TBP Industries* [1996] 2 All E.R. 573.**

10.126 In this case[78] Jacobs J. imposed what was in effect an impeccable fair-dealing requirement on a seller who wished to take advantage of a "whole agreement" exclusion clause to exclude his liability for pre-contractual misrepresentations. He said: "Unless it is manifestly made clear that a purchaser has agreed only to have a remedy for breach of warranty I am not disposed to think that a contractual term said to have this effect by a roundabout route does indeed do so. In other words, if a clause is to have the effect of excluding or reducing remedies for damaging untrue statements then *the party seeking that protection cannot be mealy-mouthed in his clause. He must bring it home that he is limiting his liability for falsehoods he may have told.*"[79]

[78] Also noted in Chap. 17, Good Faith and the Misrepresentation Act 1967, at para. 17.05.

[79] At 596. Italics supplied.

PART 3

AFTER THE CONTRACT

PART 3

INTRODUCTION

CANDOUR AND ACCURACY AFTER THE CONTRACT

11.00 The application of the twin good faith duties above is not confined to the period leading up to the formation of the contract. There is of course only need for these duties after the contract where the vendor has contingent rights, which operate only when something is or is not the case. The facts which trigger the contingent right may be within the knowledge of one party and not readily ascertainable by the other party. One example of this situation is to be seen in Chapter 12, on a vendor's right of rescission, at paragraph 12.01 *et seq*. above. Here the facts as to the title—the unexpectedness of the difficulty revealed by the purchaser's requisition, and so on, are within the vendor's knowledge but quite unavailable to the purchaser.[a] It is therefore not surprising that the assumption of candour and accuracy was often made in this sphere,[b] until the law went through the period of change adverted to above and elsewhere in this book, which caused good faith principles to fall into desuetude for the most part.

Another area where the need has been felt for the twin good faith duties has been a modern one—on-demand performance bonds. Here also the triggering facts, which give rise to the right to make a demand under the bond, are within the knowledge of the obligee, typically an employer, and not in the least within the knowledge of the obligor, typically an issuing bank. Relatively soon after these became established commercially, Lord Denning said *obiter* in *Edward Owen Ltd v. Barclay's Bank*[c] that there was a requirement that the customer make an "honest demand". In *State Trading Corporation of India Ltd v. E.D. & F. Man (Sugar) and the State Bank of India*[d] Lord Denning said, as cited, that there was an implied term "that the buyer, when giving notice of default, must honestly believe that there has been a default on the part of the seller. Honest belief is enough . . ."

[a] *c.f.* the similar basis for the duty of disclosure by the applicant for *ex parte* injunctions, and *c.f.* also the post contractual duty of disclosure in insurance cases.

[b] The duty of candour in such circumstances will often mean that a degree of spontaneous disclosure must be made, in order to deal with what the buyer's assumptions will otherwise naturally be.

[c] [1978] Q.B. 159.

[d] Unreported, but referred to in *United Trading v. Allied Arab Bank* [1985] 2 Lloyd's Rep. 554.

However, in the *United Trading*[e] case, it may be that the court translated this requirement of honesty into a formal requirement for a statement to the effect that the conditions laid down in the Bond for claiming applied.

> "I accept Mr Tugendhat's alternative submission that in addition to the beneficiary making the demand, he must also inform the bank that he does so on the basis provided for in the performance bond itself . . . A beneficiary may seek, honestly or dishonestly, to apply a performance bond to the wrong contract, and the need to inform the bank of the true basis upon which he is making his demand may be very salutary."

However, the idea that the obligee must make his demand "in good faith" surfaced again in two of the judgments of the Court of Appeal decision in *Trafalgar House Construction v. General Surety and Guarantee Co.*[f] The point did not arise in the House of Lords decision on the case since they concluded the bond in question was not an on-demand bond.

The question perhaps remains unresolved. Lord Denning's formula leaves it unclear whether the honest but wholly deluded obligor may claim.[g] This may possibly account for the suggestion of a specific requirement of "good faith" by the Court of Appeal in the *Trafalgar House*[h] case. It may have been intended to go a little beyond honesty, in requiring a small measure of diligence on the part of the obligee also. It may be that a requirement that the obligor must be satisfied after inspecting the information *within his knowledge*[i] would meet the case. No doubt, as with the doctrine of notice, the commercial context would indicate that the inquiries need not be too prolonged or exacting. Compare the statement, possibly not to be taken quite at face value, by Hirst J in *Siporex v. Banque Indosuez*[j]

> "The whole commercial purpose of a performance bond is to provide a security which is to be readily, promptly and assuredly realizable when the prescribed event occurs; a purpose reflected in the provision here that it should be payable "on first demand".

While no doubt the purpose is as stated, one must remember that he was considering the question whether in an on-demand bond the obligee had to prove his loss before being able to claim. This would take a year or two, and can readily be seen to be inconsistent with the main purpose of a bond of this kind. However, there will normally have to be some inquiries made by an obligee anyway before claiming under an on-demand bond, and the extra requirement that these should reasonably be comprehensive and *be fairly and candidly based on* the information in his possession or control is not going to cause the kind of delay which will frustrate the whole purpose of the bond. At present, it has been suggested that resort to this otherwise useful

[e] [1985] 2 Lloyd's Rep. 554.
[f] (1994) 66 Build. L.R. 47.
[g] See discussion of "grey innocence" in Chap. 5, Sale of Land.
[h] [1994] 66 Build. L.R. 47.
[i] See Chap. 5, Sale of Land for discussion of this phrase.
[j] [1986] 2 Lloyd's Rep. 146.

commercial instrument is increasingly being avoided by many, simply because of the lack of control by the courts over any wrongful exercise of it by the obligee.

The result of a duty of good faith (accuracy and candour) in on-demand performance bonds would as in other cases of breach of the duty, be that the part of the demand made in disregard of the duty would be disregarded by the court, and the demand, to that extent at least, treated as wrongfully made.

Insurance

Curiously, the operation of the post-contractual duty "of good faith" in insurance contracts has received relatively little attention. A number of questions perhaps remain to be fully worked out by the courts, *e.g.*

- (i) What *kind* of duty "of good faith" persists after the insurance contract is made? In particular, is it the duty of candour and accuracy, or is it something more—or less—ferocious?[k]
- (ii) What is the effect of its breach? In particular, does the breach render the contract voidable at the option of the insurer, in the same way as a breach of the duty of disclosure prior to the formation of the contract[l]
- (iii) To what extent is there a continuing duty of (unasked) full disclosure during the post-contractual period?[m]
- (iv) More speculatively perhaps, might the duty of loyalty (as to which see the other chapters in Part III) come into play to prevent an insurer seeking to avoid the policy in a way which runs counter to the overall purpose of the contract of insurance, i.e. to insure a particular risk?[n]

Candour, accuracy and loyalty

The role of the duty of candour and accuracy after the contract of sale is made is a real one, but it will tend to operate only where A.'s rights are affected by a statement of fact by B., but the relevant facts are only known to B. Therefore, it crops up only occasionally in Part III of this book. It has had this section to itself merely so that its existence is not forgotten. The main subject matter of Part III is what has been called the good-faith Duty of Loyalty. This is introduced and explained in the Introduction to Chapter 11, at paragraph 11.01 *et seq.*

[k] See *Black King Shipping Corporation v. Massie ("The Litsion Pride")* [1985] 1 Lloyd's Rep. 437, *Orakpo v. Barclays Insurance Services* (1964) C.L.C. 373, *New Hampshire Insurance Co. v. M.G.N.*, unreported, C.A., September 6, 1996 and *Manifest Shipping Co. v. Uni-Polaris Shipping*, unreported, C.A., January 23, 1997.

[l] See the cases cited in n. [k] and *Britton v. Royal Insurance Co.* (1866) 4 F.&F. 905; 176 E.R. 843 and *Cory v. Patton* (1872) 7 L.R. Q.B. 304.

[m] See on this and (iv), in addition to the cases already cited, the "held-covered cases—*Mentz Decker v. Maritime Insurance Co.* [1910] 1 K.B. 367, *Thames and Mersey Marine Insurance v. H.T. Van Laun & Co.*, noted at [1917] 2 K.B. 48, *Niger v. Guardian Assurance Co.* [1922] 13 Lloyd's Rep. 75, *Hood v. West End Motor Car Packing Co.* [1917] 2 K.B. 38, *Overseas Commodities v. Style* [1958] 1 Lloyd's Rep. 546 and *Liberian Insurance Agency v. Mosse* [1977] 2 Lloyd's Rep. 560.

[n] See also, where appropriate, the Unfair Contract Terms Regulations 1994: see Chap. 19.

CHAPTER 11

THE AFTER-SALE RELATIONSHIP: THE SELLER RETAINS SOMETHING AFFECTING THE THING SOLD

"The expression 'derogation from grant' conjures up images of parchment and sealing wax, of copperplate handwriting and fusty title deeds. But the principle is not based on some ancient technicality of real property. As Younger L.J. observed in Harmer v. Jumbil (Nigeria) Tin Areas Ltd[1]*, it is a principle which merely embodies in a legal maxim a rule of common honesty. It was imposed in the interest of fair dealing . . ."*[2]

"English law thinks in pigeon-holes and rarely seeks to relate one pigeon-hole to another"[3]

"I think I may safely say, as a general rule, that where in a written contract it appears that both parties have agreed that something shall be done, which cannot effectually be done unless both concur in doing it, the construction of the contract is that each agrees to do all that is necessary to be done on his part for the carrying out of that thing, though there may be no express words to that effect.[4]

INTRODUCTION

11.01 "After-sale relationship" does not mean, naturally, the kind of relationship where a salesman drops in from time to time to try and sell one something more. This chapter is about the kinds of contract where a clean break between seller and buyer on the making of the contract is not possible. Typically the seller retains something giving him *power*

[1] [1921] 1 Ch. 200 at 225, 226.
[2] Nicholls L.J. in ***Johnston v. Holland*** [1988] 1 E.G.L.R. 264.
[3] Nicholas, *The French Law of Contract*, (2nd ed.).
[4] Lord Blackburn in *Mackay v. Dick* (1881) 6 App. Cas. 251.

over the buyer: some retained land, an apparently widely-drawn right to refuse the buyer permission to do something, some common parts giving access to the buyer's flat, a roof from which rainwater can leak, or where the responsibility for the success of the contract depends on steps to be taken by one of the parties. There is thus a relationship between the two, unwilling perhaps, only for certain purposes, and needed only from time to time – but an unavoidable relationship just the same. It may remain dormant for many years before either needs to resort to the other. By then the circumstances of buyer and seller, or of the world in general, may well be considerably changed in ways no-one could have foreseen at the time of the contract. Consequently it is unusual for there to be much small print about it. Regulating the relationship in advance in detail would be a pointless exercise. The question which arises is, how are the respective rights of the seller and the buyer to be balanced in this relationship?

This question has given rise to fair dealing or good faith principles. These are to be found in a number of areas varying from the extremely ancient, such as derogation from grant, to the relatively modern, such as the law on a landlord's reasonable consent, or the suggestion that a degree of good faith in some sense may be necessary when making a demand under "on-demand" performance bonds. These areas have traditionally been treated as separate. The collecting together of these topics is probably overdue. They are collected together in this book; and an attempt has been made to show the common thread of fair-dealing principle which runs through them all.

11.02 Perhaps the current answer to the question of fairness between buyer and seller in a relationship of this kind, might nowadays be, the court will decide what is reasonable. However, for litigants the appearance of this precept is distinctly better than the reality. One may fear, with Lord Erskine, that there would be "no safety" in the law. The Latin maxim *tot homines, quot sententiae* may be loosely paraphrased as "If there are ten judges there will ten different ideas of what is "reasonable in the circumstances". If the problem before a court is whether a particular fact or proposition should be inferred, for example would X have entered into the contract if he had known the true facts which we now know, there are a lot of variables on one side. When to that is added the problem of assessing whether something is reasonable in the circumstances, another set of variables is added also, and the possibility opened up of an unconscious personal moral bias. What is reasonable to Judge A of one kind of background or simply one kind of mindset, may seem moderately unreasonable to Judge B of another. "Reasonable" has a fairly large personal-approbation content in it, inevitably, since it is an answer to the question "what would be *the right* way for a person to act in those circumstances? Hence, perhaps the current mutterings about the need for more women judges in England: the idea presumably is that at least the litigant might have a sporting chance of a different set of unconscious assumptions, tendencies, *etc.*, from a woman judge. No doubt there are indeed good reasons for a system of selecting judges in England which is fairer to women (among others) than the present one, but one must deplore the idea that we should have or encourage a system of law where a judge's personal background or sex *can* affect his or her decisions in the first place more than minimally. If we really have, or believe we are tending to have such a system, perhaps we should ask whether we really want it, before it is too late. Thus, we are fortunate in good faith, in that it is about fixed principles. Litigants are safer from unconscious bias. Equally importantly, or maybe more importantly, if the good faith rules are accepted we have in place a coherent system of business morality which the public may anticipate will be applied to these after-sale relationships, and may be guided in advance.

The thread of principle which runs through the after-sale relationship cases is, like the good faith principles governing the formation of the contract, based on the deemed reasonable expectation of the parties. There is strong emphasis on a reasonable expectation of deemed loyalty to *the paramount or characteristic, purpose of the contract.* This last, the paramount purpose of the contract, is a crucial concept which needs to be appreciated at the outset. It is explained in Part 1 below, on derogation from grant at paragraph 11.06. The concept of deemed loyalty to the paramount purpose of the contract is perhaps ripe for wider development into non-traditional spheres. For example, its use could be contemplated in some circumstances in insurance contracts within the scope of the Unfair Contract Terms Regulations 1994 where an insurer seeks to rely on a "basis of the contract" clause to an extent which is inconsistent with the paramount purpose of the contract, namely to insure a particular type of broad risk.

PART 1: THE RULE AGAINST DEROGATION FROM GRANT

1. A general contractual principle—A person may not give a thing with one hand and take away the means of enjoying it with the other

11.03 The most ancient of these after-sale fair dealing rules is the rule that a person may not derogate from his own grant, or, as Bowen L.J. put it in *Birmingham, Dudley & District Banking Co v. Ross,*[5] having given a thing with one hand, taking away the means of enjoying it with the other. Rather like the ancient rules regarding dealings with the vulnerable,[6] it has lacked the good faith or fair dealing label probably only because it was well established (in the case of the main investment in earlier times—land) before the time when the concept of good

[5] (1888) 38 Ch. D. 295.

[6] See Chap. 9, Dealings with the Vulnerable Buyer or Seller.

faith began to be fashionable in England. This, as has been mentioned elsewhere, was partly as a result of Lord Mansfield's introduction of the notion, but rather more as a result of the influence in England of "natural" lawyers such as Pothier, mainly after 1806 when his *Traité des Obligations* was translated into English and began to be regarded as both chic and influential by lawyers. "Derogation from grant" is, however, and has been labelled, a principle of common honesty, imposed in the interests of fair dealing; and like the other good-faith/fair-dealing topics in this book, also treats the paramount or ultimate purpose of the contract as something of a star to steer by. Accordingly, it qualifies to rank with these other good faith/fair dealing topics.

11.04 The principle of non-derogation from grant is now recognised to be a general one, not confined to land. It began with land. As has been noted elsewhere in this book,[7] until the latter part of the nineteenth century when shares in joint-stock companies began to be seen as a proper investment, land was the normal investment opportunity, and what affected land sales affected investment generally. It is to the credit of certain nineteenth and twentieth century judges that they have recognised the general nature of the principle despite its archaic clothing, and have been ready to apply it on occasions (they are not often asked to do so) in modern contexts far removed from the sale of land. In the House of Lords' decision in *British Leyland Motor Corporation v. Armstrong Patents*,[8] the principle was applied to preserve the right of buyers of British Leyland cars to replace their exhaust systems in the most economical way possible, whether or not this involved buying from the defendant copies of the exhaust pipes of the plaintiff. One may hope this beneficial development of the doctrine of non derogation from grant will continue into new situations of all kinds where there is an after-sale relationship between buyer and seller. There is clearly room for emphasis on a rule of fair dealing, or of common honesty outside the sale of land. Nonetheless, the cases illustrating the rule against derogation from grant do in the main involve land; and until the development of the doctrine of loyalty to the main purpose of the contract is properly under way, some imagination will no doubt be necessary to make the link from land to new forms of investment or other subject matter of ownership. Meanwhile, it is helpful to study the workings of the principle.

It should be stressed that the principle gives rights to prevent certain activities on retained land or other subject matter where this can detrimentally affect the paramount purpose for which the grantee took his land (or chattels or bundles of rights or whatever). It is something that comes with a contract to buy, in appropriate circumstances. It is absolutely powerless to prevent disagreeable or immoral conduct, or any conduct at all, on the part of those who are outsiders to the relationship conveniently labelled grantor and grantee, that is seller and purchaser, lessor and lessee, *etc.*, as the case may be. The *insiders* are described below.

[7] *Passim.*
[8] [1987] A.C. 577.

The principle

11.05 Lord Denning in *Molton Builders Ltd v. City of Westminster*[9] described it thus:

> "... if one man agrees to confer a particular benefit on another, he must not do anything which substantially deprives the other of the enjoyment of that benefit: because that would be to take away with one hand what is given with the other."

The significance of the "end", main, characteristic or paramount purpose of the contract

11.06 The cases show that the extent of the principle is found by looking to the main or paramount purpose of the contract or what Aristotle would have called the *telos* or "end". It is that which the grantor cannot derogate from, that to which he is deemed to be loyal. One does not need to trawl minutely through the small print to find it out: it is not anything specially detailed, but is broadly speaking the answer to the question "What is it being sold for?" It is better put like this than "What is he buying it for?", because we are not looking for the purchaser's reasons for buying it, but the obvious or apparent purpose which both parties would acknowledge. Quite often this purpose is not expressed, but inferred from the circumstances. If I sell a pair of shoes, their purpose is to be walked in; if I lease a timber merchants, the purpose of the lease is the carrying on business as a timber merchant. Thus, the paramount purpose of the contract is usually something like "land for building a house on", land for building a railway on, tyres to be put into people's cars, and so on. The label "paramount purpose" is used in this book for the main purpose of the contract or clause in this sense.

In *North Eastern Railway Company v. Elliot*[10] the plaintiff was a railway company which had taken land under its compulsory powers for the purpose of forming the railway. There were mineral mines under the land which were reserved to the vendor; and which were drowned at the time of the sale. A lessee of the vendor's retained land proposed to work the minerals on his leased land in such a way as to affect the stability of the railway company's land. Sir Page Wood V.C. said:

> "the common law, independently of any question of priority, gives to every landowner the right to have his own soil in its natural state supported by the adjoining soil; ... The common law gave no further right to support, and if you build upon your land you have no such right to support for the additional weight. But if a landowner conveys one of two closes to another, he cannot afterwards do anything to derogate from his grant; and *if the conveyance is made for the express purpose of having buildings*

[9] (1975) 30 P. & C.R. 182.

[10] (1860) 1 J. & H. 145; 70 E.R. 697.

erected upon the land so granted, a contract is implied on the part of the grantor to do nothing to prevent the land from being used for the purpose for which to the knowledge of the grantor the conveyance is made.[11] Thus, the lessee was not permitted to use his land in the way he proposed in so far as this caused damage to the railway bridge.

11.07 Also relevant for the understanding of "paramount purpose" is the case of *Aldin v. Latimer Clark, Muirhead & Co*[12] where it meant "land for a timber merchants". The case also shows where something stops being the paramount purpose of the contract and begins to be something ancillary, which might or might not happen, and thus could not be the main purpose of the contract. It did not mean, land for any particular kind of timber merchants: that (in the absence of clear evidence that the parties must have intended some special use of timber) would have been to stray away from the paramount purpose of the contract. Sterling J. allowed reliance on derogation from grant but confined it to the normal business of timber merchants, not "special branches of the business" which might call for "extraordinary protection. He added the qualification, at all events where these post-date the grant of the lease. It seems likely he added this because he could see that it was possible to envisage, given the right circumstances, the parties at the outset deciding or acknowledging that it *was* going to be a letting for a particular kind of timber merchants, for example for high-pressure treating of timber or the like. There would be "special circumstances", but they would need to be proved by evidence, and it would have to be shown also that the special circumstances would have needed to exist at the date of the lease.[13] Since the special drying sheds had been put in by the tenant after the date of the lease, there was no chance of this being the case.

11.08 The principle has been called a rule based on the common intention of the parties[14], and no doubt it is in a way, but it is not all kinds of intentions which are so recognised: merely what Bowen L.J. in *Myers v. Catterson*[15] called "the reason of the thing". "The reason of the thing" is, no doubt, another way of explaining the elusive Aristotelian concept of the paramount-purpose-of-the-contract.[16]

In *Myers v. Catterson*[17] Bowen L.J. said:

> "... As in the case of all other implied covenants, or implied obligations, in order to see what the measure of the obligation is we must look at the reason of the thing, and at the surrounding circumstances, in order to ascertain, if we can, what was the obvious intention of the parties, so as to give to the transaction

[11] Italics supplied.
[12] [1894] 2 Ch. 437.
[13] See below as to the importance of this.
[14] See, *e.g.* Lord Loreburn in *Lyttelton Times v. Warners* [1907] A.C. 476.
[15] (1889) 43 Ch. D. 470.
[16] For the debt owed to Aristotle and St Augustine by the natural lawyers see Gordley. *The Philosophical Origins of Modern Contract Doctrine*, Oxford, 1991.
[17] Above.

> between them that minimum of efficacy and value, which, upon any view of the case, it must have been their common intention that it should have."

Bowen L.J. then posited a situation where an ordinary landowner has two pieces of land which either adjoin or are so near to one another that the enjoyment of the one, perhaps for all purposes, at any rate for some purposes, depends upon the user to be made of the other portion of land, and continued:

> "Surely it must be in the contemplation of the parties that, in the absence of any express agreement one way or the other, *the vendor shall not so use that land which he retains as to preclude any possible use of the building or land which he sells, or to prevent that use of it for which he knows he is selling it to the purchaser. It would be contrary to common notions of justice and fair dealing if it were otherwise . . .*[18]

In *Hall v. Lund*[19] the paramount purpose of the contract was, to be used as a paper mill. An example of land to be used as a brewery was also given. Wilde B. explained that not *all* the liberties and privileges in fact enjoyed under the original grant could be relied on by the grantee by virtue of the rule. He said:

> "It seems to me that, in cases of implied grant, the implication must be confined to a reasonable use of the premises for the purpose for which, according to the obvious intention of the parties, they are demised. Some rules are obvious enough. A demise of a brewery would carry with it the right to use the premises for brewing; although that might be a nuisance to the lessor or his assigns. . . . Each case must depend on its own circumstances and the intention of the parties, to be ascertained from the character, state, and use of the premises at the time of the grant . . ."

The grantee may sometimes be restrained by the principle too

11.09 Lord Loreburn in *Lyttelton Times Co v. Warners*[20] said:

> "When it is a question of what shall be implied from the contract, it is proper to ascertain what in fact was the purpose, or what were the purposes, to which both intended the land to be put, and, having found that, both should be held to all that was implied in this common intention."

Inheriting the original intention:

The parties' presumed intentions as to the paramount purpose of the contract: successors in title or derivative owners are unwitting inheritors of these

[18] Italics supplied.
[19] (1863) 1 H. & C. 676; 158 E.R. 1055.
[20] [1907] A.C. 476.

11.10 The rule is, as has been said, a rule of presumed intention of the original grantor and grantee. It is a presumed intention which stamps permanently certain limitations upon that which is granted and that which is retained. Both (a) successors in title of the original grantor and grantee and (b) derivative owners of rights carved out of that which the original grantor retained or the original grantee received are unwilling inheritors of the knowledge of the original paramount purpose-of-the-contract which the original grantor and grantee are presumed to have had. There are various permutations shown by the cases.

(1) The grantee entitled to invoke the principle as against a purchaser from the grantor

11.11 In an early case, *Palmer v. Fletcher*[21], the purchaser of retained land of the vendor was not permitted to diminish the right to light of the owner of land purchased earlier from the same vendor, any more than the vendor himself could have done.

In *Rigby v. Bennett*[22], there had been a sale of leasehold land in lots, each purchaser being bound to take a lease and build in accordance with plans provided by the vendor local authority. The purchaser of a plot commenced to build a house with deeper foundations than shown on the plan (but without objection from the vendor). A later purchaser of an adjacent lot on the land of the vendor which had not been sold off started to build his house with even deeper foundations, endangering the first purchaser's. The first purchaser was held by the Court of Appeal to be entitled by reason of the rule against derogation from grant to prevent the later purchaser from the vendor from building so as to endanger these deeper foundations. Cotton L.J. put the applicable principle as follows:

> The Plaintiff makes this case "I took this grant of land for the purpose of building a house upon it . . . and I rely on the principle that in such a grant there is an implied obligation on the part of the grantor that he will not derogate from his own grant, *that he will not deal with his adjoining property so as to destroy the house which he intended I should build on the land when he granted it to me.*"[23]

Indeed, since the first purchaser had no strict right under his lease to build the house as he had built it, there could have been no other basis for the judgment.

Hall v. Lund[24] concerned an implied grant under the rule in *Wheeldon v. Burrows*[25]. The rule in *Wheeldon v. Burrows*[26] is itself almost certainly explicable on good faith principles. Where land is sold with "continu-

[21] in the 15th year of Charles II's reign, also noted below.
[22] (1882) 21 Ch. D. 559.
[23] Italics supplied.
[24] (1863) 1 H. & C. 676; 158 E.R. 1055.
[25] (1879) 12 Ch. D. 31.
[26] *Ibid.*

ous and apparent'' easements, and nothing is said, the purchaser's reasonable expectation that he will enjoy these with the land in the absence of express terms of the contract excluding these is upheld. See the formulation of the rule by Thesiger L.J., quoted at paragraph 11.37 below. In *Hall v. Lund*[27] a *Wheeldon v. Burrows* quasi easement was seen as a derogation from grant question. Thus the purchaser from the original grantor was held entitled to step into the shoes of the original owner as far as the ability to derogate from his grant went; so that he received the land as it were stamped with the original acceptance of that first owner that he had let nearby land to a mill which was in the habit of discharging its refuse into a stream by which the owner's land was situated. He could no more prevent that than the first owner who had let the land could have prevented it.

(2) A tenant of the grantee entitled to invoke the principle as against a tenant of the grantor:

11.12 In *Rosewell v. Pryor*[28] the principle was affirmed by Holt C.J. as applying to preserve the ''very good lights'' of a tenant of the grantee as against a tenant of contiguous land who had taken his lease from the original vendor at a later date.

(3) Contemporaneous grantees from a common grantor

11.13 The inheriting of the original intention principle has been extended to cases of contemporaneous conveyances. In *Compton v. Richards*[29] one of two joint simultaneous purchasers of building plots from a common vendor was held not entitled to obstruct the windows of the house on the other purchaser's plot by reason of the principle of derogation from grant. In *Swansborough v. Coventry*[30] Tindal C.J. applied the principle of derogation from grant to two purchasers under simultaneous conveyances, holding in effect that neither simultaneous purchaser was entitled to obstruct the light to the windows of the other.

The unimportance of notice

11.14 The benefit of the principle, that is, being able to prevent the grantor from acts detrimental to the original paramount purpose of the contract, descends to the grantee's successors in title whether or not they know of it. The burden of the principle, that is, the inability to use the land or the subject matter of the original grant in a way which is detrimental to the original main purpose of the contract between the grantor and grantee, similarly descends to successors in title of the grantor whether or not they in fact know of it.

[27] Above
[28] in the 2nd year of Queen Anne's reign.
[29] (1814) 1 Price 27; 145 E.R. 1320.
[30] (1832) 9 Bing. 305; 131 E.R. 629.

In *Cable v. Bryant*[31] the argument on behalf of the purchaser from the original grantor was that he had not had notice of the right of an adjacent tenant from his grantor to use his land as a stables. (The purchaser had blocked ventilation ducts of the stables with a hoarding.) Neville J. considered that the rule that a man may not derogate from his grant was a rule of law, and not a rule of equity. He said:

> "I do not think it depends upon an implication of a covenant on the part of a grantor. I think it is quite clear that the obligation not to derogate from a grant applies to a person deriving title from a grantor in the same way as it applies to a grantor himself; and it seems to me that that is conclusive upon the point of whether the rule depends on the implication of a covenant or whether it does not, because if it depends upon the implication of a covenant it is only those who take with notice of a covenant who would be subject to the obligation, and that would be an equitable obligation, and not a legal obligation, which I believe the obligation not to derogate from a grant to be."

Neville J.'s reasoning is distinctly hard to follow. However, since he referred to Romer L.J.'s judgment in *Quicke v. Chapman*[32] as essentially supporting this analysis, we are not without sources of assistance. In *Quicke v. Chapman*[33] Romer L.J. said this about the nature of the right.

> "Now, in order to see whether a grant of light over the adjacent land is to be implied, you must inquire into two things. You must first inquire into the title to that adjacent land, to see whether the grantor has such an estate or interest in it as will support an implied grant by him of the right to the access of light over it. That inquiry is purely as to the title, and has nothing to do with the question whether the grantee did or did not at the time of the grant know of the state of the title. For, if he did not know at that time of the state of the title, still, if he claims a right over the adjacent land, he was bound to take such title as the grantor had. He is in no better position than he would have been if he had inquired into the title to the adjacent land.
>
> "But, in my opinion, more than that must be inquired into in order to see what passed by implication by the use of the word 'lights'. In my opinion you are also entitled to inquire into the surrounding circumstances which are relevant to such a question—the circumstances affecting the two pieces of land, though this is not strictly a matter of title and might not appear on the title if it were inquired into. In order that the circumstances may be relevant they must, in my opinion, have been known to both the parties. But, if they are known to both, although therefore not strictly a matter of title, yet, in my opinion, those circumstances

[31] [1908] 1 Ch. 259.
[32] [1903] 1 Ch. 659.
[33] *Ibid.*

> must also be considered in order to see whether there is or is not an implied grant of the right to light over the adjacent land.

This seems more explicable: the right not to have one's grant derogated from is a right akin to a person's title. You either do or not have title: whether you know you have title, have investigated properly, etc makes no difference. You cannot have any better title to land or other rights than your predecessor had. Bound up with that title is the non-derogation package, which the successors in title of both vendor and purchaser take equally, one with another, and regardless of their actual state of knowledge.[34]

An exceptional case: Johnston v. Holland[35]

11.15 In this case, there was interference by a successor in title of the grantor who also had a reserved right to put up an advertising hoarding. The problem was that the interference took place on land which had been acquired by the grantor's successor after the date of the original grant. It would simply not have been possible for the interference to have taken place without this additional adjacent land. Nicholls L.J. held that "common honesty" meant that the grantor's successor in title should be restrained from the interference even though it took place on this additional land. He considered that this approach was consistent with the judgment of Younger L.J. in *Harmer v. Jumbil (Nigeria) Tin Areas Ltd*[36] in which the latter had said in particular:

> "It [the obligation] must be such as, in view of the surrounding cirumstances, was within the reasonable contemplation of the parties at the time when the transaction was entered into, and was at that time within the grantor's power to fulfil. But so limited, the obligation imposed may I think, be infinitely varied in kind, regard being had to the paramount purpose to serve which it is imposed."

It is difficult to see how Nicholls L.J. can have thought that his approach *was* consistent with Younger L.J.'s statement: it is plainly not. Younger L.J.'s judgment expressly embodies the traditional limiting of the principle to what was in the grantor's power at the time of the grant. It was plainly not in the power of the grantor in *Johnston v. Holland*[37] *at the time of the grant* to exercise any power at all over the extra land.

Is the case nonetheless a permissible extension of the law? Probably not. It is likely to be a case of hard cases making bad law. It fudges the boundaries of the ancient doctrine in a way which is difficult to reconcile with the nature of the doctrine as developed over the centuries. The principle is based on the reasonable expectation of the parties at the time of the grant. They could not have expected the Nicholls

[34] *c.f.* estoppels which bind successors in title.
[35] [1988] 1 E.G.L.R. 264.
[36] [1921] 1 Ch. 200.
[37] [1988] 1 E.G.L.R. 264.

L.J. solution, nor is it fair to suppose that any successor in title could have expected it. It causes huge difficulties with the normal method of inheriting of the grantor's original intention. Nicholls L.J. was forced to say that the extended deemed intention he had found in the case bound the successor of title of the original grantor, but would not bind any successor in title of the extra land, taken separately from the original grantor's land. One must ask how this fits with the established principles and how any owner of land is to predict such things. This is inventing law to accommodate law one has just invented. The doctrine of loyalty to the original paramount purpose of the grant is ancient and well-defined, and in need of sympathetic development into other territory. As noted above, the House of Lords has shown that it has application outside the sphere of real property. To seek to change its shape to suit the exigencies of the moment, and to do so within its established homeland of real property, seems less desirable.

Limits of the principle

Mere long enjoyment of right insufficient

11.16 Mere long enjoyment by a person of a right does not entitle him to invoke the principle if he is neither the original grantee or grantor, a successor in title or derivative owner from one of these, or at least a simultaneous purchaser from a common grantor (or successor in title, *etc.*, of the former). In *White v. Bass*[38] there was in fact a connection of sorts between the claimant and the original grantor, but it was affirmed that even so, mere long enjoyment of the right in question was insufficient for the claimant to be entitled to invoke the principle. He had to be within the original grant-relationship either originally or by descent, in effect.

The grantor must have been able to grant the implied right at the time of the original grant

11.17 In *Quicke v. Chapman*,[39] Cozens-Hardy L.J. put it simply thus: "I decline to imply a grant of light as against a man who could not have made an express grant of light over the land."

In that case, the vendor had been a developer who had had no ownership of the plots as a whole, merely the right to be given a lease of each plot to sell on to a purchaser after he had completed a house on it. No doubt the mechanism may have seemed rather unfair to the purchaser of one of these plots, when his vendor started to build a house obscuring his lights on the next-door plot with a view to obtaining a lease and selling that. However, the court, quite rightly,

[38] (1862) H. & N. 722; 158 E.R. 660.
[39] [1903] 1 Ch. 659 noted below.

refused to fudge or dilute the essential nature of the doctrine in order to relieve a hard case. Collins M.R. said:

> "the implication must rest upon the ascertained facts as to the interest of the grantor in the land out of which he is supposed to make the grant of an easement constituting that land the servient tenement."

No implied reservation of similar rights for grantor

11.18 The grantor (or vendor or lessor) may not claim a similar right against his grantee by virtue of any implied reservation yielded from the circumstances; he has to make any reservation in his own favour specifically. In *Suffield v. Brown*[40] Lord Westbury said:

> "It seems to me more reasonable and just to hold that if the grantor intends to reserve any right over the property granted it is his duty to reserve it expressly in the grant rather than to limit and cut down the operation of a plain grant . . . by the fiction of an implied reservation".

The plaintiff-grantors failed. In *Crossley & Sons v. Lightowler,*[41] the same approach was taken, even though the purchaser had in a sense "come to" the activities which were in derogation from grant. He had known that the vendor was in the habit of polluting a river, and bought some land on the river from the polluting vendor precisely in order to be in a position to take advantage of the principle of derogation from grant.

Further, if a vendor wants to reserve the right to derogate, he may not do so in ambiguous words, he must, as is the case with anyone who wishes to exclude fair dealing terms when he makes a contract, do so in plain words, which can easily be understood by the grantee. If not, his planned-for reservation will not be effective. See *Mundy v. Duke of Rutland*[42] in which the proposed operation by the landlord would have effectively destroyed the mine which he had let to the defendants.

Nature of the rule

11.19 We have seen that the rule has been regarded as giving rise to a set of rights akin to title rights[43]. Although, as with questions of interpretation of the contract, the court will look to the circumstances of the original contract, or the "matrix of facts", the non derogation rights are to be strictly differentiated from questions of interpretation of the contract. The rights have been classified as an implied covenant,

[40] (1864) 4 D.J. & S. 185; 46 E.R. 888.
[41] (1867) L.R. 2 Ch. 478.
[42] (1883) 23 Ch. D. 81.
[43] By Romer L.J. in ***Quicke v. Chapman*** [1903] 1 Ch. 659.

or in the nature of an implied covenant, but one arising from circumstances outside the deed, as an incident in the grantor-grantee post sale *relationship*. In *Birmingham, Dudley & District Banking Co v. Ross*,[44] Cotton L.J. said:

> "That obligation [not to interfere with that which the vendor has granted] arises, I repeat, not from any interpretation of the conveyance, but from *the duty* which is imposed on the grantor *in consequence of the relation which he has taken upon himself towards the grantee*."[45]

The circumstances, he went on, were looked at because the court had to have regard to all the circumstances which existed at the time when the conveyance was executed which brought the parties into that relation from which the implied obligation results. Note also the judgments of Lindley L.J. and Bowen L.J. in the same case. The latter said it was:

> "a duty that arises from the outside circumstances having regard to the relation of grantor and grantee which the deed creates ... it is only looking outside the deed that you see that such a power of protection on the part of the grantor in favour of the grantee exists."

The case of *Beddington v. Atlee*[46] shows clearly that the principle is not a question of interpretation of the contract. In that case a vendor sold to purchaser A a house which enjoyed certain lights from its windows and sold some adjoining land to purchaser B. The contract to sell the land was first in time out of the two. The conveyances were in the opposite order of time, and the conveyance of the house granted no express right to light. The pre-conveyance circumstances were considered by Chitty J., who held that the Judicature Acts compelled him to give due weight to the position in equity as had been done by the Equity Courts prior to the Judicature Acts.[47] The buyer of the house was not entitled to set up a right to light against the purchaser of the land because the circumstances of the two contracts showed that no reservation of light was intended in favour of the later purchaser.

Also relevant is the case of *Pollard v. Gare*[48] in which the pre-conveyance agreement that a house of specified character would be built on certain land gave rise to a derogation-from-grant right even though neither the lease of the plaintiff's land nor the later conveyance by the vendor to others gave any express right.

[44] (1888) 38 Ch. D. 295.
[45] Italics supplied.
[46] (1887) 35 Ch. D. 317.
[47] He cited ***Compton v. Richards*** (1814) 1 Price 27; 145 E.R. 1320 and ***Swansborough v. Coventry*** (1832) 9 Bing. 305.
[48] [1910] 1 Ch. 834.

Ascertaining the extent of the right descending to the purchaser:

Assessing the reasonable expectation of the grantee or purchaser from the circumstances of the original grant

11.20 In *Birmingham Dudley & District Banking Co v. Ross*[49] Bowen L.J. said in the Court of Appeal:

> "But coming to the amount of enjoyment of light that is supposed by the law to accompany in an ordinary case the lease or the grant of a house which is erected with window-lights, where the grantor of the house is also the owner of premises either adjoining or neighbouring, then this presumption arises, that the grantor intends the grantee to enjoy so much light unobstructed as must under the circumstances have been assumed by both parties to be reasonably necessary for the fair and comfortable use of the premises which are the subject of the grant. That seems to me to be the real definition and measure of the ordinary implication that arises. . . .
>
> Now if it is an obligation which arises from such an implication, it must be measured by all the surrounding circumstances. The presumption that arises in favour of the ordinary measure can be rebutted by shewing that the circumstances are not ordinary circumstances, or, to speak more accurately, it is not a case of rebutting a presumption, it is a question of the proper inference to be drawn from a consideration of all the facts . . ."

In that case, the effect of the surrounding circumstances went to *narrow* the purchaser's reasonable expectation, and thus his non-derogation rights against the grantor. He had known perfectly well that there would be building by the grantor on the other side of the roadway from the building land he had bought, since it had been known to all concerned that the sale had been part of an urban renewal scheme, to improve an unhealthy area of Birmingham. In effect, the main purpose of the contract had become not, to build a building, but to build a building as part of the urban renewal scheme.

11.21 The surrounding circumstances will not include evidence of negotiations between the parties prior to the contract[50], but will include any understanding or collateral agreement reached between the parties before the main contract, and will also include facts which are communicated by the vendor to the purchaser. In *Myers v. Catterson,*[51] Bowen L.J., having said that the law imposes an implied obligation on the vendor who retains land to use only such of his rights of ownership as can be used consistently with the convenient and reasonable enjoyment house he has sold as a house, continued:

[49] (1888) 38 Ch. D. 295.
[50] See, *e.g.* the preceding case.
[51] (1889) 43 Ch. D. 470.

"That is the ordinary implication. But, as is clear, this implication depends upon *what one gathers from observing the transaction and trying to find in it a clue to the mutual intention of the parties*, and as soon as you add facts which make it obvious that the intention of the parties was one way or the other, then you have facts which give a colour to the inference which the law draws, and which very often lessen the obligation which, in the absence of those facts, or that fact, would be supposed to have arisen. I keep a piece of land and sell the house as a house. The obvious intention, in the absence of anything else, is that I intend it to be used as a house. *But if at the time I sell it I make it clear to the person who is taking the house*,—or supposing the circumstances of the case make it clear to him,—that although I sell it to him as a house, *I am intending nevertheless to use the remainder of my land, which I keep, in a way which may interfere in some degree with the full enjoyment of the house as a house,—then you get a new fact or a new element introduced into the case, which shews that the intention of the parties was a limited one*,[52] and that it was not intended by the parties that the full use of the house as a house, or the full enjoyment of the lights and windows as windows, was the essence of the transaction."

In *Robinson v. Kilvert*[53] the focus was on the grantor's knowledge of the paramount purpose of the contract at the time of the grant. It was proved that they had known the letting was for the purpose of the plaintiff lessee's business as a twine and paper merchant. They had not known of his intention to deal in brown paper among other papers, or any other particular class of paper. Thus, the Court of Appeal considered the lessee was not entitled to call on the principle of non-derogation against the landlord when a boiler on the landlord's retained premises damaged this class of paper, but left other stores unaffected.

Not confined to implying easements; wider rights may be protected

11.22 It follows from the cases cited above that the non-derogation right may be wider, and may be altogether different from an easement. It is thus not confined to the implication of easements.[54]

The unimportance of more limited express covenants in the grant

11.23 Because the rule against derogation from grant is a relationship-based obligation rather than a matter of interpretation of the contract

[52] Italics supplied.

[53] (1889) 41 Ch. D. 88.

[54] See ***Johnston v. Holland*** [1988] 1 E.G.L.R. 264 below and see for examples of non-easement rights protected by the principle ***Aldin v. Latimer Clark, Muirhead & Co*** [1894] 2 Ch. 437; ***Cable v. Bryant*** [1908] 1 Ch. 259; ***Lyttelton Times Co v. Warners*** [1907] A.C. 476; and ***Harmer v. Jumbil (Nigeria) Tin Limited*** [1921] 1 Ch. 200.

or grant, it follows that an express agreement or covenant in limited terms in the contract, grant, conveyance, *etc*, will *not* have the effect of cutting down the implied agreement or covenant of non-derogation. In *Grosvenor Hotel v. Hamilton*,[55] the landlord had given his tenant of the next-door premises an express covenant for quiet enjoyment in terms too limited to cover the landlord's activities complained of. These caused damaging vibrations to the demised premises. All three members of the Court of Appeal thought the express covenant was no bar to the tenant's action. As Lindley L.J. put it:

> "The house was demised by the person who caused the vibration, and he cannot defeat the grant contained in the lease. This consideration gets rid of the difficulty that a covenant for quiet enjoyment applicable to this case cannot be implied."

They then went on to consider the remedy: this they all thought was in nuisance (Lopes L.J. thought it would also be trespass.) The reasoning seems to have been that the landlord's normal obligations were, as it were, given extended boundaries by the application of the non-derogation principle, so turning into nuisance in his case an act which would have been permitted to anyone else.

Principle not confined to physical interference by the grantor

11.24 In *Harmer v. Jumbil (Nigeria) Tin Areas Limited*[56] the Court of Appeal had little difficulty in throwing out the argument put on behalf of the grantor that the principle extended only to physical interference with land and did not extend to what in argument was rather quaintly labelled "metaphysical" interference. It was held that the implied obligation which was to be inferred from the circumstances of the lease, was based on a lease for the express purpose of an explosives magazine. All agreed on the significance of the purpose for which the premises were let, sold, *etc*. They all defined the right in slightly different but similar terms. Lord Sterndale said that the obligation was that the lessor "would not do anything which would violate the conditions of the existing [explosives] licence" because the lessor must be taken to have known that "acts that violated the conditions of the licence might cause its withdrawal". Warrington L.J. said that it was not to to do anything which would render the premises "*unfit, or materially less fit, for the purpose for which they were demised.*[57]" Younger L.J. said that the obligation must be such as:

> "In view of the surrounding circumstances, was within the reasonable contemplation of the parties at the time when the transaction was entered into, and was at that time within the grantor's power to fulfil. But so limited, the obligation imposed may, I think, be infinitely varied in kind, regard being had to the paramount purpose to serve which it is imposed."

[55] [1894] 2 Q.B. 836.
[56] [1921] 1 Ch. 200.
[57] Italics supplied.

No right to prevent mere interference with comfort and privacy; no right to prevent acts making the enjoyment of the subject matter of the grant merely more expensive

11.25 In *Browne v. Flower*[58] it was held that an outside staircase on the grantor's retained land which interfered with the comfort and privacy of the flat in the same building previously demised by the grantor could not be prevented by reliance on any non-derogation right. Parker J. thought acts which merely affected the amenities of property were generally outside the rule.

In *O'Cedar v. Slough Trading Co. Ltd*[59] the lessee of a factory failed to prevent the lessor from letting some of his retained land to a woodworker, and thereby putting up the insurance premium on the leased land greatly, but not hindering the lessee in any other way from the intended use of his land.

PART 2—RETENTION OF SOMETHING AFFECTING THE THING SOLD

The vendor's duties regarding retained common parts

The vendor (usually a landlord after sale of a lease) who retains common parts must take reasonable care to see that these are not in a condition which prevents the use of what is sold for the main purpose of the contract

11.26 This principle clearly developed from a slightly unexpected source, not from derogation from grant as might well have been the case, but from the law about terms as to fitness for purpose which became part of the Sale of Goods Act 1893. This is particularly quaint, since the case of *Francis v. Cockrell*[60] which initially gave rise to the principle, was about the supplying of a grandstand for people to view the races, and expressly disclaimed any relationship with landlord and tenant law (on the grounds that there a proper inspection would then have tended to be made first). However, one can see that there is need for a principle to cover the liability defects which become apparent during the relationship, where these are not the subject of express agreement. One cannot say that a particularly clear principle of loyalty to the main purpose of the contract has emerged in this area: judges have tended to draw back from committing themselves, and in *Liverpool City Council v. Irwin*[61], the majority at least, and perhaps all of the court thought that the principle was simply one of business efficacy. Yet even in that case there was considerable emphasis on the *ongoing*

[58] [1911] 1 Ch. 219.
[59] [1927] 2 K.B. 123.
[60] (1870) L.R. 5 Q.B. 501.
[61] [1977] A.C. 239.

relationship between landlord and tenant, and the fact that the *purpose of the letting of the flats as dwellinghouses* would be rendered virtually impossible by the unmaintained lifts, *etc.* One may perhaps say, if it was an implied term of business efficacy, at all events the implied term owed a great deal to the background of deemed loyalty to the main purpose of the contract.[62]

APPENDIX TO CHAPTER 11: SOME CASES OF INTEREST

PART 1: DEROGATION FROM GRANT

***Palmer v. Fletcher* (in the 15th year of Charles II's reign)**

11.27 The vendor built a house, and subsequently split the estate, selling the house to one purchaser and then the adjoining land to another. It was held that the purchaser of the lands, the successor in title of the vendor, could no more obstruct the windows of the house than the original vendor could have done in derogation of his own grant.

***Cox v. Matthews* (in the 24th and 25 year of Charles II's reign) 1 Vent 237; 86 E.R. 159**

11.28 A lessor was not permitted to stop up the lights of his own lessee.

***Rosewell v. Pryor* (in the 2nd year of Queen Anne's reign) 6 Mod.116; 87 E.R. 874**

11.29 The case arose purely on a pleading point, but Holt C.J. affirmed the principle that if a house built on a vacant piece of ground has very good lights, and the vendor lets this house; neither he nor his lessee of a contiguous piece of ground may build so as to obstruct these lights.

***Compton v. Richards* (1814) 1 Price 27, 145 E.R. 1320**

11.30 This was a simultaneous purchase of two plots from one vendor. The houses on each plot were nearing completion, and the window openings were made in each at the time of sale. It was held that the principle of derogation from grant applied to prevent one of the purchasers from extending his house so as to obstruct one of the windows on the other plot.

***Swansborough v. Coventry* (1832) 9 Bing.305; 131 E.R. 629**

11.31 Tindal C.J. held that the principle of derogation from grant applied so as to preserve the ancient lights to the plaintiff' house, where there had been

[62] *c.f.* the interesting Court of Appeal case of *Timeload Limited v. British Telecommunications PLC* [1995] E.M.L.R. 459 noted *in at* para. 12.43 below, for a similar approach in the case of termination of a licence to use a telephone number.

simultaneous conveyances, even though the defendant's conveyance described the latter's land as building land. Tindal C.J. took into account as part of the surrounding circumstances of the grants that there had been a house once on the defendant's land which extended up to the first storey of the plaintiff's house. He considered that on the true construction of the defendant's conveyance, building up to one storey only was permitted to the defendant. If the defendant were to be permitted to obstruct the plaintiff's lights, this would involve derogation from the vendor's grant.

***North Eastern Railway Company v. Elliot* (1860) 1 J. & H. 145; 70 E.R. 697**

11.32 The plaintiff railway company took a conveyance of land from a Mr Boulcott under its compulsory powers. The conveyance recited that the purchase was for the purpose of forming the railway, and the plans of the railway showed that the land was intended to form the foundation for the abutments of a large bridge over the river Wear. There was an old mine beneath both the land compulsorily purchased and part of the retained land. Mr Elliot was a lessee from Mr Boulcott of the mines. He proposed to work the minerals, and to pump water out of the shafts on his leased land.

Sir Page Wood V.C. (later Lord Hatherley) referred to the evidence, in particular to the fact that the mines had been drowned at the time of the plaintiff's purchase, and that the plaintiff had *proceeded on the assumption that that state of things would continue.* He explained that the case of *Caledonian Railway Company v. Sprot*[63] and other authorities determined that: "the common law, independently of any question of priority, gives to every landowner the right to have his own soil in its natural state supported by the adjoining soil ... The common law gave no further right to support, and if you build upon your land you have no such right to support for the additional weight. But if a landlowner conveys one of two closes to another, he cannot afterwards do anything to derogate from his grant; and *if the conveyance is made for the express purpose of having buildings erected upon the land so granted, a contract is implied on the part of the grantor to do nothing to prevent the land from being used for the purpose for which to the knowledge of the grantor the conveyance is made.*[64]

***White v. Bass* (1862) 7 H. & N. 722; 158 E.R. 660**

11.33 The owners of a house and land granted a 99 year lease to trustees, who covenanted to build upon it according to a certain plan. Later they also conveyed the reversion in the land but not the house to the trustees; and still later conveyed the house to a third party. The successor in title of the third party was held not entitled to maintain an action for obstruction of his lights against the trustees as owners of the land, even though the trustees had built higher than the lease covenants (merged) would have permitted. It had been argued that the existence of the house with its long-enjoyed lights was a circumstance from which the right might be implied, but this argument was rejected.

***Hall v. Lund* (1863) 1 H. & C. 676; 158 E.R. 1055**

11.34 The owner of two mills had granted a lease of one to A, and later granted a new lease on the same terms after the surrender of the original lease by A. A had been in the habit of discharging the refuse from the mill works into a stream upon which the other mill was situated. B, the purchaser of the free-

[63] 2 McQ. 449.
[64] Italics supplied.

hold of both mills from the owner (who had carried on the business of a paper maker from the un-leased mill) was not permitted by the court to prevent the lessee from continuing to discharge into the stream. He could be in no better position than the first owner, who could not have derogated from his grant.

Martin B. desired to rest his judgment on the decision of the House of Lords in *Ewart v. Cochrane*[65] "that where there is a demise of premises with which certain rights have been usually enjoyed, it must be taken that the lessor has granted those rights." He continued, "It is not necessary to consider what is appurtenant or what is not appurtenant – there is the decision of the House of Lords to the effect which I have stated." (He went on to say it did not matter whether the right was an easement in the strict sense of the term.) Channell B thought the user (on average seven times in a fortnight, was sufficiently continuous. He also relied on *Ewart v. Cochrane*[66]

Wilde B. warned that he did not think a lessee might in every case have all the liberties and privileges enjoyed by the former lessee. "It seems to me that, in cases of implied grant, the implication must be confined to a reasonable use of the premises for the purpose for which, according to the obvious intention of the parties, they are demised. Some rules are obvious enough. A demise of a brewery would carry with it the right to use the premises for brewing; although that might be a nuisance to the lessor or his assigns. . . . Each case must depend on its own circumstances and the intention of the parties, to be ascertained from the character, state, and use of the premises at the time of the grant . . ."

***Suffield v. Brown* (1864) 4 D.J. & S. 185; 46 E.R. 888**

11.35 A small strip of land beside a dock was sold off in the fullest possible manner. The dock owners were in the habit of of allowing the bowsprits of vessels in the dock to overhand the strip of land, but no express reservation of the right was made. The following passage from the judgment of Lord Westbury is significant. It was quoted in two later cases: *Crossley & Sons v Lightowler* and in *Wheeldon v Burrows*, both noted below: "It seems to me more reasonable and just to hold that if the grantor intends to reserve any right over the property granted it is his duty to reserve it expressly in the grant rather than to limit and cut down the operation of a plain grant . . . by the fiction of an implied reservation". The plaintiffs failed.

***Crossley & Sons v. Lightowler* (1867) L.R. 2 Ch.478**

11.36 The plaintiff Company wished to prevent the fouling of the river by some dye-works. He bought a piece of land on the banks of the river from the owner of the dye-works without mentioning his purpose. No reservation of the right to foul the river was made. The injunction he sought to prevent the pollution was granted by Lord Chelmsford L.C.

***Wheeldon v. Burrows* (1879) 12 Ch.D.31**

11.37 Thesiger L.J. laid down that there were two general rules governing cases of the kind before him:

(1) "that on the grant by the owner of a tenement of part of that tenement as it is then used and enjoyed, there will pass to the grantee all those continuous and apparent easements (by which I mean *quasi* easements) or, in other words, all those easements which are *necessary*

[65] 4 Macq. Sc. App. 117.
[66] (above).

to the reasonable enjoyment of the property granted, and which *have been and are at the time of the grant used by the owners of the entirety for the benefit of the part granted*".[67]

(2) "The second proposition is that, if the grantor intends to reserve any right over the tenement granted, it is his duty to reserve it expressly in the grant. [He went on to except ways of necessity, *inter alia.*]

Allen v. Taylor **(1880) 16 Ch.D.357**

11.38 Jessel M.R. merely decided in accordance with the above cases, noting that in any case the parties' intention that each should keep his ancient lights was manifest, from the fact that each was a party to the others' conveyance.

Rigby v. Bennett **(1882) 21 Ch.D.559 (Jessel M.R., Cotton L.J., Brett L.J.)**

11.39 The Corporation of Liverpool put up a piece of land for sale in lots, each purchaser to take a lease and to be bound to build upon the lots in accordance with the plans provided by the corporation. The plaintiff bought a lot and commenced to build a house. The foundations were deeper than shown on the plan, but the depth was approved by the corporation. The defendant later bought another lot, and, deciding to excavate yet deeper foundations to his house, endangered the foundations of the plaintiff's house. The plaintiff's right of support was affirmed on appeal.

Cotton L.J. said: The Plaintiff makes this case "I took this grant of land for the purpose of building a house upon it . . . and I rely on the principle that in such a grant there is an implied obligation on the part of the grantor that he will not derogate from his own grant, *that he will not deal with his adjoining property so as to destroy the house which he intended I should build on the land when he granted it to me.*"[68] He reserved the position if it had been impossible to build in a reasonable way on the adjoining land without letting down the plaintiff's house.

Mundy v. Duke of Rutland **(1883) 23 Ch.D.81 (Jessel M.R., Cotton L.J., Bowen L.J.)**

11.40 The Duke of Rutland let one of the upper strata of his coal to the trustees of a settlement of which the plaintiff was tenant for life, reserving to himself and his lessees the right of working any coal not included in that demise, and the same powers and privileges with respect to such last-mentioned coal as if that demise had not been made: provided always, that in exercising these the working of the coal then demised should not be prevented or unnecessarily interfered with, and that compensation should be made to the plaintiff for any necessary interference with the workings. The Duke afterwards demised some of the strata of coal underneath the Plaintiff's to the Manners Colliery Company. The plaintiff sought an injunction restraining certain workings on these strata, fearing that the workings would cause a large quantity of water to press against the outside of their barrier and cause injury.

It was held by the Court of Appeal that the construction of the clause contended for by the defendants would permit them to destroy the subject of the demise altogether. Where a grantor intends to reserve to himself such a right he ought to express it in clear terms, and the onus is on him to show that he has such a clause. Jessel M.R. said: "Of course you may make any kind of bargain: and it may be that these people would have agreed to pay £500 a

[67] Italics supplied.
[68] Italics supplied.

year and get nothing for it. But if you ask me to speculate as to whether rational men would be likely to enter into such a bargain I do not think they would; and therefore whatever the construction is, I cannot bring my mind to believe that the construction contended for by the Defendants was the construction intended by the parties. It is not necessary for me to say more than that. There is not to my mind in this lease a clause authorizing the landlord to do what he claims to do, and it is for him to shew that he has such a clause. As he has not made that out clearly, I think the point of construction must be decided in favour of the Respondents."

Cotton L.J. said: ". . . I have found the very greatest difficulty in understanding what the provision in favour of the landlord was intended to be or to what extent it is to go. . . . *We must deal with this case on the hypothesis that the work which the landlord intends to carry on, or which the Defendants, his lessees, intend to carry on, would destroy that barrier which the Plaintiffs were to leave, and for which they were to pay rent. Where a grantor intends to reserve to himself such a right he ought to express it in clear terms, and although I cannot say to what extent this right reserved to the landlord was intended to go, it, in my opinion, does not contain sufficiently plain terms to enable him to carry on operations which would entirely destroy, according to our present hypothesis, that which was demised to his lessees.*"[69]

Bowen L.J. said: "I have studied this clause, and at the end I remain in profound uncertainty as to what it means . . . If the landlord had meant to reserve the power which he claims he should have done so in clear terms."

The court adjourned the matter for further evidence as to the likelihood of damage, and subsequently granted the injunction sought.

***Beddington v. Atlee* (1887) 35 Ch. D. 317**

11.41 A house which enjoyed lights, and adjoining land, were each sold separately by the owner. The contract to sell the land came before that to sell the house: the conveyances were in the opposite order of time. The buyer of the house claimed a right to light as against the buyer of the other land.

Chitty J. said: "Now I go to the question which has been so much argued, as to the grant to be implied on the conveyance. The first observation I make is this: on reading the conveyance no implication whatever arises. It is not like the case of an implied grant when, upon reading the instrument, you say the terms employed mean so and so; and it is necessary, in order to give effect to the intention, as manifested by the deed, to imply something which is not expressed in so many words. In this case, *in order to raise any implied grant, it is necessary to look outside the deed of conveyance, and to consider the surrounding circumstances*. . . . It is necessary to make an inquiry in regard to the adjoining land, that is to say, the alleged servient tenement.

. . . Cases have been cited and commented upon with regard to *the doctrine of implied grant. The maxim is, that the grantor shall not derogate from his own grant. That is a compendious way of stating this head of law, it embodies the principle upon which implied grant has been founded.*[70] In the cases at law before the *Judicature Acts*, and I may say before the *Common Law Procedure Act*, a Court of Law did not recognise equitable titles. . . . Consequently, when the Court was asked to raise implication, the Court of Law did not in the cases referred to go into any question of equitable title. However in ***Compton v. Richards*** 1 Price 27 and ***Swansborough v. Coventry*** 9 Bing. 305 the Court appears to some extent to have proceeded on matters relating to the adjoining land, which were outside the grant itself.

[69] Italics supplied.
[70] Italics supplied.

Chitty J. then looked into the circumstances, and considered that if there had been any inquiry made into the title of the adjoining land it would have been the duty of the vendor and his advisers to disclose the equitable title of the defendant, to whom he had contracted to sell the land. "But there was no such investigation in this case. Therefore I think that a plea on the part of the Plaintiff that he was a purchaser of the supposed legal right without notice could not be maintained."

Note: The case is of interest for the application of the constructive (failure to investigate) principle to the pre-contractual circumstances being looked at to ascertain the extent of the principle. The purchaser here was fixed with constructive notice of the enquiries he should have made, even though he did not (it seems) make them, and was thus unable to claim that on the conveyance to him he became a purchaser for value without notice.

Birmingham Dudley & District Banking Co. v. Ross **(1888) 38 Ch.D.295**

11.42 The Birmingham Corporation had made a scheme for the improvement of an unhealthy area in the borough. It made a map of the scheme showing a main street, Corporation Street, which was to be 66 feet wide, and a number of other intended new streets. The plaintiff bought a part of the scheme land for the purpose of building shops, auction rooms, and premises. He built buildings facing Corporation St which were 48 feet high. The defendant bought a similar plot on the opposite side of Corporation Street from the Corporation, but began to build buildings which were to be about 80 feet high. The plaintiff applied at trial (by which time the defendant had finished his building) for an injunction obliging the defendant to lower them. Kekewich J. at first instance found that the plaintiff: "must be taken to have known that the corporation of *Birmingham* had made large purchases of land for the purpose of constructing a new and important thoroughfare, and that this could properly be done and that they could recoup their expenditure only by selling or letting the land for building purposes. He must be taken to have known generally what class of buildings were likely to be erected in a broad street in a commercial town."

Kekewich J. considered accordingly that the rule as to derogation from grant did not apply, by reason of the plaintiff's knowledge, inferred from the surrounding circumstances. On appeal, Cotton L.J. considered whether the right claimed was contained in the implied obligation on the vendor *not to interfere* with that which he has granted: namely, the house, and enjoyment of the house. He said:[71] "That obligation arises, I repeat, not from any interpretation of the conveyance, but from *the duty which is imposed on the grantor in consequence of the relation which he has taken upon himself towards the grantee.*"[72] However, he considered that when considering the question of an implied obligation, "we must have regard to all the circumstances which existed at the time when the conveyance was executed which brought the parties into that relation from which the implied obligation results. . ." He then defined in effect what we would now call the "factual matrix" of the lease, and concluded this was such that the plaintiff could not claim the particular right he wanted.

Lindley L.J. said: "The grant of an easement of this kind is, properly speaking, an implied covenant by the grantor not to use his own land so as to injure the rights of [the Plaintiff] and those claiming under him". He too dismissed the appeal, on the facts as to the plaintiff's knowledge.

Bowen L.J. noted that the maxim that a grantor shall not derogate from his

[71] *Ibid.* at 308.
[72] Italics supplied.

own grant was at least as old as the Year Books. He too considered the nature of the right to window-light in general. He noted that it was not necessary to presume a grant as in the case of an affirmative easement such as a right of way; but considered that no doubt it originated in some consent on the part of the person who has the right to obstruct the light; and that it was more in the nature of a right that arises from an implied covenant or an express covenant than from what is strictly speaking called a grant. He considered the obligation, if it existed here, must be an implied, not express obligation. "It is not an obligation which arises simply from the interpretation of the deed as read by the light of the circumstances outside. It is a *duty that arises from the outside circumstances having regard to the relation of grantor and grantee which the deed creates.*[73] . . . it is only by looking outside the deed that you see that such a power of protection on the part of the grantor in favour of the grantee exists."

Thus, all of the facts had to be considered, and these were fatal to the claim, since the plaintiff knew perfectly well that there must be some interference with his lights by building.

***Robinson v. Kilvert* (1889) 41 Ch.D.88**

11.43 The landlord had let premises for the purpose of a paper and twine merchant. A boiler on the landlord's ground-floor retained premises below caused heat to rise to the demised premises above which damaged the lessee's brown paper (only) which was stored on his premises. Cotton L.J. said: "Then it was contended that there was an implied contract . . . that the Defendants would not do anything to interfere with the Plaintiff's trade. Now to determine into what implied contract the Defendants can be considered to have entered, *we must consider what was known to them when they let the property.*[74] They undoubtedly knew that the Plaintiff took it for the purposes of his business as a twine and paper merchant, but it is not shewn that they knew anything as to his dealing in any particular class of paper."

Lindley L.J. explained that the grounds on which the plaintiff put his case were: nuisance, breach of the covenants for quiet enjoyment, in rendering the premises unfit for the purpose for which they were let, and thirdly, which he thought came to the same thing, that the lessors were by their own acts derogating from their grant. He felt that these grounds failed. Lopes L.J. agreed: "Then as to the contention that the Defendants have broken an implied agreement not to do anything which will make the property unfit for the purpose for which it was let, we must look to what the Defendants at the time of letting knew as to the purpose for which the demised property was to be used. [A paper warehouse, simply.]

***Myers v. Catterson* (1889) 43 Ch.D.470**

11.44 The London Chatham and Dover Railway Company sold off a piece of their surplus land together with a house to the plaintiff. The house obtained light through two brick arches supporting a viaduct on the company's land. The railway company gave no express grant of any right to light to the plaintiff, but the conveyance contained a recital that all the remainder of their retained land would actually be required by them for the construction of their railway. The defendant in the action was a successor of title of one Isaacs who had bought a part of the railway company's land opposite the plaintiff's house. Mr Isaac's conveyance was subject to any right of light which the plaintiff

[73] Italics supplied.
[74] Italics supplied.

might have. He also took a 1000 year lease of the arches. The defendant put up hoardings which the plaintiff claimed materially obstructed the access of light to the windows of his house. Cotton L.J. held that there was an implied obligation not to do anything on the adjoining land to interfere with the plaintiff's reasonable enjoyment of the land sold except that which was necessarily required for the construction of the railway.

Bowen L.J. said: " . . . *As in the case of all other implied covenants, or implied obligations, in order to see what the measure of the obligation is we must look at the reason of the thing, and at the surrounding circumstances, in order to ascertain, if we can, what was the obvious intention of the parties, so as to give to the transaction between them that minimum of efficacy and value, which, upon any view of the case, it must have been their common intention that it should have.*" He then posited a situation where an ordinary landowner has two pieces of land which either adjoin or are so near to one another that the enjoyment of the one, perhaps for all purposes, or at any rate for some purposes, depends upon the user to be made of the other portion of land . . .

"Surely it must be in the contemplation of the parties that, in the absence of any express agreement one way or the other, *the vendor shall not so use that land which he retains as to preclude any possible use of the building or land which he sells, or to prevent that use of it for which he knows he is selling it to the purchaser. It would be contrary to common notions of justice and fair dealing if it were otherwise; and the truth is that the law in such a case, when the parties have entered into the relation of vendor and purchaser, assumes from the circumstances an obligation on the part of the seller not to do anything with his own land which would defeat the known mutual intention of both parties upon the sale.*"[75]

Later, he said that the law imposes an implied obligation on the vendor who retains land to use only such of his rights of ownership as can be used consistently with the convenient and reasonable enjoyment of the house he has sold as a house. "That is the ordinary implication. But, as is clear, this implication depends upon what one gathers from observing the transaction and trying to find in it a clue to the mutual intention of the parties, and as soon as you add facts which make it obvious that the intention of the parties was one way or the other, then you have facts which give a colour to the inference which the law draws, and which very often lessen the obligation which, in the absence of those facts, or that fact, would be supposed to have arisen. I keep a piece of land and sell the house as a house. The obvious intention, in the absence of anything else, is that I intend it to be used as a house. But if at the time I sell it I make it clear to the person who is taking the house,—or supposing the circumstances of the case make it clear to him,—that although I sell it to him as a house, I am intending nevertheless to use the remainder of my land, which I keep, in a way which may interfere in some degree with the full enjoyment of the house as a house,—then you get a new fact or a new element introduced into the case, which shews that the intention of the parties was a limited one, and that it was not intended by the parties that the full use of the house as a house, or the full enjoyment of the lights and windows as windows, was the essence of the transaction." Fry L.J. concurred.

Note: The intention of the parties is looked to, but only a limited aspect of that intention, "the reason of the thing". It might be more accurate to say that the purpose (known to both parties) for which the land was to be used is ascertained. The bland expression "the intention of the parties", common as it is, is somewhat misleading. The same expression occurs in regard to discussions of damages (the first branch of Hadley v. Baxendale), and with a similar connotation of reasonable expectation, rather than any inquiry into what the parties actually intended.

[75] Italics supplied.

***Grosvenor Hotel v. Hamilton* [1894] 2 Q.B. 836**

11.45 A company let a house to an individual. The house was weak and insecure. The company ran a hotel next door, and after the tenancy commenced, sunk another well to supply the hotel with water. The water was pumped up. The vibrations damaged the tenant's house. The tenant moved out and refused to pay further rent. There was a covenant for quiet enjoyment in the tenant's lease but in terms too limited to be applicable to assist his claim. Lindley L.J. held that the tenant had a cause of action, apparently in nuisance (although it might have different had the principle of derogation from grant not applied to make the landlord's action nuisance). He said[76]: "... the cause of action being the vibration which has brought the house down... The house was demised by the person who caused the vibration, and he cannot defeat the grant contained in the lease. This consideration gets rid of the difficulty that a covenant for quiet enjoyment applicable to this case cannot be implied. Where there is an express covenant for quiet enjoyment in a lease it excludes any implied one: *Line v. Stephenson*.[77]. An action therefore will not lie on the ground of implied covenant, but it will lie on the ground I have stated. Before the Judicature Acts the action would have been an action on the case." Lopes L.J. considered the landlord's activities amounted to nuisance; Davey L.J. thought it was nuisance or trespass.[78]

***Aldin v. Latimer Clark, Muirhead & Co* [1894] 2 Ch. 437**

11.46 The lessor let land to the plaintiff for the purpose of carrying on the business of a timber merchant, and the lessee covenanted to carry on such business. The lessee had subsequently, with the lessor's permission, constructed certain ventilators for his timber-drying sheds. The defendants, assigns of the lessor, had obstructed these by building erected on the adjoining retained property. Sterling J. referred to *North Eastern Railway Co v. Elliot*[79] and *Robinson v. Kilvert*[80] He considered that the result of these was: "that where a landlord demises part of his property for carrying on a particular business, he is bound to abstain from doing anything on the remaining portion which would render the demised premises unfit for carrying on such business in the way in which it is ordinarily carried on, but that this obligation does not extend to special branches of the business which call for extraordinary protection." He granted the lessee an inquiry as to the damages suffered by him by reason of the defendants' buildings rendering the drying sheds less fit for use by him in the *ordinary* course of his business as a timber merchant.

Note: Sterling J. was in effect trying to delimit the boundaries of the non-derogation implied term. The time element, namely that the advent of the drying sheds with the landlord's permission was subsequent to the grant, was also a factor, consistently with the Court of Appeal's decision in Myers v. Catterson[81]. *Sterling J. also made it abundantly plain that the search is for a "purpose" not "purposes": that is, it is the*

[76] *Ibid.* at 840.

[77] 5 Bing (N.C.) 678.

[78] The landlord had argued that the measure of damages was only the value of the term of which the defendant had been deprived: *Lock v. Furze* 19 CB (N.S.) 96; *Rolph v. Crouch* LR. 3 Ex. 44; *Williams v. Burrell* 1 C.B. 402. The court did not agree (Lindley L.J. enquiring in the course of argument whether the party in *Lock v. Furze* had sustained any consequential damage); and awarded damages based on "whatever loss results to the injured party as a natural consequence of the wrongful act of the defendant. (Lindley L.J. at 840).

[79] above.

[80] above.

[81] above.

known "end" for which the land was to be used which has to be ascertained. If the principle was to be extended to anything permitted at any subsequent time, the inconvenience of the necessary inquiry would be enormous.

Pollard v. Gare [1901] 1 Ch. 834 (Principle not dependent on a formal deed)

11.47 Mrs Sophia Hartas contracted with the owners of a piece of land to build a house of a specified character on the land the subject matter of that agreement, and they agreed that on its completion, she would be granted a lease of the land on certain terms. The house was erected and the lease granted. The owners thereafter conveyed two plots on the land retained to the defendant Mary Ann Gare, who proceeded to erect a large hoarding which obstructed the plaintiff's light. Kekewich J. accepted for the purposes of the case that the rights of Mrs Hartas and her successors were fixed at the date of the original agreement, rather than the conveyance. "The doctrine that a grantor cannot derogate from his own grant must be applied not to the vacant piece of land, but to the land with the house on it according to the contract." He also referred to *Broomfield v. Williams*[82]

Quicke v. Chapman [1903] 1 Ch. 659

11.48 A builder had an agreement with the Ecclesiastical Commissioners whereby he might erect houses on a piece of land, and the Commissioners agreed that they would then grant 99 year leases of the houses to the purchasers. The leases were to be in a specified form, whereby the Commissioners reserved the right to erect any buildings whatsoever on the adjoining retained land whether or not such building would diminish the light enjoyed by the lessees. The builder erected a house on a plot, sold it on, and then proceeded to put up another house on an adjoining plot which obstructed the lights of the first. Collins M.R., Romer L.J. and Cozens-Hardy L.J. held that:

(1) The general words in section 6(2) of the Conveyancing Act 1881 only apply to pass on rights which the grantor had at the time;[83]
(2) The surrounding circumstances may be relevant, if known to both parties, in considering whether there is an implied grant of a right to light. These negatived the implication of any grant. The defendant had acquired the interest which was threatening the plaintiff *after* the date of the lease to the plaintiff of his plot and house: thus there could be no room for implication of a grant.

As Collins M.R. put it: "The solution, therefore, of the present case really lies in the true appreciation of what is the basis of an implication of a grant of light. As I have said, the implication must rest upon the ascertained facts as to the interest of the grantor in the land out of which he is supposed to make the grant of an easement constituting that land the servient tenement.... The defendant's interest in the adjoining plot was, as I have pointed out, only that which he had under his agreement with the Commissioners, and, unless that agreement enabled him to make that plot servient to an easement of light passing over it, there could be no grant of the easement by him and no implication of a grant.

Romer L.J.'s judgment, concurring, considered the implication of grants in a slightly broader way. He said: "Now, in order to see whether a grant of light over the adjacent land is to be implied, you must inquire into two things. You must first inquire into the title to that adjacent land, to see whether the

[82] [1897] 1 Ch. 602.
[83] *Booth v. Alcock* (1873) Ch. App. 663.

grantor has such an estate or interest in it as will support an implied grant by him of the right to the access of light over it. That inquiry is purely as to the title, and has nothing to do with the question whether the grantee did or did not at the time of the grant know of the state of the title. For, if he did not know at that time of the state of the title, still, if he claims a right over the adjacent land, he was bound to take such title as the grantor had. He is in no better position than he would have been if he had inquired into the title to the adjacent land.

But, in my opinion, more than that must be inquired into in order to see what passed by implication by the use of the word 'lights'. In my opinion you are also entitled to inquire into the surrounding circumstances which are relevant to such a question—the circumstances affecting the two pieces of land, though this is not strictly a matter of title and might not appear on the title if it were inquired into. In order that the circumstances may be relevant they must, in my opinion, have been known to both the parties. But, if they are known to both, although therefore not strictly a matter of title, yet, in my opinion, those circumstances must also be considered in order to see whether there is or is not an implied grant of the right to light over the adjacent land."

Cozens-Hardy L.J. agreed, and said: "I decline to imply a grant of light as against a man who could not have made an express grant of light over the land."

***Cable v. Bryant* [1908] 1 Ch. 259**

11.49 A brewery company owned a stable and adjacent yard. They conveyed the stable to the plaintiff. This stable was ventilated by apertures which let onto the adjacent yard. The adjacent yard was owned by the plaintiffs but let to a tenant at the time. Later the defendant acquired the freehold reversion in the yard from the company and the lease from the third party, so as to merge the latter in the freehold, and claimed that he might block up the apertures ventilating the plaintiff's stable. The defendant argued (*inter alia*) that derogation from grant was an equitable principle, and thus did not affect a purchaser for value without notice, which he claimed he was.

Neville J. held that derogation from grant was a rule of law, not a rule of equity. He relied on *Quicke v. Chapman*[84] for the proposition that there was a distinction between an implied covenant on the part of the grantor and the non-derogation rule. Accordingly, he considered that the grantor company and its successors in title could not derogate from grant "by any act which shall render the subject of the grant unfit from a reasonable point of view for the purpose for which it is granted."

***Lyttelton Times Co v. Warners* [1907] A.C. 476 (Privy Council case on appeal from the Court of Appeal of New Zealand)**

11.50 The lessees and the lessors had agreed that the lessors might rebuild their printing house adjoining the demised premises, placing their engine house and printing machinery on the ground floor, while the lessees were to have a lease of the upper floors as additional bedrooms for the hotel they ran on the demised premises. Both parties anticipated that the noise from the machinery would be slight. In the event, it was troublesome to the residents in the bedrooms above.

Lord Loreburn said:[85] "If A. lets a plot to B., he may not act so as to frustrate the purpose for which in the contemplation of both parties the land was hired.

[84] [1903] 1 Ch. 659.
[85] *Ibid*, at 481.

So also if B. takes a plot from A., he may not act so as to frustrate the purpose for which in the contemplation of both parties the adjoining plot remaining in A.'s hands was destined. The fact that one lets and the other hires does not create any presumption in favour of either in construing an expressed contract. Nor ought it to create a presumption in construing the implied obligations arising out of a contract. *When it is a question of what shall be implied from the contract, it is proper to ascertain what in fact was the purpose, or what were the purposes, to which both intended the land to be put, and, having found that, both should be held to all that was implied in this common intention.*"[86] He considered that both purposes had been intended; so that it followed neither could maintain any rights against the other which would frustrate either intention.

Note (1) The note introducing the case uses the expression "detrimental to" rather than "so as to frustrate", even though the latter expression is used in the judgment of the court. This is simply to avoid the ambiguity inherent in the word "frustrate": which can mean "operate detrimentally to but not prevent altogether; or "prevent altogether, render completely impossible". The facts of the case show that the former, wider meaning is the true one. Thus, within its relatively narrow ambit, the principle or implied term has a powerful effect on how the parties can act.

(2) See the note to Myers v. Catterson[87] on the expression "the parties' intention" as meaning the known purpose for which the land the subject matter of the grant was to be used.

***Browne v. Flower* [1911] 1 Ch.219**

11.51 Two flats had been let in the same house for residential use. The lessee of the second one to be let built an outside staircase to a part of her flat, which interfered with the comfort and privacy of the first. The plaintiffs relied on derogation from grant. Parker J. held:

(1) In the absence of anything in the terms of the grant or demise or in the circumstances of the particular case rebutting the implication, the grant would carry with it continuous and apparent quasi-easements.
(2) Further, there was an obligation on the grantor not to use the land retained by him in such a way as to render the land granted or demised unfit or materially less fit for the particular purpose for which the grant or demise was made. However, he distinguished *Lyttelton Times Co v. Warner*[88] on the facts before him. He considered that the staircase merely affected the comfort and privacy of those using the plaintiff's flat.

He said: "It is quite reasonable for a purchaser to assume that a vendor who sells land for a particular purpose will not do anything to prevent its being used for that purpose, but it would be utterly unreasonable to assume that the vendor was undertaking restrictive obligations which would prevent his using land retained by him for any lawful purpose whatsoever merely because his so doing might affect the amenities of the property he had sold. After all, a purchaser can always bargain for those rights which he deems indispensable to his comfort."

Note: There is clearly a fine line between an act merely affecting the privacy and comfort of the occupier of the land demised, as here, and the "troublesome" noise affecting the hotel bedrooms, in Lyttleton Times Co v. Warner.[89] We must suppose the answer lies in the fact that the hotel was a

[86] Italics supplied.
[87] Paragraph 11.44 above.
[88] para. 11.50 above.
[89] *Ibid.*

business, the economics of which would be affected by the noise in the hotel bedrooms; while the occupier of the flat would not suffer in the economic sense? However this explanation would not be consistent with O'Cedar v. Slough Trading Co.[90] *Perhaps the test is whether it can be said the interference renders the grantee's land less fit for its purpose.*[91]

***Harmer v. Jumbil (Nigeria) Tin Areas Limited* [1921] 1 Ch.200**

11.52 The plaintiff took a 21 year lease of land in Cornwall for the express purpose of an explosives magazine. The lessor entered into a covenant for quiet enjoyment with the tenant, but no further covenant. Both knew there had been extensive working of minerals in the past in the immediate neighbourhood. The lessee knew that any such workings, if they took place, would endanger his explosives licence. The defendant, who was a successor in title of the lessor, began to work the minerals so near to the plaintiff's land that the plaintiff was liable to lose his explosives licence. The argument was put on behalf of the defendant in the Court of Appeal that derogation from grant was confined to physical interference with the land: the interference in question was labelled "metaphysical" only.

Lord Sterndale M.R. adopted the law as stated by Eve J. in the court below[92]. He referred to certain surrounding circumstances, notably that the lessee's land was very small in relation to the retained land, and the rent was very small, though higher than agricultural rents having regard to the special purpose for which the land was let. It had been urged on the part of the defendant that this being a mining district there must be an implication that the grant did not extend so far as to interfere with the lessor's right to work his mines. Lord Sterndale did not think, however, that the working of the minerals on the retained land was contemplated by the parties. It had been claimed that the lessee "took the risk" since he had failed to obtain a covenant against mining operations. Lord Sterndale however felt that since neither party had in mind the working of the minerals, *both of them took the risk.*

"As a matter of fact I think, if the use of the expression "took the risk" is going to be relied on, both parties took the risk in this sense. The mines had not been worked for fifty years . . . as a matter of fact, it was the extraordinary change in value of minerals by reason of the influence of the late war that induced the reopening of these mines." He considered that the lessor must be taken to have known . . . "that acts that violated the conditions of the licence might cause its withdrawal." In those circumstances, there was an implied obligation on the part of the lessor that he would not do anything which would violate the conditions of the existing licence. He left open the question whether there was an obligation on the lessor in regard to any future licences.

Warrington L.J. also thought the principle was not confined to physical interference, and considered there was an implied obligation, *arising from the purposes for which these premises were demised*, that the lessor would not do anything which would render them unfit, or materially less fit for the purpose for which they were demised. He distinguished *Browne v. Flower*[93] where the premises had remained *fit* for residential purposes, although *less pleasant* to live in. He agreed with the Master of the Rolls that both took the risk.

[90] [1927] 2 K.B. 123.
[91] C.p. ***Harmer v. Jumbil Tin*** [1921] 1 Ch. 200.
[92] Who had referred to ***Aldin v. Latimer Clarke*** para. 11.46 above, and *Browne v. Flower* para. 11.51 above.
[93] para. 11.51 above.

Younger L.J. said[94]: "Now if these questions are to be answered in a sense favourable to the lessee, it must be on the principle that a grantor shall not derogate from his grant, *a principle which merely embodies in a legal maxim a rule of common honesty. . . . The rule is clear but the difficulty is, as always, in its application. For the obligation laid upon the grantor is not unqualified. If it were,. that which was imposed in the interest of fair dealing might, in unscrupulous hands, become a justification for oppression, or an instrument of extortion. The obligation therefore must in every case be construed fairly, even strictly, if not narrowly. It must be such as, in view of the surrounding circumstances, was within the reasonable contemplation of the parties at the time when the transaction was entered into, and was at that time within the grantor's power to fulfil. But so limited, the obligation imposed may, I think, be infinitely varied in kind, regard being had to the paramount purpose to serve which it is imposed.*"[95] He went further than his brethren in inferring knowledge on the part of the lessor of the terms of the licence, and for the rest, agreed with them.

Note: (1) The grantor has to have actual knowledge of the purpose (although such actual knowledge may be inferred from the circumstances): however he need then only have constructive knowledge of the detrimental effect his actions will have on the land granted (see above "must be taken to have known").

(2) The case is of interest in that the now-fashionable "allocation of risk" argument sometimes deployed against the implication of good faith was raised and firmly rejected in this context. The lessee could have obtained a specific covenant: yet the risk was allocated to the lessor by reason of the principle.

***O'Cedar Ltd v. Slough Trading Co Ltd* [1927] 2 K.B. 123**

11.53 Lessors had granted a lease of a factory which contained a covenant to reimburse the landlords for insuring the premises, and a covenant that they would not do or suffer anything which would cause an extra insurance premium to be paid. The landlord then proceeded to let some of his retained land to a woodworker, which put up the insurance premium greatly. Branson J. said, "I should be extending the application of the principle into a region quite different from that in which it has hitherto been applied if I were to hold that it applied to anything done by a lessor upon adjoining land which, while not otherwise affecting the demised premises or their user in any way, merely made it more expensive than it was before for the lessee to carry on his business on the demised premises."

***Kelly v. Battershell* [1949] 2 All E.R. 830**

11.54 The tenant of a building sub-let the top floor to the plaintiff. The tenant then sold his interest to the owners of a hotel business next door, and they incorporated the whole house apart from the plaintiff's top floor into the hotel. The Court of Appeal held that the mere fact of incorporation in a hotel did not necessarily involve a derogation from grant. There was no statement of principle on the topic.

***Molton Builders v. City of Westminster* (1975) 30 P. & C.R. 182 C.A.**

11.55 It was held by the Court of Appeal in this case that a buyer/tenant might not seek to pray in aid the principle of derogation from grant to enable him

[94] At 225.
[95] Italics supplied.

to do something which was unlawful, whether unlawful at the time of the contract, or at a later stage.

***British Leyland Motor Corporation v. Armstrong Patents* [1986] A.C. 577**

11.56 The plaintiff company were attempting to prevent the defendant company from copying their exhaust pipes. The House of Lords held that it would not be right to diminish the right of the buyer of a British Leyland car to "do whatever is necessary to keep it in running order and to effect whatever repairs may be necessary in the most economical way possible". Lord Bridge said:" To allow [B.L.] to enforce their copyright to maintain a monopoly for themselves and their licensees in the supply and replacement of exhausts is, to a greater or lesser extent, to detract from the owner's rights and, at least potentially, the value of their cars. There is an inconsistency between marketing cars and thereby creating whatever rights attach to their ownership on the one hand and acting to restrain the free exercise of those rights on the other. The law does not countenance such inconsistencies. It may be a novel application of the principle to preclude a plaintiff from enforcing a statutory right to which he is prima facie entitled. But, as my noble and learned friend, Lord Templeman, demonstrates, the application of the principle to the relationship between the mass car manufacturer and those who at any time acquire cars of his manufacture is no more than an extension to a non-contractual relationship of the considerations which underlie the classical doctrine of the law that a grantor may not derogate from his grant." . . .

Lord Templeman cited a number of derogation from grant cases, and said[96]: "I see no reason why the principle that a grantor will not be allowed to derogate from his grant by using property retained by him in such a way as to render property granted by him unfit or materially unfit for the purpose for the which the grant was made should not apply to the sale of a car. . . . The principle applied to a motor car manufactured in accordance with engineering drawings and sold with components which are bound to fail during the life of the car prohibits the copyright owner of the drawings from exercising his copyright powers in such a way as to prevent the car from functioning unless the owner of the car buys replacement parts from the copyright owner or his licensee." He based the car owner's right to repair firmly on the principle of non-derogation from grant and rejected the notion of an implied licence, which had been argued also."

***Johnston v. Holland* [1988] 1 E.G.L.R. 264 (C.A.)**

11.57 The judgment of the court was delivered by Nicholls L.J. The facts are complicated and not especially illuminating. The question was whether the appellant company was able to put up on its land a hoarding which obscured almost totally the hoardings which the defendant had been accustomed to putting up or licensing others to put up, on the adjoining land, No. 6 Queen's Parade, Green Lanes, Haringay, N8. The reservation of the right to erect hoardings had been reserved by the lessor of No. 6, Mrs Holland, in a lease of adjoining land to the company's predecessor in title. The land on which the obscuring hoarding was put up by the company, however, was not owned by the then-lessee at the time: the company had added to its land-holding by acquiring this later. The main question was, did the principle of derogation from grant apply to acts done on land not then owned by the grantor, (or, as here, technically the grantee, since the reservation operated as a re-grant by the lessee to the lessor)? The company's counsel had cited *inter alia Beddington*

[96] At p. 641.

v. Atlee.[97] Nicholls L.J. carefully considered the nature of the rule against derogation of grant, in order to ascertain whether it necessitated a rigid rule that derogation from grant could only apply to activities on land owned at the time of the grant. He thought that it did not. He emphasized that the principle of non-derogation from grant was not purely "based on some ancient technicality of real property" but was a principle embodying in a legal maxim a rule of common honesty, imposed in the interests of fair dealing. That being so, in this particular case, he could not see why the non-ownership of the additional land at the time of the grant made any difference to the principle in the case before him.

He said, "In my view common honesty permits of only one answer to that question." He said also, "Of course in considering what is necessarily implicit in a transaction in a case where the grantor owns no other land, very great weight indeed must be given to that factor. It will be a very exceptional case for it to be necessarily implicit in a lease that the activities of a lessor who owns no adjoining land, and has no plans to buy any adjoining land, are to be restricted on the adjoining land should he ever become owner or tenant of that land. Whether it is so implicit or not will depend on all the circumstances, including the purpose of the grant and the nature of the activities sought to be restrained. But if the facts in a given case point clearly to such a restriction being implicit, I can see no reason in principle why the law should treat that case differently from one where the lessor already owns the adjoining land at the time of the lease."[98]

PART 2 : RETENTION OF SOMETHING AFFECTING THE THING SOLD

***Francis v. Cockrell* (1870) L.R. 5 Q.B. 501.**

11.58 This is a licence case of considerable interest. The defendant constructed a grandstand for viewing the races. He sub-contracted the work to a competent sub-contractor, but unbeknownst to him the stand was negligently constructed, and the plaintiff was injured. It was held that there was an implied undertaking to users that due care and skill had been used, and that the stand was reasonably fit for its purpose. Kelly C.B. said: "I do not hesitate to say that I am clearly of opinion, as a general proposition of law, that when one man engages with another to supply him with a particular *article or thing*, to be applied to a certain use and purpose, in consideration of a pecuniary payment, he enters into *an implied contract that the article or thing shall be reasonably fit for the purpose for which it is to be used and to which it is to be applied.*[99] That I hold to be a general proposition of law applicable to all contracts of this nature and character."

He said there was however a qualification or exception: where there was a defect "which is unseen and unknown and undiscoverable, not only unknown to the contracting party, but undiscoverable by the exercise of any reasonable skill and diligence, or by any ordinary and reasonable means of inquiry and examination."

He dealt with the argument that the contract was similar to a lease and in a lease there was no implied term for fitness for the purpose for which it is let, as follows: "There really is no analogy at all between the case of a lessor

[97] (1887) 35 Ch. D. 317.
[98] See the text at para. 11.15 above for comment on this case.
[99] Italics supplied.

and lessee of a house, and the case of one who contracts for the supply of a carriage or for the supply of a seat in a stand upon a race-course, or for the safe passage over a railway bridge. In the case of lessor and lessee of a house, both parties, before the lease is granted and accepted, ascertain for themselves the condition of the premises, and they then enter into such express covenants as they may think fit, for the repair of the premises, or for any other purpose incidental to the enjoyment of the premises . . ."

Keating J. said that the liability or undertaking was, "that due care, that is, reasonable care, had been exercised in the erection of that stand which he so let out for the use of the public."

Montague Smith J. seems to have adopted a similar formulation to that of Kelly C.B., although the expression of it is not identical. He considered the duty was that, "due care and skill had been used in the construction of the building; or the obligation my be put in the other form, that the building was reasonably fit for the use for which it was let, so far as the exercise of reasonable care and skill could make it so."

Note: Kelly C.B.'s concept of qualified fitness for purpose is seldom applied to contracts to perform a service nowadays: the "due skill and care" alternative formulation has caught on instead. However, it might have a contribution to make in this area, since Kelly C.B.'s formulation can explain a falling short in the duty better than the widely formulated "due skill and care" formula, which leaves open the question, what is ***"due"****. A contract with a solicitor to check the title of land one is buying can tend to be regarded virtually as a contract to deliver good title (that the purchase should be fit for its purpose) if nothing is said, and it can be difficult for a solicitor to rely on the defence that many other solicitors would have missed a particular flaw too.*[1] *On the other hand a contract for services whose purpose is more diffuse tends to be less strictly regarded.*

Carstairs v. Taylor **(1871) L.R. 6 Ex. 217**

11.59 In this case (which was brought in the alternative in contract or "law", that is, negligence) water on the roof of a warehouse was collected into a box which was on the part retained by the landlord, and thence discharged into the landlord's retained drains. The landlord examined the box from time to time to see if it was in fit condition. Despite that, water flowed from the drains because rats had gnawed holes in the gutters and damage was caused to the tenant's warehouse below. It was held the landlord was under no absolute duty in regard to the common parts, merely *a duty to take reasonable care*, which he had done. Kelly C.B. referred to *Francis v. Cockrell*[2] for the proposition that "if a person hires the use of a thing, there is an implied undertaking, on the part of the person who receives the consideration, that the thing shall be reasonably fit for the purpose for which he lets it". Bromwell B. thought "it cannot be said that persons ought to anticipate that rats will enter the roof by gnawing holes in the gutters."

Miller v. Hancock **[1893] 2 Q.B. 177.**

11.60 This case was later overruled by the House of Lords in so far as it appeared to establish that a third party, the tenant's invitee, had any contractual right against the landlord.[3] The statements in the case about implied terms are nonetheless interesting. The landlord let chambers/offices on different floors

[1] *c.f. Edward Wong v. Johnson Stokes* [1984] A.C. 1296.
[2] L.R. 5 Q.B. 501.
[3] See *Fairman v. Perpetual Investment Building Society* [1932] A.C. 74.

of a building in the City, retaining a staircase by which access was gained to them. One of the stairs was defective, and a visitor to one of the tenants was injured. Lord Esher, M.R. said.[4] "[this staircase] may be called an easement, but it was, in my opinion, under the circumstances, such an easement *as the landlord was bound to keep so as to afford a reasonably safe entrance and exit to the tenants*. It seems to me that there is an implied obligation on the part of the landlord to the tenants to that effect, *or else he is letting to the tenants that which will be of no value to them*.[5] What is the use of a second floor to any one, if the staircase, by which alone there can be access to it, is to be allowed to go to ruin?

Bowen L.J. felt the parties to the demise, "must have intended by necessary implication, *as a basis without which the whole transaction would be futile*,[6] that the landlord should maintain the staircase. . . . It seems to me that it would render the whole transaction inefficacious and absurd if an implied undertaking were not assumed on the part of the landlord to maintain the staircase so far as might be necessary for the reasonable enjoyment of the demised premises."

Note: The language is strikingly couched in terms of the reasonable expectation of the parties in the light of the nature of the contract. It could be said perhaps that in a case so relatively obvious as this there is an overlap with the "business efficacy/officious bystander" type of implied term: the officious bystander would have had the same reasonable expectations.

Hargroves Aronson & Co v. Hartopp [1905] 1 K.B. 472

11.61 This case was approved by the House of Lords in *Fairman v. Perpetual Investment Building Society*.[7] The landlord retained possession and control of the roof of a building. A gutter became stopped up and overflowed. The tenants gave notice of this to the landlord. Lord Alverston C.J. considered that the landlord was liable to the tenants. An argument on behalf of the landlord had been that the mere fact of the landlord's control of the gutter brought with it no positive duty, merely a duty to refrain from rendering the premises dangerous though his active interference. It was said that the maxim "*sic utere tuo ut alienum non laedas*" which, interestingly, appears to have been agreed to be applicable, had been so confined in an American landlord and tenant case on similar facts to those in the case. Lord Alverstone said, however,[8]. "Even if it were true as contended that in such a case no duty to take care can arise, independently of covenant, except in respect of acts of commission, I think that here the defendants were guilty of an act of commission. A person who maintains an artificial thing like a gutter, *used for the very purpose*[9] of carrying off the rain-water from the roof, in an improper condition after notice may be said to be guilty of an act of commission . . .". Kennedy J. and Ridley J. concurred.

Note: (1) The landlord's knowledge is important.

(2) The fact that a blocked gutter is useless for its "very purpose" is relevant.

(3) After notice of the blockage a landlord who does nothing is presumed

[4] At 179.
[5] Italics supplied.
[6] Italics supplied.
[7] [1932] A.C. 74.
[8] At 477.
[9] Italics supplied.

to be injuring his tenant, just as if he had done so as a result of a deliberate act[10].

***Cockburn v. Smith* [1924] 2 K.B. 119**

11.62 The owner of a block of flats let one of the top flats, keeping the roof and guttering of the building under his own control. He covenanted expressly in the contract of tenancy to keep the staircases, passages and landings in good repair. The guttering became defective, so that the tenant's flat became damp. She gave the landlord notice of the defect. Greer J. at first instance held that there could be no implied term, to give the lease business efficacy, that the landlord should repair the gutter, considering the landlord's obligations were limited to those set out in the tenancy agreement.

In the Court of Appeal a different view was taken.

Bankes L.J. relied on *Hargroves v. Hartopp*.[11] He said as to the principle: "Whether this duty arises out of a contract between the parties, or whether it is an instance of the duty imposed by law upon an occupier of premises to take reasonable care that the condition of his premises does not cause damage, I prefer not to decide." He did not think the maxim *expressum facit cessare tacitum* (that is, the fact that other obligations had been expressly mentioned) applied to rule out this implied obligation.

Scrutton L.J. based his judgment mainly on *Rylands v. Fletcher*,[12] and reserved the question whether this was also a contractual liability arising out of the relation of landlord and tenant.

Sargant L.J. relied on *Hargroves v. Hartopp*[13] but as to the principle involved said "... it is not quite clear whether the landlord's duty is founded on some implied covenant or obligation in the contract of tenancy or from the circumstances that the landlord retains physical possession of the roof and lets the flat to the tenant. In my view it is not necessary to decide that difficult question. The view most favourable to the landlords is that their liability arises from an implied contract." He too felt that the maxim *expressum facit cessare tacitum* did not apply here, because, he thought, the express contract did not extend to the roof, only the staircase, *etc.*

Note: it may perhaps be thought by now that the unacknowledged thread which runs through all these cases is one of loyalty to the paramount purpose of the contract. The landlord let the flat for a dwelling house; thus, he could not, on straight derogation from grant principles (derogation from grant was not argued in any of these cases) act so as to render the inhabiting of the flat virtually impossible for this purpose.

***Liverpool City Council v. Irwin* [1977] A.C. 239**

11.63 In this well-known case the House of Lords held that it was an implied term of a lease of a 15 storey tower block that the Council landlord should keep in repair the lifts and other common parts. At least the majority of the House of Lords, and very likely all of them, considered the term was of the kind implied to give business efficacy to the lease, but did so on essentially purpose-of-the-contract grounds. Lord Wilberforce put it as follows[14]: "All these [lifts, *etc.*] are not just facilities, or conveniences provided at discretion:

[10] He discharges the duty if he employs a competent contractor to deal with the problem, even if in fact further problems ensue: *Blake v. Woolf* [1898] 2 K.B. 426.

[11] Above para. 11.61.

[12] L.R. 3 H.L. 330.

[13] Above.

[14] At 254.

they are essentials of the tenancy without which life in the dwellings, as a tenant, is not possible . . . The subject matter of the lease (high rise blocks) and the relationship created by the tenancy demand, of their nature, some contractual obligation on the landlord."

***Duke of Westminster v. Guild* [1985] Q.B. 688**

11.64 The Court of Appeal set limits to the principle, declining to apply it to the extent of making the landlord take positive steps to repair a drain in his retained property through which the tenant had an easement. The tenant was obliged under the lease to pay a fair proportion of the expenses of repairing drains relating to the premises or used jointly with the occupiers of neighbouring permises. The drain in question served only the demised premises. It became blocked. It emerged that the drain was full of earth and had not been cleared or maintained for many years before the lease. The tenant claimed the landlord was obliged to repair it. The landlord was perfectly content for the tenant to repair it. Slade L.J., giving the judgment of the Court of Appeal, held that it was not enough that the parties contemplated that in fact and in practice the landlord will do repairs, or even that the lease confers express rights of entry on him for the purpose. He held in this case there were anyway a number of pointers the other way. The lease contained a number of elaborate provisions about repairs, yet the drain was not mentioned. The repairing would be onerous to the landlord, and a number of other installations would be covered by an implied term in addition to the offending drain. Thirdly, the proposed implied term would conflict to some extent with the express provisions of the lease. Fourthly, it was not "necessary" in the *Liverpool City Council v. Irwin*[15] sense (the facts of that case were said to be distinguishable) and was inconsistent with the general law of easements, which places no duty to repair the subject matter of the easement on the servient tenement.

Note: The decision draws the line in the correct place given the existing law on easements. What is most interesting about the case is perhaps what was not argued or discussed: the relation between an easement case of this kind and the principle of derogation from grant (the tenant's case was based on an implied term to give business efficacy and in the alternative on negligence). One may suspect that even if derogation from grant had been argued it would have failed because derogation from grant requires a positive step to have been taken first which is inconsistent with the main-purpose-of-the-contract. Here the landlord had taken no positive step, merely let the drain deteriorate. The landlord's failure to repair the drain did not hinder or prevent the purpose of the lease being carried on: it could be carried on perfectly well on the footing that the tenant repaired it himself, as he had the right to do.

***Gordon v. Selico Co* [1986] 1 E.G.L.R. 71**

11.65 The Court of Appeal declined to imply a covenant as a matter of "business efficacy" to supplement the protection afforded to the tenants by the express terms of the lease.

***Barrett v. Lounova* [1990] 1 Q.B. 348**

11.66 The Court of Appeal allowed the implication of a term that the landlord would keep the outside of the demised premises in repair. The main alternative possibility was that the tenant was to keep it repair, which was thought unlikely since it was a monthly tenancy with the rent being paid weekly.

[15] [1977] A.C. 239.

Some of the earlier cases were reviewed, but there was no in-depth discussion of principle.

***King v. South Northamptonshire District Council* [1992] 1 E.G.L.R. 53, C.A.**

11.67 *Liverpool City Council v. Irwin*[16] and *Miller v. Hancock*[17] were applied to impose an implied obligation on a landlord to keep in repair an access path to the rear of the demised premises over which the tenant had a right of way. Mann L.J. with whom Waller L.J. agreed, said: "The houses could not be enjoyed or function in accord with their design without the rear access. In that circumstance, I for my part, find no difficulty in concluding that the implication of an obligation to maintain the rear access is a necessary one to fulfil the purpose of the demise. The demise is a dwelling-house, which is designed to function as such with the mechanism of rear service. In my judgment, the demise of a house which is designed to function in that way is not efficacious unless the rear surface is adequately maintained."

Note: See the note to Miller v. Hancock at paragraph 11.60.

***Hafton Properties v. Camp* [1994] 1 E.G.L.R.**

11.68 Judge Fox-Andrews Q.C. held that a term could not be implied into a lease that the lessor would be responsible for breaches of covenants by the management company.

[16] [1977] A.C. 239.
[17] [1893] 2 Q.B. 177.

CHAPTER 12

THE AFTER–SALE RELATIONSHIP: EXERCISE OF RIGHTS AFFECTING THE CONTINUED EXISTENCE OF THE CONTRACT OF SALE

PART 1

Vendor's rescission clauses

12.01 The practice sprang up during the nineteenth century of inserting clauses into contracts of sale of land which allowed the vendor to opt for rescission after contract and before completion of the sale, that is during the period of title investigation. The clause was commonly used to cover the situation where the purchaser made a request (requisition) regarding the title which the vendor was unable or unwilling to comply with. The clause was thus a wide one, and gave rise to questions about the circumstances in which it might fairly be operated by the vendor. After all, if there were no restrictions, it might be used to nullify the contract for no reason at all. The principle initially developed was a simple enough principle of loyalty to the contract—both the paramount purpose of the contract itself in the most basic sense, as an agreement binding the vendor to sell and the purchaser to purchase; and the deemed paramount *purpose of the clause itself*, in its contractual setting. The principle originally applied became transmogrified somewhat after the 1880s, with the result that the present law in this area is difficult to define. It tends towards a wide discretion, which seems to have the effect in practice of allowing the vendor to use the clause to rescind more or less when he likes. It would seem not to be too late to rediscover and redefine the old principles in this area, muddied as the waters must be admitted to be.

The principle until the 1880s

12.02 Loyalty to the paramount purpose of the contract was the first guiding principle. Rescission clauses were construed so as not to permit the contract to be terminated by "some failure" on the part of the vendor himself: in *Roberts v. Wyatt*,[1] an approach reminiscent of the early cases on "a man may not take advantage of his own wrong" was taken[2] and in *Page v. Adam*,[3] there was reference to an "escape" by the vendor from a duty which he was bound to perform. This duty will have been the deemed (rather than express) duty of loyalty to the contract—namely to progress the contract by making proper efforts to make title, *etc*. In *Morley v. Cook*,[4] what was in effect disloyalty to the contract was labelled "fraudulent" with all the connotations of disloyalty to the contract that that phrase had in the days when "equitable fraud" was a common expression. In *Greaves v. Wilson*,[5] Sir J. Romilly did use the word "reasonable", but went on at once to limit it by reference to the circumstances which will have been within the vendor's knowledge. He also spelled out the presumed paramount purpose of the *clause* itself, given this setting: it was limited to deal only with *unexpected title problems which might be expensive and troublesome for the vendor to deal with.*

Compliance with his good faith duty of accuracy assumed on the part of the vendor

12.03 A problem which could occur in the course of working out what was "unexpected" was the proper treatment of a breach by the vendor of his duty of candour or duty of accuracy in the formation of the contract. The traditional application of these good faith principles was, as has been seen, to build in the assumption of good faith to the contract. Thus, where there had been a relevant breach by the vendor of one or both of the twin good faith duties, he would often be in breach of the contract also. It was an easy step to disapply the rescission clause in such cases, on the ground that the vendor himself could have prevented the problem by compliance with the good faith duties.

In *Nelthorpe v. Holgate*[6] a vendor who had known about a title defect was not allowed to rescind upon a requisition by the purchaser about it. In *Duddell v. Simpson*[7] both strands of duty are discernible—the limiting of the clause to the paramount purpose of the contract (again the word "reasonable" is used, but immediately limited in its opera-

[1] (1810) 2 Taunton 268; 127 E.R. 1080.

[2] See the section at para. 13.09 *et seq.* below, particularly for the reasoning that permitting a party to put an end to the contract at his whim was inconsistent with the purpose of the contract as a contract to be bound to do something.

[3] (1841) 4 Beav. 269; 49 E.R. 342.

[4] (1842) 2 Hare 106; 67 E.R. 44.

[5] (1858) 25 Beav. 290; 53 E.R. 647.

[6] (1844) 1 Coll. 203; 63 E.R. 384.

[7] (1866) 2 Ch. App. 102.

tion by reference to the need to uphold the parties' intention to be *bound*); and the duty of accuracy. The latter was expressed by saying that the problem to which the purchaser's requisition was directed and which was the trigger for the vendor's rescission should have been "unforeseen"; that it should not have been something which ought to have been disclosed prior to the contract. Similarly, *Gray v. Fowler*[8] stressed the good faith element by saying that the problem must be unexpected. In *Bowman v. Hyland*[9] the vendor had never had any title at all, and consistently with the good faith duty to give good title, the clause was held not to be operable by the vendor against the purchaser. Also relevant is *Hardman v. Child*[10] in which rescission was not allowed where the problem was undisclosed by the vendor prior to the contract.

From the mid-1880s to the present day: the old principles are misconstrued by the courts and a shift of emphasis gradually takes place

12.04 As appears elsewhere in this book[11] a shift of judicial attitude began to take place in around the mid 1880's. The reasons for this, as has been discussed, are to some extent a matter of conjecture; there was certainly a period of prosperity, with rising prices and no need for good faith remedies such as rescission, characteristic of less ebullient times; the increased influence of the forerunners of the logical positivist philosophers such as Locke, Berkeley and Hume had perhaps begun to be felt, with their engaging overall message of "What you see is what there is", and no need in consequence to bother with "metaphysical" searches for the original purpose of anything; the increasing reliance on statute law as something where you knew where you were (in theory); perhaps even the Vendor and Purchaser Act 1874, which had provided a popular summary remedy in case of difficulties over land (still the main safe investment at that time other than the Funds) on terms that the only question was to be whether or not the vendor had had title; and no argument attacking the existence of the contract (for example on good faith grounds, such as inaccurate description of the subject matter, *etc.*) might be taken. The effect on the court's attitude to contractual rights of these influences, whatever they were, was noticeable. Indeed, in *In re Dames and Wood*[12] both the old good faith attitude can be seen, in the judgment of Lindley L.J., and the new, in the judgment of Cotton L.J. The latter consciously or unconsciously latched onto the word "reasonable", shorn of its original good faith limitations and taken as allowing the courts a very wide discretion. Over time the vendor was inevitably allowed much more scope for "capricious" behaviour than the old formulation

[8] (1873) L.R. 8 Exch. 249.
[9] (1878) 8 Ch. D. 588.
[10] (1885) 28 Ch. D. 712.
[11] See, *e.g.* Chap. 5, Sale of Land.
[12] (1885) 29 Ch. D. 626.

would have given him; a narrower formulation had meant the vendor's freedom to operate the clause was limited to areas where good faith permitted it. *Re Starr-Bowkett Building Society and Sibun's Contract*[13] provides a fascinating glimpse of the new fashion taking hold of the judiciary. Chitty J.'s judgment expands on the new idea—which has persisted to the present day—that given complete "freedom of contract," *economic* factors will tend to prevent "caprice" or bad behaviour on the part of the vendor; the corollary being that good faith rules were not required for the purpose. Thus, in *Ashburner v. Sewell*,[14] a vendor was allowed to use a clause of the kind being discussed to rescind, saddling the purchaser with the costs of the conveyancing, even though he had had a latent defect of title which had not been disclosed; and in *Re Deighton and Harris's Contract*,[15] the vendor was similarly held free to rescind, despite an undisclosed mortgage which one would imagine he must have known about.

12.05 *In Re Jackson and Haden's Contract*[16] the same uneasy coexistence of both approaches can be seen. The case concerned in effect, the vendor's duty of disclosure which he had not complied with. The concept of "recklessness" was adopted by Collins M.R. (it was unreasonable to be reckless). A reckless vendor, in effect, was a vendor who had not complied with his duty of accuracy. Yet in the same case, Cozens Hardy L.J.—although he came to the same decision on the facts—thought the question was simply whether it was "just and reasonable" to allow reliance on the clause.

The shift towards literalism continued, although it did so somewhat jerkily. In *Quinion v. Horne*,[17] "reasonable" was given the widest possible meaning: any conduct which had a "rational foundation"; thus approaching as nearly as might be to truly literal interpretation of the clause. "Good faith" was redefined at the same time *en passant* as the absence of "bad faith"—not at all the same thing.[18] "Bad faith" itself was defined very narrowly but no doubt rightly as equivalent to "dishonest purpose". In *Merrett v. Schuster*,[19] a vendor who had in fact believed he would be able to give title was allowed to rescind using the clause, without any consideration whether he ought not to have disclosed the evidence he had relied on more fully to the purchaser or not. Yet in In *Des Reaux and Setchfield's Contract*,[20] what was essentially breach of the good faith duty of disclosure by the vendor disentitled him from relying on the clause. It was called "recklessness" as above!

12.06 Finally, by the time of the Privy Council decision in *Selkirk v. Romar*

[13] (1889) 42 Ch. D. 386.
[14] [1891] 3 Ch. 405.
[15] [1898] 1 Ch. 464.
[16] [1906] 1 Ch. 412.
[17] [1906] 1 Ch. 596.
[18] We commonly use the expression "in bad faith" to mean, not a breach of the good faith rules, but a dishonest purpose of some kind.
[19] [1920] 2 Ch. 240.
[20] [1926] Ch. 178.

Investments[21] we see the court fixated by the wide, wide discretion in this area. The original principle is now forgotten: there is a desire for a neat defining word to look at as one looks at a statute. "Recklessness"—itself an introduction without real antecedents, as can be seen above,—was put under a new kind of microscope, but of course, being simply a word, and a word which takes colour more from such surrounding circumstances as one gives it than from any inherent limitations of its own, yielded a wide discretion. No-one should be surprised at that. Single words can be dangerous, loose things without a bedrock of known principle. It lost its—probably always somewhat tenuous—good faith connotation, and became something which was said by Lord Radcliffe, giving the judgment of the court, to derive from "some equitable principle". Since it had been, he considered, exercised only by the Courts of Equity,[22] it must have depended crucially on which equitable remedy they were exercising, typically specific performance, rescission, *etc.* No such remedy was being sought here, merely a desire to do what the words seemed to allow, so why was it not all right for the vendor to do it? The vendor, who had been guilty of less than full disclosure to the unfortunate purchaser, was thus permitted to rescind, after this highly speculative tour of the supposed law.

Sale of land—provision that contract is to come to an end if purchaser's solicitors have not approved the title ("subject to the approval of title by the purchaser's solicitors")

12.07 This provision occurs occasionally in contracts for sale of land. During the period between contract and completion by conveyance or transfer of the land, the relationship is primarily directed to matters concerning title. The buyer tries to ensure during this period that he takes good title to the land. We find in the case of clauses such as that under discussion the reverse of the situation in the previous section. This time it is the buyer who could, if literalism were allowed to prevail, simply terminate the contract at will. The response of the courts has been similarly to control the exercise of the right by the purchaser. The approval must be *"reasonable"* or *"in good faith"*. There is little exploration of the underlying reasons for any such principle, and no real explanation of the operation of the "good faith" involved. However, since "reasonable" is opposed to such things as "caprice" it may be supposed that a degree of loyalty to the purpose of the contract, as a contract whereby the vendor binds himself to sell land, is presupposed in this approach. "Good faith" would seem to have a similar meaning, confining the exercise of the right to the purpose originally envisaged at the time of the contract. This is because the alternative meaning of good faith purely as a matter of the English

[21] [1963] 1 W.L.R. 1415.

[22] That this is incorrect may be seen from the early cases in the Appendix below.

language, "honesty", has no obvious application to the circumstances here, still less "dishonesty"?

In *Hudson v. Buck,*[23] there was a contract for the sale of leasehold property which was expressed to be "subject to the approval of the title by the purchaser's solicitor". Fry J. (*obiter*) considered it to be implicit in the above that the solicitor should act "reasonably". This would seem to connote some degree of deemed loyalty to the paramount purpose of the contract, because he said:

> "It is not necessary to decide that the absence of approval by the purchaser's solicitor would be conclusive, if the purchaser himself had acted unreasonably, as, for instance, if he had declined to appoint any solicitor, or if the solicitor whom he appointed had insisted upon utterly unreasonable objections to the title. *Possibly in such cases the purchaser would not be able to enforce the condition.*"[24]

However, since it had not been suggested in the case that the solicitor had been unreasonable, he held that the condition had not been fulfilled.

In *Hussey v. Horne-Payne*[25] the Court of Appeal approved what Fry J. had said in *Hudson v. Buck*[26] In the same case in the Lords[27] the point did not, on the view they took, arise. Lord Cairns L.C. however (*obiter*) doubted whether the expression in fact added anything to the normal obligation of the vendor to show title and thus construed it as meaning that "the title must be investigated and approved of in the usual way, which would be by the solicitor of the purchaser."

12.08 In *Curtis Moffat Ltd v. Wheeler*[28], the contract contained the same provision. Maugham J. followed *Hussey v. Horne Payne*[29] and the Court of Appeal in *Hudson v. Buck*[30] despite the doubts of Lord Cairns; and noted that the Court of Appeal in *Hudson v. Buck*[31] had in any event not construed the expression as allowing the solicitors to decline the title out of mere caprice, but had considered that good faith was a necessary ingredient. Maugham J. therefore held that the solicitor had to act "reasonably" "and in good faith" when approving the title under such a provision.

Farwell J. in *Caney v. Leith*[32] considered the cases, and similarly, thought the contract which contained the words "subject to questions of title being to our approval" was enforceable if the purchaser's solicitor "*acting in good faith*" disapproved of the title.

Cross J. in *Re Longlands Farm*[33] thought the condition would be ful-

[23] (1877) 7 Ch. D. 683.
[24] Italics supplied.
[25] (1878) 8 Ch. D. 670.
[26] [1877] 7 Ch. D. 683.
[27] (1879) 4 App. Cas. 311.
[28] [1929] 2 Ch. 224.
[29] Above.
[30] Above.
[31] *ibid.*
[32] [1937] 2 All E.R. 532.
[33] [1968] 3 All E.R. 552.

filled if "the title was in order so no reasonable objections could be taken to it", in other words that the obligation was that the purchaser's solicitors was confined to taking reasonable objections.

PART 2

Apparently unrestricted rights to terminate licences to use something—restricted by virtue of the nature or purpose of the contract

12.09 The rule against derogation from grant is acknowledged to be a general principle applicable to contracts. Similarly, it may well be that the two sections discussed above in Part II, although relating to the sale of land, are merely examples of a general principle of loyalty to the original contract's purpose. The apparently unrestricted exercise of a right to terminate a licence has been restricted, both as regards land, and as regards a BT telephone number. The exercise of these retained rights to terminate a contract has been confined by the courts to an exercise which could reasonably have been expected by parties to a contract *of that nature, or for that main purpose,* at the time of its making. The actual intentions of the parties are not relevant: it is the "intent of the transaction" which is in point. Although not strictly concerned with sales, some cases have been noted in the Appendix, for comparison purposes.

APPENDIX: SOME CASES OF INTEREST

PART 1: VENDOR; RESCISSION CLAUSES

***Roberts v. Wyatt* (1810) 2 Taunt. 268; 127 E.R. 1080**

12.10 The point before the court related to the abstract of title, the question being whether the purchaser was entitled to demand it back from the vendor; and since the court thought that the purchaser had a temporary property in the abstract, for so long as the contract should continue, the question of the vendor's right to rescind arose also. There was a condition to the effect that in case the vendor could not make title, the contract should be void.

Mansfield C.J. said: "But in order to adapt that defence to the present case, the argument must be, that if the Defendant says he cannot answer the objection, it shall be absolutely void at the choice of either party. But that is not so: the meaning is, that if the seller cannot make a good title by the time mentioned, the contract shall be void as against him, and the Plaintiff has a right to be off his bargain. So, e contrá, if the Plaintiff does not pay the money, the Defendant may avoid the contract; but the Plaintiff cannot say, I am not ready with my money, therefore I will avoid the contract; nor can the seller say, my title is not good, therefore I shall be off. And the word is 'if they cannot make', so it must appear by sufficient proof that they cannot make a title."

Lawrence J. agreed. He said, "it would be a monstrous construction if either party could vitiate the agreement by refusing to perform his part of it."

Malins v. Freeman **(1838) 4 Bing** (NC) 399; 132 E.R. 839

12.11 The purchaser entered into an auction contract to purchase land, on terms that he was to pay at once a deposit of 20 per cent and half of the excise duty of seven pence in the pound and sign the agreemment to pay the remainder on a certain day.

Tindal C.J., Park J., Bosanquet J. and Coltman J. all agreed that the defendant could not take advantage of his own failure to pay the government duty in order to come within a statute making such agreements void. Tindal C.J. applied cases about advowsons which, when they were not made in accordance with a particular statutory provision, were not valid as to the successor in title, but the invalidity could not be taken advantage of by the grantor himself; and also *Doe dem Bryan v. Bancks*.[34] Tindal C.J. also thought that the construction of the statute for the benefit of the government need not destroy the contract between the parties. Coltman C.J. expressed similar sentiments.

Tanner v. Smith **(1840) 10 Sim. 410; 59 E.R. 673**

12.12 The Vice-Chancellor said that the vendor had to elect to rescind or not, and could not first try to deal with the objection and then later on rescind.

Page v. Adam **(1841) 4 Beav. 269; 49 E.R. 342**

12.13 There was a clause allowing the vendor to terminate the contract on any objection to title. The court discussed the clause, *obiter*, because in fact the case turned on the question whether the purchaser's objection was a valid one or not, the vendor by then desiring to sell the property after all. (It had been suggested in argument, incidentally, that if the vendor were allowed to rescind here it would be to allow him to rely on his wrong: *Rede v. Farr*.[35] The Master or the Rolls, Lord Langdale, said: ". . . I should have thought the notice to annul the contract invalid, if, in giving it, the Defendant had sought improperly to escape from the performance of a duty which, by the nature of the contract, he was bound to perform . . ."

Morley v Cook **(1842) 2 Hare 106; 67 E.R. 44**

12.14 There was a condition of sale allowing rescission by the vendor if the purchaser raised objections to the title which the vendor was unwilling to remove. The Vice-Chancellor, Sir James Wigram, said: "I agree that a vendor, in a case like the present, is bound to deliver the best abstract that he can; and a Court of Equity would not do a very violent act in holding that a vendor who, under conditions of this kind, having a perfect abstract, fraudulently delivered one which was imperfect, had, by such fraudulent breach of the conditions on his part, forfeited the benefit of the conditions in his favour."

He also said later ". . . I have no hesitation in saying that I think conditions

[34] (1821) 4 B. & Ald. 401; 106 E.R. 984: noted at para. 13.51.
[35] (1817) 6 M & S. 121; 125 E.R. 1188: noted at para. 13.50.

of sale like those before me (the meaning of which no purchaser knows until *ex post facto* decisions of a Court of Justice informs him of it) ought to be discouraged, and that I am but offering such discouragement by putting a strict construction upon them in favour of a purchaser, and by holding that they are not to have a construction which might subject purchasers to a great expense and inconvenience at the mere will of a vendor . . ."

***Nelthorpe v. Holgate* (1844) 1 Coll. 203; 63 E.R. 384**

12.15 There was a condition that if any dispute should arise as to the title, the same should be submitted to some eminent conveyancer, and that in case he should be of opinion that a good title could not be made the contract should be rescinded. Upon the delivery of the abstract, it appeared the vendor's mother had a life interest, which the vendor had known all about at the time of the sale. She refused to join in the conveyance to the purchaser, and the vendor was ordered to give specific performance with compensation. The Vice-Chancellor said that it might well have been different if he had not known about the life interest.

***Hoy v. Smithies* (1856) 22 Beav. 510; 52 E.R. 1205**

12.16 The vendor was in fact found to have acted properly in rescinding; but Sir John Romilly said "In these cases the conditions are to be construed most strictly against the vendor, and I shall always do so; but still a meaning must be given to them, such as they fairly bear . . ."

***Greaves v. Wilson* (1858) 25 Beav. 290; 53 E.R. 647**

12.17 There was a condition that the vendor should be at liberty to rescind the contract if the purchaser should "shew any objection of title, conveyance or otherwise, and should insist thereon".

Sir John Romilly M.R. gave the plaintiff purchaser a decree of specific performance. He said "The mode in which these conditions must be construed is explained, very clearly, in all the cases upon the subject, and nowhere more clearly than by Sir James Wigram in *Money v. Cooke.*[36] *They must be construed,* like every other instrument, *most strictly against the person who frames them, because the vendor alone can be the sole judge of the necessity or propriety of making such conditions before he offers the property for sale. In addition to that, it is to be borne in mind that a person who offers property for sale becomes subject to certain duties, in the character of vendor, and that he does not get rid of them by special conditions of sale.* For instance, he cannot, by entering into any condition of sale of this description, compel a purchaser to take a title upon an insufficient abstract if he is able to give him a complete one. He is bound to perform the duties of a vendor as fully as he is able to do, subject to this exception, that it shall be *reasonable,* for it is always a question of the reasonableness of the thing required, for although it may be in his power to do it, *it may involve him in so much expense and trouble as to make it unreasonable that he should be called upon to do it. This exception or condition of sale is introduced with a view of meeting that particular sort of case.*[37] *Page v. Adams*[38] establishes this: that a vendor cannot make use of a condition to rescind a contract for the purpose of getting rid of the duty which attaches to him, upon the rest of the contract, of making out the title. These conditions then are to be construed most strictly

[36] 2 Hare 106.
[37] Italics supplied.
[38] 4 Beav. 269.

against the vendor . . . "He then dealt with the requisition involved. The purchaser had asked for proof of insurance (the premises were leasehold and there was a covenant to insure) and had asked for a mortgagee of the premises to concur in the sale. Sir John Romilly asked, "Does this mean that if a requisition be put to the vendor which he disapproves of or dislikes, he is thereupon to be at liberty to say at once, "I will put an end to the contract?" He thought not, in that case.

He also adverted to the fact that the sale had achieved a lower price than the vendor had hoped; but thought this told *against* the vendor. "If the vendor intended to make use of this condition for the purpose of avoiding the sale in case the property should not be sold for what he considered its full value, then it was clearly fraudulent and intended to deceive a purchaser who would be wholly unable to ascertain what use the vendor intended to make of it. I think that it could not be allowed to be made use of for this purpose. The vendor ought, if he so intended, to have expressed it plainly in his conditions of sale by saying, "If the property does not sell for as much as I think it is worth, I reserve to myself a right to put an end to the contract, "and then there would have been no purchaser."

***Duddell v. Simpson* (1866) 2 Ch. App. 102**

12.18 The vendor had agreed to sell a 24 year lease when he only had that less three days, but had the promise of those entitled to the three days to concur.

Sir G.J. Turner L.J. said as to the principle that a number of earlier cases had "settled, and, I think very wisely settled, that the word unwilling, in a condition of sale of this description, is not to be considered as giving *an arbitrary power* to the vendor to annul the contract. I think that in a case where the vendor annuls the contract on the ground of unwillingness, he must shew some *reasonable ground for unwillingness; thus, for instance, he may shew that if he proceeds to comply with a requisition, he will be involved in expenses far beyond what he ever contemplated, or be involved in litigation and expense which he never contemplated, and for avoiding which he reserved to himself the power of annulling the contract.*[39] But to say that a vendor, upon a condition of that description, could annul a contract *brevi manu*, without attempting to answer any of the requisitions which are made on the part of the purchaser, would be opposed both to principle and authority; for that would, in truth, be giving to the vendor the power of saying that that which was intended as a sale, and was a sale, shall, in truth, be no sale at all." On the facts he found the vendor had acted properly, however.

***Mawson v. Fletcher* (1870) 6 Ch. App. 91**

12.19 The purchaser raised a question concerning the limestone and freestone rights of the land. The vendors were held entitled to rescind under a condition in the contract allowing this. It was said that otherwise the inquiry which would be necessary *would* involve them in very considerable trouble and expense; and they had rescinded bona fide.

***Gray v. Fowler* (1873) L.R. 8 Exch. 249**

12.20 It was said that to give a right to rescind under the condition permitting this, the objection had to *arise out of* the abstract. It was also confirmed that the vendor had to elect one way or another to rescind or not rescind, and stick by it. If he did not exercise the right at the time the objection was made

[39] Italics supplied.

it would be too late later on. He had in any event to exercise the right within a reasonable time, which would include time to take legal advice if need be.

On appeal Blackburn J. (with whose judgment the other members of the court concurred) said: "The intricacies of title, according to the law of real property, are such that a vendor who bonâ fide thinks he has a good title, and who honestly discloses a perfect abstract, may unexpectedly find that, owing to something not appearing in his abstract, and of which he had no knowledge, he has no title at all, or one which can only be made marketable at a great expense. And *it is to meet such a case that the provision in the condition is inserted*, which, I think, must be construed to mean that in case any objection to the title, whether as appearing in the abstract or otherwise, is made, the vendor may have the option to rescind.

It is objected that this construction leaves it open to a dishonest vendor to deliver an abstract concealing the defect, and take the chance of the blot not being hit; that he may with impunity put the purchaser to a great deal of expense before he discovers the blot, and then the vendor can rescind. I do not think he can do so with impunity. The purchaser, on a count framed in tort, alleging that the vendor represented to him that the abstract was a perfect abstract, which was false to his knowledge, might recover any damages resulting from his being induced to act on that representation; and on a count for the breach of the vendor's contract to deliver a true abstract, he might recover such damages as resulted from the breach: see *Steer v. Crowley*."[40,41]

Bowman v. Hyland (1878) 8 Ch.D. 588

12.21 The condition was that if the purchaser should make any objection or requisition which the vendor should be unwilling on the ground of expense or otherwise to comply with, the vendor might annul the sale. It emerged that the vendor did not have the fee simple which he had agreed to sell, but the residue of a long term of years at a peppercorn rent, expiring shortly after the date of the contract. Hall V.C. said that the plaintiff might have judgment for "such damages as he may have been put to in respect of the non-performance of this contract by the Defendants." He said of the condition, particularly interestingly,

"I hold that such a condition does not apply to a case where the vendor has not any title at all. The words 'unwilling on the ground of expense or otherwise to comply with' do not apply to a case where there has been an objection or requisition on the part of the purchaser in effect saying that the vendor has no title, and that the property belongs to someone else. The purchaser says in effect: 'I do not make an objection or requisition in respect of anything which you may cure. I don't require you to remove the objection or requisition by purchasing the interest of the freeholder which you have contracted to sell and to which you have shewn no title.' *Non constat* that the freeholder would be willing to sell. *The matter is not one capable of being complied with as between vendor and purchaser, and it is not, in my judgment, that which was within the contemplation of the parties when this clause was framed.*"[42]

Hardman v. Child (1885) 28 Ch.D. 712

12.22 There was a condition permitting the vendors to rescind if any objection or requisition as to (*inter alia*) title should be insisted on, and the vendors should be unable or unwilling to remove or comply with it. The abstract of title

[40] Italics supplied.
[41] 14 C.B. (N.S.) 337.
[42] Italics supplied.

delivered to the purchaser showed that there was an obligation to repair and keep in repair a wall on one side of the land. *This had not been mentioned* prior to the sale. The purchaser would not accept a conveyance subject to such a right to repair. The vendor rescinded. Pearson J. considered they were not entitled to do so, whether or not the obligation ran with the land. As he said, if it ran with the land, it would bind the purchaser anyway: if it did not, the vendors had no right to insist on the obligation going in the conveyance. "Neither the particulars nor the conditions of sale contained any notice of the obligation, and the purchaser was therefore entitled to say to the vendors, You have contracted to sell me the property with a free title." He considered the vendors were not entitled to rescind. He regretted that similar conditions were by then common practice. "A condition of this kind is, in my opinion, intended only to meet the case of a purchaser insisting on an objection which the vendor is absolutely unable to remove; or, if not absolutely unable, the removal of which would throw upon him such an amount of expense as it would be unjust that he should be compelled to bear." Thus the vendors had to pay the costs of the action, which was all that remained in the litigation.

***Re Dames & Wood* (1885) 29 Ch.D. 626**

12.23 There was a power for the vendor to rescind "if the purchaser should take any objection or make any requisition" which the vendor was unable or unwilling to remove or comply with. It was affirmed by the Court of Appeal that *Duddell v. Simpson*[43] which had decided that no *locus poenitentiae* had to be given to the purchaser in a case where the condition required the words "insist on", also applied to the wording of the condition here.

Cotton L.J.'s attitude to the old rule is interesting. He took it as ruling out the "*unreasonable* or arbitrary"[44] exercise of the power and said "There may be a doubt whether it is quite reasonable to say, when parties have entered into a contract, that the Court must consider whether it is unreasonable or not; but the cases do certainly lay down this, that a vendor cannot avail himself of such a condition arbitrarily, or unless he shews some reasonable ground for his unwillingness to answer the requisitions." He held that in the case the vendors *would* be put to considerable labour and expense, so it was not unreasonable.

Lindley L.J. on the other hand kept to the original spirit of the old rule. He said "The power so reserved to the vendor must be considered *with reference to the object with which it was so inserted,*[45] an object perfectly well known to everybody who has any experience in real property transactions. The vendor cannot say, 'I will not complete, and will throw up the contract for sale;' he must exercise the power *bonâ fide* for the purpose for which it was made part of the contract. As long as he does that I do not see how we can restrain him from the exercise of the power."

Fry L.J. did not determine the question on whom the burden of proof lay to show the power had not been properly exercised: he thought in any case the vendor had shown that the exercise was reasonable there.

***Re Starr-Bowkett Building Society and Sibun's Contract* (1889) 42 Ch.D. 386**

12.24 This was a purchaser's summons to ascertain whether the vendor had properly annulled the contract or not. There was a condition that if the pur-

[43] Above.
[44] Italics supplied.
[45] Italics supplied.

chaser should make any objection to or requisition on the title which the vendors should be unable or unwilling to remove or comply with, the vendors might rescind. The vendors, who were trustees, received the purchaser's requisitions and passed a resolution that as some of the requisitions could not be complied with, and as great trouble and expense would be incurred in complying with others, they would give notice to rescind. The purchasers contended that the vendors had not been entitled to rescind (1) because "making" meant the same as persisting in, and they had not persisted; (2) because they felt they were entitled to be given a *locus poenitentiae* and (3) because the vendors had acted arbitrarily or capriciously in rescinding. Both Chitty J. and the Court of Appeal rejected these contentions. Chitty J. took the opportunity for some flag-waving for the newly fashionable literalism. He said[46] *"The present rule of the Court is not to make new contracts for men, and not by means of construction indirectly to do that which the Court declines to do directly."* (This is of course a matter of definition.) He pointed out that the condition was plainly there, and there had been no case made against the contract in any way. As to the plea for fair dealing, the suggestion that there should be a dealing "on a footing of credit and trust", he merely pointed out that were good economic reasons why a vendor would normally for his part not wish his own expenditure on preparing the sale to be wasted either, so that there was no pecuniary reason in general why a vendor should penalise himself by a capricious exercise of the power. He rejected the argument that "making" should be read as if it meant "persisting in", and said that no *locus poenitentiae* could thus possibly arise, since in the case of contracts where the right arose on the purchaser "persisting", the right to rescind arose right away: *Duddell v. Simpson.*[47] Further, a vendor was not bound to state his reasons. *Glenton v. Saunders*[48] had, he thought, taken matters a step further than the earlier decision and cast doubt on the earlier case of *Re Dames & Wood.*[49] In any event he said that the latter case only contained dicta, because the court had thought the vendor acted reasonably, in the event. Thus, he held that the burden of proof of the capricious or arbitrary exercise of the power was on the *purchaser*. This capricious or arbitrary exercise he seems also to have construed *as if it was synonymous with the mala fide or corrupt exercise of a power*, or the exercise from some improper motive. The purchaser had not cross-examined the trustees on their affidavit which contained a general expression of good faith, so he held the purchasers failed.

The purchasers appealed and the Court of Appeal (Cotton L.J. Fry L.J. and Lopes L.J.) all upheld Chitty J. Cotton L.J.'s judgment emphasized the burden of proof; taking the vendors' affidavit stating that their decision was come to bona fide as prima facie conclusive, in the absence of any evidence from the purchasers.

Fry L.J. seems also to have been somewhat converted to the new literalist fashion. He said of the rule that the power must be exercised, as he put it "*reasonably* and not arbitrarily or capriciously",[50] "Whether the introduction of such a term is construing the contract, or making a fresh one, I do not say; but there is such a current of *dicta* and authorities on that point that it must be considered settled." Lopes L.J. also seems to have thought the vendors' affidavit stating that they had exercised the power bona fide was conclusive.

[46] At 389.
[47] (1866) 2 Ch. App. 102, above.
[48] 53 L.T. (N.S.) 434.
[49] Above.
[50] Italics supplied.

Ashburner v. Sewell **[1891] 3 Ch. 405**

12.25 This simply decided that the vendor might rescind where there was a latent defect as to an easement, which ranked as a title matter, whether or not it was also a misdescription question.

Re Deighton and Harris Contract **[1898] 1 Ch. 464**

12.26 There was a condition allowing the vendor to rescind if the purchaser made any objection or requisition "as to the title, particular, conditions, or any other matter or thing relating or incidental to the the sale" which the vendor was unable or unwilling to comply with. It was held this condition extended beyond matters of title and included also matters of conveyance. A mortgagee who had contracted to sell the entire mortgage term turned out to be only a mortgagee by sub-demise, and he declined to an arrange for the person entitled to the remainder of the term to join in the conveyance. There was no real discussion of principle; but it is to be noted that the vendor was treated as honest.[51] The decision was perhaps inevitable given that and the very wide wording of the condition.

Re Jackson and Haden's Contract **[1906] 1 Ch. 412**

12.27 There was a condition (in so far as material to this chapter) that if the purchaser should insist on any objection or requisition as to title or evidence of title which the vendors should be unable, or, on the ground of expense, should decline to remove or comply with, then the vendors were to be at liberty to rescind the contract. The purchaser insisted on a proof of title to the mines and minerals which had been reserved to the grantor under an earlier conveyance. The vendors replied that the purchaser knew that the mines and minerals could not be sold, having been reserved. The purchaser did not know. The purchaser took out a summons under the Vendor and Purchaser Act 1874, relying on "the conduct and knowledge of the vendors [of the fact that the mines and minerals could not be sold] and the unreasonableness of the present rescission". On the vendors' appeal to the Court of Appeal Collins M.R. said this;

"Though in my opinion this particular condition, on the face of it, might apply to the particular failure of title which arises in this case, and that the objection raised by this purchaser is an objection addressed to title, nevertheless it does seem to me that, within the principle of the cases which have been cited it is not an objection that the vendors, on this contract, can avail themselves of as justifying them in rescinding this contract. Now, it is to be noted that, in dealing with this right to rescind, the learned judges have always criticized most carefully the conduct of the parties to the contract, and the purpose for which the particular condition must be supposed to have been introduced, with a view to seeing whether or not it is, in the circumstances of the particular case, a condition that ought to be applied for the benefit of the person who has introduced it. In this particular case, there is no doubt that this clause was introduced for the benefit of the vendors. The Court considers whether or not the vendor has so acted in the matter as to be entitled to avail himself of that condition; or it may be put in other words. Can we construe this condition, in the circumstances, as applying to the particular state of facts

[51] See the judgment of Lindley M.R.

which has caused the difficulty?" He referred to *Duddell v. Simpson*[52] and *Nelthorpe v. Holgate*;[53] and said:

"Now what is the element that the Vice-Chancellor [in *Nelthorpe v. Holgate*] is seeking for there which determines the case? It seems to me to be an element of something on the part of the vendor less than the law requires of him in such cases. It may stop short of fraud, it may be consistent with honesty: but, at the same time, there must be a falling short on his part—he must have done less than an ordinarily prudent man, having regard to his relations to another person, when dealing with him, is bound to do; and therefore where, *knowing the exact facts, he has recklessly made a description of them which would mislead another person who did not know as much as himself* (even though he thought that person might know as much as himself) there is a clear failure of duty on the part of the vendor which fairly disentitles him to say that a clause introduced into the contract for his benefit is introduced to meet such a case as that which has arisen here, namely, *a reckless disregard by the vendor of his duty as to accuracy of statement when he is making a statement with a view to other people acting on it as correct.*[54] On that ground it is enough to say that this particular condition must be read (as against the persons who are taken to have introduced it and introduced it for their own benefit) as not applying to the particular case to which they seek to apply it, namely something arising wholly and solely out of their own recklessness in the manner in which they have formulated the contract . . ."

12.28 Romer L.J., also dismissed the vendors' appeal, but gave his reasons rather briefly, first calling the circumstances "special and peculiar", then saying—rather clumsily—that in the circumstances "the difficulty that has arisen is not really a matter of title, though it would have been a matter of title as between an ordinary vendor and purchaser", and finally simply referring to Rigby L.J.'s remark in *In Re Deighton and Harris's Contract*[55] that it would "not be right" to let the vendor "ride off upon a condition to rescind which was obviously not framed with reference to any such case as" that which had arisen.

Cozens-Hardy L.J. was more illuminating. He said after referring to authorities in a general way "It is not enough for the vendor to say: Here is a condition which, as a matter of construction, entitles me to rescind this contract. The answer is: No, you must look at all the circumstances; are they such as to entitle you to put an end to that contract of sale which, in form and in fact, you have entered into?" He referred to the vendors' knowledge of the true facts, and asked "Now, under those circumstances, is it just, is it reasonable, that they should be allowed to put an end to the contract . . .? . . . For the reasons given [by the other two]" he thought not.

Note: One sees the transmogrification of good faith principles already begun in the handling of this essentially good faith law by these three judges. They are groping for the relevant principle, trying to uphold the old authorities without a clear guiding thread. Of the three, Collins M.R. expresses the duty of accuracy in terms which are nearest to the principle in the older good faith cases,[56] *but even he muddies the waters by talking of "recklessness" and a "failure of duty". Romer L.J. really does not help us at all; while Cozens-Hardy L.J. seems to see the court as having a wide inquiry to make into the conduct of the vendor, followed by a decision (on what guiding principles is unclear) whether it would be just and reasonable to let him rely on the rescission clause.*

[52] Above.
[53] Above.
[54] Italics supplied.
[55] (1898) above.
[56] See e.g. Chap. 5, Sale of Land.

***Quinion v. Horne* [1906] 1 Ch.596**

12.29 There was a condition that if the purchaser should make any objection or requisition the vendor should be "unwilling to remove or comply with" the vendor might annul the sale. The purchaser made an essential requisition (on the footing that there was to be proof of title) and the vendor sought to rescind, saying that the requisition in no way affected the title.

Farwell J. referred to *In re Dames and Wood*,[57] and *In re Starr-Bowkett Building Society and Sibun's Contract*[58] but thought the only question before him, since the vendor had given reasons, was to consider whether they were "a mere arbitrary exercise of his own will, or whether they rest upon any rational foundation on which any ordinary reasonable man is entitled to rely." He thought there was no *mala fides*, which he took as meaning dishonest purpose, on the part of the vendor, but that his conduct had been entirely arbitrary, and he was not allowed to rely on the condition.

***Merrett v. Schuster* [1920] 2 Ch.240**

12.30 The vendor was allowed to rely on the rescission condition where he had *believed from the conduct of a tenant* that he would quit so as to allow the sale to be free of his tenancy.

***Re Des Reaux and Setchfield's Contract* [1926] Ch.178**

12.31 The condition was that if the purchaser should insist on any objection or requisition which the vendor shall be unable, or on the ground of expense, unwilling to remove or comply with, the vendor may by notice in writing to be given to the purchaser, and notwithstanding any intermediate negotiation or litigation, rescind the contract for sale . . ."

The abstract for title revealed that the vendor did not have title to the property, which had belonged to his late wife, merely a life interest in it. The purchaser submitted several requisitions, and finally a requisition requiring the vendor to make certain applications to the court to perfect his title. The vendor then purported to rescind. Romer J. held (after referring to *Re Jackson & Haden's Contract*[59] and *Duddell v. Simpson*,[60] that the vendor, who had not consulted any competent legal adviser as to the title, and had acted recklessly in entering into the contract, could not rescind on the grounds that it would involve him in expense: it was "not a reasonable thing for the vendor to do in reference to the purchaser." . . . "I can well understand that where, on a closer examination of the title it appears that there is some blot on it which was unknown and unsuspected by the vendor, even although that blot can be removed by the expenditure of a comparatively small sum of money, it may be quite reasonable for him to rescind the contract if the purchaser insists upon that expenditure being incurred. It is to meet such cases as that that conditions of this description are inserted."

Note: The "reckless/unreasonable" approach again here, thus continuing the process of obscuring the old principles.

***Baines v. Tweddle* [1959] Ch.679**

12.32 The vendor had agreed to sell property which was subject to mortgages. Before he signed the contract he asked his solicitor to get in touch with the

[57] Above.
[58] Above.
[59] Above.
[60] Above.

mortgagees and was told that the solicitor "had the matter in hand"; but he knew that the solicitor had not in fact been in touch with them. The vendor had been in arrear with instalments and the building society mortgagee refused to concur in the sale. The vendor served a notice purporting to rescind. On appeal, *In re Jackson and Haden's Contract*,[61] *Merrett v. Schuster*[62] and *Duddell v. Simpson*[63] were cited to the court: but *In re Jackson and Haden's Contract*[64] was taken by the court to be the foundation of the case law on the appeal. Accordingly, the question became whether the vendor had been "reckless" or not. It was accepted that he had not been dishonest "or acted otherwise than in perfect good faith" (Lord Evershed M.R.).[65] Because the original good faith principles had become obscured, we see the court unsure how to approach the condition, wondering, for example, whether the normal principles of agency really applied; but they finally decided that in any case the vendor himself had been reckless. Yet the vendor's failing was probably not really what would literally be called recklessness, but a non-compliance with the duty of candour in what he had told the purchaser—real good faith territory. As Lord Evershed put it,[66] "I cannot think that a man can be excused because he chose to take, as I think he undoubtedly did, a considerable risk when he signed the contract"; or as Romer L.J. put it "it seems to me that the evidence shows that, in the language of P.O. Lawrence J.,[67] he had "only a fanciful and unsubstantial ground for such belief"; or as Pearce L.J. put it "A reasonably prudent man would, I think, have said: "I cannot sign until you have found out for certain that an arrangement has been made and that I can convey the property".

Selkirk v. Romar Investments [1963] 1 W.L.R. 1415

12.33 This was an appeal from the Bahamas. The contract had contained a condition that if any objection or requisition whatsoever be insisted on which the vendor shall be unable or unwilling to satisfy or comply with he might (notwithstanding any attempt to remove or satisfy the same . . .) rescind the contract . . ." The purchaser complained that the vendor was not entitled to rescind because he had not been frank before the contract about the existing deficiency in the evidence of a part of the title.

Lord Radcliffe, delivering the judgment of the Privy Council, considered the nature of the court's control of the vendor's right of rescission. He thought it had to be by virtue of "some equitable principle which enures for the benefit of the purchaser; and" he continued, ". . . it is not in dispute that courts of equity have on numerous occasions intervened to restrain or control the exercise of such a right of rescission in contracts for the sale of land, despite what, on the face of the contract, its terms seem to secure for the vendor."

"It does not appear to their Lordships, any more than it did to the judge who tried the action, that there is any room for uncertainty as to the nature of the equitable principle that is invoked in these cases. It has frequently been analysed, and frequently applied, by Chancery judges, and, although the epithets that describe the vendor's offending action have shown some variety of expression, they are all related to the same underlying idea, and their variety

[61] Above.
[62] Above.
[63] Above.
[64] Above.
[65] *i.e.* he had avoided deliberate dishonesty: the expression "in good faith" does not connote compliance with the duty of accuracy or the duty of candour.
[66] In *Merrett v. Schuster* (above).
[67] At 695.

is only due to the fact that, as each case is decided according to the whole context of its circumstances and the course of conduct of the vendor, one may illustrate more vividly than another some particular aspect of that idea. Thus, it has been said that a vendor, in seeking to rescind, must not act arbitrarily, or capriciously, or unreasonably. Much less can he act in bad faith. He may not use the power of rescission to get out of a sale 'brevi manu,' since by doing so he makes a nullity of the whole elaborate and protracted transaction. Above all, perhaps, he must not be guilty of 'recklessness' in entering into his contract, a term frequently resorted to in discussions of the legal principle and which their Lordships understand to connote an unacceptable indifference to the situation of a purchaser who is allowed to enter into a contract with the expectation of obtaining a title which the vendor has no reasonable anticipation of being able to deliver. A vendor who has so acted is not allowed to call off the whole transaction by resorting to the contractual right of rescission: see *In re Jackson and Haden's Contract*;[68] *Baines v. Tweddle*."[69]

12.34 He went on as follows: "The appellant's argument before the Board concentrated upon the fact that the respondents had not before entering into the contract made known to him the existing deficiency of evidence with regard to the descent of title from Mrs Kemp to Edward Maximo Kemp, the grantor under the 1939 conveyance. This non-disclosure, it was said, was a breach of that duty of frankness in respect of matters of title which the law requires a vendor of land to observe in his dealings with his purchaser. A vendor guilty of such a breach, it was said, was necessarily precluded from taking advantage of a right of rescission. But, in their Lordships' opinion, a case of rescission cannot be determined by any general proposition about the duty of disclosure. *No doubt the law imposes upon a vendor of land certain obligations of disclosure with regard to a matter so peculiarly within his own knowledge as his title to his own land. But the extent of those obligations and their consequences have to be measured in the light of the particular rights which in the instant case vendor or purchaser is seeking to assert.*[70] The present case is not a case in which a vendor is resorting to the court for an equitable remedy, such as specific performance, or is trying to force upon his purchaser a title unexpectedly less than the good marketable title which is called for by the law. On the contrary, he stands by his contractual right to rescind the contract and asks for nothing more. Again, the court is not dealing here with a claim by a purchaser to avoid an existing contract or an executed conveyance on the ground of a material concealment or non-disclosure of want of title on the part of a vendor. Authorities or propositions of law which bear upon such situations have therefore no immediate relevance to what is now in issue, which is simply the question whether the respondent is to be held guilty of 'recklessness' in the legal sense, in not warning the appellant before the contract was signed that there were certain evidential gaps in the proof of its title that it was unlikely to be able to fill up.

12.35 Their Lordships are satisfied that recklessness is not to be attributed to the respondent for this omission. While there have indeed been instances in which a vendor has been deprived of the right of rescission for entering into his contract in circumstances in which he had no reasonable assurance that he could convey the whole title for which he was contracting, his disqualification arises out of his carelessness or lack of prudence in the particular circumstances and not out of a mere failure to disclose a defect of title, much less a defect in the evidence of title, which rendered the title that he had to offer less than complete. Had the law been otherwise, the decisions in *Duddell v.*

[68] Above.
[69] Above.
[70] Italics supplied.

Simpson[71] and *In re Deighton and Harris's Contract*[72] could never have gone, as they did, in favour of the vendor." . . .

"No doubt recklessness in entering into the contract may not be the only thing to be regarded when a vendor's right to exercise a contractual power of rescission is brought into question. It is the *use of that right*[73] that is not to be arbitrary or without reason, and courts have expressed themselves from time to time as being unwilling to allow a vendor to call the whole contract off in the face of some requisition to which he takes what is merely a capricious or fanciful objection." However, he thought here there had not been anything of that kind, so the vendor won.

Note: (1) See Chapter 10, Excluding the Fair Dealing Terms, for the idea that rescission of the contract, being the remedy which was applicable anywhere where there was a want of good faith, was a remedy more readily granted to a vendor. The argument was that he had only contracted to have what the law might have allowed him anyway.

(2) The other relevant point in the case is the question of the appropriate stance to be taken by the court where there was a rescission clause in the contract but there had been (or arguably had been) a failure of good faith (a breach of the duty of candour/accuracy).[74]

***Leominster Properties & Broadway Finance Ltd* (1981) 42 P. & C.R. 372**

12.36 There was a condition that if the purchaser persisted in any objection to the title which the vendor should be unable or unwilling, on reasonable grounds, to remove, and it was not withdrawn for 10 days after being asked to do so, the vendor might rescind by notice. The vendor was a mortgagee, unaware that there was a prior mortgage which although second in time, had been registered at HM Land Registry first, so as to take priority. The vendor sought to rescind when the purchaser required the prior mortgage to be discharged. Slade J. dealt with the matter by means of the distinction between matters of conveyance (which this was, in his opinion) and matters of title. Thus, the rescission clause was inapplicable because its ambit was narrowed by construction.

***British Gas Trading Ltd v. Eastern Electricity* (Reported in [1996] New Law Digest, November 21.)**

The plaintiff agreed to supply the defendant with gas. There was a proviso in the agreement that either party could terminate the agreement if the other party were subject to a change of control, subject to the approval of the other party, such approval not to be unreasonably refused. Colman J. adopted an approach similar to that used in the landlord and tenant cases: the question being whether the proposed assignment was for a purpose or with an effect which would be outside the mutual contemplation of the parties at the time of the original agreement.

[71] (1866) 2 Ch. App. 102.
[72] [1898] 1 Ch. 464.
[73] Italics supplied.
[74] See the comment in text above at para. 12.06.

PART 2: APPARENTLY UNRESTRICTED RIGHTS TO TERMINATE LICENCES

***Cornish v. Stubbs* (1870) L.R. 5 C.P. 334 (Licence to store goods on land—reasonable time to remove goods)**

12.37 A part of the case concerned a right (for consideration) to stack timber on a part of a wharf belonging to the defendant and adjacent to land which he rented from the defendant. Bovill C.J. said "it seems almost necessary, *from the nature of the license*[75] that the Plaintiff should have had a right to a reasonable time to remove his goods" . . . Willes J. and Montague Smith J. agreed.

***Llanelli Railway & Dock Co v. London & Northwestern Railway Co* (1875) 7 H.L. 550 (Licence to a railway company to use a sister railway company's facilities—no circumstances in which licensor could terminate)**

12.38 Two railway companies entered into an agreement whereby the Northwestern Railway Co was to have have running powers over the Llanelli Railway & Dock Co's ("Llanelli's") lines, and to have its passengers and goods carried; and each company would send by each other's lines all traffic not otherwise specifically consigned. There was no express provision for termination. Llanelli purported to terminate this agreement by six month's notice from a given date.

The House of Lords held that in the circumstances here, which included the potential heavy outlay of money on staff, *etc.*, contemplated at the date of the agreement, the statutory background which permitted contracts without limit of time, and the factual background of permanence which the subject matter of the contract evinced, the licence might *not be terminated at all.* Lord Selborne expressed it very generally, indicating that "an agreement *de futuro*, extending over a tract of time which, on the face of the instrument, is indefinite and unlimited, must (in general) throw upon any one alleging that it is not perpetual, the burden of proving that allegation, either from the nature of the subject, or from some rule of law applicable thereto."[76] He continued:

". . . In the present case, the character of perpetuity attaches both to the legal personality of each of the contracting parties, and to the legal character and use of the subject matter, the railway; and the objects of the agreement are favourably regarded by the law; all such companies having express statutory powers to contract (without any necessary limit of time) for such objects, and being (in the absence of contract) to some extent always under legal obligations, actual or potential, of a like general character.

***Hurst v. Picture Theatres Limited* [1915] 1 K.B., 1 (Ticket for theatre seat—right to stay until the performance over given normal behaviour)**

12.39 The Court of Appeal held that the purchaser of a ticket for a seat at the theatre has the right to stay till the end of performance (assuming normal behaviour); and may not be turned out at the whim of the management (who believed mistakenly he had not paid for his ticket).

Note: The evident purpose of the contract was emphasized: see for example Buckley L.J.'s judgment. It will have determined the period of irrevocability here.

[75] Italics supplied.
[76] *c.f.*, however, Lord Macdermott in *Winter Garden Theatres v. Millennium Productions.*

***Minister of Health v. Bellotti* [1944] K.B. 298 (Bare licence, notice to terminate must be reasonable having regard to the circumstances at the time of its grant: evacuees to have reasonable time to remove)**

12.40 The Minister of Health had exercised a statutory power to allow the defendants, who were evacuees, to live in certain large blocks of flats which had been requisitioned. The Ministry then attempted to terminate the licence by giving a week's notice. The Court of Appeal held that even in the case of a bare licence such as this one, there had to be a period of notice which was reasonable having regard to "all the circumstances (Mackinnon L.J.) or "reasonable" ... "so that the licensee can remove himself and his property" (Goddard L.J.). That they both probably meant, reasonable as a matter of reasonable expectation at the time of the contract, is evident from the judgment of Lord Green M.R. who said it must surely be "the implied intention of the parties that, if they were turned out by the ministry, they should be given such an opportunity as strangers in the land might require, to enable them to find other accommodation."

***Winter Garden Theatre v. Millennium Productions* [1948] A.C. 173 (Reasonable period of notice to be given, judged by the nature of the contract – a month sufficient)**

12.41 A licence was granted by the Winter Garden Theatre to Millennium Productions to use the theatre for producing plays concerts or ballets. The licence was for one year certain and thereafter weekly, terminable on one month's notice from Millennium Productions. There was no provision for termination by the Winter Garden Theatre. Millennium Productions argued that the licence was irrevocable save by it. It was held by the House of Lords that:

(1) a term was to be implied that the licence was revocable by the owners; (2) a term was to be implied that a reasonable period of notice was to be given, and (3) on the facts, Millennium Productions had not proved the period was unreasonable.

Their Lordships differed on the question whether the reasonable period of notice extended the period of the licence, or happened, theoretically, after the licence had been terminated. Lord Macdermott, with whose analysis Viscount Simon and Lord Simonds agreed, thought it did not extend the contract period, but was a "period of grace" after the contract had technically been terminated. This had to be measured "reasonably and fairly"; and Lord Macdermott *may* have thought that the contractual circumstances might separately show a longer period than would be necessary for the licensee's purposes. What he said is a little ambiguous, however, on this point. He said "... where, as for example in cases of a specialized user involving obligations to third parties or the public, the circumstances of the contract are such as to show that an immediate cessation of the authorized use or activity was not contemplated or intended, the rule of law to which I have referred may well, and notwithstanding a liberal measurement of its reasonable period, fall short of meeting the just requirements of the position." He does not seem to have shared Lord Uthwatt's idea that the circumstances to be taken into account in calculating the period included the actual user at the time of termination, since he accepted that the licensor might not be fully versed concerning all the relevant circumstances. He thought the *nature of the contract* (presumably judged at its making) was relevant, as well as its express words ("That, to my mind, is what accords best with the express terms of the contract and the nature of the transaction".). Despite this, he seems to have classified the implied term as something which "went without saying". Possibly seeing that this was a doubtful proposition here, he contented himself with saying it arose as a matter of "such business efficacy as the parties must have intended". He did not base it on any good faith principle, but none had been argued.

12.42 Lord Porter took the provisional view that the licence was prima facie terminable at once on the giving of a reasonable period of notice, but added, "I think . . . the licensee must be given a reasonable time to vacate the premises and what is a reasonable time must depend upon all the circumstances of the case. In the case of a theatre, it might even extend to the run of a play, if no suitable alternative premises could be found". However since here he found that it had not been proved the notice was insufficient, he did not reach a formal decision on the point.

Lord Uthwatt pointed out that the question whether the normal power of a licensee to determine was contained in the contract here depended on "the subject-matter of the bargain". Here, the circumstances were such that the power to determine was not barred. He considered that a reasonable time had to be given; and that this did extend the period of the licence, rather than being an extra period of grace after the licence had been terminated at once.

He thought, however, that the calculation of a reasonable period depended not only on the nature of the user authorised by the licence, but the actual user at the time of the notice. He thought an implied obligation on the licensees to give any information to the licensors about this user had to be implied therefore.[77].

***Timeload Limited v. British Telecommunications PLC* [1995] E.M.L.R. 459, C.A. (Arguable that exercise of wide licence to terminate use of a telephone line might be restricted by the nature of the contract)**

12.43 The plaintiff decided to set up a free telephone inquiry line for people needing particular professional/commercial services. The callers were to have free calls, the plaintiff being reimbursed by the professional and commercial enterprises which paid to be on his books. The plaintiff managed (possibly by a breach of duty by an employee of BT) to be allotted the freephone number it desired, which was BT's own directory inquiries service. When it discovered, which was after the plaintiff had begun to market its service, BT gave the plaintiff one month's notice under the contract, which provided that the contract could be terminated at any time on one month's notice. The matter came before the Court of Appeal on an appeal by BT against the grant of an interlocutory injunction by the judge in the court below restraining BT from so doing. The question was thus whether the plaintiff could seriously argue that the wide right apparently granted to BT to terminate was to be restricted.

The Master of the Rolls paid attention to BT's position in the market. "It is therefore correct, speaking very generally, to regard BT as a privatised company, no longer a monopoly, but still a very dominant supplier closely regulated to ensure that it operates in the interests of the public and not simply in the interests of its shareholders should those be in conflict. Against that background I am, for my part, by no means sure that the classical approach to the implication of terms is appropriate here. As Lord Cross pointed out in *Liverpool City Council v. Irwin*,[78] implied terms can find their way into contracts either because the law lays down a general rule that in contracts of a certain type a certain obligation should be implied, or on grounds of necessity for business efficacy. Thus, pure necessity is not the only ground on which a term can be implied and I can see strong grounds for the view that in the circumstances of this contract BT should not be permitted to exercise a potentially

[77] *c.f. Mackay v. Dick* (1881) 6 App. Cas. 251, noted below at 13.62.
[78] [1977] A.C. 239 at 257.

drastic power of termination without demonstrable reason or cause for doing so.

I also share the learned judge's view that it is not altogether easy to reconcile clause 6, enabling BT to suspend only for operational reasons, with clause 18, enabling it apparently to exercise the more drastic power of termination without any reason at all. It is in fact *reasonable to suppose* that Timeload would not have committed themselves to very substantial expenditure and indeed to found their business on the possession of a telephone number of which they could be deprived at a month's notice. In my judgment the courts must be wary of accepting a construction which so obviously flies in the face of what one party at least *may be taken to have* intended.[79]

He thought it was arguable that section 3(2)(b) of the Unfair Contract Terms Act 1977 also applied, in that a performance would be rendered which was different in whole or in part from that which the customer reasonably expected.

Finally, he thought the common law itself might have an answer. "It seems to me at least arguable that the common law could, if the letter of the statute does not apply, treat the clear intention of the legislature as expressed in the statute as a platform for invalidating or restricting the operation of an oppressive clause in a situation of the present, very special kind. I say no more than that there is, I think, a question here which has attracted much attention in Commonwealth jurisdictions and on the continent and may well deserve to be further explored here."

Thus, there was a very real chance that the plaintiff might be able to establish that BT could only give notice for good cause, and the interlocutory injunction was upheld, Hoffmann and Henry L.J.J. agreeing.

[79] Italics supplied.

Chapter 13

THE AFTER–SALE RELATIONSHIP: THE EXERCISE OF RETAINED RIGHTS AFFECTING THE USE OF THE THING SOLD

PART 1: VENDOR'S APPROVAL REQUIRED

Vendor/lessor/covenantee's approval required for some act to be done by on or in relation to the subject matter of the contract or the purchaser/lessee/covenantor's land: obligation to be reasonable in giving or withholding approval implied

13.01 The cases on this topic do not reveal an entirely consistent picture. There are a number of cases (all in connection with land, though this is probably pure chance) which indicate that in certain but by no means all, circumstances, where approval or consent is required to something by one party to the contract, this approval is not to be unreasonably withheld. There are also cases in which it was held that the consent *might* be withheld arbitrarily if necessary.[1]

It is not wholly clear whether "reasonable" is narrowed so as to mean "reasonable in the light of the original paramount purpose of the contract", or is of wider scope. However, both *Dallmann v. King*[2] and *Cryer v. Scott Brothers (Sunbury) Ltd*[3] give reasons for requiring the grantor to be reasonable which strongly suggest a connection with the rule against derogation from grant, or at all events with the purpose of the contract or the clause concerned. The approach of Millett J. in *Price v. Bouch*[4] is not dissimilar though overtly more widely phrased. The explanation of cases such as *Viscount Tredegar v.*

[1] See the Appendix to this chapter for cases.

[2] (1837) Bing (N.C.) 105; 132 E.R. 729.

[3] (1988) 55 P. & C.R. 183.

[4] (1987) 53 P. & C.R. 257.

Harwood[5] and *Guardian Assurance v. Gants Hill Holdings*[6] would in this event be simply that the clauses in question did not reveal any particular purpose or aim to which the consent was an ancillary matter.[7]

13.02 The courts have hitherto limited themselves in the cases below to consideration of the "matrix of facts" which would be admissible as to the construction of the contract. Facts showing the "end" or "aim" of the contract have been there purely because they were admissible as part of the surrounding circumstances or "matrix".[8] If a principle of assumed loyalty to the paramount purpose of the contract is developed over time as a general contractual principle, whether developed out of derogation from grant or as a free-standing, parallel, principle, the evidence of the "matrix" of facts would then presumably have a dual purpose. First, it would provide an aid to construction of the traditional kind, so that any implied terms based on the intention of the actual parties to the contract as shown in the words they have used, can be ascertained. Secondly, the surrounding circumstances would reveal the main purpose of the contract, and from this a limited rule governing the parties' later contractual relationship would be derived.

PART 2: LANDLORD AND TENANT—LANDLORD'S REFUSAL OF CONSENT TO ASSIGNMENT

13.03 What a landlord will think "reasonable" and what a tenant will think "reasonable", if both consult only their own interests, are frequently going to be clashing concepts. If their disputes come before the court, the court has to choose one of the rival contentions; it has not the option to say, I think both are reasonable, depending on your point of view. Accordingly, the courts in practice have had only two real choices: either always to be pro-landlord or pro-tenant, or to find some objective principles or criteria for "reasonable". They have over the years by and large chosen the second. What is particularly interesting is that no-one, as far as can be ascertained, has related these principles to the old doctrine of non-derogation from grant; or to any good faith doctrine. Yet the curious thing is that the principles on which the courts act in this sphere would probably not look all that unfamiliar, for example, to a seventeenth-century conveyancing lawyer used to applying the principles of derogation from grant. What follows concentrates on the eventual development by the courts, with ups and downs, unaided by submissions based on the rule against derogation from grant or good faith, of a doctrine of which is based essentially on loyalty to the paramount purpose of the contract or clause. For a full approach to the topic of assignment of leases generally see the

[5] [1929] A.C. 72.
[6] (1983) 267 E.G. 678.
[7] Cp. the rule that mortgagees must exercise their powers for the purposes for which they were given, and the trust doctrine of a fraud on the power.
[8] See Lord Wilberforce in *Prenn v. Simmonds* [1971] 1 W.L.R. 1381.

landlord and tenant textbooks. Because the approach adopted is one of charting historical changes in the development of the law on the topic, it has been convenient in this section to integrate rather more cases of interest into the text than usual.

13.04 First, it was held in *Lehmann v. McArthur*,[9] a pre-1927 Act case in which there was an express covenant that the lessee might assign with consent not to be unreasonably withheld, that *no tenant's estate might be defeated for the sole purpose of bringing his estate to an end*; there was an implicit right in the tenant to keep his lease. This can be seen as a recognition of the parties implicit duty of loyalty to the paramount purpose of the contract, in its basic form: I agreed to grant you a lease for x years; I may not go against that. The judge might just as well have expressed it in the classic derogation-from-grant formula: a man may not give a thing with one hand and take away the means of enjoying it with the other.

In this case the landlord had refused consent in order to get in the leasehold interests of his tenants, in order to rebuild the premises. No objection could be made to the proposed assignee. Sir John Stuart V.C. said that this *was* unreasonable and vexatious of the landlord and set aside the assignment of the lease by the tenant to the landlord which had happened after the unreasonable refusal. He said:

> "In my opinion, *no lessor has a right to use a stipulation in a covenant of this kind, so as to defeat the right of the lessee to assign*,[10] where the assignment or agreement for an assignment has been honestly made."

Next, the court began to look back more imaginatively, to put itself in the shoes of the parties, in order to make inferences about what their main purpose was, not only for the lease itself, but *for inserting the proviso*. Note the much-quoted judgment of A.L. Smith J. in *Bates v. Donaldson*[11]:

> "It is not, in my opinion, the true reading of this clause that the permission can be withheld in order to enable the lessor to regain possession of the premises before the termination of the term. It was in my judgment inserted *alio intuitu* altogether, and *in order to protect the lessor from having his premises used or occupied in an undesirable way or by an undesirable tenant or assignee*,[12] and not in order to enable the lessor to, if possible coerce a tenant to surrender the lease so that the lessor might obtain possession of the premises, which was the reason why in the present case the assent was withheld."

Later still, a further inference was drawn from the circumstances of leases about the parties' common intention: the parties entered into the lease in their capacity as landlord and tenant; that *relationship* was the one which would subsist between them; and this will have meant

[9] (1867) L.R. 3 Eq. 746.
[10] Italics supplied.
[11] [1896] 2 Q.B. 241.
[12] Italics supplied.

the reason for refusal had to have *something to do with* the subject matter of the lease. However, this was a sufficiently vague formulation to allow back in to some extent reasons which were extraneous to the lease. It was in effect halfway house between an unfettered discretion in the landlord and the stricter derogation from grant principles.

13.05 *In Re Gibbs and Houlder Bros & Co's Lease,*[13] a lease contained a covenant by the lessee not to assign without consent, such consent not to be withheld in the case of a responsible and respectable person. The proposed assignment was to an adjoining tenant of the same landlord. The landlord objected for the reason—a perfectly sensible one from his point of view—that he would lose a good tenant and would have difficulty re-letting. Pollock M.R. said:

> "... I think that one must look at these words in their relation to the premises, and *to the contract made in reference to the premises between the lessor and lessee; in other words, one must have regard to the relation of the lessor and lessee inter se*, or, perhaps one may add, to the due and proper management of the property ... But I do not think the words of the covenant can be so interpreted as to entitle the lessor to exercise the right of refusal *when his reason given is one which is independent of the relation between the lessor and lessee, and is on grounds which are entirely personal to the lessor, and wholly extraneous to the lessee.*"[14]

It is not easy to be certain that there is here any principle beyond, "It must not be wholly irrelevant to the relationship between them of landlord and tenant."

Warrington L.J. in the same case stressed the importance of looking to and drawing inferences about the parties' *likely* (or reasonable) intentions as to the purpose of the proviso. He evidently did not mean to inquire into the parties actual, but their reasonable or inferred, intentions. This is a good, traditional approach used in derogation from grant cases, and in inferring good faith terms, notably in the sale of chattels, prior to the Sale of Goods Act 1893. He said:

> "The first question that arises is: What is the inference to be drawn as to the intention of the parties in inserting in the lease a provision of this kind? What was the danger which the lessor contemplated, and against which the lessee was content to allow the lessor to protect himself?"

13.06 At this point, he and the others missed the opportunity to narrow the operation of "reasonable" to the actual landlord-tenant relations or circumstances *at the time of the lease*: for example, if the letting had been of part of a larger building belonging to the landlord, then reasons affecting that building would be relevant, if not, not. This would have been beneficial, in that it is easy to operate, and would be in accordance with the parties' reasonable expectations. There is likely to be a feeling of unfairness, if supervening circumstances which

[13] [1925] Ch. 575, C.A.
[14] Italics supplied.

could not have been foreseen are allowed to influence the operation of a covenant long afterwards.

However that may be, Warrington L.J. thought that the reason did not have to be an objection by the landlord *"as landlord* of that particular property"[15]: it had only to *relate to the personality of the assignee or the intended user of the property.*

> "Now, what is to be inferred from what may be treated as having been in the contemplation of the parties when the contract was made? I think it must be, as I have said, that it was intended to protect the lessor as against a lessee, who, although respectable and responsible, might well be reasonably objectionable in other ways, and, secondly, from the point of view of the property, to prevent the lessor from having to accept a lessee whose user of the property might again be reasonably objectionable. The user of the property to be reasonably objectionable need not necessarily be objectionable to the lessor as lessor of that particular property. The user of the property might damage the lessor in other ways, and if it did, then an objection to that user would be reasonable; but whichever way it is looked at, I think you must find in the objection something which connects it either with the personality of the intended assignee suggested as the new tenant of the property, or with the user which he is likely to make of the property to be assigned to him."

Sargant L.J. stressed the importance of considering what was *within the reasonable contemplation of the parties at the time of the lease*; yet appeared to be content with a formula which would allow objections within a much wider range, merely *affecting the subject matter of the contract* which forms the relationship between the landlord and the tenant, and that *it must not be something wholly extraneous and completely dissociated from the subject matter of the contract.*

13.07 By the late seventies, the wide formula above was causing conscious or unconscious unease. Other criteria were suggested to cover the particular situation where the assignment would give rise to rights outside the original paramount purpose-of-the-contract: whether the assignment was "normal or abnormal" or related to "the fag-end" of the lease[16] or whether the assignment was "pregnant with possibilities.[17] Both *Bickel v. Duke of Westminster*[18] and *West Layton v. Ford*[19] would have been perfectly well dealt with by a formulation of the principle that ruled out either side taking advantage of events for a purpose which could not have existed at the date of the original lease. In both cases, the tenant tried to take advantage of new legislation, respectively the Leasehold Reform Act 1967 and the Rent Act 1974, which had not existed at the date of the lease. The landlord was held entitled to refuse consent, which is surely the right result, but the

[15] Italics supplied.

[16] *Swanson v. Forton* [1949] Ch. 143, and *Dollar v. Winston* [1950] Ch. 236.

[17] *Lee v. Carter* [1949] 1 K.B. 85.

[18] [1977] Q.B. 517.

[19] [1979] Q.B. 593.

reasoning was somewhat unsatisfactory. All that can be said is that big efforts were made both to achieve a result that was fair and, which was more difficult, to justify the relevant reasoning as completely in line with previous authority.

In the later of the two cases, *West Layton v. Ford*[20] a "slide" of the boundaries of the applicable doctrine took place: Roskill L.J. attributed to Lord Denning in *Bickel*[21] an approach which one cannot be at all sure was in fact Lord Denning's approach, on a fair reading of the latter's judgment. Lord Denning had in fact favoured a not especially fettered discretion ("He [the landlord] is not limited to any particular grounds. Nor should the court limit him".) although *in practice* he had operated it within narrower, more traditional confines, by looking to the circumstances at the time of the original lease. Roskill L.J. however (with whom the other two Lord Justices agreed) favoured an approach which looked to the original main purpose of the lease. He attributed this to Lord Denning, saying:

> "I think that the right approach . . . is to look first of all at the covenant and construe that covenant in order to *see what its purpose was* when the parties entered into it; what each party, one the holder of the reversion, the other the assignee of the benefit of the relevant term, must be *taken to have understood* when they acquired the relevant interest on either side. It is plain, when one looks at this covenant, that its purpose was that the lessee should have the benefit of living accommodation for the use of any of his staff linked with the carrying on of the business of butchery; but that if he wished to go beyond that user and to use that accommodation for some purpose disconnected with butchery . . ."[22]

13.08 In *Bromley Park Garden Estates Ltd v. Moss*[23] the Lord Denning or at all events the Lord Denning-as-reinterpreted-by-Roskill L.J. approach was given the seal of approval. All three judges, Cumming Bruce, Dunn and Slade L.J.J. agreed that the guiding principle was *the original purpose of the lease.* "Reasonable" was to be judged by whether it conduced to that purpose or was "collateral" to it.[24]

So, by a route that is distinctly Birmingham-via-Beachy-Head and a bit of fudging and tweaking here and there, the law on this topic has in fact arrived right back to a position not unlike the old derogation from grant principle of loyalty to the original purpose of the contract. It could equally be expressed in derogation from grant terms: a [reasonable] man may not give a thing with one hand and take away the means of enjoying it with the other. By "the thing" is meant "the ability to fulfil the purpose of the grant or contract". The "purpose" of the lease and of the proviso is ascertained and circumscribed by looking back to the date of the original lease; it tends—as with deroga-

[20] *ibid.*
[21] [1977] Q.B. 517.
[22] Italics supplied.
[23] [1982] 1 W.L.R. 1019.
[24] Possibly they really meant "extraneous" to it.

tion from grant, to be a single, simple main or paramount purpose, as, for example, to run a butcher's shop or the like; and it is *assumed* as a doctrine of reasonable expectation[25] that both parties will wish to be loyal to this purpose while their "relationship" imposed by that original lease exists.

The debt to the old principle is not recognised, however; and the lack of recognition tends to cause confusion. In *International Drilling Fluids v. Louisville Investments*[26] Balcombe L.J. attempted to elicit guiding principles from the body of cases as a whole. Unfortunately, he did so taking the "timeless-senior-common-room approach"[27] to these, rather than recognising the shift and consequent concentration of emphasis which in fact had occurred over a period. Unsurprisingly, this approach caused him some considerable difficulty. The lease had been for the purpose of offices only, and the assignment was to be to a tenant who would use the premises for serviced offices. The landlord objected on the grounds that such use was detrimental to the investment value of the reversion, and would create a parking problem. The problem could easily have been solved by the modern approach based (consciously or unconsciously) on the rule against derogation from grant. The main purpose of the lease was to let the premises as offices; the main purpose of the lease did not include any more investment advantages for the landlord than necessarily followed from the use as offices, and certainly did not include parking considerations: thus if the landlord objected, he would be cutting down the tenant's reasonably anticipated estate. In fact, the right result was reached, as so often happens, although the theoretical basis is rather unsatisfactory. Balcombe L.J. thought that the landlord was being unreasonable because "the detriment [to the tenant] is *extreme and disproportionate* to the benefit to the landlord."[28]

PART 3: "A MAN IS NOT PERMITTED TO RELY ON HIS OWN WRONG"

13.09 This principle almost certainly originated as one of assumed loyalty by both parties to the paramount purpose of the contract or the clause in question. The early cases were concerned with leases, for example, a mining lease where there was a provision rendering the lease void if the mine was not worked. The principle was expressed to be a *universal contractual principle,* not confined to leases or mining leases. It was explained simply as a rule that where a party could himself bring about a state of affairs which would technically put an end to a contract, the court would assume, in the absence of a clear stipulation that a party might so put an end to the contract, that the contract did

[25] Whatever the parties actually think: *cf.* Roskill L.J.'s "taken to have understood".

[26] [1986] Ch. 513.

[27] See Preface for explanation of this expression if required.

[28] Italics supplied.

not apply to allow a party to the contract to take advantage of such a self-induced state of affairs.

The court in one of the earliest cases, *Rede v Farr*[29] gave weight to the fact that the parties had agreed a lease for a particular number of years, and seem to have felt that to allow a party at his whim, in effect, simply to terminate the lease would be inconsistent with the original, accepted "end" of the agreement—another derogation from grant lookalike. In another early case, *Doe d. Bryan v. Banks*[30] the original *object* of the clause itself was looked to and loyalty to this object or purpose was what informed the court's decision.

By 1917, the court in the *New Zealand Shipping*[31] case, held fast to the definition of the rule in the older cases, but expressed themselves, unfortunately as it turned out, in very slightly different moral language. The early "moral" expression of the principle (as opposed to its actual mechanics, which were as above) had been, No man may take advantage of his own wrong. In the New Zealand case the expression "*default* or wrong" crept in, in one judgment, and "own *breach of contract*" in another. This was unfortunate. The process in the New Zealand case had been first to use the same method of construction as the older cases, namely to distinguish between terminating events brought about by the party seeking to terminate, and terminating events brought about by entirely outside causes. The court then—probably quite unnecessarily—labelled the termination by the party himself "default or wrong"/"breach of contract". This is harmless perhaps, but of course not very helpful. We only know it is a "breach of contract" because we have gone through stage 1 to label it so.

13.10 Unfortunately, it paved the way for what should probably be regarded as a wrong turning, in *Cheall v. Apex.*[32] In this case Lord Diplock in the House of Lords rejected the impeccable exposition of Slade L.J. in the Court of Appeal, and insisted that the "wrong" must not only be a wrong to the other party to the contract, as opposed to a third party; but also that it must actually be a *breach of the contract*. Curiously, he appears to have thought he was applying "the well-known rule", presumably that in the early cases referred to above. Finally, in *Alghussein v. Eton College*[33], the House of Lords reintroduced into the law the old principle of loyalty to the contract/clause, as least as a principle of construction, but nonetheless appear to have seen some benefit in continuing to label the breach they had just determined to be a breach by using the old principle, a "breach of contract". The opportunity has thus been lost, for the time being, for the House of Lords to explore the true ambit of the old principle, and redefine "wrong" correctly, as a particular kind of act of disloyalty to the paramount purpose of the contract. It may be doubted also whether their tentative confining of the rule to questions of construction was particularly helpful, at least if this was intended to confine the application

[29] (1817) 6 M. & S. 121; 125 E.R. 1188.
[30] (1821) 4 B.& Ald. 401; 106 E.R. 984.
[31] [1917] 2 K.B. 717 and [1919] A.C. 1.
[32] [1983] Q.B. 126.
[33] [1988] 1 W.L.R. 587.

of the rule to ambiguous provisions only. It is difficult to see why a contract containing an ambiguous clause should allow the rule to operate, but a contract which is entirely silent on the point should allow what one might call self-operated termination by a party. There is no reason of principle why this should be so; and it would be more consistent with the operation of the other good faith rules, for example regarding the exclusion of the effect of the fair dealing terms, if the rule were held to be an additional implied term where the contract is silent, and a guiding principle for construction where the contract is ambiguous.

PART 4: A POSITIVE DUTY (WHERE RELIANCE NECESSARY) TO TAKE STEPS TO ACHIEVE THE PURPOSE OF THE CONTRACT

13.11 If in a contract of sale something the parties have agreed shall be done cannot effectually be done unless both concur in doing it, the construction of the contract is that each agrees to do all that is necessary to be done on his part for the carrying out of that thing. The contract is further construed so that if one party has completed the contract but for the thing he is prevented from doing by the other party, he is entitled to sue the other party for the full price. This may perhaps be seen as an application of the principle that a party cannot rely on his or her own wrong (see above).

Ashurst J. delivering the opinion of the King's Bench in *Hotham v. East India Company*[34] said it was evident from common sense that if the performance of a condition precedent by the plaintiff had been rendered impossible by the neglect or default of the defendant "it is equal to performance." In other words, the plaintiff is *deemed to have done his part where he has been so prevented from doing it*.

In *Sprague v. Booth*,[35] a Privy Council case on appeal from Ontario, the contract was that the respondent would sell to the appellant's assignor, a certain Meyer, all the stock of the Canada Atlantic Railway which was standing in his name, on receipt of the purchase price. He was at the same time to transfer (subject to certain deductions) two bonds to Meyer. Later it was agreed that in return for a concession on his part Meyer was to receive a deposit of $250,000 as security for the performance of the agreement which was to be forfeited in the event of any default. The bonds were not ready on the day, entirely through the default of the respondent's assignee. Meyer's assignee, the appellant was not allowed to rely on Meyer's own default to avoid forfeiture of the deposit.[36]

[34] (1787) 1 T.R. 638, referred to in *Benjamin on Sale* (6th edn.) at p. 641, referred to in *Colley v. Overseas Exporters*. [1921] 3 K.B. 302.

[35] [1909] A.C. 576.

[36] See also *Kleinert v. Abosso Gold Mining Co.* (1913) 58 S.J. 45; and *Terry v. Moss's Empires* (1915) 32 T.L.R. 92 (duty of parties to act reasonably in the carrying out of all matters which were essential for the proper performance of the obligation.).

In *Mackay v. Dick*,[37] payment was to be made for a machine after it had been tested at a properly opened up face at the appellant's cutting at Carfin. The appellant did not provide a properly opened up face, so that the machine could not be tested fairly. The Court of Appeal affirmed the judgment of the court below awarding the respondents the contract price and interest. Lord Blackburn expressed the general principle in the terms quoted at the beginning of this chapter and repeated here: **13.12**

> "I think I may safely say, as a general rule, that where in a written contract it appears that both parties have agreed that something shall be done, which cannot effectually be done unless both concur in doing it, the construction of the contract is that each agrees to do all that is necessary to be done on his part for the carrying out of that thing, though there may be no express words to that effect.

APPENDIX TO CHAPTER 13: SOME CASES OF INTEREST

PART 1: VENDOR'S APPROVAL REQUIRED

Dallman v. King (1837) Bing (N.C.) 105: 132 E.R. 729. (Capricious withholding of approval tantamount to derogation from grant)

A lessee had agreed to spend £200 within a year on certain works of building and alteration, "such erection and alterations or repairs to be inspected and approved of by [the landlor] and to be done in a substantial manner". The agreement provided that the lessee should be allowed to retain the sum out of the first year's rent of the premises. The court held that the lessee might retain the rent despite the non-fulfilment of the condition, where the lessor had capriciously refused to approve. Tindal C.J. said: "It never could have been intended that he should be allowed capriciously to withhold his approval; that would have been a condition which would *go to the destruction of the thing granted and if so, according to the well-known rule, the thing granted would pass discharged of the condition.*"[38] The other two judges gave judgments to like effect. **13.13**

Viscount Tredegar v. Harwood [1929] A.C. 72

The lessee had covenanted "the lessee shall . . . insure . . . the said messuage . . . in the joint names of the lessee and lessor in the Law Fire Office or in some other responsible insurance office to be approved by the lessor." The House of Lords refused to import into this covenant any requirement that the landlord had to be reasonable in withholding approval: they thought that he had an absolute right to withhold his approval of an alternative office. **13.14**

[37] (1881) 6 App. Cas. 25.
[38] Italics supplied.

***Guardian Assurance Company Ltd v. Gants Hill Holdings Ltd* (1983) 267 E.G. 678**

13.15 The tenant had covenanted: "not without the previous consent of the lessor to convert or use nor permit the said demised premises or any part thereof to be converted or used for any purposes whatsoever other than as offices for their business of an Assurance Corporation." Mervyn Davies J. did not construe the covenant as carrying an implication that the consent had to be reasonable.

***Wrotham Park Estate Company Ltd v. Parkside Homes Ltd* [1974] 1 W.L.R. 798**

13.16 The restrictive covenant burdening the covenantor's land was "not to develop the said land for building purposes except in strict accordance with a lay-out plan to be first submitted to and approved in writing by the vendor or the surveyors." A concession was made by the vendor's very experienced counsel that the covenantee would have no right to refuse approval unreasonably (the scope of "unreasonably" was not discussed), and Brightman J. did not question this.

***Price v. Bouch* (1986) 53 P. & C.R. 257**

13.17 Millett J. said "there is no general principle of law that, whenever a contract requires the consent of one party to be obtained by the other, there is an implied term that such consent is not to be unreasonably refused. It all depends on the circumstances of the particular contract".

***Clerical Medical and General Life Assurance Society v. Fanfare Properties Ltd* (unreported, mentioned in *Cryer v. Scott Brothers (Sunbury) Ltd*, below)**

13.18 There was a covenant in a lease not to set up any erection or building on the demised premises without the prior "approbation and consent" of certain specified persons. What follows is the resume given in *Cryer* by Slade L.J.

"Sir Robert Megarry V.C. declined to imply any term that the approbation and consent should not be unreasonably withheld because he considered that any such implication was neither obvious nor requisite to give business efficacy to the clause. However in the course of reference to certain authorities, he drew a distinction between negative covenants which are drafted in absolute terms and those which are drafted in qualified terms, requiring the giving of some consent. Later in his judgment, in referring to covenants of the latter class, he drew a distinction between those where the requirement of consent is one of "a general and unrestricted consent" (into which category, for example, he would presumably have placed a covenant precluding the carrying on without consent of any trade upon the premises) and covenants which require *"the approval of a specific matter, as when the title has to be approved, or plans of a building have to be submitted for approval."* In the latter class of case, he observed "the Courts will not permit the party whose approval is required to *misuse the requirement* by refusing to approve a title or plans which are free from any tenable objection."[39]

[39] Italics supplied.

***Cryer v. Scott Brothers (Sunbury) Ltd* (1988) 55 P. & C.R. 183, C.A.**

13.19 There was a restrictive covenant whereby no building on the land was to take place save where plans had been submitted to the transferors for their approval. The Court of Appeal held that there was to be implied a term that consent would not be unreasonably withheld. They considered this necessary for business efficacy, since if the wide, unrestricted meaning were adopted, "the covenantees could have been in a position, by the arbitrary and capricious withholding of approval of building plans, wholly to have prevented a development of the estate by the covenantors". This could not have been the intention of the parties, who clearly *did envisage development of the land in question*.

PART 2: LANDLORD AND TENANT: SOME CASES OF INTEREST

***Lehman v. McArthur* (1867) L.R. 3 Eq. 746**

13.20 There was an express covenant that the lessee might assign with consent, the landlord's consent not to be withheld unreasonably or vexatiously. The landlord refused consent in order to get in the leasehold interests of his tenants, in order to rebuild the premises. No objection could be made to the proposed assignee. Sir John Stuart V.C. said it was unreasonable and vexatious of the landlord and *set aside* the assignment of the lease by the tenant to the landlord (which had happened after the unreasonable refusal). He said "In my opinion, no lessor has a right to use a stipulation in a covenant of this kind, so as to defeat the right of the lessee to assign, where the assignment or agreement for an assignment has been honestly made." The plaintiff assignee had sought specific performance of the covenant to assign against the landlord, and thus was able to obtain in addition to the setting aside, an inquiry as to the damages he had sustained by reason of the refusal.

***Treloar v. Bigge* (1874) L.R. 9 Ex. 151**

13.21 A lessee covenanted with his lessor not to assign without the consent in writing of the lessor, such consent not to be arbitrarily withheld. The argument for the landlord that the words above were simply a qualification of the tenant's covenant,[40] not an express covenant by the landlord, was accepted. The result was that he *could not obtain damages*. However, on the facts, it was held the landlord had not arbitrarily refused consent in any case.

***Sear v. House Property and Investment Society* (1880) 16 Ch. D. 387**

13.22 A covenant by the tenant was qualified, "but such consent not to be unreasonably withheld". Hall V.C. followed *Treloar v. Bigge*[41] in holding that this did not amount to a positive covenant not to withhold, but merely operated as a qualification on the tenant's covenant. Accordingly, the tenant was free to assign if the landlord unreasonably refused consent, but *could not obtain damages*.

[40] *i.e.* a delimiting obligation: C.p. Chap. 2, The Legal Nature of the Duty of Good Faith.
[41] Above.

***Barrow v. Isaacs* [1891] 1 Q.B. 417**

13.23 The court affirmed that the consent was not to be arbitrarily withheld, but held that it had to be asked for first; and if not asked for through forgetfulness amounting to negligence on the part of the tenant's solicitor, could not be relieved against. It was held that this forgetfulness did not amount to "mistake" which equity would relieve against.

Note: See Shiloh Spinners v. Harding[42] *in which the House of Lords laid down that a deliberate breach of covenant does not necessarily bar relief.*

Section 3 of the Conveyancing Act 1892

13.24 "In all leases containing a covenant, condition, or agreement against assigning, underletting, or parting with the possession, or disposing of the land or property leased without licence or consent, such covenant, condition, or agreement shall, unless the lease contains an expressed provision to the contrary, be deemed to be subject to a proviso to the effect that no fine or sum of money in the nature of a fine shall be payable for or in respect of such licence or consent; but this proviso shall not preclude the right to require the payment of a reasonable sum in respect of any legal or other expense incurred in relation to such licence or consent."

***Bates v. Donaldson* [1896] 2 Q.B. 241 (C.A.)**

13.25 There was a covenant by the tenant not to assign without consent, such consent not to be unreasonably withheld in the case of any respectable and responsible person.

A.L. Smith L.J. (whose judgment was preferred to that of Kay L.J. by a later Court of Appeal in *Houlder Bros v. Gibbs*,[43] having commented that there was no case in the books which covered the question what was unreasonable, said: "It is not, in my opinion, the true reading of this clause that the permission can be withheld in order to enable the lessor to regain possession of the premises before the termination of the term. It was in my judgment inserted alio intuitu altogether, and in order to protect the lessor from having his premises used or occupied in an undesirable way or by an undesirable tenant or assignee, and not in order to enable the lessor to, if possible coerce a tenant to surrender the lease so that the lessor might obtain possession of the premises, which was the reason why in the present case the assent was withheld."

***Eastern Telegraph v. Dent* [1899] 1 Q.B. 835**

13.26 A tenant had covenanted not to underlet without the landlord's consent. He underlet, through forgetfulness or because he thought the provision unimportant, to a tenant to whom no objection could be taken, but without the landlord's consent. The landlord re-entered. The Court of Appeal held he was entitled to do so, and they could not give relief; and if *Hyde v. Warren*[44] was to different effect they preferred *Barrow v. Isaacs*.[45]

Note: See the note to Barrow v. Isaacs.[46]

[42] [1973] A.C. 691, noted in the Appendix to Chap 14. Penalties, Deposits and Forfeiture.
[43] [1925] Ch. 575.
[44] (1877) 3 Ex. D. 72.
[45] [1891] 1 Q.B. 417.
[46] *ibid*.

***Young v. Ashley Gardens Properties Ltd* [1903] 1 Ch. 112**

13.27 A tenant had covenanted not to assign without consent, such consent not to be unreasonably withheld. The Court of Appeal held that although the landlord is not bound to give any reason for his refusal, if he does give a reason which in the opinion of the Court is unreasonable, the lessee will be entitled to assign without consent; and the court will make a declaratory order.

***West v. Gwynne* [1911] 2 Ch. 1 (overruling earlier cases on the point)**

13.28 The Court of Appeal confirmed its previous *obiter dicta* in an earlier case, *Andrew v. Bridgman*[47] deciding *inter alia* that if the landlord refused consent unless given a fine (contrary to section 3 Conveyancing Act 1882), then the tenant might assign without consent. Cozens-Hardy M.R. commented that "... the Legislature appears to have regarded the exaction of a fine as the price of consent to an assignment as so unreasonable that it ought not to be *deemed to have been part of the bargain unless expressly mentioned* in the lease itself."[48]

***Lewis and Allenby (1909) Ltd v. Pegge* [1914] 1 Ch. 782**

13.29 There was a covenant not to assign without consent, such consent not to be withheld in the case of a respectable and responsible person. The landlord had been asked for consent within a time period which was held reasonable, but had not given it (because the secretary of the landlord forgot to communicate with the directors). Neville J. held that in that case the tenant was entitled to assign without consent, just as in the case of unreasonable refusal: it would have been quite different if the landlord had not been asked at all.

Note: The approach is a variant on that used in the case of a pre-contractual breach of good faith by the seller: here the lease is regarded as omitting the proviso-rights wrongly exercised by the landlord for the purposes of that particular exercise. However there is no permanent omission of the proviso, which remains in being for proper exercise on any future occasion.[49]

***Ideal Film Renting Co v. Nielsen* [1921] 1 Ch. 575**

13.30 The tenants covenanted not to assign without consent, and the landlord had also covenanted separately not to refuse his consent to an assignment unreasonably. It was held the tenant here had all the remedies he would have had in the absence of these express covenant, that is a right to assign without consent, if the consent was unreasonably withheld and in addition, because of the wording of the landlord's covenant, as a separate positive obligation rather than the usual qualification only, a right to damages for the landlord's breach of his covenant. On the facts, the landlord's refusal was held unreasonable.

***Re Winfrey & Chatterton's Agreement* [1921] 2 Ch. 7**

13.31 Sargant J. followed *Bates v. Donaldson*.[50]

[47] [1908] 1 K.B. 596.
[48] Italics supplied.
[49] *c.f.* the post-contractual duty of disclosure in insurance.
[50] [1896] 2 Q.B. 241.

***Re Gibbs and Houlder Bros & Co's Lease* [1925] Ch. 575 (C.A.)**

13.32 A lease contained a covenant by the lessee not to assign without consent, such consent not to be withheld in the case of a responsible and respectable person. The proposed assignment was to an adjoining tenant of the same landlord. The landlord objected because he would lose a good tenant and would have difficulty re-letting.

Pollock M.R. preferred the judgment of A.L. Smith L.J. in *Bates v. Donaldson*[51] to that of Kay L.J. He said:

"... I think that one must look at these words in their relation to the premises, and to the contract made in reference to the premises between the lessor and lessee; in other words, one must have regard to the relation of the lessor and lessee inter se, or, perhaps one may add, to the due and proper management of the property, as in *Governors of Bridewell Hospital v Fawkner*.[52] The latter case is an illustration of a withholding of consent on broad grounds bearing upon the estate of the lessor, or it may be on grounds which are important between the lessor and other lessees of that property, or that estate, of which the lessee had cognizance. But I do not think the words of the covenant can be so interpreted as to entitle the lessor to exercise the right of refusal when his reason given is one which is independent of the relation between the lessor and lessee, and is on grounds which are entirely personal to the lessor, and wholly extraneous to the lessee.[53] As an illustration of what I mean I refer to *Young v Ashley Gardens Properties Limited* where a condition was imposed, or attempted to be imposed, by the lessor, not in reference to the relation between himself and the lessee, nor in relation to the property which was the subject of the lease, but one which was wholly personal to the lessor himself, whereby he attempted to obtain immunity from possible increase in the rates."

13.33 Warrington L.J., agreeing, put it as follows:

"The question whether a particular act is reasonable or unreasonable is obviously one that cannot be determined on abstract considerations. An act must be regarded as reasonable or unreasonable *in reference to the circumstances under which it is committed*,[54] and when the question arises on the construction of a contract the outstanding circumstances to be considered are the nature of the contract to be construed, and the relations between the parties resulting from it. In the present case the contract is a lease, and the relation between the parties that of lessor and lessee.

The first question that arises is: What is the inference to be drawn as to the intention of the parties in inserting in the lease a provision of this kind? What was the danger which the lessor contemplated, and against which the lessee was content to allow the lessor to protect himself? It must, of course, be borne in mind that without this covenant the lessee would have had a free right to assing to whom he pleased the premises comprised in the lease, and the covenant, therefore, was inserted first as a protection of the lessor, and secondly, the proviso was attached to it in order to prevent the lessor making an unreasonable use of that protection.

Now, what is to be inferred from what may be treated as having been in the contemplation of the parties when the contract was made? I think it must be, as I have said, that it was intended to protect the lessor as against a lessee, who, although respectable and responsible, might well be reasonably objectionable in other ways, and, secondly, from the point of view of the property,

[51] *ibid*.
[52] 8 T.L.R. 637.
[53] [1903] 2 Ch. 112.
[54] Italics supplied.

to prevent the lessor from having to accept a lessee whose user of the property might again be reasonably objectionable. The user of the property to be reasonably objectionable need not necessarily be objectionable to the lessor as lessor of that particular property. The user of the property might damage the lessor in other ways, and if it did, then an objection to that user would be reasonable; but whichever way it is looked at, I think you must find in the objection something which connects it either with the personality of the intended assignee suggested as the new tenant of the property, or with the user which he is likely to make of the property to be assigned to him.

13.34 When you look at the authorities—. . . this, at any rate, is plain, that in the case to which an objection to an assignment has been upheld as reasonable it has always had some reference either to the personality of the tenant, or to his proposed user of the property."

He thought Kay L.J.'s judgment did not probably differ on the law from A.L. Smith L.J.'s but he preferred A.L. Smith L.J.'s judgment.

Sargant L.J. also considered A.L. Smith L.J.'s judgment preferable. He thought the phrase "alio intuitu" in A.L. Smith L.J.'s judgment was "absolutely applicable, because it recognizes that in considering the operation and effect of a clause of this kind, you have to consider what was within the reasonable contemplation of the parties to the lease. . . ." He continued: "I was very much impressed by the [tenant's counsel's] argument that in a case of this kind the reason must be something *affecting the subject matter of the contract*[55] which forms the relationship between the landlord and the tenant, and that it must not be something wholly extraneous and completely dissociated from the subject matter of the contract."

Section 19(1) of the Landlord and Tenant Act 1927

Provisions as to covenants not to assign, etc, without licence or consent —

13.35 "In all leases whether made before or after the commencement of this Act containing a covenant condition or agreement against assigning, underletting, charging or parting with the possession of demised premises or any part thereof without licence or consent, such covenant condition or agreement shall, notwithstanding any express provision to the contrary, be deemed to be subject —

(a) to a proviso to the effect that such licence or consent is not to be unreasonably withheld, but this proviso does not preclude the right of the landlord to require payment of a reasonable sum in respect of any legal or other expenses incurred in connection with such licence or consent . . ."[56]

Premier Confectionery (London) Co Ltd v. London Commercial Sale Rooms Ltd [1933] Ch. 904

13.36 It was held not unreasonable by Bennett J. that the landlord of two separate tenancies held together by the same tenant with a user covenant limited to a tobacconist's shop had refused consent to the assignment of one of them without the other. The nature of the premises was probably an important factor in the decision: they were a shop and a kiosk.

[55] Italics supplied.

[56] See now the new section 19(1)(a); See now also section 1(6) of the Landlord and Tenant Act 1988, putting the burden of proof of "reasonableness" on the landlord.

***Creery v. Summersell and Flowerdew & Co Ltd* [1949] Ch. 751**

13.37 It was held again that the landlord's consent had to be asked for, else there would be a breach of the covenant.

***Lovelock v. Margo* [1963] 2 Q.B. 786 (C.A.)**

13.38 It was held that the reasons given have to be reasons which did in fact operate on the landlord's mind at the time.

***Norfolk Capital Group v. Kitway Ltd* [1977] Q.B. 506 (C.A.)**

13.39 A refusal of consent to an assignment at the end of a lease by a company to an individual, which would enable the individual to take advantage of Leasehold Reform Act 1967 rights, was held not unreasonable.

***Bickel v. Duke of Westminster* [1977] Q.B. 517 C.A.**

13.40 The effect of the proposed assignment, in the last seven years of the term, was again to create rights under the Leasehold Reform Act 1967. Lord Denning rejected the idea that the earlier cases had laid down any proposition of law. He held that the courts should not determine the question by strict rules, but should exercise a wide discretion. "He [the landlord] is not limited by the contract to any particular grounds. Nor should the courts limit him. Not even under the guise of construing the words. The landlord has to exercise his judgment in all sorts of circumstances. It is impossible for him, or for the courts, to evenisage them all . . . The utmost that the courts can do is to give guidance to those who have to consider the problem. As one decision follows another, people will get to know the likely result in any given set of circumstances . . . It is rather like the cases where a statute gives the court a discretion." He held the landlord was entitled to refuse consent here.

Orr L.J. referred *inter alia* to the expression "pregnant with future possibilities, used in *Re Gibbs and Houlder Bros*[57] and other cases after that. He said: "On these authorities, in my judgment, the withholding of consent in the present case was reasonable because it related to an attribute of the personality of the proposed assignee in that he would be eligible in due course to acquire the freehold by virtue of the Leasehold Reform Act 1967, and to the effect of the proposed assignment on the user and occupation of the premises, and to the relationship of landlord and tenant in regard to the subject matter of the demise, and because, on the evidence, the object of the refusal was based on views which a reasonable man could well entertain as to the proper management of the lessor's estate of which the premises in question form part.

Waller L.J.'s judgment was to similar effect. Thus, by a majority, they rejected the wide discretion favoured by Lord Denning in favour of a discretion in accordance with the principles, such as they were, set out in the earlier cases.

***West Layton Ltd v. Ford* [1979] Q.B. 593 (C.A.)**

13.41 This was a 14-year business tenancy with living accommodation over, with permission to let the latter on a fully furnished tenancy or on a service occupancy to an employee. At a date after the Rent Act 1977 gave protection to tenants of furnished accommodation, the tenant sought permission to sub-let

[57] [1925] Ch. 575.

the residential accommodation. This would have given the sub-tenant the protection of the Rent Acts as against the landlord.

Roskill L.J. relied upon what he regarded as Lord Denning's approach in *Bickel v. Duke of Westminster*[58]: "I think that the right approach, as Lord Denning M.R. suggested in the *Bickel* case . . . is to look first of all at the covenant and construe that covenant in order to *see what its purpose was when the parties entered into it;*[59] what each party, one the holder of the reversion, the other the assignee of the benefit of the relevant term, must be taken to have understood when they acquired the relevant interest on either side. It is plain, when one looks at this covenant, that its purpose was that the lessee should have the benefit of living accommodation for the use of any of his staff linked with the carrying on of the business of butchery; but that if he wished to go beyond that user and to use that accommodation for some purpose disconnected with butchery, he must grant no more than a furnished tenancy for which he must obtain the landlord's written consent, which was not to be unreasonably withheld"

Whether or not this view was accurately attributed to Lord Denning, Lawton L.J. and Megaw L.J. seem to have agreed with it also.

***Bromley Park Garden Estates Ltd v. Moss* [1982] 1 W.L.R. 1019 (C.A.)**

13.42 Cumming-Bruce L.J. cited from a number of earlier cases, and held that a landlord's reason for withholding consent was not necessarily a good one merely because it had to do with good estate management. In particular he cited Roskill L.J. in *West Layton v. Ford*[60] approving Lord Denning L.J. in *Bickel v. Duke of Westminster.*[61]

Dunn L.J. agreed, relying *inter alia* on *West Layton Ltd v. Ford*[62] for the proposition that in considering whether the landlord's refusal of consent is unreasonable, "the court should look first at the covenant *in the context of the lease and ascertain the purpose of the covenant in that context.* If the refusal of the landlord was designed to achieve that purpose then it may not be unreasonable, even in the case of a respectable and responsible assignee; but if the refusal is designed to achieve some collateral purpose wholly unconnected with the terms of the lease . . . then that would be unreasonable, even though the purpose was good estate management."

All three judges agreed that the reasons relied on by the landlord had to have operated on his mind at the time. As Slade L.J. put it: "A tenant who decides to proceed with an assignment following an unqualified refusal of consent on the part of the landlord, must be entitled to take this course in the light of the facts as they exist at the date of the assignment. Even on this footing, he must still accept a degree of risk in adopting this course inasmuch as he may not be aware of all the factors which have in truth influenced the landlord in his refusal."

Slade L.J. felt constrained by authorities[63] to suppose (although he declined to decide) that the landlord might put forward reasons as reasons which had operated on his mind at the time, which he had not put forward at the time, although he thought this a bit hard.

[58] Above.
[59] Italics supplied.
[60] Para. 13.41 above.
[61] Para. 13.40 above.
[62] Para. 13.41 above.
[63] Such as *Sonnenthal v. Newton* (1965) 109 S.J. 333 and *Welch v. Birrane* (1974) 29 P. & C.R. 102.

***Anglia BS v. Sheffield City Council* (1982) 266 E.G. 311, C.A.**

13.43 The Landlord's refusal to change to a non-retail use was really because he wanted to enhance the value of his adjoining premises; and this was held to be unreasonable.

***International Drilling Fluids v Louisville Investments (Uxbridge) Ltd* [1986] Ch. 513 (C.A.)**

13.44 A 30-year lease provided that the property was not to be used for any purpose other than as offices, and that consent was required for an assignment, but was not to be unreasonably withheld. The tenants proposed an assignment which would mean that the premises would be used as serviced offices. The landlords refused consent, on the grounds that it would be detrimental to the investment value of the reversion and create a parking problem.

Balcombe L.J. (with whose judgment the rest of the court agreed) summarised a number of propositions from the cases. On the question whether regard can be had to the disproportionate consequences to the tenant of a refusal (involving, in truth rather more, the related question of the extent to which the landlord can simply consult his own interests) he said:

"... (6) There is a divergence of authority on the question, in considering whether the landlord's refusal of consent is reasonable, whether it is permissible to have regard to the consequences to the tenant if consent to the proposed assignment is withheld. In an early case at first instance, *Sheppard v. Hongkong and Shanghai Banking Corp*,[64] Malins V.C. said that by withholding their consent the lessors threw a very heavy burden on the lessees and they therefore ought to show good grounds for refusing it. In *Houlder Bros & Co Ltd v. Gibbs*[65] Warrington L.J. said:

"An act must be regarded as reasonable or unreasonable in reference to the circumstances under which it is committed, and when the question arises on the construction of a contract the outstanding circumstances to be considered are the nature of the contract to be construed, and the relations between the parties resulting from it."

In a recent decision of this court, *Leeward Securities Ltd v. Lilyheath Properties Ltd*[66] concerning a sub-letting which would attract the protection of the Rent Act, both Oliver L.J. and O'Connor L.J. made it clear in their judgments that they could envisage circumstances in which it might be unreasonable to refuse consent to an underletting, if the result would be that there was no way in which the tenant (the sub-landlord) could reasonably exploit the premises except by creating a tenancy to which the Rent Act protection would apply, and which inevitably would affect the value of the landlord's reversion. O'Connor L.J. said[67]:

13.45 "It must not be thought that, because the introduction of a Rent Act tenant inevitably has an adverse effect upon the value of the reversion, that that is a sufficient ground for the landlords to say that they can withhold consent and that the court will hold that that is reasonable."

To the opposite effect are the dicta, obiter but nevertheless weighty, of Viscount Dunedin and Lord Phillimore in *Viscount Tredegar v. Harwood*[68]. There are numerous other dicta to the effect that a landlord need consider only his own interests: see, e.g. *West Layton Ltd v. Ford*,[69] and *Bromley Park*

[64] (1872) 20 W.R. 459 at 460.
[65] [1925] Ch. 575 at 584.
[66] (1983) 271 E.G. 279.
[67] *ibid.* At 283.
[68] [1929] A.C. 72 at 78 and 82.
[69] [1979] Q.B. 593 at 605.

Garden Estates Ltd v. Moss.[70] These dicta must be qualified, since a landlord's interests, collateral to the purposes of the lease, are in any event ineligible for consideration: see proposition (2) above. But in my judgment a proper reconciliation of those two streams of authority can be achieved by saying that *while a landlord need usually only consider his own relevant interests, there may be cases where there is such a disproportion between the benefit to the landlord and the detriment to the tenant* if the landlord withholds his consent to an assignment that it is unreasonable for the landlord to refuse consent."[71]

Balcombe L.J. thought that, considering the narrow user clause in the lease, it *was* unreasonable for the landlord to refuse consent. The tenants had moved out, so would otherwise be paying rent for an empty property.

Landlord and Tenant Act 1988 section 1 **13.46**

Qualified Duty to consent to assigning underletting etc. of premises

13.47 (1) "This section applies in any case where —

(a) a tenancy includes a covenant on the part of the tenant not to enter into one or more of the following transactions, that is —

(i) assigning . . . the premises comprised in the tenancy or any part of the premises without the consent of the landlord or some other person, but

(b) the covenant is subject to the qualification that the consent is not to be unreasonably withheld. . . .

. . .

(3)

"Where there is served on the person who may consent to a proposed transaction a written application by the tenant for consent to the transaction, he owes a duty to the tenant within a reasonable time —

(a) to give consent, except in a case where it is reasonable not to give consent,

(b) to serve on the tenant written notice of his decision whether or not to give consent specifying in addition —

(i) if the consent is given subject to conditions, the conditions,

(ii) if the consent is withheld, the reasons for withholding it.

(4) Giving consent subject to any condition that is not a reasonable condition does not satisfy the duty under subsection (3)(a) above.

(5) For the purposes of this Act it is reasonable for a person not to give consent to a proposed transaction only in a case where, if he withheld consent and the tenant completed the transaction, the tenant would be in breach of covenant.

(6) It is for the person who owed any duty under subsection (3) above —

(a) if he gave consent and the question arises whether he gave it within a reasonable time, to show that he did,

(b) if he gave consent subject to any condition and the question arises whether the condition was a reasonable condition, to show that it was,

(c) if he did not give consent and the question arises whether it was reasonable for him not to do so, to show that it was reasonable, and, if the question arises whether he served notice under that subsection within a reasonable time, to show that he did.

Section 4

Breach of duty

13.48 A claim that a person has broken any duty under this Act may be made the subject of civil proceedings in like manner as any other claim in tort for breach of statutory duty.

[70] [1982] 1 W.L.R. 1019 at 1027.

[71] Italics supplied.

Other relevant cases

13.49

Fuller's Theatre & Vaudeville Co Ltd v. Rofe [1923] A.C. 435
Sheppard v. Hong Kong & Shanghai Banking Corporation (1872) 20 W.R. 459
Governors of Bridewell Hospital v. Fawkner 8 T.L.R. 637
Wilson v. Fynn [1948] 2 All E.R. 40
Re Smith's Lease [1951] 1 All E.R. 346
Rendall v. Roberts & Stacey (1959) 175 E.G. 265
Sonnenthal v. Newton (1965) 109 S.J. 333, C.A.
Rose v. Gossman (1966) 201 E.G. 767
Property and Bloodstock Ltd v. Emerton [1967] 3 W.L.R. 973, C.A.
Isow's Restaurants Ltd v. Greenhaven (Piccadilly) Properties Ltd (1969) 213 E.G. 505
Welch v. Birrane (1974) 29 P. & C.R. 102
Pearl Assurance v. Shaw (1984) 274 E.G. 490 at 492
British Bakeries (Midlands) Ltd v. Michael Testler & Co [1986] 1 E.G.L.R. 64
Orlando Investments v. Grosvenor Estate (Belgravia) [1989] 2 E.G.L.R. 74
F.W. Woolworth v. Charlwood Alliance Properties Ltd [1987] 1 E.G.L.R. 53
Midland Bank PLC v. Chart Enterprises Inc [1990] 2 E.G.L.R. 59
Sood v. Barker [1991] 1 E.G.L.R. 87 (consent to change of use, it was held *inter alia* that the tenant was obliged to give the landlord information requested which was relevant to his decision; see also on this point *City Hotels Group Ltd v. Total Property Investments Ltd* [1985] 1 E.G.L.R. 253)
Air India v. Balabel [1993] 2 E.G.L.R. 66 (on the Landlord and Tenant Act 1988)
CIN Properties v. Gill [1993] 2 E.G.L.R. 97
Olympia & York Canary Wharf Ltd and another v. Oil Property Investments Ltd [1994] 2 E.G.L.R. 48

PART 3: "A MAN IS NOT PERMITTED TO RELY ON HIS OWN WRONG"

***Rede v. Farr* (1817) 6 M. & S. 121; 125 E.R. 1188**

13.50 The lessee attempted to take advantage of a term in a lease that if the rent should be upaid for 40 dyas after the due date, the lease should be void. Lord Ellenborough C.J. said "In this case, as to this proviso, it would be contrary to an universal principle of law, that a party shall never take advantage of his own wrong, if we were to hold that a lease, which in terms is a lease for twelve years, should be a lease determinable at the will and pleasure of the lessee; and that a lessee by not paying his rent should be at liberty to say that the lease is void. On this principle, even if it were not borne out so strongly as it is by the current of authorities, it would be sufficient to hold that the lease was only void as against the lessee, not against the lessor. In Co. Litt. 206b. it is laid down:

"If a man make a feoffment in fee, upon condition that the feoffee shall re-infeoff him before such a day, and before the day the feoffor disseise the feofee, and hold him out by force until the day be past, the state of the feoffee is absolute; for the foeffor is the cause wherefore the condition cannot be performed, and therefore shall never take advantage for non-performance thereof. And so it is if A. be bound to B. that J.S. shall marry Jane G before such a day, and before the day B. marry with Jane, he shall never take advantage of the bond, for that he himself is the mean that the condition could never be performed. And this is regularly true in all cases."

***Doe d. Bryan v. Bancks* (1821) 4 B. & Ald. 401; 106 E.R. 984**

13.51 A lease of coal mines reserved a royalty rent for each ton of coals raised. It contained a proviso that the lease should be void, to all intents and purposes if the tenant should cease working at time two years.

It was held by all members of the court that the lessee could not operate the proviso himself by ceasing to work the mine. Best J. said this: "In construing this clause of the lease, *we must look to the object which the parties had in view*. The rent was to depend upon the number of tons of coals raised. In order to derive any benefit from the mine, *it was the object of the landlord, by introducing this clause, to compel his tenant to work it*. The clause therefore was introduced solely for the benefit of the landlord, to enable him in case of a cesser to work, to take possession of the mines, and either work them himself, or let them to some other tenant. *That therefore being the object of the parties in introducing this clause*, I think it will be fully answered, by holding the lease to be void at the option of the landlord. Besides, I take it to be an universal principal of law and justice, that no man can take advantage of his own wrong . . ."[72]

***Roberts v. Davey* (1833) 4 B. & Ad. 664; 110 E.R. 606**

13.52 *Doe d. Bryan v. Bancks*[73] was applied to a mining licence. The argument that the rule only applied to interests in land was rejected.

***New Zealand Shipping Co v. Société des Atéliers et Chantiers de France* [1917] 2 K.B. 717 and [1919] A.C. 1**

13.53 The agreement was for the building of a ship. It contained a provision that the contract would be void if the ship was not completed by the due date and all money paid by the purchaser should be returned with interest. The outbreak of the First World War prevented the delivery of the ship. The purchasers were not happy with this, since the price of ships had risen in the meantime, and contended that "void" meant voidable at their option (which they did not exercise), purporting to rely on cases such as *Doe d. Bryan v. Bancks*.[74] The case provided a useful opportunity for the principle that a man may not take advantage of his own wrong to be explained.

Lord Reading C.J. said that "void" was construed as "voidable" in the cases where this was necessary to prevent a man relying on his own "default or wrong" in order to bring into operation the clause making the contract void. "Unless the language of the contract constrains the Court to hold otherwise, the law of England never permits a party to take advantage of his own default or wrong." Pickford L.J. agreed, as did Scrutton L.J. The latter put it slightly differently: ". . . I think that [the clause] and all other clauses are to be read subject to an overriding condition or proviso that the party shall not take advantage of his own wrong, and therefore is estopped from alleging invalidity of which his own breach of contract is the cause."

On appeal, Lord Finlay said: "It is a principle of law that no one can in

[72] Italics supplied.
[73] Para. 13.51 above.
[74] *ibid.*

such case take advantage of the existence of a state of things which he himself produced . . .

Questions of this sort have often arisen in case of provisions that a lease should be void on non-payment of rent or non-performance of covenants by the lessee. It has always been held that the lessee could not take advantage of his own act or default to avoid the lease, and the expression generally employed has been that such proviso makes the lease voidable by the lessor, or void at the option of the lessor. The decisions on the point are uniform and are really illustrations of the very old principle laid down by Lord Coke . . . that a man shall not be allowed to take advantage of a condition which he himself brought about."

Lord Atkinson put it like this: ". . . if the stipulation be that the contract shall be void on the happening of an event which one or either of them [the parties] can by his own act or omission bring about, then the party, who by his own act or omission brings that event about, cannot be permitted either to insist upon the stipulation himself or to compel the other party, who is blameless, to insist upon it, because to permit the blameable party to do either would be to permit him to take advantage of his own wrong, in the one case directly, and in the other case indirectly in a roundabout way, but in either way putting an end to the contract." . . . "Of course, the parties may expressly or impliedely stipulate that the contract shall be voidable at the option of either party to it. I am not dealing with such a case as that." The rest of the court delivered concurring judgments. The result was that the purchasers lost, since the French shipbuilders had hardly brought about the First World War.

***Quesnel Forks Gold Mining Co Ltd v. Ward* [1920] A.C. 222**

13.54 This was a Privy Council case which applied the *New Zealand Shipping* case.[75]

***Cheall v. Association of Professional Executive Clerical and Computer Staff* [1983] Q.B. 126, C.A., and [1983] 2 A.C. 180 (H.L.).**

13.55 Mr Cheall had resigned from his union the ACTSS and applied to join the defendant union. Mr Cheall had not stated on his application form that he was a former member of the ACTSS, but the local officials were aware of this. APEX then failed, in breach of principle 2 of the T.U.C. Disputes Principles and Procedures, called the Bridlington principles, to ask the ACTSS whether they objected to Mr Cheall's transfer. The ACTSS's parent union, the TGWU, complained to the TUC, and the TUC directed APEX to exclude Mr Cheall and tell him to rejoin his former union. Mr Cheall brought an action for a declaration that this termination of his membership was invalid.

Mr Cheall lost at first instance, but won in the Court of Appeal by a majority. Lord Denning mentioned that APEX were relying on "their own misconduct" and that the law set its face against anyone taking advantage of his own wrongdoing, but the main emphasis of this judgment was on the natural justice point which was also raised on behalf of Mr Cheall. Donaldson L.J. dissented; but Slade L.J.'s interesting judgment considers the point we are concerned with in more detail. He said[76]:

"It is, of course, open to parties to a contract expressly and specifically to stipulate that one party may by his own act bring about an event which will entitle him to elect to avoid the contract. A simple example of such a provision

[75] Para. 13.53 above.
[76] At 154.

is one expressly entitling a party to avoid the contract by serving a written notice on the other side before a specified date. In the absence of an express specified provision of this nature, however, I understand it to be a fundamental principle of the interpretation of contracts that, if an agreement is expressed to be void or voidable on the happening of a contingency, which a party can by his own act or omission bring about, then the party who has by his own act or omission brought about that contingency cannot ordinarily be permitted to rely on the avoiding words." He cited from the *New Zealand Shipping*[77] case; and pointed out that what was different about the case before him was that the relevant act had already been done, before the contract was concluded. He thought the principle applied nonetheless.

He continued "These propositions seem to me inevitably to follow from the reasoning of the speeches in *New Zealand Shipping Co Ltd v. Societe des Atelier et Chantiers de France.*[78] That reasoning is not, I think, based on the implication of an additional term in the original contract. It is based on the more simple principle that, unless a contract clearly and specifically so provides, the court will not construe an avoiding provision contained in it in such manner as to permit a party to take advantage of his own wrong. . . . The point may be illustrated by this hypothetical example. A man, for motives best known to himself, agrees to buy a horse for a stated sum, completion to take place in 14 days' time, subject to an express proviso that the buyer shall have the right to rescind the contract at any time during that 14-day period if it be discovered that the horse has suffered an injury which makes it unfit to race. Unknown to the seller, the buyer, before the conclusion of the contract, has already caused his agent to maim the horse. The buyer, I would suggest, plainly could not subsequently be permitted to rely on the avoiding provision, even though the stipulated contingency would have occurred according to its precise terms. The seller would not, I think, have to rely on any implied term in the contract; it may be difficult to imply a promise by one party to a contract that he has not done something which he knows he has done. His case would be based on the simple principle affirmed by the House of Lords in *New Zealand Shipping Co Ltd v. Societe des Ateliers et Chantiers de France.*"[79]

Slade L.J. then went on to deal with certain points which had been made by Donaldson L.J. *Inter alia*, it is worth noting that both he and Donaldson L.J. treated the rule as if it was an implied term of the contract.

13.56 The defendant appealed to the House of Lords. Lord Diplock (with whose judgement the rest of the court agreed) was curiously scathing about Slade L.J.'s approach. For his part, he called the rule under discussion "the well-known rule of construction that, except in the unlikely case that the contract contains clear express provisions to the contrary, it is to be presumed that it was not the intention of the parties that either party should be entitled to rely upon his own *breaches of his primary obligations* as bringing the contract to an end, ie as terminating any further primary obligations on his part then remaining unperformed. This rule of construction, which is *paralleled by the rule of law that a contracting party cannot rely upon an event brought about by his own breach of contract as having terminated a contract* by frustration, is often expressed in broad language as: "A man cannot be permitted to take advantage of his own wrong." But this may be misleading if it is adopted without defining the breach of duty to which the pejorative word "wrong" is intended to refer and the person to whom the duty is owed."[80] He observed that the wrong concerned was not a breach of any agreement with the plaintiff, but

[77] Para. 13.53 above.
[78] *ibid.*
[79] *ibid.*
[80] Italics supplied.

of an agreement with a third party, the original union the ACTSS. Since he considered that "wrong" in the rule meant "breach of a contract with the other party" he dismissed the plaintiff's case on this ground. He said, specifically (without reference to any authority): "To attract the principle, whether it be one of construction or one of law, that a party to a contract is not permitted to take advantage of his own breach of duty, the duty must be one that is owed to the other party under that contract; breach of a duty whether contractual or non-contractual owed to a stranger to the contract does not suffice."

***Alghussein v. Eton College* [1988] 1 W.L.R. 587, H.L.**

13.57 Eton College agreed in writing to grant a lease for 99 years to the appellants on terms *inter alia* that: "the tenant shall . . . as soon as is reasonably practicable following all necessary licences . . . use its best endeavours to commence and proceed diligently with the development" of a block of flats. There was a further term "that if for any reason due to the wilful default of the tenant the development shall remain uncompleted by [a specific date] the lease shall forthwith be completed . . . in the terms provided by the agreement". The original prospective lessee later assigned its rights with the agreement of Eton to the plaintiff. No steps were taken by the developers to begin work. Eventually the Eton solicitors wrote saying they regarded the lack of progress as repudiation of the contract, which they accepted.

The developers claimed that it had not been reasonably practicable for them to begin work, and commenced an action claiming a new lease under the provision above. Lord Jauncey, with whom the rest of the court agreed, reviewed a number of authorities, and held that the principle that no man can take advantage of his own wrong applied. He held, as Lord Diplock had done, that "wrong" meant breach of contract, and that the rule applied just as much to someone who sought to obtain a benefit under the contract by their own breach as to someone who relies on his breach to avoid a contract and escape his obligations. He then dealt with the implication of the rule into the agreement as a matter of construction. He concluded as follows:

"It only remains to refer to the respondents' argument that there is an absolute rule of law and morality which prevents a party taking advantage of his own wrong whatever the terms of the contract. My Lords I do not find it necessary to deal with this. For my part I have no doubt that the weight of authority favours the view that in general the principle is embodied in a rule of construction rather than in an absolute rule of law. However, that is not to say that there cannot be situations such as self-induced frustration, to which Lord Diplock referred in the *Cheall*[81] case, where an absolute rule exists. It is neither necessary nor would it be profitable to explore the matter further in this case."

***Thompson v. ASDA* [1988] Ch. 341; [1988] 2 W.L.R. 1093**

13.58 The plaintiff was an employee of a department store which was the wholly owned subsidiary of the defendant. Because of his employment he participated in a savings-related share option scheme. Rule 5 of this provided that no person might exercise an option under the scheme unless he was an employee of the defendant or one of its subsidiaries, and that the option would lapse on his ceasing to be so employed. In 1985 the defendant caused the plaintiff not to be so employed by selling its entire shareholding to third parties. It then insisted that the plaintiff's options had lapsed.

[81] Para. 13.55 above.

Scott L.J. considered, no doubt correctly, that he was bound by *Cheall v. APEX*,[82] and thus, since he could find no implied term in the sense of one implied to give business efficacy (he was influenced by Devlin J. in *Mona Oil Equipment & Supply Co Ltd v. Rhodesian Railways Ltd*,[83] the plaintiff failed.

Note: It should be observed that the above case was decided before the House of Lords' decision in Alghussein v. Eton College ;[84] although the result would only have been different if a term could have been implied into the contract. (There was no ambiguous clause, merely a gap on the point.)

***Attorney General v. Guardian Newspapers* (No. 2) [1990] 1 A.C. 109 (H.L.)**

13.59 This was of course the well-known Spycatcher case, in which the Crown sought an injunction restraining the publication of the book in England, and an account of profits. Lord Goff may have obliquely mentioned the rule that a man may not profit from his own wrong.[85] "The statement that a man shall not be allowed to profit from his own wrong is in very general terms, and does not of itself provide any sure guidance to the solution of a problem in any particular case. That there are groups of cases in which a man is not allowed to profit from his own wrong, is certainly true. An important section of the law of restitution is concerned with cases in which a defendant is required to make restitution in respect of benefits accrued through his own wrongful act—notably cases of waiver of tort; of benefits acquired by certain criminal acts; of benefits acquired in breach of a fiduciary relationship; and, of course, of benefits acquired in breach of confidence. The plaintiff's claim to restitution is usually enforced by an account of profits made by the defendant through his wrong at the plaintiff's expense."[86]

PART 4: A POSITIVE DUTY

***Doe v. Hunt* (1836) 1 M. & W. 690; 150 E.R. 611**

13.60 There had been an argument between a landlord and a tenant about rent. The landlord then agreed the tenant might stay on at the reduced rent he had argued for, until the next Michaelmas, provided that he, the landlord could not find a tenant for the farm at the rent it appeared to him to be worth, by August 1 of the same year. The Court of Exchequer held that it was an *implied term in the above agreement that the tenant should allow persons applying for the farm to go over it*; and because he had been in breach of that implied term, the agreement was terminated. Lord Abinger said that otherwise "the tenant *practises a sort of fraud* upon his landlord".[87] Bolland B. thought the term was a condition precedent to the completion of the new agreement. Alderson B. thought it was a kind of conditional waiver by the landlord.

Note: It may be observed that none of the three had any doubt that a term was to be implied. It may be thought that what gave rise to this implication can only have been that an expressed purpose of the contract was to permit the landlord to find a tenant if he could. Refusal to permit would-be tenants to go over the farm would be

[82] *ibid.*
[83] [1949] 2 All E.R. 1014.
[84] Para. 13.57 above.
[85] At 286.
[86] See also *Micklefield v. SAC Technology Ltd* [1990] 1 W.L.R. 1002.
[87] Italics supplied.

calculated to hinder the expressed purpose. "Practises a kind of fraud" may be thought to be a nineteenth-century way of encapsulating this idea.

***Inchbald v. Western Neilgherry Coffee, Tea & Cinchona Plantation Co. Ltd* (1864) 17 C.B. (N.S.) 733; 144 E.R. 293**

13.61 The plaintiff was retained by the directors of a public company to dispose of the shares, for which he was to receive £100 down and £400 when all the shares should have been allotted. The directors for quite other reasons put the company into liquidation, so preventing him from earning the £400. The court held that he was entitled to be paid since he was prevented from carrying out the contract. Erle C.J., Willes J., Byles J., and Keating J. heard the case. Willes J. put the principle in general form. "One who enters into a contract is bound to perform his engagement in substance. This is illustrated by the case in Bulstrode, where the defendant contracted to deliver to the plaintiff a horse, but poisoned him before delivery. That was held not to be a substantial performance of the contract, because one of the contracting parties had done an act which prevented the other from having the benefit of it. I apprehend that wherever money is to be paid by one man to another upon a given event, the party upon whom is cast the obligation to pay is liable to the party who is to receive the money, if he does any act which prevents or makes it less probable that he should receive it." Byles J. and Keating J. agreed.

Later, however, in *Luxor (Eastbourne) Ltd v. Cooper*[88] this case was explained simply as a quantum meruit case.

***Mackay v. Dick* (1881) 6 App. Cas. 251 (H.L. (Sc))**

13.62 The appellant railway contractors had agreed to buy a steam excavator from the Respondents, Messrs Dick & Stevenson. The contract provided that the machine was to be fairly tested on a properly opened up face at the appellant's cutting at Carfin. The appellant did not so test it and the court held that he was in default, and affirmed the judgment of the court below awarding the respondents the contract price and interest. Lord Blackburn explained the general rule as quoted above in the text. He referred to a very early case in the Year Book of 9th Edward IV., Easter Term 4A, regarding the great bell of Mildenhall, in which he considered the point was implicit.

He also said: ". . . it would follow in point of law that the Defender, having had the machine delivered to him, was by his contract to keep it, unless on a fair test according to the contract it failed to do the stipulated quantity of work, in which case he would be entitled to call on the Pursuers to remove it. And by his own default he can now never be in a position to call upon the Pursuers to take back the machine, on the ground that the test had not been satisfied, he must, as far as regards that, keep, and consequently pay for it."

***Colley v. Overseas Exporters* [1921] 3 K.B. 302**

13.63 Unascertained goods were sent f.o.b to the port of shipment, but the buyer failed to name an effective ship. McCardie J. distinguished *Mackay v. Dick*[89] on the grounds that the property in the goods had passed there, but had not here, so that the plaintiff was not entitled to the price. He could sue instead for damages for non-acceptance.

[88] [1941] A.C. 108, para. 13.64 below.
[89] Para. 13.62 above.

***Luxor (Eastbourne) Ltd v. Cooper* [1941] A.C. 108**

13.64 The respondent, an estate agent, had been instructed on behalf of the appellant company, to sell two cinemas, for which his commission was to be £10,000. The estate agent produced a purchaser, but the company declined to sell to him.

The House of Lords held that his right to remuneration was dependent on the contract going through: there was no right to compel the company to accept the buyer. Lord Romer thought that where a person contracts with someone to perform a service, the implied condition is merely that he will do nothing to prevent him carrying out the work. "But I am under no implied obligation to help him earn the reward whether by the supply of building materials or otherwise. But there are exceptional cases where in a contract of employment the employer is under a positive obligation. If, for instance, I employ an artist to paint my portrait I subject myself to the positive obligations of giving him the requisite sittings."

Lord Wright referred to *Mackay v. Dick*[90] as follows: "Thus in *Mackay v. Dick* . . ., the maker of an excavating machine was required by the contract to send the machine for the purpose of being tested to the railway cutting which the buyer was engaged in constructing, and the buyer was only to be liable to pay for it if it there in working satisfied the test. This House held that the buyers had prevented fulfilment of the condition because they held that, it being the buyer's duty under the contract to provide the necessary facilities, he had failed to do so. Hence his default prevented the seller from satisfying the condition. The seller could therefore say that he had done all that lay on him to fulfil the condition and was to be taken to have implemented it. The test was only not satisfied because of the buyer's default."

Lord Simon L.C. put it like this. "If A employs B for reward to do a piece of work for him which requires outlay and effort on B's part and which depends on the continued existence of a given subject-matter which is under A's control (as in *Inchbald v. Western Neilgherry Coffee Co*[91]) there may be an implied term that A will not prevent B doing the work by destroying the subject matter. And, generally speaking, where B is employed by A to do a piece of work which requires A's co-operation (e.g. to paint A's portrait, it is implied that the necessary co-operation will be forthcoming (e.g. A will give sittings to the artist)".

***Mona Oil Equipment & Supply Co Ltd v. Rhodesia Railways Ltd* [1949] 2 All E.R. 1014**

13.65 The contract provided for payment to the sellers (who required immediate payment in order to be able to carry out their side of the contract) on signed confirmation by the shipping agents for the buyers that the oil tanks in question were at the disposal of the buyers. In fact the buyers' agents refused to sign when first approached because they were waiting for written instructions, but the sellers misunderstood this, and thought they were refusing outright. They brought an action for the breach of what they said was an implied duty on the sellers to do nothing to prevent or obstruct the performance of the condition of payment on which the contract depended.

Devlin J. held that there was no such duty, because it had to arise out of an implied term, and no such implied term was alleged. He thought anyway such an implied term "like all other implied terms, must be judged by the test whether or not it is necessary for the business efficacy of the contract."

[90] Para. 13.62 above.
[91] (1864) 17 C.B. (N.S.) 733.

Blackpool Aero Club v. Blackpool Borough Council [1990] 1 W.L.R. 1195 C.A.

13.66 The plaintiff's tender had been delivered to the letter box of the defendants within the specified time, but not cleared by the town clerk's staff in time to be considered with the other tenders. It was held that the request for tenders gave rise to an implied positive contractual obligation on the part of the defendants *to consider all tenders received within the time*. Bingham L.J. said: "... Had the club, before tendering, inquired of the council whether it could rely on any timely and conforming tender being considered along with others, I feel quite sure that the answer would have been "of course"....

"I readily accept that contracts are not to be lightly implied. Having examined what the parties said and did, the court must be able to conclude with confidence both that the parties intended to create contractual relations and that the agreement was to the effect contended for.... In all the circumstances of this case, and I say nothing about any other, I have no doubt that the parties did intend to create contractual relations to the limited extent contended for. Since it has never been the law that a person is only entitled to enforce his contractual rights in a reasonable way (*White and Carter (Councils) Ltd v. McGregor*),[92] Mr Shorrock was in my view right to contend for no more than a contractual duty to consider. I think it plain that the council's invitation to tender was, to this limited extent, an offer, and the club's submission of a timely and conforming tender an acceptance."

[92] [1962] A.C. 413 at 430A, *per* Lord Reid.

Part 4

WHEN THE CONTRACT BREAKS DOWN: PROPORTIONALITY OF SANCTION TO THE ORIGINAL MAIN PURPOSE OF THE CONTRACT

Chapter 14

PENALTIES, DEPOSITS AND FORFEITURE: CLAUSES COLLATERAL TO THE PARAMOUNT PURPOSE OF THE CONTRACT

"... equity lawyers are, I notice, sometimes both surprised and discomfited by the plenitude of jurisdiction, and the imprecision of rules that are attributed to 'equity' by their more enthusiastic colleagues."[1]

"A principle has been said to have been stated in several cases, the adoption of which one cannot but lament, namely, that if the sum would be very enormous and excessive considered as liquidated damages, it shall be taken to be a penalty though agreed to be paid in the form of contract ..."[2]

"... or whether ... it is simply a penalty to be held over the other party in terrorem—whether it is, what I think gave the jurisdiction to the Courts ... to interfere at all in an agreement between the parties, unconscionable and extravagant, and one which no Court ought to allow to be enforced."[3]

"The last temptation is the greatest treason.
To do the right deed for the wrong reason."[4]

[1] Lord Radcliffe in ***Bridge v. Campbell Discount*** [1962] A.C. 600.
[2] Lord Eldon in ***Astley v. Weldon*** (1801) 2 Bos. & P. 346.
[3] Lord Halsbury in the ***Clydebank*** case, [1905] A.C. 6.
[4] T.S. Eliot, Murder in the Cathedral.

1. PENALTIES: THE DISTINCTION BETWEEN "PENALTIES" AND LIQUIDATED DAMAGES

The seventeenth and eighteenth centuries

14.01 The law on penalties is ancient: cases go back at least to the seventeenth century. Even by 1801, in *Astley v. Weldon*[5], Lord Eldon, who was vastly more concerned than most to identify as clearly as possible the legal principles he was dealing with, said that he found himself, not for the first time "much embarrassed in ascertaining the principle" upon which the cases on penalties were founded. He committed himself about the principle only so far as saying that:

> "What was urged in the course of the argument has ever appeared to me to be the clearest principle, viz., that where a doubt is stated whether the sum inserted be intended as a penalty or not, if a certain damage less than that sum is made payable upon the face of the same instrument, in case the act intended to be prohibited be done, that sum shall be construed to be a penalty . . ."

14.02 Where Lord Eldon was unsure, it would be presumptuous to be sure. However, he was, one may infer, *being* unsure about a level of principle above the most basic. He did take for granted in the above passage a couple of basic points which may have seemed so obvious to him as not to need mentioning, and thus which may easily be overlooked by us now.

(1) The penalty clause was a clause offered up merely *as security for the performance of a main contractual obligation*, rather than itself a main contractual obligation.

(2) "Penal" meant not "harsh" or anything of that kind, but simply a clause that *penalised* non-performance or faulty performance of the contract: one might as well call it a "policing" or "ensuring" clause, or a "comfort-clause" in the sense in which we use "letter of comfort". In the same way one might call a mortgage or a guarantee "penal": it is a comfort to the mortgagee; neutral to the contract-keeper; and only "punishes" the contract breaker. It is contingently penal, or punishes if . . . The way it operated was either "Here is my bond for £ [often but not invariably a large, possibly astronomical sum] to show I really intend to perform my part of the contract." Then, when the obligor had contrary to his expectation failed to perform the contract, the courts held that the sum was merely a security, in very much the way that a mortgage is a security: the obligee can in many cases be put in the same position as if the contract had not been broken, by taking his compensation out of it and returning the rest. Later the same kind of thing happened without a bond: there was merely a promise to pay a stated and fairly large sum instead of a

[5] (1801) 2 Bos. & P. 346.

bond. The distinction between this old use of the word "penal" as contingent-punishing-in case-of-breach, or "as security"; and "penal" in the sense we now use the word meaning "Draconian", "harsh", "unfair" may be a particularly crucial one to the understanding of the topic.[6]

The price of the broken promise

14.03 There then began to be a problem. There had also sprung up clauses in which people estimated and agreed in advance the damages which should be paid for the breach of a particular provision in the contract: an early example was the breach of a covenant not to plough a field. The tenant who did plough had not given any security that he would not plough: it was merely that if he did, he accepted he should pay the agreed price of the breach. In at least one case, this was the price the landlord himself put on the field, rather than the loss through the ploughing. The field had not been specially valuable but the landlord had put a high price on the breach because he had wanted to keep it as cover for game.

The fact that something was the pre-agreed price of the broken promise thus did not mean it was necessarily a fair market price: for example in *Rolfe v. Peterson*[7] the tenant actually improved the value of the field by ploughing it. If one were ranking the two kinds of clauses, "penal" and liquidated damages clauses, in order of harshness, it would not have been at all impossible for this kind of liquidated but subjectively ascertained damages to come out on top.

14.04 The contrast between a clause securing the contractual obligations and a clause which is itself *part of* the contractual obligations is made with clarity in an early case by Lord Mansfield: *Lowe v. Peers*[8]—a breach of promise of marriage case in which it became important to draw the fine distinction between "I will not marry anyone else but if I do I will give you security of £x for your damages" and "I will not marry anyone else but *if I do the price* of my broken promise shall be £x". He said:

> "And upon this distinction they proceed in Courts of Equity. They will relieve against a penalty, upon a compensation: but where the covenant is "to pay a particular liquidated sum" a Court of Equity can not make a new covenant for a man; nor is there any room for compensation or relief. As in leases containing a covenant against plowing up meadow; if the covenant be "not to plow" [6 Vin 472] and there be a penalty; a court of equity will relieve against the penalty, or will even go further than that *to preserve the substance of the agreement*: but if it is worded—"to pay £5 an acre for every acre plowed up"; there is no alternative,

[6] See below: the late nineteenth and the twentieth century and the *Clydebank* case [1905] A.C. 6.
[7] (1772) 6 Brown's Parlt Cases 1E.R. 1048.
[8] (1768) 4 Burr. 229; 98 E.R. 160.

> no room for any relief against it; no compensation, it *is the substance of the agreement*."[9]
>
> Lord Macclesfield put it similarly in *Peachy v. Duke of Somerset*:[10] "The true ground of relief against penalties is from the original intent of the case, where the penalty is designed only to secure money . . ."

The distinction between the two was probably not always an easy one even in early times. Matters became considerably worse after the statute of William III gave jurisdiction in the case of penalties to the Common law courts, so that it no longer made any difference whether the action was in a Common law or Equity court. This must have meant a great deal more use of the principle, particularly since it was something the Court might raise of its own motion.

The early and mid-nineteenth century: anti evasion techniques

14.05 A practice sprang up of labelling a provision "liquidated damages" in order to evade the new jurisdiction. The courts soon decided that this could not be allowed to prevail: as Littledale J. said in *Davies v. Penton*:[11]

> "the mere alteration of the term cannot alter the nature of the thing; and if the Court see, upon the whole agreement, that the parties intended the sum to be a penalty, they ought not to allow one party to deprive the other of the benefit to be derived from the statute."

However, the fact that one could not rely on the label meant that the courts had to take considerable care over interpretation; and rules for identifying one or other type of clause began to be developed. One was that agreed liquidated damages were a method whereby the parties put an agreed figure on something inherently uncertain. Therefore, the damages had to be difficult to ascertain in the first place: otherwise there would be an inclination to judge the clause a security or "penal" clause only.

For example, Tindal C.J. in *Kemble v. Farren*[12] said

> "For we see nothing illegal or unreasonable in the parties, by their mutual agreement, settling *the amount of damages, uncertain in their nature*, at any sum upon which they may agree."[13]

Note also the three cases mentioned after *Kemble v. Farren*[14] in the Appendix to this chapter: *Green v. Price*,[15] *Galsworthy v. Strutt*[16] and

[9] Italics supplied.
[10] Str. 447; 93 E.R. 626.
[11] (1827) 6 B. & C. 216; 108 E.R. 433.
[12] (1829) 6 Bing 141; 130 E.R. 12.
[13] Italics supplied.
[14] Above.
[15] (1845) 13 M. & W. 695; 153 E.R. 291.
[16] (1848) L.R. 1Ex. 659.

Atkyns v. Kinnier.[17] These cases all concerned restraint of trade covenants the breach of which attracted a fairly harsh sum, all of which were held valid liquidated damages provisions because of the difficulty in telling what damage the breach would cause.

Another method of interpretation which emerged was to hold that a range of *differing breaches ranging from the trivial to the substantial* which attracted just the one sum on breach would be a penalty provision. Examples of this are *Betts v. Burch*,[18] *Magee v. Lavell*[19] and *In re Newman*,[20] all noted in the Appendix to this chapter.

The Late Nineteenth Century and the Twentieth Century: the new tide of literalism sweeps the penalty rules off course

14.06 As we have seen in other spheres, the period from the 1880's onwards marked a time of change in the law. Rule by literalism was the thing: the approach became, curiously, both more formulaic and more fudged. First, we have the new literalism homing in on the only descriptive *word* which crops up in the sphere of the penalty jurisdiction—"penal". This word had of course by then acquired the present meaning of "harsh"; and so a big misconception occurred more or less by accident. The idea emerged quite suddenly and without, as far as can be seen, any historical antecedents at all—fully fledged like Aphrodite from the waves or Athena from Zeus's head—that what was important about penalties was not that they were a sum meant as security for breaches of the main contract; but that they were *harsh*. This last was rationalised as "extravagant and exorbitant" *in relation to* the breaches which might give rise to them.[21] The expression "*in terrorem*" pops up to describe "penalty" clauses, the fact that it is in Latin perhaps giving it an appearance of historical authenticity it may not entirely have deserved. The judiciary begin all of a sudden to express concern over the "interference" with "the parties' intention", choosing to mean now by this their literal words rather than some underlying goal.[22] Then, finally, we have the important change of direction caused by Lord Halsbury's judgment in the *Clydebank* case.[23]

14.07 In Lord Halsbury's judgment in that case (at least one other judgment was to different effect but Lord Halsbury's was crucially influential) we see the new literalist approach more or less complete.[24] Equity is no longer seen as assisting the parties to achieve what they had really intended all along by their imperfect expression in words; the parties' words in their literal meaning have acquired a kind of

[17] (1850) L.R. 4 Ex. 775.

[18] (1859) 4 H. & N. 505; 157 E.R. 938.

[19] (1874) L.R. 9 C.P. 107.

[20] (1876) 4 Ch. D. 724.

[21] ***Lord Elphinstone v. Monkland Iron & Coal*** (1886) 11 App. Cas. 332.

[22] See, *e.g.* ***Law v. Redditch Local Board*** [1892] 1 Q.B. 127 and ***Willson v. Love*** [1896] 1Q.B. 626.

[23] [1905] A.C. 6. below

[24] Equity's role has come full circle: Florence Nightingale has become Mrs Norris, Jane Austen's disagreeable busybody in Mansfield Park.

imposed holiness; and equity is now seen, instead, as "interfering" in what the parties had agreed. Once one has accepted that, the rest follows as a matter of course. Equity can only be allowed to "interfere" relatively rarely. This, Lord Halsbury considered, it could *only* do so when the contract was "exorbitant" or "unconscionable". "Exorbitant" may be thought to be very nearly one of those words like "Good gracious". It has little meaningful content in itself beyond something subjective such as "I do not care for it" or "ugh". "Unconscionable" is a word which is thought to have had good faith roots; but one cannot think that Lord Halsbury intended a reference to these. If he had, the necessary link would have been made. So, it means very little more than "exorbitant" to modern ears. Perhaps it added nothing but an aura of ancientness. Here, then, we have the germ of the ubiquitous wide modern "discretion" given to the courts, usually by statute, that is often the other side of the literalism coin. The unheard dialogue is:

> "The parties mean what the words mean taken literally."
> "Always?"
> "Well, almost always. Of course, not when it would be a complete affront . . . er . . . that is, when it would be, er . . . extravagant or unconscionable . . ."
> "When would that be?"
> "Well, when it is extravagant or unconscionable, of course. I should have no difficult recognising it . . ."

14.08 Their Lordships were not at one in their approach. Lord Halsbury's judgment favoured a bold, wide, discretion. Lord Davey's judgment is quoted at some length below, because it is fascinating to see that for his part he manages, just, to resist the temptation of the new approach, and stays true to the classical, original approach: whether it is a penalty or damages is a question of ascertaining the parties' true intention in making the contract they did.[25] The "exorbitant", *etc.*, point appears in quite a different role: merely as a way of expressing the sledgehammer-to-crack-a nut factor (a range of breaches from the trivial to the substantial but just the one penalty) developed in the earlier cases as a way of telling a penalty from true liquidated damages.[26] Lord Robertson's short judgment appears to leave it unclear which approach he favoured.

14.09 Lord Halsbury's approach held sway for a while. In *Webster v. Bosanquet*[27] it was said that the clause in question was "unconscionable and extravagant and one which no court ought to allow to be enforced." Whether because the dangers of so wide a jurisdiction were apparent, or for other reasons, the tide receded. By the *Dunlop*[28] rubber

[25] Indeed, Lord Dunedin in the later ***Dunlop*** case stays with this analysis.

[26] The Lord President, on the other hand, whose judgment Lord Davey quotes but does not quite endorse, had evidently gone overboard for the kind of approach adopted by Lord Halsbury. The distinction Lord Davey draws between his approach and the Lord President's may look a narrow one, but it was an important one.

[27] [1912] A.C. 394.

[28] [1915] A.C. 79.

case the approach was thought, at least in that case, to be one of construction of the parties' intentions again. True, we still have the dubious imports "*in terrorem*" (one cannot believe some of the early liquidated damages provisions such as the mid-nineteenth century restraint of trade cases above were not *meant* to be excessively "*in terrorem*" nor is it easy to see why that is always wrong) and "extravagant and unconscionable". However, they are relegated to their place in the construction exercise. The wide discretion is still there in practice, but tamed a little.

Lord Halsbury's heresy did not die. His happening to use the word "unconscionable" (it may have been chance—the word was much bandied about at that time)[29] caused the most tremendous confusion in the minds of equity judges like Farwell J. and Romer L.J.[30]

Shiloh Spinners v. Harding[31]—has this reaffirmed historical principles?

14.10 In this well-known case on relief from forfeiture, the House of Lords in effect affirmed the older, narrower, historical principle in part. The quotation from Lord Wilberforce's judgment in the Appendix below stressed the importance of selecting for the exercise of the jurisdiction only cases where the forfeiture provision was designed to *secure* a different primary object. Equally importantly, their Lordships affirmed relief from forfeiture as a general contractual principle along with the penalty jurisdiction. Lord Simon said:

> "I would therefore myself hold that equity has an unlimited and unfettered jurisdiction to relieve against contractual forfeitures and penalties."[32]

They did however retain a certain amount of nineteenth century baggage. The wide late-nineteenth-century discretion favoured by Lord Halsbury remains. Lord Wilberforce said that the jurisdiction to relieve was to be exercised "in appropriate and limited cases". "The word 'appropriate' involves consideration of the conduct of the applicant for relief, in particular whether his default was wilful, of the gravity of the breaches, and of the disparity between the value of the property of which forfeiture is claimed as compared with the damage caused by the breach. By contrast, the early Courts of Equity were concerned with the simpler question whether the individual party who had the benefit of the clause could be *adequately compensated* by the defaulter, so that he was in the position *he might reasonably have expected to be in*.[33]

[29] Possibly because it was sufficiently vague to be a suitable vehicle for the new wide discretion but at the same time carried an aura of ancientness.
[30] See para. 14.21 below on Deposits.
[31] [1973] A.C. 691.
[32] Italics supplied.
[33] See the note of Lord Erskine's judgment in *Sanders v. Pope* (1806) 12 Ves. Jun. 283 at para. 14.31 *et seq*.

The future for the penalty v. liquidated damages jurisdiction?

14.11 A benign construction of security bonds is no longer necessary because people have given up the practice of providing these, no doubt in favour of commercial guarantee or performance bonds and the like instead. Do we *need* the old law on "penal" or comfort-provisions in agreements? The number of provisions in contracts which are deliberately intended as security-provisions (as opposed to forfeiture provisions of various kinds, which seem to be relatively common) must be very small indeed. It is rather difficult to see that they were ever all that useful once bonds were no longer given: the provision was after all simply a promise in the contract, nothing more. At best it simplified proof of damage. It is not surprising that deposits and forfeiture provisions became popular: they seem to be the modern equivalent of the old "penal" bonds. They are a genuine form of security.[34]

To construe huge damages provisions as comfort/security provisions or "penalties" could thus seem something of an uncomfortable fiction in modern times. As noted earlier, there really seems no good reason why the parties should not agree a large price for a particular broken promise which is seen as important.

Is there a role for the courts at all where penalties are concerned?

14.12 Perhaps there *is* a role of real value remaining for the courts in this area. While there is nothing wrong with a large price for a broken promise *per se*, and indeed, the freedom to agree one may be a valuable commercial freedom, it may be thought there *is* something wrong if there has not been fair dealing; if the high price has not been drawn to the other side's attention with accuracy and candour. The courts' role in policing the literal words of unfair contract terms relating to damages would assume even more importance if more freedom of contract were allowed by taking a stricter, more historical line over penalties. There are times when it is reasonably plain that the "penalty" provision could never have been intended by *both parties* as a real estimate of the likely damages at the time of the contract, or an agreed figure deliberately demanded by one party and deliberately accepted by the other,[35] if it comes to that. In other words, there are cases where (absent any special background such in the latter case) we can all be sure that *no reasonable person would have agreed a particular sum light years away from the anticipated damage that the parties could have contemplated* ***as the price of his broken promise***. One party has somehow slipped it in and achieved its acceptance by the other, or at all events his signature to it. There is a kind of inequality of advertence

[34] So, of course, is the power of re-entry on land in the event of a broken covenant, not discussed in this book apart from the contribution to the law made by ***Shiloh Spinners v. Harding*** [1973] A.C. 691 and which is now largely regulated by statute.

[35] As in **Rolfe v. Peterson** (1772) 6 Brown's Parlt. Cases; 1 E.R. 1048.

or intention about such a situation which one feels *ought* to call down the protection of the courts. The early Equity Courts—and after the statute of William III, the Common law courts also—did not strike down these provisions merely because the damages were ridiculously large; in their own rather different way, they were as much against "interfering" as any judge in the 1880's; but they sought to ensure the damages really were *the agreed price of the promise*. Should the modern courts therefore be able to "interfere" as the older ones did, or should the parties be left to reap the fruits of their own foolishness?

14.13 One answer is provided by statute in the cases to which the statutes apply: see the Unfair Contract Terms Act 1977, and the Unfair Contract Terms Regulations 1994 which are noted with commentary at the end of this book. There will be cases which do not fall within the purview of either statute. The common law could still come to the rescue. The concept of "interference" by the courts changed hugely between Lord Eldon's and Lord Halsbury's day, as we have seen; and it may be that it is due for a change back again. Often but not always unspoken in earlier times was the expectation that what was being construed was *the contract of reasonable people, dealing fairly with each other*. They could not, because of the rules of evidence, hope in those early days to ascertain what the parties themselves actually expected. Thus, the reasonable expectation of fair dealing pervaded the courts' attitude to vendors in contracts of sale of various kinds. The old method of construing contracts included this important element. Clauses with an exclusionary effect—which excluded a right the party may have reasonably expected, or which gave him something less than he will reasonably have expected—were scrutinised carefully and only enforced if the exclusionary effect was clearly and specifically brought to the party's attention at the time of contracting.[36]

The old method certainly has this to be said for it: that it may deal perhaps more justly with the modern form of Merchant-of-Venice bond where one party, usually the more commercially knowledgeable, meant all along to have his pound of flesh (and knowing his statistics better, knew the circumstances might arise where he would be able to have it) while the other (not always a "consumer" as defined in the Unfair Contract Terms Act 1977 or the Unfair Contract Terms Regulations 1994) simply never thought the situation would arise and thus never took the provision seriously. The actual intentions of the parties are thus different one from another. If the court gives effect to Shylock's actual intentions it is disappointing Bassanio's. The idea that construing the contract is getting at the actual intentions of the parties themselves is unworkable in such circumstances. It becomes pure fiction. One answer is of course to say, Bassanio was an idiot to sign and thereby to signify his presumptive assent to the literal words. He deserves what he gets. No doubt; but then what if he signed not realising it was to be taken literally? Is signing one's name so important a species of magic, after all? Might it perhaps be appropriate for

[36] See Chap. 10, Excluding the Effect of the Fair dealing Terms. See also the attempt, which perhaps deserved more success, to argue very much this point in ***Nutting v. Baldwin*** [1995] 1 W.L.R. 201.

the courts as inheritors of the old Equity Courts' powers to look beyond the form where necessary and to develop the old fair dealing principles[37] to protect the incautious or the trusting where appropriate. It is not as if a literal approach in modern times has prevented Bassanios from reappearing, either, as far as may be seen: most practising lawyers would agree the deterrent effect does not seem to work very well in the civil legal system.

14.14 Let us assume for the moment that the courts will be willing to assume more fully than has been done of late the old role of the Equity Courts as protectors of the reasonable expectations of the parties to contracts in the private sphere. They already protect reasonable expectations to a considerable extent in the sphere of administrative law: the contrast between the two at present is marked.[38] It may be that most of the practical problems in the "penalty"/damages area would be dealt with by the reasonable fair dealing construction approach described in the earlier chapters of this book: others might require either an application or an extension to modern situations, of the law on dealings with the vulnerable. Compare the old equitable headings of "fraud, accident, mistake or surprise" which covered breaches of fair dealing principles as well as unfair dealings with vulnerable parties, mentioned by Lord Wilberforce in *Shiloh Spinners v. Harding*.[39] Transactions have in general become less simple, more technical. The new vulnerable, or the people in need of candour and honesty of a high degree, are to be found among the technically-ignorant and those without access to special knowledge of various kinds.

It can sometimes seem, that to enter into a contract safely reading it is not enough.[40] A battery of expert advice may often be needed if we are not to be the helpless victims of our own signature.

2. FORFEITURE OF DEPOSITS, INSTALMENTS OF THE PURCHASE PRICE, *ETC*.

Introduction

14.15 The deposit has been held to be a guarantee of performance. Seen in this light, one might expect that the vendor would *always* have to prove actual damage or give back the deposit. If a "penalty" clause may be relieved against in favour of the "real" damages suffered by the vendor purely *because* it is security for the performance of the contractual obligations, it is difficult to see why the payment of a

[37] See e.g. Chap. 10 Excluding the Effect of the Fair Dealing Terms.

[38] See *Good Faith and Default in Contract Law*, ed. Beatson, Oxford which makes this point forcibly.

[39] [1973] A.C. 691.

[40] There is a Sixties song about gadget-filled kitchens which went: "Instead of a cook, One really needs A consulting engineer"...

deposit for the same purpose should not similarly achieve automatic relief.[41] However, this is not what has happened.

What *has* happened? One can definitely state that a great deal of confusion has happened. Again, a historical overview may be useful. The "timeless senior common room approach" is perhaps again less than helpful in this area.

The mid-nineteenth century

14.16 We do not hear much about deposits until the mid-nineteenth century. When we do, at first the idea that a deposit may be subject to the same rules as penalties is not in point and not discussed: as for example in *Ockendon v. Henly*[42] and *Depree v. Bedborough*.[43] Then we have two more cases where the point again did not arise: *Hinton v. Sparkes*[44] and *Lea v. Whitaker*.[45] However, in both cases the deposit and the liquidated damages (as they clearly were) happened in fact to be *the same amount*. In the first case the vendor was allowed to keep the deposit *as liquidated damages* even though his true loss was much less: in the second the vendor was not permitted to claim his true damages which were in excess of the deposit, but confined to the deposit-as-liquidated-damages.

The 1870s: recognition of the deposit as a potential penalty

14.17 In 1873 we find the Court of Appeal apparently having no qualms at all about treating a huge forfeitable deposit as a penalty.[46] The reasoning was impeccable as penalty-construction: it was a penalty because it was a huge sum which might become payable for tiny breaches of the contract, being a day late, and the like. It does not seem that the early courts necessarily drew a sharp distinction between relief from forfeiture and relief from penalties: it was possible for example, in *Sanders v. Pope*[47] for counsel for the defendant to argue ". . . and the Court is in the habit of relieving against forfeiture and penalty".

A little later, we have two cases which do not perhaps take matters much further. In *Ex parte Barrell*[48] the Court of Appeal accepted[49] that a purchaser's trustee in bankruptcy *who had disclaimed the contract*

[41] See also Farrand, *Contract and Conveyance* (4th ed.), p. 204: ". . . the present writer in all conscience must confess his difficulty in seeing how equity came to tolerate this. Why, in other words, was it not relieved against as a *penalty/forfeiture provision*?"

[42] (1858) E.B. & E. 485 120 E.R. 485.

[43] (1863) 4 Giff. 479; 66 E.R. 795.

[44] (1868) L.R. 3 C.P. 161.

[45] (1872) L.R. 8 C.P. 70.

[46] See ***In re Dagenham (Thames) Dock Co.*** (1873) L.R. 8 Ch. App. 1022.

[47] (1806) 12 Ves. Jun. 283; 33 E.R. 108.

[48] (1875) 10 Ch. App. 512.

[49] Probably accepting Lord St Leonards' suggestion in *Vendors and Purchasers* 14th ed., p. 40.

could not recover the deposit, even under a contract which failed to make provision for forfeiture in the events which had happened, since he would be profiting from his own wrong. The only point argued seems to have been whether the deposit might, in the case of that particular contract, be returned: no penalty or relief from forfeiture point was taken.

In *Wallis v. Smith*[50] a large deposit in a building contract was specifically for damages for substantial breaches only, and thus was held, not unreasonably perhaps, to be liquidated damages.

Howe v. Smith: a frustrating decision?

14.18 *Howe v. Smith*[51] was a seminal decision on the practical operation, if not the nature, of deposits, but curiously, the decision failed to make clear everything the anxious practitioner might have desired. Fry L.J. was much taken with the idea of the deposit as an ancient earnest of performance, a kind of hostage, but interestingly, after a digression about earnests which went back beyond English law to the Phoenicians, wound up supporting this supposed role of deposits not by any actual authority, but simply by his view that a term should be implied. This term was a remarkably long one: that the deposit was not repayable if the contract went off by the purchaser's default, but counted as part-payment of the purchase price otherwise. He did not explain quite how such a term came to be implied: it is unlikely to have been on the "officious bystander" test, to give the contract business efficacy, one would think.

The other two Lord Justices, Cotton and Bowen L.J.J., probably based their decision on the principle that a purchaser who brought the contract to an end by his own wrong would be benefiting thereby if he received his deposit back. This suggestion was made by Lord St Leonards in his book, *Sugden on Vendors and Purchasers*.[52] It seems also to have influenced the Court of Appeal in *Ex parte Barrell*.[53] One cannot be sure that the "a man may not rely on his own wrong" principle really works in this context: it begs the question about the construction of the deposit as the price of the broken promise, which is surely the first question to be answered before one can know whether the purchaser is gaining an *advantage* or not. If the deposit was, or was to some extent, only intended as a "comfort-provision"; how is the purchaser gaining anything at all by getting the extra back?

14.19 The result of the case is curiously unhelpful to the practitioner. It is all very well to pronounce about the Phoenicians and so on, but merely being ancient does not prove legal worth, or no doubt cannibalism would be with us yet. The unanswered question is, Does it matter if the "earnest" is just too *big* to cover the anticipated out of pocket expenses and other loss caused to the vendor by the breach?

[50] (1882) 21 Ch. D. 243.
[51] (1884) 27 Ch. D. 89.
[52] 14th ed.
[53] (1875) 10 Ch. App. 512.

Is it still an "earnest" or "guarantee" then, or does it become, might it become, a penalty or the like? The unanswered question was not tackled for more than a century, in *Workers Trust Bank Ltd v. Dojap*[54] and even then, not perhaps as fully as might have been desirable.

The immediate aftermath of Howe v. Smith: In re Dagenham (Thames) Dock Co. followed

14.20 In *John H. Kelmer v. British Columbia Orchard Lands*[55] and *Steedman v. Drinkle*[56] the penalty principle was calmly applied to instalments of the purchase price which were to be forfeited in the events which had happened, following *In re Dagenham (Thames) Dock Co.*[57] and applying it to instalments. This seems perfectly reasonable, incidentally; there is no discernible magic in the distinction between a deposit and an instalment. Both are equally sums of money whose contractual purpose has to be determined.

Clydebank: Lord Halsbury's heresy

14.21 Meanwhile, we had Lord Halsbury's heresy—or so one may label it—in the *Clydebank*[58] case, in 1905, and the arrival into the law on penalties of the interloper "unconscionable".[59] This really unsettled equity judges like Farwell J.:[60] he assumed (who would not?) that if the thing had to be unconscionable there had to be some *conduct* which was unconscionable, and the usual time at which equity lawyers assessed unconscionable conduct, especially by the 1880's, was the time of the hearing; so he then assumed that the jurisdiction to be exercised was dependent on the way the parties *had behaved since the breach*. This was not only inconsistent with the old law on penalties, which had looked only to the time of the contract, it was even inconsistent with what Lord Halsbury himself had said. The judgments in *Stockloser v. Johnson*[61] were even more deeply bedevilled by the same problem—how to *work* "unconscionable". The solution adopted by the majority was that there were now to be two conditions (where Lord Eldon had had only one): the question whether the clause was a penalty, and the question *whether it was also "unconscionable"*. Quite what this meant in practice proved problematic. The final parting from the old precedents which began it all has taken place: predictably perhaps, free fall and guesswork ensues. Somervell L.J. thought that a deposit might be a penalty, as in *In re Dagenham (Thames) Dock Co.*,[62]

[54] [1993] A.C. 573.
[55] [1913] A.C. 319.
[56] [1916] 1 A.C. 275.
[57] (1873) L.R. 8 Ch. App. 1022.
[58] [1905] A.C. 6.
[59] See above, para. 14.07 in the Penalty section of this chapter.
[60] See ***Mussen v. Van Diemens Land*** [1938] Ch. 253.
[61] [1954] 1 Q.B. 476.
[62] Above.

but the circumstances at the time of the breach had to be looked at to see if the retention would be unconscionable. Lord Denning appeared to have somehow developed a rather restrictive definition of a penalty clause, involving "acting oppressively" on the part of the vendor, and thus thought that relief from penalties and relief from forfeiture were different kinds of thing: in the case of relief from forfeiture the equity was based on the avoidance of unjust enrichment. This had the air of being something of a rabbit out of a hat—it was suddenly just there.[63]

Workers' Trust Bank Ltd v. Dojap: a step towards a good faith construction?

14.22 Finally, there has been the relatively recent decision of the Privy Council in *Workers' Trust Bank Ltd v. Dojap*[64] in which there was, undoubtedly, a thoughtful and courageous attempt to tackle the problem at least to some extent.[65] The Judicial Committee considered that the rule allowing vendors to keep deposits (customarily 10 per cent of the purchase price) on the sale of land was simply an "anomalous exception". Lord Browne-Wilkinson giving the judgment of the Committee said (without giving his sources) that this was a matter of "ancient law"—a rather ambiguous expression, one may be permitted to think—and then said:

> "However, the special treatment afforded to deposits is plainly capable of being abused if the parties to a contract, by attaching the label "deposit" to any penalty, could escape the general rule which renders penalties unenforceable . . ."

Thus, a deposit had to be "*reasonable as earnest money*", for the vendor to be allowed to keep it. The usual English 10 per cent qualified; but the Jamaican customary deposit did not.

14.23 It is hard to guess where the idea (however "reasonable" such an idea may undoubtedly be) that a deposit had to be "reasonable as earnest money" came from: it certainly does not seem to come from the original (or "ancient") law about penalties. Indeed, the whole notion of a deposit as a kind of hostage seems to have originated only from Fry L.J.'s judgment in *Howe v. Smith*,[66] and is in truth probably nothing more than speculation or judicial myth-making, however attractive. The idea of "reasonable as earnest money" is not explained: so that if it had historical antecedents at its heels to help us, we are not permitted to glimpse them. We may speculate that it stems from the wide "exorbitant and unconscionable" jurisdiction proposed by

[63] One might spare a thought for the benighted practising lawyer who is concerned to advise his or her client about what the law is, when judges are taking wild shots at it like this.

[64] [1993] A.C. 573.

[65] And any extent is welcome in this field.

[66] (1884) 27 Ch. D. 89.

Lord Halsbury in the *Clydebank*[67] case. If so, this would be judicial law-making[68] but also, no doubt, judicial law-making at a tangent, rather than in an orderly progression from past to present. The wide jurisdiction brought in, probably unintentionally, by Lord Halsbury was itself, as has been said before in this chapter, a huge transmogrification of the original penalty jurisdiction. If an even wider discretion (in practice it would be a discretion) is to be allowed in the case of deposits which are neither "extortionate" nor "unconscionable", this would open up endless possibilities of litigation: there may be umpteen reasons, subjective, tangential, peripheral, which may be prayed in aid by a desperate plaintiff to show that a deposit greater than 10 per cent was unreasonable, or unreasonable as earnest money.

14.24 There is, however, the little phrase "as earnest money". One may be heartened by it to think that the Judicial Committee perhaps did not in fact mean to bring in so wide a jurisdiction as that referred to above If they had, the expression "as earnest money" would add nothing of much use to "reasonable". If on the other hand, we assume that "as earnest money" is intended to have some useful *limiting* meaning, we are on a different quest. One may speculate whether the Judicial Committee has not perhaps done the right thing, but failed to give the most appropriate reason for it.

We do have a sense that they *have* done the right thing, at all events. It must be right, now no less than in earlier times, for the courts to devise methods to protect the public against the use of clauses which are not *within the scope of the paramount purpose of the contract*, as a contract for whatever it is. If I am in the insurance business, fine, or the betting business, but if the clause is merely meant to be ancillary to something less inherently risky—the working out of a contract of purchase—then it is perhaps entirely reasonable that it should be "construed down to size". These sort of clauses are easily underestimated by a purchaser. Perhaps because of their ancillary status they do not seem to merit the kind of attention that the main operative clauses of the contract receive.

Once these clauses are firmly put in their place as "collateral", in the old sense, to the paramount purpose of the contract, the idea that they are not intended to secure anyone a windfall benefit, but only to compensate for real anticipated out-of-pocket expenses, *etc.*, seen as at the date of the contract becomes a natural one. The clause becomes less of a trap for the trusting or careless purchaser, and more in line with his *reasonable expectations*. We shall still have achieved the same result as was achieved in the case: the balancing of the literal fruits of the clause against the detriment to the vendor which could be anticipated if the object of the contract was not achieved; but there will be, one may hope, an orderly use of the legal principles we have inherited from the past.

[67] [1905] A.C. 6; and see as to "Lord Halsbury's heresy", para. 14.07 above.
[68] Which one need have nothing against *per se*; they are perhaps better at it than Parliament.

Should the traditional 10 per cent deposit be sacrosanct?

14.25 The analysis in the *Workers' Trust Bank Ltd v. Dojap*[69] does not of course touch on the reasons for the non-returnability of the "ordinary" 10 per cent deposit; in other words, on the reasons why the deposit when it is a deposit as earnest money should be allowed. Why, in fact, should the vendor always be able to keep 10 per cent? Ten per cent of a £20,000 flat (if there are any still extant) may be a reasonable estimate of the vendor's loss: but can one really say this where the price is higher? How many deposits can be seen as no more than reasonable compensation for the likely loss caused to the vendor? Usually, unless the market is falling, the loss to the vendor will be little more than the wasted legal expenses; but how then can one justify the 10 per cent on a £600,000 or £1,000,000 property? It is questionable whether this aspect of the deposit has really been addressed by the few cases there are: it seems simply to have been assumed that the 10 per cent deposit is not returnable to the purchaser. One cannot be sure, but it may be thought perhaps that the courts simply fell into the habit, in times of more modest house prices, of letting the vendors keep deposits, taking rather the same common-sense approach as the Lord Keeper in *Tall v. Ryland*,[70] the case of the fishmongers and the allegedly stinking flounders. It probably would not exceed the real damages anyway, so it was hardly worth the exercise of proving what the damages were. If this is so—and it is pure speculation, but would at all events be a more down-to-earth explanation than a supposed link with Phoenician customs—then the way would be open for scrutinising the effect of the 10 per cent deposit more carefully. It would be possible to bring the law on deposits sensibly into line with the old law on penalties. It would also be more or less in line with the House of Lords' views on the general equitable power to relieve from forfeiture, in *Shiloh Spinners v. Harding*.[71] In this case about a tenant's breach of covenant, Lord Wilberforce said:

> "There cannot be any doubt that from the earliest times courts of equity have asserted the right to relieve against the forfeiture of property. The jurisdiction has not been confined to any particular type of case ... Although the principle is well-established, there has undoubtedly been some fluctuation of authority as to the self limitation to be imposed or accepted on this power. There has not been much difficulty as regards two heads of jurisdiction. First, where it is possible to state that the object of the transaction and of the insertion of the right to forfeit is essentially *to secure the payment of money*, equity has been willing to relieve on terms that the payment is made with interest, if appropriate, and also costs.[72] ... Secondly, there were the heads of *fraud, accident, mistake or surprise*, always a ground for equity's intervention, the

[69] [1993] A.C. 573.
[70] (1670) 1 Cha. Cas. 183; 22 E.R. 753.
[71] [1973] A.C. 691.
[72] ***Peachy v. Duke of Somerset*** (1721) 1 Stra. 447 and cases there cited.

inclusion of which entailed the exclusion of mere inadvertence and a fortiori of wilful defaults"[73] . . .

A footnote

14.26 Section 49(2) of the Law of Property Act 1925 gives the court power (without saying how and when it is to be exercised) to return a deposit to a purchaser where the court refuses to grant specific performance or in any action for the return of the deposit. It is possible that the discretion under the section could do with some thought by the courts, for example, perhaps, to bring it into line with the law on penalties, *etc*. Meanwhile, it is said to represent a wide discretion to "do justice between vendor and purchaser".[74]

3. RELIEF FROM FORFEITURE OF PROPERTY OR POSSESSORY INTERESTS UNDER A CONTRACT

Introduction

14.27 In *Shiloh Spinners v. Harding*[75] Lord Wilberforce stated *obiter*, as noted above, that there was a *general* power to relieve from forfeiture outside the landlord and tenant field. He stressed[76] that it arose when the forfeiture provision was ancillary, to secure some other primary object. Lord Wilberforce's statement was later said by the House of Lords in *Scandinavian Trading v. Flota Ecuatoriana*,[77] a time charter case, to have been confined to the forfeiture of *proprietary or possessory interests*, and *not* to extend to provisions for terminating contracts in default of punctual payment of a sum of money payable under it.[78]

The general power to relieve has been accepted in principle on several occasions since: see the references in Dillon L.J.'s judgment in *BICC v. Burndy Corporation*.[79] Not all judgments have taken up, to the same degree, the essential security-provision point from *Shiloh Spinners v. Harding*.[80] In *Sport International Bussum v. Interfootwear*,[81] the

[73] Italics supplied. He then went on to consider the specific question, which had historically been problematic, of a non-inadvertent breach of a covenant which was not just a covenant to pay money.

[74] *Universal Corporation v. Five Ways Properties Ltd* [1979] 1 All E.R. 552. Ah, to do justice . . . how subjective a notion that can be.

[75] [1973] A.C. 691.

[76] See para. 14.25 above.

[77] [1983] 2 A.C. 694.

[78] See the judgment of Lord Diplock with which the other Law Lords agreed.

[79] [1985] Ch. 232.

[80] [1973] A.C. 691.

[81] [1984] 1 W.L.R. 776.

Court of Appeal confirmed that there was jurisdiction to relieve against forfeiture of proprietary or possessory interests. In *BICC v. Burndy Corporation*[82] the Court of Appeal made clear that relief might be granted against a contractual provision for forfeiture of an interest in *personal property*. Dillon L.J., whose judgment was the fullest on the point, did not specifically mention the principles on which such relief might be given; but it seems fairly clear from the facts of the case that the forfeiture would have provided an amount for the plaintiff which was far in excess of what was needed to compensate it for the breach as at the time of the breach, and probably would have been similarly in excess of any likely compensation for the breach viewed as at the date of the contract. Thus, the basis has at least a very similar look to the original penalty jurisdiction: the value of the property transferred was more than the price of the broken promise and thus was likely to be seen as a comfort-provision or security-provision only.

14.28 More recently, the jurisdiction to relieve against forfeiture has been affirmed in principle, though possibly rather unsatisfactorily applied in practice, by Rattee J. in *Nutting v. Baldwin*,[83] as regards the forfeiture of their share in the fruits of a jointly funded action by defaulting members of a Lloyds Names action group. It is to be noted that the line between a possessory personal interest under a contract and a personal interest in having the benefit of the rest of the time charter, as in the *Scandinavian Trading*[84] case, is perhaps an unsatisfactorily narrow one.

Towards a unified doctrine of "penal" provisions?

14.29 Provided that one can give decent burial to Lord Halsbury's heresy, and the problems it generated, the time may be thought to be ripe for the emergence of a unified doctrine. Relief from forfeiture of money; interests in property of any kind (land, personal property, interests in possession); deposits: there is now no reason why these should not be plainly seen as governed by the same set of principles. Once again[84a] we may think that the law on the topic has become unnecessarily fragmented. The single thread—the distinction between "penal" provisions (or as they might preferably be called, "comfort-provisions" or "policing provisions") and the price of the broken promise—is discernible. It is seen to be quite a simple one, once we draw upon the wells of our legal past for such clarification of the principle as is available there.

[82] [1985] Ch. 232.
[83] [1995] 1 W.L.R. 204.
[84] [1983] 2 A.C. 694.
[84a] As with dealings with the vulnerable: see Chap. 9.

Australian development of *Shiloh Spinners v. Harding*[85]

14.30 See *Legione v. Hateley*[86] (1983), *Stern v. McArthur*[87] and *Federal Airports Corporation v. Makucha Developments,*[88] the first two noted briefly below, but to which a brief note cannot do full justice

(1) The Australian position is now that it may be sufficiently "unconscionable" for relief from forfeiture if the party opposing forfeiture seeks to hold the other party to the strict contractual provisions. This removes any real force from the word "unconscionable".

(2) The High Court of Australia has also held that there is a sufficient proprietory interest in the purchaser even though his contractual interest has been validly forfeited under the contract, for example because of an express provision allowing this on expiry of a period for which time was of the essence. This removes much of the real force from "proprietory interest".

The practical result cannot but be a thoroughly good thing, whatever one may think of the circularity involved in the reasoning. Further, the way may now be open, at least in Australia and perhaps in time in Britain, for a unified doctrine of penal or security-provisions based on the old equitable jurisdiction, covering relief from forfeiture and the "penalty" jurisdiction equally and including deposits in the latter. The recognition here of the interloper "unconscionable" as a historical aberration stemming from an unacknowledged change in our use of the word "penal" would also be welcome. Finally the abandonment of any attempt to perpetuate any distinction between relief from forfeiture and penalties—which is in large part based on the need to give some work to "unconscionable" to do,[89] would be similarly welcome.

The future of the wide discretion?

14.31 Even Lord Wilberforce and the other Law Lords in *Shiloh Spinners v. Harding*[90] retained, as has been noted, the wide discretion of the late nineteenth century. There may be room for this to be reconsidered, in favour perhaps of a resurrection of the old, much narrower, discretion of the Courts of Equity. This was perhaps little more than a choice between options.[91] The crucial exercise, once a security-provision had been identified, was (a) to see if compensation could be accurately assessed; and (b) to see if the individual party with the benefit of the security provision could be put in the same position in which he could

[85] [1973] A.C. 691.
[86] (1983) 46 A.L.R. 1.
[87] (1988) 81 A.L.R. 463.
[88] (1993) 115 A.L.R. 679.
[89] See, *e.g.* the joint judgment of Mason and Deane J.J. in ***Legione v. Hateley*** *ibid.* at 28.
[90] Above.
[91] Cp. Equity's options, in Chap. 5, Sale of Land.

reasonably have expected to be. They considered that (a) was what gave them jurisdiction to "interfere" and kept them this side of being "arbitrary"; (b) was what they called their "discretion". Lord Erskine gave an account of it in *Sanders v. Pope*,[92] a landlord and tenant case:

> "There is no branch of the jurisdiction of this Court more delicate than that, which goes to restrain the exercise of a legal right. That jurisdiction rests only upon this principle; that one party is taking advantage of a forfeiture; and as a rigid exercise of the legal right would produce a hardship, a great loss and injury on the one hand arising from going to the full extent of the right, while on the other *the party may have the full benefit of the contract, as originally framed*, the court will interfere; *where a clear mode of compensation can be discovered.*"
>
> . . .
>
> "If that covenant is not performed, two questions arise: which must always be kept distinct in the mind of the Court: 1st, the abstract question of jurisdiction; what the Court may do; which is a mere question of law: 2ndly, what the Court ought to do in the particular instance. . . . "Upon the general question of jurisdiction the principle is clear compensation. Whether in every such case the Court is bound to make the landlord accept it, is another consideration; depending on the discretion of the court. . . ."
>
> "In *Cage v. Russell*[93] I find it laid down, that it is a standing rule of the Court, that a forfeiture should not bind, where a thing may be done afterwards, or any compensation made for it. Forfeitures are even odious in law. Courts of Law, circumscribed as their jurisdiction is, struggle against forfeiture. . . ."

14.32 He cited other cases which he thought went even further towards the principle that where compensation was possible relief should be given, and continued:

> ". . . Undoubtedly, *unless it is plain, that full compensation can be given, so as to put the other party in the same situation precisely, a Court of Equity ought not to act: for such a jurisdiction would be arbitrary . . . The court must see, whether the damage is such, that it can be the subject of compensation. But this is payment of a specific sum of money: not general damages.*"[94]

The principle of compensation in equity is perhaps one which merits modern reassessment, in our post-Judicature Act 1893 courts.[95] And see the recent case of *Mahoney v Purnell* [1996] 3 All E.R. 61 in which May J. granted compensation in equity to a vulnerable buyer. The old, narrower "discretion", ascertaining whether or not the individual party with the benefit of the security provision can be put in essentially the same position as if the contract had not been breached,

[92] (1806) 12 Ves. Jun. 283; 33 E.R. 108.
[93] 2 Ventr. 352; 86 E.R. 481.
[94] Italics supplied.
[95] See, for what may be a step in this direction, the Court of Appeal case of ***Jobson v. Johnson*** [1989] 1 W.L.R. 1026.

has this to be said for it. It is a lot simpler and quicker for a court to operate than the wide-ranging, ample, late-nineteenth-century discretion common today. It is also easier for prospective litigants to grasp. Finally, it may provide a more sensible, commercially understandable method of distinguishing between cases where relief ought and ought not to be granted[96] than the unsatisfactorily narrow dividing line between interests in personal property (relief from forfeiture available) and forfeiture of the remaining fruits of a contract (relief not available).

APPENDIX TO CHAPTER 14: SOME CASES OF INTEREST

***Tall v. Ryland* (1670) 1 Cha. Ca. 183; 22 E.R. 753**

14.33 The plaintiff and the defendant were fishmongers, who had had differences and compromised them on terms that the plaintiff gave the defendant a bond "of £20 penalty, conditioned to behave himself civilly and like a good Neighbour to the Defendant, and not to disparage his Goods". The plaintiff however could not resist, it would seem, the temptation to disparage his rival, and told a customer of the defendant that the flounders he had bought from the defendant stank, and the defendant lost that customer. He thereupon sued the plaintiff on the Bond he had given. The plaintiff asked the court if he might be relieved from the Bond, saying "the Damage was not considerable or valuable". The defendant argued "that the Bond was not Conditioned for Payment of Money or performance of Covenants, or for any Matter for which Damages in an Action of Debt, Covenant or any other Action, was recoverable; nor was there any other way to measure the Damages but by the penalty." The Lord Keeper allowed the penalty to stand, although it is unclear how far he accepted the defendant's argument: the decision being said to be partly because the bond was only for £20 and because "the costs of Suit here and at law would exceed the Penalty"; and possibly, it was said, a different decision might have been reached if the bond had been for £100.

Note: This case, it must be admitted, does not shed great light on the principles involved; although it may be that it is a prototype of the good-behaviour bond in a case where the monetary damages would not be great or easily measured, but the inconvenience considerable. This kind of bond was allowed to stand by Lord Hardwicke in Roy v. Duke of Beaufort.[97] *It is included partly because it is one of the earliest in which the principle of relief from penal bonds is recognised, and partly simply because the squabbling City fishmongers are rather entertaining.*

***Lowe v. Peers* (1768) 4 Burr. at 2225; 98 E.R. 160**

14.34 This was a breach of promise of marriage case. The fiance had engaged by deed not to marry anyone else, and if he did, that he would pay his fiancee,

[96] C.p. perhaps cases such as the *Scandinavian Trading* case, mentioned above: "when a shipowner becomes entitled, under the terms of his contract, to withdraw a ship from the service of a time charterer, he may well wish to act swiftly and irrevocably ..." (citation from Robert Goff LJ in the court below).

[97] (1741) 2 Atk. 191; 26 E.R. 519.

a Miss Lowe, £1,000. Lord Mansfield said: "The money was payable upon a contingency, and the contingency has happened. Therefore it ought to be paid.

There is a difference between covenants in general, and covenants secured by a penalty or forfeiture. In the latter case, the obligee has his election. He may either bring an action of debt for the penalty, and recover the penalty; (after which recovery of the penalty, he can not resort to the covenant; because the penalty is to be a satisfaction for the whole:) or, if he does not choose to go for the penalty, he may proceed upon the covenant and recover more or less than the penalty, toties quoties.

And upon this distinction they proceed in Courts of Equity. They will relieve against a penalty, upon a compensation: but where the covenant is "to pay a particular liquidated sum", a Court of Equity can not make a new covenant for a man; nor is there any room for compensation or relief. As in leases containing a covenant against plowing up meadow; if the covenant be "not to plow";[98] and there be a penalty; a Court of Equity will relieve against the penalty, or will even go further than that . . . (*to preserve the substance of the agreement*:) but if it is worded—"to pay £5 an acre for every acre plowed up;" there is no alternative, no room for any relief against it; no compensation; it *is the substance of the agreement*. Here, the specified sum of £1000 is found in damages: it is the particular liquidated sum fixed and agreed upon between the parties, and is therefore the proper quantum of the damages,"[99]

Note: The above supports the idea that the original "relief" given by equity courts against bonds was in reality simply a purposive construction of the bond as security for damages rather than pre-ascertained damages. It appears Lord Mansfield is saying that where the damages are simply said to be payable upon a contingency, that is as a term of the contract itself, as opposed to being ***security for*** *the performance of some obligation), and if that contingency has happened, there is simply no room for a purposive construction and "relief" against penalties.*

The other point worth observing is the fact that Lord Mansfield, in a common law court, was applying the law on penalties at all rather than leaving it to the equity courts. There had in fact been a statute of William III which gave jurisdiction in the case of penal bonds to Common law courts also. It thus ceased early on to be stamped with any particularly "equitable" character.

Peachy v. Duke of Somerset (1721) 1 Str.447 (cited by Kay L.J. in _Law v. Redditch Local Board,_ below); 93 E.R. 626

14.35 This was an application by a copyholder for relief from a forfeiture he had himself occasioned by making leases contrary to the custom of the manor without the lord's licence; and by felling timber, digging stones, and grubbing up hedges. He offered to pay "a recompence" instead. The argument had been pressed that there was a general jurisdiction to relieve against forfeitures, Lord Macclesfield did not accept this: he thought the penalty jurisdiction was firmly linked to a right to damages; *"for it is the recompence that gives this Court a handle to grant relief"*.[1]

"The true ground of relief against penalties is from the original intent of the case, where the penalty is designed only to secure money and the Court gives him all that he expected or desired . . ."

Note: See comment as to the preceding case Lowe v. Peers.[2]

[98] 6 Vin. 472
[99] Italics supplied.
[1] Italics supplied.
[2] Para. 14.34 above.

***Roy v. Duke of Beaufort* (1741) 2 Atk. 191; 26 E.R. 519**

14.36 The plaintiff had entered into a joint bond with his son in the penalty of £100, that the son should not trespass by shooting, hunting fishing, etc., on the Duke of Beaufort's estate, save with the licence of the gamekeeper or in company with a qualified person. (The bond to the Duke had been taken after the son had been caught trespassing by the gamekeeper and taken before a justice of the peace.) The son had caught two flounders with an angling rod, but at the invitation of the gamekeeper's brother in law and another servant of the Duke. The Lord Chancellor, Lord Hardwicke, considered the question whether the bond had been obtained by oppression, and decided that in these circumstances it had not. He approved of this sort of good-behaviour bond as being not only for the benefit of lords of manors "but even of the young person who enter into them, as this sort of idleness generally leads them to worse consequences", and considered that the penalty rules did not apply to such a bond: they were given by way of "stated damages between the parties" it being "unreasonable to imagine that they could only be intended as bare security that the obligor should not offend for the future; was this the case, in what respect is a gentleman in a better condition, who has such a bond, than he was before, if, after he has obtained judgment at law, a court of equity will give him no other satisfaction than the bare value of the price of the game that is killed". However, he granted relief on the ground of what seems to have been broadly acquiescence by the Duke's servants, since the son had been enticed onto the land, and since some two years elapsed before action was brought.

***Woodhouse v. Shepley* (1742) 2 Atk. 585; 26 E.R. 721**

14.37 The plaintiff, Hannah Woodhouse (who died soon after she commenced the action) sought to be relieved from a bond she had given the defendant. The defendant was a tailor, who had courted her against the wishes of her father, who had forbidden her to give him any encouragement. The two of them met secretly from time to time, and eventually entered into a bond whereby each entered into obligations to the other, and *inter alia* Hannah promised to pay £500 to the defendant if she did not marry him within 13 months of her father's death.

The Lord Chancellor gave relief, ordering the bond to be delivered up to be cancelled. The grounds are not entirely clear, and it seems probable that the jurisdiction was not a penalty-jurisdiction at all, but something akin to the jurisdiction in dealings with the vulnerable. The Lord Chancellor adverted to the fact that Hannah was living with, and under the influence of her father, and it would be a fraud on him (*inter alia* because he made his dispositions by his will for her benefit supposing her to have been obedient to his wishes). He considered also the fact that the bond was executed in an alehouse, and Hannah had had no friends there with her; and that the defendant had had considerable influence over her, shown by the fact that he retained the bond in his hands. The Lord Chancellor also attached weight to the way the penalty operated in a case like this; in that there was no chance of mitigating the severity of such a bond by ordering the real damages to be paid, as could happen with "executory promises": it was either the whole sum or nothing.

***Benson v. Gibson* (1746) 3 Atk. 395; 26 E.R. 1027**

14.38 This bond was a type of fidelity bond,[3] for £100, given by the plaintiff who was an agent in Flanders for buying hair, to his employer the hair-merchant

[3] See Chap. 4, on Insurance and Surety transactions.

as security for his performance of the service agreement. In fact the plaintiff only bought £5 worth of hair, and returned to England before the agreed time.

The Lord Chancellor, Lord Hardwicke, said: "I cannot decree this penalty here, because this is a bond for services only, and different from a *nomine poenae in leases*, to prevent a tenant from plowing, because that is the stated damages between the parties . . . Nor is it like the case of bonds given as a security not to defraud the revenue, because there, where a person is guilty of a breach, it is considered in law as a crime, and this court will not relieve for that reason.

Here I cannot decree the penalty, but must direct an action at law upon a *quantum damnificatus*, to try how far the defendant has been damnified by the plaintiff's non-performance of the service".

Note: The reference to plowing is probably a reference to the custom of agreeing liquidated damages for breach of a covenant not to plough a particular area: see the reference to this in Lowe v. Peers above at para. 14.34 and see the next case. It would seem that the intention for the £100 to be simply a security was thought clear, so that the purposive construction obviously dictated an inquiry as to damages.

***Rolfe v. Peterson* (1772) 2 Bro. P.C. 436; 1 E.R. 1048**

14.39 There was a lease of an estate, with a covenant by the tenant *inter alia* not to plough or to cut down trees or shrubs, *etc.*, on a particular part (set aside as a cover and protection for the game, and for sheep in winter and snowy weather); with a payment of £5 an acre if the tenant ploughed and £5 a load if the tenant cut down trees. The tenant did cut down the shrubs, *etc.*, on the fields in question and began to cultivate them. The jury assessed the damages by totalling up the agreed sum: the tenant complained that this was excessive, since the profit to the landlord over the term would be about 30 times the real value of the fields which he had actually improved in value by tilling.

On appeal from the Lord Chancellor, who had allowed the tenants' claim that they should merely pay compensation for the actual damage done, the landlord won. The judgment as reported merely reverses the decree first obtained by the tenant, after hearing counsel. The winning argument is however fully reported. This had been that the £5 per acre was "a liquidated satisfaction" not "a forfeiture for the better enforcing a prohibition, or a security for the doing of some collateral *act*; the tenant had an absolute choice whether or not to plough, but if he did, he had no excuse for not paying the sum.

Note: Again, the question is seen to be a simple one: nothing to do with the excessive nature of the agreement; merely a matter of identifying whether the sum in question was the contract price, in some sense, or simply a security for performing a contractual promise.

***Hardy v. Martin* (1783) 1 Cox 26; 29 E.R. 1046 (Before the Lords Commissioners)[4]**

14.40 The plaintiff and the defendant were in partnership in a brandy business. When the plaintiff left the partnership he sold the lease and goodwill of the shop to the defendant for £300, and entered into a bond for £600 penalty not to compete within the Cities of London and Westminster or within 5 miles thereof. The defendant filed a bill, upon breach by the plaintiff, and the plaintiff sought an injunction restraining him from taking out execution on the sum

[4] See also Sir S. Romilly's citation from this case in his note to *Cocks v. Richards* 10 Ves. 429 at 436.

in the bond. The court granted the injunction, on the ground that the payment provided for in the bond was a penalty.

Lord Loughborough said: "The penalty is never considered in this court, as *the price for doing what a man has expressly agreed not to do.*[5] The court will restrain him from setting up a trade in opposition to his own agreement, although he has a paid the penalty. The case from *1 Ch. Ca*[6] is expressly in point, that the court will moderate the damages to the real injury." He distinguished *Rolfe v. Peterson,*[7] essentially as a "price" case, saying "That is a different case from an agreement *not to do a thing, with a penalty for doing it*[8]. The former is a case in which this court will not interfere; but this is the case of an agreement not to sell brandy, with a penalty for selling it. I do not say, that under all the circumstances these are excessive damages; but the court will not on motion reject an application for an injunction, while there is a jurisdiction in a court of equity to direct an issue to try *quantum damnificatus.*" The other two Lords Commissioners agreed.

Note: A clear distinction is beginning to be seen by now between a sum, excessive or otherwise, which is the price of the promise, or a part thereof, and a sum which is merely a security or earnest, of the performance of the promise. Only the latter are proper subject matter for relief in the courts.

Sloman v. Walker **(1783) 1 Bro. C.C. 418; 28 E.R. 1213**

14.41 The agreement had been to secure the use of a room for the defendant, with a penalty for non-compliance. The plaintiff obtained an injunction restraining the defendant from suing on the penalty. Lord Thurlow said: "The rule that, where a penalty is inserted merely to secure the enjoyment of a *collateral object*, the enjoyment of *the object* is considered as the principal intent of the deed, and the penalty only as accessional, and therefore, only to secure the damage really incurred, is too strongly established in equity to be shaken."[9]

Note: Kay L.J. in Law v. Redditch Local Board[10] *below. considered that in this case Lord Thurlow modified and extended the penalty doctrine. In fact Lord Thurlow seems to be doing no more than he purports to do, namely setting out the distinction which had developed between a sum which was the price of the promise and a sum which was security for the promise.*

Astley v. Weldon **(1801) 2 Bos & Pul. 346; 126 E.R. 1318**

14.42 The plaintiff agreed to pay the defendant Frances Weldon a weekly sum to perform at his theatres, and her travelling expenses: she for her part agreed that she would perform as required, attend rehearsals, and abide by other regulations. There was additionally a provision that "either of them neglecting to perform that agreement" should pay to the other £200. Frances Weldon was in breach of her part of the agreement: the question was whether the damages were £200 or whether this was merely a penalty.

Lord Eldon said he found himself, as before, "much embarrassed in ascertaining the principle upon which those cases [the cases on penalties] were founded: but it appeared to me that the articles in this case furnished a more satisfactory ground for determining whether the sum of money therein mentioned ought to be considered in the nature of a penalty or of liquidated

[5] Italics supplied.
[6] ***Tall v. Ryland***, para. 14.33 above.
[7] Para. 14.39 above.
[8] Italics supplied.
[9] Italics supplied.
[10] [1892] 1 Q.B. 127.

damages, than most others which I had met with. What was urged in the course of the argument has ever appeared to me to be the clearest principle, viz., that where a doubt is stated whether the sum inserted be intended as a penalty or not, if a certain damage less than that sum is made payable upon the face of the same instrument, in case the act intended to be prohibited be done, that sum shall be construed to be a penalty . . . A principle has been said to have been stated in several cases, the adoption of which one cannot but lament, namely, that if the sum would be very enormous and excessive considered as liquidated damages, it shall be taken to be a penalty though agreed to be paid in the form of contract." He went on to explain that this was not so. It was perfectly possible to set a price on a promise which *was* excessive, but which represented *the value to the vendor of the promise*, as in the case of *Rolfe v. Peterson*[10a] where the lessor wanted to preserve that part of the land for his own amusement; or *Lowe v. Peers*[11] He pointed out that the "grossly unequal" contracts[12] were an entirely different class of case.

Turning to the case before him, Lord Eldon accepted that the form of the contract was not that of a penal bond, but one had to look at the whole contract; and here some of the breaches could be anticipated to be trivial, being the subject of specific fines under the theatre regulations. Thus, Lord Eldon considered the plaintiff might satisfy only his actual damage out of the £200, and retain the rest against future breaches.

The rest of the court, Heath J. Rooke J. and Chambre J., agreed; both Rooke J. and Chambre J. stating that the court was attempting to ascertain the intention of the parties; and Chambre J. noting that the jurisdiction to relieve against penalties was now available in Court of Law (by statute)[13] as well as equity, and was a matter for the Court to consider even if not pleaded.

***Reilly v. Jones* (1823) 1 Bing. 302; 130 E.R. 122**

14.43 This was an agreement for the sale of a lease of a pub named the Delaware Arms in Oxford Street, which contained a provision that "either of them not fulfilling all and every part, the party not fulfilling shall pay unto the other the sum of £500 hereby settled and fixed *as liquidated damages*;[14] the deposit now paid to be considered as part of the said damages in the case of default made by [the purchaser] or returned in addition to the said damages in the case of default by [the vendor]".

Dallas C.J., Park J. and Burrough J. all agreed that the £500 was, in effect, the *price of the promise* to buy/sell; and rejected the idea that despite the express use of the word "liquidated damages" by the parties, it might nonetheless be open to the court to hold that the intention was for the sum to be a penalty. Park J. said that this was not a case of a number of promises of performance, some of which were trivial: "in substance it is for the performance of only one: the vendor was to leave, and the vendee was to take possession."

***Davies v. Penton* (1827) 6 B. & Co. 216; 108 E.R. 433**

14.44 The agreement was for the sale of the lease of a professional business[15] together with stock and goodwill, and with a covenant from the vendor not

[10a] Para. 14.39 above.
[11] Para. 14.34 above, the breach of promise case.
[12] See Chap. 9 Dealings with the Vulnerable.
[13] Of William III.
[14] Italics supplied.
[15] A business of remarkable versatility: the business of "surgeon, apothecary, and accoucheur"!

to carry on the business within 5 miles of the premises. The purchaser also agreed that he would discharge bills drawn upon and accepted by the plaintiff, for the sums of £400 and £1701.4s. There was a provision whereby both bound and obliged themselves to the other "for the true performance of" this agreement, "in the penal sum of £500, to be recoverable for breach of the said agreement in any Court or Courts of Law, as and by way of liquidated damages". The plea by the vendor was that the bills had not been duly discharged as and when payable, and he sought the entire £500.

Abbott C.J. commented adversely on the drafting of the agreement, saying: "Whoever framed this agreement does not appear to have had any very clear idea of the distinction between a penalty and liquidated damages; for the sum of £500 is described in the same sentence as a penal sum and as liquidated damages."

Looking to the whole agreement, and bearing in mind that a relatively trivial breach was possible, for example paying one of the bills a day late, and if the plaintiff were right that the entire £500 would become payable for that, he considered the provision was a penalty, or security for damages only. The rest of the court agreed. Littledale J. commented on the prevalent use of the word "liquidated damages" as a way of escaping the jurisdiction given to common law courts to deal with penalties by the statute of William III. As he said "*the mere alteration of the term cannot alter the nature of the thing;*[16] and if the Court see, upon the whole agreement, that the parties intended the sum to be a penalty, they ought not to allow one party to deprive the other of the benefit to be derived from the statute."

***Kemble v. Farren* (1829) 6 Bing 141; 130 E.R. 1234**

14.45 This was an action by the manager of Covent Garden Theatre against an actor who was in breach of his agreement. The agreement had provided that the defendant would comply with all the regulations of the theatre, and perform during four seasons as principal comedian. The agreement also contained a clause that "if either of the parties should neglect or refuse to fulfil the said agreement, or any part thereof, or any stipulation therein contained, such party should pay to the other the sum of 1000*l*., to which sum it was thereby agreed that the damages sustained by any such omission, neglect or refusal should amount; and which sum was thereby declared by the said parties to be liquidated and ascertained damages, and not a penalty or penal sum, or in the nature thereof."

Tindal C.J. noted that it would be difficult to suppose "any words more precise and explicit than those used in the agreement". He said "... if the clause had been limited to breaches which were of an uncertain nature and amount, we should have thought it would have had the effect of ascertaining the damages upon any such breach at 1000*l*. For we see nothing illegal or unreasonable in the parties, by their mutual agreement, settling the amount of damages, uncertain in their nature, at any sum upon which they may agree. In many cases, such an agreement fixes that which is almost impossible to be accurately ascertained; and in all cases, it saves the expense and difficulty of bringing witnesses to that point." However, here the sum covered the breach of any stipulation, however minute. Thus it came within the rule that "a very large sum" which should become immediately payable "in consequence of the nonpayment of a very small sum" was a penalty, that case being "precisely that in which courts of equity have always relieved, and against which courts of law have, in modern times, endeavoured to relieve, by directing

[16] Italics supplied.

juries to assess the real damages sustained by the breach of the agreement." Thus *Astley v. Weldon*[17] was applied here.

***Green v. Price* (1845) 13 M. & W. 695; 153 E.R. 291**

14.46 The plaintiff was the executor of a certain John Gosnell, who had carried on a partnership in the perfumery business with the defendant Green. Green had assigned his partnership share in the perfumery business to Gosnell, covenanting with him and his successors in title not to be concerned in the business of a perfumer, toy-man, and hair merchant within the cities of London and Westminster or within 600 miles from either, binding himself thereby in the sum of £5,000 "as and by way of liquidated damages". In fact the defendant had after the death of Gosnell set up a business in Lombard Street, in breach of the covenant.

The court (Pollock C.B., Parke B., Alderson B. and Rolfe B.) all agreed, in effect, that this particular provision was simply the price of the promise not to compete. They attached weight to the fact that there was only one stipulation which attracted this sum, and that the damages resulting from the breach of it would be altogether uncertain. Thus the words "liquidated damages" were to be read in their ordinary sense, and meant what they said.

***Galsworthy v. Strutt* (1848) L.R. 1 Ex. 659; 154 E.R. 280**

14.47 In a deed for the dissolution of the partnership between the defendant and the plaintiff as attorneys and solicitors, the defendant covenanted not to compete within 50 miles of the former partnership place of business, and not to interfere with or solicit former clients of the business; and if he infringed such covenant, to pay £1000 "as and for liquidated damages, and not by way of penalty".

The court (Parke B. Alderson B. Platt B. and Pollock C.B.) all thought this was a provision for liquidated damages and not a penalty, bearing in mind in particular that the damages would be very uncertain in the case of a breach of either covenant.

***Atkyns v. Kinnier* (1850) L.R. 4 Ex. 775; 154 E.R. 1429**

14.48 This was a decision very similar to the above, also concerning a non-competition covenant, this time by a surgeon.

***Ockendon v. Henly* (1858) E.B. & E. 485; 120 E.R. 590 (Deposit case)**

14.49 Conditions of sale at an auction provided that the purchaser of each lot was to pay a deposit of 20 per cent and sign the agreement to pay the remainder. If he should fail to comply, the deposit was to be forfeited, and if on resale any deficiency occurred, the vendor might recover this, and all expenses of the resale, "as and for liquidated damages". The purchaser failed to pay the deposit or complete the purchase. The vendor claimed the deficiency (exceeding the deposit) on the resale and also the unpaid deposit.

Lord Campbell C.J. delivered the judgment of the court as follows: "There having been an actual forfeiture of the deposit by the express words of the seventh condition, the deposit, if paid, could not in any event have been recovered back by the purchaser; and the seller would have been entitled to any additional benefit on a resale. But, the seller having obtained a right to the forfeited deposit, and making a further demand of damages sustained on the

[17] Para. 14.42 above.

resale, it becomes necessary to consider what was the nature of the deposit. Now it is well settled that, by our law, following the rule of the civil law, a pecuniary deposit upon a purchase is to be considered as a payment in part of the purchase money, and not as a mere pledge; Sugd. V. & P. ch. I sect. III art. 18 (13th ed.). Therefore in this case, had the deposit been paid, the balance only of the purchase money would have remained payable. What then, according to the seventh condition, is the deficiency arising upon the resale which the seller is entitled to recover? We think the difference between the balance of the purchase money on the first sale and the amount of the purchase money obtained on the second sale: or, in other words, the deposit, although forfeited so far as to prevent the purchaser from ever recovering it back, as, without a forfeiture, he might have done . . ., still is to be brought by the seller into account if he seeks to recover as for a deficiency on the resale." The vendor's damages were thus reduced by the amount of the deposit.

***Betts v. Burch* (1859) 4 H. & N. 505; 157 E.R. 938**

14.50 This was an agreement for the sale of the furniture fixtures and fittings of a pub, these to be valued, and possession was to be given on a certain day, and "in the event of either of the parties not complying in every particular set forth in this agreement, he should forfeit and pay the sum of 50l., and all expenses attending the same." The defendant being in default, the plaintiff claimed the £50. Martin B. (conveying also the concurrence of the Chief Baron and Watson B.) and Bramwell B. held the provision was a penalty, in the light of the fact that a very small deficiency in the price to be paid, for example, would suffice to bring in the much larger penalty obligation.

***Depree v. Bedborough* (1863) 4 Giff. 479 (Deposit case); 66 E.R. 795**

14.51 A deposit was paid on a contract for the purchase of some land, but there was no express provision for forfeiture in the event of default, merely that there should be a resale. The Vice-Chancellor, Sir John Stuart, held that the purchaser's assignee in bankruptcy had no right to the deposit, which had been exacted for the vendor's benefit, "as some security for the performance of the contract".

***Hinton v. Sparkes* (1868) L.R. 3 C.P. 161 (Deposit case)**

14.52 In an agreement for the sale of a pub with fixtures, *etc.*, the parties agreed that the purchaser should pay £50 as a deposit to the vendor. The agreement further provided that if the vendor should not complete the agreement he should return the deposit, "in addition to the damages hereinafter stated; and if the purchaser shall fail to perform his part of the agreement, then the deposit money shall become forfeited, in part of the following damages: and if either of the parties neglect or refuse to comply with any part of this agreement, he shall pay to the other 50l. hereby mutually agreed upon to be the damages ascertained and fixed, on breach hereof." The purchaser failed to complete the purchase, and further failed to deposit the £50, merely giving the vendor an IOU. The vendor (whose true loss on resale was only £10), sued for the deposit. The court (Bovill C.J. and Willes J.) considered that since there was an express provision for forfeiture of the deposit in the events which had happened, the distinction between penalty and liquidated damages had no application: the forfeiture should be given effect; and the fact that he had not actually paid the deposit was irrelevant: as Willes J. said, "I cannot see why the rights of the vendor should be affected by the purchaser's having committed two breaches of contract instead of one."

***Thompson v. Hudson* (1869) L.R. 4 H.L. 1**

14.53 Hudson had three suits pending against him by a railway company; and eventually he reached a compromise with the company whereby he agreed with the company that he would pay the sums found to be due on an account which had been ordered against him and forego any right to appeal; the company for its part agreed to give time to him to make the payments, and accepted a mortgage over an estate of his, but reserved its original rights under a court order which had been made, if the stipulations in the compromise agreement were not performed.

Hudson did not perform the agreement, and the question arose whether the originally reserved right, which gave the company a larger sum, was a penalty. The House of Lords held that the company might claim the original sum due where there had been a breach, which operated as a waiver of the compromise agreement rights.

Lord Westbury said "It is impossible to hold that money due by contract can be converted into a penalty. A penalty is a punishment, an infliction, for not doing, or for doing something; but if a man submits to receive, at a future time, and on the default of his debtor, that which he is now entitled to receive, it is impossible to understand how that can be be regarded as a penalty."

***Lea v. Whitaker* (1872) L.R. 8 C.P. 70 (referred to in *Magee v. Lavell*[18]) (Deposit case)**

14.54 This was an agreement for the sale of a pub, with goodwill, trade, fixtures, *etc.* The agreement provided that "by way of making this agreement binding, each of the above contracting parties have deposited in the hands of [a third party] the sum of 40l. each; and either party failing to complete this agreement shall forfeit to the other his deposit-money as and for liquidated damages".

The buyer brought an action under the agreement for damages at large; but the court (Keating J. and Denman J.) held he must be confined to the sum agreed as liquidated damages.

***In re Dagenham (Thames) Dock Co.* (1873) L.R. 8 Ch. App. 1022 (Deposit case)**

14.55 The company, which was incorporated by Act of Parliament to make a dock, entered into an agreement with a landowner to buy a piece of land for £4000; £2000 to be paid immediately, and the remaining £2,000 on a certain day, time to be of the essence, with a provision that if the whole and interest was not paid on that day, the vendors might retake the land, without any obligation to repay any of the deposit money.

Here the Court of Appeal had little difficulty in holding that the provision was a penalty, since it might be the case that only a very small portion of the purchase money remained unpaid.

***Magee v. Lavell* (1874) L.R. 9 C.P. 107**

14.56 The plaintiff agreed to sell his pub to the defendant, with a stipulation that if either party "shall refuse or neglect to perform all and every part of this agreement, they hereby promise and agree to pay to the other who shall be

[18] Para. 14.56 below.

willing to complete the same the sum of 100l. as damages . . ." The defendant refused to complete, saying the agreement included a coach-house to which the plaintiff could not give vacant possession. The court held that the coach-house was not included anyway; but they ruled that the £100 was nonetheless a penalty. Coleridge C.J. said that the courts: "refuse to hold themselves bound by the mere use of the words "liquidated damages". He said that the courts *"will look to what must be considered, in reason, to have been intended by the parties in relation to the subject matter. If we look to the nature of the contract* in the present case, it will be seen that it involves *several events of various degrees of importance,* and, therefore, according to the general principle governing such cases, the sum mentioned must be considered as a penalty and not liquidated damages."[19]

***Ex parte Barrell* (1875) 10 Ch. App. 512 (Deposit case)**

14.57 In a contract of sale of land there was a provision for the purchaser to pay a deposit, but no stipulation as to what should happen to it if the purchase went off through the purchaser's fault. The purchaser defaulted and then became bankrupt. The trustee in bankruptcy disclaimed the contract. The Court of Appeal held, in short judgments, that the trustee had no right to have the deposit back. In argument there had been reference to Lord St Leonards' contention in *Sugden on Vendors and Purchasers*[20] that the purchaser could not have the deposit back because if so he would be gaining a benefit by relying on his own wrong. It is probably implicit in the phrasing of the judgments that the two Lord Justices accepted this argument.

Sir W.M. James L.J. said simply: "The trustee [in bankruptcy] in this case has no legal or equitable right to recover the deposit. The money was paid to the vendor as a guarantee that the contract should be performed. The trustee refuses to perform the contract, and then says, Give me back the deposit. There is no ground for such a claim . . ."

Sir G. Mellish L.J. said: "I am of the same opinion. It appears to me clear that, even where there is no clause in the contract as to the forfeiture of the deposit, if the purchaser repudiates the contract he cannot have back the money, as the contract has gone off through his default."

***In re Newman* (1876) 4 Ch.D.724**

14.58 Some builders agreed with their employer that the work should be completed by Christmas Day, and in default, they would forfeit to the employer £10 for every week after that during which the buildings should remain unfinished. There was also a provision that if the builders became bankrupt or for any other cause could not complete the work, the employer might rescind, and the sums he had already paid were to be treated as the full value of the works. There was also a provision that if the work was not "in all things duly performed", the employer would be paid "£1000, as and for liquidated damages".

Bacon C.J. considered that he was obliged to uphold the obligation to pay £1,000. He said: "The meaning of this clause, if it means anything at all, is, that the penalty of £1000 has been incurred. I cannot alter the contract; I cannot find any circumstances to induce me to say, or to justify me in saying, that in the events which have happened a less sum than £1000 should be

[19] Italics supplied.

[20] (14th ed., p. 40).

paid. If I were to say that, I should be obliged to ask myself how much less than £1000 ought to be paid. What means have I of ascertaining that?"

The builders appealed. The employers argued that it was precisely because it was difficult to estimate the damages which would ensue from the building not being completed in time (it was a school) that the sum should be upheld.

James L.J. said that the law was satisfactorily stated in *Astley v. Weldon*[21] by Heath J: "Where articles contain covenants for the performance of several things, and then one large sum is stated at the end to be paid upon breach of performance, that must be considered a penalty. But where it is agreed that if a party do such a particular thing, such a sum shall be paid by him, there the sum stated may be treated as liquidated damages."

He thus thought the case before him, which had a range of breaches of differing importance, but which merited the same sum on breach of any, was a penalty and allowed the builders' appeal. Baggallay J.A. and Bramwell J.A. agreed. Baggallay J.A. relied on Lord Westbury in *Thompson v. Hudson*[22] and on Lord Coleridge in *Magee v. Lavell*.[23] Bramwell J.A. relied on what he had said himself in *Betts v. Burch*[24] and on *Magee v. Lavell*[25]

Note: It is to be seen that none of the three really considers the underlying principles: the approach is becoming increasingly one of fact-matching to the situations covered in the older cases.

***Wallis v. Smith* (1882) 21 Ch.D.243 (Deposit with third party)**

14.59 The plaintiff agreed to sell land to the defendant for £70,000, to be spent by the defendant on building on the land. The defendant was to pay to a joint account in the name of the plaintiff and the defendant a deposit of £5,000, £500 was to be paid on execution of the contract and the remainder within seven months. There were provisions (1) that if the plaintiff could not make a good title the deposit of £500 was to be returned and the plaintiff was to pay the defendant £5,000 as liquidated damages; (2) that if the defendant should commit a substantial breach of the contract, either in not proceeding with due diligence to carry out the works, or in failing to perform any of the provisions of the contract, his deposit of £5,000 was to be forfeited, the contract was to be void and the plaintiff was to have back the estate, giving credit for all money actually spent by the defendant. Finally, the contract also provided (3) that no breach which arose through misconstruction of the contract would count for the purposes of (2), so that, as Fry J. held at first instance, the breach had to be a wilful one.

The defendant failed to pay the £500, and completely failed in the carrying out of the contract. Both Fry J. and the Court of Appeal held that the £5,000 was not payable for failure to pay the first deposit of £500, but was intended as liquidated damages for substantial breaches as specified, and was not a penalty.

Fry J. gave some consideration to the principles which should be applied. He rejected the idea that there was any independent equitable rule which should be applied, saying: "*The question whether a sum is a penalty or liquidated damage is one of construction. That is the primary rule. Certain subordinate rules have also been laid down with regard to the mode in which the Court is to construe agreements of this description.* In the first place it is quite plain that the words "liquidated damages", describing the nature of the payment, are by no means

[21] Para. 14.42 above.
[22] Para. 14.53 above.
[23] Para. 14.56 above.
[24] Para. 14.50 above.
[25] Para. 14.56 above.

conclusive . . ."[26] He referred to earlier cases in which "the Court seems to have thought that the words had little or no operation." However he thought that whatever the true position on that was, what was paramount was "the real nature and substance of the agreement." He thought it was important that here the deposit of £5,000 had not been paid to the plaintiff but into the hands of a third party: where there was a deposit paid to a third party or a stakeholder: in those cases it had been held that the court should regard the deposit as liquidated damages and not as a penalty. (He said about that "In that there seems to me to be great good sense, and for this reason, that if a fund is set apart to meet a particular contingency which is described, and that contingency arises, it is difficult to say that the stake-holder, or other person having the fund, is not to hand it over at once to the person who claims it under the contingency which has happened.") He allowed the plaintiff his £5,000 as liquidated damages. The defendant appealed.

14.60 (1) Jessel M.R. considered the origins of the doctrine, and concluded he did not know what these were. It had been said it was an extension into the common law of the well-known doctrine of equity. He said he knew a little of equity, and he thought that wrong. An alternative origin had been suggested, the well known rule of construction that you might depart from the literal meaning if it resulted in an absurdity. Perhaps, he thought, in early days they might have thought it absurd to make a man pay a larger sum by reason of non-payment of a smaller. He did not seem terribly satisfied with these musings; he went on to say that in any event, there was at least one Court of Appeal decision on the topic which bound them.

He conducted a lengthy review of the cases, relying particularly on the judgment of Tindal C.J. in *Kemble v. Farren*,[27] among others, and finally held that the £5,000 was not a penalty but liquidated damages. He gave particular weight to the fact that the plaintiff was or had been a solicitor and the defendant had had a solicitor and counsel, and the contract in question had been carefully prepared. His judgment perhaps shows traces of the new "Leave-all-the-namby -pamby- stuff- to- Parliament" wave which was beginning to sweep through the judiciary in the 1880's and which led to the inexorable rise of the kind of literalism in contract law which is still in vogue today; although it is fair to remember[28] that there had been some judicial unease at the apparent interference with the labels attached expressly by the parties themselves in the years before this.

". . . I have always thought, and still think, that it is of the utmost importance as regards contracts between adults—persons not under disability, and at arm's length—that the Courts of Law should maintain the performance of the contracts according to the intention of the parties; that they should not overrule any clearly expressed intention on the ground that Judges know the business of the people better than the people know it themselves. I am perfectly well aware that there are exceptions, but they are exceptions of a legislative character.

One notable exception in old times was the usury law, now repealed, to prevent people bargaining as to the rate of interest they would pay for the loan of money. There have been many other laws in modern times, such as the Factory Acts, and the Mines Regulation Acts, and so on, but they are all statutes. Judges have no right to say that people shall not perform their contracts which they have entered into deliberately, and put a different meaning on the contracts from that which the parties intend . . ."

14.61 (2) Cotton L.J. said that one could not question whether the old cases were

[26] Italics supplied.
[27] Para. 14.45 above.
[28] See cases above.

right, because the decisions were there: and the court had to apply what the courts have said are rules of construction. He thought liquidated damages could include a provision which covered a number of breaches: the provision was a penalty when some were trivial, some not.

(3) Lindley L.J. referred to the rules for ascertaining the parties' intention, and said they were settled, anyway, and "the difficulty arises in exactly understanding them and understanding the principles upon which they rest." He too thought the provision was not a penalty.

Note: The unease over what is increasingly seen as "interference" with the parties' true intention, rather than assisting them to achieve their true intention, continues in this case. Jessel M.R.'s historical research into the past appears questionable: he seems ignorant of the statute of William III giving penalty jurisdiction to Common law courts. He is clearly an enthusiast for the then-new trend towards legislation as a cure for "social" evils. On the other hand, even Cotton L.J., who was sympathetic to good faith principles in general, felt that the Court was pursuing its own idea of what was reasonable, in the teeth of the parties' deliberately expressed intention, when it exercised the jurisdiction to relieve against penalties.

***Howe v. Smith* (1884) 27 Ch.D.89 (Deposit case)**

14.62 On a sale of land the purchaser paid a deposit of £500, described as "a deposit and in part-payment of the purchase money". The question was whether the purchaser, who was held not entitled to specific performance, was entitled to recover his deposit from the vendor or whether the vendor was entitled to keep it. The true nature of such a deposit came up for consideration: was it a part-payment only or was it something else?

All three Lord Justices referred to earlier cases. They referred on the one hand to *Palmer v. Temple*[29] in which it was held that the vendor could not retain the penalty and have damages, because the penalty was a part payment, not an earnest to be forfeited; and thus held the deposit on trust to return it to the purchaser when it was clear the contract was at an end;[30] *Ockenden v. Henly*,[31] and *Hinton v. Sparkes*[32]. On the other hand, they also noted Lord St Leonards in *Sugden on Vendors and Purchasers*[33] who thought that to allow the purchaser to receive back the deposit would be to allow him to take advantage of his own wrong; *Collins v. Stimson*[34] which had held that the deposit was paid as a guarantee for the performance of the contract, and that where the contract goes off by default of the purchaser the vendor *is* entitled to retain it; and *Depree v. Bedborough*[35] together with *Ex p Barrell*[36] to similar effect.

Cotton L.J. declined to lay down any general rule that in all cases where the court would refuse the purchaser specific performance the vendor would be allowed to retain his deposit, but considered that *this* vendor could keep the deposit at all events since he had "so acted as to repudiate on his part the contract, and he cannot in those circumstances take advantage of his own default . . ."

Bowen L.J. thought that the word "deposit" meant "according to the ordinary interpretation of business men, a security for the completion of the pur-

[29] 9 Ad. & E. 508; 112 E.R. 1304.
[30] Cotton L.J. distinguished this case on the wording of the provision.
[31] Para. 14.49 above.
[32] Para. 14.52 above.
[33] (14th ed.) p. 40.
[34] 11 Q.B.D. 142.
[35] Para. 14.51 above.
[36] Para. 14.57 above.

chase. He thought that: "it is obvious that the party may lose his right to insist on specific performance before an equitable tribunal, without at the same time having necessarily so acted as to justify the other side in saying the contract is altogether at an end. As I understand, speaking with a due consciousness of my own ignorance on the point, all that a Court of Equity does when it refuses specific performance on the ground of lapse of time is to leave the parties to their remedy at law. It refuses it because it would be unfair that the relief should be given. It does not follow as a matter of law on principle that because specific performance is refused therefore the whole contract is at an end in law. We have to look to the conduct of the parties and to the contract itself, and, putting the two things together, to see whether the purchaser has acted not merely so as to break his contract, but to entitle the other side to say he has repudiated and no longer stands by it."

14.63 Fry L.J. said "Money paid as a deposit must, I conceive, be paid on some terms implied or expressed. In this case no terms are expressed, and we must therefore inquire what terms are to be implied. The terms most naturally to be implied appear to me in the case of money paid on the signing of a contract to be that in the event of the contract being performed it shall be brought into account, but if the contract is not performed by the payer it shall remain the property of the payee. It is not merely a part payment, but is then also an earnest to bind the bargain so entered into, and creates by the fear of its forfeiture a motive in the payer to perform the rest of the contract.

The practice of giving something to signify the conclusion of the contract, sometimes a sum of money, sometimes a ring or other object, to be repaid or redelivered on the completion of the contract, appears to be one of great antiquity and very general prevalence . . .[37]

Note: See the text at para. 14.18 above for comment.

***Lord Elphinstone v. Monkland Iron & Coal Co.* (1886) 11 App. Cas. 332**

14.64 This was a Scottish case, but conducted on the footing that the applicable law was the same in Scotland as in England. The provision in question was a covenant by the lessees of land (who had permission to place slag from their blast furnaces on the land but to restore the land afterwards) to pay the lessor £100 per imperial acre for all land *not* restored by a certain date. This was held to be liquidated damages.

Lord Herschell L.C. said[38]: "The agreement does not provide for payment of a lump sum upon the non-performance of any one of many obligations differing in importance. It has reference to a single obligation, and the sum to be paid bears a strict proportion to the extent to which that obligation is left unfulfilled. There is nothing whatever to shew that the compensation is *inordinate or extravagant in relation to the damage sustained*, and provision is made that the payment is to bear interest from the date when the obligation is unfulfilled. I know of no authority for holding that a payment agreed to be made under such conditions as these is to be regarded as a penalty only; and I see no sound reason or principle or even convenience for so holding . . ."

Lord Fitzgerald[39] said: "We may take it, then, that by the law of Scotland the parties to any contract may fix the damages to result from a breach at a sum estimated as liquidated damages or they may *enforce the performance of*

[37] He went on to note that if the vendor had chosen to resell and sue the purchaser for the deficiency, he would have had to bring the deposit into account: ***Ockenden v. Henly*** E.B & E. 485.

[38] This was also quoted in ***Law v. Redditch Local Board***

[39] At 346.

the stipulations of the agreement by a penalty. He went on "In the first instance the pursuer is, in case of a breach, entitled to recover the estimated sum as pactional damages irrespective of the actual loss sustained. In the other, the penalty is to cover all damages actually sustained, but it does not estimate them, and the amount of loss (not, however exceeding the penalty) is to be ascertained in the ordinary way. *In determining the character of these stipulations we endeavour to ascertain what the parties* ***must reasonably be presumed to have intended,*** *having regard to the subject-matter, and certain rules have been laid down as judicial aids.*"[40]

***Law v. Redditch Local Board* [1892] 1 Q.B. 127**

14.65 This was a contract for the construction of sewerage works, the contractor to pay £100 if the work was not done by a specified date, and £5 for every seven days during which they should not be complete. This was held not to be a penalty. The case is chiefly of interest for its reference to the early historical development of the doctrine, in the judgment of Kay L.J.

"In early times it was decided by Courts of Equity that, where a sum of money was agreed to be paid as a penalty for non-performance of a collateral contract, equity would not allow the whole sum to be recovered; but, where the damages for non-performance of such contract could be estimated, would cut down the penalty to the amount of the actual damages sustained. One of the earliest cases on the subject is *Peachy v. Duke of Somerset*[41] . . ., where Lord Macclesfield says, that "the true ground of relief against penalties is from the original intent of the case, where the penalty is designed only to secure money and the Court gives him all that he expected or desired". The doctrine so stated was afterwards modified and extended to other cases than the security of money by Lord Thurlow in *Sloman v. Walker*[42] . . ., where he says: "The rule that, where a penalty is inserted merely to secure the enjoyment of a collateral object, the enjoyment of the object is considered as the principal intent of the deed, and the penalty only as accessional, and therefore only to secure the damage really incurred, is too strongly established in equity to be shaken." Kay L.J. then referred to the increasing use thereafter of the words "as and for liquidated damages" in contracts, which Kay L.J. considered was merely to avoid the *interference* of Courts of Equity.[43]

14.66 "But then the Courts of Law *interfered*, and, as it seems to me, went further than Courts of Equity had done originally. They held that, though the parties had expressly said that the sum agreed to be paid was liquidated damages and not a penalty, they would construe the agreement as meaning that it should be a penalty . . ." He referred *inter alia* to *Kemble v. Farren,*[44] and *Wallis v. Smith,*[45] commenting that "It was no doubt a *very serious interference* with the terms of a contract to say that, though the parties had expressly stipulated that a sum was to be paid as liquidated damages, the Court would not allow the words to have their ordinary effect, but would treat the sum as a penalty . . ."[46]

Note: One sees in the above judgment the kind of slightly worried re-assessment of the older doctrines which was going on at around this time: the curiously anxious

[40] Italics and bold type supplied.
[41] Above.
[42] 1 Bro. C.C. 418. para. 14.41 above.
[43] Kay L.J. seems here to overlook the jurisdiction given very early on to the common law courts to relieve against penalties by the statute of William III: see above!
[44] Para. 14.45 above.
[45] Para. 14.59 above.
[46] Italics supplied.

insistence on putting the doctrines into "equitable" and "common law" slots which we have seen elsewhere in this book. This division seems not to have troubled the early Equity and Common law courts specially: of course they had separate jurisdictions, and neither had a full choice of remedies; but where doctrines of good faith and construction of contracts were concerned, they seem to have operated on a principle of comity with each other, borrowing doctrines (as opposed to remedies) where it seemed a good idea. See for example in the judgment of Bramwell L.J. in Betts v. Burch[47] reference to the Common law courts' borrowing of the Equity Courts, approach to penalties.

The Common law courts not only had the statutory penalty jurisdiction as regards penalties, but freely used good faith principles in ascertaining the true content of contracts. Indeed, in the light of Lord Mansfield's contribution to good faith law it is doubtful that good-faith principles can really be labelled "equitable" except in the the broadest sense.

Willson v. Love [1896] 1 Q.B. 626 (C.A.)

14.67 A lease of a farm provided that all hay and straw in the last year of the lease was to be consumed on the premises and not sold, and on breach, an additional rent payable by way of penalty of £3 per ton of hay or straw so sold was to be paid. This *was* held a penalty, partly because the parties themselves used this expression in the lease. The fact that they had used it was however said not to be decisive, though not to be disregarded either. The other reason was that the damages for the use of hay and the use of straw differed a lot, while the penalty remained the same regardless. The Court of Appeal's judgments are not perhaps of great interest, save that the slight air of worry about the existence of this doctrine among the new literalist methods persists: why not give expression to "the parties' intention" in the words they have used, they wonder. (The thought that the words used, taken literally, may be a long way from expressing "the parties' intention" in many cases, is by now beginning to be a rare one.)

Clydebank Engineering and Shipbuilding Co v. Don Jose Ramos Yzquierdo y Castaneda [1905] A.C. 6 (H.L. (Sc.))

14.68 The Spanish Government contracted with Clydebank to build 4 torpedo boats, the penalty for late delivery being £500 per week per vessel. This was held not to be a penalty. Further, payment in full of the price by the buyer without reserving his position was held to be no waiver of his right to claim that it was a penalty.

Lord Halsbury expressed the question to be asked thus: "What is the agreement here? and whether this sum of money is one which can be recovered as an agreed sum as damages, or whether, as has been contended, it is simply a penalty to be held over the other party in terrorem—*whether it is, what I think gave the jurisdiction to the Courts in both countries to interfere at all in an agreement between the parties, unconscionable and extravagant, and one which no Court ought to allow to be enforced.*"[48] He said later—"The very reason why the parties do in fact agree to such a stipulation is that sometimes, although undoubtedly there is damage and undoubtedly damages ought to be recovered, the nature of the damage is such that proof of it is extremely complex, difficult, and expensive." He thought the case was just such an example—it

[47] Above, para. 14.50, but passage not quoted.
[48] Italics supplied.

would be impossible for the Spanish Government to tell how many miles of coastline it was hindered from defending, and so on, by the late-delivery.

14.69 Lord Davey put the established principle more conservatively, thus: "... if you find a sum of money made payable for the breach, not of an agreement generally which might result in either a trifling or a serious breach, but a breach of one particular stipulation in an agreement, and when you find that the sum payable is proportioned to the amount if I may so call it, or the rate of the non-performance of the agreement—for instance, if you find that it is so much per acre for ground which has been spoilt by mining operations, or if you find, as in the present case, that it is so much per week during the whole time for which the non-delivery of vessels beyond the contract time is delayed—then you infer that primâ facie the parties intended the amount to be liquidate damages and not penalty. I say "primâ facie" because *it is always open to the parties to shew that the amount named in the clause is so exorbitant and extravagant that it could not possibly have been regarded as damages for any possible breach which was in the contemplation of the parties, and that is a reason for holding it to be a penalty and not liquidate damages notwithstanding the considerations to which I have alluded.*

But, my Lords, in *Forrest & Barr v. Henderson & Co*,[49] the Lord President, (Lord Inglis) says this: "I hold it to be part of our law on this subject that, even where parties stipulate that a sum of this kind shall not be regarded as a penalty, but shall be taken as an estimate and ascertainment of the amount of damage to be sustained in a certain event, equity will interfere to prevent the claim being maintained to an exorbitant and unconscionable amount." My only criticism upon that sentence would be this—that I do not think that that is the right way of putting it. I think the fact of a claim being of an *exorbitant or of an unconsionable amount as compared with any possible damages that could have been within the contemplation of the parties, is a reason for holding it not to be liquidate damages but a penalty*. But that is only a difference of expression, and with the substance of the observation I entirely agree. But the Lord President adds this significant sentence: "But, of course, the question whether it is *exorbitant or unconscionable*[50] is to be considered with reference to the point of time at which the stipulation is made between the parties." That is to say, you are to consider whether it is extravagant, exorbitant, or unconscionable, whatever word you like to select, at the time when the stipulation is made—that is to say, in regard to any possible amount of damages or any kind of damage which may be conceived to have been within the contemplation of the parties when they made the contract." He went on to say that it would be irrelevant and inadmissible to try to prove the clause was extravagant by showing the damages actually suffered by the Spanish Government, that agreements for liquidated damages were entered into precisely in order to exclude that kind of evidence.

Lord Robertson considered that the question was whether the payment were stipulated *in terrorem*, or formed a genuine pre-estimate of the creditor's probable or possible interest in the due performance of the principal obligation. He thought that in one sense both liquidated damages and penalties were penal: both were what had been called "instruments of restraint"; but that a penal element did not in itself invalidate the stipulation. The question remained "Had the Respondents no interest to protect by that clause, or was that interest palpably incommensurate with the sums agreed on?"

Note: See the text at para. 14.06 above for comment. This case is an important watershed in the history of the penalty doctrine.

[49] 8 M. 187.
[50] Italics supplied.

***Diestal v. Stevenson* [1906] 2 K.B. 345**

14.70 This was a contract for the sale of "screened coal" and "small coal"; with a clause saying "Penalty for non-execution of this contract by either party one shilling per ton on the portion unexecuted, and the amount of proved loss, if any, on freight actually arranged by us."

Kennedy J. held that this was liquidated damages. He thought even though the damages might well prove different for the two different classes of coal, the case was to be distinguished from *Willson v. Love.*[50a] In that case the parties knew there was bound to be a difference: here the sum fluctuated, and the parties could not know as at the time of contracting whether the sum would be the same or different. Also Kennedy J. thought *Willson*[51] distinguishable because that had been a legal document, a lease drawn up by lawyers, and "there was consequently a presumption that the persons who drew it, when using the term "penalty" intended to use it in its strict legal sense"; while here the contract was in the parties' own words.

***Public Works Committee v. Hills* [1906] A.C. 368 (P.C.)**

14.71 A contract for the construction of a railway line contained a provision that if the line was not completed by a certain date the contractor should forfeit to the defendant Public Works Committee (a) certain percentages (which it retained out of monies payable under this and two other railway contracts) as a guarantee fund for defective work and (b) certain security money lodged with its Agent General "as and for liquidated damages . . ."; and that further the Public Works Committee should take possession of the incomplete line and pay the balance due in respect of its "actual cost" (which was construed by the court as the money actually expended on the line). This was held a penalty. It could not be a genuine preestimate of loss because the security sum was liable to fluctuate in amount and to do so depending on events not connected with the fulfilment of the contract.

***Pye v. British Automobile Commercial Syndicate* [1906] 1 K.B. 425 (Deposit case)**

14.72 The defendants appointed the plaintiff sole agent for the sale of their cars in a district in Yorkshire. The agent was to pay the manufacturers a deposit of £300, to be repaid upon payment of all the goods in the schedule to the greement. If the agent did not accept delivery of the goods, the deposit was to be forfeited as liquidated and ascertained damages. Held by Bigham J., without much very illuminating discussion, that the sum was not a penalty, (partly because of the fact that the deposit had been *paid*, arguing that the plaintiff did not expect to get it back if he committed a breach).

***Webster v. Bosanquet* [1912] A.C. 394 (P.C.)**

14.73 An agreement provided that the defendant might not sell any of certain tea crops without first offering the option of buying them to the plaintiff. On breach, he was to pay the sum of £500 as liquidated damages and not as a penalty. The Judicial Committee referred to the *Clydebank*[52] case, and said that whatever the label applied by the parties, the question must always be "whether the construction contended for renders the agreement *unconscionable*

[50a] Para. 14.67 above.
[51] *ibid.*
[52] Para.14.68, above.

and extravagant and one which no Court ought to allow to be enforced."[53] This was a reference in effect, to Lord Halsbury's approach in *Clydebank*,[54] while Lord Davey's more limited use of the words, simply as a factor which might be used as an aid to construction, althouth cited, was allowed to sink out of sight. As to the facts of the case, the Judicial Committee thought, impeccably no doubt, that the sale would seriously affect the plaintiff's business; while the very uncertainty of the loss likely to arise made it most reasonable for the parties to agree beforehand what the damages should be. Also, there would be difficulty of proof and the proof might entail considerable expense. Thus they thought this was not a penalty.

Note: This case has perhaps put the penalty doctrine back on course to some extent: the jurisdiction is once more seen as an exercise in construing the parties' probable intentions. We still have the new concept of "extravagant", but it is relegated to a more subordinate place as an aid to construction once again.

***John H Kilmer v. British Columbia Orchard Lands* [1913] A.C. 319 (Forfeiture of instalments paid)**

14.74 An agreement for sale of land in British Columbia provided for the price to be paid in instalments at specified dates, time to be of the essence, and if all instalments were not punctually paid, the agreement was to be at an end and all payments of past instalments were to be forfeited to the vendor.

The Judicial Committee of the Privy Council applied *Re Dagenham (Thames) Dock Co.*,[55] saying that the instant case was an even stronger one than that, because the penalty became more and more severe as the agreement reached completion and the money liable to confiscation became large.[56]

***Dunlop Pneumatic Tyre Co. v. New Garage & Motor Co.* [1915] A.C. 79**

14.75 This was a price maintenance agreement; with a payment of £5 per tyre as liquidated damages for the breach. Lord Dunedin provided a useful working analysis, presumably aimed at practitioners, of the more recent decisions on the topic. He thought the following propositions could be stated:[57]

1. Though the parties who use a label may prima facie be supposed to mean what they say, that is not conclusive. The Court looks to see whether in truth the payment is a penalty or liquidated damages;
2. The contrast is between a "payment of money stipulated as in terrorem of the offending party"; and "a genuine covenanted pre-estimate of damage": *Clydebank*[58]:
3. The question is a question of construction, to be decided upon the terms and inherent circumstances of each particular contract, *judged at the time of its making*, not the time of breach: *Public Works v. Hills*;[59] *Webster v. Bosanquet*;[60]
4. There were various tests to assist the construction, which may prove helpful, even conclusive:
   (a) It is a penalty if the sum stipulated for is "extravagant and unconscionable in amount in comparison with the greatest loss

[53] Italics supplied.
[54] *ibid.*
[55] Para. 14.55 above.
[56] See also *Ford Motor Co. v. Armstrong* (1915) 31 T.L.R. 267.
[57] The above is a summary and not a precise quotation from his judgment.
[58] Para. 14.68 above.
[59] Para. 14.71 above.
[60] Para. 14.73 above.

that could conceivably be proved to have followed from the breach: Lord Halsbury in *Clydebank*;[61]

(b) It is a penalty if the breach is not paying a sum of money, and the sum stipulated is a sum greater than the sum which ought to have been paid: *Kemble v. Farren*.[62]

(c) There is a presumption, but no more, that it is a penalty when it is a single lump sum payable on the occurrence of one or more of several events, some of which may occasion serious damage and others but trifling damage: Lord Watson in *Elphinstone v. Monkland Iron and Coal Co* (above)[63] but;

(d) It is no obstacle to the provision being a genuine pre-estimate of damage, that the consequences of the breach are such as to make precise pre-estimation almost an impossibility. On the contrary, that is just the situation when it is probable that pre-estimated damages were the true bargain between the parties: *Clydebank*,[64] *Webster v. Bosanquet*,[65] Lord Mersey. He thought here (as did the other members of the Court), that the damages were very difficult to estimate, so it would be "a bargain to assess damages" unless the figure was "extravagant". He thought it was not extravagant.

14.76 Lord Atkinson paid attention to the "object of the appellants [sic] in making this agreement"; and thought this was a single object, "to prevent the disorganisation of their trading system and the consequent injury to their trade in many directions." He pointed out that the loss to the appellant's trade could not be measured by the loss on the particular transaction.

Lord Parker of Waddington thought that the damage resulting from the breach of each stipulation was the same in *kind*; and should thus be distinguished from the case where the damage from the breaches was different in kind and could be broken in various ways and with varying amounts of damage. In the latter case, you would prima facie need a separate pre-estimate for each type of breach; and if you had just the one, it was likely to be a penalty.

Lord Parmoor said: . . . "It is too late to question whether such *interference with the language of a contract* can be justified on any rational principle." . . . "No abstract rule can be laid down without reference to the special facts of the particular case, but when competent parties by free contract are purporting to agree a sum as liquidated damages there is no reason for *refusing a wide limit of discretion*."[66]

***Steedman v. Drinkle* [1916] 1 A.C. 275 (P.C.) (Deposit case)**

14.77 Some land in Saskatchewan was sold for 16,000 dollars, 1,000 to be paid on signing of the agreement, and the balance by six annual instalments; and if the purchaser made default in any of the payments, the vendor might cancel the agreement and retain all payments made as liquidated damages. Time was to be of the essence of the agreement. The first payment was tendered 21 days late: the vendor refused to accept it; the purchasers brought an action for specific performance of the agreement or in the alternative for relief from forfeiture. The Judicial Committee held, without discussion of principle, that although the purchaser could not have specific performance, time having been

[61] Para. 14.68 above.
[62] Para. 14.45 above.
[63] Para. 14.64 above.
[64] Para. 14.68 above.
[65] Para. 14.73 above.
[66] Italics supplied. See as to "interference", the note at para. 14.61 above.

of the essence, the provision whereby the vendor might keep the money paid was a penalty, and the purchaser might be relieved against it.[67]

***Cellulose Acetate Silk Co. v. Widnes Foundry* [1933] A.C. 20**

14.78 The contract was for the delivery and erection of an acetone recovery plant. If it was not completed within a certain time, the contractors were to pay £20 per week for each week that they were in default. The actual loss was more; but the court held it was a genuine pre-estimate of damages. A clause elsewhere in the contract said "we will use our best endeavours to keep to the dates given, but will accept no liability for failure to do so."

Lord Atkin thought that this was a sum agreed as compensation in place of the no-compensation-at-all which would otherwise have been the result. It must have been obvious to either party that the damage would be much more than £20 a week. The question whether in a suitable case a plaintiff could ignore the penalty clause altogether and sue for actual damages was left open.

***Mussen v. Van Diemens Land Co* [1938] Ch. 253 (Forfeiture of instalments)**

14.79 The plaintiff agreed to buy land in Tasmania, the purchase money to be paid in instalments on certain dates, time to be of the essence. There was a provision that if the plaintiff failed to pay the instalments by the due dates the defendants could rescind the contract and keep any money paid up to that stage. The plaintiff defaulted at a time when he had received two blocks out of the land, but had paid by way of instalments some £42,000 more than their price.

Farwell J. said he could see no ground on which he could "interfere". There was nothing "unconscionable" about what the defendants sought to do, and strictly the case was not one of a penalty at all since "the payment in question was an integral part of the principal contract". He sought to distinguish *Steedman v. Drinkle*[68] on the grounds that in that case the buyer was seeking specific performance, and only seeking to be able to pay late; thus (he thought) rendering it unconscionable for the buyer to say "We will not complete, but we will retain the money". Here, on the other hand, the plaintiff had not sought specific performance, and had brought the case after the lapse of some years without any attempt to complete the contract.

Note: The case is interesting as an example of the attempt to apply the new "unconscionable" test. It is difficult to see why reliance on one's contractual rights (which is what Farwell J. thought they were) could ever be unconscionable, whatever relief the buyer was seeking. Nor is it easy to see quite why it should matter so much whether the buyer was seeking specific performance or not. Another problem is that "unconscionable" is here being judged as at the date relief is sought, while the cases on penalties are clear that the penalty v. damages question has to be answered as at the date of the contract. We may infer that the perhaps unconsidered use by Lord Halsbury of the word "unconscionable", with its train of equitable or pseudo-equitable baggage, has caused a lot of unnecessary confusion. He had been referring to "unconscionable and extravagant agreements: while "unconscionable conduct", specially in specific performance cases, is judged as at the date of the hearing; and it is probable that an equity judge, conscientiously trying to apply the new wording, would naturally make something of a mess of the exercise, as, with the greatest respect, one may think Farwell J. did here.

[67] See also *Cameron-Head v. Cameron & Co.* 1919 S.C. 627.
[68] Para. 14.77 above.

***Stockloser v. Johnson* [1954] 1 Q.B. 476**

14.80 The purchaser agreed to buy quarrying plant and machinery by instalments, on terms that if he defaulted in the instalments for more than 28 days, the vendor might rescind, forfeit the instalments already paid, and retake the plant and machinery. The purchaser made default, the vendor rescinded, took back the plant and machinery, and bought a lease of a quarry where they had previously been used. The purchaser could not or would not complete, but sought the return of the instalments on the ground that the forfeiture clause was "penal and unconscionable".

Somervell L.J. referred to the decision of the judge below, which had included the proposition that there were *two* conditions which had to be satisfied: "First, the effect of the clause must be penal, applying the principles laid down in *Dunlop's*[69] case. Secondly, the court must be satisfied that, in the circumstances of that particular case, that is, looking not merely at the contract, but *at the circumstances at the time of the breach*,[70] it would be inequitable or unconscionable to allow the recipient to retain the money notwithstanding the power to do so contained in the clause . . ." He, for his part, thought the jurisdiction was not limited (as Romer L.J. thought). "My brother Romer comes to the conclusion that after rescission by the vendor relief would only be given if there were some special circumstance, such a fraud, sharp practice, or other unconscionable conduct, and that before rescission a buyer would only get relief if willing and able to complete. In other words, the only relief would be further time. I think that the statements of the law in the cases to which I will refer indicate a wider jurisdiction. I think that they indicate that the court would have power to give relief against the enforcement of the forfeiture provisions, although there was no sharp practice by the vendor, and although the purchaser was not able to find the balance. It would, of course, have to be shown that the retention of the instalments was unconscionable, in all the circumstances." He pointed out that in *In Re Dagenham (Thames) Dock Co.*[71] the Court of Appeal had been assimilating the law on deposits with the law on penalties, so that it would not make much sense to link relief for the plaintiff to the plaintiff's readiness and willingness to complete. "It is a question of the effect of the clause and not of the defendant's conduct."

14.81 Denning L.J. thought that a "forfeiture clause" of this kind and a penalty clause were different, and different principles applied, though he did not really explain why he thought that. He seems to have assumed that a penalty clause involved "seeking to exact payment of an extravagant sum either by action at law or by appropriating to himself moneys belonging to the other party, as in *Commissioner of Public Works v. Hills*".[72] The rationale for the penalty jurisdiction was, he thought, because the courts will not assist the seller in "an act of oppression". Here, he thought: "the seller is not seeking to exact a penalty. He only wants to keep money which already belongs to him. The money was handed to him in part payment of the purchase price and, as soon as it was paid, it belonged to him absolutely. He did not obtain it by extortion or oppression or anything of that sort, and there is an express clause—a forfeiture clause, if you please—permitting him to keep it. It is not the case of a seller seeking to enforce a penalty, but a buyer seeking restitution of money paid. If the buyer is to recover it, he must, I think, have recourse to somewhat different principles from those applicable to penalties, strictly so called. It is

[69] Para. 14.75 above.
[70] Italics supplied.
[71] Para. 14.55 above.
[72] Para. 14.71 above.

not a case of a seller seeking to enforce a penalty, but a buyer seeking restitution of money paid. If the buyer is to recover it, he must, I think, have recourse to somewhat different principles from those applicable to penalties, strictly so called."

He also disagreed with Farwell J. who had sought to confine the jurisdiction to cases where the plaintiff sought time to complete. He thought the buyer's only remedy was in equity: ". . . despite the express stipulation in the contract, equity can relieve the buyer from forfeiture of the money and order the seller to repay it on such terms as the court thinks fit."

14.82 "The difficulty", he went on poignantly, "is to know what are the circumstances which give rise to this equity . . ." He then nonetheless (perhaps in desperation) agreed with Somervell L.J. as to these, presumably for Somervell L.J.'s reasons, and endorsed the proposition that two conditions were necessary: "first, the forfeiture clause must be of a penal nature, in this sense, that the sum forfeited must be out of all proportion to the damage, and second, it must be unconscionable for the seller to retain the money". He felt there was a need for the equitable jurisdiction he postulated, giving two examples. The second of these was

". . . suppose that a vendor of property, in lieu of the usual 10 per cent. deposit, stipulates for an initial payment of 50 per cent. of the price as a deposit and a part payment; and later, when the purchaser fails to complete, the vendor resells the property at a profit and in addition claims to forfeit the 50 per cent. deposit. Surely the court will relieve against the forfeiture. The vendor cannot forestall this equity by describing an extravagant sum as a deposit, any more than he can recover a penalty by calling it liquidated damages."

He described the "equity" as an equity of restitution, to avoid unjust enrichment. It was to be tested "not at the time of the contract, but by the conditions existing when it is invoked." He thought here the buyer could not show such an equity.

Romer L.J. agreed with the judgment of Farwell J. in *Mussen's*[73] case and did not agree with the other two Lord Justices that there was any equity which arose in favour of a purchaser who had paid sums under the contract and in part payment of the purchase money.

Note: See the text at paragraph 14.21 above. It can safely be said that the law on forfeiture of deposits is by this time in an extremely confused state.

***Alder v. Moore* [1961] 2 Q.B. 57**

14.83 A footballer had an insurance policy in which he declared "In consideration of the above payment I hereby declare and agree that I will take no part as a playing member of any form of professional football in the future and that in the event of infringement of this condition I will be subject to a penalty of the amount stated above." Insurance underwriters who had paid out to a disabled footballer obtained a declaration from him that if he played football again he would refund them the £500 paid.

Sellers L.J. thought the provision in question was not properly to be classified as a genuine pre-estimate of damages, but simply, as in *In Re Apex Supply Co. Ltd*[74] an agreement to pay a certain sum of money in a certain event. There was, he thought, nothing unjust or unconscionable about it. Slade J. agreed, but Devlin L.J. could not see why it was not a penalty.

[73] Para. 14.79 above.
[74] [1942] Ch. 108.

Note: The case seems puzzlingly un-illuminating. Perhaps the problem may be that the exercise of choice between damages and a penalty strikes one as inapposite when clearly the insurers had suffered no loss by reason of the breach. If no damage has been suffered it is difficult to see how the whole question of genuine preestimate, etc., can properly be considered. See Lord Mansfield's case, Lowe v. Peers[75] *which excludes pure payments on a contingency from the operation of the penalty rule. This may be the more appropriate way to tackle the footballer's problem.*

***Bridge v. Campbell Discount Co* [1962] A.C. 600**

14.84 This was a hire purchase agreement which provided that on any failure to pay instalments, the hirer was to pay a sum equal to two-thirds of the hire purchase price. The perceptive quotation from Lord Radcliffe which appears at the beginning of this chapter comes from this case.

Lord Denning's speech takes a historical approach, pointing out that the cases in which mortgagors were relieved by equity were often cases where there was no covenant by the obligor to perform the condition, no covenant on which he could be sued at law, simply a bond that if he did not perform the condition, he would pay the specified sum.[76] Thus, the courts would restrain the obligee from suing at law on the bond so long as the obligor was ready to pay him the damage he had really sustained. Similarly, even if the sum had already been paid over in the shape of a deposit to secure performance, equity would be prepared to grant restitution if it was a penal sum.[77]

Lord Devlin said that *he* thought the jurisdiction in penalty cases was because the court had always gone behind shams to get at the reality. "That indeed, is what the court is doing when it declares that what is expressed as an agreement about liquidated damages is not a genuine agreement but cloaks the imposition of a penalty."

Note: It can be problematic when judges adopt a historical approach as part of their judgments without a full note of their research and their sources. We are all used to simply accepting judgments as "the law": we inadvertently make the transition to accepting the historical part of their judgments as legal history. This may be imprudent, as can be seen from some of the late nineteenth century cases noted in this book.

What Lord Denning says above is probably true, but it is not specially helpful: where we have needed enlightenment is about the basic nature of the principle underlying the penalty rule; and he does not touch on that difficult point. As for Lord Devlin—the "sham" approach does not appear in the cases on "penal" clauses, or as they should perhaps better be called, "security"-provisions or "comfort" provisions.

***Shiloh Spinners v. Harding* [1973] A.C. 691**

14.85 This case concerned the nature of a landlord's right of re-entry for breach of covenant not being a covenant to pay rent. The House of Lords held that there might be an equitable right of re-entry and that relief from forfeiture might be granted in such a case, but would not be granted to the tenant on the facts before the court.

Lord Wilberforce's *obiter* statement of the power, which he considered to be a power of the courts of equity, has been influential. He said[78]: ". . . it remains true today that equity expects men to carry out their bargains and

[75] Para. 14.34 above.
[76] He refers to the very learned note by Mr Evans in his appendix to *Pothier on Obligations* (1806) at 92.
[77] He referred to ***Benson v. Gibson*** para. 14.38 above per Lord Hardwicke, ***Steedman v. Drinkle***, para. 14.77 above per Viscount Haldane.
[78] At 723.

will not let them buy their way out by uncovenanted payment. But it is consistent with these principles that we should reaffirm the right of courts of equity *in appropriate and limited cases* to relieve against forfeiture for breach of covenant or condition *where the primary object of the bargain is to secure a stated result which can effectively be attained when the matter comes before the court, and where the forfeiture provision is added by way of security for the production of that result.*[79] The word "appropriate" involves consideration of the conduct of the applicant for relief, in particular whether his default was wilful, of the gravity of the breaches, and of the disparity between the value of the property of which forfeiture is claimed as compared with the damage caused by the breach."

***Starside Properties v. Mustapha* [1974] 1 W.L.R. (*Deposit (instalment purchase) case*)**

14.86 The Court of Appeal allowed relief from forfeiture of all rights and of all instalments paid under an instalment-purchase, when the payer was in arrears with her payments. They allowed her an extension of time to pay, having regard to (*inter alia*) *Re Dagenham (Thames) Dock Co.*[80]

***Legione v. Hateley* (1983) 46 A.L.R. 1 (Australia)**

14.86 Mr and Mrs Legione were purchasers of land in which time was expressly made of the essence. A notice to complete was served threatening them with rescission if they did not complete by 10 August 10, 1978. On August 9 Mr and Mrs Legione's solicitor told an employee of the vendors' solicitor that his clients would be ready to settle on August 17 and the employee said "I think that'll be all right but I'll have to get instructions." On August 17 the vendors claimed the contract was rescinded on August 10.

(1) Gibbs C.J. and Murphy J. followed Lord Wilberforce in *Shiloh Spinners v. Harding*[81] and the Privy Council in *Kilmer v. British Columbia Orchard* Lands Ltd,[82] holding also that "except in the sense that a provision for forfeiture can be described as a penalty it is unnecessary that the condition which provides for forfeiture should be a penal one before the jurisdiction of equity can be invoked. They pointed out that no additional penal element was required in the case of relief from forfeiture for non-payment of rent under a lease.

(2) They rejected the decisions of *Steedman v. Drinkle*,[83] followed in *Brickles v. Snell*,[84] which had held that relief might not be given for breach of a time provision which had been of the essence; preferring the earlier Privy Council decision in *Kilmer v. British Columbia Orchard Lands Ltd*[85] and the Court of Appeal decision in *Re Dagenham (Thames) Dock Co.*[86] The Privy council in the first two cases had sought to distinguish *Kilmer's* case as a case in which the vendor had waived the provision for time to be of the essence, but this supposed distinction was doubted.

[79] Italics supplied.
[80] Para. 14.55 above.
[81] Para. 14.85 above.
[82] Para. 14.74 above.
[83] Para. 14.77 above.
[84] [1916] 2 A.C. 599.
[85] Above.
[86] Above.

(3) They also considered that *Re Dagenham (Thames) Dock Co.*[87] (and hence probably also *Kilmer's*[88] case) had probably proceeded on the basis that relief should be given not against the forfeiture of the instalments, but primarily against the forfeiture of the estate, the forfeiture of the instalments being a part of that, under the contract.

(4) Relief would only be given as a preliminary to specific performance in exceptional cases, but there was no reason in principle why it should not be granted.

14.87 Mason and Deane J.J. (1) agreed on the rejection of Kilmer's[89] case: and (2) considered that there *was* a distinction to be drawn between relief against forfeiture and relief against penalties. "A penalty, as its name suggests, is in the nature of a punishment for non-observance of a contractual stipulation; it consists of the imposition of an additional or different liability upon breach of the contractual stipulation . . . On the other hand, forfeiture involves the loss or determination of an estate or interest in property or a proprietary right, eg a lease, in consequence of a failure to perform a covenant. When non-payment of rent or a fine is made the occasion for forfeiture of an estate or interest in property it may be proper to treat the forfeiture as being similar in character to a penalty because it is designed to ensure payment of the rent or fine. There is, however, a real distinction between 'penalty' and 'forfeiture' . . .". They thought that the case before them involved a forfeiture under the general law rather than anything in the nature of a security-provision.[90] In such a case, the jurisdiction was founded on unconscionable conduct by the party opposing relief.

(3) There was a lot to be said for the view that purchaser had a sufficient proprietary interest, because her equitable interest was "commensurate, not with her ability to obtain specific performance in the strict or primary sense, but with her ability to protect her interest under the contract by injunction or otherwise. Thus, her equitable interest would depend on whether or not she could make out a case for relief from forfeiture. However, they did not decide the point, but held instead that the exercise of the jurisdiction to relieve should be extended to cases of the kind before them, where a purchaser's interest under a contract has come to an end because he has been in breach of an essential term.

(4) Should specific performance be granted of the contract as relieved against? They considered that the reason for the strict attitude in *Kilmer's*[91] case and in *Brickles v. Snell*[92] was because "in the early part of this century, overriding importance attached to the concept of freedom of contract and to the need to hold parties to their bargains." They went on: "These considerations, though still important, should not be allowed to override competing claims based on long standing heads of justice and equity." Relief would be granted in exceptional circumstances. This would hinge on the existence of unconscionable conduct. Unconscionable conduct meant unconscionable conduct on the part of a vendor. This question required the case to be remitted to the court below.

Brennan J. dissented.

***Scandinavian Trading Tanker Co v. Flota Petrolera Ecuadoriana (The Scaptrade)* [1983] 2 A.C. 694**

14.88 See the text at paragraph 14.27 above for brief comment.

[87] *ibid.*
[88] Para. 14.74 above.
[89] *ibid.*
[90] Such as ***Steedman v. Drinkle*** and *Brickles v. Snell.*
[91] Para. 14.74 above.
[92] [1916] 2 A.C. 599.

***Sport International Bussum BV v. Inter-Footwear Ltd* [1984] 1 W.L.R. 776**

14.89 In this case the House of Lords again confined the jurisdiction to grant relief against forfeiture to contracts concerning the transfer of proprietary or possessory rights.

***BICC v. Burndy Corporation* [1985] Ch. 232**

14.90 Two companies entered into a number of agreements, including an agreement for the distribution of certain intellectual property rights and responsibilities which the companies had previously held jointly. The plaintiffs were to be responsible for processing and maintaining these joint rights, while the first defendants were to reimburse the plaintiffs, upon request, half of any expenses incurred in so doing. There was a provision that in the event of default by either party the innocent party was to be entitled to require the other to assign to them all their interests in the joint rights concerned. The defendants defaulted, failing to reimburse the plaintiffs within the time limit, and the plaintiffs claimed to be entitled to specific performance of the agreement to assign the first defendants' intellectual property rights.

On appeal, all three members of the court agreed that although the clause in question was not a penalty clause, it was a forfeiture clause, and relief could be given against forfeiture. Dillon L.J. dealt fully with the point. He referred to earlier cases as follows: "In *Shiloh Spinners Ltd v. Harding*,[93] the House of Lords held that the court had jurisdiction to grant relief against forfeiture of proprietary rights in circumstances outside the ordinary landlord and tenant relationship; but the case was concerned with a claim for relief against a right of re-entry on land, and the speeches do not cast light on the extent to which jurisdiction exists to grant relief against forfeiture of property other than an interest in land. In *Barton Thompson & Co Ltd v. Stapling Machines Co*,[94] Pennycuick J. considered it to be arguable that relief could be granted against forfeiture of a lease of chattels. That view seems to have been approved by Edmund Davies L.J. in *Starside Properties Ltd v. Mustapha*[95]; and in *Stockloser v. Johnson*,[96] Romer L.J. apparently considered that the court would have power in an appropriate case to grant relief by way of extension of time to a purchaser of a diamond necklace who had failed to pay the final instalment of the price in due time.

There is no clear authority, but for my part I find it difficult to see why the jurisdiction of equity to grant relief against forfeiture should only be available where what is liable to forfeiture is an interest in land and not an interest in personal property. Relief is only available where what is in question is forfeiture of proprietary or possessory rights, but I see no reason in principle for drawing a distinction as to the type of property in which the rights subsist. The fact that the right to forfeiture arises under a commercial agreement is highly relevant to the question whether relief against forfeiture should be granted, but I do not see that it can preclude the existence of the jurisdiction to grant relief, if forfeiture of proprietary or possessory rights, as opposed to merely contractual rights, is in question. I hold, therefore, that the court has jurisdiction to grant Burndy relief."

Note: See the text at paragraph 14.27 above

[93] [1973] A.C. 691 (para. 14.85 above).
[94] [1966] Ch. 499 at 509.
[95] [1974] 1 W.L.R. 816 at 822 (para.14.86 above).
[96] [1954] 1 Q.B. 476 at 502 (para. 14.80 above).

***Lombard North Central v. Butterworth* [1987] Q.B. 527**

14.91 This was a hire purchase case in which a way, in effect, of evading the law on penalties was permitted by the Court of Appeal. It was a hire purchase of a computer, in which on repossession the plaintiff hirers became entitled not only to their damages at that date, but to all further rentals which would have fallen due, and to damages. This was declared to be a penalty. However, this did not assist the defendant since the agreement had been drafted so as to make the time for payment of instalments on time of the essence. Thus, the non-payment on time was rendered a repudiatory breach, and the plaintiff became entitled to damages for loss of the whole transaction, so allowing the plaintiff to obtain its future instalments by another route. *Steedman v. Drinkle*[97] in which relief from forfeiture was granted even though there was a provision that time should be of the essence, expressly on the ground that the forfeiture provision amounted to a penalty, was discussed, but the curious conclusion drawn from the refusal in that case of *specific performance* (as opposed to relief from forfeiture which was granted) to the late payer that: "a clause making time of the essence, and hence making prompt performance a condition, is not to be struck down merely because a breach of the obligation is not sufficient on its own to constitute a repudiation."[98]

***Jobson v. Johnson* [1989] 1 W.L.R. 1026**

14.92 In this case some at least of the Court of Appeal may be seen to have taken a tentative step towards a unified jurisdiction in forfeiture/penalty cases. The agreement for purchase of the shares in a football club contained a provision for re-transfer of the property at a fixed price on default in paying instalments of the price. It had been argued that the provision was a penalty clause and therefore unenforceable. The Court of Appeal granted relief from forfeiture, stating that the clause was not blue-pencilled, but "will not be enforced by the court beyond the sum which represents, in the events which have happened, the actual loss of the party seeking payment . . ."[99]. However, they differed in their general approach to a unified system.

Dillon L.J. could see no real reason why the courts' penalty jurisdiction and its jurisdiction to grant relief from forfeiture should be different, and referred to *Re Dagenham (Thames) Dock Co.*,[1] which he equated with penalty cases, and *Public Works Commissioners v. Hills*.[2]

Nicholls L.J. considered there was a distinction between penalties and relief from forfeiture. "A penalty clause will not be enforced beyond the sum which equals the actual loss of the innocent party. A forfeiture clause, of which a right of re-entry under a lease on non-payment of rent is the classic example, may also be penal in its effect. Such a clause frequently subjects the defaulting party, in the event of non-payment of rent or breach of some other obligation, to a sanction which damnifies the defaulting party, and benefits the other party, to an extent far greater than the actual loss of the innocent party. For instance, the lease may be exceedingly valuable and the amount of unpaid rent may be small. But in such a case the court will lend its aid in the enforcement of the forfeiture, by making an order for possession, subject to any relief which in its discretion the court may grant to the party in default." . . .

14.93 "This is not the occasion to attempt to rationalise the distinction. One pos-

[97] Para. 14.77 above.
[98] (See Mustill L.J.'s judgment.)
[99] Nicholls L.J. at 1040.
[1] Para. 14.55 above.
[2] Para. 14.71 above.

sible explanation is that the disctinction is rooted in the different forms which the relief takes. In the case of a penalty clause in a contract equity relieves by cutting down the extent to which the contractual obligation is enforceable: the 'scaling down' exercise, as I have described it. In the case of forfeiture clauses equitable relief takes the form of relieving wholly against the contractual forfeiture provision, subject to compliance with conditions imposed by the court. Be that as it may, I see no reason why the court's ability to grant discretionary relief automatically granted [sic] in respect of a penalty clause if, exceptionally, a contractual provision has characteristics which enable a defendant to pray in aid both heads of relief."

Kerr L.J. for his part thought, unlike the two equity Lord Justices, that the clause was "penal in its nature" by which he apparently meant, a penalty clause; and that "the combined effect of law and equity[3] is simply that they will not be enforced in favour of a plaintiff without first giving to the defendant a proper opportunity to obtain relief against their penal consequences." Thus, the clause was not "*necessarily* unenforceable".

***Stern v. McArthur* (1988) 81 A.C.R. 463 (Australia)**

14.94 The purchasers had taken possession of some land and built a house on it, under an instalment-purchase contract whereby they paid monthly instalments of not less than $50. After keeping up the payments for eight years they defaulted for eleven months, giving rise to the right in the vendors to demand payment of the whole of the remaining purchase price, which they did. When the purchasers proved unable to pay this, the vendors claimed to rescind the entire contract. The purchasers sought relief from forfeiture and specific performance of the contract subject to relief. What follows is an all-too-brief summary of the interesting and thoughtful judgments of the High Court of Australia. The judgments would advantageously be read in full.

The relief sought was granted by a majority of the High Court. Dean and Dawson J.J. held (first) that notwithstanding the valid exercise by the vendors of a contractual power of rescission, the purchasers retained a sufficient equitable interest or "estate" for the purposes of the relief sought. The expression "equitable interest" in so far as it applies to the purchaser under a contract of sale of land merely described the rights of the purchaser which equity would enforce; and (secondly) that the fact that time was of the essence of the payment (as in *Kilmer v. British Columbia Orchard Lands Ltd*[4] or had been validly made of the essence, as here, and that the party seeking relief was in breach of the time-provision, did not preclude the exercise of the jurisdiction to relieve from forfeiture. It had to be accepted that the law of Australia was developing along divergent lines from that of England.[5]

14.95 Thirdly *Legione v. Hateley*[6] was considered. There was said to be no difference in that case between the approaches of the two sets of majority judgments as to the treatment of the requirement that the conduct of the party opposing relief from forfeiture be "unconscionable". There did not have to be unconscionable conduct of "an exceptional kind". "Rather, what was being said was that a court will be reluctant to interfere with the contractual rights of parties who have chosen to make time of the essence of the contract. The circumstances must be such as to make it plain that it is necessary to intervene

[3] He did not explain how this combined effect came about.
[4] [1913] A.C. 319.
[5] See *Scandinavian Trading Tanker Co v. Flota Petrolera Ecuadoriana* [1983] 2 A.C. 694 and *Sport International Bussum BV v. Inter-Footwear Ltd* [1984] 1 WLR 776.
[6] (1983) 152 C.L.R. 406, para. 14.86 above.

to avoid injustice or, what is the same thing, to relieve against unconscionable—or more accurately—unconscientious—conduct."

Fourthly it was important that the forfeiture provision in the case before them was essentially by way of security for the payment of purchase moneys—a close parallel with a purchase with the aid of a mortgage. The purchasers had a reasonable expectation of benefit from any increase in the value of land with the passage of time. The vendors would gain a windfall.

Gaudron J. was in broad agreement with the first point above, considering that what mattered for present purposes was the availability of specific performance as a remedy notwithstanding rescission.

On the second point (in the Dean/Dawson judgements), what had been forfeited was not the legal interest but the equitable interest only and as the third, was it necessary to show that there was something unconscionable about the quality of the vendor's action or was it sufficient merely to "adopt the approach (of Gibbs C.J. and Murphy I in *Legione* [above]) which assimilates the consequences of that conduct to a penalty." Different approaches had been taken to this by the two sets of majority judgments in *Legione v. Hateley*.[7] He proceeded on the basis laid down in that case, however, that a contractual provision of the kind before them providing for rescission and forfeiture is neither "a penalty nor in the nature of a penalty." He referred to Lord Wilberforce's judgment in *Shiloh Spinners v. Harding*[8] and pointed out that Lord Wilberforce did not suggest that the availability of relief was there conditional upon unconscionable conduct on the part of the person against whom relief is sought, and accordingly held that in the case before him there was sufficient unconscionability in the vendors insisting on their strict legal rights.

14.96 Mason C.J. in his dissenting judgment took the opposite view on unconscionability: he considered that to show the necessary "exceptional circumstances" to justify relief, the purchaser had to show "conduct amounting to unconscionable conduct on the part of the vendor" which there was not here. He pointed out that to hold otherwise would be "to eviscerate unconscionability of its meaning."

Brennan J. took a similar view of what unconscionable conduct required. He also considered that the forfeiture under a power in the contract for non-payment of the whole of the balance of the purchase price could not be classified as a security-provision, but a "general law right to rescind", so did not come within any of the heads of jurisdiction referred to by Lord Wilberforce in *Shiloh Spinners v. Harding*.[9]

Workers' Trust & Merchant Bank Ltd v. Dojap Investments Ltd [1993] A.C. 573 (Deposit case)

14.97 Lord Browne-Wilkinson, giving the judgment of the Privy Council, mentioned that the payment of a deposit by the purchaser of land is an exception to the rule regarding penalties. "Ancient law has established that the forfeiture of such a deposit (customarily 10% of the contract price) does not fall within the general rule and can be validly forfeited even though the amount of the deposit bears no reference to the anticipated loss to the vendor flowing from the breach of contract." He cited *Howe v. Smith*[10] and Fry L.J.'s reference to the "earnest" or "arra" of Roman law.[11]

[7] Above, para. 14.86.
[8] Para. 14.85 above.
[9] *ibid.*
[10] Para. 14.62 above.
[11] Possibly it was the "arra" which Lord Browne-Wilkinson meant by "ancient law": it is not quite clear just how ancient English law on deposits is.

He (and the court) however thought that there were exceptions which prevented the deposits being abused if they were in practice penalties. He relied on *obiter dicta* to the effect that a deposit must be "not extravagant" or "reasonable" respectively.

These were (1) of Lord Denning in *Stockloser v. Johnson*[12]: "Again, suppose that a vendor of property, in lieu of the usual 10 per cent. deposit, stipulates for an initial payment of 50 per cent. of the price as a deposit and part payment; and later, when the purchaser fails to complete, the vendor resells the property at a profit and in addition claims to forfeit the 50 per cent. deposit. Surely the court will relieve against the forfeiture. The vendor cannot forestall this equity by describing an extravagant sum as a deposit, any more than he can recover a penalty by calling it liquidated damages." and of Lord Hailsham in *Linggi Plantations Ltd v. Jagatheesan*[13]

14.98 (2) "It is also no doubt possible that in a particular contract the parties may use language normally appropriate to deposits properly so-called even to [sic] forfeiture which turn out on investigation to be purely colourable and that in such a case the real nature of the transaction might turn out to be the imposition of a penalty, by purporting to render forfeit something which is in truth part payment. This no doubt explains why in some cases the irrecoverable nature of a deposit is qualified by the insertion of the adjective "reasonable" before the noun. But the truth is that a reasonable deposit has always been regarded as a guarantee of performance as well as a payment on account, and its forfeiture had never been regarded as a penalty in English law or common English usage."

He said that in the view of their Lordships those passages accurately reflected the law. "It is not possible for the parties to attach the incidents of a deposit to the payment of a sum of money unless such sum is *reasonable as earnest money*. The question therefore is whether or not the deposit of 25 per cent. in this case was reasonable as being in line with the traditional concept of earnest money or was in truth a penalty intended to act in terrorem."

The House of Lords went on to consider whether the 25 per cent deposit was, in fact, reasonable viewed as earnest money. The judge in Jamaica had held that it was, because it was of common occurrence for banks selling property at auction to demand deposits of between 15 per cent and 50 per cent. The Judicial Committee did not accept this approach: Lord Browne-Wilkinson said: "In order to be reasonable a true deposit must be *objectively* operating as "earnest money" and not as a penalty. *To allow the test of reasonableness to depend upon the practice of one class of vendor, which exercises considerable financial muscle, would be to allow them to evade the law against penalties by adopting practices of their own.*"[14]

14.99 So far, so good, but how was the court to ascertain what was reasonable? Perhaps this was an unnecessary task—having decided the sum in question was unreasonable, they might have left matters there. However they did consider the question. Having rejected the custom of banks in Jamaica, they accepted the—undoubtedly much more universal and less one-sided—practice of conveyancers in the United Kingdom of paying 10 per cent deposits on the purchase of land as reasonable, and considered that any vendor seeking to forfeit a larger deposit would have to show "special circumstances which justify such a deposit". The payment of certain tax on the sale by the vendor had been urged as such special circumstances, but the court rejected this: (a) the tax was not due in this case until after completion and (b) no tax was payable when the sale went off. The other suggested reasons for the deposit

[12] Para 14.80 above.
[13] [1972] 1 M.L.J. 89.
[14] Italics supplied.

had been "to ensure that persons do not bid frivolously at the auction, and to cover out of pocket expenses (which however it was accepted were far less than the 25 per cent. deposit). These were considered insufficient.

Could the court order the vendor to repay the deposit? In *Stockloser v. Johnson*[15] there had been an *obiter dictum* of Romer L.J. to the effect that it could not, while the other two lord justices had thought it could. The Judicial Committee pointed out that *Stockloser v. Johnson*[16] was a case where the purchaser had gone into possession and defaulted on instalment payments—a very different matter from the simple sale contract they had before them. They left open the correct solution to a *Stockloser v. Johnson*[17] situation, and relied on *Commissioner of Public Works v. Hills*[18] as authority that they could order repayment of a penalty sum, less any damages proved to have been suffered by the vendor. They thus allowed an inquiry as to any damages suffered by the bank, these to be deducted from the purchase money.

Note: See the text at paragraph 14.22 et seq. above.

***Nutting v. Baldwin* [1995] 1 W.L.R. 201**

14.100 The plaintiffs were members of an association of Lloyd's Names who had joined together for the purpose of litigating against certain managing agents and members agents. The rules provided that members of the association should pay certain subscriptions, and on failure to pay, the committee might declare them "defaulting members" in which case they were precluded from sharing in any of the fruits of the actions. Certain members had left an additional subscription unpaid for some five months despite reminders. They were declared defaulting members. Later the actions brought by the group were compromised so that a sum of money became available. The plaintiffs argued that the "defaulting member" provision amounted to a penalty and was unenforceable, alternatively was something against which they might be relieved. They also argued that the committee should first have investigated the financial means of non-paying members.

Rattee J. held that the default provision was not a penalty. "In my judgment the essence of the contract between the members of the association is that the burden and benefit of enforcement of the members' claims against the agents should be shared between all the members. There is a pooling of all such claims and a pooling of contributions in the form of subscriptions for the purpose of financing the enforcement of such claims. It is an essential part of the arrangement . . . In other words, a member who fails to shoulder his share of the burden of this essentially multilateral arrangement runs the risk of being excluded from his share of the benefit of the arrangement."

14.101 However, he thought, curiously, that the provision effected a forfeiture. He relied on Lord Wilberforce's statement in *Shiloh Spinners v. Harding*[19], but considered that it did not apply in the case before him. The object of the clause would be entirely defeated, he considered, if relief were granted to the defaulting members. He accepted the argument of counsel for the committee that "to allow a defaulting member to share in the fruits of the litigation now, even on terms that he pays the additional subscriptions with interest, would allow him to share the fruits of the litigation without having borne his share of the risk of its prosecution."

Note: Some unease may be felt at the result of the case. One would think that the

[15] Para. 14.80 above.
[16] *ibid.*
[17] *ibid.*
[18] Para. 14.71 above.
[19] [1973] A.C. 691 at 723.

provision that the defaulting members were to be excluded from all participation in the fruits of the action was as much a security provision as any. It was surely designed to secure, or ensure, that they paid up promptly. It may be that the better test to have proposed would have been the old one[20] *whether it was too late for the committee to have been put back in the position they were before, or the "end" of the clause obtained (which may or may not have been the case on the facts). For example, let us suppose (it was not the case there, but is within the scope of the clause) a member had been a day or two late in paying, but had nonetheless been declared in default. It is hard to see that relief ought not to have been granted, since the position of the committee would on this hypothesis have been virtually unaltered despite the breach.*

[20] See the text at para. 14.32 above.

CHAPTER 15

REMEDIES FOR BREACH OF THE GOOD FAITH DUTIES

1: DAMAGES AND RESCISSION

Remedies: effect of good faith/fair dealing rules

15.01 A breach of the duty of good faith will have one of two effects on the contract:

(1) It may narrow the ambit of a term or terms of the contract to that which has been properly disclosed or accurately described by the vendor. In this case when the buyer has received something defective under the contract as interpreted in the light of good faith, he may obtain damages for the defect, just as he can when there is a breach of any other term of the contract.

(2) The breach of the duty of good faith may render the contract one which it may reasonably be assumed the buyer or inquiring party would not have entered into, or one which he proves he in fact would not have entered into. This happens precisely as in (1), because the terms of the contract may themselves become narrower in scope after the application of the good faith principles to them. The terms of the contract are seen only as terms which have been properly disclosed, accurately explained, *etc*. The remedy of rescission is appropriate where there is a big gap between what has been received and what (after the application of good faith) has been provided.

In (1), since the normal contractual remedies including damages will operate the question will be simply about the extent to which the lack of good faith has diminished the seller's (or defining party's) ability to rely on terms of the contract in their literal sense, and correspondingly rendered what is supplied under the contract something which does not conform. The question may sometimes be dealt with by way of a declaration before any breach; sometimes it will arise only after a breach or alleged breach of contract. It is not really correct to call this exercise of ascertaining the extent of the contract terms a blue-pencilling exercise, striking out certain terms of the contract.

There is no striking out. The terms which would have been terms if the duty of good faith had been complied with simply never get to be terms at all: they are still-born and not there to be blue-pencilled.

15.02 Setting aside the contract, or "rescission" is the remedy where a breach of good faith has radically affected the terms of the contract. Rescission is also the remedy in cases of dealings with the vulnerable—whether the spontaneously vulnerable or those who are vulnerable because their trust has been invited. The agreement which was the basis of the parties consent to the contract has been vitiated in both cases. Rescission is also the remedy for misrepresentations which are fraudulent, for similar reasons. Some of the cases on the operation of rescission are cases of fraud. This should not worry anyone. The remedy works in much the same way whatever the reason giving rise to rescission; whether the underlying statement is a failure to give full disclosure, an inaccurate or partial description of what you know about the thing you are selling, a false, but mistaken rather than deliberate, misrepresentation of some characteristic of the thing, or a deliberately false statement about it. Instead of (or in the appropriate cases, in addition to) rescission, a vulnerable party to a sale may elect for an account of the profits made by the trusted party. Alternatively, where property has been lost by the trusted party's breach of duty, the victim may also elect for equitable compensation.[1]

There is no direct remedy in damages (tortious or contractual) for a breach of good faith in itself. See the Court of Appeal decision in *Banque Keyser SA v. Skandia (UK) Insurance*[2] affirming by implication that the remedy for a breach of good faith is to avoid the the contract. The decision on this point was not disapproved by the House of Lords. Note, however, the Misrepresentation Act 1967, aspects of which are discussed briefly in Chapter 17. This Act provides a remedy in damages for certain misrepresentations. These, which are rather a limited class as currently interpreted, may in time be recognised as including representations made in breach of a duty of good faith.

Equitable compensation/partial enforcement/partial rescission (non-fiduciaries)

15.03 Equity could if it thought fit preserve broken contracts even where the vendor had been in breach of his duty of candour or accuracy/had been guilty of a non-fraudulent misrepresentation. It offered compensation to the injured party for the shortcomings of what was sold by comparison with what the contract (construed according to the good faith rules) had promised him. In practice it only did so where the shortcomings were such that it could reasonably have been sup-

[1] See ***Nocton v. Lord Ashburton*** [1914] A.C. 932 and the important recent decision of May J., *Mahoney v. Purnell* [1996] 3 All E.R. 61, in which compensation as at the breach date was awarded to the victim, after the company whose shares had been the subject of the dealing had gone into liquidation.

[2] [1990] 1 Q.B. 665.

posed the injured party would not at the time of the contract have objected to being bound by the contract despite the undisclosed defect, provided he had compensation for the difference. The remedy was exclusive to the equity courts, but has been available to all Divisions since the Judicature Act 1873. The remedy of compensation has suffered a curious oblivion for upwards of a century. It is probable that the main reason for this will have been the late-nineteenth century notion that compensation was all part of what was seen as a wide equitable discretion habitually operated in what was thought to be a somewhat impenetrable manner by the old equity courts in actions for specific performance.[3] The fact that the remedy will normally have been granted together with specific performance is however probably better seen as fortuitous. The equity courts granted specific performance, compensation and rescission as to appropriate contracts. They often granted the first two together. Whether they saw specific performance or compensation as the more important feature in such cases is hard to say. They did not in terms grant compensation with rescission. This was perhaps purely because the two looked to inconsistent goals: compensation was intended to give the injured party what he had been promised; rescission to put him back in his pre-contractual state. In any case, rescission was, as a matter of definition, a giving back and a taking back. It therefore came ready-packaged with its own measures to prevent the remedy operating unfairly—the accounts of profits, inquiries as to improvements, and so on.

In any event the distinction between compensation as part of specific performance and as a remedy in its own right may not matter especially. This book does not attempt to deal fully with the topic of specific performance or compensation, but it is suggested that the latter in particular may well repay further modern analysis taking into account the foundation of good faith rules, so that the real workings of the remedy as granted in such cases may be exposed. Fear of the unknown may possibly underlie a reluctance in this country to use the remedy as widely as may be thought useful and reasonable. It may be, for example, that in a case where compensation is the appropriate remedy, damages will anyway be inadequate; and thus specific performance, or more simply, the preservation of the contract, may be fitting even in the case of a number of contracts to pay money. Modern courts could grant the equitable remedy of compensation either together with specific performance as the old equity courts did, or in some cases by the exercise of the statutory discretion under section 2(2) of the Misrepresentation Act 1967[4] or the Unfair Contract Terms Regulations 1994.[5] Where the breach, for example of an assured's duty of disclosure is relatively small, it may well be be open to the courts to

[3] See further Chap. 5, Sale of Land as to this. See also, on compensation, the article by McDermott, the Jurisdiction of the Court of Chancery to Award Damages, (1992) 108 L.Q.R.

[4] See further Chapter 17 for discussion of this subsection.

[5] See further Chap. 19.

refuse rescission to the insurer at the instance of the assured,[6] instead compensating the insurer by giving him the premiums which would have been reasonably expected if the facts material to the true risk had been disclosed.[7]

15.04 There has been interest taken recently in "partial enforcement" of contracts. Note for example *TSB v. Camfield*[8] and the Australian case of *Vadusz v. Pioneer Concrete.*[9] The distinction between partial enforcement (or the rescission of part of the contract on terms that another part, typically containing an obligation on the part of the inquiring party/buyer, is preserved for the benefit of the defining party/seller) and compensation (or the preservation of part of a contract on terms that compensation is paid to the inquiring party/buyer by the defining party/seller for the shortcomings in what he has received under the contract compared with what he ought to have received) is not a clear-cut one. The main feature of difference seems to be little more than that between a buyer's obligation to perform and a seller's obligation to perform. The other difference is that there is an established jurisdiction to order preservation of the contract with compensation, provided the part misrepresented is not significant in relation to the remainder; while a jurisdiction to rewrite the contract to something the parties might have, possibly accept that they would have, but in fact did not agree to, must be wholly speculative. It may be that in non-fiduciary cases the better approach, provided the breach of the duty of good faith or the misrepresentation has not been grave, is by means of the compensation jurisdiction. The courts in England have already rightly rejected the idea of a jurisdiction for partial enforcement, at least as regards dealings with a vulnerable person: note the Court of Appeal decision in *TSB v. Camfield.*[10] For comment on the divergent decision of the High Court of Australia in *Vadasz v. Pioneer Concrete Ltd* (above) see the Appendix to this chapter.[11]

Compensation and rescission are fault-based remedies: no application where the vendor has been inaccurate but blameless

15.05 It should be stressed that both (a) compensation where specific performance is granted at the instance of either buyer or seller, and (b) rescission for breach of the duty of good faith are *fault-based* remedies. There is an ambiguity about the word "misrepresentation": does it mean a wrong representation of what you know or a wrong repres-

[6] Who would seek the preservation of the contract on terms that he paid compensation.

[7] Cp. the reference to the French practice of compensation under the *Code des Assurances*, Arts. 113–9, in Law Commission Working Paper No. 73, Insurance Law Non-disclosure and Breach of Warranty, p. 31.

[8] [1995] 1 W.L.R. 430; and see as to partial enforcement at the instance of a "fiduciary" or trusted person, Chap. 9, Dealings with the Vulnerable Buyer or Seller.

[9] (1995) 130 A.L.R. p. 570.

[10] [1995] 1 W.L.R. 430.

[11] Para. 15.91.

entation of what is in fact the case? Good faith remedies are about the former only. Outside statute, there is *no remedy* for the buyer or inquiring party for the vendor or defining party's wholly blameless representation/non-disclosure/half-truth, etc., even if it subsequently turns out to have been wrong and materially wrong.

Specific performance: the circumstances in which compensation will be given

On this topic see Chapter 5, Sale of Land and the text on "Substantial Justice" at paragraph 5.47 where this aspect is touched on.[12]

"Material" and Inducement/reliance/causation

Material

15.06 "Material" has two meanings: (a) "relevant" or "material to" the contract[13] and (b) "important or significant" in relation to what is in question. The latter usage is given its chief colour by what *is* in question. So, "material *inducement*"[14] means "important, significant in causing the Plaintiff to take the shares"; and "material defect"[15] means "more serious kind of defect". Similarly, we might talk of "material leak" or "material fire". It is only when we are talking about causing another to act in a certain way that "material" can take on a connotation of "so serious as to be particularly likely to cause whatever the action is". The root meaning remains "significant", but something which is a significant inducement is going to be significant *as an inducement*. The attempt to extract a degree of independent meaning from "material" which the word will not bear may be seen to be a futile one: it is a word, a part of our language, just a means of communicating an idea, not a scientific formula.

"Induce" also lacks scientific magic. The expression is interchangeable with "give occasion to", "act in reliance upon", "act on the faith of" or just plain "cause". The Latin phrase used in some early cases[16] is "*dans locum contractui*" (giving occasion to, or causing, the contract). It is helpful, as Latin phrases can be, in that it isolates the essential element of causation. It also avoids the attempt to draw excessively fine distinctions between "inducement", "reliance", etc.

[12] Although not strictly within the scope of this book. See also the article by McDermott, The Jurisdiction of the Court of Chancery to Award Damages, (1992) 108 L.Q.R. 652, and for specific, performance generally see standard textbooks.

[13] As in "material facts"—see Chap. 4, Insurance and Surety Transactions.

[14] As used, *e.g.* by Lord Chelmsford in *Hallows v. Fernie* (1868) L.R. 3 Ch. App. 467.

[15] See Chap. 5: "materiality/significance of defect.

[16] See, *e.g.* *Pulsford v. Richards* (1853), noted at para. 7.34 of the Appendix to Chap. 7, Sale of Company Shares.

Grades of "material" (in the sense of "significant")

15.07 Any representation made which is going to ground a cause of action must be material (in the sense of relevant). Being relevant, a representation which is inaccurate or misleading, whether by reason of a sin of omission or a sin of commission, may *also* be any of the following:

(1) trivial;

(2) more than trivial, but not such that one can be sure that it is "of such a nature as would induce a person to enter into a contract or would tend to induce him to do so, or that it would be part of the inducement to enter into the contract". The quotation is from Jessel M.R. in the Court of Appeal in *Smith v. Chadwick,*[17] and Jessel M.R. gives examples of cases in which it is not obvious to the Court that the statement is material, for example ambiguous statements which may be taken in one of several meanings; or

(3) sufficiently serious that one can infer that it was "of such a nature . . . etc." as above.

If the statement is in category (1) and the plaintiff proves no more, he is plainly vulnerable to the inference by the court that the statement could not have occasioned the contract. If the statement is in category (2) and the plaintiff proves no more he will also fail. As Jessel M.R. put it "How can the Court find out that the Plaintiff has been deceived at all?" The plaintiff must go on to show that he acted on the inducement so held out, or relied on the statements made.[18] If the statement is in category (3) however, the Court is at liberty to infer[19] that the buyer/inquiring party "acted on the inducement so held out, and you want no evidence that he did so act". In this event, it is for the seller or defining party to shift the burden of proof if he can, for example by showing that the purchaser knew the truth and so could not have relied on the misstatements, or had specifically contracted by a valid exclusion clause or the like to take the particular risk or simply by extracting an admission in the witness box.[20] See also Lord Halsbury in *Aaron's Reef v. Twiss* [1896] A.C. 273. See further cases on materiality, inducement, *etc.*, in the Appendix to Chap. 7. For the special rule as to inducement in insurance cases see Chap. 4.

Perhaps Lord Blackburn's caveat should be borne in mind when considering recent cases. A statement in a case about a category (2) type of material statement[21] cannot necessarily be lifted and applied without more to a category (1) case or a category (2) case.[22] A painting-by-numbers approach simply does not work with what is essentially a factual question.

[17] (1882) 20 Ch. D. 27.

[18] Jessel M.R. uses both expressions.

[19] It is an inference of fact, not law: see Lord Blackburn in *Smith v. Chadwick* in the House of Lords (1884) 9 App. Cas. 187.

[20] Examples given by Jessel M.R.

[21] *E.g.*, it is suggested, ***Target Holdings v. Redfern*** [1996] A.C. 421.

[22] As, it is suggested, the ***Mothew*** case (1996) below or a category (3), *e.g.*, it is suggested, ***Downs v. Chappell*** [1996] 3 All E.R. 344.

RESCISSION

Introduction

15.08 Rescission means an undoing or setting aside of the contract—a giving back and a taking back as it has been called—so that both parties are put back into their original position before contracting. The expression was also used (but is much more rarely used today since *Johnson v. Agnew*[23] as another way of expressing something quite different—the accepting that a contract is at an end when the other side has committed a sufficient breach of its ordinary (that is not good faith) terms which sound in damages. This is best called acceptance of repudiation, to distinguish it from the rescission which is being discussed in this chapter. It is quite different: the act of the party who accepts a repudiation gives rise to a right to damages because the terms of the contract have not been properly carried out by the other. The act of a party who rescinds is intended to do away with the contract and its effect altogether as having been entered into under a false appreciation of its terms; and to wind back the clock for both parties to the state they were in before the contract, or what is sometimes called the *statu quo ante*.[24]

The purchaser (or inquiring party, but he is called the purchaser below, for convenience) will be able to set the contract aside if the difference between its true terms as seen in the light of the duty of good faith, that is, the duty of candour and accuracy, and its actual terms, amounted to something which (a) would have been material to a reasonable person's decision whether to enter into the contract or not, or (b) was in fact material to that person's decision. It will however be a defence in cases of (a) for a vendor or defining party to prove if he can that the buyer or inquiring party would have entered into the contract anyway, that is that it was not material to *him*. In insurance sales it is now the law that the insurer has also to prove that he would have been induced to enter into the contract. The burden of the proof is thus changed in that respect: the insured's option has become the requirement for the insurer in insurance cases.[25]

Remedy also applicable to dealings with the vulnerable

15.09 Rescission is also the remedy where a vulnerable person (whether spontaneously vulnerable or vulnerable because his trust has been invited) has entered into a contract with someone who had "made a market of" his weakness or who has put himself in a position where his duty and personal advantage may conflict, and subsequently wishes to set it aside. In this case the knowledge of the trusted party or the exploiting party is usually not really in question in practice at

[23] [1980] A.C. 367.
[24] "the state in which before".
[25] See Chap. 4, Insurance and Surety transactions.

the rescission stage of the case (it is difficult to make a market of someone's weakness without knowing they are weak); but it remains a defence to the trusted party just as it is to an ordinary vendor if he can show that the vulnerable party knew (see, however, below for the strict knowledge requirements) and agreed to the transaction. The burden of the proof is on the trusted party in this case.[26]

Sub-principles of rescission: the prevention of injustice ("bars" to rescission), relevant matters

15.10 The courts appreciated that to grant rescission for a breach of good faith or misrepresentation might work injustice if the operation of the remedy were not itself carefully controlled. Thus, sub-principles were worked out over time to prevent injustice, both to the other party and to innocent third parties. These are dealt with by the standard contract textbooks. The reason they are dealt with here also is because it is possible to think the essentially simple sub-principles involved in the "bars" may have disappeared under the mass of different labels used. Further, the Case Appendix method may be a useful way of both supporting and illustrating the account given below.

(1) Prevention of injustice to third parties: the acquisition of third party rights in the thing bought

15.11 This is an absolute bar in the case of goods, and in the case of purchasers (including mortgagees) of interests in land. Where the thing sold is a right or a bundle of rights not being interests in land, however, it does not really seem that the acquisition of rights by a third party matters specially, since the third party is bound by all the earlier equities. It is not possible to be quite sure of the rationale underlying the latter rule. It may perhaps simply be that it is not reasonable to expect rights to be as uncluttered, as it were, as a physical object. The position of a mortgagee or other derivative owner of land, for example a sub-lessee, is not specifically dealt with in this context, but on the face of it if such a third party sided with the proprietor plaintiff by, for example consenting to the action for rescission against his vendor, there ought to be no objection to rescission at the request of the plaintiff.

In *White v. Garden*[27] the court held that although there had been underlying fraud, it was nonetheless not open to the purchasers to claim back the goods from an innocent sub-purchaser. Talfourd J. said:

> ". . . it is not competent to them, after a third party has by their act been induced to part with his money, to turn round and say that the contract as between them and [the vendor] was null and void . . ."

[26] See Chap. 9, Dealings with the Vulnerable Buyer or Seller.
[27] (1851) 10 C.B. 919; 138 E.R. 364.

Jervis C.J. explained the decision in terms of public policy, saying:

> "The question is one of considerable importance, as affecting the mercantile transactions of this country; for, if the argument urged on the part of the defendants were well founded, goods at all tainted by fraud might be followed through any number of bona fide purchasers—a most inconvenient, and, as it strikes me, a most absurd doctrine."[28]

A creditor of a company which is wound up has acquired rights in the winding up which bar any application for rescission by a shareholder of an agreement to take shares in the company (unless formally commenced before the winding up). This is so even though there is no formal contract at all between the creditor and the shareholder. The gap is supplied by the *expectation deemed to be created in the creditor* by virtue of the winding up legislation. Lord Chelmsford the Lord Chancellor put it in this way in *Oakes v. Turquand*[29]:

> "It is true that there was no contract between the creditor and the shareholders, and that the creditor probably never thought of the shareholders in his dealings with the company. But he must be *taken to have known* what his rights were under the Act . . ."[30]

(2) Prevention of injustice to the other (seller or defining) party to the contract

Three relevant matters: **15.12**

(1) Acceptance of the defect by the buyer or inquiring party with knowledge;
(2) Acts of ownership by the buyer or inquiring party with knowledge; and
(3) Change in the nature of the thing by the buyer or inquiring party with or without knowledge

The following factors are in themselves irrelevant to the question whether rescission should be allowed:

15.13

(1) Possession of the subject matter of the contract by the buyer;
(2) Delay since the acquisition;
(3) A drop in the value of the thing bought caused purely by a change in the market value of the thing; or
(4) Completion or execution of the contract by conveyance, grant of a lease, registration of shares, etc.

[28] For the assignment of rights being subject to equities, see, *e.g. Mangles v. Dixon* (1852) 3 H.L.C. 702; ***Phipps v. Lovegrove*** (1873) L.R. 16 Eq. 80.
[29] (1867) L.R. 2 H.L. 325.
[30] Italics supplied.

Relevance of labels (waiver, affirmation, acquiescence, laches, delay, election)

15.14 There are a number of labels in use, all of which relate to the conduct of the party seeking to set aside. All relate either to acceptance of the defect or to acts of ownership. The primary question asked by the court is simple: has the conduct of the party (or victim, whether because of breach of good faith or because he is a vulnerable party) who wants to set aside the contract aside been such that it would be unfair (to the other party) to give him rescission? The above labels have traditionally been used from time to time for the kinds of victim-conduct. The precise difference between them is slightly confusing, and the attempt to distinguish between them not very profitable, it may be thought. As descriptive labels they are something of a failure. They do not tell one what conduct exactly they are talking about. They do not cover the ground in an orderly way.

"Waiver" probably connotes the release in some way of a right one otherwise has to complain about or insist on something. "Affirmation" probably means agreement to a state of affairs, the unwritten underlying notion being that it may be an somewhat unsatisfactory state of affairs to one; and "acquiescence" is much the same except that the state of affairs is definitely unsatisfactory to one. "Election" is simply another word for choice: usually in legal terms a choice of one of two courses of action. It seems quite often to be used when a buyer or trusting party decides that although he has a right to set aside the contract it will actually, as events have turned out, be profitable to keep it in being. "Laches" just means being slow about things, with an underlying overtone of blameworthiness. "Delay" we know means delay, or letting time go by, but without necessary overtones of blameworthiness: delay can be quite virtuous if one is using the delay to investigate, exercise proper caution, *etc.* We might usefully all agree to deny ourselves the use of any of these words *as labels*, since they do not describe in the way a good label should; and instead simply look to conduct rendering rescission unfair to the other party under either of two simple heads—(a) acts of acceptance or (b) acts of ownership.[31]

It may be noticed that since this part of the law is not modern, the conduct is assessed strictly by reference to the sub-principles. It would be wrong to suppose that these are modern "guidelines": we have here by no means an unrestricted discretion for individual judges with individual notions of fairness. Nor are they "factors" to be "taken into account" among other factors in a judicial discretion—a strangely ambiguous modern statutory usage which can give variable results.[32] The discretion is a regulated discretion by applying the sub-principles.

[31] See for an early example of labelling problems ***Duke of Leeds v. Earl Amherst***. (1846) 2 Ph. 123; 41 E.R. 886; see also ***De Bussche v. Alt*** (1878) 8 Ch. D. 286.

[32] There is at least one body which took the view for some little time that it might "take into account" the views of its members obtained by a ballot it had itself carried out by merely noting them without action.

Fairness is considered, but so as also to give "safety to mankind" in the words of Lord Erskine, or a reasonable degree of predictability about the result.

Acceptance of the defect with knowledge

15.15 *(a) Nature of the knowledge required* It will be noticed that two out of the three above prevention of injustice sub-principles (or "bars to rescission") require knowledge on the part of the party barred. This is an essential feature, given that fairness is the question here. The knowledge must be full knowledge. Nothing less will do.[33] The question of knowledge characteristically arises in the case of dealings with the vulnerable. This is perhaps simply because the vulnerable—often principals where an agent has allowed his duty and his interest to conflict—will often have known *something* about what was going on: the question is whether they knew enough. However, the principle that full knowledge is required for the buyer or inquiring party to be barred from rescission is a general one, not limited to rescission by the vulnerable.

In *Rothschild v. Brookman*[34] a dealing with a vulnerable person was set aside and Lord Wynford said this:

> "An observation has been made as to the staleness of the demand: undoubtedly if it had appeared that the Plaintiff *knew*, at a period long before that at which he thought proper to institute proceedings, *what was the real character of these transactions*, I agree that he would have been precluded by laches from coming to complain of them. But I think it is for Mr Rothschild to show that he had notice of what was the true character of the transaction. From the very nature of the transaction itself, it is very likely that the gentleman should have remained for a long time in the state of ignorance in which he had been of the circumstances under which he had been dealing with the Appellant.[35]

15.16 In *Vigers v. Pike*[36] it was stated (*obiter*, since in fact rescission was not ordered on the facts of that case) by Lord Cottenham, with whom Lord Brougham agreed:

> "The doctrine of carrying equities by acquiescence, I consider to be one of the most important to be attended to; for otherwise there is great danger of the principles of a Court of Equity, thus improperly exercised, producing great injustice. A man who, *with full knowledge of his case*, does not complain, but deals with his opponent as if he had no case against him, builds up from day to day a wall of protection for such opponent, which will probably defeat any future attack upon him . . ."[37]

[33] See, however, below as to notice, or *deemed knowledge* from lack of due diligence before the contract by the buyer.
[34] (1831) 2 Dow. & Cl. 188; 5 E.R. 273.
[35] Italics supplied.
[36] (1842) 8 Cl. & Fin. 562; 8 E.R. 220.
[37] Italics supplied.

In *Re Reese River Company v. Smith*[38] scrupulous attention was paid to the extent of knowledge acquired by the buyer. Thus, even in a share-purchase case, where the requirements were normally strict, he was allowed two months from the date when he first learned that the shares were worthless. In this period he waited for a report about the mines in question, so that he might satisfy himself that not only were the shares worthless at the date of his information; but that they had also been worthless at the date of his contract. It was only then that the court considered he had the complete knowledge required.

In *Erlanger v. New Sombrero Phosphate Co.*[39] the question was said by Lord Penzance to be:

> "How soon . . . can the company be said to have *known the material facts*, or such of them as would make it reasonably their duty to investigate the matter if they meant to take exception to the mode in which the purchase had been effected?"[40]

In *De Busche v. Alt*,[41] another dealing with the vulnerable, Thesiger L.J. giving the judgment of the court said:

> "Before the principal can be properly be said to have ratified or adopted the act of his agent or waived his right of complaint in respect of such acts, it should be shewn that he has had *full knowledge of its nature and circumstances, in other words, that he had had presented to his mind proper materials upon which to exercise his power of election* . . ."[42]

In that case too the wronged principal had some knowledge of the defect, but not, it was held, sufficient knowledge to be barred.

15.17 In *Lagunas Nitrate Co. v. Lagunas Syndicate*,[43] one question discussed was whether disclosure by the wrongdoing syndicate directors to the company of their dual role, as directors of their syndicate and directors of the company, indicated sufficient knowledge on the part of the company to bar it from seeking rescission. It was held insufficient. As Lindley L.J. put it "To impute to the nitrate company the knowledge which the directors had acquired in another capacity, and which knowledge they did not disclose to any one, is neither law nor sense." The syndicate directors could not "in equity bind the company by any contract with themselves without fully and fairly disclosing to the company all material facts which the company ought to know" though it could if the requisite full disclosure had been made.

Also perhaps relevant is Lord Goff in *The Kanchenjunga*,[44] on the subject of election generally in contract:

[38] (1867) L.R. 2 Ch. 604, C.A. and (1869) L.R. 4 H.L. 64 (noted below and in the App. to Chap. 7, Sale of Company Shares.
[39] (1878) 3 App. (Cas 1218).
[40] Italics supplied. See below as to notice.
[41] (1878) 8 Ch. D. 286.
[42] Italics supplied.
[43] [1899] 2 Ch. 392, noted below and in the Appendix to Chap. 7, Sale of Company shares.
[44] [1990] 1 Lloyd's Rep. 391 at 399.

"In the context of a contract, the principle of election applies when a state of affairs comes into existence in which one party becomes entitled to exercise a right, and has to choose whether to exercise the right or not. His election has generally to be an informed choice, made with knowledge of the facts giving rise to the right."

15.18 *(b) The role of notice (deemed knowledge because of failure to investigate properly)*[45] When knowledge is deemed, it operates in every way like actual knowledge. Thus, a buyer may be deemed to have known of the defect before purchase, by reason of his failure to make normal investigations.

In *Re Hop and Malt Exchange and Warehouse Co, ex parte Briggs*,[46] Lord Romilly M.R. said that he was strongly inclined to think that in that case, where the last clause of the share prospectus in question had invited inspection of the memorandum and articles and stated where they might be inspected, the purchaser must be deemed to have notice of the contents of the articles. However, he in fact refused rescission on another ground.[47]

In *Oakes v. Turquand*[48] the Lord Chancellor, Lord Chelmsford took the same view regarding the buyer of shares' duty to search the memorandum and articles of the company. He said:

"I think that persons who have taken shares in a company are bound to make themselves acquainted with the memorandum of association, which is the basis upon which the company is established. If they fail to do so, and the objects of the company are extended beyond those described in the prospectus (a fact which may be easily ascertained), the persons who have so taken shares on the faith of the prospectus ought, in my opinion, to be held to be bound by acquiescence."

The same kind of notice may arise after the contract, if, for example facts are presented to the victim which are sufficiently puzzling or worrying to impose a duty on him to follow up what he has learned with further inquiries.[49]

15.19 *(c)" Fobbing off" narrows the ambit of deemed notice*[50] If a purchaser who is bound to make normal inquiries is fobbed off with reassuring statements, he is entitled to rely on these: his duty of due diligence is displaced to the extent of the reassurance given. Thus, for example in *Redgrave v. Hurd*,[51] the fact that the plaintiff, who had bought into a

45 See Chapter 8, Notice and Knowledge, on this type of deemed knowledge.
46 (1866) L.R. 1 Eq. 483.
47 See Acts of Ownership With Knowledge, at para. 15.22 below.
48 (1867) L.R. 2 H.L. 325.
49 See the statement of Lord Penzance quoted above in ***Erlanger v. New Sombrero Phosphate Co.***, above.
50 See Chap. 5, Sale of Land and Chap. 8, Knowledge and Notice for further examples of this.
51 (1881) 20 Ch. D. 1 (noted elsewhere).

partnership, had not looked properly at the books and accounts of the partnership before doing so did not matter, because he had been misled by the falsely reassuring statement the vendor had made to him about the profits of the business.

15.20 *(d) "Within one's instructions": deemed consent* To be distinguished from knowledge or notice is what one might perhaps call incidents of "reasonable ancillary expectation", or "deemed consent to administrative measures *within one's instructions*", or some such thing. It operates in a very similar way to deemed knowledge, in that a buyer cannot complain of such incidents or use them as a basis for rescission. If one contracts with someone to perform a service, say, then it is to be expected, particularly if the agent is a member of some recognised body of persons carrying out the services in question, that that person will carry out the details of that service in the way in which it is normally done by members of that body. One cannot expect him to mention and seek agreement to every single administrative measure he takes in the course of carrying out the service."

In *Robinson v. Mollett*[52] Mellor J. said:

> "A person who authorizes a broker to buy in a market, the usages of which are not known to him, may reasonably expect to find that the mode of dealing in that market may not be in all respects such as he would anticipate. . . ."

In the same case Brett J. said:

> "A stranger to a locality, or trade, or market, is not be held bound by the custom of such locality, or trade, or market, because he knows the custom, but because he has elected to enter into transactions in a locality, trade or market wherein all who are not strangers do know and act upon such custom. When considerable numbers of men of business carry on one side of a particular business, they are apt to set up a custom which acts very much in favour of their side of the business."

He continued:

> "So long as they do not infringe some fundamental principle of right and wrong, they may establish such a custom; but if, on dispute before a legal forum, it is found that they are endeavouring to enforce some rule of conduct which is so entirely in favour of their side that it is fundamentally unjust to the other side, the Courts have always determined that such a custom, if sought to be enforce against a person in fact ignorant of it, is unreasonably, contrary to law, and void . . .")

15.21 *(e) Knowledge: special added requirement of independence in the case of the vulnerable* Often merely the necessary full disclosure, presenting sufficient material to the mind of the victim for him to understand the defect properly, is enough. However, where there has been a lack of

[52] (1875) L.R. 7 H.L. 810.

independence, it may also be necessary to remove that for the victim to be able to have, in a real sense, the necessary knowledge together with the power to act on it.[53]

In *Lagunas Nitrate Co. v. Lagunas Nitrate Syndicate*[54] Lindley L.J. drew a distinction[55] between the position of the company before it had acquired independent directors, that is, while it was still controlled by the syndicate directors, and after it had acquired its own independent directors. Thus, for the purpose of deciding whether the company had accepted the defect with knowledge, he disregarded those acts of the company which had taken place before the independent board was appointed.

Acts of ownership by the buyer (or inquiring party) with knowledge

15.22 In *Campbell v. Fleming*,[56] the plaintiff, who had bought shares in a mining company relying on what proved to be fraudulent representations by the defendants' agent, was nonetheless barred from rescission because after he had learned of the fraud he had consolidated the shares with some other property and sold shares in the new company, realising a considerable sum of money. It will be observed that this case falls equally well under the next category—change in the nature of the thing: there is obviously frequent overlap between the categories.[57]

In *Deposit Life Assurance v. Ayscouch*,[58] it was held that a shareholder could not seek rescission while still remaining a shareholder: so ambiguous a position could not permitted. He must first have ceased to be a shareholder, or at least taken steps to cease to be one.

In *Ormes v. Beadel*,[59] the plaintiff was held barred from rescission since he had acquiesced with the other side in the appointment of an arbitrator to settle the dispute under the agreement for building in question, and had proceeded under the arbitration.

In *Western Bank of Scotland v. Addie*,[60] the purchaser had bought shares in an unincorporated association, and two years later, had agreed to it becoming incorporated, rendering them something altogether different, it was held. Lord Cranworth (the Lord Chancellor simply reserved his position on the point) said that it would be impossible to restore the respondent to the position he was in before. The value was not the point: the nature of the thing had changed irretrievably; in a sense, it had been destroyed, to give rise to something radically different and not comparable in any way. He said:

[53] See, generally, for the importance of "competent" independent advice, Chap. 9, Dealings with the Vulnerable Buyer or Seller.
[54] Above, and in the Appendix to Chap. 7, Sale of Company Shares.
[55] As did the other Lord Justices.
[56] (1834) 1 A. & E. 40; 110 E.R. 1122.
[57] See, *e.g.* ***Western Bank of Scotland v. Addie*** (1867) L.R. 1 H.L. (Sc.) 159 for another example.
[58] (1856) 6 E. & B. 761; 119 E.R. 1048.
[59] (1860) 2 De G.F. & J. 333.
[60] Above.

> "The Respondent might in that case have given up 135 shares of the new company, and these shares might have been as valuable as, or even more valuable than, the shares which he was induced to purchase, but they would not have been shares in the same company; and unless he was in a position to restore *the very thing* which he was fraudulently induced to purchase, he cannot have relief by way of restitutio in integrum . . . The circumstances were so changed that he could not put the Appellants in the condition in which they were before the fraudulent sale to him. I agree with the learned Judges below, that *the circumstance that the shares, from mismanagement or otherwise, had become depreciated in value subsequently to the purchase by the Pursuer, would of itself have been of no importance*. He might still have been able to restore that which he was fraudulently induced to purchase. But what in fact took place was *not a depreciation but a destruction of the thing purchased:* the unincorporated company in which he had been induced to purchase shares no longer existed."[61]

Change in the nature of the thing by the buyer (with or without knowledge)

15.23 The common law courts took a strict view. Even possession, receiving rent, *etc.*, would bar a plaintiff from receiving rescission.[62] The equity courts took a more relaxed view, retaining only the common law courts' insistence on a change in the nature of the thing as a bar.

For the common law courts' strict attitude, note *Clarke v. Dickson*[63] in which the plaintiff sought in a common law court the return of the price of an agreement to buy shares in a mining company, after (among other things) he had agreed to the company being turned into a limited liability company. Erle C.J. refused him the relief he sought saying:

> "Then he has changed the nature of the article: the shares he received were shares in a company on the cost book principle; the plaintiff offers to restore them after he has converted them into shares in a company on the cost book principle."

Crompton J. agreed, saying:

> "The true doctrine is, that a party can never repudiate a contract after, by his own act, it has become out of his power to restore the parties to their original condition."

The equity courts considered that possession was unimportant, and that many of the changes to the thing bought could be the subject of compensation either to the vendor or the purchaser. For example, in *Lindsay Petroleum v. Hurd*[64] Sir Barnes Peacock said of a land purchase:

[61] Italics supplied.
[62] See ***Hunt v. Silk*** (1804) 5 East 449; 102 E.R. 1142.
[63] (1858) El. Bl. & El. 148; 120 E.R. 463.
[64] (1874) L.R. 5 P.C. 221.

"Neither were any acts done in the interval, as it appears to us, at all material to the equity between the parties. There was possession taken, no doubt, but it would be a very novel proposition that mere possession is to be a bar, so as to raise a counter equity in cases of this description. Nothing appears to have been done beyond the sinking of a single well, by way of trial, upon the ground. The sinking of that well, if the land is restored, can in no substantial way operate to the prejudice of the Respondents; and, if any profit had been derived from it, the Court of first instance offered an account of that profit; but it manifestly was known that there was none, for that account was not accepted . . ."

15.24 And in *Erlanger v. New Sombrero Phosphate Co.*[65] Lord Blackburn said:

"But a Court of Equity could not give damages, and unless it can rescind the contract, can give no relief. And on the other hand, it can take accounts of profits, and make allowances for deterioration. And I think the practice has always been for a Court of Equity to give this relief whenever, by the exercise of its powers, it can do what is *practically just*,[66] though it cannot restore the parties precisely to the state they were in before the contract."

The exception was a *change in the nature of the thing*: note Lord Penzance's statement[67] quoted above: "Lapse of time may so change the condition of the thing sold, or bring about such a state of things that justice cannot be done by rescinding the contract subject to any amount of allowances or compensations."

It may be that the statement allows room for the operation of practical justice even where the nature of the thing has changed, if justice could be done nonetheless, presumably by compensation in money in a proper case. Note *Spence v. Crawford*[68] for the suggestion that the remedy of rescission would be possible so long as "the substantial identity" of the subject matter remained.

The above passage from Lord Blackburn's judgment in *Erlanger's*[69] case was referred to by Rigby L.J. in *Lagunas Nitrate Co. v. Lagunas Syndicate*[70] who said of it:

"This important passage is, in my judgment, fully supported by the allowance for deterioration and permanent improvements made by Lord Eldon and other great equity judges in similar cases."

He continued later:

"The obligation of the vendors to take back the property in a deteriorated condition is not imposed by way of punishment for

[65] (1878) 3 App. Cas. 1218).
[66] Italics supplied.
[67] Para. 15.72, below.
[68] [1939] 3 All E.R. 271.
[69] Above.
[70] [1899] 2Ch. 392.

wrongdoing, whether fraudulent or not, but because on equitable principles it is thought more fair that they should be compelled to accept compensation than that they should go off with the full profit of their wrongdoing. Properly speaking, it is not now in the discretion of the Court to say whether compensation ought to be taken or not. If substantially compensation can be made, rescission with compensation is ex debito justitiae."

In *Thomas Witter Ltd v. TBP. Industries*,[71] rescission was refused apparently on the sole ground that the business bought relying on the misrepresentation, had been run by the plaintiff for a while. Jacob J. said:

"Although . . . kept the Witter business separate, it is unrealistic to regard it as the same as the business conveyed. There have been numerous changes of staff and personnel (including the departure of Mr Francis who had exceptional sales skills). Those personnel who have stayed have been in different pension schemes, there are mortgagees of the business and so on. Time has moved on, and third parties would, I think, be affected".

However, it does not appear from the report that either *Erlanger's*[72] case or *Lagunas Nitrate Co. v. Lagunas Syndicate*[73] was cited to the court.

Lapse of time may have the effect of changing the nature of the thing, and if so acquires an importance that "mere delay" altogether lacks. Lord Penzance in *Erlanger v. New Sombrero Phosphate*[74] said:

"Lapse of time may so change the condition of the thing sold, or bring about such a state of things that justice cannot be done by rescinding the contract subject to any amount of allowances or compensations."

Drop in value of the thing: is this a change in its nature?

15.25 Where the drop in value is caused by the buyer, it will rank as deterioration[75] and the seller will receive compensation. If it is a result of the defect as to which there has been a lack of good faith, misrepresentation, etc., by the seller, the seller has to bear the loss, because it is caused by the very defect in the thing as to which he has been at fault. For example, Rigby L.J. in the Court of Appeal in the *Lagunas Nitrate*[76] case said:

"Now no doubt it is a general rule that in order to entitle beneficiaries to rescind a voidable contract of purchase . . . they must be in a position to offer back the subject matter of the contract.

71 [1996] 2 All E.R. 573.
72 Above.
73 Above.
74 *ibid.*
75 See above.
76 Above.

> But this rule has no application to the case of the subject matter having been reduced by the mere fault of the vendors themselves . . ."

As to a drop in value which occurs simply through the operation of the market, without being caused by either buyer or seller, see paragraph 15.28, below under Irrelevant factors; and for the date at which the value is to be taken, see paragraph 15.30, below under The working out of a rescission order.

Prevention of injustice: Irrelevant factors

(1) Possession by the buyer of the thing bought

15.26 See paragraph 15.23, above as to the irrelevance of this in equity courts, and, in particular, *Lindsay Petroleum v. Hurd*.[77]

(2) Delay per se or "mere" delay

15.27 Delay is of no importance *per se*. It may be relevant in that it may have changed the nature of the thing, or (after full knowledge has been acquired) it may imply acceptance with knowledge.[78] Subject to that, the mere passage of time, particularly the passage of time during which the buyer is ignorant of the defect, is unimportant: In Lord Penzance's statement quoted above from *Erlanger v. New Sombrero Phosphate*[79] the lapse of 14 months did not disentitle the plaintiffs from relief. In the same case Lord Blackburn pointed out the relative unimportance of "mere delay", mentioning that nine years had elapsed in one case, and nearly as long in another. Lindley M.R. in the *Lagunas Nitrate*[80] case said: "Mere lapse of time whilst the original directors were in office cannot, in my opinion, avail the syndicate in this action." Also perhaps relevant are *Gillett v. Peppercorne*,[81] a dealing with the vulnerable (a principal and agent transaction) which was set aside after a lapse of 14 years; and *Armstrong v. Jackson*,[82] a six-year delay case which had a checklist of the number of years' delay in various earlier cases: six years in *Rothschild v. Brookman*[83] and in *Oelkers v. Ellis*[84]; 11 years in *York Building Co. v. Mackenzie*;[85] and 15 in *Oliver v. Court*.[86]

[77] Above.
[78] See "He must come with the utmost diligence" (at para. 15.32, below).
[79] Above.
[80] Above.
[81] (1840) 3 Beav. 78; 49 E.R. 31.
[82] [1917] 2 K.B. 822.
[83] (1831) 2 Dow. & Cl. 188; 5 E.R. 273.
[84] [1914] 2 K.B. 130.
[85] 3 Pat. App. Cas. 378.
[86] 8 Price 127; 146 E.R. 1152.

(3) A drop in value of the thing caused by a change in the market value

15.28 In *Western Bank of Scotland v. Addie*[87] Lord Cranworth said:

> "I agree with the learned Judges below, that the circumstance that the shares, from mismanagement or otherwise, *had become depreciated in value subsequently to the purchase by the Pursuer, would of itself have been of no importance.*[88] He might still have been able to restore that which he was fraudulently induced to purchase. But what took place was not a depreciation but a destruction of the thing purchased . . ."

In *Armstrong v. Jackson,*[89] another dealing with the vulnerable, it was sensibly pointed out by McCardie J. that:

> ". . . it is only in cases where the plaintiff has sustained loss by the inferiority of the subject matter or a substantial fall in its value that he will desire to exert his power of rescission."

(4) Completion or execution of the contract by conveyance, grant of a lease, registration of shares, etc.

15.29 Chapter 17, Rescission of Executed Sales, contains a full discussion of this supposed "bar" to rescission.

The act of rescission: whose is it and when does it date from?

15.30 It is the act of the party himself. He makes an election to rescind or not, and communicates it to the other side. If not accepted by the other side, a limbo period ensues before the act of rescission is either confirmed or rejected by the court. When the order confirming rescission is made, it dates back, it would seem, to the time, after the election to rescind was communicated to the vendor or defining party, when the action in court was commenced.

In *Re Reese River Silver Mining Co v. Smith*[90] Lord Hatherley L.C., said:

> "It appeared to your Lordships, and with all humility I would say it appears to me, perfectly correct to say that the agreement subsists until rescinded; that is to say, in this sense—until rescinded *by the declaration*[91] of him whom you have sought to bind by it, that he no longer accepts the agreement, but entirely rejects and repudiates it. It is not meant, I apprehend, by that expression 'until rescinded', used by any of your Lordships at the time when that case was argued before the House, to say that the rescission

[87] (1867) L.R. 1 H.L. (S.c) 159.
[88] Italics supplied.
[89] [1917] 2 K.B. 822.
[90] (1869) L.R. 4 H.L. 64.
[91] Italics supplied.

must be an act of some Court of competent authority, and that, until the rescission by that Court of competent authority takes place, the agreement is subsisting in its full rigour."

On the question of the period of validity of the original agreement, he said: "I apprehend the true view of the case is this. The agreement is valid until rescinded."

On the time question, he said:

> "If it were necessary to use the word 'rescinded' in any way in that sense, it appears to me that it would be more correct to say that the rescission by a Court of competent authority dates from the moment when proceedings were taken invoking the aid of that competent authority . . ."

15.31 The remainder of their Lordships will have agreed, since the outcome of the case depended on when exactly the share agreement ceased to be valid. It was held that it had ceased to be valid when the shareholder commenced his action, so that it did not matter that the winding up ensued.

The election whether to accept or reject the contract is a final decision by the party, and cannot be revoked. It is unclear what the status of an election to rescind is during the period after the decision has been communicated but before an action has been commenced.

The decision to affirm on the other hand only needs "express words or an unequivocal act".

In *Clough v. London & Northwestern Railway Co.*,[92] a Court of Exchequer decision, Mellor J. said, delivering the judgment of the court[93]:

> "And, as it is stated in Com Dig Election, C2, if a man once determines his election it shall be determined for ever. And consequently we agree with what seems to be the opinion of all the judges below, 'that if it can be shewn that [the company] have at any time after knowledge of the fraud, either by *express words or unequivocal acts*,[94] affirmed the contract, their election has been determined for ever.' He went on to compare the case of an election to rescind to a landlord forfeiting a lease: "if by bringing ejectment he unequivocally shews his intention to treat the lease as void, he has determined his election, and cannot afterwards waive the forfeiture."

There seems not to be any express authority on the point, unless it be the preceding case, but it appears to follow from the statements of the court about the finality of the election that once the election is made *and the action started*, the rescinding party is free from the danger that his acts may be construed as affirmation. Thus, he may probably negotiate arrangements (whether or not expressly "without

[92] (1871) L.R. 7 Ex. 26.

[93] Affirmed in 1873 by another Court of Exchequer in ***Morrison v. Universal Marine Insurance Co.*** (1873) L.R. 8 Ex. 197.

[94] Italics supplied.

prejudice") with the vendor or defining party during the limbo period, in order, for example, to limit the damages which he will have to pay if the court decides he was not, after all, entitled to rescind.

How quickly after acquiring knowledge of the defect must a person rescind to be safe?—"He must come with the utmost diligence"

15.32 The cases seem contradictory at first blush. On the one hand there are statements to the effect that one would be lucky to be allowed say, two months in which to ascertain whether one has a real cause of action[95]; on the other there are cases where a relatively relaxed attitude to time is taken, such as *Clough v. London & Northwestern Railway Co.*[96], in which it was said that a person might delay so long as he had remained neutral and not finally elected, and so long as while he was deliberating no third party had acquired rights in the property, or indeed "if in consequence of his delay the position even of the wrongdoer is affected".

There is probably no real conflict between the cases. The apparent difference of emphasis derives simply from the degree of risk of injustice inherent in the circumstances of the cases in question. The truth is that a person who does not rescind *very quickly indeed* after acquiring full knowledge of the defect, that is, not only make his declaration to the other party, but also commence his action, *is* at risk. How much he is at risk will depend on the circumstances. If he does nothing at all, that is, does not even indicate to the other party that he does rescind, he is at risk that his inaction, certainly if it continues for a long time, will be construed as acceptance of the contract. If he does communicate his decision to the other party, he remains at risk of an innocent third party acquiring rights in the subject matter of the contract, in which case an automatic bar drops down. It seems likely to follow, therefore, that the speed which the court will expect may depend a little on the likelihood of such third parties cropping up. It is noticeable that the most ferocious statements about the need for speed occur in the company cases, where the risk of a third party being prejudiced is great. In *Central Rly Co. of Venezuela v. Kisch*,[97] for example, Lord Romilly commented that while a plaintiff wanting to rescind his share agreement remained a shareholder, people might be induced to deal with the company on the faith of his remaining a member. "The result is, that it becomes necessary for him, in order to set aside *a contract of this description*, that *he should come with the utmost diligence* for that purpose, so that no person may be misled by the fact of his remaining a member."[98] It is to be noted that he limited his statement to "a contract of this description". Perhaps the best

[95] ***Re Reese River Company v. Smith***, above.
[96] Above.
[97] (1867) L.R. 2 H.L. 99.
[98] Italics supplied.

general statement, as far as it goes, is that of Lord Blackburn in *Erlanger v. New Sombrero Phosphate Company*[99]:

> "And a Court of Equity requires that those who come to it to ask its active interposition to give them relief, should use due diligence, after there has been such notice or knowledge as to make it inequitable to lie by. And any change which occurs in the position of the parties or the state of the property after such notice or knowledge should tell much more against the party *in mora* [delaying] than a similar change before he was *in mora* should do".

It should be stressed that the need for speed arises only after full knowledge (including of course constructive notice through failure to exercise due diligence or follow up puzzling features) of the defect has been acquired: the period before that is immaterial *in itself*.[1]

The working out of an order for rescission: practical justice

15.33 As has been seen, provided that "practical justice" can be achieved, and the "nature of the thing" has not been altogether changed by the buyer or inquiring party, there may be rescission. The matter which will often need some considerable attention to detail will be the accounts and inquiries needed to ensure practical justice to both sides. There may also need to be a signalling of what has happened to third parties, by means of a note to be registered at H.M. Land Registry, etc. The accounts and inquiries may be for the benefit of either the party rescinding or the party rescinded against. The main point about these is that they may vary according to the circumstances. A former Chief Chancery Master, Master Chamberlain, used to give advice to young members of the Bar and others about about drafting orders containing accounts and inquiries. You should, he said, consider what in the circumstances your client actually wanted, and ask for it in your order; there was no precedent which would deal with every case but you could be sure that if you did not ask for it you would not get it. There may be some, daunted at the imagined cobweb-shrouded mystique of Chancery accounts and inquiries, who will still find the Chief Master's prescription a liberating one.

To revert to guidance from the cases, Lord Blackburn in *Erlanger's Case*[2] said this about the exercise by Courts of Equity of their practical-justice jurisdiction:

> "It would obviously be unjust that a person who has been in possession of property under the contract which he seeks to repudiate should be allowed to throw that back on the other party's hands without accounting for any benefit he may have derived from the use of the property, or if the property, though not

[99] Above.
[1] See as to this the section at para. 15.27, above on Mere delay.
[2] Above.

> destroyed, has been in the interval deteriorated, without making compensation for that deterioration."

This might be done in the Courts of Equity by taking an account of profits, and making allowance for deterioration.

Thus, the court will provide accounts and inquiries to restore the position on both sides—not precisely to that which it was before the contract, but to the *fair equivalent*.

The working out of rescission: the distinction between a rescission order and a damages order.

15.34 The question arises, how far does practical justice extend. It would probably not be right to say, It does not extend as far as damages, because it may on occasions go further than damages: for example a property which has fallen in value since the date of the representation/breach of good faith could possibly give rise to greater compensation by way of rescission than damages. (Damages tend to be a more desirable remedy in times of rising values: while rescission (sometimes together with a claim for consequential damages) is perhaps more likely to be desired in times of falling values, and a reasonable option when prices remain stable.) Nonetheless a clear distinction must be drawn between the two. On this point, note *Newbigging v. Adam*[3] and *Whittington v. Seale-Hayne*.[4] In the latter case, Farwell J. considered the judgments in *Newbigging v. Adam*[5] and stated that he considered, in line with the judgment of Bowen LJ in that case, that:

> "the Plaintiff is entitled to an indemnity in respect of all obligations entered into under the contract when those obligations are within the necessary or reasonable expectation of both the contracting parties at the time of the contract."

It had been made clear in *Newbigging v. Adam*[6] that expressions such as "loss arising out of the contract" would be too wide, as possibly embracing damages at common law. An example of the kind of loss which would not be recovered by way of rescission (but see the Misrepresentation Act 1967) was given by Cotton L.J. in *Newbigging v. Adam*[7]—a commission in the army given up by reason of the misstatements; no relief at all could be obtained for this save by an action in deceit.

The second question is where the line is to be drawn between practical justice and making a new contract for the parties? This has been the subject of consideration by the Court of Appeal recently in *TSB v. Camfield*[8] in the course of the working out of the House of Lords

[3] (1886) 34 Ch. D. 582.
[4] (1900) 82 L.T. 49.
[5] Above.
[6] *ibid.*
[7] *ibid.*
[8] [1995] 1 W.L.R. 430.

decision in *Barclay's Bank v. O'Brien*.[9] In that case an argument had been put forward, relying on *Hanson v. Keating*[10] and *Cheese v. Thomas*[11] for the proposition that there was a wide jurisdiction to set aside "on terms", by which was meant in effect a wide discretion as to terms the court felt to be a good idea. Mrs Camfield had succeeded in setting aside a mortgage without limit of liability into which she was induced to enter by her husband's undue influence. She would have agreed to a mortgage with a maximum liability of £15,000. Thus, it was suggested, the "terms" on which it should be set aside should include partial enforcement: that is a new charge with such a limit. This novel idea was rightly, no doubt, rejected by the Court of Appeal, who affirmed that a setting-aside must be total. In fact, interestingly, *Hanson v. Keating*[12] itself destroys rather than supports the argument for partial enforcement anyway. In that case the Vice-Chancellor, Sir James Wigram had said:

> "The rule, as I have often had occasion to observe, cannot *per se* decide what terms the Court should impose upon the Plaintiff as the price of the decree it gives him. It decides in the abstract that the Court giving the Plaintiff the relief to which he is entitled will do so only upon the terms of his submitting to give the Defendant such corresponding rights (if any) as he also may be entitled to in respect of the subject-matter of the suit; what these rights are must be determined *aliunde* [elsewhere] by strict rules of law, and not by any arbitrary determination of the Court. The rule, in short, merely raises the question what those terms (if any) should be. If, for example, a Plaintiff seeks an account against a Defendant, the Court will require the Plaintiff to do equity by submitting himself to account in the same matter in which he asks an account; the reason of which is that the Court does not take accounts partially, and perhaps ineffectually, but requires that the whole subject be, once for all, settled between the parties . . . So, if a bill be filed by the obligor in an usurious bond, to be relieved against it, the Court, in a proper case, will cancel the bond, but only upon terms of the obliggor refunding to the obligee the money actually advanced. The reasoning is analogous to that in the previous cases. The equity of the obligor is to have the entire transaction rescinded. The Court will do this so as to remit both parties to their original positions: it will not relieve the obligor from his liability, leaving him in possession of the fruits of the illegal transaction he complains of. I know of no case which cannot be explained upon this or analogous reasoning; and my opinion is that the Court can never lawfully impose merely arbitrary conditions upon a Plaintiff . . ."[13]

[9] [1994] 1 A.C. 180.
[10] (1844) 4 Hare 1; 67 E.R. 537.
[11] [1994] 1 W.L.R. 129.
[12] Above.
[13] See, however, the recent Australian partial enforcement case of ***Vadusz v. Pioneer Concrete Ltd.*** (1995) 130 A.L.R. 570 in which partial enforcement was ordered and note thereto.

Some examples of types of rescission orders made

15.35 Although every case should be considered individually, as suggested above, there *are* undoubtedly certain fairly common types of order which have been made in certain categories of case, and some of these are noted below.

Real property transactions

15.36 In *Edwards v. M'Leay*[14] the order as amended by Lord Eldon on appeal was an order:

(1) setting aside the sale and ordering that the purchase money and costs be paid; and
(2) that the vendors pay to the purchaser "all costs charges and expenses, which the Plaintiff has been properly put to in consequence of, or which have been incident to, the purchase of the said house and premises, and the conveyance thereof to the Plaintiff", with an account to be taken (with directions about what evidence the parties were to produce etc) of these costs charges and expenses.

No specific mention of interest is made, but it would have been commonplace for interest on the purchase price to be paid: note the cases in Chapter 5, Sale of Land, in which specific performance was refused and rescission granted: interest was always paid in these.

In *Hart v. Swaine*[15] Fry J.

(1) set aside the sale;
(2) declared the deed inoperative, and ordered that a memorandum of the judgment be endorsed by the Registrar on the deed in question and that it then be delivered up to the defendant;
(3) ordered that the defendant repay the purchase money with interest, after deducting the amount of the rents and profits derived by the plaintiffs from their land during their occupation of it; and finall
(4) directed an account as in *Edwards v. M'Leay*[16] of the expenses incurred in consequence of the purchase of the land, the defendant to pay the amount found due and also the costs of the action.

It should be noted that the last account probably needs re-wording to take specific account of the clarification of the law in *Whittington v. Seale-Hayne*[17]: probably the addition of "provided that such expenses were within the necessary and reasonable expectation of the parties at the time of the contract" would suffice.

[14] (1815) G. Coop. 308; 35 E.R. 568, noted in the Appx to Chap. 16.
[15] (1877) 7 Ch. D. 42, cited in the Appx to Chap. 16.
[16] Above.
[17] Above.

15.37 In *Whittington v. Seale-Hayne*[18] itself the plaintiff was awarded:

(1) rescission and cancellation of the executed lease;
(2) sums to compensate him for the rents, rates and repairs he had paid for under the lease; but *not* the value of the lost poultry due to the insanitary conditions in the premises.

Also relevant are the Australian cases *Brown v. Smitt*[19] in which the purchaser of a farm was allowed the cost of repairs, the value he had added to the land by his permanent improvements (not mere matters of taste or personal enjoyment) but was refused recovery of business losses while in occupation; and *Alati v. Kruger*[20] where the fact that the purchaser had closed down the premises so that the landlord re-entered necessitated a fairly complicated working-out in the rescission order but did not prevent the grant of rescission.

In cases which have not proceeded to completion the normal order is for the agreement to be set aside and the deposit to be returned with interest[21]:

Partnership transactions

15.38 In *Rawlins v. Wickham*[22] in which the plaintiff was allowed rescission of an agreement to purchase a partnership share some four years after he had become a partner, the order was:

(1) that the agreement should be set aside and the purchase-money repaid with costs; and
(2) that the defendant's estate should indemnify the plaintiff against the partnership liabilities.

Sale of shares

15.39 In, for example *Henderson v. Lacon*[23] in the Appendix to Chapter 7, Sale of Shares. the plaintiff obtained rescission of the agreement and removal from the register of shareholders. (He also obtained an injunction restraining the Company which by then had been wound up, from proceeding against him: this would not seem to be necessary in normal circumstances nowadays.)

Contracts involving the loan of money

15.40 Where a bond for an excessive amount was set aside it was always permitted to stand as security for the amount bona fide advanced[24]:

18 *ibid.*
19 (1924) 24 C.L.R. 160.
20 (1955) 94 C.L.R. 216.
21 See Atkin, *Court Forms*, Vol 37, Specific Performance, for precedents.
22 (1858) 3 De G. & J. 304; 44 E.R. 1285.
23 (1867) L.R. 5 Eq. 249.
24 See, *e.g. How v. Weldon & Edwards* (1754) 2 Ves. Sen. 516; 28 E.R. 330, in the App. to Chap. 7; and *Gwynne v. Heaton* (1778) 1 Bro. C.C. 1; 28 E.R. 949, in which the lender was also given the costs of his redemption account. See also *Hanson v. Keating* (1844) 4 Hare 1; 67 E.R. 537.

Contracts involving the use of services, for example of a solicitor or publisher/publicity agent

15.41 There is a very long tradition of fair payment for services rendered under the agreement set aside. In *Proof v. Hines*[25] a case of legal or para-legal assistance with a claim, a bond the plaintiff was induced to give was set aside, and allowed to stand as security only for what had actually been "laid out", with interest. It would seem this was simply the defendant's expenses: it appears from the report they would have incurred expense searching registers. etc. The defendant was left "at liberty to bring his quantum meruit at law for what he deserved for his pain and trouble."

In *Walmsley v. Booth*[26] a bond in favour of an attorney was set aside but Lord Hardwicke ordered an inquiry into any extraordinary services rendered, and payment for what was justly due.

For a more modern example, see *O'Sullivan v. Management Agency*[27] in which the defendant publisher-promoters were given "reasonable remuneration including a profit element"; although this was to fall short of a real sharing of profit on the venture with the plaintiff. Although one's first impression is of a slightly imprecise distinction, it is a distinction probably fairly easy to operate in practice: the distinction being probably between being paid for one's skill, in the same way that any outsider might be (and which can be checked against outside norms), and a sharing in profits in the way a partner or true joint venturer might (which is limited only by the profits of the venture and the number of venturers).

See also the recent Australian case of *Warman v. Dwyer*,[28] exploring the proper basis on which an account of profits was to be ordered in a business conducted by a fiduciary in breach of his duty but which would or might have made some profits quite apart from those attributable to the breach of duty anyway. The High Court of Australia relied on the preceding case *inter alia*, but may have gone very slightly further, at least in cases where an account of profits was the relief sought:

> "It is for the defendant to establish that it is inequitable to order an account of the entire profits. If the defendant does not establish that that would be so, then the defendant must bear the consequences of mingling the profits attributable to the defendant's breach of fiduciary duty and the profits attributable to those earned by the defendant's efforts and investment, in the same way that a trustee of a mixed fund bears the onus of distinguishing what is his own.
>
> *Whether it is appropriate to allow an errant fiduciary a proportion of profits or to make an allowance in respect of skill, expertise and other expenses is a matter of judgment which will depend on the facts of the*

[25] (1735) Cases T. Talbot 111.
[26] (1739) 2 Atk. 25.
[27] [1985] Q.B. 428.
[28] (1995) 128 A.L.R. 201.

given case. However, as a general rule, in conformity with the principle that a fiduciary must not profit from a breach of fiduciary duty, *a court will not apportion profits in the absence of an antecedent arrangement for profit-sharing* but will make allowance for skill, expertise and other expenses."[29]

APPENDIX TO CHAPTER 15: SOME CASES OF INTEREST

Hunt v. Silk (1804) 5 East. 448; 102 E.R. 1142 (Example of strict attitude taken by common law courts)

15.42 The defendant landlord agreed to let a house to the plaintiff for a premium of £10 to be paid on execution of lease and counterpart, and the putting of the premises into repair, this all to take place in ten days time. The plaintiff tenant paid over the premium right away and moved in, then moved out again after after 12 days, when the landlord failed to put the premises into repair, and demanded his money back. Lord Ellenborough C.J. considered that the tenant had waived his right to rescind for breach of the repairing agreement by voluntarily paying over the money "giving the defendant credit for his future performance of the contract" and afterwards continuing in possession despite the default. He said "Now where a contract is to be rescinded at all, it must be rescinded in toto, and the parties put in statu quo. But here was an intermediate occupation, a part execution of the agreement, which was incapable of being rescinded. If the plaintiff might occupy the premises two days beyond the time when the repairs were to have been done and the lease executed, and yet rescind the contract, why might he not rescind it after a twelvemonth on the same account. This objection cannot be gotten rid of: the parties cannot be put in statu quo."

The other judges agreed, Lawrence J. pointing out that the tenant could have made his payment of £10 conditional on the repairs being executed, rather than generally on account of the contract.

Rothschild v. Brookman (1831) 2 Dow. & Cl. 188; 5 E.R. 273 (Acceptance of defect only after full knowledge)

15.43 This is a delightful case. It concerns a dealing with a vulnerable person. Mr Brookman informed Mr Rothschild that he had some French rentes, and was persuaded that he should buy some Prussian bonds in the market with the proceeds. Mr Rothschild gave him to understand that he had sold and purchased some Prussian bonds. In fact, Mr Rothschild supplied the bonds out of his own stock on his behalf. A number of other transactions took place under Mr Rothschild's advice.

Lord Wynford said "I am very sorry to say, that, with respect to one of the parties in this case, it is perfectly clear that he is a most desperate gambler in the funds, and he has met with that fate which most of those meet with who become such gamblers. For I believe whenever a man puts his foot into the Stock Exchange, not being a member of that Stock Exchange, his ruin is certain, and the only question is a question of time. Therefore that has hap-

[29] Italics supplied.

pened to this Plaintiff which generally happens: for, according to the statement, he has been completely ruined. That he has acted in most of these transactions under the advice of Mr Rothschild cannot be denied. But I do not mean to say that Mr Rothschild gave him that advice with any dishonest view whatever; I have no doubt he acted fairly and properly: but the ground on which I am disposed to move your lordships to affirm this judgment goes wide of that. I am firmly persuaded that many bankers and many stockbrokers in London have acted precisely in the same manner as Mr Rothschild acted on this occasion. God forbid that I should say that these gentlemen, or any of them, have taken advantage of the confidence that was reposed in them; and, under colour of proceedings such as have taken place here, that they have injured the parties who so trusted to them. But the law which your lordships are to administer is a law of jealousy: it will not allow any man to be trusted with power, that will give him an opportunity of taking advantage of his employer. If that is so, it appears to me, in every one of these transactions, Mr Rothschild has had an opportunity, from the nature of his employment, and the manner in which he conducted himself, of taking advantage of the person with whom he was dealing, if he was disposed to take that advantage; and though I am willing to say, that I do not believe Mr Rothschild to be capable of doing that, we must deal with Mr Rothschild as with any other individual, and say that he ought not to be concerned in such transactions under such circumstances."

On the question of acceptance of the defect (laches) Lord Wynford said: "An observation has been made as to the staleness of the demand: undoubtedly if it had appeared that the Plaintiff knew, at a period long before that at which he thought proper to institute proceedings, *what was the real character of these transactions*, I agree that he would have been precluded by laches from coming to complain of them. But I think it is for Mr Rothschild to show that he had *notice of what was the true character of the transaction*. From the very nature of the transaction itself, it is very likely the gentleman should have remained for a long time in the state of ignorance in which he had been of the circumstances under which he had been dealing with the Appellant. A man not conversant with that which passes in old established houses in the city of London could not suppose that when gentlemen recommended him to sell, they meant to be the buyers."[30]

***Campbell v. Fleming* (1834) 1 A. & E. 40; 110 E.R. 1122 (Acts of ownership/ acceptance of the defect)**

15.44 The plaintiff bought shares in a supposed joint stock mining company relying on representations made by agents of the defendants. However the plaintiff, after he learned of the fraud practised on him consolidated the shares with some other property, and sold shares in the new company and realised a considerable sum of money. The court (Littledale, Parke, Patteson J.J., Lord Denman C.J.) held that it was too late: he had by his actions waived his right to object to the fraud. Nor was his right revived by discovery of another facet of the fraud after the above consolidation. The new fraud, according to Patteson J., merely strengthened the evidence of the original fraud, no more.

***Gillett v. Peppercorne* (1840) 3 Beav. 78; 49 E.R. 31 (Mere delay unimportant)**

15.45 This was a sale of a broker's own shares to his principal. It was set aside after a lapse of several years. Lord Langdale M.R. said: "It is said that this is

[30] Italics supplied.

every day's practice in the city. I certainly should be very sorry to have it proved to me that such a sort of dealing is usual; for nothing can be more open to the commission of fraud than transactions of this nature. Where a man employs another as his agent, it is on the faith that such agent will act in the matter purely and disinterestedly for the benefit of his employer, and assuredly not with the notion that the person whose assistance is required as agent, has himself in the very transaction, an interest directly opposed to that of his principal. It frequently, I believe, happens that the same person is agent for both parties, in which case he holds an even hand, and acts, in one sense, as arbitrator between them; but if a person employed as agent on account of his skill and knowledge is to have, in the very same transaction, an interest directly opposite to that of his employer, it is evident that the relation between the parties then becomes of such a nature, as must inevitably lead to continued disappointment, if not to the continued practice of fraud."

***Prendergast v. Turton* (1841) 1 Y. & C. 98; 62 E.R. 807 ("He must come with due diligence")**

15.46 Relief from a declaration by a mining company forfeiting the plaintiffs' shares for refusing to pay further calls and certain other relief, was sought after nine years. The Vice-Chancellor, Sir J.L. Knight-Bruce, thought that having regard to "the peculiar nature of the property and the circumstances of the case" this was too late.

"This is a mineral property—a property, therefore, of a mercantile nature, exposed to hazard, fluctuations and contingencies of various kinds, requiring a large outlay, and producing, perhaps, a considerable amount of profit in one year, and losing it in the next. It requires, and of all properties perhaps the most requires, the parties interested in it to be vigilant and active in asserting their rights. This rule, frequently asserted by Lord Eldon, is consonant with reason and justice. Lord Eldon always acted upon it, and has been followed by subsequent Judges of great knowledge, experience and eminence."

***Vigers v. Pike* (1842) 8 Cl. & Fin. 562; 8 E.R. 220 (Acceptance of the defect—full knowledge essential)**

15.47 The chief interest of the case, in which rescission was not ordered, is the statement of Lord Cottenham (with whom Lord Brougham agreed), who found the company had there acquiesced with full knowledge of the acts on which its claim to rescission was based: "The doctrine of carrying equities by acquiescence, I consider to be one of the most important to be attended to; for otherwise there is great danger of the principles of a Court of Equity, thus improperly exercised, producing great injustice. A man who, *with full knowledge of his case*, does not complain, but deals with his opponent as if he had no case against him, builds up from day to day a wall of protection for such opponent, which will probably defeat any future attack upon him. . . ."[31]

***Duke of Leeds v. Earl Amherst* (1846) 2 Ph. 123; 41 E.R. 886 (Early labelling problems)**

15.48 Lord Cottenham explained the difference between acquiescence and the release or abandonment of a right: "Several grounds were suggested . . . First, acquiescence. Now, acquiescence is not the term which ought to be used. If a party, having a right, stands by and sees another dealing with the property

[31] Italics supplied.

in a manner inconsistent with that right, and makes no objection while the act is in progress, he cannot afterwards complain. That is the proper sense of the word acquiescence.... The defence ... which is really intended to be set up, is not acquiescence, but release or abandonment of the party's right. For that purpose, however, it is not only necessary to shew that the Plaintiff knew of the acts of waste having been committed, but that he knew of the rights which they gave him against his father, and that having such knowledge, he did some act amounting to a release of that right."

***White v. Garden* (1851) 10 C.B. 919; 138 E.R. 364 (Prevention of injustice to third parties)**

15.49 A fraudulent seller sold goods to a purchaser who sold on to another purchaser. The purchaser had already delivered to the sub-purchaser's wharf when he learned of the fraud, and sent to seize the goods back. The court held that the property in the goods had already passed to the sub-purchaser. Talfourd J. said: "A contract for the sale of goods, though obtained by fraud, is perfectly good, if the party defrauded thinks fit to ratify it. It appears to me that the defendants here intentionally parted with their property in the iron when they caused it to be delivered to the plaintiff; and it is not competent to them, after a third party has by their act been induced to part with his money, to turn round and say that the contract as between them and [the vendor] was null and void, and that [the vendor] had no property, and therefore could pass none to the plaintiff ..."

Jervis C.J. added that any other finding would be inconvenient. "The question is one of considerable importance, as affecting the mercantile transactions of this country: for, if the argument urged on the part of the defendants were well founded, goods at all tainted by fraud might be followed through any number of bona fide purchasers—a most inconvenient, and, as it strikes me, a most absurd doctrine. A vendor, who does not choose to avail himself of means of inquiry, would thus, by trusting the vendee, be giving him unlimited means of defrauding the rest of the world."

***Deposit Life Assurance v. Ayscouch* (1856) 6 E. & B. 761; 119 E.R. 1048**

15.50 In this case it was held that a shareholder could not seek rescission while still remaining a shareholder: he had to have ceased to be one, or at least taken steps to cease to be so.

***Clegg v. Edmondson* (1858) 8 De G.M. & G. 789; 44 E.R. 593 ("He must come with due diligence")**

15.51 The plaintiffs had had a right to set aside a mining lease taken by a former partner of theirs. They continually asserted their claim but commenced no action for nine years. Turner L.J. accepted that the plaintiffs had not ceased to assert their claim, but said: "... I cannot agree to a doctrine so dangerous as that the mere assertion of a claim unaccompanied by any act to give effect to it, can avail to keep alive a right which would otherwise be precluded."

Knight-Bruce L.J. agreed, saying: "A mine which a man works is in the nature of a trade carried on by him. It requires his time, care, attention and skill to be bestowed on it, besides the possible expenditure and risk of capital, nor can any degree of science, foresight and examination afford a sure guarantee against sudden losses, disappointments and reverses. In such cases a man having an adverse claim in equity on the ground of constructive trust should pursue it promptly, and not by empty words merely. He should shew himself in good time willing to participate in possible loss as well as profit, not play a game in which he alone risks nothing."

Note: The tenor of the case is that the degree of speed required depends very much on the inherent degree of risk of injustice in the situation.

***Rawlins v. Wickham* (1858) 3 De G. & J. 304; 44 E.R. 1285**

15.52 The court (Knight-Bruce and Turner L.J.J.) held that the plaintiff was entitled to set aside the partnership agreement into which he had entered and have an indemnity against the partnership liabilities from a deceased partner's, Mr Wickham's, estate even though he had been a partner for four years. Both Lord Justices held that Mr Wickham had known nothing of the fraud: where he had been wrong was in *taking upon himself to state that the accounts represented the true financial position of the bank without satisfying himself that that was in fact so.* As Turner L.J. said: "Putting the case of the representations of Mr Wickham on the most favourable ground, this was a representation by him of a fact of the truth or falsehood of which he knew nothing—and it was a representation which must have formed a material inducement to Mr Rawlins. It has turned out that this representation was contrary to the fact. *There was not as I think any moral fraud* [that is fraud as we know it, involving dishonesty], *but there was legal fraud* [ie equitable fraud or lack of good faith]". . . .[32]

Turner L.J. also said: "There has been no dispute upon the principles, and the case plainly falls within them. *If upon a treaty for purchase one of the parties to the contract makes a representation materially affecting the subject-matter of the contract, he surely cannot be heard to say that he knew nothing of the truth or falsehood of that which he represented, and still more surely he cannot be allowed to retain any benefit which he has derived if the representation he has made turns out to be untrue.* It would be most dangerous to allow any doubt to be cast upon this doctrine. To do so would be to open a door to escape in all cases of representation as to credit, and indeed in all other cases of representation."[33]

On the *delay* by the plaintiff and the means of knowledge which he had had during his four years as partner, he said: ". . . it was said that he had the means of detecting it and ought to have done so, and it was asked on what ground the Defendants were to be made liable to the Plaintiff for acts which were done during the continuance of the partnership. This argument, it is to be observed, does not proceed upon the ground of acquiescence. To the argument put on that ground it would, I think, be an answer that there was no knowledge of the right, and so far as the argument rests upon the Plaintiff's means of knowledge, the case of *Harris v. Kemble*[34] seems to me to furnish an answer to it. . . . I do not fail to observe that this was a case of specific performance, and subject to the peculiar rules applicable to such cases, in which the Court exercises a discretion, though not an arbitrary discretion, and that the case is a direct decision only upon the question whether the Court will enforce specific performance where there has been a misrepresentation; still *the remarks there made have an important bearing on all cases where the person misled might have detected the misrepresentation.* That case has also an important bearing on the question of subsequent conduct. Various acts had there been done under the agreement, tending to affirm it and to disable the Court from putting the parties in statu quo. It was held, however, that those acts were not sufficient to induce the Court to decree specific performance; and here, had there been acts by Mr Rawlins which would have made it difficult to put the estate of Mr Wickham in the same position as if the partnership had never

[32] Italics supplied.
[33] Italics supplied.
[34] 1 Sim 111; see Chap. 14.

been entered into, I think that case tends to shew that *those acts must have been strong to induce the Court to refuse relief . . .*"[35]

15.53 On rescission, he said: "It was strongly urged . . . that if the Court held the Plaintiff entitled to any relief, the proper course would be to decree the estate of Mr Wickham to make good the representations contained in the paper; that is, to pay the difference between the amount of debts there admitted and the real amount. But what are the true principles by which the Court is to be guided, where a person has been led to enter into a contract through a misrepresentation made by the other party to it? They are clearly laid down by Sir Thomas Plumer in *Clermont v. Tasburgh*[36] and are correctly stated in the marginal note: 'The effect of partial misrepresentation is not to alter or modify the agreement pro tanto, but to destroy it entirely, and to operate as a personal bar to the party who has practised it.' That, again, was a case of specific performance, and open to the same observations in that respect as *Harris v. Kemble*[37], but *Edwards v. M'Leay*[38] was a case of setting aside a contract. . . . The vendors at the time of the sale did not know that it was a part of the common, but they knew facts which gave them reason to believe that it might be so. On this ground Sir William Grant made a decree for setting aside the sale and repaying the purchase-money with costs, and the decree was affirmed by Lord Eldon. That case is conclusive to shew what is the course of the Court in cases of this description. And how should it be otherwise; for if a contract is obtained by fraud, it is for the party defrauded to elect whether he will be bound. He, perhaps, would not have entered into the contract at all if he had known the real facts; it is, therefore, impossible, with any degree of justice, to enforce the contract against him in any part. If he had discovered the misrepresentation immediately after it was made, the very fact of its having been made would, probably, in a case like the present, have deterred him from going further with the matter. It has, therefore, been rightly settled, that the party deceived has a right to have the contract wholly set aside."

Note: This case proceeds on the basis that if the reasonable purchaser had known the truth he would not have entered into the contract

***Ormes v. Beadel* (1860) 2 De. G.F. & J. 333 (Acceptance of defect)**

15.54 The plaintiff was held no longer to be in a position to rescind an agreement for building after he had acquiesced in the appointment of an arbitrator to settle the dispute under it, and by proceeding under the arbitration.

***Morley v. Attenborough* (1849), 3 Ex. 500; 154 E.R. 943 (Application of rescission to goods)**

15.55 It was said: "Unless the goods which the party could enjoy as his own, and make full use of, were delivered, the contract would not be performed. The purchaser could not be bound to accept if he discovered the defect of title before delivery; and if he did, and the goods were recovered from him, he would be not be bound to pay, or having paid, he would be entitled to recover back the price as on a consideration which had failed."

***Re Hop and Malt Exchange and Warehouse Co. ex parte Briggs* (1866) L.R. 1 Eq. 483 (Purchaser's duty of due diligence: knowledge inferred from failure)**

[35] Italics supplied.
[36] 1 Jac. & W. 1212; 57 E.R. 520.
[37] 1 Sun. 111; 57 E.R. 520.
[38] G. Coop, 308; 35 E.R. 568.

15.56 In this case a purchaser bought shares relying on the prospectus without looking at the company's memorandum. He sought to be removed from the register, complaining that the prospectus did not properly explain the articles, which went very much further than the prospectus. Lord Romilly M.R. said he was strongly inclined to think that in the light of the last clause of the prospectus, which invited inspection of the memorandum and articles and stated where they might be inspected, that the purchaser must be deemed to have notice of the contents of the articles anyway; but in any case the purchaser could not rescind here. He had acted as owner of the shares, and thus acquiesced, by giving instructions to his broker to sell the shares, and attempted to sell them, at a date after he knew the truth.

***Oakes v. Turquand* (1867) L.R. 2 H.L. 325 (Prevention of injustice to third parties)**

15.57 A shareholder induced by a false prospectus attempted to rescind, but was held too late after the winding up of the company, Overend Gurney & Co. Limited. The reason for this was explained as follows by the Lord Chancellor Lord Chelmsford. "It was said by the counsel for the Appellant that the Companies Act 1862, was to be regarded merely as adjusting the rights of the shareholders *inter se*, and that, as the liquidators represented the company, the liability of the Appellant must be determined as between himself and the company, and not as respects creditors with whom he never contracted. It is true that there was no contract between the creditor and the shareholders, and that the creditor probably never thought of the shareholders in his dealings with the company. But he must be taken to have known what his rights were under the Act, and that he had the security of all the persons whose names were to be found upon the register, and who had agreed to become shareholders. The liability of the shareholders is not under a contract with the creditors, but it is a statutable liability under which the creditors have a right which attaches upon the shareholders to compel them to contribute to the extent of their shares towards the payment of the debts of the company."

Lord Chelmsford went on to say regarding acquiescence: "I think that persons who have taken shares in a company are bound to make themselves acquainted with the memorandum of association, which is the basis upon which the company is established. If they fail to do so, and the objects of the company are extended beyond those described in the prospectus (a fact which may be easily ascertained), the persons who have so taken shares on the faith of the prospectus ought, in my opinion, to be held to be bound by acquiescence."

Lord Cranworth also considered that there had been a kind of holding out, as if the shareholder had been a partner, by having his name on the register.

***Central Rly Co. of Venezuela v. Kisch* (1867) L.R. 2 H.L. 99 ("He should come with the utmost diligence")**

15.58 This was another case in which a purchaser of shares sought rescission on the grounds of various omissions and misrepresentations in the prospectus.[39] Lord Romilly added two propositions, one regarding laches: that while a plaintiff in this position remained a shareholder, people might be induced to deal with the company on the faith of his becoming a member. "The result is, that it becomes necessary for him, in order to set aside a contract of this

[39] See also Appendix to Chap. 7.

description, that *he should come with the utmost diligence for that purpose, so that no person may be misled by the fact of his remaining a member.*"[40]

***Re Reese River Company v. Smith* (1867) L.R. 2 Ch. 604 C.A. ("He should come with the utmost diligence" (laches))**

15.59 The question of the speed with which the remedy should be sought was dealt with more fully in this case in the Court of Appeal than the House of Lords. In the Court of Appeal it was noted that Mr Smith the plaintiff received notice on December 30, 1865 that the property the company had contracted to purchase was valuless. However, in that letter the directors also said they expected in a few days to have a very elaborate report on the subject. This Mr Smith received on January 19, 1866. He commenced his action on February 6, 1866.

Sir G.J. Turner L.J. (with whom Lord Cairns agreed) said: "Now if time were to be taken as running against him from the 30th of December 1865, he possibly might be considered to have come too late. But I think improper delay cannot be imputed to him for not having filed his bill immediately after he received the letter of the 30th December 1865, and for this reason, that although that letter, or, rather, the enclosure in that letter, stated that the property was almost valueless, it said nothing as to what the state of the property had been, and therefore it might well be, that thought when the two directors got out to the country, they found the mine was valueless, it might have been a producing valuable mine at the time when the prospectus was issued; and I think he would not have been justified in filing his bill on the information which he had then received. It was not until the second report, which was received by him on the 19th of January, 1866, that the state of the property at the time when the purchase was made was made apparent to him by the statement that the workings had been abandoned for months." He noted also that in *Central Railway Company of Venezuela v. Kisch*,[41] there had been a delay of two months which was allowed.

***Re Cachar Co, Lawrence's Case* (1867) 2 Ch. App. 412**

15.60 Shares in unregistered company were bought on September 11; memorandum and articles were received on May 14 and repudiation September 27, was held to be too late.

***Re Russian (Vysounsky) Ironworks Company* (*Taite's Case*) (1867) L.R. 3 Eq. 795**

15.61 The shareholder indicated his intention of rescinding on July 2, and October 1 was held to be too late for application.

***Western Bank of Scotland v. Addie* (1867) L.R. 1 H.L. (Sc.) 159 (Change in the nature of the thing bought)**

15.62 The purchaser bought shares in an unincorporated association, and two years later agreed to its becoming incorporated. On the question whether he was in a position to give restitutio in integrum, the Lord Chancellor reserved his position; but Lord Cranworth said it was impossible to give *restitutio*. He said even if the company had not been in the course of being wound up it would still be impossible.

[40] Italics supplied.
[41] L.R. 2 H.L. 99.

"The Respondent might in that case have given up 135 shares of the new company, and these shares might have been as valuable as, or even more valuable than, the shares which he was induced to purchase, but they would not have been shares *in the same company*; and unless he was in a position to restore the very thing which he was fraudulently induced to purchase, he cannot have relief by way of restitutio in integrum . . . The circumstances were so changed that he could not put the Appellants in the condition in which they were before the fraudulent sale to him. I agree with the learned Judges below, that *the circumstance that the shares, from mismanagement or otherwise, had become depreciated in value subsequently to the purchase by the Pursuer, would of itself have been of no importance*. He might still have been able to restore that which he was fraudulently induced to purchase. But what in fact took place was *not a depreciation but a destruction of the thing purchased*; the unincorporated company in which he had been induced to purchase shares no longer existed."[42]

***Scholey v. Central Railway Co. of Venezuela* (1868) L.R. 9 Eq. 266n ("He must come with due diligence")**

15.63 In this attempted rescission of a share sale, Lord Cairns stressed the importance of due diligence in the company context. It is noted that he thought that the court would be most careful to see, in a company going on and trading, in which the rights of shareholders and others varied from day to day, that a person coming to complain of misrepresentations of this kind, and coming to avoid a voidable contract, came within the shortest limit of time which was fairly possible in such a case.

***Re Reese River v. Smith* (1869) L.R. 4 H.L. 64 (H.L.) (Nature of rescission, act of party)**

15.64 The House of Lords held that a shareholder who had a right to rescind his agreement to take shares in a company (in this case because of fraud in the prospectus) might rescind despite the winding up of the company, provided that he had put in his application to have his name removed from the list of shareholders before the winding up. The importance of the case for present purposes is simply the confirmation that rescission—whether or not it eventually comes before the court for confirmation—is the act of the party himself (he can after all elect not to exercise his right but to keep the shares) and if the court confirms his right, the rescission nonetheless dates back to the time when the party elected to rescind.

The Lord Chancellor Lord Hatherley referred to the earlier case of *Oakes v. Turquand*[43] and said: "It appeared to your Lordships, and with all humility I would say it appears to me, perfectly correct to say that the agreement subsists until rescinded; that is to say, in this sense—until rescinded by the declaration of him whom you have sought to bind by it, that he no longer accepts the agreement, but entirely rejects and repudiates it. It is not meant, I apprehend, by that expression 'until rescinded', used by any of your Lordships at the time when that case was argued before the House, to say that the rescission must be an act of some Court of competent authority, and that, until the rescission by that Court of competent authority takes place, the agreement is subsisting in its full rigour. If it were necessary to use the word 'rescinded' in any way in that sense, it appears to me that it would be more correct to say that the rescission by a Court of competent authority dates from

[42] Italics supplied.
[43] Above, para. 15.57.

the moment when proceedings were taken invoking the aid of that competent authority. . . .

I apprehend the true view of the case is this. The agreement is valid until rescinded . . ."

***Clough v. L & NW Ry* (1871) L.R. 7 Ex. 26 at 34 (Prevention of injustice)**

15.65 A company sold goods to one Adams and shipped them by the defendant's railway line to the plaintiff who was said by Adams to be his shipping agent. The company exercised its right of stoppage *in transitu*, believing that Adams was insolvent. It turned out that the transit had in fact determined before the company exercised its right, so the plaintiff sued the railway line. The company had not avoided the sale contract until after they were joined to the action. The court however held that the company had been entitled to rescind, not having done any act to affirm the contract or otherwise determine their election, and no interest having vested in any innocent third person rendering it inequitable or unjust to rescind the contract.

The judgment of the court (Byles, Blackburn, Mellor and Lush J.J.) was delivered by Mellor J. He said: "And we further agree that the contract continues valid till the party defrauded has determined his election by avoiding it. And, as is stated in Com Dig Election, C2, if a man once determines his election it shall be determined for ever; and, as is also stated in Com Dig Election C1, the determination of a man's election shall be made by express words or by act. And consequently we agree with what seems to be the opinion of all the judges below, that if it can be shewn that the [company] have at any time after knowledge of the fraud, either by express words or by unequivocal acts, affirmed the contract, their election has been determined for ever. But we differ from them in this, that we think the party defrauded may keep the question open so long as he does nothing to affirm the contract. The principle is precisely the same as that on which it is held that the landlord may elect to avoid a lease and bring ejectment, when his tenant has committed a forfeituer. If, with knowledge of the forfeiture, by the receipt of rent or other unequivocal act, he shews his intention to treat the lease as subsisting, he has determined his election for ever, and can no longer avoid the lease. On the other hand, if by bringing ejectment he unequivocally shews his intention to treat the lease as void, he has determined his election, and cannot afterwards waive the forfeiture . . . When a lessee commits a breach of covenant on which the lessor has a right of re-entry, he may elect to avoid or not avoid the lease, and he may do so by deed or by word; if, with notice, he says, under circumstances which bind him, that he will not avoid the lease, or he does an act inconsistent with his avoiding, as distraining for rent (not under the statute of Anne) or demanding subsequent rent, he elects not to avoid the lease; but if he says he will avoid, and does an act inconsistent with its continuance, as bringing ejectment, he elects to avoid it. In strictness, therefore, the question in such cases is, has the lessor, having notice of the breach, elected not to avoid the lease? or has he elected to avoid it? or has he made no election?

In all this we agree, and think that, mutatis mutandis, it is applicable to the election to avoid a contract for fraud. . . .

15.66 "We think that so long as he has made no election he retains the right to determine it either way, subject to this, that if in the interval whilst he is deliberating, an innocent third party has acquired an interest in the property, or if in consequence of his delay the position even of the wrong-doer is affected, it will preclude him from exercising his right to rescind.

"And lapse of time without rescinding will furnish evidence that he has determined to affirm the contract; and when the lapse of time is great, it probably would in practice be treated as conclusive evidence to shew that he has so determined. But we cannot see any principle, and are not aware of any authority, for saying that the mere fact that one who is a party to the fraud has issued a writ and commenced an action before the rescission, is such a *change of position*[44] as would preclude the defrauded party from exercising his election to rescind."

***Morrison v. Universal Marine Insurance Co.* (1873) L.R. 8 Ex. 197**

15.67 The case turned very much on its facts. However, the Court of Exchequer (Blackburn, Keating, Mellor, Lush, Honyman J.J.) affirmed the statement of the law in the preceeding case.

***Phipps v. Lovegrove* (1873) L.R. 16 Eq.80**

15.68 The principle that the person who takes a chose in action takes it subject to any equities which may be attached to it was affirmed.

***Lindsay Petroleum v. Hurd* (1874) L.R. 5 P.C. 221 (Prevention of injustice)**

15.69 This was a case of a dealing with a vulnerable person, a company, which was set aside. The judgment of the Privy Council was delivered by Sir Barnes Peacock.

"Now the doctrine of laches in Courts of Equity is not an arbitrary or a technical doctrine. Where it would be practically unjust to give a remedy, either because the party has, by his conduct, done that which might fairly be regarded as equivalent to a waiver of it, or where by his conduct and neglect he has, though perhaps not waiving that remedy, yet put the other party in a situation in which it would not be reasonable to place him if the remedy were afterwards to be asserted, in either of these cases, lapse of time and delay are most material. But in every case, if an argument against relief, which otherwise would be just, is founded upon mere delay, that delay of course not amounting to a bar by any statute of limitations, the validity of that defence must be tried upon principles substantially equitable. Two circumstances, always important in such cases, are, the length of the delay and the nature of the acts done during the interval, which might affect either party and cause a balance of justice or injustice in taking one course or the other, so far as relates to the remedy. In this case the delay was at all events not of very long duration, because the conveyance to the company was dated about fifteen months before the filing of the bill; the whole purchase-money was not paid before that time; and there is nothing which would justify us in reckoning the currency of time from an earlier period than that conveyance. Neither were any acts done in the interval, as it appears to us, at all material to the equity between the parties. There was possession taken, no doubt, but it would be a very novel proposition that mere possession is to be a bar, so as to raise a counter equity in cases of this description. Nothing appears to have been done beyond the sinking of a single well, by way of trial, upon the ground. The sinking of that well, if the land is restored, can in no substantial way operate to the prejudice of the Respondents; and, if any profit had been derived from it, the Court of first instance offered an account of that profit; but it manifestly was known that there was none, for that account was not accepted. The situation of the parties having, therefore, in no substantial way been altered, either by the delay or by anything done during the interval, there is in these circumstances nothing to give special importance to the defence founded on time . . .

[44] Italics supplied.

. . ."In order that the remedy should be lost by laches or delay, it is, if not universally at all events ordinarily—and certainly when the delay has been only such as in the present case—necessary that there should be sufficient knowledge of the facts constituting the title to relief."

Robinson v. Mollett (1875) L.R. 7 H.L. 810 (Implicit agreement to administrative consequences of the contract only: "within the authority conferred".)

15.70 The facts of the case were not dissimilar to *Rothschild v. Brookman*[45] Mellor J. said: "A person who authorizes a broker to buy in a market, the usages of which are not known to him, may reasonably expect to find that the mode of dealing in that market may not be in all respects such as he would anticipate, but he can hardly be supposed to contemplate that the universal acceptance of the nature and dealing of a broker to buy for him will be converted into a principal to sell to him."

Brett J. said he thought the question was what is the proper measure or limit of the control of mercantile customs by the law. He pointed out that the invocation of mercantile rules only occurred when there was a dispute. "When merchants have disputed as to what the governing rule should be, the Courts have applied to the mercantile business brought before them what have been called legal principles, which have almost always been the fundamental ethical rules of right and wrong. They have decided in favour of that course of business which was in accordance with such principles or rules, and against that course which was inconsistent with them. Thus, for example, when shipowners and underwriters disputed upon the effect of concealment of certain facts, the Courts finding that the contract of maritime insurance must be one of confidence, because the knowledge of many material facts must of necessity be confined to the shipowner, applied the principle of *uberrima fides* . . .

. . ."Customs of trade, as distinguished from other customs, are generally courses of business invented or relied upon in order to modify or evade some application which has been laid down by the Courts, of some rule of law to business, and which application has seemed irksome to some merchants. And when some such course of business is proved to exist in fact, and the binding effect of it is dispute, the question of law seems to be, whether it is in accordance with fundamental principles of right and wrong. A mercantile custom is hardly ever invoked but when one of the parties to the dispute has not, in fact, had his attention called to the course of business to be enforced by it; for if his attention had in fact been called to such course of business, his contract would be specifically made in accordance with it, and no proof of it as a custom would be necessary. A stranger to a locality, or trade, or market, is not held to be bound by the custom of such locality, trade, or market, because he knows the custom, but because he has elected to enter into transactions in a locality, trade, or market wherein all who are not strangers do know and act upon such custom. When considerable numbers of men of business carry on one side of a particular business, they are apt to set up a custom which acts very much in favour of their side of the business. So long as they do not infringe some fundamental principle of right and wrong, they may establish such a custom; but if, on dispute before a legal forum, it is found that they are endeavouring to enforce some rule of conduct which is so entirely in favour of their side that it is fundamentally unjust to the other side, the Courts have always determined that such a custom, if sought to be enforced against a person in fact ignorant of it, is unreasonable, contrary to law, and void. . . ."

[45] Para. 15.43, above.

15.71 Mr Baron Cleasby drew a distinction regarding the employment of a broker. "I quite agree that by employing a broker who acts upon a particular market you authorize him to make contracts upon all such terms as are usual upon the market, otherwise his hand would be tied and he might not be able to contract at all. Therefore as regards all such matters as the time and mode of payment, the time and mode of delivery, the various allowances to be made, the mode of adjusting disputes as to quality, and all such matters as arise upon the contract made in the market, the principal would be bound by the usage, but not I apprehend, because he must be supposed to have made inquiries and to have known them, but ... because they were within the authority conferred upon his agent ...

... "There seems to be no necessity to resort to so unreasonable a fiction as that persons who employ a broker, and who may send their instructions from all parts of the world, know the usages prevailing at the particular time upon the market where he acts. It is one thing to say that such usages adopted and prevailing at the time upon a particular market (or more correctly speaking, in a trade acrried on at a particular place) regulate all contracts made there: but quite a different thing to say that they should regulate the employment of a person to act as broker, which is not a contract made upon the exchange, but something done, as in the present case, hundreds of miles away and where the usage was never heard of."

***Erlanger v. New Sombrero Phosphate* (1878) 3 App. Cas. 1218 (Prevention of injustice)**

15.72 For a note of other aspects of this case see paragraph 9.91 of Chap. 9. Dealing with the Vulnerable Buyer or Seller. On delay, Lord Penzance said: "... I think it is clear that the company having, in the first instance, a right to relieve itself from this contract, which the promoters have unfairly fastened upon it, it is for the vendors to shew affirmatively that the company has forfeited that right. The actual lapse of time before commencing the suit was not very great. Delay, as it seems to me, has two aspects. Lapse of time may so change the condition of the thing sold, or bring about such a state of things that justice cannot be done by rescinding the contract subject to any amount of allowances or compensations. This is one aspect of delay, and it is in many cases particularly applicable to property of a mining character. But delay may also imply acquiescence, and in this aspect it equally bars the Plaintiff's right, for such a contract as is now under consideration is only voidable, not void.

"It conduces, I think, to clearness and to the exclusion of certain vagueness which is apt to hang about this doctrine of delay as a bar to relief, to keep these two different aspects of it separate and distinct when the consequences of delay come to be considered in connection with the circumstances of an individual case. And so dealing with the facts of the present case, I find myself unable to conclude affirmatively that it has been made out by the argument at the Bar that either the character of the property, or the way in which the company had dealt with it, did in point of fact preclude the possibility of justice being worked out on the basis of the contract being rescinded ...

"The substantial question, therefore, I think, is whether there was such delay as fairly imports acquiescence.

It is hardly suggested that the company or its executive knew, or had the means of knowing, the material facts before the meeting in February. ...

How soon, then, after the meeting of February, can the company be said to have known the material facts, or such of them as would make it reasonably their duty to investigate the matter if they meant to take exception to the mode in which the purchase had been effected?" He thought there was nothing to put the company on notice.

15.73 Lord Hatherley agreed, and also considered the question whether the six weeks, and then a further period of time for which they had delayed after the time they did know the true facts was to be held against the shareholders. He thought not, because they had resolved "instead of 'rushing into litigation' as they express it ... they should endeavour to ascertain all the facts concerning this contract, and endeavour to enter into negotiation with the members of the syndicate who were impugned by the report of the committee."[46]

Thus, the court decided that despite "the peculiar nature of the property, the shortness of the lease, the deterioration of the value, and the consequent difficulty of replacing the parties, on either side, in statu quo ante" (as Lord O'Hagan put it) the lapse of 14 months did not disentitle the respondents from seeking rescission.

Lord Blackburn considered that "mere delay" was relatively unimportant: he mentioned that nine years had elapsed in one case, and nearly as long in another. On the question of restoration of the parties to their original position, he said, after pointing out that a court of law had no machinery for taking accounts or estimating compensation: "But a court of equity could not give damages, and, unless it can rescind the contract, can give no relief. And, on the other hand, it can take accounts of profits, and make allowances for deterioration. And I think *the practice has always been for a court of equity to give this relief whenever, by the exercise of its powers, it can do what is practically just,* though it cannot restore the parties precisely to the state they were in before the contract."[47]

De Bussche v. Alt (1878) 8 Ch. D. 286 (Knowledge must be full knowledge)

15.74 A sub-agent bought the ship which was the subject of the agency himself, and sold on at a profit. On appeal, the court affirmed the principle that an agent cannot make a profit for himself, ordered an account, and emphasized that the principal had to know the full facts before consenting—a mere custom could not be pleaded against him.

Dealing with acquiescence, Thesiger L.J., giving the judgment of the court (James, Baggallay and Thesiger L.JJ.), said: "... before the principal can properly be said to have ratified or adopted the act of this agent or waived his right of complaint in respect of such acts, it should be shewn that *he has had full knowledge of its nature and circumstances, in other words, that he has had presented to his mind proper materials upon which to exercise his power of election,*[48] and it by no means follows that, because in a case like the present he does not repudiate the whole transaction after it has been completed, he has lost a right actually vested in him to the profits derived by his agent from it. It appears to us also that, looking to the dangers which would arise from any relaxation of the rules by which, in agency matters, the interests of principals are protected, the evidence by which in a particular case it is sought to prove that the principal has waived the protection afforded by those rules, should be clear and cogent."

Thesiger L.J. explained that the fact that the plaintiff had assented to the

[46] He went on to refer to a letter they wrote later which he thought an erroneous step, but noted it was with a full reservation of all their rights.

[47] Italics supplied.

[48] Italics supplied.

transaction being completed on the footing that the defendant had become the purchaser of the ship in question, and received the purchase money, and allowed the defendant to incur risk and expense in obtaining payment from the sub-purchaser, among other things, did not amount to acquiescence. He said: "It is necessary . . . to bring these circumstances to the test of legal principles. It is competent no doubt to a principal to ratify or adopt the act of his agent in purchasing that which such agent has been employed to sell, and to give up the right which he would otherwise be entitled to exercise of either setting aside the transaction or recovering from the agent the profits derived by him from it; and the non-repudiation for a considerable length of time of what has been done would, at least, be evidence of ratification or adoption, or might possibly by analogy to the Statute of Limitations constitute a defence; but before the principal can properly be said to have ratified or adopted the act of his agent or waived his right of complaint in respect of such acts, it should be shewn that he has had full knowledge of its nature and circumstances, in other words, that he has had presented to his mind proper materials upon which to exercise his power of election, and it by no means follows that, because in a case like the present he does not repudiate the whole transaction after it has been completed, he has lost a right actually vested in him to the profits derived by his agent from it. It appears to us also that, looking to the dangers which would arise from any relaxation of the rules by which, in agency matters, the interests of principals are protected, the evidence by which in a particular case it is sought to prove that the principal has waived the protection afforded by thos rules, should be clear and cogent."

15.75 He reviewed the evidence and essentially thought that the plaintiff had grudgingly submitted, rather than indicated he would not enforce his legal rights against the defendant. About the expression "acquiescence" itself, he said this: "The term 'acquiescence', which has been applied to his conduct, is one which was said by Lord Cottenham in [*Duke of Leeds v. Earl Amherst*][49] ought not to be used; in other words, it does not accurately express any known legal defence, but if used at all it must have attached to it a very different signification, according to whether the acquiescence alleged occurs while the act acquiesced in is in progress or only after it has been completed. If a person having a right, and seeing another person about to commit, or in the course of committing an act infringing upon that right, stands by in such a manner as really to induce the person committing the act, and who might otherwise have abstained from it, to believe that he assents to its being committed, he cannot afterwards be heard to complain of the act. This, as Lord Cottenham said in the case already cited, is the proper sense of the term 'acquiescence', and in that sense may be defined as quiescence under such circumstances as that assent may be reasonably inferred from it, and is no more than an instance of the law of estoppel by words or conduct. But when once the act is completed without any knowledge or assent upon the part of the person whose right is infringed, the matter is to be determined on very different legal considerations. A right of action has then vested in him which, at all events as a general rule, cannot be divested without accord and satisfaction, or release under seal. Mere submission to the injury for any time short of the period limited by statute for the enforcement of the right of action cannot take away such right, although under the name of laches it may afford a ground for refusing relief under some particular circumstances; and it is clear that even an express promise by the person injured that he would not take any legal proceedings to redress the injury done to him could not by itself constitute a bar to such proceedings, for the promise would be without consideration, and therefore not binding."

[49] (1846) 41 E.R. 886.

***London Assurance Co. v. Mansel* (1879) 11 Ch.D.363**

15.76 This was a case of non-disclosure prior to the taking out of a life assurance policy. Jessel M.R. asked ". . . what is the principle on which the Court acts in setting aside contracts of assurance?" He said he did not think that any real distinction was to be drawn between one kind of insurance and another, referring also to authority on the duty of disclosure in ex parte injunctions, in which Lord Cranworth, then Lord Commissioner Rolfe, had equated the good-faith principle governing an application for an ex parte "special" (ex parte) injunction with that governing insurances: both required the utmost degree of good faith."

He also referred to *Moens v. Heyworth*[50] in which Parke B. had put forward an implied contract basis for the duty of disclosure, and to *Lindenau v. Desborough*,[51] another insurance case. Having found on the facts of the case that there was material non-disclosure, he ordered that upon the plaintiffs returning the premium, the acceptance by them was to be void and of no effect, and they were not bound to deliver the policy, and that the contract be delivered up to be cancelled.

***Redgrave v. Hurd* (1881) 20 Ch. D. 1 ("Fobbing off or lulling buyer into false sense of security displaces his duty of due diligence)**

15.77 The fact that the plaintiff had not looked thoroughly at the books and documents regarding the business did not disentitle him from rescinding an agreement to buy a partnership share. The statement by the vendor about the profits of the business had misled him. The statement *being a material one*, there was sufficient ground for rescinding the contract.

***Re London and Staffordshire Fire Insurance* (1882) 24 Ch. D. 149 (Knowledge)**

15.78 This was a decision of Pearson J. that notice of a misrepresentation (relied on to show that the shareholder was guilty of delay amounting to acceptance after he knew of the misrepresentation) posted in a way which would comply with the articles was only notice for the purposes of things in the ordinary course of business of the company, which this was not.

***Newbigging v. Adam* (1886) 34 Ch. D. 582**[52]

15.79 Cotton L.J. said: "The Plaintiff here does not recover damages as in an action of deceit, but gets what is the proper consequence in equity of setting aside the contract into which he has been induced to enter. In my opinion it cannot be said that he is put back into his old position unless he is relieved from the consequences and obligations which are the result of the contract which is set aside. That is a very different thing from damages. The Plaintiff may have been induced by these misstatements to give up a commission in the army, and if the misstatements had been such that an action of deceit would lie he could have recovered damages for the loss of his commission, but he could not in such an action as the present obtain any relief in respect of it. The indemnity to which he is entitled is only an indemnity against the obligations which he has contracted under the contract which is set aside,

[50] (1842) 2 Mac. & G. 231 (see the Appendix to Chap. 2. The Legal Nature of the Duty of Good Faith).

[51] 8 B. & C. 591.

[52] See below for the House of Lords' decision.

and, in my opinion, the requiring the Defendant whose misstatements, though not fraudulent, have been the cause of setting aside the contract, to indemnify the Plaintiff from those obligations, is the only way in which the Plaintiff can be restored to his old position in an action like this, but I entirely disclaim any intention of giving damages in an action of this nature."

Bowen L.J. thought it was as outlined by the Master of the Rolls in *Redgrave v. Hurd*,[53] a giving back by the party who made the misrepresentation of the advantages he obtained by the contract. "Now those advantages may be of two kinds. He may get an advantage in the shape of an actual benefit, as when he receives money; he may also get an advantage if the party with whom he contracts assumes some burthen in consideration of the contract. In such a case it seems to me that complete rescission would not be effected unless the misrepresenting party not only hands back the benefits which he has himself received—but also *re-assumes the burthen* which under the contract the injured person has taken upon himself."[54] He thought that "loss arising out of the contract" would be a term which would be too wide, and might embrace damages at common law; and he did not think either *Redgrave v. Hurd*[55] or *Rawlins v. Wickham*,[56] went that far. Thus, the plaintiff was entitled to receive back the credit he had been obliged by the agreement to bring into the firm, and be indemnified for the amount which had been spent out of that, and indemnified against all the liabilities of the firm.

15.80 Fry L.J. agreed with the practical result each of his brethren had reached, but as to the theory of it said he inclined towards the view of Cotton L.J. rather than Bowen L.J. . . . "I am inclined to hold that the Plaintiff is entitled to an *indemnity in respect of all obligations entered into under the contract when those obligations are within the necessary or reasonable expectation of both of the contracting parties at the time of the contract*. I hesitate to adopt the view the view of Lord Justice Bowen, that the obligations must be *created by the contract*, and I feel a little doubt whether the obligation in question in the present suit can be said to have been so created.[57]

Adam v. Newbigging (1888) 13 App. Cas. 308 (Deterioration of the thing bought may be no bar if due to the undisclosed defect)

15.81 The respondent was induced by non-fraudulent misrepresentations to enter into a partnership. The partnership was in fact insolvent at the time, and subsequently failed, having become even more insolvent by reason of the undisclosed problem. The vendors' representations were held to be "somewhat deficient in candour" (Lord Watson) as to certain of the representations made which they did know about (some they did not). The respondent was thus held entitled to rely on the assurances he received as to the business; and entitled to rescission despite the insolvency of the partnership and the fact that the position had deteriorated further after the respondent had become a partner.

Lagunas Nitrate Co v. Lagunas Nitrate Syndicate [1899] 2 Ch. 392 (Knowledge; practical justice in rescission)

15.82 For a fuller note on the vulnerable-dealing aspect of the case, see Chapter 9, Dealing with the vulnerable Buyer or Seller. The plaintiff company was

[53] Para. 15.77, above.
[54] Italics supplied.
[55] Above.
[56] (1858) 3 De G. & J. 304; 44 E.R. 1285.
[57] Italics supplied.

promoted and formed by the directors of the defendant syndicate, in order to buy part of its property consisting of nitrate works in Chile. The syndicate directors were to be the directors of the company also, and they prepared the articles of the new company nominating them; also they prepared the prospectus and the purchase contract. Two years after the date of the contract and completion of the purchase, and after the nitrate had been worked from the date of the contract till the commencement of the action, the shareholders appointed a new independent board of directors, and brought an action against the syndicate and the directors for rescission of the contract, for misrepresentation, misfeasance by the directors, breach of trust, and concealment of material facts but did not allege fraud in the sense of dishonesty.

Lindley M.R. dealt with the argument that *the disclosure of the dual role by the syndicate directors to the directors of the company meant that the company could be taken to have accepted any defect*. He drew a distinction between the position of the company before and after the independent directors were appointed; and held that the knowledge of the syndicate directors could not be imputed to the company: they were the very ones under a duty to disclose the defect to the company. "To impute to the nitrate company the knowledge which the directors had acquired in another capacity, and which knowledge they did not disclose to any one, is neither law nor sense."[58] He thus took into account only acts after the independent board came into being and disregarded the "circumstances that the directors did not rescind the contract whilst they were in office", adding "Mere lapse of time whilst the original directors were in office cannot, in my opinion, avail the syndicate in this action." However, he felt the real difficulty was that the plaintiffs had worked the mine *after* acquiring knowledge.

15.83 Rigby L.J. dissented from the other two Lord Justices on the last question above. On the way the rule was applied, in a case where duty and interest conflicted, he said this. "Speaking of equity and law for convenience, as the case would have stood before the Judicature Acts, the agreement would have been voidable in equity, but would not be void at law. The rule as to equitable interference was only necessary in order to get rid of some agreement at law (by actual contract or estoppel), and in cases within its operation the agreement at law, so far as it bound the offending party, was kept alive as against him, if it were thought by the beneficiaries more advantageous that the wrongdoers should be bound. In *Ex Parte Lacey*[59] for instance, and in numberless cases which have followed it, the subject-matter of the inequitable purchase was set up for sale again on the terms that, if a larger bid were made, the beneficiaries were to have the benefit, but that if no larger sum were bid, the purchaser should be held to his bargain. It is, indeed, one of the just and salutary branches of the rule that the party subjecting himself by his misconduct to the rule cannot make any advantage to himself out of it, but is bound by what he does if it turn out to his disadvantage. In the present case there can be no doubt that if there had been an independent board of directors, their affixing the seal of the company to the purchase agreement of June 18, 1894, would have been an act intra vires, for the very object of the incorporation of the company was that it should enter into the agreement if that were approved by the directors. It would follow, therefore, that the directors who actually caused the seal to be affixed had power at law to do so, and that the agreement was not void at law, but voidable only in equity. A court of equity might not be absolutely bound in every conceivable case to set aside an agreement so obtained, but would be bound to do so if the beneficiary within a proper time brought an action setting up that it was disadvantageous. There would be no need to prove that the sale was at an excessive or undue price.

[58] *cf.* the similar position of agents in Chap. 8.
[59] 6 Ves. 625.

The question of value need never be gone into at all." [He said here the property was clearly overvalued.] ... "The rule moreover specially applies where, as in this case, there was no full disclosure of all material facts. What facts the shareholders had notice of may be important when the question whether the right to rescind has been lost is being discussed.... *The completion of the contract by assignment would not in any way affect this right, since any deeds executed for the purposes of completion would be tainted with the same weakness as the original agreement ... The obligation to make a complete and candid disclosure of all material facts existed throughout the whole time during which they had the control of the affairs of the company, and could only have been fulfilled by calling a general meeting and laying before the shareholders at such meeting a full and complete disclosure of the material facts*."[60]

15.84 Rigby L.J. agreed that nothing done by the original directors of the company could amount to acceptance of the problem: he rejected the idea that they could do by conduct what they could not do by contract.

On the question of whether deterioration: of the property prevented restoration of the parties to their original position, he said: "Now no doubt it is a general rule that in order to entitle beneficiaries to rescind a voidable contract of purchaser against the vendor, they must be in a position to offer back the subject matter of the contract. But *this rule has no application to the case of the subject matter having been reduced by the mere fault of the vendors themselves; and the rule itself is, in equity, modified by another rule, that where compensation can be made for any deterioration of the property, such deterioration shall be no bar to rescission, but only a ground for compensation*.[61] I adopt the reasoning in *Erlanger's Case*[62] ... of Lord Blackburn as to allowances for depreciation and permanent improvement.[63] He quoted the passage from Lord Blackburn's judgment quoted above, and continued: "This important passage is, in my judgment, fully supported by the allowance for deterioration and permanent improvements made by Lord Eldon and other great equity judges in similar cases. Lord Blackburn, after some observations on the duty of parties seeking relief to exercise due diligence, cites a passage from a judgment of the Judicial Committee in *Lindsay Petroleum v. Hurd*.[64]

Rigby L.J. continued: "The obligation of the vendors to take back the property in a deteriorated condition is not imposed by way of punishment for wrongdoing, whether fraudulent or not, but because on equitable principles it is thought more fair that they should be compelled to accept compensation than that they should go off with the full profit of their wrongdoing. *Properly speaking, it is not now in the discretion of the Court to say whether compensation ought to be taken or not. If substantially compensation can be made, rescission with compensation is ex debito justitiae*."[65]

Unlike the majority, he felt that the plaintiffs had not made restoration impossible, they had done no more than keep the company going.

***Whittington v. Seale-Hayne* (1900) 82 L.T. 49 (working out of an order for rescission)**

15.85 The plaintiff bought premises which they intended to use for the breeding of prize poultry, relying on statements made by the vendor's agent that they were in a thoroughly sanitary condition. Farwell J. thought that the judgment

[60] Italics supplied.
[61] Italics supplied.
[62] Para. 15.72, above.
[63] See above para. 15.73.
[64] (1874) See para. 15.69, above: passage beginning "Now, the doctrine of laches in courts of equity is not an arbitrary or a technical doctrine. . ."
[65] Italics supplied.

of Bowen L.J. in *Newbigging v. Adam*[66] in the Court of Appeal was the correct one: Bowen L.J. had said that to put the injured party *in statu quo* did not mean putting him *in statu quo* in all respects, because this would mean he would be entitled to recover damages "but is to be replaced in his position so far as regards the rights and obligations which have been created by the contract into which he has been induced to enter." Farwell J. considered that "the plaintiff is entitled to an indemnity in respect of all obligations entered into under the contract when those obligations are within the necessary or reasonable expectation of both the contracting parties at the time of the contract"[67]

***Nocton v. Lord Ashburton* [1914] A.C. 932 (Equitable fraud preserved despite Derry v Peek)**[68]

15.86 This was a vulnerable-dealing case, in which the victim sought to be indemnified against the transaction he had been advised to enter into by his solicitor, but in which the solicitor was personally interested. He claimed that the advice was fraudulent. The advice was held to be mistaken, not fraudulent, but he was allowed compensation nonetheless. Lord Haldane, with whose speech Lord Atkinson concurred, took the opportunity to make plain the very narrow scope of the earlier case of *Derry v. Peek*.[69] It was limited to the requirement that for the tort of deceit there had to be mens rea, or dishonesty. There had been no intention, as had been made plain by the Court of Appeal in *Low v. Bouverie*[70] to interfere with cases of warranty or estoppel. There had been no intention to exclude "duty of which only a Court of Equity took cognizance", which although classified by those courts as fraud, did not require an intention to deceive. *"I can hardly imagine that those who took part in the decision of Derry v. Peek*[71] imagined that they could be supposed to have cast doubt on the principle of any cases arising under the exclusive jurisdiction of the Court of Chancery."[72] It would be wrong to suppose that equitable fraud was not a general term, or that contracts for the sale and purchase of land were in any respect privileged, so as to be free from the ordinary jurisdiction of the Court to deal with them as it deals with any instrument, or any other transactions, in which the Court is of opinion that it is unconscientious for a person to avail himself of the legal advantage which he has obtained. "Indeed, the books are full of cases in which the Court has dealt with contracts of that kind—contracts obtained by persons in a fiduciary position, contracts for the sale of shares obtained by directors through misrepresentation contained in the prospectus, in respect of which it was never necessary to allege or prove that the directors were wilfully guilty of moral fraud in what they had done". In Chancery the term "fraud" thus came to be used to describe what fell short of deceit, but imported breach of a duty to which equity had attached its sanction. The fault was to violate, "however innocently because of his ignorance, an obligation which he must be taken by the Court to have known, and his conduct has in that sense always been called fraudulent, even in such a case as a technical fraud on a power . . ." Side by side with the enforcement of the *Derry v. Peek*[73] duty to be honest, were claims in

[66] Para. 15.79 above.
[67] See the text at para. 15.37, above for the precise order made.
[68] (1882) 3 App. Cas. 337.
[69] Above.
[70] [1891] 3 Ch. 82.
[71] Above.
[72] Italics supplied.
[73] Above.

Equity where the question was "*whether the circumstances and relations of the parties were such as to give rise to duties of particular obligation which have not been fulfilled . . . Such a special duty may arise from the circumstances and relations of the parties. These may give rise to an implied contract at law or to a fiduciary obligation in equity.*"[74]

***Spence v. Crawford* [1939] 3 All E.R. 271**

15.87 The appellant was induced to sell his shares in a private company by certain "gloomy and fraudulent" representations about its financial position. He sought to set aside the sale on the grounds of fraud, which was proved. The respondent however alleged that restoration was impossible because (a) the company had increased in prosperity after the pursuer had ceased to be a shareholder, and one could not be sure that that could be attributed to its "inherent virtue"; and (b) because the effect of restoration would be to alter the parties' respective share in the control of the company: it would now have the effect (which would not have been the case before) that the appellant and a Mr Richardson would together hold the controlling interest in the company, while before it had been shared between the parties to the litigation. Their Lordships rejected these arguments.

Lord Wright pointed out that there was in some respects a distinction between fraud cases and cases of innocent misrepresentation. "A case of innocent misrepresentation may be regarded rather as one of misfortune than as one of moral obliquity. There is no deceit or intention to defraud. The court will be less ready to pull a transaction to pieces where the defendant is innocent, whereas in the case of fraud the court will exercise its jurisdiction to the full in order, if possible, to prevent the defendant from enjoying the benefit of his fraud at the expense of the innocent plaintiff. Restoration, however, is essential to the idea of restitution. . . . Though the defendant has been fraudulent, he must not be robbed nor must the plaintiff be unjustly enriched . . . The purpose of the relief is not punishment but compensation." He thought that the court could "go a long way in ordering restitution if *the substantial identity of the subject-matter of the contract* remains."[75] In the case of fraud "the court will do its best to unravel the complexities of any particular case . . ."

***Watson v. Burton* [1957] 1 W.L.R. 19; [1956] 3 All E.R. 929**

15.88 This was a case of misdescription of real property. The purchaser at first attempted to agree compensation for misdescription, paying the remainder of the deposit to stakeholders during this period. He later rescinded: the vendor sought specific performance, and at the hearing, waived a clause in the contract excluding compensation. Wynn Parry J. considered that two main questions arose: "(i) Does the property which the plaintiff can convey differ materially from the property which has been agreed to be sold?" and (ii) Will the defendant be prejudiced by the existence of such a difference?"

***Laurence v. Lexcourt Holdings* [1978] 1 W.L.R. 1128 (acceptance with knowledge)**

15.89 In this case the defect (that the premises had no planning permission to be used as offices, contrary to a representation that they could) came to light in April 1974. Thereafter the parties agreed the plaintiffs should apply for planning permission. This was refused, and the plaintiffs corresponded for a while

[74] Italics supplied.
[75] Italics supplied.

with the defendants about making alternative leasehold arrangements; and only when these came to nothing did they commence proceedings in late April. Nonetheless they were allowed rescission on the grounds that they had not accepted the defect: it took them time, not unreasonably, to decide where they should move their offices to.

***O'Sullivan v. Management Agency Ltd* [1985] Q.B. 428**

15.90 This was a case of a dealing with a vulnerable person. The publishing agreement was set aside also on restraint of trade grounds. The case is most interesting on the question of the allowance to be made to the publishing companies for the skill put in which had fostered the young plaintiff's ability as a composer and performer and had yielded the profits in question which were to be returned.

All three Lord Justices agreed that the defendants should have reasonable remuneration *including a profit element* for all work done in promoting O'Sullivan. Fox L.J.'s treatment of the topic is the fullest. He said: "What the first five defendants in substance are seeking is that the parties should be put in a position in which they would have been if the agreements had been on the basis which mr Levison, an expert witness, thought might reasonably have been negotiated if Mr O'Sullivan had received independent advice from experienced persons. I do not feel able to accept that. In the first place, Mr Levison's evidence was really only directed to the question of what might reasonably have been negotiated. The question of what recompense in the circumstances of this case it would be reasonable to allow was not investigated. If, for example, there was any failure by the MAM companies or Mr Mills to promote Mr O'Sullivan's interests as vigorously or competently as they might have been expected to do, with the result that Mr O'Sullivan suffered loss that might affect the position. Secondly, an order which, in effect, would involve substantial division of the profits between the beneficiary on the one hand and the fiduciary (and persons for whom he procured benefits) on the other, goes far beyond anything hitherto permitted.

"Once it is accepted that the court can make an appropriate allowance to a fiduciary for his skill and labour I do not see why, in principle, it should not be able to give him some part of the profit of the venture if it was thought that justice as between the parties demanded that. To give the fiduciary any allowance for his skill and labour involves some reduction of the profits otherwise payable to the beneficiary. And the business reality may be that the profits could never have been earned at all, as between fully independent persons, except on a profit sharing basis. But be that as it may, it would be one thing to permit a substantial sharing of profits in a case such as *Phipps v. Boardman*[76] where the conduct of the fiduciaries could not be criticised and quite another to permit it in a case such as the present where, though fraud was not alleged, there was an abuse of personal trust and confidence. I am not satisfied that it would be proper to exclude Mr Mills and the MAM companies from all reward for their efforts. I find it impossible to believe that they did not make a significant contribution to Mr O'Sullivan's success. It would be unjust to deny them a recompense for that. I would, therefore, be prepared as was done in *Phipps v. Boardman*[77] to authorised the payment (over and above out of pocket expenses) of an allowance for the skill and labour of the first five defendants in promoting the compositions and performances and managing the business affairs of Mr O'Sullivan, and that an inquiry . . .

[76] [1967] 2 A.C. 46.
[77] *ibid*.

should be ordered for that purpose. Such an allowance could include a profit element in the way that solicitors do."

Waller L.J. agreed that there should be reasonable remuneration. It should include "all expenses and a fair profit".

Vadasz v. Pioneer Concrete (1995) 130 A.L.R. 570 (Australia)

15.91 The High Court of Australia were faced with a personal guarantee given by a director of a company, Vadipile Ltd, to secure the granting of supplies to the company. The respondent creditor had represented to him that it covered only the company's future liabilities. On this basis he had been prepared to enter into it. In fact the guarantee covered past as well as future liabilities. The respondent had however delivered supplies relying on the guarantee. The company was owned entirely by Mr Vadasz and his wife, so the court treated the benefit to the company as a benefit to Mr Vadasz. They said: "In the present case, the appellant obtained the benefit which he sought as consideration for entering the contract of guarantee, namely, the subsequent supply on credit by the respondent of goods to Vadipile. In those circumstances, a practical restoration of the status quo which existed before the execution of the guarantee and the subsequent supply of goods on credit by the respondent would involve not only a cancellation of the appellant's obligations under the guarantee but either a return of the goods subsequently supplied by the respondent or the actual payment, either by Vadipile or the appellant, of an amount equivalent to the value of the goods which were subsequently supplied in reliance upon the appellant's guarantee of payment of their price.

However, the appellant does not offer to pay the respondent the amount which Vadipile has failed to pay for those subsequently supplied goods. Nor does he offer to submit to terms or conditions which would ensure that the purchase price of those goods, which has not been suggested to exceed their true value, is received by the respondent." . . .

Portraying their order as the kind of "practical justice" which the English courts had in mind as regards *restitutio in integrum* when ordering rescission, in cases such as *Erlanger v. New Sombrero Phosphate,*[78] *Lindsay Petroleum v. Hurd*[79] and *O'Sullivan v. Management Agency v. Music Ltd*[80] they set aside the guarantee in part, leaving in being the part relating to future indebtedness only. They drew a distinction between a case of the kind before them, where the appellant would have entered the guarantee if limited to future indebtedness, and a case such as that in *Amadio*[81] where the victims would not have entered into the transaction at all had they known the true facts.

Note: (1) The decision may be open to criticism. The line between rescission with restitutio in integrum where the jurisdiction is well-established, and partial rescission, where the jurisdiction is speculative, has been fudged. The cases relied on by the court were properly seen as cases of restitutio in integrum, not cases of partial enforcement.[82] *Whether the creditors could have made out a case for preservation of the guarantee with compensation for the misrepresentation is another matter, although it may well be that the misrepresentation would have been too substantial for that.*

(2) The emphasis on what the individual would or would not have done if he had known the truth is also open to criticism as not being soundly based on authority.

[78] (1878) 3 App. Cas 1218.
[79] (1874) L.R. 5 P.C. 221.
[80] [1985] Q.B. 428.
[81] [1982] 151 C.L.R. 447.
[82] See also the section on partial enforcement in Chap. 9. Dealings with the Vulnerable Buyer or Seller.

The distinction drawn by the courts of equity for purposes of opting between compensation and rescission was subtly, but measurably different. It was between circumstances where they thought a reasonable buyer would have entered into the contract on the footing that he receive compensation for the defect, it being open to the buyer however to prove that he had had a purpose in mind for the land or other object bought which would have caused him to reject the contract; and cases where the defect was so grave that the court would presume a reasonable buyer would have rejected the contract.[83] *The key difference is thus the reasonable-expectation approach of the older courts, albeit with some opportunity for the buyer to rely on facts special to himself, but having the burden of proof of these. By contrast, the modern Australian court attempts the unrewarding task of attempting in each such case to ascertain the retrospective actual contents of the individual buyer's mind.*

Target Holdings v. Redfern **[1996] 1 A.C. 421**

15.92 Solicitors who acted for lenders (and purchasers) wrongly parted with the mortgage money in circumstances in which they had no instructions to do so. It was common ground that the payment without instructions constituted a breach of trust by the solicitors. The House of Lords held that whether as compensation for breach of trust or as damages for negligence, the plaintiff had to prove that there was a causal link between the breach of trust and the loss suffered: it had to show that it would not have advanced the money if it had known the (un-disclosed) truth.

Note: The case is a professional negligence case about the proof of causation of loss after a breach of duty; but the relevant considerations are similar to those discussed above. It is suggested that the House of Lords' formulation above is in fact a rolled-up statement. What is really being said is perhaps the much longer statement as follows:

(1) *The Society naturally supposed, given the silence from the solicitors and given their standing instructions, that there were no second charges;*
(2) *This implicit representation (from conduct and silence) was false. There was a small second charge. The question whether the Society would or would not have entered into the contract had been found to be a triable issue. In other words, the mistatement by omission was considered by the judge to have been a category (2) statement following the analysis in the text above at para. 15.07;*
(3) *It remained therefore for the Society to adduce further evidence to show that it did rely on the misstatement so as to suffer loss. If it emerged in evidence that it would have completed the contract of loan even if it had been told the truth it clearly could not have suffered any loss.*

Downs v. Chappell **[1996] 3 All E.R. 344**

15.93 A vendor of a business had made fraudulent representations regarding its profitability, and his accountants, the second defendants, had negligently confirmed to the plaintiffs the figures given without being in a position to check whether they were true or not. The judge in the court below had held that the plaintiffs were obliged to show specifically that they would not have bought if the true figures had been disclosed. On appeal, Hobhouse L.J. said: "A representation is material when its tendency, or its natural and probable result, is to induce the representee to act on the faith of it in the kind of way in which he is proved to have in fact acted. The test is objective. In the present case it is clear that the test of materiality was satisfied and the contrary has not been suggested.

"As regards inducement, this is a question of fact. The judge has found that

[83] See Chap. 5. Sale of Land.

the representations made did induce the plaintiffs to enter into the relevant transaction, . . . The plaintiffs were induced to act to their detriment. The word "reliance" used by the judge has a similar meaning, but is not the correct criterion.

"The plaintiffs have proved what they need to prove by way of the commission of the tort of deceit and causation. They have proved that they were induced to enter into the contract with Mr Chappell by his fraudulent representations. The judge was wrong to ask how they would have acted if they had been told the truth. They were never told the truth."

He went on to consider the position as against the second defendants, the accountants. "The only answer that the second defendants could have properly given was that they did not know. . . . Here again, what the judge should have done is to ask simply whether the plaintiffs entered into the contract in reliance upon the second Defendants' letter. He answered that question in the affirmative. The causative relationship between the second defendants' tort and the entry into the contract was established."

Note: "A representation is material when . . ." ushers in a statement describing one kind of material statement, and does not, it is suggested, purport to give a comprehensive definition of material statements in general. The Court had been referred to the House of Lords' decision in Smith v. Chadwick[84]*. The statement in question will plainly have been the most serious kind, type (3) in the analysis above. It was therefore able to stand alone, and to bring with it its own inference of inducement.*

***Bristol & West Building Society v. Mothew* [1996] 4 All E.R. 698.**

15.94 A firm of solicitors acted for a lender in relation to a proposed mortgage loan and for the borrower. The solicitors omitted in breach of their standing instructions to inform the Society that the borrower proposed to have a small second mortgage. The judgment of Millett L.J. is of great importance on the question of "fiduciaries."[85]

On the question of causation of loss to the lender by reason of the negligent advice given, Millett L.J. said: "In considering the issue of causation in an action for negligence brought by a client against his solicitor it appears from *Downs v. Chappell*[86] that it is necessary to distinguish between two different kinds of case.

Where a client sues his solicitor for having negligently *failed to give him proper advice*[87] he must show what advice should have been given and (on a balance of probabilities) that if such advice had been given he would not have entered into the relevant transaction or would not have entered into it on the terms he did. The same applies where the client's complaint is that the solicitor failed in his duty to give him material information. In *Sykes v. Midland Bank Executor and Trustee Co. Ltd (a firm)*,[88] which was concerned with a failure to give proper advice, the plaintiff was unable to establish this and his claim to damages for negligence failed. In *Mortgage Express Ltd v. Bowerman & Partners*,[89] which was concerned with a failure to convey information, the plaintiff was able to establish that if it had been given the information it would have withdrawn from the transaction and its claim succeeded.

Where, however, a client sues his solicitor for having negligently given him

[84] Noted in App. to Chap. 7, above.
[85] It is noted on that aspect in Chap. 9, Dealings with the Vulnerable Buyer or Seller": see "The party trusted." See also Appx to Chap. 9.
[86] Above, para. 15.93.
[87] Italics supplied.
[88] [1971] 1 Q.B. 113.]
[89] [1996] 2 All E.R. 836.

incorrect advice or for having negligently given him incorrect information, the position appears to be different. In such a case it is sufficient for the plaintiff to prove that he relied on the advice or information, that is to say, that that he would not have acted as he did if he had not been given such advice or information. It is not necessary for him to prove that he would not have acted as he did if he had been given the proper advice or the correct information. This was the position in *Downs v. Chappell*".[90]

Note: See the analysis of different levels of "material" statement in the text above. It may be thought that there are two strands of thought here which could with advantage be separated. First, where there is an omission to give certain expected or contracted-for information, what has to be looked at is the loss-causing content of the misstatement by implication. In the case of a misstatement by omission, this is a two-stage process (while it is a one-stage process where we are concerned with a positive mis-statement). The implicitly-represented or reasonably-assumed statement has first to be reconstructed and the true statement compared with it. The question has to be asked, Was it loss-causing. This is to an extent a question of how serious or significant the statment is thought to have been, not a question of whether the statement is by omission or a positive statement. The misrepresentations in the Mothew[91] *case will plainly have amounted to no more than level (2) statements. (The second mortgage was for a small amount; this might possibly not have caused a building society in those heady days to have been unduly concerned at any possible difficulty in keeping up payments.)*

Dunbar Bank P.L.C. v. Nadeem (unreported save in [1996] New Digest November 7

15.95 Mr Nadeem had a number of loan accounts with the Plaintiff Bank which were repayable on demand. At the end of 1990 the amount owed to the Bank was some £1.2 million. He and his wife lived at 152 Pavilion Road, SW1. Mr Nadeem held a lease dated May 19, 1983 which was due to expire at the end of 1996. By the beginning of 1991 Mr Nadeem was in arrears with the interest owed to the Bank under the loan. It was envisaged that Mr Nadeem would negotiate a new lease of 152 Pavilion Road, unlike the old lease to be held in joint names, and the Bank would take an all-monies charge over it. The Bank would finance the purchase of the new lease, and add an extra £50,000 which was to be put towards Mr Nadeem's debts to it. The effect in law was thus that Mrs Nadeem would give up whatever rights she would have had (if any) on the coming to an end ofthe existing lease, in order to acquire a new lease which was charged with the liability to repay Mr Nadeem's debts to the extent ofsome £1.25 million. Mrs Nadeem had no independent advice.

Robert Englehart Q.C. held that the apparent notional gain to Mrs Nadeem was no more than illusory, so that the transaction as a whole was manifestly disadvantageous to her. He held that in the circumstances the Bank had constructive notice of her claim. Following *Midland Bank v. Greene*,[92] the deputy judge set aside the transaction, but made an order for rescission only *on terms*, that she repaid the Bank half of the £210,000 financing costs of the lease put up by it. He described this as making *restitutio in integrum* on the principles set out in Lord Blackburn's speech in *Erlanger v. New Sombrero Phosphate Co.*[93] It is understood the case is to go to appeal.

[90] Above, para. 15.93.
[91] Above, para. 15.94.
[92] [1994] 2 F.L.R. 827.
[93] (1878) 3 App. Cas. 1218.

CHAPTER 16

RESCISSION OF EXECUTED SALES

"One does not see at first sight why buyers of motor cars are more liable to be duped or are more in need of protection than buyers of bungalows".[1]

Execution of a contract by registration of a share dealing

16.01 The execution of a share purchase by registration does not seem to bar rescission (although a winding-up does, but that is because the statutory provisions regarding winding up make rescission impossible and unfair). In *Armstrong v. Jackson*[2] the diligent McCardie J. listed a number of cases where the share dealing had been registered but the court nonetheless allowed rescission:

Gillett v. Peppercorne[3]
Rothschild v. Brookman[4]
York Buildings v. Mackenzie[5] referred to by Lord Cranworth in *Aberdeen Railway Co v. Blaikie Brothers*[6] and *Oliver v. Court.*[7]

Execution by conveyance, transfer, etc., of land

16.02 If it is a rule that the execution of a contract for the sale of land by conveyance or transfer bars rescission, it is a strange and rather unfair one, for which the justification is by no means obvious. As McCardie J. pointed out[8] after mentioning the so-called rule in *Wilde v. Gilbson.*[9]

> "It is curious that the doctrine should cease to apply when the formal instrument of transfer has been executed, or the formal delivery of a chattel has taken place. In many cases the misrepresentation cannot, or may not, be discovered until the purchaser has

[1] Lord Willberforce at the second reading of the Misrepresentation Bill, House of Lords, May 17, 1966.
[2] [1917] 2 K.B. 822.
[3] (1840) 3 Beav. 78; 49 E.R. 31.
[4] (1831) 2 Dow. & Cl. 188; 5 E.R. 273.
[5] (1795) 3 Pat. App. Cas. 378.
[6] 1 Macq. 474.
[7] (1820) Dan. 301.
[8] In *Armstrong v. Jackson*, above.
[9] (1848) para. 16.36.

secured his legal title and has therefore entered into possession of his newly acquired property."

As can be seen from the fact that this appears in the preceding Chapter under the head of "Irrelevant Factors"[10] it is suggested that if properly analysed, the cases do not reveal any such rule. It must no doubt be accepted that there has been considerable confusion in this area. Part of this confusion has been caused by the relatively crude focussing by some judges during the strange melting-pot period in English law of the 1870s and 1880s, on the one question—was the relief sought before or after conveyance? (Compare the recent focussing for damages purposes on the question of the drop in value after entering into a contract—as a single-faceted question, which it is not—dealt with by the Court of Appeal in *Banque Bruxelles Lambert SA v. Eagle Star Insurance SA Ltd*[11] and reviewed further by the House of Lords.) What is certainly true is that in some cases rescission was given after conveyance; while in others it was not. Attempts were made during the troubled period above to explain away the cases where rescission was given after conveyance; but these attempts were not terribly satisfactory, and not always even seen as satisfactory in their own time. Thus it follows that the answer to the question "Was it before or after conveyance?" is by no means the end of the matter. What has been overlooked is the important aspect of *fault*, on both sides. The breach of the duty of good faith or candour is not as reprehensible as a positive misrepresentation, perhaps, but it is nonetheless less than ideal behaviour on the part of a vendor or defining party to a contract: there is fault there; and this is in fact likely to be what has determined the grant or withholding of rescission. It is suggested that the four propositions below express the true position regarding rescission after completion.

The point is not a purely academic one, despite the fact that the Misrepresentation Act 1967 prevents completion being a bar in cases of misrepresentation within the Act. The Act has been restrictively interpreted[12] and it is by no means clear, in consequence, that all statements made in breach of the good faith duties of accuracy and candour are within the Act. Accordingly, in such cases, where rescission is desired and the defect could not have been discovered by normal due diligence before completion, it will be necessary for the plaintiff to rely on the pre-Act law. The analysis below does also lend support to the idea that properly speaking, the pre-Act law (and thus the Act itself) may have restricted relief to cases where there was fault of the kind discussed in Chapter 5.

(1) Rescission may be granted after completion in certain circumstances

16.03 If there has been a breach of good faith as to a matter which was not discoverable by the use of due diligence before completion, then

[10] At para. 15.13, above.
[11] [1995] 2 All E.R. 769, C.A., and [1996] 3 All E.R. 365, H.L..
[12] See Chap. 17.

rescission may be granted (subject no doubt where applicable to the usual prevention-of-injustice reasons for withholding it).

(2) Relevance of fault crucial

16.04 For there to have been a breach of good faith, there has to be a degree of fault on the part of the seller or inquiring party; if he had good reason at the time of the contract to believe his statements true, there is no breach of good faith, even if it emerges subsequently that what he said was entirely or partly incorrect.[13]

(3) Want of due diligence by buyer will fix him with deemed knowledge of the defect; title particular factor by completion stage

16.05 For the buyer to obtain rescission, he must according to normal principles[14] not have had knowledge or notice of the defect. He will have deemed knowledge (notice through lack of due diligence)[15] which will cover all title defects which could have been discovered between contract and completion. The position after contract and before completion is to be contrasted: if the purchaser discovers a title defect, even an innocent one, after the contract and before completion, he may resist specific performance or obtain rescission in the case of more significant defects or defects which were of importance to him individually. However, before completion his traditional task is precisely to investigate title. Thus, though he need not have known about title defects after the contract; by the time he comes to completion, he must have satisfied himself of the title from documents available to him. Therefore he will be bound by what such investigations would have revealed. He will not, on the other hand, be bound by *what they would not have revealed.*

(4) Merger

16.06 The doctrine of merger of the contract into the conveyance or transfer is a doctrine of presumed intention; and thus does not apply to defects which arise from a breach of good faith and which could not have been found out until after completion.[16]

Proposition (1) examined in more detail

Rescission may be granted after completion in certain circumstances

16.07 In the following (all noted below in the Appendix) rescission has been allowed after completion:

[13] See the analysis of cases at para. 16.16, below where these no-fault cases are isolated.
[14] See above.
[15] See further Chap. 8, Knowledge and Notice.
[16] See below.

Edwards v. M'Leay[17]
Hart v. Swaine[18]
Whittington v. Seale-Hayne[19]

Are these cases distinguishable?

16.08 *Edwards v. M'Leay*[20] This is clearly not, on the facts, a case of what was then called "moral"[21] fraud, that is, fraud as we use the term today. Lord Eldon, when he affirmed the considered judgment of the Master of the Rolls, made it plain that the kind of fraud in question was equitable fraud or a lack of good faith—"in the sense in which we use the term, fraudulent". The vendors had believed their statement (The Master of the Rolls had said: "What is the result of all this evidence? not indeed that Mr Prescott knew, of his own knowledge. . . but that he had so much information on the subject as made it altogether improper and unfair to represent to a purchaser . . ."), but had omitted to mention a fact which could reasonably be thought to cast doubt on its accuracy.

Hart v. Swaine[22] In *Joliffe v. Baker*[23] Watkin Williams J. attempted to explain away *Hart v. Swaine*[24] as being based on "moral" (that is dishonest) fraud. It is difficult to see that this can be so. The vendor does seem to have been rather a vague man, in that he sold the land in question as freehold land, having previously bought land which included the land sold on, then described as one fourth copyhold. There is no suggestion that he was dishonest, however, and the whole tenor of Fry J.'s judgment is otherwise: "the vendor had enough to put him on inquiry as to the facts: instead of which he relied on his own vague notion". "Put him on inquiry" is not the language to describe dishonesty; and a vague notion, however reprehensible, is not modern fraud. Further, Malins V.C. in *Manson v. Thacker*[25] took the view that the case did concern "legal" fraud, ie equitable fraud or breach of the vendor's duty of good faith.

Denman J. in *Brett v. Clowser*[26] thought that the explanation of *Hart v. Swaine*[27] was that the purchaser had not "got the thing he bargained for"; but that seems not to be either very helpful or specially true: he had the thing, one would think, but it was not as described. See also the view of Cotton L. J. in *Soper v. Arnold*.[28]

[17] (1815) G. Coop. 308; 35 E.R. 568.
[18] (1877) 7 Ch. D. 42.
[19] (1900) 82 L.T. 49.
[20] Above.
[21] Really, immoral, *i.e.* dishonest.
[22] Above.
[23] (1883) 11 Q.B.D. 255.
[24] 5 C.P.D. 376.
[25] (1877) 7 Ch. D. 620, noted below at para. 16.44.
[26] (1880).
[27] Above.
[28] (1887) 37 Ch. D. 96, noted below, para. 16.52.

Whittington v. Seale-Hayne[29] In this case Farwell J. had no difficulty in setting aside an executed lease of a poultry house, where the vendor had misrepresented that it was in a thoroughly sanitary condition—something presumably within his knowledge. This case seems to have escaped attempts to distinguish it.

It will be seen that the above cases have in fact escaped various attacks and remained unscathed. The fact that there are not many should not cause concern. These sort of cases are bound to be rare as most defects in land show up before completion.

Is there other support for the proposition?

16.09 *(1) Yes, the underlying proposition also has powerful obiter* support. In *Brownlie v. Campbell*[30] which *was a case where the purchaser sought to set aside the conveyance after completion,* Lord Hatherley said, dismissing the appeal on the facts of that case, that:

> "it is perfectly impossible to say that that [what the vendors had said and done] approaches within any appreciable distance of the cases which have been decided upon representations made, or silence kept, with regard to that which the vendor was bound, acting in good faith towards those with whom he was dealing, to have disclosed."

There was no suggestion that rescission would have been inappropriate had the purchaser proved lack of good faith.

See also similar remarks in Lord Selborne's judgment, making an exception of cases such as *Burrowes v. Lock*[31] and *Slim v. Croucher*[32] which are:

> "simply of this sort. A man is going to deal for valuable consideration with a particular subject, and the value of the return which he is to receive depends entirely upon a particular fact, which is, or ought to be, in the knowledge of a particular person".

Lord Blackburn took a more restrictive view of the operation of good faith anyway.

In *Derry v. Peek*[33] in the House of Lords Lord Herschell referred to as entirely different from the case before them:

> "those cases where a person within whose special province it lay to know a particular fact, has given an erroneous answer to an inquiry made with regard to it by a person desirous of ascertaining the fact for the purpose of determining his course accordingly, and has been held bound to make good the assurance he has given."

29 (1900).
30 (1880) 5 App. Cas. 925.
31 (1805) 10 Ves. 470; 32 E.R. 927.
32 1 De G.F. & J. 518; 45 E.R. 462.
33 (1889) 14 App. Cas. 337.

He cited not only *Burrowes v. Lock*[34] but more significantly, Lord Selborne in *Brownlie v. Campbell*.[35]

16.10 *(2) Further, the cases about compensation (as opposed to rescission) after completion lend support* These cases have not been entirely free from attempts made to explain them away, any more than the cases about rescission after completion. However, compensation after completion may be seen to have survived the attempts.

In *Bos v. Helsham*[36] a common law court decided that a compensation clause which did not specifically say it was to be relied on before completion only might be relied on after completion where the particulars of sale had misstated the rent. This case was said to have been based on (moral or modern) fraud by Malins V.C. in *Manson v. Thacker*;[37] however, Jessel M.R.[38] disagreed with Malins V.C.'s view. There is no trace of any fact from which one could infer fraud, and one would expect it to have been mentioned, given that the compensation clause was for "mistake or error". The Court of Appeal in *Palmer v. Johnson*[39] finally specifically approved this case, *Cann v. Cann*[40] and *Turner v. Skelton*.[41]

16.11 *Turner v. Skelton*[42] The purchaser in this case had not had permission, it seems, to enter the land to survey it before completion. He was thus suing for compensation for a misdescription of the land after completion. Jessel M.R. enquired rhetorically on what principle a purchaser could be said to lose his right to compensation by taking a conveyance.

> "The theory is that he has contracted to take compensation by taking a conveyance, and on what principle should he do so? The theory is that he has contracted to take compensation if there is any variation from the particulars. Why, then, should he lose it by taking a conveyance? The only reason that can be alleged is that everything is supposed to be settled between the parties, but why should that be an obstacle to the right of the purchaser when the defect is discovered afterwards? . . . When the mistake is one which a purchaser could not by due diligence discover, why should he be held not to be entitled to compensation?"

Further mention of the Court of Appeal decision in *Palmer v. Johnson*[43] which approved the above case is made at paragraph 16.25

[34] Above.
[35] Above.
[36] (1866) L.R. 2 Ex. 72.
[37] Above.
[38] See ***Turner v. Skelton*** (1879) 13 Ch. D. 130.
[39] (1884) 13 Q.B.D. 351.
[40] (1830) 3 Sim. 447; 57 E.R. 1065.
[41] Above.
[42] *ibid.*
[43] Above.

below. *Palmer v. Johnson*[44] also disapproved *Besley v. Besley*[45] and *Allen v. Richardson*,[46] and disapproved of Watkin Williams "elaborate judgment" in *Joliffe v. Baker*[47] if it conflicted with *Cann v. Cann*[48] and *Bos v. Helsham*.[49] Since *Besley v. Besley*[50] and *Allen v. Richardson*[51] were rescission cases, and *Palmer v. Johnson* was about merger, it follows that the disapproval is likely to have been not so much a comment about the facts of these cases, as disapproval of the notion that a right to rescind could not survive the conveyance or transfer in appropriate cases. Certainly the reasoning which allows a right to compensation to survive seems to apply equally well to a right to rescind. It is true that the compensation cases had centred on the construction of an express compensation clause, but that is not really a distinguishing feature of any merit. As has been seen, the good faith doctrine operates on express clauses, narrowing or expanding their ambit: thus, where it has been breached it is equally as capable of giving rise to a right to rescind after completion as any ordinary express clause.

Why then has rescission been refused after completion in so many cases?

16.12 There were four main reasons:

(1) because the case was framed in deceit only and failed on the facts;
(2) because there was no fault: that is, no breach of the duty of good faith, but a purely "innocent" misstatement;
(3) because the purchaser had deemed (*caveat emptor*) knowledge by reason of his failure to make proper investigations before completion; and
(4) more recently, simply because the court had, perhaps unsurprisingly in the circumstances, misapprehended the earlier law, and had in any case taken too simplistic a view of "after completion", failing to analyse the underlying *fault* in such cases.

(1) Examples of cases framed in deceit only[52]

16.13 *Wilde v. Gibson*[53] There was no positive representation of any kind by the vendor. It might perhaps have been found, if the case had been commenced on a contractual basis, that her agent had been guilty of a want of good faith by a partial non-disclosure. In fact no such point

44 *ibid.*
45 (1878) 9 Ch. D. 103.
46 (1879) 13 Ch. D. 524.
47 (1883) 11 Q.B.D. 255.
48 Above.
49 (1866) L.R.2 Ex. 72.
50 Above.
51 Above.
52 All noted in the Appendix below.
53 (1848) 1 H.L.C. 605; 9 E.R. 897.

could be taken because the case was brought in deceit. It was fatally flawed as such, since actual dishonesty had to be proved against the vendor herself, and she had not herself had any sufficient knowledge for this; while constructive knowledge on the part of her agent could not be imputed to her deceit.

16.14 *Kennedy v. Panama, etc., Royal Mail Co.*[54] The prospectus complained of here had been honestly prepared on the facts then known to the vendor. There was probably no breach of the duties of accuracy or candour. In any event the plaintiff's case was pleaded only in deceit in the sense of dishonesty, which failed.

16.15 *Manson v. Thacker*[55] The vendor had made no relevant representation. The case is also an example of (2): the defect would, it seems, have been discoverable by the purchaser on a survey.

(2) Examples of no-fault cases

16.16 *Besley v. Besley*[56] The agreement had not been in any way misleading, as it happened, although the purchaser had believed he was getting something different. Malins V.C. described it as "nothing more than an innocent mistake". Again, the case may well be within (2) as well: the purchaser would have found out the truth if he had troubled to inspect the lease before buying.[57] The case was also disapproved by the Court of Appeal in *Palmer v. Johnson*. There was little real discussion, and one has the impression that the disapproval was thought necessary in order to approve the earlier decision of Jessel M.R. in *Turner v. Skelton*. Thus, as has been said above, the disapproval must, probably be taken less as a detailed consideration of the factual basis, more a disapproval of the idea that a suitable term of the contract may not survive the conveyance.

16.17 *Brownlie v. Campbell*[58] The vendor had reasonably believed at the time of the contract, on perfectly good grounds, that it was accurate to say, as he did, that the land in question was held from the Crown, and it was only later that it emerged this was in fact not true.

16.18 *Saper v. Arnold*[59] The vendor in this case had disclosed everything which it was his duty to disclose. The purchaser had simply failed to use due diligence.

(3) Examples of cases where the purchaser was fixed with deemed knowledge by reason of his failure to make normal inquiries.

[54] (1867) L.R. 2 Q.B. 580.
[55] (1878) 7 Ch. D. 620.
[56] (1878) 9 Ch. D. 103.
[57] Above.
[58] (1880) 5 App. Cas. 925.
[59] (1887) 37 Ch. D. 96.

Allen v. Richardson[60] in which *caveat emptor* was applied because the purchaser had the means of knowledge and ought to have found out. Malins V.C. said "I have not heard a single scrap of information which the Defendant and his advisers acquired after [completion] which was not in their possession before".[61] **16.19**

Brett v. Clowser,[62] in which the purchaser might have been able to set aside the sale after contract, because he had been misled by the auctioneer's statement; but could not say he had been misled by the time of completion, since he had had the deeds, which made the defect perfectly clear. **16.20**

(4) Examples of cases where the court simply misunderstood the law

Seddon v. North Eastern Salt[63] There may not have been any misrepresentation in this case, as a matter of fact. However in so far as it proceeded on the basis that there had, Joyce J. wrongly relied on no-fault/deceit-only cases: *Brownlie v. Campbell*;[64] *Soper v. Arnold*[65] and *Kennedy v. Panama, etc., Royal Mail Co.*[66] **16.21**

Angel v. Jay[67] Part of the excuse for this decision may have been that the tenant's counsel took a fairly "way-out" point, namely that a lease when executed is substantially executory! At all events, Darling J. relied on *Legge v. Croker*;[68] while Bucknill J. relied on *Brett v. Clowser*[69] a lack of due diligence case and *Kennedy v. Panama, etc., Royal Mail Co*,[70] a no-fault case. **16.22**

None of these cases provide any true basis for a decision that rescission may not be had after completion where (a) there has been fault in the vendor in the sense that he has been in breach of his good faith duty of accuracy/candour or been guilty of a misrepresentation, and (b) the defect could not have been discovered by the purchaser before completion.

What about the doctrine of merger?

Merger, that is, the doctrine that a contract merges in the subsequent deed, conveyance or transfer, is, as has been said, a doctrine of presumed intention. It is also operates in a much more limited way **16.23**

[60] (1879) 13 Ch. D. 524.
[61] This case was also disapproved without real discussion: see ***Turner v. Skelton***, above.
[62] (1880) 5 C.P.D. 376.
[63] [1905] 1 Ch. 326.
[64] Above.
[65] Above.
[66] Above.
[67] [1911] 1 K.B. 666.
[68] 1 Ball & B. 506.
[69] (1880) 5 C.P.D. 376.
[70] Above.

than is sometimes thought. In so far as the deed carries out and replaces provisions in the contract, no doubt the contract is subsumed into the deed, and the contract acquires the status of a recital, providing a guide to construction, the parties' intention, etc., but no more. However, the deed may not so carry out every provision in the contract. In order to determine whether or not it does, one has to look at the contract: if there are there found provisions which are not carried into effect in the deed, then it may be that one should infer an intention on the part of the parties that these provisions are intended to live on and have force beyond the execution of the deed. Certain passages from the two main cases on merger illustrate the main point.

16.24 In *Leggott v. Barrett*,[71] a case concerning a deed of dissolution of a partnership, James L.J. said regarding merger:

> "I cannot help saying that I think it is very important, according to my view of the law of contract, both at Common Law and in Equity, that if parties have made an executory contract *which is to be carried out by a deed afterwards executed*,[72] the real completed contract between the parties is to be found in the deed, and that you have no right whatever to look at the contract, although it is recited in the deed, except for the purpose of construing the deed itself. You have no right to look at the contract either for the purpose of enlarging or diminishing or modifying the contract which is to be found in the deed itself. A recital of the agreement in such deed would have the same effect as an ordinary preamble to an Act of Parliament, or any other instrument as showing what the object of the parties was, and what they were about to do, so as to afford a guide in the construction of their words; but you have no right for any other purpose to look at anything but the deed itself, unless there be a suit for rescinding the deed on the ground of fraud, or for altering it on the ground of mistake."

In the same case Brett L.J. said:

> "I entirely agree with my Lord that where there is a preliminary contract in words which is afterwards reduced into writing, or where there is a preliminary contract in writing which is afterwards *reduced into a deed*,[73] the rights of the parties are governed in the first case entirely by the writing, and in the second case entirely by the deed; and if there be any difference between the words and the written document in the first case, or between the written agreement and the deed in the other case, the rights of the parties are entirely governed by the superior document and by the governing part of that document. If there is any doubt about the construction of the governing words of that document, the recital may be looked at in order to determine what is the true construction; but if there is no doubt about the construction,

[71] (1880 15 Ch. D. 306).
[72] Italics supplied.
[73] Italics supplied.

the rights of the parties are governed entirely by the operative part of the writing or the deed . . ."

16.25 The above was explained by the Court of Appeal in *Palmer v. Johnson.*[74] Brett M.R. said that the judge in the court below in *Palmer v. Johnson,*[75] Smith J, had correctly pointed out that:

"All that was there held was . . . that where the parties enter into a preliminary contract which is afterwards to be carried out by a deed to be executed, there the complete contract is to be found in the deed, and that the Court has no right whatever to look at the preliminary contract". "But *Bos v. Helsham*[76] has decided that *this particular contract for compensation was one which was not to be carried out by the deed of conveyance, and therefore it did not come within that principle of the law and was not merged in the deed.*"[77]

Bowen L.J. dealt with the point more fully.

". . . Therefore, the first question is, what is the interpretation of the agreement in this case. Now it is commonly said, that where there is a preliminary contract for sale which has afterwards ended in the execution of a formal sale which has afterwards ended in the execution of a formal deed, you must look to the deed only for the terms of the contract, but it seems to me one cannot lay down any rule which is to apply to all such cases, but *must endeavour to see what was the contract according to the true intention of the parties*. Suppose the parties should make a parol contract, with the intention that it should afterwards be reduced into writing; and that that which is reduced into writing shall be the only contract, then, of course, one cannot go beyond it; but if they intend, as they might, that there should be something outside such contract, they might agree that that should exist, notwithstanding it was not in the contract which was put into writing. In the same way, when one is dealing with a deed by which the property has been conveyed, *one must see if it covers the whole ground of the preliminary contract*. One must construe the preliminary contract by itself, and *see whether it was intended to go on to any, and what, extent after the formal deed had been executed.*"[78]

Fry L.J. agreed with the other two that there was no merger and that the deed in this case *"was intended to cover only a portion of the ground* covered by the contract of purchase."[79]

[74] (1884) 13 Q.B.D. 351.
[75] *ibid.*
[76] (1866) L.R. 2. Ex. 72.
[77] Italics supplied.
[78] Italics supplied.
[79] Italics supplied.

APPENDIX TO CHAPTER 16: SOME CASES OF INTEREST

***Legge v. Croker* 1 Ball & B. 506**

16.26 Colonel Legge took a lease of a house in 1808. When viewing the grounds, he observed a gravel walk across part of it, and inquired of the vendor if there were any public right of way there. The vendor told him there was not; but that there had been one until it was stopped in 1772 by a Presentment of the Grand Jury, since when he believed it had only been used with his permission, so that it could be stopped up entirely without trouble.

It subsequently transpired, after Colonel Legge had taken up possession and built a wall across the gravel walk, that there was in fact a right of way. He sued the vendor for rescission of the lease or compensation for the incumbrance. The vendor's counsel accepted the vendor had said there was no right of way, but said "this was the firm Conviction of his Mind; and from the Presentment, and the Acquiescence by the Public, he was fully justified in this Opinion." The Lord Chancellor said that the vendor had asserted there was no right of way, but "conceived himself to be, in point of Law, justified in asserting this, after the Presentment by the Grand Jury; and to be warranted in Point of Fact; when, after having erected Gates, having directed his Servants to prevent People passing, he found it acquiesced in for so many Years. This cannot be called a Misrepresentation." Colonel Legge lost.

Note: This is plainly a no-fault case. The vendor had honestly represented what he reasonably believed from the facts within his knowledge.

***Burrowes v. Lock* (1805) 10 Ves. Jun. 470; 32 E.R. 927**

16.27 The plaintiff Burrowes was intending to take an assignment of one Cartwright's beneficial interest under a trust, and applied to the trustee Lock, to find out whether it was unincumbered. In fact it was, and Lock had forgotten, and not bothered to find out before giving his answer.

The Master of the Rolls noted that it was a demand for damages, but thought that was no special objection in equity; and noted that the Lord Chancellor had said in *Evans v. Bicknell*[80] that *Pasley v. Freeman*[81] was more fit for a court of equity than a court of law; and had said "It has occurred to me, that that case upon the principles of many decisions in this Court might have been maintained here; for it is a very old head of equity; that if a representation is made to another person, going to deal in a matter of interest upon the faith of that representation, the former shall make that representation good, if he knows it to be false." The Master of the Rolls did not see how the plaintiff could be expected to "dive into the secret recesses of his [Lock's] heart"; and it was at the least "gross negligence to take upon him to aver positively and distinctly, that Cartwright was entitled to the whole fund, without giving himself the trouble to recollect, whether the fact was so or not; without thinking on the subject". Thus the order was that Lock should make up any deficiency in the depleted trust fund which Cartwright had.

Note: The case is in effect an early negligent misstatement case. It was later disapproved, although the underlying law may be said perhaps to have been revived in the

[80] 6 Ves. 174.
[81] 3 Term. Rep. 51.

negligent misstatement cases. It is cited merely because it is referred to in a number of later cases as illustrative of a type of case.

***Todd v. Gee* (1810) 17 Ves. 273; 34 E.R. 106 (Chancery courts' reluctance to give damages as opposed to compensation)**

16.28 This was a procedure question. The plaintiff sought specific performance, or if not, "satisfaction for the damages and injury sustained by the non-performance". Lord Eldon Lord Chancellor said that he was not aware "that this Court would give relief in the shape of damages; which is very different from giving compensation out of the purchase-money. . . . My opinion is, that this Court ought not, except under very particular circumstances, as there may be, upon a Bill for the specific performance of a contract to direct an issue, or a reference to the Master, to ascertain the damages. That is purely at Law. It has no resemblance to compensation. Where, for instance, an estate is held with an engagement, that a certain number of acres are tithe-free, which is not the case, and the vendee contracts to sell to another person with a similar engagement, this Court would give compensation for so much as was not tithe-free; but would not give compensation for the damage, sustained by not being able to complete the subsequent contract; which might fairly be offered to the consideration of a jury. He later confirmed this view, after reflection)

***Butcher v. Butcher* (1812), 1 Ves. & B. 79; 35 E.R. 31 (Chancery and common law jurisdiction—comment)**

16.29 Lord Eldon said *en passant* of the doctrine of the Master of the Rolls that a deed could not be fraudulent unless it was fraudulent both in law and in equity. "To that Doctrine I do not agree. Though in modern Times, and particularly during the Period, in which I have been engaged in this Hall, a strong Inclination has been evident to say, that whatever is Equity ought to be Law; an Opinion, acted upon especially by Mr Justice Buller; who persuaded Lord Mansfield to act upon it, until it was reformed by Lord Kenyon, with the Assistance of the same very able Judge, as he certainly was; yet the clear Doctrine of Lord Hardwicke and all his Predecessors was, that there are many Instances of Fraud, that would affect Instruments in Equity; of which the Law could not take Notice; and this Class of Cases is one Instance."

***Edwards v. M'Leay* (1815) G. Coop. 308; 35 E.R. 568**

16.30 The plaintiff brought his action to set aside a conveyance of land to him, since he discovered after conveyance that a part of the land had a doubtful title, having been enclosed out of Clapham Common. The Master of the Rolls gave a considered judgment as follows: "This is a bill of rather an unusual description. It is brought by the purchaser of an estate who has had a conveyance made to him for the purpose of setting aside the sale and getting back his purchase-money, on the ground of an alleged misrepresentation with regard to the title to a part of such estate.

It cannot certainly be contended that by the law of this country, the insufficiency of a title, even when producing actual eviction, necessarily furnished a ground for claiming restitution of the purchase-money. By the civil law it was otherwise. By our law a vendor is, in general, liable only to the extent of his covenants. But it has never been laid down, that on the subject of title there can be no such misrepresentation as will give the purchaser a right to claim a relief to which the covenants do not extend. In the case of *Urmston v. Pate* there was no ingredient of fraud. Both parties misapprehended the law. *The vendor had no knowledge of any fact which he withheld from the purchaser.* In the case of *Bree v. Olbech,*[82–83] *it did not at all appear that the party knew that the mortgage which he assigned was a forgery.* Lord Mansfield says, "if he had discovered the forgery, and had then got rid of the deed as a true security, the case would have been very different." And the Plaintiff had leave to amend his replication, in case upon inquiry the facts would support a charge of fraud.

"Whether it would be a fraud to offer as good a title which the vendor knows to be defective in point of law, it is not necessary to determine. *But if he knows and conceals a fact material to the validity of the title, I am not aware of any principle on which relief can be refused to the purchaser.* [He reviewed the evidence of knowledge on the part of the vendors and continued]

16.31 "What is the result of all this evidence? *not indeed that Mr Prescott [one of the vendors] knew, of his own knowledge, that this had been part of the common, or that he had, with his own eyes, seen the encroachment made, but that he had so much information on the subject as made it altogether improper and unfair to represent* to a purchaser, as it is admitted he and the other vendors did, that they were seised or entitled in fee-simple, or had full power and authority to dispose of the fee-simple and inheritance of the whole and every part without exception of the premises which they offered to the Plaintiff for sale. *Be it that he entertained the opinion, which he and Mr Malcolm expressed to Mr Copeland, that after such a length of time the parish could not support the claim which they were then making . . .*"[84] [He went on to say that the lord of the manor might yet make a claim, and the true facts might have influenced the price at least.] Therefore he made an order for rescission.

The case was appealed.[85] Lord Eldon confirmed it, saying the representation made by the vendors was "*in the sense in which we use the term, fraudulent*". He refined the rescission order regarding repairs to read "an account of all costs, charges, and expenses, which the Plaintiff has been properly put to, *in consequence of, or which have been incident to,* the purchase of the said house and premises, and the conveyance thereof to the Plaintiff; and, for the better taking of such account, the parties are to produce etc . . ."[86]

Newham v. May (1824) 13 Price 749; 147 E.R. 1142 (A common law view of "fraud" at common law and in equity)

16.32 Alexander C.B., rejected a claim brought after conveyance for compensation for the difference between the actual rental value of property and the value represented by the vendor's agent before the contract. He rejected it mainly on the evidence, but also said that if he had thought the case turned on the question of jurisdiction he would have taken time to consider it further.

"It is not in every case of fraud that relief is to be administered in a Court of Equity. In the case, for instance, of a fraudulent warranty on the sale of a horse, or any fraud upon the sale of a chattel, no one, I apprehend, ever thought of filing a bill in Equity. *The cases of compensation in Equity I consider to have grown out of the jurisdiction of the Courts of Equity as exercised in respect of contracts for the purchase of real property,*[87] where it is often ancillary, as incidentally necessary to effectuate decrees of specific performance. This, however, appears to me to be no more than a common case of fraud by means of misrepresentation, raising a dry question of damages—in effect, a mere money demand."

[82–83] Dougl. Rep. 630.
[84] Italics supplied.
[85] 2 Swans. 287.
[86] Italics supplied.
[87] Italics supplied.

***Cann v. Cann* (1830) 3 Sim. 447; 57 E.R. 1065**

16.33 The rent of some land had been misstated in the particulars. There was a compensation clause. The vendor said he would rather repay the buyer his money with interest since he had another buyer. The court however ordered compensation even though it was after conveyance. The case of *Thomas v. Powell*[88] was said by the Vice-Chancellor to be of no application, because there the purchaser had a remedy under his covenants. He thought the circumstance of having taken a conveyance did not at all affect his right.

***Clarke v. Manning* (1844) 7 Beav. 167; 49 E.R. 1025 (Exposition of the term equitable fraud**

16.34 The case had been brought in equity on the ground of fraud. The Master of the Rolls, Lord Langdale, said: "This court has clearly a concurrent jurisdiction with all other Courts in matters of fraud; but the defence which is made is this—that all the frauds which are here distinctly charged as such, that if the Plaintiffs were to make them out, they would furnish a defence at law, and therefore the Plaintiffs have no occasion to seek relief in equity. The Defendants here say, let the action be tried, you have pleaded the frauds, prove them, and you will have there the same relief which you ask for here. The answer to which is this: It is very true, that if I make out those frauds which would be a defence at law, I should succeed at law; and though I have not distinctly charged fraud of any other kind, yet I have stated and alleged facts, which shew that there has been a fraud which would not be a defence at law, not being those *direct frauds arising from falsehood, concert and combination, which will be taken notice of there,* but frauds which will only be taken cognizance of in a Court of Equity, namely, *fraud arising from the negligence or want of caution of the parties dealing with the agents, directors or managers of the Joint Stock Company*[89]—such negligence and such want of caution as have enabled them to practise a fraud on those for whom they were acting, and which they would not have been able to have practised, if the Defendants here had not been guilty of such want of attention and such negligence as they have.

"It is very true that there are courses of conduct which this Court construes to be fraudulent, and which may be used as a defence to a party sought to be charged with the consequence of them, which would not be taken notice of in a Court of law. It is very true also that those matters which have been called legal frauds might be taken notice of here; but relief is sought for on the ground of both species of fraud, namely, that which would be considered fraud in a Court of law, and that which would be held to be fraud in a Court of Equity." Later, he said the case had two distinct portions as pleaded: "the charges of direct fraud, and the charges of fraud which, though not direct and being innocently meant, might nevertheless relieve the party who is sought to be charged with the effect of it."

***Gibson v. D'Este,* (1843) 27 & C.C. 542; 63 E.R. 243**

16.35 This of course was reversed in *Wilde v. Gibson.*[90] However, the decree is worth noting: it was fully reported, and followed *Edwards v. M'Leay.*[91] It included a reconveyance and an occupation rent payable by the plaintiff.

[88] Italics supplied.
[89] Italics supplied.
[90] para., 16.36, below.
[91] Above, para. 16.30

***Wilde v. Gibson* (1848) 1 H.L.C. 605; 9 E.R. 897**

16.36 The action was in deceit, based on fraud. There had been no warranty or relevant assertion by the vendor, although her dealings were inconsistent with the existence of a right of way; and after completion the purchaser found that the property was encumbered with a right of way. It could not be proved she had knowledge of the right of way, although her agent had known about it. Lord Campbell in argument said "In an action upon contract, the representation of an agent is the representation of the principal; but in the action on the case, for deceit, the misrepresentation or concealment must be proved against the principal."

The Lord Chancellor noted that the action was based on fraud, which could not be proved; and said "It is in all cases important to consider how far the case proved is in conformity with the case alleged; but it is peculiarly so in cases founded upon alleged fraud, imputing dishonest practices to the defendants. It is in all such cases essential to prevent the proceedings from becoming instruments of unfounded slander. Plaintiffs should bear in mind that imputations which cannot be supported, will not only not profit them, but may debar them from that relief to which they might be entitled upon other grounds, if properly brought forward." Later he noted again that Mlle. D'Este had had only constructive notice and that *no representation of any kind took place*. "And the question would arise whether such circumstances would entitle the purchaser to have a completed purchase set aside. It has not been, and cannot be, contended that it could . . ."

Lord Brougham agreed, saying that "Constructive notice is only where actual knowledge is not alleged".

16.37 Lord Campbell said that "in the court below the distinction between a bill for carrying into execution an executory contract, and a bill to set aside a conveyance that has been executed, has not been very distinctly borne in mind.

With the regard to the first: If there be, in any way whatever, misrepresentation or concealment, which is material to the purchaser, a court of equity will not compel him to complete the purchase; but where the conveyance has been executed, I apprehend, my Lords, that a court of equity will set aside the conveyance only on the ground of actual fraud. And there would no safety for the transactions of mankind, if, upon a discovery being made at any distance of time of a material fact not disclosed to the purchaser, of which the vendor had merely constructive notice, a conveyance which had been executed could be set aside." He then went on to make the same point as the others, that essentially deceit had to be proved, and had not been proved.

Note: There is no good faith point here, is perhaps what is to be stressed: it is a case of "mere" non-disclosure of something known only to the agent, there having been nothing misleading said to the purchaser. Thus, the case in reality says nothing new.

***Rawlins v. Wickham* (1858) 3 De G. & J. 304; 44 E.R. 1285**

16.38 The plaintiff was induced to join a banking partnership by means of a balance sheet left with him by Wickham who was one of the partners, stating the financial position of the partnership. In fact, unbeknownst to Wickham, the statement was quite false, in that a confidential clerk who had been managing the bank had been defrauding it of huge sums of money.

The court (Lord Justice Knight Bruce and the Lord Justice Turner) held that the plaintiff was entitled to set aside the agreement even though he had been a partner for four years, and have an indemnity against the partnership liabilities from Mr Wickham's estate. Both held that Mr Wickham had known nothing of the fraud: where he had been wrong was in *taking upon himself to state that the accounts represented the true financial position of the bank without satisfying himself that that was in fact so.* As Turner L.J. said, "Putting the case of the representations of Mr Wickham on the most favourable ground, this was a representation by him of a fact of the truth or falsehood of which he knew nothing—and it was a representation which must have formed a material inducement to Mr Rawlins. It has turned out that this representation was contrary to the fact. *There was not as I think any moral fraud* [that is, fraud as we know it, involving dishonesty], *but there was legal fraud* [that is, equitable, fraud or lack of good faith]".[92]

Turner L.J. said "There has been no dispute upon those principles [that is, "the principles on which the cases on this subject have proceeded"], and the case plainly falls within them. *If upon a treaty for purchase one of the parties to the contract makes a representation materially affecting the subject-matter of the contract, he surely cannot be heard to say that he knew nothing of the truth or falsehood of that which he represented, and still more surely he cannot be allowed to retain any benefit which he has derived if the representation he has made turns out to be untrue.* It would be most dangerous to allow any doubt to be cast upon this doctrine. To do so would be to open a door to escape in all the cases of representation as to credit, and indeed in all other cases of representation."[93]

16.39 On the *delay* by the plaintiff and the means of knowledge which he had had during his four years as partner, he said: ". . . it was said that he had the means of detecting it and ought to have done so, and it was asked on what ground the Defendants were to be made liable to the Plaintiff for acts which were done during the continuance of the partnership. This argument, it is to be observed, does not proceed upon the ground of acquiescence. To the argument put on that ground it would, I think, be an answer that there was no knowledge of the right, and so far as the argument rests upon the Plaintiff's means of knowledge, the case of *Harris v. Kemble*[94] seems to me to furnish an answer to it. . . . I do not fail to observe that this was a case of specific performance, and subject to the peculiar rules applicable to such cases, in which the Court exercises a discretion, though not an arbitrary discretion, and that the case is a direct decision only upon the question whether the Court will enforce specific performance where there has been a misrepresentation; still *the remarks there made have an important bearing on all cases where the person misled might have detected the misrepresentation.* That case has also an important bearing on the question of subsequent conduct. Various acts had there been done under the agreement, tending to affirm it and to disable the Court from putting the parties in statu quo. It was held, however, that those acts were not sufficient to induce the Court to decree specific performance; and here, had there been acts by Mr Rawlins which would have made it difficult to put the estate of Mr Wickham in the same position as if the partnership had never been entered into, I think that case tends to shew that *those acts must have been strong to induce the Court to refuse relief.*"[95]

16.40 [On rescission]: "It was strongly urged . . . that if the Court held the Plaintiff entitled to any relief, the proper course would be to decree the estate of Mr Wickham to make good the representations contained in the paper; that is, to pay the difference between the amount of debts there admitted and the real amount. But what are the true principles by which the Court is to be guided, where a person has been led to enter into a contract through a misrepresentation made by the other party to it? They are clearly laid down by Sir

[92] Italics supplied.
[93] Italics supplied.
[94] 1 Sim. 111; see Chap. 14 on Penalties, Deposits and Forfeiture.
[95] Italics supplied.

Thomas Plumer in *Clermont v. Tasburgh*[96] and are correctly stated in the marginal note "The effect of partial misrepresentation is not to alter or modify the agreement *pro tanto*, but to destroy it entirely, and to operate as a personal bar to the party who has practised it." That, again, was a case of specific performance, and open to the same observations in that respect as *Harris v. Kemble*,[97] but *Edwards v. M'Leay*[98] was a case of setting aside a contract.... The vendors at the time of the sale did not know that it was a part of the common, but they knew facts which gave them reason to believe that it might be so. On this ground Sir William Grant made a decree for setting aside the sale and repaying the purchase-money with costs, and the decree was affirmed by Lord Eldon. That case is conclusive to shew what is the course of the Court in cases of this description. And how should it be otherwise; for if a contract is obtained by fraud, it is for the party defrauded to elect whether he will be bound. He, perhaps, would not have entered into the contract at all if he had known the real facts; it is, therefore, impossible, with any degree of justice, to enforce the contract against him in any part. If he had discovered the misrepresentation immediately after it was made, the very fact of its having been made would, probably, in a case like the present, have deterred him from going further with the matter. It has, therefore, been rightly settled, that the party deceived has a right to have the contract wholly set aside."

***Bos v. Helsham* (1866) L.R. 2 Ex. 72**

16.41 The contract of sale of a property provided that any mistake or error should not annul the sale but compensation was to be given. It was discovered after conveyance that the particulars had misstated the rental from the property, and the purchaser was allowed compensation. The court did not enter into the question whether in the absence of the compensation clause the courts of equity would have given the purchaser the right to raise the point after completion, but confined itself to the compensation clause.

Kelly C.B. said about this "Now, here it is to be observed that no distinction is made, though it would have been easy to make it, between an error or mistake discovered *before*, and one discovered *after*[99] the execution of the conveyance."

Channel B. agreed, saying "We need not decide, for instance, what would have been the parties' rights had there been no ninth condition of sale,—whether or not such a mistake as has occurred would or would not have annulled the sale. Here there is an express condition that it shall not annul it. Nor need we examine the authorities which are supposed to decide that the parties' rights are concluded after conveyance executed, purchase-money paid, and possession given, except where there has been fraud or circumstances (such a gross inadequacy of price) whence a court of equity would imply fraud. For we are not called upon to *rescind*[1] this contract . . ."

Note: The misrepresentation in the above case was said to have been fraudulent (that is legal fraud) by Malins V.C. in Manson v. Thacker.[2] There is in fact no trace of this in the judgment whatever; and Jessel M.R. in any event disagreed with Malins V.C.'s approach in *Turner v. Skelton*.[3]

[96] 1 Jac. & W. 1212.
[97] Above.
[98] Above, para. 16.30.
[99] Both are italicised in the original.
[1] Italics in original.
[2] (Below, para. 16.44.
[3] Below, para. 16.46.

***Kennedy v. Panama, etc., Royal Mail Co.* (1867) L.R. 2 Q.B. 580**
(Deceit-only case)

16.42 The plaintiff sought the return of instalments paid for shares in the company, pleading fraudulent misrepresentation. The company's representative had believed he had a valid contract with the New Zealand government. However at a later date, after the prospectus had been issued, an incoming New Zealand government disputed the contract alleging it to have been beyond the powers of the previous government to make it. The allegation of fraud failed on the facts.

***Hart v. Swaine* (1877) 7 Ch. D. 42**

16.43 A vendor sold and conveyed land as freehold land. He had bought the land not long before, it being then described as one fourth copyhold. Afterwards the purchaser discovered the land was really copyhold. It had not been possible to discover this from the abstract of title which he had had: this showed a perfectly good title. Fry J. held that *the vendor had enough to put him upon inquiry as to the facts; instead of which he relied on his own vague notion*, and sold the land to the purchaser. Fry J. also relied on Maule J. in *Evans v. Edmonds*[4] and Turner L.J., in *Rawlins v. Wickham*.[5] He set aside the sale, declared the deed inoperative, ordered that a memorandum of the judgment be endorsed by the Registrar on the deed, and that it then be delivered up to the defendant. He also ordered that the defendant repay the purchase money with interest, after deducting the amount of the rents and profits derived by the plaintiffs from the land during their occupation of it. Finally he directed an account as in *Edwards v. M'Leay*[6] of the expenses incurred by the plaintiffs in consequence of the purchaser of thee land; the defendant to pay the amount found due, and the costs of the action.

Note. In Soper v. Arnold[7] Cotton L.J. stated that this case was one of "legal" fraud, that is; equitable fraud or a breach of the good faith duties.

***Manson v. Thacker* (1878) 7 Ch. D. 620**

16.44 The purchaser sought compensation for misrepresentation after completion. The property had an underground culvert not disclosed or discovered (although no *representation had apparently been made about it*).

Malins V.C. denied the purchaser compensation. He said he had had "ample opportunity of examining the property, for there was no concealment, and he ought to have discovered this defect before the completed his purchase." He said that the cases where it had been allowed after completion were distinguishable: *Cann v. Cann*[8] because what was said by the vendor amounted to a species of fraudulent misrepresentation; *Bos v. Helsham*[9] again because the vendor was guilty of a fraud; and *Hart v. Swaine*[10] where "*there was legal fraud, that vitiated the whole transaction*. Here fraud is not charged."[11]

Note: This case was doubted or disapproved by the Master of the Rolls in Turner

[4] 13 C.B. 777.
[5] Above, para. 16.38.
[6] Above, para. 16.30.
[7] Below, para. 16.52.
[8] Above, para. 16.33.
[9] Above, para. 16.41.
[10] Above, para. 16.43.
[11] Italics supplied.

v. Skelton[12]*: he said Malins V.C. could not have intended to overrule earlier cases where the plaintiff's right of action survived completion.*

***Besley v. Besley* (1878) 9 Ch. D. 103 (No-fault case)**

16.45 The purchaser of an underlease claimed compensation (some years after the transaction in question), though he had not troubled to inspect the original lease nor ascertain for himself the precise term of his lease. *The agreement had not been misleading,* since it had simply been for the residue of the lessee's term less ten days. In fact the underlease was made seven years too long by mistake, and the original lease had only sixteen years to run.

Malins V.C. said that it was simply a case of mutual mistake, "because if Micklem had known he was misstating the term of the lease, it would have been a fraudulent act on his part, and fraud vitiates every transaction. No fraud is alleged here, and therefore it could be nothing more than an innocent mistake. Thus the purchaser's claim was dismissed.

***Turner v. Skelton* (1879) 13 Ch. D. 130 (Compensation granted after completion)**

16.46 The purchaser in this case was not claiming to set aside the conveyance but was claiming compensation after conveyance for a misdescription of the measurements of the land. He had not had permission from the vendor to survey the land, it appears, and thus could not by due diligence have found out the problem before conveyance.

Jessel M.R. cited *Dart on Vendors and Purchasers,*[13] to the effect that a purchaser's right to compensation or to resist specific performance before completion, and his right to compensation after conveyance depended on whether the purchaser had had knowledge or notice of the problem. "No book can be produced to shew that it was thought to be settled law that a purchaser loses his right to compensation by taking a conveyance, and on what principle should he do so? The theory is that he has contracted to take compensation by taking a conveyance, and on what principle should he do so? The theory is that he has contracted to take compensation if there is any variation from the particulars. Why, then, should he lose it by taking a conveyance? The only reason that can be alleged is that everything is supposed to be settled between the parties, but why should that be an obstacles to the right of the purchaser when the defect is discovered afterwards? . . . When the mistake is one which a purchaser could not by due diligence discover, why should he be held not to be entitled to compensation?" He relied on *Cann v. Cann*[14] in which the Vice-Chancellor had said: "The question is whether, there having been a misrepresentation as to the value of the property, in respect of which the purchaser had a right of action, the circumstance of his having taken a conveyance has destroyed the right. Now it appears to me that the right of the Petitioner in that respect is not at all affected by that circumstances."

Jessel M.R. also relied on *Bos v. Helsham*[15], in which Kelly C.B. had observed in the Court of Exchequer "No distinction is made, though it would have been easy to make it between an error or mistake discovered *before* and one discovered *after* the execution of the conveyance."

He considered Malins V.C.'s comments in *Manson v. Thacker,*[16] disagreed

[12] Below, para. 16.46.
[13] (5th ed.) at pp. 1077 and 1225.
[14] Above, para. 16.33.
[15] Above, para. 16.41.
[16] Above, para. 16.44.

with his views (possibly about both cases but certainly about *Bos v. Helsham*[17] and said "I cannot imagine that Vice-Chancellor Malins intended to overrule the previous cases." Thus, he considered that the purchaser had not waived the condition by taking a conveyance in this case (although there might be cases where that was the effect of taking a conveyance); and the purchaser was entitled to his compensation.

Allen v. Richardson (1879) 13 Ch. D. 524 (Purchaser failed to use due diligence; deemed knowledge of defect)

16.47 The purchaser agreed to buy a public house, it being represented that the freeholder had offered to release a covenant in the lease against Sunday trading for a payment of another £25 additional rent. The vendor was an underlessee. The purchaser did not appreciate until after completion that he also needed a release from the original lessee.

The case came before Malins V.C. In argument the vendors referred to the cases he had decided earlier of *Manson v. Thacker*[18] and *Besley v. Besley*.[19] The plaintiffs' counsel called *Manson v. Thacker*[20] a decision "that a purchaser cannot in the absence of fraud obtain any compensation after completion of the contract by execution of the conveyance"; but in fact described the ratio in narrower terms: "In both those cases the defect was discovered after the completion of the contract. You thought the purchaser had the means of finding out the defect before completion. So, here the purchaser had the means of knowledge, for he had notice of the outstanding interest, but it was not discovered that *Dawson* had no power to release the covenant till after completion."

Malins V.C. reviewed the facts, and said *inter alia*: "I have not heard a single scrap of information which the Defendant and his advisers acquired after the 19th of July which was not in their possession before." The Vice Chancellor applied *caveat emptor* to the case and denied the purchaser the relief he sought. He criticised *Turner v. Skelton*[21] on the grounds that the purchaser *would* have had the right to inspect the property and ought to have done so. " . . . until I find it laid down by the Court of Appeal that a purchaser is to be allowed to be lax in the conduct of his business, that he is to be allowed to lie by carelessly and discover things after the completion of the purchase which he ought to have discovered before . . . I shall adhere to my own view . . ." Nor did he think it ranked as a case of mutual mistake.

Brett v. Clowser (1880) 5 C.P.D. 376

16.48 The purchaser believed that he was to have a right of way leading to Hampstead Heath along a path at the back of the property. In fact the deeds gave him no such right, and after completion of the lease in favour of the purchaser, the way was obstructed by the new owner of the adjoining land. The vendor's auctioneer had mistakenly represented at the sale that there was such a right. Denman J. relied on *Legge v. Croker*[22] and on *Dart on Vendors and Purchasers*[23] which said that with a few exceptions, "a purchaser, after the conveyance is executed by all necessary parties, has no remedy at law or in

[17] Above.
[18] Above.
[19] Above, para. 16.45.
[20] Above.
[21] Above, para. 16.46.
[22] Above, para. 16.26.
[23] 3rd edn. at p. 503.

equity in respect of any defects either in the title to or in the quantity or quality of the estate". He also relied on *Manson v. Thacker,*[24] *Allen v. Richardson,*[25] and *Wilde v. Gibson,*[26] all above and regarded *Hart v. Swaine*[27] as a case where the purchaser had not got the thing he had bargained for, and further where the inaccuracy was on the face of the contract itself (the land was described as freehold land, but turned out to be copyhold).

***Brownlie v. Campbell* (1880) 5 App. Cas. 925 (No-fault cause)**

16.49 The purchaser had agreed to buy land "with all risks of error in the particulars". The vendors reasonably believed that the land was held from the Crown, but it emerged later that this was not so, resulting in the successful assertion of a right against the purchaser.

Lord Selborne L.C. dealing with the point regarding representation, said that the cases cited belonged to an entirely different category, cases like *Burrowes v. Lock*[28] and *Slim v. Croucher.*[29] "They are simply of this sort. A man is going to deal for valuable consideration with a particular subject, and the value of the return which he is to receive depends entirely upon a particular fact, which is, or ought to be, in the knowledge of a particular person—in one of those cases a trustee, in the other the lessor and landlord. In the one case the question was whether notice of any prior incumbrance upon the trust fund had been given to the trustee. That was a question of fact, and the whole value of the intended security depended upon it. In the other case the question was whether the landlord was in a position to grant the lease upon which money was to be lent. There also the whole value of the intended security depended upon the answer to the question, to be given by a person within whose knowledge the fact ought to have been, and in point of fact at one time or another necessarily was. If his memory had failed, still it was the case of a man who once had certain knowledge of the fact, and *who could have no right to assert one way or the other a fact as of his own knowledge upon such a subject unless he possessed that knowledge; and if he did assert it, he was bound to make the assertion good.*

The mere fact of forgetfulness by a man who has known a certain fact, who is asked whether that fact has happened or not, and says positively that it did or did not, cannot possibly be an excuse; because *if he had spoken the simple truth he would have said "I do not recollect whether it is so or not"*. If the fact be that he does not recollect, then *by saying that the fact was so, or by saying that the fact was not so, he takes upon himself the responsibility of a positive statement, upon the faith of which he knows that the other man is going to deal for valuable consideration.*"[30]

16.50 Lord Selborne said the principle of the law in such cases was perfectly clear; but had no application to a case of vendor and purchaser *like the one before them,* where the purchaser had expressly taken the risk, and thus the principle *caveat emptor* was at all events prima facie applicable. He went on to say, that assuming the errors which the purchaser was to take the risk of were unconnected with fraud in the particulars," . . . when the conveyance takes place it is not, as far as I know, in either country the principle of equity that relief should afterwards be given against that conveyance, unless there be a

[24] Above, para. 16.44.
[25] Above, para. 16.47.
[26] Above, para. 16.36.
[27] Above, para. 16.43
[28] Above, para. 16.27.
[29] 1 De G.F. & J. 518.
[30] Italics supplied.

case of fraud, or a case of misrepresentation amounting to fraud, by which the purchaser may have been deceived." (Failing that, he went on, there was also the possibility of "error in substantialibus sufficient to annul the whole contract".) Here, however, the statements were all made bona fide, and there were perfectly good grounds for believing them to be true.

Lord Hatherley agreed, and distinguished the case where a person is asked something with reference to a particular fact and says yes or no: in this case he is answerable.

"Whether or not he bonâ fide was aware and had treasured up in his memory the existence of certain facts connected with the property, *he would be answerable if he took it upon himself to say that such and such a thing had not occurred or had occurred. The only proper answer for a man to make is what he knows, and if he asserts that such a thing happened when the question is asked of him as a matter of business, he is bound to make that representation good; he is not at liberty to say afterwards, "I had no recollection on the subject. I really did not remember whether it happened or not." If that was the state of his mind he ought to have said so when he was asked the question. He ought to have said, "I have an indistinct recollection of it, but I know none of the facts."* He ought to give, in fact, the proper answer for a man to give who is speaking the truth." Thus, he thought that on the facts here, there were good reasons for the vendors thinking what they did, and "*no bad faith of any description* whatever" could be imputed to them. He said

16.51 ". . . it is perfectly impossible to say that that approaches within any appreciable distance of *the cases which have been decided upon representations made, or silence kept, with regard to that which the vendor was bound, acting in good faith towards those with whom he was dealing, to have disclosed.*"[31]

Lord Blackburn, for his part, thought that the lack of good faith would also be fraud, but found nothing here of either kind anyway; and thought, *obiter*, that the duty of *uberrima fides* was limited to insurance contracts.

Lord Watson simply said that if he were satisfied that "from the circumstances in which Mr Carment was placed at that time that the facts either within his knowledge, or which ought to have been within his knowledge, were such as reasonably to suggest to his mind that that decree was in serious peril, and that there was a serious risk of that title being challenged, I should not have come, with the same confidence at least, to the conclusion which I have formed upon this part of the case."

Soper v. Arnold (1887) 37 Ch.D.96 (No-fault case; purchaser also fails to use due diligence), C.A.

16.52 The purchaser had contracted to buy land, then failed to come up with the purchase money. On the sale by the vendor to another purchaser, it emerged there was a title defect which the first purchaser had not found, although it appeared on the face of the abstract he had had. The first purchaser tried to have the contract set aside.

The main importance of the case is perhaps that Cotton L.J. saw *Hart v. Swaine*[32] as a case of legal (equitable) fraud.[33]

Sir J. Hannen stressed that in the present case there was "no misrepresentation, no concealment of any fact, but the facts that were disclosed satisfied the advisers of the Plaintiff at that time, and the title was approved of."[34] The Court of Appeal's decision was afirmed by the House of Lords.[35]

[31] Italics supplied.
[32] Above, para. 16.43.
[33] Above, See text above at para. 16.08.
[34] *per* Sir J. Hannen.
[35] cat (1889) 14 App. (N.S.) 49.

***Derry v. Peek* (1889) 14 App. Cas. 337**

16.53 Lord Herschell affirmed that an action of deceit differed from an action "brought to obtain rescission of a contract on the ground of misrepresentation of a material fact"; and also differed from another class of actions. "I mean those cases where a person *within whose special province it lay to know a particular fact, has given an erroneous answer to an inquiry made with regard to it by a person desirous of ascertaining the fact for the purpose of determining his course accordingly,*[36] and has been held bound to make good the assurance he has given." He cited *Burrowes v. Lock*[37] (an estoppel or early negligent misrepresentation case) as an example of this kind of case, and referred to Lord Selborne in *Brownlie v. Campbell*[38] who had pointed out that such cases were in an altogether different category from actions to recover damages for false representation, such as they were dealing with.

Lord Bramwell also referred to "the equitable rule (which is not in question here) that a material misrepresentation, though not fraudulent, may give a right to avoid or rescind a contract where capable of such rescission." but went on to say "To found an action for damages there must be a contract and breach, or fraud."

***Low v. Bouverie* (1891) 3 Ch.82**

16.54 A trustee who had forgotten information which he had in his possession regarding the trust fund, gave incomplete information about charges on the trust fund to an intending mortgagee of a beneficiary. It was held by the Court of Appeal that he was not liable for this honest but inaccurate non-contracted statement. It was contrary to information in his possession, which he had failed to look at before answering; but the statement he had made was held in the circumstances to amount to a statement only to the best of his knowledge and belief.

The rather similar cases of *Burrowes v. Lock*[39] (above) (and *Slim v. Croucher*[40] were considered. It was held that in the absence of estoppel (and the statement here was held too confined in its effect to support the estoppel claimed[41]) or a warranty to someone one was intending a *contractual* relationship with, there was no duty to be careful in making statements even if one knew they were to be relied on. Although the effect of the two above cases had been expressly preserved in *Derry v. Peek,*[42] it was held that any other finding would be inconsistent with *Derry v. Peek.* It was an important part of the case that a trustee has no duty to give information at all to a stranger to the trust: there was neither an equitable nor a legal obligation to such effect. The statement could not be taken as a warranty, since, as Lindley L.J. pointed out "the Plaintiff and the Defendant were not contracting parties. There was no intention to contract, nor was there any consideration which is essential for the purpose of treating what the Defendant said as a promise or a warranty."

Bowen L.J. agreed with Lindley L.J. He added that *Derry v. Peek*[43] decided two things, and two things only: first that an action for deceit, or fraud,

[36] Italics supplied.
[37] Above para. 16.27.
[38] Above, para. 16.49.
[39] Above, para. 16.27.
[40] 1 D.F. & J. 518.
[41] See Lindley L.J. in the course of argument—"But supposing the true interpretation of the letters is, "so far as I know there is no charge . . ."
[42] Above.
[43] *ibid.*

required a statement which was not only incorrect, but in which the person making it had no genuine or honest belief; and secondly, that in such cases there is no duty to be careful in the representation which is made, or only to answer after careful inquiry. However, *Derry v. Peek*[44] left altogether untouched the case of warranty and cases of estoppel.

Kay L.J. confined himself to the estoppel aspect of the case.

***Greswolde-Williams v. Barneby* (1900) 83 L.T. 708**

16.55 This was a case where the misrepresentation to a purchaser was contained in the agreement, but there had been a conveyance thereafter pursuant to the agreement. Wills J. held that the agreement had, insofar as the matter misrepresented was concerned, merged in the conveyance.
can be maintained after conveyance." Thus the Plaintiff failed.
Note: The decision may as much as anything have been a decision that, on the facts, there had been merger.

***Whurr v. Devenish* (1904) 20 T.L.R., 385**

16.56 The Lord Chief Justice ordered the rescission of a completed agreement to sell a horse, on the grounds that the vendor, who did not own the horse, had allowed his name to be used as owner.

***Seddon v. North Eastern Salt*[45] [1905] 1 Ch. 326**

16.57 Joyce J. refused to set aside an executed contract for the sale of shares, (a) relying on *Wilde v. Gibson,*[46] *Brownlie v. Campbell*[47] *Soper v. Arnold*[48] and *Kennedy v. Panama, etc., Royal Mail Co;*[49] (b) on the grounds of the plaintiff's laches and (c) because he was not satisfied on the facts there had been any misrepresentation.

***Angel v. Jay* [1911] 1 K.B. 666**

16.58 Darling J. and Bucknill J. on an appeal from the county court refused to set aside an executed lease. Part of the reason may have been the rather odd point taken by the tenant's counsel—that a lease although executed is really in substance executory! Both judges—perhaps unsurprisingly—declined to accede to this. Darling J. relied on *Legge v. Croker*[50] and Bucknill J. also relied on *Brett v. Clowser*[51] and on *Kennedy v. Panama, etc., Royal Mail Co.*[52]

[44] *ibid.*
[45] See now the law on negligent misrepresentation from *Hedley Byrne v. Heller* [1964] A.C. 465.
[46] Above, para. 16.36.
[47] Above, para. 16.49.
[48] Above, para. 16.52.
[49] Above, para. 16.42.
[50] Above.
[51] Above, para. 16.48.
[52] Above.

CHAPTER 17

GOOD FAITH AND THE MISREPRESENTATION ACT 1967

"I do not draft bills myself, and I am sure I should make an awful hash of it if I did. They are necessarily drafted by Parliamentary draftsmen, who have had a certain training in a certain school. I have in the past expressed views suggesting that this is a style which might with advantage be simplified. I am still of that opinion. But a change in that respect is not going to come. I think easily or quickly."[1]

"I feel some reservations as to this example of piecemeal legislation. Generally on the Bill, its character is one which deals with the law of contract over a fairly wide front . . . What it does its to attempt the rather ambitious task of putting into statutory language matters which normally are dealt with by judicial development of law. That is by no means an easy thing to do."[2]

INTRODUCTION

17.01 The Misrepresentation Act 1967 Act has hitherto been applied almost exclusively to relatively clear statements, rather than the grey world of ambiguous, vague, uncandid representations patrolled by good faith. A current statement of the law contained in the Act is the following, which is taken from the judgment of Mustill L.J. in *Atlantic Estates PLC v. Ezekiel*[3]:

> ". . . the application of well-established rules to the particular circumstances of the dispute. These rules I take to be as follows.
>
> (1) The question whether one party has made a representation in the course of negotiations for a contract depends upon

[1] Lord Gardiner, Lord Chancellor, at the second reading of the Misrepresentation Bill, House of Lords, May 17, 1966.

[2] Lord Wilberforce at the second reading of the Misrepresentation Bill, House of Lords, May 17, 1966.

[3] [1991] 2 E.G.L.R. 202.

what he has actually conveyed by writing, words or conduct, such as a nod or a wink.

(2) If one party has made a representation in this sense, it is no answer to a claim or a defence founded upon it that if the representee had taken the trouble to inquire he could have discovered that it was untrue.

(3) Except in those cases where the nature of the contract is such as to require certain facts to be disclosed, for example where the contract is one of the utmost good faith, one party has no ground for complaint simply because the other has not disclosed a fact which, if disclosed, would have influenced the first party in deciding whether to enter into the contract.

(5) There may, however, be circumstances in which the true import of what was said or written is distorted by what is left unsaid, so that even if the representation is literally true in every particular it is nevertheless misleading."

17.02 The above is a general statement of the law, not specially limited to sales. There is nothing in the statement or in the Act to exclude statements made by a seller or defining party which are in breach of the duty of candour or the duty of accuracy from being misrepresentations within the Act. Indeed, the pedigree of the "nod or wink"[4] argues for the inclusion of statements made in breach of the good faith duties. It is just not possible to "convey" anything purely by a "nod or wink" in the same sense that one conveys it by writing. The "nod or wink" kind of representation, although classified as a statement made by conduct, is typically a statement of the kind referred to in *Smith v. Hughes*[5] made by silence ("conduct") where the circumstances give rise to a reasonable expectation which needs to be expressly countered. If one recognises that a statement made by conduct *can be* a statement made by silence, where silence is misleading, it is a short step to accepting that statements which breach the good faith duties are misrepresentations within the Act.

SECTION 1

"... after a misrepresentation has been made to him"

17.03 To what extent can a statement which is in breach of the duty of candour or the duty of accuracy—for example, a statement which is not properly explained so as to be understandable, a statement which is literally true but not in a sense in which the kind of purchaser to be expected would understand it, or a statement containing a half-truth or part-truth only—count as a "misrepresentation" for the pur-

[4] See Chap. 5, Sale of Land.
[5] (1871) L.R. 6 Q.B. 597.

poses of the 1967 Act? It is generally accepted that a case such as *With v. O'Flanigan*[6] where a positive representation had been made, but which later became untrue to the knowledge of the vendor, gives rise to a duty to correct the original statement.[7] There was a misrepresentation by reason of the later silence, or the later failure to disclose the changed events, it matters not which. It seems likely that there would also be liability for a statement in breach of the duty of accuracy in the sense of a statement that is literally true but only if taken in some rather specialised sense which it could not be anticipated would be known to the purchaser.[8] It would for practical purposes be a misrepresentation to the person to whom it was made. The case of a statement which was literally *un*true would be *a fortiori*.

17.04 More difficult is a breach of the good faith duty of accuracy consisting in simply conveying the information in a muddling over-technical or over-verbose way, not likely to be understood by the likely recipient.[9] Once it is accepted that there is a duty on a vendor or defining party who describes that which he is selling to do so accurately, so as to be understood, it should prima facie follow that this kind of statement also may rank as a misrepresentation, although it may well be a matter of degree whether it does or not.

There is similarly no reason why a breach of the duty of candour by part-omission, if made by a seller or defining party, who owes the good faith duty of candour and accuracy to the buyer or inquiring party, should not be regarded as a misrepresentation within the Act. Treitel in *The Law of Contract*,[10] makes the suggestion that there may be liability under the Act for a statement such as that in the (well-known good faith) case of *Nottingham Patent Brick and Tile Co v. Butler*.[11] Lord Macnaghten said memorably in *Gluckstein v. Barnes*.[12] "And everybody knows that sometimes a half truth is no better than a downright falsehood."

Incorporation of misrepresentation in the contract . . . "if otherwise he would be entitled to rescind"

17.05 It may be noted that section 1 of the Act does not in fact say that there shall *be* liability for any misrepresentation made as a result of which the representee enters into a contract. It merely makes clear that the incorporation of the misrepresentation in the contract does not bar the right to rescind for a non-fraudulent representation, assuming the right to rescind to have existed in the first place. The effect is to throw us back to the pre-Act law. The Act supplements but does not replace that law. Accordingly there is scope for argument

[6] [1936] Ch. 575.
[7] *c.f.* also *Traill v. Baring* (1864) 4 D.J. & S. 318.
[8] See, *e.g.* the examples in Chap. 5, Sale of Land.
[9] See, *e.g.* Chap. 5, Sale of Land for examples.
[10] (9th edn.) at p. 365.
[11] (1886) 16 Q.B.D. 778, noted in Chap. 10, Excluding the Effect of the Fair Dealing Terms.
[12] [1900] 2 A.C. 240.

to the effect that a wholly innocent statement, *i.e.* one which is true on the information "within the vendor's knowledge" at the time of the contract may not render the vendor liable either outside the Act or under it.

The extent to which that pre-Act law ever allowed rescission for a wholly innocent (as opposed to "grey-innocent") misrepresentation may be debatable. As can be seen above,[13] the pre-Act law, on analysis, *did* distinguish between cases where the seller was wholly innocent (or what have been labelled "no-fault" cases) and cases of "grey innocence" where the seller had conducted himself misleadingly (albeit not deliberately misleadingly) on the basis of his knowledge or what was "within his knowledge".[14] The reference to the "entitlement" to rescind may thus be a reference to the nature or classification of the statement made by the representor. This degree of blameworthiness may be viewed as a prerequisite of the representee's entitlement to seek rescission for misrepresentation. It may naturally be referred to as granting a prima facie "right" to the representee to rescind. He has after all achieved a *qualifying entitlement,* which is subject only to the court's discretion to refuse rescission on prevention-of- injustice grounds.[15] The traditional textbook explanation, usually rather despairingly given, is that "if otherwise he would be entitled to rescind" must be a reference to the claimant's surviving the court's discretion to refuse rescission. This seems less likely, purely as a matter of language. The expression "entitled" simply does not seem the most natural one if that were meant. One would expect some expression such as "held entitled". In *Thomas Witter Ltd v. TBP Industries Ltd,*[16] Jacob J. relying (pursuant to the "limited new-found freedom" given by *Pepper (Inspector of Taxes) v. Hart*[17]) on what the Solicitor-General said in the House of Commons at the time of the passing of the Act [extract quoted at para. 17.16], considered at all events that the words "if otherwise he would be entitled to rescind" meant only that the transaction concerned had to be shown to have been "rescissionable", at least by the date when the representee first claimed rescission.

Section 2(2): damages in lieu of rescission: measure of damages?

17.06 This subsection, like the abolition of the supposed bar on rescission after completion, resulted from the Tenth Report of the Law Reform Committee,[18] part of which is printed below in the Appendix to this chapter. The measure of damages to be awarded under the section is

[13] See, *e.g.* Chap. 16, Rescission of Executed Sales; and see Chap. 4, Insurance and Surety Sales.
[14] See the section "Eleven Shades of Ambiguity" in Chap. 5, Sales of Land.
[15] See Chap. 16 for comment on these.
[16] [1996] 2 All E.R. 573.
[17] [1993] A.C. 593.
[18] (1962) Cmnd. 1782.

not specified. See the quotation from Lord Wilberforce at the beginning of this chapter.[19]

We have three possible measures: the tortious measure, the contractual measure, and a measure which is perhaps not readily classifiable as either but which aims "to put the plaintiff, so far as it can be done by a money award, into the same position as he would have been if a decree of rescission had been granted to him.[20]

We have three potential clues:

(a) Section 2(3) of the Act provides that "Damages may be awarded against a person under subsection (2) of this section whether or not he is liable to damages under subsection (1) thereof, but where he is so liable any award under the said subsection (2) shall be taken into account in assessing his liability under the said subsection (1)."

This may possibly envisage that damages under subsection (2) are to be smaller.[21] On the other hand, consideration of some possible examples makes this seem unlikely, although the damages may *sometimes* be smaller. The *measure* of damages under the two subsections must at all events be intended to be different; else the damages would always be the same.[22]

17.07 *Example 1* A house has been bought following a misrepresentation regarding planning permission for use as a stud. There is in fact only planning permission for residential use. The purchaser entered into certain other commitments (known to the seller at the time of the contract) on account of the fact misrepresented, and suffered disastrous losses on these amounting to £2 million. The purchase was on a rising market, and the value of the house has increased, despite or because of the residential status.

17.08 *Example 2* A house has been bought following an actionable misrepresentation regarding the drains. The purchase was on a falling market. The purchaser would not have bought anything but would have kept his money on deposit had he not bought the house in question. He suffered some consequential losses on commitments entered into as a result of the contract, amounting to £500,000. His main loss arises as a result of the fall in value of the house by some £3 million.

17.09 In example 1 the purchaser will not be claiming rescission in practice. If he did, there would be no section 2(2) damages to set off

[19] Second Reading of the Representation Bill, H.L., May 17, 1986.

[20] *McGregor on Damages* (15th edn.) at p. 1751.

[21] See Treitel, *Law of Contract* (9th edn.) at p. 337 ("It can be inferred . . . that damages under subsection (2) are meant to be less than damages under subsection (1)".

[22] See also *per* Hoffmann L.J. in ***William Sindall PLC v. Cambridgeshire County Council*** [1994] 1 W.L.R. 1016 (noted below): ". . . section 2(3) contemplates that damages under section 2(2) may be less than damages under section 2(1) . . . This only makes sense if the measure of damages may be different".

anyway. In example 2 the purchaser needs to claim both kinds of damage. If "taking into account" means what it says, he may obtain both, since he has genuinely suffered both, and since there is no element of overlap. The alternative view is that "taking into account" means that a party who falls under both sections is limited to the excess of his section 1(1) damages over his section 2(2) damages, but there seems no reason for adopting this apparently capricious interpretation.

Thus, it may perhaps be said that the only real clue that section 2(3) gives us is that:

(a) the party who is prima facie entitled to both kinds of damage is not to be deprived of his section 2(2) damages save in the event of genuine overlap; and (b) the measure of damages in section 2(2) is different from the deceit-damages at present given in section 2(1). In *Royscot v. Rogerson,*[23] the Court of Appeal has held that the effect of section 2(1) and in particular the words "*so* liable" is not only to give damages where the contract has been made non-fraudulently, but to give these on the deceit basis. Thus, all damage flowing from the breach will be obtainable under section 2(1).)

(b) Our second potential clue is the Law Reform Committee's reference, in paragraph 11,[24] to the relative importance or unimportance of the fact misrepresented, and the "anomaly" that if the fact misrepresented were embodied in the contract and constituted a minor term of it, it would be treated as a warranty only, giving no right to rescind. This is useful as far as it goes, but it is difficult to derive much real assistance from it about the measure of damages. It is going much too far to attempt to obtain from this the concept that section 2(2) damages must never be more than breach-of-warranty damages.

(c) Our third clue is the Law Reform Committee's reference to the Lord Cairns' Act jurisdiction and *Leeds Industrial Co-operative Society Ltd v. Slack.*[25] This has perhaps not received the attention it merits in this context. Viscount Finlay's judgment, which which Lord Dunedin (and it would seem the Earl of Birkenhead) agreed, stressed the obvious but perhaps overlooked point that the damages under the Act were intended to be *a substitute in money for the equitable relief which was being withheld.*

17.10 This seems conclusive in favour of the McGregor view. It is also conclusive against the Court of Appeal's *obiter* view in *William Sindall v. Cambridgeshire County Council.*[26] Unless one assumes that damages under section 2(2) *must* always be lower than those under section 2(1),

[23] [1991] 2 Q.B. 297. But the deceit-damages basis has now been queried by the House of Lords in *Smith New Court v. Scrimgeour Vickers* [1966] 4 All E.R. 769.

[24] See para. 17.16 of the Appendix to this chapter.

[25] [1924] A.C. 851.

[26] Below, para. 17.20.

which does not follow from the wording of the Act, there is no real justification at all for the Court of Appeal's view in that case anyway. It is also difficult to see how it can be reconciled with the compensatory nature of damages[27] here awarded expressly as a substitute for rescission. It is unlikely that an assumed warranty-basis could ever provide a reliable equivalent, or financial substitute, for rescission. The warranty-basis proceeds on the footing that the contract would have been entered into but compensation paid for breaches of warranty.[28] Rescission proceeds on the contrary footing, that the contract would *not* have been entered into. Finally, the Court of Appeal's judgment in the *Sindall*[29] case probably needs to be reviewed anyway in the light of *Banque Bruxelles Lambert SA v. Eagle Star Insurance Co. Ltd*[30] and the House of Lords' further consideration of fall–in–value damages in *South Australia Asset Management Corp. v. York Montague Ltd.*[31]

"having regard to the nature of the misrepresentation and the loss that would be caused by it" . . .

17.11 As pointed out by the Court of Appeal in the *Sindall*[32] case, "it" must refer back to the misrepresentation, not the contract. However, this does not mean that loss caused by entering into the contract cannot be claimed. If the misrepresentation did not cause the representee to enter into the contract, the representee would have no case anyway, because he would not have been induced to enter into the contract thereby. If it did cause the representee to enter the contract, the contract would be a part of the chain of causation: loss caused by the contract would *be* loss caused by the representation—at least, to the extent permitted by the *South Australia* case (above).

"having regard to . . . the loss that rescission would cause to the other party"

17.12 Since the representee is to be compensated in damages under the section anyway, the "loss" in question must be caused by the fact of rescission,[33] *leaving out of account* the representor's liability to pay damages to the representee.

[27] See, *e.g. Johnson v. Agnew* [1980] A.C. 367.
[28] Cp. the old equity courts' power to award compensation, on the assumed principle that the parties would have entered into the contract but on terms that they were compensated for minor breaches which could be adequately assessed in money and where the breach did not interfere with the purchaser's purpose for the purchase.
[29] Above
[30] [1996] 3 All E.R. 365.
[31] [1995] Q.B. 214.
[32] Above.
[33] *e.g.* having to unscramble a series of subsequent commitments entered into with third parties.

"after a misrepresentation has been made to him otherwise than fraudulently"

17.13 It has been generally assumed that "otherwise than fraudulently" means "innocently". This conclusion may be questioned. It is odd if so that the section did not say so. It is arguable that the slightly curious expression "otherwise than fraudulently" taken together with "would be entitled by reason of the misrepresentation to rescind" may be construed as a reference to the nineteenth-century law on rescission for statements which are "grey untruths", that is, (a) incorrect, (b) not deliberately incorrect, but (c) where the state of mind of the maker is blameworthy.[34]

It may well be that section 2(1) "did not have reasonable grounds to believe" is an attempt to define the same state of mind. If so, section 2(1) may be seen as a statutory reversal of *Derry v. Peek*.[35] It would follow that the state of mind in a representor which would ground a right in the representee to damages under section 2(1) would be the same as the state of mind which would ground the right to rescind (subject to the prevention-of injustice "bars" to rescission).

"Where . . . he would be entitled, by reason of the misrepresentation, to rescind the contract . . ."

17.14 The point has been made frequently that it would be odd and unfair if the subsection means that the representee must not have been barred from rescission by one of the prevention-of-injustice "bars" to rescission, before he can claim damages in lieu. The section does not prima facie need to mean that. There is no reason why it should not, again, be a reference to the "qualifying right" prima facie given to the misrepresentee by the nature of the misrepresentation itself together with the necessary reliance or deemed reliance. Once the misrepresentation is seen to possess the "right" qualities, of inaccuracy, lack of candour and blameworthiness, and the misrepresentee has relied on it, on this view the representee may have damages. It does not matter that he may not be allowed to obtain rescission as such for prevention-of-injustice reasons.[36] The role of the expression "would be entitled" in the subsection, on this view, is purely in order to refer back to the pre-Act degree of blameworthiness, reliance, *etc.*, required to ground an action. Otherwise the section would confer the right on anyone who had entered a contract merely "after" a misrepresentation had been made; which it does not.

---

[34] See the discussion of "grey innocence", *etc.*, in Chap. 5, Sale of Land, in the section headed "Eleven Shades of Ambiguity".

[35] (1889) 14 App. Cas. 337).

[36] See Chap. 15, Remedies for Breech of the Good Faith Rules, for discussion of the "bars" to rescission.

APPENDIX TO CHAPTER 17: SOME MATERIALS OF INTEREST

***Leeds Industrial Co-operative Society Ltd v. Slack* [1924] A.C. 851 (Damages in lieu of an injunction against the commission or continuance of any wrongful act" under the Lord Cairns' Act jurisdiction)**

17.15 Romer J. at first instance had found that the defendant's buildings when completed would cause an actionable obstruction of the plaintiff's right to light, that the interference with the plaintiff's legal rights would be small, and could be adequately compensated in damages; but that no such obstruction had taken place. The question decided by the House of Lords was whether the section permitted damages to be awarded when no damage had yet accrued—in other words, in circumstances when common law damages could not be awarded but a quia timet injunction would be appropriate.

Viscount Finlay said: "The power conferred on a Court of Chancery by Lord Cairns's Act included power to give damages in respect of a past injury. This in itself was a useful extension of jurisdiction, as it would prevent the hardship involved by the necessity of going to another Court to get such relief. But the enactment did not stop there. In terms it gave *power to substitute damages for an injunction. Such a substitution in the very nature of things involves that the damages are to deal with what would have been prevented by the injunction if granted.*[37] In the present case the building has not proceeded far enough to constitute an actionable wrong in respect of the plaintiff's lights, and an injunction would prevent the commission of that wrong in the future. On what principle can it be said that, until there has been *some*[38] interference with the plaintiff's windows, the Court cannot give damages in lieu of an injunction against obstruction? Such a construction would impose a purely arbitrary and meaningless restriction on the relief to be given under the Act. . . . it seems to me that . . . it would in practice nullify the provision that damages may be given in substitution for an injunction."

Viscount Finlay's approach was adopted by a majority of their Lordships.

Law Reform Committee report prior to Misrepresentation Act 1967, paragraphs 11 and 12:

17.16 "11. A more fundamental objection which may be advanced against our recommendation [to abolish the bar on rescission after completion] concerns the drastic character of the remedy to which the plaintiff would be entitled. Unless the court's power to grant rescission is made more elastic than it is at present, the court will not be able to take account of the relative importance or unimportance of the facts which have been misrepresented. A car might be returned to the vendor because of a misrepresentation about the mileage done since the engine was last overhauled, or a transfer of shares rescinded on account of an incorrect statement about the right to receive the current dividend. In some cases the result could be as harsh on the representor as the

[37] Italics supplied.
[38] Italics in original.

absence of a right to rescind under the current law can be on the representee. Moreover, the conflict between remedies for misrepresentation and those for breach of contract would be aggravated. There is already the anomaly that a statement embodied in the contract and constituting a minor term of it is treated as a warranty, the breach of which gives only a right to damages, whereas the same statement as a representation inducing the contract enables the latter to be rescinded. Before the contract is executed and at a time when the parties can be relatively easily restored to their original positions, this anomaly may not matter very much, but the position would be different if the court had no option but to order rescission after the contract had been executed.

17.17 12. To meet these objections we recommend that wherever the court has power to order rescission it should, as an alternative, have a discretionary power to award damages it it is satisfied that these would afford adequate compensation to the plaintiff, having regard to the nature of the misrepresentation and the fact that the injury suffered by the plaintiff is small compared with what rescission would involve. The courts were given power to award damages in addition to or in substitution for an injunction or a decree of specific performance by section 2 of Lord Cairns's Act (the Chancery Procedure Amendment Act 1858) and since the decision of the House of Lords in *Leeds Industrial Co-operative Society Ltd v. Slack* [1924] A.C. 851, the power has been exercised on principles similar to those we have just mentioned."

***The Lucy* [1983] 1 Lloyd's Rep. 188.**

17.18 There was held to be a misrepresentation but no inducement in that case. Mustill L.J. considered section 2(2), *obiter*. He said: "The first question which would have arisen, had I found an operative misrepresentation, would have been whether the case is one where rescission is in principle available at all, having regard to an argument addressed by Atlantic to the effect that restitution in integrum is now impossible. Several cases were cited in argument . . . In the light of these decisions, I would have been disposed to hold that in the case of an innocent misrepresentation inducing a contract for the performance of services, it is not a bar to rescission that the contract has been partially performed, although the imposition of some order for the payment of money as an adjunct to the order for rescission (or a declaration that a prior rescission was valid) will often be required, in order to bring about a full adjustment of the equitable rights of the parties. I consider that in principle, therefore, it would have been open to the Court to declare that Hallam were entitled to avoid the contract.

17.19 The matter would therefore have fallen within the province of s 2(2) of the 1967 Act, which gives the Court a discretion to order damages as an alternative to rescission. There are some formidable difficulties in the partial application of this discretion to a case where the Court is not asked to order rescission as a direct and immediate remedy, but is invited to validate a rescission which has already been effected as a measure of self-help. In this particular instance, the difficulties are reduced because the performance of the contract did not cease at the moment of the purported rescission, but was kept in being until the without-prejudice agreement. It seems to me that in such a case the words "or has been rescinded" in subs 2(2) must be read as entitling the Court to annul retrospectively a rescission which has taken place in the past, and to compel the injured party to accept damages in lieu. This is a discretion which, in the circumstances of the present case, I would have thought it right to exercise. The damage to Atlantic which would ensue from having *Lucy* returned on a collapsing spot market would be great. The difference in value between a charter with a wide liberty and one with a narrow liberty would on the evidence have been slight, if anything at all. Much more to the point, there is no evidence that the rate for a sub-charter with a wide liberty fixed with a disponent owner who had chartered from the head owner on a narrow liberty would differ in the slightest from that obtainable for the same sub-charter fixed with a disponent owner who had a back to back charter. Finally, the misrepresentation, even if, contrary to my findings, it was to be regarded as inducing the contract, was of quite a trivial nature: at most it could be said to have tipped the scale, rather than striking to the root of the bargain. The balance contemplated by s 2(2) seems to me decisive in favour of awarding damages in lieu of rescission."

***William Sindall PLC v. Cambridgeshire County Council* [1994] 1 W.L.R. 1016.**

17.20 The case is noted on another aspect in the Appendix to Chapter 10, Excluding the Effect of the Fair dealing Terms. The measure of damages in section 2(2) was considered, again *obiter*, by the Court of Appeal in the course of their judgments. Hoffmann L.J. stated that:

(1) the "nature of the misrepresentation" meant "the importance of the representation in relation to the subject matter of the transaction, deriving this from the Law Reform Committee's report above; and
(2) "the loss" meant the loss that would be caused by "the misrepresentation as such", since "it" in the subsection clearly refers back to "the misrepresentation".
(3) The Law Reform Committee report had made it clear that "section 2(2) was enacted because it was thought that it might be a hardship to the representor to be deprived of the whole benefit of the bargain on account of a minor misrepresentation. It could not possibly have intended the damages in lieu to be assessed on a principle which would invariably have the same effect.
(4) It followed, he considered, that "damages under section 2(2) should never exceed the sum which would have been awarded if the representation had been a warranty." He seems to have assumed also without real discussion[39] that the damages were to be taken as at the date of the contract, ruling out the fall-in-value damages which were the main basis of the respondent's claim.

Evans L.J.

(1) noted that the measure of damages under section 2(1) was intended to compensate the representee for "all the losses which he has sustained by reason of his acting upon it at the time when he did" while the damages under section 2(2) are in lieu of rescission;
(2) adopted Hoffmann L.J.'s distinction between damages caused by the representation and caused by the contract;
(3) followed Hoffmann L.J. in excluding the fall-in-value damages claimed on the ground that these were caused by the contract and not by the misrepresentation.

Both considered that the word "equitable" gave the court a wide discretion, not limited to the specific factors mentioned.[40]

[39] Probably as a result of point (2) above, but see the text as to this.
[40] This may be debatable.

PART 5

GOOD FAITH RESURGENT?

CHAPTER 18

DO WE NEED GOOD FAITH/ FAIR DEALING TERMS ANYWAY?

ENGLAND

18.01 No-one would expect to find the answer "No" in the pages of this book. People do not as a rule write books about subjects they consider of negligible importance. But it is perhaps worth standing back and trying to consider briefly any reasons which may be advanced for the proposition that we ought to resist the rediscovery of good faith law in this country.

One reason advanced may be the feeling that good faith is a European invention, and perhaps to be eschewed therefore in a country which has not as yet found an entirely comfortable role as a member state of the European Union, and perhaps never will. Good faith is coming back to us from Europe in perhaps its least attractive and most intractable form. What could once be described as "natural law" and welcomed here as part of a civilized shared tradition of European thought has grown the characteristic barnacles of bureaucracy to a frightening degree. The wholly good intentions behind these bureaucratic emanations—rectifying inequality of bargaining position, ensuring properly informed consent to transactions throughout the length and breadth of the European Union—may seem hard to discern. If as seller or defining party in the course of a business we want to deal fairly with consumers within the law, it would seem we have first to puzzle over at least one statute, some regulations and a Directive and try to work out their joint and several impact on our proposed conduct. Alternatively, we should consult a lawyer, who will puzzle over these for us, and charge us for so doing. The cost will normally be passed on to the buyer. What were once relatively easily-acquired principles of fair dealing have become submerged.

18.02 To feel this is unsatisfactory is natural; but it is to criticise the wrapping while ignoring the content. Good faith/fair dealing principles are in themselves quite simple.

Another reason advanced against the acceptance of good faith here may be the notion that we now have in this country a settled tradition, accepted since at least the 'sixties, in which fair dealing is "a matter for Parliament". That being so, it might be difficult for judges—under attack at present by the government for "interfering" in the interests of fair dealing in administrative law—to arrogate to themselves a jurisdiction to police fairness in sales contracts.

There is in fact no reason to suppose that a collective effort on the part of the judiciary to re-impose our principles of fair dealing would bring it into conflict with anybody. Indeed, it might be welcomed by governments which seem to have less and time to process litigation through Parliament. The fact that we have had what one might call the ascendancy of statute law for some thirty years may argue a possible resistance to a new change or trend by some; but it is not per se an argument against this particular trend. It is always difficult to accustom oneself to a new way of thinking, and the practice of law leads us all to reach instinctively for the familiar and apparently time-honoured, as for a comfort blanket. However, there are other forces for change at work. There is the need for a new approach to civil justice if the courts are not to sink under the fast-increasing mass of litigation. One has only to look at the history of company legislation in the nineteenth century to see that statute law (unless the statutes are extremely short, and sometimes even then) has a tendency to spawn litigation about the meaning of the statute, followed frequently by a general recognition that the thing could have been better expressed in certain respects, followed in turn by another statute, whereupon the process is repeated. By contrast, cases in which the courts have worked out the application of an old principle to a new situation, such as the *Erlanger v. New Sombrero Phosphate Co.*[1] and *Lagunas Nitrate v. Lagunas Nitrate Syndicate*[2] may perhaps be seen to have a litigation-quieting tendency. Similarly, where a statute is based on acknowledged principles which have already been the subject of case-law development, such as the Sale of Goods Act 1893, or (apart from one clarification) the law on constructive and imputed notice codified in the Conveyancing Act 1882, relatively little litigation ensues about the meaning.

18.03 Thirdly, there are the disaster predictions: "The introduction of good faith here would be the death of contract as we know it." and the like. We may suspect that this kind of approach is based on the idea that good faith is a purely literary concept, rather than the technical legal set of fair-dealing principles that it is. It is as if a non-accountant were to consider reading company accounts without troubling to find out what the accounting definition of "fixed assets" or "material events" was.

Finally, it might be urged that the re-introduction of good faith would be bad for commercial life. Business people need to know where they are. There are perhaps two answers to this. First, good faith principles were an accepted part of commercial life, and indeed, were expanded by common law and equity courts alike during the

[1] (1878) 3 App. Cas. 1218.
[2] [1899] 2 Ch. 392.

nineteenth century when Britain was a substantial commercial power. It did not seem to do us any harm then. Secondly, it is common for bankers and brokers and other commercial men and women to deplore the mass of regulations which they have to try to observe. They complain that they do not know where they are. Indeed, recognising this, the present government runs as an annexe to the Cabinet Office, an Office of De-regulation.

A GLANCE AT SOME OTHER COUNTRIES

18.04 There seems to be quite a lot of good faith in other countries' law. What follows is a brief glance at a little of this. The application of good faith in Australia and in France, in particular, both bear striking similarities to the operation of our own good-faith principles, but may be seen to go even further than these in some respects. The similarity may perhaps be no coincidence. There is a shared tradition of thought between all three going back to the late eighteenth and early nineteenth century natural lawyers. In England and France the influence will have been a direct one. In Australia (where a good faith regime has come about in large part through appropriate judicial interpretation of a modern statute) it will have been an indirect one gained from the deeper attention paid there to the underlying principles expressed in the older cases that form our joint inheritance, themselves influenced by natural law ideas.

AUSTRALIA

18.05 We have seen that what is there termed the principle of "unconscionability", the underlying subject matter of which has been discussed in this book in Chapter 9, Dealings with the Vulnerable Buyer or Seller, has had a vigorous life in Australia. The principles underlying the old cases have been explored and applied for some time.

In ordinary contracts, including but not limited to sales, there has been a remarkable development since the seventies. It is based on a statute whose pervading influence seems to have been in inverse proportion to its remarkable terseness—a form of legislative self-denial which is little more than a memory in present-day Britain. The Australian Trade Practices Act 1974, as amended, provides by section 52 that "a corporation[3] shall not, in trade or commerce, engage in conduct that is misleading or deceptive or is likely to mislead or deceive."

18.06 This covers statements of opinion: note the judgments of Bowen C.J., Lockhart and Fitzgerald J.J. in *Global Sportsman Pty Ltd v. Mirror Newspapers Ltd*[4]:

> "A statement which involves the state of mind of the maker ordinarily conveys the meaning (expressly or by implication) that the maker of the statement had a particular state of mind when the statement was made and, commonly at least, *that there was a basis for that state of mind*."[5]

Since 1986 the new section 51A provides that where a company makes representations with respect to a future matter and where the maker does not have reasonable grounds for making the representation, the representation is taken to be misleading. The burden of the proof of reasonable grounds is on the maker.

18.07 Implied statements are not neglected. The mere giving of a warranty about a present state of affairs in existence may, if the state of affairs is not as represented, amount to conduct in contravention of section 52. Failure to speak may amount to misleading or deceptive conduct under the section.[6] Professor Harland[7] states that it is now established that silence can mislead where the circumstances are *such as to give rise to a reasonable expectation that if some relevant fact exists it would be disclosed*.[8]

Exclusion clauses are not effective to exclude section 52 liability. Acknowledgment clauses are not conclusive. Persons "involved" in the making of the statement may be liable in addition to the company that made the statement. There is a wide range of remedies under the

[3] As a result of the Act and the consequent state legislation combined, it applies to individuals as well: see the illuminating article by Professor Harland in (1995) 111 L.Q.R. 100 from which the short account here is derived.

[4] (1984) 55 A.L.R. 25.

[5] *cf.* for our own good faith principles, the section headed "Eleven Shades of Ambiguity" in Chap. 5, Sale of Land, and *Brown v. Raphael* [1958] Ch. 636 and *Smith v. Land & House Property*, (1884) 28 Ch. D. 7, noted in the Appendix thereto.

[6] See in particular *Rhone Poulenc Agrochemie SA v. UIM Chemical Services Pty Ltd* (1986) 68 A.L.R. 77 and *Kabwand Pty Ltd v. National Australia Bank Ltd* (1989) A.T.P.R. 40–950.

[7] *Op. cit.*

[8] *cf.* the parallel good faith approach as explained in *Smith v. Hughes* (1871) L.R. 6 Q.B. 597, and as exemplified in the surety cases discussed in Chap. 4, Insurance and Surety Transactions. Cp. also Pothier, *Contrat de Vente* (1806 ed.) at para. 294 who refers to "les *manoeuvres* que l'acheteur emploieroit pour porter le vendeur à vendre, ou à vendre moins cher . . ."; and Article 1116 of France's *Code Civil*, referring also to "les manoeuvres" of the seller.

Act but the most commonly sought are damages and rescission (and the "bars" to rescission have been held inapplicable to the statutory "rescission").

ISRAEL

Good faith required in the formation of the contract and in negotiating the contract

18.08 A pre-contractual duty of good faith exists in Israel which goes further than our own good faith principles, in that it imposes liability for failure to negotiate in good faith even where a contract does not result. Section 12(a) of the Contracts (General Part) Law 1973 provides that "in negotiating a contract, a person shall act in customary manner and in good faith." Section 12(b) provides "A party who does not act in customary manner and in good faith shall be liable to pay compensation to the other party for the damage caused him in consequence of the negotiations or the making of the contract."[9]

THE UNITED STATES

Good faith required during the contractual relationship

(1) Good faith in the formation of the Contract

(a) Unconscionability

18.09 *Uniform Commercial Code 2-302.*

> "If a court as a matter of law finds the contract or any clause of the contract to have been unconscionable at the time it was made the court may refuse to enforce the contract, or it may enforce the remainder of the contract without the unconscionable clause or it may so limit the application of any unconscionable clause so as to avoid any unconscionable result.
> (2) Where it is claimed or appears to the court that the contract or any clause thereof may be unconscionable the parties shall be afforded a reasonable opportunity to present evidence as to its commercial setting, purpose and effect to aid the court in making the determination."

[9] The above is derived from an article by Nili Cohen, "Pre-Contractual Duties: Two Freedoms and the Contract to Negotiate", contained in *Good Faith and Default in Contract Law*, eds. Beatson and Friedman (Oxford, 1995). *cf.* Pothier, *Contrat de Vente* (1806 edn.) who refers to "la bonne foi et l'équité qui doivent régner dans le contrat de vente".

See also American Law Institute, Restatement, Contracts, Second Section 208, which is in similar terms.

The Draftmen's comment to the Code, above states *inter alia*:

> "This section is intended to make it possible for the courts to police explicitly against the contracts or clauses which they find to be unconscionable. In the past such policing has been accomplished by adverse construction of language, by manipulation of the rules of offer and acceptance or by determinations that the clause is contrary to public policy or to the dominant purpose of the contract.
>
> This section is intended to allow the court to pass directly on the unconscionability of the contract or particular clause therein and to make a conclusion of law as to its unconscionability. The basic test is whether, in the light of the general commercial background and the commercial needs of the particular trade or case, the clauses involved are so one-sided as to be unconscionable under the circumstances existing at the time of the making of the contract. . . . The principle is one of the prevention of oppression of unfair surprise . . . and not of disturbance of allocation of risks because of superior bargaining power."

Note: Many of the illustrations given in the comment to the Restatement (not quoted here) appear not dissimilar to our own courts habitual narrow construction of exclusion clauses: e.g. a disclaimer of implied warranties did not extend to defects rendering goods not of the contract description; a clause limiting time of complaint about defects held inapplicable to latent defects in a shipment where the latent defects could only be discovered by microscopic analysis.

(b) Via a good-faith view of "misrepresentation"

See Restatement, Contracts 2nd, Section 168(2) Reliance on Assertions of Opinion "If it is reasonable to do so, the recipient of an assertion of a person's opinion as to facts not disclosed and not otherwise known to the recipient may properly interpret it as an assertion

(a) that the facts known to that person are not incompatible with his opinion, or

(b) that he knows facts sufficient to justify him in forming it."

Note: Compare Brown v. Raphael.[9a] *Smith v. Land & House Property*[9b] *and see Chapter 5, Sale of Land, paragraph 5.13.*

Section 160. When Action is Equivalent to an Assertion (Concealment).

> "Action intended or known to be likely to prevent another from learning a fact is equivalent to an assertion that the fact does not exist."

[9a] [1958] Ch. 636.

[9b] (1884) 28 Ch. D. 7.

Section 161. When Non-disclosure is Equivalent to an Assertion.

"A person's non-disclosure of a fact known to him is equivalent to an assertion that the fact does not exist in the following cases only:

(a) where he knows that disclosure of the fact is necessary to prevent some previous assertion from being a misrepresentation or from being fraudulent or material.[9c]

(b) where he knows that disclosure of the fact would correct a mistake of the other party as to a basic assumption on which that party is making the contract and if non-disclosure of the fact amounts to a failure to act in good faith and in accordance with reasonable standards of fair dealing.

(c) where he knows that disclosure of the fact would correct a mistake of the other party as to the contents or effect of a writing, evidencing or embodying an agreement in whole or in part

(d) where the other person is entitled to know the fact because of a relationship of trust and confidence between them."

Section 169. When Reliance on an Assertion of Opinion is Not justified.

"To the extent that an assertion is one of opinion only, the recipient is not justified in relying on it unless the recipient:

(a) stands in such a relation of trust and confidence to the person whose opinion is asserted that the recipient is reasonable in relying on it, or

(b) reasonably believes that, as compared with himself, the person whose opinion is asserted has special skill, judgment or objectivity with respect to the subject matter, or

(c) is for some other special reason particularly susceptible to a misrepresentation of the type involved."

Section 171. When Reliance on an Assertion of Intention is Not Justified.

"(1) To the extent that an assertion is one of intention only, the recipient is not justified in relying on it if in the circumstances a misrepresentation of intention is consistent with reasonable standards of dealing.

(2) If it is reasonable to do so, the promisee may properly interpret the promise as an assertion that the promisor intended to perform the promise."

Section 172. When Fault Makes Reliance Unjustified. A recipient's fault in not knowing or discovering the facts before making the contract does not make his reliance unjustified unless it amounts to a failure to act in good faith and in accordance with reasonable standards of fair dealing.

[9c] See section 162—"a misrepresentation is material if it would be likely to induce a reasonable person to manifest his assent, or if the maker knows it would be likely to induce the recipient to do so."

Section 173. When Abuse of a Fiduciary Relationship Makes a Contract Voidable. If a fiduciary makes a contract with his beneficiary relating to matters within the scope of the fiduciary relationship, the contract is voidable by the beneficiary, unless,

(a) it is on fair terms, and
(b) all parties beneficially interested manifest assent with full understanding of their legal rights and of all relevant facts that the fiduciary knows or should know.

Note: It may be also that the requirement of good faith in the after-sale relationship (see below as to this) includes retrospectively a degree of presumed good faith in the formation of the contract: c.p. the late nineteenth century idea that it was against conscience for a man to enforce something he now (i.e. after the contract is made) knows to be wrong. Thus, a seller who insists on an exclusion clause which was not candidly and accurately explained may be in trouble.

(c) Via the more compassionate rules on mistake

Restatement, Contracts, Second, Section 151 Mistake Defined.

"A mistake is a belief that is not in accord with the facts."

Section 152. When the Mistake of both parties Makes a Contract Voidable.

(1) Where a mistake of both parties at the time the contract was made as to a basic assumption on which the contract was made has a material effect on the agreed exchange of performances, the contract is voidable by the adversely affected party unless he bears the risk of the mistake under the rule stated in section 154.
(2) In determining whether the mistake has a material effect on the agreed exchange of performances account is taken of any relief by way of reformation, restitution or otherwise.

Section 153. When the Mistake of one Party Makes a Contract Voidable.

"Where a mistake of one party at the time a contract was made as to a basic assumption on which he made the contract has a material effect on the agreed exchange of performances that is adverse to him, the contract is voidable by him if he does not bear the risk of the mistake under the rule stated in section 154, and

(a) the effect of the mistake is such that enforcement of the contract would be unconscionable, or,
(b) the other party had reason to know of the mistake or his fault caused the mistake.

Section 154. When a Party Bears the Risk of a Mistake

"A party bears the risk of a mistake when

(a) the risk is allocated to him by agreement of the parties, or
(b) he is aware, at the time the contract is made, that he has

only limited knowledge with respect to the facts to which the mistake relates but treats his limited knowledge as sufficient

(c) the risk is allocated to him by the court on the ground that it is reasonable in the circumstances to do so.

Section 157. Effect of Fault of Party Seeking Relief.

A mistaken party's fault in failing to know or discover the facts before making a contract does not bar him from avoidance or reformation under the rules stated in this Chapter, unless his fault amounts to a failure to act in good faith and in accordance with reasonable standards of fair dealing.

Section 158. Relief Including Restitution.

(1) In any case governed by the rules stated in this Chapter either party may have a claim for relief including restitution under the rules stated in sections 240 and 376 [part performances as agreed equivalents, rules on restitution and other relief].

(2) In any case governed by the rules stated in this Chapter, if those rules together with the rules stated in Chapter 16 will not avoid injustice, the court may grant relief on such terms as justice requires including protection of the parties' reliance interests.

(2) The after-sale relationship

American law Institute, Restatement of the Law, Contracts, Second, Section 205, Duty of Good Faith and Fair Dealing: "Every contract imposes upon each party a duty of good faith and fair dealing in its performance and its enforcement."

The Comment to the Restatement contains the following:

"Good faith performance or enforcement of a contract emphasizes faithfulness to an agreed common purpose and consistency with the justified expectations of the other party; it excludes a variety of types of conduct characterized as involving "bad faith" because they violate community held standards of decency, fairness or reasonableness. The appropriate remedy for a breach of the duty of good faith also varies with the circumstances."

and later;

"Good faith performance—
Subterfuges and evasions violate the obligation of good faith performance even though the actor believes his conduct to be justified. But the obligation goes further: bad faith may be overt or may consist of inaction, and fair dealing may require more than honesty. A complete catalogue of types of bad faith is impossible, but the following types are among those which have been recognized in judicial decisions: evasion of the spirit of the bargain, lack of diligence and slacking off, wilful rendering of imperfect performance, abuse of a power to specify terms, and interference with or failure to cooperate in the other party's performance."

Note: An illustration given (from a real case as are all the illustrations) is where A,, the owner of a shopping center, leases part of it to B, giving B the exclusive right to conduct a supermarket, the rent to be a percentage of B's gross receipts. During the term of the lease A acquires adjoining land, expands the shopping center and leases part of the adjacent land to C for a competing supermarket. Unless such action was contemplated or is otherwise justified, there is a breach of contract by A.

Uniform Commercial Code

1–201 (19). Good faith is defined as "honesty in fact in the conduct or transaction concerned."

1-203 "Every contract of duty within this Act imposes an obligation of good faith in its performance or enforcement."

2-103 (1) (b) "Good faith in the case of a merchant means honesty in fact and the observance of reasonable commerciqal standards of fair dealing in the trade."

Note: Another illustration given is as follows. A suffers a loss of property covered by an insurance policy issued by B and submits to B notice and proof of loss. The notice and proof fail to comply with requirement of the policy as to form and detail, but B does not point out the defects. He remains silent and evasive, telling A broadly to perfect his claim. The defects do not bar recovery on the policy.

See also the comment to the Restatement Section 205 (above) "The obligation of good faith and fair dealing extends to the assertion, settlement and litigation of contract claims and defences."

Another illustration given is a case in which A contracts to sell and ship goods to B on credit. The contract provides that, if B's credit or financial responsiblity becomes impaired or unsatisfactory to A, A may demand cash or security before making the shipment and may cancel if the demand is not met. A may property demand cash or security only if he honestly believes, with reason, that the prospect of payment is impaired.

FRANCE

Good faith/fair dealing required both in formation of the contract[10] and during the after-sale relationship

(1) Formation of the contract: (a) "dol" vitiating consent; (b) the seller's duty to reveal latent defects

[10] See discussion of "dol" below.

(a) Dol

18.10 This concept appears to cover both fraud in its present-day sense, and conduct which is not dissimilar to a breach of our good faith duty of candour/accuracy.[11]

18.11 *Code Civil.*[12] Art 1109 Il n'y a point de consentement valable, si le consentement n'a été donné que par erreur, ou s'il a été extorqué par violence ou surpris par *dol*.

18.12 *Art 1116.* Le dol est une cause de nullité de la convention lorsque les manoeuvres pratiquées par l'une des parties sont telles, qu'il est évident que, sans ces manoeuvres, l'autre partie n'aurait par contracté.
Il ne se présume pas, et doit être prouvé.

18.13 *An intention to deceive is not a necessary ingredient of dol.*[13] The width of *dol* as a concept (and the correspondingly wide seller's duty of disclosure, may be seen from the development of *réticence dolosive*. It is in sharp contrast to our own present narrowly confined idea of fraud. Professor Nicholas[14] says:

> "... there is a greater readiness than there is in English law to see silence (as to a fact which determined the other party's consent) as reprehensible. And similarly the line between dishonest *manoeuvres* and dishonest silence seems less sharp than the line in English law between fraudulent misrepresentation and passive acquiesence in the other party's self-deception. Certainly there has been in the last twenty years a steady flow of cases in which an *attendu* such as the following has appeared:
>
> 'Dol can consist of the silence of one party concealing from the other a fact which, if he had known it, would have prevented him from contracting.'
>
> This occurs, for example, in a case in which the vendor of a house in the country had not revealed to the purchaser the existence of a plan to set up a piggery nearby."[15]

Another case Professor Nicholas cites is the following:

> "There was held to be *dol* where the seller of land, who knew that the buyer intended to build a hotel on it, did not reveal that the only water supply was from a spring which was on land retained by the seller and was in any case quite inadequate."[16]

[11] *cf.* the nineteenth century twin concept of fraud, embracing both "equitable fraud" or "legal" fraud on the one hand and "moral" or intentional/reckless fraud on the other.
[12] Quoted from Dalloz edition 1994/5.
[13] See Nicholas, *The French Law of Contract* (2nd edn., Oxford, 1992) p. 103.
[14] *Op. cit.*.
[15] Civ 2.10.1974, D. IR 252 (Mazeaud/Chabas, 189).
[16] Civ 7.5.1974, D. 1974 IR 176. *cf.* our good faith duty of candour which might lead to a similar result.

(b) Seller's duty to disclose latent defects in the thing sold

18.14 *Art 1641.*[17] "Le vendeur est tenu de la garantie à raison des défauts cachés de la chose vendue qui la rendent impropre à l'usage auquel on la destine, ou qui diminue tellement cet usage, que l'acheteur ne l'aurait pas acquise, ou n'en aurait donné qu'un moindre prix, s'il les avait connus."

18.15 *Art 1643.*[18] Il est tenu des vices cachés, quand même il ne les aurait pas connus, à moins que, dans ce cas, il n'ait stipulé qu'il ne sera obligé à aucune garantie. (The seller is liable for latent defects, even if he was unaware of them, unless, being unaware of them, he expressly stipulated that he should not be bound by any warranty [garantie].[19]

18.16 *Deemed awareness of the "professional" seller.* The professional seller is now irrebuttably presumed to be aware of the latent defect.[20] If he sells to another professional the presumption is rebuttable.[21]

If the seller has pointed the defect out to the buyer it no longer ranks as a latent or hidden defect.[22] Professor Ghestin says[23]

> "The warranty against latent defects can therefore be seen . . . as providing the sanction for *an obligation to give information, and that obligation will often be pre-contractual. The defect is not discovered, it is true, until after the contract has been performed, but it will often have been in existence before the contract was made.*"[24]

The rationale given by Professor Ghestin for French law's attitude to the obligation to disclose is as follows.

> "The obligation of disclosure has its source in the inequality of the information available to the parties. *This inequality gives to one party an advantage such as to destroy the equilibrium of the contract.*"[25]

It is perhaps implicit in the passage quoted that the lack of equilibrium prevents the kind of properly informed consent which is desirable in

[17] (Seller's duty to reveal latent defects which render the thing sold unfit for its purpose or which diminish its value for its purpose.)
[18] Seller unable to exclude liability for latent defects unless he is unaware of them (but see below for deemed awareness).
[19] Tr. Ghestin.
[20] See the article by Professor Ghestin The Obligation to Disclose Information at p. 158 in Harris & Tallon, *Contract Law Today*: Anglo-French Comparisons.
[21] See the note to the Dalloz edition of the *Code Civil*.
[22] Ghestin, *op. cit.* p. 156, and see Chap. 10, Excluding the Effect of the Fair Dealing Rules, for examples of the substantially similar approach adopted by our good faith rules.
[23] *Op. cit.*, p. 157.
[24] Italics supplied Cp. the similar operation of our good faith rules regarding the formation of the contract.
[25] Italics supplied. Ghestin, in Harris & Tallon, *op. cit.*, p. 157, quoting Ghestin, *Traite de Droit Civil: II Le Contrat* (1980).

a contract. A similar rationale has been given for our own good faith rules regarding the formation of the contract.

(2) The after-sale relationship

Art 1134[26]

"Les conventions legalement formées . . . doivent être exécutées de bonne foi." **18.17**

Art 1135

Les conventions obligent non seulement à ce qui y est exprimé, mais encore à toutes les suites que l'équité, l'usage ou la loi donnent à l'obligation d'après sa nature.[27] **18.18**

(3) Remedies for failure to disclose latent defects

Art 1644[28]

Dans le cas des articles 1641 et 1643, l'acheteur a le choix de rendre la chose et de se faire restituer le prix, ou de garder la chose et de se faire rendre une partie du prix, telle qu'elle sera arbitrée par experts. **18.19**

Art 1645[29]

Si le vendeur connaissait les vices de la chose, il est tenu, outre la restitution du prix qu'il a recu, de tous les dommage et intérêsts envers l'acheteur.[30] **18.20**

Art 1646[31]

Si le vendeur ignorait les vices de la chose, il ne sera tenu qu'à la restitution du prix, et à rembourser a l'acquéreur les frais occasionnés par la vente. **18.21**

[26] Obligation to act in good faith during the post-contractual relationship.

[27] *cf.* Pothier's reference to terms which are "of the nature of" the contract, as contrasted with "essential" terms, without which there would be no contract, and the lowest in his scale, "accidental" terms: *Traité des Obligations* (1806 ed.) Part I, Chap. I, s.5. See Nicholas (*op. cit.*) p. 153ff for comment on the use by French courts of the above sections.

[28] (The buyer has a choice whether to seek the equivalent of equitable compensation, or rescission.)

[29] (The vendor who knew (and see above for constructive knowledge) of the latent defects but did not disclose them must accept rescission at the hands of the buyer and pay damages as well.)

[30] *cf.* Pothier, *Contrat de Vente* (1806 ed.) para. 236, "La bonne foi oblige le vendeur, non-seulement à ne rien dissimuler de vices intrinsèques de la chose, mais en général à ne rien dissimuler de tout ce qui concerne la chose, qui pourroit porter l'acheteur à ne pas acheter, ou à ne pas acheter si cher."

[31] (The vendor who has made proper disclosure is only bound to accept rescission and need not pay damages as well.)

So we see that other countries have good faith elements in their contract law. In this country we are having it re-imported to us in certain areas: eg public offers of shares, and most important of all, in the contracts imposed on consumers which are covered by the New Regulations. We have our share of the kind of conduct that calls for good faith law, as much as any other country. Pockets of our original good faith jurisdiction survive as acknowledged parts of our law; other parts survive uneasily and are often misunderstood. Their role as part of a coherent body of principles is not understood. A wider use of our own original good faith principles is open to us, in order to regulate misleading or deceptive conduct in sales in a way which is consistent with the parties' reasonable expectations.

CHAPTER 19

THE UNFAIR TERMS IN CONSUMER CONTRACTS REGULATIONS 1994[1]

"There are yet other issues raised by the Directive which are put into relief by a comparison between the theories of common and civil law of what constitutes a contract, and what obligations or entitlements are created by it. The most important one is the topic of good faith. . . . It would be interesting to reflect upon the question of where this notion fits in the continental conception of contract, whether it could really coherently be introduced within a conception of contract as exchange, how it relates to the demands of Equity in English law and whether the English notion of reasonableness could meet some of the requirements inherent in it. . . . I do believe that, . . . reflection on the topic of good faith in the framework of contrasting notions of contract will help to pave the way for a smooth integration of the Directive into English law, as well as for further integration of the European laws of contract."[2]

INTRODUCTION

19.01 Our Regulations have not adopted the approach (known as "copy-out") of simply enacting the English translation of the Directive. What we have is no doubt considered, rightly or wrongly, to be in the kind of form English lawyers and the English public are more accustomed to. This has, it seems, entailed also the decision not to have the rather aspirational recitals which the Directive has. It may be their inclusion was thought likely to be unpopular with the British public, as, perhaps, emphasising the alien origins of the new law, and our partial surrender of sovereignty to the EU. Whether or not that was the case, we lack the Directive's recitals. This has meant, harmlessly enough perhaps, that we lack the lead-in which the recitals represent. They describe the nature of the problem (different laws, differ-

[1] S.I. 1994 No. 3159.

[2] Anne de Moore, "Common and Civil Law Conceptions of Contract and a European Law of Contract: the Case of the Directive on Unfair Terms in Consumer Contracts," *European Review of Private Law*, 257–271.

ent contracts to be encountered in the EU countries, inimical to the free movement of goods and services). More importantly, the recitals which explained things, for example, the meaning of good faith, or certain aspects of the scope of the Regulations, have had to be selected out, upgraded in status, and incorporated in the body of the Regulations.

19.02 One may or may not be sceptical about the wisdom of this approach, but there it is. The practical result is that virtually nothing in the Regulations can be read in the way an English statute is normally read. The English words are often simply the beginning of a trawl through the Directive, since the Regulations have to be construed in the light of it. This means that the words in the Regulations cannot be relied on with any confidence as possessing the ordinary meaning they would have to an English reader. It has been thought helpful to refer on occasion to the French-language version of the Directive for comparison purposes. First, it is sometimes clearer than the English-language version on a particular point, simply because an ambiguity in one language may not always exist in another. Secondly, it is sometimes different in meaning. One is thus alerted to potential problems of interpretation and the need to harmonise our interpretation of the Directive with that of other member states as far as possible. One example of this is the question whether the Regulations cover land,[3] which one is alerted to by the difference in meaning between "biens" and "goods".

It should be noted that the Unfair Terms in Consumer Contracts Act 1977 also offers some protection against unfair terms in a number of contracts. It has been thought that an attempt at comparing the protection offered by the Act and the New Regulations would simply compound the problems already raised by the relationship between the Regulations and the Directive, let alone those raised by the different effect of the different Community languages. However, the text of part of the 1977 Act appears in the Appendix, and reference may be made to the contract textbooks for the effect of the Act.

THE UNFAIR TERMS IN CONSUMER CONTRACTS REGULATIONS 1994[4]

19.03

Made	*8th December 1994*
Laid before Parliament	*14th December 1994*
Coming into force	*1st July 1995*

Whereas the Secretary of State is a Minister designated for the purposes of section 2(2) of the European Communities Act 1972 in relation to measures relating to consumer protection;

[3] See below.

[4] S.I. 1994 No. 3159 elsewhere in the book, referred to as "the Unfair Contract Terms Regulations 1994", and below simply called "the Regulations".

Now, the Secretary of State, in exercise of the powers conferred upon him by section 2(2) of that Act and of all other powers enabling him in that behalf hereby makes the following Regulations:—

Citation and commencement

19.04 **1.** These Regulations may be cited as the Unfair Terms in Consumer Contracts Regulations and shall come into force on 1st July 1995.

"Shall come into Force"

19.05 The Regulations have been brought into force some seven months later than envisaged by the Directive:[5] Article 10.1 states:

> "Member States shall bring into force the laws, regulations and administrative provisions necessary to comply with this Directive no later than 31 December 1994. . . .
> These provisions shall be applicable to all contracts concluded after 31 December 1994."

It is understood that the reason for the delay was the desire to complete as much consultation as possible with various bodies likely to be affected.

Do the Regulations operate retrospectively to cover contracts concluded between December 31, 1994 and July 1, 1995? It seems probable that they will be held to do so. The statute is likely to be construed (by the European Court in effect) so as to take into account the background of the Directive's requirements. See also the case of *Marleasing v. La Comercial*[6] in which the European court was dealing with the problem of the direct effect of a directive which had not yet been transposed into national law by a member-state. It held that:

> "The obligation on the part of the national courts to interpret their national law in conformity with a directive arises whenever the provision in question is to any extent open to interpretation. In those circumstances the national court must, having regard to the legal system, give precedence to the method which enables it to construe the national provision concerned in a manner consistent with the directive".

Interpretation

19.06 **2.**—(1) In these Regulations —

"business" includes a trade or profession and the activities of any government department or local or public authority;

"the Community" means the European Economic Community and the other States in the European Economic Area;

[5] See Statutory Appendix for full text of Directive.
[6] [1992] 1 C.M.L.R. 305.

"consumer" means a natural person who, in making a contract to which these Regulations apply, is acting for purposes which are outside his business;

"court" in relation to England and Wales and Northern Ireland means the High Court, and in relation to Scotland, the Court of Session;

"Director" means the Director General of Fair Trading;

"EEA AGreement" means the Agreement on the European Economic Area signed at Oporto on 2 May 1992 as adjusted by the protocol signed at Brussels on 17 March 1993

"Member State" shall mean a State which is a contracting party to the EEA Agreement but until the EEA Agreement comes into force in relation to Liechtenstein does not include the State of Liechtenstein;

"seller" means a person who sells goods and who, in making a contract to which these Regulations apply, is acting for purposes relating to his business; and

"supplier" means a person who supplies goods or services and who, in making a contract to which these Regulations apply, is acting for purposes relating to his business.

(2) In the application of these Regulations to Scotland for references to an "injunction" or an "interlocutory injunction" there shall be substituted references to an "interdict" or interim interdict" respectively.

"Activities of any Government Department"

19.07 This prima facie appears wide in scope, and may even cover activities which prove to be ultra vires the department or local or public authority, or purely social activities such as a sports club run by or for the department etc. The French phrase "*dans le cadre de son activité professionelle*" used in the French version of the Directive as applicable both to the public and the private "activities" is plainly wider than the English "for the purposes of", meaning something more like "within the framework of". It is probable that for reasons of comity the wide meaning of "activities" covering these ancillary activities will be preferred here. The relevant passage from the Directive is cited more fully below[7] which supports a wide meaning.

"Public Authority"

19.08 This is unlikely to bear the relatively narrow meaning which an English person would attribute to it. The Directive is on its face much wider, applying to all sorts of activities "of a public nature" ("*activite professionelle, qu'elle soit publique ou privée*"), whether or not carried on by bodies which ordinary English usage would define as "public authorities". It would be likely to apply to bodies such as the BBC and to quangos. If it is to be construed in a way which is truthful to the Directive, the expression "public authority" will probably also cover, for example a small charity, or similar body which may not

[7] At para. 19.12.

trade for profit (and thus is not naturally comprehended within the words "trade or profession"), but which is naturally seen as having an occupation *of a public nature*.

It would also no doubt cover the supply of "collective services" such as gas and water to consumers, or transport services. See the concern expressed about these in the second European Economic Community programme dated May 19, 1981 for a consumer protection and information policy:

> ... "a large—sometimes the largest—proportion of service activities consists of collective services where the public sector or the quasi-public sector has a near monopoly on supply and where market forces operate only partially, as regards both the fixing of prices and determination of the quality of the service offered."

Consumer means a natural person ... acting for purposes which are outside his business

19.09 This is taken from the Directive, Article 2 (b). The French version of Article 2 (b) is:

> Consommateur: toute personne physique qui, dans les contrats relevant de la présente directive, agit à des fins qui *n'entrent pas dans le cadre de* son activité professionnelle.[8]

Possibly something like "not within the every day scope of his business activities" would be an alternative translation incorporating the effect of the word "cadre" or "framework". The word "framework" has about it some slight connotation of permanence which the English "outside his business" avoids. Whether the wording in either language would let in the possibility of an individual trader or professional claiming to be within the section when he indulges in a purchase which is for his business but abnormal for it, or outside its "framework" remains to be seen.

"His [business]"

19.10 It is unclear how significant the possessive adjective "his" is. Would non-business trustees who say, held property *for* a business be within the definition of *consumer* if they entered into a contract with a *seller or supplier* even though they held the property on trust, even a bare trust, for a business? Or charitable trustees? It seems unlikely that "his" would prevent this. The same possessive adjective occurs in the expression "his trade, business or profession, whether publicly or privately owned"; and there is clearly no connotation of personal possession, or private profit, *there*.[9]

[8] Italics supplied.
[9] See also "Business", at para. 19.11 below.

"Business"

19.11 It is unclear in the English version of the Regulations whether this extends to non-profit making businesses such as sports clubs and other unincorporated associations, but it probably does: see above. The French equivalent is *"activite professionelle"*. *"Professionel"* is translated by the *Dictionnaire Economique et Juridique*[10] as "professional, vocational"; and probably does not contain the element of private profit which the English word "business" does.

Seller . . . supplier

19.12 This is taken from the Directive, Article 2 (c). (*"professionel": "toute personne physique ou morale qui, dans les contrats relevant de la présente directive, agit dans le cadre de son activité professionelle, qu-elle soit publique ou privée."*)

The "seller/supplier" label may have a conscious or unconscious limiting effect which may be misleading: see above, para. 19.08, as to charities, etc.

"For purposes relating to his business"

19.13 The English words make the Seller/Supplier equivalent to the Consumer in a way the French version of the Directive does not. As worded, both have to act for purposes which are respectively not outside and relating to (as the case may be) their respective businesses. In the French version, this is true of the Consumer only: the Seller/Supplier only has to act within the "framework" (*cadre*) of his business, and his purposes (*fins*) do not come into it at all. There is no reason however why our Regulations should not go further than the Directive in preventing unfair terms for the consumer.[11]

The arguably wider wording of the English Regulations would probably catch the Seller/Supplier who is acting *ultra vires* his business, and thus not for its purposes, because these would be purposes "relating to it". Further, a Seller/Supplier could be using his business organisation for purposes which (though not *ultra vires* necessarily) are completely outside the "framework" of his business *e.g.* a greengrocer might enter into a contract to store used cricket balls for his local cricket club. This would probably *not* be within the French Directive wording (which, it is suggested, may have some connotation of the "usual course of a business") but might, depending on the precise circumstances, be within the English Regulations. Equally, a set of barristers might enter into a contract with an individual to sell their used photocopier to a Consumer. They would rank as Seller/Suppliers for Regulation purposes, while arguably being exempted

[10] (3rd edn.)
[11] See Art. 8 of the Directive.

from the scope of the Directive at least if the French version were followed.

Terms to which these Regulations apply

19.14

3—(1) Subject to the provisions of Schedule 1, these Regulations apply to any term in a contract concluded between a seller or supplier and a consumer where the said term has not been individually negotiated.

(2) In so far as it is in plain, intelligible language, no assessment shall be made of the fairness of any term which —

(a) defines the main subject matter of the contract, or

(b) concerns the adequacy of the price or remuneration, as against the goods or services sold or supplied.

(3) For the purposes of these Regulations, a term shall always be regarded as not having been individually negotiated where it has been drafted in advance and the consumer has not been able to influence the substance of the term.

(4) Notwithstanding that a specific term or certain aspects of it in a contract has been individually negotiated, these Regulations shall apply to the rest of a contract if an overall assessment of the contract indicates that it is a pre-formulated standard contract.

(5) It shall be for any seller or supplier who claims that a term was individually negotiated to show that it was.

"a contract concluded between a seller or supplier and a consumer . . ."

19.15

What does *"a contract"* mean? (1) Does it have to be a sale of goods or a supply *of* services *by the Seller/Supplier* or can it also include purchases by a *Seller/Supplier* from a Consumer if on non-individually negotiated terms?[12] For example, there must be considerable doubt whether the bank lender who takes a guarantee from a wife for her husband's debts is really providing services: it is she who is really providing the service and the lender who is "buying" it. There is little doubt, however, that the lender is carrying on a business activity, and one which is likely indirectly to affect economic activity.

(2) Does the Contract of Adhesion have to be either a sale or a purchase of *goods* (or supply/receipt of *services*) or do the Regulations cover other types of contracts provided these are made between the right people, that is the Seller/Supplier and the Consumer? Put another way, is it the nature of the contract or the makers of the contract which is the important classifying feature? Certainly, if the Directive had been intended to bite only on sales of goods and services, one might have expected a specific exemption for, for example sales

[12] These contracts in which a term (or the whole) has not been individually negotiated will be called, as does the French version of the Directive, "Contracts of Adhesion"?

of intellectual property or other rights not really easily classified as services.[13]

19.16 The scope of the Regulations depends crucially on the answer to these questions. It is suggested the wider view on both questions is likely to be the correct one. The Directive gives no hint that the contract has to be for the sale or supply of goods/services only: on the contrary, Article 1, Recital (14) and Recital (25) are in general terms, the only limitation being that they apply to contracts (of Adhesion) entered into between a Seller/Supplier and a Consumer.[14] The ambiguity of the Regulations on the point merely brings in interpretation by our courts, and this interpretation must of necessity be in accordance with the Directive: see the *Marleasing*[15] case. Our courts will no doubt also wish to arrive at a conclusion which will be in accordance with the Directive's recitals' overall aim of preventing distortions of competition between consumers and seller/suppliers; although no doubt these interpretation problems will in practice be solved by a reference to the European court under Article 177 of the Treaty.

"Goods"

19.17 This expression may also be a great deal wider than might appear to an English reader. A current concern, for example, is whether "goods" includes land. This will not matter if the wide interpretation of "contract" is correct; but would matter if it were not. "*Biens*" in French is a wider word than our "goods": more equivalent to "property". The Dictionnaire Economique et Juridique gives as a translation of what it calls the *concept patrimonial* of "*biens*": "*estate, property, assets, goods and chattels*". It thus includes interests in land.[16] It is likely also to include sales of rights generally.[17] The expression is statutorily defined to include interests in land by French law also.[18] It is thought that there may, however, be a divergence on the point between the various European–language versions, some with a wider meaning, including land in their equivalent, some not. Thus, the mere desire for harmony with the rest of Europe will not give any clear guidance. However, it is suggested that our courts will nonetheless, pending application to the European Court of Justice, wish to give the word the wider meaning, for two reasons. First, it is safer, since if the true meaning turns out to be the wide one, this country will have failed in its duty to bring in the Directive's terms to our legislation. Secondly, it would be in accordance with the overall Community policy of building up the consumer[19] so as to be a healthy "balancing factor" in the European

[13] See para. 19.17 below as to "goods", however.
[14] See also "a contract" in Reg. 3(1).
[15] Above.
[16] *c.f.* our own older usage in "With all my worldly goods I thee endow . . ." in the marriage service.
[17] *c.f.* the pre-1893 law on sales of personal property in Chap. 3, Sales of Personal Property.
[18] See *Code Civil*, Dalloz edition. 1994/5, Art. 516.
[19] Possibly ultimately to include the small and medium sized business as well as the individual consumer: see the Council Resolution next referred to,

economy vis a vis the seller/supplier, and to this end protecting him against damage to his economic interests.[20]

19.18 In any event, many contracts involving land will also involve services and thus be within the Regulations, for example a mortgage loan which includes a charge over the land. A grey area is perhaps the situation where the loan provisions are in one document and the mortgage is in another. Given that what is covered by the Regulations is unfair terms in contracts, not *documents*, it is likely that the courts will hold that the two documents are sufficiently related in such a case to be treated as one effective contract contained in two documents.

The core terms

19.19 Subsection 3(2) defines the "core terms" which are outside the assessment required by the Regulations. They are perhaps what Pothier would have defined as "essential" terms of the contract of sale: the thing sold, and the price paid.[21]

> "Dans chaque contrat l'on doit distinguer trois choses: celles qui sont de l'essence du contrat, celles qui sont seulement de sa nature, et celles qui sont purement accidentelles.
>
> 6. Les choses qui sont de l'essence du contrat, sont celles sans lesquelles ce contrat ne peut subsister; faute de l'une de ces choses, ou il n'y'a pas du tout de contrat, ou c'est une autre espèce de contrat.
>
> Par exemple, il est de l'essence du contrat de vente qu'il y ait une chose qui soit vendue, et qu'il y ait un prix pour lequel elle soit vendue; c'est pourquoi si je vous ai vendu une chose que nous ignorions avoir cesse d'exister, il n'y aura pas de contrat . . . ne pouvant pas y' avoir de contrat de vente sans une chose pour le prix qui ait été vendue . . ."

The main subject matter of the contract

19.20 The relevant Directive wording is in Article 4(2), which in French is: "la définition de l'*objet* principal du contrat".[22] This may well be the equivalent of what elsewhere in this book is called the paramount

para. 2.3.3. expressing the desire to prohibit unfair terms in contracts generally, taking particular account of the problems experienced by small and medium sized enterprises.

[20] See the Council Resolution of April 14, 1975 on a preliminary programme for a consumer protection and information policy, setting out the former as the underlying driving force behind legislation like the Directive. See also *Aannemersbedrijf PL Kraaijeveld BV v. Gedeputeerde Staten van Zuid-Holland*, ECJ, reported *New Law Digest*, October 24, 1996, confirming that, especially in a case where a comparison of the different language versions shows a divergence between them, the provision in question is interpreted by reference to the purpose and general scheme of which it forms part.

[21] *Traité des Obligations* (1835 edn.), para. 5.

[22] Italics supplied.

purpose of the contract,[23] in the sense of the Greek word telos, and Lord Wilberforce's "end".[24] It will thus probably bear a fairly narrow meaning, if our courts pay regard, as they no doubt will, to harmony with other European countries.

"the adequacy of the price or remuneration, as against the goods or services sold or supplied"

19.21 The French wording in Article 4(2) is *"l'adéquation entre le prix et la rémunération, d'une part, et les services ou les biens à fournir en contre-partie, d'autre part"*. The latter perhaps makes clearer yet than does the English wording (although that does so too) that it is only the price seen as a balancing mechanism in exchange for the goods or services which is regarded as a core term. The point is not a merely semantic one: the only aspect of the price which is as it were safe from the Regulations is the question, Did he pay too much (little) for what he got? The price is on the hand almost certainly relevant in assessing the unfairness or otherwise of *other* terms. The exercise would be a thoroughly artificial one if the price had to be excluded.

One would expect the price to be a factor in the assessment of fairness: a low price may for example point to a contract in which an increased risk was reasonably expected to be shouldered by the consumer: cp the relevance of the price in pre-1893 sales of personal property[25] and in furnished lettings.[26] A high price may have the opposite effect. It is unclear whether this kind of exercise is or is not ruled out by the definition of this core term. One could argue either way: either, to look at the price as a factor in unfairness is simply taking it into account as background, not assessing its fairness *in itself*[27] or, to look at the price at all is indirectly to assess its fairness as an exchange for the goods to some extent.

19.22 There is perhaps a logic about the exclusion of the "core terms": the answer to the question, Is it unfair, of any given contract only makes sense if there is a constant "it" which one is talking about. Further, it is difficult to see how the so-called "blue-pencil" effect[28] could be applied to either core term sensibly.

19.23 The chief area of concern about the core terms will no doubt be their attempted use as a vehicle for unfair terms which are made part of the contract definition and thus seek to escape the impact of the Directive. A narrow interpretation of the core terms will tend to prevent avoidance.

[23] See Part III, dealing with After the Contract loyalty to the paramount purpose of the contract.

[24] See *Prenn v. Simmonds* [1971] 1 W.L.R. 1381.

[25] See Chap. 3, Sales of Personal Property.

[26] See Chap. 6, Sale of Shorter Leases.

[27] As to the latter c.p. the old controversy about the "just price", discussed in Gordley, *The Philosophical Origins of Modern Contract Doctrine* (Oxford, 1991).

[28] As to which, see below.

"Plain, intelligible language"

19.24 The Directive wording in French is "*rédigées de façon claire et compréhensible*" which differs little. To whom must it be comprehensible? There is no guidance in the Regulations or Directive, but it is suggested that the likely answer is that which was developed in English good faith law: *the Consumer (or Seller/Supplier) who is likely to be buying those goods or those services, in the circumstances of the actual sale.*[29]

Is it a question of the words being plain and intelligible as a matter of grammar, or does their *practical effect* have to be clear? It is suggested that the latter would be more consistent with our own good faith law.[30] It would also fit with the separate requirement of good faith—the duty to be honest, straightforward and fair.[31] Thus, a term which was grammatically clear but which related to undisclosed risks which were within the Seller/Supplier's knowledge[32] would be unfair as regards that contract.[33]

Jargon, *e.g.* legal or technical jargon, should be avoided at least in contracts where the consumer would not normally be expected to seek legal advice, or where if he did, it could not be guaranteed that the effect of the clause or word in question would be explained to him. For example, a clause in a standard contract for the sale of land containing conditions might be unfair even though the use of a solicitor is normal, if the clause was not an unusual one and thus one the solicitor is under a duty to explain.

The Director General of Fair Trading takes an even wider view than the above (although perhaps not adverting especially to contracts in which it would be normal to use the services of a professional such as a solicitor). The Office of Fair Trading September 1996 Bulletin states at paragraph 2.14: "Since, by their very nature, consumer contracts are intended to be read by consumers, it follows that, so far as possible, legal (and other jargon must be avoided. What is required are everyday words, used in their familiar sense."

"defines the main subject matter of the contract"[34]

19.24 To what extent are general exclusion clauses apparently aimed at the definition of what is sold permitted? Examples are to be found in Chapter 10, Excluding the Effect of the Fair-dealing Terms. Consider for example "the land is sold subject to all easements, . . . other incumbrances whatsoever", which could be thought to rank as a

[29] See for further detail on this, other chapters of the book, notably Chap. 10, Excluding the Effect of the Fair Dealing Terms.

[30] See, *e.g.* Chap. 10, Excluding the Effect of the Fair dealing Terms.

[31] See "good faith" below.

[32] *e.g.* the undisclosed contract in *Greenwood v. Leather Shod Wheel* noted in Chap. 10.

[33] See also *e.g.; Price v. Macaulay* (1852) 2 G.M. & G. 339; 42 E.R. 903, in which Knight Bruce L.J. said the purchaser must be shown clearly to have had information of the real state of facts communicated to his mind."

[34] See above.

description of what is sold; and compare on the other hand, "such title as the vendor has", which probably has a much stronger claim to be part of the description. General exclusion clauses of the type above are intelligible in the sense that the grammar and general meaning are not difficult.[35] Our own good faith law, as has been seen, has held that these general clauses, whether part of the description or overtly exclusion clauses, have to point to any specific blot or concern of the vendor's, and are only good in so far as he has complied with his duty of accuracy and candour, and mentioned anything within his knowledge which was relevant from the buyer's (or inquiring party's) point of view. This definition of intelligibility includes an element of reasonable expectation as a substratum. It is possible that the courts will wish to apply such a definition, both in order to prevent evasion of the Regulations, and in order to achieve uniformity of approach, with what one might call a high degree of truth in selling regarded as the norm. It would however, as with other parts of the Regulations, require a considerable move away from a literalist approach.

The "plain and intellible language" provision may well have significant application in the insurance sphere. For example, a consumer could probably avail himself of it to argue against a "basis-of-the-contract" provision, complaining that it was insufficiently specific for its effect to be properly understood, and that consequently it sought to define the risk in a manner he could not reasonably have expected. Another situation in which a consumer might use the provision, is if, after he had completed a detailed questionnaire accurately, the insurer sought to avoid or rescind the contract on the grounds of some other non-disclosure by the consumer.

"a contract"

19.25 It is to be noted that the contract containing the term to be scrutinised is not specifically tied to contracts *of sale*: any contract, whether or not of sale, which is made between a Seller/Supplier and a Consumer will apparently count.[36] Thus, even if it were not a sale of services, a contract between a finance house and the Consumer for a sale made by a dealer to the Consumer is likely to be caught by the Regulations. The potential mischief is seen (in what is perhaps a curiously old-fashioned way) simply in *being* a Seller/Supplier dealing with a Consumer; *c.f.* the old approach—the trustee, the guardian, the common carrier, etc.

Oral contracts are included in the scope of the Regulations: see Recital (11).

"not . . . individually negotiated"

19.26 See also subsection (4). This expression is evidently much wider than pure, undiluted standard-form contracts. A large number of con-

[35] But see above as to "plain intelligible language" probably needing to include practical intelligibility to the likely customer.

[36] See above, "a contract concluded between a seller or supplier and a consumer."

tracts not obviously standard-form as a whole at all will be subject to scrutiny. Within the ambit of the Regulations will prima facie be, in descending order of obviousness:

(a) a completely standard-form contract, for example the kind which accompanies the purchase of a railway ticket where there is no realistic opportunity of making any changes. The kind of standard conditions which are sent by post with goods may not necessarily be covered, since a contract of this kind is made by acceptance of the conditions. No doubt if it contains exclusions it will need even under the general law[37] to be clearly worded and probably should make clear that it is a contract made only on acceptance by the customer, and that the customer may object to the contract so constituted within a reasonable time and make amendments or return the goods. The various standard conditions for the sale of land are no doubt covered to the extent that land is within the Regulations anyway.

(b) a set of standard conditions of any sort which has been amended by the Consumer, or which he has been able to amend, but where the Seller/Supplier has refused to accept amendment of certain parts of it. This poses a problem for the Seller Supplier: if he refuses to accept what he regards as unreasonable amendments he must accept some risk that his view will not be regarded as fair by the court. On the other hand, he can hardly be expected to accept every amendment that the Consumer wants.

(c) a contract which is not specially standard, but which has been drafted in advance by the Seller/Supplier and offered to the Consumer on a take it or leave it basis, or where the Seller/Supplier has refused the Consumer the right to amend some part or a term thereof.

(d) A *clause* in an individually negotiated contract which the buyer has not been given the opportunity to change, even though he may have negotiated changes or been able to negotiate changes to all the rest.

19.27 A question which perhaps arises is whether the Consumer can be said to have had the opportunity to influence a term when the term has been considered and approved by some organisation acting on behalf of consumers? Could it be said that the organisation was in some sense his agent? The answer is, probably not, simply because this is stretching the concept of agency too far. However, no doubt the scrutinising by the consumer organisation will make it more likely (though how likely will no doubt depend greatly on the real equality of the bargaining position of the consumer organisation) that the courts will find the term is not unfair to the kind of Consumer to be expected for that kind of contract.

Another question to which the above examples (a) to (d) gives rise is what exactly "able to influence" means in practice. As mentioned, it should stop short of allowing the Consumer carte blanche; but

[37] See Chap. 10, Excluding the Effect of the Fair Dealing terms and see also the Unfair Contract Terms Act 1977.

where? The best answer which can be given at present is probably that the court will regard as most crucial the practical realities of bargaining power in the transaction. The real mischief aimed at in the Regulations is is perhaps the practical imbalance in bargaining power of many Consumers vis-à-vis many Seller/Suppliers. The Council Resolution of April 14, 1975[38] on a preliminary programme of the European Economic Community for a consumer protection and information policy states in paragraph 6:

19.28 "[A consumer policy] has developed in response to the abuses and frustrations arising at times from the increased abundance and complexity of goods and services afforded the consumer by an ever-widening market. Although such a market offers certain advantages, the consumer, in availing himself of the market, is no longer able properly to fulfil the role of a balancing factor. As market conditions have changed, the balance between suppliers and customer has tended to become weighted in favour of the supplier. The discovery of new materials, the introduction of new methods of manufacture, the development of means of communication, the expansion of markets, new methods of retailing—all these factors have had the effect of increasing the production, supply and demand of an immense variety of goods and services. This means that the consumer, in the past usually an individual purchaser in a small local market, has become merely a unit in a mass market, the target of advertising campaigns and of pressure by strongly organized production and distribution groups. Producers and distributors often have a greater opportunity to determine market conditions than the consumer. Mergers, cartels and certain self-imposed restrictions on competition have also created imbalances to the detriment of consumers."

... "8. ... Increasingly detailed information is therefore needed to enable consumers, as far as possible, to make better use of their resources, to have a freer choice between the various products or services offered and to influence prices and product and market trends."

19.29 The above is reminiscent of the language used by the nineteenth century courts who developed the implied terms in sales of goods, also to meet a changed commercial situation. We are no doubt at a watershed of similar proportions, as was recognised by the Council in the above Resolution.[39]

It is possible that the ready availability (which would probably need to be known actually or constructively by the Consumer) of similar products on better terms would be a factor. The degree of ability to negotiate might properly be rather less in such a case. It is also pos-

[38] Citation.

[39] One may consider the recent "mad cow disease" problems. It would appear that the farmers did not know what was in their cattle feed; while the consumers did not know what was in their gelatine, soup, etc.

sible that the importance of the purchase to the Consumer may have some bearing: a sale of land or a mortgage transaction, or a sale of pension rights may perhaps be more strictly scrutinised for ability to negotiate and a higher level of truly equal bargaining power required in it, than a sale of everyday goods.[40] This will be both because it is more important to him and because the former are, if not more unique, at least more one-off, less readily or less easily available.

Regulation 3 "(5) It shall be for any seller or supplier who claims that a term was individually negotiated to show that it was"

19.30 The situations as regards equality of bargaining will vary enormously. There may be two broad groups, and a range between them: the Seller/supplier who is in a near-monopoly position as regards the subject matter of the contract on the one hand, and ordinary Seller/suppliers on the other. One may compare the distinction drawn in our law between someone who makes a market of another's weakness, whether because of pre-existing or spontaneous vulnerability, or because he has invited trust either expressly or by placing himself in a situation which demands trust[41] and the ordinary seller. The distinction is one of burden of proof once the vulnerability is established: the former has to justify himself as having provided a good deal for the vulnerable party, essentially; while the latter has no such burden of proof. On the contrary, the burden of proof is on the ordinary buyer to show that the seller has failed in his duty of accuracy or his duty of candour. Yet the Regulations in Regulation 3 (5) place the burden of proof on *all* sellers to show the allegedly unfair term was individually negotiated, so to this limited extent have placed a fiduciary-type burden on all sellers. However, the old distinction between the two may provide a useful guide when considering unfairness.[42]

Unfair terms

19.31 **4.**—(1) In these Regulations, subject to paragraphs (2) and (3) below, "unfair term" means any term which contrary to the requirement of good faith causes a significant imbalance in the parties' rights and obligations under the contract to the detriment of the consumer.

(2) An assessment of the unfair nature of a term shall be made taking into account the nature of the goods or services for which the contract was concluded and referring, as at the time of the conclusion of the contract, to all circumstances attending the conclusion of the contract and to all the other terms of the contract or of another contract on which it is dependent.

(3) In determining whether a term satisfies the requirement of good faith, regard shall be had in particular to the matters specified in Schedule 2 to these Regulations.

[40] See also para. 19.37 under Fairness.
[41] See Chap. 9, Dealings with the Vulnerable Buyer or Seller.
[42] See below.

(4) Schedule 3 to these Regulations contains an indicative and non-exhaustive list of the terms which may be regarded as unfair.

Good faith

19.32 What is meant by good faith? Is "good faith" an *additional* requirement or is unfairness comprised in the "significant imbalance..." and "detriment to the consumer" only? Regulation 4(1) is taken verbatim from the latter part of Article 3 of the Directive. The French version of that part of Article 3 is not specially of assistance on the point: it is:

> *"Une clause d'un contrat n'ayant pas fait l'objet d'une négociation individuelle est considerée comme abusive lorsque, en dépit de l'exigence de bonne foi, elle crée au detriment du consommateur un deséquilibre significatif entre les droits et obligations des parties découlant du contrat."*

The only significant point is that the French version encloses "contrary to the requirement of good faith" in commas. This perhaps makes good faith look more like a wholly independent and thus additional requirement

We are also, by Regulation 4(3) referred to Schedule 3 to the Regulations. This contains pieces taken out of Recital (16) to the Directive, and it will be helpful to go to Recital (16) direct. Recital (16) to the Directive at first blush seems more promising. The quotation is from the possibly slightly clearer French version. Since it is something of a casserole of a paragraph in either language, it has been fragmented and numbering and lettering allotted to it in order to help differentiate the various points made in it:

19.33 "Considérant

(i) que l'appréciation, selon les critères généraux fixés, du caractère abusif des clauses notamment dans les activités professionnelles à caractère public fournissant des services collectifs prenant en compte une solidarité entre usagers, nécessite d'être complétée par un moyen d'évaluation globale des différents intérêts impliqués;

(ii) que ceci constitue l'exigence de bonne foi;

(iii) que, dans l'appréciation de la bonne foi, il faut prêter une attention particulière

(a) à la force des positions respectives de négociation des parties,

(b) à la question de savoir si le consommateur a été encouragé par quelque moyen à donner son accord à la clause et si les biens ou services ont été vendus ou fournis sur commande speciale du consommateur;

(iv) que l'exigence de bonne foi peut être satisfaite par le professionel en traitant de façon loyale et équitable avec l'autre partie dont il doit prendre en compte les intérêts légitimes."

The ambit of this is not as clear as might be wished, either. However, it would seem that the "global" or "overall" evaluation of the different interests involved is not *limited* to the public activities specifically mentioned; these are simply an area where particular attention is to be paid to the "global" evaluation of the different interests involved. The "global evaluation" is a general requirement in assessing whether a clause in a contract is unfair, within the meaning of the Regulations.

Point (ii) is perhaps more of a problem: does it mean that (i) is a *sufficient* requirement of good faith, ie that if one has globally evaluated the different interests . . ., one has by so doing also assessed good faith, or is it merely a part of the inquiry into good faith? Or is it the case that the global evaluation is merely sketched in at this stage, to be amplified in the remainder of the recital. Consideration of (iii) and (iv) would seem to indicate one of the last two.

19.34 (iii) (a) looks to the bargaining strength or weakness of the parties; (b) contains two separate branches—(y) the inducement to agree to the clause and (z) the question whether the goods or services were made or supplied to the special order of the consumer.

(y) would most naturally connote a lower price paid by the buyer: see earlier chapters of this book in which a low price is treated as a relevant feature and see above on Regulation 3(2)(b)); but might include other benefits which could be taken to balance the detrimental clause.

The meaning of (z) is perhaps a touch impenetrable. How do you "specially order" say the services of a solicitor or a surveyor? To be meaningful in this context there must be something which is the norm, not specially ordered; but in fact our instincts are to say, surely the whole service is specially ordered, individualised. It is possible (though far from certain) that (z) may include or indicate an inquiry essentially into the degree of reasonable reliance by the buyer on the Seller/Supplier: compare the inquiry in the sale of personal property cases[43] about whether the buyer relied on the seller's skill and judgment or took the relevant risk himself, for example by laying down his own specifications for manufacture; or by telling the surveyor not to bother with the attic or the solicitor not to delay things by making a local search. If so, clauses putting the risks of the defect on the Consumer will not be unfair to that extent.

19.35 (iv) tells us that the requirement of good faith is satisfied by treating the "other party" (he is not on this occasion called the "consumer") in an honest, straightforward and fair fashion.[44]

The above analysis makes it possible to conclude that good faith is defined, if somewhat allusively, in (iv), that to find out whether there has been good faith one needs to carry out the global evaluation of the different interests involved referred to in (i), including in this evaluation as factors to which particular attention should be paid, the factors in (y) and (z).

Armed with this conclusion about good faith, we revert to Regula-

[43] See Chap. 3, Sale of Personal Property and see the Sale of Goods Act 1979; see also the other chapters in Part II.

[44] The Dictionnaire Economique et Juridique translates "loyal" as "fair, honest, straightforward", so the last two have been arrogated to "loyal" leaving "fair" as the most fitting translation of "equitable".

tion 4(1). We know that to be unfair the term must be contrary to the requirement of good faith. Is the term[45] automatically contrary to good faith, as defined, if the rest of Regulation 4(1) is satisfied: that is, if there is a significant imbalance in the parties rights and obligations under the contract to the detriment of the consumer?

19.36 One might perhaps, at a pinch, call the process of finding out whether there was a significant imbalance/detriment an "overall evaluation of the different interests involved.[46] However, this exercise is nothing very out of the ordinary: it amounts to no more perhaps than looking at the circumstances of the contract and of the parties to it. Something so everyday and so obviously necessary for an assessment of anything to do with the contract is unlikely to be determinative. On the other hand, the relatively specific (y) and (z) from Recital (16) are rather more apt to the consideration of the question whether the Seller/Supplier acted honestly, straightforwardly and fairly to the consumer than to the question whether there was a significant imbalance to the detriment. . . . They are primarily directed (particularly (z)) to the question of willing, informed, *acceptance* by the Consumer of something on its face detrimental to him. This seems on the whole rather more apt for an inquiry into the seller's compliance or otherwise with his good faith duty of candour and accuracy (not far off perhaps from the Regulations duty to be honest and straightforward[47] and to be fair).

It simply does not follow that the mere finding that a term creates a significant imbalance in the parties' rights and obligations and—presumably in the context of the contract as a whole—one which was at the time of the contract to the detriment of the consumer, *is* necessarily always going to mean that the Seller/Supplier has failed in his duty to be honest, straightforward and fair to the Consumer. Compare the cases in Chapter 9, Dealings with the Vulnerable Buyer or Seller, or the cases of ordinary sellers dealt with in the specific sale, chapters such as Chapter 5, Sale of Land, *etc.*, to the effect that the mere fact that the contract was a harsh one, or at an undervalue, was not enough. There had to be something more: a failure on the part of the seller in his duty of candour and accuracy, or in the vulnerable cases, a profiting from another's bargaining weakness.

19.37 Thus, it is suggested that the requirement of good faith *is* an additional requirement, so that there are three requirements in Regulation 4(1) and not two, before a term is treated as unfair for the purpose of the Regulations. It is also perhaps properly seen as a requirement we ought to be at least as familiar with in England as other Member States—and possibly more so, since we have the advantage of the old case law to give us a practical illustration of the concepts involved at work. These are, as has been suggested, not very different from the concepts seen in earlier chapters of the book—that the seller should

[45] Not being a price or main subject-matter term: see reg. 3(2).

[46] Recital (16.).

[47] Including perhaps such reliance-based duties as those discussed in Chap. 9, Dealings with the Vulnerable Buyer or Seller.

not be in breach of his duty of candour or his duty of accuracy and his "duty of fairness".

This last no doubt includes fairness towards those in a vulnerable bargaining position. This has no doubt begun to assume rather more importance than it had in the nineteenth century, since we should probably now include, at least for the purpose of the Regulations, the profiting from the consumer's vulnerability by large organisations or groups with a huge advantage in bargaining power.[48] "Fairness" is likely also to include[49] what has in Part III of this book been called Loyalty to the paramount purpose of the contract—or the fair use of a retained power in a way which is true to the original paramount purpose-of-the-contract.

No-one should be very surprised that these principles making up the notion of good faith in the Regulations appear after all to be relatively familiar ones. We were less insular once. The European notions of good faith and our own notions of good faith were developed at about the same time as our own, and influenced by the same influences[50]. It would be odder if there were not similarities.

Regulation 4 (2)

"taking into account the nature of the goods and services"

19.38 This is consistent with our established good-faith principles, which, as has been seen[51] were developed with the nature of the contract in mind; and see also the reference to implied terms demanded by the "nature of the contract" in *Liverpool City Council v. Irwin.*[52]

"The time of conclusion of the contract"

19.39 This is again consistent with the good faith principles as seen in the earlier parts of this book: the definition of the duty is in the light of the original circumstances of the contract, not supervening events.

"In determining whether a term satisfies the requirement of good faith, regard shall be had in particular to the matters specified in Schedule 2 to these Regulations."

19.40 See the discussion of good faith at paragraph 19.32 above.

[48] See Mason J.'s reference to this likely development, noted in Chap. 9, Dealing with the Vulnerable Buyer or Seller.

[49] See Sched. 3.

[50] See Chap. 1, Introduction, and Chap. 2. The Legal Nature of the Duty of Good Faith.

[51] See Parts I and II of this book.

[52] [1977] A.C. 239.

Regulation 4 (4) "Schedule 3 to these Regulations contains an indicative and non-exhaustive list of the terms which may be regarded as unfair".

19.41 See the notes to Schedule 3, and note that the provisions listed there amount only to natural candidates for selection as unfair, and are *not necessarily* unfair.

Consequence of inclusion of unfair terms in contracts

19.42 **5.**—(1) An unfair term in a contract concluded with a consumer by a seller or supplier shall not be binding on the consumer.

(2) The contract shall continue to bind the parties if it is capable of continuing in existence without the unfair term.

"an unfair term . . . shall not be binding on the consumer"

19.43 (a) In the case of an exclusion clause of the type (discussed in Chapter 10, Excluding the Effect of the Fair-dealing terms), that is a separate add-on, qualifying the nature of the thing sold so as either to add unwelcome obligations or risks to the Consumer or to diminish the thing sold beyond what the Consumer would otherwise reasonably have expected, the practical result may often be that the clause is simply of no effect. Although as a matter of language the clause remains binding on the Seller/Supplier by virtue of the Regulations, there is no meaningful sense in which it can be binding. The only way in which he wants to use it is barred to him.

(b) Problems of interpretation are likely to occur when the unfair term is an exclusion clause in the above sense but is *also* mixed up with other essential terms of the contract, for example if it qualifies and is part of a term defining some essential (but not "core") right such as the right to vacant possession, or delivery. Does the whole term have to go (possibly against the wishes of the Consumer), or can the unfair *effect* of it be dissected out, leaving the essential right intact? The remainder of the Regulations offers no guidance on the point.

19.44 The Directive in Article 6 lays down a requirement that Member States "shall lay down that unfair terms used in a contract concluded with a consumer by a seller or supplier shall, as provided for under their national law, not be binding on the consumer and that the contract shall continue to bind the parties upon those terms if it is capable of continuing in existence without the unfair terms." The only clue one may derive from that is perhaps the phrase "as provided for under their national law"; but even that faces both ways. It might indicate that the not-being-binding should operate in a way which the Member State's law recognises already; on the other hand it might mean (and this seems the more likely on the whole) that there should be provision for it not being binding made by the national law pursuant to Article 6.

19.45 Thus the answer to the question raised in the last paragraph but one remains to be worked out by the courts. It is suggested that the preferable approach would be to exclude only the unfair effect of the term, leaving the rest of the term in being. This is consistent with the approach to oral/written contracts such as those discussed in the ticket cases; allows proper emphasis on the circumstances within the knowledge of the parties at the time of the contract;[53] is broadly consistent with the operation of our own old-established good faith principles, and is certainly consistent with the spirit of the Regulations and Directive. Seller/Suppliers will have to get it right if they cannot easily rely on a let-out. Finally, it is probably in keeping also with our own legal attitudes to the destruction of agreements intended to have legal effect, embodied in the maxim *ut magis valeat quam pereat*, to try to save the contract as far as possible. For example, a sweeping general clause about, say possible problems of delivery would be allowed to have effect as regards the events which were not within the Seller/Supplier's knowledge[54] at the time of the contract, but excluded as regards, say, difficulties with his wholesaler which he was well able to forecast from what he knew (but had not disclosed to the Consumer) at the time of the contract. This would have the salutary effect that he would be prevented from casting the predictable risk of uncertain supplies on the Consumer, and instead obliged to perform his contract.

19.46 It would no doubt have the further salutary effect (in common with the operation of our own old-established good faith principles) of ensuring that in such a case, if the Seller/Supplier cannot perform his contract, he is liable to pay damages to the Consumer.

What if a term which is part of the core definition of the subject matter of the contract (see Regulation 3(2)(a)) has been rendered subject to scrutiny because it was not expressed in "plain, intelligible language" and has been found to be unfair? Let us say, for example, that a "basis of the contract" provision in an insurance policy, rendering the proposal statements warranties so that every non-disclosure is material, has been considered, and found to be insufficiently clear in its effect to the kind of consumer to be expected to buy that particular type of insurance. The contract is perfectly capable of continuing in effect but only objectively material non-disclosures will be allowed to affect it.[55] This would, no doubt, be to rewrite the contract, in one sense, but to no greater extent than was traditionally done by the good faith rules anyway. The interference is confined to that which is reasonably to be expected, so there is no unfairness to the parties. Further, it can be said that the contract is still essentially the same contract.

The problem of material non-disclosures by the consumer to the insurer where the effect of these was not clearly explained may also perhaps arise at some stage. The term rendering the insurance contract invalid would, on this hypothesis among others, be unfair to the consumer and thus excluded; but it can hardly be right for the courts to let assureds recover for a misdescribed risk on precisely the same

[53] See reg. 4(2) for the importance of this.
[54] See Part II for "within his knowledge".
[55] See the British Insurers' Code of Practice.

terms as if the risk had been correctly described. Once again, perhaps a form of compensation to the insurer, as granted by the early equity courts in (all but the most serious) misdescribed sales of land would be an appropriate remedy, this time imposed on the assured for the benefit of the insurer. The system of compensation operated in France may have something of interest to us: where the assured has misdescribed the risk without fraud, and the problem emerges for the first time on his making a claim, he obtains the lesser cover which his description would have entitled him to, as opposed to that which a true description would have given him. *C.f., e.g.* Sicot & Margeat: *Précis de la loi sur le contrat d'assurance, Lib. Gen. de Droit et de Jurisprudence:*

> "l'omission ou la déclaration inexacte de la part de l'assuré dont la mauvaise foi n'est pas établie n'entraine pas la nullité de l'assurance. ... Dans le cas où la constatation n'a lieu qu'après un sinistre, l'indemnite est réduite en proportion du taux de primes payées par rapport des primes qui auraient été dues, si les risques avaient été complètement et exactement déclarées."

For the most serious cases, where the risk assured is rendered so different by the non-disclosure/misstatement that it could not be said still to be "the" contract, see perhaps the discussion of "the contract", below.

"The contract shall continue to bind the parties ... if it is capable of continuing in existence without the unfair term"

19.47 What however if what is found unclear and unintelligible to the Consumer is, say, a surety contract entered into by a Consumer with a lender which covers various undisclosed and not readily-to-be-expected liabilities of the debtor? The surety would have envisaged that he or she was taking on the risk of some liability, albeit more restricted liability. On the other hand, if one saves that contract, holding only the extended unforeseeable effect non-binding, it may have undesirable public policy (and Directive policy) effects. It will encourage lenders to word their contracts widely, reckoning that the term will simply be of no effect in so far as it is unfair.

The answer probably lies in the words above. It is not "a contract" but "*the contract*" which has to be "capable of continuing in existence without the unfair term". Thus, the question would be the practical one: is this essentially "the contract" if one knocks out the unfair term, or is it an altogether different contract? The approach may not be far off that adopted by the early courts of equity when granting rescission where the contract was one that the Consumer *would never have entered into*, but allowing it to continue, subject to the effect on the terms of the good faith rules, in cases where the difference was sufficiently unimportant to be properly remedied by compensation, or if the Consumer desired.[56]

[56] See in particular Chap. 5, Sale of Land, for this. See also Pothier, *Contral de Vente* (1806 edn.) who refers to "*tout ce qui concerne la chose, qui porte l'acheteur à ne pas acheter, ou à ne pas acheter si cher*". If the case fell on the "*ne pas*

It should be noted, of course, that if "the contract" *is* capable of continuing in existence, it remains binding on the Seller/Supplier, but in an altered form, without the effect of the unfair term. Therefore, in the surety example above, it would be a matter of degree whether the surety remained bound: in some cases the contract would not be the same contract, *e.g.* if the unfair part took up most of the risk-picture (as of the time of contracting): in others it would. This result seems consistent with the parties' reasonable expectations.

Construction of written contracts

19.48 "**6.** A seller or supplier shall ensure that any written term of a contract is expressed in plain, intelligible language, and if there is doubt about the meaning of a written term, the interpretation most favourable to the consumer shall prevail.

"plain, intelligible language"

19.49 See paragraph 19.24, above.

"If there is doubt about the meaning of a written term"

19.50 "If there is doubt" is likely, from the wording, to be objectively construed—doubt as felt by the court or the reasonable consumer to be expected in that contract rather than the particular Consumer.

The provision as a whole would seem to fall short of writing in an *assumption of good faith* to relevant contracts.[57] It appears to be narrower. Precisely like our ancient *contra proferentem* rule which probably pre-dates the development of good faith terms[58] there must first be uncertainty or ambiguity about the meaning, before Regulation 6 "bites".

It would seem however to provide a very broad tool indeed once the Regulation is seen to be applicable. The uncertain or ambiguous provision apparently does not merely have to be construed so that it is fair: it has to be construed in the sense *most favourable to the Consumer*, which could be more than fairness to him requires, and could involve *un*fairness to the Seller/supplier. It really does not seem possible from the wording of the provision (or the Directive, which is precisely similar) to read in any qualification to *"most favourable"*.

19.51 Thus the result seems odd: if the term is plain, it is subjected to the three-factor exercise discussed above,[59] which is by no means one-sidedly Consumer-oriented, before it is cut down. If it is ambiguous, the Consumer may demand any meaning the words will bear. It is possible the wide provision may have been public-policy driven to

acheter" side of the line, the contract would be rescinded, on this approach: if it was simply a question of "*ne pas acheter si cher*" the contact would continue, in its new cut-down form.

[57] *c.f.* Part II of this book.

[58] See Chap. 10, Excluding the Effect of the Fair Dealing Rules.

[59] See under reg. 4(1).

provide a deterrent to ambiguity on the part of Seller/suppliers. Truth–in–selling is a high priority. For example the Council Resolution of 19 May, 1981[60] on a second programme for the EEC consumer protection and information policy, paragraph 28(3) sets out a number of principles including:

> "(3) "the presentation and promotion of goods and services, including financial services, should not be designed to mislead, either directly or indirectly, the person to whom they are offered or by whom they have been requested.

If Regulation 6 is interpreted (and one can see no reason why it should not be) as including doubt arising not because of the particular phrase in itself, but the particular phrase *as it operates within the contract as a whole,* then there are even more lurking dragons for the Seller/supplier. It is all too easy, at all events with our customary rather long small-print Anglo-Saxon written contracts, for there to be doubt arising simply from the complex interaction of the various bits of small print. It may be that there will need to be a culture change, in which cautious contracts made between Seller/Suppliers and Consumers will need not only to be clear ones as to the individual provisions taken separately, but also short ones, to avoid this risk.

Choice of law clauses

19.52 **7.** These Regulations shall apply notwithstanding any contract term which applies or purports to apply the law of a non-member state, if the contract has a close connection with the territory of the member States.

This is of course an anti-avoidance provision.

Prevention of continued use of unfair terms

19.53 **8.**—(1) It shall be the duty of the Director to consider any complaint made to him that any contract term drawn up for general use is unfair, unless the complaint appears to the Director to be frivolous or vexatious.

(2) If having considered a complaint about any contract term pursuant to paragraph (1) above the Director considers that the contract term is unfair he may, if he considers it appropriate to do so, bring proceedings for an injunction (in which proceedings he may also apply for an interlocutory injunction) against any person appearing to him to be using or recommending use of such a term in contracts concluded with consumers.

(3) The Director may, if he considers it appropriate to do so, have regard to any undertakings given to him by or on behalf of any person

[60] [1981] O.J. C133/1

as to the continued use of such a term in contracts concluded with consumers.

(4) The Director shall give reasons for his decision to apply or not to apply, as the case may be, for an injunction in relation to any complaint which these Regulations require him to consider.

(5) The court on an application by the Director may grant an injunction on such terms as it thinks fit.

(6) An injunction may relate not only to use of a particular contract term drawn up for general use but to any similar term, or a term having like effect, used or recommended for use by any party to the proceedings.

(7) The Director may arrange for the dissemination in such form and manner as he considers appropriate of such information and advice concerning the operation of these Regulations as may appear to him to be expedient to give to the public and to all persons likely to be affected by these Regulations.

8th December 1994

(1) "It shall be the duty of the Director to consider any complaint made to him that any contract term drawn up for general use is unfair . . ."

It is questionable whether as matters stand Regulation 8 really complies with Article 7 of the Directive. Article 7 is, frankly, in much wider terms: "Member States shall ensure that, in the interests of consumers and of competitors, adequate and effective means exist to prevent the continued use of unfair terms in contracts concluded with consumers by sellers or suppliers".

(a) The sole means which the Regulations provide are dependent for their efficacy on a sufficiently wide range of complaints being made to the Director to cover fairly the entire range of contracts made between a Consumer and a Seller/supplier which are within the scope of the Regulations. The Director General has received complaints in the main from Trading Standards Departments and from consumers. It is difficult to be sure that this method is likely to ensure compliance with the Directive. It may be thought (although in time any emphasis of this kind—if such there is—would no doubt change) that there would perhaps be a tendency for there to be rather more references to the Director as regards sales and hire contracts of consumer goods and leisure facilities, and rather fewer covering sales of insurances, pensions, mortgages, land, legal and medical services, *etc.*—all arguably covered by the Directive if contracts of adhesion are involved. It is perhaps a pity that there is not a more positive duty put upon the Director to identify relevant abuses, by making, for example, arrangements to receive regular references from Ombudsmen (assuming their terms of reference permit this) and consumer organisations, lawyers, patients' organisations, the Securities and Investments Board, etc., and perhaps identifying sectors where there is no consumer organisation, or no wholly adequate consumer organisation[61] preventing unfairness and taking whatever steps seem fitting to him to identify abuses in the absence of these. The Office of Fair Trading's admirably clear and well set-out most recent Bulletin for September 1996, for example, does certainly contain specific details of a few insurance cases dealt with and one mortgage interest case, but leisure and sale/hire of goods cases do seem to predominate, at present at least, among the cases which receive specific mention. However, it is understood that the Director General would welcome complaints from public-spirited members of the public including the professions.

(b) Another, perhaps minor, criticism which could be levelled at the implementation of the Directive in this country is that the Director's duty is probably limited (implicitly, by the use of the words "term drawn up for general use") to written contracts or mixed oral and written contracts in which the abusive clause is in the written part, and does not cover oral contracts.[62]

(c) The Director General of Fair Trading in the September 1996 Bulletin (referred to above) has reviewed the first twelve months of operation of his Unfair Terms Unit. In two-thirds of the 817 complaints received, action was taken. He states "Our experience in these first months leads us to believe that the use of unfair terms in consumer contracts is widespread and amounts to a serious problem in the United Kingdom. This was contrary to our expectations . . ." He also notes sadly the attitude of many businesses requested to redraft potentially unfair terms:

"All too often, businesses return with replacement terms that are deeply flawed, and do so more than once. Points we have raised are ignored or wilfully misinterpreted. Sometimes new material is introduced which has obvious potential for unfairness. In effect, some businesses draft new terms where they do not accept the justice of our criticism of their old ones. This is a pointless exercise. Where any business does not accept our view, its appropriate course of action is to say so and give its reasons."

(d) The Office of Fair Trading May 1996 Bulletin lists at paragraph 1.18 the most common unfair terms encountered as at that date:
   (i) "Entire agreement clauses" excluding from the contract anything said or promised by a salesman or agent of the company:
   (ii) Hidden clauses—terms which consumers could not get to know before signing a contract:

[61] The role of "self-regulating" organisations for Directive purposes may be thought to be in need of further examination.

[62] Oral contracts are within the scope of the Regulations: see Directive, Rec. (11).

(iii) Penalty clauses, e.g. one-sided clauses which penalise consumers, for example by permitting a company to retain deposits with no counterbalancing penalties on the company if it does not comply with its obligations:

(iv) Exclusion clauses, as to which the Office of Fair Trading writes with perhaps a detectable hint of desperation "[T]hese exclude liability for every possible eventuality, and are very common."; and

(v) Variation Clauses, which are noted as typically giving the supplier the right to put up prices with no realistic right for the consumer to withdraw without penalty.

The September 1996 Bulletin additionally raises the point (among others) that clauses referring to statutory rights may be unfair if they do not give sufficient information to Consumers for them to know what their statutory rights in fact are. The idea that, for example, a wide exclusion clause may be saved by tacking on "this does not affect your statutory rights" is deprecated: the latter wording is not "a lucky charm". The whole clause without further explanation, "is simply meaningless to consumers, and cannot prevent them being misled into believing that an ineffective exclusion clause denies them redress."

(e) The Consumers Association has sought clarification of the following preliminary question from the European Court of Justice under Article 177 of the Treaty:

"Does Article 7(2) of the Council Directive 93/13/EEC of 5 April 1993 on unfair terms in consumer contracts impose obligations on Member States to ensure that national law

(1) states criteria to identify private persons or organisations having a legitimate interest in protecting consumer, and
(2) allows such private persons or organisations to take action before the courts or before competent administrative bodies for a decision as to whether contractual terms drawn up for general use are unfair?"

The referral to the European Court was made in the course of an application for judicial review of the decision about the wording of the Regulations.

The Association argues that bodies such as it is have "a legitimate interest under national law in protecting consumers", and ought to be allowed to take action "before the courts or before competent administrative bodies" for a decision as to whether contractual terms drawn up for general use are unfair" so that the government can take "appropriate and effective means to prevent the continued use of such terms."

The question presumably will be one of construction. A further question will be in practice whether it is adequate to entrust the sole responsibility under Article 7(2) to one body, the Office of Fair Trading. The wording of Article 7(2) certainly appears to envisage a number of bodies having the right to complain on behalf of the consumer. However, there may be scope for an argument that there should be some limitation at least, in the interests of administrative efficiency. It may be that the counter-argument would be that it would be sufficient if there were a duty on bodies such as the Consumers' Association to notify the Office of Fair Trading of any intended action, and to desist if it seemed that such action would duplicate any initiative of that Office which was in progress. No doubt the overriding consideration will be whether the present arrangements are within Article 7(1): that is, whether they do in fact represent "adequate and effective means . . . to prevent the continued use of unfair terms in contracts concluded with consumers by sellers or suppliers". There is perhaps room to question whether this is so, in spite of the energy and verve displayed in this field by the Office of Fair Trading, particularly given the potentially very wide scope of the Directive and thus the Regulations: see above passim. The current prevalence in England and Wales of "self-regulating" organisations of Seller/Suppliers may also be relevant. These bodies, however heavily directed from on high, may not be thought quite to amount to the same thing as a really independent body giving full force to the consumers' interests.

SCHEDULE 1 **Regulation 3(1)**

CONTRACTS AND PARTICULAR TERMS EXCLUDED FROM THE SCOPE OF THESE REGULATIONS

19.54 These Regulations do not apply to —

(a) any contract relating to employment;
(b) any contract relating to succession rights;
(c) any contract relating to rights under family law;
(d) any contract relating to the incorporation and organisation of companies or partnerships; and
(e) any term incorporated in order to comply with or which reflects —
  (i) statutory or regulatory provisions of the United Kingdom; or
  (ii) the provisions or principles of international conventions to which the member States or the Community are party.

"any term incorporated in order to comply with or which reflects— (i) statutory or regulatory provisions of the United Kingdom . . ."

19.55 Presumably the expression "the United Kingdom" is meant to connote the law applicable in the different parts of the United Kingdom, as the case may be.

Since our statutory provisions (and no doubt regulations made under them similarly) are themselves to be interpreted in accordance with relevant Directives[63] there should in theory be no problem here.[64] No doubt terms implied into contracts by statute will rank as "terms incorporated in order to comply with ... etc". An example which springs to mind is the Sale of Goods Act implied terms as to merchantability and fitness for purpose (the former now called "satisfactory quality")[65].

It is not entirely clear what is meant by "excluded from the scope of these Regulations" in a case such as that just given, where a statutory term is implied into the contract. It is to be hoped that "excluded" merely means that the term itself will not be scrutinised for unfairness; but may be taken into account as part of the contract's term, when scrutinising other terms of the contract.

Secondary legislation made by statutory instrument will operate similarly. The Regulations themselves, made under section 2(2) of the European Communities Act 1972 are one example of such a statutory instrument.

Should the word "mandatory" have been included before "statutory or regulatory provisions"? The DTI have taken the view[66] that the Directive wording, which is *"les dispositions législatives ou réglementaires imperatives'*[67]*'* means "mandatory statutory provisions or [mandatory] regulatory provisions". This plainly seems correct. It is hard to see quite why "mandatory" has therefore been left out.

If a statute lays down that a term is to apply only in default of an express contractual provision to the contrary, is that term one "to comply with or which reflects" a mandatory statutory or regulatory provision? The point admits of argument either way. On the one hand, it could be said that something you have an option to exclude by agreement is not really mandatory at all. On the other, you could say that once the default situation has arisen, *i.e.* if you have taken no steps to agree an exclusion, the term really does become mandatory. It is simply selectively mandatory. Recital 13 to the Directive includes default provisions, so these clearly are capable of ranking as "mandatory". The question may vary according to the wording of the particular statute or regulation in question. For example, the Arbitration Act 1996 has a special group of provisions expressly labelled "mandatory", which apply regardless of the parties' wishes, and a large group of default provisions, which apply only in the absence of agreement. The Act's default provisions would thus probably not rank as "mandatory" for present purposes.

Are rules made by various bodies to comply with an Act which says they have to make rules, *e.g.* the Personal Investment Authority

[63] See the *Marleasing* case, above.

[64] See also the House of Lords in *Factortame* [1990] 2 A.C. 85 at 140, to the effect that UK statutes are to be construed as if without prejudice to the directly enforceable community rights of nationals of any Member State of the EU.

[65] See the Sale and Supply of Goods Act 1994.

[66] Guidance Notes 1995.

[67] Recital 13.

under the Financial Services Act 1986[68] or the Building Societies under the Building Societies Act 1986, "mandatory regulatory provisions?

It is probable, as matter of construction of the words in their context, and in particular the operation of the expression "term" (of the contract) that the "mandatory" in question in the Regulations means "mandatory to the parties to the contract", rather than mandatory to one party. The question therefore will be, mandatory to whom? If this is right, a term may still be unfair within the meaning of the New Regulations in a particular contract even if it is a term deriving from rules of a body which that body had been obliged to make in order to comply with a particular statute. In practice it seems perhaps unlikely that such a term would be unfair in itself; but may be capable of combining with other terms of the contract to produce an unfair total effect.

The DTI[69] takes the contrary view, that terms "not laid down by a statute but nevertheless agreed with a regulator established by statute and acting under powers ultimately derived from statute would fall outside the scope of the Regulations . . .", but cites only policy reasons for this view. These are

> "Elements of fairness of transactions are reflected in these arrangements and should further cross-border approximation be required in such areas, sectoral rather than horizontal measures would be appropriate. It is implicit that those who regulate the industry are best placed to assess the needs of sellers and buyers of services in the context of the industry product. Should transactions which appear to operate against the interests of certain parties come to light, those with a detailed appreciation of the operation of such markets are best placed to take an informed view as to whether rules governing transactions need to be revised and/ or to be placed on a more binding footing."

SCHEDULE 2 **Regulation 4(3)**

ASSESSMENT OF GOOD FAITH

19.56 In making an assessment of good faith, regard shall be had in particular to —

(a) the strength of the bargaining positions of the parties;

(b) whether the consumer had an inducement to agree to the term;

(c) whether the goods or services were sold or supplied to the special order of the consumer, and

[68] See statutory appendix for Article 11 Financial Services Directive 1993 and comment.

[69] Guidance Notes 1995.

(d) the extent to which the seller or supplier has dealt fairly and equitably with the consumer.

See the discussion of this and Article (16) of the Directive under Regulation 4(1) *"good faith"* at paragraph 19.32, above.

SCHEDULE 3 **Regulation 4(4)**

INDICATIVE AND ILLUSTRATIVE LIST OF TERMS WHICH MAY BE REGARDED AS UNFAIR

19.57

1. Terms which have the object or effect of —

(a) excluding or limiting the legal liability of a seller or supplier in the event of the death of a consumer or personal injury to the latter resulting from an act or omission of that seller or supplier;

(b) inappropriately excluding or limiting the legal rights of the consumer vis-à-vis the seller or supplier or another party in the event of total or partial non-performance or inadequate performance by the seller or supplier of any of the contractual obligations, including the option of offsetting a debt owed to the seller or supplier against any claim which the consumer may have against him;

(c) making an agreement binding on the consumer whereas provision of services by the seller or supplier is subject to a condition whose realisation depends on his own will alone;

(d) permitting the seller or supplier to retain sums paid by the consumer where the latter decides not to conclude or perform the contract, without providing for the consumer to receive compensation of an equivalent amount from the seller or supplier where the latter is the party cancelling the contract;

(e) requiring any consumer who fails to fulfil his obligation to pay a disproportionately high sum in compensation;

(f) authorising the seller or supplier to dissolve the contract on a discretionary basis where the same facility is not granted to the consumer, or permitting the seller or supplier to retain the sums paid for services not yet supplied by him where it is the seller or supplier himself who dissolves the contract;

(g) enabling the seller or supplier to terminate a contract of indeterminate duration without reasonable notice except where there are serious grounds for doing so;

(h) automatically extending a contract of fixed duration where the consumer does not indicate otherwise, when the deadline fixed for the consumer to express this desire not to extend the contract is unreasonably early;

(i) irrevocably binding the consumer to terms with which he had no real opportunity of becoming acquainted before the conclusion of the contract;

(j) enabling the seller or supplier to alter the terms of the contract unilaterally without a valid reason which is specified in the contract;

(k) enabling the seller or supplier to alter unilaterally without a valid reason any characteristics of the product or service to be provided;

(l) providing for the price of goods to be determined at the time of delivery or allowing a seller of goods or supplier of services to increase their price without in both cases giving the consumer the corresponding right to cancel the contract if the final price is too high in relation to the price agreed when the contract was concluded;

(m) giving the seller or supplier the right to determine whether the goods or services supplied are in conformity with the contract, or giving him the exclusive right to interpret any term of the contract;

(n) limiting the seller's or supplier's obligation to respect commitments undertaken by his agents or making his commitments subject to compliance with a particular formality;

(o) obliging the consumer to fulfil all his obligations where the seller or supplier does not perform his;

(p) giving the seller or supplier the possibility of transferring his rights and obligations under the contract, where this may serve to reduce the guarantees for the consumer, without the latter's agreement;

(q) excluding or hindering the consumer's right to take legal action or exercise any other legal remedy, particularly by requiring the consumer to take disputes exclusively to arbitration not covered by legal provisions, unduly restricting the evidence available to him or imposing on him a burden of proof which, according to the applicable law, should lie with another party to the contract.

2. Scope of subparagraphs 1(g), (j) and (l)

(a) Subparagraph 1(g) is without hindrance to terms by which a supplier of financial services reserves the right to terminate unilaterally a contract of indeterminate duration without notice where there is a valid reason, provided that the supplier is required to inform the other contracting party or parties thereof immediately.

(b) Subparagraph 1(j) is without hindrance to terms under which a supplier of financial services reserves the right to alter the rate of interest payable by the consumer or due to the latter, or the amount of other charges for financial services without notice where there is a valid reason, provided that the supplier is required to inform the other contracting party or parties thereof at the earliest opportunity and that the latter are free to dissolve the contract immediately.

Subparagraph 1(j) is also without hindrance to terms under

which a seller or supplier reserves the right to alter unilaterally the conditions of a contract of indeterminate duration, provided that he is required to inform the consumer with reasonable notice and that the consumer is free to dissolve the contract.

(c) Subparagraphs 1(g), (j) and (l) do not apply to:
- — transactions in transferable securities, financial instruments and other products or services where the price is linked to fluctuations in a stock exchange quotation or index or a financial market rate that the seller or supplier does not control;
- — contracts for the purchase or sale of foreign currency, traveller's cheques or international money orders denominated in foreign currency;

(d) Subparagraph 1(l) is without hindrance to price indexation clauses, where lawful, provided that the method by which prices vary is explicitly described.

General note

19.58 This is grey law. We are taught by hints, or given a first-time guide to some of the areas where we can look for unfair terms. The heads contain a mixture, in no particular discernible order, of terms affecting the after-sale relationship, terms restricting the Consumer's remedies after the contract has been breached, and terms affecting the formation of the contract. The preponderance of the heads given relate, whether deliberately or not, to the after-sale relationship. Many of these appear to focus on the situation where there is a change of circumstances after the date of the contract, and their inclusion in their present form indicates that the emphasis is mostly on predictability (as far as possible) to the Consumer at the date of the contract, and removal of any element of "whim" on the part of the Seller/supplier.

We are given no guarantee that all the heads in the Schedule will *be* unfair, nor that there are not many more unfair terms or types of terms, which are *not* mentioned in the Schedule.

Schedule 3, paragraph 1(c)

19.59 Compare the sections on the refusal of consent by a landlord or by a vendor in Chapter 13, The Exercise of Retained Rights. It may be that it would be in the interests of a landlord or a vendor whose contract was within the Regulations to argue that his refusal was strictly limited so that it might not go outside the paramount purpose of the contract at the time it was made, so as to escape having the right removed altogether by a Consumer purchaser or tenant.

As to (e) compare perhaps the consideration whether a 1 per cent increase in interest payable on default might be a penalty, by Colman J. in the non-consumer case of *Lordsvale Finance PLC v. Bank of*

Zambia.[70] He considered there was "no reason in principle why a contractual provision the effect of which was to increase the consideration payable under an executory contract upon the happening of a default should be struck down as a penalty if the increase could in the circumstances be explained as commercially justifiable, provided always that its dominant purpose was not to deter the other party from breach." He noted a number of older mortgage interest cases together with some Commonwealth authority, and observed that "at least on three occasions since 1725 the courts have been prepared to enforce increased rates of interest or analogous payments where the increase applied from the date of default "[only, as opposed to retrospectively as well]. His decision was reached in part to ensure consistency between our law and that of "the other major participant in the trade in question"—in this case regarded as New York. However, there is no reason to suppose that a similarly commercially justifiable increase (because of the increase in credit risk represented by default), clearly explained, might not be equally valid in a contract governed by the Regulations.

Schedule 3, paragraph 1(d), (e)

19.60 These will presumably overlap with our existing law on penalties and relief from forfeiture to some extent.

Schedule 3, paragraph 1(g)

19.61 See, however, paragraph 2 (a) and (c) of Schedule 3.

Schedule 3, paragraph 1(i)

19.62 This head would cover, in effect, a number of breaches of the Seller/supplier's duty of accuracy and duty of candour (alias his duty to be honest, straightforward and fair) affecting the formation of the contract.[71]

Schedule 3, paragraph 1(j)

19.63 See, however, paragraphs 2(b) and (c) of Schedule 3.

Schedule 3, paragraph 1(l)

19.64 See, however, paragraph 2(c) of Schedule 3.

Schedule 3, paragraph 1(m)

19.65 This head will prima facie cover a large number of "deeming" provisions in contracts: see Chapter 10, Excluding the Effect of the Fair-

[70] [1996] 3 W.L.R. 688.
[71] See Part II of this book.

dealing terms, for examples of these. Also included would probably be "conclusively presumed to be . . ." clauses, which in effect give the Seller/supplier the right to decide what the interpretation should be.

Schedule 3, paragraph 1(n)

19.66 Time-limits for claims which are unreasonable, whether because the time is simply not enough for the practicalities of claiming, or because they may "bite" before the Consumer has the relevant knowledge, are one example which comes to mind.

Schedule 3, paragraph 1(p)

19.67 It is not quite clear what is meant by "the guarantees"[72] It presumably means the practical worth of the guarantees or security the Consumer had at the date of the contract, since the contractual obligation on his part will be precisely the same before and after transfer. An example might be the transfer of service or warranty obligations, including perhaps the transfer of the reversion by a landlord with service and repair obligations. The transfer of mortgages may possibly be within the head, actually or by parallel reasoning, if the new mortgagee had a radically different policy or relevant standing.

2. Scope of subparagraphs 1(g) (j) and (l)

Subparagraph (a) "without notice where there is a valid reason."

Does there have to be a valid reason for the unilateral termination, or a valid reason for the absence of notice, or both? This point has been raised by Professor Trevor C. Hartley in Uncertainty in European Community Law[73] The English text leaves the matter entirely open. The French text which has an extra comma perhaps supports the latter. It would be safer to assume that the valid reason applies to both for the present. See Chapters 11–13 for the potential importance of the original paramount purpose of the contract or clause. It may be that the reason has to be valid as seen in the light of that paramount purpose. Thus, a perfectly good reason based on some supervening event not envisaged at the time of contracting might not be valid; nor a reason based on some factor which existed at the time of contracting, but was quite extraneous to the contract itself, *e.g.* some other contracts of the lender or seller.

Subparagraph 1(b)

"Without notice where there is a valid reason". See discussion above.

[72] The French: *"les garanties"*, is translated as "guarantee, security", by the Dictionnaire Economique et Juridique.
[73] [1996] C.L.J. 265.

It is difficult to see that it could be necessary in all cases for the contract to give the right to the Consumer to terminate the contract on being told ("at the earliest opportunity"). If the alteration in the rate of interest was fairly explained, in terms which could be understood by the kind of customer expected, and the effect of any reasonably anticipated conditions explained, and if there was a paramount purpose for the clause in question to which the alteration could be seen as ancillary (*i.e.* so that it could not be said the alteration was a matter of pure caprice or opportunism on the part of the seller/supplier—why should the clause not be perfectly fair within the meaning of the Regulations? The answer is that it probably could. When all is said and done, it remains the case that the subparagraphs in Schedule 2, despite being heavily qualified as above,[74] are still merely descriptions of contracts which may be objectionable, not which *must* be.

Schedule 3, paragraph 1(q)

19.68 Arbitration agreements, that is "agreements to submit to arbitration present or future disputes or differences (whether or not contractual)" which are terms of a contract within the Regulations may be scrutinised for unfairness within the meaning of the Regulations like any other term.[75]

Section 91 Arbitration Act 1996 renders unfair a term in a contract within the Regulations constituting an arbitration agreement in so far as it relates to a claim for a pecuniary remedy not exceeding certain limits to be specified by Order. The aim is no doubt to prevent the cost of arbitration proceedings operating as a deterrent to complaint on the part of Consumers where the cost would be disproportionate in relation to the claim.

One can only guess at the meaning of the obscure "arbitration not covered by legal provisions". It may be that it would include arbitration "ex aequo et bono", and perhaps a "review" of the dispute by a nominated person who was in effect permitted to exercise an unregulated discretion.

Schedule 3 paragraph 2(b)

19.69 The French Directive equivalent has a comma after the second "financial services" and before "without notice".

[74] In a way which can perhaps be misleading to English lawyers used to reading literalist English statutes.

[75] See sections 89–91 of the Arbitration Act 1996 affirming this.

PART 6

STATUTORY AND OTHER MATERIAL

Council Directive 93/13 of April 5, 1993 on unfair terms in consumer contracts

[1993] O.J. L95/25

THE COUNCIL OF THE EUROPEAN COMMUNITIES,

Having regard to the Treaty establishing the European Economic Community, and in particular Article 100 A thereof,

Having regard to the proposals from the Commission,

In cooperation with the European Parliament,

Having regard to the opinion of the Economic and Social Committee,

Whereas it is necessary to adopt measures with the aim of progressively establishing the internal market before 31 December 1992; whereas the internal market comprises an area without internal frontiers in which goods, persons, services and capital move freely;

Whereas the laws of Member States relating to the terms of contract between the seller of goods or supplier of services, on the one hand, and the consumer of them, on the other hand, show many disparities, with the result that the national markets for the sale of goods and services to consumers differ from each other and that distortions of competition may arise amongst the sellers and suppliers, notably when they sell and supply in other Member States;

Whereas, in particular, the laws of Member States relating to unfair terms in consumer contracts show marked divergences;

Whereas it is the responsibility of the Member States to ensure that contracts concluded with consumers do not contain unfair terms;

Whereas, generally speaking, consumers do not know the rules of law which, in Member States other than their own, govern contracts for the sale of goods or services; whereas this lack of awareness may deter them from direct transactions for the purchase of goods or services in another Member State;

Whereas, in order to facilitate the establishment of the internal market and to safeguard the citizen in his role as consumer when acquiring goods and services under contracts which are governed by the laws of Member States other than his own, it is essential to remove unfair terms from those contracts;

Whereas sellers of goods and suppliers of services will thereby be helped in their task of selling goods and supplying services, both at home and throughout the internal market; whereas competition will thus be stimulated, so contributing to increased choice for Community citizens as consumers;

Whereas the two Community programmes for a consumer protection and information policy underlined the importance of safeguarding consumers in the matter of unfair terms of contract; whereas this protection ought to be provided by laws and regulations which are either harmonized at Community level or adopted directly at that level;

Whereas in accordance with the principle laid down under the heading "Protection of the economic interests of the consumers", as stated in those programmes: "acquirers of goods and services should be protected against the abuse of power by the seller or supplier, in particular against one-sided standard contracts and the unfair exclusion of essential rights in contracts";

Whereas more effective protection of the consumer can be achieved by adopting uniform rules of law in the matter of unfair terms; whereas those rules should apply to all contracts concluded between sellers or suppliers and consumers; whereas as a result *inter alia* contracts relating to employment, contracts relating to succession rights, contracts relating to rights under family law and contracts relating to the incorporation and organization of companies or partnership agreements must be excluded from this Directive;

Whereas the consumer must receive equal protection under contracts concluded by word of mouth and written contracts regardless, in the latter case, of whether the terms of the contract are contained in one or more documents;

Whereas, however, as they now stand, national laws allow only partial harmonization to be envisaged; whereas, in particular, only contractual terms which have not been individually negotiated are covered by this Directive; whereas Member States should have the option, with due regard for the Treaty, to afford consumers a higher level of protection through national provisions that are more stringent than those of this Directive;

Whereas the statutory or regulatory provisions of the Member States which directly or indirectly determine the terms of consumer contracts are presumed not to contain unfair terms; whereas, therefore, it does not appear to be necessary to subject the terms which reflect mandatory statutory or regulatory provisions and the principles or provisions of international conventions to which the Member States or the Community are party; whereas in that respect the wording "mandatory statutory or regulatory provisions" in Article 1 (2) also covers rules which, according to the law, shall apply between the contracting parties provided that no other arrangements have been established;

Whereas Member States must however ensure that unfair terms are not included, particularly because this Directive also applies to trades, business or professions of a public nature;

Whereas it is necessary to fix in a general way the criteria for assessing the unfair character of contract terms;

Whereas the assessment, according to the general criteria chosen, of the unfair character of terms, in particular in sale or supply activities of a public nature providing collective services which take account of solidarity among users, must be supplemented by a means of making an overall evaluation of the different interests involved; whereas this constitutes the requirement of good faith; whereas, in making an assessment of good faith, particular regard shall be had to the strength of the bargaining positions of the parties, whether the consumer had an inducement to agree to the term and whether the goods or services were sold or supplied to the special order of the consumer; whereas the requirement of good faith may be satisfied by the seller or supplier where he deals fairly and equitably with the other party whose legitimate interests he has to take into account;

Whereas, for the purposes of this Directive, the annexed list of terms can be of indicative value only and, because of the cause of the minimal character of the Directive, the scope of these terms may be the subject of amplification or more restrictive editing by the Member States in their national laws;

Whereas the nature of goods or services should have an influence on assessing the unfairness of contractual terms;

Whereas, for the purposes of this Directive, assessment of unfair character shall not be made of terms which describe the main subject matter of the contract nor the quality/price ratio of the goods or services supplied; whereas the main subject matter of the contract and the price/quality ratio may nevertheless be taken into account in assessing the fairness of other terms; whereas it follows, *inter alia*, that in insurance contracts, the terms which clearly define or circumscribe the insured risk and the insurer's liability shall not be subject to such assessment since these restrictions are taken into account in calculating the premium paid by the consumer;

Whereas contracts should be drafted in plain, intelligible language, the consumer should actually be given an opportunity to examine all the terms and, if in doubt, the interpretation most favourable to the consumer should prevail;

Whereas Member States should ensure that unfair terms are not used in contracts concluded with consumers by a seller or supplier and that if, nevertheless, such terms are so used, they will not bind the consumer, and the contract will continue to bind the parties upon those terms if it is capable of continuing in existence without the unfair provisions;

Whereas there is a risk that, in certain cases, the consumer may be deprived of protection under this Directive by designating the law of a non-Member country as the law applicable to the contract; whereas provisions should therefore be included in this Directive designed to avert this risk;

Whereas persons or organizations, if regarded under the law of a Member State as having a legitimate interest in the matter, must have facilities for initiating proceedings concerning terms of contract drawn up for general use in contracts concluded with consumers, and in particular unfair terms, either before a court or before an administrative authority competent to decide upon complaints or to initiate appropriate legal proceedings; whereas this possibility does not, however, entail prior verification of the general conditions obtaining in individual economic sectors;

Whereas the courts or administrative authorities of the Member States must have at their disposal adequate and effective means of preventing the continued application of unfair terms in consumer contracts,

HAS ADOPTED THIS DIRECTIVE:

Article 1

1. The purpose of this Directive is to approximate the laws, regulations and administrative provisions of the Member States relating to unfair terms in contracts concluded between a seller or supplier and a consumer.

2. The contractual terms which reflect mandatory statutory or regulatory provisions and the provisions or principles of international conventions to which the Member States or the Community are party, particularly in the transport area, shall not be subject to the provisions of this Directive.

Article 2

For the purposes of this Directive:

(a) "unfair terms" means the contractual terms defined in Article 3;

(b) "consumer" means any natural person who, in contracts covered by this Directive, is acting for purposes which are outside his trade, business or profession;

(c) "seller or supplier" means any natural or legal person who, in contracts covered by this Directive, is acting for purposes relating to his trade, business or profession, whether publicly owned or privately owned.

Article 3

1. A contractual term which has not been individually negotiated shall be regarded as unfair if, contrary to the requirement of good faith, it causes a significant imbalance in the parties' rights and obligations arising under the contract, to the detriment of the consumer.

2. A term shall always be regarded as not individually regotiated where it has been drafted in advance and the consumer has therefore not been able to influence the substance of the term, particularly in the context of a pre-formulated standard contract.

The fact that certain aspects of a term or one specific term have been individually negotiated shall not exclude the application of this Article to the rest of a contract if an overall assessment of the contract indicates that it is nevertheless a pre-formulated standard contract.

Where any seller or supplier claims that a standard term has been individually negotiated, the burden of proof in this respect shall be incumbent on him.

3. The Annex shall contain an indicative and non-exhaustive list of the terms which may be regarded as unfair.

Article 4

1. Without prejudice to Article 7, the unfairness of a contractual term shall be assessed, taking into account the nature of the goods or services for which the contract was concluded and by referring, at the time of conclusion of the contract, to all the circumstances attending the conclusion of the contract and to all the other terms of the contract or of another contract on which it is dependent.

2. Assessment of the unfair nature of the terms shall relate neither to the definition of the main subject matter of the contract nor to the adequacy of the price and remuneration, on the one hand, as against the services or goods supplies in exchange, on the other, in so far as these terms are in plain, intelligible language.

Article 5

In the case of contracts where all or certain terms offered to the consumer are in writing, these terms must always be drafted in plain, intelligible language. Where there is doubt about the meaning of a term, the interpretation most favourable to the consumer shall prevail. This rule on interpretation shall not apply in the context of the procedures laid down in Article 7 (2).

Article 6

1. Member States shall lay down that unfair terms used in a contract concluded with a consumer by a seller or supplier shall, as provided for under their national law, not be binding on the consumer and that the contract shall continue to bind the parties upon those terms if it is capable of continuing in existence without the unfair terms.

2. Member States shall take the necessary measures to ensure that the consumer does not lose the protection granted by this Directive by virtue of the

choice of the law of a non-Member country as the law applicable to the contract if the latter has a close connection with the territory of the Member States.

Article 7

1. Member States shall ensure that, in the interests of consumers and of competitors, adequate and effective means exist to prevent the continued use of unfair terms in contracts concluded with consumers by sellers or suppliers.

2. The means referred to in paragraph 1 shall include provisions whereby persons or organizations, having a legitimate interest under national law in protecting consumers, may take action according to the national law concerned before the courts or before competent administrative bodies for a decision as to whether contractual terms drawn up for general use are unfair, so that they can apply appropriate and effective means to prevent the continued use of such terms.

3. With due regard for national laws, the legal remedies referred to in paragraph 2 may be directed separately or jointly against a number of sellers or suppliers from the same economic sector or their associations which use or recommend the use of the same general contractual terms or similar terms.

Article 8

Member States may adopt or retain the most stringent provisions compatible with the Treaty in the area covered by this Directive, to ensure a maximum degree of protection for the consumer.

Article 9

The Commission shall present a report to the European Parliament and to the Council concerning the application of this Directive five years at the latest after the date in Article 10 (1).

Article 10

1. Member States shall bring into force the laws, regulations and administrative provisions necessary to comply with this Directive no later than 31 December 1994. They shall forthwith inform the Commission thereof.

These provisions shall be applicable to all contracts concluded after 31 December 1994.

2. When Member States adopt these measures, they shall contain a reference to this Directive or shall be accompanied by such reference on the occasion of their official publication. The methods of making such a reference shall be laid down by the Member States.

3. Member States shall communicate the main provisions of national law which they adopt in the field covered by this Directive to the Commission.

Article 11

This Directive is addressed to the Member States.

Done at Luxembourg, 5 April 1993.

For the Council
The President
N. HELVEG PETERSEN

Annex

Terms referred to in Article 3 (3)

1. Terms which have the object or effect of:
    - (a) excluding or limiting the legal liability of a seller or supplier in the event of the death of a consumer or personal injury to the latter resulting from an act of omission of that seller or supplier;
    - (b) inappropriately excluding or limiting the legal rights of the consumer *vis-à-vis* the seller or supplier or another party in the event of total or partial non-performance or inadequate performance by the seller or supplier of any of the contractual obligations, including the option of offsetting a debt owed to the seller or supplier against any claim which the consumer may have against him;
    - (c) making an agreement binding on the consumer whereas provision of services by the seller or supplier is subject to a condition whose realization depends on his own will alone;
    - (d) permitting the seller or supplier to retain sums paid by the consumer where the latter decides not to conclude or perform the contract, without providing for the consumer to receive compensation of an equivalent amount from the seller or supplier where the latter is the party cancelling the contract;
    - (e) requiring any consumer who fails to fulfil his obligation to pay a disporportionately high sum in compensation;
    - f) authorizing the seller or supplier to dissolve the contract on a discretionary basis where the same facility is not granted to the consumer, or permitting the seller or supplier to retain the sums paid for services not yet supplied by him where it is the seller or supplier himself who dissolves the contract;
    - (g) enabling the seller or supplier to terminate a contract of indeterminate duration without reasonable notice except where there are serious grounds for doing so;
    - (h) automatically extending a contract of fixed duration where the consumer does not indicate otherwise, when the deadline fixed for the consumer to express this desire not to extend the contract is unreasonably early;
    - (i) irrevocably binding the consumer to terms with which he had no real opportunity of becoming acquainted before the conclusion of the contract;
    - (j) enabling the seller or supplier to alter the terms of the contract unilaterally without a valid reason which is specified in the contract;
    - (k) enabling the seller or supplier to alter unilaterally without a valid reason any characteristics of the product or service to be provided;
    - (l) providing for the price of goods to be determined at the time of delivery or allowing a seller of goods or supplier of services to increase their price without in both cases giving the consumer the corresponding right to cancel the contract if the final price is too high in relation to the price agreed when the contract was concluded;
    - (m) giving the seller or supplier the right to determine whether the goods or services supplied are in conformity with the contract, or giving him the exclusive right to interpret any term of the contract;
    - (n) limiting the seller's or supplier's obligation to respect commitments undertaken by his agents or making his commitments subject to compliance with a particular formality;
    - (o) obliging the consumer to fulfil all his obligations where the seller or supplier does not perform his;

(p) giving the seller or supplier the possibility of transferring his rights and obligations under the contract, where this may serve to reduce the guarantees for the consumer, without the latter's agreement;

(q) excluding or hindering the consumer's right to take legal action or exercise any other legal remedy, particularly by requiring the consumer to take disputes exclusively to arbitration not covered by legal provisions, unduly restricting the evidence available to him or imposing on him a burden of proof which, according to the applicable law, should lie with another party to the contract.

2. Scope of subparagraphs (g), (j) and (l)

(a) Subparagraph (g) is without hindrance to terms by which a supplier of financial services reserves the right to terminate unilaterally a contract of indeterminate duration without notice where there is a valid reason, provided that the supplier is required to inform the other contracting party or parties thereof immediately.

(b) Subparagraph (j) is without hindrance to terms under which a supplier of financial services reserves the right to alter the rate of interest payable by the consumer or due to the latter, or the amount of other charges for financial services without notice where there is a valid reason, provided that the supplier is required to inform the other contracting party or parties thereof at the earliest opportunity and that the latter are free to dissolve the contract immediately.

Subparagraph (j) is also without hindrance to terms under which a seller or supplier reserves the right to alter unilaterally the conditions of a contract of indeterminate duration, provided that he is required to inform the consumer with reasonable notice and that the consumer is free to dissolve the contract.

(c) Subparagraphs (g), (j) and (l) do not apply to:

— transactions in transferable securities, financial instruments and other products or services where the price is linked to fluctuations in a stock exchange quotation or index or a financial market rate that the seller or supplier does not control;

— contracts for the purchase or sale of foreign currency, traveller's cheques or international money orders denominated in foreign currency;

(d) Subparagraph (l) is without hindrance to price-indexation clauses, where lawful, provided that the method by which prices vary is explicitly described.

Investment Services Directive

[1993] O.J. L141/27

Article 11 of the Investment Services Directive deals with certain broadly good-faith requirements of investment firms which carry on home-regulated investment business in the United Kingdom. Article 11 appears below. It has been thought useful to add some comment also, if only because the relationship between Rules made under Article 11 and the New Regulations will require examination. Article 11, however, applies to Consumer and non-Consumer contracts alike (although the way it applies to a professional investor is likely to be wholly different: see below). The Securities and Investment Board "SIB" has the power under section 47A of the Financial Services Act 1986 as amended to "issue statements of principle with respect to the conduct and financial standing expected of persons authorized to carry on investment business". The SIB Statement of Principles has been effectively incorporated into, *inter alia,* the current Personal Investment Authority ("PIA") Rules and the corresponding Rules are noted below after each of the relevant Article 11 heads. The PIA Rules have been chosen as the most likely to affect Consumers within the meaning of the Unfair Contract Terms Regulation, 1994. Contracts made by members of the PIA with their customers incorporate the PIA Rules. The status of the Statement of Principle within the PIA Rules is rather curious. The Introduction states that "the Principles are intended to form a universal statement of the standards expected", and that they "apply directly to the conduct of investment business . . . of all authorized persons . . ." It is also explained that the principles are not exhaustive of the standards expected. "Conformity with the principles does not absolve a failure to observe other requirements, while the observance of other requirements does not necessarily amount to conformity with the principles." On the other hand, the Introduction to the PIA Rules also states, "The principles do not give rise to actions for damages, but will be available for purposes of discipline and other intervention." This is perfectly understandable as coming from the SIB which only has the duty to make the rules for others to observe, but makes little sense as coming from the PIA. More importantly, it makes little sense in the light of the Investment Services Directive itself, which simply states that rules of conduct are to be drawn up incorporating the points from Article 11, which the investment firms are to observe at all times. "At all times" prima facie means when dealing with the public as well as when dealing with the regulator. One rationalization would no doubt be that the Principles do not give rise to an action for damages on the part of the investor unless and until incorporated in a contract for investment business which is breached. A further alternative, suggested by the possible good-faith ancestry of certain of the Principles, would be that they should be treated as implied terms of the contract made by the investor with the investment firm, but implied terms which do not sound directly in damages: compare Chapter 2, The Legal Nature of Good Faith and the duty "of utmost good faith" in insurance law there discussed in this context. In this event, the express terms of the contract would fall to be construed in the light of the Principles and gaps would be filled in so far as appropriate by reading in the Principles. However, on this view it would be possible for the express terms of the investment contract to exclude the application of one or more Principles, provided this is done fairly and in good faith (compare Chapter 10: Excluding the Effect of the Fair Dealing Terms). This is, however, arguably inconsistent with Article 11 of the Directive which provides that the rules of conduct therein are to be observed "at all times".

If broken, the Principles in the PIA Rules thus may afford an indirect claim for breach of contract by the client. The contract with the customer incorporating the PIA Rules will in any event be a Contract of Adhesion for the purposes of the New Regulations. The terms will therefore be subject to scrutiny for unfairness: see above. A separate problem which may arise is whether certain parts of the SIB Statement of Principle may not be somewhat narrower in scope than Article 11 of the Investment Services Directive. A consequent question may be whether a Marleasing-type construction, *i.e.* a wide, purposive one, taking into account the objectives of the Directive, will be sufficient to cure any defect of this kind which may exist.

The SIB is plainly alive to the interesting possibilities to which the Investment Services Directive gives rise for development by national regulatory bodies of their own standards as to relevant matters, in broad conformity with the continental ones: see the speech by the Chairman on October 29, 1996, "Standards of Market Integrity in the New World", in which the desire of the SIB over the last few years was expressed for "a set of overarching principles that we could apply in shaping our response to markets as they developed and new issues as they arose". It may be hoped, perhaps, that our own home-grown good-faith rules, married with the unparalleled experience of financial markets which London has to offer the rest of Europe, may provide a key to the spirit behind the Investment Services Directive, and to a simpler and more imaginative use of the good-faith/fair dealing principles discernible in that Directive: see in particular the note below on the link between "loyalement et équitablement" and good faith. The United Kingdom, which already has a plethora of statutes and currently at least, a highly literalist approach to contract terms, has perhaps suffered particularly from the influx of prescriptive rules which have been imposed from the E.U.: it would be pleasant to think that the United Kingdom might also take a lead in providing the way out of the morass.

Article 11

1. Member States shall draw up rules of conduct which investment firms shall observe at all times. Such rules must implement at least the principles set out in the following indents and must be applied in such a way as to take account of the profesional nature of the person for whom the service is provided. The Member States shall also apply these rules where appropriate for the non-core services listed in Section C of the Annex. These principles shall ensure that an investment firm:

[1]—acts honestly and fairly [loyalement et équitablement] in conducting its business activities in the best interests of its clients and [of] the integrity of the market,

(**PIA Rule 1**: A firm should observe high standards of integrity and fair dealing.)

Note: The same expression "loyalement et équitablement" occurs in the Unfair Contract Terms Regulations 1994, where it is used to describe the requirement of good faith. See the comment on good faith in the Regulations, above. It seems possible that the requirement is not dissimilar to that of our own original judge-made good-faith/fair-dealing principles, and at all events could most fruitfully be so interpreted. Thus, the requirement of good faith would require the investment firm to comply with its duty of accuracy (e.g. no swamping with verbiage that requires several hours and a wet towel for the unsophisticated investor to understand); and candour (no part-true statements, so that e.g. disclosure to the investor of the effect of the first five years' commission on a life assurance policy would be insufficient compliance, if the firm remained silent about any latent defects such as the effect of commission on the remaining years of the policy. Latent defects would mean defects which the kind of investigation reasonably to be expected of that investor (in the case of non-professionals, probably not much if any) would not reveal. A similar duty of accuracy and candour would apply to exclusion clauses: see Chapter 10 for these.

If interpreted as above, there would be no relevant conflict between the Unfair Contract Terms Regulations 1994 and the Investment Services Directive. Further, the customer would be in a much better position than at present, in that he could more readily prove a specific breach of the Directive and PIA Rule provision and thus breach of contract on the part of the investment firm. If not, we shall no doubt be faced with the unsatisfactory position that the PIA Rules may themselves potentially fall to be treated as unfair; see comment to Regulations, above.

"in the best interests of its clients and the integrity of the market"

This twin duty is not explained, nor is there any explanation of the concept "integrity" of the market. It may be that the expression is intended to mean something like "the uprightness" of the market.[1] *There should be no real conflict between the two duties, provided one presupposes or implies into the contract a desire by both parties to do what they ought. We may compare a barrister's twin duty to do his or her level best for the client, and on the other hand, to inform and give a fair picture to, the court. The twin duty to the client and the market might perhaps equally have been put as "in the best interests of the client provided always that that is consistent with the firm's upholding the integrity of the market at all times".*

The PIA Rule may in any event be thought a milk and water affair by comparison with the Directive. "Be good", or as here, "Observe high standards of integrity and fair dealing" does not tell the firm what it has to do, nor the customer what to expect. "Be accurate, be candid", especially with the illustrations provided by the nineteenth-century cases[2] *does away with the need for a myriad of detailed rules, and gives both sides a reasonably clear picture. The reason is that the more abstract expression has a greater subjective content and correspondingly less objective meaning. "High standards" does not really help in this regard since we have nothing objective to which they are to apply: compare "Be* very *good". See, however, Rule 6 below, which supplements this Rule.*

[2]—acts with due skill, care and diligence, in the best interests of its clients and the integrity of the market,

(**PIA Rule 2**: A firm should act with due skill, care and diligence.)

The question, diligence, etc., in doing what, arises and is left unspecified. Since the Directive leaves the matter open, we must assume that it covers anything done for the customer. If the firm is giving advice, e.g. what kind of investment will suit the client best, we have few problems: the traditional duty of a professional person arises. But what if the investment firm is, say, an insurance or other company selling through its own employees? What does it have to be skilled, careful and diligent about? It is not giving advice about a range of different products, only about its own. It is suggested the answer in this case is the lesser duty on a seller—to describe what

[1] See paper delivered by the Chairman of the SIB, on October 29, 1966, "Standards of Market Integrity in the New World" noting the absence of elucidation about the meaning of the concept of market integrity, but suggesting a meaning of "a marketplace operating to high standards for the benefit of all market users".

[2] See *e.g.* Chaps. 5, 7 and 10.

it is selling with accuracy and candour, utilizing information "within its knowledge".[3] *The skill, care and diligence may be seen as exercisable on that.*

[3]—has and employs effectively the resources and procedures that are necessary for the proper performance of its business activities,

(**PIA Rule 8**: A firm should ensure that it maintains adequate financial resources to meet its investment business commitments and to withstand the risks to which its business is subject.)

Note: The PIA Rule no doubt seeks to apply the Directive to the nature of the contract in question, which must be the right approach for rules made under the Directive. However, one may query whether Rule 8 would not be better seen as an application of the Directive principle to investment rather than an enunciation of it. The old good-faith rule that a business is deemed to keep the kind of records reasonably to be expected, and to make proper arrangements to have sufficient access to them so that it can comply with its duty of accuracy and candour would seem to be included in the Directive principle but is absent from the PIA Rule.

[4]—seeks from its clients information regarding their financial situations, investment experience [leur expérience en matière d'investissement] and objectives as regards the services requested.

(**PIA Rule 4**: A firm should seek from customers it advises or for whom it exercises discretion any information about their circumstances and investment objectives which might reasonably be expected to be relevant in enabling it to fulfil its responsibilities to them.)

Note: There are a number of ways in which the PIA Rule is arguably narrower than the Directive here.

- *(i) The Directive Principle is not limited to circumstances when the firm advises or exercises discretions: it appears in effect to place the responsibility for fitness for purposes in all cases on the firm—at least where the investor is insufficiently experienced (in practice, probably any investor who is not an investment professional) to perform this job himself. In the latter case, the information would not "reasonably be expected to be relevant . . ." because the investor could shoulder the responsibility.*[4]
- *(ii) there is no reference to the customer's "investment experience" in the PIA Rule. In fact even if the expression had found its way into the Rule, the English expression is probably itself a little ambiguous: the French perhaps puts across better the notion that the investor might not have any investment experience at all.*
- *(iii) "which might reasonably be expected to be relevant in fulfilling its responsibilities towards them" in the PIA Rule probably narrows the Directive slightly ("expected to be relevant . . ." is substituted for simply "as regards", but the alteration is unlikely to make much practical difference.*
- *(iv) It is a little difficult to see why "the services requested" which is a good understandable expression, has been replaced with "its responsibilities towards them" which merely raises the question, what are its responsibilities.*
- *(v) "Investment objectives" in the PIA Rule has a prima facie more limited scope than "objectives". The former is liable to be thought (by some, at least) limited to matters such as medium risk, high income, capital growth, etc., while the Directive covers what you might call the "raw" version; e.g. I want to go round the world when I am 85, or, I want a fund to pay for my grandchildren's education, which needs a bit of translating to become an*

[3] See for this expression, earlier chapters of this book, *passim*.

[4] Compare the Sale of Goods Act 1979 reference to reliance on the skill and judgment of the seller as regards fitness for purpose.

investment objective. This translating is prima facie the responsibility of the investment firm.

[5]—makes adequate disclosure of relevant material information in its dealings [les informations utiles dans le cadre de négociations] with its clients,

(**PIA Rule 6**: A firm should take reasonable steps to give a customer it advises, in a comprehensible and timely way, any information needed to enable him to make a balanced and informed decision. A firm should similarly be ready to provide a customer with a full and fair account of the fulfilment of its responsibilities to him.)

Note: (i) "reasonable steps to give" is a watering down of the Directive duty which is simply to "make adequate disclosure". The PIA wording prima facie leaves open to the firm the argument that there was useful information which it was not reasonable to give the investor.

(ii) Subject as above, the PIA Rule draws out and explains admirably the two duties which may well be comprised in the Directive: to give relevant and useful information in the pre-formation stage of the contract (the duty to describe, in the case of a seller: no doubt the duty to advise in the case of an adviser hardly needs mention); and further imposes a duty to explain, presumably after the contract, what the seller/adviser, etc., has done. Again, the somewhat uncertain expression "fulfilment of his responsibilities" could usefully be replaced with something more concrete. (What if he has not fulfilled them: does he have a duty to explain what he has omitted? He probably does: see "full and fair"; but why have this unnecessary uncertainty in the first place?)

[6]—tries to avoid conflicts of interests and, when they cannot be avoided, ensures that its clients are fairly treated, and

(**PIA Rule 6**: A firm should either avoid any conflict of interest arising or, where conflicts arise, should ensure fair treatment to all its customers by disclosure, internal rules of confidentiality, declining to act, or otherwise. A firm should not unfairly place its interests above those of its customers and, where a properly informed customer would reasonably expect that the firm would place his interests above its own, the firm should live up to that expectation.)

Note: (i) The Directive only allows conflicts of interest to exist in a transaction when they cannot be avoided. The PIA Rule, by contrast, appears to allow them readily, subject to "disclosure, internal rules about confidentiality [Chinese walls?], declining to act, or otherwise".

(ii) Some definition of a "conflict of interest" is desirable. A simple sale of goods, say, is not normally thought of as giving rise to a "conflict of interest" in any sense. Nor, inherently, does a sale of an assurance policy (assuming that all forms of latent profit such as commission arrangements, surrender penalties, etc., are properly explained (and where appropriate, these and other terms comply with the Unfair Contract Terms Regulations 1994). Consequently it would seem to arise where the firm is acting as agent rather than straight seller. The distinction between the good-faith duty of a seller and the "fiduciary" duty of an agent could do with more attention in this context.

(1) An agent will have a ("fiduciary") duty not to make a separate personal profit out of the way he structures the client transaction, unless that is properly (and specifically: see Chapter 9: Dealings with the Vulnerable Buyer or Seller) explained to the client. The line between this kind of disclosure and disclosure of latent defects not likely to be discovered by the buyer is not a clear-cut one, given the nature of the contracts we are talking about.

The propriety of licensing "Chinese walls" requires further consideration in this context.[5] *Why are they not something which "can be avoided"? What they can amount to is a licence to an organization as a whole to make an undisclosed personal profit provided the right-hand part of the organization that makes the investment is kept separate and ignorant of the decisions being made by the left-hand part that makes the personal profit. But this does not mean that the right hand cannot guess what decisions by it will help the left hand: e.g. if it invests in a certain fund, part-owned or part-managed by the left hand, it must be evident to it this will bring in useful payments to the left hand. True, all this will be information that is useful and relevant and should be disclosed to the client under [5] above; but there is still a conflict of interest. The Directive does not in terms say that there may be a conflict of interest provided full and specific disclosure is made.*

(2) *The other meaning, in which a degree of "conflict" is both permissible, if properly managed, and "cannot" be avoided, in a more real sense of the word, is where an agent carries out the same type of transaction for clients whose interests differ: to take an obvious example, an agent for the buying and selling of shares will have among his clients both sellers of shares who will want a high price, and buyers who will want a low price. This is certainly a case for disclosure, and for specific rules about how transactions can be carried out in a manner calculated to be fair and acceptable to both.*[6]

[7]—complies with all regulatory requirements applicable to the conduct of its business activities so as to promote the best interests of its clients and the integrity of the market.

(**PIA Rule 3**: A firm should observe high standards of market conduct. It should also, to the extent endorsed for the purpose of this principle, comply with any code or standard as in force from time to time and as it applies to the firm either according to its terms or by ruling made under it.)

See above for comment on the use of abstract expressions which do not tell the firm what to do or the customer what to expect. Further, the purpose manner of compliance, i.e. in order to promote the best interests of the customer and the integrity of the market, have disappeared. The Directive itself is rather more clearly worded.

2. Without prejudice to any decisions to be taken in the context of the harmonization of the rules of conduct, their implementation and the supervision of compliance with them shall remain the responsibility of the Member State in which a service is provided.

3. Where an investment firm executes an order, for the purposes of applying the rules referred to in paragraph 1 the professional nature of the investor shall be assessed with respect to the investor from whom the order originates, regardless of whether the order was placed directly by the investor himself or indirectly through an investment firm providing the service referred to in Section A(1)(a) of the Annex.[7]

[5] See for much interesting discussion of this and other related questions, The Law Commission Consultation Paper No. 124 Fiduciary Duties and Regulatory Rules 1992.

[6] Compare the Privy Council case of *Kelly v. Cooper* [1993] A.C. 205, in which it was held to be an implied term of an estate agency contract (because the principal would know that the agent acted for numerous buyers, all of whose affairs had to be kept confidential) that the agent might keep confidential from client A relevant information which he had received as confidential information from client B. The probably more stringent duties of disclosure of the Directive make the implied-term solution of that case less likely in the financial services context without more, however.

[7] General note: The PIA Rules disapply the above "Principles" in the case of European Members: see Lomnicka and Powell, *Financial Services Encyclopaedia*, 8-1115.

Misrepresentation Act 1967

(1967 c. 7)

An Act to amend the law relating to innocent misrepresentations and to amend sections 11 and 35 of the Sale of Goods Act 1893

[March 22, 1967]

Northern Ireland. This Act does not apply; see s 6(4) post.

1. Removal of certain bars to rescission for innocent misrepresentation

Where a person has entered into a contract after a misrepresentation has been made to him, and—

(a) the misrepresentation has become a term of the contract; or

(b) the contract has been performed;

or both, then, if otherwise he would be entitled to rescind the contract without alleging fraud, he shall be so entitled, subject to the provisions of this Act, notwithstanding the matters mentioned in paragraphs (a) and (b) of this section.

2. Damages for misrepresentation

(1) Where a person has entered into a contract after a misrepresentation has been made to him by another party thereto and as a result thereof has suffered loss, then, if the person making the misrepresentation would be liable to damages in respect thereof had the misrepresentation been made fraudulently, that person shall be so liable notwithstanding that the misrepresentation was not made fraudulently, unless he proves that he had reasonable ground to believe and did believe up to the time the contract was made that the facts represented were true.

(2) Where a person has entered into a contract after a misrepresentation has been made to him otherwise than fraudulently, and he would be entitled, by reason fo the misrepresentation, to rescind the contract, then, if it is claimed, in any proceedings arising out of the contract, that the contract ought to be or has been rescinded the court or arbitrator may declare the contract subsisting and award damages in lieu of rescission, if of opinion that it would be equitable to do so, having regard to the nature of the misrepresentation and the loss that would be caused by it if the contract were upheld, as well as to the loss that rescission would cause to the other party.

(3) Damages may be awarded against a person under subsection (2) of this section whether or not he is liable to damages under subsection (1) thereof, but where he is so liable any award under the said subsection (2) shall be taken into account in assessing his liability under the said subsection (1).

[3. Avoidance of provision excluding liability for misrepresentation

If a contract contains a term which would exclude or restrict—

(a) any liability to which a party to a contract may be subject by reason of any misrepresentation made by him before the contract was made; or

(b) any remedy available to another party to the contract by reason of such a misrepresentation, that term shall be of no effect except in so far as it satisfies the requirement of reasonableness as stated in section 11(1) of the Unfair Contract Terms Act 1977; and it is for those claiming that the term satisfies that requirement to show that it does.]*

4. (Repealed by the Sale of Goods Act 1979, s 63(2), Sch 3.)

5. Saving for past transactions

Nothing in this Act shall apply in relation to any misrepresentation or contract of sale which is made before the commencement of this Act.

6. Short title, commencement and extent

(1) This Act may be cited as the Misrepresentation Act 1967.

(2) This Act shall come into operation at the expiration of the period of one month beginning with the date on which it is passed.

(3) (*Applies to Scotland only.*)

(4) This Act does not extend to Northern Ireland.

* This section was substituted by the Unfair Contract Terms Act 1977, s 8(1).

Unfair Contract Terms Act 1977

(1977 c. 50)

ARRANGEMENT OF SECTIONS

PART I

AMENDMENT OF LAW FOR ENGLAND AND WALES AND NORTHERN IRELAND

Introductory

SECT.
1. Scope of Part I.

Avoidance of liability for negligence, breach of contract, etc.

2. Negligence liability.
3. Liability arising in contract.
4. Unreasonable indemnity clauses.

Liability arising from sale or supply of goods

5. "Guarantee" of consumer goods.
6. Sale and hire-purchase.
7. Miscellaneous contracts under which goods pass.

Other provisions about contracts

8. Misrepresentation.
9. Effect of breach.
10. Evasion by means of secondary contract.

Explanatory provisions

11. The "reasonableness" test.
12. "Dealing as consumer".
13. Varieties of exemption clause.
14. Interpretation of Part I.

PART II

AMENDMENT OF LAW FOR SCOTLAND

15. Scope of Part II.
16. Liability for breach of duty.
17. Control of unreasonable exemptions in consumer or standard form contracts.
18. Unreasonable indemnity clauses in consumer contracts.
19. "Guarantee" of consumer goods.
20. Obligations implied by law in sale and hire-purchase contracts.

An Act to impose further limits on the extent to which under the law of England and Wales and Northern Ireland civil liability for breach of contract, or for negligence or other breach of duty, can be avoided by means of contract terms and otherwise, and under the law of Scotland civil liability can be avoided by means of contract terms. [October 26, 1977]

PART I

AMENDMENT OF LAW FOR ENGLAND AND WALES AND NORTHERN IRELAND

Introductory

Scope of Part I

1.—(1) For the purposes of this Part of this Act, "negligence" means the breach—

(a) of any obligation, arising from the express or implied terms of a contract, to take reasonable care or exercise reasonable skill in the performance of the contract;
(b) of any common law duty to take reasonable care or exercise reasonable skill (but not any stricter duty);
(c) of the common duty of care imposed by the Occupiers' Liability Act 1957 or the Occupiers' Liability Act (Northern Ireland) 1957.

(2) This Part of this Act is subject to Part III; and in relation to contracts, the operation of sections 2 to 4 and 7 is subject to the exceptions made by Schedule 1.

(3) In the case of both contract and tort, sections 2 to 7 apply (except where

the contrary is stated in section 6 (4)) only to business liability, that is liability for breach of obligations or duties arising—

(a) from things done or to be done by a person in the course of a business (whether his own business or another's); or

(b) from the occupation of premises used for business purposes of the occupier;

and references to liability are to be read accordingly.

(4) In relation to any breach of duty or obligation, it is immaterial for any purpose of this Part of this Act whether the breach was inadvertent or intentional, or whether liability for it arises directly or vicariously.

Avoidance of liability for negligence, breach of contract, etc.

Negligence liability

2.—(1) A person cannot by reference to any contract term or to a notice given to persons generally or to particular persons exclude or restrict his liability for death or personal injury resulting from negligence.

(2) In the case of other loss or damage, a person cannot so exclude or restrict his liability for negligence except in so far as the term or notice satisfies the requirement of reasonableness.

(3) Where a contract term or notice purports to exclude or restrict liability for negligence a person's agreement to or awareness of it is not of itself to be taken as indicating his voluntary acceptance of any risk.

Liability arising in contract

3.—(1) This section applies as between contracting parties where one of them deals as consumer or on the other's written standard terms of business.

(2) As against that party, the other cannot by reference to any contract term—

(a) when himself in breach of contract, exclude or restrict any liability of his in respect of the breach; or

(b) claim to be entitled—

(i) to render a contractual performance substantially different from that which was reasonably expected of him, or

(ii) in respect of the whole or any part of his contractual obligation, to render no performance at all,

except in so far as (in any of the cases mentioned above in this subsection) the contract term satisfies the requirement of reasonableness.

Unreasonable indemnity clauses

4.—(1) A person dealing as consumer cannot by reference to any contract term be made to indemnify another person (whether a party to the contract or not) in respect of liability that may be incurred by the other for negligence or breach of contract, except in so far as the contract term satisfies the requirement of reasonableness.

(2) This section applies whether the liability in question—

(a) is directly that of the person to be indemnified or is incurred by him vicariously;

(b) is to the person dealing as consumer or to someone else.

Liability arising from sale or supply of goods

"Guarantee" of consumer goods

5.—(1) In the case of goods of a type ordinarily supplied for private use or consumption, where loss or damage—

(a) arises from the goods proving defective while in consumer use; and
(b) results from the negligence of a person concerned in the manufacture or distribution of the goods,

liability for the loss or damage cannot be excluded or restricted by reference to any contract term or notice contained in or operating by reference to a guarantee of the goods.

(2) For these purposes—

(a) goods are to be regarded as "in consumer use" when a person is using them, or has them in his possession for use, otherwise than exclusively for the purposes of a business; and
(b) anything in writing is a guarantee if it contains or purports to contain some promise or assurance (however worded or presented) that defects will be made good by complete or partial replacement, or by repair, monetary compensation or otherwise.

(3) This section does not apply as between the parties to a contract under or in pursuance of which possession or ownership of the goods passed.

Sale and hire-purchase

6.—(1) Liability for breach of the obligations arising from—

(a) section 12 of the Sale of Goods Act 1893 (seller's implied undertakings as to title, etc.);
(b) section 8 of the Supply of Goods (Implied Terms) Act 1973 (the corresponding thing in relation to hire-purchase),

cannot be excluded or restricted by reference to any contract term.

(2) As against a person dealing as consumer, liability for breach of the obligations arising from—

(a) section 13, 14 or 15 of the 1893 Act (seller's implied undertakings as to conformity of goods with description or sample, or as to their quality or fitness for a particular purpose);
(b) section 9, 10 or 11 of the 1973 Act (the corresponding things in relation to hire-purchase),

cannot be excluded or restricted by reference to any contract term.

(3) As against a person dealing otherwise than as consumer, the liability specified in subsection (2) above can be excluded or restricted by reference to a contract term, but only in so far as the term satisfies the requirement of reasonableness.

(4) The liabilities referred to in this section are not only the business liabilities defined by section 1 (3), but include those arising under any contract of sale of goods or hire-purchase agreement.

Miscellaneous contracts under which goods pass

7.—(1) Where the possession or ownership of goods passes under or in pursuance of a contract not governed by the law of sale of goods or hire-purchase, subsections (2) to (4) below apply as regards the effect (if any) to be given to contract terms excluding or restricting liability for breach of obligation arising by implication of law from the nature of the contract.

(2) As against a person dealing as consumer, liability in respect of the goods' correspondence with description or sample, or their quality or fitness for any particular purpose, cannot be excluded or restricted by reference to any such term.

(3) As against a person dealing otherwise than as consumer, that liability can be excluded or restricted by reference to such a term, but only in so far as the term satisfies the requirement of reasonableness.

(4) Liability in respect of—

(a) the right to transfer ownership of the goods, or give possession; or

(b) the assurance of quiet possession to a person taking goods in pursuance of the contract,

cannot be excluded or restricted by reference to any such term except in so far as the term satisfies the requirement of reasonableness.

(5) This section does not apply in the case of goods passing on a redemption of trading stamps within the Trading Stamps Act 1964 or the Trading Stamps Act (Northern Ireland) 1965.

Other provisions about contracts

Misrepresentation

8.—(1) In the Misrepresentation Act 1967, the following is substituted for section 3—

"**Avoidance of provision excluding liability for misrepresentation**

3. If a contract contains a term which would exclude or restrict—

(a) any liability to which a party to a contract may be subject by reason of any misrepresentation made by him before the contract was made; or

(b) any remedy available to another party to the contract by reason of such a misrepresentation,

that term shall be of no effect except in so far as it satisfies the requirement of reasonableness as stated in section 11 (1) of the Unfair Contract Terms Act 1977; and it is for those claiming that the term satisfies that requirement to show that it does."

(2) The same section is substituted for section 3 of the Misrepresentation Act (Northern Ireland) 1967.

Effect of breach

9.—(1) Where for reliance upon it a contract term has to satisfy the requirement of reasonableness, it may be found to do so and be given effect accordingly notwithstanding that the contract has been terminated either by breach or by a party electing to treat it as repudiated.

(2) Where on a breach the contract is nevertheless affirmed by a party entitled to treat it as repudiated, this does not of itself exclude the requirement of reasonableness in relation to any contract term.

Evasion by means of secondary contract

10. A person is not bound by any contract term prejudicing or taking away rights of his which arise under, or in connection with the performance of, another contract, so far as those rights extend to the enforcement of another's liability which this Part of this Act prevents that other from excluding or restricting.

Explanatory provisions

The "reasonableness" test

11.—(1) In relation to a contract term, the requirement of reasonableness for the purposes of this Part of this Act, section 3 of the Misrepresentation Act 1967 and section 3 of the Misrepresentation Act (Northern Ireland) 1967 is that the term shall have been a fair and reasonable one to be included having regard to the circumstances which were, or ought reasonably to have been, known to or in the contemplation of the parties when the contract was made.

(2) In determining for the purposes of section 6 or 7 above whether a contract term satisfies the requirement of reasonableness, regard shall be had in

particular to the matters specified in Schedule 2 to this Act; but this subsection does not prevent the court or arbitrator from holding, in accordance with any rule of law, that a term which purports to exclude or restrict any relevant liability is not a term of the contract.

(3) In relation to a notice (not being a notice having contractual effect), the requirement of reasonableness under this Act is that it should be fair and reasonable to allow reliance on it, having regard to all the circumstances obtaining when the liability arose or (but for the notice) would have arisen.

(4) Where by reference to a contract term or notice a person seeks to restrict liability to a specified sum of money, and the question arises (under this or any other Act) whether the term or notice satisfies the requirement of reasonableness, regard shall be had in particular (but without prejudice to subsection (2) above in the case of contract terms) to—

(a) the resources which he could expect to be available to him for the purpose of meeting the liability should it arise; and

(b) how far it was open to him to cover himself by insurance.

(5) It is for those claiming that a contract term or notice satisfies the requirement of reasonableness to show that it does.

"Dealing as consumer"

12.—(1) A party to a contract "deals as consumer" in relation to another party if—

(a) he neither makes the contract in the course of a business nor holds himself out as doing so; and

(b) the other party does make the contract in the course of a business; and

(c) in the case of a contract governed by the law of sale of goods or hire-purchase, or by section 7 of this Act, the goods passing under or in pursuance of the contract are of a type ordinarily supplied for private use or consumption.

(2) But on a sale by auction or by competitive tender the buyer is not in any circumstances to be regarded as dealing as consumer.

(3) Subject to this, it is for those claiming that a party does not deal as consumer to show that he does not.

Varieties of exemption clause

13.—(1) To the extent that this Part of this Act prevents the exclusion or restriction of any liability it also prevents—

(a) making the liability or its enforcement subject to restrictive or onerous conditions;

(b) excluding or restricting any right or remedy in respect of the liability, or subjecting a person to any prejudice in consequence of his pursuing any such right or remedy;

(c) excluding or restricting rules of evidence or procedure;

and (to that extent) sections 2 and 5 to 7 also prevent excluding or restricting liability by reference to terms and notices which exclude or restrict the relevant obligation or duty.

(2) But an agreement in writing to submit present or future differences to arbitration is not to be treated under this Part of this Act as excluding or restricting any liability.

Interpretation of Part I

14. In this Part of this Act—

"business" includes a profession and the activities of any government department or local or public authority;

"goods" has the same meaning as in the Sale of Goods Act 1893;
"hire-purchase agreement" has the same meaning as in the Consumer Credit Act 1974;
"negligence" has the meaning given by section 1 (1);
"notice" includes an announcement, whether or not in writing, and any other communication or pretended communication; and
"personal injury" includes any disease and any impairment of physical or mental condition.

PART II

AMENDMENT OF LAW FOR SCOTLAND

Scope of Part II

15.—(1) This Part of this Act applies only to contracts, is subject to Part III of this Act and does not affect the validity of any discharge or indemnity given by a person in consideration of the receipt by him of compensation in settlement of any claim which he has.

(2) Subject to subsection (3) below, sections 16 to 18 of this Act apply to any contract only to the extent that the contract—

(a) relates to the transfer of the ownership or possession of goods from one person to another (with or without work having been done on them);
(b) constitutes a contract of service or apprenticeship;
(c) relates to services of whatever kind, including (without prejudice to the foregoing generality) carriage, deposit and pledge, care and custody, mandate, agency, loan and services relating to the use of land;
(d) relates to the liability of an occupier of land to persons entering upon or using that land;
(e) relates to a grant of any right or permission to enter upon or use land not amounting to an estate or interest in the land.

(3) Notwithstanding anything in subsection (2) above, sections 16 to 18—

(a) do not apply to any contract to the extent that the contract—
    (i) is a contract of insurance (including a contract to pay an annuity on human life);
    (ii) relates to the formation, constitution or dissolution of any body corporate or unincorporated association or partnership;
(b) apply to—
    a contract of marine salvage or towage;
    a charter party of a ship or hovercraft;
    a contract for the carriage of goods by ship or hovercraft; or
    a contract to which subsection (4) below relates,
  only to the extent that—
    (i) both parties deal or hold themselves out as dealing in the course of a business (and then only in so far as the contract purports to exclude or restrict liability for breach of duty in respect of death or personal injury); or
    (ii) the contract is a consumer contract (and then only in favour of the consumer).

(4) This subsection relates to a contract in pursuance of which goods are carried by ship or hovercraft and which either—

(a) specifies ship or hovercraft as the means of carriage over part of the journey to be covered; or
(b) makes no provision as to the means of carriage and does not exclude ship or hovercraft as that means,

in so far as the contract operates for and in relation to the carriage of the goods by that means.

Liability for breach of duty

16.—(1) Where a term of a contract purports to exclude or restrict liability for breach of duty arising in the course of any business or from the occupation of any premises used for business purposes of the occupier, that term—

(a) shall be void in any case where such exclusion or restriction is in respect of death or personal injury;

(b) shall, in any other case, have no effect if it was not fair and reasonable to incorporate the term in the contract.

(2) Subsection (1) (a) above does not affect the validity of any discharge and indemnity given by a person, on or in connection with an award to him of compensation for pneumoconiosis attributable to employment in the coal industry, in respect of any further claim arising from his contracting that disease.

(3) Where under subsection (1) above a term of a contract is void or has no effect, the fact that a person agreed to, or was aware of, the term shall not of itself be sufficient evidence that he knowingly and voluntarily assumed any risk.

Control of unreasonable exemptions in consumer or standard form contracts

17.—(1) Any term of a contract which is a consumer contract or a standard form contract shall have no effect for the purpose of enabling a party to the contract—

(a) who is in breach of a contractual obligation, to exclude or restrict any liability of his to the consumer or customer in respect of the breach;

(b) in respect of a contractual obligation, to render no performance, or to render a performance substantially different from that which the consumer or customer reasonably expected from the contract;

if it was not fair and reasonable to incorporate the term in the contract.

(2) In this section "customer" means a party to a standard form contract who deals on the basis of written standard terms of business of the other party to the contract who himself deals in the course of a business.

Unreasonable indemnity clauses in consumer contracts

18.—(1) Any term of a contract which is a consumer contract shall have no effect for the purpose of making the consumer indemnify another person (whether a party to the contract or not) in respect of liability which that other person may incur as a result of breach of duty or breach of contract, if it was not fair and reasonable to incorporate the term in the contract.

(2) In this section "liability" means liability arising in the course of any business or from the occupation of any premises used for business purposes of the occupier.

"Guarantee" of consumer goods

19.—(1) This section applies to a guarantee—

(a) in relation to goods which are of a type ordinarily supplied for private use or consumption; and

(b) which is not a guarantee given by one party to the other party to a contract under or in pursuance of which the ownership or possession of the goods to which the guarantee relates is transferred.

(2) A term of a guarantee to which this section applies shall be void in so

far as it purports to exclude or restrict liability for loss or damage (including death or personal injury)—

(a) arising from the goods proving defective while—

(i) in use otherwise than exclusively for the purposes of a business; or

(ii) in the possession of a person for such use; and

(b) resulting from the breach of duty of a person concerned in the manufacture or distribution of the goods.

(3) For the purposes of this section, any document is a guarantee if it contains or purports to contain some promise or assurance (however worded or presented) that defects will be made good by complete or partial replacement, or by repair, monetary compensation or otherwise.

Obligations implied by law in sale and hire-purchase contracts

20.—(1) Any term of a contract which purports to exclude or restrict liability for breach of the obligation arising from—

(a) section 12 of the Sale of Goods Act 1893 (seller's implied undertakings as to title, etc.);

(b) section 8 of the Supply of Goods (Implied Terms) Act 1973 (implied terms as to title in hire-purchase agreements),

shall be void.

(2) Any term of a contract which purports to exclude or restrict liability for breach of the obligations arising from—

(a) section 13, 14 or 15 of the said Act of 1893 (seller's implied undertakings as to conformity of goods with description or sample, or as to their quality or fitness for a particular purpose);

(b) section 9, 10 or 11 of the said Act of 1973 (the corresponding provisions in relation to hire-purchase),

shall—

(i) in the case of a consumer contract, be void against the consumer;

(ii) in any other case, have no effect if it was not fair and reasonable to incorporate the term in the contract.

Obligations implied by law in other contracts for the supply of goods

21.—(1) Any term of a contract to which this section applies purporting to exclude or restrict liability for breach of an obligation—

(a) such as is referred to in subsection (3) (a) below—

(i) in the case of a consumer contract, shall be void against the consumer, and

(ii) in any other case, shall have no effect if it was not fair and reasonable to incorporate the term in the contract;

(b) such as is referred to in subsection (3) (b) below, shall have no effect if it was not fair and reasonable to incorporate the term in the contract.

(2) This section applies to any contract to the extent that it relates to any such matter as is referred to in section 15 (2) (a) of this Act, but does not apply to—

(a) a contract of sale of goods or a hire-purchase agreement; or

(b) a charterparty of a ship or hovercraft unless it is a consumer contract (and then only in favour of the consumer).

(3) An obligation referred to in this subsection is an obligation incurred under a contract in the course of a business and arising by implication of law from the nature of the contract which relates—

(a) to the correspondence of goods with description or sample, or to the quality or fitness of goods for any particular purpose; or

(b) to any right to transfer ownership or possession of goods, or to the enjoyment of quiet possession of goods.

(4) Nothing in this section applies to the supply of goods on a redemption of trading stamps within the Trading Stamps Act 1964.

Consequence of breach

22. For the avoidance of doubt, where any provision of this Part of this Act requires that the incorporation of a term in a contract must be fair and reasonable for that term to have effect—

(a) if that requirement is satisfied, the term may be given effect to notwithstanding that the contract has been terminated in consequence of breach of that contract;

(b) for the term to be given effect to, that requirement must be satisfied even where a party who is entitled to rescind the contract elects not to rescind it.

Evasion by means of secondary contract

23. Any term of any contract shall be void which purports to exclude or restrict, or has the effect of excluding or restricting—

(a) the exercise, by a party to any other contract, of any right or remedy which arises in respect of that other contract in consequence of breach of duty, or of obligation, liability for which could not by virtue of the provisions of this Part of this Act be excluded or restricted by a term of that other contract;

(b) the application of the provisions of this Part of this Act in respect of that or any other contract.

The "reasonableness" test

24.—(1) In determining for the purposes of this Part of this Act whether it was fair and reasonable to incorporate a term in a contract, regard shall be had only to the circumstances which were, or ought reasonably to have been, known to or in the contemplation of the parties to the contract at the time the contract was made.

(2) In determining for the purposes of section 20 or 21 of this Act whether it was fair and reasonable to incorporate a term in a contract, regard shall be had in particular to the matters specified in Schedule 2 to this Act; but this subsection shall not prevent a court or arbiter from holding in accordance with any rule of law, that a term which purports to exclude or restrict any relevant liability is not a term of the contract.

(3) Where a term in a contract purports to restrict liability to a specified sum of money, and the question arises for the purposes of this Part of this Act whether it was fair and reasonable to incorporate the term in the contract, then, without prejudice to subsection (2) above, regard shall be had in particular to—

(a) the resources which the party seeking to rely on that term could expect to be available to him for the purpose of meeting the liability should it arise;

(b) how far it was open to that party to cover himself by insurance.

(4) The onus of proving that it was fair and reasonable to incorporate a term in a contract shall lie on the party so contending.

Interpretation of Part II

25.—(1) In this Part of this Act—

"breach of duty" means the breach—

(a) of any obligation, arising from the express or implied terms of a contract, to take reasonable care or exercise reasonable skill in the performance of the contract;
(b) of any common law duty to take reasonable care or exercise reasonable skill;
(c) of the duty of reasonable care imposed by section 2 (1) of the Occupiers' Liability (Scotland) Act 1960;

"business" includes a profession and the activities of any government department or local or public authority;
"consumer" has the meaning assigned to that expression in the definition in this section of "consumer contract";
"consumer contract" means a contract (not being a contract of sale by auction or competitive tender) in which—

(a) one party to the contract deals, and the other party to the contract ("the consumer") does not deal or hold himself out as dealing, in the course of a business, and
(b) in the case of a contract such as is mentioned in section 15 (2) (a) of this Act, the goods are of a type ordinarily supplied for private use or consumption;

and for the purposes of this Part of this Act the onus of proving that a contract is not to be regarded as a consumer contract shall lie on the party so contending;
"goods" has the same meaning as in the Sale of Goods Act 1893;
"hire-purchase agreement" has the same meaning as in section 189 (1) of the Consumer Credit Act 1974;
"personal injury" includes any disease and any impairment of physical or mental condition.

(2) In relation to any breach of duty or obligation, it is immaterial for any purpose of this Part of this Act whether the act or omission giving rise to that breach was inadvertent or intentional, or whether liability for it arises directly or vicariously.

(3) In this Part of this Act, any reference to excluding or restricting any liability includes—

(a) making the liability or its enforcement subject to any restrictive or onerous conditions;
(b) excluding or restricting any right or remedy in respect of the liability, or subjecting a person to any prejudice in consequence of his pursuing any such right or remedy;
(c) excluding or restricting any rule of evidence or procedure;
(d) excluding or restricting any liability by reference to a notice having contractual effect,

but does not include an agreement to submit any questions to arbitration.

(4) In subsection (3) (d) above "notice" includes an announcement, whether or not in writing, and any other communication or pretended communication.

(5) In sections 15 and 16 and 19 to 21 of this Act, any reference to excluding or restricting liability for breach of an obligation or duty shall include a reference to excluding or restricting the obligation or duty itself.

PART III

PROVISIONS APPLYING TO WHOLE OF UNITED KINGDOM

Miscellaneous

International supply contracts

26.—(1) The limits imposed by this Act on the extent to which a person may exclude or restrict liability by reference to a contract term do not apply to liability arising under such a contract as is described in subsection (3) below.

(2) The terms of such a contract are not subject to any requirement of reasonableness under section 3 or 4: and nothing in Part II of this Act shall require the incorporation of the terms of such a contract to be fair and reasonable for them to have effect.

(3) Subject to subsection (4), that description of contract is one whose characteristics are the following—

(a) either it is a contract of sale of goods or it is one under or in pursuance of which the possession or ownership of goods passes; and

(b) it is made by parties whose places of business (or, if they have none, habitual residences) are in the territories of different States (the Channel Islands and the Isle of Man being treated for this purpose as different States from the United Kingdom).

(4) A contract falls within subsection (3) above only if either—

(a) the goods in question are, at the time of the conclusion of the contract, in the course of carriage, or will be carried, from the territory of one State to the territory of another; or

(b) the acts constituting the offer and acceptance have been done in the territories of different States; or

(c) the contract provides for the goods to be delivered to the territory of a State other than that within whose territory those acts were done.

Choice of law clauses

27.—(1) Where the proper law of a contract is the law of any part of the United Kingdom only by choice of the parties (and apart from that choice would be the law of some country outside the United Kingdom) sections 2 to 7 and 16 to 21 of this Act do not operate as part of the proper law.

(2) This Act has effect notwithstanding any contract term which applies or purports to apply the law of some country outside the United Kingdom, where (either or both)—

(a) the term appears to the court, or arbitrator or arbiter to have been imposed wholly or mainly for the purpose of enabling the party imposing it to evade the operation of this Act; or

(b) in the making of the contract one of the parties dealt as consumer, and he was then habitually resident in the United Kingdom, and the essential steps necessary for the making of the contract were taken there, whether by him or by others on his behalf.

(3) In the application of subsection (2) above to Scotland, for paragraph (b) there shall be substituted—

"(b) the contract is a consumer contract as defined in Part II of this Act, and the consumer at the date when the contract was made was habitually resident in the United Kingdom, and the essential steps necessary for the making of the contract were taken there, whether by him or by others on his behalf."

Temporary provision for sea carriage of passengers

28.—(1) This section applies to a contract for carriage by sea of a passenger or of a passenger and his luggage where the provisions of the Athens Convention (with or without modification) do not have, in relation to the contract, the force of law in the United Kingdom.

(2) In a case where—

(a) the contract is not made in the United Kingdom, and

(b) neither the place of departure nor the place of destination under it is in the United Kingdom,

a person is not precluded by this Act from excluding or restricting liability for loss or damage, being loss or damage for which the provisions of the

Convention would, if they had the force of law in relation to the contract, impose liability on him.

(3) In any other case, a person is not precluded by this Act from excluding or restricting liability for that loss or damage—

(a) in so far as the exclusion or restriction would have been effective in that case had the provisions of the Convention had the force of law in relation to the contract; or

(b) in such circumstances and to such extent as may be prescribed, by reference to a prescribed term of the contract.

(4) For the purposes of subsection (3) (a), the values which shall be taken to be the official values in the United Kingdom of the amounts (expressed in gold francs) by reference to which liability under the provisions of the Convention is limited shall be such amounts in sterling as the Secretary of State may from time to time by order made by statutory instrument specify.

(5) In this section,—

(a) the references to excluding or restricting liability include doing any of those things in relation to the liability which are mentioned in section 13 or section 25 (3) and (5); and

(b) "the Athens Convention" means the Athens Convention relating to the Carriage of Passengers and their Luggage by Sea, 1974; and

(c) "prescribed" means prescribed by the Secretary of State by regulations made by statutory instrument;

and a statutory instrument containing the regulations shall be subject to annulment in pursuance of a resolution of either House of Parliament.

Saving for other relevant legislation

29.—(1) Nothing in this Act removes or restricts the effect of, or prevents reliance upon, any contractual provision which—

(a) is authorised or required by the express terms or necessary implication of an enactment; or

(b) being made with a view to compliance with an international agreement to which the United Kingdom is a party, does not operate more restrictively than is contemplated by the agreement.

(2) A contract term is to be taken—

(a) for the purposes of Part I of this Act, as satisfying the requirement of reasonableness; and

(b) for those of Part II, to have been fair and reasonable to incorporate,

if it is incorporated or approved by, or incorporated pursuant to a decision or ruling of, a competent authority acting in the exercise of any statutory jurisdiction or function and is not a term in a contract to which the competent authority is itself a party.

(3) In this section—

"competent authority" means any court, arbitrator or arbiter, government department or public authority;

"enactment" means any legislation (including subordinate legislation) of the United Kingdom or Northern Ireland and any instrument having effect by virtue of such legislation; and

"statutory" means conferred by an enactment.

Obligations under Consumer Protection Acts

30.—(1) In section 3 of the Consumer Protection Act 1961 (provisions against marketing goods which do not comply with safety requirements), after subsection (1) there is inserted—

"(1A) Any term of an agreement which purports to exclude or restrict, or has the effect of excluding or restricting, any obligation imposed by or by virtue of that section, or any liability for breach of such an obligation, shall be void."

(2) The same amendment is made in section 3 of the Consumer Protection Act (Northern Ireland) 1965.

General

Commencement; amendments; repeats

31.—(1) This Act comes into force on 1st February 1978.

(2) Nothing in this Act applies to contracts made before the date on which it comes into force; but subject to this, it applies to liability for any loss or damage which is suffered on or after that date.

(3) The enactments specified in Schedule 3 to this Act are amended as there shown.

(4) The enactments specified in Schedule 4 to this Act are repealed to the extent specified in column 3 of that Schedule.

Citation and extent

32.—(1) This Act may be cited as the Unfair Contract Terms Act 1977.

(2) Part I of this Act extends to England and Wales and to Northern Ireland; but it does not extend to Scotland.

(3) Part II of this Act extends to Scotland only.

(4) This Part of this Act extends to the whole of the United Kingdom.

Schedules

Section 1 (2)

Schedule 1

SCOPE OF SECTIONS 2 TO 4 AND 7

1. Sections 2 to 4 of this Act do not extend to—

(a) any contract of insurance (including a contract to pay an annuity on human life);

(b) any contract so far as it relates to the creation or transfer of an interest in land, or to the termination of such an interest, whether by extinction, merger, surrender, forfeiture or otherwise;

(c) any contract so far as it relates to the creation or transfer of a right or interest in any patent, trade mark, copyright, registered design, technical or commercial information or other intellectual property, or relates to the termination of any such right or interest;

(d) any contract so far as it relates—

(i) to the formation or dissolution of a company (which means any body corporate or unincorporated association and includes a partnership), or

(ii) to its constitution or the rights or obligations of its corporators or members;

(e) any contract so far as it relates to the creation or transfer of securities or of any right or interest in securities.

2. Section 2 (1) extends to—

(a) any contract of marine salvage or towage;

(b) any charterparty of a ship or hovercraft; and

(c) any contract for the carriage of goods by ship or hovercraft;

but subject to this sections 2 to 4 and 7 do not extend to any such contract except in favour of a person dealing as consumer.

3. Where goods are carried by ship or hovercraft in pursuance of a contract which either—

(a) specifies that as the means of carriage over part of the journey to be covered, or

(b) makes no provisions as to the means of carriage and does not exclude that means,

then sections 2 (2), 3 and 4 do not, except in favour of a person dealing as consumer, extend to the contract as it operates for and in relation to the carriage of the goods by that means.

4. Section 2 (1) and (2) do not extend to a contract of employment, except in favour of the employee.

5. Section 2 (1) does not affect the validity of any discharge and indemnity given by a person, on or in connection with an award to him of compensation for pneumoconiosis attributable to employment in the coal industry, in respect of any further claim arising from his contracting that disease.

Sections 11 (2) and 24 (2)

Schedule 2

"GUIDELINES" FOR APPLICATION OF REASONABLENESS TEST

The matters to which regard is to be had in particular for the purposes of sections 6 (3), 7 (3) and (4), 20 and 21 are any of the following which appear to be relevant—

(a) the strength of the bargaining positions of the parties relative to each other, taking into account (among other things) alternative means by which the customer's requirements could have been met;

(b) whether the customer received an inducement to agree to the term, or in accepting it had an opportunity of entering into a similar contract with other persons, but without having to accept a similar term;

(c) whether the customer knew or ought reasonably to have known of the existence and extent of the term (having regard, among other things, to any custom of the trade and any previous course of dealing between the parties);

(d) where the term excludes or restricts any relevant liability if some condition is not complied with, whether it was reasonable at the time of the contract to expect that compliance with that condition would be practicable;

(e) whether the goods were manufactured, processed or adapted to the special order of the customer.

Section 31 (3)

Schedule 3

AMENDMENT OF ENACTMENTS

In the Sale of Goods Act 1893—

(a) in section 55 (1), for the words "the following provisions of this section" substitute "the provisions of the Unfair Contract Terms Act 1977";

(b) in section 62 (1), in the definition of "business", for "local authority or statutory undertaker" substitute "or local or public authority".

In the Supply of Goods (Implied Terms) Act 1973 (as originally enacted and as substituted by the Consumer Credit Act 1974)—

(a) in section 14 (1) for the words from "conditional sale" to the end substitute "a conditional sale agreement where the buyer deals as consumer within Part I of the Unfair Contract Terms Act 1977 or, in Scotland, the agreement is a consumer contract within Part II of that Act";

(b) in section 15 (1), in the definition of "business", for "local authority or statutory undertaker" substitute "or local or public authority".

Section 31 (4)

Schedule 4

REPEALS

Chapter	Short title	Extent of repeal
56 & 57 Vict. c. 71.	Sale of Goods Act 1893.	In section 55, subsections (3) to (11). Section 55A. Section 61 (6). In section 62 (1) the definition of "contract for the international sale of goods".
1962 c. 46.	Transport Act 1962.	Section 43 (7).
1967 c. 45.	Uniform Laws on International Sales Act 1967.	In section 1 (4), the words "55 and 55A".
1972 c. 33.	Carriage by Railway Act 1972.	In section 1 (1), the words from "and shall have" onwards.
1973 c. 13.	Supply of Goods (Implied Terms) Act 1973.	Section 5 (1). Section 6. In section 7 (1), the words from "contract for the international sale of goods" onwards. In section 12, subsections (2) to (9). Section 13. In Section 15 (1), the definition of "consumer sale".

The repeals in sections 12 and 15 of the Supply of Goods (Implied Terms) Act 1973 shall have effect in relation to those sections as originally enacted and as substituted by the Consumer Credit Act 1974.

Sale of Goods Act 1979

(1979 c. 54)

12. Implied terms about title, etc.

(1) In a contract of sale, other than one to which subsection (3) below applies, there is an implied [term] on the part of the seller that in the case of a sale he has a right to sell the goods, and in the case of an agreement to sell he will have such a right at the time when the property is to pass.

(2) In a contract of sale, other than one to which subsection (3) below applies, there is also an implied [term] that—

(a) the goods are free, and will remain free until the time when the property is to pass, from any charge or encumbrance not disclosed or known to the buyer before the contract is made, and

(b) the buyer will enjoy quiet possession of the goods except so far as it may be disturbed by the owner or other person entitled to the benefit of any charge or encumbrance so disclosed or known.

(3) This subsection applies to a contract of sale in the case of which there appears from the contract or is to be inferred from its circumstances an intention that the seller should transfer only such title as he or a third person may have.

(4) In a contract to which subsection (3) above applies there is an implied [term] that all charges or encumbrances known to the seller and not known to the buyer have been disclosed to the buyer before the contract is made.

(5) In a contract to which subsection (3) above applies there is also an implied [term] that none of the following will disturb the buyer's quiet possession of the goods, namely—

(a) the seller;

(b) in a case where the parties to the contract intend that the seller should transfer only such title as a third person may have, that person;

(c) anyone claiming through or under the seller or that third person otherwise than under a charge or encumbrance disclosed or known to the buyer before the contract is made.

[(5A) As regards England and Wales and Northern Ireland, the term implied by subsection (1) above is a condition and the terms implied by subsections (2), (4) and (5) above are warranties.]

(6) Paragraph 3 of Schedule 1 below applies in relation to a contract made before 18 May 1973.

The words in square brackets in sub-ss (1), (2), (4), (5) were substituted, and sub-s (5A) was inserted, by the Sale and Supply of Goods Act 1994, s 7(1), Sch 2, para 5(1), (3).

13. Sale by description

(1) Where there is a contract for the sale of goods by description, there is an implied [term] that the goods will correspond with the description.

[(1A) As regards England and Wales and Northern Ireland, the term implied by subsection (1) above is a condition.]

(2) If the sale is by sample as well as by description it is not sufficient that the bulk of the goods corresponds with the sample if the goods do not also correspond with the description.

(3) A sale of goods is not prevented from being a sale by description by reason only that, being exposed for sale or hire, they are selected by the buyer.

(4) Paragraph 4 of Schedule 1 below applies in relation to a contract made before 18th May 1973.

The words in square brackets in sub-s (1) was substituted, and sub-s (1A) was inserted, by the Sale and Supply of Goods Act 1994, s 7(1), Sch 2, para 5(1), (4).

14. Implied terms about quality or fitness

(1) Except as provided by this section and section 15 below and subject to any other enactment, there is no implied [term] about the quality or fitness for any particular purpose of goods supplied under a contract of sale.

[(2) Where the seller sells goods in the course of a business, there is an implied term that the goods supplied under the contract are of satisfactory quality.

(2A) For the purposes of this Act, goods are of satisfactory quality if they meet the standard that a reasonable person would regard as satisfactory, taking account of any description of the goods, the price (if relevant) and all the other relevant circumstances.

(2B) For the purposes of this Act, the quality of goods includes their state and condition and the following (among others) are in appropriate cases aspects of the quality of goods—

(a) fitness for all the purposes for which goods of the kind in question are commonly supplied,
(b) appearance and finish,
(c) freedom from minor defects,
(d) safety, and
(e) durability.

(2C) The term implied by subsection (2) above does not extend to any matter making the quality of goods unsatisfactory—

(a) which is specifically drawn to the buyer's attention before the contract is made,
(b) where the buyer examines the goods before the contract is made, which that examination ought to reveal, or
(c) in the case of a contract for sale by sample, which would have been apparent on a reasonable examination of the sample.]

(3) Where the seller sells goods in the course of a business and the buyer, expressly or by implication, makes known—

(a) to the seller, or
(b) where the purchase price or part of it is payable by instalments and the goods were previously sold by a credit-broker to the seller, to that credit-broker,

any particular purpose for which the goods are being bought, there is an implied [term] that the goods supplied under the contract are reasonably fit for that purpose, whether or not that is a purpose for which such goods are commonly supplied, except where the circumstances show that the buyer does not rely, or that it is unreasonable for him to rely, on the skill or judgment of the seller or credit-broker.

(4) An implied [term] about quality or fitness for a particular purpose may be annexed to a contract of sale by usage.

(5) The preceding provisions of this section apply to a sale by a person who in the course of a business is acting as agent for another as they apply to a sale by a principal in the course of a business, except where that other is not selling in the course of a business and either the buyer knows that fact or reasonable steps are taken to bring it to the notice of the buyer before the contract is made.

[(6) As regard England and Wales and Northern Ireland, the terms implied by subsections (2) and (3) above are conditions.]

(7) Paragraph 5 of Schedule 1 below applies in relation to a contract made on or after 18 May 1973 and before the appointed day, and paragraph 6 in relation to one made before 18th May 1973.

(8) In subsection (7) above and paragraph 5 of Schedule 1 below references to the appointed day are to the day appointed for the purposes of those provisions by an order of the Secretary of State made by statutory instrument.

The words in square brackets in sub-ss (1), (3), (4) and the whole of sub-s (6) were substituted, and sub-ss (2), (2A)–(2C) were substituted for the original sub-s (2), by the Sale and Supply of Goods Act 1994, ss 1(1), 7(1), Sch 2. para 5(1), (5).

Sale by sample

15. Sale by sample

(1) A contract of sale is a contract for sale by sample where there is an express or implied term to that effect in the contract.

(2) In the case of a contract for sale by sample there is an implied [term]—

(a) that the bulk will correspond with the sample in quality;

(b) . . .

(c) that the goods will be free from any defect, [making their quality unsatisfactory], which would not be apparent on reasonable examination of the sample.

[(3) As regards England and Wales and Northern Ireland, the term implied by subsection (2) above is a condition.]

(4) Paragraph 7 of Schedule 1 below applies in relation to a contract made before 18 May 1973.

The words in square brackets in sub-s (2) and the whole of sub-s (3) were substituted, and sub-s (2)(b) was repealed, by the Sale and Supply of Goods Act 1994, ss 1(2), 7, Sch 2, para 5(1), (6), Sch 3.

[Miscellaneous

15A. Modificatios of remedies for breach of condition in non-consumer cases

(1) Where in the case of a contract of sale—

(a) the buyer would, apart from this subsection, have the right to reject goods by reason of a breach on the part of the seller of a term implied by section 13, 14 or 15 above, but

(b) the breach is so slight that it would be unreasonable for him to reject them,

then, if the buyer does not deal as consumer, the breach is not to be treated as a breach of condition but may be treated as a breach of warranty.

(2) This section applies unless a contrary intention appears in, or is to be implied from, the contract.

(3) It is for the seller to show that a breach fell within subsection (1)(b) above.

(4) This section does not apply to Scotland.]

This section, and the cross-heading preceding it, were inserted by the Sale and Supply of Goods Act 1994, s 4(1).

55. Exclusion of implied terms

(1) Where a right, duty or liability would arise under a contract of sale of goods by implication of law, it may (subject to the Unfair Contract Terms Act 1977) be negatived or varied by express agreement, or by the course of dealing between the parties, or by such usage as binds both parties to the contract.

(2) An express [term] does not negative a [term] implied by this Act unless inconsistent with it.

(3) Paragraph 11 of Schedule 1 below applies in relation to a contract made on or after 18th May 1973 and before 1st February 1978, and paragraph 12 in relation to one made before 18th May 1973.

The words in square brackets in sub-s (2) were substituted by the Sale and Supply of Goods Act 1994, s 7(1), Sch 2, para 5(1), (8).

Financial Services Act 1986

(1986 c. 60)

Applications for listing

143.—(1) An application for listing shall be made to the competent authority in such manner as the listing rules may require.

(2) No application for the listing of any securities shall be made except by or with the consent of the issuer of the securities.

(3) No application for listing shall be made in respect of securities to be issued by a private company or by an old public company within the meaning of section 1 of the Companies Consolidation (Consequential Provisions) Act 1985 or the corresponding Northern Ireland provision.

COMMENCEMENT

January 12, 1987 for certain purposes and February 16, 1987 otherwise for all purposes, see S.I. 1986 No. 2246 (c. 88), Art. 5.

Admission to list

144.—(1) The competent authority shall not admit any securities to the Official List except on an application duly made in accordance with section 143 above and unless satisfied that—

(a) the requirements of the listing rules made by the authority for the purposes of this section and in force when the application is made; and

(b) any other requirements imposed by the authority in relation to that application,

are complied with.

[(2) Listing rules shall require as a condition of the admission to the Official List of any securities for which application for admission has been made and which are to be offered to the public in the United Kingdom for the first time before admission—

(a) the submission to, and approval by, the authority of a prospectus in such form and containing such information as may be specified in the rules; and

(b) the publication of that prospectus.

(2A) Listing rules may require as a condition of the admission to the Official List of any other securities—

(a) the submission to, and approval by, the authority of a document (in this Act referred to as "listing particulars") in such form and containing such information as may be specified in the rules; and

(b) the publication of that document;

or, in such cases as may be specified by the rules, the publication of a document other than listing particulars or a prospectus.

(2B) Subsections (2) and (2A) have effect without prejudice to the generality of the power of the competent authority to make listing rules for the purposes of this section.]

(3) The competent authority may refuse an application—

(a) if it considers that by reason of any matter relating to the issuer the admission of the securities would be detrimental to the interests of investors; or

(b) in the case of securities already officially listed in another member State, if the issuer has failed to comply with any obligations to which he is subject by virtue of that listing.

(4) The competent authority shall notify the applicant of its decision on the application within six months from the date on which the application is received or, if within that period the authority has required the applicant to furnish further information in connection with the application, from the date on which that information is furnished.

(5) If the competent authority does not notify the applicant of its decision within the time required by subsection (4) above it shall be taken to have refused the application.

(6) When any securities have been admitted to the Official List their admission shall not be called in question on the ground that any requirement or condition for their admission has not been complied with.

AMENDMENT

Subsection (2) was substituted by, and subss. (2A) and (2B) inserted by, S.I. 1995 No. 1537, Sched. 2, Pt. 1, para. 2(1).

COMMENCEMENT

January 12, 1987 for certain purposes and February 16, 1987 otherwise for all purposes, S.I. 1986 No. 2246 (c. 88) Art. 5.

Discontinuance and suspension of listing

145.—(1) The competent authority may, in accordance with the listing rules, discontinue the listing of any securities if satisfied that there are special circumstances which preclude normal regular dealings in the securities.

(2) The competent authority may in accordance with the listing rules suspend the listing of any securities.

(3) Securities the listing of which is suspended under subsection (2) above shall nevetheless be regarded as listed for the purposes of sections 153 and 155 below.

(4) This section applies to securities included in the Official List at the coming into force of this Part of this Act as it applies to securities included by virtue of this Part.

COMMENCEMENT

January 12, 1987 for certain purposes and February 16, 1987 otherwise for all purposes, see S.I. 1986 No. 2246 (c. 88), Art. 5.

General duty of disclosure in listing particulars

146.—(1) In addition to the information specified by listing rules or required by the competent authority as a condition of the admission of any securities to the Official List any listing particulars submitted to the competent authority under secrtion 144 above shall contain all such information as investors and their professional advisers would reasonably require, and reasonably expect to find there, for the purpose of making an informed assessment of—

(a) the assets and liabilities, financial position, profits and losses, and prospects of the issuer of the securities; and

(b) the rights attaching to those securities.

(2) The information to be included by virtue of this section shall be such information as is mentioned in subsection (1) above which is within the knowledge of any person responsible for the listing particulars or which it would be reasonable for him to obtain by making enquiries.

(3) In determining what information is required to be included in listing particulars by virtue of this section regard shall be had—

(a) to the nature of the securities and of the issuer of the securities;

(b) to the nature of the persons likely to consider their acquisition;

(c) to the fact that certain matters may reasonably be expected to be within the knowledge of professional advisers of any kind which those persons may reasonably be expected to consult; and

(d) to any information available to investors or their professional advisers by virtue of requirements imposed under section 153 below or by or under any other enactment or by virtue of requirements imposed by a recognised investment exchange for the purpose of complying with paragraph 2(2)(b) of Schedule 4 to this Act.

COMMENCEMENT

January 12, 1987 for certain purposes and February 16, 1987 otherwise for all purposes, see S.I. 1986 No. 2246, Art. 5.

Supplementary listing particulars

147.—(1) If at any time after the preparation of listing particulars for submission to the competent authority under section 144 above and before the commencement of dealings in the securities following their admission to the Official List—

(a) there is a significant change affecting any matter contained in those particulars whose inclusion was required by section 146 above or by listing rules or by the competent authority; or

(b) a significant new matter arises the inclusion of information in respect of which would have been so required if it had arisen when the particulars were prepared,

the issuer of the securities shall, in accordance with listing rules made for the purposes of this section, submit to the competent authority for its approval and, if approved, publish supplementary listing particulars of the change or new matter.

(2) In subsection (1) above "significant" means significant for the purpose of making an informed assessment of the matters mentioned in section 146(1) above.

(3) Where the issuer of the securities is not aware of the change or new matter in question he shall not be under any duty to comply with subsection (1) above unless he is notified of it by a person responsible for the listing particulars; but it shall be the duty of any person responsible for those particulars who is aware of such a matter to give notice of it to the issuer.

(4) Subsection (1) above applies also as respects matters contained in any supplementary listing particulars previously published under this section in respect of the securities in question.

COMMENCEMENT

January 12, 1987 for certain purposes and February 16, 1987 otherwise for all purposes, see S.I. 1986 No. 2246 (c. 88), Art. 5.

Registration of listing particulars

149.—(1) On or before the date on which listing particulars or supplementary listing particulars are published as required by listing rules a copy of the particulars shall be delivered for registration to the registrar of companies and a statements that a copy has been delivered to him shall be included in the particulars.

(2) In subsection (1) above "the registrar of companies" means—

(a) if the securities in question are or are to be issued by a company incorporated in Great Britain, the registrar of companies in England and Wales or the registrar of companies in Scotland according to whether the company's registered office is in England and Wales or in Scotland;

(b) if the securities in question are or are to be issued by a company incorporated in Northern Ireland, the registrar of companies for Northern Ireland;

(c) in any other case, any of those registrars.

(3) If any particulars are published without a copy of them having been delivered as required by this section the issuer of the securities in question and any person who is knowingly a party to the publication shall be guilty of an offence and liable—

(a) on conviction on indictment, to a fine;

(b) on summary conviction, to a fine not exceeding the statutory maximum.

COMMENCEMENT

January 12, 1987 for certain purposes and February 16, 1987 otherwise for all purposes: S.I. 1986 No. 2246, Art. 5.

Compensation for false or misleading particulars

150.—(1) Subject to section 151 below, the person or persons responsible for any listing particulars or supplementary listing particulars shall be liable to pay compensation to any person who has acquired any of the securities in question and suffered loss in respect of them as a result of any untrue or misleading statement in the particulars or the omission from them of any matter required to be included by section 146 or 147 above.

(2) Where listing rules require listing particulars to include information as to any particular matter on the basis that the particulars must include a statement either as to that matter or, if such is the case, that there is no such matter, the omission from the particulars of the information shall be treated for the purposes of subsection (1) above as a statement that there is no such matter.

(3) Subject to section 151 below, a person who fails to comply with section 147 above shall be liable to pay compensation to any person who has acquired any of the securities in question and suffered loss in respect of them as a result of the failure.

(4) This section does not affect any liability which any person may incur apart from this section.

(5) References in this section to the acquisition by any person of securities include references to his contracting to acquire them or an interest in them.

(6) No person shall by reason of being a promoter of a company or otherwise incur any liability for failing to disclose any information which he would not be required to disclose in listing particulars in respect of a company's

securities if he were responsible for those particulars or, if he is responsible for them, which he is entitled to omit by virtue of section 148 above.

[The reference above to a person incurring liability includes a reference to any other person being entitled as against that person to be granted any civil remedy or to rescind or repudiate any agreement.]

AMENDMENT

The words in square brackets in subsection (6) were added by Companies Act 1989, s.197(1) from March 15, 1990 (see S.I. 1990 No. 354, Art. 3).

COMMENCEMENT

January 12, 1987 for certain purposes and February 16, 1987 otherwise for all purposes, see S.I. 1986 No. 2246, Art. 5.

Exemption from liability to pay compensation

151.—(1) A person shall not incur any liability under section 150(1) above for any loss in respect of securities caused by any such statement or omission as is there mentioned if he satisfies the court that at the time when the particulars were submitted to the competent authority he reasonably believed, having made such enquiries (if any) as were reasonable, that the statement was true and not misleading or that the matter whose omission caused the loss was properly omitted and—

(a) that he continued in that belief until the time when the securities were acquired; or

(b) that they were acquired before it was reasonably practicable to bring a correction to the attention of persons likely to acquire the securities in question; or

(c) that before the securities were acquired he had taken all such steps as it was reasonable for him to have taken to secure that a correction was brought to the attention of those persons; or

(d) that he continued in that belief until after the commencement of dealings in the securities following their admission to the Official List and that the securities were acquired after such a lapse of time that he ought in the circumstances to be reasonably excused.

(2) A person shall not incur any liability under section 150(1) above for any loss in respect of securities caused by a statement purporting to be made by or on the authority of another person as an expert which is, and is stated to be, included in the particulars with that other person's consent if he satisfies the court that at the time when the particulars were submitted to the competent authority he believed on reasonable grounds that the other person was competent to make or authorise the statement and had consented to its inclusion in the form and context in which it was included and—

(a) that he continued in that belief until the time when the securities were acquired; or

(b) that they were acquired before it was reasonably practicable to bring the fact that the expert was not competent or had not consented to the attention of persons likely to acquire the securities in question; or

(c) that before the securities were acquired he had taken all such steps as it was reasonable for him to have taken to secure that that fact was brought to the attention of those persons; or

(d) that he continued in that belief until after the commencement of dealings in the securities following their admission to the Official List and that the securities were acquired after such a lapse of time that he ought in the circumstances to be reasonably excused.

(3) Without prejudice to subsections (1) and (2) above, a person shall not incur any liability under section 150(1) above for any loss in respect of any securities caused by any such statement or omissions as is there mentioned if he satisfies the court—

(a) that before the securities were acquired a correction, or where the statement was such as is mentioned in subsection (2), the fact that the expert was not competent or had not consented had been published in a manner calculated to bring it to the attention of persons likely to acquire the securities in question; or

(b) that he took all such steps as it was reasonable for him to take to secure such publication and reasonably believed that it had taken place before the securities were acquired.

(4) A person shall not incur any liability under section 150(1) above for any loss resulting from a statement made by an official person or contained in a public official document which is included in the particulars if he satisfies the court that the statement is accurately and fairly reproduced.

(5) A person shall not incur any liability under section 150(1) or (3) above if he satisfies the court that the person suffering the loss acquired the securities in question with knowledge that the statement was false or misleading, of the omitted matter or of the change or new matter, as the case may be.

(6) A person shall not incur any liability under section 150(3) above if he satisfies the court that he reasonably believed that the change or new matter in question was not such as to call for supplementary listing particulars.

(7) In this section "expert" includes any engineer, valuer, accountant or other person whose profession, qualifications or experience give authority to a statement made by him; and references to the acquisition of securities include references to contracting to acquire them or an interest in them.

COMMENCEMENT

January 12, 1987 for certain purposes and February 16, 1987 otherwise for all purposes, see S.I. 1986 No. 2246, Art. 5.

Persons responsible for particulars

152.—(1) For the purposes of this Part of this Act the persons responsible for listing particulars or supplementary listing particulars are—

(a) the issuer of the securities to which the particulars relate;

(b) where the issuer is a body corporate, each person who is a director of that body at the time when the particulars are submitted to the competent authority;

(c) where the issuer is a body corporate, each person who has authorised himself to be named, and is named, in the particulars as a director or as having agreed to become a director of that body either immediately or at a future time;

(d) each person who accepts, and is stated in the particulars as accepting, responsibility for, or for any part of, the particulars;

(e) each peson not falling within any of the foregoing paragraphs who has authorised the contents of, or any part of, the particulars.

(2) A person is not responsible for any particulars by virtue of subsection (1)(b) above if they are published without his knowledge or consent and on becoming aware of their publication he forthwith gives reasonable public notice that they were published without his knowledge or consent.

(3) Where a person has accepted responsibility for, or authorised, only part of the contents of any particulars, he is responsible under subsection (1)(d) or (e) above for only that part and only if it is included in (or substantially in) the form and context to which he has agreed.

(4) Where the particulars relate to securities which are to be issued in connection with an offer by (or by a wholly-owned subsidiary of), the issuer for, or an agreement for the acquisition by (or by a wholly-owned subsidiary of) the issuer of, securities issued by another person or in connection with any arrangement whereby the whole of the undertaking of another person is to become the undertaking of the issuer (of a wholly-owned subsidiary of the issuer or of a body corporate which will become such a subsidiary by virtue of the arrangement) then if—

(a) that other person; and

(b) where that other person is a body corporate, each person who is a director of that body at the time when the particulars are submitted to the competent authority and each other person who has authorised himself to be named, and is named, in the particulars as a director of that body,

is responsible by virtue of paragraph (d) of subsection (1) above for any part of the particulars relating to that other person or to the securities or undertaking to which the offer, agreement or arrangement relates, no person shall be responsible for that part under paragraph (a), (b) or (c) of that subsection but without prejudice to his being responsible under paragraph (d).

(5) Neither paragraph (b) nor paragraph (c) of subsection (1) above applies in the case of an issuer of international securities of a class specified by listing rules for the purposes of section 148(1)(c) above; and neither of those paragraphs nor paragraph (b) of subsection (4) above applies in the case of any director certified by the competent authority as a person to whom that paragraph should not apply by reason of his having an interest, or of any other circumstances, making it inappropriate for him to be responsible by virtue of that paragraph.

(6) In subsection (5) above "international securities" means any investment falling within paragraph 2 of Schedule 1 to this Act as modified by section 142(3)(b) above which is of a kind likely to be dealt in by bodies incorporated in or persons resident in a country or territory outside the United Kingdom, is denominated in a currency other than sterling or is otherwise connected with such a country or territory.

(7) In this section "wholly-owned subsidiary", in relation to a person other than a body corporate, means any body corporate that would be his wholly-owned subsidiary if he were a body corporate.

(8) Nothing in this section shall be construed as making a person responsible for any particulars by reason of giving advice as to their contents in a professional capacity.

(9) Where by virtue of this section the issuer of any shares pays or is liable to pay compensation under section 150 above for loss suffered in respect of shares for which a person has subscribed no account shall be taken of that liability or payment in determining any question as to the amount paid on subscription for those shares or as to the amount paid up or deemed to be paid up on them.

COMMENCEMENT

January 12, 1987 for certain purposes and February 16, 1987 otherwise for all purposes, see S.I. 1986 No. 2246, Art. 5.

Obligations of issuers of listed securities

153.—(1) Listing rules may specify requirements to be complied with by issuers of listed securities and make provision with respect to the action that may be taken by the competent authority in the event of non-compliance, including provision—

(a) authorising the authority to publish the fact that an issuer has contravened any provision of the rules; and
(b) if the rules require an issuer to publish any information, authorising the authority to publish it in the event of his failure to do so.

(2) This section applies to the issuer of securities included in the Official List at the coming into force of this Part of this Act as it applies to the issuer of securities included by virtue of this Part.

COMMENCEMENT

January 12, 1987 for certain purposes and February 16, 1987 otherwise for all purposes, see S.I. 1986 No. 2246, Art. 5.

Advertisements etc., in connection with listing applications

154.—(1) Where listing particulars are or are to be published in connection with an application for the listing of any securities no advertisement or other information of a kind specified by listing rules shall be issued in the United Kingdom unless the contents of the advertisement or other information have been submitted to the competent authority and that authority has either—
(a) approved those contents; or
(b) authorised the issue of the advertisement or information without such approval.

(2) An authorised person who contravenes this section shall be treated as having contravened rules made under Chapter V of Part I of this Act or, in the case of a person who is an authorised person by virtue of his membership of a recognised self-regulating organisation or certification by a recognised professional body, the rules of that organisation or body.

(3) Subject to subsection (4) below, a person other than an authorised person, who contravenes this section shall be guilty of an offence and liable—
(a) on conviction on indictment, to imprisonment for a term not exceeding two years or to a fine or to both;
(b) on summary conviction, to a fine not exceeding the statutory maximum.

(4) A person who in the ordinary course of a business other than investment business issues an advertisement or other information to the order of another person shall not be guilty of an offence under this section if he proves that he believed on reasonable grounds that the advertisement or information had been approved or its issue authorised by the competent authority.

(5) Where information has been approved, or its issue has been authorised, under this section neither the person issuing it nor any person responsible for, or for any part of, the listing particulars shall incur any civil liability by reason of any statement in or omission from the information if that information and the listing particulars, taken together, would not be likely to mislead persons of the kind likely to consider the acquisition of the securities in question.

[The reference above to a person incurring civil liability includes a reference to any other person being entitled as against that person to be granted any civil remedy or to rescind or repudiate any agreement.]

Application of Part IV to prospectuses

154A. Sections 146 to 152 and 154 above shall apply in relation to a prospectus required by listing rules in accordance with section 144(2) above as they apply in relation to listing particulars, but as if—
(a) any reference to listing particulars were a reference to a prospectus

and any reference to supplementary listing particulars were a reference to a supplementary prospectus; and

(b) notwithstanding section 142(7) above, any reference in section 152 above (other than in subsection (1)(b) of that section) to the issuer of securities included a reference to the person offering or proposing to offer them.

AMENDMENTS

The words in square brackets in subs. (5) were added by Companies Act 1989, s.197(2) from March 15, 1990 (see (S.I. 1990 No. 354), Art. 3).

Section 154A was added by (S.I. 1995 No. 1537), Sched. 2, Pt. 1, s. 2(3).

COMMENCEMENT

Subss. (1), (5); January 12, 1987 for certain purposes and February 16, 1987 otherwise for all purposes, see (S.I. 1986 No. 2246), Art. 5.

April 29, 1988 in so far as not yet in force (S.I. 1988 No. 740).

Fees

155. Listing rules may require the payment of fees to the competent authority in respect of applications for listing and the retention of securities in the Official List.

COMMENCEMENT

January 12, 1987 for certain purposes and February 16, 1987 otherwise for all purposes, see (S.I. 1986 No. 2246), Art. 5.

Listing rules: general provisions

156.—(1) Listing rules may make different provision for different cases.

(2) Listing rules may authorise the competent authority to disperse with or modify the application of the rules in particular cases and by reference to any circumstances.

(3) Listing rules shall be made by an instrument in writing.

(4) Immediately after an instrument containing listing rules is made it shall be printed and made available to the public with or without payment.

(5) A person shall not be taken to have contravened any listing rule if he shows that at the time of the alleged contravention the instrument containing the rule had not been made available as required by subsection (4) above.

(6) The production of a printed copy of an instrument purporting to be made by the competent authority on which is endorsed a certificate signed by an officer of the authority authorised by it for that purpose and stating—

(a) that the instrument was made by the authority;

(b) that the copy is a true copy of the instrument; and

(c) that on a specified date the instrument was made available to the public as required by subsection (4) above,

shall be prima facie evidence or, in Scotland, sufficient evidence of the facts stated in the certificate.

(7) Any certificate purporting to be signed as mentioned in subsection (6) above shall be deemed to have been signed unless the contrary is shown.

(8) Any person wishing in any legal proceedings to cite an instrument made by the competent authority may require the authority to cause a copy of it to be endorsed with such a certificate as is mentioned in subsection (6) above.

Approval of prospectus where no application for listing

156A.—(1) Listing rules may also provide for a prospectus to be submitted to and approved by the competent authority where—

(a) securities are to be offered to the public in the United Kingdom for the first time;

(b) no application for listing of the securities has been made under this Part of this Act; and

(c) the prospectus is submitted by or with the consent of the issuer of the securities.

(2) Listing rules made under subsection (1) above may make provision—

(a) as to the information to be contained in, and the form of, a prospectus submitted under any such rules; and

(b) subject to the provisions of the Public Offers of Securities Regulations 1995, as to the timing and manner of publication of such a prospectus.

(3) Sections 146 to 152 and 154 above shall apply in relation to such a prospectus as they apply in relation to listing particulars but as if—

(a) any reference to listing particulars were a reference to a prospectus and any reference to supplementary listing particulars were a reference to a supplementary prospectus;

(b) in section 146(1) above—

(i) the words "as a condition of the admission of any securities to the Official List" were omitted; and

(ii) for the words "section 144 above" there were substituted "section 156A(1) below";

(c) in section 147(1) above, for the words "under section 144 above and before the commencement of dealings in the securities following their admission to the Official List" there were substituted "under section 156A(1) below and before the end of the period during which the offer to which the prospectus relates remains open";

(d) in subsections (1)(d) and (2)(d) of section 151 above—

(i) the words "that he continued in that belief until after the commencement of dealings in the securities following their admissions to the Official List and" were omitted; and

(ii) the words "and, if the securities are dealt in on an approved exchange, that he continued in that belief until after the Commencement of dealings in the securities on that exchange" were added at the end;

(e) notwithstanding section 142(7) above, any reference in section 152 above (other than in subsection (1)(b) of that section) to the issuer of securities included a reference to the person offering or proposing to offer them; and

(f) in section 154(1) above, for the words "Where listing particulars are or are to be published in connection with an application for the listing of any securities" there were substituted "Where a prospectus is or is to be published in connection with an application for approval, then, until the end of the period during which the offer to which the prospectus relates remains open,".

(4) Listing rules made under this section may require the payment of fees to the competent authority in respect of a prospectus submitted for approval under the rules.

Publication of prospectus

156B.—(1) Where listing rules made under section 144(2) above require the publication of a prospectus, it shall not be lawful, before the time of publication of the prospectus, to offer the securities in question to the public in the United Kingdom.

(2) An authorised person who contravenes subsection (1) above shall be treated as contravening rules made under Chapter V of Part I of this Act or, in the case of a person who is an authorised person by virtue of his membership of a recognised self-regulating organisation or certification by a recognised professional body, the rules of that organisation or body.

(3) A person, other than an authorised person, who contravenes subsection (1) above shall be guilty of an offence and liable—

(a) on conviction on indictment, to imprisonment for a term not exceeding two years or to a fine or to both;

(b) on summary conviction, to imprisonment for a term not exceeding three months or a fine not exceeding level 5 on the standard scale.

(4) Without prejudice to any liability under section 150 above, a person shall not be regarded as contravening subsection (1) above by reason only of a prospectus not having fully complied with this [sic] requirements of listing rules as to its form or content.

(5) Any contravention of subsection (1) above shall be actionable at the suit of a person who suffers loss as a result of the contravention subject to the defences and other incidents applying to actions for breach of statutory duty.

COMMENCEMENT

January 12, 1987 for certain purposes and February 16, 1987 otherwise for all purposes, see (S.I. 1986 No. 2246), Art. 5.

Sections 156A and 156B were inserted by (S.I. 1995 No. 1537), Sched. 2, Pt. I, para. 2.

Some Philosophical Source Material: The influence of Aristotle, Aquinas and the "natural lawyers" on English good faith law

English good faith law is based on some ideas of conduct so ancient that they may sometimes seem oddly familiar, hardly like legal ideas at all. As explained in Chapter 2, ideas which were originally Aristotelian were considered and given a more practical appearance by Thomas Aquinas. Later, by a circuitous route, these ideas surfaced again in the "natural lawyers", writers such as Grotius and Pothier. These, in turn, were taken up by the courts in England in the eighteenth and early to mid-nineteenth century, and formed the basis of English good faith law. This book has attempted to describe that good faith law. Its philosophical origins may seem utterly unimportant to some. "A busy lawyer just needs to know what the law is" is no doubt true. However, there may be some, busy or not, who feel that if an area of law owes something to earlier ideas, it is as well to have some slight nodding acquaintance with the way those ideas were expressed by some of those who wrote about them.

Another point about seeing these ideas simply as part of an ancient framework of ideas may be the avoidance, on occasion, of easy misconceptions. For example, there may be those who, with the author, had vaguely entertained the notion that *caveat emptor*, despite being in Latin, was a robust notion of particular Englishness, a real John Bull of an idea. It is then perhaps a surprise to find it a topic of discussion by Thomas Aquinas and Grotius, not as a sturdy, free-standing idea, but as part of a system of rules of proper conduct for ensuring "equality in exchange", a system that gives no special preeminence to *caveat emptor*, but balances it against the corresponding duty of good faith on the part of the seller.

What follows may serve to indicate, however crudely and broadly, some of the particularly influential natural law ideas whcih were applied in England.[1]

(1) *The idea that a contract derives from the will of the parties to be bound*[2]

"Because of the obligation of decency based upon natural law, man is bound by any promise made." *Thomas Aquinas*

[1] The author acknowledges with gratitude the great debt she owes to Professor Gordley's book, *The Philosophical Origins of Modern Contract Doctrine*. All references save the passages from Domat and Baldus have been checked in the original context, and all save those from Aristotle and Grotius (which are respectively in an English and French translation) in the original language. Subject to that, there is no claim made for accuracy of philosophical exposition in what follows, and Professor Gordley is certainly not responsible for any errors of that kind that there may be. Nor is the account a comprehensive one: for reasons of space and time the quotations in this section focus on Aristotle, Thomas Aquinas, Grotius and Pothier; there is little or no reference to other influential natural lawyers such as Pufendorf, Dormat and Barbeyrac.

[2] *Summa Theologica* Vol. 18 2a2ae, 88.3 (tr. Gilby). The notion that an act of liberality was similarly binding was rejected in England, and the additional requirement of consideration added, before a contract could be binding.

Grotius,[3] referred with approval to Cicero,[4] as placing so much emphasis on the act of promising that he called "la Fidelité à les tenir, le fondement de Justice".

"Le contrat renferme le concours des volontés de deux personnes, dont l'une promet quelque chose à l'autre, etl'autre accepte la promesse qui lui est faite." *Pothier*[5]

Note: The idea that the parties will the contract has been with us for a long time. What is perhaps interesting is the way the whole apparatus of what is actually meant by the parties' "will" has changed. The original natural law approach to the concept of willing an agreement (see below as to the "natural terms" deemed to have been willed) has been forgotten and replaced by present-day will theories. These presuppose no natural law basis; the parties are seen as making their own law, as and when they choose. "The whole doctrine of contract is formal and external" as Oliver Wendell Holmes put it, writing at the beginning of the period of doctrinal change, in 1881.[6] *Yet these "classical" will theories do not explain—or at least, explain only at the cost of ignoring the rationale given by the older judgments themselves—the large parts of our law which were developed by our courts in the nineteenth century by applying the natural-law principles to practical situations. Nor do they really explain how it is that, for example, the victims of unequal bargains are often released from them even where they have in fact willed the unequal bargain expressly; nor how any terms at all, even "officious bystander" ones, come to be implied. Nor do they sit easily with the reality of the parties' consent where contracts of adhesion are concerned. As Eric Holmes puts it*[7] *"though concern with objective, external conduct may simplify factual inquiry, it ignores what the parties really wanted and erects pure doctrinal cathedrals purged of social facts and duties. . . . Sophisticated businessmen, supported by the classical contract myth, imposed their will on those unequal in sophistication through impersonal, mass-standardised contracts. Serious questions arose regarding the reality of equal knowledge, voluntary choice, and genuine assent in the agreement process . . ."*

(2) Equality in exchange

This is a composite concept, including the following:

Step (i) "Commutative justice"

Justice is done by taking the amount necessary to restore equality from one party and giving to the other.[8] Commutative justice is to be aimed at in bargains. It is to be distinguished from the exercise of liberality (or giving "to the right people, the right amounts, and at the right time".[9] The latter is the relevant quality when making gifts.

[3] *De Iure Belli et Pacis* (tr. Barbeyrac, Paris, 1924), Liv. II, Ch. XI. The quotations from Grotius in this appendix are taken from this edition.

[4] De Offic. Lib. I Cap. 7.

[5] *Traité des Obligations*, para. 4. The quotations from this book in this appendix are taken from the 1835 edition.

[6] The Common Law, 230, quoted in "A Contextual Study of Commercial Good Faith: Good-faith disclosure in Contract Formation", by Eric M. Holmes, *University of Pittsburgh Law Review*, 1978, vol. 39, p. 381.

[7] *op. cit.*

[8] Aristotle, *Nicomachean Ethics* IV 1119–1120. This quotation is as it appears in Gordley, *op. cit.* The remaining quotations from Aristotle in this appendix are taken from the O.U.P. edition, ed. Ross, 1915.

[9] Aristotle, *Nichomachean Ethics* V iv 1131–1132. See also Thomas Aquinas, *Summa Theologica* II–IIq 61a2.

Step (ii) The will or consent of the parties to be bound by a contract presupposes a reasonable degree of equality of knowledge

"Since that which is done under compulsion or by reason of ignorance is involuntary, the voluntary would seem to be that of which the moving principle is the agent himself, he being aware of the particular circumstances of the action."[10]

"Besides, knowledge is essential to voluntariness, as we have seen, and knowledge involves activity."[11]

"Mais dans tous les Contracts intéressez de part & d'autre, comme on s'y propose directement & essentiellement un échange de services, l'égalité, dont il s'agit, doit être observée avec beaucoup d'exactitude. En vain prétendroit-on, que ce qu'une des Parties promet au delà de ce à quoi l'autre s'engage à son tour, est regardé comme un don. Ce n'est point là pour l'ordinaire l'intention de ceux qui font de tels Contracts; & on ne doit jamais le présumer, tant qu'il n'y en a point de preuve évidente. Car ce qu'ils promettent ou qu'ils donnent, ils sont censez le promettre ou le donner comme équivalent à ce qu'ils doivent recevoir, & comme dû à cause de cette égalité même."[12]

Step (iii) A reasonable equality of knowledge requires some disclosure of latent defects

The idea that Aristotle's principle of "equality in exchange" required a degree of equivalence of knowledge about the subject matter of the sale appears in Thomas Aquinas. "... any contract between two parties should, therefore, be based on an equality of material exchange".[13] He regarded it as a violation of this equality when a seller sold a thing with a fault in it:

"An object of sale can have three sorts of flaw in it ... And the third sort of flaw is in relation to the quality of a thing, as in the case where somebody sells a sickly animal as if it were healthy. If this is done knowingly, the sale is vitiated by fraud, and rendered illicit.

In all these cases a person who makes an unjust sale not only commits a sin, but is bound to make restitution. Of course, if the seller is unaware of any of these defects in the thing sold, he personally commits no sin since the injustice is only material and not willed and does not make the sale unjust as we have already explained, although he is bound to make restitution when he does discover the facts."[14]

See also Grotius for the same idea. He gave it the label "good faith", which was taken up in England by Lord Mansfield. Grotius also focused on the idea that contracting parties must exercise good faith because they are in a "special relationship" with each other. Grotius says:

"Le Droit Naturel veut qu'il aît de l'*égalité* dans tous les Contracts, en sorte que, du moment qu'il paroit quelque inégalité, celui qui a moins acquiert par là le droit d'exiger qu'on y supplée. Cette égalité regarde en partie les actes des Contractans, en partie la chose sur quoi ils traitent.

Par rapport aux *actes qui précédent l'engagement*, l'égalité demande que

[10] Aristotle, *Nicomachean Ethics* III 1111.

[11] Thomas Aquinas, *Summa Theologica* 1a2ae, 6.3.

[12] Grotius, *op. cit.*, Liv. II Ch. XII, XI.

[13] *op. cit.*, 2a2ae, 77.2.

[14] *op. cit.*, 2a2ae, 77.1.

quiconque traite avec un autre, lui déclare de bonne foi les défauts qu'il connoit dans la chose dont il s'agit. Cela est non-seulement établi par les Loix Civiles, mais encore conforme à la nature même de l'affaire. Car il y a entre les Contractans une société [relationship] plus particulière, que celle qui unit généralement tous les Hommes.[15]

See Lord Mansfield's reference to it: "Good faith forbids either party by concealing what he privately knows, to draw the other into a bargain, from his ignorance of that fact, and his believing the contrary . . ."' *Carter v. Boehm*[16] Other probable references to the same concept may be found in the various Chapter Appendices, *passim*.

Pothier, like Grotius, labelled this kind of disclosure-to-ensure-equality "good faith". He explained the inequality in terms of the superior means of knowledge possessed by the vendor. He also, like Grotius before him, narrowed the scope of disclosure somewhat, by means of the idea that the disclosure had to be about that which was "intrinsic" to the thing sold. (This may well have derived from the Aristotelian idea of the characteristic "end" of a contract: see below at page 790.)

"Quoique dans plusieurs affaires de la société civile, les règles de la bonne foi se bornent à nous défendre de mentir, et nous permettent de ne pas découvrir aux autres ce qu'ils auroient intérêt de savoir, lorsque nous avons un égal intérêt de ne le leur pas découvrir, néanmoins dans les contrats interessés, du nombre desquels est le contrat de vente, la bonne foi ne défend pas seulement tout mensonge, mais toute réticence de tout ce que celui avec qui nous contractons a intérêt de savoir touchant la chose qui fait l'objet du contrat.

La raison est que la justice et l'équité dans ces contrats consiste dans l'égalité: tout ce qui tend à la blesser est donc contraire a l'équité. Il est évident que toute réticence de la part d'un des contractans, de tout ce que l'autre auroit intérêt de savoir touchant la chose qui fait l'objet du contrat, blesse cet égalité: car dés que l'un a plus de connoissance que l'autre touchant cette chose, il a plus d'avantage que l'autre à contracter; il sait mieux ce qu'il fait que l'autre, et par-conséquent l'égalité ne se trouve plus dans le contrat. . . .

Suivant ces principes, un vendeur est obligé de ne rien dissimuler des défauts de la chose qu'il vend, qui sont à sa connoissance . . .

. . . 236 "La bonne foi oblige le vendeur, non-seulement à ne rien dissimuler des vices intrinsèques de la chose, mais en général à ne rien dissimuler de tout ce qui concerne la chose, qui pourroit porter l'acheteur à ne pas acheter, ou à ne pas acheter si cher."[17]

Step (iv) The "just price" as a proper market price (provided there was also equality of access to information)

Thomas Aquinas had also thought it was a violation to sell at an "unjust price". The idea of the just price eventually evolved into that of a properly achieved market price, on the footing that proper *equality of knowledge* had been achieved. This "passed for" equality of exchange. See, *e.g.* Grotius:

"Tout ce que nous avons dit jusqu'ici, est conforme au Droit Naturel. Il ne paroît pas que le Droit des Gens arbitraire y aît rien changé, hormis en ce

[15] Grotius, *op. cit.*, Liv. II Ch. XII, VIII. Italics in original. Barbeyrac's edition gives references also to Pufendorf.

[16] (1766) 3 Burr. 1905; 97 E.R. 1162.

[17] Pothier, *Traité de Contrat de Vente* (Paris, 1806), paras. 233 ff. As to this last distinction, note the similar test used by the early Lord Chancellors in making their decision to rescind or to permit the contract to stand with compensation: see Chapter 5, Sale of Land.

qui regarde une seule maxime qu'il établit; C'est que, par rapport aux actions extérieures, une inégalité à laquelle on a consenti de part et d'autre, sans qu'il y aît eu ni mensonge, ni suppression de ce que l'on devoit déclarer, passe pour égalité . . .[18]

Note: The idea of any different form of "just price" will not have been seriously suggested, since obviously commerce would be impossible if the adequacy of the price was always to be subject to scrutiny by the courts. The concept of an undistorted market may have some relevance to modern sales of investment services: see perhaps now also the reference to the "integrity of the market" in Article 11 of the Investment Services Directive 1993.[19]

Step (v) *Caveat emptor* relevant to what has to be disclosed

Caveat emptor was seen by Aquinas and Grotius as part and parcel of the rules for proper conduct in sales. The buyer (or inquiring party) must take reasonable steps to protect himself. He could be assumed to have seen obvious flaws. He could buy something "with all faults" provided the seller had been candid about the faulty object.

Aquinas said, "Where, on the other hand, the flaw is obvious, as where a horse has only one eye, or where other people might find a use for the object of sale even though the buyer could not, and where, moreover, the seller takes a fair amount off the price, he is not bound to disclose the flaw."[20]

Grotius extended the scope of *caveat emptor* beyond actual knowledge, to knowledge which it was reasonably to be expected the buyer had. "Il n'est pas même necessaire de parler de ces sortes de défauts [those which were connected with the thing sold] lors que l'autre Contractant les connoît aussi bien que nous. . . . He then gives an example of a man who repurchases a house he had once owned, and thus is deemed to know its incumbrances. In other words, he has introduced a degree of constructive knowledge into *caveat emptor*. "En effet, *la connoissance qu l'on suppose de part & d'autre rend les Contractans parfaitement égaux à cet égard . . .*"[21]

Note: See in particular Chapter 8, Knowledge and Notice, for the careful balance achieved by the English courts between the caveat emptor *or buyer/inquiring party to-do-his-homework principle, and the seller/describing party's duty of candour and accuracy. Contrast also the stringent* caveat emptor *duty in sales of land*[22] *with that in sales of personal property.*[23] *In the latter, the duty of candour eventually took on the form of a duty to controvert a misleading silence where necessary: see* e.g. *the powerful obiter statement in* Smith v. Hughes.[24] *Silence is less likely to be blameworthy or risky for a vendor where the buyer can be expected to find out most of the relevant facts for himself. The result in sales of personal property was that* caveat emptor *was all but eaten up by this large, positive seller's duty of candour. This will no doubt have been because in the circumstances of most sales of personal prop-*

[18] *op. cit.*, Liv. II Ch. XII, XXVI.

[19] See Statutory Appendix for commentary on Article 11. See also Grotius' view that price-fixing monopolies were a wrong done to the buyer (and thus contrary to equality): *op. cit.*, Liv. II Ch. XII, XVI "Mais ceux qui . . . s'accordent entr'eux, de ne vendre leurs denrées et leurs marchandises qu'au delà du plus haut degré du prix courant . . . ceux-la, dis-je, font du tort à autrui, et par conséquent sont obligez de le réparer."

[20] Thomas Aquinas, *op. cit.*, 2a2ae, 77.4.

[21] Grotius, *op. cit.*, Liv. II Ch. XII, IX.

[22] See Chap. 5, Sale of Land.

[23] See Chap. 3, Sale of Personal Property.

[24] (1871) L.R. 6 Q.B. 597.

erty[25] *there was little scope for the* caveat emptor *principle. The most that could be expected by way of "homework" from the buyer was that he would examine the goods where possible.*

(3) The Aristotelian idea that things might be defined or classified according to their "final cause" or "end", or characteristic behaviour/evolution towards a usual purpose

Thomas Aquinas applied this idea to human actions: "... each act draws its specific nature from its objective. And so it should be a difference there that gives rise to the specific difference in the act."[26] He also categorizes contracts of sale, hire, deposit, pledge, surety, etc., by means of their characteristic "end" or main purpose as well as retaining his two overall distinctions between acts of liberality and of commutative justice.[27]

Grotius, speaking about the fundamental nature of insurance contracts in particular says:

"Le Contract d'Assurance est entiérement nul, si l'un des Contractans sait ou que la chose dont il s'agit est arrivée à bon port dans le lieu qu'on souhaitoit; ou qu'elle a péri. Cette connoissance est non seulement contraire à l'égalité qu'il doit y avoir dans tous les Contracts intéressez de part et d'autre, mais encore à la nature propre du Contract d'Assurance, qui roule sur un danger incertain. L'estimation de ce danger doit se régler sur l'estimation commune."[28]

Pothier developed the idea in various ways, one being the useful distinction between principal obligations, which seem to be connected with the "end" or paramount purpose of the contract, and ancillary obligations.

"L'obligation *principale* est l'obligation de ce qui fait le principal objet de l'engagement, qui a été contracté entre les parties.

On appelle obligations *accessoires*, celles qui sont comme des suites et des dépendances de l'obligation principale.

Par exemple, dans le contrat de vente d'un héritage, l'obligation principale, que le vendeur contracte, est l'obligation de livrer cet héritage à l'acheteur, et de le garantir de tous troubles et de toutes evictions . . .[29]

The distinction between "essential", "natural" and "accidental" terms of a contract probably also stems from the idea of a characteristic "end" or purpose of a contract. See for this, the opening quotation at the beginning of Chapter 2 from Pothier. Allied to this distinction was the idea that a term of a contract that would remove the "natural" effect of the type of contract the parties had entered into would be void since "to remove the natural effect is to remove the species": see, *e.g.* Gordley[30] citing Baldus, a medieval Glossator.

Note: The concept of the "nature of the contract" as giving rise to various subcategories of contract, each with their own special implied terms, has been endorsed

[25] But compare now sales of pensions, endowment policies, etc., where a *caveat emptor* duty corresponding to the real expectations (if any) we have of the buyer has yet to be developed.

[26] *op. cit.*, 1a2ae, 18.5.

[27] *op. cit.*, 2a2ae, 61.3.

[28] *op. cit.*, Liv. II Ch. XII, XXIII.

[29] *Traité des Obligations*, Part II Chap. I para. 165. Italics in original.

[30] *op. cit.*, p. 64.

by the House of Lords in Liverpool City Council v. Irwin.[31] *It is probably inherent in the implications of fitness for purpose terms.*

Further, the concept of the characteristic "end" or what in this book has been labelled the "paramount purpose" of the contract (to be distinguished both from ancillary purposes and from any actual purpose of either party) has also been (and continues to be) influential in the development of means of restraining within bounds the powers exercisable by the parties during the after-sale period, e.g. *by cutting down the arbitrary exercise by the seller of retained powers to that which is to be expected in the light of that original paramount purpose or "end", or by similarly restraining the parties' afer the contract has broken down: see Parts III and IV of this book.*

It may well be that the narrowing of the scope of disclosure (above) to that which was "intrinsic" derived from the Aristotelian concept of the "end" of a contract also. See also Grotius' definition of "intrinsic" as concerned with the quality and the circumstances which in themselves (i.e. without adding any special circumstances, such as those of Cicero's famine: see below) have some relationship with the basic subject matter of the sale.[32] *The distinction attracted most attention in England in connection with surety contracts: see Chapter 4, Insurance and Surety Contracts.*

(4) "Natural terms" of a contract as something the parties are deemed to have intended (unless there is a clear express exclusion).

The idea of "natural terms" of a contract was linked not only to equality of exchange but in turn (because equality of exchange was itself a part of the assumed substructure of the parties' consent: see above) also to the concept of the way the parties willed a contract. Domat, another "natural lawyer" took the view that once one enters into an agreement of a certain type, one is bound "not only by what is expressed, but also to everything that is required by the nature of the agreement, and to all the consequences that equity, statute and usage give to the obligation one has undertaken."[33]

See also Pothier:[34]

"C'est encore un effet général commun à toutes les conventions, qu'elles doivent être executées *de bonne foi*, c'est à dire, que le juge peut condamner les parties à donner non-seulement ce qui a été expressement promis et stipulé, mais encore à toutes les suites que *l'équité, l'usage ou la loi* donnent à l'obligation d'après sa nature."

Compare Article 1135 of the French Code Civil[35] (cited in Chapter 18, Do we need Good Faith anyway?) which remains virtually in Pothier's wording.

See also Gordley[36] who says:

"To Thomas [Aquinas], the late scholastics, Grotius, or Domat, the requirement of equality was not something imposed on the parties against their will. The parties to an exchange could only have intended that the contract preserve equality. ... For Grotius then, as for the late scholastics, to require equality in an onerous contract in which neither party wished to make a gift was to honour and not to thwart the intention of the contracting parties."

[31] [1977] A.C. 239. See comment and quotation from the case in Chapter 1, Introduction.
[32] *op. cit.*, Liv. II Ch. XII.
[33] Les Lois Civiles, Paris, I i iii i, quoted in Gordley, *op. cit.*, at p. 110.
[34] *Traité des Obligations, Part I Chap. II (De l'effet des obligations) paragraph 123. Italics in original.*
[35] Dalloz edition, 1994–5.
[36] *op. cit.*, at p. 110.

Note: The mechanism of good faith implied terms developed by the courts in England depended entirely upon the classification of good faith terms as "natural" and thus something the parties might properly be deemed *to have intended.*

(6) A particular kind of extra fairness required in dealings with the vulnerable buyer or seller

The idea that special vulnerability calls forth an extra duty from the other side appears at all events in Grotius. He said,[37] "Outre l'égalité, dont nous venons de parler, qui regard les connoissances nécessaires pour l'affaire dont il s'agit; les Contractans doivent garder entr'eux quelque égalité par rapport à l'usage de leur volonté. Ce n'est pas que, si l'on a été porté à traiter par une crainte juste, l'autre Contractant soit tenu de faire cesser cette crainte; car c'est-là une circonstance extérieure, qui n'entre pour rien dans le Contract: mais il ne faut jamais user d'une crainte injuste, pour porter quelcun à traiter; et si on l'a fait, on doit ôter le sujet de crainte." A little later he said also, possibly not specially in regard to dealings with the vulnerable, "L'égalité, qu'il doit y avoir dans *l'acte principal du Contract*, consiste à ne rien demander au delà de ce qui est juste et raisonnable."

Note: The idea that the impugned dealing with a vulnerable party must be justified as being "fair, just and reasonable" may be traced in the cases on this topic.

[37] *op. cit.*, Liv.II Ch. XII, X.

SELECT BIBLIOGRAPHY

General — mainly works the author has found helpful in seeking to understand the development of good faith in England[1]

Aquinas, T., *Summa Theologiae*, vol 18, *Principles of Morality* (tr. T. Gilby).
Aristotle, *Ethica Nicomachea* (tr. W. D. Ross).
Atiyah, P. S., *The Rise and Fall of Freedom of Contract* (1979).
Beatson, J. and Friedmann, D., (ed) *Good Faith and Default in Contract Law* (1995).
Clarke, *The Law of Insurance Contracts* (2nd ed., 1994).
Fry, *Specific Performance* (1st ed., 1858).
Finn, P. D. (ed) *Equity and Commercial Relationships* (1987).
— *Essays on Contract* (1987).
Gordley, *The Philosophical Origins of Modern Contract Doctrine* (1991).
Grotius, *De Jure Belli et Pacis* (tr. Barbeyrac, 1724).
Harpum, C. "Exclusion Clauses and Contracts for the Sale of Land," [1992] C.L.J. 263.
Harpum, C. [1992] 108 L.Q.R. 280.
Harris, D. and Tallon, D. (ed) *Contract Law Today, Anglo-French Comparisons* (1989).
Mansfield, Lord, judgment in *Carter v. Boehm* (1766) 3 Burr. 1905; 97 E.R. 1162.
Mason, Sir Anthony, *Unfairness in Contracting: The Role of Equity and Good Conscience in Commercial Transactions* (paper given at Gray's Inn Hall on July 5, 1995).
Meagher, Gummow & Lehane, *Equitable Doctrines and Remedies* (3rd ed., 1992).
Nicholas, B. *Introduction to French Law* (2nd ed., 1992).
Pothier, *Traité du Contrat de Vente* (1806).
Pothier, *Traité des Obligations* (1835).
Simpson, "Innovation in Nineteenth Century Contract Law" (1975) 91 L.Q.R. 247.

Unfair Terms in Consumer Contracts Regulations 1994 — some useful articles

Bright, S. and Bright, C. 'Unfair Terms in Land Contracts: Copy out or cop out?" [1995] 111 L.Q.R. 655.
Brownsword, R. and Howells, G., "The Implementation of the EC Directive on Unfair Terms in Consumer Contracts — Some Unresolved Questions", [1995] J.B.B.L. 243.
de Burca, G., "Giving Effect to European Community Directives", (1992) 55 M.L.R. 215.

[1] It does not include all works referred to in the text.

Department of Trade and Industry, *The Unfair Terms in Consumer Contracts Regulations 1994*, Guidance Notes (July 1995).
Hartley, T., "Uncertainty in European Community Law", [1996] C.L.J. 265.
Hunter, R., *The Effect of 1994 E.U. Based Regulations on Product Liability and Service Law* (paper given at Gray's Inn Hall, July 5, 1995).
Merkin, R., *The Unfair Terms in Consumer Contracts Regulations and Insurance Contracts* (paper given at Gray's Inn Hall, July 5, 1995).
de Moor, A., *Common and Civil Law Conceptions of Contract and a European Law of Contract: the Case of the Directive on Unfair Terms in Consumer Contracts, European Review of Private Law* (1995).

INDEX

(All references are to paragraph number)